Street by Street

BIG ATLAS LONDON

3rd edition May 2007

© Automobile Association Developments Limited 2007

Original edition printed 2001

This product includes map data licensed from Ordnance Survey® with the permission of the Controller of Her Majesty's Stationery Office. © Crown copyright 2007. All rights reserved. Licence number: 100021153.

The copyright in all PAF is owned by Royal Mail Group plc.

Published by AA Publishing (a trading name of Automobile Association Developments Limited, whose registered office is Fanum House, Basing View, Basingstoke, Hampshire RG21 4EA. Registered number 1878835).

Produced by the Mapping Services Department of The Automobile Association. (A03278)

A CIP Catalogue record for this book is available from the British Library.

Printed by Oriental Press in Dubai

The contents of this atlas are believed to be correct at the time of the latest revision. However, the publishers cannot be held responsible or liable for any loss or damage occasioned to any person acting or refraining from action as a result of any use or reliance on any material in this atlas, nor for any errors, omissions or changes in such material. This does not affect your statutory rights. The publishers would welcome information to correct any errors or omissions and to keep this atlas up to date. Please write to Publishing, The Automobile Association, Fanum House (FH12), Basing View, Basingstoke, Hampshire, RG21 4EA.
E-mail: *streetbystreet@theaa.com*

Ref: BA041y

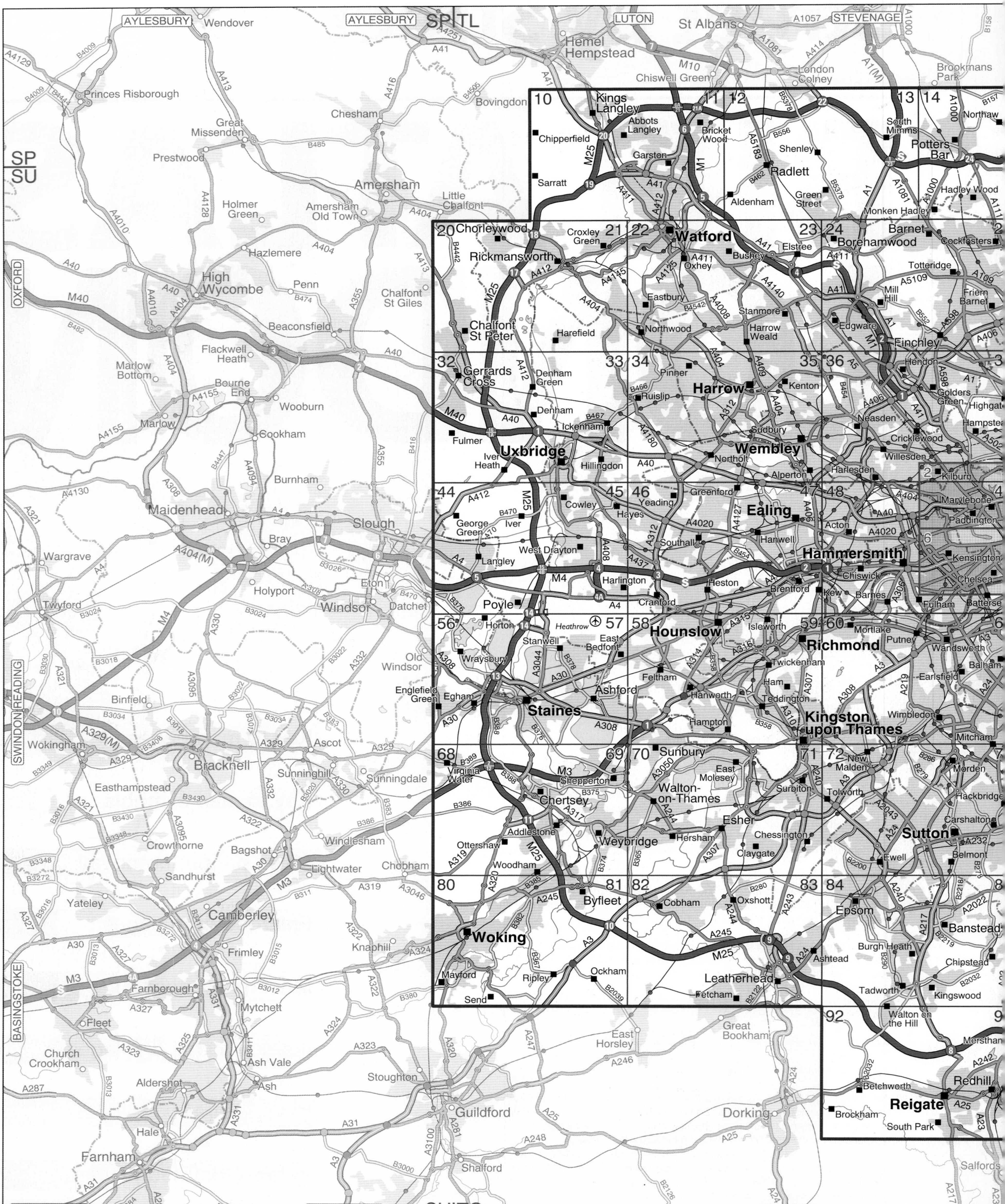

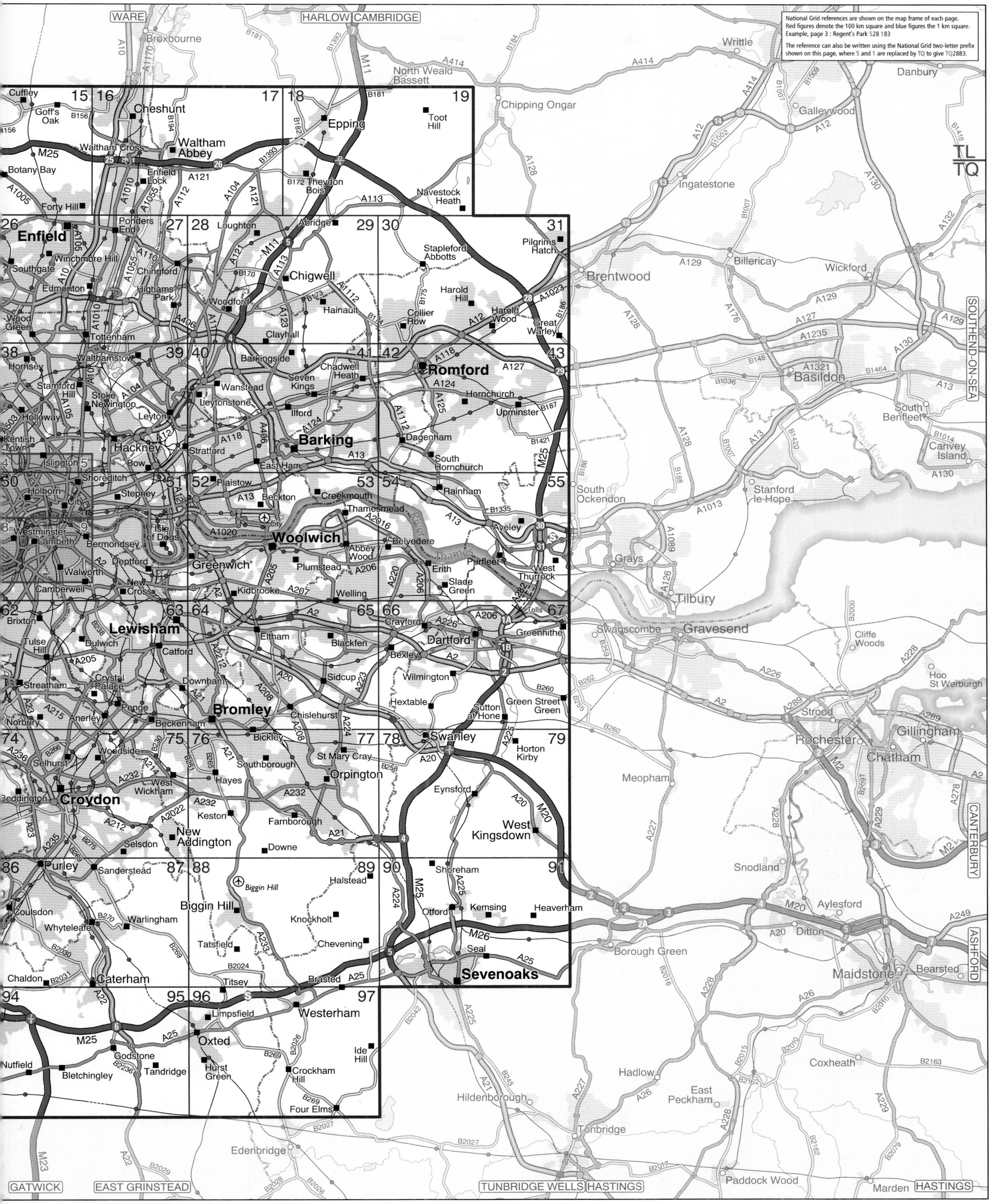

National Grid references are shown on the map frame of each page.
Red figures denote the 100 km square and blue figures the 1 km square.
Example, page 3 : Regent's Park 528 183

The reference can also be written using the National two-letter prefix
shown on this page, where 5 and 1 are replaced by TQ to give TQ2883.

3.2 inches to 1 mile   **Scale of main map pages** 1:20,000

Junction 9 Motorway & junction	**151** Page continuation 1:20,000	Cinema
Services Motorway service area	**17** Page continuation to enlarged scale 1:10,000	Golf course
J58 Primary road single/dual carriageway & junction	River/canal, lake, pier	Camping AA inspected
Services Primary road service area	Aqueduct, lock, weir	Caravan site AA inspected
A road single/dual carriageway	Beach	Camping & caravan site AA inspected
B road single/dual carriageway	Woodland	Theme park
Other road single/dual carriageway	Park	Abbey, cathedral or priory
Minor/private road, access may be restricted	Cemetery	Castle
One-way street	Built-up area	Historic house or building
Pedestrian area	Industrial / business building	Wakehurst Place NT National Trust property
Track or footpath	Leisure building	Museum or art gallery
Road under construction	Retail building	Roman antiquity
Road tunnel	Other building	Ancient site, battlefield or monument
P Parking	City wall	Industrial interest
P+ Park & Ride	**A&E** Hospital with 24-hour A&E department	Garden
Bus/coach station	**PO** Post Office	Garden Centre Garden Centre Association Member
Railway & main railway station	Public library	Garden Centre Wyevale Garden Centre
Railway & minor railway station	**i** Tourist Information Centre	Arboretum
Underground station	**i** Seasonal Tourist Information Centre	Farm or animal centre
Docklands Light Railway (DLR) station	Petrol station, 24 hour Major suppliers only	Zoological or wildlife collection
Light railway & station	**†** Church/chapel	Bird collection
LC Level crossing	Public toilets	Nature reserve
Tramway	Toilet with disabled facilities	Aquarium
Ferry route	**PH** Public house AA recommended	Visitor or heritage centre
Airport runway	Restaurant AA inspected	Country park
County, administrative boundary	Madeira Hotel Hotel AA inspected	Cave
Congestion Charging Zone *	Theatre or performing arts centre	Distillery, brewery or vineyard
Charge-free route through the Charging Zone	**IKEA** IKEA store	Windmill

* The AA central London congestion charging map is also available

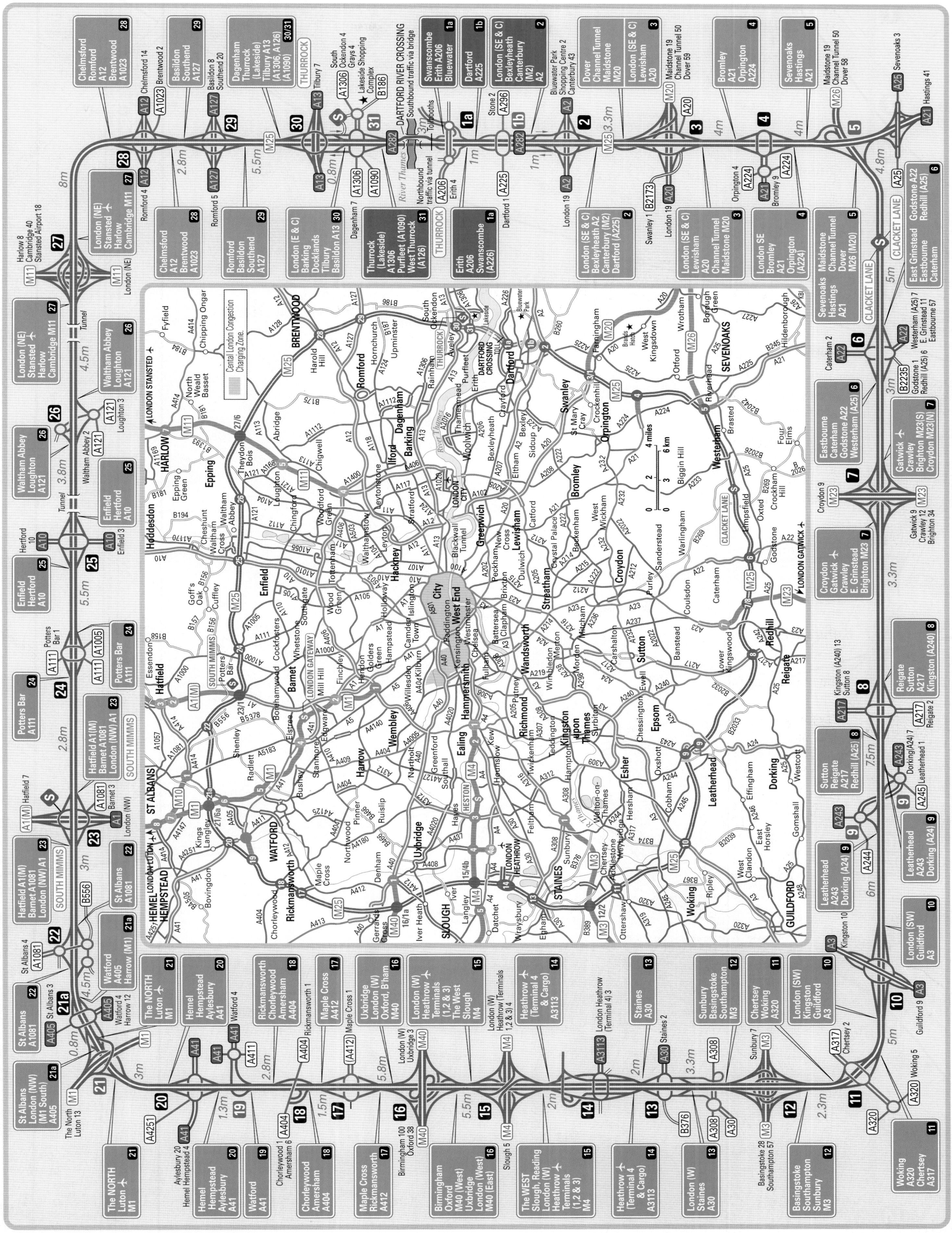

M25 London Orbital Motorway — junction and destination map with surrounding road network.

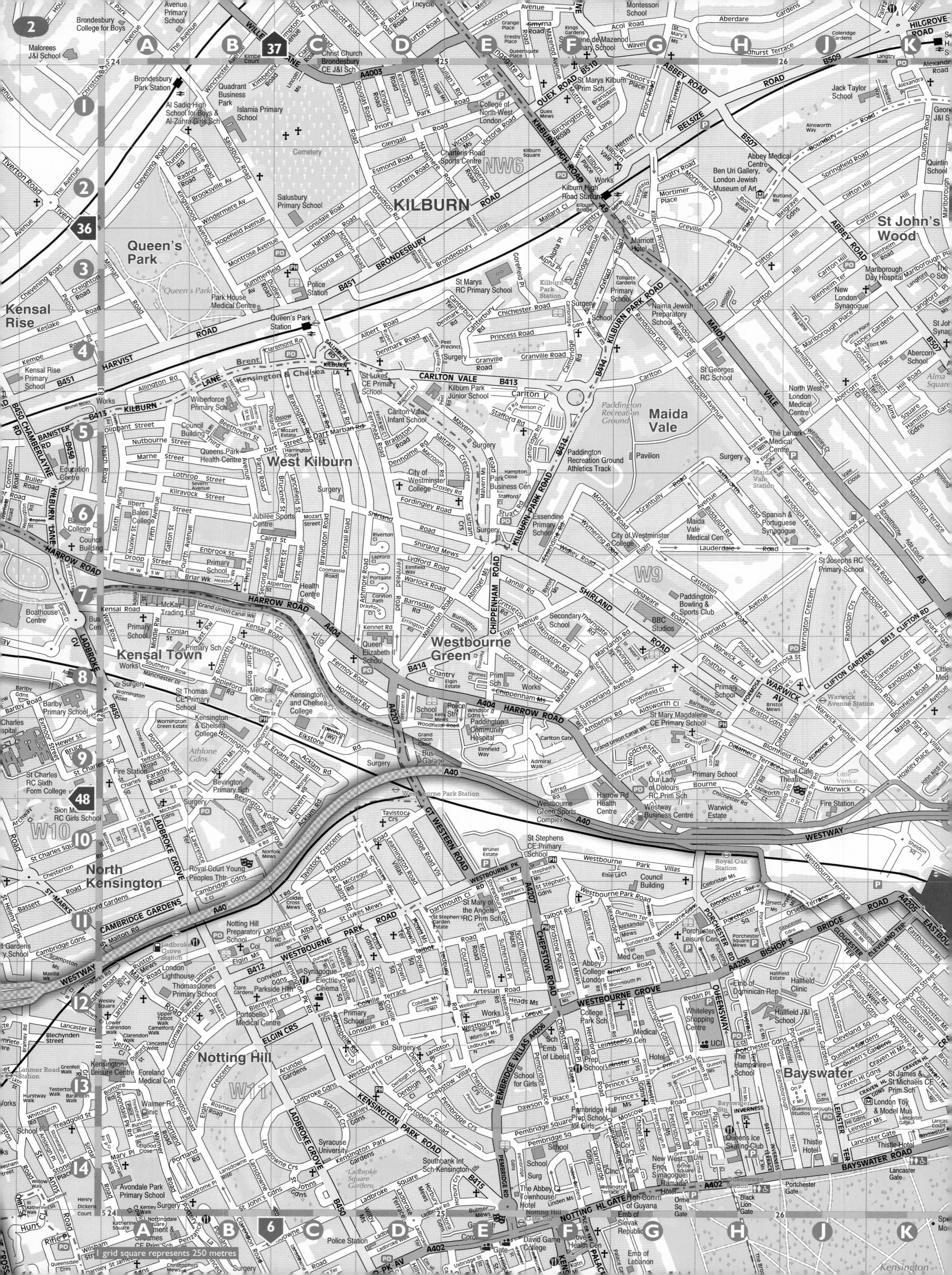
2
KILBURN
Queen's Park
Kensal Rise
West Kilburn
Maida Vale
St John's Wood
Westbourne Green
Kensal Town
North Kensington
Notting Hill
Bayswater
NW6
W9
W10
W11
36
37
48
6
A
B
C
D
E
F
G
H
J
K
1
2
3
4
5
6
7
8
9
10
11
12
13
14
Brondesbury Park Station
Kilburn High Road Station
Queen's Park Station
Kilburn Park Station
Maida Vale Station
Warwick Avenue Station
Westbourne Park Station
Royal Oak Station
Ladbroke Grove Station
Latimer Road Station
Bayswater Stn
Queensway Station
Notting Hill Gate Stn
KILBURN HIGH ROAD
BRONDESBURY VILLAS
KILBURN PARK ROAD
MAIDA VALE
ABBEY ROAD
HARROW ROAD
HARVIST ROAD
CARLTON VALE
SHIRLAND ROAD
CHIPPENHAM ROAD
WESTWAY
WESTBOURNE GROVE
WESTBOURNE PARK ROAD
LADBROKE GROVE
KENSINGTON PARK ROAD
PEMBRIDGE VILLAS
CHEPSTOW ROAD
QUEENSWAY
BISHOP'S BRIDGE ROAD
BAYSWATER ROAD
NOTTING HL GATE
CLIFTON GARDENS
WARWICK AV
ELGIN CRS
CAMBRIDGE GARDENS
A5
A40
A404
A402
A4206
A4207
B413
B414
B450
B451
B507
B509
B510
Grand Union Canal
Paddington Recreation Ground
Cemetery
Queen's Park
Ladbroke Square Gardens
Little Venice
1 grid square represents 250 metres

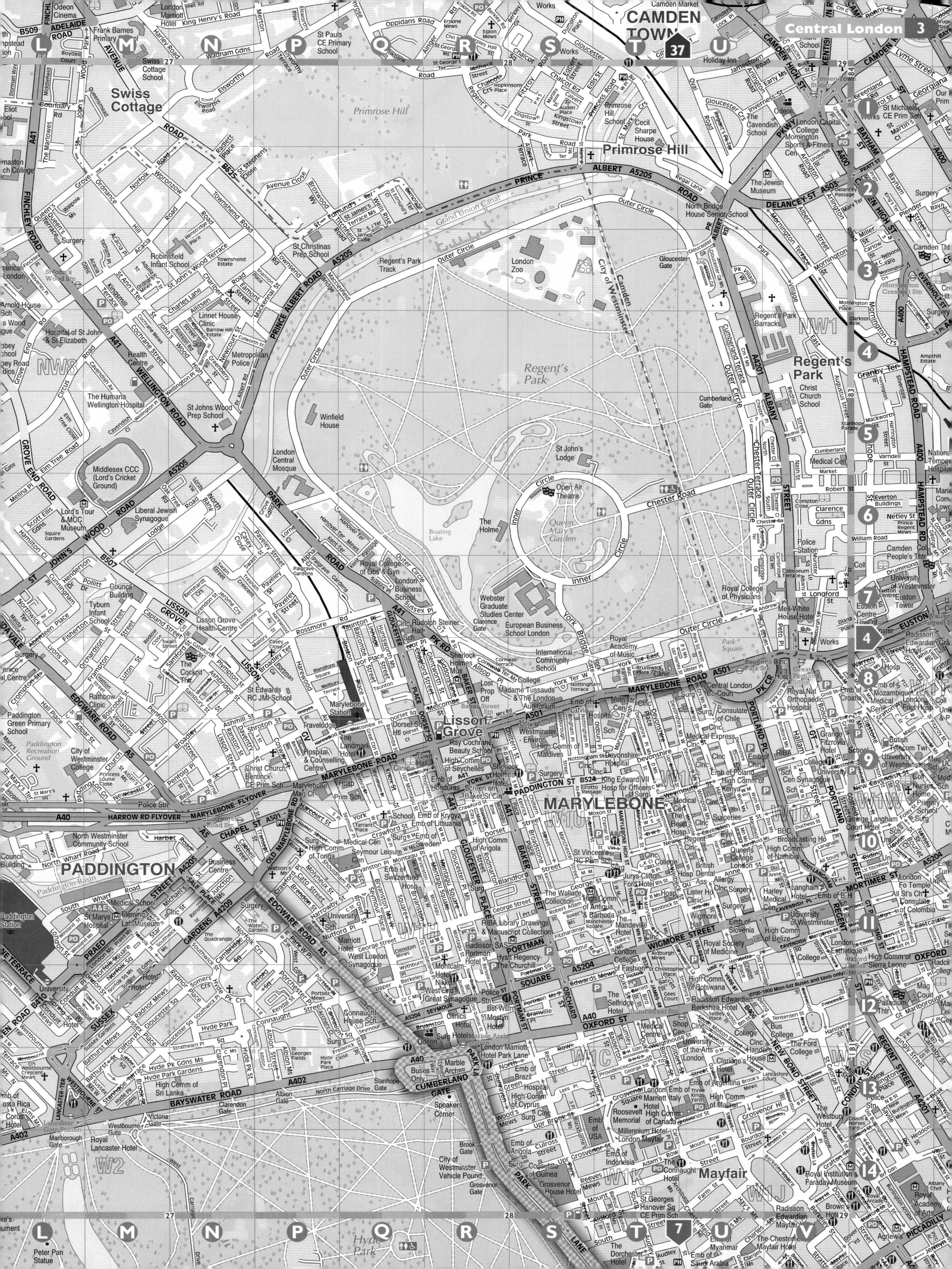
CAMDEN TOWN
37
Swiss Cottage
Primrose Hill
Primrose Hill
Regent's Park
Regent's Park
London Zoo
PRINCE ALBERT ROAD A5205
Grand Union Canal
Outer Circle
Inner Circle
Queen Mary's Garden
Open Air Theatre
Boating Lake
The Holme
Winfield House
London Central Mosque
St John's Lodge
Regent's Park Barracks
Camden
City of Westminster
NW1
NW8
Middlesex CCC (Lord's Cricket Ground)
Lord's Tour & MCC Museum
ST JOHN'S WOOD ROAD
WELLINGTON ROAD
FINCHLEY ROAD
GROVE END ROAD
EDGWARE ROAD
LISSON GROVE
PARK ROAD
GLOUCESTER PLACE
BAKER STREET
MARYLEBONE ROAD
MARYLEBONE FLYOVER
HARROW RD FLYOVER
A40
Marylebone Station
Madame Tussauds & The London Auditorium
Royal Academy of Music
Lisson Grove
MARYLEBONE
PADDINGTON
Paddington Basin
Paddington Station
PRAED STREET
SUSSEX GARDENS
BAYSWATER ROAD
OXFORD STREET
PORTMAN SQUARE
WIGMORE STREET
CAVENDISH PL
MORTIMER ST
PORTLAND PL
GREAT PORTLAND STREET
ALBANY STREET
HAMPSTEAD ROAD
EUSTON ROAD
CAMDEN HIGH ST
DELANCEY ST A503
REGENT STREET
NEW BOND STREET
PARK LANE
CUMBERLAND GATE
Marble Arch
Speakers Corner
Mayfair
Hyde Park
W1
W1B
W1C
W1G
W1H
W1J
W1K
W1S
W1U
W1W
W2
L M N P Q R S T U V
1 2 3 4 5 6 7 8 9 10 11 12 13 14
27 28 29
7

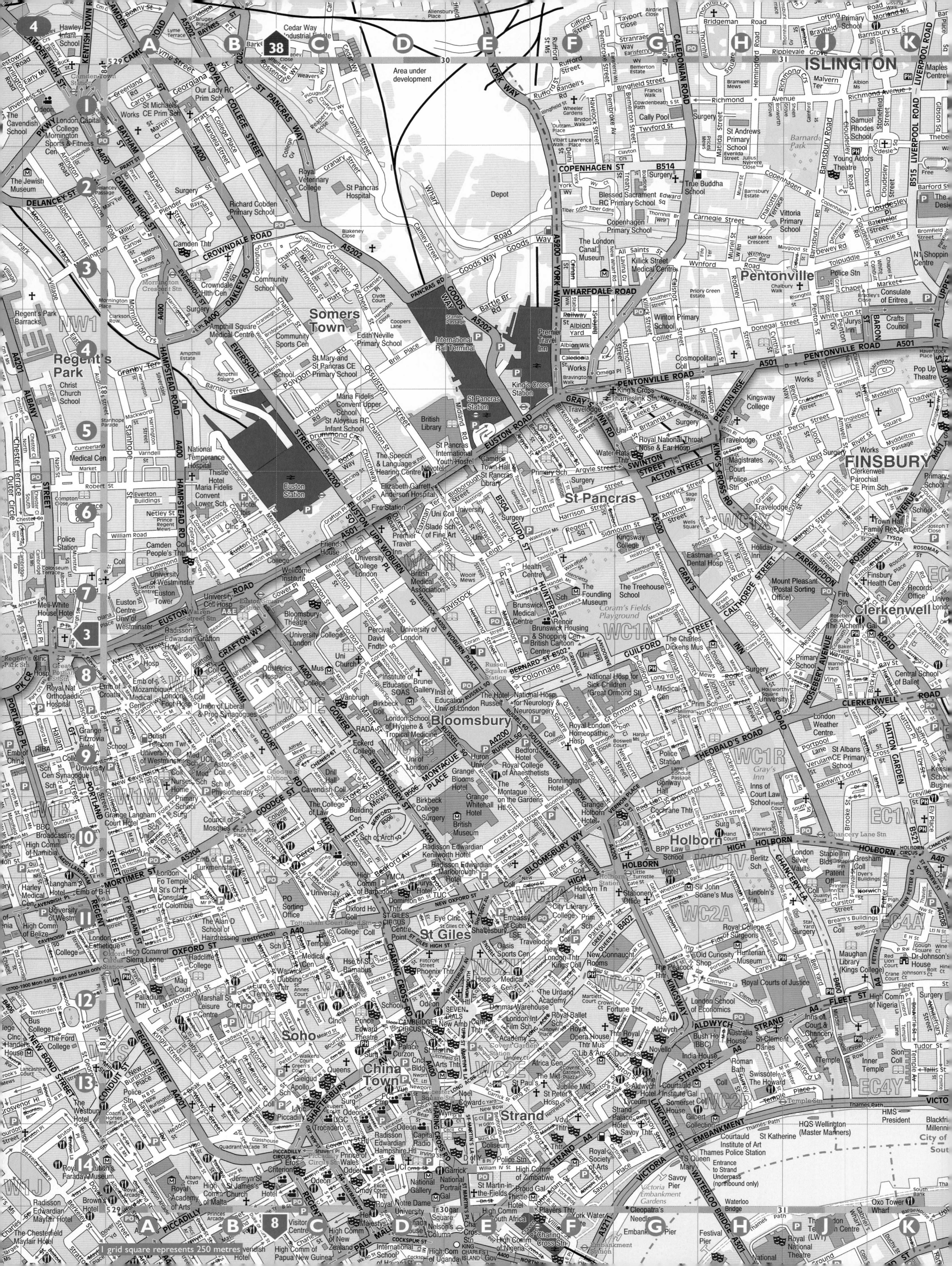

4
38
3
8
A
B
C
D
E
F
G
H
J
K
1
2
3
4
5
6
7
8
9
10
11
12
13
14
ISLINGTON
Somers Town
Regent's Park
Pentonville
St Pancras
FINSBURY
Clerkenwell
Bloomsbury
Holborn
St Giles
Soho
China Town
Strand
NW1
WC1X
WC1H
WC1N
WC1E
WC1B
WC1R
WC1V
WC1A
WC2A
WC2H
WC2B
WC2E
WC2R
W1T
W1W
W1B
W1F
W1S
W1J
EC1R
EC1N
EC4A
EC4Y
Area under development
Depot
Euston Station
King's Cross Station
St Pancras Station
British Library
International Rail Terminal
Mount Pleasant (Postal Sorting Office)
British Museum
Royal Courts of Justice
Victoria Embankment Gardens
EUSTON ROAD
PENTONVILLE ROAD
OXFORD ST
HIGH HOLBORN
CLERKENWELL ROAD
THEOBALD'S ROAD
FARRINGDON ROAD
GRAY'S INN ROAD
KING'S CROSS ROAD
CALEDONIAN ROAD
YORK WAY
CAMDEN HIGH ST
HAMPSTEAD RD
TOTTENHAM COURT RD
CHARING CROSS RD
SHAFTESBURY AV
REGENT STREET
PICCADILLY
STRAND
FLEET ST
KINGSWAY
ALDWYCH
VICTORIA EMBANKMENT
WATERLOO BRIDGE
1 grid square represents 250 metres

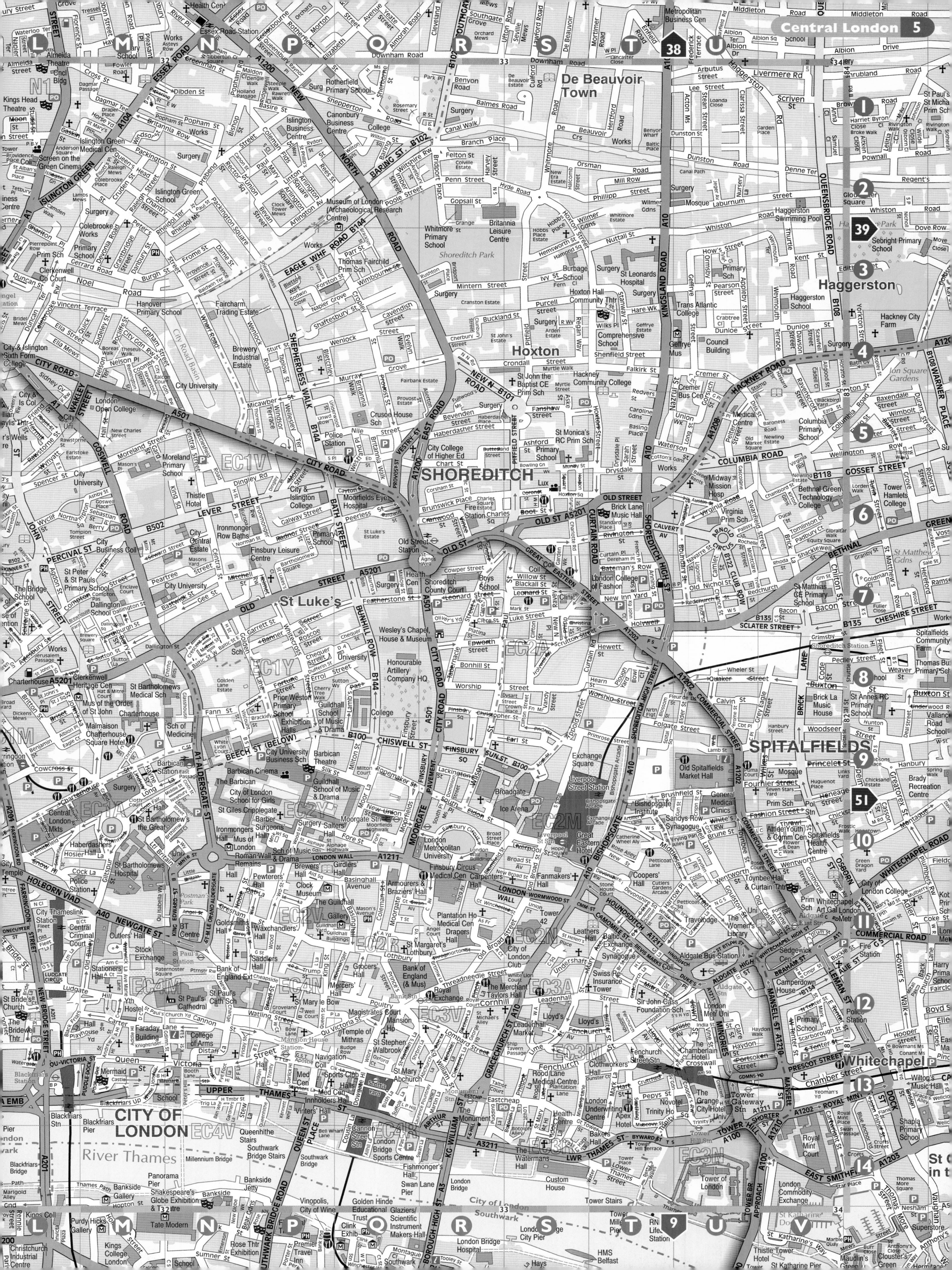
De Beauvoir Town
Haggerston
Hoxton
SHOREDITCH
St Luke's
SPITALFIELDS
Whitechapel
CITY OF LONDON
River Thames
EC1V
EC1Y
EC2A
EC2M
EC2Y
EC2V
EC2R
EC2N
EC3A
EC3V
EC3M
EC3R
EC3N
EC4M
EC4N
EC4R
EC4V
EC1A
N1
CITY ROAD
OLD STREET
GOSWELL ROAD
ESSEX ROAD
NEW NORTH ROAD
KINGSLAND ROAD
SHOREDITCH HIGH ST
COMMERCIAL STREET
HACKNEY ROAD
COLUMBIA ROAD
BISHOPSGATE
LONDON WALL
MOORGATE
FINSBURY PAVEMENT
CHISWELL ST
BEECH ST (BELOW)
ALDERSGATE ST
NEWGATE ST
HOLBORN VIAD
FARRINGDON ST
NEW BRIDGE STREET
QUEEN VICTORIA ST
UPPER THAMES ST
LWR THAMES ST
CANNON
GRACECHURCH ST
KING WILLIAM ST
FENCHURCH
LEADENHALL
HOUNDSDITCH
MINORIES
ALDGATE HIGH ST
WHITECHAPEL HIGH ST
WHITECHAPEL ROAD
COMMERCIAL ROAD
MANSELL ST
LEMAN ST
ROYAL MINT ST
EAST SMITHFIELD
TOWER HILL
SOUTHWARK BRIDGE ROAD
BOROUGH HIGH ST
Liverpool Street Station
Old Spitalfields Market Hall
Barbican Theatre
Barbican Cinema
The Barbican
Museum of London
Guildhall
Bank of England (& Mus)
St Paul's Cathedral
The Monument
Tower of London
Tate Modern
Shakespeare's Globe Exhibition & Theatre
Moorfields Eye Hospital
St Bartholomews Hospital
Wesley's Chapel, House & Museum
Honourable Artillery Company HQ
Brick Lane Music Hall
Shoreditch Park
Geffrye Mus
Hackney City Farm
L
M
N
P
Q
R
S
T
U
V
32
33
34
38
39
51
9
1
2
3
4
5
6
7
8
9
10
11
12
13
14

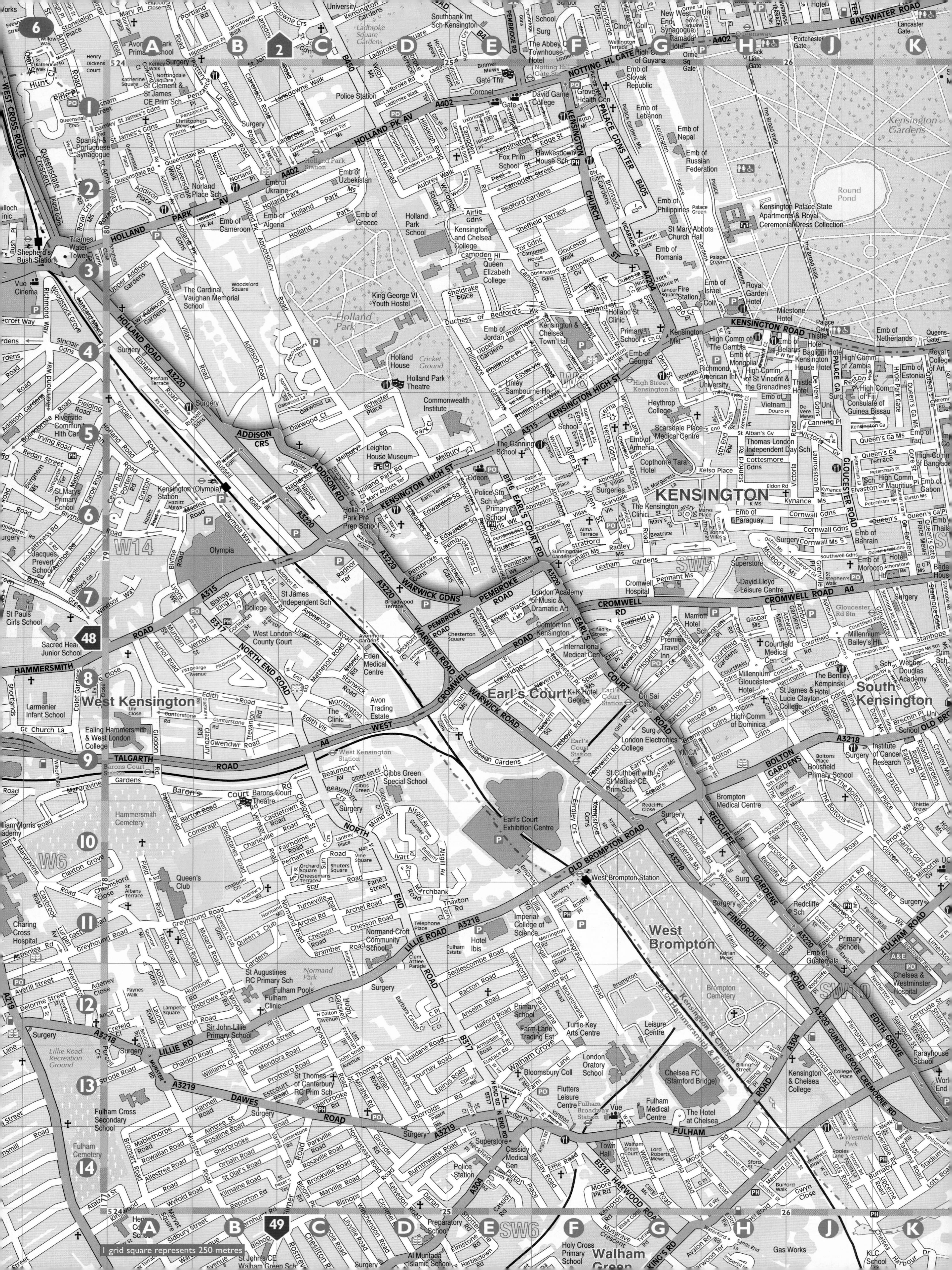
A B C D E F G H J K
1 2 3 4 5 6 7 8 9 10 11 12 13 14
2
48
49
KENSINGTON
Earl's Court
West Kensington
South Kensington
West Brompton
Kensington Gardens
Holland Park
Round Pond
Hammersmith Cemetery
Brompton Cemetery
Fulham Cemetery
W14
W8
W6
SW5
SW6
SW10
BAYSWATER ROAD
NOTTING HL GATE
HOLLAND PK AV
HOLLAND PARK
HOLLAND ROAD
KENSINGTON HIGH ST
KENSINGTON ROAD
KENSINGTON CHURCH ST
CROMWELL ROAD
WARWICK ROAD
EARL'S COURT RD
OLD BROMPTON ROAD
TALGARTH ROAD
NORTH END ROAD
LILLIE ROAD
FULHAM ROAD
REDCLIFFE GARDENS
FINBOROUGH ROAD
DAWES ROAD
GLOUCESTER ROAD
WEST CROSS ROUTE
HAMMERSMITH
Olympia
Kensington (Olympia) Station
Shepherd's Bush Station
Earl's Court Exhibition Centre
West Brompton Station
Chelsea FC (Stamford Bridge)
Commonwealth Institute
Holland Park Theatre
Leighton House Museum
Kensington Palace State Apartments & Royal Ceremonial Dress Collection
Chelsea & Westminster Hospital
Fulham Broadway Station
Barons Court Station
West Kensington Station
High Street Kensington Stn
Gloucester Rd Stn
1 grid square represents 250 metres

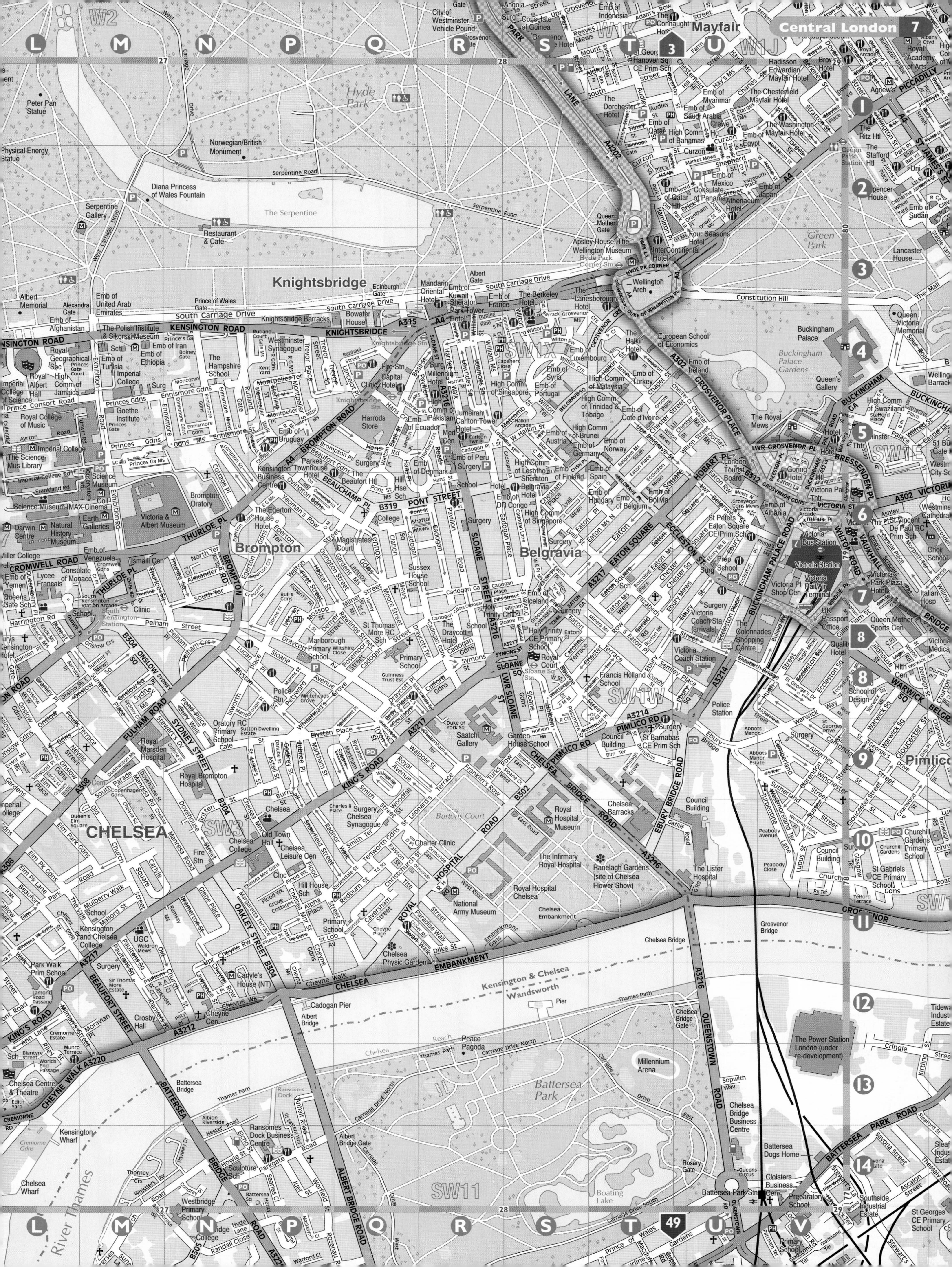
Mayfair
Hyde Park
Knightsbridge
The Serpentine
Diana Princess of Wales Fountain
Serpentine Gallery
Peter Pan Statue
Norwegian/British Monument
Albert Memorial
Royal Albert Hall
Imperial College
Victoria & Albert Museum
Natural History Museum
Brompton Oratory
Brompton
Belgravia
Harrods Store
Wellington Arch
Apsley House, The Wellington Museum
Green Park
Buckingham Palace
Buckingham Palace Gardens
Constitution Hill
Victoria Station
Victoria Coach Station
CHELSEA
Royal Hospital Chelsea
National Army Museum
Chelsea Physic Garden
Chelsea Barracks
Ranelagh Gardens (site of Chelsea Flower Show)
Saatchi Gallery
Battersea Park
Peace Pagoda
Millennium Arena
The Power Station London (under re-development)
Battersea Dogs Home
Chelsea Bridge
Albert Bridge
Battersea Bridge
River Thames
Kensington & Chelsea
Wandsworth
KENSINGTON ROAD
KNIGHTSBRIDGE
BROMPTON ROAD
CROMWELL ROAD
SLOANE STREET
KING'S ROAD
FULHAM ROAD
CHELSEA EMBANKMENT
CHEYNE WALK
GROSVENOR PLACE
PICCADILLY
PARK LANE
BUCKINGHAM PALACE ROAD
QUEENSTOWN ROAD
BATTERSEA PARK ROAD
ALBERT BRIDGE ROAD
SW1X
SW1W
SW3
SW11
W1K
W1J
W2
Pimlico

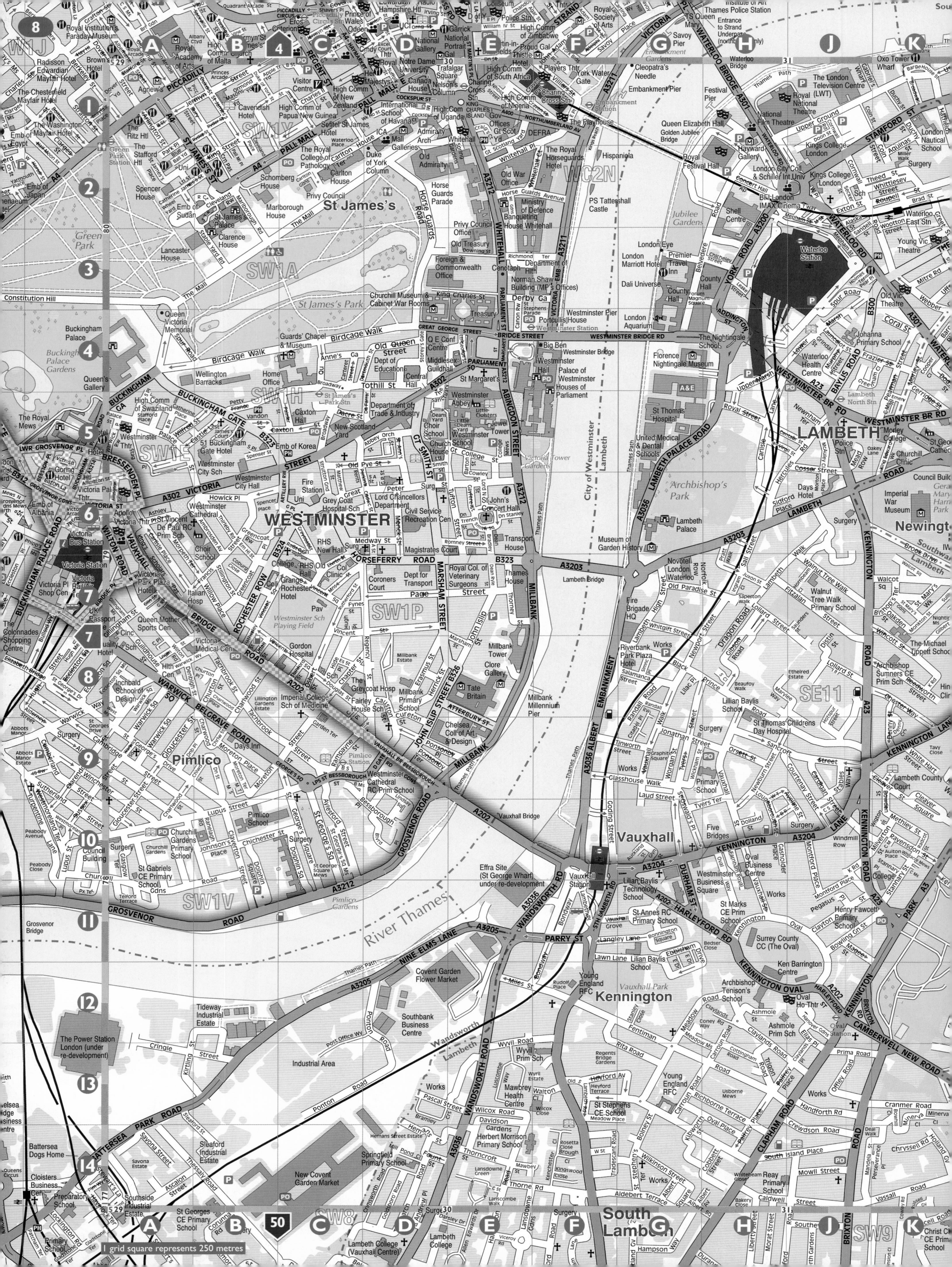

4
50
A
B
C
D
E
F
G
H
J
K
1
2
3
4
5
6
7
8
9
10
11
12
13
14
W1J
SW1Y
WC2N
SW1A
SW1H
SW1E
SW1P
SW1V
SE11
SW8
SW9
St James's
Green Park
St James's Park
Buckingham Palace
Buckingham Palace Gardens
Piccadilly
Pall Mall
Regent St
Trafalgar Square
Whitehall
Strand
Victoria Embankment
Waterloo Bridge
Westminster Bridge
Lambeth Bridge
Vauxhall Bridge
Grosvenor Bridge
River Thames
Westminster
Lambeth
Pimlico
Vauxhall
Kennington
South Lambeth
Newington
Victoria Station
Waterloo Station
Charing Cross Stn
Vauxhall Station
Houses of Parliament
Westminster Abbey
Big Ben
London Eye
Tate Britain
Imperial War Museum
Lambeth Palace
Archbishop's Park
Surrey County CC (The Oval)
The Power Station London (under re-development)
New Covent Garden Market
Covent Garden Flower Market
Battersea Dogs Home
Nine Elms Lane
Wandsworth Road
Kennington Lane
Kennington Road
Kennington Oval
Harleyford Rd
Camberwell New Road
Clapham Road
Grosvenor Road
Millbank
Horseferry Road
Vauxhall Bridge Road
Belgrave Road
Warwick Way
Albert Embankment
Lambeth Palace Road
Westminster Bridge Rd
Lambeth Road
Battersea Park Road
1 grid square represents 250 metres

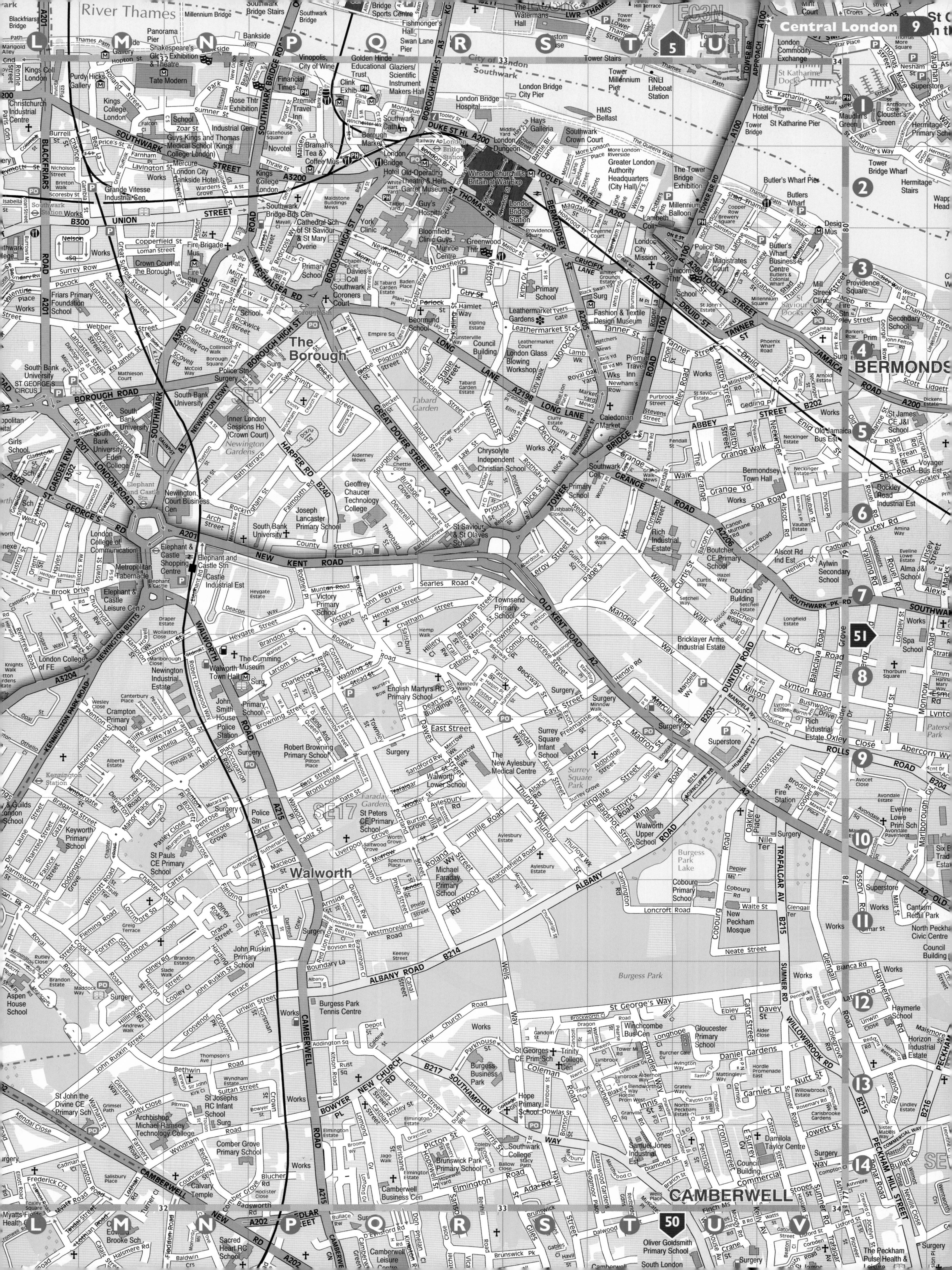
River Thames
City of London
Southwark
The Borough
SE1
BERMONDSEY
SE17
Walworth
CAMBERWELL
Tate Modern
Shakespeare's Globe Exhibition & Theatre
Southwark Cathedral
London Bridge Station
London Dungeon
Winston Churchill's Britain at War Exp
City Hall
HMS Belfast
Tower Bridge
Guy's Hospital
Borough Market
Elephant and Castle Stn
Elephant & Castle Shopping Centre
Imperial War Museum
Cuming Museum
Walworth Town Hall
Burgess Park
Burgess Park Lake
Fashion & Textile Design Museum
Southwark Bridge Road
Borough High St
Blackfriars Road
Southwark Street
Union Street
Borough Road
Great Dover Street
Long Lane
Tower Bridge Road
Jamaica Road
Abbey Street
Grange Road
New Kent Road
Old Kent Road
Walworth Road
Kennington Park Road
Camberwell Road
Albany Road
Southampton Way
Peckham Hill Street
Trafalgar Av
Tooley Street
Bermondsey St
St George's Way
Wells Way
Camberwell Business Cen
Oliver Goldsmith Primary School
L
M
N
P
Q
R
S
T
U
V
1
2
3
4
5
6
7
8
9
10
11
12
13
14
5
50
51

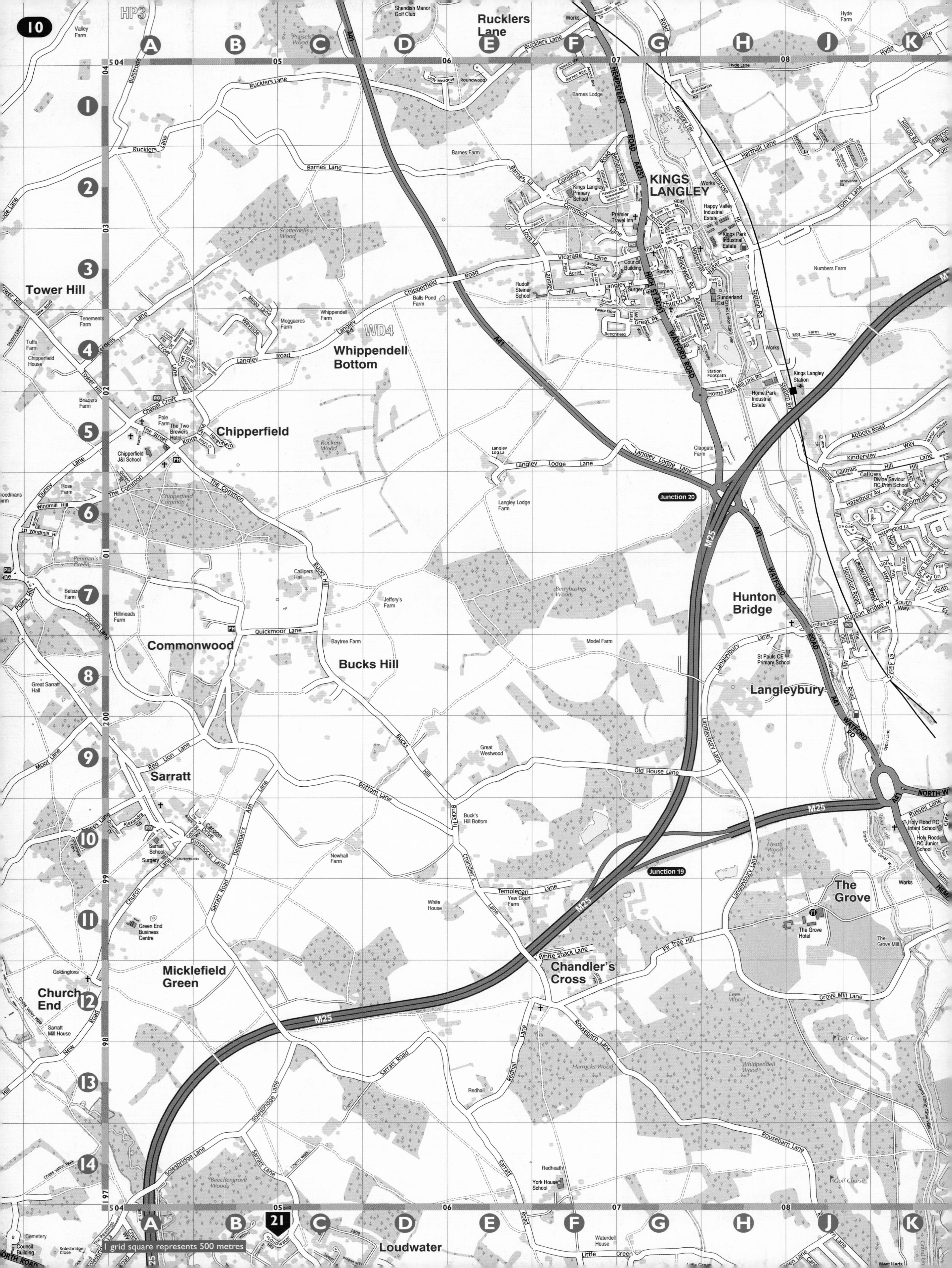

HP3
WD4
A
B
C
D
E
F
G
H
J
K
1
2
3
4
5
6
7
8
9
10
11
12
13
14
504
05
06
07
08
04
03
02
01
200
99
98
97
21
Valley Farm
Shendish Manor Golf Club
Rucklers Lane
Praisels Wood
Works
Hyde Farm
Hyde Lane
Rucklers Lane
Lady Meadow
Roundwood
Abbots Rise
Barnes Rise
Barnes Lodge
HEMPSTEAD ROAD
Railway Ter
Woodlands Rd
Barnes Farm
Barnes Lane
Hartnall Lane
Grand Union Canal
Coniston Road
Kings Langley Primary School
KINGS LANGLEY
Works
Happy Valley Industrial Estate
Kings Park Industrial Estate
Premier Travel Inn
Common Lane
Love La
Tom's Lane
Scatterdells Wood
Vicarage Lane
Council Building
Surgery
Waterside
Water La
Numbers Farm
Tower Hill
Tenements Farm
Chipperfield Road
Balls Pond Farm
Rudolf Steiner School
Langley Hill
HIGH ST
Sunderland Estate
Station Rd
Whippendell Farm
Meggacres Farm
Wayside
Beechfield
WATFORD ROAD
Egg Farm Lane
Tuffs Farm
Chipperfield House
Langley Road
Whippendell Bottom
A41
Station Footpath
Home Park Mill Link Rd
Home Park Industrial Estate
Kings Langley Station
Braziers Farm
Chapel Croft
Pale Farm
The Two Brewers Hotel
Chipperfield
The Street
Rockery Wood
Abbots Road
Chipperfield J&I School
Langley Lodge Lane
Clapgate Farm
Kindersley Way
Gallows Hill
Divine Saviour RC Prim School
Rose Farm
The Common
Chipperfield Common
Junction 20
Hazelbury Av
Broomfield Rise
Windmill Hill
Langley Lodge Farm
M25
A41
Penman's Green
Callipers Hall
Bucks Hill
Berrybushes Wood
Hamilton Road
Belsize Farm
Jeffery's Farm
Hunton Bridge
Hillmeads Farm
Plough Lane
Quickmoor Lane
Bridge Road
Baytree Farm
Model Farm
Commonwood
Bucks Hill
St Pauls CE Primary School
Mill Road
Great Sarratt Hall
Langleybury
Langleybury Lane
Great Westwood
Moor Lane
Red Lion Lane
Old House Lane
Sarratt
Bottom Lane
NORTH W
Buck's Hill Bottom
Deadman's Ash Lane
Russell Lane
Holy Rood RC Infant School
Holy Rood RC Junior School
Alexandra Rd
Sarratt School
Surgery
Dimmocks Lane
Newhall Farm
Chandler's Lane
Heath Wood
Junction 19
Works
Templepan Lane
Yew Court Farm
White House
The Grove
Church Lane
Green End Business Centre
Sarratt Road
The Grove Hotel
The Grove Mill
White Shack Lane
Fir Tree Hill
Goldingtons
Micklefield Green
Chandler's Cross
Lees Wood
Church End
Grove Mill Lane
Chess Valley Walk
Sarratt Mill House
New Road
Rousebarn Lane
Golf Course
Sarratt Road
Harrocks Wood
Whippendell Wood
Redhall Lane
Redhall
Solesbridge Lane
Cherry Walk
Sarratt Lane
Beechengrove Wood
Redheath
York House School
Grand Union Canal Walk
Cemetery
Council Building
Solesbridge Close
Loudwater
Waterdell House
Little Green
West Herts
1 grid square represents 500 metres

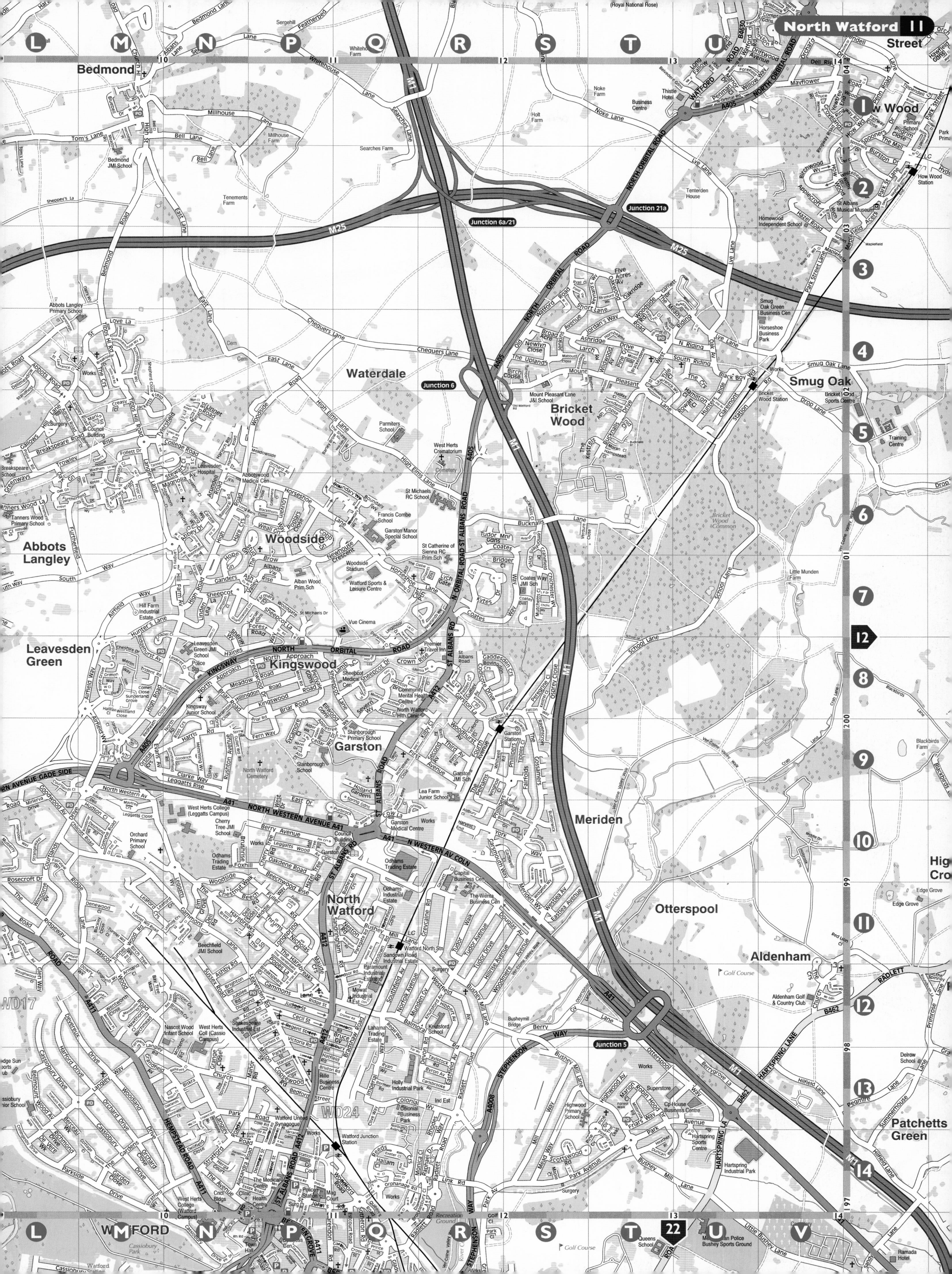
Bedmond
Waterdale
Bricket Wood
Smug Oak
How Wood
Abbots Langley
Leavesden Green
Woodside
Kingswood
Garston
North Watford
Meriden
Otterspool
Aldenham
Patchetts Green
Watford
Junction 6a/21
Junction 21a
Junction 6
Junction 5
M25
M1
A405
A41
A412
A411
A4008
B462
North Orbital Road
North Western Avenue
St Albans Road
Hempstead Road
Stephenson Way
Radlett Road
Hartspring Lane
Chequers Lane
High Elms Lane
Bucknalls Lane
School Lane
Smug Oak Lane
Park Street Lane
Bushey Mill Lane
Berrygrove La
Searches Farm
Tenements Farm
Holt Farm
Noke Farm
Thistle Hotel
Business Centre
Tenterden House
St Albans Musical Museum
Homewood Independent School
How Wood Station
Bricket Wood Station
Bricket Wood Common
Training Centre
Little Munden Farm
Blackbirds Farm
Mount Pleasant Lane J&I School
West Herts Crematorium
Parmiters School
St Michaels RC School
Francis Combe School
Garston Manor Special School
St Catherine of Sienna RC Prim Sch
Woodside Stadium
Watford Sports & Leisure Centre
Alban Wood Prim Sch
Vue Cinema
Coates Way JMI Sch
Leavesden Green JMI School
Kingsway Junior School
Stanborough Primary School
Stanborough School
North Watford Cemetery
Garston Station
Garston JMI Sch
Lea Farm Junior School
Garston Medical Centre
West Herts College (Leggatts Campus)
Cherry Tree JMI School
Orchard Primary School
Odhams Trading Estate
Odhams Industrial Estate
Capital Business Cen
The Wenta Business Cen
Beechfield JMI School
Watford North Stn
Sandown Road Industrial Estate
Paramount Industrial Estate
Mowat Industrial Est
Laham Trading Estate
Knutsford School
Holly Industrial Park
Colonial Business Park
Nascot Wood Infant School
West Herts Coll (Cassio Campus)
Shakespeare Industrial Est
Watford Junction Station
Watford United Synagogue
Highwood Primary School
Superstore
Cp House Business Centre
Hartspring Sports Centre
Hartspring Industrial Park
Aldenham Golf & Country Club
Golf Course
Delrow School
Edge Grove
Bushey Mill Bridge
Queens School
Metropolitan Police Bushey Sports Ground
Ramada Hotel
Recreation Ground
Cassiobury Park
WD17
WD24

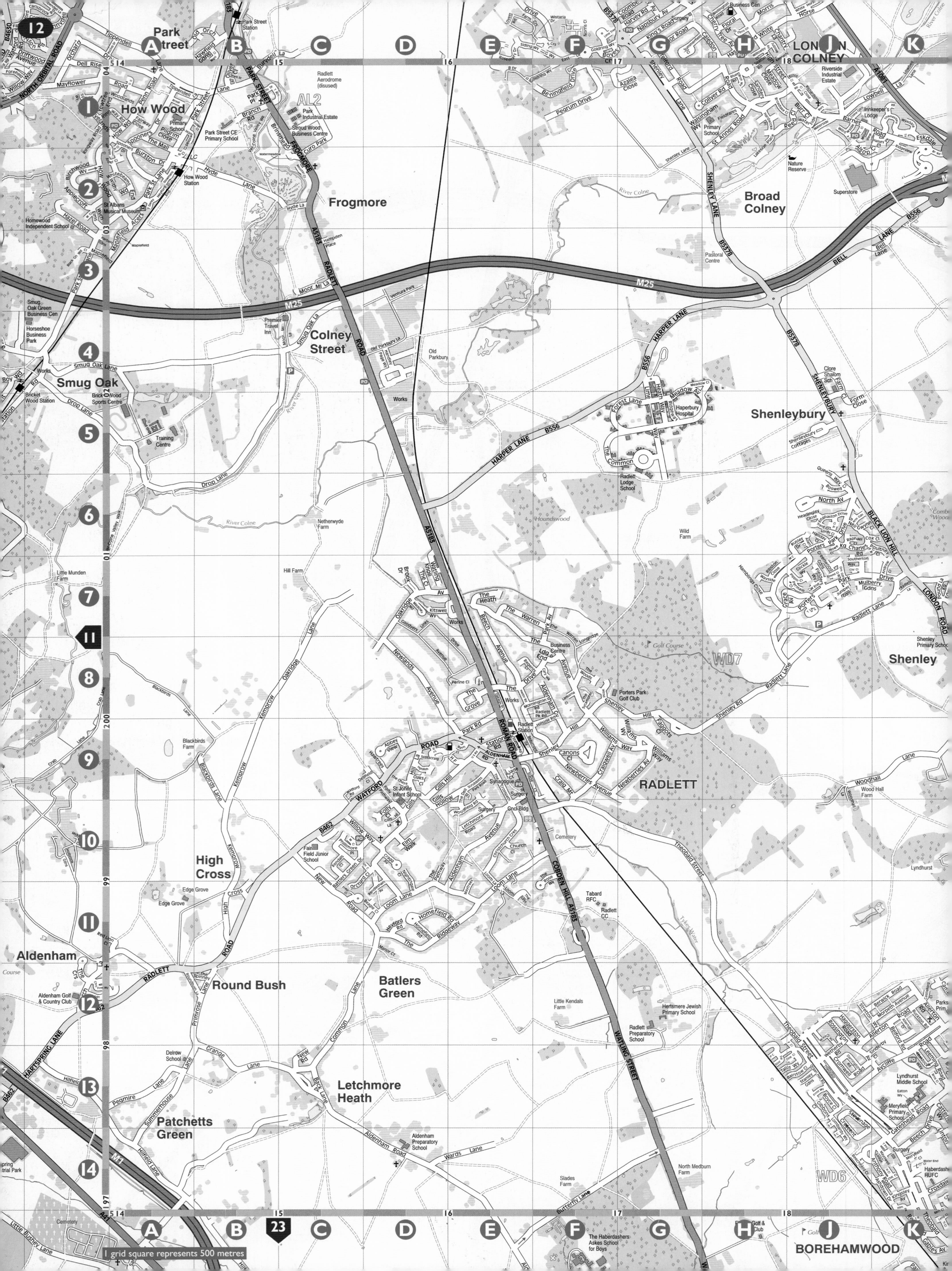
12
11
23
Park Street
How Wood
Frogmore
Colney Street
Smug Oak
London Colney
Broad Colney
Shenleybury
Shenley
RADLETT
High Cross
Aldenham
Round Bush
Batlers Green
Letchmore Heath
Patchetts Green
BOREHAMWOOD
AL2
WD7
WD6
M25
M1
A5183
B5378
B556
B462
A1081
NORTH ORBITAL ROAD
PARK STREET
FROGMORE
RADLETT ROAD
WATLING STREET
COBDEN HILL
HARPER LANE
SHENLEY LANE
SHENLEYBURY
BLACK LION HILL
LONDON ROAD
WATFORD ROAD
RADLETT ROAD
HARTSPRING LANE
Radlett Aerodrome (disused)
Park Street Station
How Wood Station
Bricket Wood Station
Radlett Station
River Colne
River Ver
Tykes Water
Porters Park Golf Club
Haperbury Hospital
Radlett Lodge School
Aldenham Golf & Country Club
Aldenham Preparatory School
Hertsmere Jewish Primary School
Radlett Preparatory School
The Haberdashers Askes School for Boys
Lyndhurst Middle School
Meryfield Primary School
Shenley Primary School
1 grid square represents 500 metres

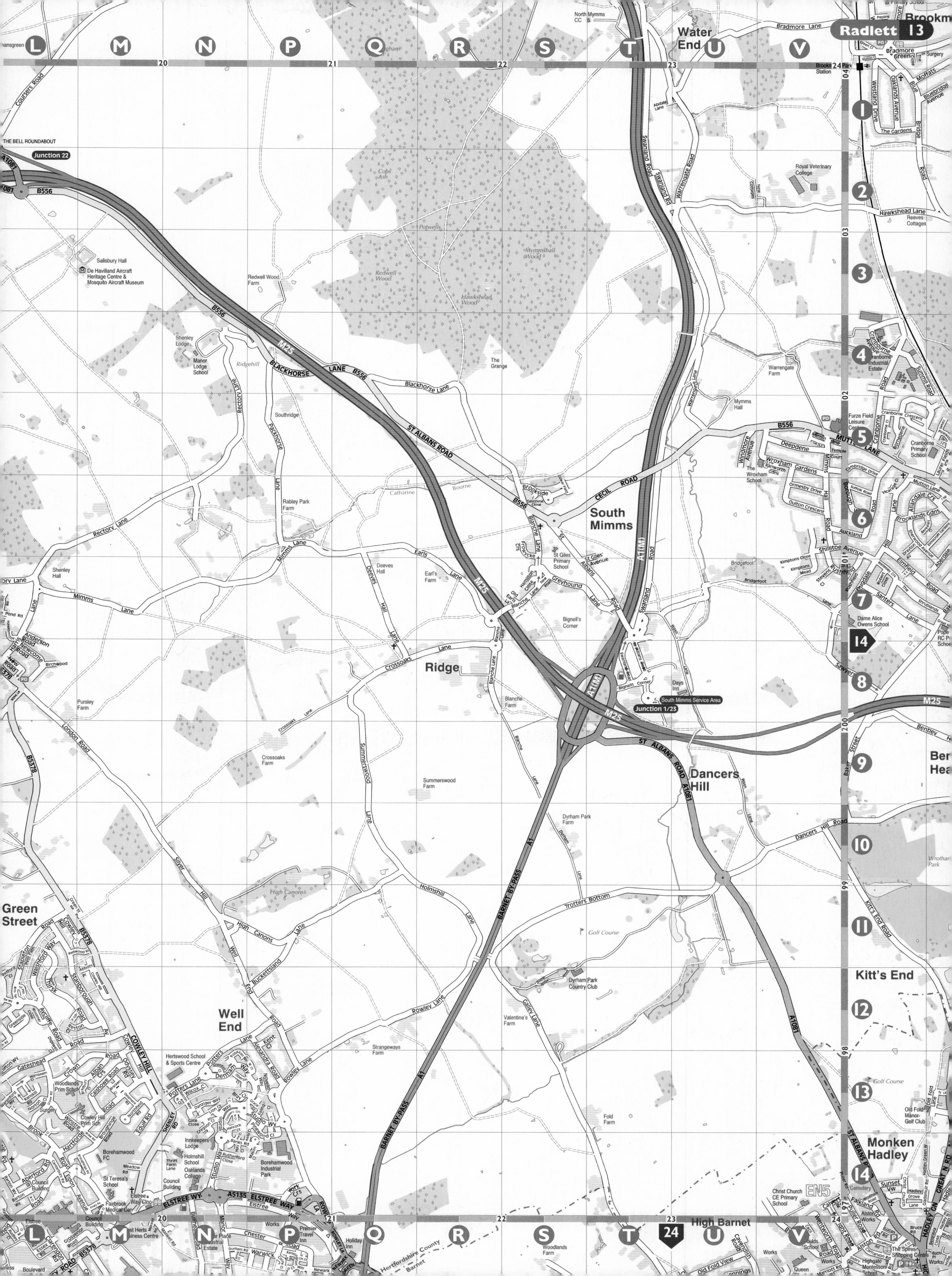
Radlett 13
L
M
N
P
Q
R
S
T
U
V
20
21
22
23
24
Water End
North Mymms CC
Bradmore Lane
Brookmans Park Station
Bradmore Green
Surgery
Moffats
Bluebridge Avenue
Oaklands Avenue
Westland Drive
The Gardens
Bridge Road
Abdale Lane
Swanland Road
Warrengate Road
Royal Veterinary College
Hawkshead Lane
Reeves Cottages
THE BELL ROUNDABOUT
Junction 22
A1081
B556
Cobs Ash
Potwells
Mymmshall Wood
Redwell Wood
Hawkshead Wood
Salisbury Hall
De Havilland Aircraft Heritage Centre & Mosquito Aircraft Museum
Redwell Wood Farm
Mymmshall Brook
Shenley Lodge
Manor Lodge School
Ridgehill
BLACKHORSE LANE
M25
Blackhorse Lane
The Grange
Warrengate Farm
Warrengate Lane
Mymms Hall
Cranborne Avenue
Cranborne Industrial Estate
Summit Road
Rectory Lane
Packhorse Lane
Southridge
ST ALBANS ROAD
Furze Field Leisure Centre
Cranborne Road
Cranborne Crescent
Cranborne Primary School
MUTTON LANE
Deepdene
Windmore Avenue
Wroxham Gardens
The Wroxham School
Mimms Hall Road
Cambridge Drive
Ormesby Drive
Oulton Crescent
Borough Road
Auckland Road
Mutton Lane
Allandale Crs
Brooklands Gdns
CECIL ROAD
Brookside
South Mimms
A1(M)
Catharine Bourne
Rabley Park Farm
Rectory Lane
Mimms Lane
Earls Lane
Deeves Hall
Deeves Hall Lane
Earl's Farm
Blanche Lane
St Giles Primary School
St Giles Avenue
Greyhound Lane
Bignell's Corner
Shillitoe Avenue
Rushfield
Bridgefoot
Kimptons Close
Kimptons Mead
Dugdale Hill Lane
Santers Lane
Dame Alice Owens School
Shenley Hall
Mimms Lane
Anderson Road
Newcome Road
Birchwood
Crossoaks Lane
Ridge
Sawyers Lane
14
Days Inn
South Mimms Service Area
Junction 1/23
Blanche Farm
Pursley Farm
London Road
B5378
Crossoaks Farm
Summerswood Lane
Summerswood Farm
ST ALBANS ROAD
Dancers Hill
A1081
Bentley Heath
Baker Street
Wash Lane
Dyrham Park Farm
Dyrham Lane
Dancers Hill Road
Wrotham Park
A1
BARNET BY-PASS
Silver Hill
High Canons
Holmshill Lane
Trotters Bottom
Golf Course
Kitt's End Road
Green Street
High Canons Lane
Well End
Buckettsland Lane
Dyrham Park Country Club
Kitt's End
Well End Road
Rowley Lane
Galley Lane
Valentine's Farm
Hertswood School & Sports Centre
Potters Lane
Alexandra Road
Strangeways Farm
COWLEY HILL
Woodlands Prim Sch
Cowley Hill Prim Sch
Golf Course
Old Fold Manor Golf Club
Fold Farm
Monken Hadley
Borehamwood FC
Innkeepers Lodge
Holmshill School
Oaklands College
Borehamwood Industrial Park
St Teresa's School
Council Building
Fairbrook Medical Ctr
ELSTREE WAY
A5135
Elstree Way
Christ Church CE Primary School
EN5
High Barnet
24
Hertfordshire County
Barnet
Holiday Inn
Premier Travel Inn
Chester
Warwick
Woodlands Farm
Wentworth Road
Cavendish Road
Old Fold View
Works
Queen
The Spires Shopping Centre
Highgate Montessori School
Hadley Green
Sunset Vw
GREAT N RD
Cemetery
Falkland Rd
Alston Rd
Lucan Rd
Carnarvon Rd
Boulevard
Newark

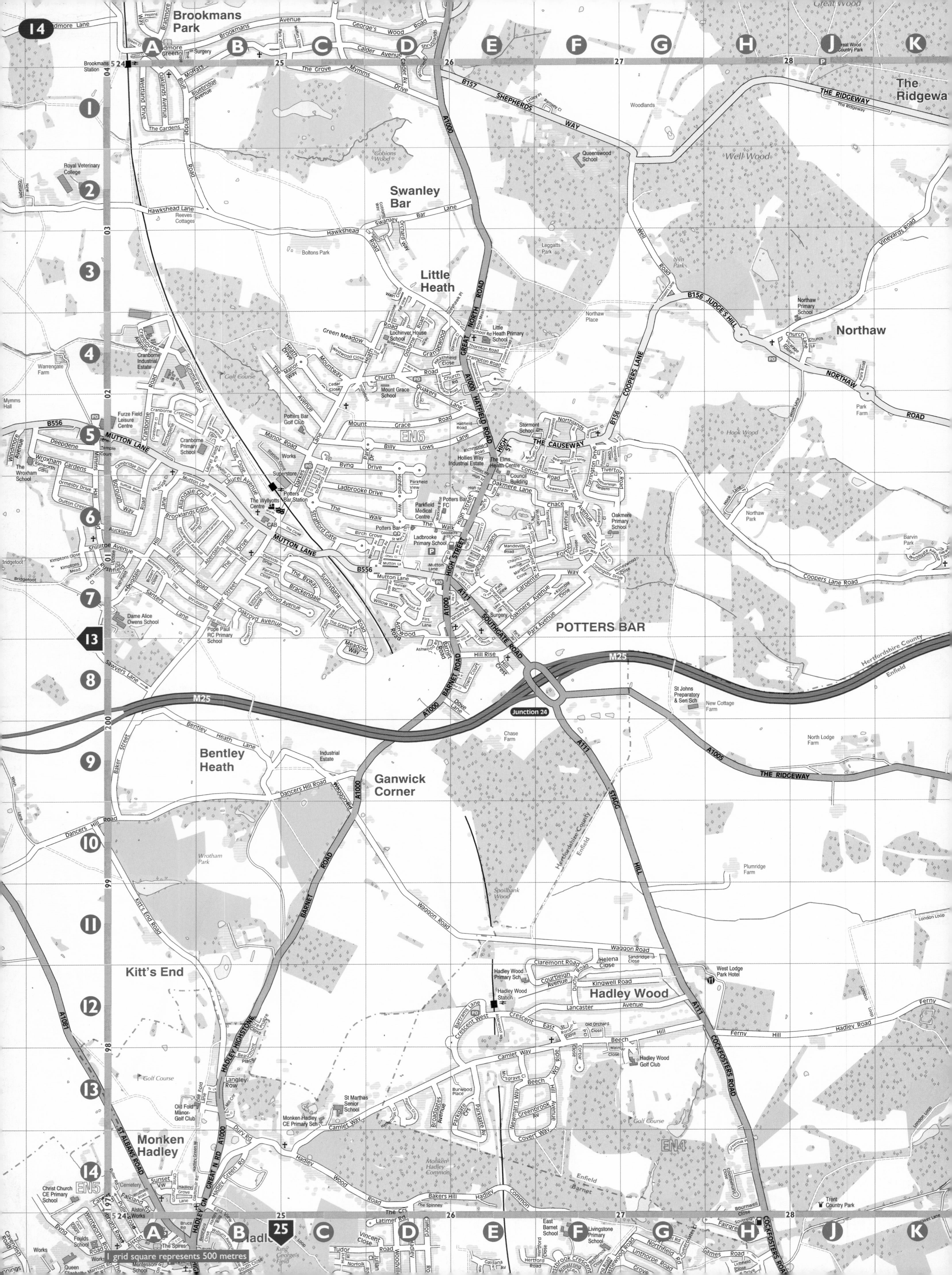
14
Brookmans Park
Brookmans Park Station
A
B
C
D
E
F
G
H
J
K
24
25
26
27
28
The Ridgeway
THE RIDGEWAY
Great Wood
Great Wood Country Park
B157 SHEPHERDS WAY
Woodlands
Queenswood School
Well Wood
Gobions Wood
Royal Veterinary College
Swanley Bar
Swanley Bar Lane
Hawkshead Lane
Hawkshead Road
Reeves Cottages
Boltons Park
Leggatts Park
Nyn Park
Little Heath
GREAT NORTH ROAD
A1000 HATFIELD ROAD
B156 JUDGE'S HILL
COOPERS LANE
Northaw Place
Northaw Primary School
Northaw
NORTHAW ROAD
Park Farm
Hook Wood
Vineyards Road
Warrengate Farm
Mymms Hall
Cranborne Industrial Estate
Golf Course
Green Meadow
Lochinver House School
Little Heath Primary School
Mount Grace School
Potters Bar Golf Club
Furze Field Leisure Centre
B556 MUTTON LANE
Deepdene
Wroxham Gardens
The Wroxham School
Cranborne Primary School
Stormont School
THE CAUSEWAY
Hollies Way Industrial Estate
The Elms Health Centre
Council Building
Oakmere Lane
Oakmere Primary School
Tiverton Road
Northaw Park
Barvin Park
Coopers Lane Road
Potters Bar Station
The Wyllyotts Centre
Parkfield Medical Centre
Potters Bar FC
Ladbrooke Primary School
Ladbrooke Drive
Mount Grace Road
Billy Lows Lane
EN6
HIGH STREET
SOUTHGATE ROAD
POTTERS BAR
Dame Alice Owens School
Pope Paul RC Primary School
Oakroyd Avenue
Sawyers Lane
13
M25
Junction 24
Hertfordshire County
Enfield
St Johns Preparatory & Sen Sch
New Cottage Farm
Chase Farm
North Lodge Farm
A1005 THE RIDGEWAY
Bentley Heath
Bentley Heath Lane
Baker Street
Industrial Estate
Dancers Hill Road
Ganwick Corner
A1000 BARNET ROAD
Wrotham Park
Spoilbank Wood
Plumridge Farm
A111 STAGG HILL
Waggon Road
Kitt's End Road
Kitt's End
A1081 ST ALBANS ROAD
Hadley Wood Primary Sch
Hadley Wood Station
Claremont Road
Kingwell Road
Hadley Wood
Lancaster Avenue
Crescent West
Crescent East
Ferny Hill
Hadley Road
West Lodge Park Hotel
London Loop
A111 COCKFOSTERS ROAD
Camlet Way
Beech Hill
Hadley Wood Golf Club
HADLEY HIGHSTONE
Langley Row
Old Fold Manor Golf Club
St Marthas Senior School
Monken Hadley CE Primary Sch
Monken Hadley
Monken Hadley Common
Covert Way
Greenbrook Av
EN4
EN5
Christ Church CE Primary School
Trent Country Park
Bakers Hill
Hadley Common
Livingstone Primary School
East Barnet School
1 grid square represents 500 metres

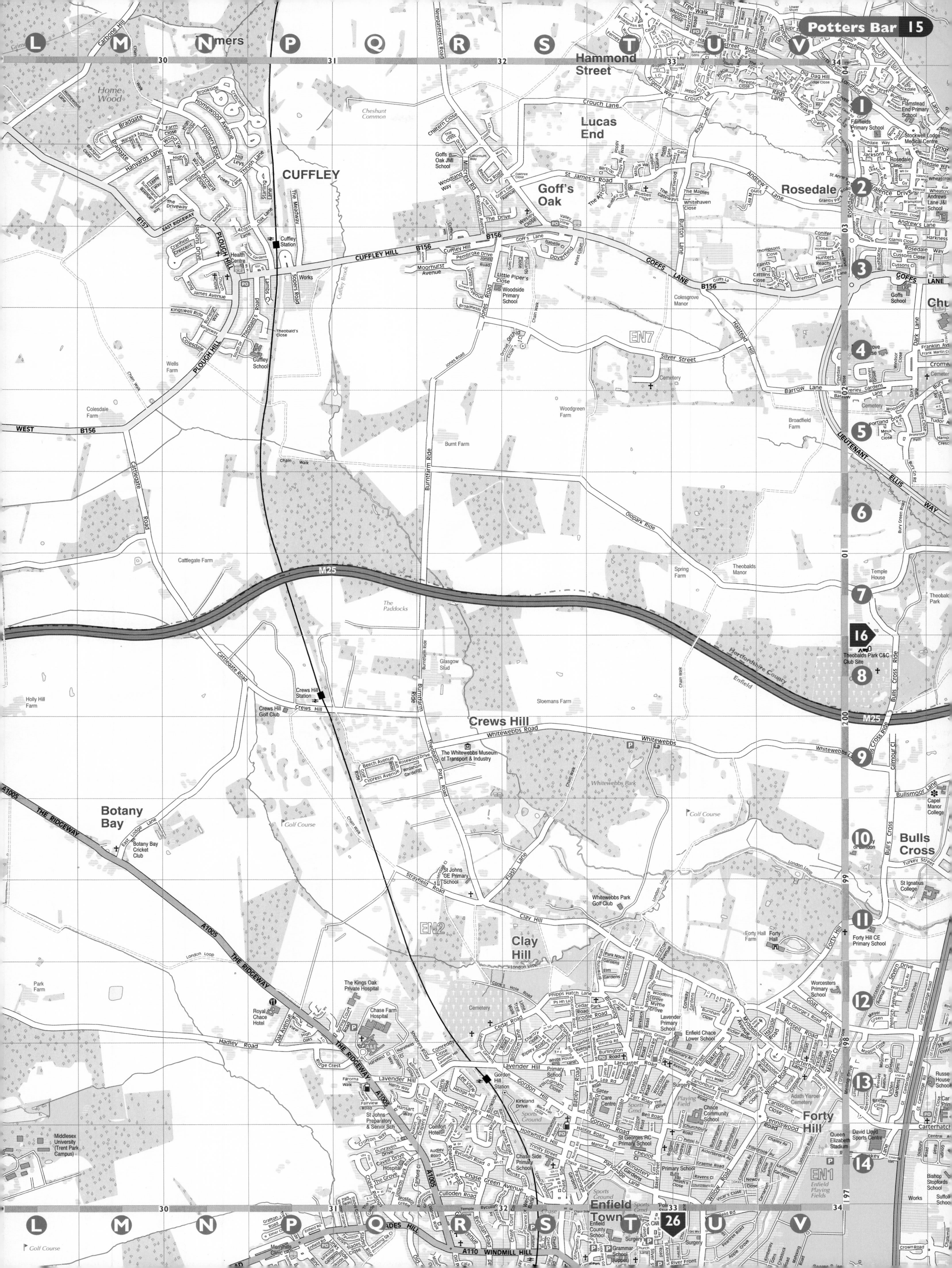
L
M
N
P
Q
R
S
T
U
V
Hammond Street
Lucas End
CUFFLEY
Goff's Oak
Rosedale
Home Wood
Cheshunt Common
Crouch Lane
St James's Road
Cuffley Station
CUFFLEY HILL
B156
GOFFS LANE
PLOUGH HILL
EAST RIDGEWAY
B157
Silver Street
EN7
Barrow Lane
LIEUTENANT ELLIS WAY
Colesdale Farm
Wells Farm
WEST
Burnt Farm
Woodgreen Farm
Broadfield Farm
Oldpark Ride
Cattlegate Road
Cattlegate Farm
Spring Farm
Theobalds Manor
Temple House
M25
The Paddocks
Glasgow Stud
Crews Hill Station
Crews Hill
Crews Hill Golf Club
Holly Hill Farm
Sloemans Farm
Whitewebbs Road
The Whitewebbs Museum of Transport & Industry
Whitewebbs Park
Golf Course
Botany Bay
Botany Bay Cricket Club
THE RIDGEWAY
A1005
Bulls Cross
Capel Manor College
St Ignatius College
Whitewebbs Park Golf Club
Clay Hill
EN2
Forty Hall Farm
Forty Hall
Forty Hill CE Primary School
Park Farm
Royal Chace Hotel
The Kings Oak Private Hospital
Chase Farm Hospital
Hadley Road
Middlesex University (Trent Park Campus)
Gordon Hill Station
Cemetery
Forty Hill
Enfield Town
EN1
Queen Elizabeth Stadium
David Lloyd Sports Centre
A110 WINDMILL HILL
Theobalds Park C&C Club Site
16
26
1
2
3
4
5
6
7
8
9
10
11
12
13
14
30
31
32
33
34

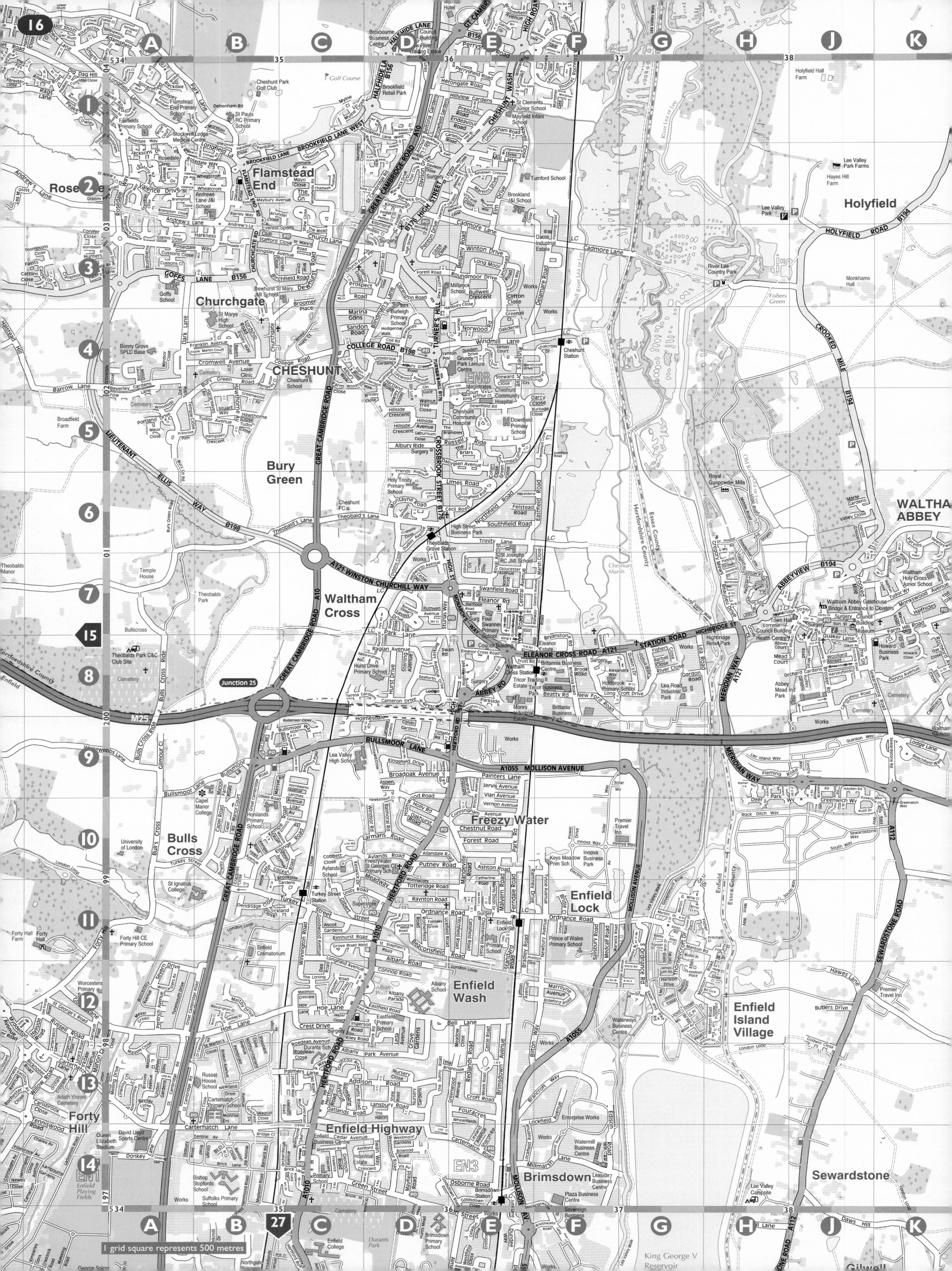

16
A B C D E F G H J K
1 2 3 4 5 6 7 8 9 10 11 12 13 14
15
27
Flamstead End
Churchgate
CHESHUNT
Bury Green
Waltham Cross
Holyfield
WALTHAM ABBEY
Bulls Cross
Freezy Water
Enfield Lock
Enfield Wash
Enfield Island Village
Forty Hill
Enfield Highway
Brimsdown
Sewardstone
EN8
EN3
EN1
GREAT CAMBRIDGE ROAD
A10
M25
Junction 25
A121 WINSTON CHURCHILL WAY
BULLSMOOR LANE
A1055 MOLLISON AVENUE
HERTFORD ROAD
A1010
CROOKED MILE
B194
HOLYFIELD ROAD
SEWARDSTONE ROAD
A112
MERIDIAN WAY
ELEANOR CROSS ROAD
STATION ROAD
COLLEGE ROAD
B198
LIEUTENANT ELLIS WAY
BROOKFIELD LANE WEST
GOFFS LANE
B156
HIGH STREET
B176
Cheshunt Station
Theobalds Grove Station
Waltham Cross Station
Turkey Street Station
Enfield Lock Station
Brimsdown Station
River Lee Country Park
Lee Valley Park
Royal Gunpowder Mills
King George V Reservoir
1 grid square represents 500 metres

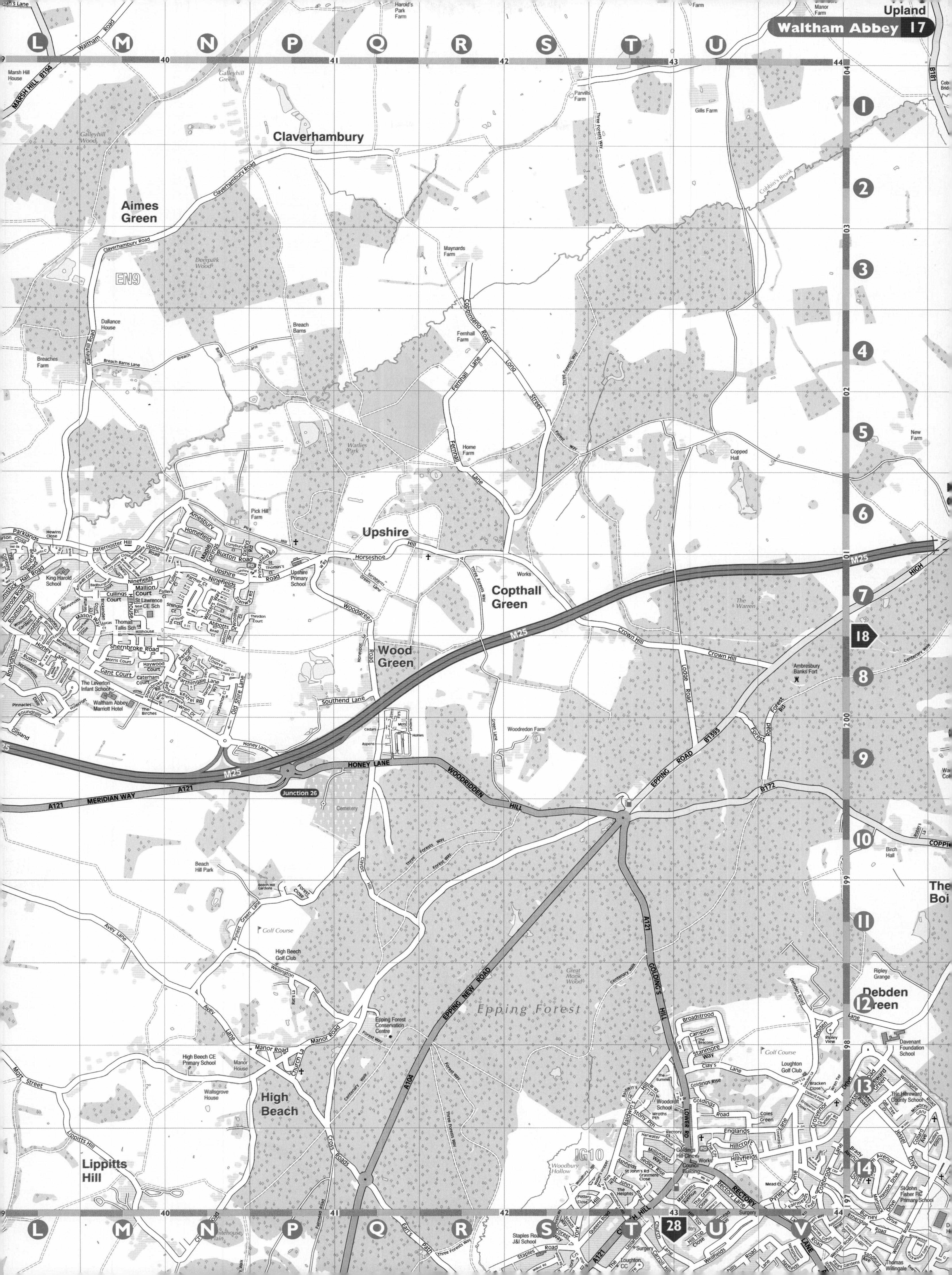
Upland
Claverhambury
Aimes Green
EN9
Deerpark Wood
Galleyhill Wood
Galleyhill Green
Marsh Hill House
MARSH HILL B194
Waltham Road
Claverhambury Road
Galleyhill Road
Dallance House
Breaches Farm
Breach Barns Lane
Breach Barns
Parvills Farm
Gills Farm
Cobbin's Brook
Three Forests Way
Maynards Farm
Cobbinsend Road
Fernhall Farm
Fernhall Lane
Long Street
Home Farm
Warlies Park
Copped Hall
New Farm
Pick Hill Farm
Upshire
Horseshoe Hill
Upshire Primary School
Copthall Green
Works
The Warren
Crown Hill
Wood Green
Woodgreen Road
Paternoster Hill
Ninefields
King Harold School
Mallion Court
Cullings Court
St Lawrence CE Sch
Thomas Tallis Sch
Shernbroke Road
Honey Lane
The Leverton Infant School
Waltham Abbey Marriott Hotel
Southend Lane
Lodge Road
Ambresbury Banks Fort
Woodredon Farm
Green Lane
EPPING ROAD B1393
Forest Road
M25
Junction 26
A121 MERIDIAN WAY
HONEY LANE
WOODRIDDEN HILL
Cemetery
B172
Birch Hall
COPPICE
Beach Hill Park
Beech Hill Gardens
Forest Close
Avey Lane
Golf Course
High Beech Golf Club
Wellington Hill
Great Monk Wood
Epping Forest
EPPING NEW ROAD
A104
A121 GOLDING'S HILL
Epping Forest Conservation Centre
Manor Road
High Beech CE Primary School
Manor House
Church La
High Beach
Wallsgrove House
Mott Street
Lippitts Hill
Cross Roads
Debden Road
Ripley Grange
Debden Green
Davenant Foundation School
Broadstrood
Campions
Stanmore Way
Loughton Golf Club
Clay's Lane
Goldings Rise
Woodcroft School
Coles Green
Englands
Hillcroft
Hillyfields
IG10
Woodbury Hollow
Council Building
Rectory Lane
LOWER RD
CHURCH HILL
The Hereward County School
St John Fisher RC Primary School
Staples Road J&I School
Earl's Path
28
18

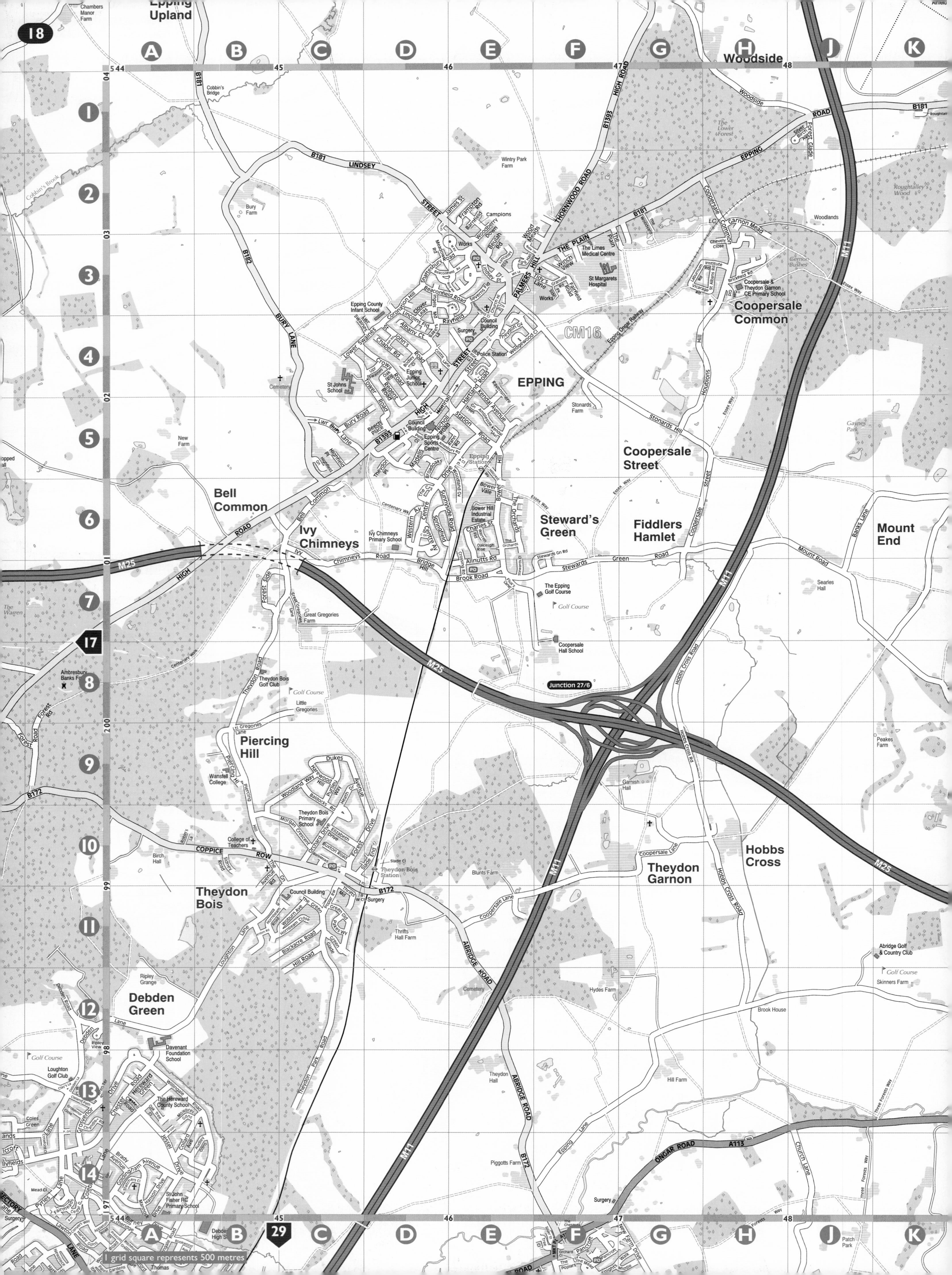
18
17
29
A
B
C
D
E
F
G
H
J
K
1
2
3
4
5
6
7
8
9
10
11
12
13
14
Epping Upland
Chambers Manor Farm
Woodside
Cobbin's Bridge
Cobbin's Brook
B181
B1393
B182
B172
M25
M11
A113
Lindsey Street
High Road
Thornwood Road
Bury Lane
Bury Farm
Wintry Park Farm
Campions
The Plain
Palmers Hill
The Limes Medical Centre
St Margarets Hospital
Coopersale Common
Coopersale & Theydon Garnon CE Primary School
Epping Road
Roughtalley's Wood
The Lower Forest
Woodlands
Garnon Bushes
Gaynes Park
Epping County Infant School
Epping Junior School
St Johns School
Council Building
Police Station
Surgery
Cemetery
EPPING
CM16
Epping Ongar Railway
Stonards Farm
Stonards Hill
Epping Sports Centre
Epping Station
New Farm
Bell Common
Ivy Chimneys
Ivy Chimneys Primary School
Coopersale Street
Steward's Green
Fiddlers Hamlet
Mount End
Mount Road
Searles Hall
The Epping Golf Course
Golf Course
Coopersale Hall School
Great Gregories Farm
Junction 27/6
The Warren
Ambresbury Banks Fort
Theydon Bois Golf Club
Little Gregories
Piercing Hill
Wansfell College
Garnish Hall
Peakes Farm
Theydon Bois Primary School
College of Teachers
Birch Hall
Coppice Row
Theydon Bois Station
Blunts Farm
Theydon Bois
Theydon Garnon
Hobbs Cross
Hobbs Cross Road
Coopersale Lane
Thrifts Hall Farm
Abridge Road
Abridge Golf & Country Club
Skinners Farm
Ripley Grange
Debden Green
Hydes Farm
Brook House
Davenant Foundation School
Loughton Golf Club
Theydon Hall
Hill Farm
The Hereward County School
St John Fisher RC Primary School
Piggotts Farm
Ongar Road
Church Lane
Three Forests Way
Surgery
Patch Park
1 grid square represents 500 metres

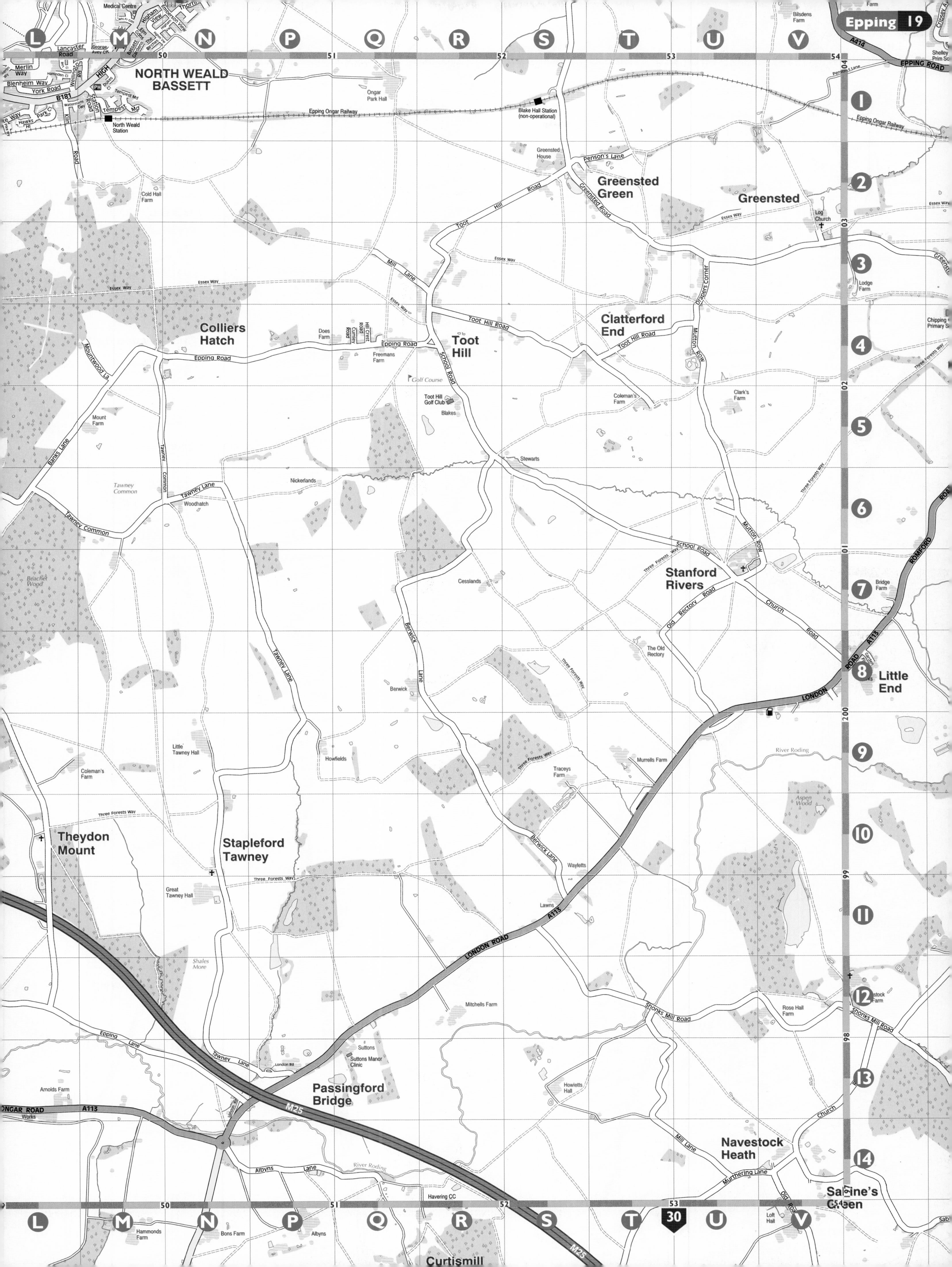
L
M
N
P
Q
R
S
T
U
V
50
51
52
53
54
NORTH WEALD BASSETT
North Weald Station
Epping Ongar Railway
Ongar Park Hall
Blake Hall Station (non-operational)
Medical Centre
Lancaster Road
Merlin Way
Blenheim Way
York Road
B181
HIGH
Station Road
Kiln Road
Tempest Md
Hawks Hl
Park Ct
Bilsdens Farm
A414
EPPING ROAD
Penson's Lane
Shelley Prim Sch
Greensted House
Greensted Green
Greensted Road
Greensted
Log Church
Essex Way
Toot Hill Road
Cold Hall Farm
Mill Lane
Lodge Farm
Chipping Primary S
Drapers Corner
Colliers Hatch
Does Farm
Epping Road
Freemans Farm
Toot Hill
School Road
Clatterford End
Mutton Row
Golf Course
Toot Hill Golf Club
Blakes
Coleman's Farm
Clark's Farm
Mountwood La
Mount Farm
Banks Lane
Three Forests Way
Stewarts
Tawney Common
Tawney Lane
Woodhatch
Nickerlands
Beacher Wood
Cesslands
Stanford Rivers
Old Rectory Road
Church Road
Bridge Farm
ROMFORD ROAD
A113
The Old Rectory
Berwick Lane
Berwick
Little End
LONDON ROAD
Little Tawney Hall
Howfields
Coleman's Farm
Traceys Farm
Murrells Farm
River Roding
Aspen Wood
Theydon Mount
Stapleford Tawney
Great Tawney Hall
Waylets
Lawns
Shales More
Mitchells Farm
Shonks Mill Road
Rose Hall Farm
Suttons
Suttons Manor Clinic
London Rd
Epping Lane
Passingford Bridge
Howletts Hall
Arnolds Farm
ONGAR ROAD
Works
M25
Albyns Lane
Mill Lane
Navestock Heath
Murthering Lane
Church
Havering CC
Saxine's Green
Hammonds Farm
Bons Farm
Albyns
Loft Hall
Old Road
Curtismill
Green
01
02
03
04
200
99
98
97
1
2
3
4
5
6
7
8
9
10
11
12
13
14
30

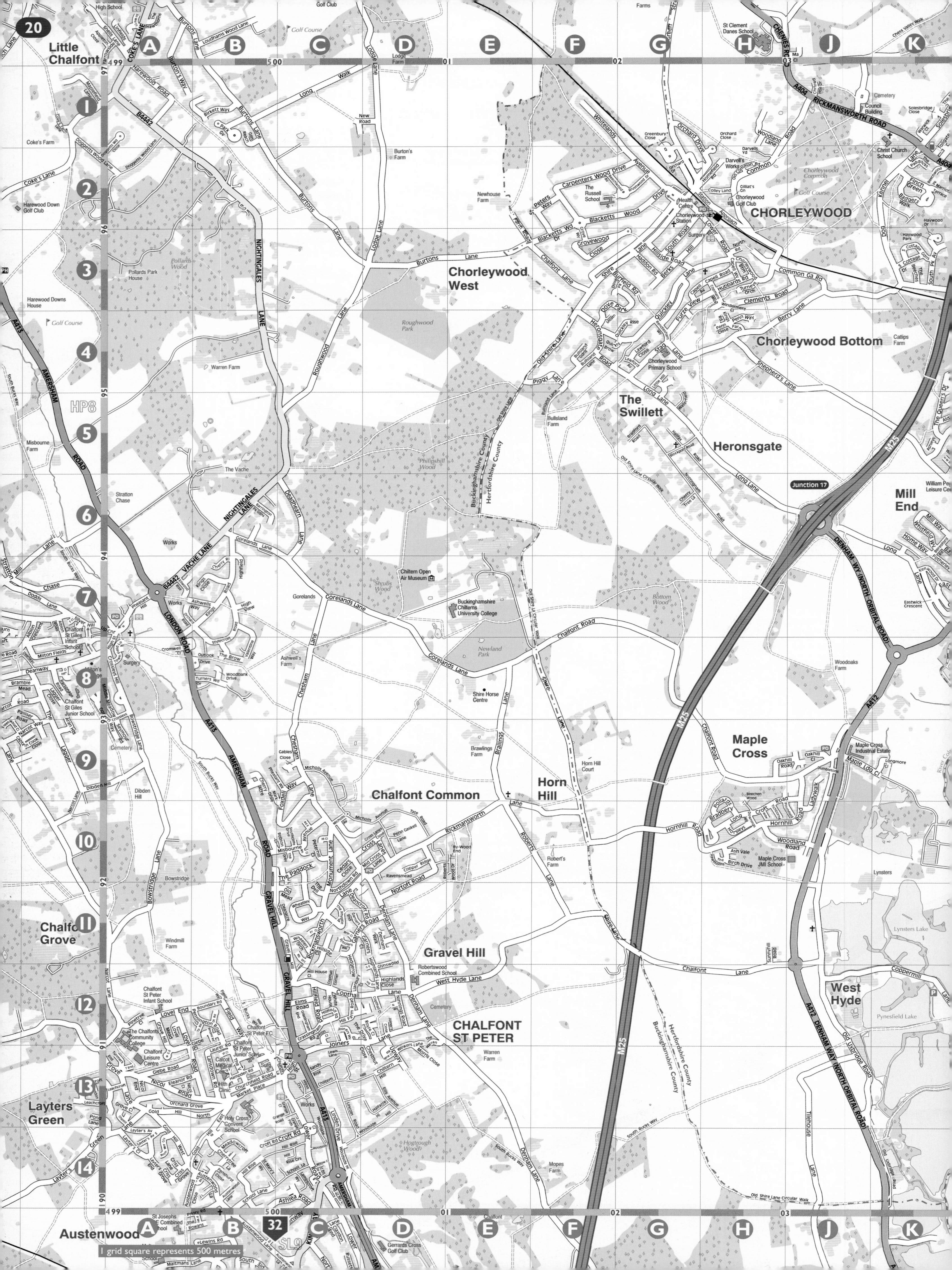
20
Little Chalfont
Chorleywood West
CHORLEYWOOD
Chorleywood Bottom
The Swillett
Heronsgate
Junction 17
Mill End
Maple Cross
Horn Hill
Chalfont Common
Gravel Hill
CHALFONT ST PETER
West Hyde
Layters Green
Austenwood
HP8
SL9
AMERSHAM ROAD
LONDON ROAD
GRAVEL HILL
NIGHTINGALES LANE
VACHE LANE
RICKMANSWORTH ROAD
DENHAM WAY (NORTH ORBITAL ROAD)
A404
A413
A412
B4442
M25
Chiltern Open Air Museum
Buckinghamshire Chilterns University College
Newland Park
Shire Horse Centre
Roughwood Park
Philipshill Wood
Shrubs Wood
Bottom Wood
Hogtrough Wood
Pollards Wood
Lynsters Lake
Pynesfield Lake
Buckinghamshire County
Hertfordshire County
Old Shire Lane Circular Walk
South Bucks Way
32
1 grid square represents 500 metres

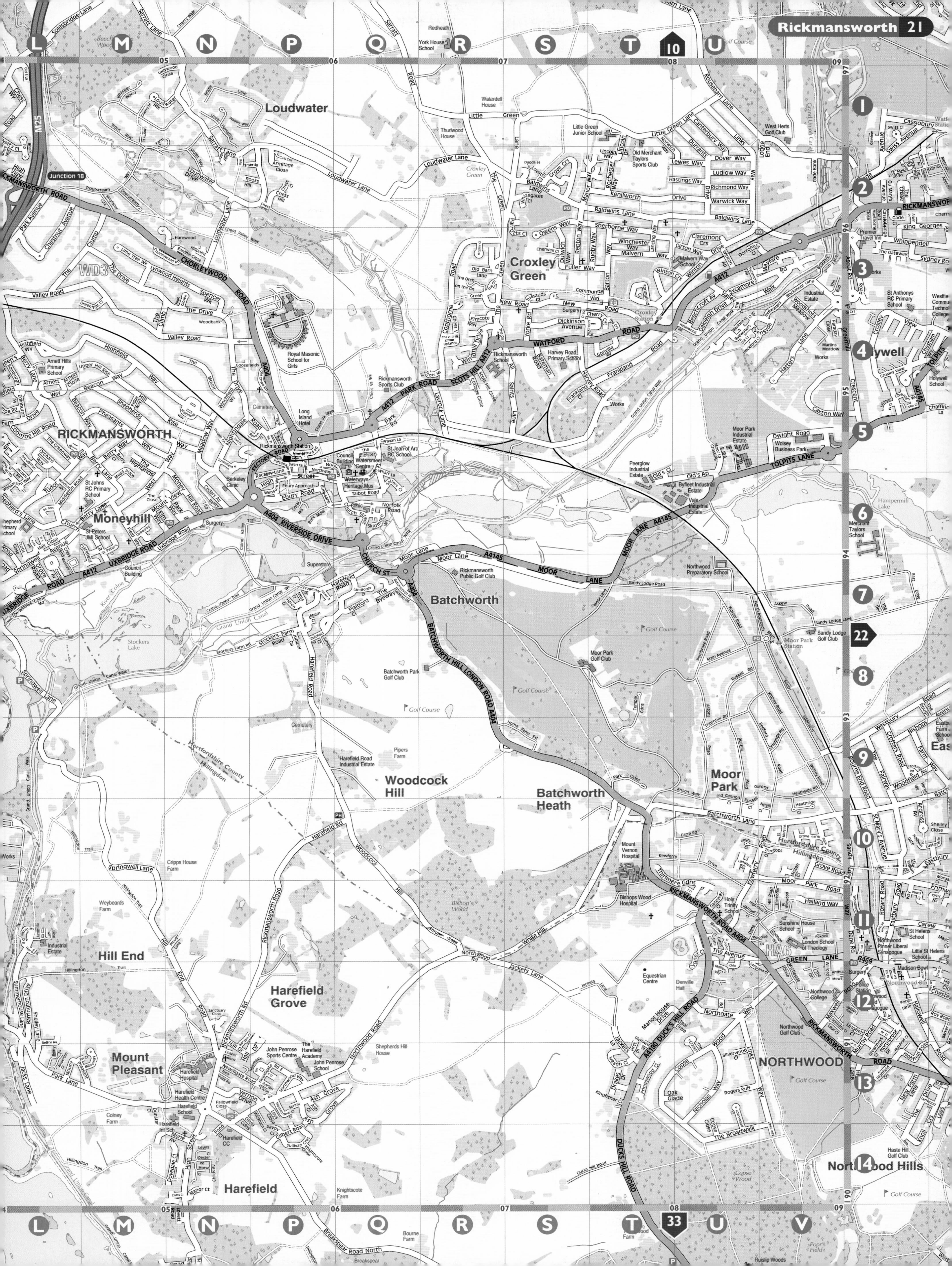
L
M
N
P
Q
R
S
T
U
V
10
33
22
05
06
07
08
09
Loudwater
Croxley Green
RICKMANSWORTH
Moneyhill
Batchworth
Woodcock Hill
Batchworth Heath
Moor Park
NORTHWOOD
Hill End
Harefield Grove
Mount Pleasant
Harefield
Northwood Hills
WD3
HA6
Junction 18
M25
RICKMANSWORTH ROAD
CHORLEYWOOD ROAD
A404
A412
PARK ROAD
SCOTS HILL
WATFORD ROAD
TOLPITS LANE
MOOR LANE
A4145
A404 RIVERSIDE DRIVE
UXBRIDGE ROAD
CHURCH ST
BATCHWORTH HILL LONDON ROAD
RICKMANSWORTH ROAD A404
GREEN LANE
B469
A4180 DUCKS HILL ROAD
DUCKS HILL ROAD
Royal Masonic School for Girls
Rickmansworth Station
Croxley Station
Moor Park Station
Rickmansworth Public Golf Club
Moor Park Golf Club
Batchworth Park Golf Club
Sandy Lodge Golf Club
Northwood Golf Club
Haste Hill Golf Club
West Herts Golf Club
Mount Vernon Hospital
Bishops Wood Hospital
Harefield Hospital
Stockers Lake
Grand Union Canal
River Colne
River Chess
River Gade
Hampermill Lake
Bishop's Wood
Copse Wood
Hertfordshire County
Hillingdon

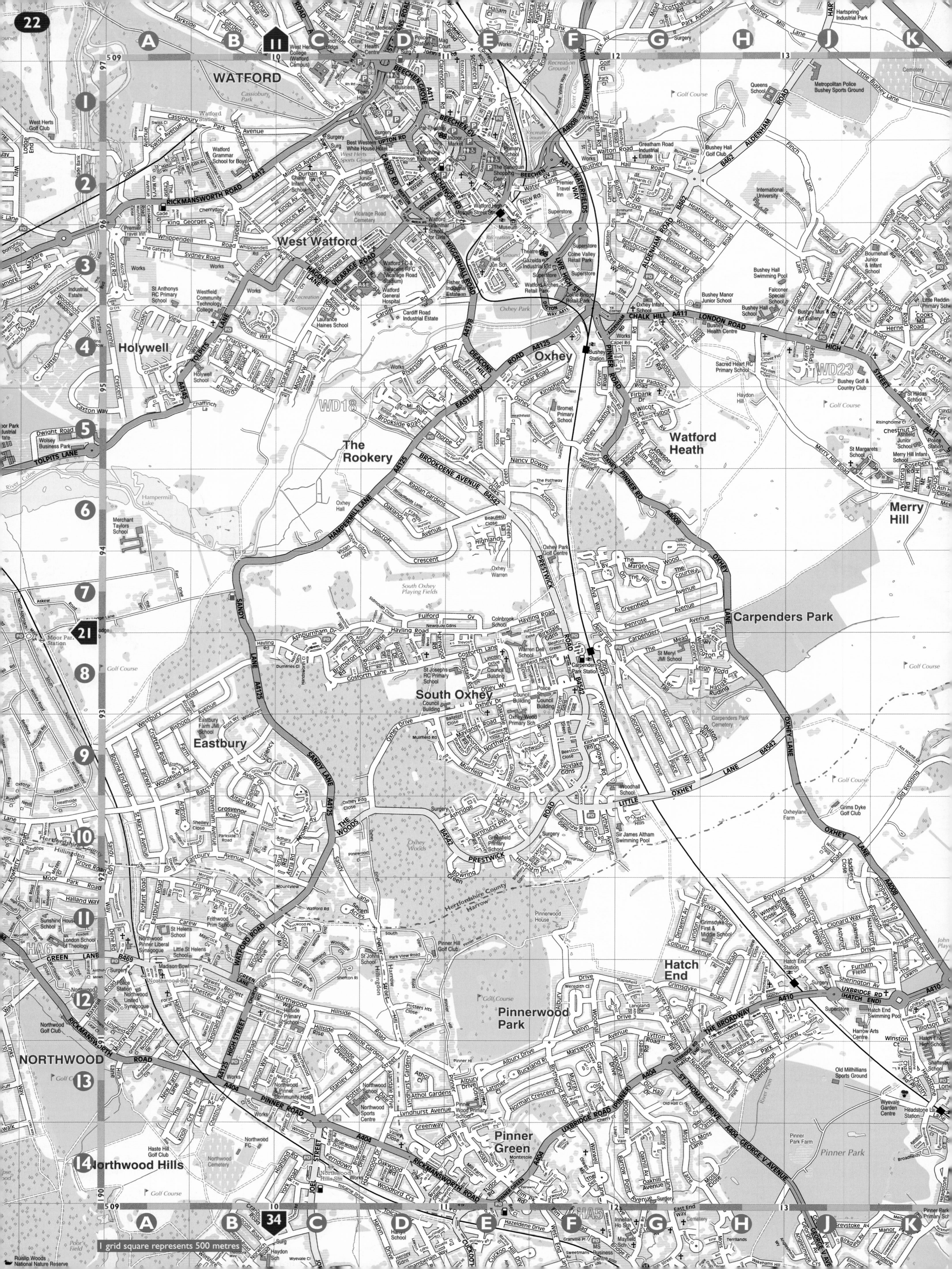
WATFORD
West Watford
Holywell
Oxhey
The Rookery
Watford Heath
Merry Hill
Carpenders Park
South Oxhey
Eastbury
Hatch End
Pinnerwood Park
NORTHWOOD
Northwood Hills
Pinner Green
Pinner Park
WD18
WD23
HA6
HA5
11
21
34
1 grid square represents 500 metres

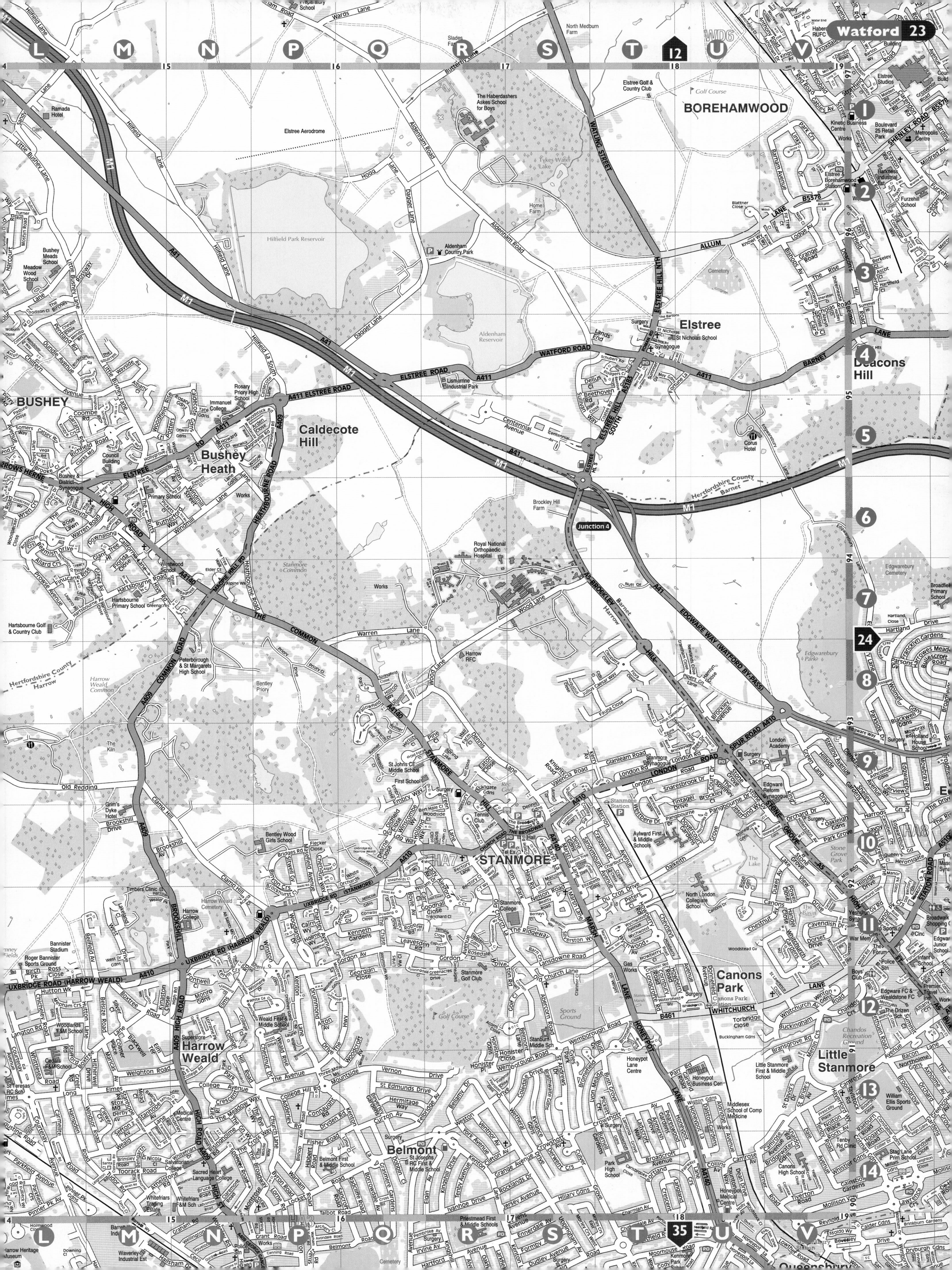
BOREHAMWOOD
Elstree
Deacons Hill
BUSHEY
Bushey Heath
Caldecote Hill
STANMORE
Canons Park
Little Stanmore
Harrow Weald
Belmont
Elstree Aerodrome
Hilfield Park Reservoir
Aldenham Reservoir
Aldenham Country Park
The Haberdashers Askes School for Boys
Elstree Golf & Country Club
Royal National Orthopaedic Hospital
Stanmore Common
Harrow Weald Common
Bentley Priory
Edgwarebury Park
Junction 4
M1
A41
A411 ELSTREE ROAD
WATFORD ROAD
WATLING STREET
ELSTREE HILL NTH
BROCKLEY HILL
EDGWARE WAY (WATFORD BY-PASS)
SPUR ROAD A410
LONDON ROAD
STANMORE HILL
UXBRIDGE ROAD (HARROW WEALD)
HIGH ROAD
COMMON ROAD
HONEYPOT LANE
WHITCHURCH LANE
THE BROADWAY
Hertfordshire County
Barnet
Harrow
Stanmore Station
Canons Park Station
Elstree & Borehamwood Station
Stanmore Golf Club
William Ellis Sports Ground

12
24
35

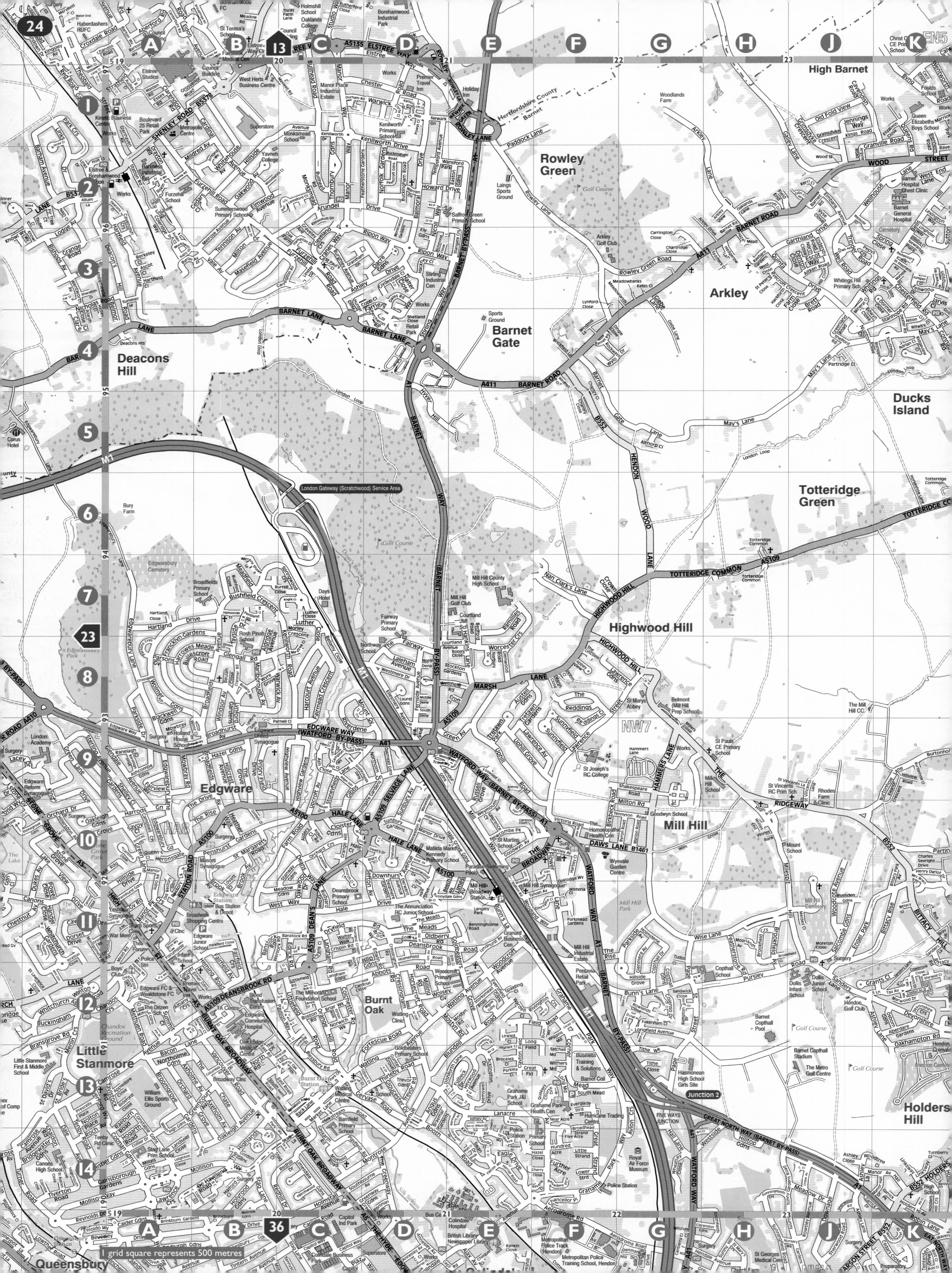
13
23
36
A
B
C
D
E
F
G
H
J
K
EN5
NW7
HA8
High Barnet
Rowley Green
Barnet Gate
Arkley
Deacons Hill
Ducks Island
Totteridge Green
Highwood Hill
Edgware
Mill Hill
Burnt Oak
Little Stanmore
Holders Hill
Queensbury
ELSTREE WAY
SHENLEY ROAD B5378
BARNET LANE
BARNET BY-PASS
BARNET ROAD
A411
WOOD STREET
ROWLEY LANE
BARNET WAY
HENDON WOOD LANE
TOTTERIDGE COMMON
A5109
HIGHWOOD HILL
MARSH LANE
EDGWARE WAY (WATFORD BY-PASS)
A41
WATFORD WAY (BARNET BY-PASS)
HALE LANE
A5100
SELVAGE LANE
STATION ROAD
DEANSBROOK RD
BURNT OAK BROADWAY
DAWS LANE B1461
THE BROADWAY
RIDGEWAY
HAMMERS LANE
GREAT NORTH WAY (BARNET BY-PASS)
M1
A1
B552
London Gateway (Scratchwood) Service Area
Hertfordshire County
Barnet
Golf Course
Mill Hill Broadway Station
Edgware Station
Burnt Oak Station
Junction 2
FIVE WAYS JUNCTION
Royal Air Force Museum
1 grid square represents 500 metres

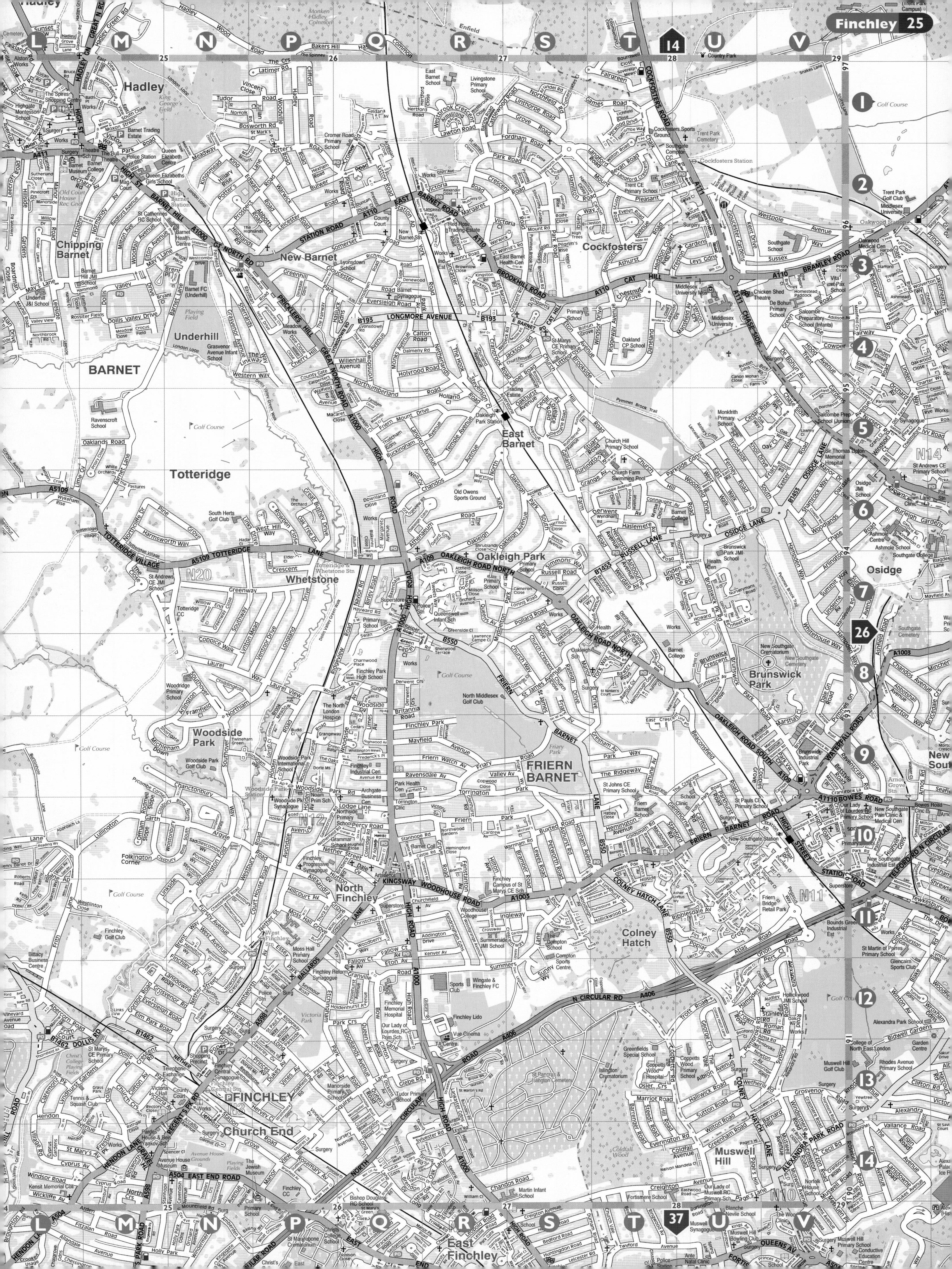
L M N P Q R S T U V
14
25 26 27 28 29
Hadley
Chipping Barnet
New Barnet
Cockfosters
BARNET
Underhill
Totteridge
East Barnet
Oakleigh Park
Whetstone
N20
Osidge
N14
26
Brunswick Park
Woodside Park
FRIERN BARNET
N12
North Finchley
N11
Colney Hatch
FINCHLEY
N3
Church End
Muswell Hill
N10
East Finchley
37
1 2 3 4 5 6 7 8 9 10 11 12 13 14
STATION ROAD
GREAT NORTH ROAD
HIGH ROAD
OAKLEIGH ROAD NORTH
OAKLEIGH ROAD SOUTH
N CIRCULAR RD
TOTTERIDGE VILLAGE
TOTTERIDGE LANE
COCKFOSTERS ROAD
CAT HILL
CHASE SIDE
BRAMLEY ROAD
BOWES ROAD
OSIDGE LANE
RUSSELL LANE
LONGMORE AVENUE
FRIERN BARNET LANE
FRIERN BARNET ROAD
COLNEY HATCH LANE
WOODHOUSE ROAD
KINGSWAY
BALLARDS LANE
REGENT'S PK RD
EAST END ROAD
DOLLIS RD
ALEXANDRA PARK ROAD
QUEENS AV
Golf Course
Cockfosters Station
Oakwood Station
High Barnet Station
New Southgate Cemetery
St Pancras & Islington Cemetery
Finchley Golf Club
North Middlesex Golf Club

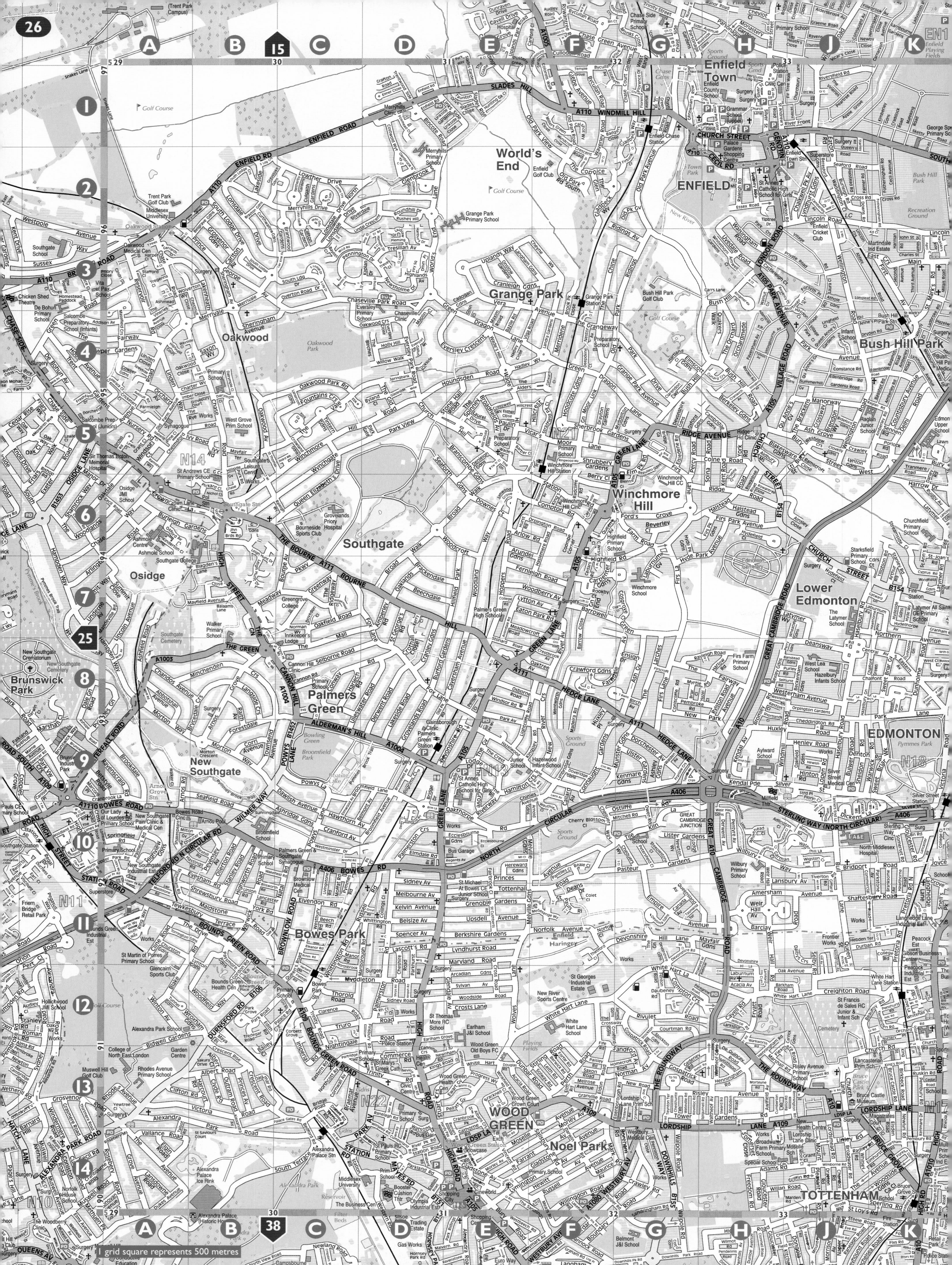

15
25
38
A
B
C
D
E
F
G
H
J
K
1
2
3
4
5
6
7
8
9
10
11
12
13
14
EN1
N14
N21
N13
N18
N11
N22
N10
N17
Enfield Town
ENFIELD
World's End
Grange Park
Oakwood
Bush Hill Park
Winchmore Hill
Southgate
Osidge
Lower Edmonton
EDMONTON
Palmers Green
New Southgate
Brunswick Park
Bowes Park
WOOD GREEN
Noel Park
TOTTENHAM
SLADES HILL
ENFIELD ROAD
ENFIELD RD
WINDMILL HILL
CHURCH STREET
CECIL RD
GREEN LANES
RIDGE AVENUE
HEDGE LANE
THE BOURNE
BOURNE HILL
ALDERMAN'S HILL
BOWES ROAD
NORTH CIRCULAR
STERLING WAY (NORTH CIRCULAR)
GREAT CAMBRIDGE ROAD
CAMBRIDGE ROAD
GREAT CAMBRIDGE JUNCTION
THE ROUNDWAY
LORDSHIP LANE
BOUNDS GREEN ROAD
BROWNLOW ROAD
HIGH ROAD
HIGH STREET
CANNON HILL
WILMER WAY
TELFORD RD N CIRCULAR RD
STATION ROAD
ALEXANDRA PARK ROAD
WESTBURY AV
DOWNHILLS WAY
BRUCE GROVE
VILLAGE ROAD
LONDON ROAD
CHASE SIDE
OSIDGE LANE
Golf Course
Trent Park Golf Club
Oakwood Park
Grovelands Priory Hospital
Broomfield Park
Bush Hill Park Golf Club
Edmonton Cemetery
Pymmes Park
Alexandra Palace
Alexandra Park
Alexandra Palace Ice Rink
North Middlesex Hospital
Bruce Castle Museum
1 grid square represents 500 metres

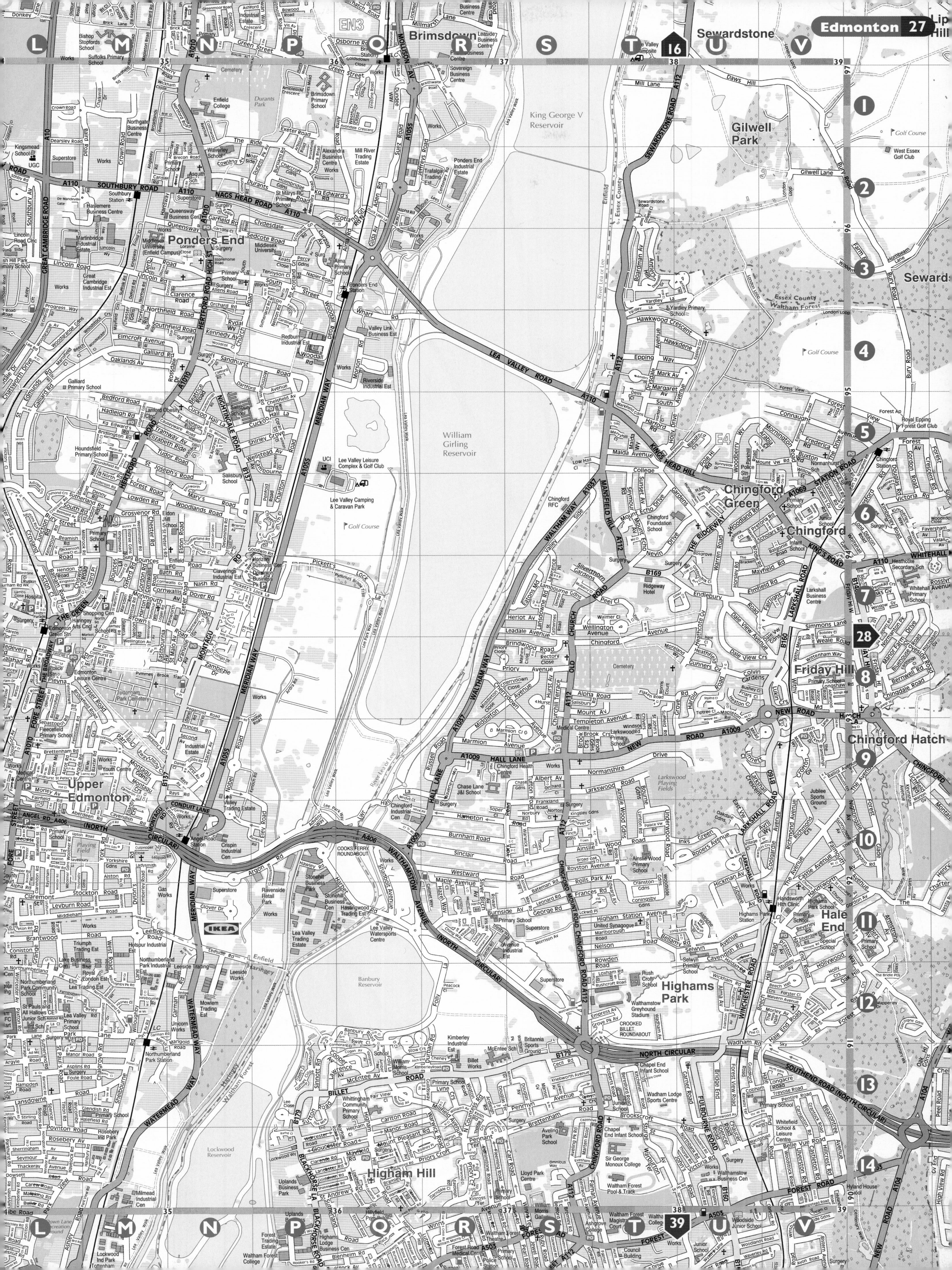
Brimsdown
Sewardstone
Gilwell Park
King George V Reservoir
Ponders End
William Girling Reservoir
Lee Valley Leisure Complex & Golf Club
Lee Valley Camping & Caravan Park
Chingford Green
Chingford
Friday Hill
Chingford Hatch
Upper Edmonton
Highams Park
Hale End
Banbury Reservoir
Lockwood Reservoir
Higham Hill
LEA VALLEY ROAD
MERIDIAN WAY
HERTFORD ROAD
SOUTHBURY ROAD
NAGS HEAD ROAD
KINGS HEAD HILL
STATION ROAD
WALTHAM WAY
SEWARDSTONE ROAD
NORTH CIRCULAR
SOUTHEND ROAD (NORTH CIRCULAR)
CHINGFORD MOUNT ROAD
FOREST ROAD
LARKSHALL ROAD
NEW ROAD
HALL LANE
ANGEL RD
FORE STREET
WATERMEAD WAY
BLACKHORSE LA
MOLLISON AV
Essex County
Waltham Forest
Enfield
Haringey
West Essex Golf Club
Royal Epping Forest Golf Club
Ponders End Station
Angel Road Station
Northumberland Park Station
Chingford Station
Highams Park Station
Edmonton Green Station
CROOKED BILLET ROUNDABOUT
COOKS FERRY ROUNDABOUT
Walthamstow Greyhound Stadium
Sir George Monoux College
IKEA
EN3
E4
N9
L M N P Q R S T U V
35 36 37 38 39
1 2 3 4 5 6 7 8 9 10 11 12 13 14
16 28 39

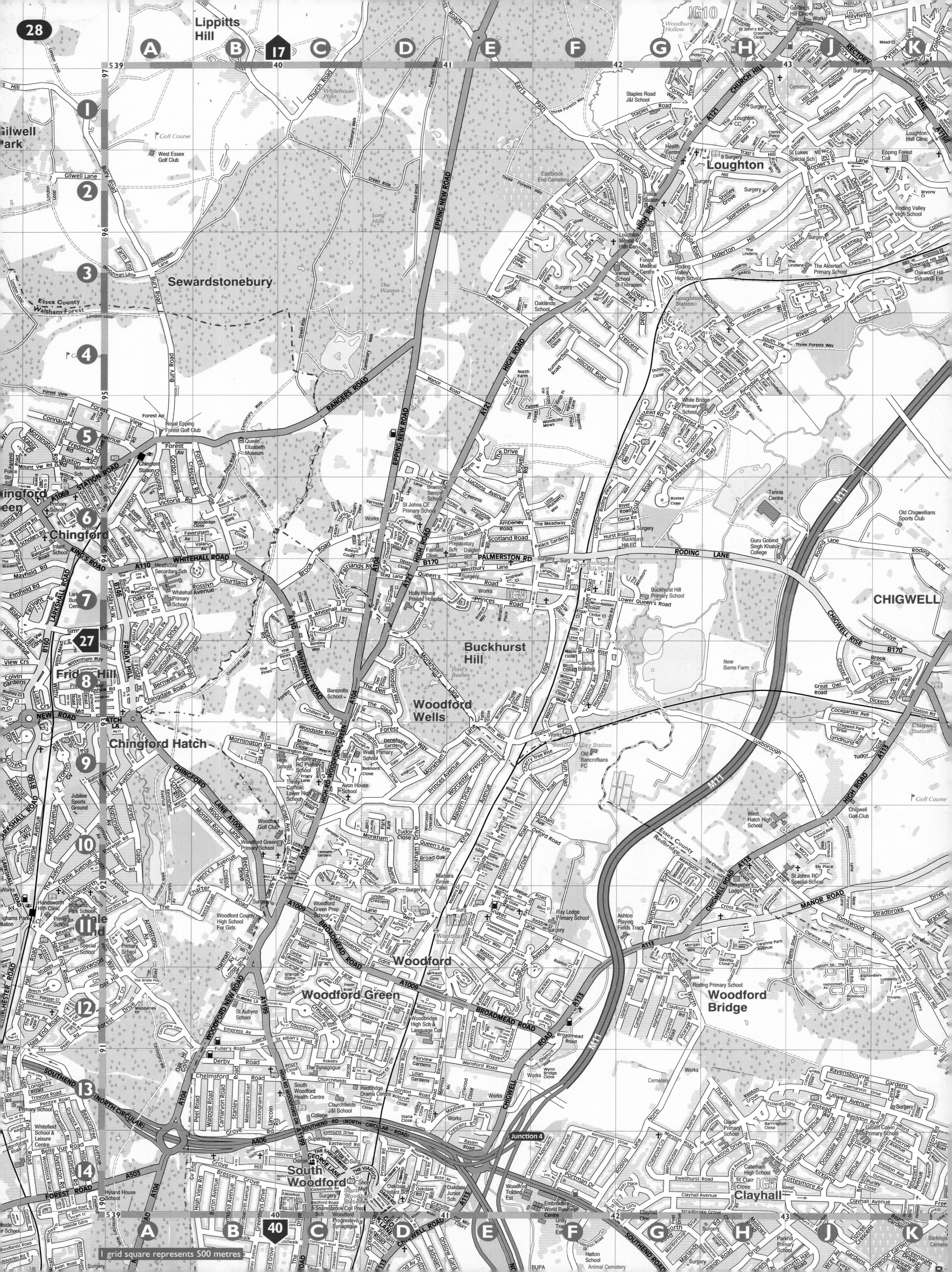
Lippitts Hill
17
Gilwell Park
Sewardstonebury
Essex County
Waltham Forest
Loughton
Chingford
Chingford Hatch
Friday Hill
Buckhurst Hill
Woodford Wells
Woodford
Woodford Green
Woodford Bridge
CHIGWELL
South Woodford
Clayhall
27
40
EPPING NEW ROAD
HIGH ROAD
RANGERS ROAD
WHITEHALL ROAD
PALMERSTON RD
RODING LANE
CHIGWELL RISE
MANOR ROAD
BROADMEAD ROAD
WOODFORD NEW ROAD
SOUTHEND ROAD (NORTH CIRCULAR)
FOREST ROAD
NEW ROAD
STATION ROAD
CHINGFORD LANE
M11
A104
A121
A113
A110
A1009
A1199
A406
A503
B170
Junction 4
Roding Valley Station
Buckhurst Hill Station
Loughton Station
Chigwell Station
Chingford Station
Woodford Station
South Woodford Station
Royal Epping Forest Golf Club
West Essex Golf Club
Chigwell Golf Club
Queen Elizabeth Museum
IG10
IG9
IG8
IG5
E18

1 grid square represents 500 metres

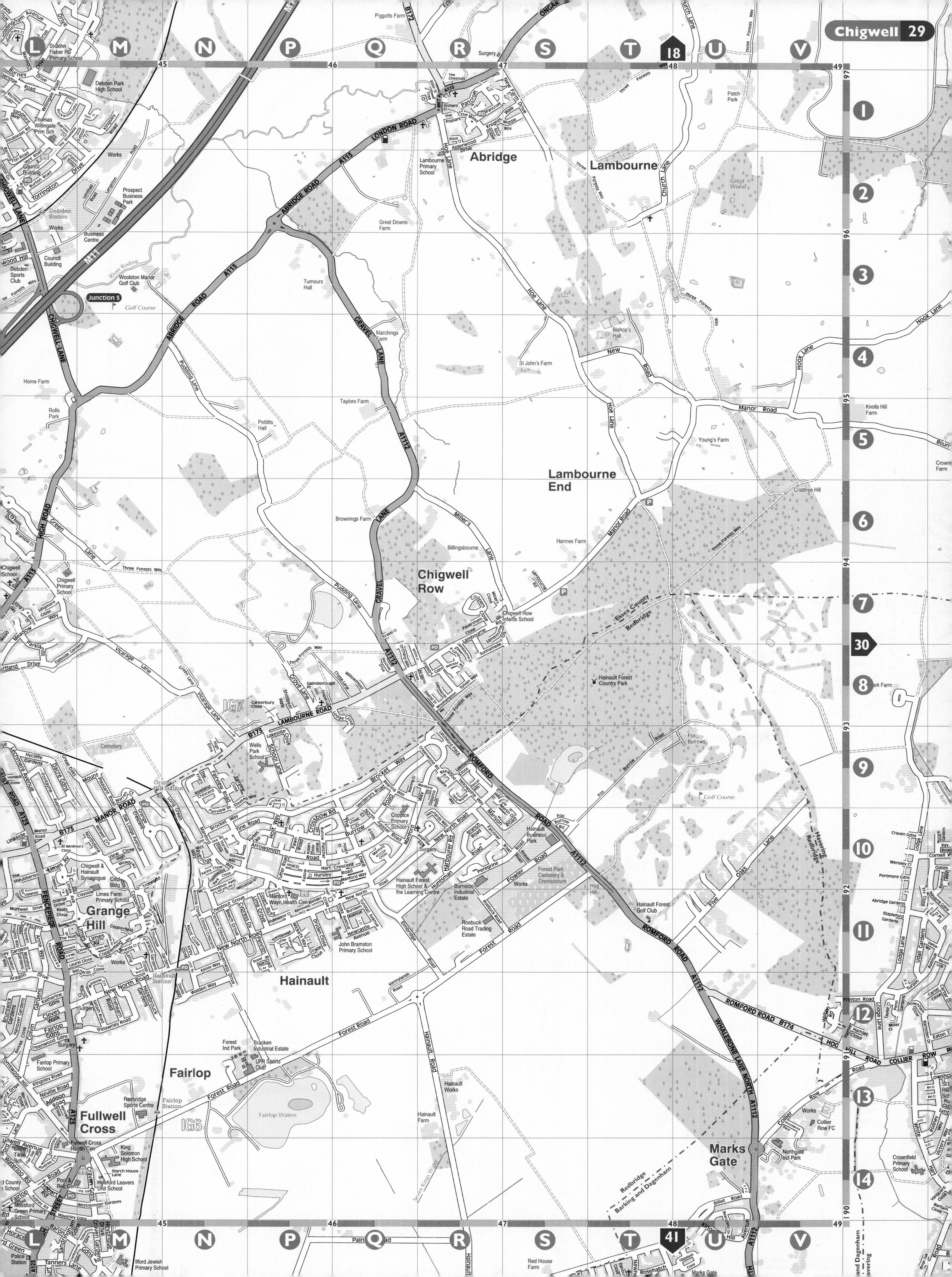
Abridge
Lambourne
Lambourne End
Chigwell Row
Grange Hill
Hainault
Fairlop
Fullwell Cross
Marks Gate
ABRIDGE ROAD
LONDON ROAD
GRAVEL LANE
ROMFORD ROAD
WHALEBONE LANE NORTH
CHIGWELL LANE
HIGH ROAD
MANOR ROAD
LAMBOURNE ROAD
FENCEPIECE ROAD
ROMFORD ROAD B174
HOG HILL ROAD
COLLIER ROW
Forest Road
Hainault Road
Hoe Lane
Manor Road
Hook Lane
Church Lane
Pudding Lane
Vicarage Lane
Miller's Lane
Three Forests Way
Fox Burrow Road
Five Oaks Lane
Fowler Road
Debden Station
Woolston Manor Golf Club
Junction 5
Golf Course
Turnours Hall
Great Downs Farm
Marchings Farm
Taylors Farm
Pettits Hall
Brownings Farm
Billingsbourne
Harmes Farm
Bishop's Hall
St John's Farm
Knolls Hill Farm
Young's Farm
Crabtree Hill
Great Wood
Patch Park
Home Farm
Rolls Park
Hainault Forest Country Park
Chigwell How Infants School
Hainault Forest Golf Club
Hainault Forest High School & the Learning Centre
Forest Park Cemetery & Crematorium
Roebuck Road Trading Estate
Burnside Industrial Estate
Hainault Business Park
Fairlop Waters
Redbridge Sports Centre
Fairlop Station
Hainault Station
Grange Hill Station
Forest Ind Park
Bracken Industrial Estate
LPR Sports Club
Hainault Works
Hainault Farm
Collier Row FC
Northgate Ind Park
Crownfield Primary School
Red House Farm
Essex County
Redbridge
Havering
Barking and Dagenham
IG7
IG6
M11
A113
A1112
A123
B173
B172
18
41
30
L M N P Q R S T U V
45 46 47 48 49
1 2 3 4 5 6 7 8 9 10 11 12 13 14
97 96 95 94 93 92 91 90

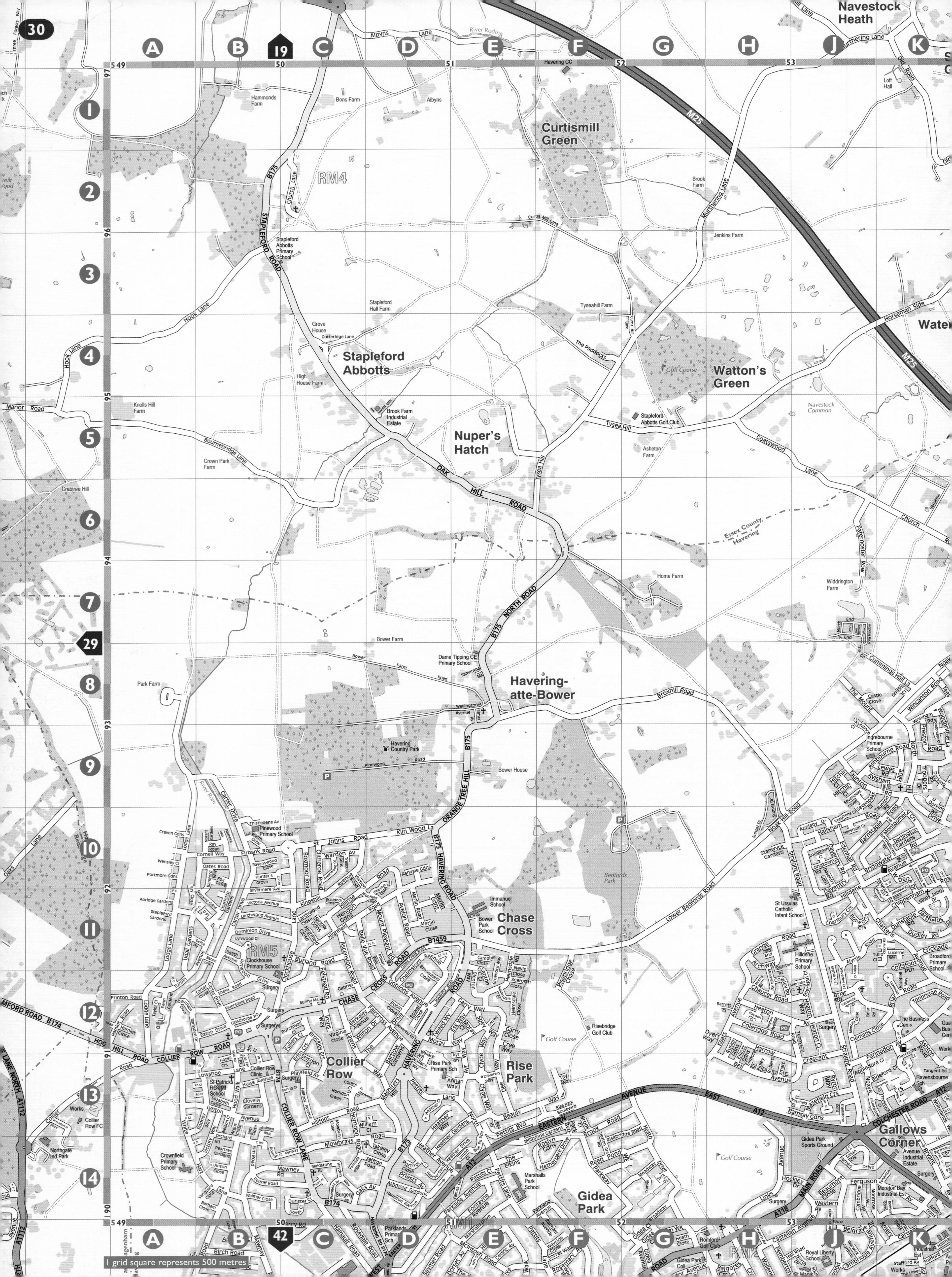
Navestock Heath
Albyns Lane
River Roding
Havering CC
M25
Hammonds Farm
Bons Farm
Albyns
Curtismill Green
Loft Hall
RM4
Church Lane
B175
Stapleford Road
Stapleford Abbotts Primary School
Curtis Mill Lane
Brook Farm
Murthering Lane
Jenkins Farm
Hook Lane
Stapleford Hall Farm
Tyseahill Farm
Grove House
Cutteridge Lane
Stapleford Abbotts
The Paddocks
Golf Course
Watton's Green
High House Farm
Horseman Side
Manor Road
Knolls Hill Farm
Brook Farm Industrial Estate
Nuper's Hatch
Stapleford Abbotts Golf Club
Tysea Hill
Navestock Common
Asheton Farm
Bournebridge Lane
Crown Park Farm
Coatswood Lane
Oak Hill Road
Crabtree Hill
Church Road
Essex County
Havering
Home Farm
Paternoster Row
Widdrington Farm
North Road
Bower Farm
Dame Tipping CE Primary School
Bower Farm Road
Park Farm
Havering-atte-Bower
Broxhill Road
Cummings Hall La
Havering Country Park
Pinewood Road
Bower House
Orange Tree Hill
Ingrebourne Primary School
Noak Hill Road
Carter Drive
Pinewood Primary School
St Johns Road
Kiln Wood La
Havering Road
Bedfords Park
Lower Bedfords Road
Stanwyck Gardens
St Ursulas Catholic Infant School
Straight Road
Immanuel School
Chase Cross
Bower Park School
B1459
RM5
Clockhouse Primary School
Hilldene Primary School
Cross Road
Chase
Risebridge Chase
Frinton Road
Romford Road B174
Risebridge Golf Club
Collier Row Road
Hog Hill Road
Collier Row
Rise Park
Rise Park Primary Sch
St Patricks RC Prim School
B174
Collier Row Lane
Eastern Avenue
A12
Eastern Avenue East
Colchester Road
Gallows Corner
Gidea Park Sports Ground
Crownfield Primary School
Marshalls Park School
Gidea Park
Main Road
A118
Northgate Ind Park
Collier Row FC
Romford Golf Club
RM2
RM1
Royal Liberty School
Hainault Road
Lane North A1112
A112
A
B
C
D
E
F
G
H
J
K
19
29
42
49
50
51
52
53
97
96
95
94
93
92
91
90

1 grid square represents 500 metres

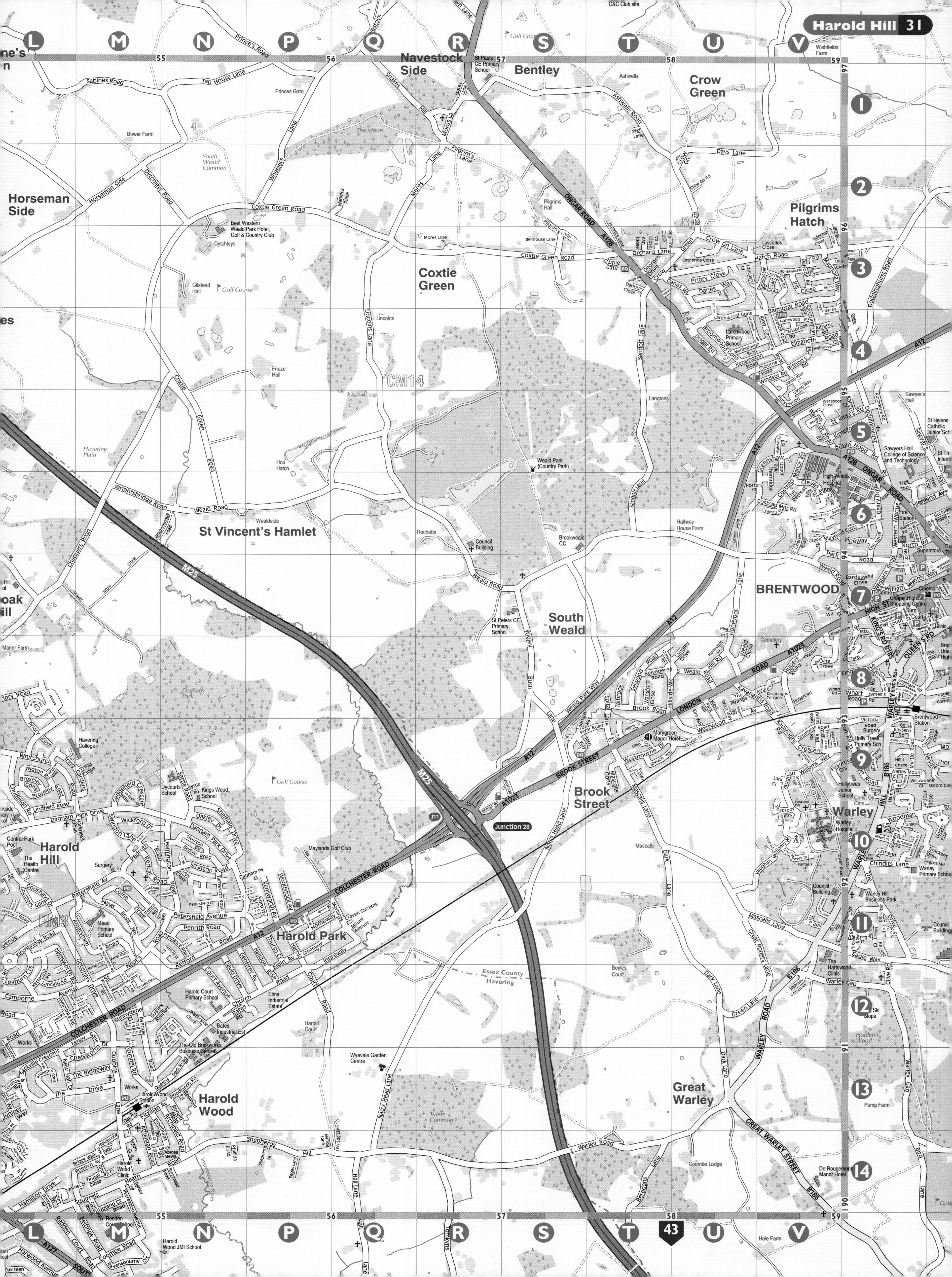

L
M
N
P
Q
R
S
T
U
V
55
56
57
58
59
Navestock Side
Bentley
Crow Green
Horseman Side
Pilgrims Hatch
Coxtie Green
CM14
St Vincent's Hamlet
South Weald
BRENTWOOD
Harold Hill
Harold Park
Brook Street
Warley
Harold Wood
Great Warley
RM3
C&C Club site
Wishfields Farm
St Pauls CE Primary School
Ashwells
Princes Gate
Bower Farm
The Mores
South Weald Common
Best Western Weald Park Hotel, Golf & Country Club
Dytchleys
Gilstead Hall
Golf Course
Lincolns
Frieze Hall
Havering Plain
Hou Hatch
Weald Park (Country Park)
Rochetts
Council Building
Brookweald CC
Halfway House Farm
Langtons
St Peters CE Primary School
Manor Farm
Dagnam Park
Havering College
Dycourts School
Kings Wood School
Central Park Pool
The Health Centre
Surgery
Maylands Golf Club
Junction 28
Marygreen Manor Hotel
Mascalls
Harold Court Primary School
Elms Industrial Estate
Bates Industrial Est
The Old Brickworks Business Centre
Harold Court
Wyevale Garden Centre
Boyles Court
Essex County
Havering
Tylers Common
Coombe Lodge
De Rougemont Manor Hotel
Hole Farm
Pump Farm
Holden's Wood
Ski Slope
The Hartswood Clinic
Warley Hill Business Park
Warley Hospital
Hollytrees Junior School
Holly Trees Primary Sch
Brentwood Station
Cemetery
Chapel High Shopping Centre
Cinema
Superstore
Sawyers Hall College of Science and Technology
St Helens Catholic Junior Sch
High Wood Hospital
Larchwood Primary School
Harold Wood Station
Harold Wood JMI School
Harold Wood Clinic
Mead Primary School
Prince's Road
Sabines Road
Tan House Lane
Snakes Hill
Mores Lane
Pilgrim's Lane
Wheelers Lane
Dytchleys Road
Horseman Side
Coxtie Green Road
Ongar Road
A128
Ashwells Road
Days Lane
Crow Green Road
Crow Gn Lane
Orchard Lane
Hatch Road
Priory Close
Danes Way
Balmoral Road
Larchwood Gdns
Broomwood Gdns
Kensington Road
Windsor Rd
Doddinghurst Road
Lincolns Lane
Coxtie Green Road
Wrightsbridge Road
Weald Road
Chequers Road
Sandpit Lane
M25
A12
A1023
London Road
Brook Street
Weald Park Way
Wigley Bush Lane
Nag's Head Lane
Mascalls Lane
Dark Lane
Colchester Road
Dagnam Park Drive
Petersfield Avenue
Warley Road
Warley Hill
Great Warley Street
B186
Warley Gap
Eagle Way
Chindits Lane
Green Lane
Great Ropers Lane
Shepherds Hill
Hall Lane
Tomkyns Lane
Bird Lane
Lake Rise
Court Avenue
Gubbins Lane
Squirrels Heath Road
Hamilton Drive
Harwood Avenue
43

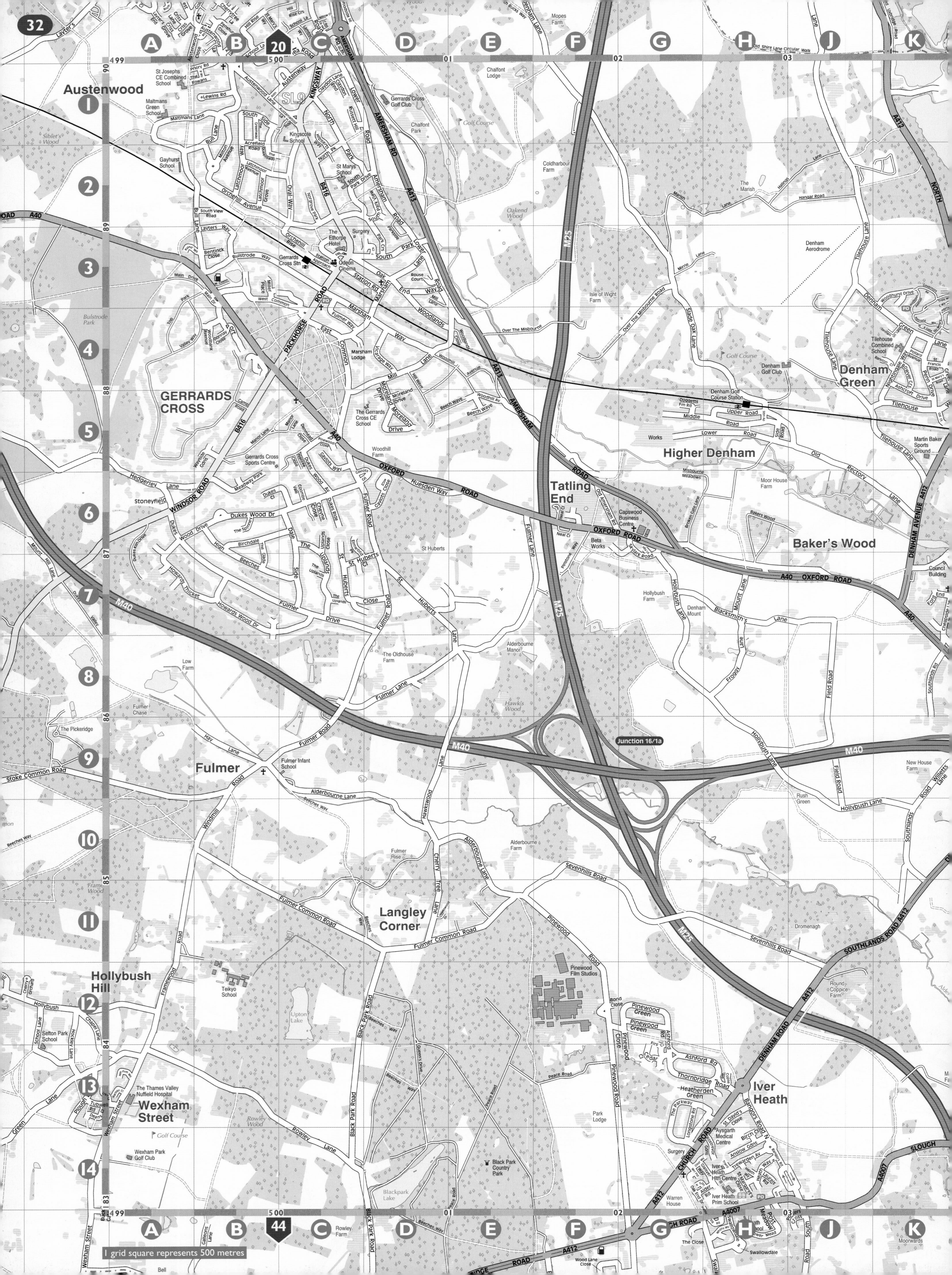
20
44
A
B
C
D
E
F
G
H
J
K
499
500
01
02
03
90
89
88
87
86
85
84
83
1
2
3
4
5
6
7
8
9
10
11
12
13
14
Austenwood
GERRARDS CROSS
Tatling End
Higher Denham
Baker's Wood
Denham Green
Fulmer
Langley Corner
Hollybush Hill
Wexham Street
Iver Heath
SL9
Junction 16/1a
M40
M25
A40
A413
A412
A4007
B416
AMERSHAM RD
AMERSHAM ROAD
OXFORD ROAD
PACKHORSE ROAD
WINDSOR ROAD
KINGSWAY
DENHAM AVENUE
DENHAM ROAD
SOUTHLANDS ROAD
CHURCH ROAD
SLOUGH
Old Shire Lane Circular Walk
Chalfont Lodge
Chalfont Park
Gerrards Cross Golf Club
Golf Course
Coldharbour Farm
Oakend Wood
Isle of Wight Farm
Over The Misbourne
Denham Golf Club
Denham Golf Course Station
Denham Aerodrome
The Marish
Hangar Road
Tilehouse Lane
Tilehouse Combined School
Martin Baker Sports Ground
Moor House Farm
Rectory Lane
Old Rectory Lane
Upper Road
Middle Road
Lower Road
Works
Misbourne Meadows
Capswood Business Centre
Beta Works
Skylark Road
Hollybush Farm
Denham Mount
Blacksmith's Lane
Mount Lane
Froggy Lane
Field Road
Hollybush Lane
New House Farm
Rush Green
Council Building
Southlands Road
Alderbourne Manor
Hawk's Wood
St Huberts
The Oldhouse Farm
Fulmer Lane
Fulmer Road
Fulmer Infant School
Fulmer Chase
Low Farm
The Pickeridge
Stoke Common Road
Hay Lane
Alderbourne Lane
Beeches Way
Windmill Road
Hawkswood Lane
Fulmer Rise
Cherry Tree Lane
Alderbourne Farm
Sevenhills Road
Fulmer Common Road
Dromenagh
Round Coppice Farm
Pinewood Road
Pinewood Film Studios
Pinewood Green
Pinewood Close
Ashford Rd
Thornbridge Road
Heatherden Green
Peace Road
Park Lodge
Teikyo School
Upton Lake
Black Park Road
Black Park Country Park
Blackpark Lake
Rowley Lane
Rowley Farm
Framewood Road
Hollybush Hill
Sefton Park School
The Thames Valley Nuffield Hospital
Wexham Park Golf Club
Wexham Street
Frame Wood
Rowley Wood
Aysgarth Medical Centre
Surgery
Iver Heath Hlth Centre
Iver Heath Prim School
Warren House
The Close
Swallowdale
Wood Lane Close
Moorwards
Bulstrode Park
Siblet's Wood
St Josephs CE Combined School
Maltmans Green School
Maltmans Lane
Kingscote School
St Marys School
Gayhurst School
Orchehill Avenue
The Ethorpe Hotel
Odeon Cinema
Gerrards Cross Stn
Station Road
Bulstrode Way
Marsham Lodge
Marsham Way
Woodlands
The Gerrards Cross CE School
Woodhill Farm
Huesden Way
Gerrards Cross Sports Centre
Hedgerley Lane
Stoneyfield
Dukes Wood Drive
Howards Thicket
Howards Wood Dr
Fulmer Drive
Mount Hill Lane
1 grid square represents 500 metres

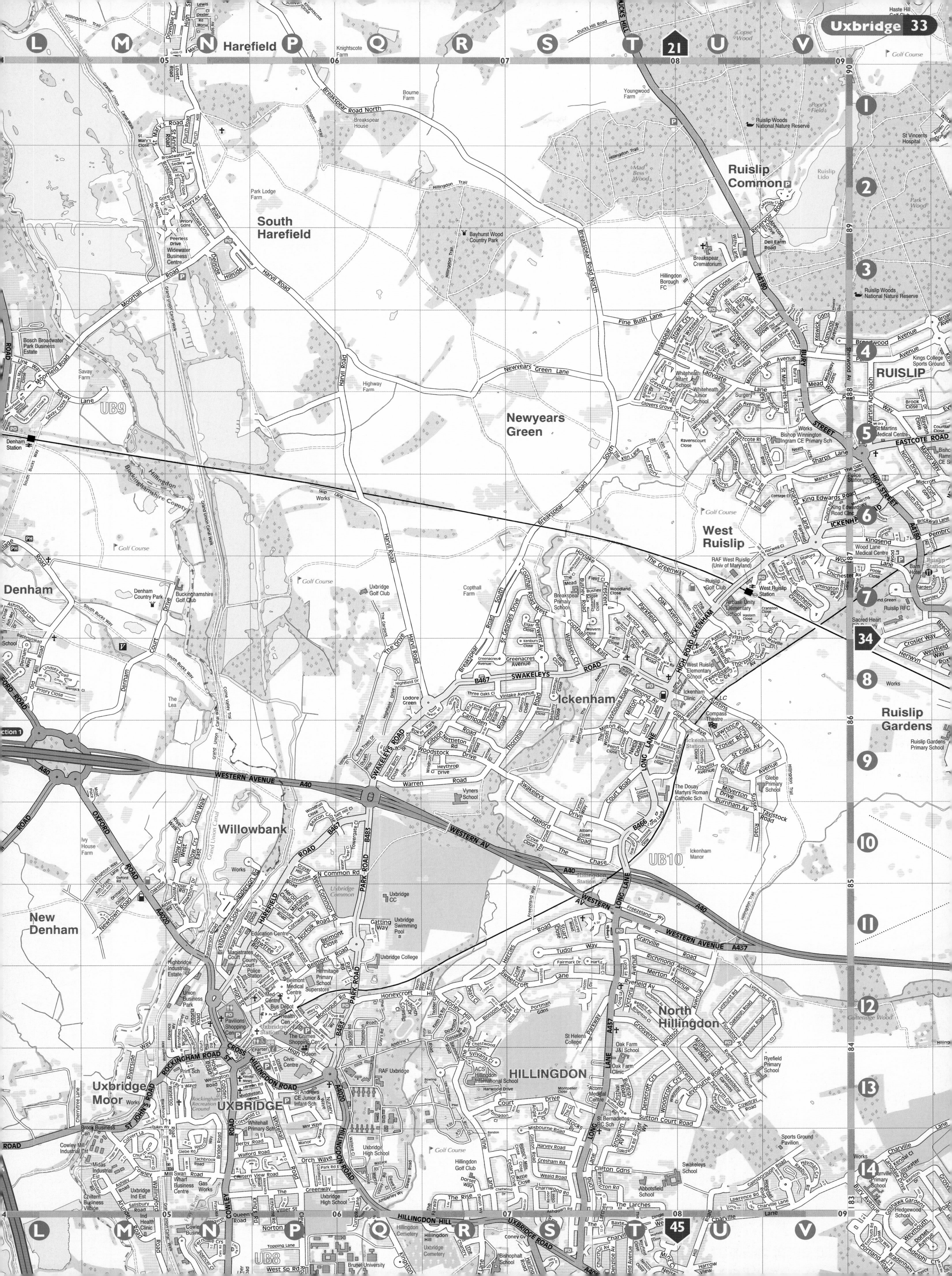
Harefield
South Harefield
Ruislip Common
RUISLIP
Newyears Green
West Ruislip
Denham
Ickenham
Ruislip Gardens
Willowbank
New Denham
North Hillingdon
HILLINGDON
Uxbridge Moor
UXBRIDGE
UB9
UB10
UB8
WESTERN AVENUE
A40
Breakspear Road North
Harvil Road
Swakeleys Road
Long Lane
High Street
Eastcote Road
Hillingdon Hill
Uxbridge Road
Park Road
Oxford Road
Moorhall Road
Grand Union Canal
Ruislip Woods National Nature Reserve
Bayhurst Wood Country Park
Uxbridge Golf Club
Hillingdon Golf Club
Brunel University
21
34
45

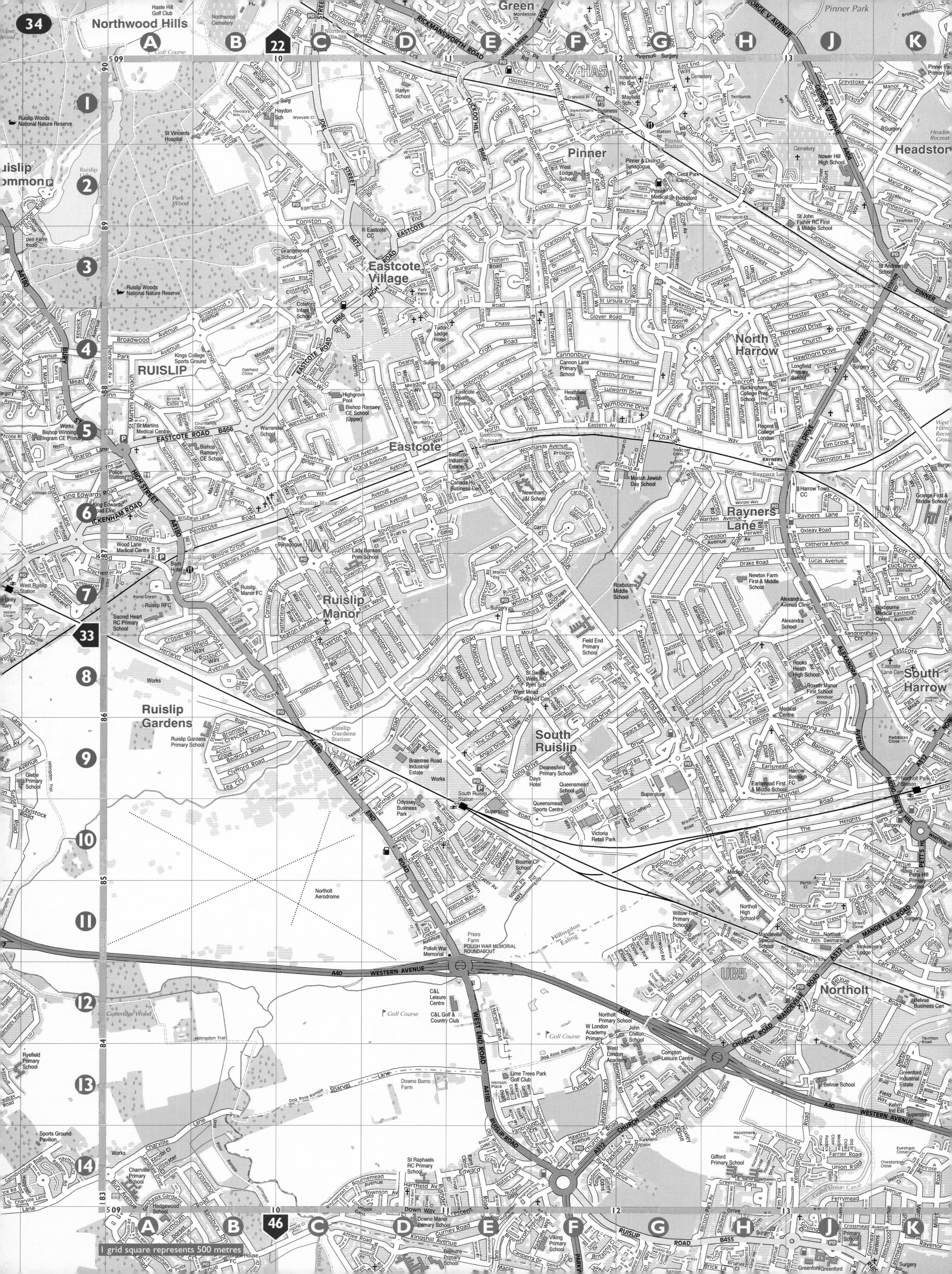
Northwood Hills
Pinner
Pinner Park
Headstone
Ruislip Common
Ruislip Woods National Nature Reserve
Eastcote Village
North Harrow
RUISLIP
Eastcote
Rayners Lane
Ruislip Manor
South Harrow
Ruislip Gardens
South Ruislip
Northolt Aerodrome
Northolt
Polish War Memorial Roundabout
Western Avenue
West End Road
HA5
HA4
HA2
UB5
22
33
46
1 grid square represents 500 metres

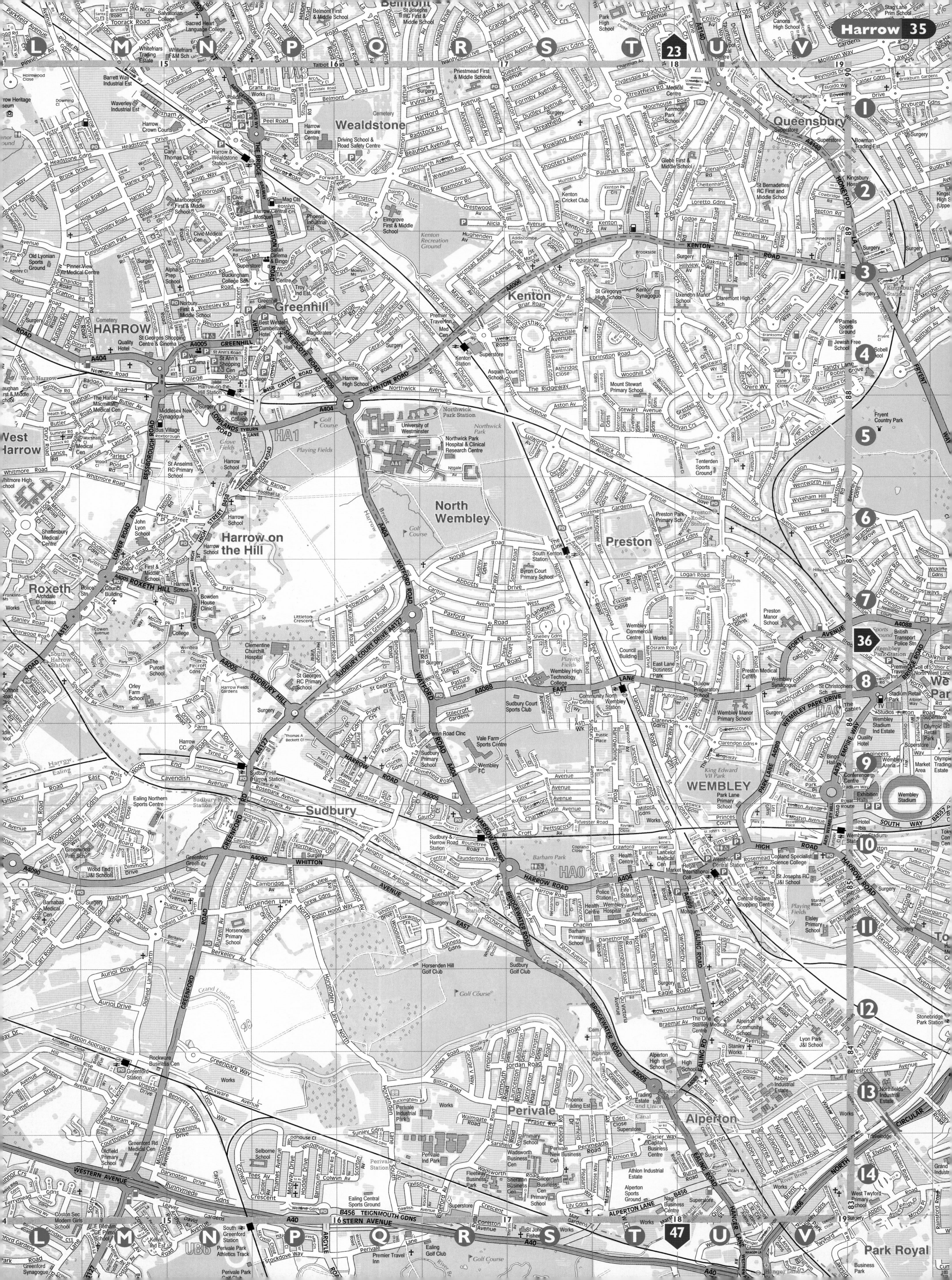
HARROW
West Harrow
Roxeth
Harrow on the Hill
Greenhill
Wealdstone
Kenton
Queensbury
North Wembley
Preston
WEMBLEY
Sudbury
Perivale
Alperton
Park Royal
Wembley Stadium
Northwick Park Hospital & Clinical Research Centre
University of Westminster
Fryent Country Park
Horsenden Hill Golf Club
Sudbury Golf Club
Grand Union Canal
WESTERN AVENUE
HARROW ROAD
WATFORD ROAD
KENTON ROAD
EALING ROAD
BRIDGEWATER ROAD
GREENFORD ROAD
WHITTON AVENUE
NORTH CIRCULAR

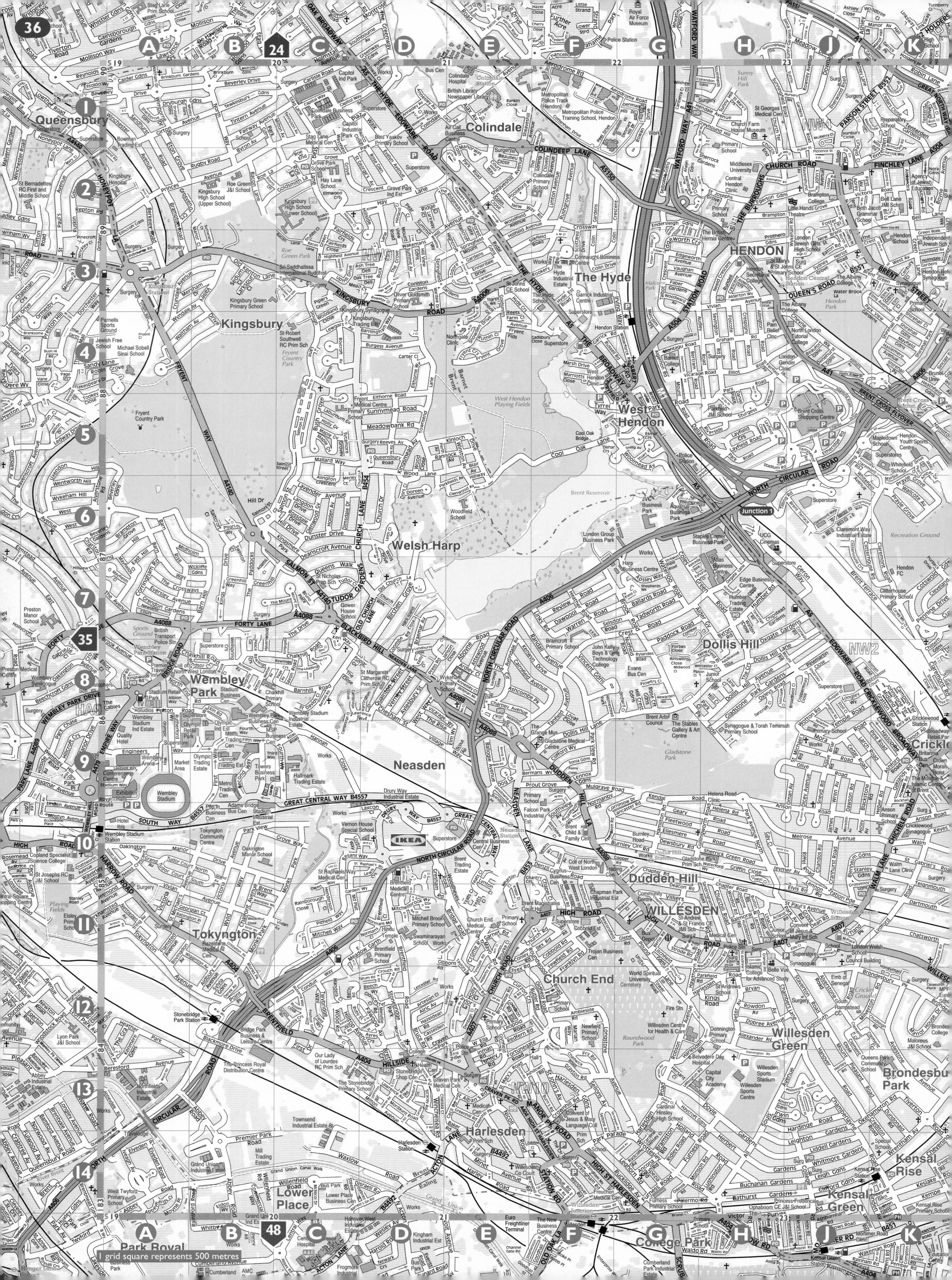
24
35
48
A
B
C
D
E
F
G
H
J
K
Queensbury
Colindale
Kingsbury
The Hyde
HENDON
NW4
NW9
West Hendon
Welsh Harp
Brent Reservoir
Junction 1
Dollis Hill
NW2
Wembley Park
Wembley Stadium
Neasden
IKEA
Dudden Hill
WILLESDEN
Cricklewood
Tokyngton
Church End
Willesden Green
Brondesbury Park
Harlesden
NW10
Kensal Rise
Kensal Green
Lower Place
College Park
Park Royal
NORTH CIRCULAR ROAD
EDGWARE ROAD
WATFORD WAY
KINGSBURY ROAD
FORTY LANE
HARROW ROAD
GREAT CENTRAL WAY B4557
BRENT CROSS FLYOVER
Brent Cross Shopping Centre
Royal Air Force Museum
Fryent Country Park
West Hendon Playing Fields
Gladstone Park
Roundwood Park
Willesden New Cemetery
Grand Union Canal
1 grid square represents 500 metres

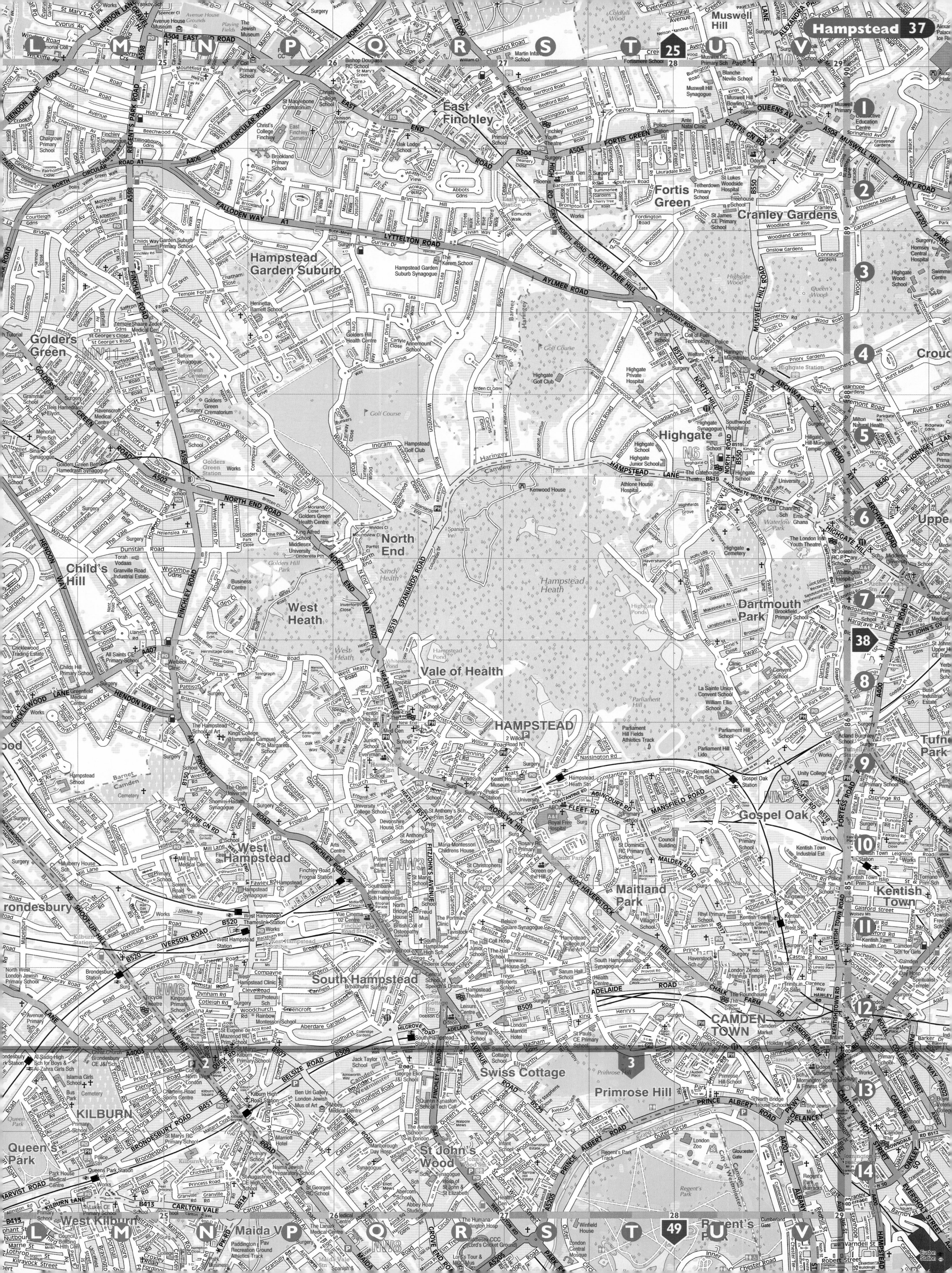
Muswell Hill
East Finchley
Fortis Green
Cranley Gardens
Hampstead Garden Suburb
Golders Green
Highgate
North End
Child's Hill
West Heath
Hampstead Heath
Vale of Health
HAMPSTEAD
Dartmouth Park
Gospel Oak
West Hampstead
Maitland Park
Kentish Town
South Hampstead
CAMDEN TOWN
Swiss Cottage
Primrose Hill
KILBURN
Queen's Park
St John's Wood
West Kilburn
Maida Vale
Regent's Park
25
38
3
49

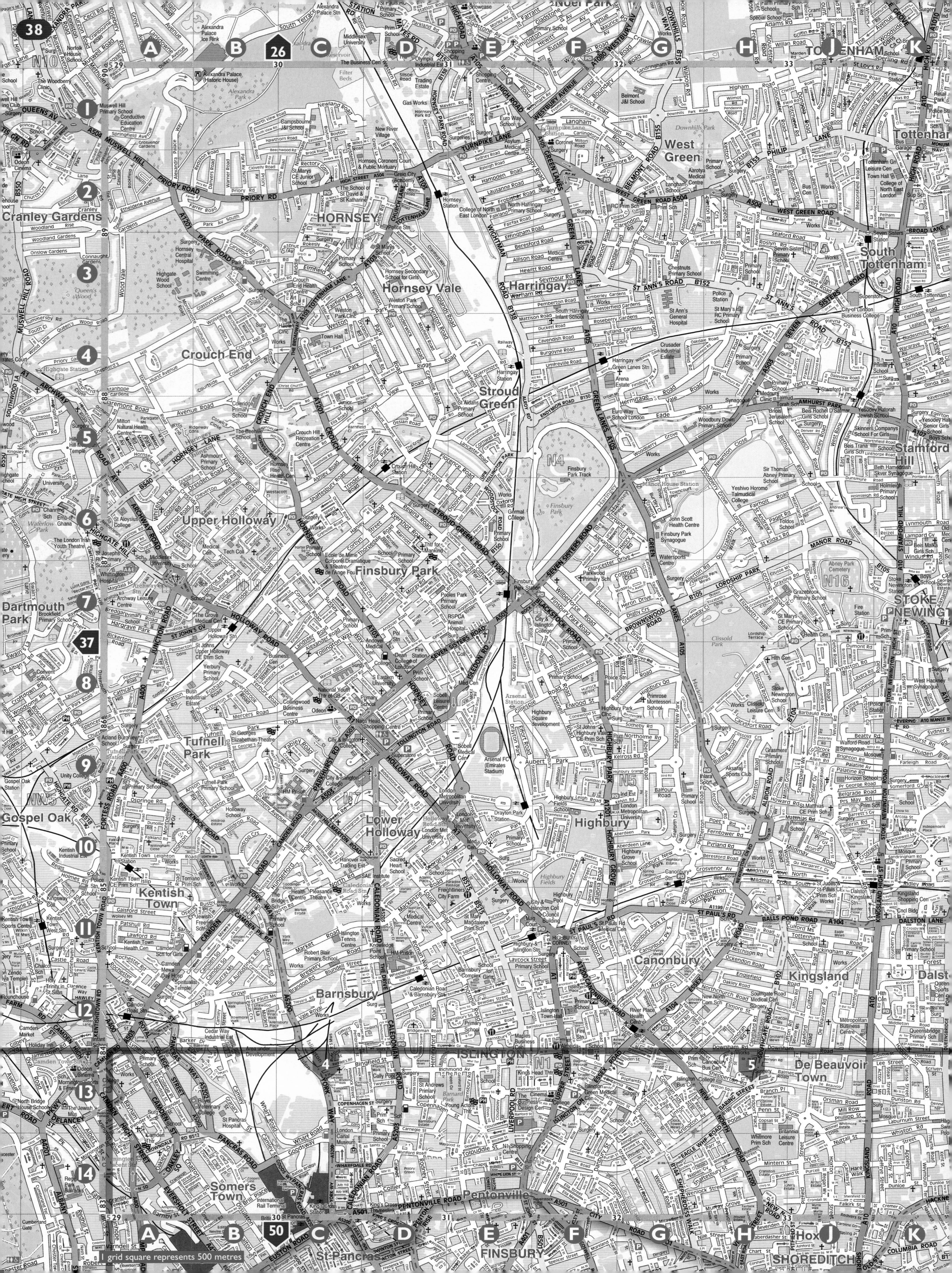

38
26
37
50
A
B
C
D
E
F
G
H
J
K
1
2
3
4
5
6
7
8
9
10
11
12
13
14
TOTTENHAM
Tottenham
West Green
Cranley Gardens
HORNSEY
Hornsey Vale
Harringay
South Tottenham
Crouch End
Stroud Green
Stamford Hill
Upper Holloway
Finsbury Park
STOKE NEWINGTON
Dartmouth Park
Tufnell Park
Gospel Oak
Lower Holloway
Highbury
Kentish Town
Canonbury
Kingsland
Barnsbury
ISLINGTON
De Beauvoir Town
Somers Town
Pentonville
St Pancras
FINSBURY
SHOREDITCH
Hoxton
N10
N8
N4
N15
N16
N19
N5
N7
NW5
N1
1 grid square represents 500 metres

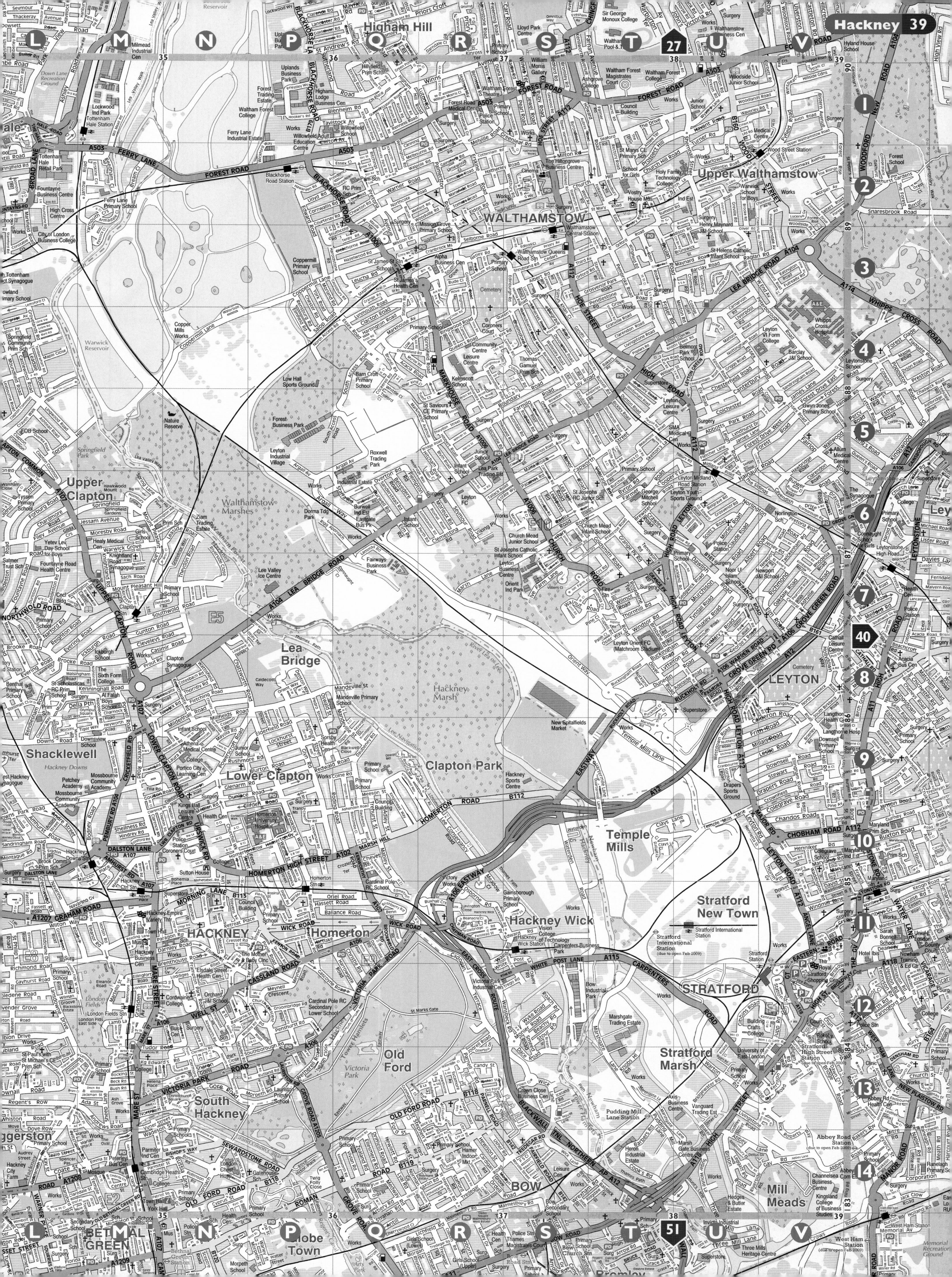
Higham Hill
Upper Walthamstow
WALTHAMSTOW
Upper Clapton
Walthamstow Marshes
Lea Bridge
Hackney Marsh
Shacklewell
Lower Clapton
Clapton Park
Temple Mills
LEYTON
Stratford New Town
HACKNEY
Homerton
Hackney Wick
STRATFORD
Old Ford
Stratford Marsh
South Hackney
BOW
Mill Meads
Globe Town
Bethnal Green
Haggerston
Warwick Reservoir
Victoria Park
Leyton Orient FC (Matchroom Stadium)
New Spitalfields Market
A104 LEA BRIDGE ROAD
A503 FOREST ROAD
A12
A102
A11
E5
E10
E9
E15
E8
E2
27
40
51

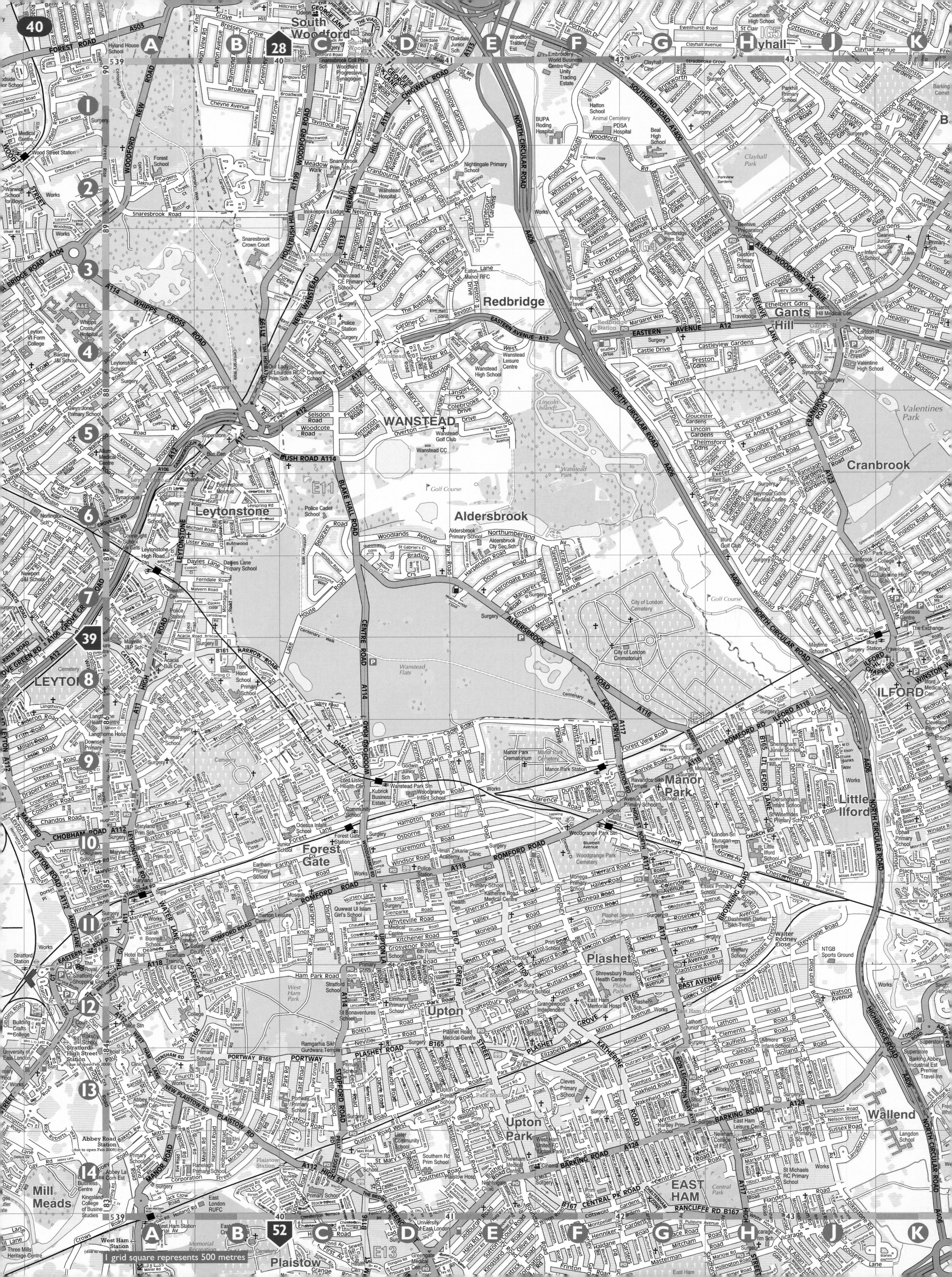

South Woodford
Redbridge
Gants Hill
Hyhall
WANSTEAD
Aldersbrook
Cranbrook
Leytonstone
LEYTON
ILFORD
Manor Park
Little Ilford
Forest Gate
Plashet
Upton
Upton Park
EAST HAM
Wallend
Mill Meads
Plaistow
Wanstead Flats
City of London Cemetery
Valentines Park
NORTH CIRCULAR ROAD
EASTERN AVENUE
ROMFORD ROAD
WOODFORD AVENUE
SOUTHEND ROAD A1400
WHIPPS CROSS ROAD
BARKING ROAD
CENTRAL PK ROAD
RANCLIFFE RD B167
PORTWAY B165
PLASHET ROAD
HIGH STREET NORTH
WOODGRANGE ROAD
CENTRE ROAD A114
BLAKE HALL ROAD
ALDERSBROOK
FOREST DRIVE
HARROW ROAD
CHOBHAM ROAD
LEYTON ROAD
NEW PLAISTOW ROAD
CHIGWELL ROAD
HOLLYBUSH HILL
NEW WANSTEAD
FOREST ROAD
Stratford Station
Wanstead Park Stn
Manor Park Station
Woodgrange Park Stn
Forest Gate Station
Wood Street Station
West Ham Station
Ilford Station
E11
E7
E12
E13
IG1
IG4
IG5
A B C D E F G H J K
1 2 3 4 5 6 7 8 9 10 11 12 13 14
28
39
52
40
41
42
43
539
1 grid square represents 500 metres

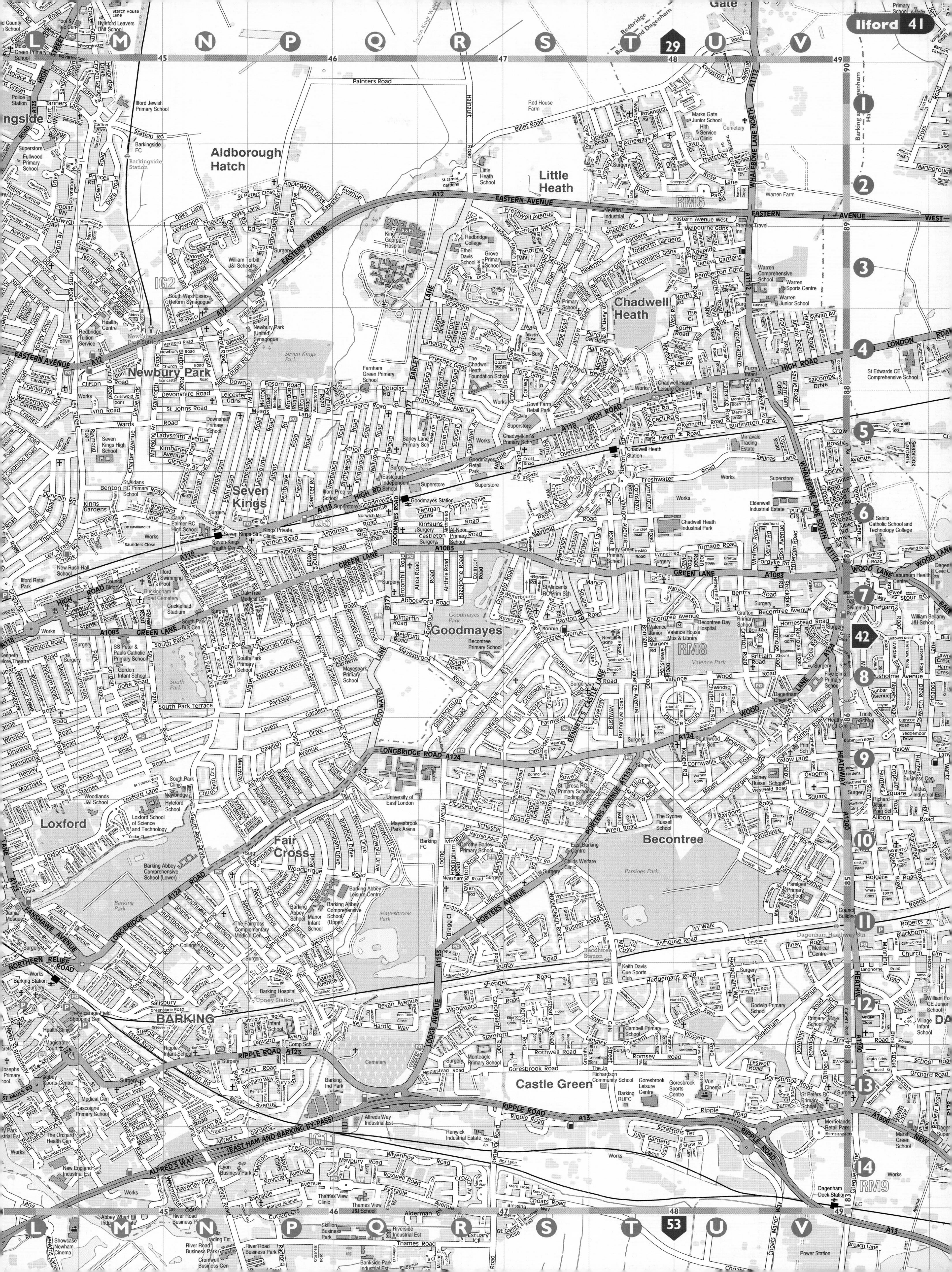
Aldborough Hatch
Little Heath
Chadwell Heath
Newbury Park
Seven Kings
Goodmayes
Loxford
Fair Cross
Becontree
BARKING
Castle Green
EASTERN AVENUE
HIGH ROAD
GREEN LANE
LONGBRIDGE ROAD
RIPPLE ROAD
ALFRED'S WAY (EAST HAM AND BARKING BY-PASS)
WHALEBONE LANE NORTH
WHALEBONE LANE SOUTH
HEATHWAY
PORTERS AVENUE
LODGE AVENUE
King George Hospital
Valence Park
Parsloes Park
Mayesbrook Park
Goodmayes Park
South Park
Barking Park
RM6
RM8
RM9
IG2
IG3
IG11
L M N P Q R S T U V
29
42
53

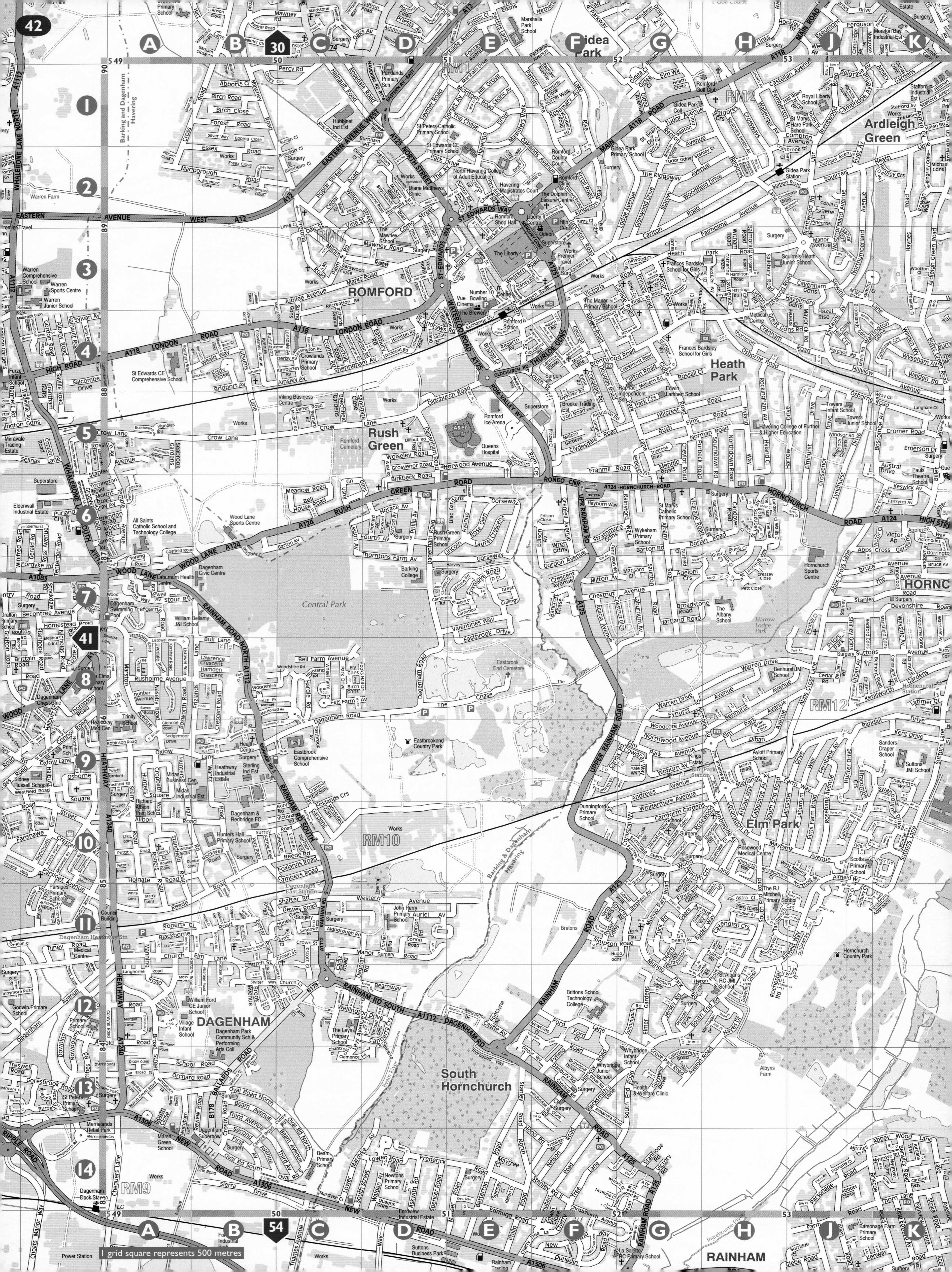
A
B
C
D
E
F
G
H
J
K
30
41
54
Gidea Park
Ardleigh Green
ROMFORD
Heath Park
Rush Green
Central Park
Eastbrookend Country Park
RM1
RM2
RM7
RM10
RM12
RM9
Elm Park
DAGENHAM
South Hornchurch
RAINHAM
HORNC
Hornchurch Country Park
EASTERN AVENUE WEST
A12
A118 LONDON ROAD
MAIN ROAD
A124 RUSH GREEN ROAD
A124 HORNCHURCH ROAD
A125 UPPER RAINHAM ROAD
RAINHAM ROAD NORTH A1112
RAINHAM RD SOUTH
A1112 DAGENHAM RD
A1306 NEW ROAD
A1240 HEATHWAY
WHALEBONE LANE NORTH
A1083 WOOD LANE
WATERLOO ROAD
ST EDWARDS WAY
RIPPLE ROAD
Romford Station
Gidea Park Station
Dagenham East Station
Elm Park Station
Dagenham Heathway Stn
Dagenham Dock Stn
Hornchurch Station
Queens Hospital
Romford Ice Arena
Barking and Dagenham
Havering
1 grid square represents 500 metres

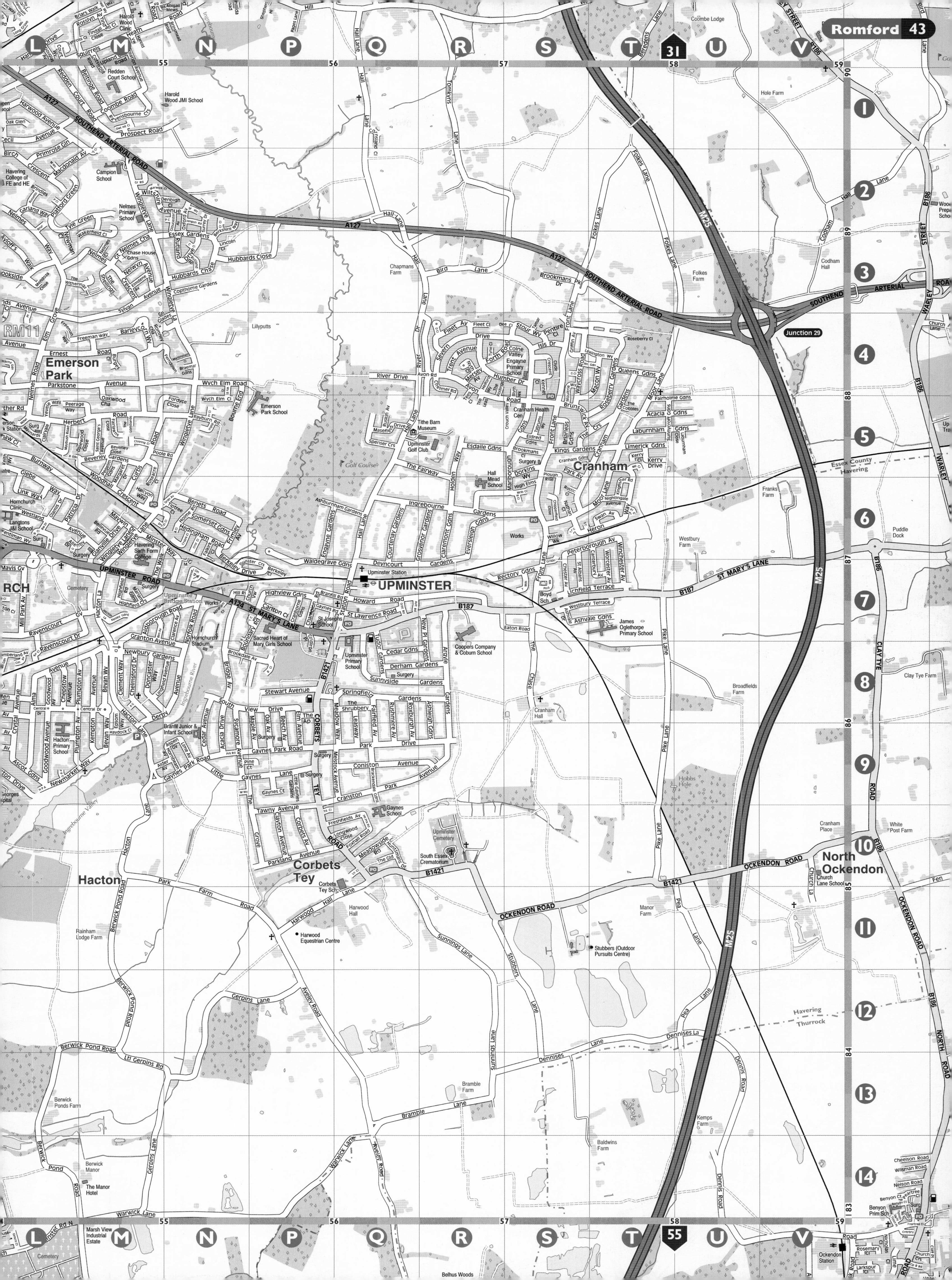

Emerson Park
UPMINSTER
Cranham
Hacton
Corbets Tey
North Ockendon
SOUTHEND ARTERIAL ROAD
A127
M25
Junction 29
UPMINSTER ROAD
A124 ST MARY'S LANE
B187 ST MARY'S LANE
B1421
OCKENDON ROAD
B186
CLAY TYE ROAD
WARLEY STREET
NORTH ROAD
Hall Lane
Bird Lane
Folkes Lane
Front Lane
Pike Lane
Aveley Road
Sunnings Lane
Stubbers Lane
Dennises Lane
Dennis Road
Bramble Lane
Warwick Lane
Berwick Pond Road
Gerpins Lane
Harwood Hall Lane
Park Farm Road
Upminster Station
Emerson Park School
Tithe Barn Museum
Upminster Golf Club
Hall Mead School
Coopers Company & Coburn School
James Oglethorpe Primary School
Sacred Heart of Mary Girls School
Gaynes School
Hacton Primary School
Havering Sixth Form College
Campion School
Nelmes Primary School
Upminster Cemetery
South Essex Crematorium
Stubbers (Outdoor Pursuits Centre)
Harwood Equestrian Centre
Berwick Ponds Farm
Berwick Manor
The Manor Hotel
Marsh View Industrial Estate
Ockendon Station
Belhus Woods
Essex County
Havering
Thurrock
RM11

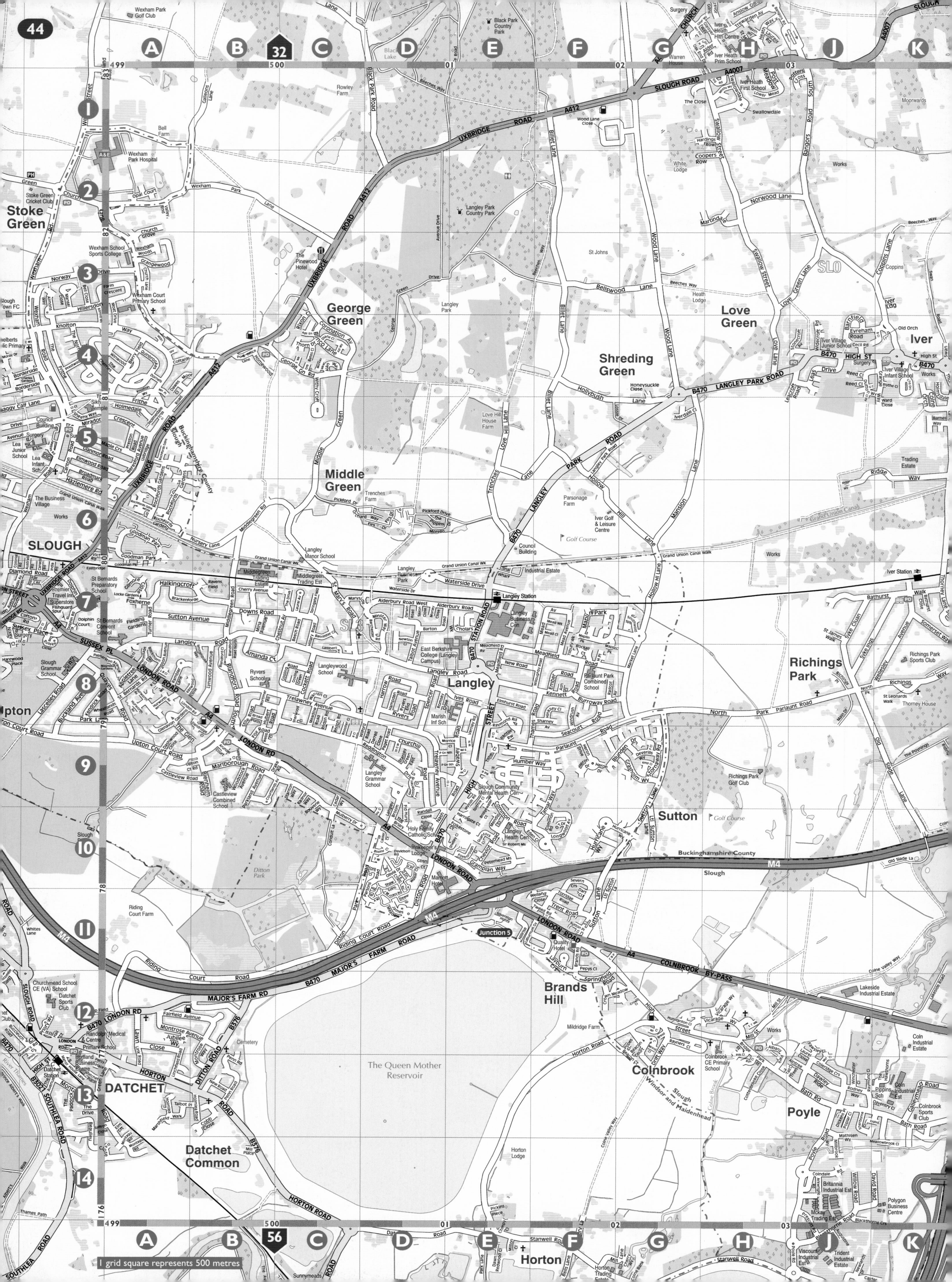
A
B
32
C
D
E
F
G
H
J
K
Wexham Park Golf Club
Black Park Country Park
Black Lake
Rowley Farm
Beeches Way
Black Park Road
SLOUGH ROAD
A4007
Surgery
Iver Heath
Iver Heath Hlth Centre
Iver Heath Prim School
Iver Heath First School
Warren House
Swallowdale
The Close
Wood Lane Close
Bell Farm
Wexham Park Hospital
A&E
UXBRIDGE ROAD
A412
Wexham Park Lane
Opal Court
Church Grove
Stoke Green Cricket Club
Stoke Green
Wexham School Sports College
Wexham Court Primary School
Norway Drive
Hillersdon
Knolton Way
Slough Town FC
Langley Park Country Park
Avenue Drive
The Pinewood Hotel
St Johns
Bellswood Lane
Beeches Way
Heath Lodge
Hardings Row
Coopers Row
White Lodge
Norwood Lane
Works
Moorwards
Swallow Street
Bangors Road South
Love Green Lane
Coppins Lane
SL0
Coppins
Iver Ldg
Old Orch
Iver
High St
HIGH ST
B470
Iver Village Junior School
Iver Village Infant School
Evreham Road
Barnfield
Cecil Rd
George Green
Coronation Av
George Gn Rd
Wilton Croft
Langley Park
Love Green
Shreding Green
Billet Lane
Wood Lane
Honeysuckle Close
Hollybush Lane
B470 LANGLEY PARK ROAD
Iverdale Cl
Love Hill House Farm
Love Hill Lane
Trenches Lane
LANGLEY PARK ROAD
Hollow Hill Lane
Mansion Lane
Parsonage Farm
Iver Golf & Leisure Centre
Golf Course
Council Building
Grand Union Canal
Grand Union Canal Wk
Trading Estate
Ridge Way
Works
Middle Green
Trenches Farm
Pickford Dr
Pickford Drive
Nursery Lane
Middlegreen Rd
Langley Manor School
Langley Business Park
Waterside Drive
Industrial Estate
Iver Station
Langley Station
Bathurst Walk
Buckinghamshire County
SLOUGH
Holmedale
Crescent
Mirador Crescent
Elmwood Road
Hazlemere Rd
Sikh Temple
Council Building
Lea Junior School
Lea Infant Sch
The Business Village
Works
Goodman Park
Grand Union Canal Walk
Rochford Gardens
Halkingcroft
Middlegreen Trading Estate
Middlegreen Trading Est
Cherry Avenue
Ravens Field
Brackenforde
Foxherne
St Bernards Preparatory School
Premier Travel Inn
Superstore
Fishguard Spur
Dolphin Court
St Bernards Convent School
Fielding Gardens
Sutton Avenue
Downs Road
Alderbury Road West
Alderbury Road
STATION ROAD
B470
Langley Business Cen
SL3
Barton
Meadfield Rd
Meadfield
Mead Av
Sussex Place
SUSSEX PL
A4
LONDON ROAD
Langley Road
Amanda Ct
Lambert Av
East Berkshire College (Langley Campus)
Slough Grammar School
Harewood Place
Upton
Ryvers School
Langleywood School
Langley Road
Langley
New Road
Parlaunt Park Combined School
Kennett Rd
Burroway Road
Richings Park
Richings Park Sports Club
St Leonards Walk
Thorney House
Richings Way
North Park
Parlaunt Road
Upton Court Road
Lascelles Road
Buckland Av
Kendrick Road
Park Lane
Trelawney Avenue
Churchill Road
Ivers Road
Marish Inf Sch
Elmhurst Road
Parlaunt Road
Seacourt Rd
Humber Way
Thames Road
Upton Court Road
Castleview Road
Marlborough Road
Castleview Combined School
Blenheim Road
Redington
Langley Grammar School
Trelawney Avenue
Slough Community Mental Health Cen
Common Road
Langley Health Cen
Sutton
Lt Sutton Lane
Golf Course
Richings Park Golf Club
Old Slade Lane
The Poynings
Slough
Ditton Park
Riding Court Farm
Mulberry Dr
Conduit La
Cedar Wy
Holy Family Catholic Sch
Kingpeeper's Lodge
Marriott Hotel
Grampian Way
Peterhead Ms
Sir Robert Ms
Tamar Way
Hurricane Wy
Buckinghamshire County
Slough
M4
Old Slade La
Ditton Road
Riding Court Road
Junction 5
Severn Cres
Trent Road
Tweed Rd
Quality Hotel
LONDON ROAD
A4
COLNBROOK BY-PASS
Pepys Cl
Springfield Road
Brands Hill
Colne Valley Way
Lakeside Industrial Estate
Whites Lane
Riding Court Road
B470 MAJOR'S FARM ROAD
MAJOR'S FARM RD
Churchmead School CE (VA) School
Datchet Sports Club
SLOUGH ROAD
B470 LONDON RD
Fairfield Avenue
Montrose Avenue
Jubilee Wy
B376
Cemetery
Randolph Medical Centre
Primary School
Datchet Station
Close
HORTON
DITTON ROAD
Penn Rd
New Road
Talbot Pl
DATCHET
Mildridge Farm
Horton Road
Vicarage Way
Mill St
Albany
Works
Raymers Cl
Colnbrook CE Primary School
Colnbrook
Slough
Windsor and Maidenhead
Colne Brook
Coln Industrial Estate
Pippins Sch
Coln Industrial Est
Colnbrook Sports Club
Bath Rd
Bath Road
Galleymead Road
Poyle
Mathisen Wy
Meadowbrook Cl
The Queen Mother Reservoir
Horton Lodge
Datchet Common
Mill Place
B376
River Thames
B3021 SOUTHLEA ROAD
HORTON ROAD
Colndale Rd
Britannia Industrial Est
Willow Road
David Road
Polygon Business Centre
Mckay Trading Est
Pickins Piece
Blackthorne Road
Blackthorne Cres
Thames Path
499
500
01
02
03
56
Datchet Road
Stanwell Road
Horton
Stanwell Road
Park Lane
Horton Trading Estate
Viscount Industrial Est
Trident Industrial Estate
SOUTHLEA ROAD
Sunnymeads
ROAD
1 grid square represents 500 metres
1
2
3
4
5
6
7
8
9
10
11
12
13
14
83
82
81
80
79
78
77
176

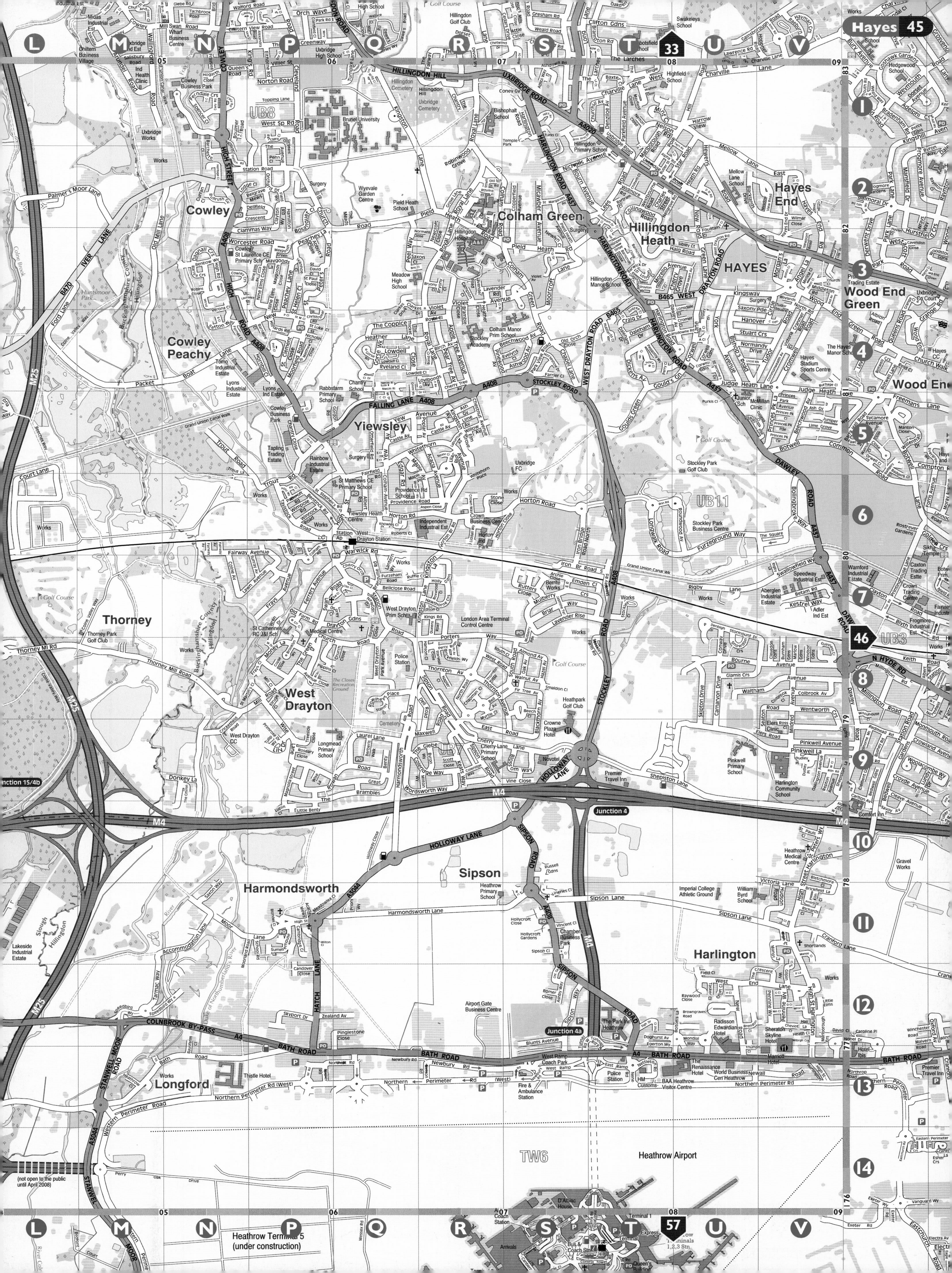
Cowley
Cowley Peachy
Yiewsley
Colham Green
Hillingdon Heath
Hayes End
HAYES
Wood End Green
Thorney
West Drayton
Harmondsworth
Sipson
Harlington
Longford
Heathrow Airport
Brunel University
Hillingdon Hill
Uxbridge Road
High Street
Harlington Road
West Drayton Road
Stockley Road
Falling Lane A408
Dawley Road
Holloway Lane
Sipson Road
Hatch Lane
Bath Road
Colnbrook By-Pass
Stanwell Moor Road
Northern Perimeter Rd
Western Perimeter Road
Iver Lane
Packet Boat Lane
Thorney Mill Road
Sipson Lane
Harmondsworth Lane
N Hyde Rd
Stockley Park Golf Club
Thorney Park Golf Club
Heathpark Golf Club
West Drayton Station
Grand Union Canal Walk
M4
M25
A4
Junction 4
Junction 4a
Junction 15/4b
UB8
UB7
UB11
UB3
TW6
Heathrow Terminal 5 (under construction)
Heathrow Terminals 1,2,3 Stn
(not open to the public until April 2008)
33
46
57
L M N P Q R S T U V
05 06 07 08 09
1 2 3 4 5 6 7 8 9 10 11 12 13 14
76 77 78 79 80 81 82 83

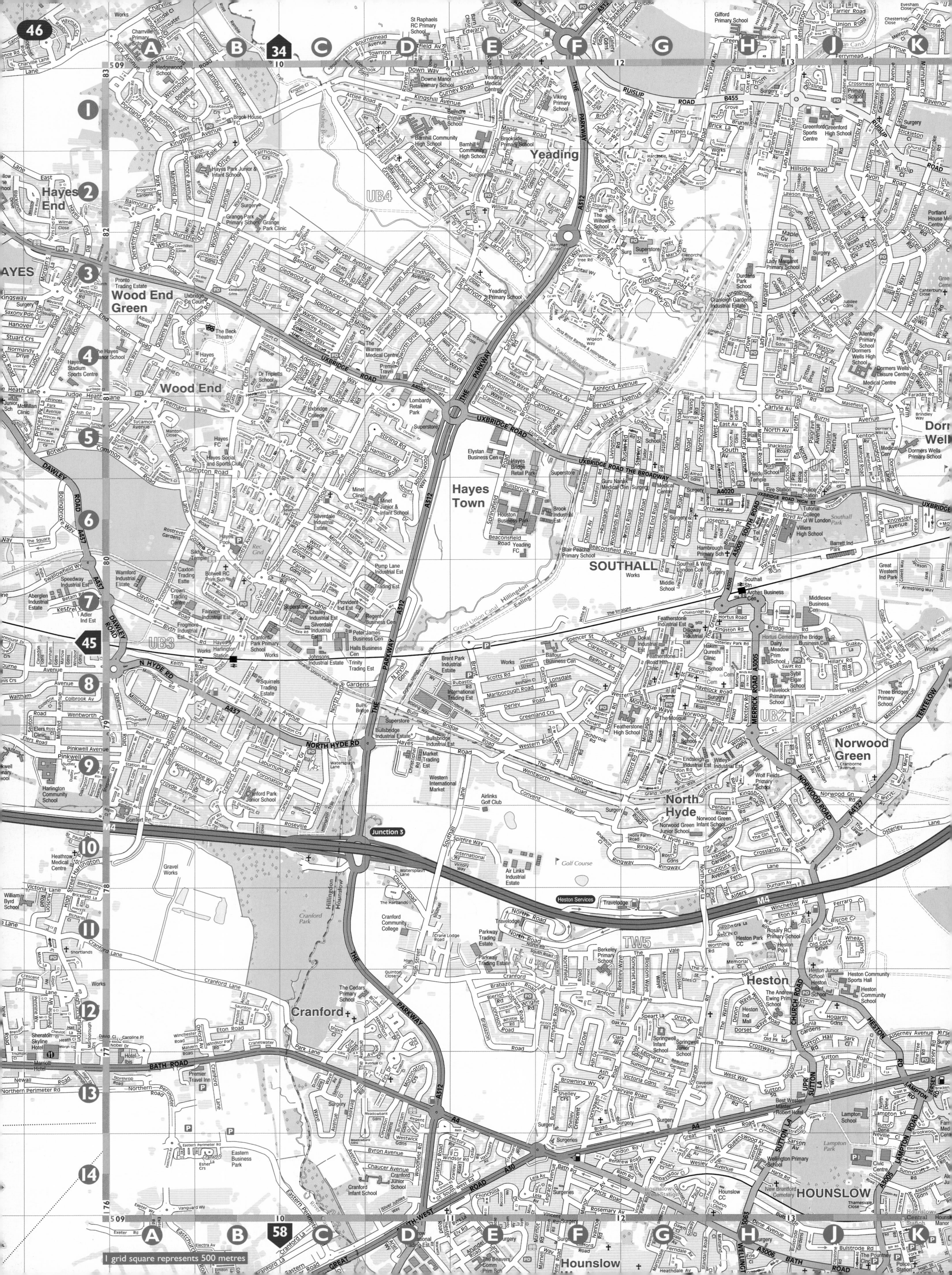

46
34
58
45
A B C D E F G H J K
1 2 3 4 5 6 7 8 9 10 11 12 13 14
Hayes End
Wood End Green
Wood End
Yeading
Hayes Town
SOUTHALL
Norwood Green
North Hyde
Heston
Cranford
HOUNSLOW
Hounslow
UB4
UB3
UB1
UB2
TW5
UXBRIDGE ROAD
THE PARKWAY
NORTH HYDE RD
BATH ROAD
M4
Junction 3
Heston Services
Grand Union Canal
1 grid square represents 500 metres

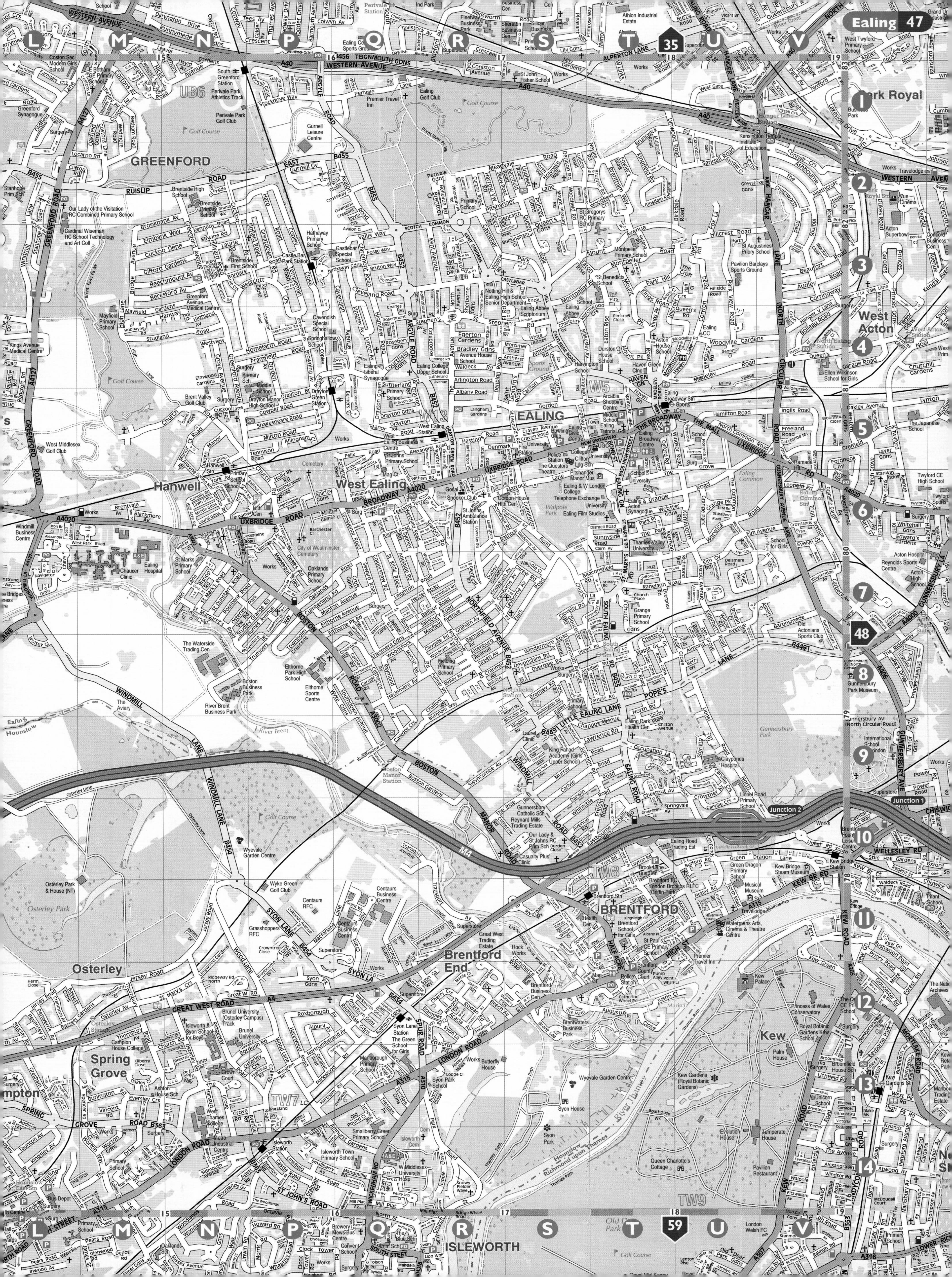
GREENFORD
Hanwell
West Ealing
EALING
West Acton
Park Royal
BRENTFORD
Brentford End
Osterley
Spring Grove
Kew
ISLEWORTH
W5
W13
TW7
TW8
TW9
UB6
WESTERN AVENUE
A40
RUISLIP ROAD
UXBRIDGE ROAD
BOSTON ROAD
NORTHFIELD AVENUE
SOUTH EALING RD
GUNNERSBURY AVENUE
NORTH CIRCULAR ROAD
HANGER LANE
GREAT WEST ROAD
LONDON ROAD
KEW ROAD
M4
Osterley Park
Gunnersbury Park
Kew Gardens (Royal Botanic Gardens)
Syon Park
Walpole Park
Ealing Common
35
48
59

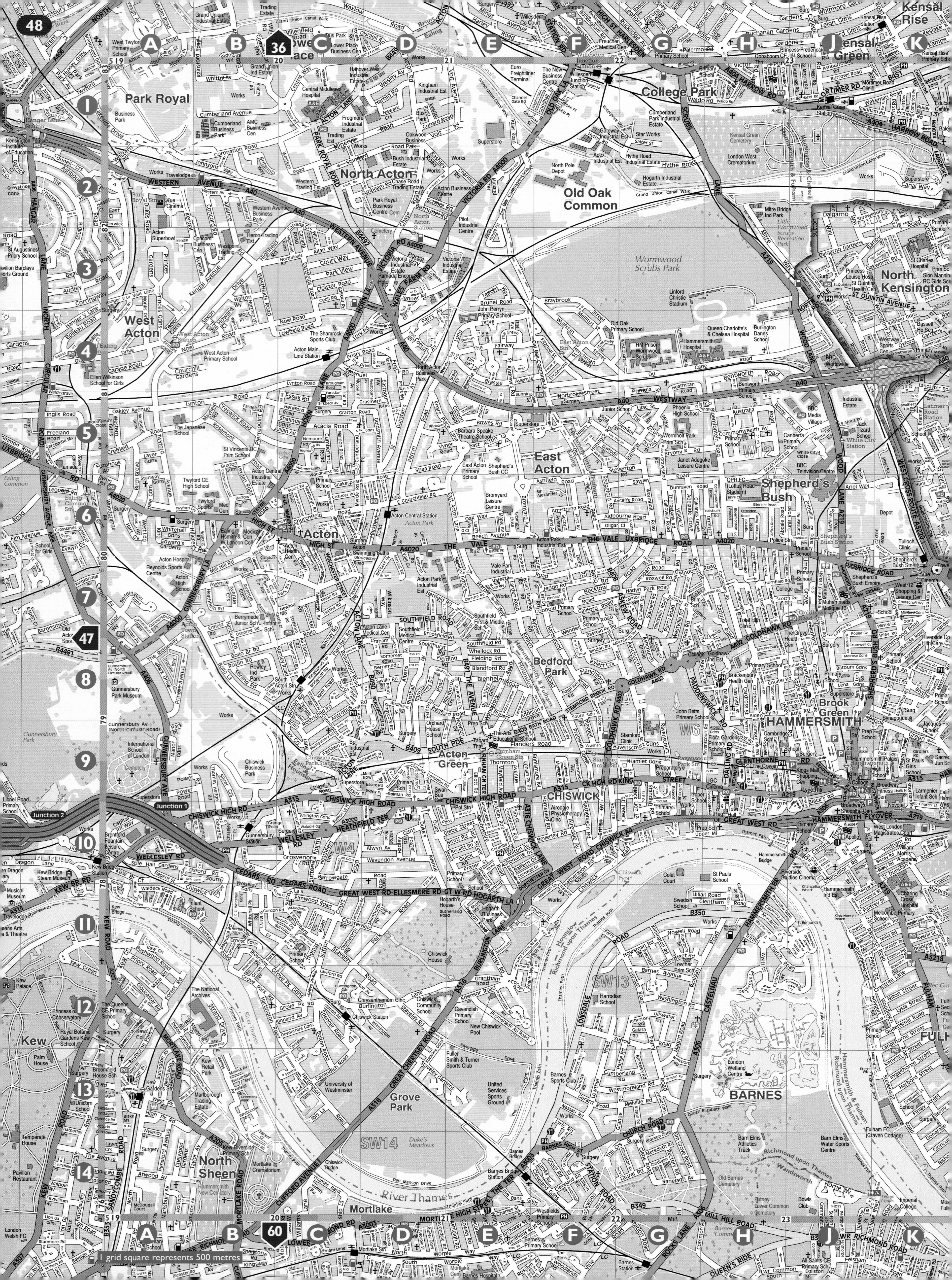
Park Royal
North Acton
Old Oak Common
College Park
Kensal Rise
Kensal Green
North Kensington
West Acton
Wormwood Scrubs Park
East Acton
Shepherd's Bush
Acton
Bedford Park
Acton Green
Chiswick
Brook Green
HAMMERSMITH
Kew
North Sheen
Grove Park
Mortlake
BARNES
FULH
River Thames
SW14
SW13
W3
W4
W6
W12
WESTERN AVENUE
WESTWAY
NORTH CIRCULAR ROAD
UXBRIDGE ROAD
CHISWICK HIGH ROAD
GREAT WEST ROAD
HAMMERSMITH FLYOVER
WEST CROSS ROUTE
WOOD LANE
SCRUBS LANE
HARROW ROAD
GOLDHAWK RD
KING STREET
CASTELNAU
UPPER RICHMOND ROAD
Junction 1
Junction 2
Gunnersbury Park
London Wetland Centre
Kew Gardens
Chiswick House
36
47
60
A
B
C
D
E
F
G
H
J
K
1
2
3
4
5
6
7
8
9
10
11
12
13
14
1 grid square represents 500 metres

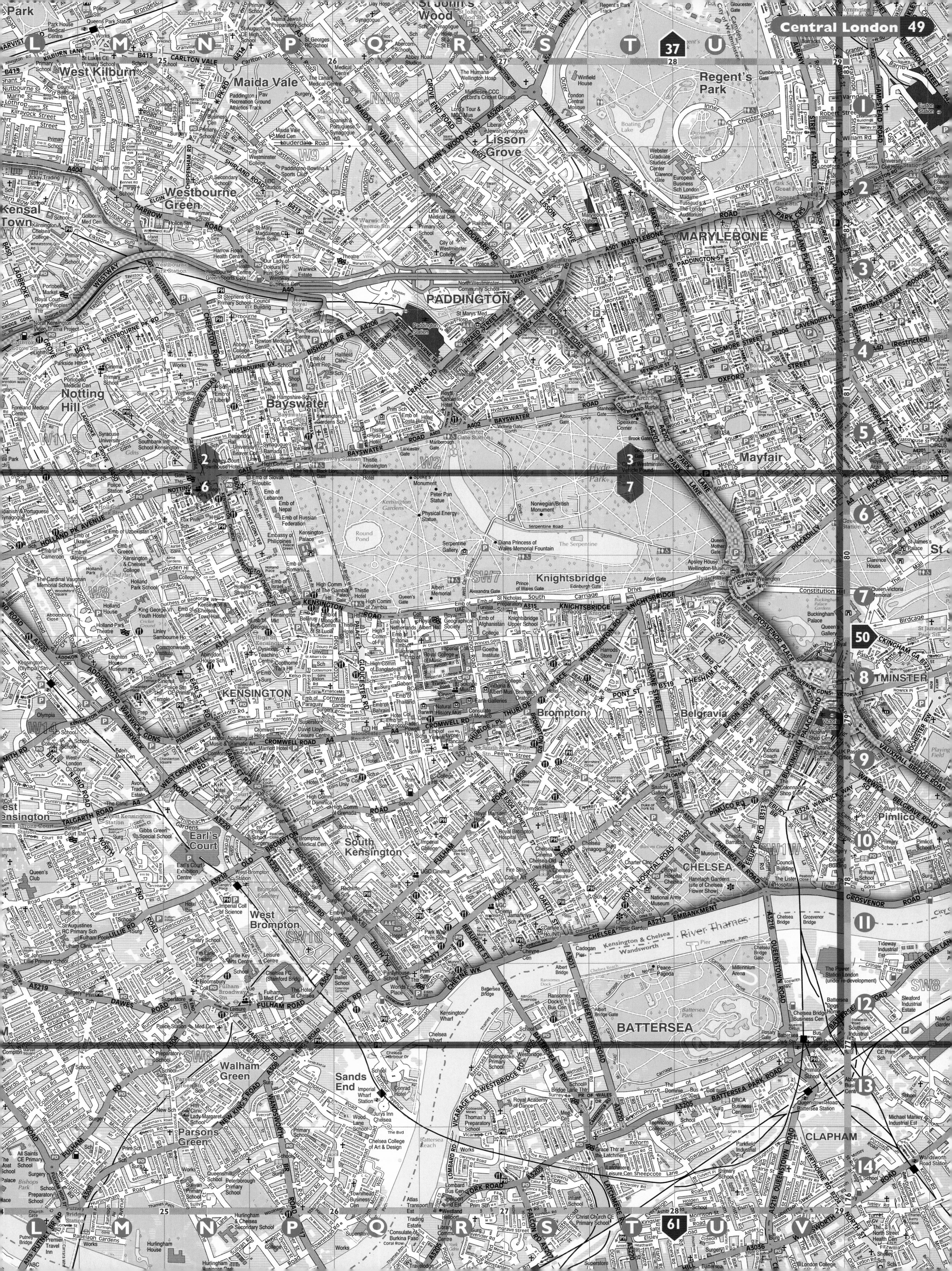
West Kilburn
Maida Vale
St John's Wood
Regent's Park
Lisson Grove
Westbourne Green
Kensal Town
Marylebone
Paddington
Notting Hill
Bayswater
Mayfair
Hyde Park
Kensington Gardens
Knightsbridge
Kensington
Brompton
Belgravia
Earl's Court
South Kensington
Chelsea
West Brompton
Pimlico
Battersea
Walham Green
Sands End
Parsons Green
Clapham
River Thames

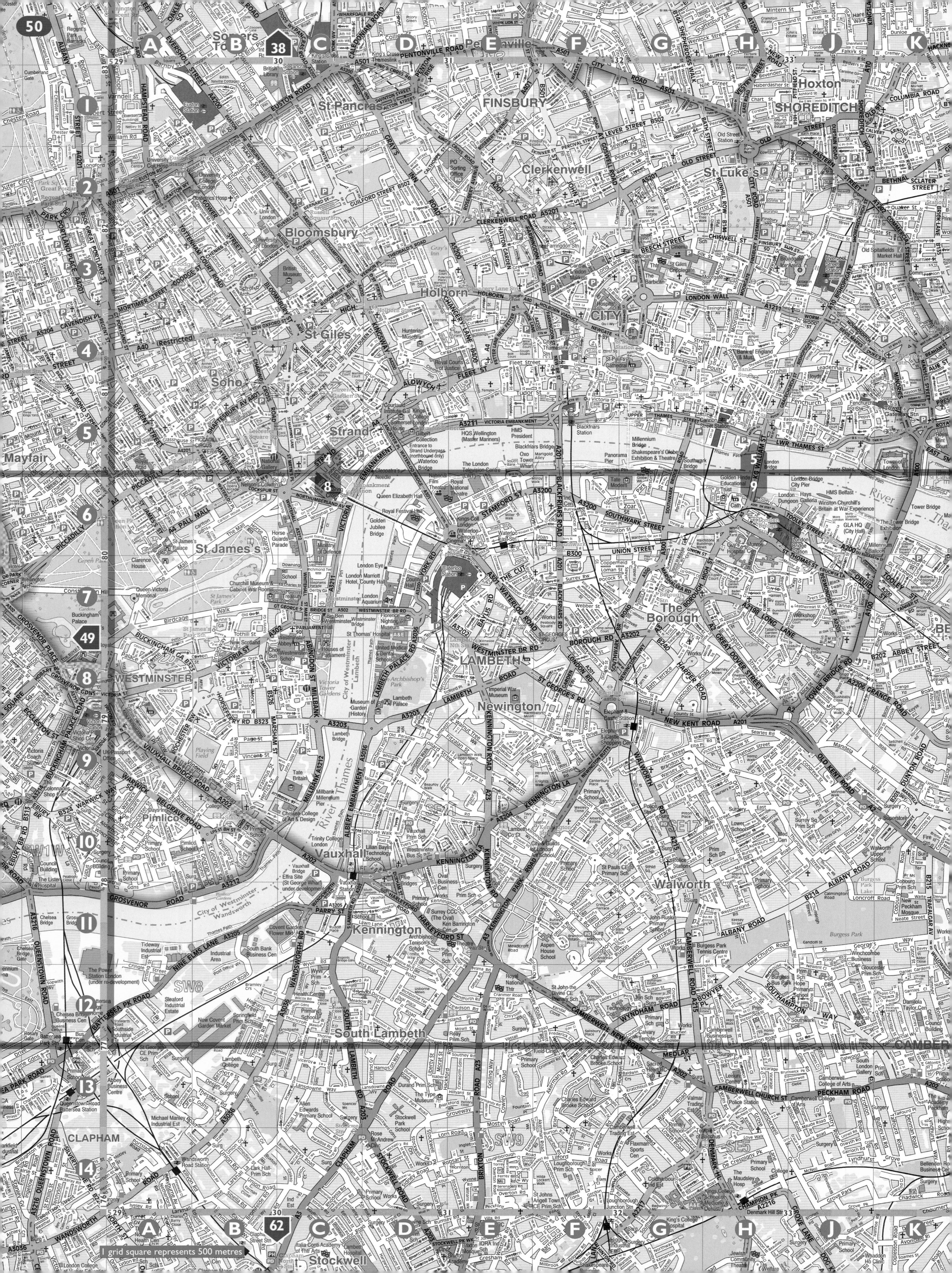
50
38
49
62
A B C D E F G H J K
1 2 3 4 5 6 7 8 9 10 11 12 13 14
Somers Town
Pentonville
St Pancras
FINSBURY
Hoxton
SHOREDITCH
Clerkenwell
St Luke's
Bloomsbury
Holborn
CITY
St Giles
Soho
Mayfair
Strand
St James's
WESTMINSTER
LAMBETH
The Borough
Newington
Pimlico
Vauxhall
Kennington
Walworth
South Lambeth
CLAPHAM
Stockwell
SW1W
SE11
SE17
SW8
SW9
SE5
River Thames
Euston Station
King's Cross Station
British Library
British Museum
Waterloo Station
Victoria Station
Burgess Park
Buckingham Palace
Houses of Parliament
London Eye
Tower of London
Elephant & Castle Station
1 grid square represents 500 metres

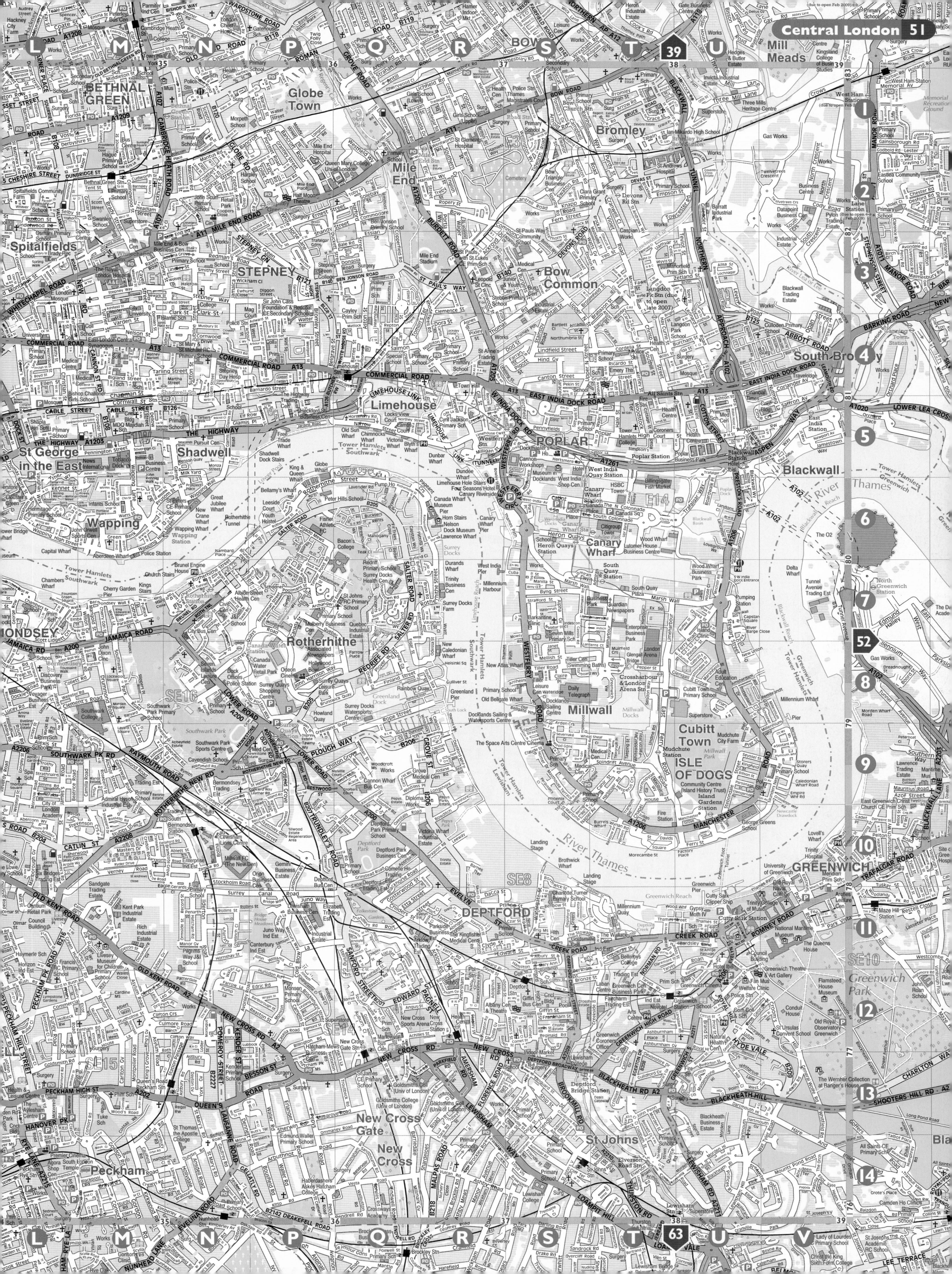
BETHNAL GREEN
Globe Town
Mile End
Bromley
Mill Meads
Spitalfields
STEPNEY
Bow Common
South Bromley
Limehouse
POPLAR
St George in the East
Shadwell
Wapping
Blackwall
Canary Wharf
River Thames
Rotherhithe
Millwall
Cubitt Town
ISLE OF DOGS
DEPTFORD
GREENWICH
Greenwich Park
New Cross Gate
New Cross
St Johns
Peckham
The O2
COMMERCIAL ROAD
EAST INDIA DOCK ROAD
MILE END ROAD
THE HIGHWAY
JAMAICA ROAD
LOWER ROAD
OLD KENT ROAD
NEW CROSS RD
EVELYN ST
CREEK ROAD
BLACKHEATH HILL
SHOOTERS HILL RD
LEWISHAM WAY
BLACKWALL TUNNEL NORTHERN APPROACH
BARKING ROAD
MANCHESTER ROAD
WESTFERRY ROAD
SALTER ROAD
ROTHERHITHE NEW RD
PECKHAM HIGH ST
QUEEN'S ROAD

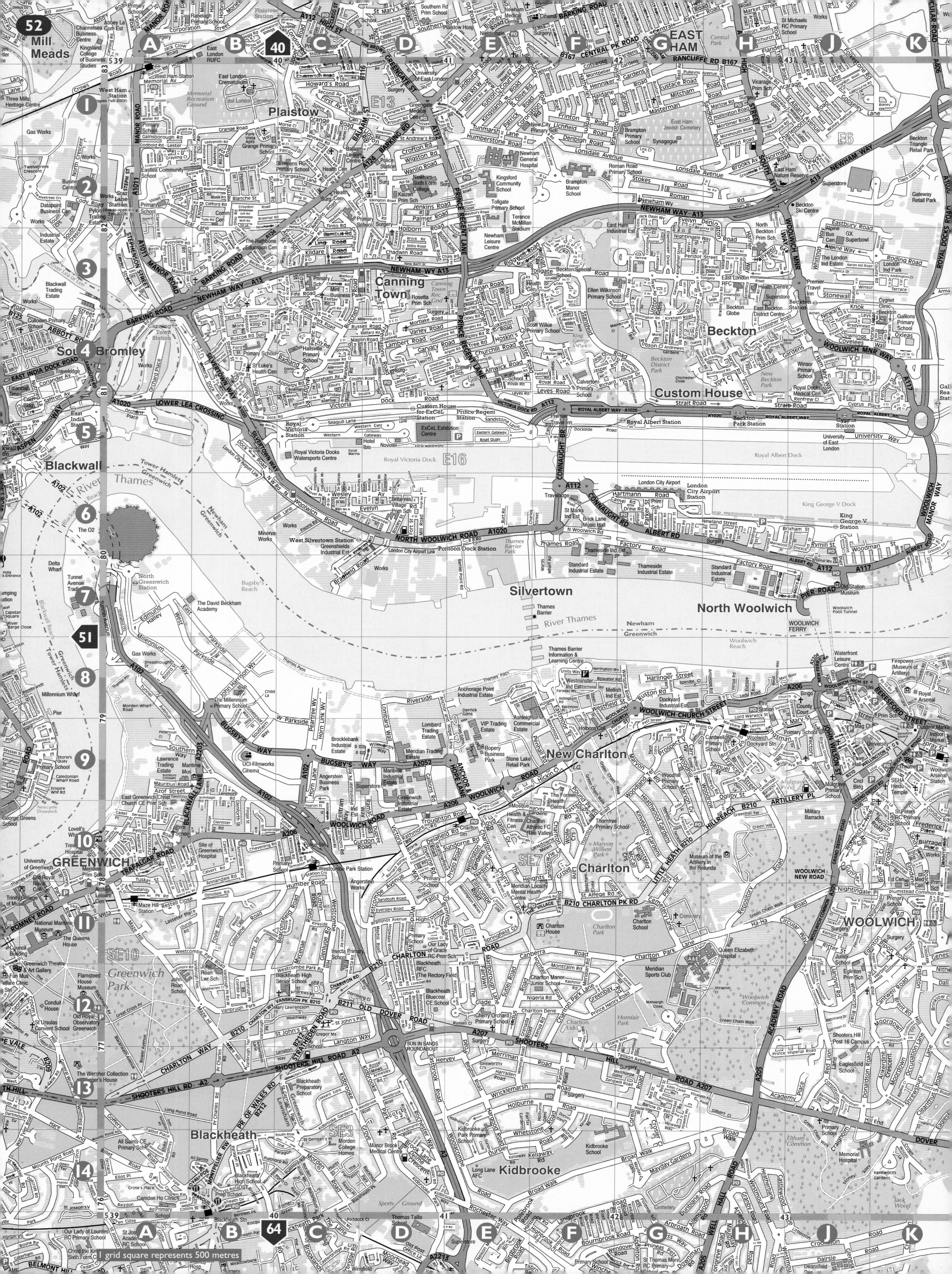
Mill Meads
Plaistow
East Ham
Canning Town
Beckton
South Bromley
Custom House
Blackwall
Silvertown
North Woolwich
River Thames
Royal Victoria Dock
Royal Albert Dock
King George V Dock
London City Airport
The O2
New Charlton
Greenwich
Charlton
Woolwich
Greenwich Park
Blackheath
Kidbrooke
E13
E6
E16
SE10
SE7
SE3
NEWHAM WAY A13
NORTH WOOLWICH ROAD A1020
WOOLWICH ROAD A206
SHOOTERS HILL ROAD A2
ROYAL ALBERT WAY A1020
LOWER LEA CROSSING
BARKING ROAD
PRINCE REGENT LANE
WOOLWICH CHURCH STREET
ACADEMY ROAD
A
B
C
D
E
F
G
H
J
K
1
2
3
4
5
6
7
8
9
10
11
12
13
14

40
51
64

1 grid square represents 500 metres

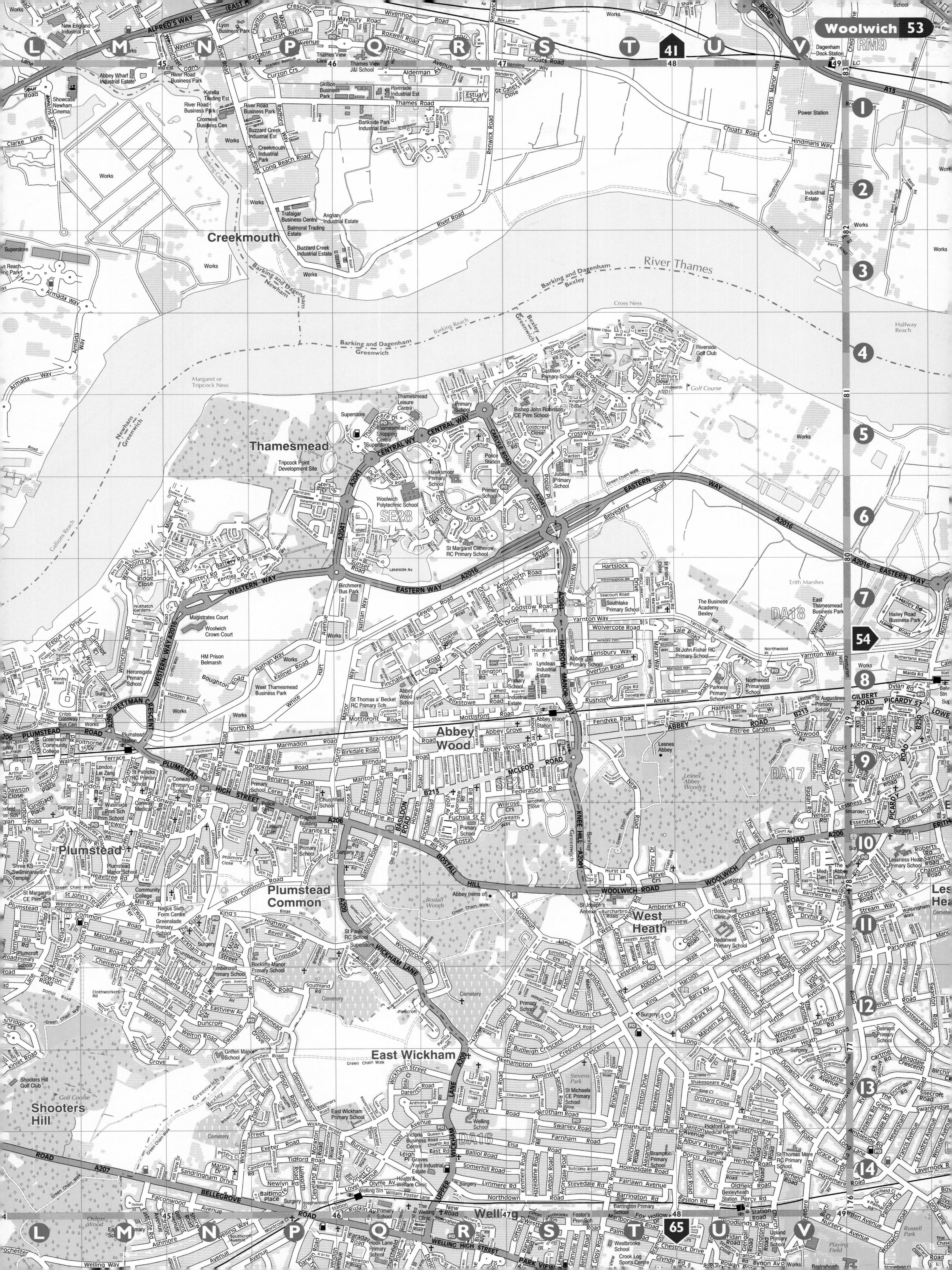

Creekmouth
River Thames
Thamesmead
SE28
Abbey Wood
SE2
DA18
DA17
Plumstead
SE18
Plumstead Common
West Heath
East Wickham
Shooters Hill
Welling
DA16
RM9
Barking and Dagenham
Newham
Greenwich
Bexley
Cross Ness
Barking Reach
Margaret or Tripcock Ness
Halfway Reach
Gallions Reach
Erith Marshes
Lesnes Abbey Woods
Bostall Woods
EASTERN WAY
WESTERN WAY
PLUMSTEAD HIGH STREET
WOOLWICH ROAD
HARROW MANOR WAY
RIVER ROAD
41
54
65
L
M
N
P
Q
R
S
T
U
V
1
2
3
4
5
6
7
8
9
10
11
12
13
14

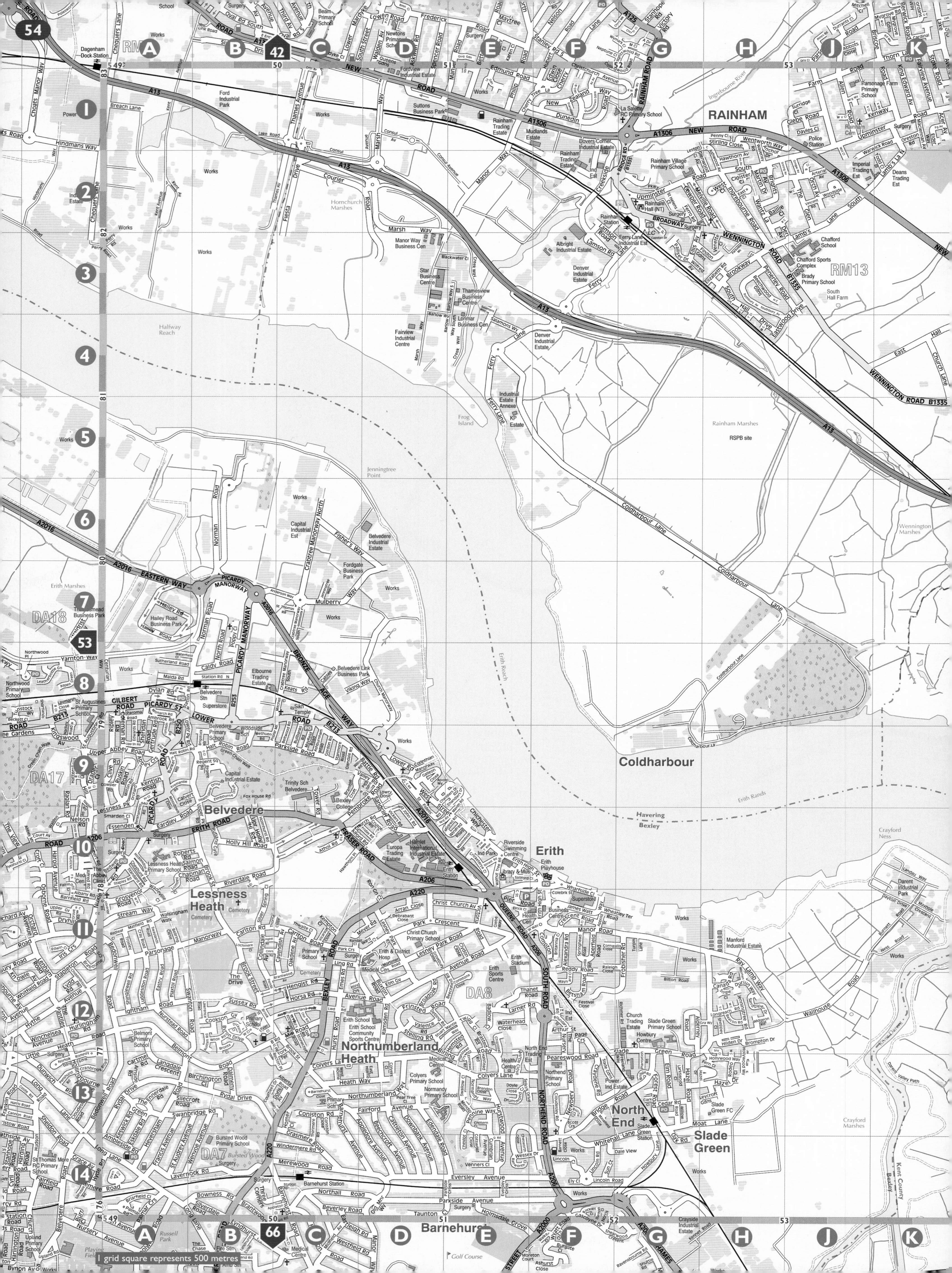
54
42
53
66
RAINHAM
RM13
Rainham Marshes
RSPB site
Wennington Marshes
Ingrebourne River
NEW ROAD
A1306
A13
WENNINGTON ROAD B1335
RAINHAM ROAD
BROADWAY
Rainham Station
Rainham Hall (NT)
Chafford School
Chafford Sports Complex
Brady Primary School
South Hall Farm
Hornchurch Marshes
Halfway Reach
Frog Island
Jenningtree Point
Erith Reach
Coldharbour Lane
Coldharbour
Erith Rands
Havering
Bexley
Crayford Ness
Darent Industrial Park
Crayford Marshes
Dagenham Dock Station
Ford Industrial Park
Suttons Business Park
Rainham Trading Estate
Fairview Industrial Centre
Thamesview Business Centre
Erith Marshes
DA18
EASTERN WAY
A2016
PICARDY MANORWAY
BRONZE AGE WAY
Belvedere Stn
DA17
Belvedere
ERITH ROAD
Lessness Heath
Erith
Erith Station
Erith Playhouse
Riverside Swimming Centre
DA8
Erith Stadium
SOUTH ROAD
NORTHEND ROAD
Northumberland Heath
North End
Slade Green
Slade Green Station
Manford Industrial Estate
Kent County
DA7
Bursted Wood
Barnehurst Station
Barnehurst
Golf Course
1 grid square represents 500 metres

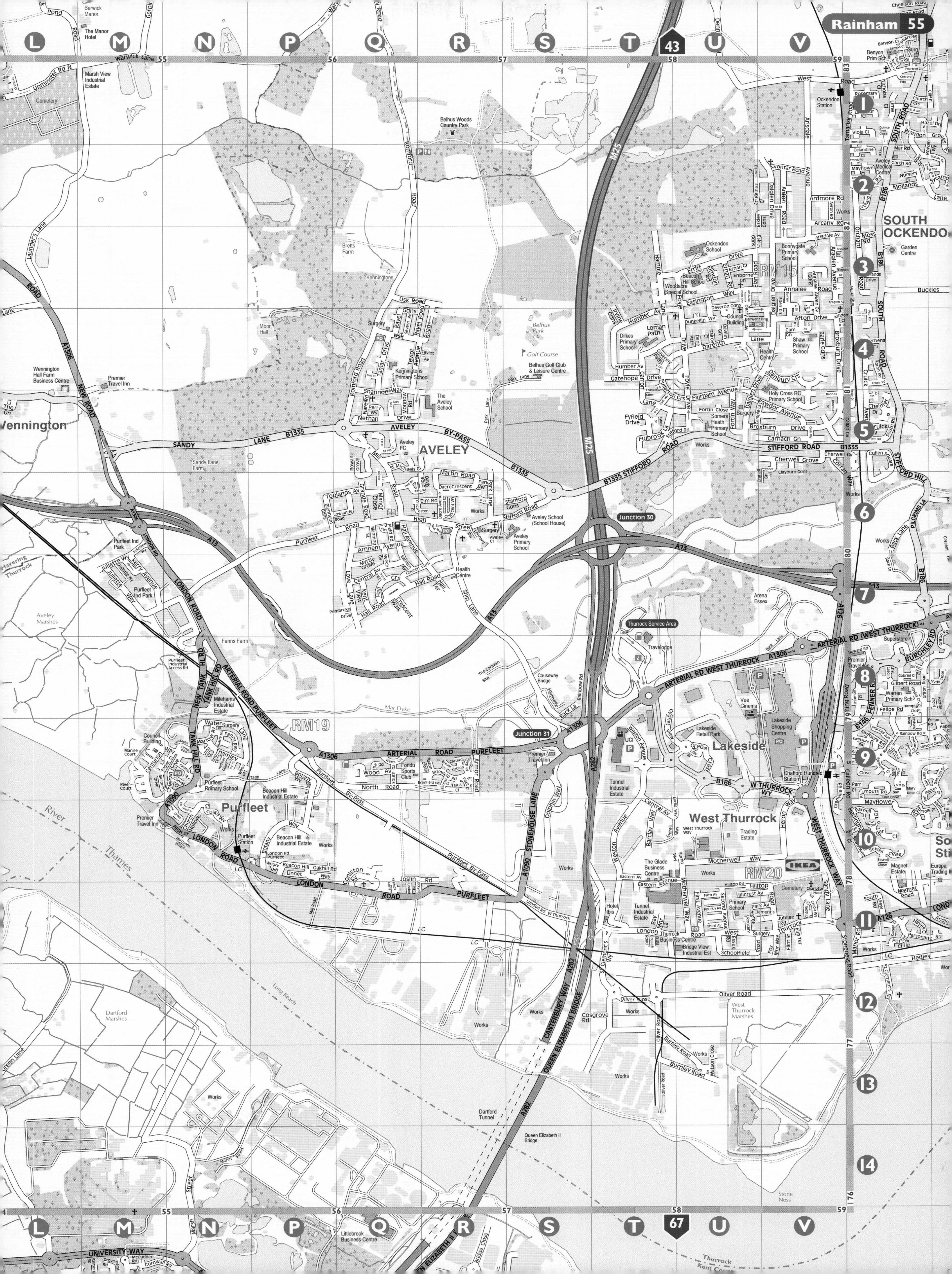
AVELEY
SOUTH OCKENDON
Purfleet
West Thurrock
Lakeside
Wennington
RM15
RM19
RM20
Junction 30
Junction 31
M25
A13
A1306
A126
A282
B186
B1335
A1090
ARTERIAL ROAD PURFLEET
ARTERIAL RD WEST THURROCK
STIFFORD ROAD
SANDY LANE
AVELEY BY-PASS
LONDON ROAD
NEW ROAD
QUEEN ELIZABETH II BRIDGE
CANTERBURY WAY
STONEHOUSE LANE
Purfleet By-Pass
Belhus Woods Country Park
Belhus Park
Belhus Golf Club & Leisure Centre
Ockendon Station
Purfleet Station
Chafford Hundred Station
Thurrock Service Area
Lakeside Shopping Centre
Lakeside Retail Park
Tunnel Industrial Estate
Milehams Industrial Estate
Beacon Hill Industrial Estate
Purfleet Ind Park
Marsh View Industrial Estate
Wennington Hall Farm Business Centre
Aveley Marshes
Dartford Marshes
West Thurrock Marshes
Dartford Tunnel
Queen Elizabeth II Bridge
River Thames
Long Reach
Stone Ness
Arena Essex
IKEA
Littlebrook Business Centre
UNIVERSITY WAY
L M N P Q R S T U V
55 56 57 58 59
43
67
1 2 3 4 5 6 7 8 9 10 11 12 13 14
76 77 78 79 80 81 82 83

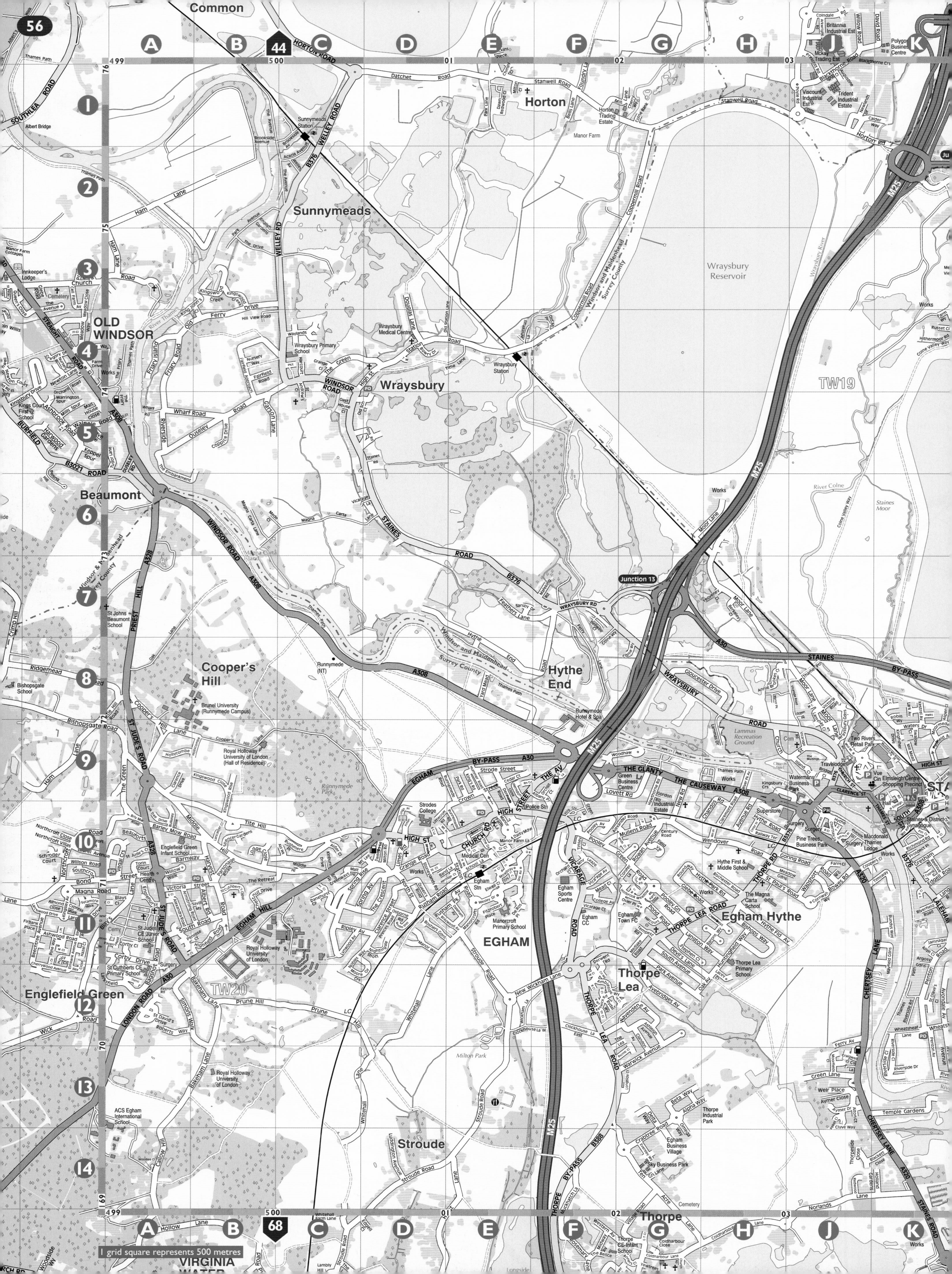
Common
44
68
Horton
Sunnymeads
Wraysbury
Wraysbury Reservoir
OLD WINDSOR
Beaumont
Cooper's Hill
Hythe End
Junction 13
EGHAM
Egham Hythe
Thorpe Lea
Englefield Green
Stroude
Thorpe
VIRGINIA WATER
TW19
TW20
Staines Moor
Milton Park
Runnymede Park
Runnymede (NT)
Magna Carta Island
Manor Farm
Horton Trading Estate
Sunnymeads Station
Wraysbury Station
Egham Stn
Wraysbury Primary School
Wraysbury Medical Centre
St Johns Beaumont School
Bishopsgate School
Brunel University (Runnymede Campus)
Royal Holloway University of London (Hall of Residence)
Royal Holloway University of London
Englefield Green Infant School
Strodes College
Manorcroft Primary School
Egham Sports Centre
Egham CC
Egham Town FC
Thorpe Lea Primary School
The Magna Carta School
Hythe First & Middle School
Runnymede Hotel & Spa
Green Business Centre
Gordon Rd Industrial Estate
Pine Trees Business Park
Lammas Recreation Ground
Two Rivers Retail Park
Watermans Business Park
Thorpe Industrial Park
Egham Business Village
Sky Business Park
ACS Egham International School
Thorpe CE Infant School
Britannia Industrial Est
Mckay Trading Est
Viscount Industrial Est
Trident Industrial Estate
Polygon Business Centre
M25
A30
A308
A328
B376
B388
B3021
STAINES BY-PASS
EGHAM BY-PASS
WINDSOR ROAD
WELLEY ROAD
STAINES ROAD
WRAYSBURY RD
PRIEST HILL
ST JUDE'S ROAD
EGHAM HILL
LONDON ROAD
HIGH ST
THE CAUSEWAY
THE GLANTY
THORPE LEA ROAD
THORPE BY-PASS
CHERTSEY LANE
Datchet Road
Stanwell Road
Horton Rd
Coppermill Road
Hythe End Road
River Thames
Wraysbury River
River Colne
Windsor and Maidenhead
Surrey County
499
500
01
02
03
A B C D E F G H J K
1 2 3 4 5 6 7 8 9 10 11 12 13 14
76
75
74
73
72
71
70
69
1 grid square represents 500 metres

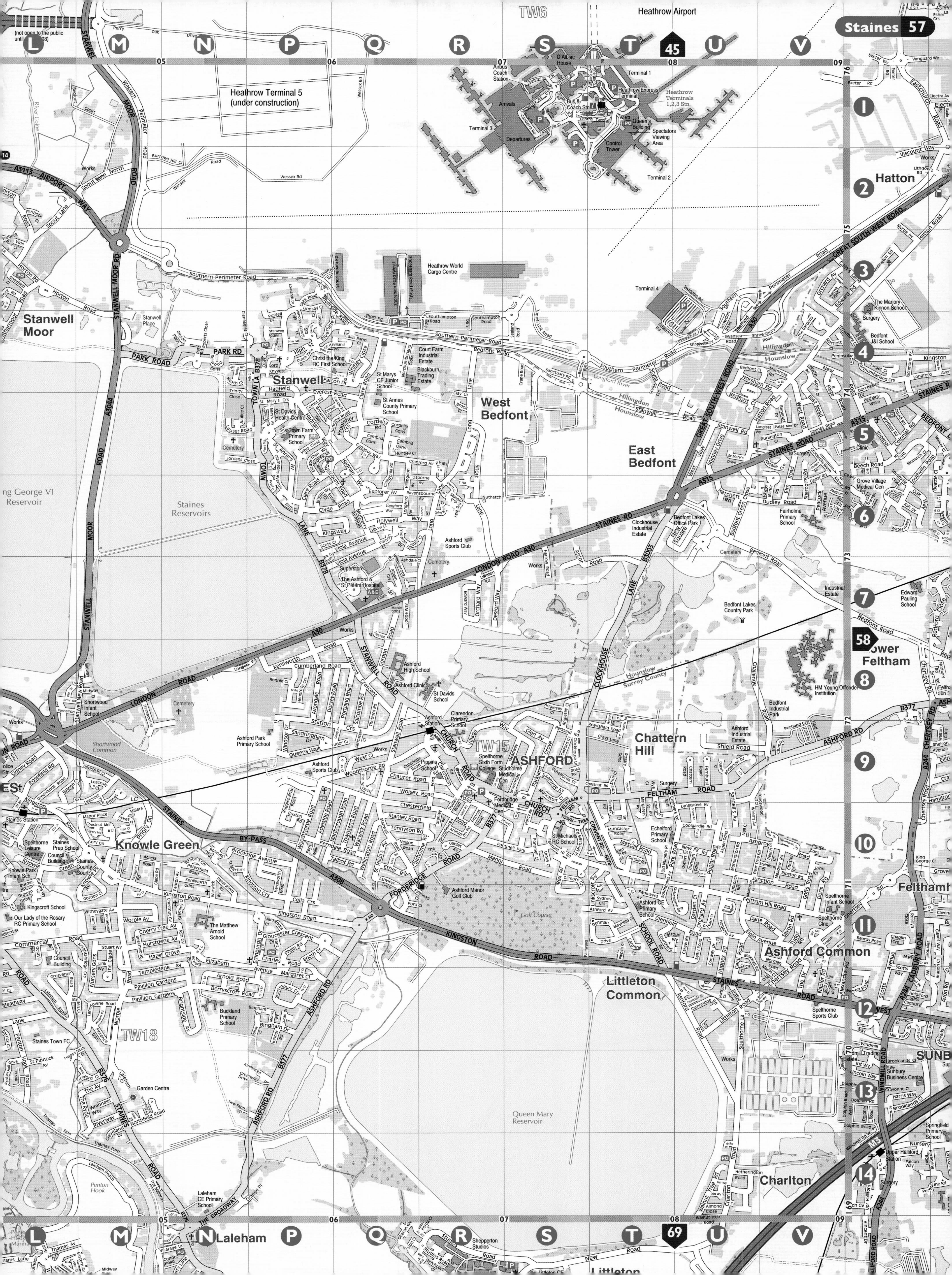
Heathrow Airport
TW6
Heathrow Terminal 5
(under construction)
Terminal 1
Terminal 2
Terminal 3
Terminal 4
Heathrow Terminals 1,2,3 Stn.
Heathrow Express Terminal
Control Tower
Queen's Building
Spectators Viewing Area
Arrivals
Departures
Airbus Coach Station
Heathrow World Cargo Centre
Southern Perimeter Road
45
Hatton
Stanwell Moor
Stanwell
West Bedfont
East Bedfont
King George VI Reservoir
Staines Reservoirs
GREAT SOUTH-WEST ROAD
STAINES ROAD
LONDON ROAD A30
STANWELL MOOR ROAD
A3113 AIRPORT WAY
CLOCKHOUSE LANE
Bedfont Lakes Country Park
HM Young Offender Institution
58
Lower Feltham
The Ashford & St Peters Hospital
Ashford
TW15
Chattern Hill
Knowle Green
Staines Station
Ashford Station
Shortwood Common
Ashford Manor Golf Club
KINGSTON ROAD
STAINES BY-PASS
Littleton Common
Ashford Common
Feltham
Queen Mary Reservoir
Charlton
Upper Halliford Station
Sunbury
TW18
Staines Town FC
Penton Hook
Laleham
Shepperton Studios
69
Littleton
M3
L M N P Q R S T U V
05 06 07 08 09
1 2 3 4 5 6 7 8 9 10 11 12 13 14
76 75 74 73 72 71 70 69

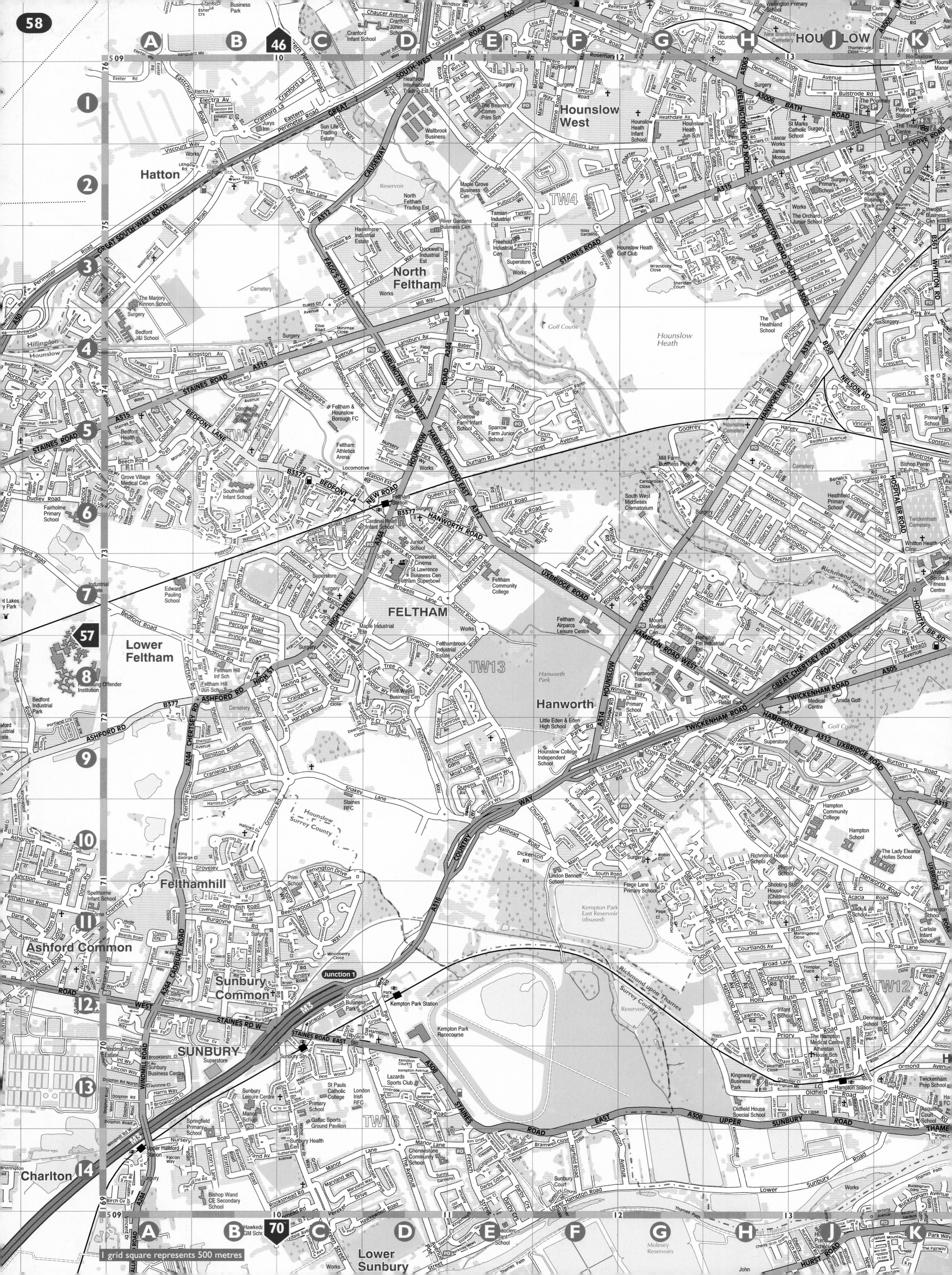
A
B
46
C
D
E
F
G
H
J
K
Hatton
Hounslow West
North Feltham
FELTHAM
Lower Feltham
Hanworth
Felthamhill
Ashford Common
Sunbury Common
SUNBURY
Charlton
Lower Sunbury
HOUNSLOW
TW4
TW14
TW13
TW12
TW16
57
70
Hounslow Heath
Golf Course
Hanworth Park
Kempton Park Racecourse
Kempton Park Station
Kempton Park East Reservoir (disused)
Junction 1
M3
GREAT SOUTH-WEST ROAD
STAINES ROAD
BATH ROAD
HANWORTH ROAD
HOUNSLOW ROAD
HARLINGTON ROAD WEST
HARLINGTON ROAD EAST
HIGH STREET
BEDFONT LANE
BEDFONT LA
NEW ROAD
ASHFORD RD
CHERTSEY RD
UXBRIDGE ROAD
HAMPTON ROAD WEST
GREAT CHERTSEY ROAD
TWICKENHAM ROAD
COUNTRY WAY
WINDMILL ROAD
STAINES ROAD EAST
UPPER SUNBURY ROAD
WELLINGTON ROAD NORTH
WELLINGTON ROAD SOUTH
HOSPITAL BR ROAD
NELSON RD
FAGG'S ROAD
CAUSEWAY
A30
A315
A312
A244
A314
A316
A308
A305
B377
B3377
1 grid square represents 500 metres

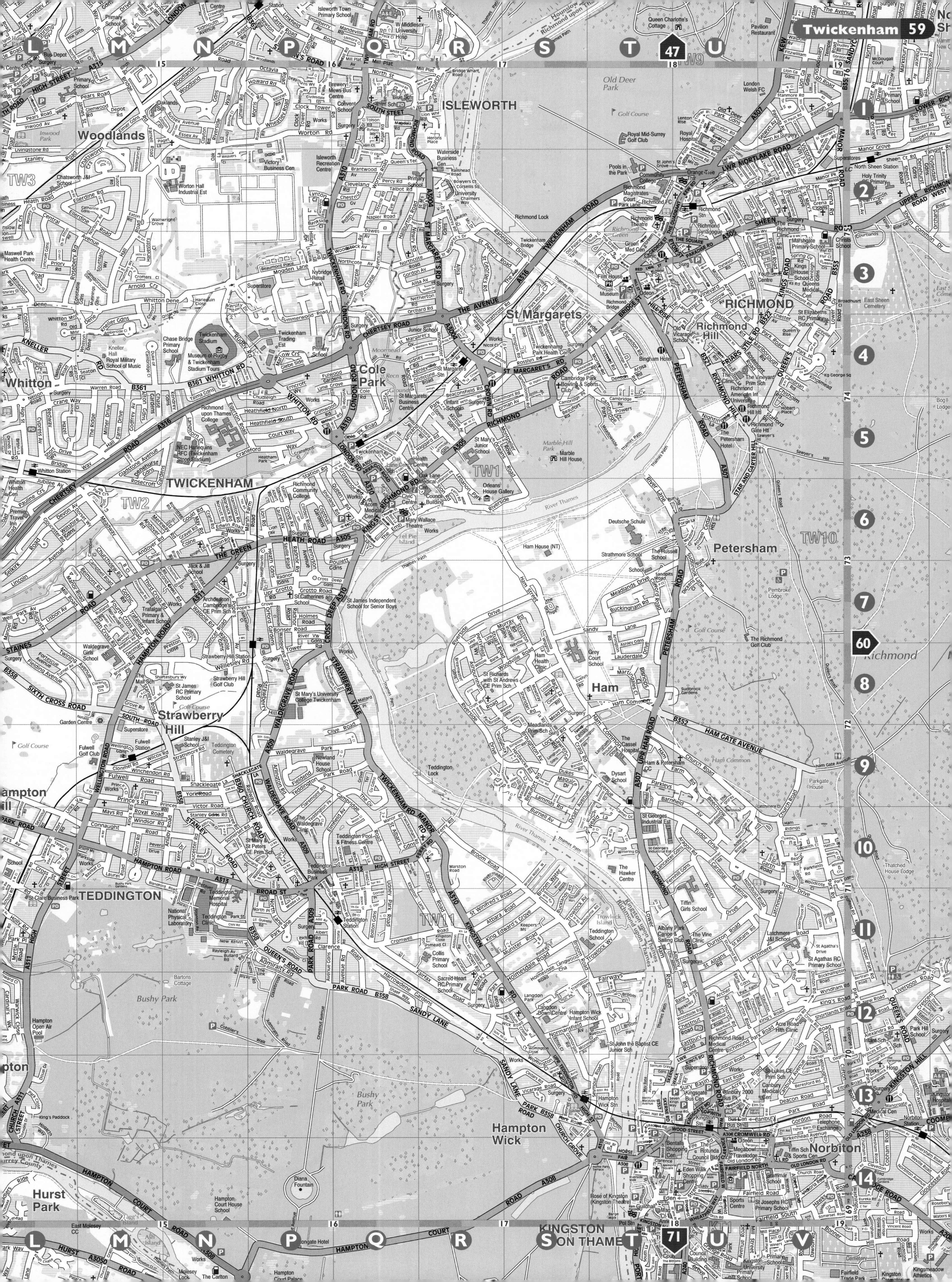
ISLEWORTH
Woodlands
Whitton
TWICKENHAM
St Margarets
Cole Park
RICHMOND
Richmond Hill
Petersham
Ham
Strawberry Hill
TEDDINGTON
Hampton Wick
Hurst Park
Bushy Park
KINGSTON UPON THAMES
Norbiton
Old Deer Park
River Thames
Marble Hill Park
Ham House (NT)
Eel Pie Island
Teddington Lock
Twickenham Stadium
TW1
TW2
TW3
TW9
TW10
TW11
KT1
47
60
71

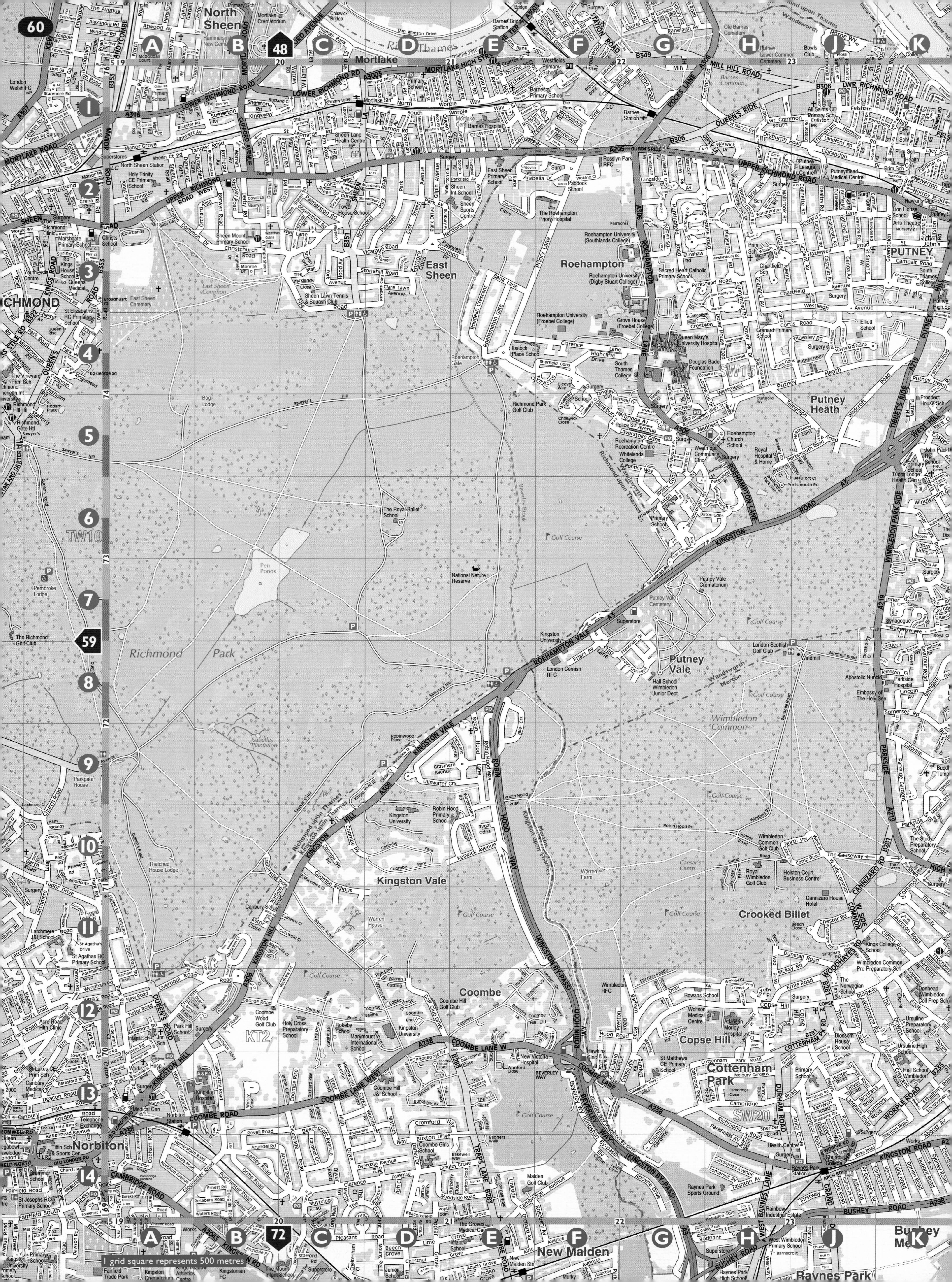
60
48
59
72
North Sheen
Mortlake
River Thames
Old Barnes Cemetery
Putney Lower Common Cemetery
Barnes Common
LOWER RICHMOND RD
MORTLAKE HIGH ST
MORTLAKE ROAD
UPPER RICHMOND ROAD WEST
UPPER RICHMOND ROAD
SHEEN ROAD
QUEEN'S RIDE
ROCKS LANE
MILL HILL ROAD
CLIFFORD AVENUE
LWR RICHMOND ROAD
PUTNEY
RICHMOND
QUEEN'S ROAD
KINGS ROAD
MANOR ROAD
East Sheen
East Sheen Cemetery
East Sheen Common
Roehampton
ROEHAMPTON LANE
Roehampton University (Southlands College)
Roehampton University (Digby Stuart College)
Roehampton University (Froebel College)
Queen Mary's University Hospital
Douglas Bader Foundation
Roehampton Gate
Richmond Park Golf Club
Putney Heath
SW15
TW10
Sawyer's Hill
Bog Lodge
The Royal Ballet School
Pen Ponds
National Nature Reserve
Beverley Brook
Golf Course
Richmond Park
Pembroke Lodge
The Richmond Golf Club
KINGSTON ROAD
A3
ROEHAMPTON VALE
Putney Vale Crematorium
Putney Vale Cemetery
Putney Vale
Kingston University
London Cornish RFC
London Scottish Golf Club
Windmill
Wimbledon Common
Wandsworth
Merton
Richmond upon Thames
Kingston upon Thames
Isabella Plantation
Parkgate House
Robinwood Place
KINGSTON VALE
ROBIN HOOD WAY
Robin Hood Primary School
Kingston Vale
Thatched House Lodge
Warren Farm
Caesar's Camp
Royal Wimbledon Golf Club
Wimbledon Common Golf Club
Crooked Billet
Cannizaro House Hotel
TIBBET'S RIDE
WIMBLEDON PARK SIDE
PARKSIDE
CANNIZARO RD
KINGSTON HILL
KINGSTON BY-PASS
Coombe
Coombe Hill Golf Club
Coombe Wood Golf Club
KT2
Wimbledon RFC
Copse Hill
Cottenham Park
SW20
COMBE LANE WEST
COOMBE ROAD
A238
Kingston Hospital
Norbiton
CAMBRIDGE ROAD
Malden Golf Club
BEVERLEY WAY
Raynes Park
Raynes Park Sports Ground
KINGSTON ROAD
WORPLE ROAD
DURHAM ROAD
WEST BARNES LANE
BUSHEY ROAD
New Malden
Kingston Crematorium
A B C D E F G H J K
1 2 3 4 5 6 7 8 9 10 11 12 13 14
19 20 21 22 23
74 73 72 71 70 69
1 grid square represents 500 metres

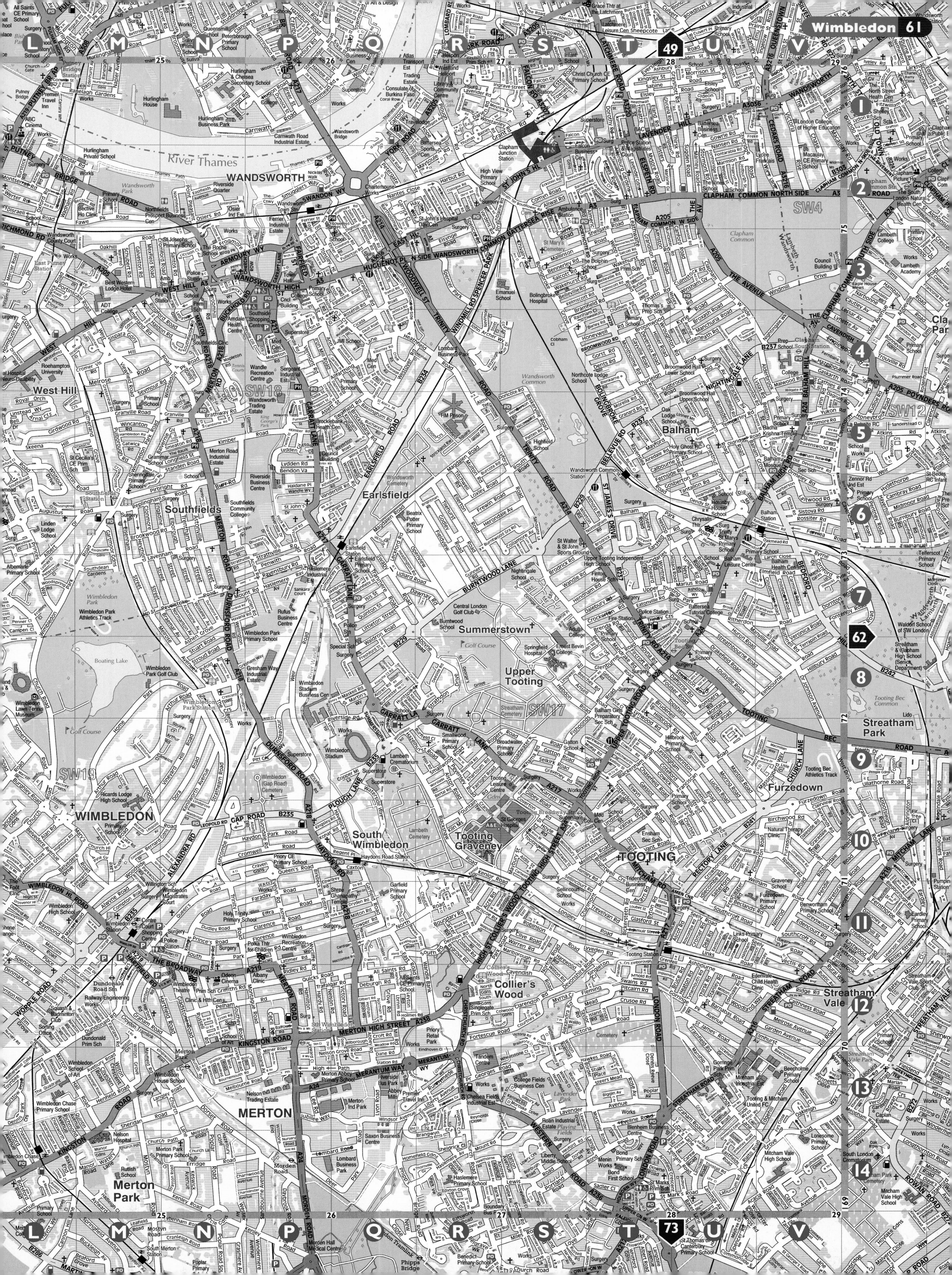
River Thames
WANDSWORTH
Putney Bridge
West Hill
Southfields
Earlsfield
Summerstown
Upper Tooting
Balham
WIMBLEDON
South Wimbledon
Tooting Graveney
TOOTING
Collier's Wood
MERTON
Merton Park
Furzedown
Streatham Park
Streatham Vale
Wandsworth Common
Clapham Common
Wimbledon Park
Boating Lake
SW4
SW12
SW17
SW18
SW19
49
62
73
L
M
N
P
Q
R
S
T
U
V

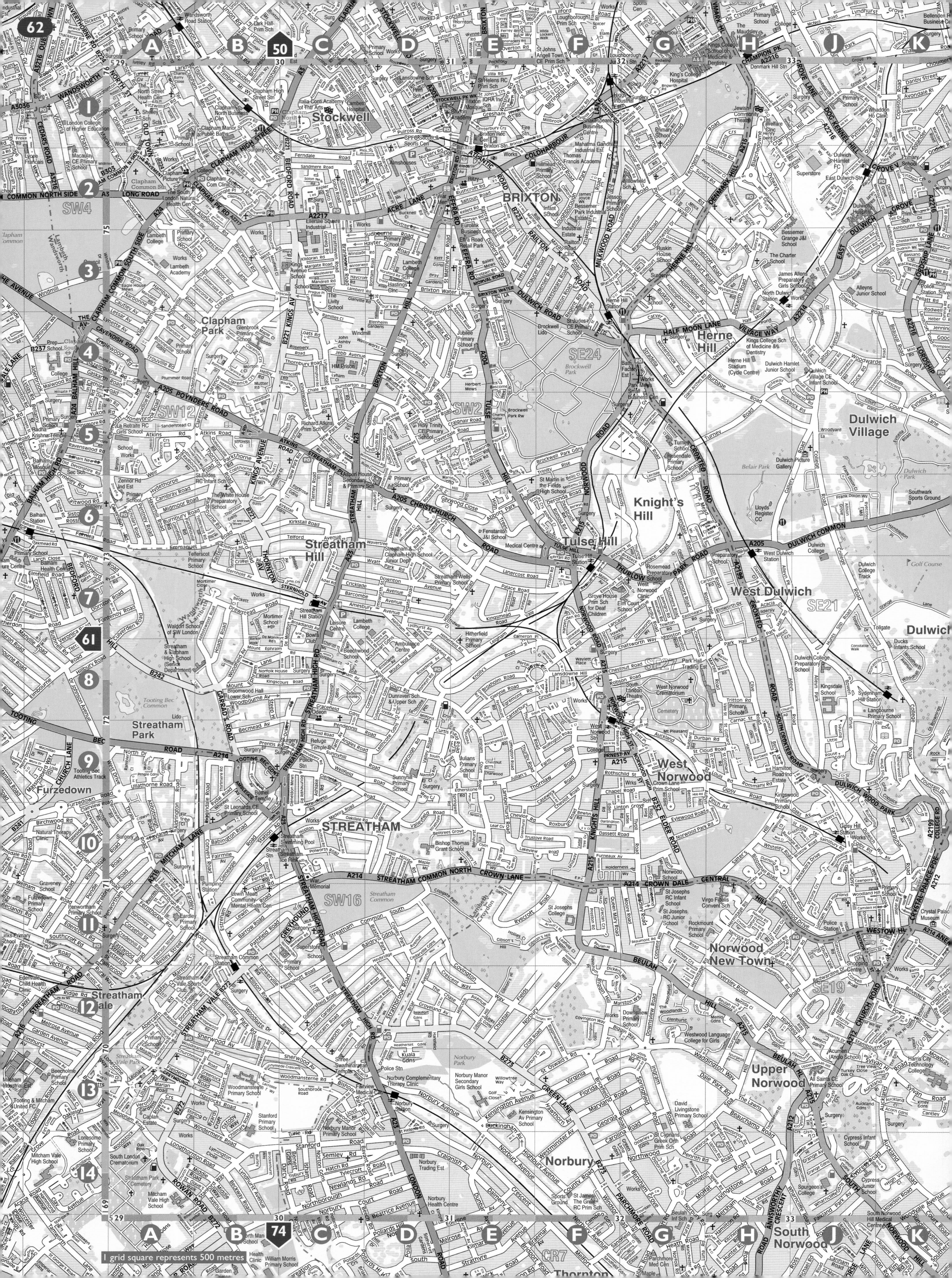
50
Stockwell
BRIXTON
Clapham Park
SW4
SW12
SW2
SE24
Brockwell Park
Herne Hill
Dulwich Village
Knight's Hill
Tulse Hill
Streatham Hill
West Dulwich
SE21
Dulwich
SE27
West Norwood
Streatham Park
Furzedown
STREATHAM
SW16
Streatham Common
Norwood New Town
SE19
Streatham Vale
Upper Norwood
Norbury
South Norwood
CR7
61
74
A
B
C
D
E
F
G
H
J
K
1
2
3
4
5
6
7
8
9
10
11
12
13
14

1 grid square represents 500 metres

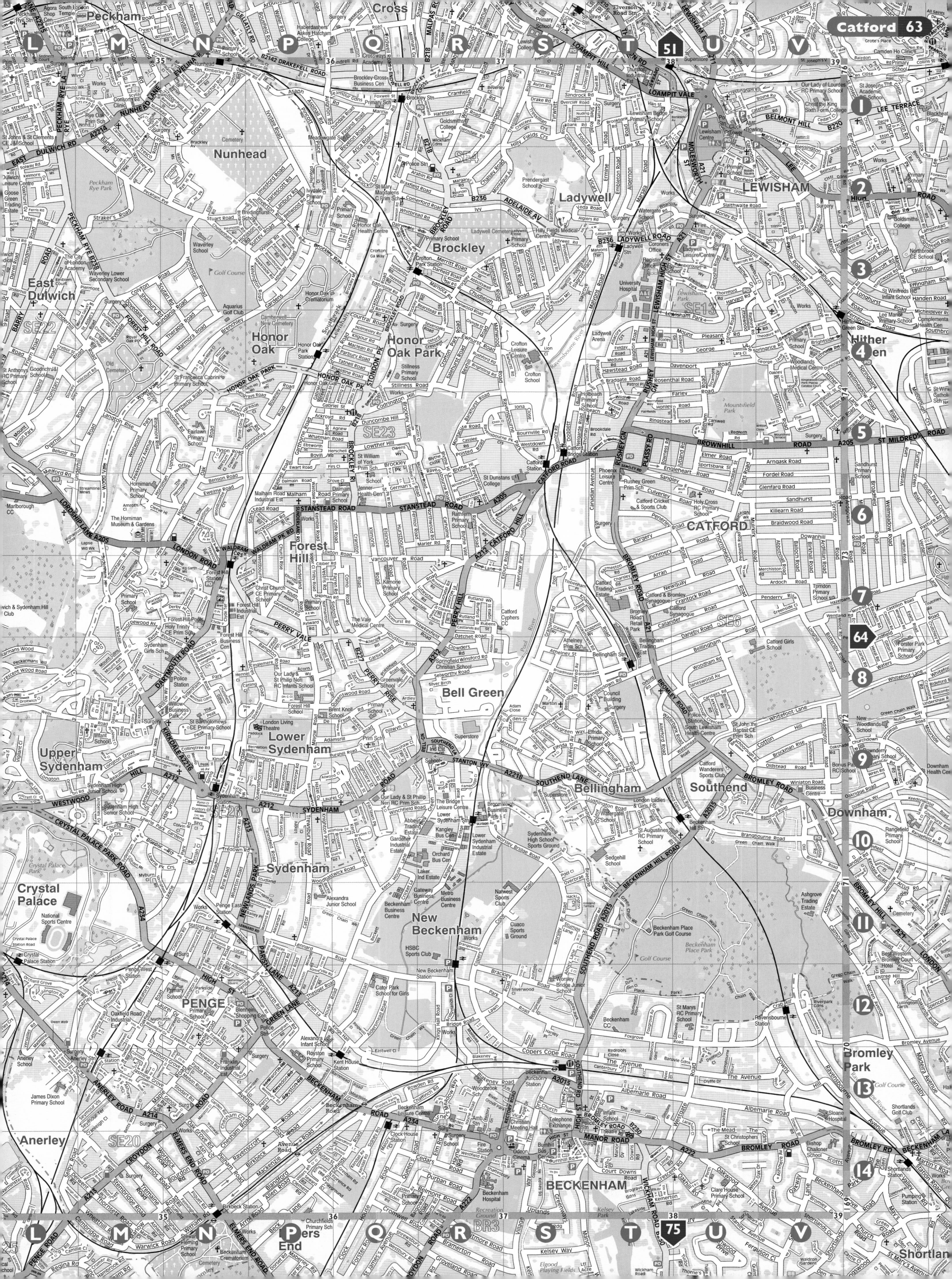
Peckham
Nunhead
East Dulwich
Honor Oak
Honor Oak Park
Brockley
Ladywell
LEWISHAM
Hither Green
Forest Hill
CATFORD
Bell Green
Lower Sydenham
Upper Sydenham
Sydenham
Bellingham
Southend
Downham
Crystal Palace
New Beckenham
PENGE
Anerley
BECKENHAM
Bromley Park
Elmers End
SE4
SE13
SE22
SE23
SE6
SE26
SE20
BR3
STANSTEAD ROAD
BROMLEY ROAD
BROWNHILL ROAD
LORDSHIP LANE
CRYSTAL PALACE PARK ROAD
BECKENHAM HILL ROAD
SOUTHEND LANE
LADYWELL ROAD
ADELAIDE AV
BROCKLEY RISE
PERRY VALE
KIRKDALE
DARTMOUTH ROAD
LONDON ROAD
WESTWOOD HILL
HONOR OAK PARK
PECKHAM RYE
NUNHEAD LANE
EAST DULWICH RD
LOAMPIT VALE
LOAMPIT HILL
BELMONT HILL
LEE TERRACE
RUSHEY GREEN
CATFORD HILL
PERRY HILL
SYDENHAM ROAD
BROMLEY HILL
ANERLEY ROAD
ELMERS END ROAD
CROYDON ROAD
MANOR ROAD
SOUTHEND ROAD
WICKHAM ROAD
PARISH LANE
GREEN LANE
HIGH ST
DRAKEFELL ROAD
ST MILDREDS ROAD
L
M
N
P
Q
R
S
T
U
V
1
2
3
4
5
6
7
8
9
10
11
12
13
14
51
64
75

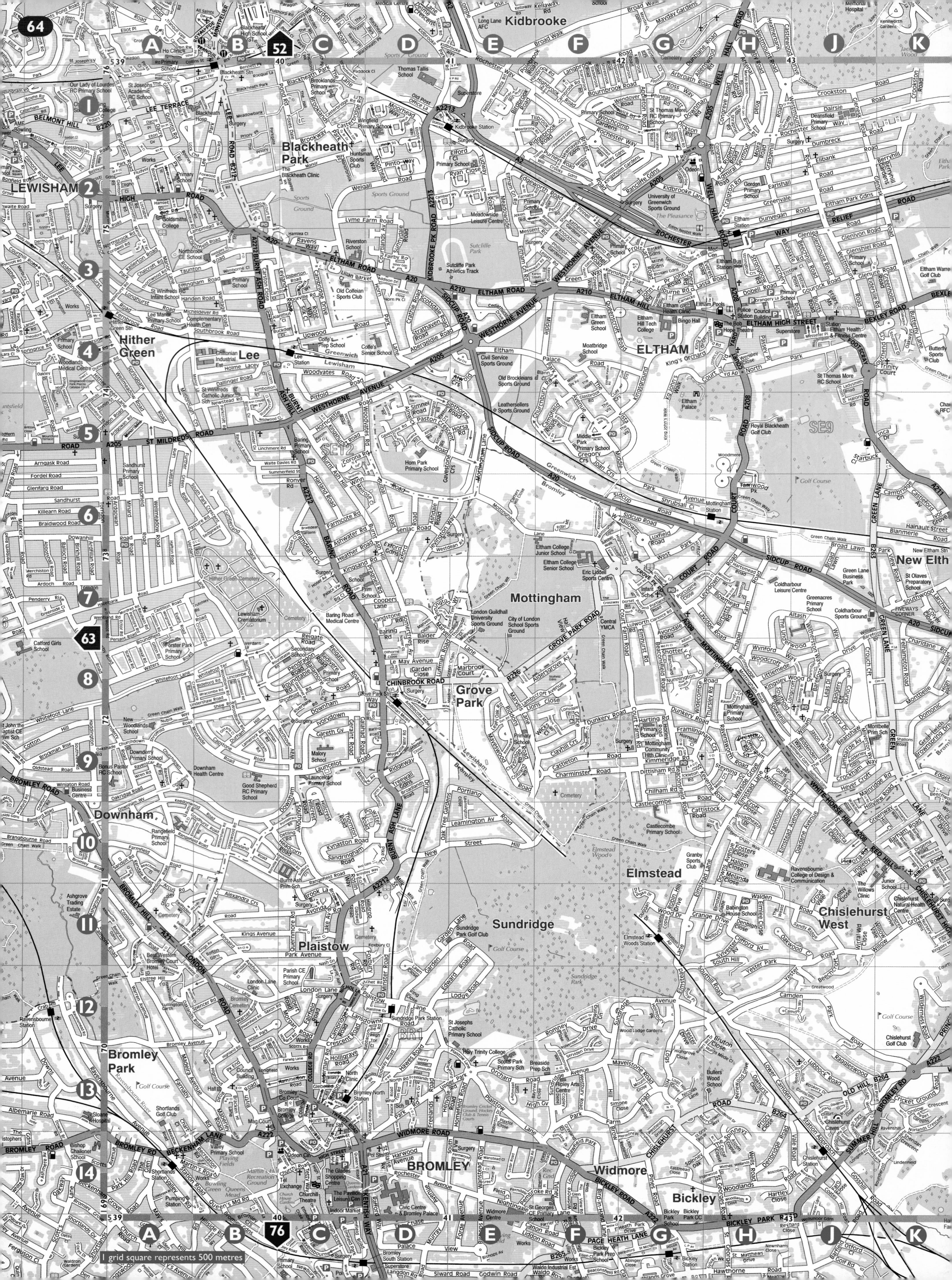
A
B
C
D
E
F
G
H
J
K
52
Kidbrooke
Blackheath Park
LEWISHAM
Lee
Hither Green
ELTHAM
Mottingham
Grove Park
Downham
Elmstead
Sundridge
Plaistow
Chislehurst West
New Elth
Bromley Park
BROMLEY
Widmore
Bickley
63
76
1
2
3
4
5
6
7
8
9
10
11
12
13
14
1 grid square represents 500 metres

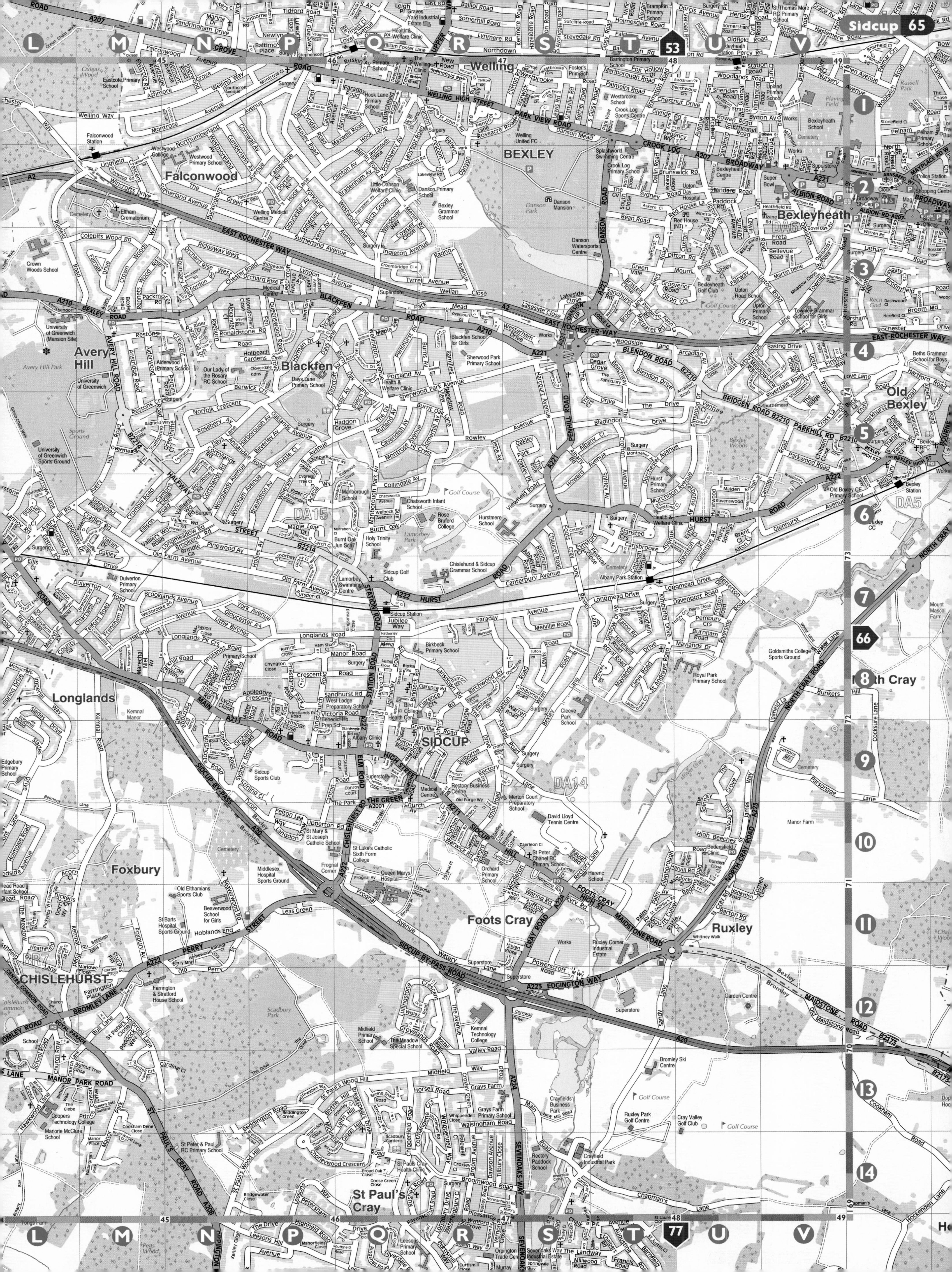
Welling
BEXLEY
Falconwood
Bexleyheath
Avery Hill
Blackfen
Old Bexley
Longlands
SIDCUP
North Cray
Foxbury
Foots Cray
Ruxley
CHISLEHURST
St Paul's Cray
EAST ROCHESTER WAY
SIDCUP BY-PASS ROAD
MAIDSTONE ROAD
NORTH CRAY ROAD
STATION ROAD
BLENDON ROAD
BRIDGEN ROAD B2210
HURST ROAD
DA5
DA6
DA14
DA15
BR7
53
66
77

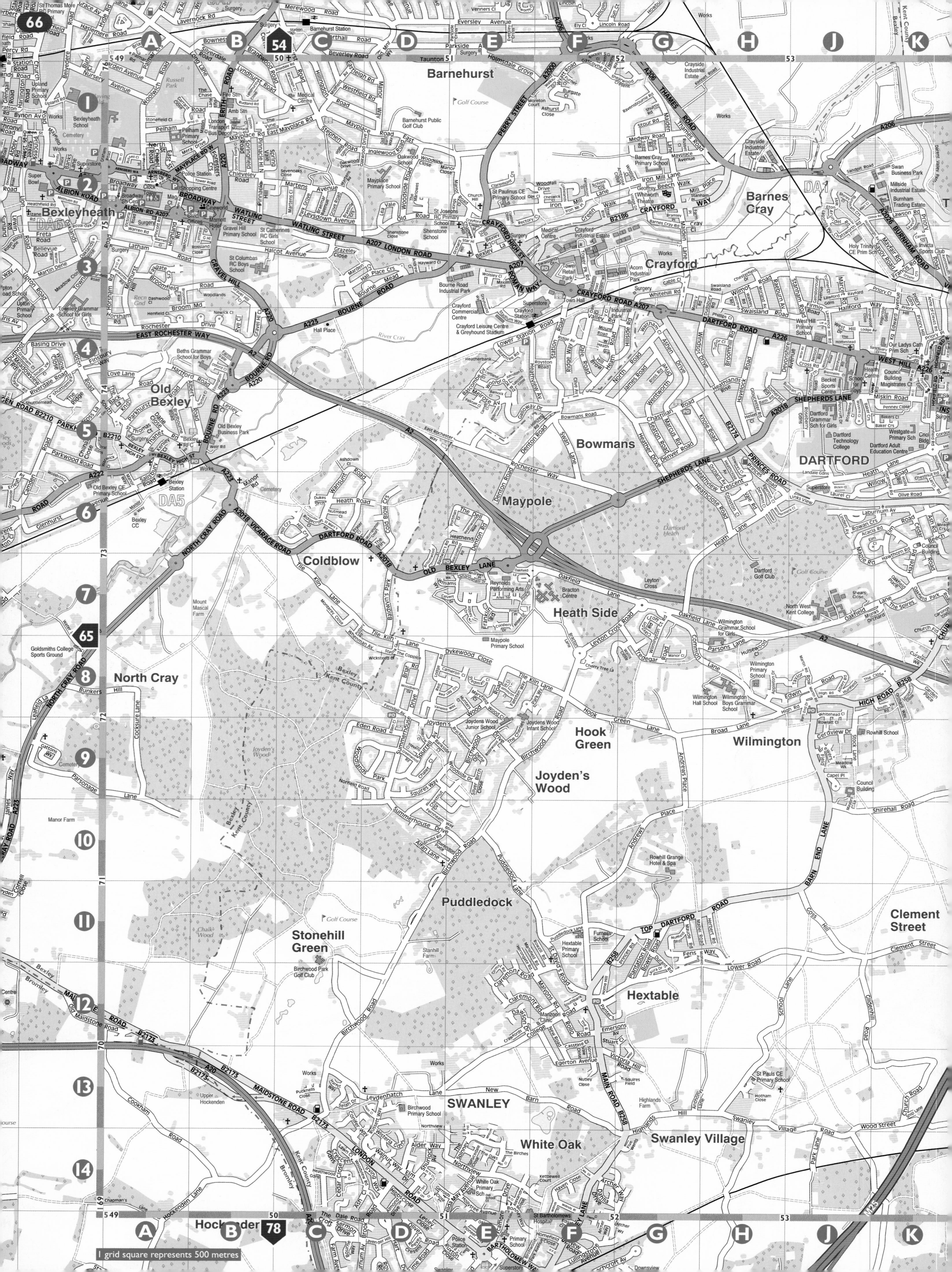

54
78
65
A
B
C
D
E
F
G
H
J
K
1
2
3
4
5
6
7
8
9
10
11
12
13
14
Barnehurst
Bexleyheath
DA6
Old Bexley
DA5
Barnes Cray
DA1
Crayford
Bowmans
DARTFORD
Maypole
Coldblow
Heath Side
North Cray
Hook Green
Wilmington
Joyden's Wood
Puddledock
Stonehill Green
Clement Street
Hextable
SWANLEY
White Oak
Swanley Village
Hockenden
WATLING STREET
A207 LONDON ROAD
EAST ROCHESTER WAY
BOURNE ROAD
A223
A220
A2
A206
THAMES ROAD
CRAYFORD ROAD A207
DARTFORD ROAD
A226
WEST HILL
SHEPHERDS LANE
PRINCES ROAD
NORTH CRAY ROAD
A2018 VICARAGE ROAD
DARTFORD ROAD A2018
OLD BEXLEY LANE
HIGH ROAD B258
TOP DARTFORD ROAD
BARN END LANE
MAIN ROAD B258
MAIDSTONE ROAD B2173
LONDON ROAD
M25
Golf Course
Dartford Heath
Dartford Golf Club
Birchwood Park Golf Club

1 grid square represents 500 metres

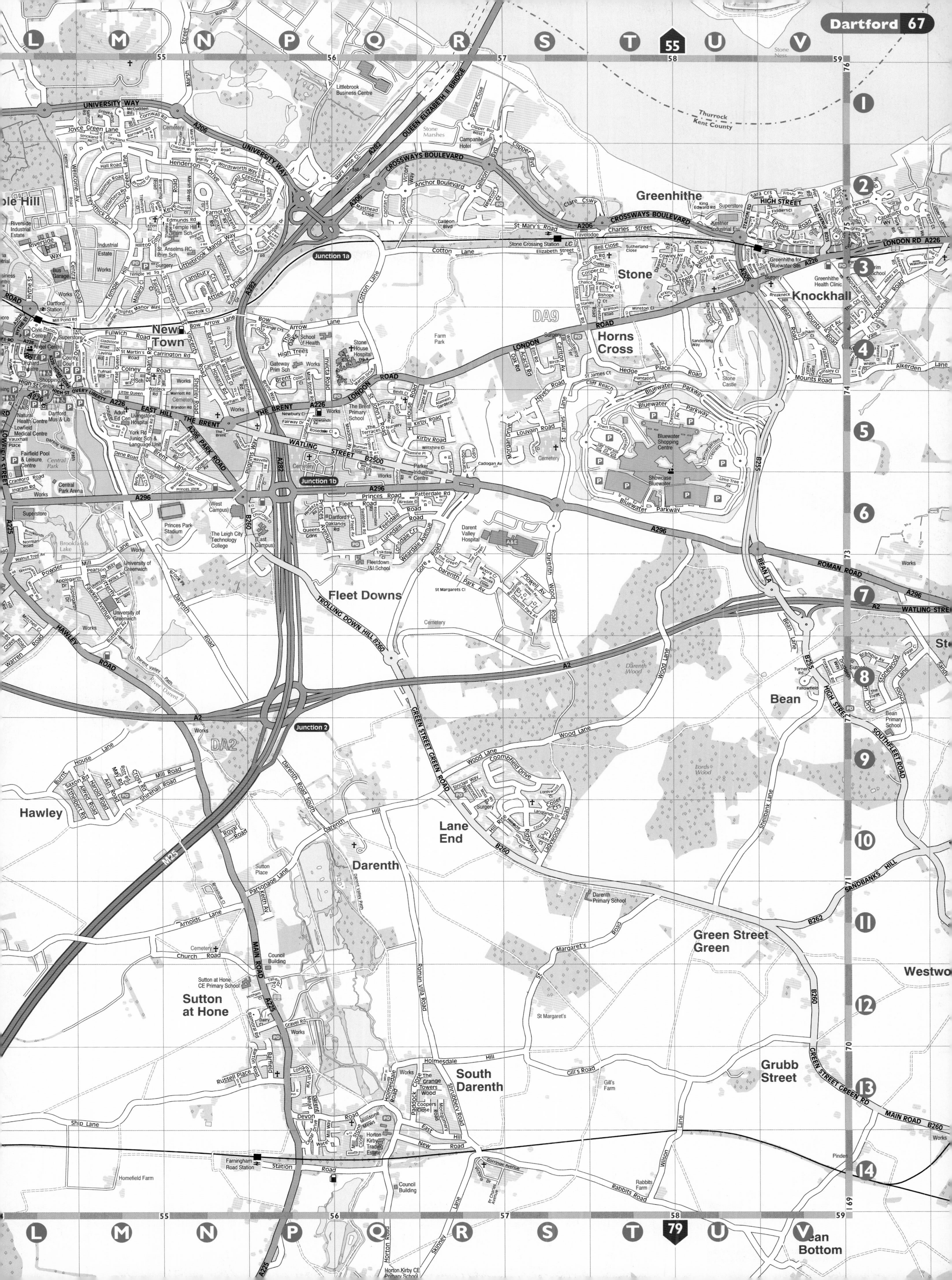
L
M
N
P
Q
R
S
T
55
U
V
55
56
57
58
59
Stone Ness
Thurrock
Kent County
Littlebrook Business Centre
QUEEN ELIZABETH II BRIDGE
UNIVERSITY WAY
A206
Joyce Green Lane
Cemetery
Henderson Drive
Stone Marshes
Campanile Hotel
Bridge Close
Clipper Blvd
CROSSWAYS BOULEVARD
Anchor Boulevard
Galleon Blvd
Greenhithe
HIGH STREET
King Edward Rd
Superstore
Kestner Industrial Est
STATION RD
THE AVENUE
Capability Wy
LONDON RD A226
Riverside Industrial Estate
Industrial Estate
Bus Garage
Dartford Station
Central Road
Temple Hill
St Anselms RC Prim Sch
Littlebrook Manor Way
Junction 1a
St Mary's Road
Travelodge
Charles Street
Stone Crossing Station
Cotton Lane
Elizabeth Street
Bell Close
Stone
Greenhithe for Bluewater Stn
Greenhithe Health Clinic
Knockhall
DA9
Fulwich Road
New Town
Bow Arrow Lane
School of Health
High Trees
Stone House Hospital
Farm Park
Horns Cross
LONDON ROAD
Hedge Place Road
Stone Castle
Mounts Road
Alkerden Lane
Angel Centre
Orchard Theatre
Shopping Centre
County Court
HIGH STREET
A226
EAST HILL
THE BRENT
A296 PARK ROAD
Dartford Mus & Lib
Livingstone Hospital
Fairfield Pool & Leisure Centre
Central Park
Central Park Arena
WATLING STREET
B2500
Bluewater Parkway
Bluewater Shopping Centre
Showcase Bluewater
Cemetery
Junction 1b
A296
Princes Road
Parker Industrial Centre
Superstore
Princes Park Stadium
The Leigh City Technology College
East Campus
West Campus
Darent Valley Hospital
A&E
Fleet Downs
TROLLING DOWN HILL B260
Brooklands Lake
University of Greenwich
HAWLEY ROAD
Darenth Road
River Darent
A2
Junction 2
DA2
Darenth Wood
BEAN LA
ROMAN ROAD
WATLING STREET
Bean
HIGH STREET
SOUTHFLEET ROAD
Bean Primary School
Wood Lane
Hawley
Mill Road
Lane End
Coombfield Drive
Lords Wood
Darenth
B260
Sutton Place
M25
Parsonage Lane
Arnolds Lane
Darenth Primary School
SANDBANKS HILL
B262
Green Street Green
Cemetery
Church Road
MAIN ROAD
Council Building
Sutton at Hone CE Primary School
Sutton at Hone
Roman Villa Road
St Margaret's
Westwood
A225
Holmesdale Hill
South Darenth
Gill's Road
Gill's Farm
Grubb Street
GREEN STREET GREEN RD
MAIN ROAD
B260
Russell Place
Ship Lane
Horton Kirby Trading Estate
New Road
Farningham Road Station
Station Road
Homefield Farm
Council Building
Wilson Lane
Rabbits Farm
Rabbits Road
Gorringe Avenue
Pinden
Works
Skinney Lane
Horton Road
Horton Kirby CE Primary School
79
Bean Bottom
1
2
3
4
5
6
7
8
9
10
11
12
13
14
76
75
74
73
72
71
70
169

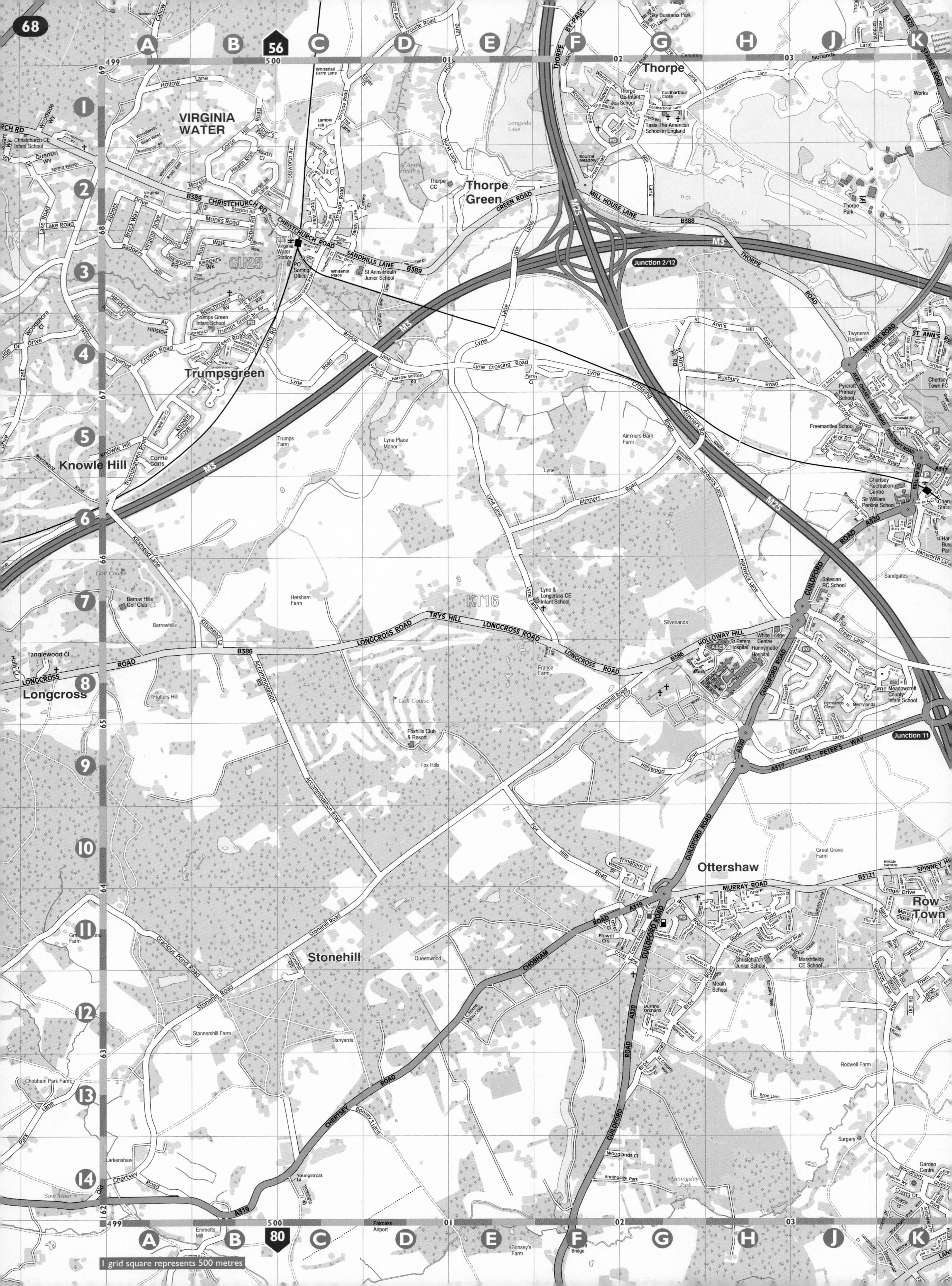

56
80
A
B
C
D
E
F
G
H
J
K
1
2
3
4
5
6
7
8
9
10
11
12
13
14
499
500
01
02
03
69
68
67
66
65
64
63
62
VIRGINIA WATER
Thorpe
Thorpe Green
Trumpsgreen
Knowle Hill
Longcross
Stonehill
Ottershaw
Row Town
GU25
KT16
CHRISTCHURCH ROAD
B389
SANDHILLS LANE
GREEN ROAD
MILL HOUSE LANE
B388
THORPE BY-PASS
M25
M3
Junction 2/12
Junction 11
Lyne Crossing Road
Almners Road
Hardwick Lane
Lyne Lane
LONGCROSS ROAD
TRYS HILL
B386
HOLLOWAY HILL
GUILDFORD ROAD
A320
ST PETER'S WAY
A317
MURRAY ROAD
B3121
CHOBHAM ROAD
A319
CHERTSEY ROAD
Stonehill Road
Accommodation Road
Kitsmead Lane
Gracious Pond Road
Fox Hills Road
Brox Lane
STAINES ROAD
PYRCROFT ROAD
Virginia Water Station
St Anns Heath Junior School
Trumps Green Infant School
Christchurch CE Infant School
Thorpe CE Infant School
TASIS The American School in England
Thorpe Park
Longside Lake
Lyne Place Manor
Almners Barn Farm
Lyne & Longcross CE Infant School
Hersham Farm
Barrow Hills Golf Club
Golf Course
Foxhills Club & Resort
Fox Hills
St Peters Hospital
Runnymede Hospital
Silverlands
France Farm
Salesian RC School
Meadowcroft County Infant School
Chertsey Recreation Centre
Sir William Perkins School
Freemantles School
Pyrcroft Primary School
Christchurch Junior School
Marshfields CE School
Meath School
Queenwood
Stannershill Farm
Stanyards
Chobham Park Farm
Larkenshaw
Sow Moor
Emmetts Mill
Fairoaks Airport
Bonsey's Farm
Anningsley Park
Great Grove Farm
Rodwell Farm
Sandgates
Twynersh House

1 grid square represents 500 metres

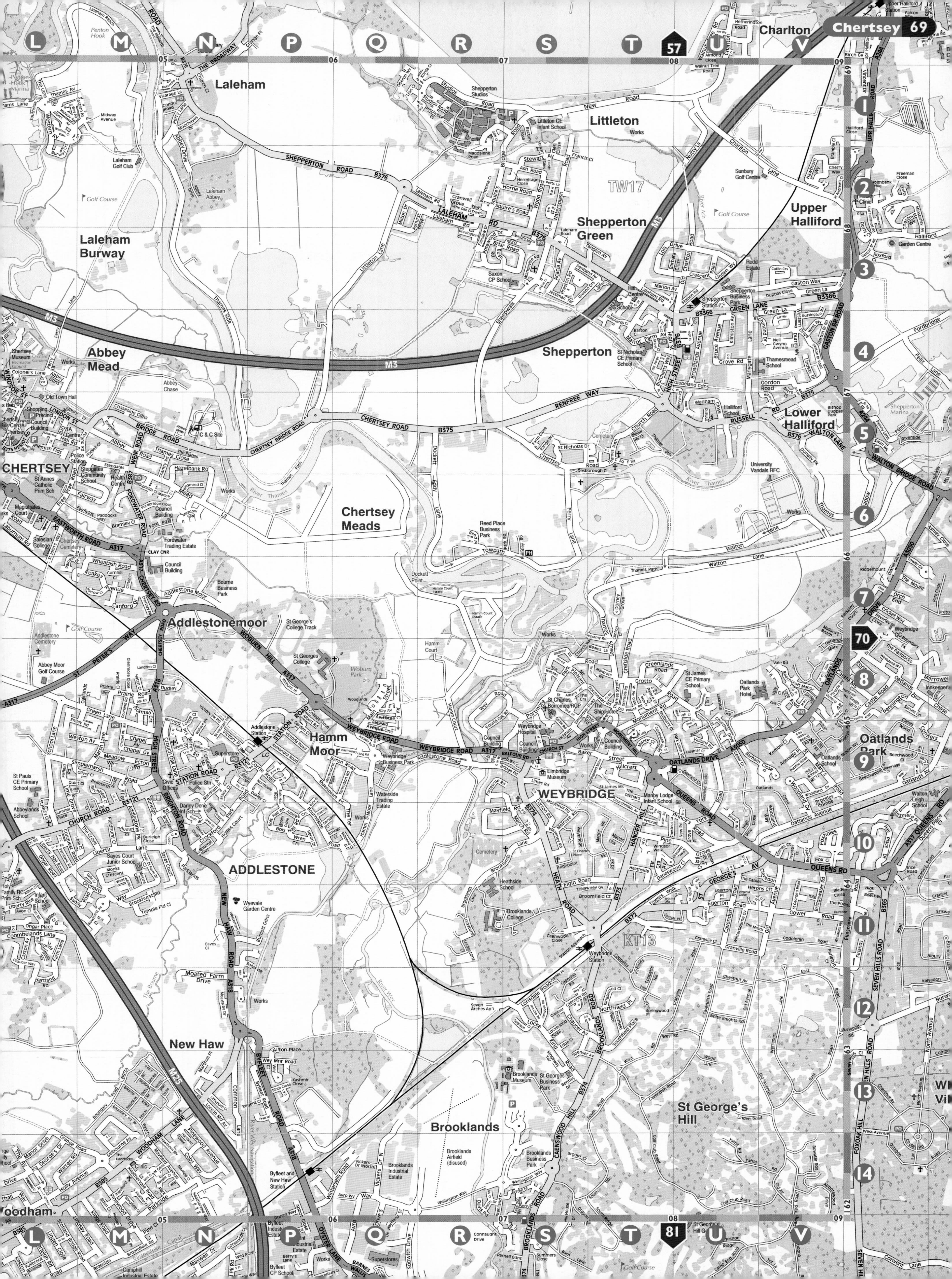
Laleham
Littleton
Charlton
Shepperton Studios
Laleham Burway
Shepperton Green
Upper Halliford
TW17
Abbey Mead
Shepperton
Lower Halliford
CHERTSEY
Chertsey Meads
Addlestonemoor
Hamm Moor
WEYBRIDGE
Oatlands Park
ADDLESTONE
New Haw
Brooklands
St George's Hill
KT13
Woodham
M3
M25
SHEPPERTON ROAD
CHERTSEY ROAD
RENFREE WAY
WOBURN HILL
WEYBRIDGE ROAD
QUEENS ROAD
OATLANDS DRIVE
WALTON BRIDGE ROAD
SEVEN HILLS ROAD
BROOKLANDS ROAD
CAENSWOOD HILL
HEATH ROAD
BYFLEET ROAD
NEW HAW ROAD
BRIGHTON ROAD
HIGH STREET
CHURCH ROAD
STATION ROAD
ST PETER'S WAY
EASTWORTH ROAD
GUILDFORD STREET
WEIR ROAD
BRIDGE ROAD
LONDON ST
GREEN LANE
HIGH STREET
GASTON BR ROAD
RUSSELL RD
WALTON LANE
Weybridge Station
Addlestone Station
Shepperton Station
Byfleet and New Haw Station
Elmbridge Museum
Brooklands Museum
River Thames
River Wey
57
70
81
L M N P Q R S T U V
05 06 07 08 09
1 2 3 4 5 6 7 8 9 10 11 12 13 14
69 68 67 66 65 64 63 62

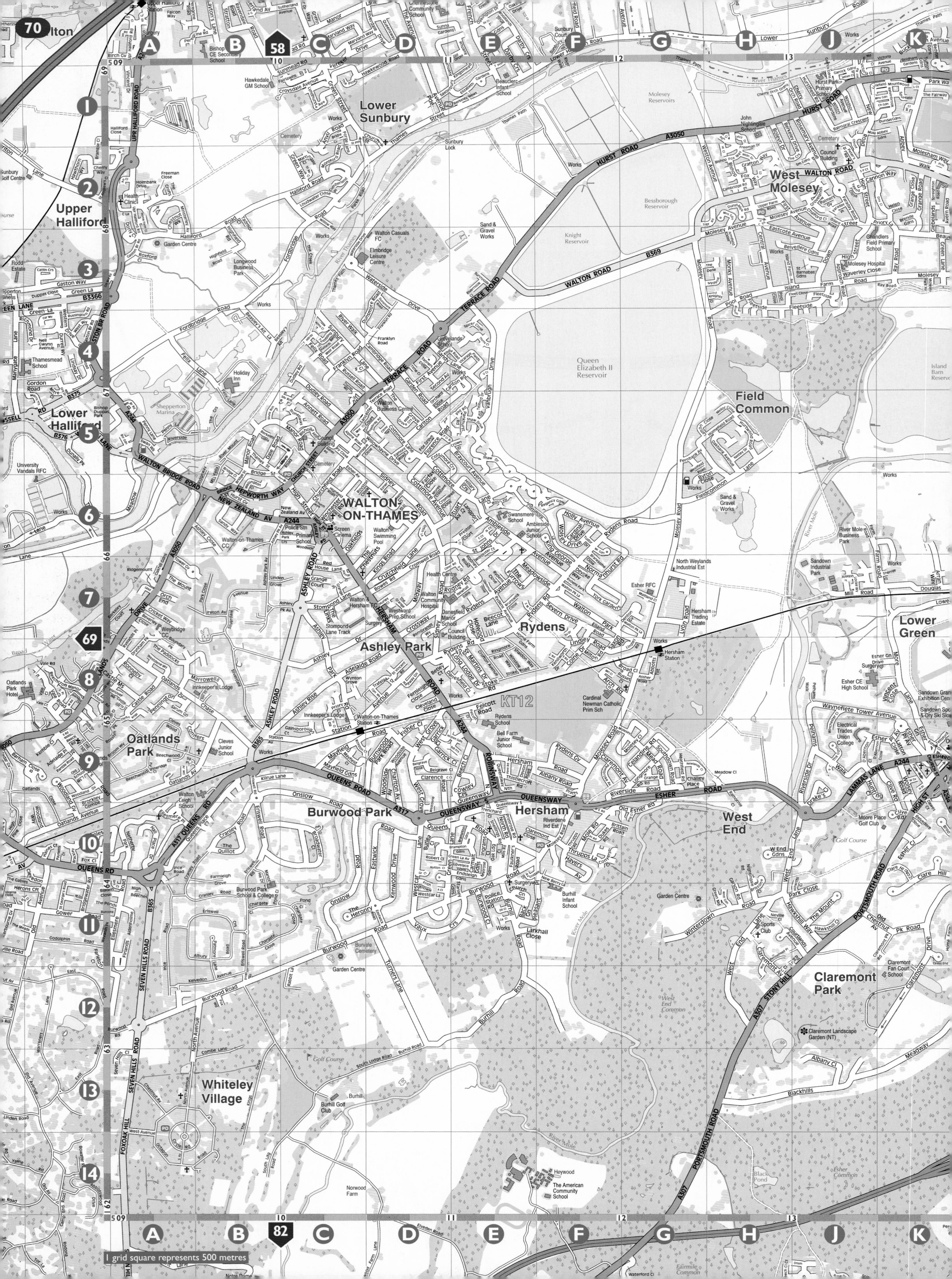

70
58
69
82
A B C D E F G H J K
1 2 3 4 5 6 7 8 9 10 11 12 13 14
509 10 11 12 13
69 68 67 66 65 64 63 62
Upper Halliford
Lower Halliford
Lower Sunbury
West Molesey
Walton-on-Thames
Field Common
Rydens
Ashley Park
Oatlands Park
Burwood Park
Hersham
West End
Lower Green
Claremont Park
Whiteley Village
Queen Elizabeth II Reservoir
Knight Reservoir
Bessborough Reservoir
Molesey Reservoirs
River Thames
River Mole
Shepperton Marina
Walton-on-Thames Station
Hersham Station
Upper Halliford Station
KT12
HURST ROAD
TERRACE ROAD
WALTON ROAD
WALTON BRIDGE ROAD
NEW ZEALAND AV
QUEENS ROAD
QUEENSWAY
ESHER ROAD
LAMMAS LANE
PORTSMOUTH ROAD
STONY HILL
SEVEN HILLS ROAD
FOXOAK HILL
HERSHAM ROAD
ASHLEY ROAD
CHURCH STREET
HEPWORTH WAY
ROBINSWAY
UPR HALLIFORD ROAD
A3050
A244
A317
A307
B365
B369
B3366
B375
B376
Burwood Road
Burhill Road
Molesey Road
Claremont Landscape Garden (NT)
Burhill Golf Club
Heywood
The American Community School
1 grid square represents 500 metres

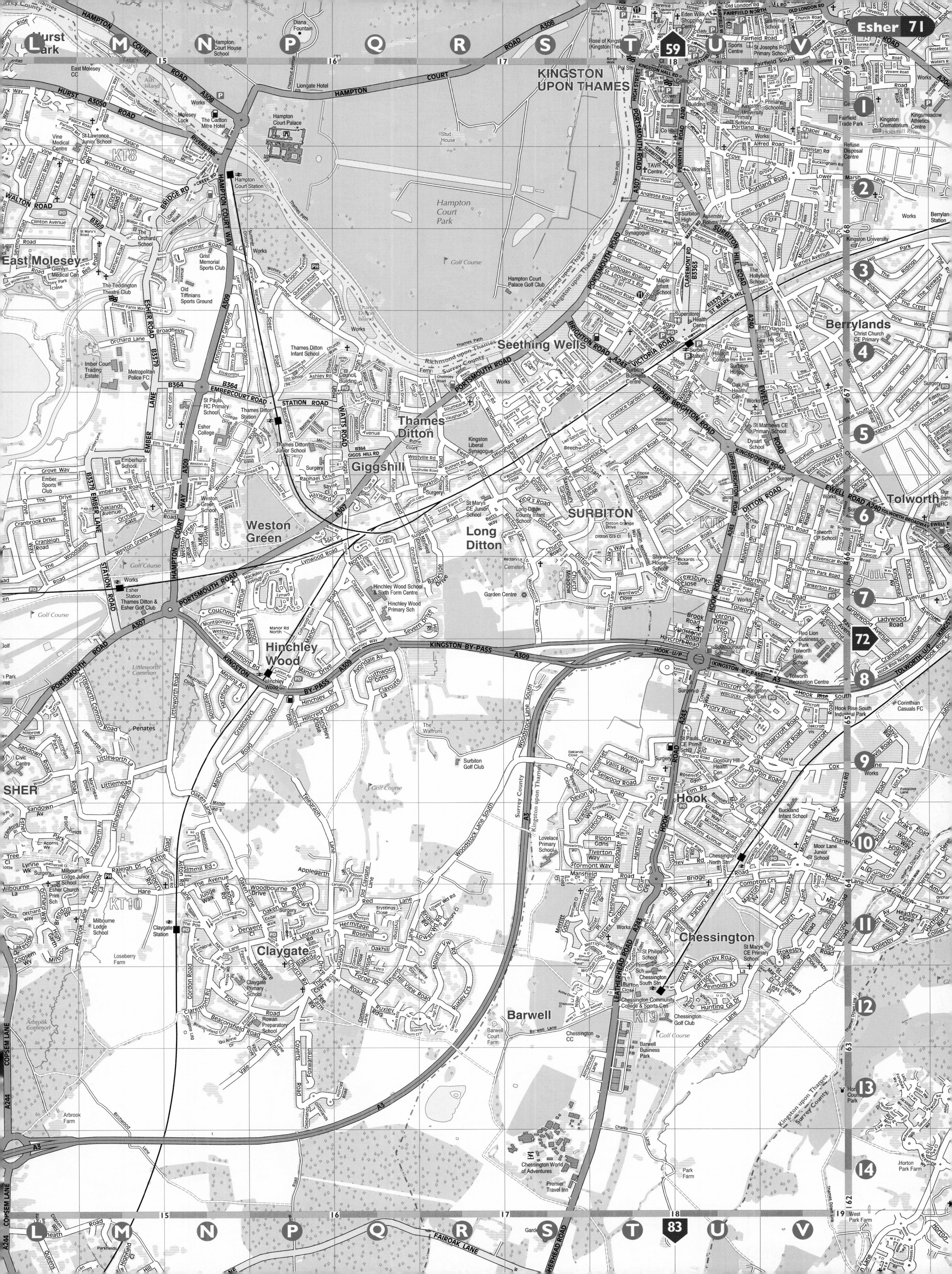

KINGSTON UPON THAMES
Hampton Court Park
East Molesey
Hurst Park
Seething Wells
Thames Ditton
Giggshill
Weston Green
Long Ditton
SURBITON
Berrylands
Tolworth
Hinchley Wood
Hook
Claygate
Chessington
Barwell
KT8
KT7
KT6
KT10
KT9
PORTSMOUTH ROAD
HAMPTON COURT WAY
KINGSTON BY-PASS
EWELL ROAD
HOOK ROAD
LEATHERHEAD ROAD
Chessington World of Adventures
Hampton Court Palace
Surbiton Golf Club
59
72
83

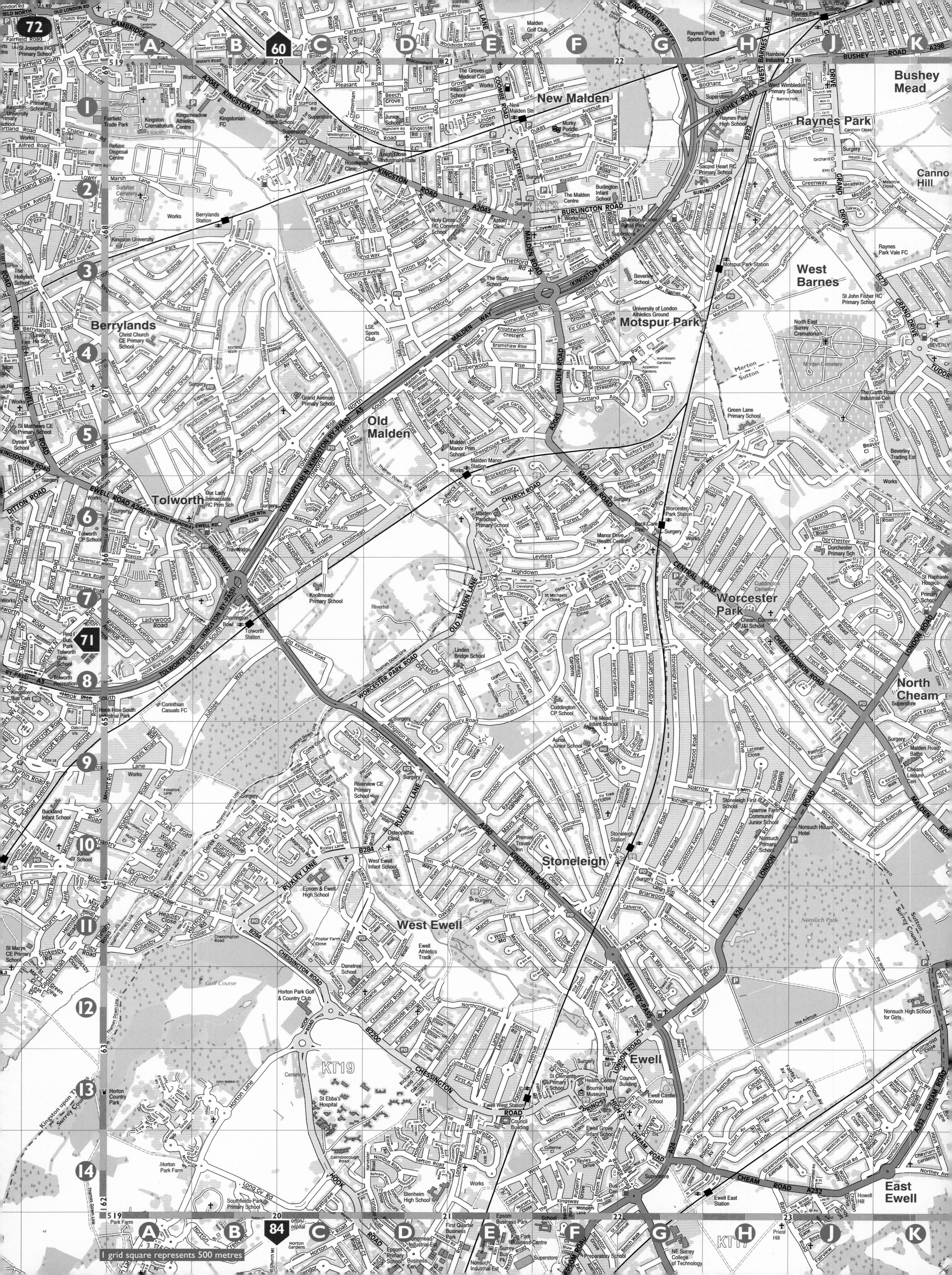

72
60
71
84
New Malden
Bushey Mead
Raynes Park
West Barnes
Motspur Park
Berrylands
Old Malden
Tolworth
Worcester Park
North Cheam
Stoneleigh
West Ewell
Ewell
East Ewell
Canno Hill
KT3
KT4
KT5
KT19
KT17
KINGSTON ROAD
MALDEN ROAD
KINGSTON BY-PASS
CENTRAL ROAD
CHEAM COMMON ROAD
LONDON ROAD
CHESSINGTON ROAD
EWELL BY-PASS
CHEAM ROAD
BURLINGTON ROAD
BUSHEY ROAD
WORCESTER PARK ROAD
EWELL ROAD
TOLWORTH BROADWAY
HOOK ROAD
Nonsuch Park
Nonsuch High School for Girls
Morden Cemetery
Horton Park Golf & Country Club
Golf Course
Merton
Sutton
Surrey County
Hogsmill River
1 grid square represents 500 metres

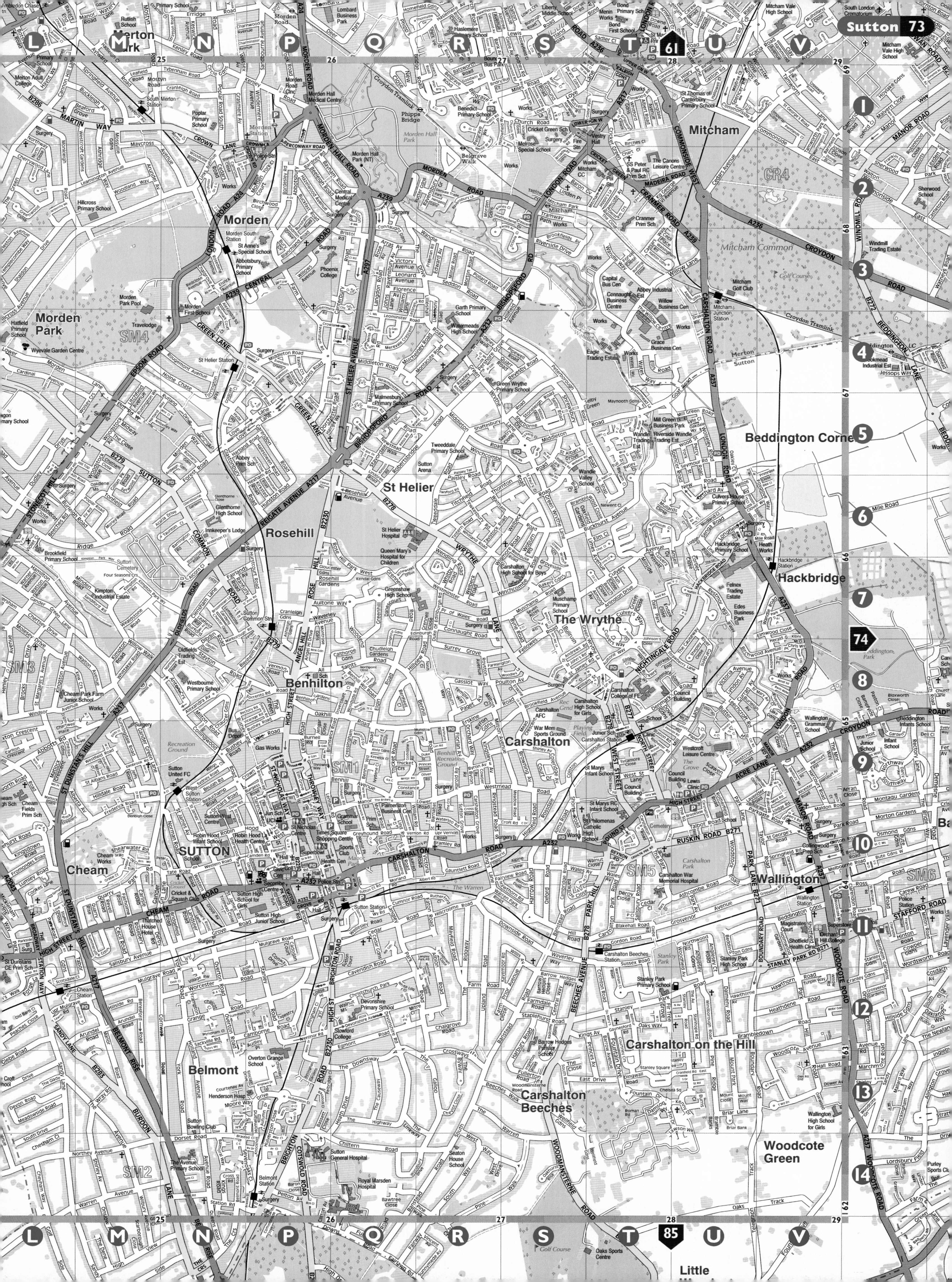
Merton Park
Morden
Morden Park
Mitcham
Mitcham Common
St Helier
Rosehill
Beddington Corner
Hackbridge
The Wrythe
Benhilton
Carshalton
SUTTON
Cheam
Wallington
Carshalton on the Hill
Belmont
Carshalton Beeches
Woodcote Green
Little
SM1
SM2
SM3
SM4
SM5
SM6
CR4

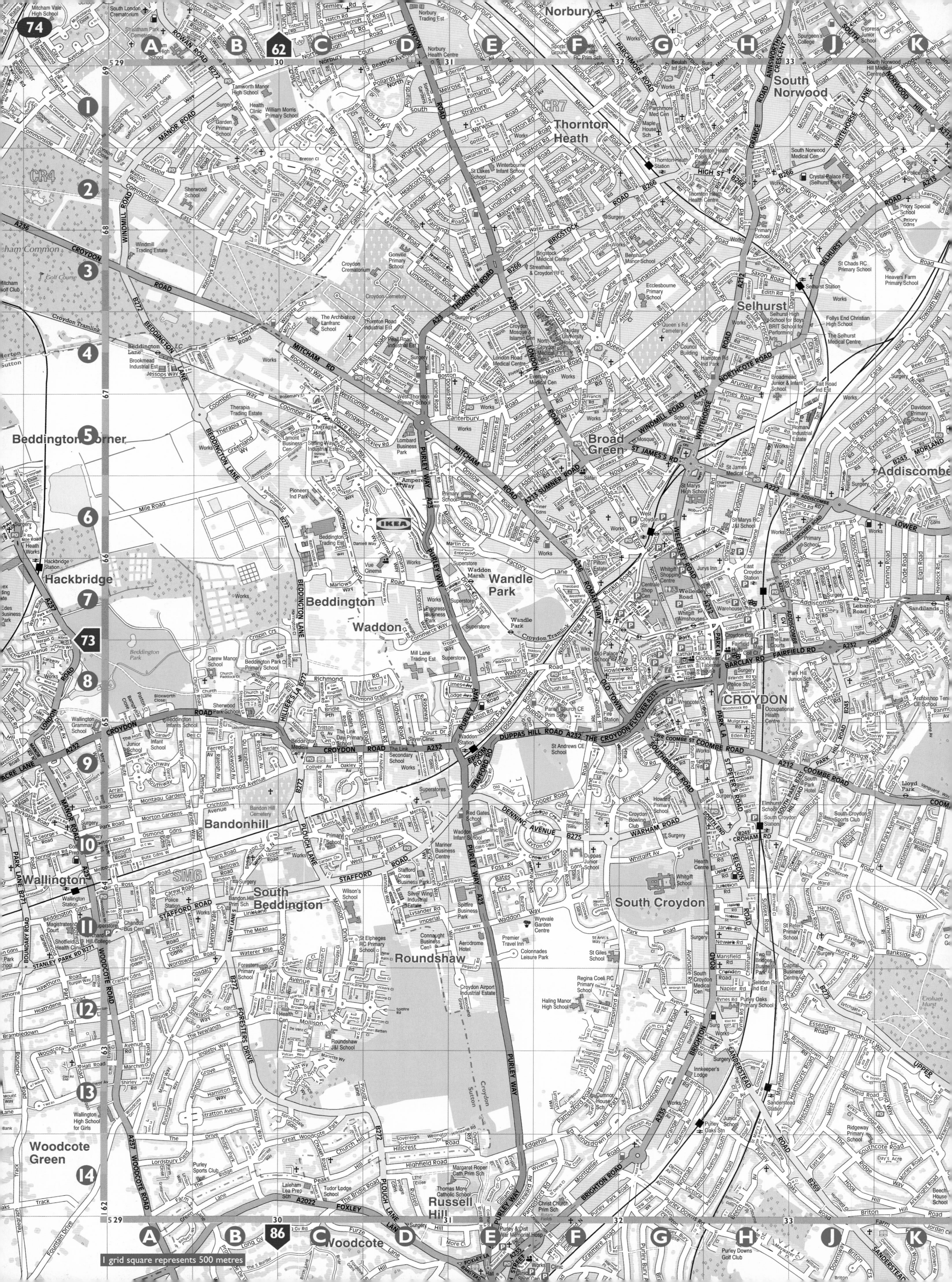
Norbury
South Norwood
Thornton Heath
Selhurst
Beddington Corner
Hackbridge
Broad Green
Addiscombe
Wandle Park
Beddington
Waddon
CROYDON
Bandonhill
Wallington
South Beddington
South Croydon
Roundshaw
Woodcote Green
Russell Hill
Woodcote
62
73
86
1 grid square represents 500 metres

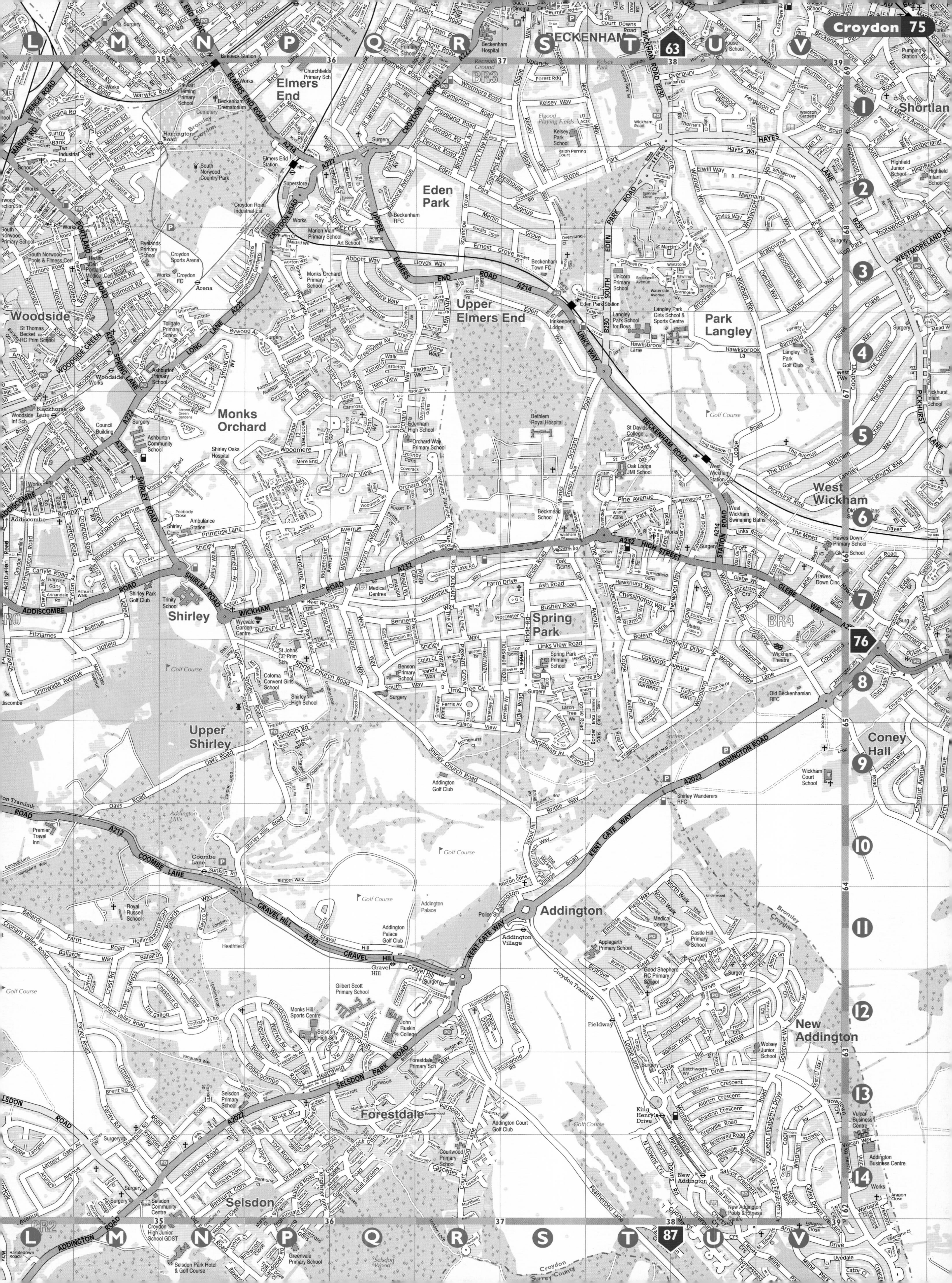
Beckenham
Elmers End
Eden Park
Upper Elmers End
Park Langley
Shortlan
Woodside
Monks Orchard
West Wickham
Shirley
Spring Park
Coney Hall
Upper Shirley
Addington
New Addington
Forestdale
Selsdon
Elmers End Road
Croydon Road
Upper Elmers End Road
Long Lane
Spring Lane
Shirley Road
Addiscombe Road
Wickham Road
High Street
Glebe Way
Beckenham Road
Links Way
Station Road
South Eden Park Road
Hayes Lane
Pickhurst Lane
Westmoreland Road
Addington Road
Kent Gate Way
Coombe Lane
Gravel Hill
Selsdon Park Road
Addington Road
Portland Road
Woodside Green
Shirley Church Road
Oaks Road
Featherbed Lane
Croham Valley Road
Birkbeck Station
Elmers End Station
Eden Park Station
West Wickham Station
Woodside Station
Bethlem Royal Hospital
Addington Palace
Golf Course
Croydon Tramlink
Bromley
Croydon
Surrey County
BR3
BR4
CR2
63
76
87
L
M
N
P
Q
R
S
T
U
V
1
2
3
4
5
6
7
8
9
10
11
12
13
14
35
36
37
38
39
62
63
64
65
66
67
68
69

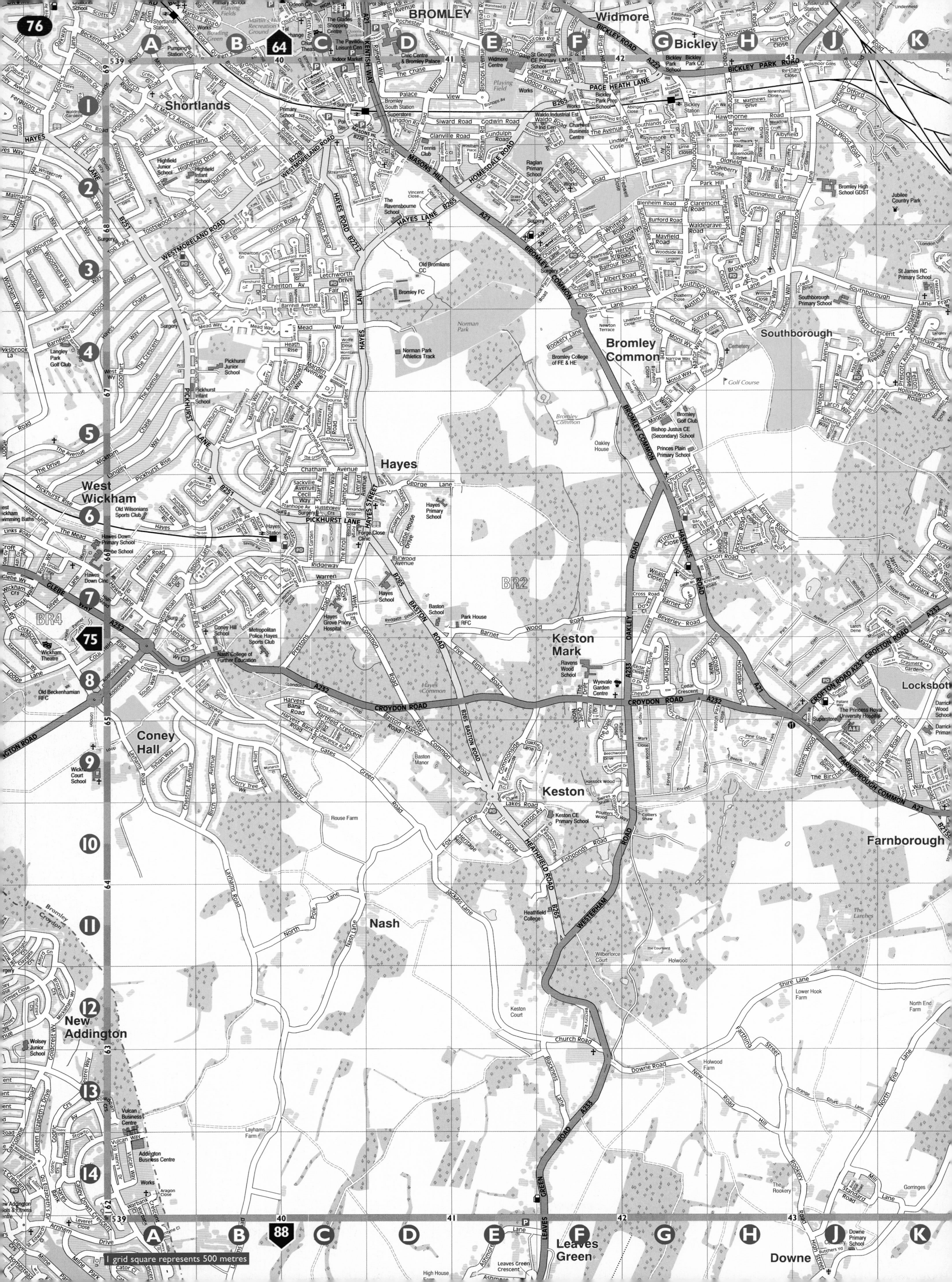
BROMLEY
Widmore
Bickley
Shortlands
Hayes
West Wickham
Bromley Common
Southborough
Keston Mark
Keston
Coney Hall
Nash
Farnborough
Locksbottom
New Addington
Leaves Green
Downe
BR2
BR4
MASONS HILL
KENTISH WAY
WESTMORELAND ROAD
HAYES LANE
HAYES ROAD
BROMLEY COMMON
BICKLEY ROAD
BICKLEY PARK ROAD
PAGE HEATH LANE
PICKHURST LANE
HAYES STREET
BASTON ROAD
CROYDON ROAD
OAKLEY ROAD
HASTINGS ROAD
WESTERHAM ROAD
HEATHFIELD ROAD
LEAVES GREEN ROAD
FARNBOROUGH COMMON
CROFTON ROAD
Norman Park
Bromley Common
Hayes Common
The Princess Royal University Hospital
64
75
88
A B C D E F G H J K
1 2 3 4 5 6 7 8 9 10 11 12 13 14
1 grid square represents 500 metres

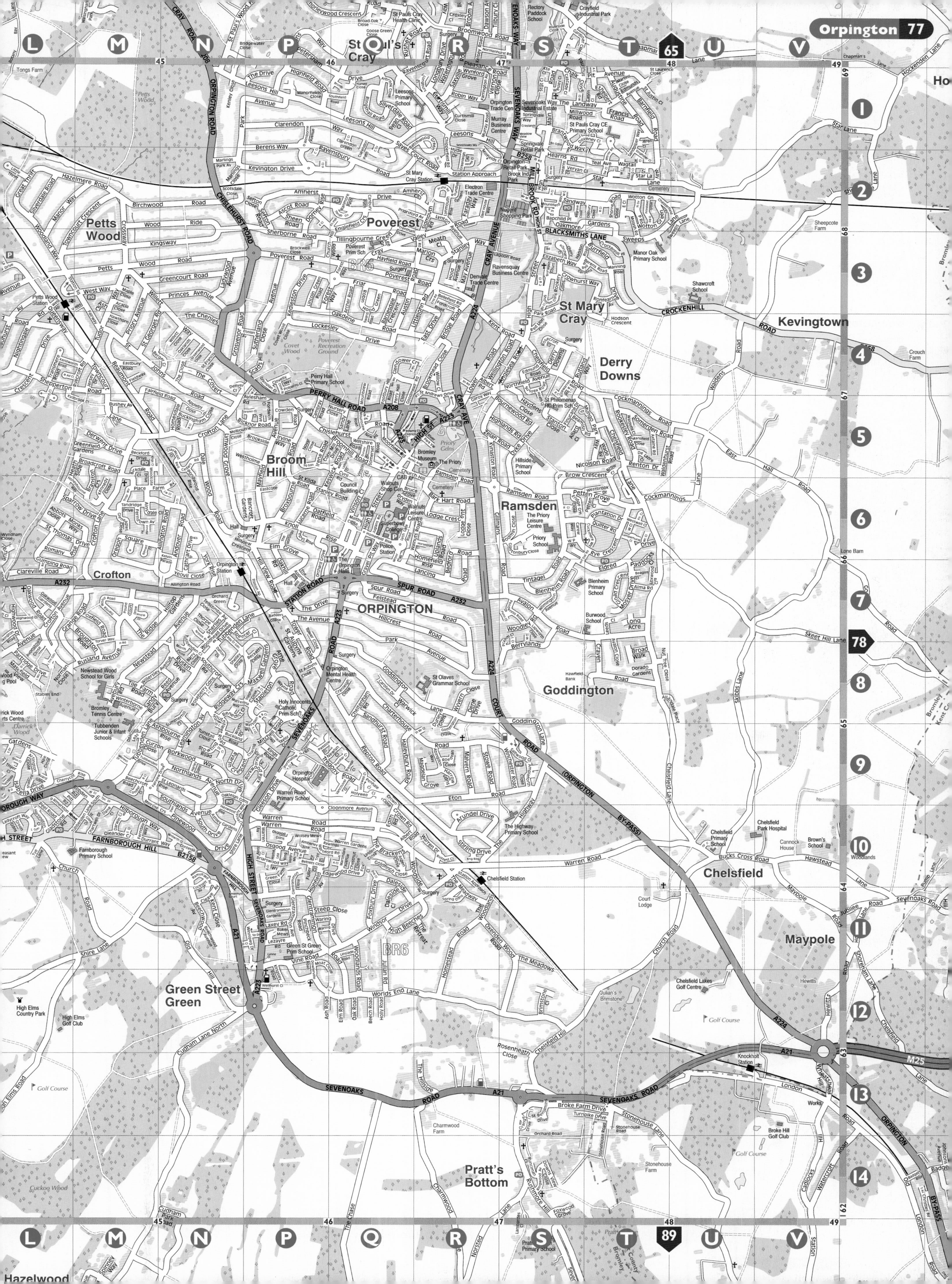

St Paul's Cray
Poverest
Petts Wood
St Mary Cray
Kevingtown
Derry Downs
Broom Hill
Ramsden
Crofton
ORPINGTON
Goddington
Chelsfield
Maypole
Green Street Green
Pratt's Bottom
Hazelwood
CHISLEHURST ROAD
ORPINGTON ROAD
SEVENOAKS WAY
CRAY AVENUE
PERRY HALL ROAD
SPUR ROAD
STATION ROAD
HIGH STREET
FARNBOROUGH HILL
SEVENOAKS ROAD
COURT ROAD
ORPINGTON BY-PASS
CROCKENHILL ROAD
BLACKSMITHS LANE
Orpington Station
Petts Wood Station
Chelsfield Station
St Mary Cray Station
Knockholt Station
Orpington Hospital
Chelsfield Park Hospital
Chelsfield Lakes Golf Centre
High Elms Country Park
High Elms Golf Club
Broke Hill Golf Club
M25
A224
A232
A223
A21
A208
B258
B2158
BR5
BR6
65
78
89
L
M
N
P
Q
R
S
T
U
V
1
2
3
4
5
6
7
8
9
10
11
12
13
14
45
46
47
48
49
62
63
64
65
66
67
68
69

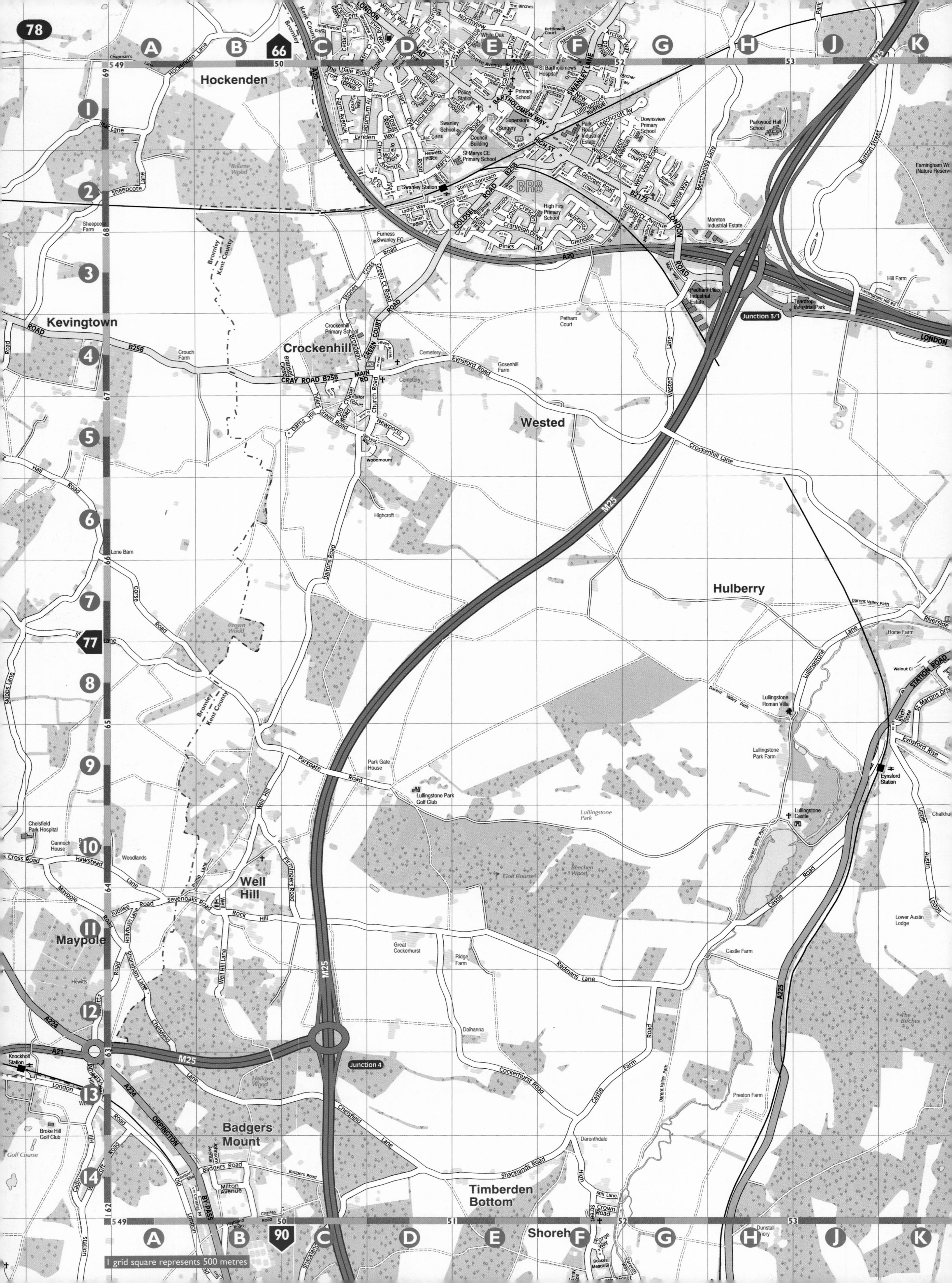

Hockenden
Hockenden Lane
Chapman's Lane
Star Lane
Sheepcote Lane
Bourne Wood
Sheepcote Farm
Bromley
Kent County
Kevingtown
Crouch Farm
Crockenhill
Crockenhill Primary School
CRAY ROAD B258
MAIN RD
Green Court Road
Stones Cross Road
Furness Swanley FC
Cemetery
Evnsford Road
Gosenhill Farm
Petham Court
Wested
Wested Lane
Crockenhill Lane
Newports
Woodmount
Highcroft
Daltons Road
Lone Barn
Gorse Road
Crown Wood
Hall Road
Skibbs Lane
M25
Hulberry
Darent Valley Path
Lullingstone Lane
Lullingstone Roman Villa
Lullingstone Park Farm
Lullingstone Park
Lullingstone Castle
Lullingstone Park Golf Club
Park Gate House
Parkgate Road
Beechen Wood
Golf Course
Riverside
Home Farm
Walnut Cl
STATION ROAD
St Martins Drive
Birch Close
Eynsford Rise
Eynsford Station
Upper Austin Lodge
Lower Austin Lodge
Chalkhu
Castle Road
Castle Farm
A225
The Birches
Preston Farm
Chelsfield Park Hospital
Cannock House
Woodlands
Hawstead Lane
Maypole Road
Jubilee Road
Hollybush Lane
Sevenoaks Road
Well Hill
Well Hill Lane
Firmingers Road
Rock Hill
Maypole
Hewitts
Shoreham Lane
Great Cockerhurst
Ridge Farm
Redmans Lane
Dalhanna
Cockerhurst Road
Castle Farm Road
Darenthdale
Junction 4
A224
A21
Knockholt Station
London Road
Hollows Wood
Chelsfield Lane
Badgers Mount
Badgers Road
Milton Avenue
Johnsons Avenue
ORPINGTON BY-PASS
Shacklands Road
Timberden Bottom
Mill Lane
Crown Road
High Street
Forge Way
Shoreh
Dunstall Priory
Broke Hill Golf Club
Golf Course
Station Road
Swanley Station
BR8
B2173
HIGH ST
BARTHOLOMEW WAY
SWANLEY LANE
LONDON ROAD
A20
St Bartholomews Hospital
Primary School
Swanley School
Police Station
Council Building
Superstore
Surgery
St Marys CE Primary School
High Firs Primary School
Park Road Industrial Estate
Downsview Primary School
Leechcroft Av
Kettlewell Court
White Oak
Moreton Industrial Estate
Pedham Place Industrial Estate
Teardrop Industrial Park
Junction 3/1
Beechenlea Lane
Manse Way
Parkwood Hall School
Button Street
Farningham Hill Rd
Hill Farm
Farningham Wo (Nature Reserv
Pinks Hill
Glendale
Goldsel Road
Station Approach
Azalea Drive
Cranleigh Drive
Salisbury Avenue
Kent County
A B C D E F G H J K
1 2 3 4 5 6 7 8 9 10 11 12 13 14
66
77
90
49 50 51 52 53
62 63 64 65 66 67 68 69
1 grid square represents 500 metres

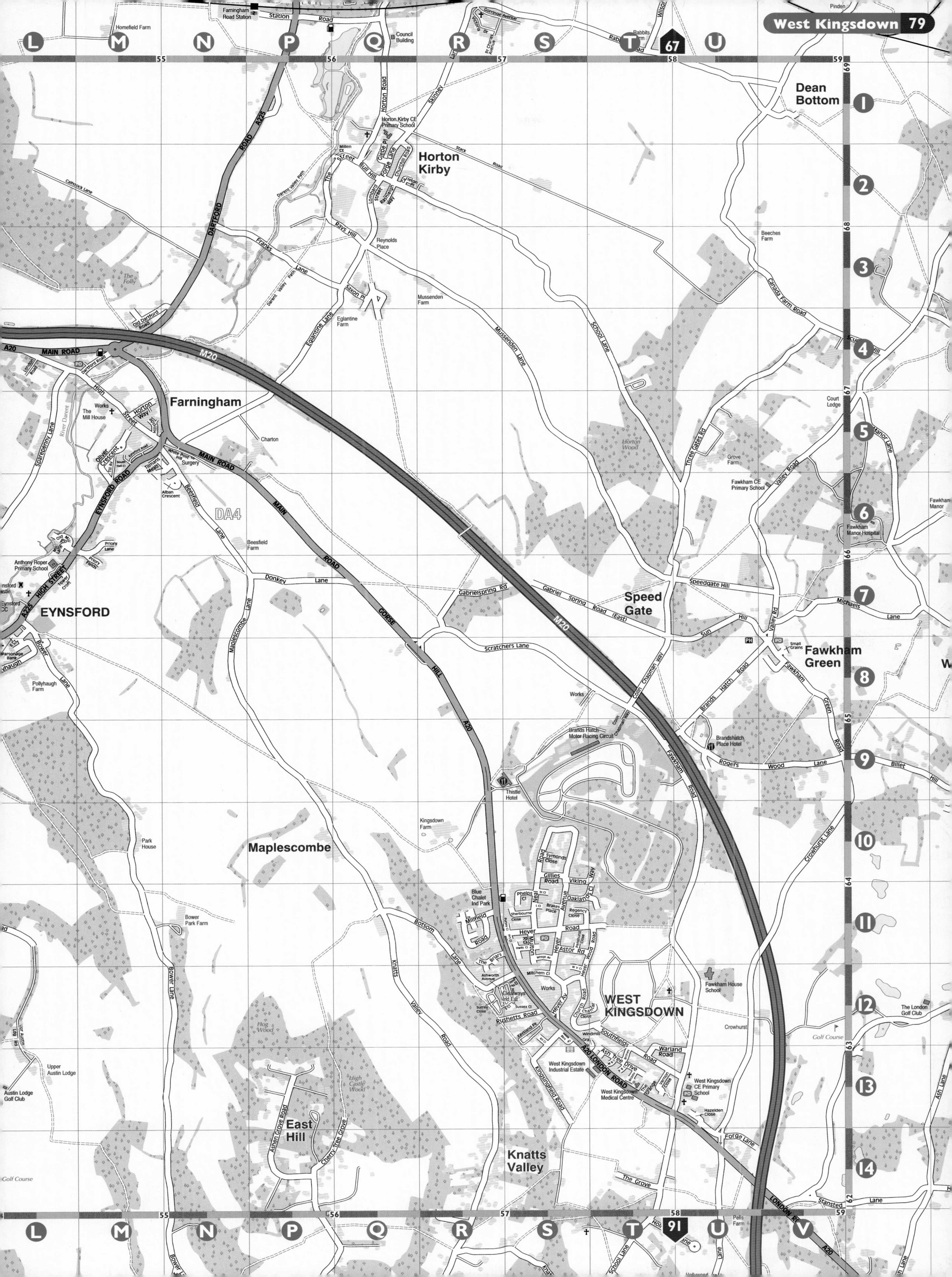
Farningham Road Station
Station Road
Homefield Farm
Council Building
Gorringe Avenue
Rabbits Farm
67
Pinden
Dean Bottom
Horton Kirby CE Primary School
Horton Road
Skinney Lane
Horton Kirby
Stack Road
Bull Hill
Forge Lane
Churchill Road
The Street
Millen Ct
Glebe Pl
Lombard Street
Raleigh Way
Darent Valley Path
Calfstock Lane
DARTFORD ROAD
A225
Rays Hill
Reynolds Place
Franks Lane
The Folly
Saxon Pl
Beeches Farm
Canada Farm Road
Mussenden Farm
Mussenden Lane
School Lane
Eglantine Lane
Eglantine Farm
Old Dartford Road
A20 MAIN ROAD
M20
Farningham
High Street
Horton Way
Works
The Mill House
River Darent
Sparepenny Lane
Charton
Oliver Crescent
EYNSFORD ROAD
MAIN ROAD
Surgery
Alban Crescent
Beesfield Lane
DA4
Beesfield Farm
Priory Lane
Priory Fields
Anthony Roper Primary School
HIGH STREET
EYNSFORD
Donkey Lane
GORSE HILL
Maplescombe Lane
Gabrielspring Rd
Gabriel Spring Road (East)
Speed Gate
Speedgate Hill
Three Gates Rd
Horton Wood
Grove Farm
Fawkham CE Primary School
Valley Road
Court Lodge
Manor Lane
Fawkham Manor
Fawkham Manor Hospital
Michaels Lane
Sun Hill
Fawkham Green
Small Grains
Scratchers Lane
Colin Chapman Way
Brands Hatch Road
Fawkham Green Road
Pollyhaugh Farm
Bower Lane
Parsonage Bank
Works
Brands Hatch Motor Racing Circuit
Brandshatch Place Hotel
Rogers Wood Lane
Billet Hill
Fawkham Road
Thistle Hotel
Kingsdown Farm
Crowhurst Lane
Park House
Maplescombe
Blue Chalet Ind Park
Symonds Close
Gillies Road
Viking Way
Oaklands Cl
Neal Road
Phelps Cl
Sherbourne Close
Brakes Place
Regency Close
Millfield Road
Hever Road
Astor Rd
Botsom Lane
Bower Park Farm
Knatts Valley Road
The Briars
Ashworth Avenue
Mitchem Cl
Works
Clearways Ind Est
Surrey Close
Sussex Ct
Rusherts Road
Hever Av
Church Road
Chancel Close
WEST KINGSDOWN
Fawkham House School
Crowhurst
The London Golf Club
Golf Course
Southfields
Warland Road
Ash Tree Drive
A20 LONDON ROAD
West Kingsdown Industrial Estate
Kingsingfield Road
Hog Wood
Upper Austin Lodge
Austin Lodge Golf Club
High Castle Wood
West Kingsdown CE Primary School
West Kingsdown Medical Centre
The Grange
Hazelden Close
Ashen Grove Road
East Hill
Cherry Tree Grove
Forge Lane
Knatts Valley
The Grove
Stansted Lane
Golf Course
Pells Farm
London Rd
A20
School Lane
91
L M N P Q R S T U V
55 56 57 58 59
62 63 64 65 66 67 68 69
1 2 3 4 5 6 7 8 9 10 11 12 13 14

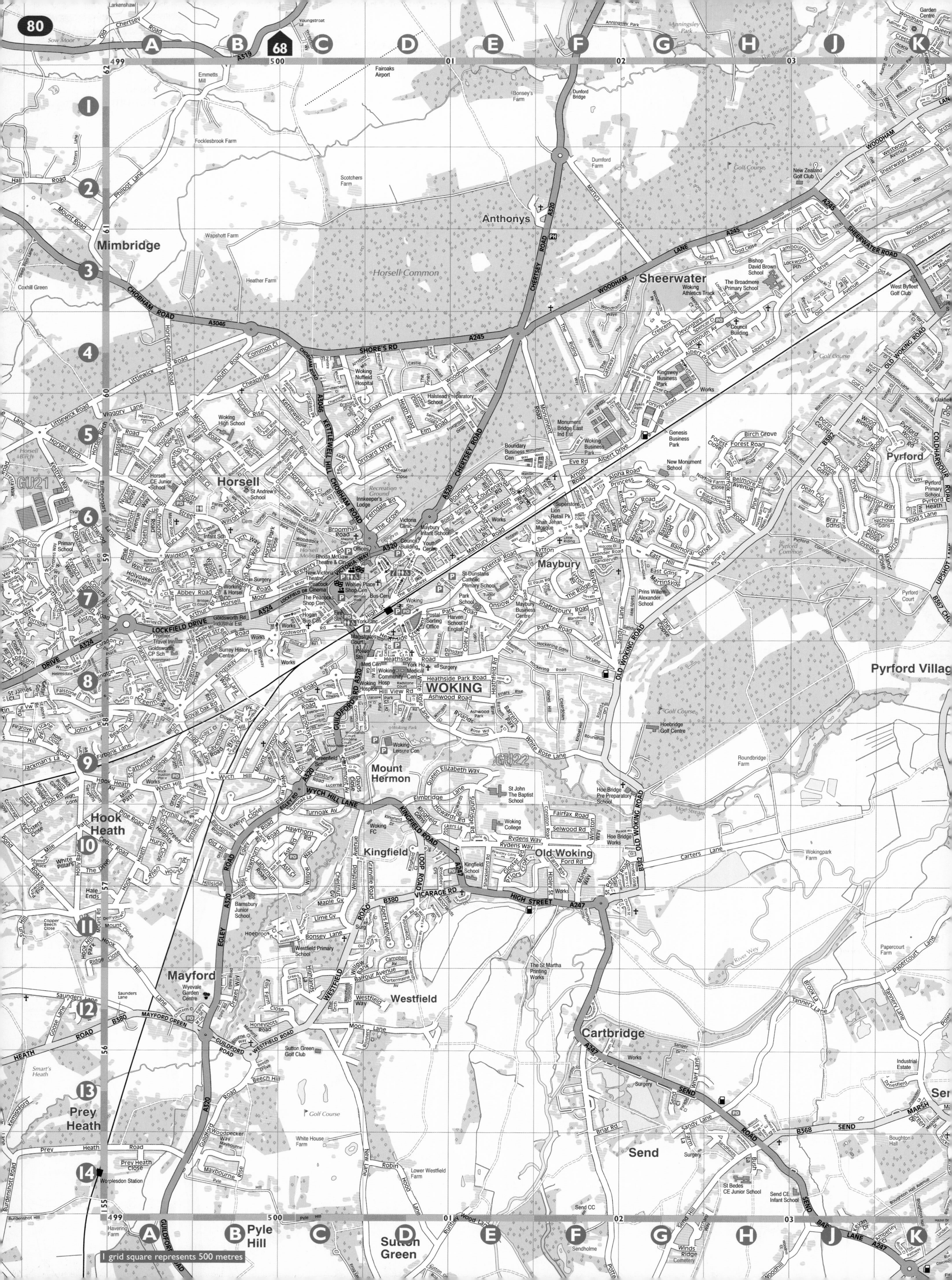
68
Fairoaks Airport
Anthonys
Horsell Common
Mimbridge
Sheerwater
Horsell
WOKING
Maybury
Pyrford
Pyrford Village
Mount Hermon
Hook Heath
Kingfield
Old Woking
Mayford
Westfield
Cartbridge
Prey Heath
Send
Pyle Hill
Sutton Green
Worplesdon Station
CHOBHAM ROAD
CHERTSEY ROAD
WOODHAM LANE
SHORE'S RD
VICTORIA WAY
LOCKFIELD DRIVE
GUILDFORD ROAD
EGLEY ROAD
HIGH STREET
SEND ROAD
OLD WOKING ROAD
WYCH HILL LANE
KINGFIELD ROAD
SHEERWATER ROAD
MAYFORD GREEN
GU21
GU22
1 grid square represents 500 metres

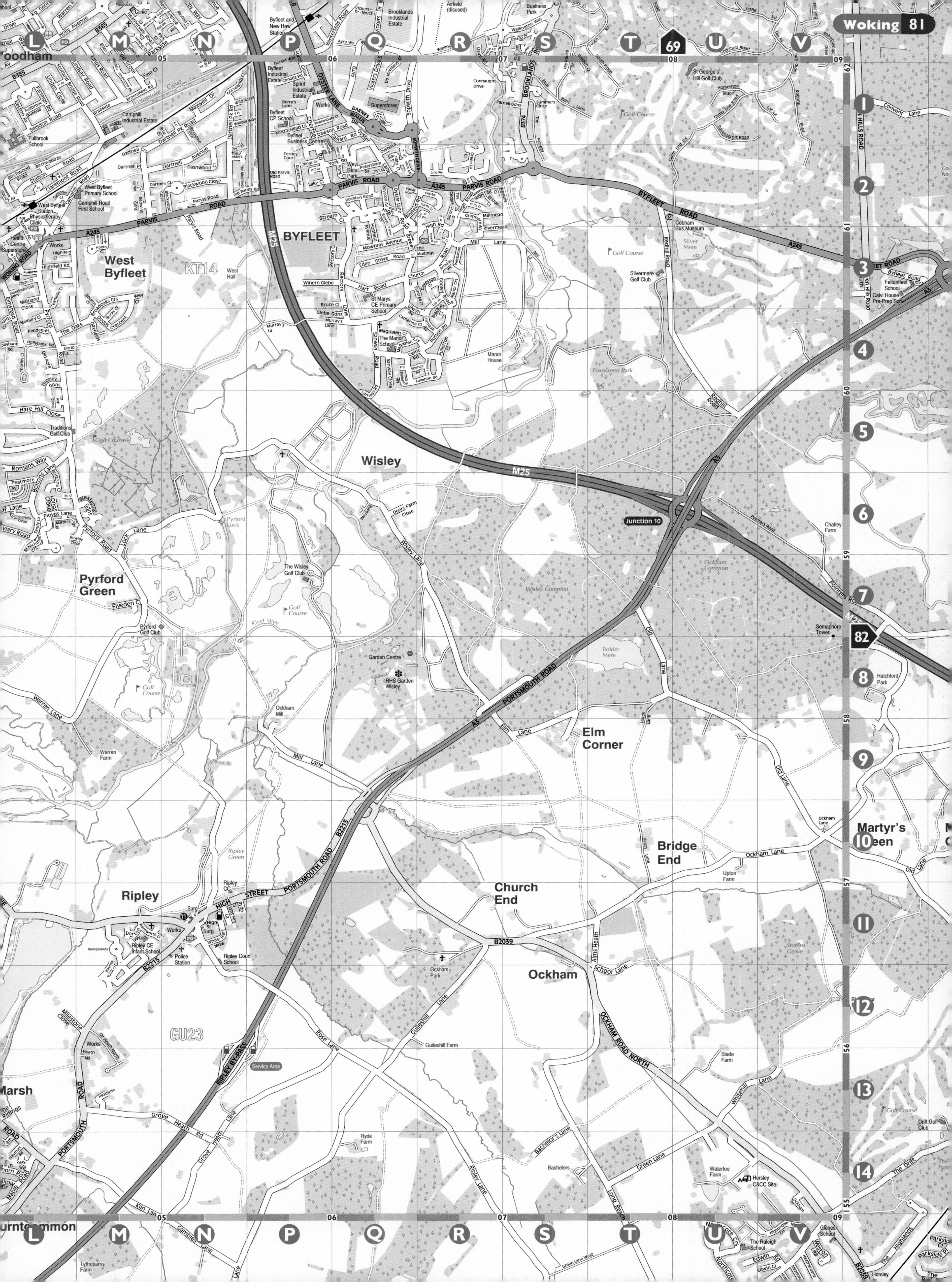
BYFLEET
West Byfleet
Wisley
Pyrford Green
Ripley
Elm Corner
Bridge End
Church End
Ockham
Martyr's Green
Marsh
M25
A3
A245
B2215
B2039
B374
B385
PARVIS ROAD
BYFLEET ROAD
PORTSMOUTH ROAD
OCKHAM ROAD NORTH
RIPLEY BY-PASS
HIGH STREET
OYSTER LANE
BROOKLANDS
Junction 10
KT14
GU23
RHS Garden Wisley
Garden Centre
The Wisley Golf Club
Pyrford Golf Club
Pyrford Lock
Ockham Mill
Warren Farm
Ripley Green
Ripley Court School
Police Station
Ripley CE Infant School
Service Area
Guileshill Farm
Ryde Farm
Bachelors
Waterloo Farm
Horsley C&CC Site
Slade Farm
Upton Farm
Stumps Grove
Ockham Park
Bolder Mere
Wisley Common
Ockham Common
Chatley Farm
Hatchford Park
Semaphore Tower
Foxwarren Park
Manor House
Silvermere Golf Club
Silver Mere
Cobham Bus Museum
St George's Hill Golf Club
Drift Golf Club
Feltonfleet School
Calvi House Pre-Prep Sch
Brooklands Industrial Estate
Byfleet Industrial Estate
Camphill Industrial Estate
Fullbrook School
West Byfleet Primary School
Camphill Road First School
West Byfleet Station
Byfleet and New Haw Station
St Marys CE Primary School
The Manor School
Traditions Golf Club
Tythebarns Farm
The Raleigh School
Glenesk School
Mill Lane
Old Lane
Ockham Lane
Wisley Lane
Rose Lane
Ripley Lane
Long Reach
Green Lane
Whitehill Lane
Pointers Road
Redhill Road
Warren Lane
Hare Hill Close
Grove Heath Road
Kiln Lane
Convent Lane
69
82
L
M
N
P
Q
R
S
T
U
V
05
06
07
08
09
1
2
3
4
5
6
7
8
9
10
11
12
13
14

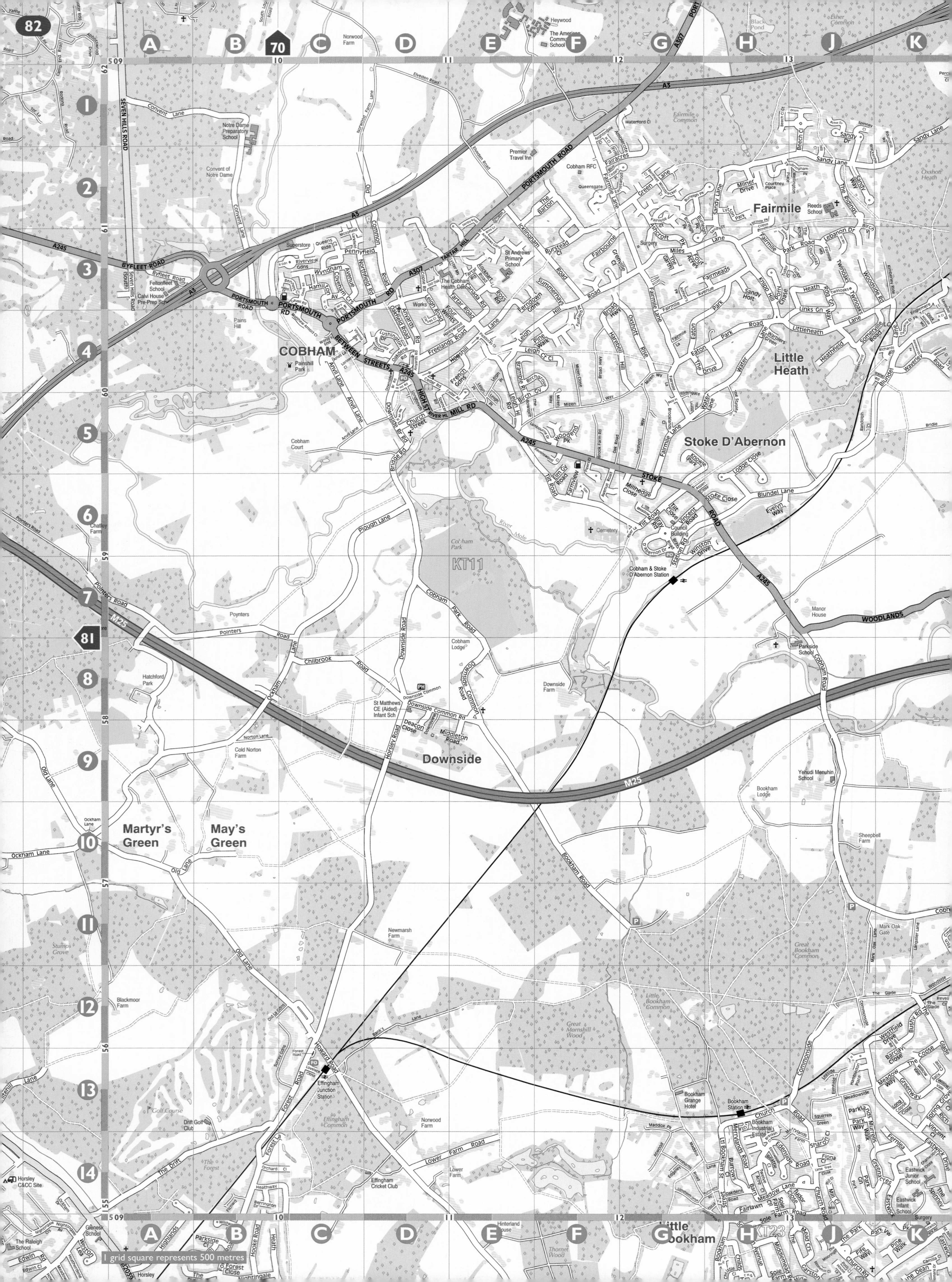
70
81
A
B
C
D
E
F
G
H
J
K
1
2
3
4
5
6
7
8
9
10
11
12
13
14
COBHAM
Fairmile
Little Heath
Stoke D'Abernon
Downside
Martyr's Green
May's Green
Little Bookham
KT11
KT23
PORTSMOUTH ROAD
BYFLEET ROAD
SEVEN HILLS ROAD
A3
A245
A307
M25
Convent Lane
Notre Dame Preparatory School
Convent of Notre Dame
Norwood Farm
Heywood
The American Community School
Black Pond
Esher Common
Elveden Road
Premier Travel Inn
Cobham RFC
Fairmile Common
Waterford Cl
Sandy Lane
Oxshott Heath
Reeds School
Feltonfleet School
Calvi House Pre-Prep Sch
Pains Hill
Painshill Park
Superstore
The Cobham Health Centre
St Andrews Primary School
Surgery
TARTAR HILL
BETWEEN STREETS
HIGH ST
MILL RD
RIVER HL
Church Street
Bridge Rd
Anvil Lane
Cobham Court
Chatley Farm
Pointers Road
Poynters
Plough Lane
River Mole
Cobham Park
Cemetery
STOKE ROAD
Blundel Lane
Council Building
Cobham & Stoke D'Abernon Station
WOODLANDS
Manor House
Parkside School
Cobham Road
Cobham Lodge
Cobham Park Road
Downside Road
Downside Common
Downside Farm
Hatchford Park
Chilbrook Road
Ockham Lane
St Matthews CE (Aided) Infant Sch
Downside Common Rd
Deacon Close
Middleton Road
Norton Lane
Cold Norton Farm
Old Lane
Horsley Road
Yehudi Menuhin School
Bookham Lodge
Sheepbell Farm
Bookham Road
Mark Oak Gate
Great Bookham Common
Little Bookham Common
Great Mornshill Wood
Newmarsh Farm
Stumps Grove
Blackmoor Farm
Howard Road
Effingham Junction Station
Effingham Common
Golf Course
Drift Golf Club
The Drift
The Forest
Forest Rd
Norwood Farm
Effingham Cricket Club
Lower Farm Road
Lower Farm
Bookham Grange Hotel
Bookham Station
Church Road
Bookham Industrial Estate
Maddox Pk
Hinterland House
Thornet Wood
Eastwick Junior School
Eastwick Infant School
Horsley C&CC Site
The Raleigh School
Glenesk School
Horsley
Surgery
I grid square represents 500 metres

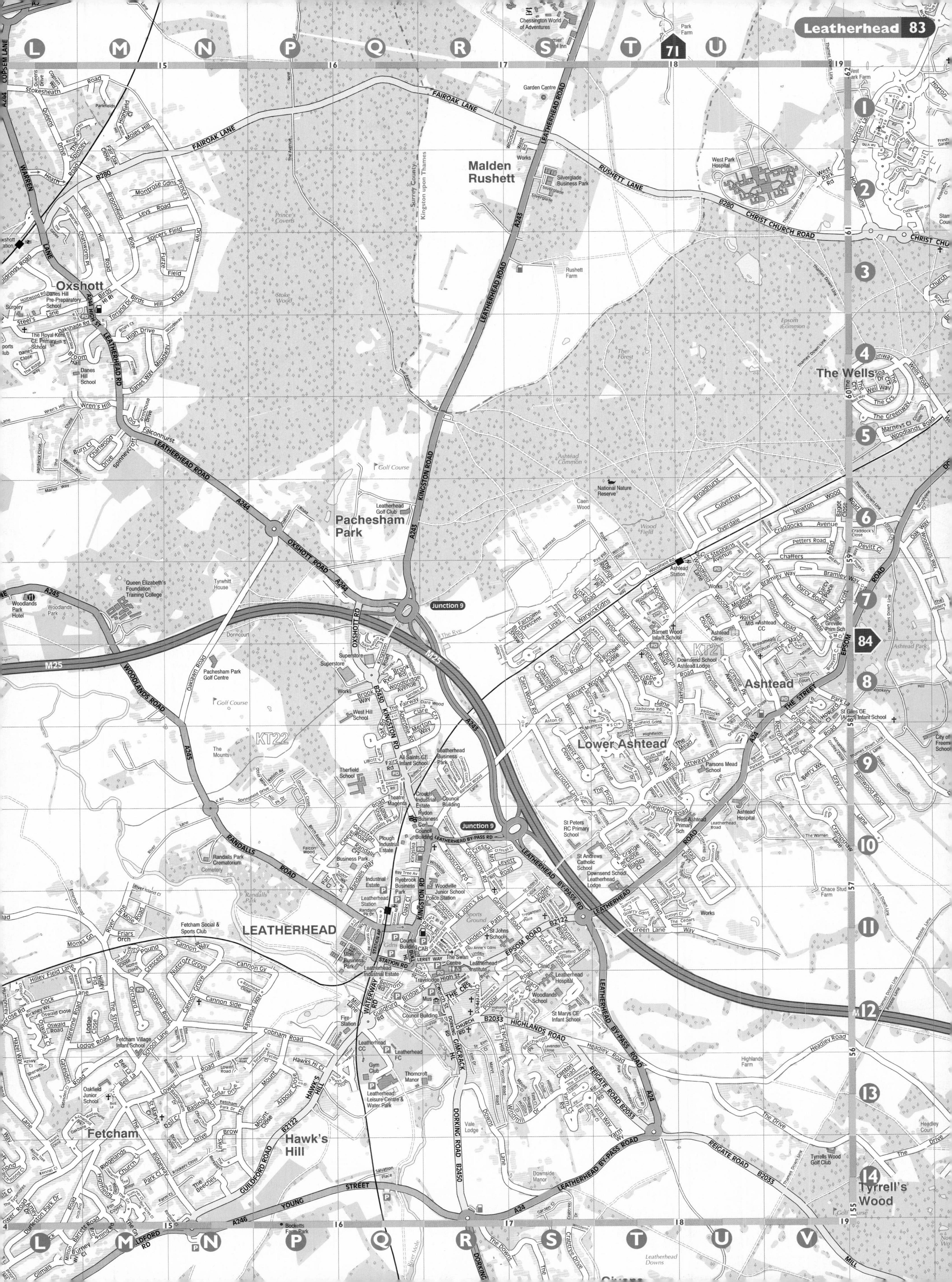
Malden Rushett
Oxshott
Pachesham Park
The Wells
Ashtead
Lower Ashtead
LEATHERHEAD
Fetcham
Hawk's Hill
Tyrrell's Wood
Chessington World of Adventures
West Park Hospital
Silverglade Business Park
Epsom Common
Ashtead Common
National Nature Reserve
Leatherhead Golf Club
Pachesham Park Golf Centre
Queen Elizabeth's Foundation Training College
Randalls Park Crematorium
Leatherhead Hospital
Leatherhead Leisure Centre & Water Park
Thorncroft Manor
Tyrrells Wood Golf Club
Junction 9
M25
FAIROAK LANE
RUSHETT LANE
CHRIST CHURCH ROAD
LEATHERHEAD ROAD
KINGSTON ROAD
OXSHOTT ROAD
WOODLANDS ROAD
RANDALLS ROAD
LEATHERHEAD BY-PASS ROAD
REIGATE ROAD
DORKING ROAD
GUILDFORD ROAD
YOUNG STREET
THE STREET
EPSOM ROAD
HIGHLANDS ROAD
WARREN LANE
KT21
KT22
71
84

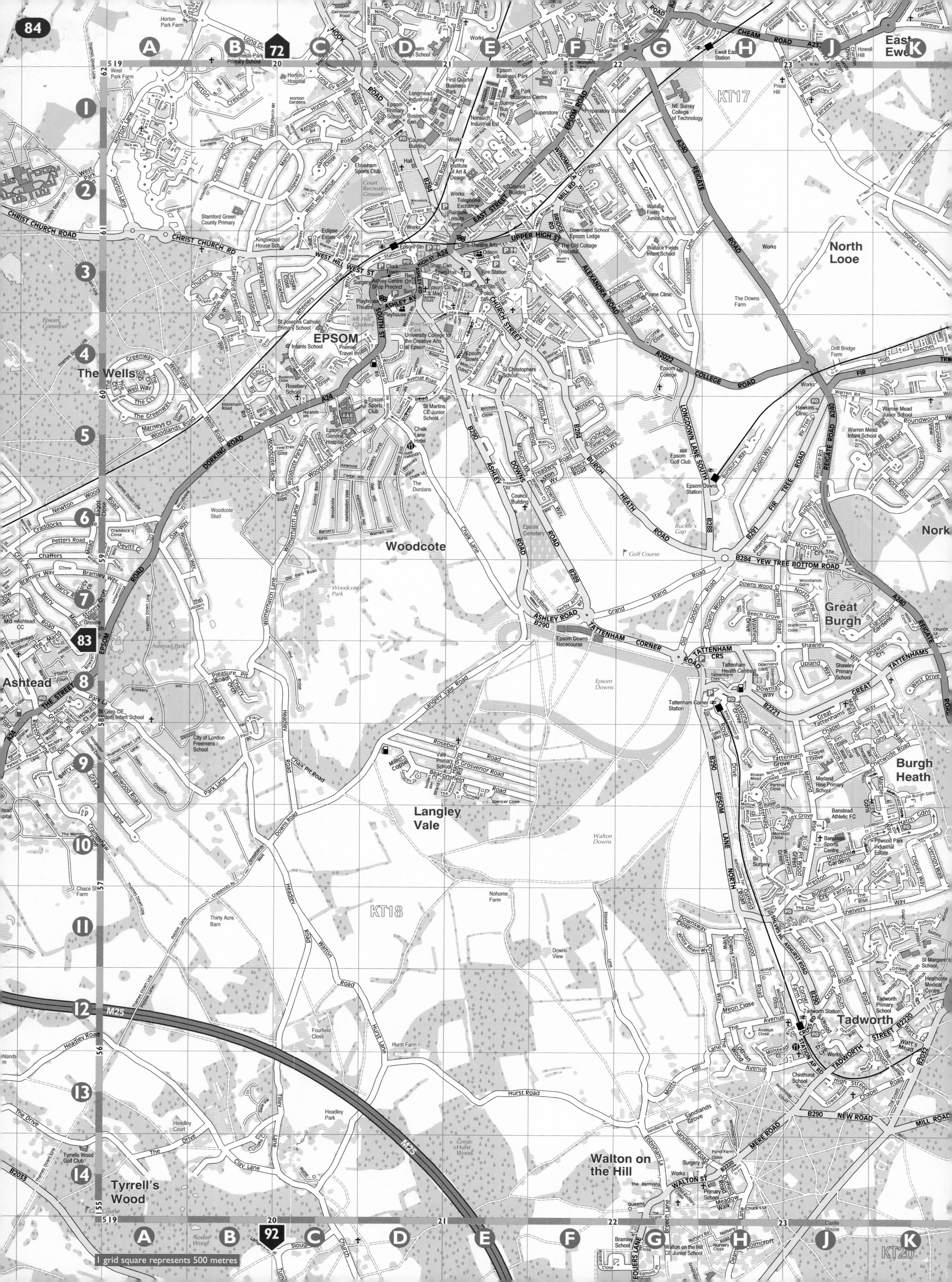
EPSOM
The Wells
Woodcote
Langley Vale
North Looe
Great Burgh
Burgh Heath
Tadworth
Walton on the Hill
Tyrrell's Wood
Ashtead
East Ewell
KT17
KT18
KT20
Epsom Common
Epsom Downs
Walton Downs
Epsom Downs Racecourse
Epsom Downs Station
Tattenham Corner Station
Tadworth Station
Epsom Stn
Ewell East Station
Epsom General Hospital
Epsom College
Epsom Golf Club
Tyrrells Wood Golf Club
City of London Freemens School
NE Surrey College of Technology
University College for the Creative Arts at Epsom
CHRIST CHURCH ROAD
DORKING ROAD
ASHLEY ROAD
EPSOM ROAD
REIGATE ROAD
COLLEGE ROAD
TATTENHAM CORNER ROAD
YEW TREE BOTTOM ROAD
WEST HILL
WEST ST
SOUTH ST
HIGH ST
EAST STREET
UPPER HIGH ST
CHURCH STREET
ALEXANDRA ROAD
LONGDOWN LANE SOUTH
BURGH HEATH ROAD
FIR TREE ROAD
EPSOM LANE NORTH
TADWORTH STREET
NEW ROAD
MILL ROAD
MERE ROAD
WALTON ST
CHEAM ROAD
HOOK ROAD
M25
A24
A240
A2022
B280
B284
B288
B289
B290
B291
B2032
B2033
B2220
B2221
72
83
92
1 grid square represents 500 metres

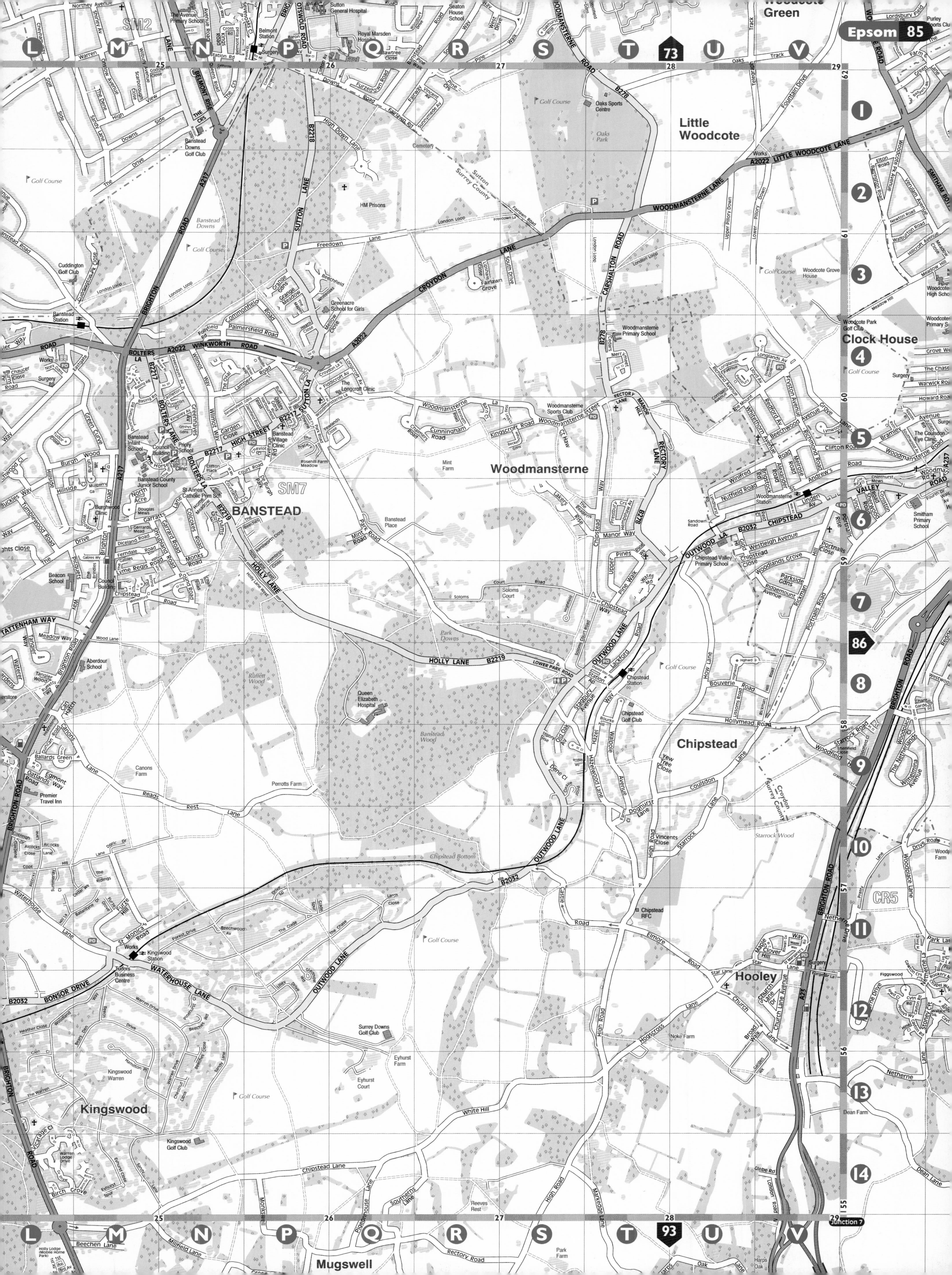
Epsom 85
73
86
93
Junction 7
L M N P Q R S T U V
25 26 27 28 29
62 61 60 59 58 57 56 55
1 2 3 4 5 6 7 8 9 10 11 12 13 14
SM2
SM7
CR5
Woodcote Green
Little Woodcote
Clock House
Woodmansterne
BANSTEAD
Chipstead
Hooley
Kingswood
Mugswell
Belmont Station
Sutton General Hospital
Royal Marsden Hospital
Seaton House School
The Avenue Primary School
Banstead Downs Golf Club
Banstead Downs
Golf Course
Cuddington Golf Club
Banstead Station
HM Prisons
Cemetery
Sutton
Surrey County
Oaks Sports Centre
Oaks Park
Greenacre School for Girls
Woodmansterne Primary School
Woodmansterne Sports Club
The Longcroft Clinic
Rosehill Farm Meadow
Mint Farm
Banstead Place
Banstead Village Clinic
Priory School
Banstead Infant School
Council Building
Banstead County Junior School
St Anne's Catholic Prim Sch
Burghwood Clinic
Douglas Mews
Beacon School
Aberdour School
Solorns Court
Park Downs
Ruffett Wood
Queen Elizabeth Hospital
Banstead Wood
Perrotts Farm
Canons Farm
Premier Travel Inn
Chipstead Station
Chipstead Golf Club
Chipstead Valley Primary School
Woodmansterne Station
Smitham Primary School
The Coulsdon Eye Clinic
Woodcote Park Golf Club
Woodcote Grove House
Starrock Wood
Chipstead Bottom
Chipstead RFC
Kingswood Station
Tudors Business Centre
Surrey Downs Golf Club
Eyhurst Farm
Eyhurst Court
Kingswood Warren
Kingswood Golf Club
Reeves Rest
Park Farm
Noke Farm
Dean Farm
Holly Lodge (Mobile Home Park)
Croydon
Surrey County
A217
A2022
A23
A237
B2217
B2218
B2219
B2032
B278
BRIGHTON ROAD
BELMONT RISE
SUTTON LANE
COTSWOLD ROAD
WOODMANSTERNE ROAD
WOODMANSTERNE LANE
LITTLE WOODCOTE LANE
CROYDON LANE
CARSHALTON ROAD
BOLTERS LANE
WINKWORTH ROAD
HIGH STREET
HOLLY LANE
OUTWOOD LANE
LOWER PARK ROAD
CHIPSTEAD VALLEY ROAD
RECTORY LANE
MANOR HILL
TATTENHAM WAY
WATERHOUSE LANE
BONSOR DRIVE
Freedown Lane
Chipstead Lane
Woodmansterne Street
Reads Rest Lane
Hollymead Road
Coulsdon Lane
Starrock Lane
Elmore Road
Castle Road
High Road
Hogscross Lane
White Hill
Rectory Road
Netherne Lane
Dean Lane
Beechen Lane
Millfield Lane

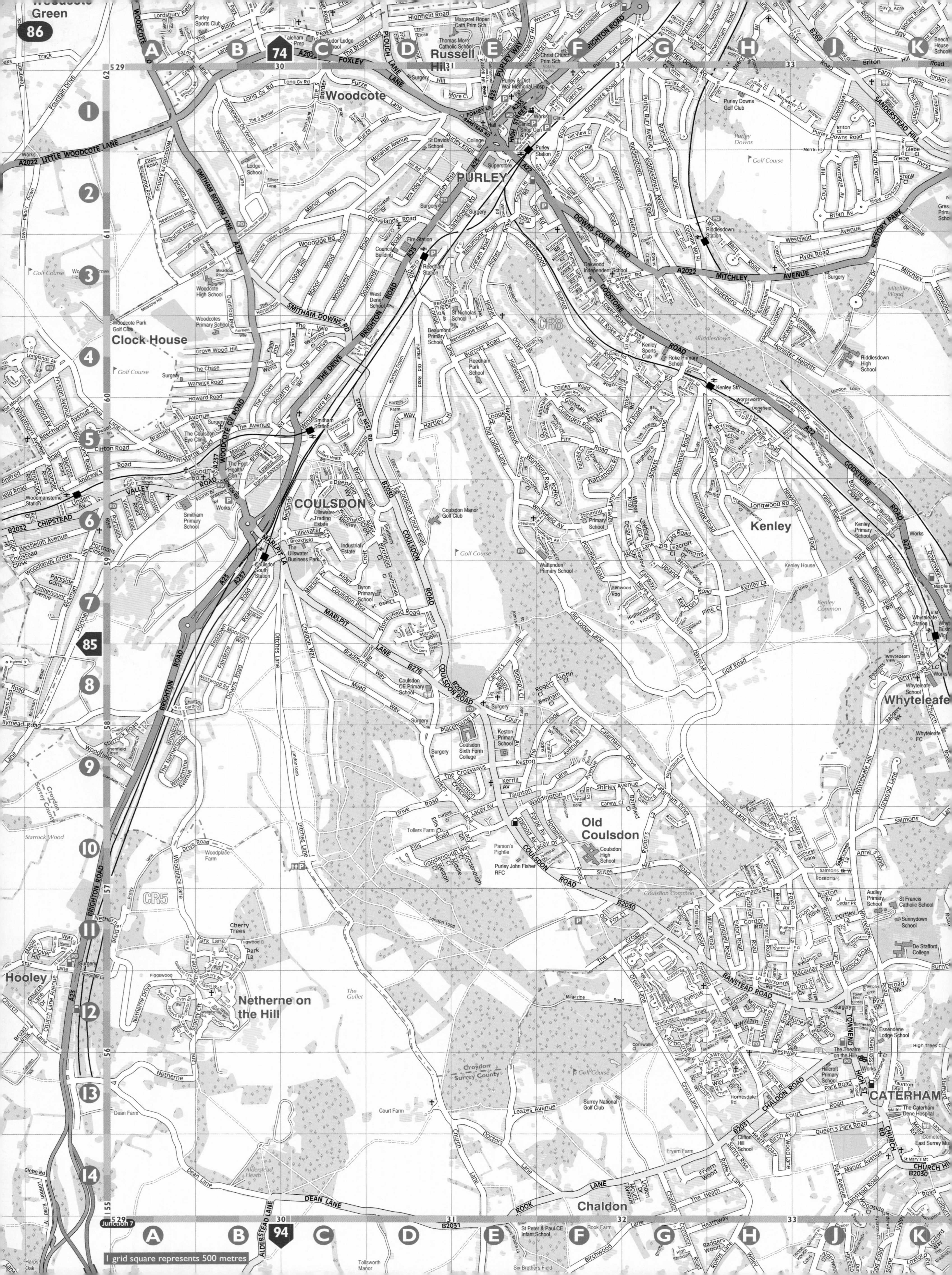
86
74
85
94
Woodcote
Russell Hill
PURLEY
Clock House
COULSDON
Kenley
Whyteleafe
Old Coulsdon
Hooley
Netherne on the Hill
CATERHAM
Chaldon
CR8
CR5
Purley Downs Golf Club
Coulsdon Manor Golf Club
Surrey National Golf Club
Riddlesdown
Kenley Common
Coulsdon Common
Croydon Surrey County
Starrock Wood
The Gullet
Aldersted Heath
Purley Station
Reedham Station
Smitham Station
Coulsdon South Station
Woodmansterne Station
Kenley Stn
Riddlesdown Station
Whyteleafe Station
BRIGHTON ROAD
SMITHAM BOTTOM LANE
LITTLE WOODCOTE LANE
FOXLEY LANE
PLOUGH LANE
PURLEY WAY
BRIGHTON ROAD
DOWNS COURT ROAD
MITCHLEY AVENUE
GODSTONE ROAD
SANDERSTEAD HILL
RECTORY PARK
SMITHAM DOWNS RD
WOODCOTE GV ROAD
CHIPSTEAD VALLEY ROAD
THE DRIVE
MARLPIT LA
MARLPIT LANE
COULSDON ROAD
STOATS NEST RD
COULSDON COURT ROAD
BANSTEAD ROAD
CHALDON ROAD
DEAN LANE
ROOK LANE
CHURCH HILL
TOWNEND
Junction 7
1 grid square represents 500 metres

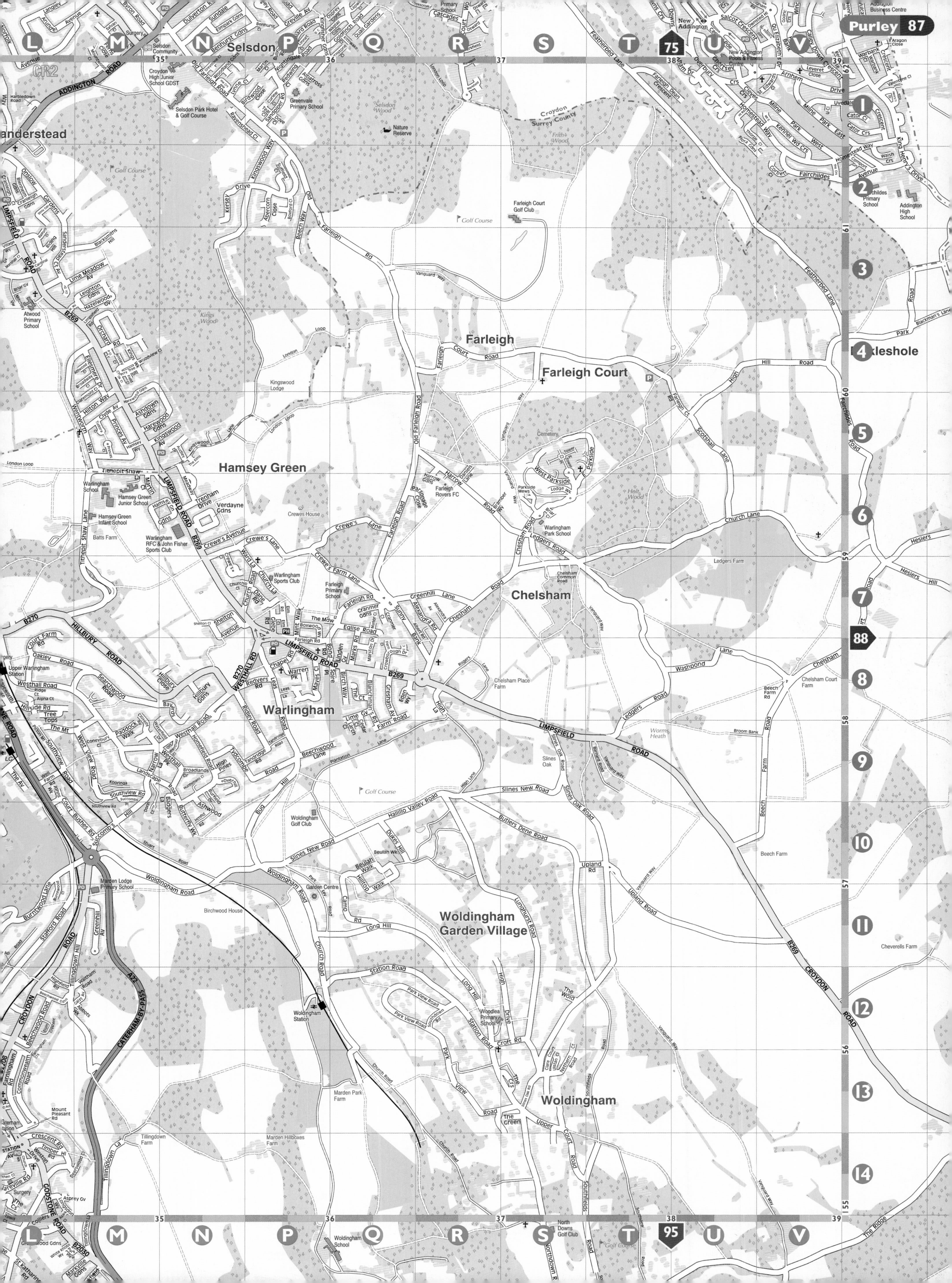
Selsdon
Sanderstead
Farleigh
Farleigh Court
Hamsey Green
Chelsham
Warlingham
Woldingham Garden Village
Woldingham
Croydon
Surrey County
Farleigh Court Golf Club
Golf Course
Kings Wood
Frith Wood
Selsdon Wood
Nature Reserve
Crewes House
Batts Farm
Ledgers Farm
Chelsham Place Farm
Chelsham Court Farm
Beech Farm
Cheverells Farm
Marden Park Farm
Marden Hillboxes Farm
Tillingdown Farm
Woldingham Golf Club
Woldingham Station
Woldingham School
North Downs Golf Club
Warlingham School
Hamsey Green Junior School
Hamsey Green Infant School
Atwood Primary School
Farleigh Primary School
Warlingham Park School
Marden Lodge Primary School
Woodlea Primary School
Greenvale Primary School
Croydon High Junior School GDST
Selsdon Park Hotel & Golf Course
Addington High School
LIMPSFIELD ROAD
CROYDON ROAD
ADDINGTON ROAD
HILLBURY ROAD
WESTHALL RD
CATERHAM-BY-PASS
Featherbed Lane
Old Farleigh Road
Farleigh Rd
Church Lane
Slines New Road
Slines Oak Road
Upland Road
Butlers Dene Road
Station Road
Long Hill
Church Road
B269
B270
A22
75
88
95

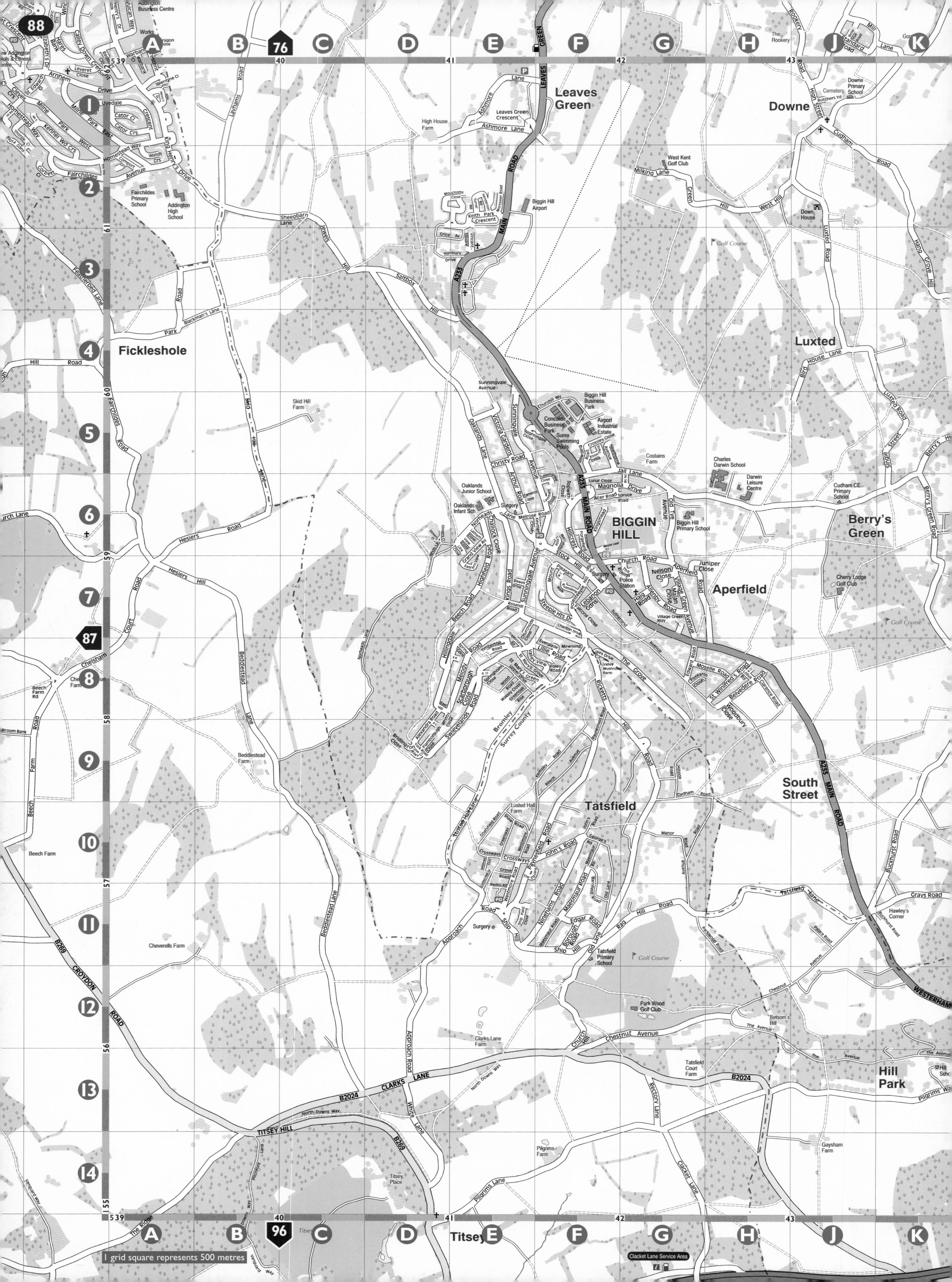
76
87
96
Leaves Green
Downe
Fickleshole
Luxted
Biggin Hill Airport
BIGGIN HILL
Berry's Green
Aperfield
South Street
Tatsfield
Hill Park
Titsey
A233 MAIN ROAD
LEAVES GREEN
Jail Lane
Church Road
Hesiers Road
Hesiers Hill
Skid Hill Lane
Beddlestead Lane
Approach Road
Clarks Lane
B2024
B269
CROYDON ROAD
TITSEY HILL
North Downs Way
Chestnut Avenue
Rectory Lane
Clacket Lane
Pilgrims Lane
Saltbox Hill
Sheepbarn Lane
Milking Lane
West Hill
Luxted Road
Cudham Road
Downe Primary School
West Kent Golf Club
Down House
Charles Darwin School
Darwin Leisure Centre
Cudham CE Primary School
Cherry Lodge Golf Club
Biggin Hill Primary School
Oaklands Junior School
Oaklands Infant Sch
Biggin Hill Business Park
Airport Industrial Estate
Concorde Business Park
Surex Swimming Pools
Tatsfield Primary School
Park Wood Golf Club
Golf Course
Costains Farm
Skid Hill Farm
High House Farm
Beddlestead Farm
Beech Farm
Cheverells Farm
Clarks Lane Farm
Tatsfield Court Farm
Pilgrims Farm
Gaysham Farm
Titsey Place
Lusted Hall Farm
Fairchildes Primary School
Addington High School
Hawley's Corner
Clacket Lane Service Area
WESTERHAM
Bromley
Surrey County
1 grid square represents 500 metres

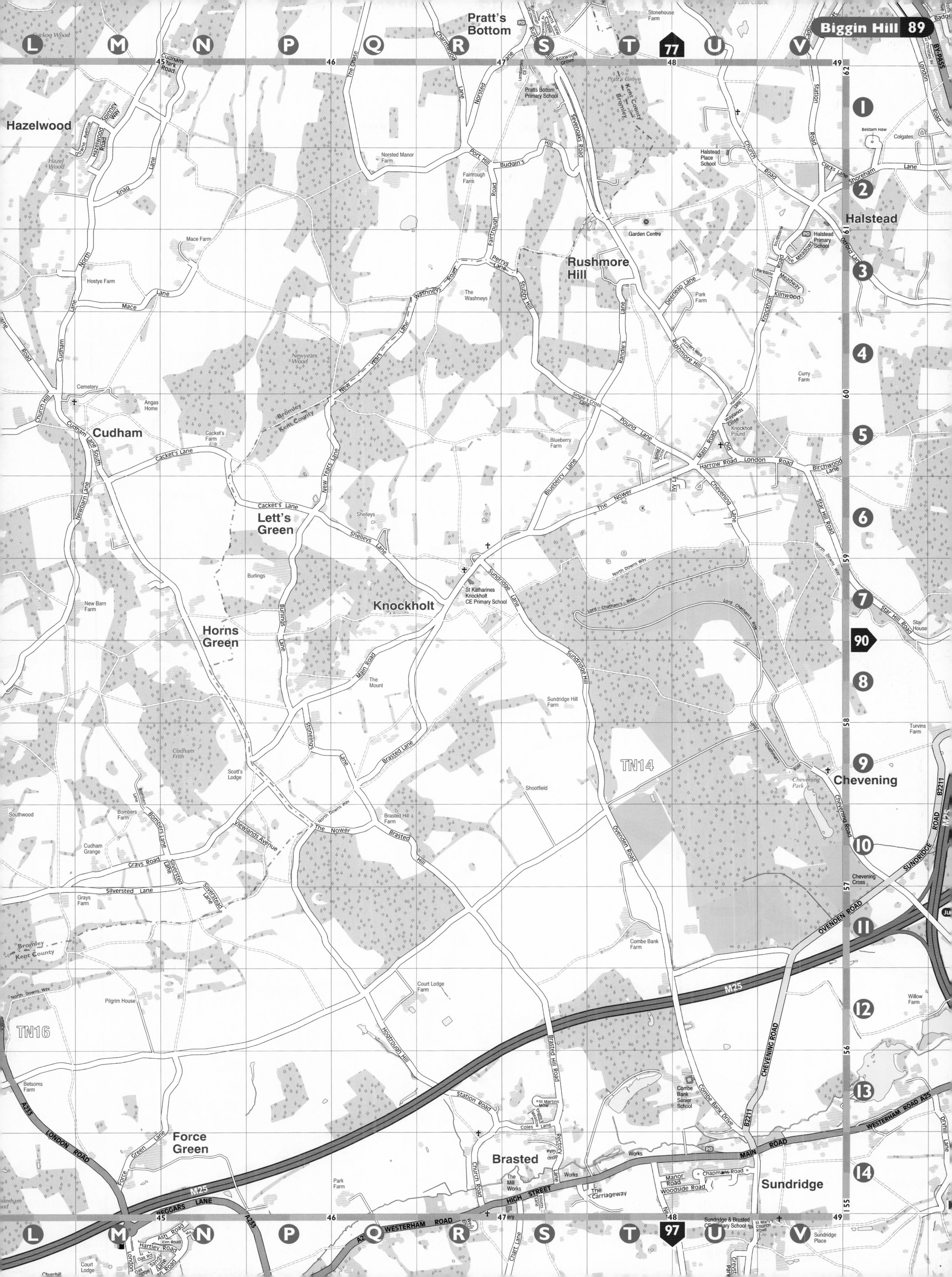

Biggin Hill 89
Pratt's Bottom
Stonehouse Farm
77
97
90
Hazelwood
Hazel Wood
Cudham Park Road
Spinney Way
Downe Avenue
Hazelwood Road
Snag Lane
North Lane
Mace Farm
Hostye Farm
Mace Lane
Cudham Lane
Cemetery
Church Hill
Angas Home
Cudham
Cudham Lane South
Cacket's Farm
Cacket's Lane
Newbarn Lane
New Barn Farm
Horns Green
Lett's Green
Burlings
Burlings Lane
Knockholt
St Katharines Knockholt CE Primary School
Shelleys
Shelleys Lane
New Years Lane
Newyears Wood
Washneys Road
The Washneys
Norsted Manor Farm
Norsted Lane
Charmwood Lane
The Chase
Port Hill
Budgin's Hill
Fairtrough Farm
Fairtrough Road
Perrys Lane
Stubbs Hill
Pratts Bottom Primary School
Sevenoaks Road
Foxwood Grove
Pratt's Grove
Bromley
Kent County
Rushmore Hill
Garden Centre
Rushmore Hill
Randle's Lane
Deerleap Lane
Park Farm
Single's Cross Lane
Pound Lane
Blueberry Farm
Blueberry Lane
The Nower
Ivy La
Harrow Road
London Road
Chevening Lane
Main Road
Old Road
Knockholt Pound
Waylands Close
Knockholt Road
Halstead
Halstead Place School
Halstead Primary School
Church Road
Station Road
Shoreham Lane
Clarks Lane
Beldam Haw
Colgates
Otford Lane
Meadway
Kilnwood
Parkside
The Meadows
Curry Farm
Birchwood Lane
Star Hill Road
North Downs Way
Lord Chatham's Ride
Star House
Sundridge Lane
Sundridge Hill
Sundridge Hill Farm
Main Road
The Mount
Stonelings
Brasted Lane
Brasted Hill Farm
Brasted Hill
The Nower
Cudham Frith
Scott's Lodge
Shootfield
TN14
Chevening
Chevening Park
Chevening Road
Turvins Farm
Chevening Cross
Sundridge Road
B2211
Ovenden Road
Combe Bank Farm
Southwood
Bombers Farm
Bombers Lane
Cudham Grange
Grays Road
Silversted Lane
Viewlands Avenue
Grays Farm
Pilgrim House
TN16
Court Lodge Farm
Hogtrough Hill
M25
Willow Farm
Brasted Hill Road
Station Road
St Martins Mow
Coles Lane
Rectory Lane
Combe Bank Senior School
Combe Bank Drive
Chevening Road
Westerham Road A25
Main Road
Dryhill Lane
Betsoms Farm
A233
London Road
Force Green
Force Green Lane
Beggars Lane
Brasted
Church Road
The Mill Works
High Street
The Carriageway
Works
Manor Road
Woodside Road
Chapmans Road
Sundridge
Park Farm
A25 Westerham Road
Chart Lane
Sundridge & Brasted CE Primary School
St Mary's Church Road
Sundridge Place
Ash Road
Elm Road
Hartley Road
Oak Road
London
Court Lodge
Churchill
L M N P Q R S T U V
1 2 3 4 5 6 7 8 9 10 11 12 13 14
45 46 47 48 49
62 61 60 59 58 57 56 155

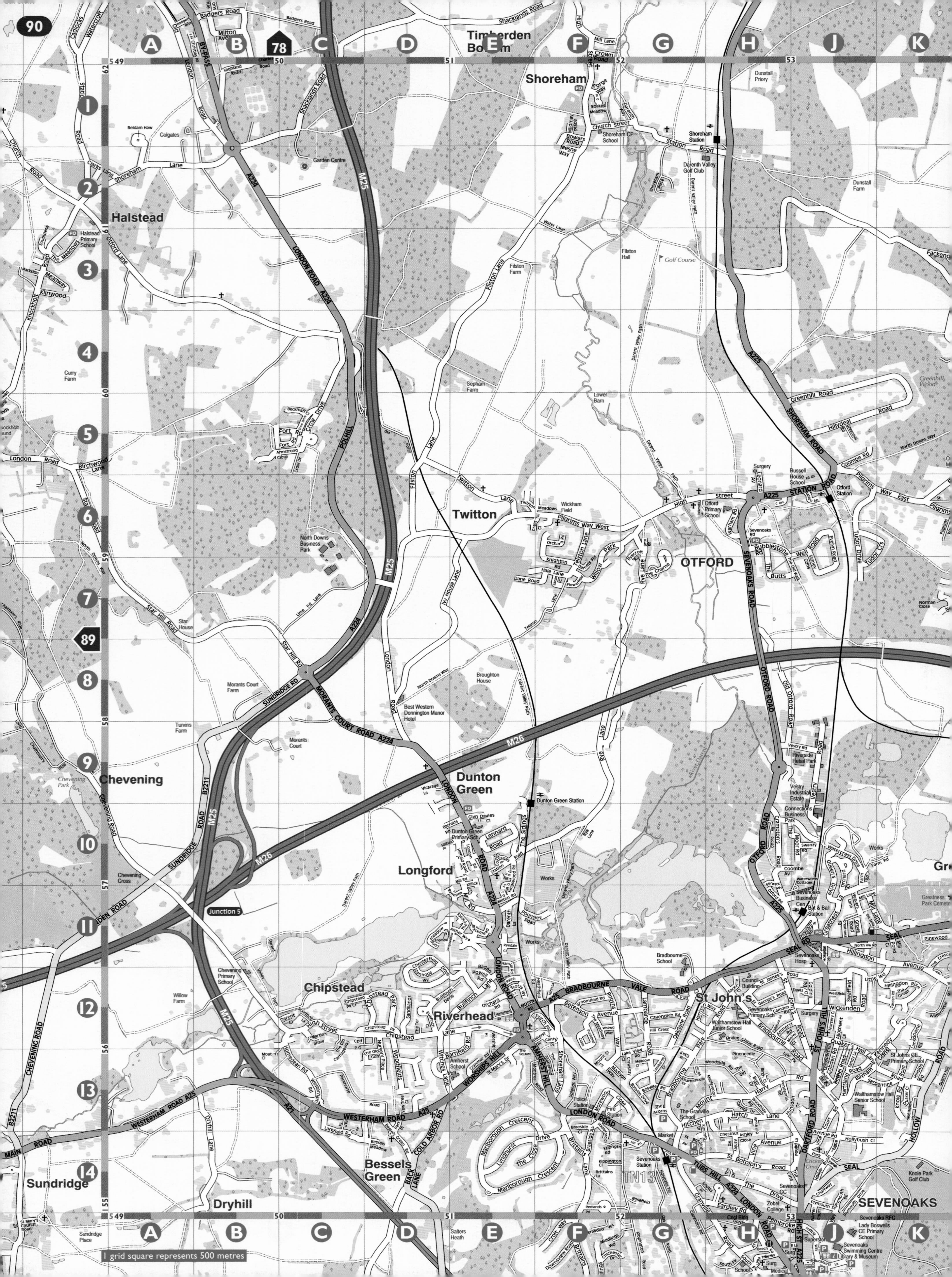
78
89
A B C D E F G H J K
1 2 3 4 5 6 7 8 9 10 11 12 13 14
Timberden Bottom
Shoreham
Halstead
Twitton
OTFORD
Chevening
Dunton Green
Longford
Chipstead
Riverhead
St John's
Bessels Green
Sundridge
Dryhill
SEVENOAKS
Badgers Road
Shacklands Road
Shoreham Lane
London Road
Otford Lane
Filston Lane
Pilgrims Way West
High Street
Station Road
Shoreham Road
Greenhill Road
Hillydeal Road
Coombe Rd
Pilgrims Way East
Sevenoaks Road
Otford Road
Old Otford Road
Star Hill Road
Sundridge Rd
Morants Court Road A224
Chevening Road
Sundridge Road
Westerham Road A25
Main Road
Cold Arbor Rd
Back Lane
Bradbourne Vale Road
Amherst Hill
Tubs Hill
Dartford Road
Seal Road
Hillingdon Avenue
London Road A224
Polhill
M25
M26
A225
Junction 5
Shoreham Station
Otford Station
Dunton Green Station
Bat & Ball Station
Sevenoaks Station
Darenth Valley Golf Club
Golf Course
Knole Park Golf Club
Chevening Primary School
Amherst School
Bradbourne School
Walthamstow Hall Senior School
Sevenoaks Swimming Centre
Sevenoaks Library & Museum
Best Western Donnington Manor Hotel
North Downs Business Park
Riverside Retail Park
Vestry Industrial Estate
Sevenoaks Business Cen
TN13
1 grid square represents 500 metres

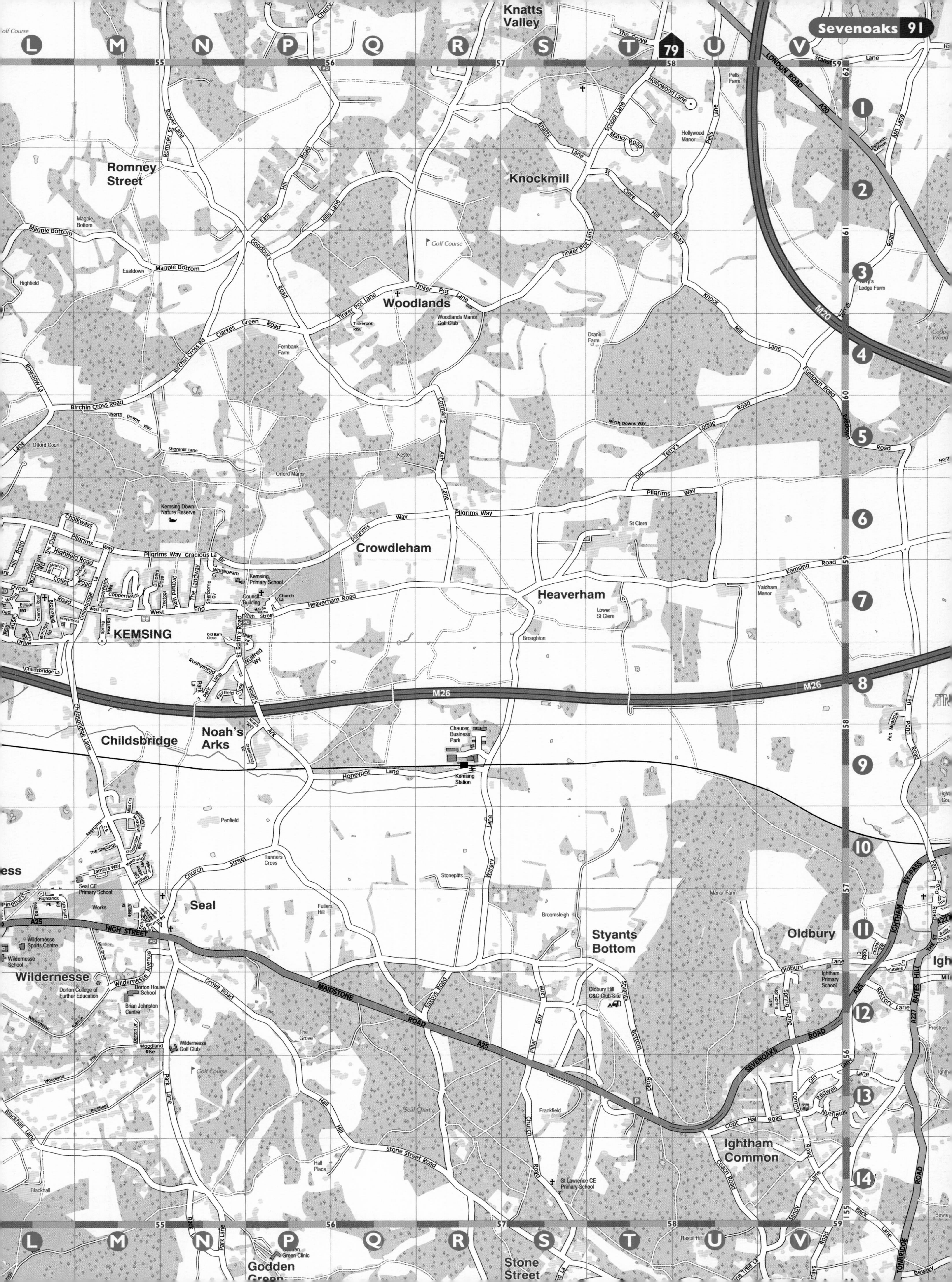
Knatts Valley
Romney Street
Knockmill
Woodlands
Woodlands Manor Golf Club
Crowdleham
Heaverham
KEMSING
Childsbridge
Noah's Arks
Kemsing Station
Seal
Styants Bottom
Oldbury
Wildernesse
Ightham Common
Godden Green
Stone Street
M26
M20
A25
MAIDSTONE ROAD
HIGH STREET
LONDON ROAD
Pilgrims Way
Magpie Bottom
Birchin Cross Road
Clarkes Green Road
Tinker Pot Lane
Knock Mill Lane
Exedown Road
Terry's Lodge Road
Kemsing Road
Heaverham Road
Honeypot Lane
Watery Lane
Church Street
Childsbridge Lane
Grove Road
Park Lane
Stone Street Road
Hall Hill
Pillar Box Lane
Church Road
Styants Bottom Road
Coach Road
Copt Hall Road
Rectory Lane
Oldbury Lane
Fen Pond Road
Seal Chart
Golf Course

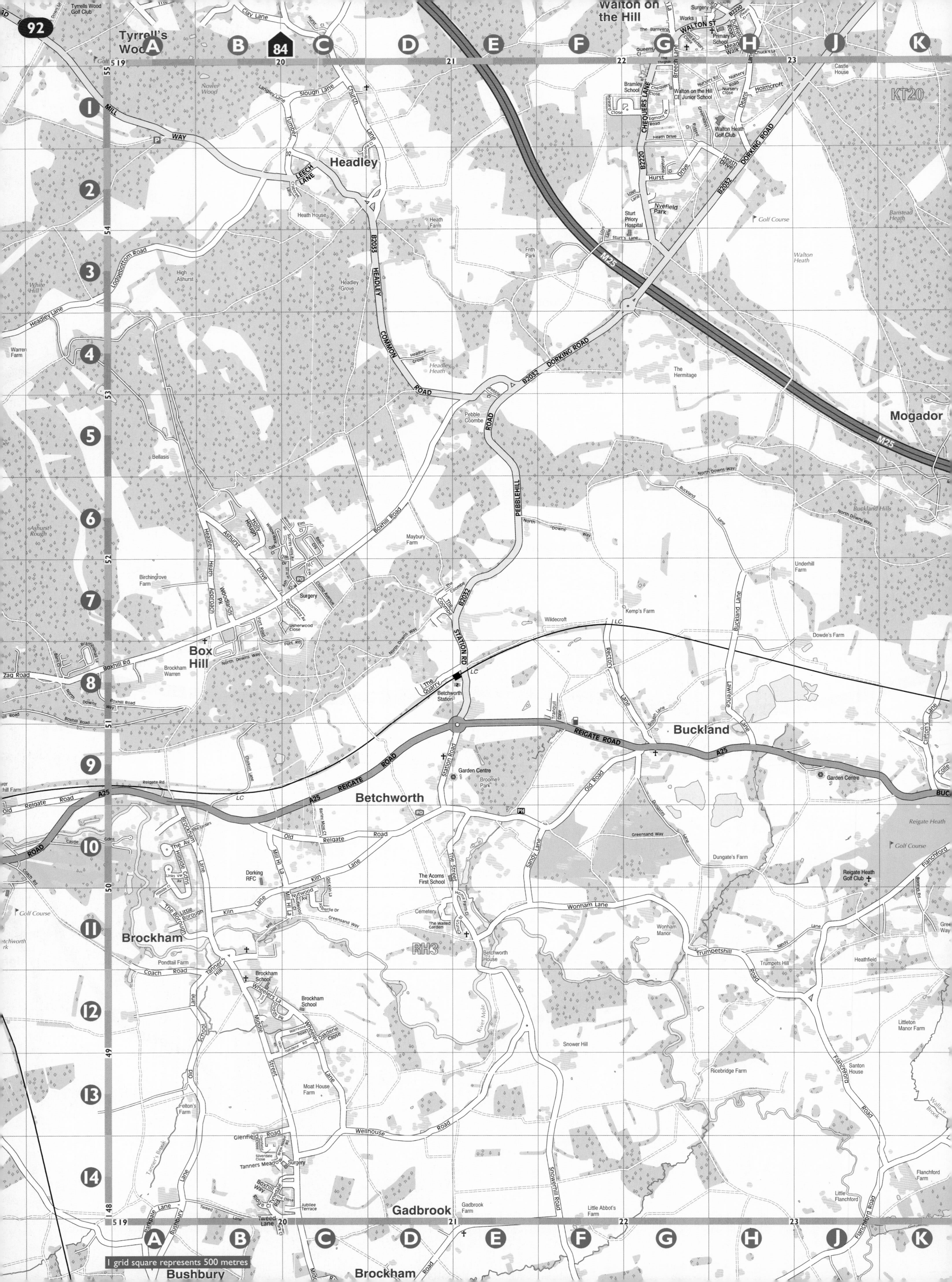
92
84
Tyrrells Wood Golf Club
Tyrrell's Wood
Walton on the Hill
Headley
Box Hill
Betchworth
Buckland
Brockham
Gadbrook
Mogador
Bushbury
Brockham
KT20
RH3
M25
B2033 HEADLEY COMMON ROAD
B2032 DORKING ROAD
B2220 CHEQUERS LANE
WALTON ST
PEBBLEHILL ROAD
B2032 STATION RD
A25 REIGATE ROAD
MILL WAY
LEECH LANE
Slough Lane
Clay Lane
Church Lane
Lodgebottom Road
Headley Lane
Headley Heath Approach
Boxhill Road
Boxhill Rd
Zag Road
Old Reigate Road
Reigate Rd
Brockham Lane
Kiln Lane
Coach Road
Tanners Hill
Wheelers Lane
Middle Street
Wellhouse Road
Wonham Lane
Trumpetshill Road
Sandy Lane
Old Road
Rectory Lane
Buckland Lane
Lawrence Lane
Dungates Lane
Snowerhill Road
Flanchford Road
Station Road
The Street
Tweed Lane
Parkpale Lane
School Lane
Pondtail Farm
Warren Farm
Bellasis
Birchingrove Farm
High Ashurst
Ashurst Rough
Heath House
Headley Grove
Heath Farm
Frith Park
Headley Heath
Pebble Coombe
Maybury Farm
Sturt Priory Hospital
Nyefield Park
Bramley School
Walton on the Hill CE Junior School
Walton Heath Golf Club
Walton Heath
The Hermitage
Castle House
Banstead Heath
Buckland Hills
North Downs Way
Underhill Farm
Kemp's Farm
Wildecroft
Dowde's Farm
Betchworth Station
Brockham Warren
Garden Centre
Broome Park
Dorking RFC
The Acorns First School
Cemetery
The Walled Garden
Betchworth House
Wonham Manor
Trumpets Hill
Heathfield
Dungate's Farm
Reigate Heath
Reigate Heath Golf Club
Golf Course
Greensand Way
Brockham School
Moat House Farm
Felton's Farm
Snower Hill
Ricebridge Farm
Santon House
Littleton Manor Farm
Little Flanchford
Flanchford Farm
Gadbrook Farm
Little Abbot's Farm
Jubilee Terrace
Glenfield Road
Tanners Meadow
Surgery
Tanner's Brook
River Mole
Wallace Brook
1 grid square represents 500 metres

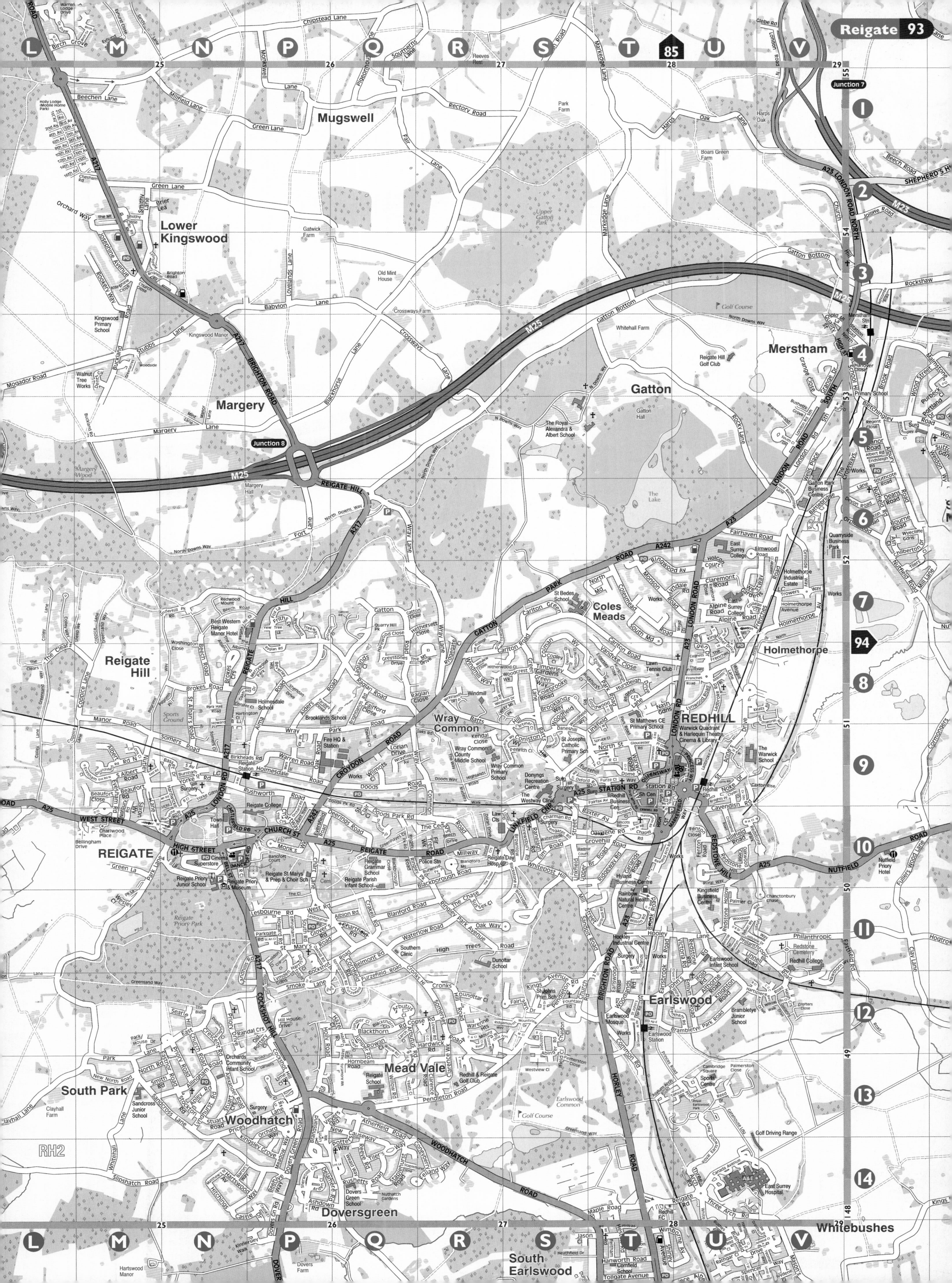
L
M
N
P
Q
R
S
T
U
V
85
94
25
26
27
28
29
Mugswell
Lower Kingswood
Margery
Gatton
Merstham
Coles Meads
Holmethorpe
Reigate Hill
Wray Common
REDHILL
REIGATE
Earlswood
Mead Vale
South Park
Woodhatch
Doversgreen
South Earlswood
Whitebushes
Junction 7
Junction 8
M25
M23
A217
A25
A23
A242
BRIGHTON ROAD
REIGATE HILL
GATTON PARK ROAD
CROYDON ROAD
LONDON ROAD
STATION RD
HIGH STREET
CHURCH ST
REIGATE ROAD
WEST STREET
COCKSHOT HILL
WOODHATCH ROAD
BRIGHTON ROAD
HORLEY ROAD
NUTFIELD ROAD
LONDON ROAD NORTH
Chipstead Lane
Rectory Road
Babylon Lane
Green Lane
Margery Lane
Mogador Road
Gatton Bottom
North Downs Way
Upper Gatton Park
The Lake
Gatton Hall
The Royal Alexandra & Albert School
Reigate Hill Golf Club
Golf Course
Reigate Priory Park
Earlswood Common
East Surrey Hospital
Earlswood Station
Reigate Station
Redhill Stn
Merstham Stn
Kingswood Primary School
Reigate College
Reigate Grammar School
Dunottar School
Reigate School
Redhill College
Golf Driving Range
RH2

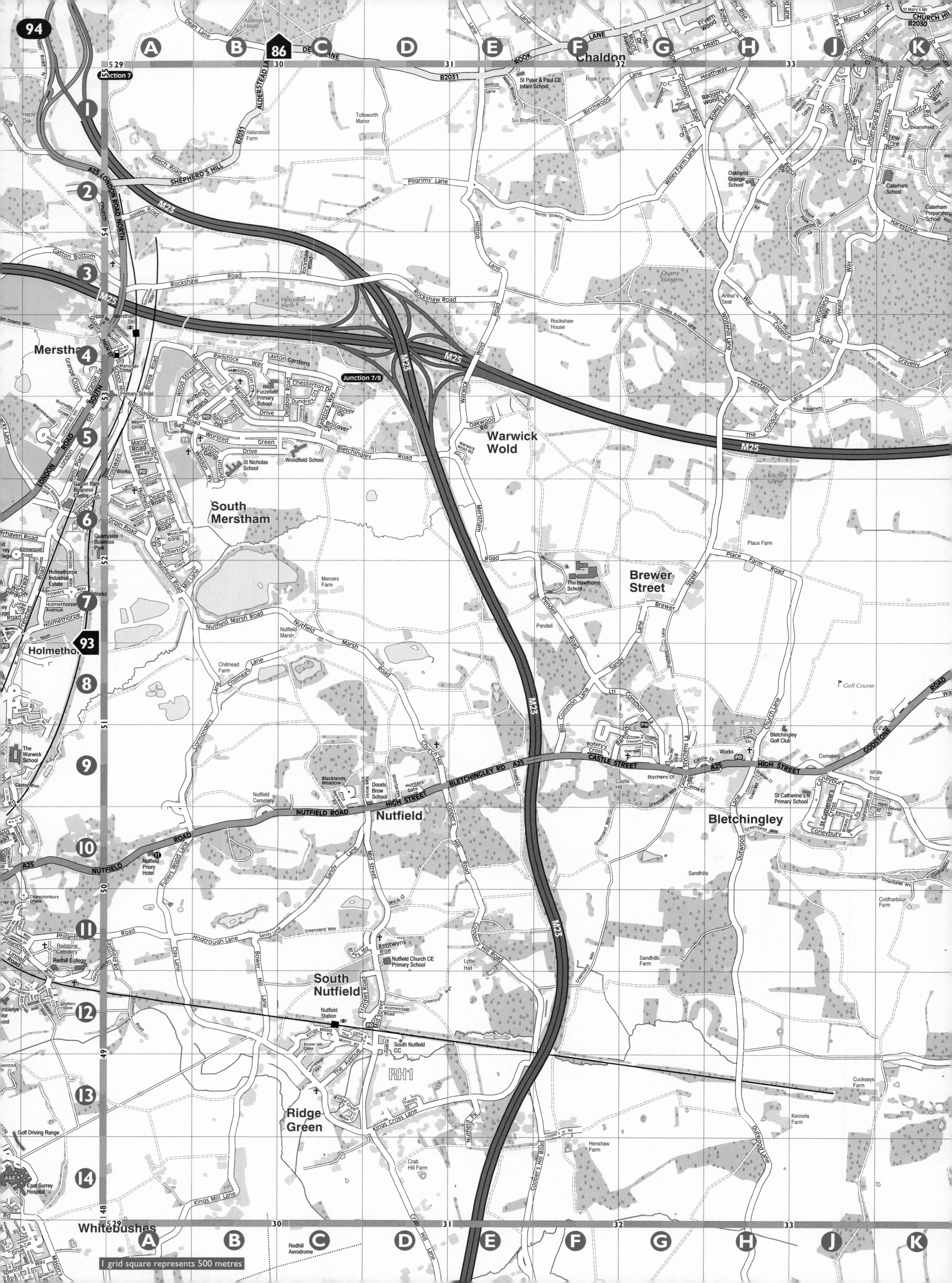
94
86
93
Chaldon
Merstham
Warwick Wold
South Merstham
Brewer Street
Holmethorpe
Nutfield
Bletchingley
South Nutfield
Ridge Green
Whitebushes
M25
M23
A23 LONDON ROAD NORTH
A25
B2031
B2030
Junction 7
Junction 7/8
SHEPHERD'S HILL
Rockshaw Road
Pilgrims' Lane
North Downs Way
NUTFIELD ROAD
HIGH STREET
CASTLE STREET
BLETCHINGLEY RD
Nutfield Marsh Road
Hogtrough Lane
Kings Mill Lane
Outwood Lane
Cooper's Hill Road
Greensand Way
Tollsworth Manor
Alderstead Farm
Rockshaw House
Place Farm
Mercers Farm
Chilmead Farm
Nutfield Priory Hotel
Nutfield Station
South Nutfield CC
Redhill College
East Surrey Hospital
Golf Driving Range
Redhill Aerodrome
Sandhills Farm
Coldharbour Farm
Cuckseys Farm
Kennels Farm
Henshaw Farm
Crab Hill Farm
Lyttel Hall
The Hawthorns School
Furzefield Primary School
St Nicholas School
Woodfield School
Nutfield Church CE Primary School
St Catherine's Primary School
Oakhyrst Grange School
Caterham School
Caterham Preparatory School
Bletchingley Golf Club
Golf Course
Kitchen Copse
Quarry Hangers
Arthur's Seat
RH1
1 grid square represents 500 metres

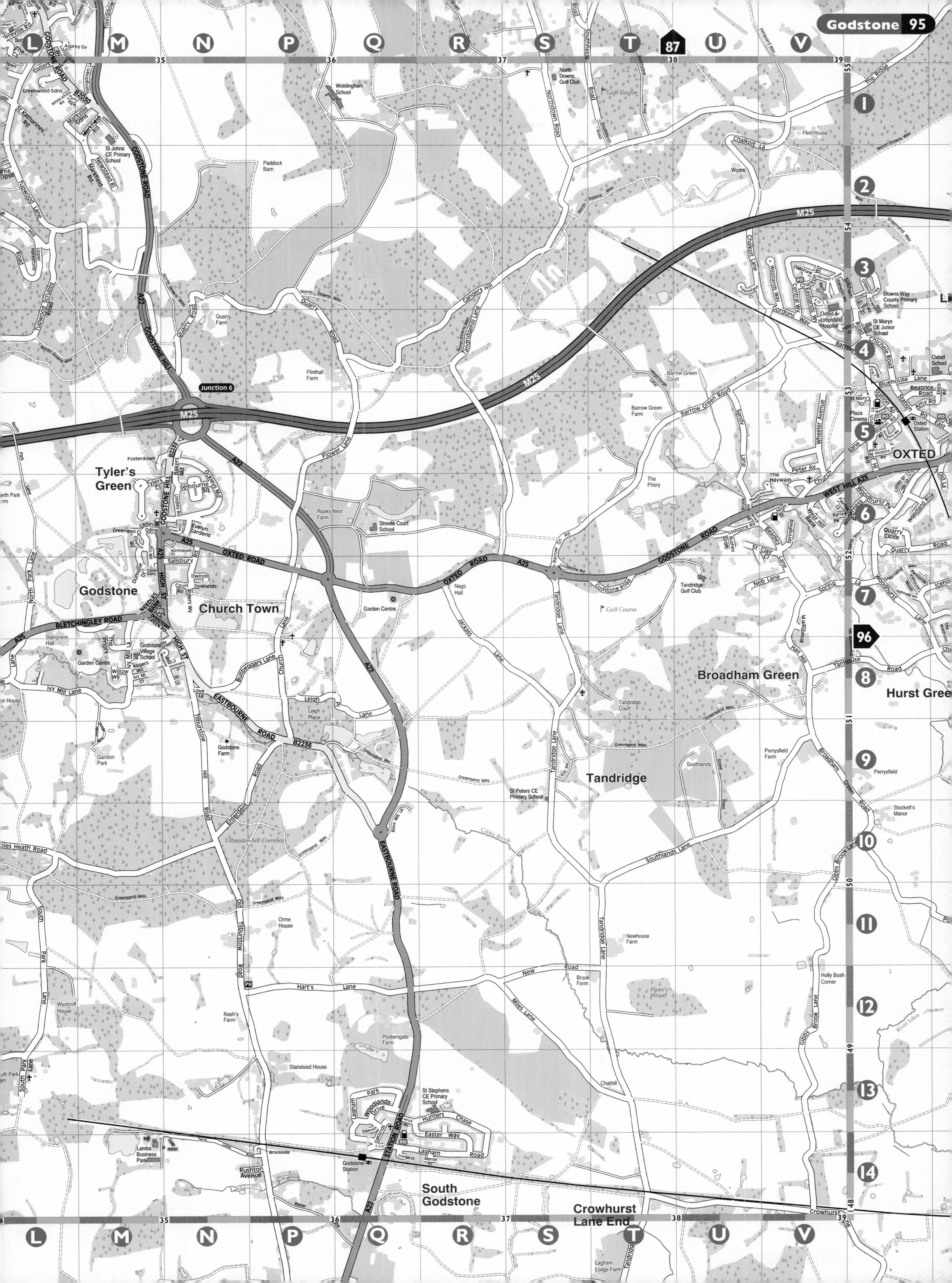
L
M
N
P
Q
R
S
T
U
V
87
96
35
36
37
38
39
55
54
53
52
51
50
49
48
1
2
3
4
5
6
7
8
9
10
11
12
13
14
GODSTONE ROAD
B2030
Greenwood Gdns
St Katharines Rd
Markville Gdns
St Johns CE Primary School
Newstead Rl
Tupwood Lane
Tupwood Scrubbs Road
GODSTONE HILL
A22
Woldingham School
North Downs Golf Club
Golf Course
Northdown Road
Southfields
Flint House
Chalkpit La
Works
The Ridge
North Downs Way
Paddock Barn
Quarry Farm
Quarry Road
Flinthall Farm
Gangers Hill
Tandridgehill Lane
M25
Junction 6
Chalkpit Lane
Westlands Way
Central Wy
Gordons Way
Oxted & Limpsfield Hospital
St Marys CE Junior School
Downs Way County Primary School
Chichele Road
Barrow Green Court
Barrow Green Farm
Barrow Green Road
Sandy Lane
Oxted School
Bluehouse Lane
Beatrice Road
Amy Rd
Station Rd
Oxted Station
Plaza Cinema
OXTED
Wheeler Avenue
Peter Av
The Haywain
WEST HILL A25
Woodhurst Pk
Woodland Rise
Quarry Close
Tyler's Green
Fosterdown
Selbourne Sq
Evelyn Gardens
Greenwell
Godstone
Salisbury
Dwinds
Dewlands
Church Town
OXTED ROAD
A25
Rooks Nest Farm
Streete Court School
The Priory
Nags Hall
Garden Centre
GODSTONE ROAD
Godstone Rd
Tandridge Golf Club
Golf Course
Springfield
Beadles
St Clair Cl
Neb Lane
Spring
Broadham Pl
Hall Hill
Tanhouse Road
Broadham Green
Hurst Gree
BLETCHINGLEY ROAD
NEEDLES BANK
HIGH ST
Stangrave Hall
The Priory
Godstone Village School
Garden Centre
Willow Wy
Rogers
Ivy Mill Cl
Ivy Mill Lane
Bullbeggars Lane
Church Lane
Leigh Place
Leigh Pl
Jackass Lane
Tandridge Lane
Tandridge Court
Greensand Way
EASTBOURNE ROAD
B2236
Godstone Farm
Garston Park
Tilburstow Hill Road
Enterdent Road
Tilburstowhill Common
St Peters CE Primary School
Tandridge
Southlands
Perrysfield Farm
Perrysfield
Broadham Green Road
Stockett's Manor
Gibbs Brook
Gibbs Brook Lane
Southlands Lane
EASTBOURNE ROAD
South Park Lane
Orme House
Old Tilburstow Road
Newhouse Farm
Hart's Lane
New Road
Brook Farm
Miles Lane
Piper's Wood
Holly Bush Corner
River Eden
Wychcroft House
Nash's Farm
Posterngate Farm
Stanstead House
Chathill
St Stephens CE Primary School
Lagham Park
Woodlands Drive
Hunters Chase
Easter Way
Lagham Road
STATION ROAD
Godstone Station
Lambs Business Park
Rushton Avenue
Brookside
South Godstone
Crowhurst Lane End
Crowhurst
Lagham Lodge Farm
Tandridge

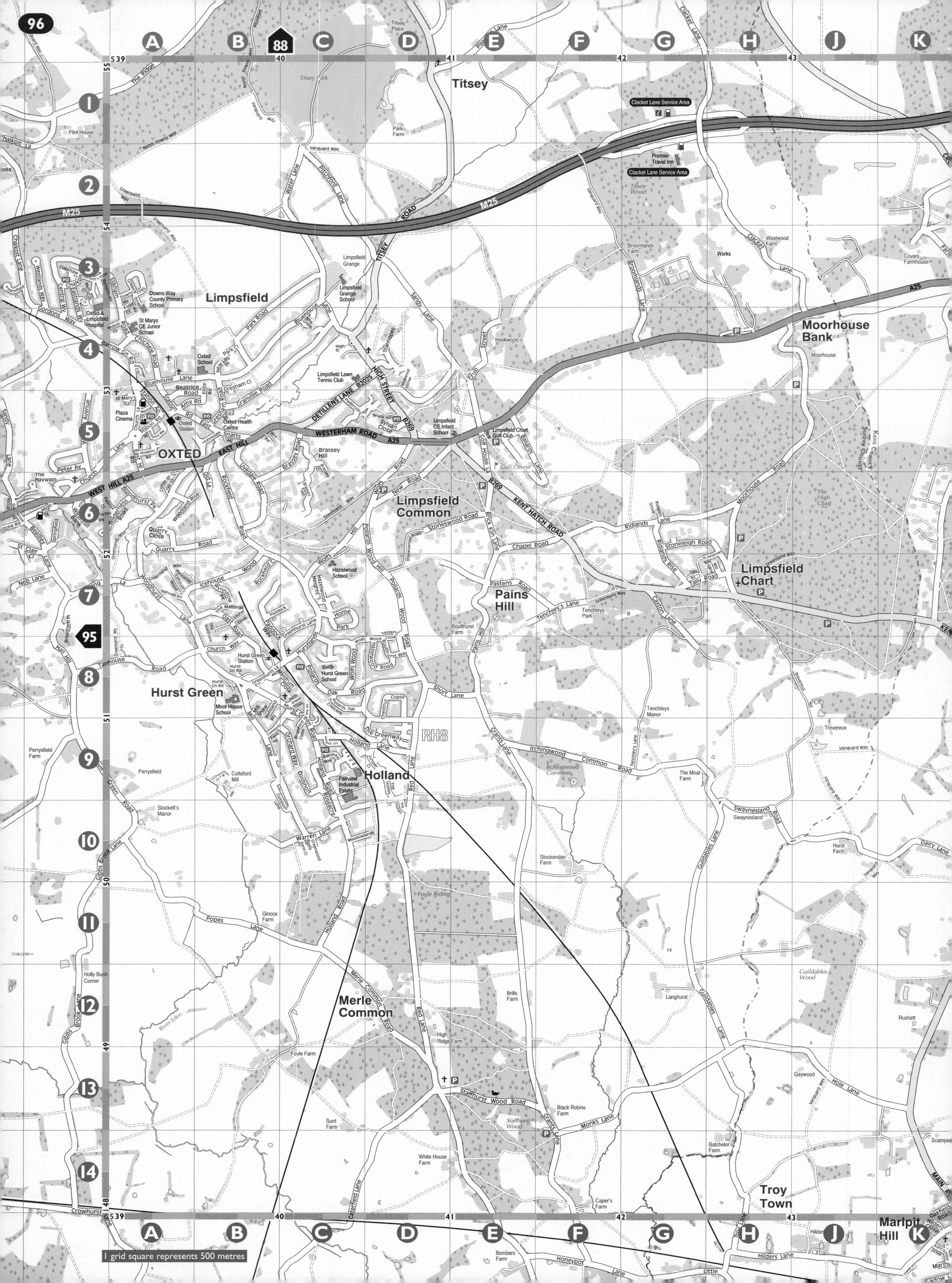
88
95
A
B
C
D
E
F
G
H
J
K
Titsey
Titsey Place
Titsey Park
Park Farm
Clacket Lane Service Area
Premier Travel Inn
Titsey Wood
M25
Flint House
Limpsfield
Limpsfield Grange
Limpsfield Grange School
Downs Way County Primary School
Oxted & Limpsfield Hospital
St Marys CE Junior School
Oxted School
Limpsfield Lawn Tennis Club
Limpsfield CE Infant School
Limpsfield Chart Golf Club
Golf Course
Plaza Cinema
Oxted Station
Oxted Health Centre
OXTED
Brassey Hill
Limpsfield Common
Hookwood
Broomlands Farm
Works
Westwood Farm
Covers Farmhouse
Moorhouse Bank
Moorhouse
The High Chart
Limpsfield Chart
Pains Hill
Tenchleys Park
Boulthurst Farm
Hazelwood School
Home Park
Hurst Green Station
Hurst Green School
Hurst Green
Moor House School
Holland
Fairview Industrial Estate
RH8
Coltsford Mill
Perrysfield Farm
Perrysfield
Stockett's Manor
Tenchleys Manor
Itchingwood Common
The Moat Farm
Swaynesland
Trevereux
Stockenden Farm
Hurst Farm
Foyle Riding
Gincox Farm
Holly Bush Corner
Merle Common
Brills Farm
High Ridge Farm
Langhurst
Guildables Wood
Rushett
Foyle Farm
Gaywood
Sunt Farm
Staffhurst Wood
Black Robins Farm
White House Farm
Batchelor's Farm
Caper's Farm
Troy Town
Marlpit Hill
Bombers Farm
River Eden
Kent County
Surrey County
A25
B269
B2025
WEST HILL A25
EAST HILL
WESTERHAM ROAD
DETILLENS LANE
HIGH STREET
TITSEY ROAD
KENT HATCH ROAD
Staffhurst Wood Road
Clacket Lane
Broomlands Lane
Vanguard Way
Greensand Way
North Downs Way
Pilgrims Lane
Water Lane
Pitchfont Lane
Sandy Lane
Grub Street
Chalkpit Lane
Barrow Grn Rd
Bluehouse Lane
Station Rd
Snatts Hill
Rockfield Road
Uvedale Road
Wolfs Hill
Pollards Wood Hill
Stoneswood Road
Chapel Road
Brick Kiln Lane
Ridlands Lane
Stoneleigh Road
Tally Road
Pastens Road
Tenchley's Lane
Caxton Lane
Moorhouse Road
Icehouse Wood
Woodhurst Lane
Tanhouse Road
Church Way
Hurst Green Road
Holland Road
Holland Lane
Red Lane
Short Lane
Grants Lane
Itchingwood Common Road
Swaynesland Road
Guildables Lane
Dairy Lane
Hole Lane
Popes Lane
Merle Common Road
Warren Lane
Gibbs Brook Lane
Green Road
Monks Lane
Caterfield Lane
Crowhurst
Hilders Lane
Honeypot Lane
Troy Lane
Neb Lane
St Clair Cl
Hall Hill
Peter Av
The Haywain
Quarry Close
Quarry Road
Chichele Road
Granville Road
Park Road
Beatrice Road
Gresham Cl
Amy Rd
Westerham Road
Golf House La
Ballards Lane
1 grid square represents 500 metres

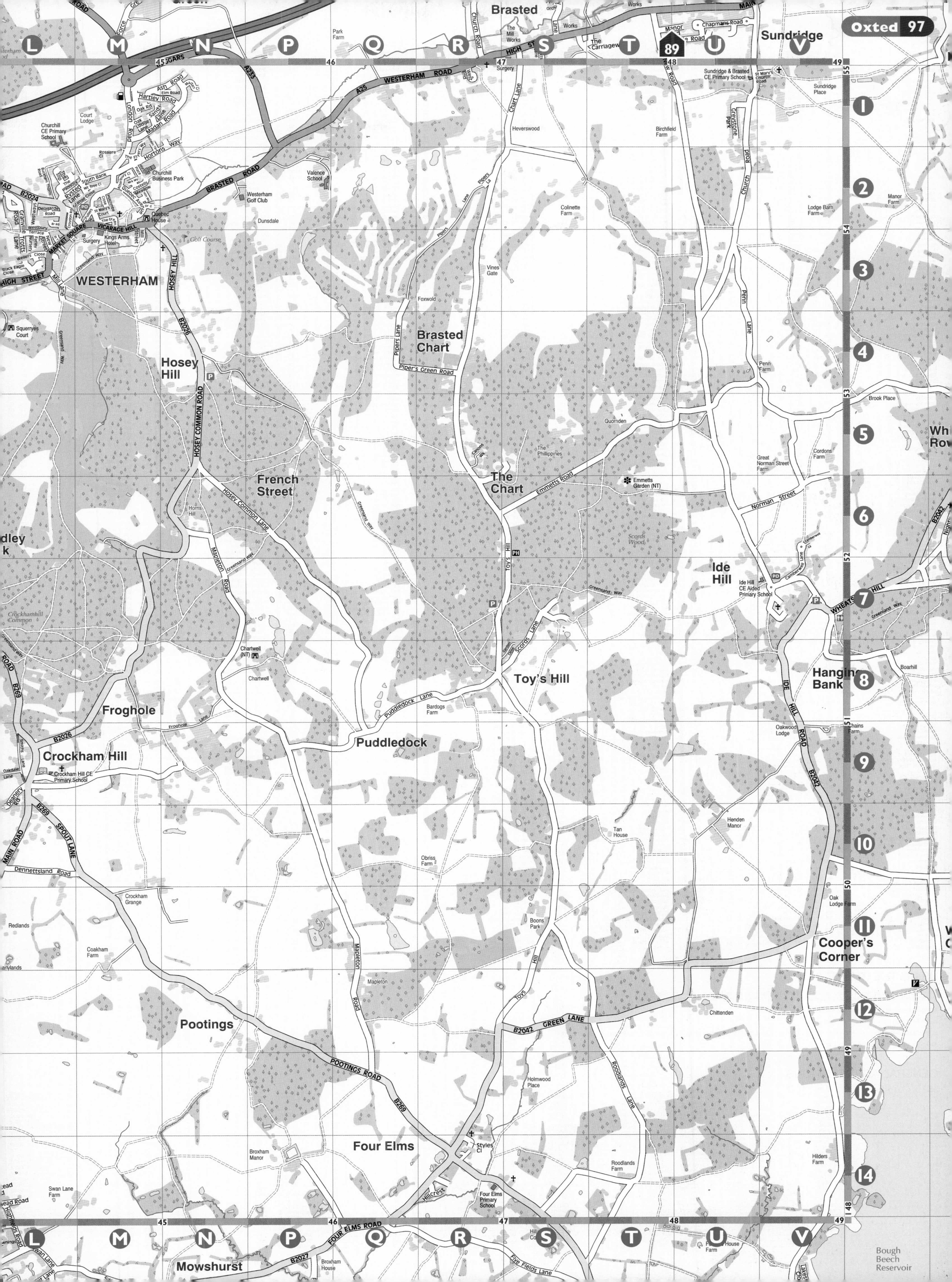
Brasted
Sundridge
WESTERHAM
Hosey Hill
French Street
Brasted Chart
The Chart
Ide Hill
Toy's Hill
Hanging Bank
Froghole
Crockham Hill
Puddledock
Cooper's Corner
Pootings
Four Elms
Mowshurst
Westerham Road
Brasted Road
Hosey Common Road
Hosey Common Lane
Mapleton Road
Puddledock Lane
Froghole Lane
Pipers Lane
Piper's Green Road
Emmetts Road
Emmetts Garden (NT)
Scords Wood
Scords Lane
Toys Hill
Church Road
Penn Lane
Norman Street
Ide Hill Road
Green Lane
Pootings Road
Four Elms Road
Spout Lane
Main Road
Dennettsland Road
Hollybush Lane
Chartwell (NT)
Chartwell
Westerham Golf Club
Valence School
Squerryes Court
Crockham Hill CE Primary School
Ide Hill CE Aided Primary School
Four Elms Primary School
Crockhamhill Common
Greensand Way
Bough Beech Reservoir
Chart Lane
Heverswood
Quornden
The Phillipines
Colinette Farm
Penn Farm
Cordons Farm
Brook Place
Great Norman Street Farm
Bardogs Farm
Obriss Farm
Tan House
Henden Manor
Oak Lodge Farm
Chittenden
Boons Park
Mapleton
Holmwood Place
Roodlands Farm
Broxham Manor
Crockham Grange
Coakham Farm
Redlands
Hilders Farm
Swan Lane Farm
Boarhill
Oakwood Lodge
L M N P Q R S T U V
1 2 3 4 5 6 7 8 9 10 11 12 13 14

USING THE STREET INDEX

Street names are listed alphabetically. Each street name is followed by its postal town or area locality, the Postcode District, the page number, and the reference to the square in which the name is found.

Standard index entries are shown as follows:

Aaron Hill Rd *EHAM* E6 .... 52 J3

Street names and selected addresses not shown on the map due to scale restrictions are shown in the index with an asterisk:

Abbeville Ms *CLAP* SW4 * 62 B3

GENERAL ABBREVIATIONS

ACC ACCESS	CNR CORNER	E EAST	GRG GARAGE	LDG LODGE	OFF OFFICE	R RIVER
ALY ALLEY	CO COUNTY	EMB EMBANKMENT	GT GREAT	LGT LIGHT	ORCH ORCHARD	RBT ROUNDABOUT
AP APPROACH	COLL COLLEGE	EMBY EMBASSY	GTWY GATEWAY	LK LOCK	OV OVAL	RD ROAD
AR ARCADE	COM COMMON	ESP ESPLANADE	GV GROVE	LKS LAKES	PAL PALACE	RDG RIDGE
ASS ASSOCIATION	COMM COMMISSION	EST ESTATE	HGR HIGHER	LNDG LANDING	PAS PASSAGE	REP REPUBLIC
AV AVENUE	CON CONVENT	EX EXCHANGE	HL HILL	LTL LITTLE	PAV PAVILION	RES RESERVOIR
BCH BEACH	COT COTTAGE	EXPY EXPRESSWAY	HLS HILLS	LWR LOWER	PDE PARADE	RFC RUGBY FOOTBALL CLUB
BLDS BUILDINGS	COTS COTTAGES	EXT EXTENSION	HO HOUSE	MAG MAGISTRATE	PH PUBLIC HOUSE	RI RISE
BND BEND	CP CAPE	F/O FLYOVER	HOL HOLLOW	MAN MANSIONS	PK PARK	RP RAMP
BNK BANK	CPS COPSE	FC FOOTBALL CLUB	HOSP HOSPITAL	MD MEAD	PKWY PARKWAY	RW ROW
BR BRIDGE	CR CREEK	FK FORK	HRB HARBOUR	MDW MEADOWS	PL PLACE	S SOUTH
BRK BROOK	CREM CREMATORIUM	FLD FIELD	HTH HEATH	MEM MEMORIAL	PLN PLAIN	SCH SCHOOL
BTM BOTTOM	CRS CRESCENT	FLDS FIELDS	HVN HAVEN	MKT MARKET	PLNS PLAINS	SE SOUTH EAST
BUS BUSINESS	CSWY CAUSEWAY	FLS FALLS	HWY HIGHWAY	MKTS MARKETS	PLZ PLAZA	SER SERVICE AREA
BVD BOULEVARD	CT COURT	FM FARM	IMP IMPERIAL	ML MILL	POL POLICE STATION	SH SHORE
BY BYPASS	CTRL CENTRAL	FT FORT	IN INLET	MNR MANOR	PR PRINCE	SHOP SHOPPING
CATH CATHEDRAL	CTS COURTS	FTS FLATS	IND EST INDUSTRIAL ESTATE	MS MEWS	PREC PRECINCT	SKWY SKYWAY
CEM CEMETERY	CTYD COURTYARD	FWY FREEWAY	INF INFIRMARY	MSN MISSION	PREP PREPARATORY	SMT SUMMIT
CEN CENTRE	CUTT CUTTINGS	GA GATE	INFO INFORMATION	MT MOUNT	PRIM PRIMARY	SOC SOCIETY
CFT CROFT	CYN CANYON	GAL GALLERY	INT INTERCHANGE	MTN MOUNTAIN	PROM PROMENADE	SP SPRING
CH CHURCH	DEPT DEPARTMENT	GDN GARDEN	IS ISLAND	MTS MOUNTAINS	PRS PRINCESS	SPR SPUR
CHA CHASE	DL DALE	GDNS GARDENS	JCT JUNCTION	MUS MUSEUM	PRT PORT	SQ SQUARE
CHYD CHURCHYARD	DM DAM	GLD GLADE	JTY JETTY	MWY MOTORWAY	PT POINT	ST STREET
CIR CIRCLE	DR DRIVE	GLN GLEN	KG KING	N NORTH	PZ PIAZZA	STN STATION
CIRC CIRCUS	DRO DROVE	GN GREEN	KNL KNOLL	NE NORTH EAST	QD QUADRANT	STR STREAM
CLFS CLIFFS	DRY DRIVEWAY	GND GROUND	L LAKE	NW NORTH WEST	QU QUEEN	STRD STRAND
CMP CAMP	DWGS DWELLINGS	GRA GRANGE	LA LANE	O/P OVERPASS	QY QUAY	SW SOUTH WEST
						TDG TRADING

TER ... TERRACE	TPK ... TURNPIKE	U/P ... UNDERPASS	VA ... VALLEY	VLG ... VILLAGE	WD ... WOOD	WLS ... WELLS
THWY ... THROUGHWAY	TR ... TRACK	UNI ... UNIVERSITY	VIAD ... VIADUCT	VIADS ... VIADUCTS	WHF ... WHARF	WY ... WAY
TNL ... TUNNEL	TRL ... TRAIL	UPR ... UPPER	VIL ... VILLA	VW ... VIEW	WLK ... WALK	YD ... YARD
TOLL ... TOLLWAY	TWR ... TOWER	V ... VALE	VIS ... VISTA	W ... WEST	WKS ... WALKS	YHA ... YOUTH HOSTEL

POSTCODE TOWNS AND AREA ABBREVIATIONS

ABLGY	Abbots Langley
ABR/ST	Abridge/Stapleford Abbotts
ABYW	Abbey Wood
ACT	Acton
ADL/WDHM	Addlestone/Woodham
ALP/SUD	Alperton/Sudbury
AMSS	Amersham South
ARCH	Archway
ASHF	Ashford (Surrey)
ASHTD	Ashtead
BAL	Balham
BANK	Bank
BAR	Barnet
BARB	Barbican
BARK	Barking
BARK/HLT	Barkingside/Hainault
BAY/PAD	Bayswater/Paddington
BCTR	Becontree
BECK	Beckenham
BELMT	Belmont
BELV	Belvedere
BERM/RHTH	Bermondsey/Rotherhithe
BETH	Bethnal Green
BF/WBF	Byfleet/West Byfleet
BFN/LL	Blackfen/Longlands
BGR/WK	Borough Green/West Kingsdown
BGVA	Belgravia
BH/WHM	Biggin Hill/Westerham
BKHH	Buckhurst Hill
BKHTH/KID	Blackheath/Kidbrooke
BLKFR	Blackfriars
BMLY	Bromley
BMSBY	Bloomsbury
BNSTD	Banstead
BORE	Borehamwood
BOW	Bow
BRKHM/BTCW	Brockham/Betchworth
BRKMPK	Brookmans Park
BROCKY	Brockley
BROX	Broxbourne
BRW	Brentwood
BRWN/ST	Brixton north/Stockwell
BRXS/STRHM	Brixton south/Streatham Hill
BRYLDS	Berrylands
BTFD	Brentford
BTSEA	Battersea
BUSH	Bushey
BXLY	Bexley
BXLYHN	Bexleyheath north
BXLYHS	Bexleyheath south
CAMTN	Camden Town
CAN/RD	Canning Town/Royal Docks
CANST	Cannon Street Station
CAR	Carshalton
CAVSQ/HST	Cavendish Square/Harley Street
CDALE/KGS	Colindale/Kingsbury
CDW/CHF	Chadwell St Mary/Chafford Hundred
CEND/HSY/T	Crouch End/Hornsey/Turnpike Lane
CFSP/GDCR	Chalfont St Peter/Gerrards Cross
CHARL	Charlton
CHCR	Charing Cross
CHDH	Chadwell Heath
CHEAM	Cheam
CHEL	Chelsea
CHERT	Chertsey
CHES/WCR	Cheshunt/Waltham Cross
CHIG	Chigwell
CHING	Chingford
CHOB/PIR	Chobham/Pirbright
CHONG	Chipping Ongar
CHSGTN	Chessington
CHST	Chislehurst
CHSWK	Chiswick
CITYW	City of London west
CLAP	Clapham
CLKNW	Clerkenwell
CLPT	Clapton
CMBW	Camberwell
COND ST	Conduit Street
COUL/CHIP	Coulsdon/Chipstead
COVGDN	Covent Garden
CRICK	Cricklewood
CROY/NA	Croydon/New Addington
CRW	Collier Row
CSTG	Chalfont St Giles
CTHM	Caterham
DAGE	Dagenham east
DAGW	Dagenham west
DART	Dartford
DEN/HRF	Denham/Harefield
DEPT	Deptford
DORK	Dorking
DTCH/LGLY	Datchet/Langley
DUL	Dulwich
E/WMO/HCT	East & West Molesey/Hampton Court
EA	Ealing
EBAR	East Barnet
EBED/NFELT	East Bedfont/North Feltham
ECT	Earl's Court
EDEN	Edenbridge
EDGW	Edgware
EDUL	East Dulwich
EFNCH	East Finchley
EGH	Egham
EHAM	East Ham
EHSLY	East Horsley
ELTH/MOT	Eltham/Mottingham
EMB	Embankment
EMPK	Emerson Park
EN	Enfield
ENC/FH	Enfield Chase/Forty Hill
EPP	Epping
EPSOM	Epsom
ERITH	Erith
ERITHM	Erith Marshes
ESH/CLAY	Esher/Claygate
EW	Ewell
EYN	Eynsford
FBAR/BDGN	Friern Barnet/Bounds Green
FELT	Feltham
FENCHST	Fenchurch Street
FITZ	Fitzrovia
FLST/FETLN	Fleet Street/Fetter Lane
FNCH	Finchley
FSBYE	Finsbury east
FSBYPK	Finsbury Park
FSBYW	Finsbury west
FSTGT	Forest Gate
FUL/PGN	Fulham/Parsons Green
GDMY/SEVK	Goodmayes/Seven Kings
GDST	Godstone
GFD/PVL	Greenford/Perivale
GLDGN	Golders Green
GNTH/NBYPK	Gants Hill/Newbury Park
GNWCH	Greenwich
GPK	Gidea Park
GSTN	Garston
GT/LBKH	Great Bookham/Little Bookham
GWRST	Gower Street
HACK	Hackney
HAMP	Hampstead
HARH	Harold Hill
HART	Hartley
HAYES	Hayes
HBRY	Highbury
HCH	Hornchurch
HCIRC	Holborn Circus
HDN/ICK	Hillingdon/Ickenham
HEST	Heston
HGDN/ICK	Hillingdon/Ickenham
HGT	Highgate
HHS/BOV	Hemel Hempstead
HMSMTH	Hammersmith
HNHL	Herne Hill
HNWL	Hanwell
HOL/ALD	Holborn/Aldwych
HOLWY	Holloway
HOM	Homerton
HOR/WEW	Horton/Ewell
HPTN	Hampton
HRW	Harrow
HSLW	Hounslow
HSLWW	Hounslow west
HTHAIR	Heathrow Airport
HYS/HAR	Hayes/Harlington
IL	Ilford
IS	Islington
ISLW	Isleworth
KBOROVD	Kings Boro/vd
KENS	Kensington
KGLGY	Kings Langley
KIL/WHAMP	Kilburn/West Hampstead
KTBR	Knightsbridge
KTN/HRWW/WS	Kenton/Harrow Weald/Wealdstone
KTTN	Kentish Town
KUT/HW	Kingston upon Thames
KUTN/CMB	Kingston upon Thames
KWD/TDW/WH	Kingswood/Tadworth/Walton on the Hill
LBTH	Lambeth
LCOL/BKTW	London Colney/Bricket Wood
LEE/GVPK	Lee/Grove Park
LEW	Lewisham
LEY	Leyton
LHD/OX	Leatherhead/Oxshott
LING	Lingfield
LIT	Lincoln's Inn
LOTH	Lothbury
LOU	Loughton
LSQ/SEVD	Leicester Square/Seven Dials
LVPST	Liverpool Street
MANHO	Mansion House
MBLAR	Marble Arch
MHST	Marylebone High Street
MLHL	Mill Hill
MNPK	Manor Park
MON	Monument
MORT/ESHN	Mortlake/East Sheen
MRDN	Morden
MTCM	Mitcham
MUSWH	Muswell Hill
MV/WKIL	Maida Vale/West Kilburn
MYFR/PICC	Mayfair/Piccadilly
MYFR/PKLN	Mayfair/Park Lane
NFNCH/WDSPK	North Finchley/Woodside Park
NKENS	North Kensington
NOXST/BSQ	New Oxford Street/Bloomsbury Square
NRWD	Norwood
NTGHL	Notting Hill
NTHLT	Northolt
NTHWD	Northwood
NWCR	New Cross
NWDGN	Norwood Green
NWMAL	New Malden
OBST	Old Broad Street
ORP	Orpington
OXHEY	Oxhey
OXSTW	Oxford Street west
OXTED	Oxted
PECK	Peckham
PEND	Ponders End
PGE/AN	Penge/Anerley
PIM	Pimlico
PIN	Pinner
PLMGR	Palmers Green
PLSTW	Plaistow
POP/IOD	Poplar/Isle of Dogs
POTB/CUF	Potters Bar/Cuffley
PUR	Purfleet
PUR/KEN	Purley/Kenley
PUT/ROE	Putney/Roehampton
RAD	Radlett
RAIN	Rainham
RCH/KEW	Richmond/Kew
RDART	Rural Dartford
RDKG	Rural Dorking
REDBR	Redbridge
REDH	Redhill
REGST	Regent Street
REIG	Reigate
RKW/CH/CXG	Rickmansworth/Chorleywood/Croxley Green
ROM	Romford/Rush Green
RPLY/SEND	Ripley/Send
RSEV	Rural Sevenoaks
RSLP	Ruislip
RSQ	Russell Square
RYLN/HDSTN	Rayners Lane/Headstone
RYNPK	Raynes Park
SAND/SEL	Sanderstead/Selsdon
SCUP	Sidcup
SDTCH	Shoreditch
SEV	Sevenoaks
SEVS/STOTM	Seven Sisters/Tottenham
SHB	Shepherd's Bush
SHPTN	Shepperton
SKENS	South Kensington
SLN	Slough north
SLN	Slough
SOHO/CST	Soho/Carnaby Street
SOHO/SHAV	Soho/
SRTFD	Stratford
STA	Staines
STALE/WH	St Albans east/Wheathampstead
STAN	Stanmore
STBT	St Bart's
STHGT/OAK	Southgate/Oakwood
STHL	Southall
STHWK	Southwark
STJS	St James's Park
STJSPK	St James's Park
STJWD	St John's Wood
STKPK	Stockley Park
STLK	St Luke's
STMC/STPC	St Mary Cray/St Paul's Cray
STNW/STAM	Stoke Newington/Stamford Hill
STP	St Pancras
STRHM/NOR	Streatham/Norbury
STWL/WRAY	Stanwell/Wraysbury
SURB	Surbiton
SUT	Sutton
SWCM	Swanscombe
SWFD	South Woodford
SWLY	Swanley
SYD	Sydenham
TEDD	Teddington
THDIT	Thames Ditton
THHTH	Thornton Heath
THMD	Thamesmead
TOOT	Tooting
TPL/STR	Temple/Strand
TOTTENHAM	...
TRDG/WHET	Totteridge/Whetstone
TWK	Twickenham
TWRH	...
UED	Upper Edmonton
UPMR	Upminster
UX/CGN	Uxbridge/Colham Green
VW	Virginia Water
VX/NE	Vauxhall/Nine Elms
WAB	Waltham Abbey
WALTH	Walthamstow
WALW	Walworth
WAP	Wapping
WAND/EARL	Wandsworth/Earlsfield
WAT	Watford
WATN	Watford north
WATW	Watford west
WBLY	Wembley
WBPTN	West Brompton
WCHMH	Winchmore Hill
WCHPL	Whitechapel
WDGN	Wood Green
WDR/YW	West Drayton/Yiewsley
WDSR	Windsor
WEA	West Ealing
WELL	Welling
WEST	Westminster
WESTW	Westminster west
WFD	Woodford
WHALL	Whitehall
WIM/MER	Wimbledon/Merton
WKENS	West Kensington
WLGTN	Wallington
WLSDN	Willesden
WNWD	West Norwood
WOKN/KNAP	Woking north/Knaphill
WOKS/MYFD	Woking south/Mayford
WOOL/PLUM	Woolwich/Plumstead
WOT/HER	Walton-on-Thames/Hersham
WPK	Worcester Park
WTHK	West Thurrock
WWKM	West Wickham
YEAD	Yeading

Barnaby Pl SKENS SW7 7 L8
Barnaby Wy CHIG IG7 28 J8
Barnacre Cl UX/CGN UB8 45 P4
Barnard Cl CHST BR7 65 M13
SUN TW16 58 D12
WLGTN SM6 74 B12
WOOL/PLUM SE18 52 J9
Barnard Gdns NWMAL KT3 72 G2
YEAD UB4 46 D2
Barnard Hl MUSWH N10 25 V14
Barnard Ms BTSEA SW11 61 S2
Barnardo Dr BARK/HLT IG6 41 L2
Barnardo Gdns WCHPL E1 * 51 P4
Barnardo St WCHPL E1 51 P4
Barnard Pl EW KT17 72 J14
Barnard Rd BTSEA SW11 61 S2
EN EN1 16 B14
MTCM CR4 73 U1
WARL CR6 87 T9
Barnards Pl SAND/SEL CR2 74 F13
Barnato Cl BF/WBF KT14 81 Q2
Barnby St CAMTN NW1 4 B4
SRTFD E15 40 A13
Barn Cl ASHF TW15 57 T10
BNSTD SM7 85 R5
KTTN NW5 * 38 B10
NTHLT UB5 34 E14
RAD WD7 12 E9
Barn Crs PUR/KEN CR8 86 H3
STAN HA7 23 S11
Barncroft Cl LOU IG10 28 J3
UX/CGN UB8 45 T3
Barncroft Gn LOU IG10 28 J3
Barncroft Rd LOU IG10 28 J3
Barneby Cl WHTN TW2 59 N6
Barnehurst Av BXLYHN DA7 54 C13
Barnehurst Cl ERITH DA8 54 C13
Barnehurst Rd BXLYHN DA7 54 C14
Barn End Dr RDART DA2 66 J9
Barn End La RDART DA2 66 J11
Barnes Av BARN SW13 48 G12
NWDGN UB2 46 H9
Barnes Br CHSWK W4 48 E14
Barnes Cl MNPK E12 40 F9
Barnes Cray Rd DART DA1 66 G2
Barnesdale Crs STMC/STPC BR5 77 Q4
Barnes End NWMAL KT3 72 G3
Barnes High St BARN SW13 48 F14
Barnes La KGLGY WD4 10 C2
Barnes Ri KGLGY WD4 10 F1
Barnes Rd IL IG1 41 L10
UED N18 27 N9
Barnes St POP/IOD E14 51 Q4
Barnes Ter DEPT SE8 51 R10
Barnes Wallis Dr BF/WBF KT14 81 Q1
Barnes Wy IVER SL0 44 K5
Barnet By-Pass BORE WD6 24 E3
Barnet Dr HAYES BR2 76 G7
Barnet Gate La BAR EN5 24 G5
Barnet Gv BETH E2 51 L1
Barnet Hl BAR EN5 25 M2
Barnet La BORE WD6 23 V4
TRDG/WHET N20 25 M6
Barnet Rd BAR EN5 14 C11
BAR EN5 24 F4
LCOL/BKTW AL2 12 K2
Barnett Cl ERITH DA8 54 F14
LHD/OX KT22 83 R9
Barnetts Ct RYLN/HDSTN HA2 * 34 K8
Barnett's Shaw OXTED RH8 95 V3
Barnett St WCHPL E1 51 M4
Barnetts Wy OXTED RH8 95 V3
Barnett Wood La LHD/OX KT22 83 R9
Barnet Wy (Barnet By-Pass)
MLHL NW7 24 D6
Barnet Wood Rd HAYES BR2 76 F7
Barney Cl CHARL SE7 52 E10
Barn Fld BNSTD SM7 85 P4
Barnfield EPP CM16 18 E2
Barn Fld HAMP NW3 * 37 T10
Barnfield IVER SL0 44 J4
NWMAL KT3 72 E4
Barnfield Av CROY/NA CR0 75 N7
KUTN/CMB KT2 59 T9
MTCM CR4 73 V2
Barnfield Cl COUL/CHIP CR5 86 G9
FSBYPK N4 38 C5
RDART DA2 67 T4
SWLY BR8 78 C5
TOOT SW17 61 Q8
Barnfield Crs BGR/WK TN15 91 L7
Barnfield Gdns KUTN/CMB KT2 59 U10
WOOL/PLUM SE18 * 52 K11
Barnfield Pl POP/IOD E14 51 T9
Barnfield Rd BELV DA17 53 V11
BH/WHM TN16 88 F11
EA W5 47 S2
EDGW HA8 24 C13
SAND/SEL CR2 74 J13
SEV TN13 90 D13
STMC/STPC BR5 77 T1
WOOL/PLUM SE18 52 K11
Barnfield Wy OXTED RH8 96 C9
Barnfield Wood Cl BECK BR3 75 V4
Barnfield Wood Rd BECK BR3 75 V4
Barnham Dr THMD SE28 53 P6
Barnham Rd GFD/PVL UB6 47 L1
Barnham St STHWK SE1 9 T3
Barnhill PIN HA5 34 E3
Barn Hl WBLY HA9 36 B7
Barnhill Av HAYES BR2 76 C3
Barnhill La YEAD UB4 46 D1
Barnhill Rd WBLY HA9 36 C8
YEAD UB4 46 D2
Barnhurst Pth OXHEY WD19 22 E10
Barningham Wy CDALE/KGS NW9 36 C4
Barn Lea RKW/CH/CXG WD3 21 L6
Barnlea Cl FELT TW13 58 G7
Barnmead EPP CM16 18 C10
Barnmead Gdns DAGW RM9 41 V10
Barn Meadow La GT/LBKH KT23 82 H14
Barnmead Rd BECK BR3 63 P13
DAGW RM9 41 V10
Barnock Cl DART DA1 66 E5
Barn Ri WBLY HA9 36 A6
Barn Rd ADL/WDHM KT15 69 M13
Barnsbury Cl NWMAL KT3 72 C2
Barnsbury Crs BRYLDS KT5 72 C6
Barnsbury Est IS N1 4 H2
Barnsbury Gv HOLWY N7 38 D12
Barnsbury La BRYLDS KT5 72 C6
Barnsbury Pk IS N1 38 E12
Barnsbury Rd IS N1 4 J3
Barnsbury Sq IS N1 38 E12
Barnsbury St IS N1 38 E12
Barnsbury Ter IS N1 38 D12
Barnscroft RYNPK SW20 72 H1
Barnsdale Av POP/IOD E14 51 T9
Barnsdale Cl BORE WD6 12 K13
Barnsdale Rd MV/WKIL W9 2 D7
Barnsfield Pl UX/CGN UB8 33 N13
Barnsley Rd HARH RM3 31 M12
Barnsley St WCHPL E1 51 M2
Barnstaple La LEW SE13 63 U2
Barnstaple Rd HARH RM3 30 J10
RSLP HA4 34 E8
Barnston Wk IS N1 * 5 N1
Barn St STNW/STAM N16 38 J7
Barnsway KGLGY WD4 10 E2
Barnway EGH TW20 56 A10
Barn Wy WBLY HA9 36 A6
Barnwell Rd BRXS/STRHM SW2 62 E3
DART DA1 67 M1
Barnwood Cl MV/WKIL W9 2 G8
RSLP HA4 33 V7
The Barnyard KWD/TDW/WH KT20 84 G14
Baron Cl BELMT SM2 73 P14
FBAR/BDGN N11 25 U10
Baron Ct HARH RM3 31 M13
Baroness Rd BETH E2 5 V5
Baronet Gv TOTM N17 27 L13
Baronet Rd TOTM N17 27 L13
Baron Gdns BARK/HLT IG6 41 M1
Baron Gv MTCM CR4 73 S2
Baron Rd BCTR RM8 41 T6
Barons Cl IS N1 * 4 J3
Baron's Court Rd WKENS W14 6 A9
Baronsfield Rd TWK TW1 * 59 R4
Barons Ga EBAR EN4 25 S4
Baron's Hurst EPSOM KT18 84 C6
Barons Md HRW HA1 35 N2
Baronsmead Rd BARN SW13 48 G13
Baronsmede EA W5 47 V7
Baronsmere Ct BAR EN5 * 25 L2
Baronsmere Rd EFNCH N2 37 S2
Baron's Pl STHWK SE1 8 K4
The Barons TWK TW1 59 R4
Baron St IS N1 4 K4
Baron's Wk CROY/NA CR0 75 Q4
Barons Wy EGH TW20 56 H11
REIG RH2 93 N14
Barque Ms DEPT SE8 51 S11
Barrack Rd HSLWW TW4 58 F2
Barra Hall Rd HYS/HAR UB3 46 A5
Barrass Cl PEND EN3 16 G11
Barratt Av WDGN N22 26 D14
Barratt Wy KTN/HRWW/WS HA3 35 M1
Barrenger Rd MUSWH N10 25 T13
Barrens Brae WOKS/MYFD GU22 80 E8
Barrens Cl WOKS/MYFD GU22 80 E9
Barrens Pk WOKS/MYFD GU22 80 E8
Barrett Cl HARH RM3 30 H12
Barrett Rd WALTH E17 39 U2
Barrett's Green Rd WLSDN NW10 36 C14
Barrett's Gv STNW/STAM N16 38 J10
Barretts Rd SEV TN13 90 D10
Barrett St MHST W1U 3 T12
Barrhill Rd BRXS/STRHM SW2 62 C7
Barrie Cl COUL/CHIP CR5 86 A6
Barriedale NWCR SE14 51 Q13
Barrier Point Rd CAN/RD E16 52 E7
Barringer Sq TOOT SW17 61 U9
Barrington Cl CLAY IG5 28 H13
KTTN NW5 37 U10
Barrington Dr DEN/HRF UB9 21 L12
Barrington Gn LOU IG10 29 L2
Barrington Ldg WEY KT13 69 U10
Barrington Park Gdns CSTG HP8 20 B6
Barrington Rd BRXN/ST SW9 62 F1
BXLYHN DA7 53 T14
CEND/HSY/T N8 38 B3
CHEAM SM3 73 N6
LOU IG10 29 L1
MNPK E12 40 J11
PUR/KEN CR8 86 A2
Barrington Vls WOOL/PLUM SE18 52 J13
Barrington Wk NRWD SE19 * 62 J11
Barrow Av CAR SM5 73 T12
Barrow Cl WCHMH N21 26 F8
Barrowdene Cl PIN HA5 22 G14
Barrowell Gn WCHMH N21 26 F7
Barrowgate Rd CHSWK W4 48 C10
Barrow Green Rd OXTED RH8 95 S7
Barrow Hedges Cl CAR SM5 73 S12
Barrow Hedges Wy CAR SM5 73 S12
Barrow Hl WPK KT4 72 E7
Barrow Hill Cl WPK KT4 72 E7
Barrow Hill Est STJWD NW8 3 N4
Barrow Hill Rd STJWD NW8 3 N4
Barrow La CHESW EN7 15 V5
Barrow Point Av PIN HA5 22 G14
Barrow Point La PIN HA5 22 G14
Barrow Rd CROY/NA CR0 74 E10
STRHM/NOR SW16 62 B11
Barr Rd POTB/CUF EN6 14 E7
Barrsbrook Farm Rd CHERT KT16 68 J6
Barrs Rd WLSDN NW10 36 D12
Barry Av BXLYHN DA7 53 U12
SEVS/STOTM N15 38 K4
Barry Cl ORP BR6 77 N8
Barry Pde EDUL SE22 * 63 L2
Barry Rd EDUL SE22 63 L4
EHAM E6 52 G4
WLSDN NW10 36 C12
Barry Ter ASHF TW15 * 57 R7
Barset Rd PECK SE15 63 N1
Barsons Cl PGE/AN SE20 63 N12
Barston Rd WNWD SE27 62 G7
Barstow Crs BRXS/STRHM SW2 62 D6
Barter St NOXST/BSQ WC1A 4 F10
Barth Ms WOOL/PLUM SE18 53 N9
Bartholomew Cl STBT EC1A 5 N10
WAND/EARL SW18 61 Q2
Bartholomew Dr HARH RM3 30 K14
Bartholomew La OBST EC2N 5 R11
Bartholomew Rd KTTN NW5 38 A11
Bartholomew Sq FSBYE EC1V 5 P7
Bartholomew St STHWK SE1 9 Q6
Bartholomew Vls KTTN NW5 38 A11
Bartholomew Wy SWLY BR8 78 E1
Barth Rd WOOL/PLUM SE18 53 N9
Bartle Av EHAM E6 40 G14
Bartle Rd NTGHL W11 48 K4
Bartlett Cl POP/IOD E14 51 S4
Bartlett Ct FLST/FETLN EC4A * 4 K11
Bartlett Rd BH/WHM TN16 97 L2
Bartlett St SAND/SEL CR2 74 H10
Bartlow Gdns CRW RM5 30 D13
Barton Av ROMW/RG RM7 42 C6
Barton Cl ADL/WDHM KT15 69 L11
BXLYHS DA6 65 U3
CHIG IG7 29 L7
EHAM E6 52 H4
HDN NW4 36 G3
HOM E9 39 N10
PECK SE15 63 M1
SHPTN TW17 69 T4
Barton Gn NWMAL KT3 60 D14
Barton Mdw BARK/HLT IG6 40 K2
Barton Rd DTCH/LGLY SL3 44 D7
EYN DA4 67 P13
HCH RM12 42 G6
SCUP DA14 65 U11
WKENS W14 6 A10
The Bartons BORE WD6 23 T4
Barton St WEST SW1P 8 E6
The Barton COB KT11 82 F2
Barton Wy BORE WD6 13 L14
RKW/CH/CXG WD3 21 T3
Bartram Cl UX/CGN UB8 45 T2
Bartram Rd BROCKY SE4 63 Q3
Bartrams La EBAR EN4 14 E12
Bartrip St HOM E9 39 Q11
Bartrop Cl CHESW EN7 15 T2
Barts Cl BECK BR3 75 S3
Barwell Ct CHSGTN KT9 * 71 S12
Barwell La CHSGTN KT9 71 S12
Barwick Dr UX/CGN UB8 45 T3
Barwick Rd FSTGT E7 40 D9
Barwood Av WWKM BR4 75 T6
Bascombe Gv DART DA1 66 E5
Bascome St BRXS/STRHM SW2 62 E5
Basden Gv FELT TW13 58 J7
Basedale Rd DAGW RM9 41 R12
Baseing Cl EHAM E6 52 J5
Basevi Wy DEPT SE8 51 S11
Bashley Rd WLSDN NW10 48 D2
Basil Av EHAM E6 52 G1
Basildene Rd HSLWW TW4 58 F1
Basildon Av CLAY IG5 28 J13
Basildon Cl BELMT SM2 73 P13
WATW WD18 21 U4
Basildon Rd ABYW SE2 53 Q10
Basil Gdns CROY/NA CR0 75 P6
WNWD SE27 62 G10
Basilon Rd BXLYHN DA7 53 U14
Basil St CHEL SW3 7 Q5
Basin Ap POP/IOD E14 51 Q4
Basing Cl THDIT KT7 71 P5
Basing Ct PECK SE15 50 K13
Basingdon Wy CMBW SE5 62 H2
Basing Dr BXLY DA5 65 V4
Basingfield Rd THDIT KT7 71 P5
Basinghall Av CITYW EC2V 5 Q11
Basinghall Gdns BELMT SM2 73 P13
Basinghall St CITYW EC2V 5 Q11
Basing Hl GLDGN NW11 37 M6
WBLY HA9 35 V7
Basing Pl BETH E2 5 T5
Basing Rd BNSTD SM7 85 M5
RKW/CH/CXG WD3 20 K6
Basing St NTGHL W11 2 C11
Basing Wy FNCH N3 37 N1
THDIT KT7 71 P5
Basire St IS N1 5 P1
Baskerville Gdns WLSDN NW10 36 E9
Baskerville Rd WAND/EARL SW18 61 S5
Basket Gdns ELTH/MOT SE9 64 G3
Baslow Cl KTN/HRWW/WS HA3 23 M13
Baslow Wk CLPT E5 39 P9
Basnett Rd BTSEA SW11 * 61 U1
Bassano St EDUL SE22 62 K3
Bassant Rd WOOL/PLUM SE18 53 P11
Bassein Park Rd SHB W12 48 F7
Basset Cl ADL/WDHM KT15 69 M14
Basset Dr REIG RH2 93 N9
Bassett Cl BELMT SM2 73 P13
Bassett Gdns ISLW TW7 47 L12
Bassett Rd NKENS W10 48 K4
UX/CGN UB8 33 N12
WOKS/MYFD GU22 80 G6
Bassetts Cl ORP BR6 76 K9
Bassett St KTTN NW5 37 U11
Bassetts Wy ORP BR6 76 K9
Bassett Wy GFD/PVL UB6 46 K4
Bassingham Rd ALP/SUD HA0 35 T11
WAND/EARL SW18 61 Q5
Basswood Cl PECK SE15 63 M1
Bastable Av BARK IG11 41 Q14
Bastion Rd ABYW SE2 53 Q10
Baston Manor Rd WWKM BR4 76 D8
Baston Rd HAYES BR2 76 D7
Bastwick St FSBYE EC1V 5 M7
Basuto Rd FUL/PGN SW6 49 N13
Batavia Rd NWCR SE14 51 Q12
SUN TW16 58 D13
Batchelor St IS N1 4 J3
Batchwood Gn STMC/STPC BR5 77 Q2
Batchworth Hl RKW/CH/CXG WD3 * 21 Q7
Batchworth Hill London Rd
RKW/CH/CXG WD3 21 R8
Batchworth La NTHWD HA6 21 U10
Bateman Cl BARK IG11 41 L11
Bateman Rd CHING E4 27 S11
RKW/CH/CXG WD3 21 S4
Bateman's Buildings SOHO/SHAV W1D 4 C12
Batemans Cnr CHSWK W4 * 48 D10
Bateman's Rw SDTCH EC2A 5 T7
Bateman St SOHO/SHAV W1D 4 D12
Bates Cl DTCH/LGLY SL3 44 C4
Bates Crs CROY/NA CR0 74 E11
STRHM/NOR SW16 62 A12
Bateson Wy WOKN/KNAP GU21 80 G4
Bates Rd HARH RM3 31 N12
Bate St POP/IOD E14 51 R5
Bates Wk ADL/WDHM KT15 69 N11
Bath Cl PECK SE15 51 N13
Bathgate Rd WIM/MER SW19 60 K8
Bath Gv BETH E2 39 L14
Bath House Rd CROY/NA CR0 74 C6
Bath Pas KUT/HW KT1 59 T14
Bath Pl BAR EN5 25 M1
SDTCH EC2A * 5 S6
Bath Rd CHSWK W4 48 E9
DART DA1 66 H5
DTCH/LGLY SL3 44 K13
ED N9 27 M7
FSTGT E7 40 F11
HSLW TW3 58 K1
WDR/YW UB7 45 M13
Bath St FSBYE EC1V 5 P6
Bath Ter STHWK SE1 9 N6
Bathurst Av WIM/MER SW19 61 P13
Bathurst Cl WDR/YW UB7 44 K7
Bathurst Gdns WLSDN NW10 36 H14
Bathurst Ms BAY/PAD W2 3 M13
Bathurst Rd IL IG1 40 K6
Bathurst St BAY/PAD W2 3 M13
Bathurst Wk DTCH/LGLY SL3 44 J7
Bathway WOOL/PLUM SE18 52 J9
Batley Cl CAR SM5 73 T5
Batley Pl STNW/STAM N16 38 K8
Batley Rd ENC/FH EN2 15 S13
STNW/STAM N16 38 K8
Batman Cl SHB W12 48 H6
Baton Cl PUR RM19 55 R9
Batoum Gdns HMSMTH W6 48 J8
Batson St SHB W12 48 G7
Batsworth Rd MTCM CR4 73 R1
Batten Cl EHAM E6 52 H4
Batten Cottages POP/IOD E14 * 51 Q3
Batten St BTSEA SW11 61 S1
Battersby Rd CAT SE6 63 V7
Battersea Br BTSEA SW11 7 N13
Battersea Bridge Rd BTSEA SW11 7 M13
Battersea Church Rd BTSEA SW11 49 R13
Battersea High St BTSEA SW11 49 R14
Battersea Park Rd BTSEA SW11 49 U13
VX/NE SW8 7 V14
Battersea Ri BTSEA SW11 61 S3
Battersea Sq BTSEA SW11 7 N14
Battery Rd THMD SE28 53 N7
Battishill St IS N1 38 F12
Battlebridge La REDH RH1 93 V6
Battle Bridge La STHWK SE1 9 S2
Battle Bridge Rd CAMTN NW1 4 E4
Battle Cl WIM/MER SW19 61 Q11
Battledean Rd HBRY N5 38 F10
Battle Rd ERITH DA8 54 C9
Battlers Green Dr RAD WD7 12 C11
Batts Hl REIG RH2 93 S9
Batty St WCHPL E1 51 L4
Baudwin Rd CAT SE6 64 A7
Baugh Rd SCUP DA14 65 S10
The Baulk WAND/EARL SW18 61 N5
Bavant Rd STRHM/NOR SW16 62 C14
Bavaria Rd ARCH N19 38 C7
Bavdene Ms HDN NW4 36 H2
Bavent Rd CMBW SE5 50 G14
Bawdale Rd EDUL SE22 62 K3
Bawdsey Av GNTH/NBYPK IG2 41 P2
Bawtree Cl BELMT SM2 73 Q14
Bawtree Rd NWCR SE14 51 Q12
UX/CGN UB8 33 N11
Bawtry Rd TRDG/WHET N20 25 T8
Baxendale TRDG/WHET N20 25 Q7
Baxendale St BETH E2 51 L1
Baxter Av REDH RH1 93 S10
Baxter Cl HGDN/ICK UB10 45 T1
NWDGN UB2 46 K8
Baxter Rd CAN/RD E16 52 E4
IL IG1 40 K10
IS N1 38 H11
UED N18 27 M9
Bayards WARL CR6 87 N8
Bay Ct EA W5 * 47 U8
Baycroft Cl PIN HA5 * 34 E1
Bayeux KWD/TDW/WH KT20 84 K12
Bayfield Rd ELTH/MOT SE9 64 F2
Bayford Ms HACK E8 * 39 M12
Bayford Rd WLSDN NW10 48 K1
Bayford St HACK E8 39 M12
Bayham Pl CAMTN NW1 4 A2
Bayham Rd CHSWK W4 48 D8
MRDN SM4 73 P2
SEV TN13 90 J13
WEA W13 47 R5
Bayham St CAMTN NW1 4 A2
Bayhurst Dr NTHWD HA6 22 B11
Bayleaf Cl HPTN TW12 59 M10
Bayley St FITZ W1T 4 C10
Baylis Ms TWK TW1 59 Q5
Baylis Rd STHWK SE1 8 J5
Bayliss Av THMD SE28 53 T5
Bayliss Cl ENC/FH EN2 26 C3
Bayly Rd DART DA1 67 N4
Bay Manor La WTHK RM20 55 T11
Bayne Cl EHAM E6 52 H4
Baynes Cl EN EN1 16 A13
Baynes Ms HAMP NW3 37 R11
Baynes St CAMTN NW1 38 A12
Baynham Cl BXLY DA5 65 V4
Bayonne Rd HMSMTH W6 6 A12
Bays Cl SYD SE26 63 N10
Baysfarm Ct WDR/YW UB7 45 N13
Bayshill Ri NTHLT UB5 34 K11
Bayston Rd STNW/STAM N16 38 K8
Bayswater Rd BAY/PAD W2 2 K14
Baythorne St BOW E3 51 R3
Bay Tree Av LHD/OX KT22 83 Q10
Baytree Cl BFN/LL DA15 65 P6
BMLY BR1 64 F13
Bay Tree Cl CHESW EN7 * 15 V1
LCOL/BKTW AL2 11 V1
Baytree Rd BRXS/STRHM SW2 62 D2
Bay Tree Wk WAT WD17 11 N12
Baywood Sq CHIG IG7 29 R9
Bazalgette Cl NWMAL KT3 72 C3
Bazalgette Gdns NWMAL KT3 72 D3
Bazely St POP/IOD E14 51 U5
Bazile Rd WCHMH N21 26 E4
Beacham Cl CHARL SE7 52 F11
Beachborough Rd BMLY BR1 63 U9
Beachcroft Rd WAN E11 40 A8
Beach Gv FELT TW13 58 J8
Beachy Rd BOW E3 39 S12
Beacon Cl BNSTD SM7 84 K6
CFSP/GDCR SL9 20 C12
UX/CGN UB8 33 P10
Beacon Ct DTCH/LGLY SL3 44 G12
Beaconfield Av EPP CM16 18 E3
Beaconfield Rd EPP CM16 18 D3
Beaconfield Wy EPP CM16 18 D3
Beacon Ga NWCR SE14 63 P1
Beacon Hl HOLWY N7 38 C10
PUR RM19 55 P10
WOKN/KNAP GU21 80 A9
Beacon Pl CROY/NA CR0 74 C8
Beacon Rd ERITH DA8 54 H12
HTHAIR TW6 57 S4
LEW SE13 63 V4
Beaconsfield Cl BKHTH/KID SE3 52 C11
CHSWK W4 48 C10
Beaconsfield Cottages
TRDG/WHET N20 * 25 N8
Beaconsfield Gdns ESH/CLAY KT10 71 N12
Beaconsfield Pl EW KT17 84 E2
Beaconsfield Rd BKHTH/KID SE3 52 C11
BMLY BR1 76 F1
BXLY DA5 66 E7
CAN/RD E16 52 B2
CHSWK W4 48 D8
CROY/NA CR0 74 H4
EA W5 47 S7
ED N9 27 L8
ELTH/MOT SE9 64 G8
EPSOM KT18 84 D9
ESH/CLAY KT10 71 N12
FBAR/BDGN N11 25 U8
LEY E10 * 39 U8
NWMAL KT3 72 D1
PEND EN3 16 D11
SEVS/STOTM N15 38 J2
SURB KT6 71 V5
TWK TW1 59 R5
WALTH E17 39 R5
WALW SE17 9 R11
WLSDN NW10 36 F11
WOKS/MYFD GU22 80 D10
YEAD UB4 46 E6
Beaconsfield Wk FUL/PGN SW6 49 M13
The Beacons LOU IG10 17 U12
Beacontree Av WALTH E17 27 V13
Beacontree Rd WAN E11 40 B6
Beacon Wy BNSTD SM7 84 K6
RKW/CH/CXG WD3 21 M5
Beadles La OXTED RH8 95 V6
Beadlow Cl CAR SM5 73 R4
Beadman Pl WNWD SE27 * 62 F9
Beadman St WNWD SE27 62 F9
Beadnell Rd FSTH SE23 63 P6
Beadon Rd HAYES BR2 76 C2
HMSMTH W6 48 J9
Beads Hall La BRWN CM15 31 V2
Beaford Gv RYNPK SW20 73 L1
Beagle Cl FELT TW13 58 D9
RAD WD7 12 D11
Beagles Cl STMC/STPC BR5 77 T7
Beak St REGST W1B 4 A13
Beal Cl WELL DA16 53 Q13
Beale Cl PLMGR N13 26 F10
Beale Pl BOW E3 39 R14
Beale Rd BOW E3 39 R13
Beales La WEY KT13 69 T8
Beal Rd IL IG1 40 J7
Beam Av DAGE RM10 42 B13
Beames Rd WLSDN NW10 36 D13
Beaminster Gdns BARK/HLT IG6 40 K1
Beamish Dr BUSH WD23 23 L6
Beamish Rd ED N9 27 L6
STMC/STPC BR5 77 S5
Beamway DAGE RM10 42 D12
Beanacre Cl HOM E9 39 R11
Bean La RDART DA2 67 V8
Bean Rd BXLYHS DA6 65 T2
SWCM DA10 67 V4
Beanshaw ELTH/MOT SE9 64 J9
Beansland Gv CHDH RM6 29 U14
Bear Cl ROMW/RG RM7 42 B4
Beardell St NRWD SE19 62 K11
Beardow Gv STHGT/OAK N14 * 26 A4
Beard Rd KUTN/CMB KT2 59 V10
Beardsfield PLSTW E13 40 C13
Beard's Hl HPTN TW12 58 J13
Beard's Hill Cl HPTN TW12 58 J13
Beardsley Wy ACT W3 48 D7
Beards Rd ASHF TW15 58 A11
Bearfield Rd KUTN/CMB KT2 59 U12
Bear Gdns STHWK SE1 9 N1
Bearing Cl CHIG IG7 29 Q9
Bearing Wy CHIG IG7 29 Q9
Bear La STHWK SE1 9 M1
Bear Rd FELT TW13 58 F9
Bears Den KWD/TDW/WH KT20 85 M12
Bearstead Ri BROCKY SE4 63 R3
Bearstead Ter BECK BR3 * 63 S13
Bear St LSQ/SEVD WC2H 4 D13
Bearwood Cl ADL/WDHM KT15 69 L11
POTB/CUF EN6 14 F5
Beasant House WATN WD24 * 11 R14
Beasley's Ait SUN TW16 70 C4
Beasley's Ait La SUN TW16 70 B4
Beaton Cl SWCM DA10 67 V3
Beatrice Av STRHM/NOR SW16 74 D1
WBLY HA9 35 U10
Beatrice Cl PIN HA5 34 C2
PLSTW E13 52 C2
Beatrice Pl KENS W8 6 G6
Beatrice Rd ED N9 27 N5
FSBYPK N4 38 E5
OXTED RH8 96 A5
RCHPK/HAM TW10 59 V3
STHL UB1 46 H6
STHWK SE1 51 L9
WALTH E17 39 S3
Beattie Cl EBED/NFELT TW14 58 B6
GT/LBKH KT23 82 H14
Beattock Ri MUSWH N10 37 V2
Beatty Rd CHES/WCR EN8 16 F8
STAN HA7 23 S11
STNW/STAM N16 38 J9
Beatty St CAMTN NW1 * 4 A3
Beattyville Gdns CLAY IG5 40 J1
Beauchamp Cl RKW/CH/CXG WD3 21 L6
Beauchamp Pl CHEL SW3 7 P6
Beauchamp Rd BTSEA SW11 61 S2
E/WMO/HCT KT8 70 K3
FSTGT E7 40 D12
NRWD SE19 62 H13
SUT SM1 73 N10
TWK TW1 59 Q5
Beauchamp St HCIRC EC1N 4 J10
Beauchamp Ter BARN SW13 60 H1
Beauclare Cl LHD/OX KT22 83 T11
Beauclerc Rd HMSMTH W6 48 H8
Beauclerk Cl FELT TW13 58 D6
Beaufort EHAM E6 52 J3
Beaufort Av KTN/HRWW/WS HA3 35 Q2
Beaufort Cl CHING E4 27 T11
EA W5 47 V3
EPP CM16 19 L1
PUT/ROE SW15 60 J6
REIG RH2 93 M9
ROMW/RG RM7 42 C2
WOKS/MYFD GU22 80 G6
Beaufort Ct RCHPK/HAM TW10 59 S9
Beaufort Dr GLDGN NW11 37 N2
Beaufort Gdns CHEL SW3 7 P5
HDN NW4 36 J4
HEST TW5 46 G13
IL IG1 40 J6
STRHM/NOR SW16 62 D12
Beaufort Rd EA W5 47 V3
KUT/HW KT1 71 U2
RCHPK/HAM TW10 59 S9
REIG RH2 93 M9
RSLP HA4 * 33 V7
WOKS/MYFD GU22 80 G6
Beauforts EGH TW20 56 A10
Beaufort St CHEL SW3 7 M12
Beaufort Wy EW KT17 72 G12
Beaufoy Rd TOTM N17 26 K12
Beaufoy Wk LBTH SE11 8 H8
Beaulieu Av CAN/RD E16 52 D6
SYD SE26 63 M9
Beaulieu Cl CDALE/KGS NW9 36 E2
CMBW SE5 62 H1
DTCH/LGLY SL3 44 A14
HSLWW TW4 58 H3
MTCM CR4 61 U13
OXHEY WD19 22 E6
TWK TW1 59 T4
Beaulieu Dr PIN HA5 34 F4
WAB EN9 16 H7
Beaulieu Gdns WCHMH N21 26 G5
Beaulieu Pl CHSWK W4 48 C8
Beauly Ct ROM RM1 30 E13
Beauly Wy ROM RM1 30 E13
Beaumaris Gn CDALE/KGS NW9 * 36 E4
Beaumont ALP/SUD HA0 35 S10
RCH/KEW TW9 59 V1
RYLN/HDSTN HA2 34 K4
WKENS W14 6 C9
Beaumont Cl GPK RM2 30 J14
KUTN/CMB KT2 60 A12
Beaumont Ct ALP/SUD HA0 35 S10
Beaumont Crs RAIN RM13 42 G11
WKENS W14 6 C9
Beaumont Dr ASHF TW15 57 V10
Beaumont Gdns HAMP NW3 37 N7
Beaumont Ga RAD WD7 12 E9
Beaumont Gv WCHPL E1 51 P2
Beaumont Ms MHST W1U * 3 T9
PIN HA5 * 34 G1
Beaumont Pl BAR EN5 14 B13
FITZ W1T 4 B7
ISLW TW7 59 P3
Beaumont Ri ARCH N19 38 C6
Beaumont Rd CHSWK W4 48 C8
LEY E10 39 U5
NRWD SE19 62 G11
PLSTW E13 52 E1
PUR/KEN CR8 86 E3
STMC/STPC BR5 77 M4
WIM/MER SW19 61 L5
Beaumont Sq WCHPL E1 51 P3
Beaumont St CAVSQ/HST W1G 3 T9
Beaumont Ter LEW SE13 * 64 A5
Beaumont Wk HAMP NW3 37 T12
Beauvais Ter NTHLT UB5 46 F1
Beauval Rd EDUL SE22 62 K4
Beaverbank Rd ELTH/MOT SE9 65 M6
Beaver Cl HPTN TW12 58 K13
MRDN SM4 72 J5
PGE/AN SE20 * 63 L12
Beaver Rd BARK/HLT IG6 29 S10
Beavers Crs HSLWW TW4 58 F2
Beavers La HSLWW TW4 58 E1
Beaverwood Rd CHST BR7 65 N10
Beavor La HMSMTH W6 48 G10
Bebbington Rd WOOL/PLUM SE18 * 53 N9
Beblets Cl ORP BR6 77 P10
Beccles Dr BARK IG11 41 P11
Beccles St POP/IOD E14 51 R4
Bec Cl RSLP HA4 34 F8
Beck Cl LEW SE13 51 T13
Beckenham Gdns ED N9 26 J8
Beckenham Gv HAYES BR2 63 V14
Beckenham Hill Rd BECK BR3 63 T11
Beckenham La HAYES BR2 64 A14
Beckenham Place Pk BECK BR3 63 T12
Beckenham Rd BECK BR3 63 P13
BECK BR3 75 T5
Beckenshaw Gdns BNSTD SM7 85 S5
Becket Av EHAM E6 52 J1
Becket Cl SNWD SE25 75 L4
WIM/MER SW19 * 61 P13
Becket Fold HRW HA1 * 35 P3
Becket Rd UED N18 27 N9
Becket St STHWK SE1 9 Q5
Beckett Av PUR/KEN CR8 86 F5
Beckett Cha DTCH/LGLY SL3 44 D10
Beckett Cl BELV DA17 53 U8
STRHM/NOR SW16 62 B7
WLSDN NW10 36 D11
Becketts Cl EBED/NFELT TW14 58 D4
ORP BR6 77 P8
Becketts Pl KUT/HW KT1 59 T13
Beckett Wk BECK BR3 63 Q11
Beckford Cl WKENS W14 6 D8
Beckford Dr STMC/STPC BR5 77 M5
Beckford Pl WALW SE17 * 9 P10
Beckford Rd CROY/NA CR0 74 K4
Beck La BECK BR3 75 P1
Becklow Rd SHB W12 48 F7
Beckman Cl RSEV TN14 90 C5
Beck River Pk BECK BR3 63 R13
Beck Rd HACK E8 39 M13
Becks Rd SCUP DA14 65 Q8
Beckton Rd CAN/RD E16 52 B3
Beck Wy BECK BR3 75 R1
Beckway Rd STRHM/NOR SW16 62 B14
Beckway St WALW SE17 9 S8
Beckwith Rd HNHL SE24 62 H4
Beclands Rd TOOT SW17 61 U11
Becmead Av KTN/HRWW/WS HA3 35 R3
STRHM/NOR SW16 62 B9
Becondale Rd NRWD SE19 62 J10
Becontree Av BCTR RM8 41 R9
Bective Rd FSTGT E7 40 C9
PUT/ROE SW15 61 M2
Becton Pl ERITH DA8 54 B13
Bedale Rd ENC/FH EN2 15 S12
HARH RM3 31 N10
Bedale St STHWK SE1 * 9 Q2
Beddington Cross CROY/NA CR0 74 C5
Beddington Farm Rd CROY/NA CR0 74 C7
Beddington Gdns CAR SM5 73 U11
Beddington Gn STMC/STPC BR5 65 P13
Beddington Gv WLGTN SM6 74 B10
Beddington La CROY/NA CR0 74 B6
Beddington Rd GDMY/SEVK IG3 41 P5
STMC/STPC BR5 65 N13
Beddington Ter CROY/NA CR0 * 74 D5
Beddlestead La WARL CR6 88 B8
Bede Cl PIN HA5 22 F13
Bedens Rd SCUP DA14 65 U11
Bede Rd CHDH RM6 41 S4
Bedevere Rd ED N9 27 L8
Bedfont Cl EBED/NFELT TW14 57 U5
MTCM CR4 61 U14
Bedfont Ct STWL/WRAY TW19 57 M1
Bedfont Court Est
STWL/WRAY TW19 * 57 M2
Bedfont Green Cl EBED/NFELT TW14 57 U6
Bedfont La EBED/NFELT TW14 58 A5
Bedfont Rd FELT TW13 58 A7
STWL/WRAY TW19 57 R4
Bedford Av BAR EN5 25 M3
RSQ WC1B 4 D10
YEAD UB4 46 D4
Bedfordbury CHCR WC2N 4 E13
Bedford Cl CHSWK W4 48 F12
MUSWH N10 25 U12
WOKN/KNAP GU21 80 A5
Bedford Cnr CHSWK W4 * 48 E9
Bedford Ct CHCR WC2N 4 E14
Bedford Crs PEND EN3 16 E9
Bedford Gdns HCH RM12 42 J7
KENS W8 6 E2
Bedford Hl BAL SW12 61 V7
Bedford Pk CROY/NA CR0 74 G6
Bedford Pl CROY/NA CR0 74 H6
RSQ WC1B 4 E9
Bedford Rd BFN/LL DA15 65 N8
CEND/HSY/T N8 38 B4
CHSWK W4 48 D8
CLAP SW4 62 C2
DART DA1 67 N5
ED N9 27 M5
EFNCH N2 37 S1
EHAM E6 40 J13
HRW HA1 35 L4
IL IG1 40 K8
MLHL NW7 24 E7
NTHWD HA6 21 V9
ORP BR6 77 R7
RSLP HA4 34 B9
SEVS/STOTM N15 38 H2
SWFD E18 28 C14
WALTH E17 27 S14
WDGN N22 26 C13
WEA W13 47 R5
WHTN TW2 59 M8
WPK KT4 72 J7
Bedford Rw GINN WC1R 4 H9
Bedford Sq RSQ WC1B 4 D10
Bedford St COVGDN WC2E 4 E13
WATN WD24 11 P13
Bedford Vls KUT/HW KT1 * 59 V14
Bedford Wy STPAN WC1H 4 D8
Bedgebury Gdns WIM/MER SW19 61 L7
Bedgebury Rd ELTH/MOT SE9 64 F2
Bedivere Rd BMLY BR1 64 C8
Bedlow Cl STJWD NW8 3 M8
Bedlow Wy CROY/NA CR0 74 D9
Bedmond Rd ABLGY WD5 11 M3
Bedonwell Rd BXLYHN DA7 53 V13
Bedser Cl LBTH SE11 8 H11
THHTH CR7 74 G1
WOKN/KNAP GU21 80 E6
Bedser Dr GFD/PVL UB6 35 M10
Bedster Gdns E/WMO/HCT KT8 58 K14
Bedwardine Rd NRWD SE19 62 J12
Bedwell Gdns HYS/HAR UB3 46 A10
Bedwell Rd BELV DA17 54 A10
TOTM N17 26 J13
Beeby Rd CAN/RD E16 52 D3
Beech Av ACT W3 48 E6
BFN/LL DA15 65 Q5
BH/WHM TN16 88 F9
BKHH IG9 28 D7
BTFD TW8 47 R12
ENC/FH EN2 15 Q9
RAD WD7 12 E7
RSLP HA4 34 D6
SAND/SEL CR2 86 H1
SWLY BR8 78 G2
TRDG/WHET N20 25 S6
UPMR RM14 43 P8
Beech Cl ASHF TW15 57 V10
BF/WBF KT14 81 Q2
CAR SM5 73 T7
COB KT11 82 J2
DEPT SE8 51 R11
ED N9 27 L4
HCH RM12 42 H8
LOU IG10 28 K1
PUT/ROE SW15 60 G5
SUN TW16 58 F14
WDR/YW UB7 45 S8
WIM/MER SW19 60 J11
WOT/HER KT12 70 E9
Beech Close Ct COB KT11 82 H1
Beech Copse BMLY BR1 64 H14
SAND/SEL CR2 74 J10
Beech Ct ELTH/MOT SE9 * 64 G4
Beech Crs KWD/TDW/WH KT20 92 C6
Beechcroft ASHTD KT21 83 V9
CHST BR7 64 J12
Beechcroft Av BXLYHN DA7 54 D14
GLDGN NW11 37 M5
NWMAL KT3 60 C13
PUR/KEN CR8 86 H5
RKW/CH/CXG WD3 21 U4
RYLN/HDSTN HA2 34 J5
STHL UB1 46 H6
Beechcroft Cl HEST TW5 46 G12
ORP BR6 77 M9
STRHM/NOR SW16 62 D10
Beechcroft Gdns WBLY HA9 35 V8
Beechcroft Mnr WEY KT13 69 V8
Beechcroft Rd BUSH WD23 22 G3
CHSGTN KT9 71 V9
MORT/ESHN SW14 * 60 C1
ORP BR6 77 M9
SWFD E18 28 D14
TOOT SW17 61 T8
Beechdale WCHMH N21 26 D7
Beechdale Rd BRXS/STRHM SW2 62 D4
Beech Dell HAYES BR2 76 H9
Beechdene KWD/TDW/WH KT20 84 H12
Beech Dr BORE WD6 12 K14
EFNCH N2 37 T1
KWD/TDW/WH KT20 85 M12
REIG RH2 93 R10
RPLY/SEND GU23 80 K14
Beechen Cliff Wy ISLW TW7 47 P14
Beechengrove PIN HA5 34 H1
Beechen Gv WAT WD17 22 D1
Beechen La KWD/TDW/WH KT20 93 M1
Beechenlea La SWLY BR8 78 G2
Beechen Pl FSTH SE23 63 N7
Beechen Wd RKW/CH/CXG WD3 20 H9
Beeches Av CAR SM5 73 S12
Beeches Cl KWD/TDW/WH KT20 85 N13
PGE/AN SE20 63 N13
Beeches Rd CHEAM SM3 73 L6
TOOT SW17 61 T8
The Beeches BNSTD SM7 85 P6
BRW CM14 31 V8
CHING E4 * 27 V6
HNWL W7 * 47 P7
LCOL/BKTW AL2 12 B1
LHD/OX KT22 83 N14
RKW/CH/CXG WD3 20 K3
STA TW18 * 57 L10
SWLY BR8 66 F12
WATW WD18 * 22 D1
Beeches Wk BELMT SM2 73 R13
Beeches Wy DTCH/LGLY SL3 32 D11
Beeches Wd KWD/TDW/WH KT20 85 N12
Beech Farm Rd WARL CR6 87 V10
Beechfield BNSTD SM7 85 P3
KGLGY WD4 10 F4
Beechfield Cl BORE WD6 12 J14
Beechfield Gdns ROMW/RG RM7 42 C5
Beechfield Rd BMLY BR1 64 E14
CAT SE6 63 R6
ERITH DA8 54 E12
FSBYPK N4 38 G4
Beechfield Wk WAB EN9 16 K9
Beech Gdns DAGE RM10 42 B12
EA W5 47 U7
WOKN/KNAP GU21 80 C5
Beech Gv ADL/WDHM KT15 69 M9
BARK/HLT IG6 29 N11
CTHM CR3 94 H2
EPSOM KT18 84 H7
MTCM CR4 74 B3
NWMAL KT3 72 D1
SOCK/AV RM15 55 Q7
WOKS/MYFD GU22 80 B13
Beech Hall CHERT KT16 * 68 G12
Beech Hall Crs CHING E4 27 V12
Beech Hall Rd CHING E4 27 U12
Beech Hl EBAR EN4 14 F12
WOKS/MYFD GU22 80 B13
Beech Hill Av EBAR EN4 14 F13
Beech Hill Gdns WAB EN9 17 P11
Beechhill Rd ELTH/MOT SE9 64 J3
Beech Holt LHD/OX KT22 83 S12
Beech House Rd CROY/NA CR0 74 H8
Beech Lawns NFNCH/WDSPK N12 * 25 R10
Beechmeads COB KT11 * 82 F3
Beechmont Av VW GU25 68 B4
Beechmont Cl BMLY BR1 64 A10
Beechmore Gdns CHEAM SM3 72 K7
Beechmore Rd BTSEA SW11 49 T13
Beechmount Av HNWL W7 47 M3
Beecholme BNSTD SM7 * 85 L4
Beecholme Av MTCM CR4 61 V13
Beecholme Est CLPT E5 * 39 N8
Beechpark Wy WAT WD17 11 L11
Beech Pl EPP CM16 18 D5
Beech Rd BH/WHM TN16 88 E7
DART DA1 66 K6
DTCH/LGLY SL3 44 C7
EBED/NFELT TW14 58 A5
EW KT17 84 F5
FBAR/BDGN N11 26 C11
ORP BR6 77 Q12
REDH RH1 94 A2
REIG RH2 93 N8
STRHM/NOR SW16 62 C14
WATN WD24 11 N11
WEY KT13 69 V9
Beechrow KUTN/CMB KT2 59 U9
Beech St ROMW/RG RM7 42 C2
Beech St (Below) BARB EC2Y 5 N9
Beech Tree Cl IS N1 38 E12
STAN HA7 23 S10
Beech Tree Gld CHING E4 28 B6
Beech Tree La STA TW18 * 57 M14
Beech Tree Pl SUT SM1 73 P10
Beech V WOKS/MYFD GU22 * 80 C8
Beechvale Cl NFNCH/WDSPK N12 25 S10
Beech Wk DART DA1 66 G2
EW KT17 84 G1
MLHL NW7 24 D11
Beechway BXLY DA5 65 T4
Beech Wy EW KT17 84 F5
SAND/SEL CR2 87 P3
WHTN TW2 58 J8
WLSDN NW10 36 D12
Beech Waye CFSP/GDCR SL9 32 E5
Beechwood KWD/TDW/WH KT20 * 92 B7
Beechwood Av COUL/CHIP CR5 85 V5
FNCH N3 37 M1
GFD/PVL UB6 46 K1
HYS/HAR UB3 45 V5
KWD/TDW/WH KT20 85 N11
ORP BR6 77 N11
POTB/CUF EN6 14 D7
RCH/KEW TW9 48 A13
RKW/CH/CXG WD3 20 F2
RSLP HA4 34 B7
RYLN/HDSTN HA2 34 K8
STA TW18 57 M11
SUN TW16 58 C11
THHTH CR7 74 F2
UX/CGN UB8 45 R4
WEY KT13 70 A9
Beechwood Cl EFNCH N2 * 37 T2
MLHL NW7 24 E10
SURB KT6 71 S5
WEY KT13 70 A9
Beechwood Crs BXLYHN DA7 65 T1
Beechwood Dr COB KT11 82 J1
HAYES BR2 76 F9
WFD IG8 28 B10
Beechwood Gdns CLAY IG5 40 H3
CTHM CR3 87 L12
RAIN RM13 54 H3
RYLN/HDSTN HA2 34 K8
Beechwood Gv ACT W3 48 E5
Beechwood La WARL CR6 87 P9
Beechwood Mnr WEY KT13 70 A9
Beechwood Ms ED N9 27 L7
Beechwood Pk LHD/OX KT22 83 S12
RKW/CH/CXG WD3 20 K2
SWFD E18 40 C1
Beechwood Ri CHST BR7 64 K10
WATN WD24 11 P10
Beechwood Rd CEND/HSY/T N8 38 B2
CTHM CR3 87 L12
HACK E8 38 K11
SAND/SEL CR2 74 J13
Beechworth Cl HAMP NW3 37 P7
Beechy Lees Rd RSEV TN14 90 K7
Beecot La WOT/HER KT12 70 E7
Beecroft La BROCKY SE4 63 Q3
Beecroft Ms BROCKY SE4 63 Q3
Beecroft Rd BROCKY SE4 63 Q3
Beehive Cl BORE WD6 23 T4
HACK E8 38 K12
HGDN/ICK UB10 33 R12
Beehive La REDBR IG4 40 H3
Beehive Pl BRXN/ST SW9 62 E1
Beehive Rd CHESW EN7 15 R2
STA TW18 56 K10
Beehive Wy REIG RH2 93 P14
Beeken Dene ORP BR6 77 L9
Beeleigh Rd MRDN SM4 73 P2
Beesfield La EYN DA4 79 N6
Beeston Cl HACK E8 39 L10
OXHEY WD19 22 F9
Beeston Dr CHES/WCR EN8 16 D1
Beeston Pl BGVA SW1W 7 V6
Beeston Rd EBAR EN4 25 R4
Beeston Wy EBED/NFELT TW14 58 E4
Beethoven Rd BORE WD6 23 S5
Beethoven St NKENS W10 2 B5
Beeton Cl PIN HA5 22 J12
Begbie Rd BKHTH/KID SE3 52 E13
Beggars Bush La WATW WD18 21 V3
Beggars La BH/WHM TN16 97 M1
Beggar's Roost La SUT SM1 73 N11
Begonia Cl EHAM E6 52 G3
Begonia Pl HPTN TW12 58 J11
Beira St BAL SW12 61 V5
Beken Ct GSTN WD25 * 11 Q9
Bekesbourne St POP/IOD E14 * 51 Q4
Belcroft Cl BMLY BR1 64 B12
Beldam Haw RSEV TN14 90 A1
Beldham Gdns E/WMO/HCT KT8 70 K1
Belfairs Dr CHDH RM6 41 S5
Belfairs Gdn OXHEY WD19 22 F10
Belfairs Gn OXHEY WD19 22 F10
Belfast Rd SNWD SE25 75 M2
STNW/STAM N16 38 K7
Belfield Rd HOR/WEW KT19 72 D13
Belford Gv WOOL/PLUM SE18 52 J9
Belford Rd BORE WD6 12 K12
Belfort Rd PECK SE15 51 N14
Belfry Av DEN/HRF UB9 21 L13
Belfry Cl BERM/RHTH SE16 51 M10
BMLY BR1 76 K2
Belfry La RKW/CH/CXG WD3 21 N6
The Belfry REDH RH1 93 T9
Belgrade Rd HPTN TW12 58 K13
STNW/STAM N16 38 J9
Belgrave Av GPK RM2 42 J1
Belgrave Cl ACT W3 48 C7
MLHL NW7 24 D10
STHGT/OAK N14 26 A3
STMC/STPC BR5 77 S2
WOT/HER KT12 70 D9
Belgrave Crs SUN TW16 58 D13
Belgrave Dr KGLGY WD4 10 J2
Belgrave Gdns STAN HA7 23 S10
STHGT/OAK N14 26 B3
STJWD NW8 2 J2
Belgrave Mnr WOKS/MYFD GU22 80 C9
Belgrave Ms UX/CGN UB8 45 P2
Belgrave Ms South KTBR SW1X 7 T5
Belgrave Ms West KTBR SW1X 7 S5
Belgrave Pl KTBR SW1X 7 T6
Belgrave Rd BARN SW13 48 F12
HSLWW TW4 58 H1
IL IG1 40 H6
MTCM CR4 73 R1
PIM SW1V 8 B8
PLSTW E13 52 E2
SNWD SE25 74 K2
SUN TW16 58 D13
WALTH E17 39 S4
WAN E11 40 C6
Belgrave Sq KTBR SW1X 7 S5
Belgrave St WCHPL E1 51 P4
Belgrave Wk MTCM CR4 73 R1
Belgravia Cl BAR EN5 25 M1
Belgravia Gdns BMLY BR1 64 A11
Belgravia Ms KUT/HW KT1 71 T2
Belgrove St CAMTN NW1 4 E5
Belham Rd KGLGY WD4 10 F2
Belinda Rd BRXN/ST SW9 62 F1
Belitha Vls IS N1 38 E12
Bellamaine Cl THMD SE28 53 P7
Bellamy Cl EDGW HA8 24 C8
HGDN/ICK UB10 33 S9
POP/IOD E14 51 S7
WAT WD17 11 N13
WKENS W14 6 D10
Bellamy Dr STAN HA7 23 R13
Bellamy Rd CHES/WCR EN8 16 E3
CHING E4 27 T11
ENC/FH EN2 * 15 T14
Bellamy St BAL SW12 61 V5
Bel La FELT TW13 58 G8
Bellarmine Cl THMD SE28 53 P6
Bellasis Av BRXS/STRHM SW2 62 C6
Bell Av HARH RM3 30 H13
WDR/YW UB7 45 R8
Bell Bridge Rd CHERT KT16 68 K6
Bell Cl ABLGY WD5 11 M1
PIN HA5 34 E1
RDART DA2 67 T3
Bellclose Rd WDR/YW UB7 45 Q7
Bell Common EPP CM16 18 C6
Bell Crs COUL/CHIP CR5 85 V11
Bell Dr WAND/EARL SW18 61 L5
Bellefield Rd STMC/STPC BR5 77 R3
Bellefields Rd BRXN/ST SW9 62 D1
Bellegrove Cl WELL DA16 53 P14
Bellegrove Rd WELL DA16 53 N14
Bellenden Rd PECK SE15 50 K14
Belle Staines Pleasaunce CHING E4 27 S7
Belleville Rd BTSEA SW11 61 T3
Belle Vue GFD/PVL UB6 35 M13
Belle Vue Cl STA TW18 57 L13
Belle Vue La BUSH WD23 23 M6
Bellevue Pk THHTH CR7 74 G1
Bellevue Pl WCHPL E1 * 51 N2
Belle Vue Rd CRW RM5 30 C11
HDN NW4 36 K2
ORP BR6 76 J14
WALTH E17 27 V14
Bellevue Rd BARN SW13 48 G14
BXLYHS DA6 65 V3
EMPK RM11 43 M6
FBAR/BDGN N11 25 U9
KUT/HW KT1 71 U1
TOOT SW17 61 T5
WEA W13 47 R2
Belle Vue Ter DEN/HRF UB9 * 21 L12
Bellew St TOOT SW17 61 Q8
Bell Farm Av DAGE RM10 42 C8
Bellfield CROY/NA CR0 75 Q13
Bellfield Av KTN/HRWW/WS HA3 23 M11
Bellfield Cl BKHTH/KID SE3 52 D12
Bell Gdns LEY E10 * 39 S6
STMC/STPC BR5 77 S3
Bellgate Ms KTTN NW5 37 V9
Bell Gn SYD SE26 63 R9
Bell Green La SYD SE26 63 R10
Bellhouse La BRW CM14 31 S3
Bell House Rd ROMW/RG RM7 42 C6
Bellina Ms KTTN NW5 37 V9
Bellingham Dr REIG RH2 93 M10
Bellingham Gn CAT SE6 63 S8
Bellingham Rd CAT SE6 63 U8
Bell La ABLGY WD5 11 N2
CAN/RD E16 52 B6
HDN NW4 36 K2
LCOL/BKTW AL2 12 K3
LHD/OX KT22 83 M13
PEND EN3 16 D12
TWK TW1 59 Q6
WBLY HA9 * 35 T7
WCHPL E1 5 U10
Bell Lane Cl LHD/OX KT22 83 M13
Bellmarsh Rd ADL/WDHM KT15 69 M9
Bell Meadow GDST RH9 95 N8
NRWD SE19 62 J9
Bellmount Wood Av WAT WD17 11 L13
Bello Cl HNHL SE24 62 F6
Bellot St GNWCH SE10 52 A10
Bell Pde HSLW TW3 * 58 K2
WWKM BR4 * 75 U7
Bellring Cl BELV DA17 54 A11
Bell Rd E/WMO/HCT KT8 71 M3
EN EN1 15 T13
HSLW TW3 58 K2
The Bell Rbt LCOL/BKTW AL2 13 L1
Bells Hl BAR EN5 24 K3
Bells La DTCH/LGLY SL3 56 F1
Bell St BAY/PAD W2 3 N9
REIG RH2 93 N10
WOOL/PLUM SE18 52 G13
Bellswood La IVER SL0 44 F3
Belltrees Gv STRHM/NOR SW16 62 D10
Bell Water Ga WOOL/PLUM SE18 52 J8
Bellweir Cl STWL/WRAY TW19 56 F7
Bell Wharf La CANST EC4R 5 P14
Bellwood Rd PECK SE15 63 P2
Bell Yd LINN WC2A 4 J12
Bell Yard Ms STHWK SE1 9 T4
Belmont Av ALP/SUD HA0 35 V13
EBAR EN4 25 T3
ED N9 27 L6
NWDGN UB2 46 G8
NWMAL KT3 72 G3
PLMGR N13 26 C10
TOTM N17 38 G1
UPMR RM14 43 M7
WELL DA16 53 N14
Belmont Cir KTN/HRWW/WS HA3 * 23 R13
Belmont Cl CHING E4 27 V10
CLAP SW4 62 A1
EBAR EN4 25 T2
TRDG/WHET N20 25 P6
UX/CGN UB8 33 P11
WFD IG8 28 D9
Belmont Gv CHSWK W4 48 D9
LEW SE13 63 V1
Belmont Hl LEW SE13 63 V1
Belmont La CHST BR7 65 L10
STAN HA7 23 S12
Belmont Pde CHST BR7 * 64 K10
GLDGN NW11 * 37 M3
Belmont Pk LEW SE13 63 V2
Belmont Park Cl LEW SE13 64 A2
Belmont Park Rd LEY E10 39 T4
Belmont Ri BELMT SM2 85 N1
Belmont Rd BECK BR3 63 Q14
BELMT SM2 73 N14
BUSH WD23 22 G3
CHST BR7 64 K10
CLAP SW4 62 A1
ERITH DA8 54 B12
HCH RM12 42 K8
IL IG1 41 L8
KTN/HRWW/WS HA3 35 P1
LHD/OX KT22 83 Q12
REIG RH2 93 Q11
SEVS/STOTM N15 38 G2
SNWD SE25 75 M3
UX/CGN UB8 33 P12
WHTN TW2 59 M7
WLGTN SM6 74 A10
Belmont St CAMTN NW1 37 U12
Belmont Ter CHSWK W4 48 D9
Belmor BORE WD6 24 A3
Belmore Av WOKS/MYFD GU22 80 H6
YEAD UB4 46 C4
Belmore La HOLWY N7 38 B10
Belmore St VX/NE SW8 50 B13
Beloe Cl PUT/ROE SW15 60 G2
Belsham St HOM E9 39 N11
Belsize Av HAMP NW3 37 S10
PLMGR N13 26 D11
WEA W13 47 R8
Belsize Court Gdns HAMP NW3 37 R10
Belsize Crs HAMP NW3 37 R10
Belsize Gdns SUT SM1 73 P9
Belsize Gv HAMP NW3 37 S11
Belsize La HAMP NW3 37 R11
Belsize Ms HAMP NW3 * 37 R11
Belsize Pk HAMP NW3 37 R11
Belsize Park Gdns HAMP NW3 37 R11
Belsize Park Ms HAMP NW3 37 R11
Belsize Pl HAMP NW3 37 R10
Belsize Rd KIL/WHAMP NW6 2 G1
KIL/WHAMP NW6 37 Q12
KTN/HRWW/WS HA3 23 M12
Belsize Sq HAMP NW3 37 R11
Belsize Ter HAMP NW3 37 R11
Belson Rd WOOL/PLUM SE18 52 H9
Beltane Dr WIM/MER SW19 60 K8
Belthorn Crs BAL SW12 62 A5
Beltinge Rd HARH RM3 43 M1
Beltona Gdns CHES/WCR EN8 16 D1
Belton Rd FSTGT E7 40 D12
SCUP DA14 65 Q9
TOTM N17 38 J1
WAN E11 40 A9
WLSDN NW10 36 G11
Belton Wy BOW E3 51 S3
Beltran Rd FUL/PGN SW6 49 P14
Beltwood Rd BELV DA17 54 C9
Belvedere Av BARK/HLT IG6 28 K14
WIM/MER SW19 61 L10
Belvedere Buildings STHWK SE1 9 M4
Belvedere Cl ESH/CLAY KT10 70 K10
TEDD TW11 59 N10
WEY KT13 69 S10
Belvedere Ct BELV DA17 53 V8
OXHEY WD19 22 G4
Belvedere Dr WIM/MER SW19 61 L10
Belvedere Gdns E/WMO/HCT KT8 70 H3
LCOL/BKTW AL2 11 T1
Belvedere Gv WIM/MER SW19 61 L10
Belvedere Ms PECK SE15 63 N1
Belvedere Pl BRXS/STRHM SW2 62 D2
Belvedere Rd ABYW SE2 53 T6
BH/WHM TN16 88 H8
BRW CM14 31 T8
BXLYHN DA7 65 V1
HNWL W7 47 N8
LEY E10 39 Q6
NRWD SE19 62 K12
STHWK SE1 8 G3
Belvedere Sq WIM/MER SW19 61 L10
Belvedere Strd CDALE/KGS NW9 24 F14
The Belvedere WBPTN SW10 * 49 Q13
Belvedere Wy KTN/HRWW/WS HA3 35 U4
Belvoir Rd EDUL SE22 63 L5
Belvue Cl NTHLT UB5 34 J12
Belvue Rd NTHLT UB5 34 J12
Bembridge Cl KIL/WHAMP NW6 37 L12
Bembridge Gdns RSLP HA4 33 V7
Bembridge Pl GSTN WD25 * 11 N7
Bemerton Est IS N1 4 G1
Bemerton St IS N1 4 G1
Bemish Rd PUT/ROE SW15 60 K1
Bempton Dr RSLP HA4 34 D7
Bemsted Rd WALTH E17 39 R1
Benares Rd WOOL/PLUM SE18 53 P9
Benbow Moorings UX/CGN UB8 * 45 N3
Benbow Rd HMSMTH W6 48 H8
Benbow St DEPT SE8 51 S11
Benbow Wy UX/CGN UB8 45 N3
Benbury Cl BMLY BR1 63 U10
The Bence EGH TW20 68 F1
Bench Fld SAND/SEL CR2 74 K11
Bench Manor Crs CFSP/GDCR SL9 20 A14
The Bench RCHPK/HAM TW10 * 59 S8
Bencombe Rd PUR/KEN CR8 86 E4
Bencroft Rd STRHM/NOR SW16 62 A12
Bencurtis Pk WWKM BR4 75 V8
Bendall Ms CAMTN NW1 3 P9
Bendemeer Rd PUT/ROE SW15 60 K1
Bendish Rd EHAM E6 40 G12
Bendmore Av ABYW SE2 53 Q10
Bendon Va WAND/EARL SW18 61 P5
Bendysh Rd BUSH WD23 22 G1
Benedict Cl ORP BR6 77 N8
Benedict Dr EBED/NFELT TW14 57 V5
Benedictine Ga CHES/WCR EN8 16 E1
Benedict Rd BRXN/ST SW9 62 D1
MTCM CR4 73 R1
Benedict Wy EFNCH N2 * 37 Q1
Benedict Whf MTCM CR4 73 S1
Benenden Gn HAYES BR2 76 C3
Benen-Stock Rd STWL/WRAY TW19 57 L4
Benets Rd EMPK RM11 43 N6
Benett Gdns STRHM/NOR SW16 62 C14
Benfleet Cl COB KT11 82 G2
SUT SM1 73 Q8
Benfleet Wy FBAR/BDGN N11 25 U7
Bengal Rd IL IG1 40 K9
Bengarth Dr KTN/HRWW/WS HA3 23 M14
Bengarth Rd NTHLT UB5 34 F13
Bengeworth Rd CMBW SE5 62 G1
HRW HA1 35 Q7
Ben Hale Cl STAN HA7 23 Q10
Benham Cl CHSGTN KT9 71 S11
COUL/CHIP CR5 86 F8
Benham Gdns HSLWW TW4 58 H3
Benham Rd HNWL W7 47 N3
Benhill Av SUT SM1 73 Q9
Benhill Rd CMBW SE5 9 R14
SUT SM1 73 R8
Benhill Wood Rd SUT SM1 73 Q9
Benhilton Gdns SUT SM1 73 P8
Benhurst Av HCH RM12 42 H9
Benhurst Cl SAND/SEL CR2 75 P14
Benhurst Gdns SAND/SEL CR2 75 N14
Benhurst La STRHM/NOR SW16 62 E10
Beningfield Dr LCOL/BKTW AL2 12 F1
Benin St LEW SE13 63 V5
Benjafield Cl UED N18 27 M9
Benjamin Cl EMPK RM11 42 G4
HACK E8 39 L13
Benjamin Ms BAL SW12 62 A5
Benjamin St FARR EC1M 5 L9
Ben Jonson Rd WCHPL E1 51 Q3
Benledi St POP/IOD E14 51 V4
Benn Cl OXTED RH8 96 C10
Bennelong Cl SHB W12 48 H5
Bennerley Rd BTSEA SW11 61 T3
Bennet Cl KUT/HW KT1 59 S13
Bennetsfield Rd STKPK UB11 45 T6
Bennet's Hl BLKFR EC4V 5 M13
Bennett Cl COB KT11 82 C3
HSLWW TW4 58 G3
NTHWD HA6 22 B12
WELL DA16 53 Q14
Bennett Gv LEW SE13 51 T13
Bennett Pk BKHTH/KID SE3 64 B1
Bennett Rd BRXN/ST SW9 50 E14
CHDH RM6 41 U4
PLSTW E13 52 E2
Bennetts Av CROY/NA CR0 75 Q7
GFD/PVL UB6 35 N13
Bennett's Castle La BCTR RM8 41 S9
Bennetts Cl MTCM CR4 61 V13
TOTM N17 26 K11
Bennetts Copse CHST BR7 64 G11
Bennett St CHSWK W4 48 E11
WHALL SW1A 8 A1
Bennetts Wy CROY/NA CR0 75 Q7
Bennetts Yd UX/CGN UB8 33 P12
Bennett Wy RDART DA2 67 R9
Benningholme Rd EDGW HA8 24 E11
Bennington Rd TOTM N17 26 J13

WFD IG8 * 28 A12
Bennions Cl HCH RM12 42 K11
Bennison Dr HARH RM3 30 K14
Benn St HOM E9 39 Q11
Benrek Cl BARK/HLT IG6 29 L12
Bensbury Cl PUT/ROE SW15 60 H5
Bensham Cl THHTH CR7 74 G2
Bensham Gv THHTH CR7 62 G14
Bensham La THHTH CR7 74 F4
Bensham Manor Rd THHTH CR7 74 H3
Benskin Rd WATW WD18 22 C3
Benskins La ABR/ST RM4 30 K6
Bensley Cl FBAR/BDGN N11 25 T10
Ben Smith Wy BERM/RHTH SE16 51 L8
Benson Av PLSTW E13 40 E14
Benson Cl HSLW TW3 58 J2
UX/CGN UB8 45 Q3
Benson Quay WAP E1W 51 N5
Benson Rd CROY/NA CR0 74 E8
FSTH SE23 63 N6
Benthall Gdns PUR/KEN CR8 86 G6
Benthal Rd STNW/STAM N16 38 K7
Bentham Av WOKN/KNAP GU21 80 G5
Bentham Rd HOM E9 39 P11
THMD SE28 53 R6
Ben Tillet Cl BARK IG11 41 Q12
CAN/RD E16 * 52 H6
Bentinck Cl CFSP/GDCR SL9 32 B3
Bentinck Ms MHST W1U 3 T11
Bentinck Rd WDR/YW UB7 45 P6
Bentinck St MHST W1U 3 T11
Bentley Cl WIM/MER SW19 61 N9
Bentley Dr CRICK NW2 37 M8
GNTH/NBYPK IG2 41 L4
WEY KT13 69 S13
Bentley Heath La BAR EN5 14 A9
Bentley Ms EN EN1 26 H4
Bentley Rd IS N1 38 J11
Bentley's Meadow BGR/WK TN15 91 M10
Bentley Wy STAN HA7 23 Q10
WFD IG8 28 C8
Benton Rd IL IG1 41 M6
OXHEY WD19 22 F10
Benton's La WNWD SE27 62 G9
Benton's Ri WNWD SE27 62 H10
Bentry Cl BCTR RM8 41 U7
Bentry Rd BCTR RM8 41 U7
Bentworth Rd SHB W12 48 H4
Benwell Ct SUN TW16 * 58 C13
Benwell Rd HOLWY N7 38 E9
Benwick Cl BERM/RHTH SE16 51 M9
Benwood Ct SUT SM1 73 Q8
Benworth St BOW E3 51 R1
Benyon Rd IS N1 5 R1
Benyon Whf IS N1 5 T1
Beomonds Rw CHERT KT16 69 L5
Berberis Wk WDR/YW UB7 45 Q9
Berber Pde WOOL/PLUM SE18 * 52 G12
Berber Rd BTSEA SW11 * 61 T3
Berceau Wk WAT WD17 11 L13
Bercta Rd ELTH/MOT SE9 65 L7
Beredens La RBRW/HUT CM13 31 T14
Berenger Wk WBPTN SW10 * 7 L13
Berens Rd STMC/STPC BR5 77 S3
WLSDN NW10 48 K1
Berens Wy CHST BR7 77 P2
Beresford Av ALP/SUD HA0 36 A13
BRYLDS KT5 72 B6
HNWL W7 47 M3
SLN SL2 44 A5
TRDG/WHET N20 25 T7
TWK TW1 59 S4
Beresford Dr BMLY BR1 76 G1
WFD IG8 28 E9
Beresford Gdns CHDH RM6 41 U3
EN EN1 26 J2
HSLWW TW4 58 H3
Beresford Rd BELMT SM2 73 M12
CEND/HSY/T N8 38 E3
CHING E4 28 A6
EFNCH N2 37 S1
HBRY N5 38 H10
HRW HA1 35 M3
KUTN/CMB KT2 59 V13
NWMAL KT3 72 C2
RKW/CH/CXG WD3 20 K7
STHL UB1 46 F5
WALTH E17 27 T13
Beresford Sq WOOL/PLUM SE18 52 K9
Beresford St WOOL/PLUM SE18 52 K8
Beresford Ter HBRY N5 38 G10
Berestede Rd HMSMTH W6 48 F10
Bere St WAP E1W 51 P5
Berger Cl STMC/STPC BR5 77 M4
Berger Rd HOM E9 39 P11
Berghem Ms WKENS W14 48 K8
Bergholt Av REDBR IG4 40 G3
Bergholt Crs STNW/STAM N16 38 J5
Bergholt Ms CAMTN NW1 38 A12
Bering Sq POP/IOD E14 51 S10
Bering Wk CAN/RD E16 52 F4
Berisford Ms WAND/EARL SW18 61 Q4
Berkeley Av BXLYHN DA7 53 T13
CLAY IG5 28 J14
CRW RM5 30 C12
GFD/PVL UB6 35 N11
HSLWW TW4 46 C13
Berkeley Cl ABLGY WD5 11 M6
BORE WD6 24 A3
EMPK RM11 43 P7
KUTN/CMB KT2 59 U12
POTB/CUF EN6 14 B6
RSLP HA4 34 C8
STMC/STPC BR5 77 N5
STWL/WRAY TW19 56 H7
Berkeley Ct RKW/CH/CXG WD3 * 21 V3
WEY KT13 69 V7
WLGTN SM6 74 A8
Berkeley Crs DART DA1 67 M6
EBAR EN4 25 R3
Berkeley Dr E/WMO/HCT KT8 70 H1
EMPK RM11 43 N6
Berkeley Gdns BF/WBF KT14 80 K4
ESH/CLAY KT10 71 Q12
KENS W8 6 F2
WCHMH N21 26 H5
WOT/HER KT12 70 B5
Berkeley Ms MBLAR W1H 3 R11
SUN TW16 70 E1
Berkeley Pl EPSOM KT18 84 D6
WIM/MER SW19 60 K11
Berkeley Rd BARN SW13 48 G13
CDALE/KGS NW9 36 A2
CEND/HSY/T N8 38 B3
HGDN/ICK UB10 33 U12
MNPK E12 40 G10
SEVS/STOTM N15 38 H4
Berkeley Sq MYFR/PICC W1J 3 V14
The Berkeleys LHD/OX KT22 83 N14
SNWD SE25 * 75 L2
Berkeley St MYFR/PICC W1J 3 V14
Berkeley Waye HEST TW5 46 G12
Berkhampstead Rd BELV DA17 54 A10
Berkhamsted Av WBLY HA9 35 V11
Berkley Av CHES/WCR EN8 16 D8
Berkley Cl WHTN TW2 * 59 N8
Berkley Pl CHES/WCR EN8 * 16 D8
Berkley Rd CAMTN NW1 37 T12
Berks Hl RKW/CH/CXG WD3 20 G3
Berkshire Cl CTHM CR3 86 H12
Berkshire Gdns PLMGR N13 26 E11
UED N18 27 M10
Berkshire Rd HOM E9 39 R11
Berkshire Wy EMPK RM11 43 N3
MTCM CR4 74 C2
Bermans Wy WLSDN NW10 36 F9
Bermer Rd WATN WD24 11 Q13
Bermondsey St STHWK SE1 9 S2
Bermondsey Wall East
BERM/RHTH SE16 51 M7
Bermondsey Wall West STHWK SE1 51 L7
Bernal Cl THMD SE28 53 T5
Bernard Ashley Dr CHARL SE7 52 D10
Bernard Av WEA W13 47 R8
Bernard Cassidy St CAN/RD E16 52 B3
Bernard Gdns WIM/MER SW19 61 M10
Bernard Gv WAB EN9 16 H7
Bernard Rd ROMW/RG RM7 42 C5
SEVS/STOTM N15 38 K3
WLGTN SM6 73 V10
Bernards Cl BARK/HLT IG6 29 L12
Bernard St BMSBY WC1N 4 E8
Bernays Cl STAN HA7 23 S11
Bernay's Gv BRXN/ST SW9 62 D2
Bernel Dr CROY/NA CR0 75 R8
Berne Rd THHTH CR7 74 F3
Berners Dr WEA W13 47 Q5
Berners Ms FITZ W1T 4 B10
Berners Pl FITZ W1T 4 B11
Berners Rd IS N1 5 L3
WDGN N22 26 E13
Berners St FITZ W1T 4 B10
Berner Ter WCHPL E1 * 51 L4
Berney Rd CROY/NA CR0 74 H5
Bernhardt Crs STJWD NW8 3 N7
Bernhart Cl EDGW HA8 24 C12
Bernice Cl RAIN RM13 54 J2
Bernwell Rd CHING E4 28 A8
Berridge Gn EDGW HA8 24 A12
Berridge Ms KIL/WHAMP NW6 37 N10
Berridge Rd NRWD SE19 62 H10
Berriman Rd HOLWY N7 38 D8
Berrington Dr EHSLY KT24 82 B14
Berriton Rd RYLN/HDSTN HA2 34 H6
Berry Av WATN WD24 11 P10
Berrybank Cl CHING E4 27 U7
Berry Cl DAGE RM10 42 A10
HCH RM12 42 J10
RKW/CH/CXG WD3 21 M5
WCHMH N21 26 F6
Berry Cottages POP/IOD E14 * 51 Q4
Berry Ct HSLWW TW4 58 H3
Berrydale Rd YEAD UB4 46 G2
Berry Fld SLN SL2 44 A4
Berryfield Cl BMLY BR1 64 G13
Berry Field Cl WALTH E17 39 T2
Berryfield Rd WALW SE17 9 M9
Berry Grove La GSTN WD25 11 T12
Berrygrove La GSTN WD25 11 U13
Berryhill ELTH/MOT SE9 64 K2
Berry Hl STAN HA7 23 T9
Berryhill Gdns ELTH/MOT SE9 64 K2
Berrylands BRYLDS KT5 72 A3
ORP BR6 77 S8
RYNPK SW20 72 J1
Berrylands Rd BRYLDS KT5 71 V4
Berry La DUL SE21 62 H9
RKW/CH/CXG WD3 20 H4
RKW/CH/CXG WD3 21 M6
Berryman Cl BCTR RM8 41 S8
Berryman's La SYD SE26 63 P9
Berry Meade ASHTD KT21 83 V7
Berry Meade Cl ASHTD KT21 83 V7
Berrymead Gdns ACT W3 48 C6
Berrymede Rd CHSWK W4 48 D8
Berry Pl FSBYE EC1V 5 M6
Berryscroft Rd STA TW18 57 N12
Berry's Green Rd BH/WHM TN16 88 K6
Berry's Hl BH/WHM TN16 88 K5
Berry's La BF/WBF KT14 81 P1
Berry St FSBYE EC1V 5 M8
Berry Wk ASHTD KT21 83 V9
Berry Wy EA W5 47 U8
RKW/CH/CXG WD3 21 M5
Bertal Rd TOOT SW17 61 R9
Berther Rd EMPK RM11 43 L5
Berthold Ms WAB EN9 16 H7
Berthons Gdns WALTH E17 * 39 V3
Berthon St DEPT SE8 51 S12
Bertie Rd SYD SE26 63 P11
WLSDN NW10 36 G11
Bertram Rd EN EN1 27 L2
HDN NW4 36 G4
KUTN/CMB KT2 60 A12
Bertram St KTTN NW5 37 V8
Bertrand St LEW SE13 63 T1
Bertrand Wy THMD SE28 53 R5
Bert Rd THHTH CR7 74 G3
Bert Wy EN EN1 26 K2
Berwick Av YEAD UB4 46 F5
Berwick Cl CHES/WCR EN8 16 G8
STAN HA7 23 P11
WHTN TW2 58 J6
Berwick Crs BFN/LL DA15 65 N4
Berwick Gdns SUT SM1 73 Q8
Berwick La CHONG CM5 19 Q7
Berwick Pond Cl RAIN RM13 42 K14
Berwick Pond Rd RAIN RM13 43 L14
Berwick Rd BORE WD6 12 K12
CAN/RD E16 52 D4
RAIN RM13 42 K14
WDGN N22 26 F13
WELL DA16 53 R13
Berwick St SOHO/CST W1F 4 B12
Berwick Wy RSEV TN14 90 H11
Berwyn Av HSLW TW3 46 K13
Berwyn Rd HNHL SE24 62 F6
RCHPK/HAM TW10 60 B2
Beryl Av EHAM E6 52 G3
Beryl Rd HMSMTH W6 48 K10
Berystede KUTN/CMB KT2 60 B12
Besant Cl CRICK NW2 * 37 L8
Besant Pl EDUL SE22 62 K2
Besant Rd CRICK NW2 37 L9
Besant Wy WLSDN NW10 36 C10
Besley St STRHM/NOR SW16 62 A11
Bessant Dr RCH/KEW TW9 48 B13
Bessborough Gdns PIM SW1V 8 D9
Bessborough Pl PIM SW1V 8 C10
Bessborough Rd HRW HA1 35 M6
PUT/ROE SW15 60 G6
Bessborough St PIM SW1V 8 C9
Bessels Green Rd SEV TN13 90 D14
Bessels Meadow SEV TN13 90 D14
Bessemer Cl DTCH/LGLY SL3 44 D10
Bessemer Rd CMBW SE5 50 G14
Bessie Lansbury Cl EHAM E6 52 J4
Bessingby Rd RSLP HA4 34 C7
Besson St NWCR SE14 51 N13
Bessy St BETH E2 * 51 N1
Best Ter SWLY BR8 * 78 C3
Bestwood St DEPT SE8 51 P9
Beswick Ms KIL/WHAMP NW6 37 P10
Betam Rd HYS/HAR UB3 45 V7
Beta Rd WOKS/MYFD GU22 80 F6
Beta Wy EGH TW20 56 G13
Betchworth Cl SUT SM1 73 R10
Betchworth Rd GDMY/SEVK IG3 41 N7
Betchworth Wy CROY/NA CR0 75 U13
Betenson Av SEV TN13 90 F12
Betham Rd GFD/PVL UB6 47 M1
Bethany Pl WOKN/KNAP GU21 * 80 B8
Bethany Waye EBED/NFELT TW14 58 A5
Bethecar Rd HRW HA1 35 N3
Bethel Cl HDN NW4 36 K3
Bethell Av CAN/RD E16 52 B2
IL IG1 40 J5
Bethel Rd SEV TN13 90 J13
WELL DA16 65 S1
Bethersden Cl BECK BR3 63 R12
Bethnal Green Rd BETH E2 5 V7
Bethune Av FBAR/BDGN N11 25 T9
Bethune Rd STNW/STAM N16 38 H5
WLSDN NW10 48 D2
Bethwin Rd CMBW SE5 9 N13
Betjeman Cl CHESW EN7 16 A2
COUL/CHIP CR5 86 D7
RYLN/HDSTN HA2 34 J2
Betjeman Ct WDR/YW UB7 * 45 P6
Betley Ct WOT/HER KT12 70 D8
Betony Cl CROY/NA CR0 75 P6
Betoyne Av CHING E4 28 A9
Betsham Rd ERITH DA8 54 F12
Betstyle Rd FBAR/BDGN N11 25 V9
Betterton Dr SCUP DA14 65 U7
Betterton Rd RAIN RM13 42 E14
Betterton St LSQ/SEVD WC2H 4 E12
Bettles Cl UX/CGN UB8 33 N14
Bettons Pk SRTFD E15 40 A13
Bettridge Rd FUL/PGN SW6 49 M14
Betts Cl BECK BR3 63 Q14
Betts Ms WALTH E17 39 R4
Betts Rd CAN/RD E16 52 D4
Betts St WAP E1W 51 M5
Betts Wy PGE/AN SE20 63 M14
SURB KT6 71 R6
Betula Cl PUR/KEN CR8 86 H5
Betula Ter CHES/WCR EN8 * 16 E6
Between Streets COB KT11 82 D4
Beulah Av THHTH CR7 * 62 G14
Beulah Cl EDGW HA8 24 B8
Beulah Crs THHTH CR7 62 G14
Beulah Gv CROY/NA CR0 74 G4
Beulah Hl NRWD SE19 62 F11
Beulah Rd EPP CM16 18 E3
HCH RM12 42 J8
SUT SM1 73 N9
THHTH CR7 74 G1
WALTH E17 39 T3
WIM/MER SW19 61 M12
Beulah Wk CTHM CR3 87 Q10
Beult Rd DART DA1 66 G1
Bevan Av BARK IG11 41 Q12
Bevan Ct CROY/NA CR0 74 E10
Bevan House WATN WD24 11 R14
Bevan Pk EW KT17 84 F1
Bevan Pl SWLY BR8 78 F2
Bevan Rd ABYW SE2 53 R10
EBAR EN4 25 T2
Bevan St IS N1 5 P2
Bevan Wy HCH RM12 43 M9
Bev Callender Cl VX/NE SW8 61 V1
Bevenden St IS N1 5 R5
Beveridge Rd WLSDN NW10 36 E12
Beverley Av BFN/LL DA15 65 P5
HSLWW TW4 58 H2
RYNPK SW20 60 F13
Beverley Cl ADL/WDHM KT15 69 P10
BARN SW13 48 G14
BTSEA SW11 61 R2
CHSGTN KT9 71 S9
EMPK RM11 43 M5
EW KT17 84 J1
WCHMH N21 26 G6
WEY KT13 70 A7
Beverley Ct BROCKY SE4 63 R1
Beverley Crs WFD IG8 28 D13
Beverley Dr EDGW HA8 35 V1
Beverley Gdns BARN SW13 60 F1
CHESW EN7 15 V5
EMPK RM11 43 M5
GLDGN NW11 37 L5
STAN HA7 23 Q13
WBLY HA9 35 V6
WPK KT4 72 G6
Beverley Hts REIG RH2 93 P8
Beverley La KUTN/CMB KT2 60 E12
Beverley Rd BARN SW13 60 F1
BXLYHN DA7 54 C14
CHING E4 27 V11
CHSWK W4 48 F10
CTHM CR3 86 J7
DAGW RM9 41 U9
EHAM E6 52 F1
HAYES BR2 76 G7
KUT/HW KT1 59 S13
MTCM CR4 74 B2
NWDGN UB2 46 G9
NWMAL KT3 72 G2
PGE/AN SE20 63 M14
RSLP HA4 34 D7
SUN TW16 58 B13
WPK KT4 72 J7
Beverley Wy KUTN/CMB KT2 60 F13
Beverley Way (Kingston By-Pass)
RYNPK SW20 60 F13
The Beverly MRDN SM4 72 K4
Beversbrook Rd ARCH N19 38 B8
Beverstone Rd BRXS/STRHM SW2 62 D3
THHTH CR7 74 E2
Beverston Ms MBLAR W1H 3 Q10
Bevill Allen Cl TOOT SW17 61 T11
Bevill Cl SNWD SE25 75 L1
Bevin Cl BERM/RHTH SE16 51 Q6
Bevington Rd BECK BR3 63 T14
NKENS W10 2 B9
Bevington St BERM/RHTH SE16 51 L7
Bevin Rd YEAD UB4 46 C1
Bevin Sq TOOT SW17 61 T8
Bevin Wy FSBYW WC1X 4 J4
Bevis Cl RDART DA2 67 Q5
Bevis Marks HDTCH EC3A 5 T11
Bewcastle Gdns ENC/FH EN2 26 C2
Bewdley St IS N1 38 E12
Bewick Ms PECK SE15 51 M12
Bewick St VX/NE SW8 49 V14
Bewley Cl CHES/WCR EN8 16 D5
Bewley St WCHPL E1 51 M5
WIM/MER SW19 61 R11
Bewlys Rd WNWD SE27 62 F10
Bexhill Cl FELT TW13 58 G7
Bexhill Rd BROCKY SE4 63 R4
FBAR/BDGN N11 26 B10
MORT/ESHN SW14 60 C1
Bexley Cl DART DA1 66 E3
Bexley Gdns CHDH RM6 41 R3
ED N9 26 H8
Bexley High St BXLY DA5 66 A5
Bexley La DART DA1 66 E3
SCUP DA14 65 S7
Bexley Rd ELTH/MOT SE9 64 J4
ERITH DA8 54 C12
Beynon Rd CAR SM5 73 T10
Bianca Rd PECK SE15 9 V12
Bibsworth Rd FNCH N3 25 M14
Bibury Cl PECK SE15 9 T12
Bicester Rd RCH/KEW TW9 60 A1
Bickenhall St MHST W1U 3 R9
Bickersteth Rd TOOT SW17 61 T11
Bickerton Rd ARCH N19 37 V7
Bickles Yd STHWK SE1 9 T4
Bickley Crs BMLY BR1 76 G2
Bickley Park Rd BMLY BR1 76 H1
Bickley Rd BMLY BR1 64 F14
LEY E10 39 T5
Bickley St TOOT SW17 61 T10
Bicknell Rd CMBW SE5 62 G1
Bickney Wy LHD/OX KT22 83 L12
Bicknoller Cl BELMT SM2 73 P14
Bicknoller Rd EN EN1 15 V13
Bicknor Rd ORP BR6 77 N5
Bidborough Cl HAYES BR2 76 B3
Bidborough St STPAN WC1H 4 E6
Biddenden Wy ELTH/MOT SE9 64 J9
Biddenham Turn GSTN WD25 11 Q9
Bidder St CAN/RD E16 52 A3
Biddestone Rd HOLWY N7 38 D9
Biddulph Rd MV/WKIL W9 2 H6
SAND/SEL CR2 74 G13
Bideford Av GFD/PVL UB6 47 R1
Bideford Cl EDGW HA8 24 A13
FELT TW13 58 H8
HARH RM3 30 K13
Bideford Gdns EN EN1 26 J5
Bideford Rd BMLY BR1 64 B8
PEND EN3 16 F12
RSLP HA4 34 D8
WELL DA16 53 R12
Bidhams Crs KWD/TDW/WH KT20 84 J11
Bidwell Gdns FBAR/BDGN N11 26 A13
Bidwell St PECK SE15 * 51 M13
The Bield REIG RH2 93 N12
Big Common La REDH RH1 94 F9
Biggerstaff Rd SRTFD E15 39 U13
Biggerstaff St FSBYPK N4 38 E7
Biggin Av MTCM CR4 61 T13
Biggin Hl NRWD SE19 62 F12
Biggin Wy NRWD SE19 62 F12
Bigginwood Rd STRHM/NOR SW16 62 F12
Biggs Grove Rd CHESW EN7 15 U1
Bigg's Rw PUT/ROE SW15 60 K1
Bigland St WCHPL E1 51 M4
Bignell Rd WOOL/PLUM SE18 52 K10
Bignells Cnr POTB/CUF EN6 13 T8
Bignold Rd FSTGT E7 40 C9
Big St CLPT E5 39 M6
Bigwood Rd GLDGN NW11 37 P4
Biko Cl UX/CGN UB8 45 N4
Billet La DTCH/LGLY SL3 44 F4
EMPK RM11 42 K6
Billet Rd CHDH RM6 41 S1
WALTH E17 27 P13
Billetts Hart Cl HNWL W7 47 N7
Bill Hamling Cl ELTH/MOT SE9 64 H7
Billingford Cl BROCKY SE4 63 P2
Billing Pl WBPTN SW10 6 H13
Billing Rd WBPTN SW10 6 H13
Billings Cl DAGW RM9 41 S12
Billing St WBPTN SW10 6 H13
Billington Hl CROY/NA CR0 74 H7
Billington Rd NWCR SE14 51 P12
Billiter Sq FENCHST EC3M * 5 T12
Billiter St FENCHST EC3M 5 T12
Bill Nicholson Wy TOTM N17 26 K12
Billockby Cl CHSGTN KT9 71 V11
Billson St POP/IOD E14 51 U9
Billy Lows La POTB/CUF EN6 14 E5
Bilton Centre LHD/OX KT22 * 83 P9
Bilton Rd ERITH DA8 54 G12
GFD/PVL UB6 35 R13
Bilton Wy HYS/HAR UB3 46 D7
PEND EN3 16 F13
Bina Gdns ECT SW5 6 J8
Bincote Rd ENC/FH EN2 26 D1
Binden Rd SHB W12 48 F8
Binfield Rd BF/WBF KT14 81 Q2
CLAP SW4 50 C13
SAND/SEL CR2 74 K10
Bingfield St IS N1 4 G1
Bingham Cl SOCK/AV RM15 55 V4
Bingham Ct IS N1 * 38 F12
Bingham Dr STA TW18 57 P12
Bingham Pl CAMTN NW1 3 S8
Bingham Rd CROY/NA CR0 75 L6
Bingham St IS N1 38 H11
Bingley Rd CAN/RD E16 52 E4
GFD/PVL UB6 47 L2
SUN TW16 58 C12
Binney St MYFR/PKLN W1K 3 T13
Binns Rd CHSWK W4 48 E10
Binsey Wk ABYW SE2 53 S7
Binstead Cl YEAD UB4 46 G3
Binyon Crs STAN HA7 23 P10
Birbetts Rd ELTH/MOT SE9 64 H7
Birchanger Rd SNWD SE25 75 L3
Birch Av CTHM CR3 86 H14
LHD/OX KT22 83 P10
PLMGR N13 26 G8
WDR/YW UB7 45 R4
Birch Cl ADL/WDHM KT15 69 P13
BKHH IG9 28 F8
BTFD TW8 47 R12
CAN/RD E16 52 A3
EYN DA4 78 K8
HSLW TW3 59 M1
IVER SL0 32 H14
ROMW/RG RM7 42 B1
SEV TN13 90 H13
TEDD TW11 59 Q10
WOKN/KNAP GU21 80 A9
Birch Copse LCOL/BKTW AL2 11 S4
Birch Ct WLGTN SM6 73 V9
Birch Crs EMPK RM11 43 L2
HGDN/ICK UB10 33 R13
Birchcroft Cl CTHM CR3 94 G1
Birchdale CFSP/GDCR SL9 32 B6
Birchdale Cl BF/WBF KT14 81 N1
Birchdale Gdns CHDH RM6 41 T5
Birchdale Rd FSTGT E7 40 E10
Birchdene Dr THMD SE28 53 Q7
Birch Dr RKW/CH/CXG WD3 20 H10
Birchen Cl CDALE/KGS NW9 36 D7
Birchend Cl SAND/SEL CR2 74 H11
Birchen Gv CDALE/KGS NW9 36 D7
Birches Cl EPSOM KT18 84 E5
MTCM CR4 73 T1
PIN HA5 34 G3
The Birches BUSH WD23 23 L3
CHARL SE7 52 D11
CMBW SE5 * 62 J1
HSLWW TW4 * 58 H5
ORP BR6 76 J9
SWLY BR8 66 E14
WAB EN9 17 M8
WCHMH N21 26 D4
WOKS/MYFD GU22 80 D8
Birchfield Cl ADL/WDHM KT15 69 M9
COUL/CHIP CR5 86 D6
Birchfield Gv EW KT17 72 J14
Birchfield Rd CHES/WCR EN8 16 B3
Birchfield St POP/IOD E14 51 S5
Birch Gdns DAGE RM10 42 C8
Birchgate Ms KWD/TDW/WH KT20 * 84 J11
Birch Gn STA TW18 56 K9
Birch Gv ACT W3 48 A6
Birchgrove COB KT11 82 E4
Birch Gv COB KT11 82 F5
KWD/TDW/WH KT20 85 M14
LEE/GVPK SE12 64 B5
POTB/CUF EN6 14 C6
SHPTN TW17 58 A14
WAN E11 40 A8
WELL DA16 65 Q2
WOKS/MYFD GU22 80 H5
Birch Hl CROY/NA CR0 75 P10
Birchin Cross Rd RSEV TN14 91 L5
Birchington Cl BXLYHN DA7 54 B13
Birchington Rd BRYLDS KT5 71 V5
CEND/HSY/T N8 38 B4
KIL/WHAMP NW6 2 F1
Birchin La BANK EC3V 5 R12
Birchlands Av BAL SW12 61 T5
Birch La PUR/KEN CR8 86 C1
Birch Md ORP BR6 76 J7
Birchmead WAT WD17 11 M12
Birchmead Av PIN HA5 34 E2
Birchmere Rw BKHTH/KID SE3 52 B14
Birchmore Wk HBRY N5 38 G8
Birch Pk KTN/HRWW/WS HA3 23 L12
Birch Pl RDART DA2 67 S4
Birch Rd FELT TW13 58 F10
ROMW/RG RM7 42 B1
Birch Rw HAYES BR2 76 J5
Birch Tree Av WWKM BR4 76 B10
Birch Tree Wk WAT WD17 11 M11
Birch Tree Wy CROY/NA CR0 75 M7
Birch V COB KT11 82 J3
Birch Wk BORE WD6 * 13 L13
MTCM CR4 61 V13
Birchway BGR/WK TN15 79 T13
HYS/HAR UB3 46 C6
Birch Wy LCOL/BKTW AL2 12 H1
Birchway REDH RH1 93 V12
Birch Wy WARL CR6 87 Q8
Birchwood RAD WD7 13 L8
Birchwood Av BECK BR3 75 R2
MUSWH N10 37 U1
SCUP DA14 65 R8
WLGTN SM6 73 U8
Birchwood Cl MRDN SM4 73 P2
Birchwood Ct EDGW HA8 24 C14
Birchwood Dr BF/WBF KT14 81 L2
HAMP NW3 37 P8
RDART DA2 66 E9
Birchwood Gv HPTN TW12 58 J11
Birchwood La CTHM CR3 94 F1
ESH/CLAY KT10 71 M13
RSEV TN14 89 V5
Birchwood Park Av SWLY BR8 78 F1
Birchwood Rd BF/WBF KT14 81 L2
STMC/STPC BR5 77 M2
SWLY BR8 66 C12
TOOT SW17 61 V10
Birchwood Ter SWLY BR8 * 66 C13
Birchwood Wy LCOL/BKTW AL2 11 V2
Birdbrook Cl DAGE RM10 42 C12
Birdbrook Rd BKHTH/KID SE3 64 E1
Birdcage Wk WESTW SW1E 8 B4
Birdham Cl BMLY BR1 76 G3
Bird House La ORP BR6 88 J4
Birdhurst Av SAND/SEL CR2 74 H9
Birdhurst Gdns SAND/SEL CR2 74 H9
Birdhurst Ri SAND/SEL CR2 74 J10
Birdhurst Rd SAND/SEL CR2 74 J10
WAND/EARL SW18 61 Q3
WIM/MER SW19 61 S11
Bird in Bush Rd PECK SE15 51 L12
Bird-in-Hand La BMLY BR1 64 F14
Bird-in-Hand Ms FSTH SE23 63 N7
Bird-in-Hand Pas FSTH SE23 63 N7
Bird La UPMR RM14 43 R3
Birds Farm Av CRW RM5 30 B13
Birdsfield La BOW E3 39 R13
Birds Hill Dr LHD/OX KT22 83 N3
Birds Hill Ri LHD/OX KT22 83 M3
Birds Hill Rd LHD/OX KT22 83 M2
Bird St MHST W1U 3 T12
Bird Wk WHTN TW2 58 H6
Birdwood Cl SAND/SEL CR2 87 N1
TEDD TW11 59 N9
Birkbeck Av ACT W3 48 C5
GFD/PVL UB6 35 L13
Birkbeck Gv ACT W3 48 D7
Birkbeck Hl DUL SE21 62 F7
Birkbeck Ms ACT W3 * 48 D5
HACK E8 38 K10
Birkbeck Pl DUL SE21 62 F6
Birkbeck Rd ACT W3 48 D6
BECK BR3 63 P14
CEND/HSY/T N8 38 C2
EA W5 47 S9
ENC/FH EN2 15 T13
GNTH/NBYPK IG2 41 M3
HACK E8 38 K10
MLHL NW7 24 F10
NFNCH/WDSPK N12 25 Q10
ROMW/RG RM7 42 D6
SCUP DA14 65 Q8
TOTM N17 26 K13
WIM/MER SW19 61 P11
Birkbeck St BETH E2 51 M1
Birkbeck Wy GFD/PVL UB6 35 M13
Birkdale Av HARH RM3 31 N12
PIN HA5 34 J1
Birkdale Cl BERM/RHTH SE16 51 M10
ORP BR6 77 M6
THMD SE28 53 S4
Birkdale Gdns CROY/NA CR0 75 P9
OXHEY WD19 22 F8
Birkdale Rd ABYW SE2 53 Q9
EA W5 47 U2
Birkenhead Av KUTN/CMB KT2 59 V14
Birkenhead St CAMTN NW1 4 F5
Birkett Wy CSTG HP8 20 B1
Birkhall Rd CAT SE6 63 V6
Birkheads Rd REIG RH2 93 N9
Birkwood Cl BAL SW12 62 B5
Birley Rd TRDG/WHET N20 25 Q7
Birley St BTSEA SW11 49 U14
Birling Rd ERITH DA8 54 D12
Birnam Rd FSBYPK N4 38 D7
Birnham Cl RPLY/SEND GU23 81 L14
Birse Crs WLSDN NW10 36 E9
Birstal Gn OXHEY WD19 22 F9
Birstall Rd SEVS/STOTM N15 38 J3
Biscay Rd HMSMTH W6 48 K10
Biscoe Cl HEST TW5 46 J11
Biscoe Wy LEW SE13 * 63 V2
Bisenden Rd CROY/NA CR0 74 J7
Bisham Cl CAR SM5 73 T6
Bisham Gdns HGT N6 37 U6
Bishop Butt Cl ORP BR6 77 P8
Bishop Ct ABLGY WD5 11 M5
Bishop Duppas Pk SHPTN TW17 69 V5
Bishop Fox Wy E/WMO/HCT KT8 70 H2
Bishop Ken Rd KTN/HRWW/WS HA3 23 P14
Bishop Kings Rd WKENS W14 6 B7
Bishop Rd STHGT/OAK N14 25 V6
Bishops Av BMLY BR1 76 E1
BORE WD6 23 V3
CHDH RM6 41 S4
FUL/PGN SW6 48 K14
NTHWD HA6 22 A9
PLSTW E13 40 D13
The Bishops Av EFNCH N2 37 R4
Bishop's Bridge Rd BAY/PAD W2 2 H11
Bishop's Cl ARCH N19 38 A8
BAR EN5 24 K4
CHSWK W4 48 C10
COUL/CHIP CR5 86 E8
ELTH/MOT SE9 65 L7
EN EN1 16 B14
HGDN/ICK UB10 33 S14
RCHPK/HAM TW10 59 T8
SUT SM1 73 N8
WALTH E17 39 T2
Bishops Ct CHES/WCR EN8 * 16 B4
RDART DA2 67 T3
STP EC4M 5 L11
Bishops Dr EBED/NFELT TW14 57 V4
NTHLT UB5 34 G13
Bishopsford Rd MRDN SM4 73 R4
Bishopsgate LVPST EC2M 5 T10
Bishopsgate Ar LVPST EC2M 5 S10
Bishops Gn BMLY BR1 * 64 E13
Bishops Gv EFNCH N2 37 S4
HPTN TW12 58 H9
Bishop's Hall KUT/HW KT1 59 T14
Bishop's Hall Rd BRWN CM15 31 V4
Bishops Hl WOT/HER KT12 70 C5
Bishopsmead Cl HOR/WEW KT19 72 D14
Bishop's Park Rd FUL/PGN SW6 48 K14
STRHM/NOR SW16 62 C13
Bishop's Pl SUT SM1 73 Q10
Bishop's Rd CROY/NA CR0 74 F5
FUL/PGN SW6 6 C14
FUL/PGN SW6 49 M13
HGT N6 37 U4
HNWL W7 47 N7
HYS/HAR UB3 45 U4
Bishops Ter LBTH SE11 8 K7
Bishopsthorpe Rd SYD SE26 63 N9
Bishop St IS N1 5 N1
Bishops Wk CHST BR7 65 L13
CROY/NA CR0 75 P10
Bishop's Wy BETH E2 39 N14
EGH TW20 56 H11
Bishopswood Rd HGT N6 37 T5
Bishop Wy WLSDN NW10 36 E12
Biskra WAT WD17 11 N13
Bisley Cl CHES/WCR EN8 16 D7
WPK KT4 72 J6
Bispham Rd WLSDN NW10 47 V1
Bisson Rd SRTFD E15 39 U14
Bistern Av WALTH E17 39 V1
Bittacy Cl MLHL NW7 24 K11
Bittacy Hl MLHL NW7 24 K11
Bittacy Park Av MLHL NW7 24 K11
Bittacy Ri MLHL NW7 24 K11
Bittacy Rd MLHL NW7 24 K11
Bittams La CHERT KT16 68 H9
Bittern Cl YEAD UB4 46 F3
Bittern Pl WDGN N22 * 26 D14
Bittern St STHWK SE1 9 N3
Bittoms Ct KUT/HW KT1 * 71 T1
The Bittoms KUT/HW KT1 71 T1
Bixley Cl NWDGN UB2 46 H9
Blackacre Rd EPP CM16 18 C11
Blackall St SDTCH EC2A 5 S7
Blackberry Cl SHPTN TW17 70 A2
Blackberry Farm Cl HEST TW5 46 G12
Blackberry Fld STMC/STPC BR5 65 Q13
Blackbird Hl WBLY HA9 36 C7
Blackbirds La GSTN WD25 12 B9
Blackbird Yd BETH E2 5 V5
Blackborne Rd DAGE RM10 42 A11
Blackborough Cl REIG RH2 93 Q10
Blackborough Rd REIG RH2 93 R10
Black Boy La SEVS/STOTM N15 38 G3
Black Boy Wd LCOL/BKTW AL2 11 U4
Blackbridge Rd WOKS/MYFD GU22 80 B10
Blackbrook La HAYES BR2 76 J3
Blackburne's Ms MYFR/PKLN W1K 3 S13
Blackburn Rd KIL/WHAMP NW6 37 P11
The Blackburn GT/LBKH KT23 82 H14
Blackbury Cl POTB/CUF EN6 14 E5
Blackbush Av CHDH RM6 41 T3
Blackbush Cl BELMT SM2 73 P12
Blackdale CHESW EN7 16 A1
Black Ditch Rd WAB EN9 * 16 J10
Black Ditch Wy WAB EN9 16 H10
Blackdown Av WOKS/MYFD GU22 80 J5
Blackdown Cl EFNCH N2 25 Q14
WOKS/MYFD GU22 80 G6
Blackdown Ter WOOL/PLUM SE18 * 52 H13
Black Eagle Cl BH/WHM TN16 97 L3
Blackenham Rd TOOT SW17 61 T9
Blackett Cl EGH TW20 56 K14
Blackett St PUT/ROE SW15 60 K1
Blacketts Wood Dr RKW/CH/CXG WD3 20 G2
Black Fan Cl ENC/FH EN2 15 S13
Blackfen Pde BFN/LL DA15 * 65 Q4
Blackfen Rd BFN/LL DA15 65 P3
Blackford Cl SAND/SEL CR2 74 F13
Blackford Rd OXHEY WD19 22 F10
Blackfriars Br STHWK SE1 5 L14
Black Friars La BLKFR EC4V 5 L12
Blackfriars Pas BLKFR EC4V 5 L13
Blackfriars Rd STHWK SE1 9 L1
Blackfriars U/P BLKFR EC4V 5 M13
Black Green Wood Cl LCOL/BKTW AL2 11 V3
Blackhall La BGR/WK TN15 91 L13
Blackheath Av GNWCH SE10 51 V12
Blackheath Gv BKHTH/KID SE3 52 B14
Blackheath Hl GNWCH SE10 51 U13
Blackheath Pk BKHTH/KID SE3 64 B1
Blackheath Ri LEW SE13 51 U14
Blackheath Rd GNWCH SE10 51 T13
Blackheath V BKHTH/KID SE3 52 A14
Blackhills ESH/CLAY KT10 70 H13
Black Horse Ct STHWK SE1 * 9 R6
Blackhorse La CROY/NA CR0 75 L5
KWD/TDW/WH KT20 93 P5
POTB/CUF EN6 13 Q4
WALTH E17 39 P1
Black Horse Pde PIN HA5 * 34 D3
Blackhorse Pl UX/CGN UB8 33 M13
Blackhorse Rd DEPT SE8 51 Q11
Black Horse Rd SCUP DA14 65 Q9
Blackhorse Rd WALTH E17 39 P2
Blacklands Dr YEAD UB4 45 U2
Blacklands Meadow REDH RH1 94 C9
Blacklands Rd CAT SE6 63 U9
Blacklands Ter CHEL SW3 7 Q8
Blackley Cl WAT WD17 11 M11
Black Lion Ga BAY/PAD W2 2 H14
Black Lion Hl RAD WD7 12 J6
Black Lion La HMSMTH W6 48 G9
Blackmans Cl DART DA1 66 J6
Blackman's La WARL CR6 88 A4
Blackmans Yd WCHPL E1 * 5 V7
Blackmead SEV TN13 90 E11
Blackmoor La WATW WD18 21 V3
Blackmore Av STHL UB1 47 M6
Blackmore Ct WAB EN9 17 N7
Blackmore Crs WOKN/KNAP GU21 80 G4
Blackmore Dr WLSDN NW10 36 B12
Blackmore Rd BKHH IG9 28 G5
Blackmore's Gv TEDD TW11 59 Q11
Blackmore Wy UX/CGN UB8 33 P11
Blackness Cottages HAYES BR2 * 76 F13
Blackness La HAYES BR2 76 F13
WOKS/MYFD GU22 80 C9
Black Park Rd DTCH/LGLY SL3 44 D1
Blackpool Gdns YEAD UB4 46 A2
Blackpool Rd PECK SE15 51 M14
Black Prince Cl BF/WBF KT14 81 R4
Black Prince Rd LBTH SE11 8 H8
Black Rod Cl HYS/HAR UB3 46 B8
Blackrurn Wy HSLWW TW4 58 G3
Blackshaw Rd TOOT SW17 61 R10
Blacksmith Cl ASHTD KT21 83 V9
CHDH RM6 41 S4
Blacksmith Rw DTCH/LGLY SL3 44 E9
Blacksmiths Hl SAND/SEL CR2 87 M3
Blacksmiths La CHERT KT16 69 L5
DEN/HRF UB9 32 H7
RAIN RM13 42 F13
STA TW18 69 M1
STMC/STPC BR5 77 S3
Black's Rd HMSMTH W6 48 J10
Blackstock Rd FSBYPK N4 38 F7
Blackstone Cl REDH RH1 93 S11
Blackstone Est HACK E8 39 L12
Blackstone Hl REDH RH1 93 S10
Blackstone Rd CRICK NW2 36 J10
Black Swan Yd STHWK SE1 9 S3
Blackthorn Av WDR/YW UB7 45 S9
Blackthorn Cl BGR/WK TN15 79 T13
GSTN WD25 11 P6
REIG RH2 93 Q12
Blackthorn Ct HEST TW5 46 G12
Blackthorn Dell DTCH/LGLY SL3 44 A8
Blackthorne Av CROY/NA CR0 75 N6
Blackthorne Crs DTCH/LGLY SL3 44 J14
Blackthorne Dr CHING E4 27 V9
Blackthorne Rd DTCH/LGLY SL3 56 J1
Blackthorn Gv BXLYHN DA7 65 U1
Blackthorn Rd BH/WHM TN16 88 G6
IL IG1 41 M10
REIG RH2 93 Q12
Blackthorn St BOW E3 51 S2
Blacktree Ms BRXN/ST SW9 * 62 E1
Blackwall La GNWCH SE10 52 A10
Blackwall Tunnel Ap POP/IOD E14 51 U5
Blackwall Tunnel Northern Ap
BOW E3 39 S13
BOW E3 51 T1
POP/IOD E14 51 U4
Blackwall Wy POP/IOD E14 51 U5
Blackwater Cl FSTGT E7 40 B9
RAIN RM13 54 D3
Blackwater St EDUL SE22 62 K3
Blackwell Cl CLPT E5 39 Q9
KTN/HRWW/WS HA3 23 M12
Blackwell Dr OXHEY WD19 22 E4
Blackwell Gdns EDGW HA8 24 A9
Blackwell Rd KGLGY WD4 10 G3
Blackwood Cl BF/WBF KT14 81 N2
Blackwood St WALW SE17 9 Q9
Bladen Cl WEY KT13 69 V11
Blades Cl LHD/OX KT22 83 T10
Bladindon Dr BXLY DA5 65 T5
Bladon Gdns RYLN/HDSTN HA2 34 K4
Blagden's La STHGT/OAK N14 26 B7
Blagdon Rd CAT SE6 63 T4
NWMAL KT3 72 F2
Blagdon Wk TEDD TW11 59 S11
Blagrove Rd NKENS W10 2 B10
Blair Av CDALE/KGS NW9 36 E5
ESH/CLAY KT10 71 L7
Blair Cl BFN/LL DA15 65 N3
HYS/HAR UB3 46 C9
IS N1 38 G11
Blairderry Rd BRXS/STRHM SW2 62 C7
Blair Dr SEV TN13 90 H13
Blairhead Dr OXHEY WD19 22 D8
Blair St POP/IOD E14 51 U4
Blake Av BARK IG11 41 N13
Blake Cl CAR SM5 73 S6
NKENS W10 48 J3
RAIN RM13 42 F13
WELL DA16 53 N13
Blakeden Dr ESH/CLAY KT10 71 P12
Blake Gdns DART DA1 67 M2
FUL/PGN SW6 49 N13
Blakehall Rd CAR SM5 73 T11
Blake Hall Rd WAN E11 40 C6
Blake Ms RCH/KEW TW9 48 A13
Blakemore Gdns BARN SW13 48 H11
Blakemore Rd STRHM/NOR SW16 62 C8
THHTH CR7 74 D3
Blakemore Wy BELV DA17 53 U8
Blakeney Av BECK BR3 63 R13
Blakeney Cl CAMTN NW1 4 C3
HACK E8 39 L10
HOR/WEW KT19 84 D1
TRDG/WHET N20 25 Q6
Blakeney Rd BECK BR3 63 R13
Blaker Ct CHARL SE7 * 52 E12
Blake Rd CAN/RD E16 52 B2
CROY/NA CR0 74 J7
FBAR/BDGN N11 26 A12
MTCM CR4 73 S1
Blaker Rd SRTFD E15 39 U13
Blakes Av NWMAL KT3 72 F3
Blakes Cl WLSDN NW10 36 G11
Blake's Gn WWKM BR4 75 U6
Blakes La NWMAL KT3 72 F3
Blakesley Av EA W5 47 S4
Blake's Rd PECK SE15 9 T13
Blakes Ter NWMAL KT3 72 G3
Blakesware Gdns ED N9 26 H5
Blakewood Cl FELT TW13 58 E9
Blanchard Cl ELTH/MOT SE9 64 G8
Blanchard Dr WATW WD18 22 A2
Blanchard Gv PEND EN3 16 G12
Blanchard Ms HARH RM3 31 M12
Blanchard Wy HACK E8 * 39 L11
Blanch Cl PECK SE15 51 N12
Blanchedowne CMBW SE5 62 H2
Blanche La BAR EN5 13 S9
Blanche St CAN/RD E16 52 B2
Blanchland Rd MRDN SM4 73 P3
Blanchman's Rd WARL CR6 87 Q8
Blandfield Rd BAL SW12 61 U5
Blandford Av BECK BR3 63 Q14
WHTN TW2 58 K6
Blandford Cl CROY/NA CR0 74 C8
DTCH/LGLY SL3 44 B8
EFNCH N2 37 Q3
ROMW/RG RM7 42 B2
WOKS/MYFD GU22 80 F7
Blandford Crs CHING E4 27 U5
Blandford Ms REIG RH2 93 R10
Blandford Rd BECK BR3 63 P14
CHSWK W4 48 E8
EA W5 47 T7
NWDGN UB2 46 H9
TEDD TW11 59 M10
Blandford Rd North DTCH/LGLY SL3 44 B8
Blandford Rd South DTCH/LGLY SL3 44 B9
Blandford Sq CAMTN NW1 3 P8
Blandford St MHST W1U 3 R11
Blandford Waye YEAD UB4 46 E4
Bland St ELTH/MOT SE9 64 F2
Blaney Crs EHAM E6 52 K1
Blanford Rd REIG RH2 93 Q11
Blanmerle Rd ELTH/MOT SE9 64 K6
Blann Cl ELTH/MOT SE9 64 F4
Blantyre St WBPTN SW10 7 L13
Blantyre Wk WBPTN SW10 * 7 L13
Blashford St CAT SE6 63 V5
Blattner Cl BORE WD6 23 U2
Blawith Rd HRW HA1 35 N2
Blaydon Cl RSLP HA4 34 A5
TOTM N17 * 27 M12
Blaydon Wk TOTM N17 27 M12
Blays Cl EGH TW20 56 A11
Bleak Hill La WOOL/PLUM SE18 53 P11
Blean Gv PGE/AN SE20 63 N12
Bleasdale Av GFD/PVL UB6 35 Q14
Blechynden Gdns NKENS W10 48 K5
Blechynden St NKENS W10 * 48 K5
Bledlow Cl THMD SE28 53 S5
Bledlow Ri GFD/PVL UB6 35 L14
Bleeding Heart Yd HCIRC EC1N * 4 K10
Blegborough Rd STRHM/NOR SW16 62 A11
Blendon Dr BXLY DA5 65 T4
Blendon Rd BXLY DA5 65 T4
Blendon Ter WOOL/PLUM SE18 53 L11
Blendworth Wy PECK SE15 9 T13
Blenheim CDALE/KGS NW9 * 24 F14
Blenheim Av GNTH/NBYPK IG2 40 J4
Blenheim Cl BF/WBF KT14 80 K3
DART DA1 66 J4
GFD/PVL UB6 * 35 M14
OXHEY WD19 22 F5
ROMW/RG RM7 42 C2
RYNPK SW20 72 J1
UPMR RM14 43 S6
WCHMH N21 26 G6
WLGTN SM6 74 A12
Blenheim Ct ARCH N19 38 C7
BFN/LL DA15 65 M8
WFD IG8 28 D12
Blenheim Crs NTGHL W11 2 B12
RSLP HA4 33 V7
SAND/SEL CR2 74 G12
Blenheim Dr WELL DA16 53 P13
Blenheim Gdns BRXS/STRHM SW2 62 D4
CRICK NW2 36 J10
KUTN/CMB KT2 60 B13
SAND/SEL CR2 87 L2
SOCK/AV RM15 55 P6
WBLY HA9 35 U8
WLGTN SM6 74 A11
Blenheim Gv PECK SE15 50 K14
Blenheim Pde HGDN/ICK UB10 * 45 T2
Blenheim Park Rd SAND/SEL CR2 74 G13
Blenheim Pas STJWD NW8 * 2 J3
Blenheim Pl TEDD TW11 59 P10
Blenheim Ri SEVS/STOTM N15 * 38 K2
Blenheim Rd BAR EN5 24 K1
BFN/LL DA15 65 S6
BMLY BR1 76 G2
BRWN CM15 31 U4
CHSWK W4 48 E8
DART DA1 66 J4
DTCH/LGLY SL3 44 B9
EHAM E6 52 F1
HOR/WEW KT19 84 D1
NTHLT UB5 34 K11
ORP BR6 77 S7
PGE/AN SE20 63 N12
RYLN/HDSTN HA2 34 K4
RYNPK SW20 72 J1
SRTFD E15 40 A9
STJWD NW8 2 K3
SUT SM1 73 N8
WALTH E17 39 P1
Blenheim St CONDST W1S 3 U12
Blenheim Ter STJWD NW8 2 J3
Blenheim Wy EPP CM16 19 L1
ISLW TW7 47 Q13
Blenhiem Rd ABLGY WD5 11 N7
Blenkarne Rd BTSEA SW11 61 T4
Bleriot Rd HEST TW5 46 E12
Blessbury Rd EDGW HA8 24 C13
Blessington Rd LEW SE13 63 V2
Blessing Wy BARK IG11 41 S14
Bletchingley Cl REDH RH1 94 A5
THHTH CR7 74 F2
Bletchingley Rd GDST RH9 95 L7
REDH RH1 94 A5
Bletchley St IS N1 5 P4
Bletchmore Cl HYS/HAR UB3 45 V11
Bletsoe Wk IS N1 5 P3
Blincoe Cl WIM/MER SW19 60 K7
Blinco La DTCH/LGLY SL3 44 C4
Blindman's La CHES/WCR EN8 16 D4
Blissett St GNWCH SE10 51 U13
Bliss Ms NKENS W10 * 2 B5
Blisworth Cl YEAD UB4 46 G2
Blithbury Rd DAGW RM9 41 R11
Blithdale Rd ABYW SE2 53 Q9
Blithfield St KENS W8 6 G6
Blockley Rd ALP/SUD HA0 35 R7
Bloemfontein Av SHB W12 48 H6
Bloemfontein Rd SHB W12 48 H5
Blomfield Rd MV/WKIL W9 2 H9
Blomfield St LVPST EC2M 5 R10
Blomfield Vls BAY/PAD W2 2 H10
Blomville Rd BCTR RM8 41 U7
Blondell Cl WDR/YW UB7 45 P11
Blondel St BTSEA SW11 49 U14
Blondin Av EA W5 47 S9
Blondin St BOW E3 39 S14
Bloomfield Crs GNTH/NBYPK IG2 40 K4
Bloomfield Pl MYFR/PKLN W1K 3 V13
Bloomfield Rd HAYES BR2 76 F3
HGT N6 37 U4
KUT/HW KT1 71 U2
WOOL/PLUM SE18 52 K10
Bloomfield Ter BGVA SW1W 7 T9
Bloom Gv WNWD SE27 62 F8
Bloomhall Rd NRWD SE19 62 H10
Bloom Park Rd FUL/PGN SW6 6 C14
Bloomsbury Cl EA W5 47 V5
HOR/WEW KT19 72 D14
Bloomsbury Pl NOXST/BSQ WC1A 4 F10
Bloomsbury Sq NOXST/BSQ WC1A 4 F10
Bloomsbury St GWRST WC1E 4 D9
Bloomsbury Wy NOXST/BSQ WC1A 4 E10
Blore Cl VX/NE SW8 50 B13
Blossom Cl DAGW RM9 41 V13
EA W5 47 U7
SAND/SEL CR2 74 K10
Blossom La ENC/FH EN2 15 S13
Blossom St WCHPL E1 5 T8
Blossom Wy HGDN/ICK UB10 33 R12
WDR/YW UB7 45 S9
Blossom Waye HEST TW5 46 G11
Blount St POP/IOD E14 51 Q4
Bloxam Gdns ELTH/MOT SE9 64 G3
Bloxhall Rd LEY E10 39 R6
Bloxham Crs HPTN TW12 58 H13
Bloxworth Cl WLGTN SM6 74 A8
Blucher Rd CMBW SE5 9 P14
Blue Anchor La BERM/RHTH SE16 51 L9
Blue Anchor Yd WCHPL E1 51 L5
Blue Ball La EGH TW20 56 D10
Blue Ball Yd WHALL SW1A 8 A2
Blue Barn La WEY KT13 81 S1
Bluebell Av MNPK E12 40 G10
Bluebell Cl HOM E9 39 N13
NTHLT UB5 34 H11
ORP BR6 77 L7
ROMW/RG RM7 42 E7
SYD SE26 62 K9
WLGTN SM6 73 V6
Bluebell Ct WOKS/MYFD GU22 80 B9
Bluebell Dr ABLGY WD5 11 M1
CHESW EN7 15 T2
Bluebell Wy IL IG1 40 K11
Blueberry Cl WFD IG8 28 C11
Blueberry Gdns COUL/CHIP CR5 86 D6
Blueberry La RSEV TN14 89 S6
Bluebird La DAGE RM10 42 A12
Bluebird Wy LCOL/BKTW AL2 11 T4
THMD SE28 53 M7
Bluebridge Av BRKMPK AL9 14 A1
Blue Bridge Rd BRKMPK AL9 14 A2
Blue Cedars BNSTD SM7 84 K4
Blue Cedars Pl COB KT11 82 F2
Bluefield Cl HPTN TW12 58 J10
Bluegates EW KT17 72 G12
Bluehouse Gdns OXTED RH8 96 C4
Bluehouse La OXTED RH8 96 A4
Bluehouse Rd CHING E4 28 A8
Blue Leaves Av COUL/CHIP CR5 86 B12
Blue Lion Pl STHWK SE1 9 S5
Blue Riband Est CROY/NA CR0 * 74 F7
Bluett Rd LCOL/BKTW AL2 12 H1
Bluewater Pkwy RDART DA2 67 U5
Blundel La COB KT11 82 H6
Blundell Cl HACK E8 39 L9
Blundell Rd EDGW HA8 24 E12
Blundell St HOLWY N7 38 C12
Blunden Cl BCTR RM8 41 S6
Blunden Dr DTCH/LGLY SL3 44 F9
Blunesfield POTB/CUF EN6 14 F5
Blunt Rd SAND/SEL CR2 74 H10
Blunts Av WDR/YW UB7 45 S12
Blunts Rd ELTH/MOT SE9 64 J3
Blurton Rd CLPT E5 39 P9
Blyth Cl BORE WD6 12 K13
TWK TW1 59 P4
Blythe Cl CAT SE6 63 R5
IVER SL0 44 K4
Blythe Hl CAT SE6 63 R5
STMC/STPC BR5 65 P13
Blythe Hill La CAT SE6 63 R5
Blythe Hill Pl FSTH SE23 * 63 Q5
Blythe Ms WKENS W14 * 48 K8
Blythe Rd WKENS W14 48 K8
Blythe St BETH E2 51 M1
Blytheswood Pl STRHM/NOR SW16 62 D9
Blythe V CAT SE6 63 R6
Blyth Rd BMLY BR1 64 B13
HYS/HAR UB3 46 A7
THMD SE28 53 S5
WALTH E17 39 R5
Blyth's Whf POP/IOD E14 * 51 Q5
Blythswood Rd GDMY/SEVK IG3 41 Q6
Blyth Wk UPMR RM14 43 S5
Blythwood Rd FSBYPK N4 38 C5
PIN HA5 22 F13
Boadicea St IS N1 4 G2
Boakes Cl CDALE/KGS NW9 36 C2
Boakes Meadow RSEV TN14 90 F1
Boardman Av CHING E4 27 T3
Boardman Cl BAR EN5 25 L3
Board School Rd WOKN/KNAP GU21 80 D6
Boardwalk Pl POP/IOD E14 51 U6
Boar's Head Yd BTFD TW8 47 T12
Boathouse Wk PECK SE15 9 V13
RCH/KEW TW9 47 T13
Boat Lifter Wy BERM/RHTH SE16 51 Q9
Boat Quay CAN/RD E16 52 E5
Bob Anker Cl PLSTW E13 52 C1
Bobbin Cl CLAP SW4 62 A1
Bob Marley Wy HNHL SE24 62 E2
Bockhampton Rd KUTN/CMB KT2 59 V12
Bocking St HACK E8 39 M13
Boddicott Cl WIM/MER SW19 61 L7
Boddington Gdns ACT W3 48 A7
Bodiam Cl EN EN1 15 T14
Bodiam Rd STRHM/NOR SW16 62 B13
Bodiam Wy WLSDN NW10 47 V1
Bodicea Ms HSLWW TW4 58 H4
Bodley Cl EPP CM16 18 D4
NWMAL KT3 72 E3
Bodley Rd NWMAL KT3 72 E4
Bodmin Cl RYLN/HDSTN HA2 34 H8
STMC/STPC BR5 77 S6
Bodmin Gv MRDN SM4 73 P3
Bodmin St WAND/EARL SW18 61 N7
Bodnant Gdns RYNPK SW20 72 G1
Bodney Rd CLPT E5 39 M10
Boeing Wy NWDGN UB2 46 D8
Bofors House CHARL SE7 * 52 G12
Bognor Gdns OXHEY WD19 * 22 E10
Bognor Rd WELL DA16 53 T13
Bohemia Pl HACK E8 39 N11
Bohn Rd WCHPL E1 51 Q3
Bohun Gv EBAR EN4 25 S4
Boileau Rd BARN SW13 48 G12
EA W5 47 V4
Bois Hall Rd ADL/WDHM KT15 69 P10
Bolden St DEPT SE8 51 T14
Boldero Pl STJWD NW8 * 3 N8
Bolderwood Wy WWKM BR4 75 T7
Boldmere Rd PIN HA5 34 E5
Boleyn Av EN EN1 16 B13
EW KT17 72 H14
Boleyn Cl LOU IG10 28 G4
STA TW18 56 J10
WALTH E17 39 S2
Boleyn Ct BKHH IG9 28 D6
Boleyn Dr E/WMO/HCT KT8 70 H1
RSLP HA4 34 F7
Boleyn Gdns DAGE RM10 42 C12
WWKM BR4 75 T7
Boleyn Rd BGR/WK TN15 91 L7
FSTGT E7 40 C12
STNW/STAM N16 38 J10
Boleyn Wk LHD/OX KT22 83 P10
Boleyn Wy BAR EN5 25 Q1
BARK/HLT IG6 29 L11
Bolina Rd BERM/RHTH SE16 51 N10
Bolingbroke Gv BTSEA SW11 61 S3
Bolingbroke Rd WKENS W14 48 K8
Bolingbroke Wk BTSEA SW11 7 M14
Bolingbroke Wy HYS/HAR UB3 45 V6
Bollo Bridge Rd ACT W3 48 C7
Bollo La ACT W3 48 B8
Bolney Ga SKENS SW7 7 N4
Bolney St VX/NE SW8 8 G14
Bolsover Gv REDH RH1 94 C5
Bolsover St GTPST W1W 3 V8
Bolstead Rd MTCM CR4 61 V13
Bolster Gv WDGN N22 * 26 B13
Bolt Ct FLST/FETLN EC4A 4 K12
Bolters La BNSTD SM7 85 M4
Boltmore Cl HDN NW4 36 K1
Bolton Cl CHSGTN KT9 71 T11
Bolton Crs CMBW SE5 8 K12
Bolton Dr MRDN SM4 73 R5
Bolton Gdns BMLY BR1 64 B11
ECT SW5 6 H9
TEDD TW11 59 Q11
WLSDN NW10 36 K14
Bolton Gardens Ms WBPTN SW10 6 H10
Bolton Pl IS N1 * 38 F12
Bolton Rd CHSGTN KT9 71 T11
CHSWK W4 48 C12
HRW HA1 35 L2
SRTFD E15 40 B11
STJWD NW8 2 H2
UED N18 26 K10
WLSDN NW10 36 E13
Boltons Cl WOKS/MYFD GU22 81 L5
Bolton's La HYS/HAR UB3 45 U12
WOKS/MYFD GU22 81 L6
Boltons Pl ECT SW5 6 J9
The Boltons ALP/SUD HA0 35 P9
WBPTN SW10 6 J9
WFD IG8 * 28 C9
Bolton St MYFR/PICC W1J 7 V1
Bombay St BERM/RHTH SE16 51 M9
Bombers La BH/WHM TN16 89 M10
Bomer Cl WDR/YW UB7 45 S12
Bomore Rd NTGHL W11 2 A13
NTGHL W11 48 K5
Bonaparte Ms PIM SW1V 8 C9
Bonar Pl CHST BR7 64 G12
Bonar Rd PECK SE15 51 L12
Bonchester Cl CHST BR7 64 J12
Bonchurch Cl BELMT SM2 73 P12
Bonchurch Rd NKENS W10 2 A9
WEA W13 47 R6
Bond Cl IVER SL0 32 F12
RSEV TN14 89 T5
WDR/YW UB7 45 R4
Bondfield Av YEAD UB4 46 C1
Bond Gdns WLGTN SM6 74 A9
Bond Rd MTCM CR4 61 T14
SURB KT6 71 V7
WARL CR6 87 P8
Bond St EA W5 47 T5
SRTFD E15 40 A10
Bondway VX/NE SW8 8 F12
Bone Mill La GDST RH9 95 Q10
Boneta Rd WOOL/PLUM SE18 52 H8
Bonfield Rd LEW SE13 63 U2
Bonham Gdns BCTR RM8 41 T7
Bonham Rd BCTR RM8 41 T7
BRXS/STRHM SW2 62 D3
Bonheur Rd CHSWK W4 48 D7
Bonhill St SDTCH EC2A 5 R8
Boniface Gdns KTN/HRWW/WS HA3 22 K12
Boniface Rd HGDN/ICK UB10 33 T8
Boniface Wk KTN/HRWW/WS HA3 22 K12
Bonington Rd HCH RM12 42 K10
Bonita Ms BROCKY SE4 63 P1
Bonner Hill Rd KUT/HW KT1 71 V1
Bonner Rd BETH E2 39 N14
Bonners Cl WOKS/MYFD GU22 80 D12
Bonnersfield Cl HRW HA1 35 Q4
Bonnersfield La HRW HA1 35 Q4
Bonner St BETH E2 * 39 N14
Bonneville Gdns CLAP SW4 62 A4
Bonney Gv CHESW EN7 16 A4
Bonney Wy SWLY BR8 66 E14
Bonnington Sq VX/NE SW8 8 G11
Bonnys Rd REIG RH2 92 K10
Bonny St CAMTN NW1 38 A12
Bonser Rd TWK TW1 59 P7
Bonsey Cl WOKS/MYFD GU22 80 C11
Bonsey La WOKS/MYFD GU22 80 C11
Bonsey's La CHOB/PIR GU24 68 C13
Bonsor Dr KWD/TDW/WH KT20 85 L12
Bonsor St CMBW SE5 9 S14
Bonville Gdns HDN NW4 36 G2
Bonville Rd BMLY BR1 64 B10
Booker Rd UED N18 27 L10
Bookham Ct GT/LBKH KT23 82 H13
Bookham Rd COB KT11 82 F10
Boones Rd LEW SE13 64 A2
Boone St LEW SE13 64 A2
Boord St GNWCH SE10 52 A8
Boothby Rd ARCH N19 38 B7
Booth Cl HOM E9 39 M13
THMD SE28 53 R6
Booth Dr STA TW18 57 P11
Booth La BLKFR EC4V 5 N13
Booth Rd CDALE/KGS NW9 24 D13
CROY/NA CR0 * 74 F7
Boot Pde EDGW HA8 * 24 A11
Boot St FSBYE EC1V 5 S6
Bordars Rd HNWL W7 47 N3
Bordars Wk HNWL W7 47 N3
Borden Av EN EN1 26 H4
Border Crs SYD SE26 63 M10
Border Gdns CROY/NA CR0 75 T9
Border Ga MTCM CR4 61 S13
Border Rd SYD SE26 63 N10
Border's La LOU IG10 28 J2
Bordesley Rd MRDN SM4 73 P2
Bordon Wk PUT/ROE SW15 60 G5
Boreas Wk IS N1 5 M4
Boreham Av CAN/RD E16 52 C4
Boreham Cl WAN E11 39 U6
Boreham Rd WDGN N22 26 G13
Borgard House CHARL SE7 * 52 G12
Borgard Rd WOOL/PLUM SE18 52 H9
Borkwood Pk ORP BR6 77 P9
Borkwood Wy ORP BR6 77 N9
Borland Cl RDART DA2 67 U3
Borland Rd PECK SE15 63 N2
TEDD TW11 59 R11
Bornedene POTB/CUF EN6 14 A5
Borneo St PUT/ROE SW15 60 J1
Borough High St STHWK SE1 9 P4
Borough Hl CROY/NA CR0 74 F8
Borough Rd BH/WHM TN16 88 F11
ISLW TW7 47 N13
KUTN/CMB KT2 60 A13
MTCM CR4 61 S14
STHWK SE1 9 L5
Borough Sq STHWK SE1 9 N4
The Borough BRKHM/BTCW RH3 92 A11
Borough Wy POTB/CUF EN6 14 A6
Borrett Cl WALW SE17 9 N10
Borrodaile Rd WAND/EARL SW18 61 P4
Borrowdale Av KTN/HRWW/WS HA3 23 Q14
Borrowdale Cl EGH TW20 56 F12
REDBR IG4 40 G2
SAND/SEL CR2 86 K3
Borrowdale Dr SAND/SEL CR2 86 K2
Borthwick Ms WAN E11 * 40 A9
Borthwick Rd CDALE/KGS NW9 36 F4
SRTFD E15 40 A9
Borthwick St DEPT SE8 51 S10
Borwick Av WALTH E17 39 R1
Bosanquet Cl UX/CGN UB8 45 P3
Bosbury Rd CAT SE6 63 U8
Boscastle Rd KTTN NW5 37 V8
Boscobel Cl BMLY BR1 64 H14
Boscobel Pl BGVA SW1W 7 T7
Boscobel St BAY/PAD W2 3 M9
Boscombe Av EMPK RM11 42 K5
LEY E10 39 V5
Boscombe Cl CLPT E5 39 Q10
EGH TW20 56 G13
Boscombe Rd SHB W12 48 G7

WIM/MER SW19 61 N13
WPK KT4 72 J6
Bose Cl FNCH N3 25 L13
Bosgrove CHING E4 27 U6
Boshers Gdns EGH TW20 56 D11
Boss St STHWK SE1 9 U3
Bostall Heath ABYW SE2 * 53 S10
Bostall Hl ABYW SE2 53 R10
Bostall La ABYW SE2 53 R10
Bostall Manorway ABYW SE2 53 R9
Bostall Park Av BXLYHN DA7 53 U12
Bostall Rd STMC/STPC BR5 65 R12
Boston Gdns BTFD TW8 47 Q9
CHSWK W4 48 E11
Boston Gv RSLP HA4 33 U4
Boston Manor Rd BTFD TW8 47 Q9
Boston Pde HNWL W7 * 47 Q9
Boston Park Rd BTFD TW8 * 47 S11
Boston Pl CAMTN NW1 3 Q8
Boston Rd CROY/NA CR0 74 D4
EDGW HA8 24 C12
EHAM E6 52 G1
HNWL W7 47 N6
Bostonthorpe Rd HNWL W7 * 47 N7
Boston V HNWL W7 47 Q9
Bosville Dr SEV TN13 90 G13
Bosville Rd SEV TN13 90 G13
Boswell Cl RAD WD7 12 J6
STMC/STPC BR5 77 S4
Boswell Ct BMSBY WC1N 4 F9
Boswell Rd THHTH CR7 74 G2
Boswell St BMSBY WC1N 4 F9
Bosworth Cl WALTH E17 27 R13
Bosworth Crs HARH RM3 30 J11
Bosworth Rd BAR EN5 25 N1
DAGE RM10 42 A9
FBAR/BDGN N11 26 B11
NKENS W10 2 B8
Botany Bay La CHST BR7 65 L14
Botany Cl EBAR EN4 25 S2
Botany Ter PUR RM19 * 55 N10
Botany Wy PUR RM19 55 P10
Boteley Cl CHING E4 27 V7
Botery's Cross REDH RH1 94 F9
Botham Cl EDGW HA8 24 C12
Botha Rd PLSTW E13 52 D3
Bothwell Cl CAN/RD E16 52 C3
Bothwell Rd CROY/NA CR0 75 U14
Bothwell St HMSMTH W6 48 K11
Botleys Pk CHERT KT16 * 68 G10
Botolph Aly MON EC3R 5 S14
Botolph La MON EC3R 5 S14
Botsford Rd RYNPK SW20 61 L14
Botsom La BGR/WK TN15 79 Q11
Bottom La KGLGY WD4 10 C9
Bott Rd RDART DA2 67 M9
Bott's Ms BAY/PAD W2 2 F12
Botwell Common Rd HYS/HAR UB3 45 V5
Botwell Crs HYS/HAR UB3 46 A4
Botwell La HYS/HAR UB3 46 A5
Boucher Cl TEDD TW11 59 P10
Boughton Av HAYES BR2 76 B5
Boughton Hall Av RPLY/SEND GU23 80 K14
Boughton Rd THMD SE28 53 N8
Boulcott St WCHPL E1 51 P4
Boulevard WATW WD18 * 21 V3
The Boulevard FUL/PGN SW6 49 Q14
WATW WD18 21 V3
WFD IG8 28 J12
Boulmer Rd UX/CGN UB8 45 N1
Boulogne Rd CROY/NA CR0 74 H4
Boulter Gdns RAIN RM13 42 G11
Boulthurst Wy OXTED RH8 96 D8
Boulton Rd BCTR RM8 41 U7
Boultwood Rd EHAM E6 52 H4
Bounces La ED N9 27 M7
Bounces Rd ED N9 27 M7
Boundaries Rd BAL SW12 61 T7
FELT TW13 58 E6
Boundary Av WALTH E17 39 R5
Boundary Business Ct MTCM CR4 73 R1
Boundary Cl BAR EN5 14 B13
GDMY/SEVK IG3 41 N9
KUT/HW KT1 72 A1
NWDGN UB2 46 J10
Boundary La CMBW SE5 9 P12
PLSTW E13 52 F2
Boundary Ms STJWD NW8 * 2 K1
Boundary Pk WEY KT13 70 A8
Boundary Pass WCHPL E1 5 T7
Boundary Rd ASHF TW15 57 N10
BARK IG11 41 L14
BFN/LL DA15 65 N3
CAR SM5 73 U13
CFSP/GDCR SL9 20 B12
ED N9 27 N4
EFNCH N2 25 R13
PIN HA5 34 F4
PLSTW E13 40 E14
ROM RM1 42 G4
STJWD NW8 2 J2
UPMR RM14 43 N8
WALTH E17 39 R5
WBLY HA9 35 U8
WDGN N22 26 G14
WIM/MER SW19 61 R11
WOKN/KNAP GU21 80 E6
Boundary Rd East ADL/WDHM KT15 69 M13
Boundary Rd North ADL/WDHM KT15 69 M13
Boundary Rd West ADL/WDHM KT15 69 M13
Boundary Rw STHWK SE1 9 L3
Boundary St BETH E2 5 U6
ERITH DA8 54 F12
Boundary Wy CROY/NA CR0 75 S10
GSTN WD25 11 Q6
WOKN/KNAP GU21 80 F5
Boundfield Rd CAT SE6 64 B7
Bounds Green Rd FBAR/BDGN N11 26 C12
Bourchier St SOHO/SHAV W1D 4 C13
Bourdon Pl MYFR/PKLN W1K 3 V13
Bourdon Rd PGE/AN SE20 63 N14
Bourdon St MYFR/PKLN W1K 3 V13
Bourke Cl CLAP SW4 62 C4
WLSDN NW10 36 E11
Bourke Hl COUL/CHIP CR5 85 T8
Bourlet Cl FITZ W1T 4 A10
Bourn Av EBAR EN4 25 R3
SEVS/STOTM N15 38 H2
UX/CGN UB8 45 S2
Bournbrook Rd BKHTH/KID SE3 64 F1
Bourne Av CHERT KT16 69 L1
HYS/HAR UB3 45 U8
RSLP HA4 34 E10
STHGT/OAK N14 26 C7
Bournebridge La ABR/ST RM4 30 B5
Bourne Cl BF/WBF KT14 81 M3
ISLW TW7 59 N1
THDIT KT7 71 P7
Bourne Ct BF/WBF KT14 * 81 Q3
RSLP HA4 34 D10
Bourne Dr MTCM CR4 61 R14
Bourne End EMPK RM11 43 N5
Bourne End Rd NTHWD HA6 22 A9
Bourne Est HCIRC EC1N * 4 J9
Bournefield Rd CTHM CR3 86 K8
Bourne Gdns CHING E4 27 T9
Bourne Gv ASHTD KT21 83 T9
Bournehall BUSH WD23 22 J4
Bournehall Av BUSH WD23 22 J3
Bournehall La BUSH WD23 22 J4
Bournehall Rd BUSH WD23 22 J4
Bourne Hl PLMGR N13 26 C7
Bourne Hill Cl PLMGR N13 * 26 D7
Bourne La CTHM CR3 86 H11
Bourne Md BXLY DA5 66 C3
Bournemead Av NTHLT UB5 34 C14
Bournemead Cl NTHLT UB5 46 C1
Bourne Meadow EGH TW20 68 F2
Bournemouth Cl PECK SE15 51 L14
Bournemouth Rd PECK SE15 51 L14
WIM/MER SW19 61 N13
Bourne Pde BXLY DA5 * 66 B5
Bourne Park Cl PUR/KEN CR8 86 J6
Bourne Rd ADL/WDHM KT15 69 M13
BUSH WD23 22 J3
BXLY DA5 66 C4
CEND/HSY/T N8 38 C4
HAYES BR2 76 F2
REDH RH1 94 A6
VW GU25 68 B3
WAN E11 40 B8
Bourneside Crs STHGT/OAK N14 26 B6
Bourneside Gdns CAT SE6 63 U10
Bourneside Rd ADL/WDHM KT15 69 P10
Bourne St BGVA SW1W 7 S8
CROY/NA CR0 74 F7
Bourne Ter BAY/PAD W2 2 G9
The Bourne STHGT/OAK N14 26 C6
Bourne V HAYES BR2 76 C6
Bournevale Rd STRHM/NOR SW16 62 C9
Bourne Vw GFD/PVL UB6 35 P11
PUR/KEN CR8 86 H5
Bourne Wy ADL/WDHM KT15 69 N10
HAYES BR2 76 C7
HOR/WEW KT19 72 C9
SUT SM1 73 M10
SWLY BR8 78 C1
WOKS/MYFD GU22 80 B12
Bournewood Rd STMC/STPC BR5 77 R5
WOOL/PLUM SE18 53 Q12
Bournville Rd CAT SE6 63 S5
Bournwell Cl EBAR EN4 25 T1
Bourton Cl HYS/HAR UB3 46 C6
Bousfield Rd NWCR SE14 51 P14
Bousley Ri CHERT KT16 68 H12
Boutflower Rd BTSEA SW11 61 S2
Boutique Hall LEW SE13 * 63 U2
Bouverie Gdns KTN/HRWW/WS HA3 35 T4
PUR/KEN CR8 86 C4
Bouverie Ms STNW/STAM N16 38 J7
Bouverie Pl BAY/PAD W2 3 M11
Bouverie Rd COUL/CHIP CR5 85 U8
HRW HA1 35 L4
STNW/STAM N16 38 J7
Bouverie St EMB EC4Y 4 K12
Bouverie Wy DTCH/LGLY SL3 44 C10
Bouvier Rd PEND EN3 16 C12
Boveney Rd FSTH SE23 63 P5
Bovey Wy SOCK/AV RM15 55 V3
Bovill Rd FSTH SE23 63 P5
Bovingdon Av WBLY HA9 36 A11
Bovingdon Crs GSTN WD25 11 R8
Bovingdon La CDALE/KGS NW9 24 E13
Bovingdon Rd FUL/PGN SW6 49 P13
Bovington Dr ARCH N19 38 A7
Bow Arrow La DART DA1 67 N4
Bowater Cl BRXS/STRHM SW2 62 C4
CDALE/KGS NW9 36 D3
Bowater Gdns SUN TW16 58 E13
Bowater Pl BKHTH/KID SE3 52 D12
Bowater Rdg WEY KT13 69 V14
Bowater Rd WBLY HA9 36 B8
WOOL/PLUM SE18 52 F8
Bow Bridge Est BOW E3 51 T1
Bow Churchyard STP EC4M * 5 P12
Bow Common La BOW E3 51 R2
Bowden Cl EBED/NFELT TW14 58 A6
Bowden Dr EMPK RM11 43 L6
Bowden St LBTH SE11 8 K9
Bowditch DEPT SE8 51 R10
Bowdon Rd WALTH E17 39 S5
Bowen Dr DUL SE21 62 J8
Bowen Rd HRW HA1 35 L5
Bowen St POP/IOD E14 51 T4
Bowens Wd CROY/NA CR0 * 75 R13
Bowenswood CROY/NA CR0 75 R13
Bowen Wy COUL/CHIP CR5 86 B12
Bower Av GNWCH SE10 52 A13
Bower Cl CRW RM5 30 D12
NTHLT UB5 34 E14
Bower Ct WOKS/MYFD GU22 80 F6
Bowerdean St FUL/PGN SW6 49 P14
Bower Farm Rd ABR/ST RM4 30 C8
Bower Hl EPP CM16 18 E6
Bower Hill Cl REDH RH1 94 C12
Bower Hill La REDH RH1 94 B11
Bower La BGR/WK TN15 91 N1
EYN DA4 79 L8
Bowerman Av NWCR SE14 51 Q11
Bower Rd SWLY BR8 66 G12
Bowers Rd RSEV TN14 90 F1
Bower St WCHPL E1 * 51 P4
Bower V EPP CM16 18 E6
Bowes Cl BFN/LL DA15 65 R4
Bowes Rd ACT W3 48 E5
BCTR RM8 41 S9
FBAR/BDGN N11 25 V10
STA TW18 56 J11
WOT/HER KT12 70 D7
Bowes Rd (North Circular)
PLMGR N13 26 C10
Bowfell Rd HMSMTH W6 48 J11
Bowford Av BXLYHN DA7 53 U13
Bowhill Cl BRXN/ST SW9 8 K13
Bowie Cl CLAP SW4 62 B5
Bowland Rd CLAP SW4 62 B2
WFD IG8 28 E11
Bowland Yd KTBR SW1X * 7 R4
Bow La NFNCH/WDSPK N12 25 Q12
STP EC4M 5 P12
Bowl Ct WCHPL E1 5 T8
Bowles Gdn EN EN1 16 B10
Bowley Cl NRWD SE19 62 K11
Bowley La NRWD SE19 62 K10
Bowley St POP/IOD E14 51 R5
Bowling Cl HGDN/ICK UB10 33 R13
Bowling Green Cl PUT/ROE SW15 60 H5
Bowling Green Ct WBLY HA9 35 V7
Bowling Green La CLKNW EC1R 4 K8
Bowling Green Pl STHWK SE1 * 9 Q3
Bowling Green Rw
WOOL/PLUM SE18 * 52 H9
Bowling Green St LBTH SE11 8 J11
Bowling Green Wk IS N1 5 S6
Bowls Cl STAN HA7 23 R10
Bowman Av CAN/RD E16 52 C4
Bowman Ms WAND/EARL SW18 61 M6
Bowmans Cl POTB/CUF EN6 14 F6
WEA W13 47 R6
Bowmans Gn GSTN WD25 11 S10
Bowmans Lea FSTH SE23 63 N5
Bowman's Meadow WLGTN SM6 73 V8
Bowman's Ms HOLWY N7 38 C8
WCHPL E1 51 L5
Bowman's Pl HOLWY N7 38 C8
Bowmans Rd DART DA1 66 F5
Bowmead ELTH/MOT SE9 64 H7
Bowmore Wk CAMTN NW1 38 B12
Bowness Cl HACK E8 * 38 K11
Bowness Crs PUT/ROE SW15 60 E10
Bowness Dr HSLWW TW4 58 G2
Bowness Rd BXLYHN DA7 54 B14
CAT SE6 63 T5
Bowness Wy HCH RM12 42 G10
Bowood Rd CLAP SW4 61 U2
PEND EN3 16 D14
Bowring Gn OXHEY WD19 22 E10
Bow Rd BOW E3 51 S1
Bowrons Av ALP/SUD HA0 35 T12
Bowry Dr STWL/WRAY TW19 56 D4
Bowsley Ct FELT TW13 58 C7
The Bowsprit COB KT11 82 E5
Bow St COVGDN WC2E 4 F12
SRTFD E15 40 A10
Bowstridge La CSTG HP8 20 A11
Bowyer Cl EHAM E6 52 H3
Bowyer Crs DEN/HRF UB9 32 K4
Bowyer Pl CMBW SE5 9 Q13
Bowyers Cl ASHTD KT21 83 V8
Bowyers Ct TWK TW1 59 R2
Bowyer St CMBW SE5 9 P13
Boxall Rd DUL SE21 62 J4
Boxelder Cl EDGW HA8 24 C10
Boxford Cl SAND/SEL CR2 87 P2
Boxgrove Rd ABYW SE2 53 S8
Boxhill Rd KWD/TDW/WH KT20 92 D6
Boxhill Wy BRKHM/BTCW RH3 92 B14
Box La BARK IG11 41 S14
Boxley Rd MRDN SM4 73 Q2
Boxley St CAN/RD E16 52 D6
Boxmoor Rd CRW RM5 30 C10
KTN/HRWW/WS HA3 35 R2
Boxoll Rd DAGW RM9 41 V9
Box Ridge Av PUR/KEN CR8 86 D2
Boxted Cl BKHH IG9 28 G6
Boxtree La KTN/HRWW/WS HA3 23 L13
Boxtree Rd KTN/HRWW/WS HA3 23 M12
Box Tree Wk REDH RH1 93 R13
Boxwood Cl WDR/YW UB7 45 R7
Boxwood Wy WARL CR6 87 P7
Boxworth Cl NFNCH/WDSPK N12 25 R10
Boxworth Gv IS N1 4 H1
Boyard Rd WOOL/PLUM SE18 52 K10
Boyce Cl BORE WD6 12 J13
Boyce Wy PLSTW E13 52 C2
Boycroft Av CDALE/KGS NW9 36 C4
Boyd Av STHL UB1 46 H6
Boyd Cl KUTN/CMB KT2 60 A12
Boydell Ct STJWD NW8 37 R12
Boyd Rd WIM/MER SW19 61 R11
Boyd St WCHPL E1 51 L4
Boyfield St STHWK SE1 9 M4
Boyland Rd BMLY BR1 64 B10
Boyle Av STAN HA7 23 Q11
Boyle Cl HGDN/ICK UB10 33 R14
Boyle Farm Rd THDIT KT7 71 Q4
Boyne Av HDN NW4 36 K2
Boyne Rd DAGE RM10 42 A8
LEW SE13 63 V1
Boyne Terrace Ms NTGHL W11 6 C1
Boyson Rd WALW SE17 9 P11
Boyton Cl CEND/HSY/T N8 38 C1
WCHPL E1 51 P2
Boyton Rd CEND/HSY/T N8 38 C1
Brabant Rd WDGN N22 26 D14
Brabazon Av WLGTN SM6 74 C12
Brabazon Rd HEST TW5 46 E12
NTHLT UB5 34 J14
Brabazon St POP/IOD E14 51 T4
Brabourne Cl NRWD SE19 62 J10
Brabourne Crs BXLYHN DA7 53 V11
Brabourne Ri BECK BR3 75 V3
Brabourn Gv PECK SE15 51 N14
Bracewell Av GFD/PVL UB6 35 P10
Bracewell Rd NKENS W10 48 J3
Bracewood Gdns CROY/NA CR0 74 K8
Bracey St FSBYPK N4 * 38 C7
Bracken Av BAL SW12 61 U4
CROY/NA CR0 75 S8
Brackenbridge Dr RSLP HA4 34 F8
Brackenbury Gdns HMSMTH W6 48 H8
Brackenbury Rd EFNCH N2 37 Q1
HMSMTH W6 48 H8
Bracken Cl BORE WD6 13 M13
EHAM E6 52 H3
GT/LBKH KT23 82 H14
LOU IG10 17 V14
WHTN TW2 58 J5
WOKS/MYFD GU22 80 D8
Brackendale POTB/CUF EN6 14 C7
WCHMH N21 26 D7
Brackendale Cl HSLW TW3 46 K13
Brackendale Gdns UPMR RM14 43 Q9
Brackendene LCOL/BKTW AL2 11 T4
RDART DA2 66 E9
Brackendene Cl WOKN/KNAP GU21 80 E5
Bracken Dr CHIG IG7 28 K11
Bracken End ISLW TW7 59 M3
Brackenforde DTCH/LGLY SL3 44 A7
Bracken Gdns BARN SW13 48 G14
Brackenhill COB KT11 82 J2
RSLP HA4 * 34 G9
Bracken Hill Cl BMLY BR1 64 B13
Bracken Hill La BMLY BR1 64 B13
Bracken Ms ROMW/RG RM7 42 B4
Bracken Pth EPSOM KT18 84 B3
The Brackens EN EN1 26 J5
ORP BR6 77 Q10
The Bracken CHING E4 27 U7
Brackenwood SUN TW16 58 C13
Brackley WEY KT13 69 V10
Brackley Av PECK SE15 63 N1
Brackley Cl WLGTN SM6 74 C12
Brackley Rd BECK BR3 63 R12
CHSWK W4 48 E10
Brackley Sq WFD IG8 28 F12
Brackley St BARB EC2Y 5 P9
Brackley Ter CHSWK W4 48 E10
Bracklyn St IS N1 5 Q3
Bracknell Cl WDGN N22 26 E13
Bracknell Gdns HAMP NW3 37 P10
Bracknell Wy HAMP NW3 37 P9
Bracondale ESH/CLAY KT10 71 L10
Bracondale Rd ABYW SE2 53 Q9
Bracton La RDART DA2 66 F8
Bradbery RKW/CH/CXG WD3 20 H10
Bradbourne Park Rd SEV TN13 90 G13
Bradbourne Rd BXLY DA5 66 A5
SEV TN13 90 H12
Bradbourne St FUL/PGN SW6 49 N14
Bradbourne Vale Rd SEV TN13 90 G12
Bradbury Cl BORE WD6 13 M13
NWDGN UB2 46 H9
Bradbury St STNW/STAM N16 38 J10
Braddock Cl CRW RM5 30 C11
ISLW TW7 59 P1
Braddon Ct BAR EN5 * 25 L1
Braddon Rd RCH/KEW TW9 59 V1
Braddyll St GNWCH SE10 52 A10
Bradenham Av WELL DA16 65 Q2
Bradenham Cl WALW SE17 9 Q11
Bradenham Rd KTN/HRWW/WS HA3 35 R2
YEAD UB4 46 A1
Bradenhurst Cl CTHM CR3 94 K2
Braden St MV/WKIL W9 * 2 G8
Bradfield Cl WOKS/MYFD GU22 80 C8
Bradfield Dr BARK IG11 41 Q10
Bradfield Rd CAN/RD E16 52 C7
RSLP HA4 34 G10
Bradford Cl HAYES BR2 76 H6
SYD SE26 63 M9
TOTM N17 26 K11
Bradford Dr HOR/WEW KT19 72 F11
Bradford Rd ACT W3 48 E7
IL IG1 41 M6
RKW/CH/CXG WD3 20 G5
Bradgate POTB/CUF EN6 15 M1
Bradgate Cl POTB/CUF EN6 15 M2
Bradgate Rd CAT SE6 63 T4
Brading Crs WAN E11 40 D7
Brading Rd BRXS/STRHM SW2 62 D5
CROY/NA CR0 74 D4
Brading Ter SHB W12 48 G8
Bradiston Rd MV/WKIL W9 2 D5
Bradley Cl BELMT SM2 73 P14
HOLWY N7 38 C12
Bradley Gdns WEA W13 47 R4
Bradley Rd NRWD SE19 62 G11
PEND EN3 16 E12
WAB EN9 16 J10
WDGN N22 26 D14
Bradley's Cl IS N1 4 J3
Bradley Stone Rd EHAM E6 52 H4
Bradman Rw EDGW HA8 * 24 C12
Bradmead VX/NE SW8 * 49 V13
Bradmore Park Rd HMSMTH W6 48 H8
Bradmore Wy COUL/CHIP CR5 86 C8
Bradshaw Cl WIM/MER SW19 61 N11
Bradshaw Cottages POP/IOD E14 * 51 Q4
Bradshaw Dr MLHL NW7 24 K12
Bradshaw Rd WATN WD24 11 Q13
Bradshaws Cl SNWD SE25 75 L1
Bradstock Rd EW KT17 72 H10
HOM E9 39 P11
Brad St STHWK SE1 8 K2
Bradwell Av DAGE RM10 42 A7
Bradwell Cl HCH RM12 42 H11
SWFD E18 40 B2
Bradwell Ms UED N18 27 L9
Bradwell Rd BKHH IG9 28 G6
Brady Av LOU IG10 18 A14
Brady Dr BMLY BR1 76 J1
Bradymead EHAM E6 52 J4
Brady St WCHPL E1 51 M2
Braemar Av ALP/SUD HA0 35 T12
BXLYHN DA7 66 C2
SAND/SEL CR2 74 G14
THHTH CR7 74 F1
WDGN N22 26 C13
WIM/MER SW19 61 N7
WLSDN NW10 36 D8
Braemar Gdns BFN/LL DA15 65 M8
CDALE/KGS NW9 24 D13
EMPK RM11 43 N4
WWKM BR4 75 U6
Braemar Rd BTFD TW8 47 T11
PLSTW E13 52 B2
SEVS/STOTM N15 38 J3
WPK KT4 72 H8
Braeside ADL/WDHM KT15 81 M1
BECK BR3 63 S10
Braeside Av RYNPK SW20 61 L13
SEV TN13 90 F14
Braeside Cl PIN HA5 22 J12
SEV TN13 90 F14
Braeside Crs BXLYHN DA7 66 C2
Braeside Rd STRHM/NOR SW16 62 A12
Braes Md REDH RH1 94 C11
Braes St IS N1 38 F12
Braesyde Cl BELV DA17 53 V9
Brafferton Rd CROY/NA CR0 74 G9
Braganza St WALW SE17 9 L10
Bragg Cl BCTR RM8 41 R11
Bragg Rd TEDD TW11 59 N12
Braham St WCHPL E1 5 V12
Braid Av ACT W3 48 E4
Braid Cl FELT TW13 58 H7
Braidwood Rd CAT SE6 63 V6
Braidwood St STHWK SE1 9 S2
Brailsford Cl WIM/MER SW19 61 S12
Brailsford Rd BRXS/STRHM SW2 62 E4
Brainton Av EBED/NFELT TW14 58 D5
Braintree Av REDBR IG4 40 G3
Braintree Rd DAGE RM10 42 A8
RSLP HA4 34 D9
Braintree St BETH E2 * 51 N1
Braithwaite Av ROMW/RG RM7 42 A5
Braithwaite Gdns STAN HA7 23 S13
Braithwaite Rd PEND EN3 27 R1
Brakes Pl BGR/WK TN15 79 S11
Brakey Hl REDH RH1 94 J10
Brallings La CFSP/GDCR SL9 20 E9
Bramalea Cl HGT N6 37 U4
Bramall Cl SRTFD E15 40 B10
Bramber Ct BTFD TW8 47 U9
Bramber Rd NFNCH/WDSPK N12 25 S10
WKENS W14 6 C11
Bramber Wy WARL CR6 87 R6
Bramble Acres Cl BELMT SM2 73 N12
Bramble Banks CAR SM5 73 U13
Bramblebury Rd WOOL/PLUM SE18 53 M10
Bramble Cl BECK BR3 75 U3
CFSP/GDCR SL9 20 C11
CHIG IG7 29 L6
CROY/NA CR0 75 S9
GSTN WD25 11 N8
REDH RH1 93 U12
SEVS/STOTM N15 39 L2
SHPTN TW17 69 V2
STAN HA7 23 T12
UX/CGN UB8 45 R3
Bramble Cft ERITH DA8 54 C9
Brambledene Cl WOKN/KNAP GU21 80 A8
Brambledown STA TW18 57 M13
Brambledown Cl WWKM BR4 76 A4
Brambledown Rd CAR SM5 73 U12
SAND/SEL CR2 74 J13
Bramble Gdns SHB W12 48 F5
Bramble La HPTN TW12 58 H11
UPMR RM14 43 Q13
Bramble Ri COB KT11 82 E4
Brambles Cl CTHM CR3 86 J12
ISLW TW7 47 R12
Brambles Farm Dr HGDN/ICK UB10 45 T1
The Brambles CHES/WCR EN8 16 D5
CHIG IG7 29 L11
SUT SM1 73 R7
WDR/YW UB7 45 P10
WIM/MER SW19 * 61 M10
Brambletye Park Rd REDH RH1 93 T12
Bramble Wk EPSOM KT18 84 B4
REDH RH1 * 93 U12
Bramble Wy RPLY/SEND GU23 80 K14
Bramblewood REDH RH1 93 V5
Bramblewood Cl CAR SM5 73 S6
Brambling Cl BUSH WD23 22 G2
The Bramblings CHING E4 27 V9
Bramcote Av MTCM CR4 73 T2
Bramcote Gv BERM/RHTH SE16 51 N10
Bramcote Rd PUT/ROE SW15 60 H2
Bramdean Crs LEE/GVPK SE12 64 C6
Bramdean Gdns LEE/GVPK SE12 64 C6
Bramerton Rd BECK BR3 75 R1
Bramerton St CHEL SW3 7 N11
Bramfield GSTN WD25 11 S8
Bramfield Rd BTSEA SW11 61 S4
Bramford Rd WAND/EARL SW18 61 Q2
Bramham Ct NTHWD HA6 * 22 A10
Bramham Gdns CHSGTN KT9 * 71 T10
ECT SW5 6 G9
Bramhope La CHARL SE7 52 D11
Bramlands Cl BTSEA SW11 61 S1
Bramleas WATW WD18 22 B3
Bramley Av COUL/CHIP CR5 86 A5
Bramley Cl CHERT KT16 69 M6
HYS/HAR UB3 46 C5
ORP BR6 76 K6
PIN HA5 34 B1
REDH RH1 93 S12
SAND/SEL CR2 74 G10
STA TW18 57 N11
STHGT/OAK N14 25 V3
SWLY BR8 78 E2
WALTH E17 27 Q14
WFD IG8 28 E12
WHTN TW2 59 L4
Bramley Ct GSTN WD25 11 P6
Bramley Crs GNTH/NBYPK IG2 40 J4
VX/NE SW8 8 E13
Bramley Gdns OXHEY WD19 22 E11
Bramley Gv ASHTD KT21 83 U9
Bramley Hl SAND/SEL CR2 74 G9
Bramley House Ct ENC/FH EN2 * 15 T11
Bramley Hyrst SAND/SEL CR2 * 74 G10
Bramley Ldg ALP/SUD HA0 35 T10
Bramley Pde STHGT/OAK N14 26 A2
Bramley Pl DART DA1 66 G2
Bramley Rd BELMT SM2 72 K13
EA W5 47 S8
NKENS W10 48 K4
STHGT/OAK N14 25 V3
SUT SM1 73 R10
Bramley Shaw WAB EN9 17 M7
Bramley Wy ASHTD KT21 83 V7
HSLWW TW4 58 H3
WWKM BR4 75 T7
Brampton Cl CHESW EN7 16 A2
CLPT E5 39 M7
Brampton Gdns WOT/HER KT12 70 E10
Brampton Gv HDN NW4 36 H2
KTN/HRWW/WS HA3 35 Q2
WBLY HA9 36 A6
Brampton La HDN NW4 36 J2
Brampton Park Rd WDGN N22 38 E1
Brampton Rd BXLYHN DA7 65 T1
CDALE/KGS NW9 36 A2
CROY/NA CR0 74 K5
EHAM E6 52 F2
HGDN/ICK UB10 33 T14
OXHEY WD19 22 C8
SEVS/STOTM N15 38 G3
Brampton Ter BORE WD6 13 L12
Bramshaw Gdns OXHEY WD19 22 F10
Bramshaw Ri NWMAL KT3 72 E4
Bramshaw Rd HOM E9 39 P11
Bramshill Gdns KTTN NW5 37 V8
Bramshill Rd WLSDN NW10 36 E14
Bramshot Av CHARL SE7 52 D11
Bramshot Wy OXHEY WD19 22 C7
Bramston Cl BARK/HLT IG6 29 P11
Bramston Rd MTCM CR4 61 T12
WLSDN NW10 36 G14
Bramwell Cl SUN TW16 58 F14
Bramwell Ms IS N1 4 H1
Brancaster Dr MLHL NW7 24 G12
Brancaster La PUR/KEN CR8 86 G1
Brancaster Rd GNTH/NBYPK IG2 41 N4
STRHM/NOR SW16 62 C8
Brancepeth Gdns BKHH IG9 28 C7
Branch Hl HAMP NW3 37 Q8
Branch Pl IS N1 5 R1
Branch Rd BARK/HLT IG6 29 R10
LCOL/BKTW AL2 12 B1
POP/IOD E14 51 Q4
Branch St CMBW SE5 9 T14
Brancker Rd KTN/HRWW/WS HA3 35 T1
Brancroft Wy PEND EN3 16 E13
Brand Cl FSBYPK N4 38 F6
Brandesbury Sq WFD IG8 28 J12
Brandlehow Rd PUT/ROE SW15 61 M2
Brandon Est WALW SE17 9 L12
Brandon Ms BARB EC2Y * 5 Q9
Brandon Rd DART DA1 67 N5
HOLWY N7 38 C12
NWDGN UB2 46 H10
SUT SM1 73 P9
WALTH E17 39 U2
Brandon St WALW SE17 9 P8
Brandram Ms LEW SE13 * 64 A2
Brandram Rd LEW SE13 64 A1
Brandreth Ct HRW HA1 * 35 P4
Brandreth Rd EHAM E6 52 H4
TOOT SW17 61 V7
The Brandries WLGTN SM6 74 B8
Brands Hatch Pk HART DA3 * 79 T8
Brands Hatch Rd HART DA3 79 U8
Brandsland REIG RH2 93 P14
Brands Rd DTCH/LGLY SL3 44 F11
Brand St GNWCH SE10 51 U12
Brandville Gdns BARK/HLT IG6 40 K2
Brandville Rd WDR/YW UB7 45 Q7
Brandy Wy BELMT SM2 73 N12
Branfill Rd UPMR RM14 43 P7
Brangbourne Rd BMLY BR1 63 U10
Brangton Rd LBTH SE11 8 H10
Brangwyn Crs WIM/MER SW19 61 R14
Branksome Av UED N18 26 K11
Branksome Cl TEDD TW11 59 M9
WOT/HER KT12 70 F7
Branksome Rd BRXS/STRHM SW2 62 C3
WIM/MER SW19 61 N13
Branksome Wy KTN/HRWW/WS HA3 35 V4
NWMAL KT3 60 C14
Bransby Rd CHSGTN KT9 71 U12
Branscombe Gdns WCHMH N21 26 E5
Branscombe St LEW SE13 63 T1
Bransdale Cl KIL/WHAMP NW6 2 F1
Bransell Cl SWLY BR8 78 C4
Bransgrove Rd EDGW HA8 23 V13
Branston Crs STMC/STPC BR5 77 M6
Branstone Rd RCH/KEW TW9 47 V13
Branton Rd RDART DA2 67 T4
Brants Wk HNWL W7 47 N2
Brantwood Av ERITH DA8 54 C12
ISLW TW7 59 Q2
Brantwood Cl WALTH E17 * 39 T1
Brantwood Dr BF/WBF KT14 80 K3
Brantwood Gdns BF/WBF KT14 80 K3
ENC/FH EN2 26 C3
REDBR IG4 40 G3
Brantwood Rd BXLYHN DA7 54 B14
HNHL SE24 62 G3
SAND/SEL CR2 74 G13
TOTM N17 27 L11
Brantwood Wy STMC/STPC BR5 77 S1
Brasenose Dr BARN SW13 48 J11
Brasher Cl GFD/PVL UB6 35 M10
Brassey Cl EBED/NFELT TW14 * 58 C6
OXTED RH8 96 C5
Brassey Hl OXTED RH8 96 C6
Brassey Rd KIL/WHAMP NW6 37 M11
OXTED RH8 96 C5
Brassey Sq BTSEA SW11 61 U1
Brassie Av ACT W3 48 E4
Brasted Cl BELMT SM2 73 N14
BXLYHS DA6 65 T3
SYD SE26 63 N9
Brasted Hl RSEV TN14 89 Q10
Brasted Hill Rd BH/WHM TN16 89 S13
Brasted La RSEV TN14 89 Q9
Brasted Rd BH/WHM TN16 97 N2
ERITH DA8 54 E12
Brathway Rd WAND/EARL SW18 61 N5
Bratley St WCHPL E1 51 L2
Braund Av GFD/PVL UB6 46 K2
Braundton Av BFN/LL DA15 65 P6
Braunston Dr YEAD UB4 46 G2
Bravington Cl SHPTN TW17 69 R3
Bravington Pl MV/WKIL W9 * 2 C7
Bravington Rd MV/WKIL W9 2 C5
Bravingtons Wk IS N1 4 F4
Braxfield Rd BROCKY SE4 63 Q2
Braxted Pk STRHM/NOR SW16 62 D11
Brayard's Rd PECK SE15 51 M14
Braybourne Cl UX/CGN UB8 33 N11
Braybourne Dr ISLW TW7 47 P12
Braybrooke Gdns NRWD SE19 62 J12
Braybrook St SHB W12 48 F3
Brayburne Av VX/NE SW8 50 A14
Bray Cl BORE WD6 13 N13
Braycourt Av WOT/HER KT12 70 E5
Bray Crs BERM/RHTH SE16 51 P7
Braydon Rd STNW/STAM N16 38 K6
Bray Dr CAN/RD E16 52 B5
Brayfield Ter IS N1 38 E12
Brayford Sq WCHPL E1 * 51 N4
Bray Gdns WOKS/MYFD GU22 80 J6
Bray Ldg CHES/WCR EN8 * 16 E1
Bray Pl CHEL SW3 7 Q9
Bray Rd COB KT11 82 G6
MLHL NW7 24 K11
Brayton Gdns ENC/FH EN2 26 B2
Braywood Av EGH TW20 56 D11
Braywood Rd ELTH/MOT SE9 65 M2
Brazil Cl CROY/NA CR0 74 C5
Breach Barns La WAB EN9 17 N4
Breach La DAGW RM9 54 A1
Breach Rd WTHK RM20 55 T11
Bread St STP EC4M 5 P12
Breakfield COUL/CHIP CR5 86 C6
Breakneck Hl RDART DA2 67 V3
Breakspear Ct ABLGY WD5 11 M4
Breakspeare Cl WATN WD24 11 P12
Breakspeare Rd ABLGY WD5 11 L5
Breakspear Rd RSLP HA4 33 T4
Breakspear Rd North DEN/HRF UB9 33 Q1
Breakspear Rd South HGDN/ICK UB10 33 R8
Breakspears Dr STMC/STPC BR5 65 Q13
Breakspears Ms BROCKY SE4 51 S14
Breakspears Rd BROCKY SE4 63 R1
Bream Cl TOTM N17 39 M2
Bream Gdns EHAM E6 52 J1
Breamore Cl PUT/ROE SW15 60 G6
Breamore Rd GDMY/SEVK IG3 41 P7
Bream's Buildings LINN WC2A 4 J11
Bream St BOW E3 39 S12
Breamwater Gdns RCHPK/HAM TW10 59 R8
Brearley Cl EDGW HA8 24 C12
UX/CGN UB8 33 Q11
Breasley Cl PUT/ROE SW15 60 H2
Breasy Pl HDN NW4 * 36 H2
Brechin Pl SKENS SW7 6 K9
Brecknock Rd ARCH N19 38 A9
Brecknock Road Est ARCH N19 * 38 B10
Brecon Cl MTCM CR4 74 C2
WPK KT4 72 J7
Brecon Gn CDALE/KGS NW9 * 36 E4
Brecon Ms HOLWY N7 38 B10
Brecon Rd HMSMTH W6 6 A12
PEND EN3 27 N2
Brede Cl EHAM E6 52 J1
Bredgar Rd ARCH N19 37 V7
Bredhurst Cl PGE/AN SE20 63 N11
Bredon Rd CROY/NA CR0 74 K5
Bredune PUR/KEN CR8 86 H5
Breech La KWD/TDW/WH KT20 92 C1
Breer St FUL/PGN SW6 61 P1
Breezer's Hl WAP E1W * 51 L5
Bremans Rw WAND/EARL SW18 61 Q7
Brember Rd RYLN/HDSTN HA2 35 L7
Bremer Ms WALTH E17 39 T2
Bremer Rd STA TW18 57 L8
Bremner Cl SWLY BR8 78 G2
Bremner Rd SKENS SW7 6 K5
Brenchley Cl CHST BR7 64 J13
HAYES BR2 76 B3
Brenchley Gdns EDUL SE22 63 N4
Brenchley Rd STMC/STPC BR5 65 N14
Brendans Cl EMPK RM11 43 L6
Brenda Rd TOOT SW17 61 T7
Brende Gdns E/WMO/HCT KT8 70 K3
Brendon SCUP DA14 * 65 Q9
Brendon Av WLSDN NW10 36 E9
Brendon Cl ERITH DA8 54 E13
ESH/CLAY KT10 71 L11
HYS/HAR UB3 45 U12
Brendon Ct RAD WD7 * 12 F8
Brendon Dr ESH/CLAY KT10 71 L11
Brendon Gdns RYLN/HDSTN HA2 34 K9
Brendon Gv EFNCH N2 25 Q14
Brendon Rd BCTR RM8 41 V6
ELTH/MOT SE9 65 M7
Brendon St MBLAR W1H 3 P11
Brendon Vls WCHMH N21 * 26 G6
Brendon Wy EN EN1 26 J5
Brenley Cl MTCM CR4 73 U1
Brenley Gdns ELTH/MOT SE9 64 F2
Brent Cl BXLY DA5 65 U6
RDART DA2 67 P4
Brentcot Cl WEA W13 47 R2
Brent Crs WLSDN NW10 35 V14
Brent Cross F/O HDN NW4 36 J4
Brentfield WLSDN NW10 36 B12
Brentfield Cl WLSDN NW10 36 D11
Brentfield Gdns CRICK NW2 * 36 K5
Brentfield Rd DART DA1 67 N4
WLSDN NW10 36 D11
Brentford Cl YEAD UB4 46 F2
Brent Gn HDN NW4 36 K3
Brentham Wy EA W5 47 T2
Brenthouse Rd HACK E8 39 M12
Brenthurst Rd WLSDN NW10 36 F11
Brentlands Dr DART DA1 67 N6
Brent La DART DA1 67 M5
Brent Lea BTFD TW8 47 S12
Brentmead Cl HNWL W7 47 N5
Brentmead Gdns WLSDN NW10 35 V14
Brenton St POP/IOD E14 51 Q4
Brent Park Rd CDALE/KGS NW9 36 G6
Brent Pl BAR EN5 25 N3
Brent River Park Wk GFD/PVL UB6 47 R1
Brent Rd BTFD TW8 47 S11
CAN/RD E16 52 C4
NWDGN UB2 46 E8
SAND/SEL CR2 75 M13
WOOL/PLUM SE18 52 K12
Brentside BTFD TW8 47 S11
Brentside Cl WEA W13 47 P2
Brent St HDN NW4 36 K3
Brent Ter CRICK NW2 36 J7
The Brent DART DA1 67 N5
Brentvale Av ALP/SUD HA0 35 V13
STHL UB1 47 M6
Brent View Rd CDALE/KGS NW9 36 G4
Brent Wy BTFD TW8 47 T12
FNCH N3 25 N11
RDART DA2 67 P4
WBLY HA9 36 B11
Brentwick Gdns BTFD TW8 47 U9
Brentwood Cl ELTH/MOT SE9 65 L6
Brentwood Rd GPK RM2 42 J3
ROM RM1 42 F4
Brereton Rd TOTM N17 26 K12
Bressenden Pl WESTW SW1E 7 V5
Bressey Av EN EN1 16 A13
Bressey Gv SWFD E18 28 B14
Bretlands Rd CHERT KT16 68 J7
Brett Cl NTHLT UB5 46 F1
STNW/STAM N16 38 J7
Brett Crs WLSDN NW10 36 D13
Brettell St WALW SE17 9 R10
Brettenham Av WALTH E17 27 S13
Brettenham Rd UED N18 27 L9
WALTH E17 27 S14
Brett Gdns DAGW RM9 41 U12
Brettgrave HOR/WEW KT19 72 C14
Brett Pas HACK E8 39 M10
Brett Pl WATN WD24 11 N11
Brett Rd BAR EN5 24 J3
HACK E8 39 M10
Brett Vls ACT W3 * 48 D3
Brevet Cl PUR RM19 55 R9
Brewers Fld RDART DA2 66 J9
Brewer St REDH RH1 94 G7
REGST W1B 4 B13
Brewery Cl ALP/SUD HA0 35 Q10
Brewery La BF/WBF KT14 81 Q3
Brewery Rd HAYES BR2 76 G6
HOLWY N7 38 C12
WOKN/KNAP GU21 80 C7
WOOL/PLUM SE18 53 M10
Brewery Sq FSBYE EC1V 5 M8
STHWK SE1 9 U2
Brewhouse La WAP E1W 51 M6
Brew House Rd BRKHM/BTCW RH3 92 C14
Brewhouse Rd WOOL/PLUM SE18 52 H9
Brewhouse St PUT/ROE SW15 61 L2
Brewhouse Wk BERM/RHTH SE16 51 Q6
Brewhouse Yd FSBYE EC1V 5 L7
Brewood Rd BCTR RM8 41 R11
Brewster Gdns NKENS W10 48 J3
Brewster Rd LEY E10 39 T6
Brian Av SAND/SEL CR2 86 J2
Brian Cl HCH RM12 42 H9
Briane Rd HOR/WEW KT19 72 C14
Brian Rd CHDH RM6 41 S3
Briants Cl PIN HA5 22 G14
Briant St NWCR SE14 51 P13
Briar Av STRHM/NOR SW16 62 D12
Briar Bank CAR SM5 73 U13
Briarbank Rd WEA W13 47 Q4
Briar Cl BF/WBF KT14 81 M1
BKHH IG9 28 F7
CHES/WCR EN8 16 C3
EFNCH N2 * 37 P1
HPTN TW12 58 H10
ISLW TW7 59 P3
PLMGR N13 26 G8
WARL CR6 87 S6
Briar Crs NTHLT UB5 34 K11
Briardale Gdns HAMP NW3 37 N8
Briarfield Av EFNCH N2 37 P1
FNCH N3 25 P14
Briarfield Cl BXLYHN DA7 54 A14
Briar Gdns HAYES BR2 76 B6
Briar Gv SAND/SEL CR2 87 L3
Briar Hl PUR/KEN CR8 86 C1
Briar La CAR SM5 73 U13
CROY/NA CR0 75 T9
Briarleas Gdns UPMR RM14 43 S5
Briar Rd BXLY DA5 66 D8
CRICK NW2 36 J9
GSTN WD25 11 N8
HARH RM3 30 K12
KTN/HRWW/WS HA3 35 S3
RPLY/SEND GU23 80 F14
SHPTN TW17 69 R3
STRHM/NOR SW16 74 C1
WHTN TW2 59 N6
Briars Ct LHD/OX KT22 83 M4
The Briars BGR/WK TN15 79 R11
CHES/WCR EN8 16 E5
DTCH/LGLY SL3 44 D10
RKW/CH/CXG WD3 10 A10
Briars Wk HARH RM3 31 L14
Briarswood CHESW EN7 15 U2
Briarswood Wy ORP BR6 77 P10
Briar Wk BF/WBF KT14 81 L2
EDGW HA8 24 C12
NKENS W10 2 A7
PUT/ROE SW15 60 H2
Briar Wy WDR/YW UB7 45 S7
Briarwood Cl CDALE/KGS NW9 * 36 C4
FELT TW13 58 A8
Briarwood Ct WPK KT4 * 72 G6
Briarwood Dr NTHWD HA6 22 C14
Briarwood Rd CLAP SW4 62 B3
EW KT17 72 G11
Briary Cl EDGW HA8 24 B14
HAMP NW3 * 37 S12
Briary Ct SCUP DA14 65 R10
Briary Gdns BMLY BR1 64 D10
Briary La ED N9 26 J8
Brick Ct EMB EC4Y * 4 J12
Brickenden Ct WAB EN9 17 M7
Brickett Cl RSLP HA4 33 U3
Brick Farm Cl RCH/KEW TW9 48 B13
Brickfield Cl BTFD TW8 47 S12
Brickfield Cottages
WOOL/PLUM SE18 53 P11
Brickfield Farm Gdns ORP BR6 77 L9
Brickfield La BAR EN5 24 F4
HYS/HAR UB3 45 V11
Brickfield Rd BOW E3 51 T2
EPP CM16 18 H3
THHTH CR7 62 F13
WIM/MER SW19 61 P9
Brickfields RYLN/HDSTN HA2 35 M7
Brickfields Wy WDR/YW UB7 45 R8
Brickfield Vls CAR SM5 * 73 S8
Brick Kiln Cl OXHEY WD19 22 G4
Brick Kiln La OXTED RH8 96 E6
Brick La BETH E2 5 V6
EN EN1 16 B14
NTHLT UB5 46 H1
STAN HA7 23 T12
Brick St MYFR/PKLN W1K 7 U2
Brickwall La RSLP HA4 34 A6
Brickwood Cl SYD SE26 63 M8
Brickwood Rd CROY/NA CR0 74 J7
Brideale Cl PECK SE15 9 V12
Bride Ct EMB EC4Y 5 L12
Bride La EMB EC4Y 5 L12
Bridel Ms FSBYE EC1V 5 L4
Bridewain St STHWK SE1 9 U5
Bridewell Pl BLKFR EC4V 5 L12
WAP E1W 51 M6
Bridford Ms GTPST W1W 3 V9
Bridge Av HMSMTH W6 48 J10
HNWL W7 47 M3
UPMR RM14 43 N8
Bridge Barn La WOKN/KNAP GU21 80 A8
Bridge Cl BF/WBF KT14 81 R2
EN EN1 16 B14
NKENS W10 48 K4
RDART DA2 67 R1
ROMW/RG RM7 42 E4
STA TW18 56 J9
WOKN/KNAP GU21 80 A7
WOT/HER KT12 70 B5
Bridge Ct RAD WD7 * 12 F9
WOKN/KNAP GU21 80 B7
Bridge Dr PLMGR N13 26 D9
Bridge End WALTH E17 27 U13
Bridge End Cl KUTN/CMB KT2 60 A13
Bridgefield Cl BNSTD SM7 84 J5
Bridgefield Rd SUT SM1 73 N11
Bridgefoot La POTB/CUF EN6 13 V7
Bridge Gdns ASHF TW15 57 U12
E/WMO/HCT KT8 71 M2
Bridge Ga WCHMH N21 26 G5
Bridgeham Cl WEY KT13 69 S10
Bridge Hl EPP CM16 18 D7
Bridge House Quay POP/IOD E14 51 U6
Bridgeland Rd CAN/RD E16 52 C5
Bridgelands Cl BECK BR3 63 R12
Bridge La BTSEA SW11 49 S13
GLDGN NW11 37 L3
HDN NW4 36 K2
VW GU25 68 C4
Bridgeman Rd IS N1 38 D12
TEDD TW11 59 Q11
Bridgeman St STJWD NW8 3 N4
Bridge Mdw NWCR SE14 51 P11
Bridge Ms WOKN/KNAP GU21 80 B7
Bridgend Rd EN EN1 16 C9
Bridgenhall Rd EN EN1 15 V13
Bridgen Rd BXLY DA5 65 U5
Bridge Pde STRHM/NOR SW16 * 62 C10
WCHMH N21 * 26 G5
Bridge Pk WAND/EARL SW18 61 N3
Bridge Pl CROY/NA CR0 74 H6
PIM SW1V 7 V7
WAT WD17 22 F3
Bridgepoint Pl HGT N6 37 V6
Bridgeport Pl WAP E1W * 51 L6
Bridger Cl GSTN WD25 11 R7
Bridge Rd BECK BR3 63 R12
BXLYHN DA7 65 U1
CHERT KT16 69 M5
CHSGTN KT9 71 U10
COB KT11 82 D5
E/WMO/HCT KT8 71 N2
ED N9 27 L8
EHAM E6 40 H12
ERITH DA8 54 G13
EW KT17 84 F2
HSLW TW3 59 M1
KGLGY WD4 10 J7
NWDGN UB2 46 H7
RAIN RM13 54 G2
SRTFD E15 39 V13
STMC/STPC BR5 77 R4
SUT SM1 73 P11
TWK TW1 59 R4
UX/CGN UB8 33 N14
WALTH E17 39 R5
WBLY HA9 36 A8
WDGN N22 26 C13
WEY KT13 69 R9
WLGTN SM6 73 V10
WLSDN NW10 36 E11
Bridge Rw CROY/NA CR0 * 74 H6
Bridges Ct BTSEA SW11 61 R1
Bridges Dr DART DA1 67 P3
Bridges La CROY/NA CR0 74 C9
Bridges Rd STAN HA7 23 P10
Bridges Road Ms WIM/MER SW19 61 P11
Bridge St CHSWK W4 48 D9
DTCH/LGLY SL3 44 H12
LHD/OX KT22 83 Q12
PIN HA5 34 F1
TWK TW1 59 T4
WHALL SW1A 8 E4
WOT/HER KT12 70 B6
Bridge Ter LEW SE13 * 63 V2
SRTFD E15 39 V12
The Bridge EA W5 * 47 V6
KTN/HRWW/WS HA3 35 P1
Bridgetown Cl NRWD SE19 62 J10
Bridgeview HMSMTH W6 48 J10
Bridge Vw SWCM DA10 67 V2
Bridge Vls WIM/MER SW19 * 61 N10
Bridgewater Cl STMC/STPC BR5 65 N14
Bridgewater Ct DTCH/LGLY SL3 44 E10
Bridgewater Gdns EDGW HA8 23 V14
Bridgewater Rd ALP/SUD HA0 35 S12
SRTFD E15 39 U13
WEY KT13 69 V11
Bridgewater Sq BARB EC2Y * 5 N9
Bridgewater St BARB EC2Y 5 N9
Bridgewater Wy BUSH WD23 22 K4
Bridgeway ALP/SUD HA0 35 U12
BARK IG11 41 P12
Bridge Wy COUL/CHIP CR5 85 S9
GLDGN NW11 37 M3
HGDN/ICK UB10 33 T10
WHTN TW2 59 L5
Bridgeway St CAMTN NW1 4 B4
Bridge Wharf Rd ISLW TW7 59 R1
Bridgewood Cl PGE/AN SE20 63 M12
Bridgewood Rd STRHM/NOR SW16 62 B12
WPK KT4 72 G9
Bridgford St WAND/EARL SW18 61 Q8
Bridgman Rd CHSWK W4 48 C8
Bridgwater Rd HARH RM3 30 J10
RSLP HA4 34 C9
Bridgwater Wk HARH RM3 30 K10
Bridle Cl HOR/WEW KT19 72 C9
KUT/HW KT1 71 T2
PEND EN3 16 F11
SUN TW16 70 C1
Bridle La COB KT11 82 K5
LHD/OX KT22 83 L5
RKW/CH/CXG WD3 21 N1
SOHO/CST W1F 4 B13
TWK TW1 59 R4
Bridle Pth CROY/NA CR0 74 C8
WAT WD17 11 P14
The Bridle Pth EW KT17 72 J14
WFD IG8 28 A12
Bridlepath Wy EBED/NFELT TW14 58 A5
Bridle Rd CROY/NA CR0 75 S9
ESH/CLAY KT10 71 R11
EW KT17 84 F3
PIN HA5 34 E4
The Bridle Rd PUR/KEN CR8 74 C14
Bridle Wy CROY/NA CR0 75 S10
ORP BR6 77 L9
Bridleway Cl EW KT17 72 J14
The Bridle Wy WLGTN SM6 74 A10
Bridlington Cl BH/WHM TN16 88 D9
Bridlington Rd ED N9 27 M5
OXHEY WD19 22 F8
Bridport Av ROMW/RG RM7 42 B4
Bridport Pl IS N1 5 R3
Bridport Rd GFD/PVL UB6 34 K13
THHTH CR7 74 E1
UED N18 26 J10
Bridstow Pl BAY/PAD W2 2 F11
Brief St BRXN/ST SW9 50 F13
Brier Lea KWD/TDW/WH KT20 93 M2
Brierley CROY/NA CR0 75 T11
Brierley Av ED N9 27 N6
Brierley Cl EMPK RM11 42 J4
SNWD SE25 75 L2
Brierley Rd BAL SW12 62 A7
WAN E11 39 V9
Brierly Gdns BETH E2 * 39 N14
Brier Rd KWD/TDW/WH KT20 84 H9
Briery Fld RKW/CH/CXG WD3 21 L2
Brigade Cl RYLN/HDSTN HA2 35 M7
Brigade Pl CTHM CR3 86 G12
Brigade St BKHTH/KID SE3 * 52 B14
Brigadier Av ENC/FH EN2 15 S13
Brigadier Hl ENC/FH EN2 15 S12
Briggeford Cl CLPT E5 39 L7
Briggs Cl MTCM CR4 61 V13
Bright Cl BELV DA17 53 T9
Brightfield Rd LEE/GVPK SE12 64 A3
Brightlands Rd REIG RH2 93 Q8
Brightling Rd BROCKY SE4 63 R4
Brightlingsea Pl POP/IOD E14 51 R5
Brightman Rd WAND/EARL SW18 61 R6
Brighton Av WALTH E17 39 R3
Brighton Cl ADL/WDHM KT15 69 N10
HGDN/ICK UB10 33 T12
Brighton Dr NTHLT UB5 * 34 J11
Brighton Rd ADL/WDHM KT15 69 N9
BELMT SM2 73 P14
BNSTD SM7 85 M4
COUL/CHIP CR5 85 V11
COUL/CHIP CR5 86 A8
EFNCH N2 25 Q14
EHAM E6 52 J1
KWD/TDW/WH KT20 85 L8
KWD/TDW/WH KT20 93 N3
PUR/KEN CR8 74 F14
PUR/KEN CR8 86 C4
STNW/STAM N16 38 J9
SURB KT6 71 S4
WATN WD24 11 N12
Brighton Ter BRXN/ST SW9 62 D2
REDH RH1 * 93 T11
Brights Av RAIN RM13 54 H2
Brightside Av STA TW18 57 N12
Brightside Rd LEW SE13 63 V4
The Brightside PEND EN3 16 D13
Bright St POP/IOD E14 51 T4
Brightview Cl LCOL/BKTW AL2 11 S3
Brightwell Cl CROY/NA CR0 74 E6
Brightwell Crs TOOT SW17 61 T10
Brightwell Rd WATW WD18 22 C3
Brig Ms DEPT SE8 51 S11
Brigstock Rd BELV DA17 54 B9
COUL/CHIP CR5 85 V5
THHTH CR7 74 F3
Brill Pl CAMTN NW1 4 D4
Brimfield Rd PUR RM19 55 R9
Brim Hl EFNCH N2 37 Q2
Brimpsfield Cl ABYW SE2 53 R8
Brimsdown Av PEND EN3 16 E13
Brimstone Cl ORP BR6 77 S12
Brindle Ga BFN/LL DA15 65 N7
Brindles EMPK RM11 43 L2
The Brindles BNSTD SM7 85 M7
Brindley Cl ALP/SUD HA0 35 S13
BXLYHN DA7 66 A1
Brindley St BROCKY SE4 51 R13
Brindley Wy BMLY BR1 64 C10
STHL UB1 46 K5
Brindwood Rd CHING E4 27 S8
Brinkburn Cl ABYW SE2 53 Q9
EDGW HA8 36 B1
Brinkburn Gdns EDGW HA8 36 A1
Brinkley Rd WPK KT4 72 H7
Brinklow Crs WOOL/PLUM SE18 52 K12
Brinkworth Rd CLAY IG5 40 G1
Brinkworth Wy HOM E9 39 R11
Brinley Cl CHES/WCR EN8 16 D5
Brinsdale Rd HDN NW4 36 K1
Brinsley Rd KTN/HRWW/WS HA3 23 M14
Brinsley St WCHPL E1 * 51 M4
Brinsmead LCOL/BKTW AL2 12 B1
Brinsmead Rd HARH RM3 31 N14
Brinsworth Cl WHTN TW2 59 M7
Brinton Wk STHWK SE1 9 L2
Brion Pl POP/IOD E14 51 U3
Brisbane Av WIM/MER SW19 61 P13
Brisbane Rd IL IG1 41 L5
LEY E10 39 T7
Brisbane St CMBW SE5 9 Q14
Briscoe Cl WAN E11 40 B7
Briscoe Rd RAIN RM13 42 J14
WIM/MER SW19 61 R11
Briset Rd ELTH/MOT SE9 64 F1
Briset St FARR EC1M 5 L9
Briset Wy HOLWY N7 38 D7
Brisson Cl ESH/CLAY KT10 70 H11
Bristol Cl STWL/WRAY TW19 57 Q4
WLGTN SM6 74 C13
Bristol Gdns MV/WKIL W9 2 H8
Bristol Ms MV/WKIL W9 2 H8
Bristol Park Rd WALTH E17 * 39 Q2
Bristol Rd FSTGT E7 40 E11
GFD/PVL UB6 34 K13
MRDN SM4 73 Q3
Briston Gv CEND/HSY/T N8 38 C4
Bristowe Cl BRXS/STRHM SW2 62 E4
Bristow Rd BXLYHN DA7 53 U13
CROY/NA CR0 74 C9
HSLW TW3 58 K1
NRWD SE19 62 J10
Britannia Cl CLAP SW4 62 B2
ERITH DA8 54 F11
NTHLT UB5 46 F1
Britannia Ga CAN/RD E16 52 C6
Britannia La WHTN TW2 59 L5
Britannia Rd BRYLDS KT5 71 V5
CHES/WCR EN8 16 F8
FUL/PGN SW6 6 G14
IL IG1 40 K8
NFNCH/WDSPK N12 25 Q9
POP/IOD E14 51 S9
Britannia Rw IS N1 5 M1
Britannia St FSBYW WC1X 4 G5
Britannia Wk IS N1 5 Q5
Britannia Wy FUL/PGN SW6 6 H14
STWL/WRAY TW19 57 P5
WLSDN NW10 48 B2
British Est BOW E3 51 R1
British Gv HMSMTH W6 48 F10
British Grove Pas CHSWK W4 * 48 F10
British Legion Rd CHING E4 28 B7
British St BOW E3 51 R1
Briton Cl SAND/SEL CR2 86 J1
Briton Crs SAND/SEL CR2 86 J1
Briton Hill Rd SAND/SEL CR2 74 K14
Brittain Rd BCTR RM8 41 U8
WOT/HER KT12 70 F10
Brittains La SEV TN13 90 F14
Britten Cl BORE WD6 23 T4
GLDGN NW11 37 P6
Brittenden Pde ORP BR6 * 77 P11
Britten Dr STHL UB1 46 J4
Britten St CHEL SW3 7 N10
Brittidge Rd WLSDN NW10 * 36 E12
Britton Cl CAT SE6 63 V5
Britton St FARR EC1M 5 L8
Brixham Crs RSLP HA4 34 C6
Brixham Gdns GDMY/SEVK IG3 41 N10
Brixham Rd WELL DA16 53 T13
Brixham St CAN/RD E16 52 H6
Brixton Hl BRXS/STRHM SW2 62 D4
Brixton Hill Pl BRXS/STRHM SW2 62 C5
Brixton Ov BRXS/STRHM SW2 62 E2
Brixton Rd BRXN/ST SW9 62 E2
LBTH SE11 8 J12
WATN WD24 11 P13
Brixton Station Rd BRXN/ST SW9 62 E1
Brixton Water La BRXS/STRHM SW2 62 D3
Broad Acre LCOL/BKTW AL2 11 S4
Broadacre STA TW18 57 L10
Broadacre Cl HGDN/ICK UB10 33 T8
Broadbent Cl HGT N6 37 V6
Broadbent St MYFR/PKLN W1K * 3 U13
Broadberry Ct UED N18 27 M10
Broad Bridge Cl BKHTH/KID SE3 52 C12
Broad Cl WOT/HER KT12 70 F8
Broad Common Est
STNW/STAM N16 * 39 L6
Broadcoombe SAND/SEL CR2 75 P12
Broad Ct COVGDN WC2E * 4 F12
Broadcroft Av STAN HA7 23 T14
Broadcroft Rd STMC/STPC BR5 77 M5
Broadeaves Cl SAND/SEL CR2 74 J10
Broadfield Cl CRICK NW2 36 J8
KWD/TDW/WH KT20 84 J10
ROM RM1 42 F3
Broadfield Ct BUSH WD23 23 N7
Broadfield La CAMTN NW1 38 C12
Broadfield Pde EDGW HA8 * 24 B8
Broadfield Rd CAT SE6 64 A6
Broadfields CHESW EN7 15 R3
E/WMO/HCT KT8 71 M4
RYLN/HDSTN HA2 22 K14
Broadfields Av EDGW HA8 24 B9
WCHMH N21 26 E5
Broadfields Hts EDGW HA8 24 B9
Broadfields La OXHEY WD19 22 D6
Broadfield Sq EN EN1 27 M1
Broadfields Wy WLSDN NW10 36 F10
Broadfield Wy BKHH IG9 28 E8
Broadgate WAB EN9 17 M7
Broadgates Av EBAR EN4 14 D13
Broadgates Rd WAND/EARL SW18 61 R6
Broad Green Av CROY/NA CR0 74 F5
Broadham Green Rd OXTED RH8 95 V9
Broadham Pl OXTED RH8 95 V8
Broadhead Strd CDALE/KGS NW9 24 F14
Broadheath Dr CHST BR7 64 H10
Broad Hwy COB KT11 82 F4
Broadhinton Rd CLAP SW4 61 V1
Broadhurst ASHTD KT21 83 U6
Broadhurst Av EDGW HA8 24 B9
GDMY/SEVK IG3 41 P9
Broadhurst Cl KIL/WHAMP NW6 37 Q11
Broadhurst Gdns KIL/WHAMP NW6 37 Q11
REIG RH2 93 P13
RSLP HA4 34 E7
Broadhusrt Cl RCHPK/HAM TW10 59 V3
Broadlake Cl LCOL/BKTW AL2 12 H1
Broadlands FELT TW13 58 H8
Broadlands Av PEND EN3 27 M1
SHPTN TW17 69 U4
STRHM/NOR SW16 62 C7
Broadlands Cl HGT N6 37 U5
PEND EN3 27 M1
STRHM/NOR SW16 62 C7
Broadlands Dr WARL CR6 87 N9
Broadlands Rd BMLY BR1 64 D9
HGT N6 37 T5
Broadlands Wy NWMAL KT3 72 F4
Broad La CEND/HSY/T N8 38 D3
HPTN TW12 58 H12
RDART DA2 66 H9
SEVS/STOTM N15 38 K3
Broad Lawn ELTH/MOT SE9 64 J7
Broadlawns Ct KTN/HRWW/WS HA3 23 P13
Broadley St STJWD NW8 3 N9
Broadley Ter CAMTN NW1 3 P8
Broadmead ASHTD KT21 83 U8
CAT SE6 63 S8
REDH RH1 * 94 A4
Broadmead Av WPK KT4 72 G5
Broadmead Cl HPTN TW12 58 J11
PIN HA5 * 22 G12
Broadmead Rd WFD IG8 28 C11
YEAD UB4 46 C2
Broadmeads RPLY/SEND GU23 80 F12
Broad Oak SUN TW16 58 B11
WFD IG8 28 D10
Broadoak Av PEND EN3 16 D9
Broad Oak Cl CHING E4 27 T10
Broadoak Cl EYN DA4 67 N11
Broad Oak Cl STMC/STPC BR5 65 Q14
Broadoak Rd ERITH DA8 54 D12
Broadoaks EPP CM16 18 D6
Broad Oaks SURB KT6 72 B6
Broadoaks Crs BF/WBF KT14 81 M4
Broad Oaks Wy HAYES BR2 76 B3
Broad Platts DTCH/LGLY SL3 44 B8
Broadstone Pl MHST W1U 3 S10
Broadstone Rd HCH RM12 42 G7
Broad St DAGE RM10 42 A12
TEDD TW11 59 P11
Broad Street Av LVPST EC2M 5 S10
Broad Street Pl LVPST EC2M 5 R10
Broadstrood LOU IG10 17 U12
Broadview CDALE/KGS NW9 36 A4
Broadview Rd STRHM/NOR SW16 62 B12
Broad Wk BKHTH/KID SE3 52 E14
COUL/CHIP CR5 85 U12
CTHM CR3 86 K12
EPSOM KT18 84 J9
HEST TW5 46 F13
ORP BR6 77 T8
RCH/KEW TW9 47 V12
WCHMH N21 26 E6
Broadwalk RYLN/HDSTN HA2 * 34 K3
SWFD E18 40 C1
Broadwalk La GLDGN NW11 37 M5
The Broad Wk BAY/PAD W2 6 H1
The Broadwalk NTHWD HA6 21 U14
Broadwall STHWK SE1 8 K1
Broadwater POTB/CUF EN6 14 D4
Broadwater Cl WOKN/KNAP GU21 80 J2
WOT/HER KT12 70 C10
Broadwater Gdns DEN/HRF UB9 33 N2
ORP BR6 76 K9
Broadwater La DEN/HRF UB9 33 M2
Broadwater Pk DEN/HRF UB9 * 33 L4
Broadwater Rd THMD SE28 53 M8
TOOT SW17 61 S9
TOTM N17 26 J14
Broadway BARK IG11 41 L13
BXLYHS DA6 65 U2

DEN/HRF UB9 * 33 L5
GPK RM2 42 G1
HNWL W7 47 N6
RAIN RM13 54 G2
SRTFD E15 39 V12
STA TW18 * 57 M10
STJSPK SW1H 8 C5
SURB KT6 72 B6
SWLY BR8 78 C4
WEA W13 47 Q6
Broadway Av CROY/NA CR0 74 H3
TWK TW1 59 R4
Broadway Cl SAND/SEL CR2 87 M4
WFD IG8 28 D11
Broadway Ct WIM/MER SW19 61 N11
Broadway Gdns MTCM CR4 73 S2
Broadway Market HACK E8 39 M13
Broadway Market Ms HACK E8 * 39 L13
Broadway Ms PLMGR N13 26 D10
STNW/STAM N16 38 K5
WCHMH N21 26 F6
Broadway Pde CHING E4 * 27 U11
HYS/HAR UB3 * 46 B7
RYLN/HDSTN HA2 * 34 K3
WDR/YW UB7 * 45 Q7
The Broadway ACT W3 * 48 A7
ADL/WDHM KT15 69 L14
BCTR RM8 41 V7
CDALE/KGS NW9 36 F4
CEND/HSY/T N8 38 C4
CFSP/GDCR SL9 20 C13
CHEAM SM3 73 L11
EA W5 47 T5
ED N9 27 L8
FBAR/BDGN N11 * 25 T10
HCH RM12 42 H9
KTN/HRWW/WS HA3 23 N14
LOU IG10 29 L1
MLHL NW7 24 E10
PIN HA5 22 H12
PLSTW E13 40 C14
POTB/CUF EN6 14 B6
RYLN/HDSTN HA2 * 35 M7
STA TW18 69 N1
STAN HA7 23 S10
SUT SM1 73 Q9
THDIT KT7 71 N6
WAT WD17 22 E1
WFD IG8 28 D11
WIM/MER SW19 61 M11
WOKN/KNAP GU21 80 D7
Broadwell Pde KIL/WHAMP NW6 * 37 Q11
Broadwick St SOHO/CST W1F 4 B13
Broadwood Av RSLP HA4 34 B4
Broadwood Rd COUL/CHIP CR5 86 B11
Broadwood Ter WKENS W14 6 D7
Broad Yd FARR EC1M 5 L8
Brocas Cl HAMP NW3 37 S12
Brockdene Dr HAYES BR2 76 F9
Brockdish Av BARK IG11 41 P10
Brockenhurst E/WMO/HCT KT8 70 H3
Brockenhurst Av WPK KT4 72 E6
Brockenhurst Cl WOKN/KNAP GU21 80 D4
Brockenhurst Gdns IL IG1 41 L10
MLHL NW7 24 E11
Brockenhurst Ms UED N18 27 L9
Brockenhurst Rd CROY/NA CR0 75 M5
Brockenhurst Wy STRHM/NOR SW16 62 B14
Brocket Cl CHIG IG7 29 P9
Brocket Wy CHIG IG7 29 N10
Brock Gn SOCK/AV RM15 55 V4
Brockham Cl WIM/MER SW19 61 M10
Brockham Crs CROY/NA CR0 75 V12
Brockham Dr BRXS/STRHM SW2 62 D5
GNTH/NBYPK IG2 41 L4
Brockham Hill Pk KWD/TDW/WH KT20 92 C7
Brockham La BRKHM/BTCW RH3 92 A10
Brockham St STHWK SE1 9 P5
Brockhurst Cl STAN HA7 23 P11
Brockill Crs BROCKY SE4 63 Q2
Brocklebank Rd CHARL SE7 52 D9
WAND/EARL SW18 61 Q5
Brocklehurst St NWCR SE14 51 P12
Brocklesbury Cl WATN WD24 22 E1
Brocklesby Rd SNWD SE25 75 M2
Brockley Av STAN HA7 23 U8
Brockley Cl STAN HA7 23 U10
Brockley Combe WEY KT13 69 V10
Brockley Crs CRW RM5 30 C12
Brockley Cross BROCKY SE4 63 R1
Brockley Gv BROCKY SE4 63 R3
Brockley Hall Rd BROCKY SE4 63 Q4
Brockley Hl STAN HA7 23 S7
Brockley Ms BROCKY SE4 63 Q3
Brockley Pk FSTH SE23 63 Q5
Brockley Ri FSTH SE23 63 Q5
Brockley Rd BROCKY SE4 63 R3
Brockleyside STAN HA7 23 T9
Brockley Vw FSTH SE23 63 Q5
Brockley Wy FSTH SE23 63 P3
Brockman Ri BMLY BR1 63 V9
Brock Pl BOW E3 51 T2
Brock Rd PLSTW E13 52 D3
Brocks Dr CHEAM SM3 73 L8
Brockshot Cl BTFD TW8 47 T11
Brock St PECK SE15 63 N1
Brockton Cl ROM RM1 42 F2
Brock Wy VW GU25 68 A3
Brockway Cl WAN E11 40 A7
Brockwell Av BECK BR3 75 T3
Brockwell Cl STMC/STPC BR5 77 P3
Brockwell Park Gdns HNHL SE24 62 F5
Brockwell Park Rw BRXS/STRHM SW2 62 E5
Brockworth Cl PECK SE15 9 S12
Brodewater Rd BORE WD6 13 M14
Brodia Rd STNW/STAM N16 38 J8
Brodie Rd CHING E4 27 U6
ENC/FH EN2 15 S12
Brodie St STHWK SE1 9 V9
Brodlove La WAP E1W 51 P5
Brodrick Gv ABYW SE2 53 R9
Brodrick Rd TOOT SW17 61 T6
Brograve Gdns BECK BR3 63 T14
Broke Farm Dr ORP BR6 77 S13
Broken Gate La DEN/HRF UB9 32 G6
Broken Whf BLKFR EC4V 5 N13
Brokes Crs REIG RH2 93 N8
Brokesley St BOW E3 51 R2
Brokes Rd REIG RH2 93 N8
Broke Wk HACK E8 * 39 L13
Bromar Rd CMBW SE5 62 J1
Bromborough Gn OXHEY WD19 22 E10
Bromefield STAN HA7 23 T12
Bromefield Ct WAB EN9 17 N7
Bromehead St WCHPL E1 51 N4
Brome House CHARL SE7 * 52 G12
Bromell's Rd CLAP SW4 62 A2
Brome Rd ELTH/MOT SE9 64 H1
Bromet Cl WAT WD17 11 M12
Bromfelde Rd CLAP SW4 62 B1
Bromfield St IS N1 4 K3
Bromford Cl OXTED RH8 96 C9
Bromhall Rd BCTR RM8 41 R11
Bromhedge ELTH/MOT SE9 64 H8
Bromholm Rd ABYW SE2 53 R8
Bromleigh Cl CHES/WCR EN8 16 E2
Bromley Av BMLY BR1 64 A12
Bromley Common HAYES BR2 76 G5
Bromley Ct BMLY BR1 64 A12
Bromley Crs HAYES BR2 76 B1
RSLP HA4 34 B9
Bromley Gdns HAYES BR2 64 B14
Bromley Gv HAYES BR2 63 V14
Bromley Hall Rd POP/IOD E14 51 U3
Bromley High St BOW E3 51 T1
Bromley Hl BMLY BR1 64 A11
Bromley La CHST BR7 65 L12
Bromley Rd BECK BR3 63 S13
CAT SE6 63 T8
CHST BR7 64 K13
LEY E10 39 T4
TOTM N17 26 K13
UED N18 26 H9
WALTH E17 39 S1
Bromley St WCHPL E1 51 P3
Brompton Ar CHEL SW3 * 7 Q4
Brompton Cl HSLWW TW4 58 H3
Brompton Dr ERITH DA8 54 H12
Brompton Gv EFNCH N2 37 S2
Brompton Park Crs FUL/PGN SW6 6 G12
Brompton Pl CHEL SW3 7 Q5
Brompton Rd CHEL SW3 7 N7
Brompton Sq CHEL SW3 7 N5
Brompton Ter WOOL/PLUM SE18 * 52 J13
Bromwich Av HGT N6 37 U7
Bromyard Av ACT W3 48 E6
Brondesbury Ms KIL/WHAMP NW6 * 37 N12
Brondesbury Pk KIL/WHAMP NW6 36 J12
Brondesbury Rd KIL/WHAMP NW6 2 D3
Brondesbury Vls KIL/WHAMP NW6 2 D3
Bronhill Ter TOTM N17 * 27 L13
Bronsart Rd FUL/PGN SW6 6 A14
Bronson Rd RYNPK SW20 60 K14
Bronte Cl ERITH DA8 54 B13
FSTGT E7 40 C9
GNTH/NBYPK IG2 40 J3
Bronte Gv DART DA1 67 M2
Bronti Cl WALW SE17 9 P9
Bronze Age Wy BELV DA17 54 C8
Bronze St DEPT SE8 51 S12
Brook Av DAGE RM10 42 B12
EDGW HA8 24 B11
WBLY HA9 35 V8
Brookbank Av HNWL W7 47 M3
Brookbank Rd LEW SE13 63 T1
Brook Cl ACT W3 48 A6
BORE WD6 13 M14
BORE WD6 24 B1
GPK RM2 30 F13
HOR/WEW KT19 72 E13
RSLP HA4 34 A5
RYNPK SW20 72 H1
STWL/WRAY TW19 57 R5
TOOT SW17 61 U7
Brook Ct BECK BR3 * 63 R13
RAD WD7 * 12 E7
Brook Crs CHING E4 27 S9
ED N9 27 M9
Brookdale FBAR/BDGN N11 26 A9
Brookdale Av UPMR RM14 43 N8
Brookdale Cl UPMR RM14 43 P8
Brookdale Rd BXLY DA5 65 U4
CAT SE6 63 T5
WALTH E17 39 S1
Brookdene Av OXHEY WD19 22 D5
Brookdene Dr NTHWD HA6 22 B12
Brookdene Rd WOOL/PLUM SE18 53 N9
Brook Dr HRW HA1 35 L2
LBTH SE11 8 K6
RAD WD7 12 D7
RSLP HA4 34 A5
Brooke Av RYLN/HDSTN HA2 35 L8
Brooke Cl BUSH WD23 23 L5
Brooke End OXTED RH8 * 96 C9
Brookehowse Rd CAT SE6 63 T8
Brookend Rd BFN/LL DA15 65 N6
Brooker Cl POP/IOD E14 51 R3
Brooke Rd STNW/STAM N16 39 L8
WALTH E17 39 U2
Brooker Rd WAB EN9 16 J8
Brookers Cl ASHTD KT21 83 S7
Brooke St HCIRC EC1N 4 J10
Brooke Wy BUSH WD23 23 L5
Brook Farm Rd COB KT11 82 F5
Brookfield BGR/WK TN15 91 L7
Brookfield Av EA W5 47 T2
MLHL NW7 24 H11
SUT SM1 73 S8
WALTH E17 39 U2
Brookfield Cl ASHTD KT21 83 U10
CHERT KT16 68 H11
MLHL NW7 24 H11
Brookfield Crs KTN/HRWW/WS HA3 35 T3
MLHL NW7 24 H11
Brookfield Gdns CHES/WCR EN8 16 D1
ESH/CLAY KT10 71 P11
Brookfield La CHES/WCR EN8 16 B2
Brookfield La East CHES/WCR EN8 16 D2
Brookfield La West CHES/WCR EN8 16 C2
Brookfield Pk KTTN NW5 37 V8
Brookfield Pth WFD IG8 27 V11
Brookfield Pl COB KT11 82 G5
Brookfield Rd CHSWK W4 48 E8
ED N9 27 L8
HOM E9 39 Q11
Brookfields PEND EN3 27 P2
Brookfields Av MTCM CR4 73 S3
Brook Gdns BARN SW13 60 F1
CHING E4 27 T9
KUTN/CMB KT2 60 C13
Brook Ga MYFR/PKLN W1K 3 R14
Brook Gn HMSMTH W6 48 J8
Brook Hl OXTED RH8 95 U6
Brookhill Cl EBAR EN4 25 S3
Brook Hill Cl WOOL/PLUM SE18 52 K10
Brookhill Rd EBAR EN4 25 R3
WOOL/PLUM SE18 52 K10
Brookhouse Gdns CHING E4 28 A9
Brookhurst Rd ADL/WDHM KT15 69 M11
Brooking Cl BCTR RM8 41 S8
Brooking Rd FSTGT E7 40 C10
Brookland Cl GLDGN NW11 37 N2
Brookland Garth GLDGN NW11 37 N2
Brookland Hl GLDGN NW11 37 N2
Brookland Ri GLDGN NW11 37 N2
Brooklands DART DA1 67 L6
Brooklands Ap ROM RM1 42 D2
Brooklands Av BFN/LL DA15 65 M7
WIM/MER SW19 61 P7
Brooklands Cl COB KT11 82 C5
ROMW/RG RM7 42 D2
SUN TW16 58 A13
Brooklands Ct KIL/WHAMP NW6 * 37 M12
WCHMH N21 26 H3
Brooklands Dr GFD/PVL UB6 35 S13
Brooklands Gdns EMPK RM11 42 J3
POTB/CUF EN6 14 A6
Brooklands La ROMW/RG RM7 42 D2
WEY KT13 69 R11
Brooklands Pk BKHTH/KID SE3 64 C1
Brooklands Pl HPTN TW12 58 K10
Brooklands Rd ROMW/RG RM7 42 D2
THDIT KT7 71 P6
WEY KT13 81 S1
Brooklands Ter SUN TW16 * 70 C2
The Brooklands ISLW TW7 * 47 M13
Brooklands Wy REDH RH1 93 S8
Brook La BKHTH/KID SE3 52 D14
BMLY BR1 64 C11
BXLY DA5 65 T4
RPLY/SEND GU23 80 J12
Brook La North BTFD TW8 47 T10
Brooklea Cl CDALE/KGS NW9 24 E13
Brooklyn Av LOU IG10 28 C2
SNWD SE25 75 M2
Brooklyn Cl CAR SM5 73 S7
WOKS/MYFD GU22 80 C9
Brooklyn Gv SNWD SE25 75 M2
Brooklyn Rd HAYES BR2 76 F3
SNWD SE25 75 M2
WOKS/MYFD GU22 80 C8
Brooklyn Wy WDR/YW UB7 45 P8
Brookmans Cl UPMR RM14 43 S5
Brookmans Park Dr UPMR RM14 43 S3
Brookmead CROY/NA CR0 74 A4
Brook Md HOR/WEW KT19 72 E11
Brookmead Av BMLY BR1 76 H3
Brookmead Cl STMC/STPC BR5 77 R5
Brook Meadow NFNCH/WDSPK N12 25 P9
Brook Meadow Cl WFD IG8 28 A11
Brookmead Rd CROY/NA CR0 74 A4
Brook Ms North BAY/PAD W2 2 K13
Brookmill Cl OXHEY WD19 * 22 D5
Brookmill Rd DEPT SE8 51 S13
Brook Pk DART DA1 67 N7
Brook Park Cl WCHMH N21 26 F4
Brook Pl BAR EN5 25 N3
Brook Ri CHIG IG7 28 J8
Brook Rd BKHH IG9 28 C7
BORE WD6 13 L13
BRW CM14 31 T8
CEND/HSY/T N8 38 C2
CHES/WCR EN8 16 F8
CRICK NW2 36 G7
EPP CM16 18 E7
GNTH/NBYPK IG2 41 N4
GPK RM2 30 F14
REDH RH1 93 T11
REDH RH1 94 A4
SURB KT6 71 U7
SWLY BR8 78 D1
THHTH CR7 74 G2
TWK TW1 59 Q4
WDGN N22 * 26 D14
Brook Rd South BTFD TW8 47 U11
Brooks Av EHAM E6 52 H2
Brooksbank St HOM E9 * 39 P11
Brooksby Ms IS N1 38 E12
Brooksby St IS N1 38 E12
Brooksby's Wk HOM E9 39 P10
Brooks Cl WEY KT13 69 S14
Brookscroft CROY/NA CR0 75 R14
Brookscroft Rd WALTH E17 27 T13
Brookshill KTN/HRWW/WS HA3 23 N11
Brookshill Av KTN/HRWW/WS HA3 23 M10
Brookshill Dr KTN/HRWW/WS HA3 23 M10
Brookside BARK/HLT IG6 29 L11
CAR SM5 73 U10
CHERT KT16 68 J5
DTCH/LGLY SL3 44 G12
EBAR EN4 25 S4
EMPK RM11 43 L3
GDST RH9 95 P14
HGDN/ICK UB10 33 R12
ORP BR6 77 P5
POTB/CUF EN6 13 S6
WAB EN9 17 L6
WATN WD24 * 11 R10
WCHMH N21 26 D4
Brookside Av ASHF TW15 57 N10
STWL/WRAY TW19 56 C1
Brookside Cl BAR EN5 24 K4
FELT TW13 58 C8
KTN/HRWW/WS HA3 35 T3
RSLP HA4 34 G9
Brookside Crs POTB/CUF EN6 15 N1
WPK KT4 72 G6
Brookside Gdns EN EN1 16 B11
Brookside Rd ARCH N19 38 A7
ED N9 27 M9
GLDGN NW11 37 L4
OXHEY WD19 22 D5
YEAD UB4 46 E5
Brookside South EBAR EN4 25 U5
Brookside Wy CROY/NA CR0 75 P4
Brooks La CHSWK W4 48 A11
Brook's Ms MYFR/PKLN W1K 3 U13
Brooks Rd CHSWK W4 48 A10
PLSTW E13 40 C13
Brook St BAY/PAD W2 3 M13
BELV DA17 54 B10
BRW CM14 31 S9
ERITH DA8 54 C12
KUT/HW KT1 59 U14
MYFR/PKLN W1K 3 T13
TOTM N17 26 K14
Brooksville Av KIL/WHAMP NW6 2 B2
Brookview Rd STRHM/NOR SW16 61 V10
Brookville Rd FUL/PGN SW6 6 C14
Brook Wk EDGW HA8 24 D11
EFNCH N2 25 R13
Brook Water La HDN NW4 * 36 K3
Brook Wy CHIG IG7 28 J8
LHD/OX KT22 83 Q8
Brookway BKHTH/KID SE3 64 C1
RAIN RM13 54 H3
Brookwood Av BARN SW13 60 F1
Brookwood Cl HAYES BR2 76 B2
Brookwood Rd HSLW TW3 46 K14
WAND/EARL SW18 61 M6
Broom Av STMC/STPC BR5 65 R14
Broom Bank WARL CR6 87 U9
Broom Cl CHESW EN7 16 A1
ESH/CLAY KT10 70 K10
HAYES BR2 76 G4
TEDD TW11 59 T12
Broomcroft Av NTHLT UB5 46 E1
Broomcroft Dr WOKS/MYFD GU22 80 H5
Broome Cl EPSOM KT18 92 D2
Broome Pl SOCK/AV RM15 55 R6
Broome Rd HPTN TW12 58 H13
Broomer Pl CHES/WCR EN8 16 C4
Broome Wy CMBW SE5 9 Q14
Broomfield LCOL/BKTW AL2 12 A1
SUN TW16 58 C13
WALTH E17 39 R5
Broomfield Av LOU IG10 28 H4
PLMGR N13 26 D10
Broomfield Cl CRW RM5 30 D12
WOKS/MYFD GU22 80 H6
Broomfield Cottages WEA W13 * 47 R6
Broomfield Ct WEY KT13 69 S11
Broomfield La PLMGR N13 26 C9
Broomfield Pl WEA W13 47 R6
Broomfield Ride LHD/OX KT22 83 M2
Broomfield Ri ABLGY WD5 10 K6
Broomfield Rd ADL/WDHM KT15 81 M1
BECK BR3 75 Q2
BXLYHS DA6 66 A3
CHDH RM6 41 T5
PLMGR N13 26 C10
RCH/KEW TW9 47 V13
SEV TN13 90 F12
SURB KT6 71 V6
TEDD TW11 59 S11
WEA W13 47 R6
Broomfields ESH/CLAY KT10 71 L10
Broomfield St POP/IOD E14 51 S3
Broom Gdns CROY/NA CR0 75 S8
Broom Gv WAT WD17 11 N12
Broomgrove Gdns EDGW HA8 24 A13
Broomgrove Rd BRXN/ST SW9 50 D14
Broom Hall LHD/OX KT22 83 L4
Broomhall End WOKN/KNAP GU21 80 C6
Broomhall La WOKN/KNAP GU21 80 C6
Broomhall Rd SAND/SEL CR2 74 H13
WOKN/KNAP GU21 80 C6
Broomhill Ri BXLYHS DA6 66 A3
Broomhill Rd DART DA1 66 H4
GDMY/SEVK IG3 41 Q7
ORP BR6 77 Q5
WAND/EARL SW18 61 N3
WFD IG8 28 C11
Broomhouse La FUL/PGN SW6 49 N14
Broomhouse Rd FUL/PGN SW6 49 N14
Broomlands La OXTED RH8 96 G3
Broomloan La SUT SM1 73 N7
Broom Lock TEDD TW11 * 59 S10
Broom Md BXLYHS DA6 66 A4
Broom Pk TEDD TW11 59 T12
Broom Rd CROY/NA CR0 75 S8
TEDD TW11 59 S11
Broomsleigh St KIL/WHAMP NW6 * 37 N10
Broomstick Hall Rd WAB EN9 17 L7
Broom Water TEDD TW11 59 S11
Broom Water West TEDD TW11 59 S10
Broom Wy WEY KT13 69 V9
Broomwood Cl BXLY DA5 66 D7
CROY/NA CR0 75 P3
Broomwood Gdns BRWN CM15 31 U4
Broomwood Rd BTSEA SW11 61 T4
STMC/STPC BR5 65 R14
Broseley Gdns HARH RM3 31 L9
Broseley Gv SYD SE26 63 Q10
Broseley Rd HARH RM3 31 L9
Broster Gdns SNWD SE25 74 K1
Brougham Rd ACT W3 48 C4
HACK E8 39 L13
Brougham St BTSEA SW11 49 T14
Brough Cl KUTN/CMB KT2 * 59 T10
VX/NE SW8 8 F14
Broughinge Rd BORE WD6 13 M14
Broughton Av FNCH N3 37 L1
RCHPK/HAM TW10 59 S9
Broughton Dr BRXN/ST SW9 62 E2
Broughton Gdns HGT N6 38 A4
Broughton Rd FUL/PGN SW6 49 P14
ORP BR6 77 M7
RSEV TN14 90 G6
THHTH CR7 74 E4
WEA W13 47 R5
Broughton Road Ap FUL/PGN SW6 * 49 P14
Broughton St VX/NE SW8 49 V14
Broughton Wy RKW/CH/CXG WD3 21 L5
Brouncker Rd ACT W3 48 C7
Brow Cl STMC/STPC BR5 77 T5
Brow Crs STMC/STPC BR5 77 S6
Browell's La FELT TW13 58 E7
Brown Cl WLGTN SM6 74 C12
Browne Cl BRW CM14 31 V6
Brownfield St POP/IOD E14 51 U4
Browngraves Rd HYS/HAR UB3 45 U12
Brown Hart Gdns MYFR/PKLN W1K 3 T13
Brownhill Rd CAT SE6 63 U5
Browning Av HNWL W7 47 P4
SUT SM1 73 S9
WPK KT4 72 H6
Browning Cl HPTN TW12 58 H9
MV/WKIL W9 * 2 K8
WALTH E17 39 U2
WELL DA16 53 N13
Browning Ms CAVSQ/HST W1G * 3 T10
Browning Rd DART DA1 67 M2
ENC/FH EN2 15 T12
MNPK E12 40 H11
WAN E11 40 B5
Browning St WALW SE17 9 P9
Browning Wy HEST TW5 46 F13
Brownlea Gdns GDMY/SEVK IG3 41 Q7
Brownlow Cl EBAR EN4 25 R3
Brownlow Ms BMSBY WC1N 4 H7
Brownlow Rd BORE WD6 24 A2
CROY/NA CR0 74 J9
FBAR/BDGN N11 26 C11
FNCH N3 25 P12
FSTGT E7 40 C9
HACK E8 5 V1
REDH RH1 93 S10
WEA W13 * 47 Q6
WLSDN NW10 36 E12
Brownlow St GINN WC1R 4 H10
Brownrigg Rd ASHF TW15 57 S9
Brownspring Dr ELTH/MOT SE9 64 K9
Brown's Rd BRYLDS KT5 71 V5
WALTH E17 39 S1
Brown St MBLAR W1H 3 Q11
Brownswell Rd EFNCH N2 25 R14
Brownswood Rd FSBYPK N4 38 G7
The Brow CSTG HP8 20 B8
GSTN WD25 11 P7
Broxash Rd BTSEA SW11 61 U4
Broxbourne Av SWFD E18 40 D2
Broxbourne House BOW E3 51 T2
Broxbourne Rd FSTGT E7 40 C8
ORP BR6 77 P6
Broxburn Dr SOCK/AV RM15 55 V5
Broxhill Rd ABR/ST RM4 30 G8
Broxholm Rd WNWD SE27 62 E8
Brox La CHERT KT16 68 H13
Brox Rd CHERT KT16 68 G13
Broxted Rd CAT SE6 63 R7
Broxwood Wy STJWD NW8 3 P2
Bruce Av HCH RM12 42 K7
SHPTN TW17 69 U4
Bruce Castle Rd TOTM N17 26 K13
Bruce Cl BF/WBF KT14 81 P3
NKENS W10 48 K3
WELL DA16 53 R13
Bruce Dr SAND/SEL CR2 75 P13
Bruce Gdns TRDG/WHET N20 25 T8
Bruce Gv ORP BR6 77 Q6
TOTM N17 26 K14
WATN WD24 11 Q12
Bruce Rd BAR EN5 25 L1
BOW E3 51 T1
KTN/HRWW/WS HA3 23 N14
MTCM CR4 61 U12
SNWD SE25 74 H2
WLSDN NW10 36 D12
Bruce Wy CHES/WCR EN8 16 D7
Bruckner St NKENS W10 2 C6
Brudenell Rd TOOT SW17 61 T8
Bruffs Meadow NTHLT UB5 34 G11
Bruford Ct DEPT SE8 51 S11
Bruges Pl CAMTN NW1 38 A12
Brumana Cl WEY KT13 69 T11
Brumfield Rd HOR/WEW KT19 72 C10
Brunel Cl HEST TW5 46 D12
NRWD SE19 62 K11
NTHLT UB5 46 H1
ROM RM1 42 E2
Brunel Ct WLSDN NW10 48 G1
Brunel Est BAY/PAD W2 2 E10
Brunel House WOOL/PLUM SE18 * 52 G12
Brunel Ms NKENS W10 48 K1
Brunel Rd ACT W3 48 E3
BERM/RHTH SE16 51 N7
WALTH E17 39 Q4
WFD IG8 28 H10
Brunel St CAN/RD E16 52 B4
Brunel Wk WHTN TW2 58 J5
Brune St WCHPL E1 5 U10
Brunner Cl GLDGN NW11 37 P3
Brunner Ct CHERT KT16 68 G10
Brunner Rd EA W5 47 T2
WALTH E17 39 R3
Bruno Pl CDALE/KGS NW9 36 C7
Brunswick Av FBAR/BDGN N11 25 U8
UPMR RM14 43 S5
Brunswick Cl BXLYHS DA6 65 T2
PIN HA5 34 H5
THDIT KT7 71 P6
WHTN TW2 59 M8
WOT/HER KT12 70 E7
Brunswick Ct STHWK SE1 9 T4
Brunswick Crs FBAR/BDGN N11 25 U8
Brunswick Gdns BARK/HLT IG6 29 L12
EA W5 47 U2
KENS W8 6 F2
Brunswick Gv COB KT11 82 E3
FBAR/BDGN N11 25 U8
Brunswick Ms MBLAR W1H 3 R11
STRHM/NOR SW16 62 B11
Brunswick Pk CMBW SE5 50 H13
Brunswick Park Gdns
FBAR/BDGN N11 25 U7
Brunswick Park Rd FBAR/BDGN N11 25 V8
Brunswick Pl CAMTN NW1 3 T8
IS N1 5 R6
NRWD SE19 63 L12
Brunswick Quay BERM/RHTH SE16 51 Q8
Brunswick Rd BXLYHS DA6 65 T2
EA W5 47 T2
KUTN/CMB KT2 60 A13
LEY E10 39 U6
PEND EN3 16 G12
SEVS/STOTM N15 38 J3
SUT SM1 73 P9
Brunswick Sq BMSBY WC1N 4 F7
TOTM N17 26 K11
Brunswick St WALTH E17 39 U3
Brunswick Vls CMBW SE5 50 J13
Brunswick Wy FBAR/BDGN N11 25 V9
Brunton Pl POP/IOD E14 51 Q4
Brushfield St WCHPL E1 5 T9
Brushrise WATN WD24 11 N10
Brushwood Cl POP/IOD E14 51 T3
Brushwood Dr RKW/CH/CXG WD3 20 G2
Brussels Rd BTSEA SW11 61 R2
Bruton Cl CHST BR7 64 H12
Bruton La MYFR/PICC W1J 3 V14
Bruton Pl MYFR/PICC W1J 3 V14
Bruton Rd MRDN SM4 73 Q2
Bruton St MYFR/PICC W1J 3 V14
Bruton Wy WEA W13 47 Q3
Bryan Av WLSDN NW10 36 H12
Bryan Cl SUN TW16 58 C12
Bryan Rd BERM/RHTH SE16 51 R7
Bryanston Av WHTN TW2 58 K6
Bryanston Cl NWDGN UB2 46 H9
Bryanstone Rd CEND/HSY/T N8 38 B3
CHES/WCR EN8 16 F8
Bryanston Ms East MBLAR W1H 3 Q10
Bryanston Ms West MBLAR W1H 3 Q10
Bryanston Pl MBLAR W1H 3 Q10
Bryanston Sq MBLAR W1H 3 Q11
Bryanston St MBLAR W1H 3 Q12
Bryant Av HARH RM3 30 K14
Bryant Cl BAR EN5 25 M3
Bryant Rd NTHLT UB5 46 E1
Bryant Rw HARH RM3 30 J7
Bryant St SRTFD E15 39 V12
Bryantwood Rd HOLWY N7 38 E10
Brycedale Crs STHGT/OAK N14 26 B9
Bryce Rd BCTR RM8 41 S9
Bryden Cl SYD SE26 63 Q10
Brydges Pl CHCR WC2N 4 E14
Brydges Rd SRTFD E15 39 V10
Brydon Wk IS N1 4 F1
Bryett Rd HOLWY N7 38 C8
Brymay Cl BOW E3 39 S14
Brynford Cl WOKN/KNAP GU21 80 C5
Brynmaer Rd BTSEA SW11 49 T13
Bryn-y-Mawr Rd EN EN1 26 K2
Bryony Cl LOU IG10 28 K2
UX/CGN UB8 45 R3
Bryony Rd SHB W12 48 G5
Bryony Wy SUN TW16 58 C11
Bubblestone Rd RSEV TN14 90 H6
Buchanan Cl SOCK/AV RM15 55 Q5
WCHMH N21 26 D3
Buchanan Ct BORE WD6 * 13 N14
Buchanan Gdns WLSDN NW10 36 H14
Buchan Cl UX/CGN UB8 45 N1
Buchan Rd PECK SE15 63 N1
Bucharest Rd WAND/EARL SW18 61 Q5
Buckden Cl LEE/GVPK SE12 64 B4
Buckettsland La BORE WD6 13 P12
Buckfast Rd MRDN SM4 73 P2
Buckfast St BETH E2 51 L1
Buckham Thorns Rd BH/WHM TN16 97 L2
Buckhold Rd WAND/EARL SW18 61 N4
Buckhurst Av CAR SM5 73 S6
Buckhurst Cl REDH RH1 93 S8
Buckhurst Rd BH/WHM TN16 88 K11
Buckhurst St WCHPL E1 51 M2
Buckhurst Wy BKHH IG9 28 F8
Buckingham Av E/WMO/HCT KT8 58 K14
EBED/NFELT TW14 58 D4
GFD/PVL UB6 35 Q13
THHTH CR7 62 E13
TRDG/WHET N20 25 Q5
WELL DA16 65 N2
Buckingham Cl EA W5 47 S3
EMPK RM11 42 K3
EN EN1 15 U14
HPTN TW12 58 H10
STMC/STPC BR5 77 N5
Buckingham Ct BELMT SM2 * 73 N13
Buckingham Dr CHST BR7 64 K10
Buckingham Gdns E/WMO/HCT KT8 58 K14
STAN HA7 23 U12
THHTH CR7 62 E14
Buckingham Ga WESTW SW1E 8 A5
Buckingham Gv HGDN/ICK UB10 33 S14
Buckingham La FSTH SE23 63 Q5
Buckingham Ms IS N1 38 J11
WESTW SW1E * 8 A5
WLSDN NW10 36 F14
Buckingham Palace Rd BGVA SW1W 7 U7
Buckingham Pde CFSP/GDCR SL9 20 C13
STAN HA7 * 23 S10
Buckingham Pl WESTW SW1E 8 A5
Buckingham Rd BORE WD6 24 D2
EDGW HA8 23 V12
HPTN TW12 58 H9
HRW HA1 35 M3
IL IG1 41 M7
IS N1 38 J11
KUT/HW KT1 71 V2
LEY E10 39 T8
MTCM CR4 74 C3
RCHPK/HAM TW10 59 T7
SRTFD E15 40 B10
SWFD E18 28 B13
WAN E11 40 E3
WATN WD24 11 Q11
WDGN N22 26 C13
WLSDN NW10 36 F14
Buckingham St CHCR WC2N 4 F14
Buckingham Wy WLGTN SM6 74 A13
Buckland Crs HAMP NW3 37 R12
Buckland La BRKHM/BTCW RH3 92 H7
Buckland Ri PIN HA5 22 E13
Buckland Rd BELMT SM2 72 J14
CHSGTN KT9 71 V10
KWD/TDW/WH KT20 93 M5
LEY E10 39 U7
ORP BR6 77 N9
REIG RH2 92 K9
Bucklands OXHEY WD19 * 22 F8
Bucklands Rd TEDD TW11 59 S11
Buckland St IS N1 5 R4
Bucklands Whf KUT/HW KT1 * 59 T14
Buckland Wk MRDN SM4 73 Q2
Buckland Wy WPK KT4 72 J6
Buck La CDALE/KGS NW9 36 D3
Buckleigh Av RYNPK SW20 73 M1
Buckleigh Rd STRHM/NOR SW16 62 C12
Buckleigh Wy NRWD SE19 62 K13
Bucklersbury MANHO EC4N * 5 Q12
Bucklers' Wy CAR SM5 73 T8
Buckle St WCHPL E1 5 V11
Buckles Wy BNSTD SM7 85 L6
Buckley Cl DART DA1 54 F14
FSTH SE23 63 M5
Buckley Rd KIL/WHAMP NW6 37 M12
Buckmaster Cl BRXN/ST SW9 62 E1
Buckmaster Rd BTSEA SW11 61 S2
Bucknalls Cl GSTN WD25 11 S6
Bucknalls Dr LCOL/BKTW AL2 11 T5
Bucknalls La GSTN WD25 11 S6
Bucknall St NOXST/BSQ WC1A 4 E11
Bucknall Wy BECK BR3 75 U2
Bucknell Cl BRXS/STRHM SW2 62 D2
Buckner Rd BRXS/STRHM SW2 62 D2
Bucknills Cl EPSOM KT18 84 C4
Buckrell Rd CHING E4 27 V7
Bucks Av OXHEY WD19 22 G5
Bucks Cl BF/WBF KT14 81 M4
Bucks Cross Rd ORP BR6 77 U10
Bucks Hl KGLGY WD4 10 C7
Buckstone Cl FSTH SE23 63 N4
Buckstone Rd UED N18 27 L11
Buck St CAMTN NW1 3 V1
Buckters Rents BERM/RHTH SE16 51 Q6
Buckthorne Rd BROCKY SE4 63 Q4
Buckton Rd BORE WD6 12 K12
Budd Cl NFNCH/WDSPK N12 25 P9
Buddings Cir WBLY HA9 36 C8
Budebury Rd STA TW18 56 K10
Bude Cl WALTH E17 39 R3
Budge La MTCM CR4 73 T5
Budgen Dr REDH RH1 93 U7
Budge Rw MANHO EC4N 5 Q13
Budgin's Hl ORP BR6 89 R2
Budleigh Crs WELL DA16 53 S13
Budoch Dr GDMY/SEVK IG3 41 Q7
Buer Rd FUL/PGN SW6 49 L14
Buff Av BNSTD SM7 85 P5
Buffers La LHD/OX KT22 83 Q9
Bug Hl WARL CR6 87 P10
Bugsby's Wy GNWCH SE10 52 B9
Bulganak Rd THHTH CR7 74 G2
Bulinca St WEST SW1P * 8 E8
Bulkeley Cl EGH TW20 56 A10
Bullace Rw CMBW SE5 50 H13
Bull Aly WELL DA16 65 R1
Bullard Rd TEDD TW11 59 N11
Bullards Pl BETH E2 51 P1
Bullbanks Rd BELV DA17 54 C9
Bullbeggars La GDST RH9 95 N8
Bulleid Wy BGVA SW1W 7 V8
Bullen St BTSEA SW11 49 S14
Buller Cl PECK SE15 51 L12
Buller Rd BARK IG11 41 N12
THHTH CR7 74 H1
TOTM N17 27 L14
WDGN N22 26 E14
WLSDN NW10 48 K1
Bullers Cl SCUP DA14 65 U10
Bullers Wood Dr CHST BR7 64 G13
Bullescroft Rd EDGW HA8 24 B8
Bullfinch Cl SEV TN13 90 D12
Bullfinch Dene SEV TN13 90 D12
Bullfinch La SEV TN13 90 E12
Bullfinch Rd SAND/SEL CR2 75 P14
Bullhead Rd BORE WD6 13 N14
BORE WD6 24 C2
Bull Hl EYN DA4 79 Q2
LHD/OX KT22 83 Q11
Bullivant Cl RDART DA2 67 U3
Bullivant St POP/IOD E14 51 U5
Bull La CFSP/GDCR SL9 32 B2
CHST BR7 65 M12
DAGE RM10 42 B8
UED N18 26 J10
Bull Rd SRTFD E15 40 B14
Bullrush Cl CAR SM5 73 S7
CROY/NA CR0 74 J4
Bullrush Gv UX/CGN UB8 45 N2
Bulls Aly MORT/ESHN SW14 * 60 D1
Bull's Br NWDGN UB2 46 C8
Bulls Bridge Rd NWDGN UB2 46 D8
Bullsbrook Rd YEAD UB4 46 E6
Bull's Cross EN EN1 16 A10
Bulls Cross Ride CHESW EN7 16 A8
Bull's Gdns CHEL SW3 7 P7
Bullsland Gdns RKW/CH/CXG WD3 20 F4
Bullsland La RKW/CH/CXG WD3 20 F5
Bullsmoor Cl CHES/WCR EN8 16 C9
Bullsmoor Gdns CHES/WCR EN8 16 B9
Bullsmoor La PEND EN3 16 D9
Bullsmoor Ride CHES/WCR EN8 16 C9
Bullsmoor Wy CHES/WCR EN8 16 B9
Bullwell Crs CHES/WCR EN8 16 E3
Bull Yd PECK SE15 51 L13
Bulmer Gdns KTN/HRWW/WS HA3 35 T5
Bulmer Ms NTGHL W11 6 E1
Bulstrode Av HSLW TW3 58 H1
Bulstrode Gdns HSLW TW3 58 J1
Bulstrode Pl MHST W1U 3 T10
Bulstrode Rd HSLW TW3 58 J1
Bulstrode St MHST W1U 3 T11
Bulstrode Wy CFSP/GDCR SL9 32 B3
Bulwer Court Rd WAN E11 39 V6
Bulwer Gdns BAR EN5 25 Q2
Bulwer Rd BAR EN5 25 P2
UED N18 26 J9
WAN E11 39 V6
Bulwer St SHB W12 48 J6
Bunbury Wy EW KT17 84 H6
Bunce Dr CTHM CR3 86 H13
Bunces La WFD IG8 28 B12
Bundys Wy STA TW18 56 K11
Bungalow Rd SNWD SE25 74 J2
The Bungalows RYLN/HDSTN HA2 * 34 H8
STRHM/NOR SW16 61 V12
WTHK RM20 * 55 U11
Bunhill Rw STLK EC1Y 5 Q7
Bunhouse Pl BGVA SW1W 7 S9
Bunker's Hl BELV DA17 54 A9
GLDGN NW11 37 Q5
SCUP DA14 65 V8
Bunning Wy HOLWY N7 * 38 C12
Bunn's La MLHL NW7 24 E11
Bunsen St BOW E3 39 Q14
Buntingbridge Rd BARK/HLT IG6 41 M3
Bunting Cl ED N9 27 P6
MTCM CR4 73 T3
Bunton St WOOL/PLUM SE18 52 J8
Bunyan Rd WALTH E17 39 Q1
Bunyard Dr WOKN/KNAP GU21 80 G4
Burbage Cl CHES/WCR EN8 16 E5
HYS/HAR UB3 45 V4
STHWK SE1 9 Q6
Burbage Rd HNHL SE24 62 H4
Burberry Cl NWMAL KT3 60 E14
Burbidge Rd SHPTN TW17 69 S2
Burbridge Wy TOTM N17 27 L14
Burcham St POP/IOD E14 51 T4
Burcharbro Rd ABYW SE2 53 T11
Burchell Ct BUSH WD23 23 L5
Burchell Rd LEY E10 39 T6
PECK SE15 51 M13
Burcher Gale Gv PECK SE15 9 T13
Burchetts Wy SHPTN TW17 69 T4
Burchwall Cl CRW RM5 30 C12
Burcote WEY KT13 69 V11
Burcote Rd WAND/EARL SW18 61 R6
Burcott Gdns ADL/WDHM KT15 69 P11
Burcott Rd PUR/KEN CR8 86 E4
Burden Cl BTFD TW8 47 S10
Burdenshott Av RCHPK/HAM TW10 60 B2
Burden Wy WAN E11 40 D7
Burder Cl IS N1 38 J11
Burder Rd IS N1 38 J11
Burdett Av RYNPK SW20 60 G13
Burdett Cl HNWL W7 * 47 P6
SCUP DA14 65 U10
Burdett Rd BOW E3 51 R2
CROY/NA CR0 74 H4
RCH/KEW TW9 59 V1
Burdetts Rd DAGW RM9 41 V13
Burdock Cl CROY/NA CR0 75 P6
Burdock Rd TOTM N17 39 L1
Burdon La BELMT SM2 85 N1
Burdon Pk BELMT SM2 73 M13
Burfield Cl TOOT SW17 61 Q9
Burfield Dr WARL CR6 87 N9
Burfield Rd RKW/CH/CXG WD3 20 F3
Burford Cl BARK/HLT IG6 41 L2
BCTR RM8 41 S8
HGDN/ICK UB10 33 Q9
Burford Gdns PLMGR N13 26 D8
Burford La EW KT17 84 J1
Burford Rd BMLY BR1 76 G2
BTFD TW8 47 U10
CAT SE6 63 R7
EHAM E6 52 G1
SRTFD E15 39 V12
SUT SM1 73 N7
WPK KT4 72 G5
Burford Wk FUL/PGN SW6 6 H14
Burford Wy CROY/NA CR0 75 U12
Burgate Cl DART DA1 66 F1
Burges Cl EMPK RM11 43 M4
Burges Gv BARN SW13 48 H12
Burges Rd EHAM E6 40 J12
STA TW18 57 L11
Burgess Av CDALE/KGS NW9 36 D4
Burgess Cl FELT TW13 58 G9
Burgess Hl CRICK NW2 37 N9
Burgess Ms WIM/MER SW19 61 P11
Burgess Rd SRTFD E15 40 A9
SUT SM1 73 P9
Burgess St POP/IOD E14 51 S3
Burge St STHWK SE1 9 R6
Burges Wy STA TW18 57 L10
Burghfield EW KT17 84 F5
Burgh Heath Rd EW KT17 84 G6
Burghill Rd SYD SE26 63 P9
Burghley Av BORE WD6 24 C3
NWMAL KT3 60 D13
Burghley Hall Cl WIM/MER SW19 * 61 L6
Burghley Pl MTCM CR4 73 T2
Burghley Rd CEND/HSY/T N8 38 E1
KTTN NW5 37 V9
WAN E11 * 40 A6
WIM/MER SW19 60 K9
Burgh Mt BNSTD SM7 85 M5
Burgh St IS N1 5 N3
Burgh Wd BNSTD SM7 85 L5
Burgon St BLKFR EC4V 5 M12
Burgos Cl CROY/NA CR0 74 E11
Burgos Gv GNWCH SE10 51 T13
Burgoyne Rd BRXN/ST SW9 62 D1
FSBYPK N4 38 F4
SNWD SE25 74 K2
SUN TW16 58 B11
Burham Cl PGE/AN SE20 63 N12
Burhill Gv PIN HA5 22 G14
Burhill Rd WOT/HER KT12 70 D13
Burke Cl PUT/ROE SW15 60 E2
Burke St CAN/RD E16 52 B3
Burket Cl NWDGN UB2 46 G9
Burland Rd BTSEA SW11 61 T3
CRW RM5 30 C11
Burlea Cl WOT/HER KT12 70 D10
Burleigh Av BFN/LL DA15 65 P3
WLGTN SM6 73 U8
Burleigh Cl ADL/WDHM KT15 69 M10
Burleigh Ct BUSH WD23 * 22 G2
Burleigh Gdns ASHF TW15 57 U10
STHGT/OAK N14 26 A6
WOKN/KNAP GU21 80 D7
Burleigh Pde STHGT/OAK N14 * 26 B6
Burleigh Pk COB KT11 82 G2
Burleigh Pl PUT/ROE SW15 60 K3
Burleigh Rd ADL/WDHM KT15 69 M9
CHEAM SM3 73 L6
CHES/WCR EN8 * 16 E6
EN EN1 26 J2
HGDN/ICK UB10 33 T13
Burleigh St COVGDN WC2E 4 F13
Burleigh Wk CAT SE6 63 U6
Burleigh Wy ENC/FH EN2 26 H1
POTB/CUF EN6 15 N4
Burley Cl CHING E4 27 S10
STRHM/NOR SW16 62 B14
Burley Rd CAN/RD E16 52 E4
Burlings La RSEV TN14 89 P7
Burlington Ar CONDST W1S 4 A14
Burlington Av RCH/KEW TW9 48 A13
ROMW/RG RM7 42 B4
Burlington Cl EBED/NFELT TW14 57 V5
EHAM E6 52 G4
MV/WKIL W9 2 E7
ORP BR6 76 K7
PIN HA5 34 D1
Burlington Gdns ACT W3 48 C6
CHDH RM6 41 U5
CHSWK W4 48 C10
CONDST W1S 4 A14
Burlington La CHSWK W4 48 C12
Burlington Ms ACT W3 48 C6
Burlington Pde CRICK NW2 * 36 K8
Burlington Pl FUL/PGN SW6 49 L14
REIG RH2 93 N9
WFD IG8 28 C8
Burlington Ri EBAR EN4 25 S6
Burlington Rd CHSWK W4 * 48 C10
ENC/FH EN2 15 T13
FUL/PGN SW6 49 L14
ISLW TW7 47 M13
MUSWH N10 37 U1
NWMAL KT3 72 F2
THHTH CR7 62 G14
TOTM N17 27 L13
Burman Cl RDART DA2 67 Q5
Burma Rd STNW/STAM N16 38 H9
Burma Ter NRWD SE19 * 62 J10
Burmester Rd TOOT SW17 61 Q8
Burnaby Crs CHSWK W4 48 C11
Burnaby Gdns CHSWK W4 48 B11
Burnaby St WBPTN SW10 6 J14
Burnbrae Cl NFNCH/WDSPK N12 25 P11
Burnbury Rd BAL SW12 62 A6
Burn Cl ADL/WDHM KT15 69 P9
GSTN WD25 * 23 M2
LHD/OX KT22 83 L5
Burncroft Av PEND EN3 16 C14
Burndell Wy YEAD UB4 46 F3
Burnell Av RCHPK/HAM TW10 59 S10
WELL DA16 53 Q14
Burnell Gdns STAN HA7 23 T14
Burnell Rd SUT SM1 73 P9
Burnell Wk STHWK SE1 * 9 V9
Burnels Av EHAM E6 52 J1
Burness Cl HOLWY N7 38 D11
UX/CGN UB8 33 P14
Burne St CAMTN NW1 3 N9
Burnet Cl HOM E9 39 N10
Burnet Gv HOR/WEW KT19 84 C3
Burnett La BARK/HLT IG6 28 K12
Burnett Rd ERITH DA8 54 K11
Burney Av BRYLDS KT5 71 V3
Burney Dr LOU IG10 29 L1
Burney St GNWCH SE10 51 U12
Burnfoot Av FUL/PGN SW6 49 L13
Burnham Av HGDN/ICK UB10 33 U9
Burnham Cl EN EN1 15 U12
KTN/HRWW/WS HA3 35 Q2
MLHL NW7 24 G12
STHWK SE1 9 V9
Burnham Crs DART DA1 66 J2
WAN E11 40 E2
Burnham Dr REIG RH2 93 N9
WPK KT4 72 K7
Burnham Gdns CROY/NA CR0 74 K5
HSLWW TW4 46 D13
HYS/HAR UB3 45 V8
Burnham Rd CHING E4 27 R10
DAGW RM9 41 R12
DART DA1 66 K3
MRDN SM4 73 P3
ROMW/RG RM7 42 C1
SCUP DA14 65 U8
Burnhams Rd GT/LBKH KT23 82 H14
Burnham St BETH E2 51 N1
KUTN/CMB KT2 60 A13
Burnham Ter DART DA1 * 66 K3
Burnham Wy SYD SE26 63 R10
WEA W13 47 R9
Burnhill Rd BECK BR3 63 S14
Burnley Cl OXHEY WD19 22 E10
Burnley Rd BRXN/ST SW9 50 D14
WLSDN NW10 36 F10
WTHK RM20 55 T13
Burnsall St CHEL SW3 7 P10
Burns Av BFN/LL DA15 65 R4
CHDH RM6 41 S5
EBED/NFELT TW14 58 C4
STHL UB1 46 J5
Burns Cl CAR SM5 73 U13
ERITH DA8 54 F13
WALTH E17 39 U2
WELL DA16 53 P13
WIM/MER SW19 61 R11
YEAD UB4 46 C3
Burns Dr BNSTD SM7 85 L4
Burnside ASHTD KT21 83 V8
Burnside Av CHING E4 27 R11
Burnside Cl BAR EN5 25 N1
BERM/RHTH SE16 51 P6
TWK TW1 59 Q4
Burnside Crs ALP/SUD HA0 35 T13
Burnside Rd BCTR RM8 41 S7
Burns Rd ALP/SUD HA0 35 U14
BTSEA SW11 49 T14
WEA W13 * 47 R7
WLSDN NW10 36 F13
Burns Wy HEST TW5 46 F13
Burnt Ash Hl LEE/GVPK SE12 64 B4
Burnt Ash La BMLY BR1 64 C11
Burnt Ash Rd LEE/GVPK SE12 64 B4
Burntfarm Ride ENC/FH EN2 15 R8
Burnt House La RDART DA2 67 M9
Burnthwaite Rd FUL/PGN SW6 6 E14
Burnt Oak Broadway EDGW HA8 24 B13
Burnt Oak Flds EDGW HA8 24 C13
Burnt Oak La BFN/LL DA15 65 R5
Burntwood Av EMPK RM11 42 K4
Burntwood Cl CTHM CR3 87 L11
WAND/EARL SW18 * 61 R6
Burntwood Grange Rd
WAND/EARL SW18 61 R6
Burntwood La CTHM CR3 87 L11
TOOT SW17 61 R7
Burntwood Vw NRWD SE19 * 62 K10
Burnway EMPK RM11 43 L5
Burnwood Park Rd WOT/HER KT12 70 D9
Buross St WCHPL E1 51 M4
Burpham Cl YEAD UB4 46 F3
Burrage Gv WOOL/PLUM SE18 53 L9
Burrage Pl WOOL/PLUM SE18 52 K10
Burrage Rd WOOL/PLUM SE18 53 L10
Burrard Rd CAN/RD E16 52 C4
KIL/WHAMP NW6 37 N10
Burr Bank Ter RDART DA2 * 66 J9
Burr Cl BXLYHN DA7 65 V1
LCOL/BKTW AL2 12 J1
WAP E1W 51 L6
Burrell Cl CROY/NA CR0 75 Q4
EDGW HA8 24 B7
Burrell Rw BECK BR3 63 S14
Burrell St STHWK SE1 9 L1
Burrels Whf POP/IOD E14 51 T10
Burrfield Dr STMC/STPC BR5 77 T3
Burritt Rd KUT/HW KT1 60 A14
Burroughs Cottages POP/IOD E14 * 51 Q3
Burroughs Gdns HDN NW4 36 H2
The Burroughs HDN NW4 36 H2
Burroway Rd DTCH/LGLY SL3 44 F8
Burrow Gn CHIG IG7 29 P10
Burrow Rd CHIG IG7 29 Q10
EDUL SE22 62 J2
Burrows Cha WAB EN9 16 K10
Burrows Cl GT/LBKH KT23 82 H14
Burrows Hill Cl STWL/WRAY TW19 57 N2
Burrows Ms STHWK SE1 9 L3
Burrows Rd WLSDN NW10 48 J1
Burr Rd WAND/EARL SW18 61 N6
Bursar St STHWK SE1 * 9 S2
Bursdon Cl BFN/LL DA15 65 P7
Bursland Rd PEND EN3 27 P2
Burslem Av BARK/HLT IG6 29 Q11
Burslem St WCHPL E1 * 51 M4
Burstead Cl COB KT11 82 F3
Burstock Rd PUT/ROE SW15 61 L2
Burston Dr LCOL/BKTW AL2 12 A2
Burston Rd PUT/ROE SW15 60 K3
Burstow Rd RYNPK SW20 61 L13
Burtenshaw Rd THDIT KT7 71 Q5
Burtley Cl FSBYPK N4 38 G6
Burton Av WATW WD18 22 C2
Burton Bank IS N1 * 38 H12
Burton Cl CHSGTN KT9 71 T12
THHTH CR7 74 H1
Burton Dr PEND EN3 16 G11
Burton Gdns HEST TW5 46 H13
Burton Gv WALW SE17 9 Q10
Burtonhole Cl MLHL NW7 24 K9
Burtonhole La MLHL NW7 24 K10
Burton La BRXN/ST SW9 * 50 E14
CHESW EN7 15 U2
Burton Ms BGVA SW1W 7 T8
Burton Pl STPAN WC1H 4 D7
Burton Rd BRXN/ST SW9 50 F14
KIL/WHAMP NW6 37 M12
KUTN/CMB KT2 59 U12
LOU IG10 29 L2
SWFD E18 40 D1
Burtons Ct SRTFD E15 39 V12
Burtons La CSTG HP8 20 D3
Burton's Rd HPTN TW12 58 K9
Burton St STPAN WC1H 4 D7
Burt Rd CAN/RD E16 52 E6
Burtwell La DUL SE21 62 H9
Burvale Ct WATW WD18 22 D1
Burwash Ct STMC/STPC BR5 77 S3
Burwash Rd WOOL/PLUM SE18 53 M10
Burway Crs CHERT KT16 69 L2
Burwell Av GFD/PVL UB6 35 N11
Burwell Cl WCHPL E1 51 M4
Burwell Rd LEY E10 39 Q6
Burwood Av HAYES BR2 76 D7
PIN HA5 34 E3
PUR/KEN CR8 86 F4
Burwood Cl REIG RH2 93 R10
SURB KT6 72 A6
WOT/HER KT12 70 E11
Burwood Gdns RAIN RM13 54 F1
Burwood Pl BAY/PAD W2 3 P11
EBAR EN4 14 E13
Burwood Rd WEY KT13 69 V12
Bury Av RSLP HA4 33 U4
YEAD UB4 34 A14
Bury Cl BERM/RHTH SE16 51 P6
WOKN/KNAP GU21 80 B6
Bury Ct HDTCH EC3A 5 T11
Burydell La LCOL/BKTW AL2 12 B1
Bury Green Rd CHESW EN7 16 A6
Bury Gv MRDN SM4 73 P3
Bury La EPP CM16 18 B4
RKW/CH/CXG WD3 21 P6
WOKN/KNAP GU21 80 A6
Bury Mdw RKW/CH/CXG WD3 21 P6
Bury Pl NOXST/BSQ WC1A 4 E10
Bury Rd CHING E4 27 V2
DAGE RM10 42 C10
EPP CM16 18 C5
WDGN N22 38 E1
Buryside Cl GNTH/NBYPK IG2 41 P3
Bury St ED N9 26 K5
HDTCH EC3A 5 T12
RSLP HA4 33 V4
STJS SW1Y 8 A1
Bury St West ED N9 26 J5
Bury Wk CHEL SW3 7 N8
Busby Pl KTTN NW5 38 B11
Busch Cl ISLW TW7 47 R13
Bushbaby Cl STHWK SE1 9 S6
Bushbarns CHESW EN7 16 A3
Bushberry Rd HOM E9 39 Q11
Bush Cl ADL/WDHM KT15 69 N10
GNTH/NBYPK IG2 41 M3
Bush Cottages WAND/EARL SW18 61 N3
Bushell Cl BRXS/STRHM SW2 62 D7
Bushell Gn BUSH WD23 23 M7
Bushell Wy CHST BR7 64 J10
Bush Elms Rd EMPK RM11 42 G5
Bushetts Gv REDH RH1 93 V5
Bushey Av STMC/STPC BR5 77 M5
SWFD E18 40 B1
Bushey Cl CHING E4 27 U8
HGDN/ICK UB10 33 S7
PUR/KEN CR8 86 K6
Bushey Cft OXTED RH8 95 U6
Bushey Grove Rd BUSH WD23 22 G2
Bushey Hall Dr BUSH WD23 22 G2
Bushey Hall Pk BUSH WD23 * 22 G2
Bushey Hall Rd BUSH WD23 22 G2
Bushey Hill Rd CMBW SE5 50 K13
Bushey La SUT SM1 73 N8
Bushey Lees BFN/LL DA15 * 65 P4
Busheymill Br WATN WD24 11 S12
Bushey Mill Crs WATN WD24 11 Q11
Bushey Mill La WATN WD24 11 R12
Bushey Rd CROY/NA CR0 75 S7
HGDN/ICK UB10 33 S7
HYS/HAR UB3 46 A9
PLSTW E13 40 E14
RYNPK SW20 60 J14
SEVS/STOTM N15 38 J4
SUT SM1 73 N9
Bushey Wy BECK BR3 75 V4
Bushfield Cl EDGW HA8 24 B7
Bushfield Crs EDGW HA8 24 B7
Bushfields LOU IG10 28 J3
Bush Gv CDALE/KGS NW9 36 C5
STAN HA7 23 T13
Bushgrove Rd BCTR RM8 41 T9
Bush Hl WCHMH N21 26 G5
Bush Hill Pde ED N9 26 H5
Bush Hill Rd KTN/HRWW/WS HA3 35 V4
WCHMH N21 26 H5
Bush House WOOL/PLUM SE18 * 52 G12
Bush La CANST EC4R 5 Q13
RPLY/SEND GU23 80 H14
Bushmead Cl SEVS/STOTM N15 * 38 K2
Bushmoor Crs WOOL/PLUM SE18 52 K13
Bushnell Rd TOOT SW17 61 V7
Bush Rd BKHH IG9 28 F9
DEPT SE8 51 P9
HACK E8 39 M13
RCH/KEW TW9 47 V11
SHPTN TW17 69 R3
WAN E11 40 B5
Bushway BCTR RM8 41 T9
Bushwood WAN E11 40 B6
Bushwood Dr STHWK SE1 9 V8
Bushwood Rd RCH/KEW TW9 48 A11
Bushy Park Gdns HPTN TW12 59 M10
Bushy Park Rd TEDD TW11 59 R12
Bushy Rd LHD/OX KT22 82 K12
TEDD TW11 59 N11
Bushy Shaw ASHTD KT21 83 S7
Butcher Rw WAP E1W 51 P4
Butchers Rd CAN/RD E16 52 C4
Butchers Yd ORP BR6 88 J1
Bute Av RCHPK/HAM TW10 59 U7
Bute Gdns HMSMTH W6 48 K9
RCHPK/HAM TW10 * 59 U6
WLGTN SM6 74 A10
Bute Gdns West WLGTN SM6 74 A10
Bute Ms GLDGN NW11 37 P3
Bute Rd BARK/HLT IG6 40 K3
CROY/NA CR0 74 E6
WLGTN SM6 74 A9
Bute St SKENS SW7 7 L7
Bute Wk IS N1 * 38 H11
Butler Av HRW HA1 35 M5
Butler Cl EDGW HA8 24 B14
Butler Rd BCTR RM8 41 R9
HRW HA1 35 L5
WLSDN NW10 36 F12
Butlers Cl HSLWW TW4 58 H2
Butlers & Colonial Whf STHWK SE1 9 V3
Butlers Dene Rd CTHM CR3 87 S10
Butlers Dr CHING E4 16 J12
Butler St BETH E2 * 51 N1
HGDN/ICK UB10 45 T2
Buttercross La EPP CM16 * 18 E4
Buttercup Cl HARH RM3 30 K13
NTHLT UB5 34 H11
Buttercup Sq STWL/WRAY TW19 * 57 P6
Butterfield Cl BERM/RHTH SE16 * 51 L7
TOTM N17 26 G11
TWK TW1 59 P4
Butterfield House CHARL SE7 * 52 G12
Butterfields WALTH E17 39 U3
Butterfield Sq EHAM E6 52 H4
Butterfly Av DART DA1 67 M8
Butterfly La BORE WD6 23 R1
ELTH/MOT SE9 64 K4
Butterfly Wk CMBW SE5 * 50 H13
WARL CR6 87 N10
Butter Hl CAR SM5 73 U8
Butteridges Cl DAGW RM9 41 V13
Butterly Av DART DA1 * 67 M7
Buttermere Cl EBED/NFELT TW14 58 B6
MRDN SM4 72 K4
SRTFD E15 39 V9
STHWK SE1 9 U8
Buttermere Dr PUT/ROE SW15 61 L3
Buttermere Gdns PUR/KEN CR8 86 H4
Buttermere Pl GSTN WD25 * 11 N7
Buttermere Rd STMC/STPC BR5 77 T2
Buttermere Wk HACK E8 38 K11
Buttermere Wy EGH TW20 56 F12
Butterwick GSTN WD25 11 S10
HMSMTH W6 48 J9
Butterworth Gdns WFD IG8 28 C11
Buttesland St IS N1 5 R5
Buttfield Cl DAGE RM10 42 B11
Buttlehide RKW/CH/CXG WD3 20 H10
Buttmarsh Cl WOOL/PLUM SE18 52 K10
Button St SWLY BR8 78 J2
Buttsbury Rd IL IG1 41 L10
Butts Crs FELT TW13 58 J8
Butts Green Rd EMPK RM11 42 K4
Buttsmead NTHWD HA6 21 U12
Butts Piece NTHLT UB5 34 D14
Butts Rd BMLY BR1 64 A10
WOKN/KNAP GU21 80 C8
The Butts BTFD TW8 47 T11
RSEV TN14 90 H7
Buxhall Crs HOM E9 39 R11
Buxted Rd EDUL SE22 62 J2
HACK E8 38 K12
NFNCH/WDSPK N12 25 S10
Buxton Av CTHM CR3 86 J11
Buxton Cl HOR/WEW KT19 84 B1
WFD IG8 28 F11
Buxton Crs CHEAM SM3 73 L9
Buxton Dr NWMAL KT3 60 D14
WAN E11 40 A2
Buxton Gdns ACT W3 48 B5
Buxton La CTHM CR3 86 J11
Buxton Ms CLAP SW4 50 C14
Buxton Pth OXHEY WD19 * 22 E8
Buxton Rd ARCH N19 38 B6
ASHF TW15 57 P10
CHING E4 27 V5
CRICK NW2 36 H11
EHAM E6 52 G1
EPP CM16 18 C10
ERITH DA8 54 D12
GNTH/NBYPK IG2 41 N4
MORT/ESHN SW14 60 E1
SRTFD E15 40 A10
THHTH CR7 74 F3
WAB EN9 17 N6
WALTH E17 39 Q2
Buxton St WCHPL E1 5 V8
Byam St FUL/PGN SW6 49 Q14
Byards Cft STRHM/NOR SW16 62 B13
Bychurch End TEDD TW11 * 59 P10
Bycroft Rd STHL UB1 46 J3
Bycroft St PGE/AN SE20 63 P12
Bycullah Av ENC/FH EN2 26 F1
Bycullah Rd ENC/FH EN2 26 F1
Byelands Cl BERM/RHTH SE16 51 P6
Byers Cl POTB/CUF EN6 14 E8
The Bye ACT W3 48 E4
Byewaters WATW WD18 21 V4
Bye Ways WHTN TW2 58 K8
The Byeways BRYLDS KT5 72 A3
The Bye Wy KTN/HRWW/WS HA3 23 N13
The Byeway MORT/ESHN SW14 60 C1
RKW/CH/CXG WD3 21 Q7
Byfeld Gdns BARN SW13 48 G13
Byfield Cl BERM/RHTH SE16 51 Q7
Byfield Rd ISLW TW7 59 Q1
Byfleet Rd ADL/WDHM KT15 69 P13
COB KT11 81 T2
Byford Cl SRTFD E15 40 A12
Bygrove CROY/NA CR0 75 T11
Bygrove Rd WIM/MER SW19 61 R11
Bygrove St POP/IOD E14 51 T4
Byland Cl ABYW SE2 53 R8
CAR SM5 73 R5
STHGT/OAK N14 26 D5
Bylands WOKS/MYFD GU22 80 E8
Byne Rd CAR SM5 73 S7
SYD SE26 63 N11
Bynes Rd SAND/SEL CR2 74 H12
Byng Dr POTB/CUF EN6 14 C5
Byng Pl GWRST WC1E 4 D8
Byng Rd BAR EN5 24 K1
Byng St POP/IOD E14 51 S7
Bynon Av BXLYHN DA7 65 U1
Byre Rd STHGT/OAK N14 25 V4
Byrne Rd BAL SW12 61 V6
Byron Av BORE WD6 24 A3
CDALE/KGS NW9 36 B2
COUL/CHIP CR5 86 C5
HSLWW TW4 46 D14
MNPK E12 40 G11
NWMAL KT3 72 G3
SUT SM1 73 R9
SWFD E18 40 B1
WATN WD24 11 R13
Byron Av East SUT SM1 73 R9
Byron Cl CHESW EN7 15 V1
HACK E8 39 L13

HPTN TW12 58 H9
PGE/AN SE20 * 75 M1
STRHM/NOR SW16 62 C11
SYD SE26 * 63 Q9
THMD SE28 53 S6
WOT/HER KT12 70 G6
Byron Ct ENC/FH EN2 15 R14
Byron Dr EFNCH N2 37 R4
ERITH DA8 54 B12
Byron Gdns SUT SM1 73 R9
Byron Hill Rd RYLN/HDSTN HA2 35 N7
Byron Ms HAMP NW3 37 S10
MV/WKIL W9 2 F7
Byron Pde HGDN/ICK UB10 * 45 T2
Byron Pl LHD/OX KT22 83 R12
Byron Rd ADL/WDHM KT15 69 P9
ALP/SUD HA0 35 S7
CRICK NW2 36 H7
DART DA1 67 P2
EA W5 47 V6
HRW HA1 35 N4
KTN/HRWW/WS HA3 23 P14
LEY E10 39 T6
MLHL NW7 24 G10
SAND/SEL CR2 75 M14
WALTH E17 39 S1
Byron St POP/IOD E14 51 U4
Byron Ter ED N9 * 27 N5
Byron Wy HARH RM3 30 J13
NTHLT UB5 46 G1
WDR/YW UB7 45 R9
YEAD UB4 46 B2
Bysouth Cl CLAY IG5 28 K13
SEVS/STOTM N15 38 H2
By The Wd OXHEY WD19 22 G7
Bythorn St BRXN/ST SW9 62 D1
Byton Rd TOOT SW17 61 T11
Byward Av EBED/NFELT TW14 58 E4
Byward St MON EC3R 5 T14
Bywater Pl BERM/RHTH SE16 51 Q6
Bywater St CHEL SW3 7 Q9
The Byway BELMT SM2 73 R13
HOR/WEW KT19 72 F9
POTB/CUF EN6 14 C7
Bywell Pl GTPST W1W * 4 A10
Bywood Av CROY/NA CR0 75 N4
Bywood Cl PUR/KEN CR8 86 F5
By-wood End CFSP/GDCR SL9 20 E10

C

Cabbell Pl ADL/WDHM KT15 69 N9
Cabbell St BAY/PAD W2 3 N10
Caberfeigh Cl REDH RH1 93 S10
Caberfeigh Pl REDH RH1 * 93 R10
Cabinet Wy CHING E4 27 R11
Cable Pl GNWCH SE10 51 U13
Cables Cl ERITH DA8 54 C8
Cable St WCHPL E1 51 M5
Cable Trade Pk CHARL SE7 * 52 C10
Cabot Sq POP/IOD E14 51 S6
Cabot Wy EHAM E6 40 F13
Cabrera Av VW GU25 68 B3
Cabrera Cl VW GU25 68 A4
Cabul Rd BTSEA SW11 49 S14
Cacket's La RSEV TN14 89 M5
Cactus Cl CMBW SE5 * 50 J14
Cadbury Cl ISLW TW7 47 Q13
SUN TW16 58 A12
Cadbury Rd SUN TW16 58 A12
Cadbury Wy BERM/RHTH SE16 9 V7
Caddington Cl EBAR EN4 25 S3
Caddington Rd CRICK NW2 37 L8
Caddis Cl STAN HA7 * 23 P12
Caddy Cl EGH TW20 56 E10
Cadell Cl BETH E2 5 V4
Cade Rd GNWCH SE10 51 V13
Cader Rd WAND/EARL SW18 61 Q4
Cadet Dr STHWK SE1 9 V9
Cadet Pl GNWCH SE10 52 A10
Cadiz Rd DAGE RM10 42 C12
Cadiz St WALW SE17 9 P10
Cadlocks Hl RSEV TN14 77 V14
Cadman Cl BRXN/ST SW9 9 L14
Cadmer Cl NWMAL KT3 72 E2
Cadmore La CHES/WCR EN8 16 F3
Cadmus Cl CLAP SW4 62 B2
Cadogan Av RDART DA2 67 R5
Cadogan Cl HOM E9 * 39 R12
RYLN/HDSTN HA2 34 K9
TEDD TW11 59 N10
Cadogan Ct BELMT SM2 73 P11
Cadogan Gdns CHEL SW3 7 R8
FNCH N3 * 25 P13
SWFD E18 40 D1
WCHMH N21 26 E3
Cadogan Ga KTBR SW1X 7 R7
Cadogan La KTBR SW1X 7 S6
Cadogan Pl KTBR SW1X 7 R6
PUR/KEN CR8 86 G7
Cadogan Rd SURB KT6 71 T3
WOOL/PLUM SE18 53 L8
Cadogan Sq KTBR SW1X 7 Q6
Cadogan St CHEL SW3 7 Q8
Cadogan Ter HOM E9 39 R11
Cadoxton Av SEVS/STOTM N15 38 K4
Cadwallon Rd ELTH/MOT SE9 64 K7
Caedmon Rd HOLWY N7 38 D9
Caenshill Pl WEY KT13 * 69 S12
Caenshill Rd WEY KT13 69 S12
Caenswood Hl WEY KT13 69 S14
Caenwood Cl WEY KT13 69 S11
Caen Wood Rd ASHTD KT21 83 S8
Caerleon Cl ESH/CLAY KT10 71 R12
SCUP DA14 65 S10
Caernarvon Cl EMPK RM11 43 N6
MTCM CR4 74 C1
Caernarvon Dr CLAY IG5 28 J13
Caesars Wk MTCM CR4 73 T3
Caesar's Wy SHPTN TW17 69 V4
Cage Farm Cottages OXTED RH8 * 95 T10
Cage Pond Rd RAD WD7 13 L7
Cage Yd REIG RH2 * 93 N10
Cahill St STLK EC1Y * 5 P8
Cahir St POP/IOD E14 51 T9
Caillard Rd BF/WBF KT14 81 P1
Cain's La EBED/NFELT TW14 57 V3
Caird St NKENS W10 2 B6
Cairn Av EA W5 47 T6
Cairndale Cl BMLY BR1 64 B12
Cairnfield Av CRICK NW2 36 E8
Cairngorm Cl TEDD TW11 59 Q10
Cairns Av WFD IG8 28 H11
Cairns Cl DART DA1 66 K3
Cairns Rd BTSEA SW11 61 S3
Cairn Wy STAN HA7 23 P11
Cairo New Rd CROY/NA CR0 74 F7
Cairo Rd WALTH E17 * 39 S2
Caishowe Rd BORE WD6 13 M13
Caister Ms BAL SW12 61 V5
Caistor Park Rd SRTFD E15 40 B13
Caistor Rd BAL SW12 61 V5
Caithness Dr EPSOM KT18 84 D4
Caithness Gdns BFN/LL DA15 65 P4
Caithness Rd MTCM CR4 61 V12
WKENS W14 48 K8
Calabria Rd HBRY N5 38 F11
Calais St CMBW SE5 50 F13
Calbourne Av HCH RM12 42 H10
Calbourne Rd BAL SW12 61 T5
Calcott Cl BRW CM14 31 V6
Caldbeck WAB EN9 16 K8
Caldbeck Av WPK KT4 72 H7
Caldecot Av CHESW EN7 15 V3
Caldecote Gdns BUSH WD23 23 N4
Caldecote La BUSH WD23 23 P5
Caldecot Rd CMBW SE5 50 C14
Caldecot Wy CLPT E5 39 P8
Calder Av GFD/PVL UB6 35 P14
Calder Ct DTCH/LGLY SL3 44 D10
Calder Gdns EDGW HA8 36 A1
Calderon Rd WAN E11 39 U9
Calder Rd MRDN SM4 73 Q3
Caldervale Rd CLAP SW4 62 B3
Calder Wy DTCH/LGLY SL3 56 J1
Calderwood St WOOL/PLUM SE18 52 J9
Caldew St CMBW SE5 9 Q13
Caldicote Gn CDALE/KGS NW9 * 36 E4
Caldwell Rd OXHEY WD19 22 F9
Caldwell St BRXN/ST SW9 8 H14
Caldy Rd BELV DA17 54 B8
Caldy Wk IS N1 * 38 G11
Caledonian Cl GDMY/SEVK IG3 * 41 R6
Caledonian Rd HOLWY N7 38 D10
Caledonian Sq CAMTN NW1 38 B11
Caledonian Wharf Rd POP/IOD E14 51 V9
Caledonia Rd STWL/WRAY TW19 57 Q6
Caledonia St IS N1 4 F4
Caledon Rd EHAM E6 40 H13
WLGTN SM6 73 U9
Cale St CHEL SW3 7 N9
Calfstock La EYN DA4 79 L2
Calidore Cl BRXS/STRHM SW2 * 62 D4
California Cl BELMT SM2 73 N14
California La BUSH WD23 23 M6
California Rd NWMAL KT3 72 C2
Callaby Ter IS N1 * 38 H11
Callaghan Cl LEW SE13 64 A2
Callaghan Cottages WCHPL E1 * 51 N3
Callander Rd CAT SE6 63 T7
The Callanders BUSH WD23 * 23 N6
Callard Av PLMGR N13 26 F10
Callcott Rd KIL/WHAMP NW6 37 M12
Callcott St KENS W8 6 E1
Callendar Rd SKENS SW7 7 L5
Calley Down Crs CROY/NA CR0 75 V14
Callingham Cl POP/IOD E14 51 R3
Callis Farm Cl STWL/WRAY TW19 57 Q4
Callisons Pl GNWCH SE10 52 A10
Callis Rd WALTH E17 39 R4
Callow Fld PUR/KEN CR8 86 E3
Callow Hl VW GU25 56 A14
Callowland Pl WATN WD24 11 P12
Callow St CHEL SW3 7 L11
Calluna Ct WOKS/MYFD GU22 80 D8
Calmington Rd CMBW SE5 9 T11
Calmont Rd BMLY BR1 63 V11
Calmore Cl HCH RM12 42 J10
Calne Av CLAY IG5 28 K13
Calonne Rd WIM/MER SW19 60 K9
Calshot Rd HTHAIR TW6 45 T14
Calshot St IS N1 4 G3
Calshot Wy ENC/FH EN2 26 F1
HTHAIR TW6 45 T14
Calthorpe Gdns EDGW HA8 23 V10
SUT SM1 73 Q8
Calthorpe St FSBYW WC1X 4 H7
Calton Av DUL SE21 62 J4
Calton Rd BAR EN5 25 Q4
Calverley Cl BECK BR3 63 T11
Calverley Crs DAGE RM10 42 A7
Calverley Gv ARCH N19 38 B6
Calverley Rd EW KT17 72 G11
Calvert Av WCHPL E1 5 T6
Calvert Cl BELV DA17 54 A9
SCUP DA14 65 U11
Calvert Dr RDART DA2 66 E7
Calverton Rd EHAM E6 40 J13
Calvert Rd BAR EN5 13 V14
GNWCH SE10 52 B10
Calvert St CAMTN NW1 3 S1
Calvin Cl STMC/STPC BR5 77 T1
Calvin St WCHPL E1 5 U8
Calydon Rd CHARL SE7 52 D10
Calypso Crs PECK SE15 9 U13
Calypso Wy BERM/RHTH SE16 51 R8
Camac Rd WHTN TW2 59 M7
Camarthen Gn CDALE/KGS NW9 * 36 E4
Cambalt Rd PUT/ROE SW15 60 K3
Camberley Av EN EN1 26 J2
RYNPK SW20 60 H14
Camberley Cl CHEAM SM3 72 K8
Camberley Rd HTHAIR TW6 57 S1
Cambert Wy BKHTH/KID SE3 64 D2
Camberwell Church St CMBW SE5 50 H13
Camberwell Glebe CMBW SE5 50 H13
Camberwell Gn CMBW SE5 50 H13
Camberwell Gv CMBW SE5 50 H13
Camberwell La RSEV TN14 97 V7
Camberwell New Rd CMBW SE5 9 M14
Camberwell Rd CMBW SE5 9 P12
Camberwell Station Rd CMBW SE5 50 G13
Cambeys Rd DAGE RM10 42 C10
Camborne Av HARH RM3 31 L12
WEA W13 47 S7
Camborne Cl HTHAIR TW6 57 S1
Camborne Crs HTHAIR TW6 57 S1
Camborne Ms WAND/EARL SW18 61 N5
Camborne Rd BELMT SM2 73 N12
CROY/NA CR0 75 L5
MRDN SM4 72 K4
SCUP DA14 65 S8
WAND/EARL SW18 61 N5
WELL DA16 53 N14
Camborne Wy HARH RM3 31 M12
HEST TW5 46 J13
Cambourne Av ED N9 27 P5
Cambourne Ms NTGHL W11 2 A12
Cambourne Wy HARH RM3 31 L12
Cambray Rd BAL SW12 62 A6
ORP BR6 77 P5
Cambria Cl BFN/LL DA15 65 N6
HSLW TW3 58 J2
Cambria Ct EBED/NFELT TW14 58 D5
Cambria Gdns STWL/WRAY TW19 57 Q5
Cambrian Av GNTH/NBYPK IG2 41 N3
Cambrian Cl WNWD SE27 62 F8
Cambrian Gn CDALE/KGS NW9 36 E3
Cambrian Rd LEY E10 39 S5
RCHPK/HAM TW10 59 V4
Cambria Rd CMBW SE5 62 G1
Cambria St FUL/PGN SW6 6 H14
Cambridge Av GFD/PVL UB6 35 P11
GPK RM2 42 J1
KIL/WHAMP NW6 2 F3
NWMAL KT3 60 F14
WELL DA16 65 P2
Cambridge Barracks Rd
WOOL/PLUM SE18 52 H9
Cambridge Circ SOHO/SHAV W1D 4 D12
Cambridge Cl CHES/WCR EN8 16 C3
HSLWW TW4 58 G2
RYNPK SW20 60 H13
WALTH E17 39 R4
WDGN N22 * 26 E13
WDR/YW UB7 45 P11
WLSDN NW10 36 C8
Cambridge Crs BETH E2 39 M14
TEDD TW11 * 59 Q10
Cambridge Dr LEE/GVPK SE12 64 C3
POTB/CUF EN6 14 A5
RSLP HA4 34 F7
Cambridge Gdns EN EN1 16 A14
KIL/WHAMP NW6 2 F3
KUT/HW KT1 60 A14
MUSWH N10 25 U13
NKENS W10 2 B11
NKENS W10 48 K4
TOTM N17 26 H12
WCHMH N21 26 H5
Cambridge Ga CAMTN NW1 3 U7
Cambridge Gate Ms CAMTN NW1 3 V7
Cambridge Gn ELTH/MOT SE9 64 K6
Cambridge Gv HMSMTH W6 48 H9
PGE/AN SE20 * 63 M13
Cambridge Grove Rd KUT/HW KT1 72 A1
Cambridge Heath Rd BETH E2 51 M1
Cambridge Pde EN EN1 * 16 A14
Cambridge Pk TWK TW1 59 T5
WAN E11 40 C4
Cambridge Park Rd WAN E11 40 C5
Cambridge Pas HOM E9 39 N12
Cambridge Pl KENS W8 * 6 H4
Cambridge Rd ASHF TW15 57 U12
BARK IG11 41 L12
BARN SW13 48 F14
BMLY BR1 64 C12
BTSEA SW11 49 T13
CAR SM5 73 S11
CHING E4 27 V6
E/WMO/HCT KT8 70 H2
GDMY/SEVK IG3 41 N6
HNWL W7 47 P7
HPTN TW12 58 H12
KIL/WHAMP NW6 2 F5
KUT/HW KT1 60 A14
MTCM CR4 74 A1
NWMAL KT3 72 D2
PGE/AN SE20 75 L1
RCH/KEW TW9 48 A12
RYLN/HDSTN HA2 34 J3
RYNPK SW20 60 H13
SCUP DA14 65 N9
STHL UB1 * 46 H6
TEDD TW11 59 Q9
TWK TW1 59 T4
UX/CGN UB8 33 P11
WAN E11 40 B5
WATW WD18 * 22 E2
WOT/HER KT12 70 D4
Cambridge Rd North CHSWK W4 48 B10
Cambridge Rd South CHSWK W4 48 B10
Cambridge Rw WOOL/PLUM SE18 52 K10
Cambridge Sq BAY/PAD W2 3 N11
REDH RH1 93 U13
Cambridge St PIM SW1V 7 V9
Cambridge Ter CAMTN NW1 3 U6
ED N9 * 26 K5
Cambridge Terrace Ms CAMTN NW1 * 3 V6
Cambridge Yd HNWL W7 * 47 P7
Cambus Cl YEAD UB4 46 G3
Cambus Rd CAN/RD E16 52 C3
Camdale Rd WOOL/PLUM SE18 53 P12
Camden Av FELT TW13 58 E7
YEAD UB4 46 E5
Camden Cl CHST BR7 65 L13
Camden Gdns CAMTN NW1 * 37 V12
SUT SM1 73 P10
THHTH CR7 74 F1
Camden Gv CHST BR7 64 K11
Camden High St CAMTN NW1 4 A2
Camden Hill Rd NRWD SE19 62 J11
Camdenhurst St POP/IOD E14 51 Q4
Camden Lock Pl CAMTN NW1 37 V12
Camden Ms CAMTN NW1 38 B11
Camden Park Rd CAMTN NW1 38 B11
CHST BR7 64 H12
Camden Pas IS N1 5 L3
Camden Rd BXLY DA5 65 V6
CAMTN NW1 38 B11
SEV TN13 90 H12
SUT SM1 73 P10
WALTH E17 39 R4
WAN E11 40 D4
Camden Rd Permanent Wy
CAMTN NW1 * 4 C2
Camden Rw BKHTH/KID SE3 52 A14
PIN HA5 * 34 E1
Camden Sq CAMTN NW1 38 B12
Camden St CAMTN NW1 37 V12
Camden Ter CAMTN NW1 38 B11
Camden Wk IS N1 5 L2
Camden Wy CHST BR7 64 H12
THHTH CR7 74 F1
Camelford Wk NTGHL W11 2 A12
Camel Gv KUTN/CMB KT2 59 T10
Camellia Cl HARH RM3 31 L13
Camellia Pl WHTN TW2 58 K5
Camellia St VX/NE SW8 8 E14
Camelot Cl BH/WHM TN16 88 E6
THMD SE28 53 M8
WIM/MER SW19 61 M9
Camel Rd CAN/RD E16 52 G6
Camera Pl WBPTN SW10 7 L12
Cameron Cl BXLY DA5 66 E8
TRDG/WHET N20 25 S7
UED N18 27 M10
Cameron Dr CHES/WCR EN8 16 D8
Cameron Pl STRHM/NOR SW16 62 E8
Cameron Rd CAT SE6 * 63 R7
CROY/NA CR0 74 F4
GDMY/SEVK IG3 41 N6
HAYES BR2 76 C3
Cameron Sq MTCM CR4 61 S13
Cameron Ter LEE/GVPK SE12 * 64 D8
Camerton Cl HACK E8 38 K11
Cam Gn SOCK/AV RM15 55 V4
Camilla Cl SUN TW16 58 B11
Camilla Rd BERM/RHTH SE16 51 M9
Camille Cl SNWD SE25 75 L1
Camlan Rd BMLY BR1 64 B9
Camlet St BETH E2 5 U7
Camlet Wy EBAR EN4 14 C14
Camley St CAMTN NW1 4 D2
Camm Gdns KUT/HW KT1 * 59 V14
THDIT KT7 71 N5
Camomile Av MTCM CR4 61 T13
Camomile St HDTCH EC3A 5 T11
Camomile Wy WDR/YW UB7 45 Q4
Camomile Rd ROMW/RG RM7 42 D7
Campana Rd FUL/PGN SW6 49 N13
Campbell Av BARK/HLT IG6 41 L2
WOKS/MYFD GU22 80 D11
Campbell Cl BF/WBF KT14 81 P2
ROM RM1 30 E11
RSLP HA4 34 C4
STRHM/NOR SW16 * 62 B10
WHTN TW2 59 M6
WOOL/PLUM SE18 52 J13
Campbell Cottages MTCM CR4 * 61 U14
Campbell Cft EDGW HA8 24 A10
Campbell Gordon Wy CRICK NW2 36 H9
Campbell Rd BOW E3 51 S1
CROY/NA CR0 74 F5
CTHM CR3 86 H11
EHAM E6 40 G13
HNWL W7 47 N5
SRTFD E15 40 A9
TOTM N17 26 K13
WALTH E17 39 R2
WEY KT13 69 S12
WHTN TW2 59 M7
Campbell Wk IS N1 * 4 F1
Campdale Rd HOLWY N7 38 B8
Campden Crs ALP/SUD HA0 35 R8
BCTR RM8 41 S9
Campden Gv KENS W8 6 F3
Campden Hl KENS W8 6 E3
Campden Hill Gdns KENS W8 6 E1
Campden Hill Pl NTGHL W11 6 D1
Campden Hill Rd KENS W8 6 E2
Campden Hill Sq KENS W8 6 D2
Campden House Cl KENS W8 6 F3
Campden House Ter KENS W8 * 6 F2
Campden Rd HGDN/ICK UB10 33 R8
SAND/SEL CR2 74 J10
Campden St KENS W8 6 E2
Campden Ter CHSWK W4 * 48 E10
Campen Cl WIM/MER SW19 61 L7
Camp End Rd WEY KT13 81 T2
Camperdown St WCHPL E1 5 V12
Campfield Rd ELTH/MOT SE9 64 F5
Camphill Ct BF/WBF KT14 81 L2
Camphill Rd BF/WBF KT14 81 M2
Campine Cl CHES/WCR EN8 16 D2
Campion Cl CROY/NA CR0 74 J9
DEN/HRF UB9 33 L8
EHAM E6 52 H5
GSTN WD25 11 N7
KTN/HRWW/WS HA3 35 V4
ROMW/RG RM7 42 D7
UX/CGN UB8 45 R3
Campion Ct ALP/SUD HA0 * 35 U14
Campion Dr KWD/TDW/WH KT20 84 H10
Campion Gdns WFD IG8 28 C10
Campion Pl THMD SE28 53 R6
Campion Rd ISLW TW7 47 P13
PUT/ROE SW15 60 J2
Campions EPP CM16 18 E2
LOU IG10 17 U12
The Campions BORE WD6 12 K12
Campion Ter CRICK NW2 36 K8
Campion Wy EDGW HA8 24 C9
Cample La SOCK/AV RM15 55 U5
Camplin Rd KTN/HRWW/WS HA3 35 U3
Camplin St NWCR SE14 51 P12
Camp Rd CFSP/GDCR SL9 32 B5
CTHM CR3 87 Q11
WIM/MER SW19 60 H10
Campsbourne Pde CEND/HSY/T N8 * 38 C2
Campsbourne Rd CEND/HSY/T N8 38 C1
The Campsbourne CEND/HSY/T N8 38 C2
Campsey Gdns DAGW RM9 41 R12
Campsey Rd DAGW RM9 41 R12
Campshill Pl LEW SE13 63 U3
Campshill Rd LEW SE13 63 U3
Campus Rd WALTH E17 39 R4
Camp Vw WIM/MER SW19 60 H10
Cam Rd SRTFD E15 39 V13
Camrose Av ERITH DA8 54 C11
FELT TW13 58 D9
STAN HA7 23 U14
Camrose Cl CROY/NA CR0 75 Q5
MRDN SM4 73 N2
Camrose St WOOL/PLUM SE18 53 Q10
Canada Av REDH RH1 93 U14
UED N18 26 G11
Canada Crs ACT W3 48 C3
Canada Dr REDH RH1 93 U14
Canada Farm Rd EYN DA4 79 V3
Canada Park Pde EDGW HA8 * 24 B13
Canada Rd ACT W3 48 C3
BF/WBF KT14 81 P1
COB KT11 82 E3
ERITH DA8 54 H12
Canada Sq POP/IOD E14 51 T6
Canada St BERM/RHTH SE16 51 P7
Canada Wy SHB W12 48 H5
Canadian Av CAT SE6 63 T6
Canal Ap DEPT SE8 51 Q11
Canal Bvd KTTN NW5 38 B11
Canal Cl NKENS W10 48 K2
WCHPL E1 51 Q2
Canal Est DTCH/LGLY SL3 * 44 E7
Canal Gv PECK SE15 51 L11
Canal Pth BETH E2 5 U2
Canal St CMBW SE5 9 Q12
Canal Wk CROY/NA CR0 74 J4
IS N1 5 R1
WLSDN NW10 * 36 C12
Canal Wy DEN/HRF UB9 21 L11
NKENS W10 48 K2
Canal Whf DTCH/LGLY SL3 44 E7
GFD/PVL UB6 * 35 Q13
Canal Yd NWDGN UB2 * 46 D9
Canberra Cl DAGE RM10 42 D12
HCH RM12 42 J9
HDN NW4 36 G1
Canberra Crs DAGE RM10 42 D12
Canberra Dr NTHLT UB5 46 E1
Canberra Rd HTHAIR TW6 57 S1
ABYW SE2 53 T11
CHARL SE7 52 E11
EHAM E6 40 H13
WEA W13 47 Q6
Canbury Av KUTN/CMB KT2 59 V13
Canbury Ms SYD SE26 63 L8
Canbury Park Rd KUTN/CMB KT2 59 U13
Canbury Pth STMC/STPC BR5 77 Q2
Cancell Rd BRXN/ST SW9 9 L14
BRXN/ST SW9 50 E13
Candahar Rd BTSEA SW11 49 S14
Cander Wy SOCK/AV RM15 55 V5
Candle Gv PECK SE15 63 M1
Candlelight Ct SRTFD E15 40 B11
Candler Ms TWK TW1 59 Q5
Candler St SEVS/STOTM N15 * 38 H4
Candlerush Cl WOKS/MYFD GU22 80 F7
Candover Cl WDR/YW UB7 45 P12
Candover Rd HCH RM12 42 H6
Candover St GTPST W1W * 4 A10
Candy St BOW E3 39 R13
Cane Hl HARH RM3 30 K14
Canewden Cl WOKS/MYFD GU22 80 C9
Caney Ms CRICK NW2 36 K7
Canfield Dr RSLP HA4 34 D10
Canfield Gdns KIL/WHAMP NW6 37 Q11
Canfield Pl KIL/WHAMP NW6 37 Q11
Canfield Rd RAIN RM13 42 F13
WFD IG8 28 G12
Canford Av NTHLT UB5 34 H13
Canford Cl ENC/FH EN2 15 Q14
Canford Dr ADL/WDHM KT15 69 M7
Canford Gdns NWMAL KT3 72 E4
Canford Pl TEDD TW11 59 S11
Canford Rd CLAP SW4 61 U2
Canham Rd CHSWK W4 48 E7
SNWD SE25 74 J1
Can Hatch KWD/TDW/WH KT20 85 L8
Canmore Gdns STRHM/NOR SW16 62 A12
Cann Hall Rd WAN E11 40 B9
Canning Crs WDGN N22 26 D13
Canning Cross CMBW SE5 50 J14
Canning Pas KENS W8 * 6 J5
Canning Pl KENS W8 6 J5
Canning Place Ms KENS W8 * 6 J5
Canning Rd CROY/NA CR0 74 K7
HBRY N5 38 F8
KTN/HRWW/WS HA3 35 N1
SRTFD E15 40 A14
WALTH E17 39 Q2
Cannington Rd DAGW RM9 41 S11
Cannizaro Rd WIM/MER SW19 60 J11
Cannonbury Av PIN HA5 34 F4
Cannon Cl HPTN TW12 58 K11
RYNPK SW20 72 J1
Cannon Dr POP/IOD E14 51 S5
Cannon Ga SLN SL2 44 A5
Cannon Gv LHD/OX KT22 83 N12
Cannon Hl KIL/WHAMP NW6 37 P10
STHGT/OAK N14 26 C8
Cannon Hill La RYNPK SW20 72 K3
Cannon Hill Ms STHGT/OAK N14 26 C8
Cannon La HAMP NW3 37 R8
PIN HA5 34 G3
Cannon Ms WAB EN9 16 H7
Cannon Pl CHARL SE7 52 G10
HAMP NW3 37 Q8
Cannon Rd BXLYHN DA7 53 V13
STHGT/OAK N14 26 C8
WATW WD18 22 E3
Cannon Side LHD/OX KT22 83 N12
Cannon St BLKFR EC4V 5 N12
Cannon Street Rd WCHPL E1 51 M4
Cannon Wy E/WMO/HCT KT8 70 J2
LHD/OX KT22 83 N11
Canon Av CHDH RM6 41 S3
Canon Beck Rd BERM/RHTH SE16 51 N7
Canonbie Rd FSTH SE23 63 N5
Canonbury Crs IS N1 38 G12
Canonbury Gv IS N1 38 G12
Canonbury La IS N1 38 F12
Canonbury Pk North IS N1 38 G11
Canonbury Pk South IS N1 38 G11
Canonbury Rd EN EN1 15 U13
IS N1 38 F12
Canonbury Sq IS N1 38 F12
Canonbury St IS N1 38 G12
Canonbury Vls IS N1 38 F12
Canonbury Yd East IS N1 38 F11
Canon Mohan Cl STHGT/OAK N14 25 U4
Canon Murnane Rd STHWK SE1 9 U6
Canon Rd BMLY BR1 76 E1
Canon Rw WHALL SW1A 8 E4
Canons Cl EDGW HA8 23 V11
EFNCH N2 37 R5
RAD WD7 12 F9
REIG RH2 93 M9
Canons Cottages EDGW HA8 * 23 V11
Canons Ct EDGW HA8 * 23 V11
Canons Dr EDGW HA8 23 V11
Canon's Hl COUL/CHIP CR5 86 E8
Canons La KWD/TDW/WH KT20 85 L9
Canonsleigh Rd DAGW RM9 41 R12
Canon St IS N1 5 N2
Canons Wk BH/WHM TN16 97 R5
CROY/NA CR0 75 P8
Canopus Wy NTHWD HA6 22 C9
STWL/WRAY TW19 57 Q5
Canrobert St BETH E2 * 51 M1
Cantelowes Rd CAMTN NW1 38 B12
Canterbury Av BFN/LL DA15 65 S7
IL IG1 40 G5
UPMR RM14 43 T6
Canterbury Cl BECK BR3 63 T13
CHIG IG7 29 P8
CMBW SE5 * 50 G14
DART DA1 67 N5
EHAM E6 52 H4
GFD/PVL UB6 46 K3
NTHWD HA6 22 B11
Canterbury Crs BRXN/ST SW9 62 E1
Canterbury Gv WNWD SE27 62 F8
Canterbury Pl WALW SE17 9 M8
Canterbury Rd BORE WD6 13 L14
CROY/NA CR0 74 D5
FELT TW13 58 G7
KIL/WHAMP NW6 2 E4
LEY E10 39 U5
MRDN SM4 73 Q4
RYLN/HDSTN HA2 34 K3
WAT WD17 * 11 P14
Canterbury Ter KIL/WHAMP NW6 2 E3
Canterbury Wy RKW/CH/CXG WD3 21 U1
WTHK RM20 55 S12
Cantley Gdns GNTH/NBYPK IG2 41 L4
NRWD SE19 62 K13
Cantley Rd HNWL W7 47 Q8
Canton St POP/IOD E14 51 S4
Cantrell Rd BOW E3 51 S2
Cantwell Rd WOOL/PLUM SE18 52 K12
Canvey St STHWK SE1 9 N1
Cape Cl BARK IG11 40 K12
Capel Av WLGTN SM6 74 D10
Capel Cl HAYES BR2 76 G6
TRDG/WHET N20 25 Q8
Capel Gdns GDMY/SEVK IG3 41 P9
PIN HA5 34 H2
Capella Rd NTHWD HA6 22 B10
Capell Av RKW/CH/CXG WD3 20 G3
Capell Rd RKW/CH/CXG WD3 20 H3
Capell Wy RKW/CH/CXG WD3 20 H3
Capel Pl RDART DA2 66 J9
Capel Rd EBAR EN4 25 S4
EN EN1 16 B10
FSTGT E7 40 D9
OXHEY WD19 22 G4
Capelvere Wk WAT WD17 11 L13
Capener's Cl KTBR SW1X 7 S4
Capern Rd WAND/EARL SW18 61 Q6
Cape Rd TOTM N17 39 L1
Cape Yd WAP E1W 51 L6
Capital Interchange Wy BTFD TW8 48 A10
Capitol Wy CDALE/KGS NW9 36 C1
Capland St STJWD NW8 3 N7
Caple Pde WLSDN NW10 * 36 F14
Caple Rd WLSDN NW10 36 F14
Capon Cl BRW CM14 31 V6
Caprea Cl YEAD UB4 46 F3
Capri Rd CROY/NA CR0 74 K5
Capstan Cl CHDH RM6 41 R4
Capstan Ct RDART DA2 67 Q2
Capstan Dr RAIN RM13 54 G3
Capstan Ride ENC/FH EN2 15 Q14
Capstan Rd DEPT SE8 51 R9
Capstan Sq POP/IOD E14 51 U7
Capstan Wy BERM/RHTH SE16 51 Q6
Capstone Rd BMLY BR1 64 B9
Capthorne Av RYLN/HDSTN HA2 34 G6
Capuchin Cl STAN HA7 23 R11
Capulet Ms CAN/RD E16 52 C6
Capworth St LEY E10 39 T5
Caractacus Cottage Vw WATW WD18 22 C5
Caractacus Gn WATW WD18 22 B4
Caradoc Cl BAY/PAD W2 2 E11
Caradoc Evans Cl FBAR/BDGN N11 * 25 V10
Caradoc St GNWCH SE10 52 A10
Caradon Ct WAN E11 40 A6
Caradon Wy SEVS/STOTM N15 38 H2
Caravan La RKW/CH/CXG WD3 21 Q5
The Caravan Site PUR RM19 55 R8
Caravel Ms DEPT SE8 * 51 S11
Caraway Cl PLSTW E13 52 D3
Caraway Pl WLGTN SM6 73 V8
Carberry Rd NRWD SE19 62 J11
Carbery Av ACT W3 47 V7
Carbis Cl CHING E4 27 V6
Carbis Rd POP/IOD E14 51 R4
Carburton St GTPST W1W 3 V9
Carbury Cl HCH RM12 42 J11
Cardale St POP/IOD E14 51 U8
Carden Rd PECK SE15 63 M1
Cardiff Rd HNWL W7 47 Q8
PEND EN3 27 M2
WATW WD18 22 D4
Cardiff St WOOL/PLUM SE18 53 N12
Cardiff Wy ABLGY WD5 11 N6
Cardigan Gdns GDMY/SEVK IG3 41 Q7
Cardigan Pl LEW SE13 * 51 V14
Cardigan Rd BARN SW13 48 G14
BOW E3 39 R14
RCHPK/HAM TW10 59 U4
WIM/MER SW19 61 Q11
Cardigan St LBTH SE11 8 J9
Cardigan Wk IS N1 * 38 G12
Cardinal Av BORE WD6 24 B1
KUTN/CMB KT2 59 U10
MRDN SM4 73 L4
Cardinal Bourne St STHWK SE1 * 9 R6
Cardinal Cl CHST BR7 65 M13
EDGW HA8 24 C12
MRDN SM4 73 L4
SAND/SEL CR2 87 L3
WPK KT4 72 G9
Cardinal Crs NWMAL KT3 60 C14
Cardinal Dr BARK/HLT IG6 29 L11
WOT/HER KT12 70 F6
Cardinal Hinsey Cl WLSDN NW10 36 G14
Cardinal Pl PUT/ROE SW15 60 K2
Cardinal Rd FELT TW13 58 D6
RSLP HA4 34 F6
Cardinal's Wk HPTN TW12 59 L12
SUN TW16 58 A11
Cardinals Wy ARCH N19 38 B6
Cardinal Wy KTN/HRWW/WS HA3 * 35 N1
RAIN RM13 42 K14
Cardine Ms PECK SE15 51 M12
Cardington Sq HSLWW TW4 58 F2
Cardington St CAMTN NW1 4 B6
Cardozo Rd HOLWY N7 38 C10
Cardrew Av NFNCH/WDSPK N12 25 R10
Cardross St HMSMTH W6 48 H8
Cardwell Rd HOLWY N7 * 38 C9
Cardwell Ter HOLWY N7 * 38 C9
Carew Cl COUL/CHIP CR5 86 F9
HOLWY N7 38 D7
Carew Rd ASHF TW15 57 U11
MTCM CR4 61 U14
NTHWD HA6 22 A11
THHTH CR7 74 F1
TOTM N17 27 L14
WEA W13 47 S7
WLGTN SM6 74 A11
Carew St CMBW SE5 50 G14
Carew Wy OXHEY WD19 22 H8
STMC/STPC BR5 77 S6
Carey Gdns VX/NE SW8 50 A13
Carey La CITYW EC2V 5 N11
Carey Pl PIM SW1V 8 C9
Carey Rd DAGW RM9 41 U9
Carey's Fld SEV TN13 90 E10
Carey St LINN WC2A 4 H12
Carey Wy WBLY HA9 36 C9
Carfax Pl CLAP SW4 62 B2
Carfax Rd HCH RM12 42 F9
HYS/HAR UB3 46 C10
The Carfax SYD SE26 * 63 N8
Carfree Cl IS N1 38 E12
Cargill Rd WAND/EARL SW18 61 Q6
Cargreen Rd SNWD SE25 74 K2
Carholme Rd FSTH SE23 63 R6
Carisbrook Cl EN EN1 15 V13
Carisbrooke Av BXLY DA5 65 T6
WATN WD24 11 R13
Carisbrooke Cl EMPK RM11 43 N6
HSLWW TW4 58 G6
STAN HA7 23 T14
Carisbrooke Ct NTHLT UB5 * 34 H13
Carisbrooke Gdns PECK SE15 9 V13
Carisbrooke Rd HAYES BR2 76 E2
MTCM CR4 74 C2
WALTH E17 * 39 Q2
Carisbrook Rd BRWN CM15 31 V4
Carker's La KTTN NW5 37 V10
Carleton Av WLGTN SM6 74 B13
Carleton Cl ESH/CLAY KT10 71 M6
Carleton Gdns ARCH N19 * 38 A10
Carleton Pl EYN DA4 79 Q2
Carleton Rd CHES/WCR EN8 16 D1
DART DA1 67 N5
HOLWY N7 38 B10
Carleton Vls KTTN NW5 * 38 A10
Carlile Cl BOW E3 39 R14
Carlina Gdns WFD IG8 28 D10
Carlingford Rd HAMP NW3 37 R9
MRDN SM4 72 K4
SEVS/STOTM N15 38 F1
Carlisle Av ACT W3 48 E4
TWRH EC3N 5 U12
Carlisle Cl KUTN/CMB KT2 60 A13
PIN HA5 34 G5
Carlisle Gdns IL IG1 40 G4
KTN/HRWW/WS HA3 35 T5
Carlisle La STHWK SE1 8 H5
Carlisle Pl FBAR/BDGN N11 25 V9
WEST SW1P 8 A6
Carlisle Rd CDALE/KGS NW9 36 C1
DART DA1 67 N4
FSBYPK N4 38 E6
HPTN TW12 58 K12
KIL/WHAMP NW6 2 B1
LEY E10 39 S6
ROM RM1 42 F3
SUT SM1 73 M11
Carlisle St SOHO/SHAV W1D 4 C12
Carlisle Wk HACK E8 38 K11
Carlisle Wy TOOT SW17 61 U10
Carlos Pl MYFR/PKLN W1K 3 T14
Carlow St CAMTN NW1 4 A3
Carlton Av EBED/NFELT TW14 58 E4
HYS/HAR UB3 46 A9
KTN/HRWW/WS HA3 35 R3
RDART DA2 67 S4
SAND/SEL CR2 74 H12
STHGT/OAK N14 26 B3
Carlton Av East WBLY HA9 35 U7
Carlton Av West ALP/SUD HA0 35 S7
Carlton Cl BORE WD6 24 D2
CHSGTN KT9 71 T11
EDGW HA8 24 A10
HAMP NW3 37 N7
UPMR RM14 43 P7
WOKN/KNAP GU21 80 D4
Carlton Crs CHEAM SM3 73 L9
Carlton Dene EW KT17 * 72 H10
Carlton Dr BARK/HLT IG6 41 M1
PUT/ROE SW15 60 K3
Carlton Gdns EA W5 47 S4
STJS SW1Y 8 C2
Carlton Ga MV/WKIL W9 2 F9
Carlton Gn REDH RH1 93 S7
SCUP DA14 * 65 P9
Carlton Gv PECK SE15 51 M13
Carlton Hl STJWD NW8 2 J3
Carlton House Ter STJS SW1Y 8 C2
Carlton Ms KIL/WHAMP NW6 * 37 N10
Carlton Pde SEV TN13 * 90 J12
WBLY HA9 * 35 U6
Carlton Park Av RYNPK SW20 60 J14
Carlton Pl WEY KT13 * 69 T9
Carlton Rd CHSWK W4 48 D7
EA W5 47 S5
ERITH DA8 54 C11
FBAR/BDGN N11 25 U10
FSBYPK N4 38 E5
GPK RM2 42 G3
MNPK E12 40 F9
MORT/ESHN SW14 60 C1
NWMAL KT3 60 E14
REIG RH2 93 R8
SAND/SEL CR2 74 H12
SCUP DA14 65 P10
SUN TW16 58 B12
WALTH E17 27 Q13
WAN E11 40 B6
WELL DA16 65 R1
WOKN/KNAP GU21 80 E4
WOT/HER KT12 70 D5
Carlton Sq WCHPL E1 * 51 P2
Carlton St STJS SW1Y 4 C14
Carlton Ter SYD SE26 63 N9
UED N18 * 26 H9
WAN E11 40 D3
Carlton Tower Pl KTBR SW1X 7 R5
Carlton V KIL/WHAMP NW6 2 E5
Carlwell St TOOT SW17 61 S10
Carlyle Av BMLY BR1 76 F1
STHL UB1 46 H5
Carlyle Cl E/WMO/HCT KT8 58 K14
E/WMO/HCT KT8 70 K1
EFNCH N2 37 Q4
WLSDN NW10 36 D13
Carlyle Ct WBPTN SW10 * 49 Q13
Carlyle Gdns STHL UB1 46 H5
Carlyle Rd CROY/NA CR0 75 L7
EA W5 47 S9
MNPK E12 40 G9
STA TW18 56 K12
THMD SE28 53 R5
Carlyle Sq CHEL SW3 7 M10
Carlyon Av RYLN/HDSTN HA2 34 H9
Carlyon Cl ALP/SUD HA0 35 U13
Carlyon Rd ALP/SUD HA0 35 U14
YEAD UB4 46 E4
Carlys Cl BECK BR3 63 P14
Carmalt Gdns PUT/ROE SW15 60 J2
WOT/HER KT12 70 E10
Carmel Cl WOKS/MYFD GU22 * 80 C8
Carmel Ct KENS W8 6 G3
Carmelite Rd KTN/HRWW/WS HA3 23 L13
Carmelite St EMB EC4Y 4 K13
Carmel Wy RCH/KEW TW9 48 A14
Carmen St POP/IOD E14 51 T4
Carmichael Cl BTSEA SW11 * 61 R1
RSLP HA4 34 C9
Carmichael Ms WAND/EARL SW18 61 R5
Carmichael Rd SNWD SE25 75 L3
Carminia Rd TOOT SW17 61 V7
Carnaby St SOHO/CST W1F 4 A12
Carnach Gn SOCK/AV RM15 55 V5
Carnac St WNWD SE27 62 H9
Carnanton Rd WALTH E17 27 V13
Carnarvon Av EN EN1 15 V14
Carnarvon Dr HYS/HAR UB3 45 U8
Carnarvon Rd BAR EN5 25 L1
LEY E10 39 U4
SRTFD E15 40 B11
SWFD E18 28 B13
Carnation Cl ROMW/RG RM7 42 E7
Carnation St ABYW SE2 53 R10
Carnbrook Rd BKHTH/KID SE3 64 F1
Carnecke Gdns ELTH/MOT SE9 64 G3
Carnegie Cl PEND EN3 16 H12
SURB KT6 71 V7
Carnegie Pl WIM/MER SW19 60 K8
Carnegie St IS N1 4 G2
Carnet Cl DART DA1 66 E5
Carnforth Cl HOR/WEW KT19 72 B11
Carnforth Gdns HCH RM12 42 G10
Carnforth Rd STRHM/NOR SW16 62 B12
Carnoustie Dr IS N1 38 D12
Carnoustie Cl THMD SE28 53 T4
Carnwath Rd FUL/PGN SW6 61 N1
Carol Cl HDN NW4 36 K2
Carolina Cl SRTFD E15 40 A10
Carolina Rd THHTH CR7 62 F14
Caroline Cl BAY/PAD W2 2 H14
CROY/NA CR0 74 J9
ISLW TW7 47 N12
MUSWH N10 25 V14
STRHM/NOR SW16 62 D8
WDR/YW UB7 45 P7
Caroline Ct ASHF TW15 57 T11
STAN HA7 * 23 Q11
Caroline Gdns BETH E2 5 T5
PECK SE15 * 51 M12
Caroline Pl BAY/PAD W2 2 H13
BTSEA SW11 49 U14
HYS/HAR UB3 46 A12
OXHEY WD19 22 G4
Caroline Place Ms BAY/PAD W2 * 2 H14
Caroline Rd WIM/MER SW19 61 M12
Caroline St WCHPL E1 51 P4
Caroline Ter BGVA SW1W 7 S8
Caroline Wk FUL/PGN SW6 * 6 A12
Carol St CAMTN NW1 4 A1
Carolyn Dr ORP BR6 77 Q8
Caroon Dr RKW/CH/CXG WD3 10 B10
Carpenders Av OXHEY WD19 22 C8
Carpenter Cl EW KT17 72 F13
Carpenter Gdns WCHMH N21 26 F7
Carpenters Cl BAR EN5 25 P4
Carpenters Ms HOLWY N7 * 38 C10
Carpenter's Pl CLAP SW4 62 B2
Carpenters Rd EN EN1 16 C10
SRTFD E15 39 T12
Carpenter St MYFR/PKLN W1K 3 U14
Carpenters Wood Dr
RKW/CH/CXG WD3 20 F2
Carpenter Wy POTB/CUF EN6 14 E7
Carrara Ms HACK E8 39 L10
Carrara Whf FUL/PGN SW6 61 L1
Carr Cl STAN HA7 23 Q11
Carre Ms CMBW SE5 50 F13
Carr Gv WOOL/PLUM SE18 52 G9
Carriage Dr East BTSEA SW11 7 U13
Carriage Dr North BTSEA SW11 7 Q13
Carriage Dr South BTSEA SW11 49 T13
Carriage Dr West BTSEA SW11 7 Q14
BTSEA SW11 49 T13
Carriage Ms IL IG1 41 L7
The Carriageway BH/WHM TN16 89 T14
Carrick Cl ISLW TW7 59 Q1
Carrick Dr BARK/HLT IG6 29 L13
SEV TN13 90 H13
Carrick Gdns TOTM N17 26 J12
Carrick Ga ESH/CLAY KT10 71 L8
Carrick Ms DEPT SE8 51 S11
Carrill Wy BELV DA17 53 T9
Carrington Av BORE WD6 24 B3
HSLW TW3 58 K3
Carrington Cl BAR EN5 24 G3
CROY/NA CR0 75 Q5
REDH RH1 93 T9
Carrington Gdns FSTGT E7 40 C9
Carrington Pl ESH/CLAY KT10 * 70 K9
Carrington Rd DART DA1 67 M4
RCHPK/HAM TW10 60 A2
Carrington Sq KTN/HRWW/WS HA3 23 L12
Carrington St MYFR/PICC W1J 7 U2
Carrol Cl KTTN NW5 37 V9
Carroll Cl SRTFD E15 40 B10
Carroll Hl LOU IG10 28 H1
Carronade Pl THMD SE28 53 L8
Carron Cl POP/IOD E14 51 T4
Carroun Rd VX/NE SW8 8 H13
Carroway La GFD/PVL UB6 47 M1
Carrow Rd DAGW RM9 41 R12
WOT/HER KT12 70 F8
Carr Rd NTHLT UB5 34 K12
WALTH E17 27 R14
Carrs La WCHMH N21 26 H3
Carr St POP/IOD E14 51 Q4
Carshalton Gv SUT SM1 73 R9
Carshalton Park Rd CAR SM5 73 T11
Carshalton Pl CAR SM5 73 U10
Carshalton Rd BNSTD SM7 85 T3
MTCM CR4 73 U3
SUT SM1 73 Q10
Carsington Gdns DART DA1 66 K7
Carslake Rd PUT/ROE SW15 60 J4
Carson Rd CAN/RD E16 52 C3
DUL SE21 62 H7
EBAR EN4 25 T2
Carstairs Rd CAT SE6 63 U8
Carston Cl LEE/GVPK SE12 64 B3
Carswell Cl REDBR IG4 40 F2
Carswell Rd CAT SE6 63 U5
Cartbridge Cl RPLY/SEND GU23 80 F13
Cartel Cl PUR RM19 55 R9
Carter Av BGR/WK TN15 * 79 S12
Carter Cl CDALE/KGS NW9 36 D4
CRW RM5 30 B12
WLGTN SM6 74 B12
Carter Dr CRW RM5 30 B9
Carteret St STJSPK SW1H 8 C4
Carteret Wy DEPT SE8 51 Q9
Carterhatch La EN EN1 15 V13
Carterhatch Rd PEND EN3 16 E14
Carter La BLKFR EC4V 5 M12
Carter Pl WALW SE17 9 P10
Carter Rd PLSTW E13 40 D13
WIM/MER SW19 61 R11
Carters Cl KTTN NW5 * 38 B11
WPK KT4 72 K7
Cartersfield Rd WAB EN9 16 J8
Carters Hill Cl ELTH/MOT SE9 64 E6
Carters La WOKS/MYFD GU22 80 G10
Carter's Rd EW KT17 84 F5
Carter St WALW SE17 9 N11
Carter's Yd WAND/EARL SW18 61 N3
Carthew Rd HMSMTH W6 48 H8
Carthew Vls HMSMTH W6 48 H8
Carthusian St FARR EC1M 5 N9
Carting La TPL/STR WC2R 4 F14
Cart La CHING E4 28 A6
Cartmel Cl REIG RH2 93 S9
TOTM N17 27 M12
Cartmel Ct NTHLT UB5 34 G11
Cartmel Gdns MRDN SM4 73 Q3
Cartmel Rd BXLYHN DA7 54 A13
Cart Pth GSTN WD25 11 Q7
Cartwright Gdns STPAN WC1H 4 E6
Cartwright St WCHPL E1 5 V13
Cartwright Wy BARN SW13 48 H12
Carver Cl CHSWK W4 48 C8
Carver Rd HNHL SE24 62 G4
Carville Crs BTFD TW8 47 U10
Cary Rd WAN E11 40 A9
Carysfort Rd CEND/HSY/T N8 38 B3
STNW/STAM N16 38 H8
Cary Wk RAD WD7 12 F8
Cascade Av MUSWH N10 38 A2
Cascade Cl STMC/STPC BR5 77 S1
Cascade Rd BKHH IG9 28 F7
Cascades CROY/NA CR0 75 R14
Caselden Cl ADL/WDHM KT15 69 N10
Casella Rd NWCR SE14 51 P12
Casewick Rd WNWD SE27 62 F10
Casey Cl STJWD NW8 3 N6
Casimir Rd CLPT E5 39 M8
Casino Av HNHL SE24 62 G3
Caspian St CMBW SE5 9 Q13
Caspian Wk CAN/RD E16 52 F4
Caspian Wy PUR RM19 55 N10
Cassandra Cl NTHLT UB5 35 M9
Cassandra Ga CHES/WCR EN8 16 F1
Casselden Rd WLSDN NW10 36 D12
Cassidy Rd FUL/PGN SW6 6 E14
Cassilda Rd ABYW SE2 53 Q9
Cassilis Rd POP/IOD E14 51 S7
TWK TW1 59 R4
Cassiobridge Rd WATW WD18 22 A2
Cassiobridge Ter RKW/CH/CXG WD3 * 21 V3
Cassiobury Av EBED/NFELT TW14 58 B5
Cassiobury Dr WAT WD17 22 C1
Cassiobury Park Av WATW WD18 22 B1
Cassiobury Rd WALTH E17 39 P3
Cassio Pl WATW WD18 22 A2
Cassio Rd WATW WD18 22 D2
Cassio Whf WATW WD18 * 21 V3
Cassland Rd HOM E9 39 Q11
THHTH CR7 74 H2
Casslee Rd CAT SE6 63 R5
Casson St WCHPL E1 51 L3
Casstine Cl SWLY BR8 66 F13
Castellain Rd MV/WKIL W9 2 G7
Castellan Av GPK RM2 42 H1
Castellane Cl STAN HA7 23 P12
Castello Av PUT/ROE SW15 60 J3
Castell Rd LOU IG10 18 A13
Castelnau BARN SW13 48 H12
Casterbridge Rd BKHTH/KID SE3 64 C1
Casterton St HACK E8 39 M11
Castile Gdns KGLGY WD4 10 F3
Castile Rd WOOL/PLUM SE18 52 J9
Castillon Rd CAT SE6 64 A7
Castlands Rd CAT SE6 63 R7
Castle Av CHING E4 27 V10
EW KT17 72 G13
RAIN RM13 42 E12
WDR/YW UB7 45 R5
Castlebar Hl EA W5 47 S3
Castlebar Ms EA W5 47 R3
Castlebar Pk EA W5 47 R3
Castlebar Rd WEA W13 47 S4
Castle Baynard St BLKFR EC4V 5 N13
Castlebrook Cl LBTH SE11 9 L7
Castle Cl ACT W3 48 B7
BUSH WD23 22 K4
HARH RM3 30 J8
HAYES BR2 76 A1
REDH RH1 94 G9
REIG RH2 93 P14
SUN TW16 58 A12
WIM/MER SW19 60 K8
Castlecombe Dr WIM/MER SW19 60 K5
Castlecombe Rd ELTH/MOT SE9 64 G10
Castle Ct BANK EC3V * 5 R12
SYD SE26 63 Q9
Castledine Rd PGE/AN SE20 63 M12
Castle Dr BGR/WK TN15 91 L8
REDBR IG4 40 G4
REIG RH2 93 N14
Castle Farm Rd RSEV TN14 78 G13
Castlefield Rd REIG RH2 93 N9
Castleford Av ELTH/MOT SE9 64 K6
Castleford Cl BORE WD6 12 K12
TOTM N17 26 K11
Castlegate RCH/KEW TW9 59 V1
Castle Gn WEY KT13 70 A8
Castlehaven Rd CAMTN NW1 37 V12
Castle Hill Av CROY/NA CR0 75 T13
Castle Hill Pde WEA W13 * 47 R5
Castle La WESTW SW1E 8 A5
Castleleigh Ct ENC/FH EN2 26 H3
Castlemaine Av EW KT17 72 H13
SAND/SEL CR2 74 K10
Castlemaine St WCHPL E1 51 M3
Castle Ms CAMTN NW1 37 V11
NFNCH/WDSPK N12 25 Q10
TOOT SW17 61 S9
WEY KT13 69 V8
Castle Pde EW KT17 * 72 G12
Castle Pl CAMTN NW1 37 V11
Castlereagh St MBLAR W1H 3 Q11
Castle Rd CAMTN NW1 37 V11
COUL/CHIP CR5 85 S10
DAGW RM9 41 R13
EPSOM KT18 84 B5
EYN DA4 78 H11
ISLW TW7 47 P14
NFNCH/WDSPK N12 25 Q10
NTHLT UB5 34 K11
NWDGN UB2 * 46 H8
PEND EN3 16 E13
WEY KT13 70 A8
WOKN/KNAP GU21 80 D4
Castle Rw CHSWK W4 * 48 D10
Castle Sq REDH RH1 94 G9
Castle St EHAM E6 40 E14
KUT/HW KT1 * 59 U14
RDART DA2 67 U3
REDH RH1 94 G9
Castleton Av BXLYHN DA7 54 D13
WBLY HA9 35 U9
Castleton Cl BNSTD SM7 85 N5
CROY/NA CR0 75 Q4
Castleton Dr BNSTD SM7 85 N5
Castleton Gdns WBLY HA9 35 U8
Castleton Rd ELTH/MOT SE9 64 F9
GDMY/SEVK IG3 41 R6
MTCM CR4 74 B2
RSLP HA4 34 F6
WALTH E17 27 V14
Castletown Rd WKENS W14 6 B10
Castleview Cl FSBYPK N4 38 G7
Castleview Gdns IL IG1 40 G4
Castleview Rd DTCH/LGLY SL3 44 A9
WEY KT13 69 T9
Castle Vls CRICK NW2 * 36 G11
Castle Wk SUN TW16 * 70 E1
Castle Wy EW KT17 72 G14
FELT TW13 58 E9
WIM/MER SW19 60 K8
Castlewood Dr ELTH/MOT SE9 52 H14
Castlewood Rd EBAR EN4 25 R1
STNW/STAM N16 39 L4
Castle Yd HGT N6 37 U5
RCH/KEW TW9 59 T3
STHWK SE1 * 9 M1
Castor La POP/IOD E14 51 T5
Catalina Rd HTHAIR TW6 57 T1
Catalpa Ct LEW SE13 63 V4
Caterham Av CLAY IG5 28 J14
Caterham-By-Pass CTHM CR3 87 M12
Caterham Ct WAB EN9 17 M8
Caterham Dr COUL/CHIP CR5 86 G9
Caterham Rd LEW SE13 63 U1
Catesby St WALW SE17 9 R8
Catford Broadway CAT SE6 63 T5
Catford Hl CAT SE6 63 R6
Catford Island CAT SE6 * 63 T5
Catford Rd CAT SE6 63 S6
Cathall Rd WAN E11 40 A8
Cathay St BERM/RHTH SE16 51 M7
Cathcart Dr ORP BR6 77 N7
Cathcart Hl ARCH N19 38 A8
Cathcart Rd WBPTN SW10 6 J11
Cathcart St KTTN NW5 37 V11
Cathedral St STHWK SE1 9 Q1
Catherall Rd HBRY N5 38 G8
Catherine Cl BF/WBF KT14 81 R4
BRWN CM15 31 U3
LOU IG10 28 H4
Catherine Ct STHGT/OAK N14 26 A3
Catherine Dr RCH/KEW TW9 59 U2
SUN TW16 58 B12
Catherine Gdns HSLW TW3 59 M2
Catherine Griffiths Ct CLKNW EC1R 4 K7
Catherine Gv GNWCH SE10 51 T13
Catherine Howard Ct WEY KT13 69 T8
Catherine Pl HRW HA1 35 P3
WESTW SW1E 8 A5
Catherine Rd GPK RM2 42 H3
PEND EN3 16 E11
SURB KT6 71 T3
Catherines Cl WDR/YW UB7 * 45 P7
Catherine St HOL/ALD WC2B * 4 G13
Catherine Vls RYNPK SW20 * 60 H12
Catherine Wheel Aly LVPST EC2M 5 T10
Catherine Wheel Rd BTFD TW8 47 T12
Catherine Wheel Yd WHALL SW1A 8 A2
Cat Hl EBAR EN4 25 S4
Cathles Rd BAL SW12 61 V4
Cathnor Rd SHB W12 48 H7
Catisfield Rd PEND EN3 16 E11
Catlin Crs SHPTN TW17 69 V3
Catlin Gdns GDST RH9 95 M7
Catling Cl FSTH SE23 63 N8
Catlin's La PIN HA5 34 D1
Catlin St BERM/RHTH SE16 51 M10
Cator Cl CROY/NA CR0 88 A1
Cator Crs CROY/NA CR0 88 A1
Cator La BECK BR3 63 R14
Cato Rd CLAP SW4 62 B1
Cator Rd CAR SM5 73 T10
SYD SE26 63 P11
Cator St PECK SE15 9 U12
Cato St MBLAR W1H 3 P11
Catsey La BUSH WD23 23 L5
Catsey Wd BUSH WD23 23 L5
Catterick Cl FBAR/BDGN N11 25 U11
Catterick Wy BORE WD6 12 K13
Cattistock Rd ELTH/MOT SE9 64 G10
Cattlegate Rd POTB/CUF EN6 15 M5
Cattley Cl BAR EN5 25 L2
Cattlins Cl CHESW EN7 15 U3
Catton St RSQ WC1B 4 G10
Caudwell Ter WAND/EARL SW18 * 61 R4
Caulfield Rd EHAM E6 40 H12
PECK SE15 51 M14
Causeway EBED/NFELT TW14 58 D2
Causeway Br PUR RM19 55 S8
Causeway Cl POTB/CUF EN6 14 F5
The Causeway BELMT SM2 73 Q13
CAR SM5 73 U8
CHSGTN KT9 71 U9
EFNCH N2 37 R2
ESH/CLAY KT10 71 P12
POTB/CUF EN6 14 E5
STA TW18 56 G9
TEDD TW11 59 P11
WAND/EARL SW18 61 P3
WIM/MER SW19 60 J10
Causeyware Rd ED N9 27 N5
Causton Cottages POP/IOD E14 * 51 Q3
Causton Rd HGT N6 * 37 V5
Causton Sq DAGE RM10 42 A12
Causton St WEST SW1P 8 D8
Cautley Av CLAP SW4 62 A3
Cavalier Cl CHDH RM6 41 S2
Cavalier Gdns HYS/HAR UB3 45 V4
Cavalry Crs HSLWW TW4 58 F2
Cavalry Gdns PUT/ROE SW15 61 M3
Cavan Pl PIN HA5 * 22 H13
Cavaye Pl WBPTN SW10 6 K10
Cavell Crs DART DA1 67 N2
Cavell Dr ENC/FH EN2 15 Q14
Cavell Rd CHESW EN7 15 V1
TOTM N17 26 H12
Cavell St WCHPL E1 51 M3
Cavell Wy HOR/WEW KT19 84 A1
Cavendish Av BFN/LL DA15 65 Q5
ERITH DA8 54 C11
FNCH N3 37 N1
HCH RM12 42 H11
HRW HA1 35 M9
NWMAL KT3 72 H3
RSLP HA4 34 D10
SEV TN13 90 G12
STJWD NW8 3 M4
WEA W13 47 Q3
WELL DA16 65 Q1
WFD IG8 28 D12
Cavendish Cl KIL/WHAMP NW6 37 M11
STJWD NW8 3 M5
SUN TW16 58 B11
UED N18 * 27 M10
YEAD UB4 46 A3
Cavendish Ct RKW/CH/CXG WD3 * 21 V3
SUN TW16 58 B11
Cavendish Crs BORE WD6 24 A2
HCH RM12 42 H11
Cavendish Dr EDGW HA8 23 V11
ESH/CLAY KT10 71 N10
WAN E11 39 V6
Cavendish Gdns BARK IG11 41 P10
CHDH RM6 41 U3
CLAP SW4 * 62 A4
IL IG1 40 J6
REDH RH1 93 U9
Cavendish Ms North GTPST W1W 3 V9
Cavendish Ms South GTPST W1W * 3 V10
Cavendish Pde CLAP SW4 * 62 A2
HSLWW TW4 * 46 G14
Cavendish Pl BMLY BR1 76 H1
CAVSQ/HST W1G 3 V11
KIL/WHAMP NW6 36 K12
Cavendish Rd BAR EN5 24 J1
BELMT SM2 73 Q12
CHING E4 27 U11
CHSWK W4 48 C13
CLAP SW4 61 V4
CROY/NA CR0 74 F6
FSBYPK N4 38 F4
KIL/WHAMP NW6 37 L12
NWMAL KT3 72 F3
REDH RH1 93 U10
SUN TW16 58 B11
UED N18 27 M10
WEY KT13 69 U12
WIM/MER SW19 61 S12
WOKS/MYFD GU22 80 B9
Cavendish Sq CAVSQ/HST W1G 3 V11
Cavendish St IS N1 5 Q4
Cavendish Ter BOW E3 * 51 R1
FELT TW13 * 58 C7
Cavendish Wk HOR/WEW KT19 84 B1
Cavendish Wy WWKM BR4 75 T6
Cavenham Cl WOKS/MYFD GU22 80 C9
Cavenham Gdns EMPK RM11 42 J3
IL IG1 41 M8
Caverleigh Wy WPK KT4 72 G6
Caverley Gdns KTN/HRWW/WS HA3 35 T5
Cave Rd PLSTW E13 40 D14
RCHPK/HAM TW10 59 S9
Caversham Av CHEAM SM3 73 L7
PLMGR N13 26 E8
Caversham Rd KTTN NW5 * 38 A11
KUT/HW KT1 59 V14
SEVS/STOTM N15 38 G2
Caversham St CHEL SW3 7 Q11
Caverswall St SHB W12 48 J4
Cawdor Av SOCK/AV RM15 55 U5
Cawdor Crs HNWL W7 47 Q9
Cawnpore St NRWD SE19 62 J10
Cawsey Wy WOKN/KNAP GU21 80 C7
Caxton Av ADL/WDHM KT15 69 L11
Caxton Dr UX/CGN UB8 33 N14
Caxton Gv BOW E3 51 S1
Caxton La OXTED RH8 96 G7
Caxton Ms BTFD TW8 47 T12
Caxton Ri REDH RH1 93 U9
Caxton Rd NWDGN UB2 46 F8
SHB W12 48 K6
WDGN N22 26 D14
WIM/MER SW19 61 Q10
Caxton St STJSPK SW1H 8 B5
Caxton St North CAN/RD E16 52 B4
Caxton Wy ROM RM1 42 E2
WATW WD18 21 V5
Cayenne Ct STHWK SE1 9 T3
Caygill Cl HAYES BR2 76 B2
Cayley Rd NWDGN UB2 46 K8
Cayton Rd COUL/CHIP CR5 86 B12
GFD/PVL UB6 35 N14
Cayton St FSBYE EC1V 5 Q6
Cazenove Rd STNW/STAM N16 38 K7
WALTH E17 27 S14
Cdiamond Ter GNWCH SE10 51 U13
Cearn Wy COUL/CHIP CR5 86 D6
Cecil Av BARK IG11 41 M12
EMPK RM11 43 L1
EN EN1 26 K2
WBLY HA9 35 V10
Cecil Cl ASHF TW15 57 U12
CHSGTN KT9 71 T9
EA W5 * 47 T3
Cecil Ct BAR EN5 24 K1
CHCR WC2N 4 E14
Cecile Pk CEND/HSY/T N8 38 C4
Cecilia Cl EFNCH N2 37 Q1
Cecilia Rd HACK E8 38 K10

Clove St PLSTW E13 52 C2
Clowders Rd CAT SE6 63 R8
Clowser Cl SUT SM1 73 Q10
Cloysters Gn WAP E1W * 51 L6
Cloyster Wd EDGW HA8 23 T12
Club Gardens Rd HAYES BR2 76 C5
Club Rw BETH E2 5 U7
Clump Av KWD/TDW/WH KT20 92 C7
The Clumps ASHF TW15 57 V9
The Clump RKW/CH/CXG WD3 21 L3
Clunas Gdns GPK RM2 42 K1
Clunbury Av HEST TW5 46 H10
Clunbury St IS N1 5 R4
Cluny Est STHWK SE1 9 S5
Cluny Ms ECT SW5 6 E8
Cluny Pl STHWK SE1 9 S5
Clutterbucks RKW/CH/CXG WD3 10 A10
Clutton St POP/IOD E14 51 T3
Clydach Rd EN EN1 26 K2
Clyde Av SAND/SEL CR2 87 M5
Clyde Circ SEVS/STOTM N15 38 J2
Clyde Cl REDH RH1 93 U9
Clyde Ct CAMTN NW1 4 D3
Clyde Crs UPMR RM14 43 S4
Clyde Pl LEY E10 39 T5
Clyde Rd CROY/NA CR0 74 K7
SEVS/STOTM N15 38 J2
STWL/WRAY TW19 57 P6
SUT SM1 73 N10
WDGN N22 26 B13
WLGTN SM6 74 A10
Clydesdale PEND EN3 27 P2
Clydesdale Av STAN HA7 35 T1
Clydesdale Cl BORE WD6 24 D3
ISLW TW7 59 P1
Clydesdale Gdns RCHPK/HAM TW10 60 B2
Clydesdale Pth BORE WD6 * 24 D3
Clydesdale Rd EMPK RM11 42 F5
NTGHL W11 2 C11
Clyde St DEPT SE8 51 R11
Clyde Ter FSTH SE23 63 N7
Clyde V FSTH SE23 63 N7
Clyde Wy ROM RM1 30 E13
Clydon Cl ERITH DA8 54 E11
Clyfford Rd RSLP HA4 34 B9
Clymping Dene EBED/NFELT TW14 58 D5
Clyston Rd WATW WD18 22 B4
Clyston St VX/NE SW8 50 A14
Clyve Wy STA TW18 56 J13
Coach & Horses Yd CONDST W1S 3 V13
Coach House La HBRY N5 * 38 F9
WIM/MER SW19 60 K9
Coach House Ms FSTH SE23 63 N4
NWCR SE14 * 51 P13
REDH RH1 * 93 T11
Coach House Yd WAND/EARL SW18 * 61 P2
Coach Rd BGR/WK TN15 91 U14
BRKHM/BTCW RH3 92 A12
CHERT KT16 68 G11
Coalecroft Rd PUT/ROE SW15 60 J3
Coal Post Cl ORP BR6 * 77 P12
Coates Av WAND/EARL SW18 61 S4
Coates Cl THHTH CR7 74 G1
Coates Dell GSTN WD25 11 S7
Coates Hill Rd BMLY BR1 64 J14
Coates Rd BORE WD6 23 T5
Coate St BETH E2 39 L14
Coates Wy GSTN WD25 11 R7
Cobalt Cl BECK BR3 75 P2
Cobb Cl BORE WD6 24 C3
DTCH/LGLY SL3 44 B13
Cobbett Cl PEND EN3 16 C10
Cobbett Rd ELTH/MOT SE9 64 G1
WHTN TW2 58 J6
Cobbetts Av REDBR IG4 40 F3
Cobbetts Hl WEY KT13 69 T12
Cobbett St VX/NE SW8 8 H14
Cobb Gn GSTN WD25 11 P6
Cobbinsbank WAB EN9 * 16 K7
Cobbin's Br EPP CM16 18 B1
Cobbinsend Rd WAB EN9 17 R3
The Cobbins WAB EN9 17 L7
Cobble La IS N1 38 F12
Cobble Ms HBRY N5 38 G8
Cobbler's Wk TEDD TW11 59 N12
The Cobbles UPMR RM14 43 T5
Cobblestone Pl CROY/NA CR0 74 G6
Cobbold Ms SHB W12 * 48 F7
Cobbold Rd SHB W12 48 F7
WAN E11 40 B8
WLSDN NW10 36 F11
Cobb's Rd HSLWW TW4 58 H2
Cobb St WCHPL E1 5 U11
Cobden Cl UX/CGN UB8 33 N13
Cobden Hl RAD WD7 12 F10
Cobden Ms SYD SE26 63 M10
Cobden Rd ORP BR6 77 M9
SEV TN13 90 J13
SNWD SE25 75 L3
WAN E11 40 A8
Cobham Av NWMAL KT3 72 G3
Cobham Cl BFN/LL DA15 65 R4
BTSEA SW11 61 S4
EDGW HA8 24 B14
EN EN1 27 L1
HAYES BR2 76 G5
SWCM DA10 67 V4
WLGTN SM6 74 C11
Cobham Ms CAMTN NW1 38 B12
Cobham Park Rd COB KT11 82 E7
Cobham Pl BXLYHS DA6 65 T3
Cobham Rd COB KT11 82 J8
GDMY/SEVK IG3 41 N7
HEST TW5 46 E12
KUT/HW KT1 60 A14
WALTH E17 27 U13
Cobham Ter SWCM DA10 * 67 V3
Cobill Cl GPK RM2 42 J2
Cobland Rd LEE/GVPK SE12 64 E9
Coborn Rd BOW E3 51 R1
Coborn St BOW E3 51 R1
Cobourg Rd CMBW SE5 9 U11
Cobourg St CAMTN NW1 4 B6
Cobs Wy ADL/WDHM KT15 69 N14
Coburg Cl WEST SW1P 8 B7
Coburg Crs BRXS/STRHM SW2 62 D6
Coburg Dwellings WCHPL E1 * 51 N5
Coburg Gdns CLAY IG5 28 F14
Coburg Rd WDGN N22 26 D14
Cochrane Ms STJWD NW8 3 M4
Cochrane Rd WIM/MER SW19 61 L12
Cochrane St STJWD NW8 3 M4
Cockcrow Hl SURB KT6 * 71 T6
Cockerell Rd WALTH E17 39 Q5
Cockerhurst Rd RSEV TN14 78 E13
Cocker Rd EN EN1 16 B10
Cockett Rd DTCH/LGLY SL3 44 C8
Cockfosters Pde EBAR EN4 * 25 U2
Cockfosters Rd EBAR EN4 25 U2
Cock La LHD/OX KT22 83 L12
STBT EC1A 5 L10
Cockle Wy RAD WD7 12 J7
Cockmannings La STMC/STPC BR5 77 T6
Cockmannings Rd STMC/STPC BR5 77 T5
Cocks Crs NWMAL KT3 72 F2
Cocksett Av ORP BR6 77 N11
Cockshot Hl REIG RH2 93 P12
Cockshot Rd REIG RH2 93 Q11
Cockspur Ct WHALL SW1A 8 D1
Cockspur St STJS SW1Y 8 D1
Cocksure La SCUP DA14 66 A9
The Coda Centre FUL/PGN SW6 * 49 L13
Code St WCHPL E1 5 V8
Codham Hall La RBRW/HUT CM13 43 V3
Codicote Dr GSTN WD25 11 R8
Codling Cl WAP E1W 51 L6
Codling Wy ALP/SUD HA0 35 T9
Codrington Hl FSTH SE23 63 Q5
Codrington Ms NTGHL W11 2 B12
Cody Cl KTN/HRWW/WS HA3 35 T1
WLGTN SM6 74 B12
Cody Rd CAN/RD E16 51 V2
Coe Av SNWD SE25 75 L4
Coe's Aly BAR EN5 25 L2
Coffey St DEPT SE8 51 S12
Coftards SLN SL2 44 A4
Cogan Av WALTH E17 27 Q13
Cohen Cl CHES/WCR EN8 16 E6
Coin St STHWK SE1 8 K2
Coity Rd KTTN NW5 37 U11
Cokers La DUL SE21 62 G6
Coke St WCHPL E1 51 L4
Colbeck Ms SKENS SW7 6 H8
Colbeck Rd HRW HA1 35 L5
Colberg Pl STNW/STAM N16 * 38 K5
Colborne Wy WPK KT4 72 J8
Colbrook Av HYS/HAR UB3 45 V8
Colbrook Cl HYS/HAR UB3 45 V8
Colburn Av CTHM CR3 86 K14
PIN HA5 22 H12
Colburn Wy SUT SM1 73 R8
Colby Rd NRWD SE19 62 J10
WOT/HER KT12 70 C6
Colchester Dr PIN HA5 34 F3
Colchester Rd EDGW HA8 24 C12
HARH RM3 31 L12
LEY E10 39 U5
NTHWD HA6 22 C14
WALTH E17 39 S4
Colchester St WCHPL E1 5 V11
Colcokes Rd BNSTD SM7 85 N6
Cold Arbor Rd SEV TN13 90 D14
Coldbath Sq CLKNW EC1R 4 J8
Coldbath St LEW SE13 51 T14
Cold Blow Crs BXLY DA5 66 D6
Cold Blow La NWCR SE14 51 P12
Coldershaw Rd WEA W13 47 Q7
Coldfall Av MUSWH N10 25 T14
Coldham Gv PEND EN3 16 E11
Coldharbour POP/IOD E14 51 U6
Coldharbour Cl EGH TW20 68 G1
Coldharbour Crest ELTH/MOT SE9 * 64 J8
Coldharbour La BRXN/ST SW9 62 E2
BUSH WD23 22 K4
EGH TW20 68 H1
HYS/HAR UB3 46 C6
PUR/KEN CR8 86 E1
RAIN RM13 54 G9
REDH RH1 94 K10
WOKS/MYFD GU22 80 K5
Coldharbour Pl CMBW SE5 50 G14
Coldharbour Rd CROY/NA CR0 74 E10
WOKS/MYFD GU22 80 K5
Coldharbour Wy CROY/NA CR0 74 E10
Coldshott OXTED RH8 96 C9
Coldstream Gdns WAND/EARL SW18 61 M4
Coldstream Rd CTHM CR3 86 G12
Colebeck Ms IS N1 38 F11
Colebert Av WCHPL E1 51 N2
Colebrook CHERT KT16 68 H11
Colebrook Cl MLHL NW7 24 K12
Colebrooke Av WEA W13 47 R4
Colebrooke Dr WAN E11 40 E5
Colebrooke Pl CHERT KT16 * 68 G12
IS N1 5 M2
Colebrooke Rd REDH RH1 93 S8
Colebrooke Rw IS N1 5 L4
Colebrook Gdns LOU IG10 17 V14
Colebrook La LOU IG10 17 V14
Colebrook Ri HAYES BR2 64 A14
Colebrook Rd STRHM/NOR SW16 62 C13
Colebrook St ERITH DA8 54 F11
Colebrook Wy FBAR/BDGN N11 25 V10
Coleby Pth WALW SE17 9 R14
Cole Cl THMD SE28 53 R6
Coledale Dr STAN HA7 23 S13
Coleford Rd WAND/EARL SW18 61 Q3
Cole Gdns HEST TW5 46 C13
Colegrave Rd SRTFD E15 39 V10
Colegrove Rd PECK SE15 9 V13
Coleherne Ms WBPTN SW10 6 G10
Coleherne Rd WBPTN SW10 6 G10
Colehill Gdns FUL/PGN SW6 * 49 L13
Colehill La FUL/PGN SW6 49 L13
Coleman Cl SNWD SE25 63 L14
Coleman Flds IS N1 5 P1
Coleman Rd BELV DA17 54 A8
CMBW SE5 9 S13
Colemans Heath ELTH/MOT SE9 64 J8
Coleman St CITYW EC2V 5 Q11
Colenso Dr MLHL NW7 24 G12
Colenso Rd CLPT E5 39 N9
GNTH/NBYPK IG2 41 N6
Cole Park Gdns TWK TW1 59 Q4
Cole Park Rd TWK TW1 59 Q5
Colepits Wood Rd ELTH/MOT SE9 65 M3
Coleraine Rd BKHTH/KID SE3 52 B11
CEND/HSY/T N8 38 E1
Coleridge Av MNPK E12 40 G11
SUT SM1 73 S9
Coleridge Cl CHESW EN7 15 V1
VX/NE SW8 49 V14
Coleridge Crs DTCH/LGLY SL3 44 J13
Coleridge Gdns KIL/WHAMP NW6 37 Q12
Coleridge Rd ASHF TW15 57 Q9
CEND/HSY/T N8 38 B4
CROY/NA CR0 75 N5
DART DA1 67 N2
FSBYPK N4 38 E7
HARH RM3 30 H12
NFNCH/WDSPK N12 25 Q10
WALTH E17 39 R2
Coleridge Sq WEA W13 47 Q4
Coleridge Wk GLDGN NW11 37 N2
Coleridge Wy BORE WD6 24 A2
ORP BR6 77 Q4
WDR/YW UB7 45 R9
YEAD UB4 46 C4
Cole Rd TWK TW1 59 Q4
WAT WD17 11 P13
Colesburg Rd BECK BR3 75 R1
Coles Crs RYLN/HDSTN HA2 34 K7
Colescroft Hl PUR/KEN CR8 86 E5
Colesdale POTB/CUF EN6 15 N4
Coles Gn BUSH WD23 23 L6
LOU IG10 17 V13
Coles Green Rd CRICK NW2 36 H7
Coleshill Rd TEDD TW11 59 N11
Coles La BH/WHM TN16 89 S13
Colesmead Rd REDH RH1 93 T7
Colestown St BTSEA SW11 49 S14
Cole St STHWK SE1 9 P4
Colet Cl PLMGR N13 26 F11
Colet Gdns WKENS W14 48 K10
Colets Orch RSEV TN14 90 H6
Coley Av WOKS/MYFD GU22 80 E8
Coley St FSBYW WC1X 4 H8
Colfe & Hatcliffe Glebe LEW SE13 * 63 T3
Colfe Rd FSTH SE23 63 Q6
Colgate Pl PEND EN3 16 G11
Colham Av WDR/YW UB7 45 Q6
Colham Green Rd UX/CGN UB8 45 S4
Colham Mill Rd WDR/YW UB7 45 P7
Colham Rd UX/CGN UB8 45 R2
Colina Ms SEVS/STOTM N15 38 F2
Colina Rd CEND/HSY/T N8 38 F3
Colin Chapman Wy HART DA3 79 T9
Colin Cl CDALE/KGS NW9 36 E2
CROY/NA CR0 75 R8
RDART DA2 67 P4
WWKM BR4 76 B8
Colin Crs CDALE/KGS NW9 36 F3
Colindale Av CDALE/KGS NW9 36 D1
Colindeep Gdns HDN NW4 36 G3
Colindeep La CDALE/KGS NW9 36 F2
Colin Dr CDALE/KGS NW9 36 F3
Colinette Rd PUT/ROE SW15 60 J2
Colin Gdns CDALE/KGS NW9 36 F3
Colin Park Rd CDALE/KGS NW9 36 E1
Colin Rd CTHM CR3 87 L13
Colinton Rd GDMY/SEVK IG3 41 R7
Coliston Rd WAND/EARL SW18 61 N5
Collamore Av WAND/EARL SW18 61 S6
Collapit Cl HRW HA1 34 K4
Collard Av LOU IG10 18 A14
Collard Cl PUR/KEN CR8 86 H10
Collard Pl CAMTN NW1 37 V12
College Ap GNWCH SE10 51 U11
College Av EGH TW20 56 F11
EW KT17 84 F4
KTN/HRWW/WS HA3 23 N13
College Cl ADL/WDHM KT15 69 P8
KTN/HRWW/WS HA3 23 N12
UED N18 26 K10
WHTN TW2 59 M6
College Ct CHES/WCR EN8 16 C4
EA W5 * 47 U5
College Crs HAMP NW3 37 Q11
REDH RH1 93 U7
College Cross IS N1 38 E12
College Dr RSLP HA4 34 C5
THDIT KT7 71 N5
College East WCHPL E1 * 5 V10
College Gdns CHING E4 27 T5
ENC/FH EN2 15 T13
NWMAL KT3 72 F3
REDBR IG4 40 G3
TOOT SW17 61 S7
UED N18 * 26 K10
College Gn NRWD SE19 62 J12
College Gv CAMTN NW1 4 C2
College Hl CANST EC4R * 5 P13
College Hill Rd KTN/HRWW/WS HA3 23 N12
College La KTTN NW5 37 V9
WOKS/MYFD GU22 80 A9
College Ms IS N1 38 E12
WEST SW1P 8 E5
College Pde KIL/WHAMP NW6 * 2 B1
College Park Cl LEW SE13 63 U2
College Pl CAMTN NW1 4 B1
WALTH E17 40 A2
WBPTN SW10 6 J13
College Rd ABLGY WD5 11 N5
BMLY BR1 64 C13
CHES/WCR EN8 16 B4
CROY/NA CR0 74 H7
DUL SE21 62 J5
ENC/FH EN2 15 T14
EW KT17 84 G4
HRW HA1 35 N4
ISLW TW7 47 P13
KTN/HRWW/WS HA3 23 N13
SWLY BR8 66 E12
TOTM N17 26 K11
WALTH E17 39 U3
WBLY HA9 35 T6
WCHMH N21 26 E7
WEA W13 47 R4
WIM/MER SW19 61 R11
WLSDN NW10 36 J14
WOKS/MYFD GU22 80 F6
College St CANST EC4R * 5 P13
College Ter FNCH N3 25 M13
The College EW KT17 * 84 G5
College Vw ELTH/MOT SE9 64 F6
College Wy ASHF TW15 57 R9
HYS/HAR UB3 46 C5
NTHWD HA6 21 V11
College Yd KIL/WHAMP NW6 * 2 B1
KTTN NW5 37 V9
Collent St HOM E9 39 N11
Coller Crs RDART DA2 67 S10
Colless Rd SEVS/STOTM N15 38 K3
Collet Cl CHES/WCR EN8 16 D2
Collet Rd BGR/WK TN15 91 L7
Collett Rd BERM/RHTH SE16 51 L8
Collett Wy NWDGN UB2 46 K7
Colley Land RKW/CH/CXG WD3 20 H2
Colley La REIG RH2 93 L9
Colley Manor Dr REIG RH2 92 K9
Colley Wy REIG RH2 93 L7
Collier Cl EHAM E6 52 K5
HOR/WEW KT19 72 A11
Collier Dr EDGW HA8 24 A14
Collier Row La CRW RM5 30 C14
Collier Row Rd CRW RM5 29 V13
CRW RM5 30 A13
Colliers CTHM CR3 95 L1
Colliers Shaw HAYES BR2 76 G10
Collier St IS N1 4 G4
Colliers Water La THHTH CR7 74 F2
Collindale Av BFN/LL DA15 65 Q6
CDALE/KGS NW9 36 E1
ERITH DA8 54 B11
Collingbourne Rd SHB W12 48 H6
Collingham Gdns ECT SW5 6 H8
Collingham Pl ECT SW5 6 G8
Collingham Rd ECT SW5 6 H7
Collingsbourne ADL/WDHM KT15 * 69 M9
Collings Cl WDGN N22 26 D11
Collington St GNWCH SE10 * 51 V10
Collingtree Rd SYD SE26 63 N9
Collingwood Av BRYLDS KT5 72 C6
MUSWH N10 37 U1
Colling Wood Cl PGE/AN SE20 63 M13
Collingwood Cl WHTN TW2 58 J5
Collingwood Rd MTCM CR4 61 S14
RAIN RM13 42 F14
SEVS/STOTM N15 38 J2
SUT SM1 73 N9
UX/CGN UB8 45 T2
Collingwood St WCHPL E1 51 M2
Collins Av STAN HA7 23 U14
Collins Dr RSLP HA4 34 E7
Collinson St STHWK SE1 9 N4
Collinson Wk STHWK SE1 9 N4
Collins Rd HBRY N5 38 G9
Collins St BKHTH/KID SE3 52 A14
Collinwood Av PEND EN3 27 N1
Collinwood Gdns GNTH/NBYPK IG2 40 H3
Collyer Av CROY/NA CR0 74 C9
Collyer Pl PECK SE15 51 L13
Collyer Rd CROY/NA CR0 74 C9
LCOL/BKTW AL2 12 H1
Colman Cl EPSOM KT18 84 J7
Colman Pde EN EN1 * 26 J1
Colman Rd CAN/RD E16 52 E3
Colman Wy REDH RH1 93 S8
Colmar Cl WCHPL E1 51 P2
Colmer Pl KTN/HRWW/WS HA3 23 M12
Colmer Rd STRHM/NOR SW16 62 C12
Colmore Ms PECK SE15 51 M13
Colmore Rd PEND EN3 27 N2
Colnbrook By-Pass DTCH/LGLY SL3 44 G11
WDR/YW UB7 45 M12
Colnbrook Cl LCOL/BKTW AL2 12 J1
Colnbrook St STHWK SE1 9 L6
Colndale Rd DTCH/LGLY SL3 44 J14
Colne Av OXHEY WD19 22 D4
RKW/CH/CXG WD3 21 L7
WDR/YW UB7 45 N7
Colne Bank DTCH/LGLY SL3 56 G1
Colne Ct HOR/WEW KT19 72 C9
Colnedale Rd UX/CGN UB8 33 P10
Colne Dr HARH RM3 31 M11
WOT/HER KT12 70 F8
Colne Gdns LCOL/BKTW AL2 12 J1
Colne Ldg BUSH WD23 * 22 F2
Colne Md RKW/CH/CXG WD3 21 L7
Colne Orch IVER SL0 44 K4
Colne Rd CLPT E5 39 Q9
WCHMH N21 26 H5
WHTN TW2 59 N6
Colne St PLSTW E13 52 C1
Colne Va UPMR RM14 43 S4
Colne Valley Trail HGDN/ICK UB10 33 N8
RKW/CH/CXG WD3 21 N7
Colne Valley Wy IVER SL0 45 L4
STWL/WRAY TW19 56 J6
Colne Wy STWL/WRAY TW19 56 G8
Colne Way Ct WATN WD24 * 11 R11
Colney Hatch La FBAR/BDGN N11 25 T11
Colney Rd DART DA1 67 M4
Cologne Rd BTSEA SW11 61 R2
Colombo Rd IL IG1 41 L6
Colombo St STHWK SE1 9 L2
Colomb St GNWCH SE10 52 A10
Colonel's La CHERT KT16 69 L4
Colonels Wk ENC/FH EN2 15 R14
Colonial Av WHTN TW2 59 L4
Colonial Dr CHSWK W4 48 C9
Colonial Rd EBED/NFELT TW14 58 A5
Colonial Wy WATN WD24 11 Q13
Colonnade BMSBY WC1N 4 E8
The Colonnade CHES/WCR EN8 16 D2
DEPT SE8 * 51 R9
Colosseum Ter CAMTN NW1 3 V7
Colson Pth LOU IG10 28 J2
Colson Rd CROY/NA CR0 74 H7
LOU IG10 28 K2
Colson Wy STRHM/NOR SW16 62 A9
Colsterworth Rd SEVS/STOTM N15 38 K2
Colston Av CAR SM5 73 S9
Colston Crs CHESW EN7 15 R1
Colston Rd FSTGT E7 40 F11
MORT/ESHN SW14 60 C2
Colthurst Crs FSBYPK N4 38 G7
Colthurst Dr ED N9 27 M8
Coltishall Rd HCH RM12 42 J11
Coltness Crs ABYW SE2 53 R10
Colton Gdns TOTM N17 38 G1
Colton Rd HRW HA1 35 N3
Coltsfoot Dr WDR/YW UB7 45 Q4
Coltsfoot La OXTED RH8 96 B10
Coltsfoot Pth HARH RM3 30 K12
Colts Yd WAN E11 * 40 B6
Columbas Dr HAMP NW3 37 R7
Columbia Av EDGW HA8 24 B13
RSLP HA4 34 D6
WPK KT4 72 F5
Columbia Rd BETH E2 5 V5
PLSTW E13 * 52 B2
Columbia Whf PEND EN3 * 27 Q3
Columbine Av EHAM E6 52 G3
SAND/SEL CR2 74 F12
Columbine Wy HARH RM3 31 L13
LEW SE13 * 51 U14
Columbus Gdns NTHWD HA6 22 C13
Colveiw Ct ELTH/MOT SE9 64 F6
Colvestone Crs HACK E8 38 K10
Colville Est IS N1 5 R2
Colville Gdns NTGHL W11 2 D12
Colville Houses NTGHL W11 2 C11
Colville Ms NTGHL W11 2 D12
Colville Pl FITZ W1T 4 B10
Colville Rd ACT W3 48 B8
ED N9 27 M6
NTGHL W11 2 D12
WALTH E17 27 Q14
WAN E11 39 U8
Colville Sq NTGHL W11 2 C12
Colville Square Ms NTGHL W11 2 C12
Colville Ter NTGHL W11 2 D12
Colvin Cl SYD SE26 63 N10
Colvin Gdns BARK/HLT IG6 29 L12
CHES/WCR EN8 16 D9
CHING E4 27 U8
SWFD E18 40 D2
Colvin Rd EHAM E6 40 G12
THHTH CR7 74 E3
Colwall Gdns WFD IG8 28 C10
Colwell Rd EDUL SE22 62 K3
Colwick Cl HGT N6 38 B5
Colwith Rd HMSMTH W6 48 J11
Colwood Gdns WIM/MER SW19 61 S12
Colworth Gv WALW SE17 9 P8
Colworth Rd CROY/NA CR0 75 L6
WAN E11 40 A4
Colwyn Av GFD/PVL UB6 35 P14
Colwyn Cl STRHM/NOR SW16 62 A10
Colwyn Crs HSLW TW3 47 L13
Colwyn Gn CDALE/KGS NW9 * 36 E4
Colwyn Rd CRICK NW2 36 H8
Colyer Cl ELTH/MOT SE9 64 K7
Colyers Cl ERITH DA8 54 D13
Colyers La ERITH DA8 54 C13
Colyton Cl ALP/SUD HA0 35 S11
WELL DA16 53 T13
WOKN/KNAP GU21 80 A8
Colyton La STRHM/NOR SW16 62 E10
Colyton Rd EDUL SE22 63 M3
Colyton Wy UED N18 27 L10
Combe Av BKHTH/KID SE3 52 B12
Combe Bank Dr RSEV TN14 89 U13
Combedale Rd GNWCH SE10 52 C10
Combe La WOT/HER KT12 70 B13
Combemartin Rd WAND/EARL SW18 61 L5
Comber Cl CRICK NW2 36 H7
Combermere Rd BRXN/ST SW9 62 D1
MRDN SM4 73 P4
Combe Rd WATW WD18 22 B4
Comberton Rd CLPT E5 39 M7
Combeside WOOL/PLUM SE18 53 P12
Combes Rd DAGW RM9 41 V13
Combwell Crs ABYW SE2 53 Q8
Comely Bank Rd WALTH E17 39 U3
Comeragh Ms WKENS W14 6 B9
Comeragh Rd WKENS W14 6 A10
Comerford Rd BROCKY SE4 63 Q2
Comet Cl GSTN WD25 11 M8
MNPK E12 40 F9
PUR RM19 55 N9
Comet Pl DEPT SE8 51 S12
Comet Rd STWL/WRAY TW19 57 P5
Comet St DEPT SE8 51 S12
Comforts Farm Av OXTED RH8 96 B9
Commerce Rd BTFD TW8 47 S11
WDGN N22 26 D13
Commerce Wy CROY/NA CR0 74 D8
Commercial Rd POP/IOD E14 51 Q4
STA TW18 57 L11
UED N18 26 J10
WCHPL E1 51 L4
Commercial St WCHPL E1 5 U10
Commercial Wy CMBW SE5 50 K13
PECK SE15 9 U14
PECK SE15 51 L12
WLSDN NW10 36 B14
WOKN/KNAP GU21 80 D7
Commerell Pl GNWCH SE10 52 B10
Commerell St GNWCH SE10 52 A10
Commodore Pde STRHM/NOR SW16 * 62 D12
Commodore St WCHPL E1 51 Q2
Common Cl WOKN/KNAP GU21 80 B4
Commondale PUT/ROE SW15 48 J14
Commonfield Rd BNSTD SM7 85 N4
Common Gate Rd RKW/CH/CXG WD3 20 J3
Common La ADL/WDHM KT15 69 N13
ESH/CLAY KT10 71 Q12
GSTN WD25 12 C12
KGLGY WD4 10 F2
RDART DA2 66 G7
Common Rd BARN SW13 60 G1
BGR/WK TN15 91 V13
DTCH/LGLY SL3 44 E9
ESH/CLAY KT10 71 Q11
REDH RH1 93 T12
RKW/CH/CXG WD3 20 H2
STAN HA7 23 M8
Common Side EPSOM KT18 84 A5
Commonside GT/LBKH KT23 82 J13
HAYES BR2 76 E9
Commonside Cl BELMT SM2 85 P1
COUL/CHIP CR5 86 F10
Commonside East MTCM CR4 73 U1
Commonside West MTCM CR4 73 U1
The Common EA W5 47 U6
KGLGY WD4 10 A6
NWDGN UB2 46 F9
RAD WD7 12 F5
RKW/CH/CXG WD3 * 20 J3
SRTFD E15 40 B11
STAN HA7 23 P7
WDR/YW UB7 45 N10
Commonwealth Av HYS/HAR UB3 45 V4
SHB W12 48 H5
Commonwealth Rd CTHM CR3 87 L13
TOTM N17 27 L12
Commonwealth Wy ABYW SE2 53 R10
Community Cl HEST TW5 46 D13
HGDN/ICK UB10 * 33 T8
Community La HOLWY N7 38 B10
Community Rd GFD/PVL UB6 35 L13
SRTFD E15 39 V10
Community Wy RKW/CH/CXG WD3 21 T3
Como Rd FSTH SE23 63 Q7
Como St ROMW/RG RM7 42 D3
Compass Cl ASHF TW15 57 U12
EDGW HA8 23 V9
Compass Hl RCHPK/HAM TW10 59 T4
Compayne Gdns KIL/WHAMP NW6 37 P12
Comport Gn CROY/NA CR0 88 A2
Compton Av ALP/SUD HA0 35 R9
EHAM E6 40 F14
GPK RM2 42 H1
HGT N6 37 S5
IS N1 38 F11
Compton Cl CAMTN NW1 3 V6
EDGW HA8 24 C12
ESH/CLAY KT10 71 M11
GLDGN NW11 36 K8
PECK SE15 9 V14
PECK SE15 51 L12
WEA W13 47 Q4
Compton Crs CHSGTN KT9 71 U11
CHSWK W4 48 C11
NTHLT UB5 34 F13
TOTM N17 26 G12
Compton Pas FSBYE EC1V 5 M7
Compton Pl ERITH DA8 54 F11
OXHEY WD19 22 G9
STPAN WC1H 4 E7
Compton Ri PIN HA5 34 G3
Compton Rd CROY/NA CR0 75 M6
HYS/HAR UB3 46 A5
IS N1 38 F11
WCHMH N21 26 F6
WIM/MER SW19 61 M11
WLSDN NW10 48 K1
Compton St FSBYE EC1V 5 L7
Compton Ter IS N1 38 F11
WCHMH N21 * 26 E6
Comreddy Cl ENC/FH EN2 15 R13
Comus Pl WALW SE17 9 S8
Comyne Rd WATN WD24 11 M10
Comyn Rd BTSEA SW11 61 S2
Comyns Cl CAN/RD E16 52 B3
Comyns Rd DAGW RM9 42 A12
The Comyns BUSH WD23 23 L6
Conant Ms WCHPL E1 51 L5
Conaways Cl EW KT17 72 G14
Concanon Rd BRXS/STRHM SW2 62 D2
Concert Hall Ap STHWK SE1 8 H2
Concord Cl NTHLT UB5 46 F1
Concorde Cl HGDN/ICK UB10 33 Q14
HSLW TW3 46 K14
Concorde Dr EHAM E6 52 H3
Concord Rd ACT W3 48 B2
PEND EN3 27 N3
Concord Wy BERM/RHTH SE16 51 P9
Condell Rd VX/NE SW8 50 A13
Conder St POP/IOD E14 51 Q4
Condor Rd STA TW18 69 N1
Condover Crs WOOL/PLUM SE18 52 K12
Condray Pl BTSEA SW11 7 N14
Conduit Ct COVGDN WC2E * 4 E13
Conduit La DTCH/LGLY SL3 44 C10
SAND/SEL CR2 75 L10
UED N18 27 N10
Conduit Ms BAY/PAD W2 3 L12
Conduit Pas BAY/PAD W2 3 L12
Conduit Pl BAY/PAD W2 3 L12
Conduit Rd WOOL/PLUM SE18 52 K10
Conduit St CONDST W1S 3 V13
The Conduit REDH RH1 94 H5
Conduit Wy WLSDN NW10 36 C12
Conewood St HBRY N5 38 F8
Coneyberry REIG RH2 93 Q14
Coney Burrows CHING E4 28 A7
Coneybury REDH RH1 94 J10
Coneybury Cl WARL CR6 87 M9
Coney Gv HGDN/ICK UB10 45 R1
Coney Hall Pde WWKM BR4 * 76 A8
Coney Hill Rd WWKM BR4 76 A7
Coney Wy VX/NE SW8 8 G12
Conference Cl CHING E4 27 U7
Conference Rd ABYW SE2 53 S9
Congleton Gv WOOL/PLUM SE18 53 L10
Congo Dr ED N9 27 N8
Congo Rd WOOL/PLUM SE18 53 M10
Congress Rd ABYW SE2 53 S9
Congreve Rd ELTH/MOT SE9 64 H1
WAB EN9 17 L7
Congreve St WALW SE17 9 S8
Conical Cnr ENC/FH EN2 15 S14
Conifer Av CRW RM5 30 B10
Conifer Cl CHESW EN7 15 V3
ORP BR6 77 M9
REIG RH2 93 N8
Conifer Gdns EN EN1 26 H4
STRHM/NOR SW16 62 D8
SUT SM1 73 P7
Conifer La EGH TW20 56 G10
Conifer Pk EW KT17 84 E1
Conifers WEY KT13 70 A9
Conifers Cl TEDD TW11 59 S12
The Conifers GSTN WD25 11 Q9
Conifer Wy ALP/SUD HA0 35 S8
HYS/HAR UB3 46 C5
SWLY BR8 66 C13
Coniger Rd FUL/PGN SW6 49 N14
Coningesby Dr WAT WD17 11 L13
Coningham Ms SHB W12 48 G6
Coningham Rd SHB W12 48 H7
Coningsby Av CDALE/KGS NW9 24 E14
Coningsby Cottages EA W5 47 T7
Coningsby Ct RAD WD7 * 12 E10
Coningsby Dr POTB/CUF EN6 14 F7
Coningsby Gdns CHING E4 27 T11
Coningsby Rd EA W5 47 S7
FSBYPK N4 38 F5
SAND/SEL CR2 74 G13
Conington Rd LEW SE13 51 T14
Conisbee Ct STHGT/OAK N14 26 A3
Conisborough Crs CAT SE6 63 U8
Coniscliffe Cl CHST BR7 64 J13
Coniscliffe Rd PLMGR N13 26 G8
Coniston Av BARK IG11 41 N12
GFD/PVL UB6 47 R1
PUR RM19 55 Q11
UPMR RM14 43 Q9
WELL DA16 65 N1
Coniston Cl BARN SW13 48 F12
BXLYHN DA7 54 C13
CHSWK W4 48 C13
DART DA1 66 H6
ERITH DA8 54 E12
MRDN SM4 72 K4
Coniston Ct BAY/PAD W2 * 3 P12
Conistone Wy HOLWY N7 38 C12
Coniston Gdns BELMT SM2 * 73 R11
CDALE/KGS NW9 36 D3
ED N9 27 N6
PIN HA5 34 C2
REDBR IG4 40 G2
WBLY HA9 35 S6
Coniston Rd BMLY BR1 64 A11
BXLYHN DA7 54 C13
COUL/CHIP CR5 86 A6
CROY/NA CR0 75 L5
KGLGY WD4 10 F2
MUSWH N10 25 V14
TOTM N17 27 L11
WHTN TW2 58 K4
WOKS/MYFD GU22 80 F10
Coniston Wk HOM E9 39 N10
Coniston Wy CHSGTN KT9 71 U8
EGH TW20 56 F12
HCH RM12 42 G10
REIG RH2 93 S9
Conlan St NKENS W10 2 A8
Conley Rd WLSDN NW10 36 E11
Conley St GNWCH SE10 * 52 A10
Connaught Av ASHF TW15 57 Q9
CHING E4 27 V5
EBAR EN4 25 T6
EN EN1 15 U14
HSLWW TW4 58 G3
LOU IG10 28 F2
MORT/ESHN SW14 60 C1
Connaught Br CAN/RD E16 52 F5
Connaught Cl BAY/PAD W2 3 N12
EN EN1 15 U14
LEY E10 39 Q7
SUT SM1 73 R7
UX/CGN UB8 * 45 U3
Connaught Dr GLDGN NW11 37 N2
WEY KT13 81 R1
Connaught Gdns MRDN SM4 73 Q3
MUSWH N10 37 V3
PLMGR N13 26 F9
Connaught Hl LOU IG10 28 F2
Connaught La IL IG1 41 L7
Connaught Ms FUL/PGN SW6 * 49 L13
HAMP NW3 * 37 S10
WOOL/PLUM SE18 52 J10
Connaught Rd BAR EN5 24 K4
CAN/RD E16 52 F6
CHING E4 28 A5
FSBYPK N4 38 E5
HCH RM12 42 K8
IL IG1 41 M7
KTN/HRWW/WS HA3 23 P13
NWMAL KT3 72 E2
RCHPK/HAM TW10 * 59 V3
SUT SM1 73 R7
TEDD TW11 59 M10
WAN E11 39 V6
WEA W13 47 R5
WLSDN NW10 36 E14
WOOL/PLUM SE18 52 J10
Connaught Sq BAY/PAD W2 3 P12
Connaught St BAY/PAD W2 3 P12
Connaught Wy PLMGR N13 26 F9
Connell Crs EA W5 47 V2
Connemara Cl BORE WD6 * 24 C4
Connington Crs CHING E4 27 V8
Connop Rd PEND EN3 16 D12
Connor Cl BARK/HLT IG6 29 L13
WAN E11 40 A6
Connor Rd DAGW RM9 41 V9
Connor St HOM E9 * 39 P13
Conolly Rd HNWL W7 47 N6
Conquest Rd ADL/WDHM KT15 69 L10
Conrad Dr WPK KT4 72 J6
Conroy Ct SCUP DA14 65 Q9
Consfield Av NWMAL KT3 72 C2
Consort Cl FBAR/BDGN N11 25 T10
Consort Ms ISLW TW7 59 M4
Consort Rd PECK SE15 51 M14
Consort Wy DEN/HRF UB9 32 K4
Cons St STHWK SE1 * 8 K3
Constable Av CAN/RD E16 52 D6
Constable Cl GLDGN NW11 37 P4
YEAD UB4 33 U14
Constable Crs SEVS/STOTM N15 39 L3
Constable Gdns EDGW HA8 24 A13
ISLW TW7 59 M3
Constable Ms BCTR RM8 41 R10
Constable Wk DUL SE21 62 K8
Constance Crs HAYES BR2 76 B6
Constance Rd CROY/NA CR0 74 F5
EN EN1 26 J4
SUT SM1 73 Q9
WHTN TW2 58 K5
Constance St CAN/RD E16 52 G6
Constantine Rd HAMP NW3 37 S10
Constitution Hl MYFR/PICC W1J 7 U3
WOKS/MYFD GU22 80 C8
Constitution Ri WOOL/PLUM SE18 52 J13
Consul Av DAGW RM9 54 C2
Consul Gdns SWLY BR8 * 66 G12
Content St WALW SE17 9 P8
Contessa Cl ORP BR6 77 N10
Control Tower Rd HTHAIR TW6 57 T1
Convent Cl BECK BR3 63 U12
Convent Gdns EA W5 47 S9
NTGHL W11 2 C12
Convent Hl NRWD SE19 62 G11
Convent La COB KT11 82 B2
Convent Rd ASHF TW15 57 T10
Convent Wy NWDGN UB2 46 E9
Conway Cl RAIN RM13 42 G12
STAN HA7 23 Q11
Conway Crs CHDH RM6 41 S5
GFD/PVL UB6 35 N14
Conway Dr ASHF TW15 57 U11
BELMT SM2 73 P11
HYS/HAR UB3 45 U8
Conway Gdns ENC/FH EN2 15 U12
MTCM CR4 74 B2
WBLY HA9 35 S5
Conway Gv ACT W3 48 D3
Conway Ms FITZ W1T 4 A9
Conway Rd CRICK NW2 36 J7
HSLWW TW4 58 H5
RYNPK SW20 60 J13
SEVS/STOTM N15 38 G3
STHGT/OAK N14 26 C8
WOOL/PLUM SE18 53 M9
Conway St FITZ W1T 4 A8
Conybeare HAMP NW3 37 S12
Conybury Cl WAB EN9 17 N6
Cony Cl CHESW EN7 15 U1
Conyers Cl WOT/HER KT12 70 F10
Conyers Rd STRHM/NOR SW16 62 B10
Conyer St BOW E3 * 39 Q14
Conyers Wy LOU IG10 28 K1
Cooden Cl BMLY BR1 64 D12
Cookes Cl WAN E11 40 B7
Cookes La CHEAM SM3 73 L11
Cookham Cl NWDGN UB2 46 K8
Cookham Dene Cl CHST BR7 65 M13
Cookham Rd SCUP DA14 66 A13
Cookhill Rd ABYW SE2 53 R7
Cook's Cl CRW RM5 30 C13
Cooks Ferry Rbt UED N18 27 Q10
Cook's Hole Rd ENC/FH EN2 15 S12
Cooks Md BUSH WD23 22 K4
Cookson Gv ERITH DA8 54 B12
Cook's Rd SRTFD E15 39 T14
WALW SE17 9 L11
Coolfin Rd CAN/RD E16 52 C4
Coolgardie Av CHIG IG7 28 J8
CHING E4 27 V10
Coolgardie Rd ASHF TW15 57 U10
Coolhurst Rd HGT N6 38 B4
Cool Oak Br CDALE/KGS NW9 36 F5
Cool Oak La CDALE/KGS NW9 36 F5
Coomassie Rd MV/WKIL W9 2 C7
Coombe Av CROY/NA CR0 74 J9
RSEV TN14 90 H10
Coombe Bank NWMAL KT3 60 E13
Coombe Cl EDGW HA8 23 V14
HSLW TW3 58 J2
Coombe Cnr WCHMH N21 26 F6
Coombe Crs HPTN TW12 58 G12
Coombe Dr ADL/WDHM KT15 68 K11
RSLP HA4 34 D6
Coombe End KUTN/CMB KT2 60 D12
Coombefield Cl NWMAL KT3 72 E3
Coombe Gdns NWMAL KT3 72 F2
RYNPK SW20 60 G14
Coombe Hill Gld KUTN/CMB KT2 60 E12
Coombe Hill Rd KUTN/CMB KT2 60 E12
RKW/CH/CXG WD3 21 L5
Coombe House Cha NWMAL KT3 60 D13
Coombehurst Cl EBAR EN4 14 H14
Coombelands La ADL/WDHM KT15 69 L11
Coombe La CROY/NA CR0 75 M10
RYNPK SW20 60 F13
Coombe La West KUTN/CMB KT2 60 C13
Coombe Lea BMLY BR1 76 G1
Coombe Ldg CHARL SE7 52 E11
Coombe Neville KUTN/CMB KT2 60 C12
Coombe Pk KUTN/CMB KT2 60 C10
Coombe Ridings KUTN/CMB KT2 60 C10
Coombe Ri KUTN/CMB KT2 60 C13
Coombe Rd BUSH WD23 23 M5
CHSWK W4 48 E10
HARH RM3 43 M1
HPTN TW12 58 H12
KUTN/CMB KT2 60 A13
NWMAL KT3 72 E1
RSEV TN14 90 J5
SAND/SEL CR2 74 K9
SYD SE26 63 M9
WDGN N22 26 E14
WEA W13 47 R8
WLSDN NW10 36 D7
Coomber Wy CROY/NA CR0 74 C5
The Coombe BRKHM/BTCW RH3 92 D7
Coombe V CFSP/GDCR SL9 32 C6
Coombe Vls WAND/EARL SW18 * 61 N5
Coombe Wy BF/WBF KT14 81 R2
Coombewood Dr CHDH RM6 41 V4
Coombe Wood Hl PUR/KEN CR8 86 G2
Coombe Wood Rd KUTN/CMB KT2 60 C10
Coombfield Dr RDART DA2 67 R9
Coombs St IS N1 5 M4
Coomer Pl FUL/PGN SW6 6 D12
Cooms Wk EDGW HA8 24 B13
Cooperage Cl TOTM N17 26 K11
Cooper Av WALTH E17 27 P13
Cooper Cl RDART DA2 67 S3
STHWK SE1 8 K4
Cooper Crs CAR SM5 73 T8
Cooperdale Cl WFD IG8 28 E12
Cooper Rd CROY/NA CR0 74 E10
HDN NW4 36 K4
WLSDN NW10 36 G10
Coopersale Cl WFD IG8 28 E12
Coopersale Common EPP CM16 18 H2
Coopersale La EPP CM16 18 E11
Coopersale Rd HOM E9 39 P10
Coopersale St EPP CM16 18 G6
Coopers Cl CHIG IG7 29 R7
DAGE RM10 42 B11
EYN DA4 67 Q13
STA TW18 56 K10
WCHPL E1 51 N2
Coopers Crs BORE WD6 13 N13
Coopers Dr RDART DA2 66 E7
Cooper's Hill La EGH TW20 56 B9
Cooper's Hill Rd REDH RH1 94 D9
Coopers La CAMTN NW1 4 D4
LEE/GVPK SE12 64 D7
LEY E10 39 T6
POTB/CUF EN6 14 G5
Coopers Lane Rd POTB/CUF EN6 14 J7
Coopers Ms BECK BR3 63 S14
Coopers Rd POTB/CUF EN6 14 E4
STHWK SE1 9 V10
Coopers Rw IVER SL0 44 G2
TWRH EC3N 5 U13
Cooper St CAN/RD E16 52 B3
Coopers Yd IS N1 * 38 F12
NRWD SE19 62 J11
Coote Rd BCTR RM8 41 V8
BXLYHN DA7 53 V13
Copeland Rd PECK SE15 51 L14
WALTH E17 39 T3
Copeman Cl SYD SE26 63 N10
Copenhagen Gdns CHEL SW3 7 M9
CHSWK W4 48 D7
Copenhagen Pl POP/IOD E14 51 R4
Copenhagen St IS N1 4 F2
Copenhagen Wy WOT/HER KT12 70 D8
Cope Pl KENS W8 6 E6
Copers Cope Rd BECK BR3 63 S11
Cope St BERM/RHTH SE16 51 P9
Copford Wk IS N1 * 5 N1
Copgate Pth STRHM/NOR SW16 62 D11
Copland Av ALP/SUD HA0 35 T10
Copland Cl ALP/SUD HA0 35 S10
Copland Ms ALP/SUD HA0 35 U11
Copland Rd ALP/SUD HA0 35 U11
Copleigh Dr KWD/TDW/WH KT20 85 L10
Copleston Rd PECK SE15 62 K1
Copley Cl CMBW SE5 9 N12
HNWL W7 47 P3
REDH RH1 93 S8
Copley Dene BMLY BR1 64 F13
Copley Pk STRHM/NOR SW16 62 D11
Copley Rd STAN HA7 23 S10
Copley Wy KWD/TDW/WH KT20 84 K10
Copmans Wick RKW/CH/CXG WD3 20 H3
Coppard Gdns CHSGTN KT9 71 S11
Coppelia Rd BKHTH/KID SE3 64 B2
Coppen Rd BCTR RM8 41 V5
Copperas St DEPT SE8 51 T11
Copper Beech Cl CLAY IG5 28 J13
STMC/STPC BR5 77 S3
Copper Cl NRWD SE19 62 K12
TOTM N17 27 M12
Copperdale Rd HYS/HAR UB3 46 C7
Copperfield BARK/HLT IG6 29 M11
Copperfield Av UX/CGN UB8 45 S2
Copperfield Cl SAND/SEL CR2 86 G1
Copperfield Dr SEVS/STOTM N15 38 K2
Copperfield Gdns BRW CM14 31 V6
Copperfield Ri ADL/WDHM KT15 68 K11
Copperfield Rd BOW E3 51 Q2
THMD SE28 53 S4
Copperfields BGR/WK TN15 91 M7
LHD/OX KT22 83 L12
SUN TW16 * 58 B11
Copperfield St STHWK SE1 9 M3
Copperfields Wk BGR/WK TN15 91 M7
Copperfields Wy HARH RM3 30 K13
Copperfield Wy CHST BR7 65 L11
PIN HA5 34 H2
Coppergate Cl BMLY BR1 64 D13
Coppermead Cl CRICK NW2 36 J8
Copper Mill Dr ISLW TW7 47 P14
Coppermill La RKW/CH/CXG WD3 20 K12
Copper Mill La TOOT SW17 61 Q9
Coppermill La WALTH E17 39 N4
Coppermill Lock DEN/HRF UB9 * 21 L12
Coppermill Rd STWL/WRAY TW19 56 F4
Copper Rdg CFSP/GDCR SL9 20 D10
Copper Rw STHWK SE1 9 U2
Coppetts Cl NFNCH/WDSPK N12 25 T12
Coppetts Rd MUSWH N10 25 T13
Coppice Cl BECK BR3 75 T2
RSLP HA4 * 33 U4
RYNPK SW20 72 J1
STAN HA7 23 P11
Coppice Dr PUT/ROE SW15 60 G4
STWL/WRAY TW19 56 B5
Coppice End WOKS/MYFD GU22 80 J6
Coppice La REIG RH2 93 L9
Coppice Pth BARK/HLT IG6 29 R9
Coppice Rw EPP CM16 18 B10
The Coppice ASHF TW15 57 T11
BAR EN5 * 25 P4
BXLY DA5 66 D8
ENC/FH EN2 26 F2
OXHEY WD19 22 E4
WDR/YW UB7 45 Q4
Coppice Wk TRDG/WHET N20 25 N8
Coppice Wy SWFD E18 40 B2
Coppies Gv FBAR/BDGN N11 25 V9
Copping Cl CROY/NA CR0 74 J9
Coppins La IVER SL0 44 K3
The Coppins CROY/NA CR0 75 T11
KTN/HRWW/WS HA3 23 N11
Coppock Cl BTSEA SW11 49 S14
Coppsfield E/WMO/HCT KT8 70 J1
Copse Av WWKM BR4 75 T8
Copse Bank BGR/WK TN15 91 M10
Copse Cl CHARL SE7 52 D11
NTHWD HA6 21 U13
WDR/YW UB7 45 P8
Copse Edge Av EW KT17 84 F4
Copse Gld SURB KT6 71 T5
Copse Hl BELMT SM2 73 P12
PUR/KEN CR8 86 C3
RYNPK SW20 60 G13
RYNPK SW20 60 J12
Copsem Dr ESH/CLAY KT10 70 K11
Copsem La ESH/CLAY KT10 70 K11
LHD/OX KT22 83 L1
Copsem Wy ESH/CLAY KT10 71 L11
Copsen Wd LHD/OX KT22 83 L1
Copse Rd COB KT11 82 D3
REDH RH1 93 Q12
The Copse CHING E4 28 B6
CTHM CR3 95 L2
EFNCH N2 * 37 T1
LHD/OX KT22 82 K13
REDH RH1 94 C12
Copse Vw SAND/SEL CR2 75 Q13
Copse Wd IVER SL0 32 H13
Copsewood Cl BFN/LL DA15 65 N4
Copsewood Rd WATN WD24 11 P13
Copse Wood Wy NTHWD HA6 21 U13
Coptefield Dr BELV DA17 53 T8
Copthall Av LOTH EC2R 5 R11
Copthall Cl CFSP/GDCR SL9 20 D12
Copthall Cnr CFSP/GDCR SL9 20 C12
Copthall Dr MLHL NW7 24 G12
Copthall Gdns MLHL NW7 24 G12
TWK TW1 59 Q6
Copthall La CFSP/GDCR SL9 20 C12
Copt Hall Rd BGR/WK TN15 91 V13
Copthall Rd East HGDN/ICK UB10 33 S7
Copthall Rd West HGDN/ICK UB10 33 S7
Copthall Wy ADL/WDHM KT15 68 K14
Copt Hill La KWD/TDW/WH KT20 85 M10
Copthorne Av BAL SW12 62 B5
BARK/HLT IG6 28 K11
HAYES BR2 76 H7
Copthorne Cl RKW/CH/CXG WD3 21 R3
SHPTN TW17 69 U4
Copthorne Ct LHD/OX KT22 * 83 Q11
Copthorne Gdns EMPK RM11 43 N3
Copthorne Ms HYS/HAR UB3 46 A9
Copthorne Ri SAND/SEL CR2 86 H3
Copthorne Rd LHD/OX KT22 83 R10
RKW/CH/CXG WD3 21 R4
Coptic St NOXST/BSQ WC1A 4 E11
Copton Cl BOW E3 51 T3
Copwood Cl NFNCH/WDSPK N12 25 R9
Coral Cl CHDH RM6 41 S1
Coraline Cl STHL UB1 46 H1
Coralline Wk ABYW SE2 53 S7
Coral Rw BTSEA SW11 61 Q1
Coral St STHWK SE1 8 K4
Coram St BMSBY WC1N 4 E8
Coran Cl ED N9 27 P5
Corban Rd HSLW TW3 58 J1
Corbar Cl EBAR EN4 14 F12
Corbet Cl WLGTN SM6 73 U7
Corbet Pl WCHPL E1 5 U9
Corbet Rd EW KT17 72 E14
Corbets Av UPMR RM14 43 P10
Corbets Tey Rd UPMR RM14 43 P10
Corbett Cl CROY/NA CR0 87 V2
Corbett Gv FBAR/BDGN N11 26 C12
Corbett Rd WALTH E17 27 V14
WAN E11 40 E4
Corbett's La BERM/RHTH SE16 51 N10
Corbicum WAN E11 40 A5
Corbiere Ct WIM/MER SW19 60 K11
Corbin's La RYLN/HDSTN HA2 34 K8
Corbridge Crs BETH E2 39 M14
Corbridge Ms ROM RM1 42 F3
Corby Cl EGH TW20 56 A11
Corby Crs ENC/FH EN2 26 C2
Corby Dr EGH TW20 56 A11
Corbylands Rd BFN/LL DA15 65 N6
Corbyn St FSBYPK N4 38 C6
Corby Rd WLSDN NW10 36 C14
Corcorans BRWN CM15 31 V4
Cordelia Cl HNHL SE24 62 F2
Cordelia Gdns STWL/WRAY TW19 57 Q5
Cordelia Rd STWL/WRAY TW19 57 Q5
Cordelia St POP/IOD E14 51 T4
Cordell Cl CHES/WCR EN8 16 E2
Corderoy Pl CHERT KT16 68 J4
Cordingley Rd RSLP HA4 33 V7
Cording St POP/IOD E14 51 T3
Cordrey Gdns COUL/CHIP CR5 86 C5
Cordwell Rd LEW SE13 63 V3
Corelli Rd BKHTH/KID SE3 52 G13
Corfe Av RYLN/HDSTN HA2 34 J9
Corfe Cl ASHTD KT21 83 S8
BORE WD6 24 D1
HSLWW TW4 58 G6
YEAD UB4 46 E4
Corfield Rd WCHMH N21 26 D3
Corfield St BETH E2 51 M2
Corfton Rd EA W5 47 U4
Coriander Av POP/IOD E14 51 V4
Cories Cl BCTR RM8 41 T7
Corinium Cl WBLY HA9 35 V9
Corinne Rd ARCH N19 38 A9
Corinthian Manorway ERITH DA8 54 D9
Corinthian Rd ERITH DA8 54 D9
Corkran Rd SURB KT6 71 T5
Cork St Ms CONDST W1S 4 A14
Corkscrew Hl WWKM BR4 75 U7
Cork Sq WAP E1W 51 L6
Cork St CONDST W1S 4 A14
Cork Tree Wy CHING E4 27 Q10
Corlett St CAMTN NW1 3 N9
Cormongers La REDH RH1 94 B9
Cormont Rd CMBW SE5 50 F13
Cormorant Cl WALTH E17 27 P13
Cormorant Rd FSTGT E7 40 B10
Cornbury Rd EDGW HA8 23 T12
Cornelia Dr YEAD UB4 46 E3
Cornelia St HOLWY N7 38 D11
Cornell Cl SCUP DA14 65 U11
Cornell Wy CRW RM5 30 B10
Corner Farm Cl KWD/TDW/WH KT20 84 J12
Corner Fielde BRXS/STRHM SW2 * 62 D6
Corner Gn BKHTH/KID SE3 52 C14
Corner Md CDALE/KGS NW9 24 F12
Cornerside ASHF TW15 57 U12
The Corner EA W5 * 47 U6
Corney Reach Wy CHSWK W4 48 F12
Corney Rd CHSWK W4 48 E11
Cornfield Cl UX/CGN UB8 33 P14
Cornfield Rd BUSH WD23 22 K2
REIG RH2 93 Q11
Cornflower La CROY/NA CR0 75 P6
Cornflower Ter EDUL SE22 63 M4
Cornflower Wy HARH RM3 31 L13
Cornford Cl HAYES BR2 76 C3
Cornford Gv BAL SW12 61 V7
Cornhill BANK EC3V 5 R12
Cornhill Cl ADL/WDHM KT15 69 M7
Cornhill Dr PEND EN3 16 E11
Cornish Ct ED N9 27 M5
Cornish Gv PGE/AN SE20 63 M13
Cornmill WAB EN9 16 H7
Corn Mill Dr ORP BR6 77 P5
Cornmill La LEW SE13 63 T1
Cornmow Dr WLSDN NW10 36 F10
Cornshaw Rd BCTR RM8 41 T6
Cornsland Cl UPMR RM14 43 Q1
Cornthwaite Rd CLPT E5 39 N8
Cornwall Av BETH E2 51 N1
BF/WBF KT14 81 R4
ESH/CLAY KT10 71 P12
FNCH N3 25 N12
STHL UB1 46 H3
WDGN N22 26 C13
WELL DA16 65 N1
Cornwall Cl BARK IG11 41 P11
CHES/WCR EN8 16 E7
EMPK RM11 43 N2
Cornwall Crs NTGHL W11 2 A13
Cornwall Dr STMC/STPC BR5 65 S12
Cornwall Gdns SKENS SW7 6 J6
SNWD SE25 * 74 K2
WLSDN NW10 36 H11
Cornwall Gardens Wk SKENS SW7 6 H6
Cornwall Gv CHSWK W4 48 E10
Cornwallis Av ED N9 27 N7
ELTH/MOT SE9 65 M7
Cornwallis Cl CTHM CR3 86 G12
ERITH DA8 54 F11
Cornwallis Gv ED N9 27 M7
Cornwallis Rd ARCH N19 38 C7
DAGW RM9 41 U9
ED N9 27 M7
WALTH E17 39 P2
WOOL/PLUM SE18 52 K8
Cornwallis Sq ARCH N19 38 C7
Cornwallis Wk ELTH/MOT SE9 64 H1
Cornwall Ms South SKENS SW7 6 J6
Cornwall Ms West SKENS SW7 * 6 H6
Cornwall Rd BELMT SM2 73 M12
BRWN CM15 31 V3
CROY/NA CR0 74 F7
DART DA1 67 M1
FSBYPK N4 38 E5
HRW HA1 35 L4
PIN HA5 22 H12
RSLP HA4 34 B7
SEVS/STOTM N15 38 H3
STHWK SE1 8 J2
TWK TW1 59 Q5
UED N18 27 L10
UX/CGN UB8 33 P11
Cornwall St WCHPL E1 51 M5
Cornwall Ter CAMTN NW1 3 R8
Cornwall Terrace Ms CAMTN NW1 3 R8
Cornwall Wy STA TW18 56 J11
Corn Wy WAN E11 39 V8
Cornwood Cl EFNCH N2 37 R3
Cornwood Dr WCHPL E1 51 N4
Cornworthy Rd BCTR RM8 41 S10
Corona Rd LEE/GVPK SE12 64 C5
Coronation Av DTCH/LGLY SL3 44 C4
Coronation Cl BARK/HLT IG6 41 M2
BXLY DA5 65 T4
Coronation Dr HCH RM12 42 H10
Coronation Hl EPP CM16 18 D4
Coronation Rd HYS/HAR UB3 46 B9
PLSTW E13 52 E1
WLSDN NW10 48 B2
Coronation Vls WLSDN NW10 * 48 B2
Coronet Pde ALP/SUD HA0 * 35 U11
Coronet St IS N1 5 S6
Corporation Av HSLWW TW4 58 G2
Corporation Rw CLKNW EC1R 4 K7
Corporation St HOLWY N7 38 C10
SRTFD E15 40 A14
Corrance Rd BRXS/STRHM SW2 62 C2
Corran Wy SOCK/AV RM15 55 V5
Corri Av STHGT/OAK N14 26 B9
Corrib Dr SUT SM1 73 S10
Corrie Gdns VW GU25 68 A5
Corrie Rd ADL/WDHM KT15 69 P9
WOKS/MYFD GU22 80 F10
Corrigan Av COUL/CHIP CR5 85 U5
Corrigan Cl HDN NW4 36 J1
Corringham Rd GLDGN NW11 37 N5
WBLY HA9 36 A7
Corringway EA W5 47 V3
GLDGN NW11 37 P5
Corris Gn CDALE/KGS NW9 * 36 E4
Corry Dr BRXN/ST SW9 62 F2
Corsair Cl STWL/WRAY TW19 57 P5
Corsair Rd STWL/WRAY TW19 57 Q5
Corscombe Cl KUTN/CMB KT2 60 C10
Corsehill St STRHM/NOR SW16 62 A11
Corsellis Sq TWK TW1 59 R2
Corsham St IS N1 5 R6
Corsica St HBRY N5 38 F11
Cortayne Rd FUL/PGN SW6 * 49 M14
Cortina Dr DAGW RM9 54 C1
Cortis Rd PUT/ROE SW15 60 H4
Cortis Ter PUT/ROE SW15 60 H3
Cortland Cl DART DA1 66 E4
Corunna Rd VX/NE SW8 50 A13
Corunna Ter VX/NE SW8 50 A13
Corve La SOCK/AV RM15 55 V6
Corwell Gdns UX/CGN UB8 45 U4
Corwell La UX/CGN UB8 45 U4
Coryton Pth MV/WKIL W9 2 D7
Cosbycote Av HNHL SE24 62 G3
Cosdach Av WLGTN SM6 74 B12
Cosedge Crs CROY/NA CR0 74 E10
Cosgrove Cl WCHMH N21 26 G7
YEAD UB4 46 F2
Cosgrove Rd WTHK RM20 55 S12
Cosmo Pl BMSBY WC1N 4 F9
Cosmur Cl SHB W12 48 F8
Cossall Wk PECK SE15 51 M13
Cossar Ms BRXS/STRHM SW2 62 E4
Cosser St STHWK SE1 8 J5
Costa St PECK SE15 51 L14
Costead Manor Rd BRW CM14 31 V6
Costells Meadow BH/WHM TN16 97 M2
Costons Av GFD/PVL UB6 47 M1
Costons La GFD/PVL UB6 47 M1
Cosway St CAMTN NW1 3 P9
Cotall St POP/IOD E14 51 S4
Coteford Cl LOU IG10 17 V14
PIN HA5 34 C3
Coteford St TOOT SW17 61 T9
Cotelands CROY/NA CR0 74 J8
Cotesbach Rd CLPT E5 39 N8
Cotesmore Gdns BCTR RM8 41 S9
Cotford Rd THHTH CR7 74 G2
Cotham St WALW SE17 9 P8
Cotherstone HOR/WEW KT19 72 D13
Cotherstone Rd BRXS/STRHM SW2 62 D6
Cotland Acres REDH RH1 93 R12
Cotleigh Av BXLY DA5 65 T7
Cotleigh Rd KIL/WHAMP NW6 37 N12
ROMW/RG RM7 42 D4
Cotman Cl GLDGN NW11 37 Q4
Cotmandene Crs STMC/STPC BR5 65 R14
Cotman's Ash La BGR/WK TN15 91 R6
Cotmans Cl HYS/HAR UB3 46 C6
Coton Rd WELL DA16 65 Q1
Cotsford Av NWMAL KT3 72 C3
Cotswold Av BUSH WD23 23 L4
Cotswold Cl BXLYHN DA7 54 E14
ESH/CLAY KT10 71 P7
KUTN/CMB KT2 60 C11
STA TW18 57 L10
UX/CGN UB8 33 N13
Cotswold Gdns CRICK NW2 36 K7
EHAM E6 40 G14
EHAM E6 52 F1
GNTH/NBYPK IG2 41 M5
Cotswold Ga CRICK NW2 37 L6
Cotswold Gn ENC/FH EN2 26 D2
Cotswold Ms BTSEA SW11 49 R13
Cotswold Ri ORP BR6 77 P4
Cotswold Rd BELMT SM2 73 P14
HARH RM3 31 M14
HPTN TW12 58 J11
Cotswold St WNWD SE27 62 F9
Cotswold Wy ENC/FH EN2 26 D1
WPK KT4 72 J7
Cottage Av HAYES BR2 76 G6
Cottage Cl CHERT KT16 68 G11
RKW/CH/CXG WD3 21 R4
RSLP HA4 33 V6
RYLN/HDSTN HA2 35 M7
WAT WD17 11 M14
Cottage Farm Wy EGH TW20 * 68 G1
Cottage Field Cl SCUP DA14 65 S6
Cottage Gdns CHES/WCR EN8 16 D3
Cottage Gn CMBW SE5 9 S13
Cottage Gv BRXN/ST SW9 62 C1
SURB KT6 71 T4
Cottage Pl CHEL SW3 7 N5
Cottage Rd HOLWY N7 38 D10
HOR/WEW KT19 72 D12
The Cottages EDGW HA8 * 24 B12
Cottage St POP/IOD E14 51 T5
Cottenham Dr CDALE/KGS NW9 36 F1
RYNPK SW20 60 H12
Cottenham Park Rd RYNPK SW20 60 H13
Cottenham Pl RYNPK SW20 60 H12
Cottenham Rd WALTH E17 39 R2
Cotterill Rd SURB KT6 71 V7
Cottesbrooke Cl DTCH/LGLY SL3 44 H13
Cottesbrook St NWCR SE14 51 Q12
Cottesloe Ms STHWK SE1 8 K5
Cottesmore Av CLAY IG5 28 H14
Cottesmore Gdns KENS W8 6 H5
Cottimore Av WOT/HER KT12 70 D6
Cottimore Crs WOT/HER KT12 70 D5
Cottimore La WOT/HER KT12 70 E6
Cottimore Ter WOT/HER KT12 70 D5
Cottingham Cha RSLP HA4 34 C8
Cottingham Rd PGE/AN SE20 63 P12

VX/NE SW8 8 H13
Cottington Rd FELT TW13 58 F9
Cottington St LBTH SE11 8 K9
Cottis La EPP CM16 18 D4
Cotton Av ACT W3 48 D4
Cotton Cl DAGW RM9 41 S12
WAN E11 40 A7
Cotton Gardens Est LBTH SE11 9 L8
Cottongrass Cl CROY/NA CR0 75 P6
Cotton Hl BMLY BR1 63 V9
Cotton La RDART DA2 67 R3
Cotton Rd POTB/CUF EN6 14 E5
Cotton Rw BTSEA SW11 61 R1
Cottons Ap ROMW/RG RM7 42 D3
Cottons Centre STHWK SE1 9 S1
Cotton's Gdns BETH E2 5 T5
Cotton St POP/IOD E14 51 U5
Couchmore Av CLAY IG5 28 H14
ESH/CLAY KT10 71 N7
Coulgate St BROCKY SE4 63 Q1
Coulsdon Court Rd COUL/CHIP CR5 86 D6
Coulsdon La COUL/CHIP CR5 85 U9
Coulsdon Pl CTHM CR3 86 H12
Coulsdon Ri COUL/CHIP CR5 86 C7
Coulsdon Rd COUL/CHIP CR5 86 D8
Coulson Cl BCTR RM8 41 S6
Coulson St CHEL SW3 7 Q9
Coulter Cl POTB/CUF EN6 15 M1
YEAD UB4 46 G2
Coulter Rd HMSMTH W6 48 H8
Councillor St CMBW SE5 9 N14
Counter St STHWK SE1 9 S1
Countess Cl DEN/HRF UB9 21 N14
Countess Rd KTTN NW5 38 A10
Countisbury Av EN EN1 26 K5
Countisbury Gdns ADL/WDHM KT15 69 M10
Country Wy FELT TW13 58 E10
County Ga BAR EN5 25 P4
ELTH/MOT SE9 65 L8
County Gv CMBW SE5 50 G13
County Pde BTFD TW8 * 47 T12
County Rd EHAM E6 52 K3
THHTH CR7 62 F14
County St STHWK SE1 9 P6
Coupland Pl WOOL/PLUM SE18 53 L10
Courage Cl EMPK RM11 42 J4
Courcy Rd CEND/HSY/T N8 38 E1
Courier Rd DAGW RM9 54 C2
Courland Gv VX/NE SW8 50 B14
Courland Rd ADL/WDHM KT15 69 M8
Courland St VX/NE SW8 50 B13
Coursers Rd LCOL/BKTW AL2 13 L1
The Course ELTH/MOT SE9 64 J8
Courtauld Rd ARCH N19 38 B6
Courtaulds KGLGY WD4 10 B4
Courtaulds Cl THMD SE28 53 Q6
Court Av BELV DA17 53 V10
COUL/CHIP CR5 86 E8
HARH RM3 31 N12
Court Bushes Rd CTHM CR3 87 L10
Court Cl KTN/HRWW/WS HA3 35 T1
STJWD NW8 * 37 R12
WHTN TW2 58 K8
WLGTN SM6 74 B12
Court Close Av WHTN TW2 58 K8
Court Crs CHSGTN KT9 71 T11
SWLY BR8 78 E2
Court Downs Rd BECK BR3 63 T14
Court Dr CROY/NA CR0 74 D9
HGDN/ICK UB10 33 R13
STAN HA7 23 U9
SUT SM1 73 S9
Courtenay Av BELMT SM2 73 N13
HGT N6 37 S5
KTN/HRWW/WS HA3 22 K12
Courtenay Dr BECK BR3 63 V14
Courtenay Gdns UPMR RM14 43 Q7
Courtenay Ms WALTH E17 39 Q3
WOKN/KNAP GU21 80 E6
Courtenay Pl WALTH E17 39 Q3
Courtenay Rd PGE/AN SE20 63 P12
WALTH E17 39 P3
WAN E11 * 40 B8
WBLY HA9 * 35 T8
WOKN/KNAP GU21 80 E6
WPK KT4 72 J8
Courtenay Sq LBTH SE11 8 J10
Courtenay St LBTH SE11 8 H9
Courten Ms STAN HA7 23 S12
Court Farm Av HOR/WEW KT19 72 E10
Court Farm Gdns HOR/WEW KT19 * 84 D1
Court Farm Pk WARL CR6 * 87 L6
Court Farm Rd ELTH/MOT SE9 64 F7
NTHLT UB5 34 J12
WARL CR6 87 L8
Courtfield Av HRW HA1 * 35 P3
Courtfield Crs HRW HA1 35 P3
Courtfield Gdns DEN/HRF UB9 33 L8
ECT SW5 6 H8
RSLP HA4 34 B7
WEA W13 47 Q4
Courtfield Ms ECT SW5 6 J8
Courtfield Ri WWKM BR4 75 V8
Courtfield Rd ASHF TW15 57 T11
SKENS SW7 6 J8
Court Gdns HOLWY N7 38 E11
Courtgate Cl MLHL NW7 24 F11
Court Green Hts WOKS/MYFD GU22 80 A10
Court Haw BNSTD SM7 85 S5
Court Hl SAND/SEL CR2 86 J2
Courthill Rd LEW SE13 63 U3
Courthope Rd GFD/PVL UB6 35 M14
HAMP NW3 37 T9
WIM/MER SW19 61 L10
Courthope Vls WIM/MER SW19 61 L12
Courthouse La STNW/STAM N16 38 K9
Court House Rd FNCH N3 25 P11
Courtland Av CHING E4 28 B7
IL IG1 40 H7
MLHL NW7 24 D8
STRHM/NOR SW16 62 D12
Courtland Dr CHIG IG7 29 L8
Courtland Gv THMD SE28 53 T5
Courtland Rd EHAM E6 40 G13
Courtlands CHST BR7 64 K12
RCHPK/HAM TW10 60 A3
Courtlands Av DTCH/LGLY SL3 44 B9
ESH/CLAY KT10 70 H11
HAYES BR2 76 A6
HPTN TW12 58 H11
LEE/GVPK SE12 64 D3
RCH/KEW TW9 48 B14
Courtlands Cl RSLP HA4 34 B5
SAND/SEL CR2 74 K14
WATN WD24 11 L9
Courtlands Crs BNSTD SM7 85 N6
Courtlands Dr HOR/WEW KT19 72 E11
WAT WD17 11 L10
Courtlands Rd BRYLDS KT5 72 A5
Court La DUL SE21 62 K5
HOR/WEW KT19 84 C3
IVER SL0 45 L6
Court Lane Gdns DUL SE21 62 J5
Courtleas COB KT11 82 J3
Courtleet Dr BXLYHN DA7 54 B13
Courtleigh Av EBAR EN4 14 F12
Courtleigh Gdns GLDGN NW11 37 L2
Court Ldg RAD WD7 * 13 L8
Courtman Rd TOTM N17 26 G12
Court Md NTHLT UB5 46 H1
Courtmead Cl HNHL SE24 62 G4
Courtnell St BAY/PAD W2 2 E11
Courtney Cl NRWD SE19 62 J11
Courtney Crs CAR SM5 73 T12
Courtney Pl COB KT11 82 H2
CROY/NA CR0 74 E8
Courtney Rd CROY/NA CR0 74 E8
HOLWY N7 38 E10
HTHAIR TW6 57 S1
WIM/MER SW19 61 S12
Courtney Wy HTHAIR TW6 57 S1
Courtrai Rd FSTH SE23 63 Q4
Court Rd BNSTD SM7 85 N5
CTHM CR3 86 H13
ELTH/MOT SE9 64 H6
GDST RH9 95 N7
HGDN/ICK UB10 33 T10
NWDGN UB2 46 H9
RDART DA2 67 S10
SNWD SE25 62 K14
Court Rd (Orpington By-Pass)
ORP BR6 77 S9
Courtside HGT N6 38 B4
SYD SE26 * 63 N8
The Courts STRHM/NOR SW16 62 C12
Courtstreet BMLY BR1 64 C14
Court St WCHPL E1 51 M3
The Court MUSWH N10 * 38 A2
RSLP HA4 34 G9
WARL CR6 87 Q8
Court Vw HGT N6 * 37 V7
Court Wy ACT W3 48 C3
BARK/HLT IG6 41 L1
CDALE/KGS NW9 36 E2
HARH RM3 31 L14
WHTN TW2 59 P5
The Courtway OXHEY WD19 22 G7
Court Wood La CROY/NA CR0 75 R14
Court Yd ELTH/MOT SE9 64 H4
Courtyard Ms STMC/STPC BR5 65 Q12
The Courtyards WATW WD18 * 21 V5
The Courtyard BF/WBF KT14 81 L2
BH/WHM TN16 * 97 M2
BRWN CM15 31 V5
HAYES BR2 76 G11
IS N1 38 D12
Cousin La CANST EC4R 5 Q14
Cousins Cl WDR/YW UB7 45 Q5
Couthurst Rd BKHTH/KID SE3 52 D11
Coutts Av CHSGTN KT9 71 U10
Coutts Crs KTTN NW5 * 37 U8
Coval Gdns MORT/ESHN SW14 60 B2
Coval La MORT/ESHN SW14 60 B2
Coval Rd MORT/ESHN SW14 60 C2
Coveham Crs COB KT11 82 C3
Covelees Wall EHAM E6 52 J4
Covent Gdn COVGDN WC2E 4 F13
Covent Gdn Piazza COVGDN WC2E 4 F13
Coventry Cl EHAM E6 52 H4
KIL/WHAMP NW6 2 F3
Coventry Cross Est BOW E3 51 U2
Coventry Rd IL IG1 40 K6
SNWD SE25 75 L2
WCHPL E1 51 M2
Coventry St SOHO/SHAV W1D 4 C14
Coverack Cl CROY/NA CR0 75 Q6
STHGT/OAK N14 26 A4
Coverdale Gdns CROY/NA CR0 74 K8
Coverdale Rd CRICK NW2 37 L12
FBAR/BDGN N11 25 U11
SHB W12 48 H6
The Coverdales BARK IG11 41 L14
Coverley Cl WCHPL E1 * 51 L3
Coverton Rd TOOT SW17 61 S9
Covert Rd BARK/HLT IG6 29 P11
Coverts Rd ESH/CLAY KT10 71 P12
The Covert NRWD SE19 * 62 K12
NTHWD HA6 21 U13
ORP BR6 77 N4
Covert Wy EBAR EN4 14 E14
Covet Wood Cl STMC/STPC BR5 77 P4
Covey Cl WIM/MER SW19 61 P14
Covington Gdns STRHM/NOR SW16 62 F12
Covington Wy STRHM/NOR SW16 62 F12
Cowbridge La BARK IG11 40 K12
Cowbridge Rd KTN/HRWW/WS HA3 35 V2
Cowcross St FARR EC1M 5 L9
Cowdenbeath Pth IS N1 4 G1
Cowden Rd ORP BR6 77 P5
Cowden St CAT SE6 63 S9
Cowdray Rd HGDN/ICK UB10 33 U13
Cowdray Wy HCH RM12 42 G9
Cowdrey Cl EN EN1 15 U14
Cowdrey Ct DART DA1 66 H5
Cowdrey Rd WIM/MER SW19 61 P11
Cowen Av HRW HA1 35 M7
Cowgate Rd GFD/PVL UB6 47 M1
Cowick Rd TOOT SW17 61 T9
Cowings Md NTHLT UB5 34 G12
Cowland Av PEND EN3 27 N2
Cow La BUSH WD23 * 22 J4
GSTN WD25 11 Q10
Cow Leaze EHAM E6 52 J4
Cowleaze Rd KUTN/CMB KT2 59 U13
Cowles CHESW EN7 15 V1
Cowley Av CHERT KT16 68 K5
RDART DA2 67 T3
Cowley Cl SAND/SEL CR2 75 N14
Cowley Ct WAN E11 * 40 A8
Cowley Crs UX/CGN UB8 45 N3
WOT/HER KT12 70 E9
Cowley Hl BORE WD6 13 M12
Cowley La CHERT KT16 68 K5
WAN E11 * 40 A8
Cowley Mill Rd UX/CGN UB8 33 M14
Cowley Pl HDN NW4 36 J3
Cowley Rd ACT W3 48 F6
BRXN/ST SW9 50 E13
HARH RM3 30 H12
IL IG1 40 H5
MORT/ESHN SW14 60 E1
UX/CGN UB8 45 N1
WAN E11 40 D3
Cowley St WEST SW1P 8 E6
Cowling Cl NTGHL W11 2 A14
Cowper Av EHAM E6 40 G12
SUT SM1 73 R9
Cowper Cl CHERT KT16 68 K4
HAYES BR2 76 F2
WELL DA16 65 Q3
Cowper Ct WATN WD24 11 N11
Cowper Gdns STHGT/OAK N14 25 V4
WLGTN SM6 74 A11
Cowper Rd ACT W3 48 D6
BELV DA17 53 V9
HAYES BR2 76 F2
HNWL W7 47 P5
KUTN/CMB KT2 59 V10
RAIN RM13 54 G2
STHGT/OAK N14 25 V6
STNW/STAM N16 38 J9
UED N18 27 L10
WIM/MER SW19 61 Q11
Cowper St STLK EC1Y 5 R7
Cowper Ter NKENS W10 * 48 K3
Cowslip Cl HGDN/ICK UB10 33 Q12
Cowslip Rd SWFD E18 40 D1
Cowthorpe Rd VX/NE SW8 50 B13
Cox Cl RAD WD7 12 J6
Coxdean EPSOM KT18 84 J9
Coxe Pl KTN/HRWW/WS HA3 35 Q2
Coxes Av SHPTN TW17 * 70 A1
Cox La CHSGTN KT9 71 V9
HOR/WEW KT19 72 C10
Coxley Ri PUR/KEN CR8 86 G3
Coxmount Rd CHARL SE7 52 F10
Coxs Cottages WARL CR6 * 88 A4
Coxson Wy STHWK SE1 9 U4
Coxtie Green Rd BRW CM14 31 N5
Coxwell Rd NRWD SE19 62 J12
WOOL/PLUM SE18 53 M10
Crabbs Croft Cl ORP BR6 * 77 L10
Crab Hl BECK BR3 63 V12
Crab Hill La REDH RH1 94 D14
Crab La GSTN WD25 11 V9
Crabtree Av ALP/SUD HA0 35 U14
CHDH RM6 41 T2
Crabtree Cl BETH E2 5 U4
BUSH WD23 22 K3
Crabtree Dr LHD/OX KT22 83 S14
Crabtree La EPSOM KT18 92 C2
FUL/PGN SW6 48 K12
Crabtree Manorway North
BELV DA17 54 C7
Crabtree Manorway South
BELV DA17 54 C8
Crabtree Rd EGH TW20 56 G14
Cracknell Cl EN EN1 16 B11
Craddock Rd EN EN1 26 K1
Craddocks Av ASHTD KT21 83 V6
EPSOM KT18 84 B11
Craddock's Cl ASHTD KT21 84 A6
Craddock St KTTN NW5 * 37 U11
Cradley Rd ELTH/MOT SE9 65 M6
Cragg Av RAD WD7 12 D10
Cragie Lea MUSWH N10 * 25 V14
Craigdale Rd EMPK RM11 42 F4
Craig Dr UX/CGN UB8 45 T4
Craigen Av CROY/NA CR0 75 M6
Craigerne Rd BKHTH/KID SE3 52 D12
Craig Gdns SWFD E18 28 B14
Craigholm WOOL/PLUM SE18 52 J14
Craig Mt RAD WD7 12 F9
Craigmuir Pk ALP/SUD HA0 35 V13
Craignair Rd BRXS/STRHM SW2 62 D5
Craignish Av STRHM/NOR SW16 62 D14
Craig Park Rd UED N18 27 M9
Craig Rd RCHPK/HAM TW10 59 S9
Craig's Ct WHALL SW1A 8 E1
Craigs Wk CHES/WCR EN8 16 D2
Craigton Rd ELTH/MOT SE9 64 H2
Craigweil Av RAD WD7 12 F9
Craigweil Cl STAN HA7 23 T10
Craigweil Dr STAN HA7 23 T10
Craigwell Av FELT TW13 58 C8
Craigwell Cl STA TW18 56 J13
Crail Rw WALW SE17 9 R8
Crakell Rd REIG RH2 93 Q11
Crakers Md WATW WD18 * 22 D1
Cramer St MHST W1U 3 T10
Crammond Cl HMSMTH W6 * 6 A11
Cramond Ct EBED/NFELT TW14 58 A6
Crampshaw La ASHTD KT21 83 V10
Crampton Rd PGE/AN SE20 63 N11
Crampton's Rd RSEV TN14 90 H10
Crampton St WALW SE17 9 N9
Cranberry Cl NTHLT UB5 34 F14
Cranberry La CAN/RD E16 52 A2
Cranborne Av NWDGN UB2 46 J9
SURB KT6 72 A8
Cranborne Cl POTB/CUF EN6 14 A5
Cranborne Crs POTB/CUF EN6 14 A5
Cranborne Gdns UPMR RM14 43 P7
Cranborne Pde POTB/CUF EN6 * 13 V5
Cranborne Rd BARK IG11 41 M13
CHES/WCR EN8 16 D6
POTB/CUF EN6 14 A5
Cranborne Waye YEAD UB4 46 E5
Cranbourne Av POTB/CUF EN6 14 A4
WAN E11 40 D2
Cranbourne Cl ESH/CLAY KT10 70 K11
STRHM/NOR SW16 74 C1
WOT/HER KT12 70 E11
Cranbourne Dr PIN HA5 34 F3
Cranbourne Gdns BARK/HLT IG6 41 M1
GLDGN NW11 37 M3
Cranbourne Rd MNPK E12 40 G10
MUSWH N10 25 V14
NTHWD HA6 34 B1
SRTFD E15 39 U9
Cranbourn St LSQ/SEVD WC2H 4 D13
Cranbrook Cl HAYES BR2 76 C4
Cranbrook Dr ESH/CLAY KT10 71 L6
GPK RM2 42 J2
WHTN TW2 58 K6
Cranbrook La FBAR/BDGN N11 25 V9
Cranbrook Ms WALTH E17 39 R3
Cranbrook Pk WDGN N22 26 E13
Cranbrook Ri IL IG1 40 H4
Cranbrook Rd BXLYHN DA7 53 V13
CHSWK W4 48 E10
DEPT SE8 51 S14
EBAR EN4 25 R4
HSLWW TW4 58 H2
IL IG1 40 J5
THHTH CR7 62 H14
WIM/MER SW19 61 L12
Cranbrook St BETH E2 39 P14
Cranbury Rd FUL/PGN SW6 49 P14
Crandon Wk EYN DA4 * 67 S14
Crane Av ACT W3 48 C5
ISLW TW7 59 Q3
Cranebank Ms TWK TW1 * 59 R3
Cranebrook WHTN TW2 59 L7
Crane Cl DAGE RM10 42 A11
Crane Ct FLST/FETLN EC4A 4 K12
MORT/ESHN SW14 * 60 C2
Cranefield Dr GSTN WD25 11 S7
Craneford Cl WHTN TW2 59 P5
Craneford Wy WHTN TW2 59 N5
Crane Gdns HYS/HAR UB3 46 B9
Crane Gv HOLWY N7 38 E11
Cranell Gn SOCK/AV RM15 55 V6
Crane Lodge Rd HEST TW5 46 D11
Crane Md BERM/RHTH SE16 51 P10
Crane Park Rd WHTN TW2 58 K7
Crane Rd STWL/WRAY TW19 57 S4
WHTN TW2 59 N6
Cranesbill Cl CDALE/KGS NW9 36 D1
Cranes Dr BRYLDS KT5 71 U2
Cranes Pk BRYLDS KT5 71 U2
Cranes Park Av BRYLDS KT5 71 V2
Cranes Park Crs BRYLDS KT5 71 V2
Crane St PECK SE15 50 K13
Craneswater HYS/HAR UB3 46 B12
Craneswater Pk NWDGN UB2 46 H10
Cranes Wy BORE WD6 24 C3
Crane Wy WHTN TW2 59 L5
Cranfield Crs POTB/CUF EN6 15 N3
Cranfield Dr CDALE/KGS NW9 24 E13
Cranfield Rd BROCKY SE4 63 R1
Cranfield Rd East CAR SM5 73 U13
Cranfield Rd West CAR SM5 * 73 T13
Cranford Av PLMGR N13 26 C10
STWL/WRAY TW19 57 Q5
Cranford Cl PUR/KEN CR8 86 G3
RYNPK SW20 * 60 H13
STWL/WRAY TW19 57 Q5
Cranford Cottages WAP E1W * 51 P5
Cranford Dr HYS/HAR UB3 46 B9
Cranford La HEST TW5 46 F12
HTHAIR TW6 58 B1
HYS/HAR UB3 45 V11
Cranford Park Rd HYS/HAR UB3 46 B9
Cranford Ri ESH/CLAY KT10 71 L10
Cranford Rd DART DA1 67 L6
Cranford St WAP E1W 51 P5
Cranford Wy CEND/HSY/T N8 38 D3
Cranham Gdns UPMR RM14 43 T5
Cranham Rd EMPK RM11 42 H4
Cranhurst Rd CRICK NW2 36 J10
Cranleigh Cl BXLY DA5 * 66 B4
CHESW EN7 16 A2
ORP BR6 77 Q8
PGE/AN SE20 63 M14
SAND/SEL CR2 87 L2
Cranleigh Dr SWLY BR8 78 E2
Cranleigh Gdns BARK IG11 41 M12
KTN/HRWW/WS HA3 35 U3
KUTN/CMB KT2 59 V11
LOU IG10 28 H4
SAND/SEL CR2 87 L2
SNWD SE25 74 J1
STHL UB1 46 H4
SUT SM1 73 P7
WCHMH N21 26 E3
Cranleigh Ms BTSEA SW11 49 T14
Cranleigh Rd ESH/CLAY KT10 71 L6
FELT TW13 58 B9
SEVS/STOTM N15 38 G3
WIM/MER SW19 73 N1
Cranleigh St CAMTN NW1 4 B4
Cranley Dr GNTH/NBYPK IG2 41 L5
RSLP HA4 34 B7
Cranley Gdns MUSWH N10 37 V2
PLMGR N13 26 D8
SKENS SW7 6 K9
WLGTN SM6 74 A12
Cranley Ms SKENS SW7 6 K9
Cranley Pl SKENS SW7 7 L8
Cranley Rd GNTH/NBYPK IG2 41 L4
PLSTW E13 52 D3
WOT/HER KT12 70 B11
Cranley Ter HDN NW4 * 24 K14
Cranmer Av WEA W13 47 R8
Cranmer Cl MRDN SM4 72 K4
POTB/CUF EN6 14 E4
RSLP HA4 34 F6
STAN HA7 23 S12
WARL CR6 87 Q7
WEY KT13 69 S12
Cranmer Ct HPTN TW12 58 K10
KUTN/CMB KT2 59 T9
Cranmer Farm Cl MTCM CR4 73 T2
Cranmer Gdns DAGE RM10 42 C9
WARL CR6 87 Q7
Cranmer Rd BRXN/ST SW9 8 K13
CROY/NA CR0 74 G8
EDGW HA8 24 B8
FSTGT E7 40 D9
HPTN TW12 58 K10
HYS/HAR UB3 45 V4
KUTN/CMB KT2 59 U10
MTCM CR4 73 T2
SEV TN13 90 E13
Cranmer Ter TOOT SW17 61 R10
Cranmore Av ISLW TW7 47 L12
Cranmore Rd BMLY BR1 64 A8
CHST BR7 64 H10
Cranmore Wy MUSWH N10 38 A2
Cranston Cl HGDN/ICK UB10 33 V7
HSLW TW3 46 G14
REIG RH2 93 P11
Cranston Est IS N1 5 R3
Cranston Gdns CHING E4 27 T11
Cranston Park Av UPMR RM14 43 R9
Cranston Rd FSTH SE23 63 Q6
Cranswick Rd BERM/RHTH SE16 51 M10
Crantock Rd CAT SE6 63 U7
Cranwell Cl BOW E3 51 T2
Cranwell Gv SHPTN TW17 69 R2
Cranwich Av WCHMH N21 26 H5
Cranwich Rd STNW/STAM N16 38 J5
Cranwood St FSBYE EC1V 5 R6
Cranworth Crs CHING E4 27 V6
Cranworth Gdns BRXN/ST SW9 50 E13
Craster Rd BRXS/STRHM SW2 62 D5
Crathie Rd LEE/GVPK SE12 64 D4
Cravan Av FELT TW13 58 C7
Craven Av EA W5 47 S5
STHL UB1 46 H4
Craven Cl STNW/STAM N16 * 39 L5
YEAD UB4 46 C4
Craven Gdns BARK IG11 41 N14
BARK/HLT IG6 29 M14
CRW RM5 30 A10
HARH RM3 31 Q11
WIM/MER SW19 61 P10
Craven Hl BAY/PAD W2 2 K13
Craven Hill Gdns BAY/PAD W2 2 J13
Craven Hill Ms BAY/PAD W2 2 K13
Craven Ms BTSEA SW11 61 U1
Craven Pk WLSDN NW10 36 D13
Craven Park Ms WLSDN NW10 36 E13
Craven Park Rd SEVS/STOTM N15 38 K4
WLSDN NW10 36 E13
Craven Pas CHCR WC2N 8 E1
Craven Rd BAY/PAD W2 2 K13
CROY/NA CR0 75 M6
KUTN/CMB KT2 59 V13
ORP BR6 77 T8
WEA W13 47 S5
WLSDN NW10 36 D13
Craven St CHCR WC2N 8 E1
Craven Ter BAY/PAD W2 2 K13
Craven Wk CLPT E5 39 L5
Crawford Av ALP/SUD HA0 35 T10
Crawford Cl ISLW TW7 47 N14
Crawford Gdns NTHLT UB5 46 H1
PLMGR N13 26 F8
Crawford Pas CLKNW EC1R 4 J8
Crawford Pl MBLAR W1H 3 P11
Crawford Rd CMBW SE5 50 G14
Crawfords SWLY BR8 66 E12
Crawford St MBLAR W1H 3 Q10
WLSDN NW10 36 D12
Crawley Rd ED N9 26 K5
LEY E10 39 T6
WDGN N22 26 G14
Crawshaw Rd CHERT KT16 68 H11
Crawshay Cl SEV TN13 90 G13
Crawthew Gv EDUL SE22 62 K2
Cray Av ASHTD KT21 83 U6
STMC/STPC BR5 77 R3
Craybrooke Rd SCUP DA14 65 R9
Craybury End ELTH/MOT SE9 65 L7
Cray Cl DART DA1 66 G3
Craydene Rd ERITH DA8 54 F13
Crayford High St DART DA1 66 E3
Crayford Rd DART DA1 66 F3
HOLWY N7 38 C9
Crayford Wy DART DA1 66 G2
Crayke Hl CHSGTN KT9 71 U12
Craylands STMC/STPC BR5 77 S1
Crayleigh Ter SCUP DA14 * 65 S11
Crayonne Cl SUN TW16 58 A13
Cray Rd BELV DA17 54 A11
SCUP DA14 65 S11
SWLY BR8 78 C4
Crays Pde STMC/STPC BR5 * 65 S14
Cray Valley Rd STMC/STPC BR5 77 Q3
Crealock Gv WFD IG8 28 B10
Crealock St WAND/EARL SW18 61 P4
Creasey Cl EMPK RM11 42 H7
Creasy Cl ABLGY WD5 11 M5
Crebor St EDUL SE22 63 L4
Credenhall Dr HAYES BR2 76 H6
Credenhill St STRHM/NOR SW16 62 A11
Crediton Hl KIL/WHAMP NW6 37 P10
Crediton Rd WLSDN NW10 36 J13
Crediton Wy ESH/CLAY KT10 71 Q10
Credon Rd BERM/RHTH SE16 51 M10
PLSTW E13 40 E14
Credo Wy WTHK RM20 55 V11
Creechurch La HDTCH EC3A 5 T12
Creechurch Pl HDTCH EC3A * 5 T12
Creed La BLKFR EC4V 5 M12
Creek Cottages E/WMO/HCT KT8 * 71 N2
Creek Rd BARK IG11 53 P1
DEPT SE8 51 S11
E/WMO/HCT KT8 71 N2
Creekside DEPT SE8 51 T12
RAIN RM13 54 F2
The Creek SUN TW16 70 C3
Creek Wy RAIN RM13 54 E3
Creeland Gv CAT SE6 63 R6
Cree Wy ROM RM1 30 E12
Crefeld Cl HMSMTH W6 6 A12
HMSMTH W6 48 K11
Creffield Rd EA W5 48 A5
Creighton Av EFNCH N2 25 T14
EHAM E6 40 F14
Creighton Cl SHB W12 48 H5
Creighton Rd EA W5 47 T8
KIL/WHAMP NW6 36 K14
TOTM N17 26 J12
Creigton Av EFNCH N2 37 S1
Cremer St BETH E2 5 U4
Cremorne Est WBPTN SW10 7 L12
Cremorne Gdns HOR/WEW KT19 72 D13
Cremorne Rd WBPTN SW10 6 J13
Crescent TWRH EC3N 5 U13
Crescent Ar GNWCH SE10 51 U11
Crescent Av HCH RM12 42 F7
Crescent Cottages SEV TN13 90 E10
Crescent Dr STMC/STPC BR5 77 L4
Crescent East EBAR EN4 14 E12
Crescent Gdns RSLP HA4 34 D5
SWLY BR8 66 C14
WIM/MER SW19 61 N8
Crescent Gv CLAP SW4 62 A2
MTCM CR4 73 S2
Crescent La CLAP SW4 62 B3
Crescent Pde HGDN/ICK UB10 * 45 S1
Crescent Pl CHEL SW3 7 N7
Crescent Ri EBAR EN4 25 S3
WDGN N22 26 B13
Crescent Rd BECK BR3 63 T14
BFN/LL DA15 65 P8
BMLY BR1 64 C12
BRW CM14 31 V9
CEND/HSY/T N8 38 B4
CHING E4 28 A5
CTHM CR3 87 L14
DAGE RM10 42 B9
EBAR EN4 25 S4
ED N9 27 L6
ENC/FH EN2 26 F2
ERITH DA8 54 F11
FBAR/BDGN N11 25 T9
FNCH N3 25 M13
KUTN/CMB KT2 60 A12
LEY E10 39 T7
PLSTW E13 40 C13
REDH RH1 94 G9
REIG RH2 93 N12
RYNPK SW20 60 K13
SEVS/STOTM N15 * 38 F1
SHPTN TW17 69 U3
SOCK/AV RM15 55 Q7
SWFD E18 28 E14
WDGN N22 26 B13
WOOL/PLUM SE18 52 K10
Crescent Rw STLK EC1Y 5 N8
Crescent St IS N1 * 38 D12
The Crescent ABLGY WD5 11 M4
ACT W3 48 E4
ALP/SUD HA0 35 R7
ASHF TW15 57 R10
BAR EN5 25 P1
BARN SW13 48 F14
BECK BR3 63 S13
BELMT SM2 85 N1
BXLY DA5 65 S5
CHERT KT16 69 L1
CRICK NW2 36 H8
CROY/NA CR0 74 H4
CTHM CR3 87 S13
E/WMO/HCT KT8 70 H2
EGH TW20 56 D11
EPP CM16 18 D6
EPSOM KT18 84 A5
FBAR/BDGN N11 25 T9
GNTH/NBYPK IG2 40 J4
GSTN WD25 11 V12
HYS/HAR UB3 45 U12
LCOL/BKTW AL2 11 U4
LHD/OX KT22 83 R12
LOU IG10 28 F4
NWMAL KT3 60 C14
REDH RH1 * 93 R13
REIG RH2 93 P10
RKW/CH/CXG WD3 21 T4
RYLN/HDSTN HA2 35 L6
SCUP DA14 65 P9
SEV TN13 90 K12
SHPTN TW17 70 B5
STHL UB1 46 G7
SURB KT6 71 U3
SUT SM1 73 R10
UPMR RM14 43 S5
WALTH E17 39 Q3
WATW WD18 22 E2
WEY KT13 69 S8
WIM/MER SW19 61 N8
WWKM BR4 76 A4
Crescent Vw LOU IG10 28 F4
Crescent Wk SOCK/AV RM15 55 Q7
Crescent Wy BROCKY SE4 63 S1
ORP BR6 77 N10
SOCK/AV RM15 55 R6
STRHM/NOR SW16 62 D12
Crescentway NFNCH/WDSPK N12 25 S11
Crescent West EBAR EN4 14 E12
Crescent Wood Rd SYD SE26 63 L8
Cresford Rd FUL/PGN SW6 49 P13
Crespigny Rd HDN NW4 36 H4
Cressage Cl STHL UB1 46 J2
Cressall Cl LHD/OX KT22 83 R10
Cressall Md LHD/OX KT22 83 R10
Cress End RKW/CH/CXG WD3 21 L6
Cresset Rd HOM E9 39 N11
Cresset St CLAP SW4 62 B1
Cressfield Cl KTTN NW5 37 U10
Cressida Rd ARCH N19 38 A6
Cressingham Gv SUT SM1 73 Q9
Cressingham Rd EDGW HA8 24 D12
LEW SE13 63 U1
The Cressinghams EPSOM KT18 84 D3
Cressington Cl STNW/STAM N16 38 J10
Cresswell Gdns ECT SW5 * 6 J9
Cresswell Pk BKHTH/KID SE3 64 B1
Cresswell Pl WBPTN SW10 6 J9
Cresswell Rd FELT TW13 58 G9
SNWD SE25 75 M2
TWK TW1 59 T4
Cresswell Wy WCHMH N21 26 E5
Cressy Ct HMSMTH W6 48 H8
WCHPL E1 51 N3
Cressy Houses WCHPL E1 * 51 N3
Cressy Pl WCHPL E1 51 N3
Cressy Rd HAMP NW3 37 T9
Cressys Cnr HSLW TW3 * 58 K1
Cresta Dr ADL/WDHM KT15 68 K14
Crestbrook Av PLMGR N13 26 F8
Crestbrook Pl PLMGR N13 * 26 E8
Crest Cl RSEV TN14 90 B1
Crest Dr PEND EN3 16 C12
Crestfield St CAMTN NW1 4 F5
Crest Gdns RSLP HA4 34 E8
Creston Wy WPK KT4 72 K6
Crest Rd CRICK NW2 36 G7
HAYES BR2 76 B5
SAND/SEL CR2 75 M12
The Crest BRYLDS KT5 72 A3
CHESW EN7 15 R1
HDN NW4 36 J3
HOLWY N7 * 38 B10
PLMGR N13 26 E9
POTB/CUF EN6 * 14 E5
Crest Vw PIN HA5 34 F2
RDART DA2 67 J8
Crest View Dr STMC/STPC BR5 76 K3
Crestway PUT/ROE SW15 60 G4
Crestwood Wy HSLWW TW4 58 H3
Creswell Dr BECK BR3 75 T3
Creswick Rd ACT W3 48 B5
Creswick Wk GLDGN NW11 37 M2
Creukhorne Rd WLSDN NW10 * 36 E12
Crewdson Rd BRXN/ST SW9 8 J13
Crewe Pl WLSDN NW10 48 F1
Crewe's Av WARL CR6 87 N6
Crewe's Cl WARL CR6 87 N6
Crewe's Farm La WARL CR6 87 Q7
Crewe's La WARL CR6 87 Q6
Crews Hl ENC/FH EN2 15 P8
Crews St POP/IOD E14 51 S9
Crewys Rd CRICK NW2 37 M7
PECK SE15 51 M14
Crichton Av WLGTN SM6 74 B10
Crichton Rd CAR SM5 73 T12
Crichton St VX/NE SW8 * 50 A14
Cricketers Arms Rd ENC/FH EN2 * 15 S14
Cricketers Cl CHSGTN KT9 71 T10
ERITH DA8 54 E10
STHGT/OAK N14 26 A5
Cricketers Ms BAL SW12 61 V5
WAND/EARL SW18 61 P3
Cricketers Wk SYD SE26 63 N10
Cricketfield Rd CLPT E5 39 M9
Cricket Field Rd UX/CGN UB8 33 P13
Cricketfield Rd WDR/YW UB7 45 N9
Cricket Gn MTCM CR4 73 T2
Cricket Ground Rd CHST BR7 64 K13
Cricket Hl REDH RH1 94 D13
Cricket La BECK BR3 63 Q11
Cricket Rw EFNCH N2 * 37 R1
Cricket Vw WEY KT13 69 T10
Cricket Wy WEY KT13 70 A7
Cricklade Av BRXS/STRHM SW2 62 C7
HARH RM3 30 K11
Cricklewood Broadway CRICK NW2 36 K9
Cricklewood La CRICK NW2 37 L9
Cridland St SRTFD E15 40 B13
Crieff Ct TEDD TW11 59 S12
Crieff Rd WAND/EARL SW18 61 Q4
Criffel Av BRXS/STRHM SW2 62 B7
Crimscott St STHWK SE1 9 T6
Crimsworth Rd VX/NE SW8 8 D14
VX/NE SW8 50 B13
Crinan St IS N1 4 F3
Cringle St VX/NE SW8 8 B13
Cripplegate St BARB EC2Y * 5 N9
Crispen Rd FELT TW13 58 G9
Crispian Cl WLSDN NW10 36 E9
Crispin Crs CROY/NA CR0 74 B7
Crispin Rd EDGW HA8 24 C11
Crispin St WCHPL E1 5 U10
Crispin Wy UX/CGN UB8 45 R2
Crisp Rd HMSMTH W6 48 J10
Criss Gv CFSP/GDCR SL9 20 A14
Criss La CFSP/GDCR SL9 20 A14
Cristowe Rd FUL/PGN SW6 * 49 M14
Criterion Ms ARCH N19 38 B7
Crockenhill Hl STMC/STPC BR5 77 T3
Crockenhill La SWLY BR8 78 G5
Crockenhill Rd STMC/STPC BR5 77 T4
Crockerton Rd TOOT SW17 61 T7
Crockford Cl ADL/WDHM KT15 69 N9
Crockford Park Rd ADL/WDHM KT15 69 N10
Crockham Wy ELTH/MOT SE9 64 J9
Crocus Cl CROY/NA CR0 75 P6
Crocus Fld BAR EN5 25 M4
Croffets KWD/TDW/WH KT20 84 K11
Croft Av WWKM BR4 75 U6
Croft Cl ABYW SE2 53 V10
CHST BR7 64 H10
HGDN/ICK UB10 33 S12
HYS/HAR UB3 45 U12
KGLGY WD4 10 A4
MLHL NW7 24 E8
Croft Ct BORE WD6 24 D1
RSLP HA4 * 34 B6
SUT SM1 * 73 R7
Croftdown Rd KTTN NW5 37 U8
Croft End Rd KGLGY WD4 10 A4
Crofters Cl ISLW TW7 59 M3
REDH RH1 93 V12
Crofters Ct DEPT SE8 51 Q9
Crofters Md CROY/NA CR0 * 75 R13
Crofters Rd NTHWD HA6 22 A9
Crofters Wy CAMTN NW1 4 C1
Croft Fld KGLGY WD4 10 A4
Croft Gdns HNWL W7 47 Q7
RSLP HA4 34 A6
Croft La KGLGY WD4 10 A4
Croftleigh Av PUR/KEN CR8 86 E6
Croft Lodge Cl WFD IG8 28 D11
Croft Meadow KGLGY WD4 10 A4
Croft Ms NFNCH/WDSPK N12 25 Q8
Crofton ASHTD KT21 83 U8
Crofton Av BXLY DA5 65 T5
CHSWK W4 48 C12
ORP BR6 77 L7
WOT/HER KT12 70 E8
Crofton Cl CHERT KT16 68 G12
Crofton Gate Wy BROCKY SE4 63 Q3
Crofton Gv CHING E4 27 V9
Crofton La STMC/STPC BR5 77 M6
Crofton Park Rd BROCKY SE4 63 R4
Crofton Rd CMBW SE5 50 J14
ORP BR6 76 J9
PLSTW E13 52 D2
Crofton Ter RCH/KEW TW9 59 V2
Crofton Wy BAR EN5 * 25 P4
ENC/FH EN2 15 Q14
Croft Rd BH/WHM TN16 96 K2
BMLY BR1 64 C11
CFSP/GDCR SL9 20 C14
CTHM CR3 87 R12
PEND EN3 16 E13
STRHM/NOR SW16 62 E12
SUT SM1 73 R10
WIM/MER SW19 61 Q12
Crofts Rd HRW HA1 35 Q4
The Crofts SHPTN TW17 70 A2
Croft St DEPT SE8 51 Q9
WCHPL E1 51 L5
The Croft ALP/SUD HA0 35 S10
BAR EN5 25 L2
CHING E4 28 A7
EA W5 47 U3
EDGW HA8 24 B13
HEST TW5 46 G12
LOU IG10 17 U14
PIN HA5 34 H5
RSLP HA4 34 E9
SWLY BR8 78 C1
WLSDN NW10 36 F14
Croft Wy BFN/LL DA15 65 N8
RCHPK/HAM TW10 59 R8
Crogsland Rd CAMTN NW1 37 U12
Croham Cl SAND/SEL CR2 74 J12
Croham Manor Rd SAND/SEL CR2 74 J12
Croham Mt SAND/SEL CR2 74 J12
Croham Park Av SAND/SEL CR2 74 K10
Croham Rd SAND/SEL CR2 74 H10
Croham Valley Rd SAND/SEL CR2 75 M12
Croindene Rd STRHM/NOR SW16 62 C13
Cromartie Rd ARCH N19 38 B5
Cromarty Rd EDGW HA8 24 B7
Cromarty Vls BAY/PAD W2 * 2 J13
Crombie Cl REDBR IG4 40 H3
Crombie Ms BTSEA SW11 * 49 S14
Crombie Rd BFN/LL DA15 65 M6
Cromer Cl UX/CGN UB8 45 U4
Cromer Hyde MRDN SM4 * 73 P3
Crome Rd WLSDN NW10 36 E11
Cromer Rd BAR EN5 25 Q2
CHDH RM6 41 U4
EMPK RM11 42 K5
HTHAIR TW6 57 S1
LEY E10 39 V5
ROMW/RG RM7 42 C4
SNWD SE25 75 M1
TOOT SW17 61 U11
TOTM N17 27 L14
WATN WD24 11 Q12
Cromer Rd West HTHAIR TW6 57 S1
Cromer St STPAN WC1H 4 F6
Cromer Ter HACK E8 39 L10
Cromer Villas Rd WAND/EARL SW18 61 M4
Cromford Cl ORP BR6 77 N8
Cromford Rd PUT/ROE SW15 61 M3
Cromford Wy NWMAL KT3 60 D13
Cromlix Cl CHST BR7 64 K14
Crompton Pl PEND EN3 16 G12
Crompton St BAY/PAD W2 3 L8
Cromwell Av CHESW EN7 16 B4
HAYES BR2 76 D1
HGT N6 37 V6
HMSMTH W6 48 H10
NWMAL KT3 72 F3
Cromwell Cl CHSWK W4 * 48 B10
CSTG HP8 20 A8
EFNCH N2 37 R2
HAYES BR2 76 D2
WOT/HER KT12 70 D6
Cromwell Ct ALP/SUD HA0 35 U14
Cromwell Crs ECT SW5 6 E7
Cromwell Gdns SKENS SW7 7 M7
Cromwell Gv CTHM CR3 86 G11
HMSMTH W6 48 J8
Cromwell Ms SKENS SW7 7 M7
Cromwell Pde ALP/SUD HA0 * 35 U14
Cromwell Pl ACT W3 48 C6
HGT N6 * 37 V6
MORT/ESHN SW14 60 C1
SKENS SW7 7 M7
Cromwell Rd ALP/SUD HA0 35 T14
BECK BR3 63 Q14
BORE WD6 12 J13
BRW CM14 31 V9
BRXN/ST SW9 50 F13
CHESW EN7 16 B2
CROY/NA CR0 74 H5
CTHM CR3 86 G11
ECT SW5 6 F7
FELT TW13 58 D6
FNCH N3 25 Q14
FSTGT E7 40 E12
HSLW TW3 58 J2
HYS/HAR UB3 45 V4
KUTN/CMB KT2 59 U13
MUSWH N10 25 U12
REDH RH1 93 T10
SKENS SW7 7 L7
TEDD TW11 59 Q11
WALTH E17 39 U3
WIM/MER SW19 61 N10
WOT/HER KT12 70 D7
WPK KT4 72 D8
Cromwell St HSLW TW3 58 J2
Cromwell Ter HSLW TW3 * 58 J2
Crondace Rd FUL/PGN SW6 49 N13
Crondall St IS N1 5 R4
Cronin St PECK SE15 9 U14
Cronks Hl REIG RH2 93 Q11
Cronks Hill Cl REDH RH1 93 R12
Cronks Hill Rd REDH RH1 93 R12
Crooked Billet Rbt CHING E4 27 T12
Crooked Mile WAB EN9 16 J7
Crooked Usage FNCH N3 37 L1
Crooke Rd DEPT SE8 51 Q10
Crookham Rd FUL/PGN SW6 49 M13
Crook Log BXLYHS DA6 65 T1
Crookston Rd ELTH/MOT SE9 64 K1
Croombs Rd CAN/RD E16 52 E3
Croom's Hl GNWCH SE10 51 V12
Croom's Hill Gv GNWCH SE10 51 U12
Cropley St IS N1 5 Q3
Croppath Rd DAGE RM10 42 A9
Cropthorne Ct MV/WKIL W9 2 K6
Crosby Cl FELT TW13 58 G9
Crosby Rd DAGE RM10 42 B14
FSTGT E7 40 C11
Crosby Rw STHWK SE1 9 Q4
Crosby Sq HDTCH EC3A 5 S12
Crosby Wk HACK E8 38 K11
Crosier Cl BKHTH/KID SE3 52 G13
Crosier Rd HGDN/ICK UB10 33 U9
Crosier Wy RSLP HA4 34 A8
Crosland Pl BTSEA SW11 61 U1
Crossacres WOKS/MYFD GU22 80 J6
Crossbow Rd CHIG IG7 29 P10
Crossbrook Rd BKHTH/KID SE3 52 G14
Crossbrook St CHES/WCR EN8 16 D5
Cross Deep TWK TW1 59 P8
Cross Deep Gdns TWK TW1 59 P7
Crossfield Est DEPT SE8 51 S12
Crossfield Pl WEY KT13 69 T12
Crossfield Rd HAMP NW3 37 R11
TOTM N17 38 G1
Crossfield St DEPT SE8 51 S12
Crossford St BRXN/ST SW9 50 D14
Crossgate EDGW HA8 24 A8
GFD/PVL UB6 35 R11
Crossing Rd EPP CM16 18 E6
Cross Keys Cl ED N9 27 L7
MHST W1U 3 T10
Cross Lances Rd HSLW TW3 58 K2
Crossland Rd REDH RH1 93 U10
THHTH CR7 74 F4
Crosslands CHERT KT16 68 J8
Crosslands Av EA W5 47 V6
NWDGN UB2 46 H10
Crosslands Pde NWDGN UB2 * 46 J10
Crosslands Rd HOR/WEW KT19 72 D11
Cross La BXLY DA5 65 V5
CEND/HSY/T N8 38 D1
CHERT KT16 68 F11
MON EC3R 5 S14
Cross Lanes CFSP/GDCR SL9 20 D10
Cross Lanes Cl CFSP/GDCR SL9 20 D10
Crosslet St WALW SE17 9 R7
Crosslet V GNWCH SE10 51 T13
Crossley Cl BH/WHM TN16 88 F5
Crossleys CSTG HP8 20 A9
Crossleys Hl CSTG HP8 20 A8
Crossley St HOLWY N7 38 E11
Crossmead ELTH/MOT SE9 64 H6
OXHEY WD19 22 D4
Crossmead Av GFD/PVL UB6 46 J1
Crossness Rd BARK IG11 53 P1
Crossoaks La BORE WD6 13 P9
The Crosspath RAD WD7 12 E9
Cross Rd BELMT SM2 73 N14
CHDH RM6 41 S5
CHES/WCR EN8 16 E7
CHING E4 27 V6
CMBW SE5 50 J14
CROY/NA CR0 74 H6
DART DA1 66 J4
EN EN1 26 K2
FBAR/BDGN N11 25 V10
FELT TW13 58 G9
HAYES BR2 76 G7
HRW HA1 35 M2
KTN/HRWW/WS HA3 23 Q14
KUTN/CMB KT2 59 V12
KWD/TDW/WH KT20 84 J12
OXHEY WD19 22 G4
PUR/KEN CR8 86 F3
RDART DA2 67 M9
ROMW/RG RM7 42 A1
RYLN/HDSTN HA2 34 J8
SCUP DA14 65 R9
STMC/STPC BR5 77 R3
SUT SM1 73 R10
WDGN N22 26 E11
WEY KT13 * 69 V8
WFD IG8 28 H11
WIM/MER SW19 61 N12
Cross Roads LOU IG10 17 P14
Cross St BARN SW13 48 E14
ERITH DA8 54 E11
HPTN TW12 59 L10
IS N1 5 M1
UED N18 27 L10
UX/CGN UB8 33 N13
WAT WD17 22 E1
Crossthwaite Av HNHL SE24 62 H2
Crosswall TWRH EC3N 5 U13
Cross Wy HYS/HAR UB3 46 C7
Crossway BCTR RM8 41 S8
CDALE/KGS NW9 36 F2
EN EN1 26 J5
NFNCH/WDSPK N12 25 R11
NWMAL KT3 72 J2
PIN HA5 22 D14
RSLP HA4 34 E9
STMC/STPC BR5 77 M2
STNW/STAM N16 38 J10
THMD SE28 53 S5
WEA W13 47 P2
WOT/HER KT12 70 D7
Crossway Pde WDGN N22 * 26 F12
Crossways BELMT SM2 73 R13
BH/WHM TN16 88 E10
EGH TW20 56 H11
GPK RM2 42 H1
SAND/SEL CR2 75 R12
SUN TW16 58 B13
Crossways Bvd RDART DA2 67 Q2
Crossways La REIG RH2 93 Q4
Crossways Rd BECK BR3 75 S2
MTCM CR4 73 V1
Crossways Ter CLPT E5 * 39 N9
The Crossways BRYLDS KT5 * 72 B6
COUL/CHIP CR5 86 D9
HEST TW5 46 H12
REDH RH1 93 V5
WBLY HA9 36 A7
The Cross Wy KTN/HRWW/WS HA3 23 N14
The Crossway ELTH/MOT SE9 64 F7
WDGN N22 26 F12
Crosswell Cl SHPTN TW17 57 U14
Croston St HACK E8 39 L13
Crosts La WDGN N22 26 E12
Crothall Cl PLMGR N13 26 D8
Crouch Av BARK IG11 41 R14
Crouch Cl BECK BR3 63 S11
Crouch Cft ELTH/MOT SE9 64 J8
Crouch End Hl CEND/HSY/T N8 38 B5
Crouch Hall Rd CEND/HSY/T N8 38 B4
Crouch Hl CEND/HSY/T N8 38 C5
Crouch La CHESW EN7 15 S1
Crouchmans Cl SYD SE26 62 K8
Crouch Oak La ADL/WDHM KT15 69 N9
Crouch Rd WLSDN NW10 36 D12
Crouch Va UPMR RM14 43 S5
Crowborough Cl WARL CR6 87 Q8
Crowborough Dr WARL CR6 87 Q8
Crowborough Pth OXHEY WD19 22 F9
Crowborough Rd TOOT SW17 61 U10
Crowden Wy THMD SE28 53 S5
Crowder Cl NFNCH/WDSPK N12 25 Q12
Crowder St WCHPL E1 51 M5
Crow Dr RSEV TN14 90 C5
Crowfoot Cl HOM E9 39 R10
THMD SE28 53 N6
Crow Gn BRWN CM15 31 U2
Crow Green La BRWN CM15 31 U3
Crow Green Rd BRWN CM15 31 U3
Crow Hl ORP BR6 * 76 H14
Crowhurst Cl BRXN/ST SW9 50 E14
Crowhurst La BGR/WK TN15 79 V10
OXTED RH8 95 V14
Crowhurst Md GDST RH9 95 N6
Crowhurst Wy STMC/STPC BR5 77 S3
Crowland Av HYS/HAR UB3 46 A9
Crowland Gdns STHGT/OAK N14 26 C5
Crowland Rd SEVS/STOTM N15 38 K3
THHTH CR7 * 74 H2
Crowlands Av ROMW/RG RM7 42 B4
Crowland Ter IS N1 38 H12
Crowland Wk MRDN SM4 73 P4
Crow La ROMW/RG RM7 41 V5
Crowley Crs CROY/NA CR0 74 E10
Crowline Wk IS N1 * 38 G11
Crowmarsh Gdns FSTH SE23 63 N5
Crown Ar KUT/HW KT1 * 59 T14
Crownbourne Ct SUT SM1 * 73 P9
Crown Buildings CHING E4 * 27 V6
Crown Cl BOW E3 39 S13
DTCH/LGLY SL3 44 G12
HYS/HAR UB3 46 B7
KIL/WHAMP NW6 37 P11
MLHL NW7 24 F7
ORP BR6 77 Q9
WOT/HER KT12 70 E5
Crown Ct HOL/ALD WC2B 4 F12
Crown Dl NRWD SE19 62 G11
Crowndale Rd CAMTN NW1 4 B3
Crownfield Av GNTH/NBYPK IG2 41 N3
Crownfield Rd SRTFD E15 39 V10
Crown Hl CROY/NA CR0 * 74 G7
WAB EN9 17 T7
Crownhill Rd WFD IG8 28 G12
WLSDN NW10 36 F13
Crown La CHST BR7 65 L13
HAYES BR2 76 F3
MRDN SM4 73 N1
STHGT/OAK N14 26 A6
STRHM/NOR SW16 62 E10
VW GU25 68 B4
Crown Lane Gdns
STRHM/NOR SW16 * 62 E10
Crown Lane Sp HAYES BR2 76 F4
Crown Meadow DTCH/LGLY SL3 44 F12
Crownmead Wy ROMW/RG RM7 42 B2
Crown Office Rw EMB EC4Y 4 J13
Crown Pde MRDN SM4 * 73 P2
STHGT/OAK N14 * 26 A6
Crown Pas STJS SW1Y 8 B2
Crown Pl KTTN NW5 37 V11
SDTCH EC2A 5 S8
Crown Ri CHERT KT16 68 K6
GSTN WD25 11 Q8
Crown Rd BARK/HLT IG6 41 M2
BORE WD6 13 L13
EN EN1 27 M2
KUTN/CMB KT2 60 C13
MRDN SM4 73 N2
MUSWH N10 25 U12
ORP BR6 77 Q10
RSEV TN14 78 F14
RSLP HA4 34 F10
TWK TW1 59 R4
VW GU25 68 A4
Crown Sq WOKN/KNAP GU21 80 D7
Crownstone Rd BRXS/STRHM SW2 62 E3
Crown St ACT W3 48 B6
CMBW SE5 9 P13
DAGE RM10 42 C11
EGH TW20 56 E10
RYLN/HDSTN HA2 35 M6
Crown Ter CRICK NW2 * 36 K9
RCH/KEW TW9 59 V2
STHGT/OAK N14 * 26 B6
Crowntree Cl ISLW TW7 47 P11
Crown Vls ACT W3 * 48 C7
Crown Wk WBLY HA9 35 V8
Crown Wy WDR/YW UB7 45 R6
Crown Woods La WOOL/PLUM SE18 52 K14
Crown Woods Wy ELTH/MOT SE9 65 M3
Crown Yd HSLW TW3 59 L1
Crowshott Av STAN HA7 23 S14
Crows Rd BARK IG11 40 K11
BOW E3 51 V1
EPP CM16 18 D4
Crowther Av BTFD TW8 47 U10
Crowther Cl FUL/PGN SW6 6 D12
Crowther Rd SNWD SE25 75 L2
Crowthorne Cl WAND/EARL SW18 61 M5
Crowthorne Rd NKENS W10 48 K4
Croxdale Rd BORE WD6 12 K14
Croxden Cl EDGW HA8 36 A1
Croxden Wk MRDN SM4 73 Q4
Croxford Gdns WDGN N22 26 F12
Croxford Wy ROMW/RG RM7 42 D6
Croxley Cl STMC/STPC BR5 65 R14
Croxley Gn STMC/STPC BR5 65 R13
Croxley Rd MV/WKIL W9 2 D6
Croxley Vw WATW WD18 22 A4
Croxted Cl DUL SE21 62 G5
Croxted Ms HNHL SE24 62 G4
Croxted Rd DUL SE21 62 H7
Croyde Av GFD/PVL UB6 47 L1
HYS/HAR UB3 46 A9
Croyde Cl BFN/LL DA15 65 M5
The Croydon F/O CROY/NA CR0 74 F9
Croydon Gv CROY/NA CR0 74 F6
Croydon La BNSTD SM7 85 R3
Croydon La South BNSTD SM7 85 P4
Croydon Rd BECK BR3 75 P3
BH/WHM TN16 96 K2
CTHM CR3 87 L12
MTCM CR4 73 V3
PGE/AN SE20 63 M14
PLSTW E13 52 B2
REIG RH2 93 Q9
WARL CR6 87 V12
WLGTN SM6 73 V9
WWKM BR4 76 A8
Croyland Rd ED N9 27 L6
Croylands Dr SURB KT6 71 U5
Croysdale Av SUN TW16 70 C1
Crozier Dr SAND/SEL CR2 75 M14
Crozier Ter HOM E9 39 Q10
Crucible Cl CHDH RM6 41 R4
Crucifix La STHWK SE1 9 S3
Cruden St IS N1 5 M2
Cruickshank St FSBYW WC1X 4 J5
Cruikshank Rd SRTFD E15 40 A9
Crummock Gdns CDALE/KGS NW9 36 E3
Crumpsall St ABYW SE2 53 S9
Crundale Av CDALE/KGS NW9 36 A3
Crunden Rd SAND/SEL CR2 74 H12
Crusader Cl PUR RM19 55 N9
Crusader Gdns CROY/NA CR0 74 J8
Crusader Wy WATW WD18 22 B4
Crusoe Ms STNW/STAM N16 38 H7
Crusoe Rd ERITH DA8 54 D10
MTCM CR4 61 T12
Crutched Friars TWRH EC3N 5 T13
Crutchfield La WOT/HER KT12 70 D7
Crutchley Rd CAT SE6 64 B7
Crystal Av HCH RM12 43 L9
Crystal Palace NRWD SE19 * 63 L12
Crystal Palace Pde NRWD SE19 62 K11
Crystal Palace Park Rd SYD SE26 63 M10
Crystal Palace Rd EDUL SE22 62 K4
Crystal Palace Station Rd NRWD SE19 63 L11
Crystal Ter NRWD SE19 62 H11
Crystal Wy BCTR RM8 41 S6
HRW HA1 35 P3
Cuba Dr PEND EN3 16 C14
Cuba St POP/IOD E14 51 S7
Cubitt Sq NWDGN UB2 * 47 L6
Cubitt St FSBYW WC1X 4 H6
Cubitt Ter CLAP SW4 62 A1
Cuckmere Wy STMC/STPC BR5 77 T6
Cuckoo Av HNWL W7 47 N2
Cuckoo Dene HNWL W7 47 M3
Cuckoo Hall La ED N9 27 N5
Cuckoo Hl PIN HA5 34 E2
Cuckoo Hill Dr PIN HA5 34 E1
Cuckoo Hill Rd PIN HA5 34 F2
Cuckoo La HNWL W7 47 N5
Cuda's Cl HOR/WEW KT19 72 F9
Cuddington Av WPK KT4 72 F8
Cuddington Cl KWD/TDW/WH KT20 84 J10
Cuddington Gld HOR/WEW KT19 84 A2
Cuddington Park Cl BNSTD SM7 85 M3
Cuddington Wy BELMT SM2 84 K2
Cudham Cl BELMT SM2 73 N14
Cudham Dr CROY/NA CR0 75 T14
Cudham La North ORP BR6 77 N13
RSEV TN14 89 M3
Cudham La South RSEV TN14 89 M5
Cudham Park Rd RSEV TN14 89 M1
Cudham Rd BH/WHM TN16 88 G9
ORP BR6 88 J1
Cudham St CAT SE6 63 T5
Cudworth St WCHPL E1 51 M2
Cuff Crs ELTH/MOT SE9 64 G4
Cuffley Av GSTN WD25 11 R8
Cuffley Hl CHESW EN7 15 R3
Cugley Rd RDART DA2 67 Q5
Culford Gdns CHEL SW3 7 R8
Culford Gv IS N1 38 J11
Culford Ms IS N1 38 H11
Culford Rd IS N1 5 S1
IS N1 38 J12
Culgaith Gdns ENC/FH EN2 26 C2
Cullera Cl NTHWD HA6 22 B11
Cullerne Cl EW KT17 72 F14
Cullesden Rd PUR/KEN CR8 86 F5
Culling Rd BERM/RHTH SE16 51 N8
Cullings Ct WAB EN9 17 M7
Cullington Cl KTN/HRWW/WS HA3 35 Q2
Cullingworth Rd WLSDN NW10 36 H10
Culloden Cl BERM/RHTH SE16 51 L10
Culloden Rd ENC/FH EN2 15 R14
Culloden St POP/IOD E14 51 U4
Cullum St FENCHST EC3M 5 S13
Culmington Pde WEA W13 * 47 S5
Culmington Rd SAND/SEL CR2 74 G13
WEA W13 47 S6
Culmore Rd PECK SE15 51 M12
Culmstock Rd BTSEA SW11 61 U3
Culpepper Cl CHIG IG7 28 K11
UED N18 27 M10
Culross Cl SEVS/STOTM N15 38 G2
Culross St MYFR/PKLN W1K 3 S14
Culsac Rd SURB KT6 71 U7
Culverden Rd BAL SW12 62 A8
OXHEY WD19 22 D8
Culverden Ter WEY KT13 * 69 V8
Culver Dr OXTED RH8 96 A6
Culver Gv STAN HA7 23 S14
Culverhay ASHTD KT21 83 U6
Culverhouse Gdns STRHM/NOR SW16 62 D9
Culverlands Cl STAN HA7 23 R9
Culverley Rd CAT SE6 63 T6
Culvers Av CAR SM5 73 T7
Culvers Retreat CAR SM5 73 T6
Culverstone Cl HAYES BR2 76 B4
Culvers Wy CAR SM5 73 T8
Culvert La UX/CGN UB8 33 M14
Culvert Pl BTSEA SW11 49 U14
Culvert Rd BTSEA SW11 49 T14
SEVS/STOTM N15 38 J3
Culworth St STJWD NW8 3 N4
Cumberland Av HCH RM12 43 L8
WELL DA16 65 N1
WLSDN NW10 48 B1
Cumberland Cl BARK/HLT IG6 29 L13
HACK E8 38 K11
HOR/WEW KT19 72 E14
RYNPK SW20 60 K12
TWK TW1 59 R4
Cumberland Crs WKENS W14 6 B7
Cumberland Dr BXLYHN DA7 53 U12
CHSGTN KT9 71 U8
DART DA1 67 M5
ESH/CLAY KT10 71 Q7
Cumberland Gdns FSBYW WC1X 4 H5
HDN NW4 * 24 K14
Cumberland Ga BAY/PAD W2 3 R13
Cumberland House KUTN/CMB KT2 60 B12
Cumberland Market CAMTN NW1 3 V5
Cumberland Ms LBTH SE11 8 K10
Cumberland Pk ACT W3 48 C5
Cumberland Pl CAMTN NW1 3 U5
CAT SE6 64 B6
SUN TW16 70 C2
Cumberland Rd ACT W3 48 C5
ASHF TW15 57 P8
BARN SW13 48 F13
ED N9 27 N6
HAYES BR2 76 A2
HNWL W7 47 P7
HRW HA1 34 K3
MNPK E12 40 F9
PLSTW E13 52 D3
RCH/KEW TW9 48 A13
SNWD SE25 75 M4
STAN HA7 35 V1
WALTH E17 27 Q14
WDGN N22 26 D14
Cumberlands PUR/KEN CR8 86 H5
Cumberland St PIM SW1V 7 V9
STA TW18 56 H10
Cumberland Ter CAMTN NW1 3 U4
PGE/AN SE20 * 63 M12
Cumberland Terrace Ms CAMTN NW1 3 U4
Cumberlow Av SNWD SE25 75 L1
Cumbernauld Gdns SUN TW16 58 B10
Cumberton Rd TOTM N17 26 H13
Cumbrae Gdns SURB KT6 71 T7
Cumbrian Av BXLYHN DA7 54 E14
Cumbrian Gdns CRICK NW2 36 K7
Cumbrian Wy UX/CGN UB8 33 P13
Cumley Rd CHONG CM5 19 Q4
Cummings Hall La HARH RM3 30 J8
Cumming St IS N1 4 H4
Cumnor Cl BRXN/ST SW9 * 50 D14
Cumnor Gdns EW KT17 72 G11
Cumnor Ri PUR/KEN CR8 86 G7
Cumnor Rd BELMT SM2 73 Q11
Cunard Crs WCHMH N21 26 H4
Cunard Rd WLSDN NW10 48 D1
Cundy Rd CAN/RD E16 52 E4
Cundy St BGVA SW1W 7 T8
Cunliffe Cl EPSOM KT18 84 B14
Cunliffe Rd HOR/WEW KT19 72 F9
Cunliffe St STRHM/NOR SW16 62 A11
Cunningham Av PEND EN3 16 E10
Cunningham Cl CHDH RM6 41 S3
WWKM BR4 75 T7
Cunningham Pk HRW HA1 35 M3
Cunningham Pl STJWD NW8 3 L7
Cunningham Rd BNSTD SM7 85 R5
CHES/WCR EN8 16 E1
SEVS/STOTM N15 * 39 L2

Cunnington St CHSWK W4 48 C9
Cupar Rd BTSEA SW11 49 U13
Cupola Cl BMLY BR1 64 D10
Curates Wk RDART DA2 66 K8
Cureton St WEST SW1P 8 D9
Curfew Bell Rd CHERT KT16 68 K5
Curlew Cl SAND/SEL CR2 87 P1
THMD SE28 53 T5
Curlew St STHWK SE1 9 U3
Curlew Wy YEAD UB4 46 F3
Curling Cl COUL/CHIP CR5 86 D10
Curnick's La WNWD SE27 62 G9
Curo Pk LCOL/BKTW AL2 12 C2
Curran Av BFN/LL DA15 65 P3
WLGTN SM6 73 U8
Curran Cl UX/CGN UB8 45 N2
Currey Rd NTHLT UB5 35 L11
Curricle St ACT W3 48 E6
Currie Hill Cl WIM/MER SW19 61 M9
Curry Ri MLHL NW7 24 K11
Cursitor St FLST/FETLN EC4A 4 J11
Curtain Pl SDTCH EC2A 5 T7
Curtain Rd SDTCH EC2A 5 S8
Curthwaite Gdns ENC/FH EN2 26 B2
Curtis Cl RKW/CH/CXG WD3 21 L6
Curtis Dr ACT W3 48 D4
Curtis Field Rd STRHM/NOR SW16 62 D9
Curtis La ALP/SUD HA0 35 U11
Curtismill Cl STMC/STPC BR5 77 R1
Curtis Mill La ABR/ST RM4 30 F2
Curtismill Wy STMC/STPC BR5 77 R1
Curtis Rd EMPK RM11 43 M6
HOR/WEW KT19 72 C9
HSLWW TW4 58 H5
Curtiss Dr GSTN WD25 11 M8
Curtis St STHWK SE1 9 U7
Curtis Wy STHWK SE1 9 U7
Curvan Cl EW KT17 72 F14
The Curve SHB W12 48 G5
Curwen Av FSTGT E7 40 D9
Curwen Rd SHB W12 48 G7
Curzon Av PEND EN3 27 P3
STAN HA7 23 Q13
Curzon Cl ORP BR6 77 M9
WEY KT13 69 S9
Curzon Crs BARK IG11 53 P1
WLSDN NW10 36 E12
Curzon Pl PIN HA5 34 E3
Curzon Rd EA W5 47 R2
MUSWH N10 25 V14
THHTH CR7 74 E4
WEY KT13 69 S9
Curzon Sq MYFR/PICC W1J 7 T2
Curzon St MYFR/PKLN W1K 7 T2
Cusack Cl TWK TW1 * 59 P9
Cussons Cl CHESW EN7 16 A3
Custom House Reach
BERM/RHTH SE16 * 51 R8
Cutcombe Rd CMBW SE5 50 G14
Cuthberga Cl BARK IG11 41 L12
Cuthbert Cl CHESW EN7 15 V3
Cuthbert Gdns SNWD SE25 74 J1
Cuthbert Rd CROY/NA CR0 74 F7
UED N18 27 L10
WALTH E17 39 U1
Cuthbert St BAY/PAD W2 3 L8
Cutlers Gardens Ar LVPST EC2M 5 T11
Cutler St HDTCH EC3A 5 T11
The Cut STHWK SE1 8 K3
Cutty Sark Ct RDART DA2 * 67 U3
Cuxton Cl BXLYHS DA6 65 U3
Cyclamen Cl HPTN TW12 58 J11
Cyclamen Rd SWLY BR8 78 D2
Cyclamen Wy HOR/WEW KT19 72 C10
Cygnet Av EBED/NFELT TW14 58 F5
Cygnet Cl BORE WD6 13 N13
NTHWD HA6 21 U12
WLSDN NW10 36 D10
Cygnets Cl REDH RH1 93 U8
The Cygnets FELT TW13 58 G9
STA TW18 56 K10
Cygnet St WCHPL E1 5 V7
Cygnet Vw WTHK RM20 55 T9
Cygnet Wy YEAD UB4 46 F4
Cymbeline Ct HRW HA1 * 35 P4
Cynthia St IS N1 4 H4
Cypress Av ENC/FH EN2 15 Q9
WHTN TW2 59 L5
Cypress Cl CLPT E5 39 L7
WAB EN9 * 16 K8
Cypress Ct VW GU25 68 D2
Cypress Gdns BROCKY SE4 63 Q3
Cypress Gv BARK/HLT IG6 29 N11
Cypress Rd KTN/HRWW/WS HA3 23 M14
SNWD SE25 62 J14
Cypress Tree Cl BFN/LL DA15 65 P6
Cypress Wk GSTN WD25 * 11 P9
Cypress Wy BNSTD SM7 84 K4
Cyprus Av FNCH N3 25 L14
Cyprus Cl FSBYPK N4 38 E4
Cyprus Gdns FNCH N3 25 L14
Cyprus Pl BETH E2 39 N14
EHAM E6 52 J5
Cyprus Rd ED N9 26 K7
FNCH N3 25 M14
Cyprus St BETH E2 39 N14
Cyrena Rd EDUL SE22 62 K4
Cyril Rd BXLYHN DA7 53 U14
ORP BR6 77 Q5
Cyrus St FSBYE EC1V 5 M7
Czar St DEPT SE8 51 S11

D

Dabbling Cl ERITH DA8 * 54 H12
Dabbs Hill La NTHLT UB5 34 J10
D'Abernon Cl ESH/CLAY KT10 70 J9
D'Abernon Dr COB KT11 82 G6
Dabin Crs GNWCH SE10 51 U13
Dacca St DEPT SE8 51 R11
Dace Rd BOW E3 39 S13
Dacre Av CLAY IG5 28 J14
SOCK/AV RM15 55 R6
Dacre Cl CHIG IG7 29 L9
GFD/PVL UB6 34 K14
Dacre Crs SOCK/AV RM15 55 R6
Dacre Gdns BORE WD6 24 D3
CHIG IG7 29 L9
LEW SE13 * 64 A2
Dacre Pk LEW SE13 64 A1
Dacre Pl LEW SE13 64 A1
Dacre Rd CROY/NA CR0 74 C5
PLSTW E13 40 D13
WAN E11 40 B6
Dacres Est FSTH SE23 * 63 P8
Dacres Rd FSTH SE23 63 P8
Dacre St STJSPK SW1H 8 C5
Dade Wy NWDGN UB2 46 H10
Daerwood Cl HAYES BR2 76 H6
Daffodil Av BRWN CM15 31 V3
Daffodil Cl CROY/NA CR0 75 P6
HPTN TW12 58 J11
Daffodil Gdns IL IG1 40 K10
Daffodil St SHB W12 48 F5
Dafforne Rd TOOT SW17 61 T8
Dagenham Av DAGW RM9 41 U13
Dagenham Rd DAGE RM10 42 C9
LEY E10 39 R6
RAIN RM13 42 D12
ROMW/RG RM7 42 D5
Dagger La BORE WD6 23 Q4
Dagmar Av WBLY HA9 35 V9
Dagmar Gdns WLSDN NW10 36 K14
Dagmar Ms NWDGN UB2 46 G8
Dagmar Pas IS N1 5 L1
Dagmar Rd CMBW SE5 50 J14
DAGE RM10 42 C12
FSBYPK N4 38 E5
KUTN/CMB KT2 59 V13
NWDGN UB2 46 G8
SEVS/STOTM N15 38 H2
SNWD SE25 74 J2
WDGN N22 26 B13
Dagmar Ter IS N1 5 M1
Dagnall Crs UX/CGN UB8 45 N3
Dagnall Pk SNWD SE25 74 J3
Dagnall Rd SNWD SE25 74 J3
Dagnall St BTSEA SW11 49 T14
Dagnam Park Cl HARH RM3 31 N10
Dagnam Park Dr HARH RM3 31 L10
Dagnam Park Gdns HARH RM3 31 N11
Dagnam Park Sq HARH RM3 31 N11
Dagnan Rd BAL SW12 61 V5
Dagonet Rd BMLY BR1 64 C8
Dahlia Dr SWLY BR8 66 F14
Dahlia Gdns IL IG1 40 K11
MTCM CR4 74 B2
Dahlia Rd ABYW SE2 53 R10
Dahomey Rd STRHM/NOR SW16 62 A11
Daiglen Dr SOCK/AV RM15 55 U5
Daimler Wy WLGTN SM6 74 C12
Daines Cl MNPK E12 40 H8
SOCK/AV RM15 55 U2
Dainford Cl BMLY BR1 63 V10
Daintry Cl KTN/HRWW/WS HA3 35 Q2
Dairsie Rd ELTH/MOT SE9 64 J1
Dairy Cl BMLY BR1 * 64 D12
EYN DA4 67 P12
THHTH CR7 62 G14
WLSDN NW10 36 G13
Dairyglen Av CHES/WCR EN8 16 D5
Dairy La EDEN TN8 96 K10
WOOL/PLUM SE18 52 H9
Dairyman Cl CRICK NW2 * 36 K9
Dairy Wy ABLGY WD5 11 M3
Daisy Cl CROY/NA CR0 75 P6
Daisy La FUL/PGN SW6 61 N1
Daisy Meadow EGH TW20 56 E10
Daisy Rd SWFD E18 28 D14
Dakin Pl WCHPL E1 51 Q3
Dakota Cl WLGTN SM6 74 D12
Dalberg Rd BRXS/STRHM SW2 62 E3
Dalberg Wy ABYW SE2 53 T8
Dalby Rd WAND/EARL SW18 61 Q2
Dalbys Crs TOTM N17 26 J11
Dalby St KTTN NW5 37 V11
Dalcross Rd HSLWW TW4 46 G14
Dale Av EDGW HA8 23 V13
HSLWW TW4 58 G1
Dalebury Rd TOOT SW17 61 T7
Dale Cl ADL/WDHM KT15 69 M10
BAR EN5 25 P4
BKHTH/KID SE3 64 C1
DART DA1 66 F4
PIN HA5 22 D13
SOCK/AV RM15 55 U4
Dale Ct GSTN WD25 * 11 N7
Dale Dr YEAD UB4 46 B2
Dale Gdns WFD IG8 28 D9
Dalegarth Gdns PUR/KEN CR8 86 H3
Dale Green Rd FBAR/BDGN N11 25 V8
Dale Gv NFNCH/WDSPK N12 25 Q10
Daleham Av EGH TW20 56 E11
Daleham Dr UX/CGN UB8 45 T4
Daleham Gdns HAMP NW3 37 R10
Daleham Ms HAMP NW3 * 37 R11
Dalemain Ms CAN/RD E16 52 C6
Dale Park Av CAR SM5 73 T7
Dale Park Rd NRWD SE19 62 G13
Dale Rd DART DA1 66 F4
KTTN NW5 37 U10
PUR/KEN CR8 86 E2
STHL UB1 46 K3
SUN TW16 * 58 B12
SUT SM1 73 M9
SWLY BR8 78 C1
WALW SE17 9 M12
WOT/HER KT12 70 B5
Dale Rw NTGHL W11 * 2 B12
Dale Side CFSP/GDCR SL9 32 C6
Daleside ORP BR6 77 Q10
Daleside Cl ORP BR6 77 Q11
Daleside Dr POTB/CUF EN6 14 B7
Daleside Gdns CHIG IG7 29 L8
Daleside Rd HOR/WEW KT19 72 D11
STRHM/NOR SW16 61 V10
Dales Pth BORE WD6 * 24 D3
Dales Rd BORE WD6 24 D3
Dalestone Ms HARH RM3 30 H12
Dale St CHSWK W4 48 E10
The Dale HAYES BR2 76 F9
WAB EN9 17 L8
Dale Vw BAR EN5 * 25 M1
EPSOM KT18 84 B13
ERITH DA8 54 G14
Dale View Av CHING E4 27 U7
Dale View Crs CHING E4 27 U8
Dale View Gdns CHING E4 27 V8
Daleview Rd SEVS/STOTM N15 38 J4
Dalewood Cl EMPK RM11 43 M5
Dalewood Gdns WPK KT4 72 H7
Dale Wood Rd ORP BR6 77 N6
Daley St HOM E9 39 P11
Daley Thompson Wy VX/NE SW8 61 V1
Dalgarno Gdns NKENS W10 48 J3
Dalgarno Wy NKENS W10 48 J2
Dalkeith Gv STAN HA7 23 T10
Dalkeith Rd DUL SE21 62 G6
IL IG1 41 L8
Dallas Rd CHEAM SM3 73 L11
EA W5 47 V3
HDN NW4 36 G5
SYD SE26 63 M9
Dallas Ter HYS/HAR UB3 46 B8
Dallega Cl HYS/HAR UB3 45 V5
Dallinger Rd LEE/GVPK SE12 64 B4
Dalling Rd HMSMTH W6 48 H9
Dallington Cl WOT/HER KT12 70 E11
Dallington Sq FSBYE EC1V 5 M7
Dallington St FARR EC1M 5 M8
Dallin Rd BXLYHS DA6 65 T2
WOOL/PLUM SE18 52 K12
Dalmain Rd FSTH SE23 63 P6
Dalmally Rd CROY/NA CR0 74 K5
Dalmeny Av HOLWY N7 38 B9
STRHM/NOR SW16 62 E14
Dalmeny Cl ALP/SUD HA0 35 S11
Dalmeny Crs HSLW TW3 59 M2
Dalmeny Rd BAR EN5 25 Q4
CAR SM5 73 U12
ERITH DA8 54 B13
HOLWY N7 38 B9
WPK KT4 72 H8
Dalmeyer Rd WLSDN NW10 36 F11
Dalmore Av ESH/CLAY KT10 71 P11
Dalmore Rd DUL SE21 62 G7
Dalroy Cl SOCK/AV RM15 55 U4
Dalrymple Cl STHGT/OAK N14 26 B5
Dalrymple Rd BROCKY SE4 63 R3
Dalston Gdns STAN HA7 23 U13
Dalston La HACK E8 38 K11
Dalton Av MTCM CR4 61 S14
Dalton Cl ORP BR6 77 N8
YEAD UB4 45 V2
Dalton Gn DTCH/LGLY SL3 44 D10
Daltons Rd SWLY BR8 78 C7
Dalton St WNWD SE27 62 F7
Dalton Wy WAT WD17 22 F4
Daltrey Wk WBPTN SW10 * 6 K13
Dalwood St CMBW SE5 50 J13
Dalyell Rd BRXN/ST SW9 62 D1
Damask Crs CAN/RD E16 52 A2
Damer Ter WBPTN SW10 6 K14
Dames Rd FSTGT E7 40 C9
Dame St IS N1 5 N3
Damien St WCHPL E1 51 M3
Damon Cl SCUP DA14 65 R8
Damsel Ct BERM/RHTH SE16 * 51 L7
Damson Dr HYS/HAR UB3 46 C5
Damson Wy CAR SM5 73 T13
Damsonwood Rd NWDGN UB2 46 J8
Danbrook Rd STRHM/NOR SW16 62 C13
Danbury Cl BRWN CM15 31 T3
CHDH RM6 41 T1
Danbury Crs SOCK/AV RM15 55 V4
Danbury Ms WLGTN SM6 73 V9
Danbury Rd LOU IG10 28 G4
RAIN RM13 42 F13
Danbury St IS N1 5 M3
Danbury Wy WFD IG8 28 E11
Danby St PECK SE15 62 K1
Dancer Rd FUL/PGN SW6 49 M13
RCH/KEW TW9 60 A1
Dancers Hill Rd BAR EN5 13 V10
BAR EN5 14 C9
Dandelion Cl ROMW/RG RM7 42 E7
Dando Crs BKHTH/KID SE3 64 D1
Dandridge Cl DTCH/LGLY SL3 44 B9
GNWCH SE10 52 B10
Danebury CROY/NA CR0 75 T11
Danebury Av PUT/ROE SW15 60 F5
Daneby Rd CAT SE6 63 U8
Dane Cl BXLY DA5 66 A5
ORP BR6 77 M10
Dane Ct WOKS/MYFD GU22 80 K5
Danecourt Gdns CROY/NA CR0 74 K8
Danecroft Rd HNHL SE24 62 G3
Danehurst Cl EGH TW20 56 C11
Danehurst Gdns REDBR IG4 40 G3
Danehurst St FUL/PGN SW6 49 L13
Daneland EBAR EN4 25 T4
Danemead Gv NTHLT UB5 34 K10
Danemere St PUT/ROE SW15 60 J1
Dane Pl BOW E3 39 Q14
Dane Rd ASHF TW15 57 U11
IL IG1 41 L10
RSEV TN14 90 E7
STHL UB1 46 G5
UED N18 27 N9
WARL CR6 87 P7
WEA W13 47 S5
WIM/MER SW19 61 Q13
Danesbury Rd FELT TW13 58 E7
Danes Cl LHD/OX KT22 83 L4
Danescombe LEE/GVPK SE12 64 C6
Danescourt Crs SUT SM1 73 Q7
Danescroft Av HDN NW4 * 36 K3
Danescroft Gdns HDN NW4 36 K3
Danesdale Rd HOM E9 39 Q11
Danesfield RPLY/SEND GU23 80 K13
Danesfield Cl WOT/HER KT12 70 D8
Danes Ga HRW HA1 35 N1
Daneshill REDH RH1 93 S9
Danes Hl WOKS/MYFD GU22 80 F8
Daneshill Cl REDH RH1 93 S9
Danes Hill School Dr LHD/OX KT22 * 83 M4
Danesmead COB KT11 82 J1
Danes Rd ROMW/RG RM7 42 C5
The Danes LCOL/BKTW AL2 12 A2
Dane St GINN WC1R 4 G10
Danes Wy BRWN CM15 31 U3
LHD/OX KT22 83 M4
Daneswood Av CAT SE6 63 U8
Daneswood Cl WEY KT13 69 T10
Danethorpe Rd ALP/SUD HA0 35 T11
Danetree Cl HOR/WEW KT19 72 C12
Danetree Rd HOR/WEW KT19 72 C12
Danette Gdns DAGE RM10 41 V7
Daneville Rd CMBW SE5 50 H13
Dangan Rd WAN E11 40 C4
Daniel Bolt Cl POP/IOD E14 51 T3
Daniel Cl HSLWW TW4 58 H5
TOOT SW17 61 S11
UED N18 27 N9
Daniel Gdns PECK SE15 9 U13
Daniell Wy CROY/NA CR0 74 C6
Daniel Pl HDN NW4 36 H4
Daniel Rd EA W5 47 V5
Daniels La WARL CR6 87 R6
Daniel's Rd PECK SE15 63 N1
Daniel Wy BNSTD SM7 85 P4
Dan Leno Wk FUL/PGN SW6 * 6 G14
Dan Manson Dr CHSWK W4 48 D14
Dansey Pl SOHO/SHAV W1D 4 C13
Dansington Rd WELL DA16 65 Q2
Danson Crs WELL DA16 65 R1
Danson La WELL DA16 65 R2
Danson Md WELL DA16 65 S1
Danson Rd BXLYHS DA6 65 T3
Danson U/P BFN/LL DA15 65 S4
Dante Rd LBTH SE11 9 L7
Danube St CHEL SW3 7 P9
Danvers Rd CEND/HSY/T N8 38 B2
Danvers St CHEL SW3 7 M12
Danvers Wy CTHM CR3 86 G13
Danyon Cl RAIN RM13 42 J14
Danziger Wy BORE WD6 13 N13
Daphne Gdns CHING E4 27 U8
Daphne St WAND/EARL SW18 61 Q4
Daplyn St WCHPL E1 51 L3
D'Arblay St SOHO/CST W1F 4 B12
Darby Cl CTHM CR3 86 G12
Darby Crs SUN TW16 58 E14
Darby Dr WAB EN9 16 J7
Darby Gdns SUN TW16 58 E14
Darcy Av WLGTN SM6 74 A9
Darcy Cl CHES/WCR EN8 16 E5
COUL/CHIP CR5 86 F9
TRDG/WHET N20 25 R7
D'Arcy Dr KTN/HRWW/WS HA3 35 T2
D'Arcy Gdns DAGW RM9 41 V13
KTN/HRWW/WS HA3 35 U2
Darcy Pl ASHTD KT21 83 V7
D'Arcy Pl HAYES BR2 76 C2
Darcy Rd ASHTD KT21 83 V7
D'Arcy Rd CHEAM SM3 72 K9
Darcy Rd ISLW TW7 47 Q13
STRHM/NOR SW16 62 C14
Darell Rd RCH/KEW TW9 60 A1
Darent Cl SEV TN13 90 C12
Darenth Gdns BH/WHM TN16 97 M2
Darenth Hl RDART DA2 67 P10
Darenth La SEV TN13 90 E11
SOCK/AV RM15 55 U4
Darenth Park Av RDART DA2 67 S7
Darenth Pl RDART DA2 * 67 R10
Darenth Rd DART DA1 67 N7
STNW/STAM N16 38 K5
WELL DA16 53 Q13
Darenth Rd South RDART DA2 67 P9
Darenth Wy RSEV TN14 90 G1
Darenth Wood Rd RDART DA2 67 S7
Darent Md EYN DA4 67 P13
Darent Valley Pth ERITH DA8 54 K13
EYN DA4 78 H10
SEV TN13 90 C11
Darfield Rd BROCKY SE4 63 R3
Darfield Wy NKENS W10 48 K5
Darfur St PUT/ROE SW15 60 K1
Dargate Cl NRWD SE19 62 K12
Darien Rd BTSEA SW11 61 R1
Darkes La POTB/CUF EN6 14 C6
Dark La BRW CM14 31 T11
CHESW EN7 16 A5
Darlands Dr BAR EN5 24 K3
Darlan Rd FUL/PGN SW6 6 D14
Darlaston Rd WIM/MER SW19 60 K12
Darley Cl ADL/WDHM KT15 69 N10
CROY/NA CR0 75 P4
Darley Cft LCOL/BKTW AL2 * 11 V2
Darley Dene Ct ADL/WDHM KT15 * 69 N9
Darley Dr NWMAL KT3 60 D14
Darley Gdns MRDN SM4 73 P4
Darley Rd BTSEA SW11 61 T4
ED N9 26 K6
Darling Rd BROCKY SE4 63 S1
Darling Rw WCHPL E1 51 M2
Darlington Ct BRWN CM15 31 U4
Darlington Gdns HARH RM3 30 K10
Darlington Rd WNWD SE27 62 F10
Darlton Cl DART DA1 66 F1
Darmaine Cl SAND/SEL CR2 74 G12
Darndale Cl WALTH E17 27 R14
Darnets Fld RSEV TN14 90 F7
Darnley Pk WEY KT13 69 T8
Darnley Rd HACK E8 39 M11
WFD IG8 28 C13
Darnley Ter NTGHL W11 48 K6
Darns Hl SWLY BR8 78 C5
Darrell Cl DTCH/LGLY SL3 44 D9
Darrell Rd EDUL SE22 63 L3
Darren Cl FSBYPK N4 38 D5
Darrick Wood Rd ORP BR6 77 M7
Darrington Rd BORE WD6 12 J13
Darris Cl YEAD UB4 46 G2
Darsley Dr VX/NE SW8 50 B13
Dart Cl DTCH/LGLY SL3 44 F11
UPMR RM14 43 R4
Dartfields HARH RM3 30 K11
Dartford Av ED N9 27 N4
Dartford Gdns CHDH RM6 41 R3
Dartford Rd BXLY DA5 66 C6
DART DA1 66 G4
EYN DA4 79 N3
SEV TN13 90 J14
Dartford St WALW SE17 9 P11
Dart Gn SOCK/AV RM15 55 V4
Dartmoor Wk POP/IOD E14 * 51 S9
Dartmouth Av WOKN/KNAP GU21 80 G4
Dartmouth Cl NTGHL W11 2 D11
Dartmouth Gv GNWCH SE10 51 U13
Dartmouth Hl GNWCH SE10 51 U13
Dartmouth Park Av KTTN NW5 37 V8
Dartmouth Park Hl KTTN NW5 37 V8
Dartmouth Park Rd KTTN NW5 37 V8
Dartmouth Pl CHSWK W4 48 E11
FSTH SE23 63 N7
Dartmouth Rd CRICK NW2 36 K11
HAYES BR2 76 C5
HDN NW4 36 G4
RSLP HA4 34 C8
SYD SE26 63 M8
Dartmouth Rw GNWCH SE10 51 U14
Dartmouth St STJSPK SW1H 8 C4
Dartmouth Ter GNWCH SE10 51 V13
Dartnell Av BF/WBF KT14 81 N2
Dartnell Cl BF/WBF KT14 81 N2
Dartnell Ct BF/WBF KT14 81 N2
Dartnell Crs BF/WBF KT14 81 M2
Dartnell Park Rd BF/WBF KT14 81 M2
Dartnell Pl BF/WBF KT14 81 M2
Dartnell Rd CROY/NA CR0 74 K5
Dart St MV/WKIL W9 2 C5
Darvells Yd RKW/CH/CXG WD3 20 H2
Darville Rd STNW/STAM N16 38 K8
Darwell Cl EHAM E6 40 J14
Darwin Cl FBAR/BDGN N11 25 V8
ORP BR6 77 M10
Darwin Dr STHL UB1 46 K4
Darwin Gdns OXHEY WD19 22 E10
Darwin Rd DTCH/LGLY SL3 44 D7
EA W5 47 S10
WDGN N22 26 F13
WELL DA16 65 P1
Darwin St WALW SE17 9 R7
Daryngton Dr GFD/PVL UB6 35 M14
Dashwood Cl BF/WBF KT14 81 N2
BXLYHS DA6 66 A3
DTCH/LGLY SL3 44 A9
Dashwood Lang Rd ADL/WDHM KT15 69 Q9
Dashwood Rd CEND/HSY/T N8 38 D4
Dassett Rd WNWD SE27 62 F10
Datchelor Pl CMBW SE5 * 50 H13
Datchet Rd CAT SE6 63 R8
DTCH/LGLY SL3 56 D1
Date St WALW SE17 9 Q10
Daubeney Gdns TOTM N17 26 G12
Daubeney Rd CLPT E5 39 Q10
TOTM N17 26 G12
Dault Rd WAND/EARL SW18 61 Q4
Davema Cl CHST BR7 64 J13
Davenant Rd ARCH N19 38 B7
Davenant St WCHPL E1 51 L3
Davenham Av NTHWD HA6 22 B9
Davenport Cl TEDD TW11 * 59 Q11
Davenport Rd CAT SE6 63 T4
SCUP DA14 65 T7
Daventer Dr STAN HA7 23 P12
Daventry Av WALTH E17 39 S4
Daventry Cl DTCH/LGLY SL3 44 K13
Daventry Gdns HARH RM3 30 J10
Daventry Rd HARH RM3 30 J10
Daventry St CAMTN NW1 3 N9
Davern Cl GNWCH SE10 52 B9
Davey Cl HOLWY N7 38 D11
PLMGR N13 26 D10
Davey Rd HOM E9 39 S12
Davey St PECK SE15 9 V12
David Av GFD/PVL UB6 47 N1
David Cl HYS/HAR UB3 45 V12
David Dr HARH RM3 31 N11
Davidge St STHWK SE1 9 L4
David Ms MHST W1U 3 R9
David Rd BCTR RM8 41 U7
DTCH/LGLY SL3 44 K14
Davidson Gdns VX/NE SW8 8 E14
Davidson Rd CROY/NA CR0 74 J6
DTCH/LGLY SL3 44 D10
Davidson Wy ROMW/RG RM7 42 E4
David's Rd FSTH SE23 63 N6
David St SRTFD E15 39 V11
Davids Wy BARK/HLT IG6 29 N12
David Twigg Cl KUTN/CMB KT2 59 U13
Davies Cl CROY/NA CR0 74 K4
RAIN RM13 54 J1
Davies La WAN E11 40 A7
Davies Ms MYFR/PKLN W1K 3 U13
Davies St MYFR/PKLN W1K 3 U13
Davies Wk ISLW TW7 47 M13
Davington Gdns BCTR RM8 41 R10
Davington Rd BCTR RM8 41 R11
Davinia Cl WFD IG8 28 H11
Davis Cl SEV TN13 90 J12
Davison Cl CHES/WCR EN8 16 D2
Davison Dr CHES/WCR EN8 16 D2
Davis Rd ACT W3 48 F6
CHSGTN KT9 72 A9
SOCK/AV RM15 55 R6
WEY KT13 69 R14
Davis St PLSTW E13 40 D14
Davisville Rd SHB W12 48 G7
Davos Cl WOKS/MYFD GU22 80 C9
Dawell Dr BH/WHM TN16 88 E7
Dawes Av HCH RM12 42 K8
ISLW TW7 59 Q3
Dawe's Cl HGDN/ICK UB10 33 Q14
RDART DA2 67 T3
Dawes Ct ESH/CLAY KT10 70 K10
Dawes Moor Cl SLN SL2 44 A4
Dawes Rd FUL/PGN SW6 6 B13
HGDN/ICK UB10 33 Q14
Dawes St WALW SE17 9 R9
Dawley Av UX/CGN UB8 45 T3
Dawley Gn SOCK/AV RM15 55 U4
Dawley Pde HYS/HAR UB3 45 V5
Dawley Ride DTCH/LGLY SL3 44 J13
Dawley Rd HYS/HAR UB3 45 V5
HYS/HAR UB3 46 A8
Dawlish Av GFD/PVL UB6 35 Q14
PLMGR N13 26 C9
WAND/EARL SW18 61 P7
Dawlish Dr GDMY/SEVK IG3 41 P9
PIN HA5 34 G3
RSLP HA4 34 C7
Dawlish Rd CRICK NW2 36 K11
LEY E10 39 U7
TOTM N17 39 L1
Dawnay Gdns WAND/EARL SW18 61 R7
Dawnay Rd WAND/EARL SW18 61 Q7
Dawn Cl HSLWW TW4 58 G1
Dawn Crs SRTFD E15 39 V13
Dawn Redwood Cl DTCH/LGLY SL3 56 E1
Dawpool Rd CRICK NW2 36 F7
Daws Hl CHING E4 27 U1
Daws La MLHL NW7 24 F10
Dawson Av BARK IG11 41 P12
STMC/STPC BR5 65 R14
Dawson Cl HYS/HAR UB3 45 V3
WOOL/PLUM SE18 53 L9
Dawson Dr RAIN RM13 42 H12
SWLY BR8 66 E12
Dawson Gdns BARK IG11 41 P12
Dawson Pl BAY/PAD W2 2 E13
Dawson Rd BF/WBF KT14 81 P1
CRICK NW2 36 J10
KUT/HW KT1 71 V1
Dawson St BETH E2 5 V4
Dawson Ter ED N9 * 27 N5
Daybrook Rd WIM/MER SW19 61 P14
Daylesford Av PUT/ROE SW15 60 G2
Daylop Dr CHIG IG7 29 R8
Daymer Gdns PIN HA5 34 E2
Daymerslea Rdg LHD/OX KT22 83 S11
Day's Acre SAND/SEL CR2 74 K14
Daysbrook Rd BRXS/STRHM SW2 62 D6
Days La BFN/LL DA15 65 N5
BRWN CM15 31 U2
Dayton Dr ERITH DA8 54 K11
Dayton Gv PECK SE15 51 N13
Deacon Cl COB KT11 82 D9
PUR/KEN CR8 74 C13
The Deacon Est CHING E4 * 27 R11
Deacon Ms IS N1 38 H12
Deacon Pl CTHM CR3 86 G13
Deacon Rd CRICK NW2 36 G11
KUTN/CMB KT2 59 V13
Deacons Cl BORE WD6 24 A2
PIN HA5 22 D14
Deacons Hts BORE WD6 24 A4
Deacons Hl OXHEY WD19 22 E4
Deacon's Hill Rd BORE WD6 23 V3
Deacons Leas ORP BR6 77 M9
Deacons Ri EFNCH N2 37 R3
Deacons Ter IS N1 * 38 G11
Deacons Wk HPTN TW12 58 J9
Deacon Wy WALW SE17 9 N7
WFD IG8 28 H12
Deadhearn La CSTG HP8 20 C6
Deadman's Ash La RKW/CH/CXG WD3 10 B10
Deakin Cl WATW WD18 22 A5
Deakins Ter ORP BR6 77 Q5
Deal Porters Wy BERM/RHTH SE16 51 N8
Deal Rd TOOT SW17 61 U11
Deals Gtwy LEW SE13 51 T13
Deal St WCHPL E1 51 L3
Dealtry Rd PUT/ROE SW15 60 J2
Deal Wk BRXN/ST SW9 8 J14
Deanacre Cl CFSP/GDCR SL9 20 C11
Dean Bradley St WEST SW1P 8 E6
Dean Cl BERM/RHTH SE16 51 P6
HGDN/ICK UB10 33 R12
HOM E9 39 N10
WOKS/MYFD GU22 80 J6
Dean Ct ALP/SUD HA0 35 R8
GSTN WD25 * 11 R7
Deancroft Rd CFSP/GDCR SL9 20 C11
Deancross St WCHPL E1 51 N4
Dean Dr STAN HA7 23 U14
Deane Av RSLP HA4 34 D10
Deane Ct NTHWD HA6 * 22 A13
Deane Croft Rd PIN HA5 34 E4
Deanery Cl EFNCH N2 37 S2
Deanery Ms MYFR/PKLN W1K * 7 T1
Deanery Rd EDEN TN8 97 L10
SRTFD E15 40 A11
Deanery St MYFR/PKLN W1K 7 T1
Deane Wy RSLP HA4 34 D4
Dean Farrar St STJSPK SW1H 8 D5
Deanfield Gdns CROY/NA CR0 * 74 H10
Dean Gdns WALTH E17 39 V2
Deanhill Ct MORT/ESHN SW14 * 60 B2
Deanhill Rd MORT/ESHN SW14 60 B2
Dean La REDH RH1 86 A14
Dean Rd CRICK NW2 36 J11
CROY/NA CR0 74 H9
HPTN TW12 58 J10
HSLW TW3 58 K3
THMD SE28 53 Q5
Dean Ryle St WEST SW1P 8 E7
Deansbrook Cl EDGW HA8 24 C12
Deansbrook Rd EDGW HA8 24 B12
Dean's Buildings WALW SE17 9 R9
Deans Cl ABLGY WD5 10 K6
CHSWK W4 48 B11
CROY/NA CR0 74 K8
EDGW HA8 24 C11
KWD/TDW/WH KT20 84 H14
Dean's Ct STP EC4M 5 M12
Deanscroft Av CDALE/KGS NW9 36 C7
Dean's Dr EDGW HA8 24 D10
PLMGR N13 26 F11
Deansfield CTHM CR3 94 K1
Deans Gate Cl FSTH SE23 63 P8
Dean's La EDGW HA8 24 C11
KWD/TDW/WH KT20 92 H1
REDH RH1 94 E9
Dean's Ms CAVSQ/HST W1G * 3 V11
Deans Rd BRW CM14 31 V8
HNWL W7 47 P7
REDH RH1 94 A6
SUT SM1 73 P8
Dean Stanley St WEST SW1P 8 E6
Dean St FSTGT E7 40 C10
SOHO/SHAV W1D 4 C11
Deans Wk COUL/CHIP CR5 86 E8
Deans Wy EDGW HA8 24 C10
Deansway ED N9 26 J8
EFNCH N2 37 R2
Deans Yd WEST SW1P 8 D5
Dean Trench St WEST SW1P 8 E6
Dean Vls COB KT11 * 82 E3
Dean Wy NWDGN UB2 46 K7
Dearne Cl STAN HA7 23 Q10
De'Arn Gdns MTCM CR4 73 S1
Dearsley Rd EN EN1 27 L1
Deason St SRTFD E15 * 39 U13
De Barowe Ms HBRY N5 38 F9
Debden Cl CDALE/KGS NW9 24 E13
KUTN/CMB KT2 59 T10
WFD IG8 28 F12
Debden La LOU IG10 17 V13
Debden Rd LOU IG10 17 V12
De Beauvoir Crs IS N1 5 S1
De Beauvoir Est IS N1 5 S1
De Beauvoir Rd IS N1 38 J12
De Beauvoir Sq IS N1 38 J12
Debenham Rd CHESW EN7 16 B1
Debnams Rd BERM/RHTH SE16 51 N9
De Bohun Av STHGT/OAK N14 25 V4
Deborah Cl ISLW TW7 47 N13
Deborah Crs RSLP HA4 33 V5
Debrabant Cl ERITH DA8 54 D11
De Broome Rd FELT TW13 58 E6
De Burgh Gdns KWD/TDW/WH KT20 84 K9
De Burgh Pk BNSTD SM7 85 P6
Deburgh Rd WIM/MER SW19 61 Q12
Decima St STHWK SE1 9 S5
Decimus Cl THHTH CR7 74 H2
Deck Cl BERM/RHTH SE16 51 P6
Decoy Av GLDGN NW11 37 L3
De Crespigny Pk CMBW SE5 50 H14
Dee Cl UPMR RM14 43 S4
Deeley Rd VX/NE SW8 50 B13
Deena Cl ACT W3 47 V4
Deepdale WIM/MER SW19 60 K9
Deepdale Av HAYES BR2 76 B2
Deepdale Cl FBAR/BDGN N11 25 U11
Deepdene POTB/CUF EN6 13 V5
Deepdene Av CROY/NA CR0 74 K8
Deepdene Cl WAN E11 40 C2
Deepdene Ct WCHMH N21 26 F4
Deepdene Gdns BRXS/STRHM SW2 62 D5
Deepdene Pth LOU IG10 28 K2
Deepdene Rd HNHL SE24 62 G2
LOU IG10 28 J2
WELL DA16 65 Q1
Deepfield Wy COUL/CHIP CR5 86 C6
Deepwell Cl ISLW TW7 47 Q13
Deepwood La GFD/PVL UB6 47 M1
Deerbrook Rd HNHL SE24 62 F6
Deerdale Rd HNHL SE24 62 G2
Deere Av RAIN RM13 42 G11
Deerfield Cl CDALE/KGS NW9 36 F3
Deerhurst Cl FELT TW13 58 C9
Deerhurst Crs HPTN TW12 59 L10
Deerhurst Rd KIL/WHAMP NW6 36 K12
STRHM/NOR SW16 62 D10
Deerings Dr PIN HA5 34 C3
Deerings Rd REIG RH2 93 P10
Deerleap Gv CHING E4 27 T3
Deerleap La RSEV TN14 89 T3
Dee Rd RCH/KEW TW9 59 V2
Deer Park Cl KUTN/CMB KT2 60 B12
Deer Park Gdns MTCM CR4 * 73 R2
Deer Park Rd WIM/MER SW19 61 Q14
Deer Park Wy WAB EN9 16 H10
WWKM BR4 76 B7
Deers Farm Cl RPLY/SEND GU23 81 Q6
Deerswood Cl CTHM CR3 87 L14
Deeside Rd TOOT SW17 61 R8
Dee St POP/IOD E14 51 U4
Deeves Hall La POTB/CUF EN6 13 Q7
Dee Wy HOR/WEW KT19 72 E14
ROM RM1 30 E13
Defence Cl THMD SE28 53 N6
Defiant Wy WLGTN SM6 74 C12
Defoe Av RCH/KEW TW9 48 A12
Defoe Cl TOOT SW17 61 S11
Defoe Pl TOOT SW17 61 S7
Defoe Rd BERM/RHTH SE16 51 R7
STNW/STAM N16 38 J7
Defoe Wy CRW RM5 30 A11
De Frene Rd SYD SE26 63 Q9
Degema Rd CHST BR7 64 K10
Dehar Crs CDALE/KGS NW9 36 F5
De Havilland Dr WOOL/PLUM SE18 52 K11
Dehavilland Cl NTHLT UB5 46 F1
De Havilland Ct IL IG1 41 M6
RAD WD7 * 12 J6
De Havilland Dr WEY KT13 81 Q1
De Havilland Rd EDGW HA8 24 B14
HEST TW5 46 E12
De Havilland Wy ABLGY WD5 11 M6
STWL/WRAY TW19 57 P4
Dekker Rd DUL SE21 62 J4
Delabole Rd REDH RH1 94 C5
Delacourt Rd BKHTH/KID SE3 52 D12
Delafield Rd CHARL SE7 52 D10
Delaford Cl IVER SL0 * 44 K4
Delaford Rd BERM/RHTH SE16 51 M10
Delaford St FUL/PGN SW6 6 B13
Delagarde Rd BH/WHM TN16 97 L2
Delamare Crs CROY/NA CR0 75 N4
Delamare Rd CHES/WCR EN8 16 F3
Delamere Gdns MLHL NW7 24 D10
Delamere Rd BORE WD6 13 M13
EA W5 47 U7
REIG RH2 93 P14
RYNPK SW20 60 K13
YEAD UB4 46 F5
Delamere St BAY/PAD W2 2 J10
Delamere Ter BAY/PAD W2 2 H9
Delancey Pas CAMTN NW1 3 V2
Delancey St CAMTN NW1 3 V2
Delaporte Cl EW KT17 84 E2
De Lapre Cl STMC/STPC BR5 77 T5
De Lara Wy WOKN/KNAP GU21 80 B8
De Laune St WALW SE17 9 L10
Delaware Rd MV/WKIL W9 2 G7
Delawyk Crs HNHL SE24 62 H4
Delcombe Av WPK KT4 72 J6
Delderfield ASHTD KT21 83 T10
Delhi Rd EN EN1 26 K5
Delhi St IS N1 4 F2
Delia St WAND/EARL SW18 61 P5
Delisle Rd THMD SE28 53 N7
Delius Cl BORE WD6 23 S4
Delius Gv SRTFD E15 39 U14
Della Pth CLPT E5 39 L8
Dellbow Rd EBED/NFELT TW14 58 D3
Dell Cl LHD/OX KT22 83 M13
SRTFD E15 39 V13
WFD IG8 28 D8
WLGTN SM6 74 A9
Dell Farm Rd RSLP HA4 33 V3
Dellfield Cl BECK BR3 63 U13
RAD WD7 12 C9
WAT WD17 11 N14
Dellfield Crs UX/CGN UB8 45 N2
Dellfield Pde UX/CGN UB8 * 45 N2
Dell La EW KT17 72 G10
Dellmeadow ABLGY WD5 11 L4
Dellors Cl BAR EN5 24 K3
Dellow Cl GNTH/NBYPK IG2 41 M5
Dellow St WCHPL E1 51 M5
Dell Rd EW KT17 72 G11
PEND EN3 16 C12
WATN WD24 11 N11
WDR/YW UB7 45 R8
Dells Cl CHING E4 27 T5
TEDD TW11 59 P11
Dellside DEN/HRF UB9 33 N3
Dell Side WATN WD24 11 N11
Dell's Ms PIM SW1V * 8 B8
The Dell ABYW SE2 53 Q10
ALP/SUD HA0 35 R10
BECK BR3 * 63 S12
BTFD TW8 47 S11
BXLY DA5 66 E6
CFSP/GDCR SL9 20 C11
EBED/NFELT TW14 58 D5
KWD/TDW/WH KT20 84 J11
NRWD SE19 62 K13
NTHWD HA6 22 A7
PIN HA5 22 F14
RAD WD7 12 E10
RBRW/HUT CM13 31 V11
REIG RH2 * 93 N9
SWCM DA10 67 V3
WAB EN9 16 J10
WFD IG8 28 D8
WOKN/KNAP GU21 80 A9
Dell Wk NWMAL KT3 60 E14
Dell Wy WEA W13 47 S4
Dellwood RKW/CH/CXG WD3 21 M6
Dellwood Gdns CLAY IG5 40 J1
Delme Crs BKHTH/KID SE3 52 D14
Delmey Cl CROY/NA CR0 74 K8
Deloraine St DEPT SE8 51 S13
Delorme St HMSMTH W6 48 K11
Delta Centre ALP/SUD HA0 * 35 V13
Delta Cl WPK KT4 72 E8
Delta Est BETH E2 * 51 L1
Delta Gain OXHEY WD19 22 F7
Delta Gv NTHLT UB5 46 F1
Delta Rd WOKN/KNAP GU21 80 E6
WPK KT4 72 E8
Delta St BETH E2 * 51 L1
Delta Wy EGH TW20 56 G13
De Luci Rd ERITH DA8 54 C10
De Lucy St ABYW SE2 53 R9
Delvers Md DAGE RM10 42 C9
Delverton Rd WALW SE17 9 M10
Delves KWD/TDW/WH KT20 84 K11
Delvino Rd FUL/PGN SW6 49 N13
De Mandeville Ga EN EN1 27 L2
Demesne Rd WLGTN SM6 74 B9
Demeta Cl WBLY HA9 36 C8
De Montfort Pde STRHM/NOR SW16 * 62 C8
De Montfort Rd STRHM/NOR SW16 62 C8
De Morgan Rd FUL/PGN SW6 61 P1
Dempster Cl SURB KT6 71 S6
Dempster Rd WAND/EARL SW18 61 Q3
Denbar Pde ROMW/RG RM7 42 C2
Denberry Dr SCUP DA14 65 R8
Denbigh Cl CHST BR7 64 H11
EMPK RM11 43 N2
NTGHL W11 2 D13
STHL UB1 46 H4
SUT SM1 73 M10
WLSDN NW10 36 E12
Denbigh Dr HYS/HAR UB3 45 U7
Denbigh Gdns RCHPK/HAM TW10 59 V3
Denbigh Pl PIM SW1V 8 A9
Denbigh Rd EHAM E6 52 F1
HSLW TW3 46 K14
NTGHL W11 2 D13
STHL UB1 46 H4
WEA W13 47 R5
Denbigh St PIM SW1V 8 B9
Denbigh Ter NTGHL W11 2 D13
Denbridge Rd BMLY BR1 64 H14
Denby Rd COB KT11 82 E2
Dencliffe ASHF TW15 * 57 S10
Den Cl BECK BR3 75 V2
Dendridge Cl EN EN1 16 B11
Dendy St BAL SW12 61 U6
Dene Av BFN/LL DA15 65 R5
HSLW TW3 58 H1
Dene Cl BROCKY SE4 63 Q1
COUL/CHIP CR5 85 S9
HAYES BR2 76 B6
RDART DA2 66 E9
WPK KT4 72 F7
Denecroft Crs HGDN/ICK UB10 33 T13
Dene Dr ORP BR6 77 R8
Denefield Dr PUR/KEN CR8 86 H5
Dene Gdns STAN HA7 23 S10
THDIT KT7 71 Q7
Denehurst Gdns ACT W3 48 B6
HDN NW4 36 J4
RCHPK/HAM TW10 60 A2
WFD IG8 28 D9
WHTN TW2 59 M5
Dene Pth SOCK/AV RM15 55 U4
Dene Rd ASHTD KT21 83 V9
BKHH IG9 28 G6
DART DA1 67 M5
NTHWD HA6 21 U11
TRDG/WHET N20 25 T6
The Dene BELMT SM2 85 M1
CROY/NA CR0 75 P9
E/WMO/HCT KT8 70 H3
WBLY HA9 35 U9
WEA W13 47 R3
Denewood BAR EN5 25 Q3
EW KT17 * 84 E3
Denewood Cl WAT WD17 11 M11
Denewood Rd HGT N6 37 T4
Dengie Wk IS N1 5 N1
Denham Av DEN/HRF UB9 32 K7
Denham Cl DEN/HRF UB9 33 L8
Denham Court Dr DEN/HRF UB9 33 N7
Denham Crs MTCM CR4 73 T2
Denham Dr GNTH/NBYPK IG2 41 L4
Denham Garden Village
DEN/HRF UB9 * 32 K4
Denham Green Cl DEN/HRF UB9 33 L5
Denham Green La DEN/HRF UB9 32 K4
Denham La CFSP/GDCR SL9 20 D11
Denham Ldg DEN/HRF UB9 * 33 N11
Denham Pde DEN/HRF UB9 * 32 K8
Denham Pl DEN/HRF UB9 * 33 L6
Denham Rd EBED/NFELT TW14 58 E5
EGH TW20 56 E9
EW KT17 84 F2
IVER SL0 32 J12
TRDG/WHET N20 25 T8
Denham Wk CFSP/GDCR SL9 20 D11
Denham Wy BARK IG11 41 N13
BORE WD6 13 N13
DEN/HRF UB9 33 L8
Denham Wy (North Orbital Rd)
RKW/CH/CXG WD3 20 J12
Denholme Rd MV/WKIL W9 2 D5
Denholme Wk RAIN RM13 42 F11
Denison Cl EFNCH N2 37 Q1
Denison Rd EA W5 47 S2
FELT TW13 58 B9
WIM/MER SW19 61 R11
Deniston Av BXLY DA5 65 T6
Denleigh Gdns THDIT KT7 * 71 N4
WCHMH N21 26 E5
Denman Dr ASHF TW15 57 T11
ESH/CLAY KT10 71 Q11
GLDGN NW11 37 N3
Denman Dr North GLDGN NW11 37 N3
Denman Dr South GLDGN NW11 37 N3
Denman Rd PECK SE15 50 K13
Denman St SOHO/SHAV W1D 4 B14
Denmark Av WIM/MER SW19 61 L12
Denmark Ct MRDN SM4 73 N3
Denmark Gdns CAR SM5 73 T8
Denmark Gv IS N1 4 J3
Denmark Hl HNHL SE24 62 H2
Denmark Hill Dr CDALE/KGS NW9 36 G1
Denmark Rd BMLY BR1 64 D13
CAR SM5 73 T8
CEND/HSY/T N8 38 D2
CMBW SE5 50 G13
KIL/WHAMP NW6 2 E4
KUT/HW KT1 71 U1
SNWD SE25 75 M3
WEA W13 47 R5
WHTN TW2 59 M8
WIM/MER SW19 60 K11
Denmark St LSQ/SEVD WC2H 4 D12
PLSTW E13 52 D3
TOTM N17 27 M13
WAN E11 40 A8
WAT WD17 11 P14
Denmark Ter EFNCH N2 * 37 T1
Denmead Cl CFSP/GDCR SL9 32 C5
Denmead Rd CROY/NA CR0 74 F6
Dennan Rd SURB KT6 71 V6
Denner Rd CHING E4 27 S7
Denne Ter HACK E8 5 V2
Dennett Rd CROY/NA CR0 74 E5
Dennett's Gv NWCR SE14 51 P14
Dennettsland Rd EDEN TN8 97 L10
Dennett's Rd NWCR SE14 51 N13
Denning Av CROY/NA CR0 74 E10
Denning Cl HPTN TW12 58 H11
STJWD NW8 2 K5
Denning Rd HAMP NW3 37 R9
Dennington Park Rd
KIL/WHAMP NW6 37 N11
The Denningtons WPK KT4 72 E7
Dennis Av WBLY HA9 35 V10
Dennis Cl ASHF TW15 57 V12
REDH RH1 93 S8
Dennises La UPMR RM14 43 T12
Dennis Gdns STAN HA7 23 S10
Dennis La STAN HA7 23 R9
Dennis Pde STHGT/OAK N14 * 26 B6
Dennis Park Crs RYNPK SW20 61 L13
Dennis Reeve Cl MTCM CR4 61 T13
Dennis Rd E/WMO/HCT KT8 71 L2
UPMR RM14 43 U13
Dennis Wy CLAP SW4 62 B1
Denny Av WAB EN9 16 K8
Denny Crs LBTH SE11 8 K9
Denny Gdns DAGW RM9 41 R12
Denny Ga CHES/WCR EN8 16 F1
Denny Rd DTCH/LGLY SL3 * 44 D9
ED N9 27 M6
Denny St LBTH SE11 8 K9
Den Rd HAYES BR2 75 V1
Densham Dr PUR/KEN CR8 86 E4
Densham Rd SRTFD E15 40 A13
Densole Cl BECK BR3 * 63 Q13
Densworth Gv ED N9 27 N7
Dent Cl SOCK/AV RM15 55 U4
Denton Cl BAR EN5 24 J3
Denton Gv WOT/HER KT12 70 G7
Denton Rd CEND/HSY/T N8 38 D3
DART DA1 66 E5
TWK TW1 59 T4
UED N18 26 K9
WELL DA16 53 S12
Denton St WAND/EARL SW18 61 P4
Denton Ter BXLY DA5 * 66 E7
Denton Wy CLPT E5 39 P8
Dents Gv KWD/TDW/WH KT20 93 M4
Dents Rd BTSEA SW11 61 T4
Denvale Trade Pk MTCM CR4 73 R2
Denver Cl ORP BR6 77 N4
Denver Rd DART DA1 66 G5
STNW/STAM N16 38 J5
Denyer St CHEL SW3 7 P7
Denziloe Av HGDN/ICK UB10 45 T1
Denzil Rd WLSDN NW10 36 F10
Deodar Rd PUT/ROE SW15 61 M2
Deodora Cl TRDG/WHET N20 25 T8
Depot Ap CRICK NW2 36 K9
Depot Rd EW KT17 84 E3
HSLW TW3 59 M1
Depot St CMBW SE5 9 Q12
Deptford Br DEPT SE8 51 S13
Deptford Broadway NWCR SE14 51 S13
Deptford Church St DEPT SE8 51 S11
Deptford Gn DEPT SE8 51 S11
Deptford High St DEPT SE8 51 S11
Deptford Whf DEPT SE8 51 R9
De Quincey Ms CAN/RD E16 52 C6
De Quincey Rd TOTM N17 26 H13
Derby Arms Rd EPSOM KT18 84 F7
Derby Av KTN/HRWW/WS HA3 23 M13
NFNCH/WDSPK N12 25 Q10
ROMW/RG RM7 42 C4
UPMR RM14 43 M8
Derby Cl EPSOM KT18 84 H9
Derby Ga WHALL SW1A 8 E3
Derby Hl FSTH SE23 63 N7
Derby Hill Crs FSTH SE23 63 N7
Derby Rd CROY/NA CR0 74 F7
FSTGT E7 40 F12
GFD/PVL UB6 34 K13
HOM E9 39 P13
HSLW TW3 58 K2
MORT/ESHN SW14 60 B2
PEND EN3 27 M3
SURB KT6 72 A6
SUT SM1 73 M11
SWFD E18 28 B13
UED N18 27 N10
UX/CGN UB8 33 N14
WAT WD17 22 E2
WIM/MER SW19 61 N12
Derbyshire St BETH E2 51 M1
Derby Stables Rd EPSOM KT18 84 E7
Derby St MYFR/PICC W1J 7 T2
Dereham Pl CRW RM5 30 B11
SDTCH EC2A 5 T7
Dereham Rd BARK IG11 41 P11
Derek Av HOR/WEW KT19 72 A11
WBLY HA9 36 B12
WLGTN SM6 73 V8
Derek Cl HOR/WEW KT19 72 B10
Derek Walcott Cl HNHL SE24 * 62 F3
Derham Gdns UPMR RM14 43 Q8
Deri Av RAIN RM13 54 H2
Dericote St HACK E8 39 L13
Deri Dene Cl STWL/WRAY TW19 * 57 Q4
Derifall Cl EHAM E6 52 H3
Dering Pl CROY/NA CR0 74 G9
Dering Rd CROY/NA CR0 74 G9
Dering St OXSTW W1C 3 U12
Derinton Rd TOOT SW17 61 U9
Derley Rd NWDGN UB2 46 E8
Dermody Gdns LEW SE13 * 63 V3
Dermody Rd LEW SE13 63 V3
Deronda Rd HNHL SE24 62 F6
De Ros Pl EGH TW20 56 E11
Deroy Cl CAR SM5 73 T11
Derrick Av SAND/SEL CR2 74 G14
Derrick Gdns CHARL SE7 52 E8
Derrick Rd BECK BR3 75 R1
Derry Av SOCK/AV RM15 55 U3
Derry Downs STMC/STPC BR5 77 S4
Derry Rd CROY/NA CR0 74 C8
Derry St KENS W8 6 G4
Dersingham Av MNPK E12 40 H9
Dersingham Rd CRICK NW2 37 L8
Derwent Av CDALE/KGS NW9 36 E3
EBAR EN4 25 T6
HGDN/ICK UB10 33 S7
MLHL NW7 24 D10
PIN HA5 22 G11
PUT/ROE SW15 60 E9
UED N18 26 H10
Derwent Cl ADL/WDHM KT15 69 P10
DART DA1 66 H6
EBED/NFELT TW14 58 B6
ESH/CLAY KT10 71 N11
GSTN WD25 11 Q7
Derwent Crs BXLYHN DA7 54 A14
NFNCH/WDSPK N12 25 Q8
STAN HA7 23 S14
Derwent Dr PUR/KEN CR8 86 H4
STMC/STPC BR5 77 M5
YEAD UB4 46 A3
Derwent Gdns REDBR IG4 40 G2
WBLY HA9 35 S6
Derwent Gv EDUL SE22 62 K2
Derwent Pde SOCK/AV RM15 55 U4
Derwent Ri CDALE/KGS NW9 36 E4
Derwent Rd EA W5 47 S8
EGH TW20 56 F11
PGE/AN SE20 63 L14
PLMGR N13 26 D9
RYNPK SW20 72 K4
STHL UB1 46 H3
WHTN TW2 58 K4
Derwent St GNWCH SE10 52 A10
Derwentwater Rd ACT W3 48 C6
Derwent Wy HCH RM12 42 H10
Derwent Yd EA W5 * 47 S8
De Salis Rd HGDN/ICK UB10 45 U2
Desborough Cl SHPTN TW17 69 S5
Desenfans Rd DUL SE21 62 J4
Deseronto Est DTCH/LGLY SL3 * 44 C7
Desford Rd CAN/RD E16 52 A2
Desford Wy ASHF TW15 57 R7
Desmond Rd WATN WD24 11 M10
Desmond St NWCR SE14 51 Q11
Desmond Tutu Dr FSTH SE23 63 Q6
Despard Rd ARCH N19 38 A6
Detillens La OXTED RH8 96 C5
Detling Cl HCH RM12 42 J10
Detling Rd BMLY BR1 64 C10
ERITH DA8 54 D12
Detmold Rd CLPT E5 39 N7
Devalls Cl EHAM E6 52 K5
Devana End CAR SM5 73 T8
Devas Rd RYNPK SW20 60 J13
Devas St BOW E3 51 T2
Devenay Rd SRTFD E15 40 B12
Devenish Rd ABYW SE2 53 Q7
Deveraux Cl BECK BR3 75 U3
De Vere Cl WLGTN SM6 74 C12
De Vere Gdns IL IG1 40 H6
KENS W8 6 J4
Deverell St STHWK SE1 9 Q6
De Vere Ms KENS W8 6 J5
Devereux Ct TPL/STR WC2R 4 J13
Devereux Dr WAT WD17 11 L12
Devereux La BARN SW13 48 H12
Devereux Rd BTSEA SW11 61 T4
De Vere Wk WAT WD17 11 L14
Deverills Wy DTCH/LGLY SL3 44 G9
Deveron Gdns SOCK/AV RM15 55 U4
Deveron Wy ROM RM1 30 E13
Devey Cl KUTN/CMB KT2 60 F12
Devil's La EGH TW20 56 G11
Devitt Cl ASHTD KT21 84 A6
Devizes St IS N1 * 5 R2
Devoke Wy WOT/HER KT12 70 F7
Devon Av WHTN TW2 59 L6
Devon Cl BKHH IG9 28 D7
GFD/PVL UB6 35 S13
HOR/WEW KT19 84 A2
PUR/KEN CR8 86 J6
TOTM N17 38 K1
Devon Crs REDH RH1 93 R10
Devoncroft Gdns TWK TW1 59 Q5
Devon Gdns FSBYPK N4 38 F4
Devonhurst Pl CHSWK W4 * 48 D10
Devonia Gdns UED N18 26 G11
Devonia Rd IS N1 5 M3
Devon Man KTN/HRWW/WS HA3 * 35 S3
Devonport Gdns IL IG1 40 H4
Devonport Ms SHB W12 * 48 H6
Devonport Rd SHB W12 48 H7
Devonport St WCHPL E1 51 N4
Devon Ri EFNCH N2 37 R2
Devon Rd BARK IG11 41 N13
BELMT SM2 73 L13
EYN DA4 67 P13
REDH RH1 94 A6
WATN WD24 11 R13
WOT/HER KT12 70 E9
Devons Est BOW E3 51 T1
Devonshire Av BELMT SM2 73 Q12
DART DA1 66 H4
KWD/TDW/WH KT20 92 C7
WOKN/KNAP GU21 80 G4
Devonshire Cl CAVSQ/HST W1G 3 U9
SRTFD E15 40 A9
Devonshire Ct FELT TW13 * 58 D7
Devonshire Crs MLHL NW7 24 K12
Devonshire Dr GNWCH SE10 51 T13
SURB KT6 71 T6
Devonshire Gdns CHSWK W4 48 C12
TOTM N17 26 G11
WCHMH N21 26 G5
Devonshire Gv PECK SE15 51 M11
Devonshire Hill La TOTM N17 26 H12
Devonshire Ms South CAVSQ/HST W1G 3 U9
Devonshire Ms West CAVSQ/HST W1G 3 T9
Devonshire Pl CAVSQ/HST W1G 3 T8
CRICK NW2 37 N8
KENS W8 * 6 G6
Devonshire Place Ms CAVSQ/HST W1G 3 T8
Devonshire Rd BELMT SM2 73 Q12
BXLYHS DA6 65 U2
CAN/RD E16 52 E4
CAR SM5 73 U9
CHSWK W4 48 E10
CROY/NA CR0 74 H5
EA W5 47 S8
ED N9 27 N6
ELTH/MOT SE9 64 G7
FELT TW13 58 G8
FSTH SE23 63 P5
GNTH/NBYPK IG2 41 M5
HCH RM12 42 K7
HRW HA1 35 M4
MLHL NW7 24 K12
ORP BR6 77 Q5
PIN HA5 22 H13
PIN HA5 34 E5
PLMGR N13 26 D9
STHL UB1 46 J3
TOTM N17 26 G11
WALTH E17 39 S4
WEY KT13 * 69 S9
WIM/MER SW19 61 S12
Devonshire Rw LVPST EC2M 5 T10
Devonshire Row Ms GTPST W1W 3 V8
Devonshire Sq HAYES BR2 76 D2
LVPST EC2M 5 T11
Devonshire St CAVSQ/HST W1G 3 U9
CHSWK W4 48 E11
Devonshire Ter BAY/PAD W2 2 K12
EDUL SE22 * 63 L2
Devonshire Wy CROY/NA CR0 75 R7
YEAD UB4 46 D4
Devons Rd BOW E3 51 S3
Devon St PECK SE15 51 M11
Devon Wy CHSGTN KT9 71 S9
HGDN/ICK UB10 33 R14
HOR/WEW KT19 72 B10
Devon Waye HEST TW5 46 H12
De Walden St CAVSQ/HST W1G 3 T10
Dewar Sp DTCH/LGLY SL3 44 D11
Dewar St PECK SE15 63 L1
Dewberry Gdns EHAM E6 52 G3
Dewberry St POP/IOD E14 51 U4
Dewey La BRXS/STRHM SW2 62 E4
Dewey Rd DAGE RM10 42 C11
IS N1 4 J3
Dewey St TOOT SW17 61 T10
Dewgrass Gv CHES/WCR EN8 16 D9
Dewhurst Rd CHES/WCR EN8 16 C3
HMSMTH W6 48 K8
Dewlands GDST RH9 95 N7
Dewlands Av RDART DA2 67 P5
Dewsbury Cl PIN HA5 34 G4
Dewsbury Gdns HARH RM3 30 K11
WPK KT4 72 G8
Dewsbury Rd HARH RM3 31 L11
WLSDN NW10 36 G10
Dexter Rd BAR EN5 24 K4
DEN/HRF UB9 21 N14
Deyncourt Gdns UPMR RM14 43 Q7
Deyncourt Rd TOTM N17 26 G13
Deynecourt Gdns WAN E11 40 E2
D'Eynsford Rd CMBW SE5 50 H13
Dharam Marg GSTN WD25 * 12 C13
Diadem Ct SOHO/CST W1F 4 C11
Diamedes Av STWL/WRAY TW19 57 P5
Diameter Rd STMC/STPC BR5 76 K5
Diamond Cl BCTR RM8 41 S6
Diamond Rd RSLP HA4 34 F9
WATN WD24 11 N12
Diamond St PECK SE15 9 T14
WLSDN NW10 36 D12
Diana Cl DEPT SE8 51 R11
DTCH/LGLY SL3 44 C4
SCUP DA14 65 U7
SWFD E18 28 D13
Diana Gdns SURB KT6 71 V7
Diana Pl CAMTN NW1 3 V7
Diana Rd WALTH E17 39 R1
Dianne Wy EBAR EN4 25 S2
Dianthus Cl ABYW SE2 * 53 R10
CHERT KT16 68 J5
Dianthus Ct WOKS/MYFD GU22 80 B8
Diban Av HCH RM12 42 H9
Dibden St IS N1 5 N1
Dibdin Cl SUT SM1 73 N8
Dibdin Rd SUT SM1 73 N8
Diceland Rd BNSTD SM7 85 M6
Dicey Av CRICK NW2 36 J10
Dickens Av DART DA1 67 N2
FNCH N3 25 Q13
UX/CGN UB8 45 T4
Dickens Cl ERITH DA8 54 B12
HYS/HAR UB3 46 A9
RCHPK/HAM TW10 59 U7
Dickens Dr ADL/WDHM KT15 68 K11
CHST BR7 65 L11
Dickens Est BERM/RHTH SE16 * 51 L8
Dickens La UED N18 26 J10
Dickens Ms FARR EC1M 5 L8
Dickenson Cl ED N9 27 L6
Dickenson Rd CEND/HSY/T N8 38 C5
FELT TW13 58 E10
Dickenson's La SNWD SE25 75 L4
Dickenson's Pl SNWD SE25 75 L4
Dickens Pl DTCH/LGLY SL3 44 J13
Dickens Ri CHIG IG7 28 J8
Dickens Rd EHAM E6 40 F14
Dickens Sq STHWK SE1 9 P5
Dickens St VX/NE SW8 49 V14
Dickens Wy ROM RM1 42 E2
Dickens Wood Cl NRWD SE19 62 F12
Dickerage La NWMAL KT3 72 C1
Dickerage Rd KUT/HW KT1 60 C13
Dickins Cl CHESW EN7 16 A1
Dickinson Av RKW/CH/CXG WD3 21 S4
Dickinson Sq RKW/CH/CXG WD3 21 T4
Dickson CHESW EN7 15 V1
Dickson Fold PIN HA5 34 F2
Dickson House CHARL SE7 * 52 G12
Dickson Rd ELTH/MOT SE9 64 G1
Dick Turpin Wy EBED/NFELT TW14 58 B2
Didsbury Cl EHAM E6 40 H13
Digby Crs FSBYPK N4 38 G7
Digby Gdns DAGE RM10 42 A13
Digby Pl CROY/NA CR0 74 K8
Digby Rd BARK IG11 41 P12
HOM E9 39 P11
Digby St BETH E2 51 N1
Digby Wy BF/WBF KT14 81 R2
Dig Dag Hl CHESW EN7 15 V1
Digdens Ri EPSOM KT18 84 C5
Diggon St WCHPL E1 51 P3
Dighton Rd WAND/EARL SW18 61 Q3
Dignum St IS N1 * 4 J3
Digswell Cl BORE WD6 13 L12
Digswell St HOLWY N7 * 38 E11
Dilhorne Cl LEE/GVPK SE12 64 D8

Dilke St CHEL SW3 7 R11
Dillwyn Cl SYD SE26 63 Q9
Dilston Cl NTHLT UB5 46 E1
Dilston Rd LHD/OX KT22 83 Q9
Dilton Gdns PUT/ROE SW15 60 G6
Dimes Pl HMSMTH W6 48 H9
Dimmock Dr GFD/PVL UB6 35 M10
Dimmocks La RKW/CH/CXG WD3 10 A10
Dimond Cl FSTGT E7 40 C10
Dimsdale Dr CDALE/KGS NW9 36 C6
EN EN1 27 L5
Dimson Crs BOW E3 51 S2
Dingle Cl BAR EN5 24 F4
Dingle Gdns POP/IOD E14 * 51 S5
Dingle Rd ASHF TW15 57 T10
The Dingle HGDN/ICK UB10 45 T1
Dingley La STRHM/NOR SW16 62 B7
Dingley Pl FSBYE EC1V 5 P6
Dingley Rd FSBYE EC1V 5 N6
Dingwall Av CROY/NA CR0 74 G7
Dingwall Gdns GLDGN NW11 37 N4
Dingwall Rd CAR SM5 73 T13
CROY/NA CR0 74 H7
WAND/EARL SW18 61 Q5
Dinmont St BETH E2 39 M14
Dinsdale Cl WOKS/MYFD GU22 80 D8
Dinsdale Gdns BAR EN5 25 P3
SNWD SE25 74 J3
Dinsdale Rd BKHTH/KID SE3 52 B11
Dinsmore Rd BAL SW12 61 V5
Dinton Rd KUTN/CMB KT2 59 V12
WIM/MER SW19 61 R11
Diploma Av EFNCH N2 37 S2
Dippers Cl BGR/WK TN15 91 M7
Dirdene Cl EW KT17 84 F2
Dirdene Gdns EW KT17 84 F2
Dirdene Gv EW KT17 84 E2
Dirleton Rd SRTFD E15 40 B13
Disbrowe Rd HMSMTH W6 6 A12
Discovery Wk WAP E1W 51 M5
Dishforth La CDALE/KGS NW9 24 E13
Disney Pl STHWK SE1 9 P3
Disney St STHWK SE1 9 P3
Dison Cl PEND EN3 16 D13
Disraeli Cl THMD SE28 53 R6
Disraeli Ct DTCH/LGLY SL3 44 F11
Disraeli Rd EA W5 47 T6
FSTGT E7 40 C11
PUT/ROE SW15 61 L2
WLSDN NW10 36 C14
Diss St BETH E2 5 U5
Distaff La BLKFR EC4V 5 N13
Distillery La HMSMTH W6 48 J10
Distillery Rd HMSMTH W6 48 J10
Distin St LBTH SE11 8 J8
District Rd ALP/SUD HA0 35 R10
Ditchburn St POP/IOD E14 51 U5
Ditches La COUL/CHIP CR5 86 B7
Ditchfield Rd YEAD UB4 46 G2
Dittisham Rd ELTH/MOT SE9 64 G9
Ditton Cl THDIT KT7 71 Q5
Dittoncroft Cl CROY/NA CR0 74 J9
Ditton Grange Cl SURB KT6 71 T6
Ditton Grange Dr SURB KT6 71 T6
Ditton Hl SURB KT6 71 S6
Ditton Hill Rd SURB KT6 71 S6
Ditton Lawn THDIT KT7 71 Q6
Ditton Park Rd DTCH/LGLY SL3 44 D10
Ditton Pl PGE/AN SE20 * 63 M13
Ditton Reach THDIT KT7 71 R4
Ditton Rd BXLYHS DA6 65 T3
DTCH/LGLY SL3 44 B13
NWDGN UB2 46 H10
SURB KT6 71 U6
Dixey Cottages EFNCH N2 * 37 S3
Dixon Cl EHAM E6 52 H4
Dixon Dr WEY KT13 69 R14
Dixon Pl WWKM BR4 75 T6
Dixon Rd NWCR SE14 51 Q13
SNWD SE25 74 J1
Dobbin Cl KTN/HRWW/WS HA3 23 Q14
Dobell Rd ELTH/MOT SE9 64 H3
Dobree Av WLSDN NW10 36 H12
Dobson Cl KIL/WHAMP NW6 37 R12
Dockers Tanner Rd POP/IOD E14 51 S9
Dockett Eddy La SHPTN TW17 69 R5
Dockett Moorings CHERT KT16 * 69 R6
Dockhead STHWK SE1 9 V4
Dock Hill Av BERM/RHTH SE16 51 P7
Dockland St CAN/RD E16 52 J7
Dockley Rd BERM/RHTH SE16 51 L8
Dock Rd BTFD TW8 * 47 T12
CAN/RD E16 52 B5
Dockside Rd CAN/RD E16 52 F5
Dock St WCHPL E1 51 L5
Dockwell Cl EBED/NFELT TW14 58 C2
Doctors Cl SYD SE26 63 N10
Doctors La CTHM CR3 86 E14
Docwra's Buildings IS N1 38 J11
Dodbrooke Rd WNWD SE27 62 E8
Doddington Gv WALW SE17 9 L11
Doddington Pl WALW SE17 9 L11
Dodds Crs BF/WBF KT14 81 M4
Dodd's La WOKS/MYFD GU22 81 L4
Dodds Pk BRKHM/BTCW RH3 92 B12
Dodsley Pl ED N9 27 N8
Dodson St STHWK SE1 8 K4
Dod St POP/IOD E14 51 S4
Doebury Wk WOOL/PLUM SE18 53 Q11
Doel Cl WIM/MER SW19 61 Q12
Doggett Rd CAT SE6 63 S5
Doggetts Ct EBAR EN4 25 S3
Doggetts Farm Rd DEN/HRF UB9 32 G5
Doggetts Wood Cl CSTG HP8 20 A2
Doggetts Wood La CSTG HP8 20 A2
Doghurst Av WDR/YW UB7 45 T12
Doghurst Dr WDR/YW UB7 45 T12
Doghurst La COUL/CHIP CR5 85 T10
Dog Kennel Hl EDUL SE22 62 J1
Dog Kennel La RKW/CH/CXG WD3 20 K3
Dog La WLSDN NW10 36 E9
Dog Rose Ramble YEAD UB4 34 C13
Dog Rose Ramble & Hillingdon Trail
YEAD UB4 34 B13
YEAD UB4 46 F4
Doherty Rd PLSTW E13 52 C2
Dolben Ct DEPT SE8 * 51 R9
Dolben St STHWK SE1 * 9 M2
Dolby Rd FUL/PGN SW6 49 M14
Doldens Cottages EYN DA4 * 79 P2
Dolland St LBTH SE11 8 H10
Dollary Pde KUT/HW KT1 * 72 B1
Dollis Av FNCH N3 25 M13
Dollis Crs RSLP HA4 34 E6
Dollis Hill Av CRICK NW2 36 H8
Dollis Hill Est CRICK NW2 * 36 G8
Dollis Hill La CRICK NW2 36 F9
Dollis Pk FNCH N3 25 M13
Dollis Rd MLHL NW7 25 L13
Dollis Valley Dr BAR EN5 25 M3
Dollis Valley Green Wk BAR EN5 25 P5
FNCH N3 37 L2
HDN NW4 25 L14
Dollis Valley Wy EBAR EN4 25 R2
Dolman Cl FNCH N3 25 Q14
Dolman Rd CHSWK W4 48 D9
Dolman St CLAP SW4 62 D2
Dolphin Ap ROM RM1 42 F2
Dolphin Cl BERM/RHTH SE16 51 P7
SURB KT6 71 T4
THMD SE28 53 T4
Dolphin Ct STA TW18 57 L8
Dolphin Ct North STA TW18 * 57 L8
Dolphin Est SUN TW16 * 58 A13
Dolphin La POP/IOD E14 51 T5
Dolphin Rd NTHLT UB5 34 H14
SUN TW16 58 A13
Dolphin Rd North SUN TW16 57 V13
Dolphin Rd South SUN TW16 57 V13
Dolphin Rd West SUN TW16 58 A13
Dolphin Sq CHSWK W4 * 48 E12
PIM SW1V 8 C10
Dolphin St KUT/HW KT1 59 U14
Dolphin Wy PUR RM19 55 S10
Dombey St BMSBY WC1N 4 G9
Dome Buildings RCH/KEW TW9 * 59 T3
Dome Hl CTHM CR3 94 J3
Dome Hill Pk SYD SE26 62 K9
Dome Hill Peak CTHM CR3 94 J2
Domett Cl CMBW SE5 62 H2
Dome Wy REDH RH1 93 T9
Domingo St FSBYE EC1V 5 N7
Dominica Cl PLSTW E13 52 F1
Dominic Ct WAB EN9 16 H7
Dominion Cl HSLW TW3 47 M14
Dominion Dr CRW RM5 30 B11
Dominion Pde HRW HA1 * 35 P3
Dominion Rd CROY/NA CR0 74 K5
NWDGN UB2 46 G8
Dominion St LVPST EC2M 5 R9
Dominion Wy RAIN RM13 54 G1
Domonic Dr ELTH/MOT SE9 64 K8
Domville Cl TRDG/WHET N20 25 R7
Donald Dr CHDH RM6 41 S3
Donald Rd CROY/NA CR0 74 D4
PLSTW E13 40 D13
Donaldson Rd KIL/WHAMP NW6 2 D2
WOOL/PLUM SE18 52 J13
Donald Woods Gdns BRYLDS KT5 72 B7
Doncaster Dr NTHLT UB5 34 H10
Doncaster Gdns FSBYPK N4 * 38 G4
NTHLT UB5 34 H10
Doncaster Gn OXHEY WD19 22 E10
Doncaster Rd ED N9 27 M5
Doncaster Wy UPMR RM14 43 M8
Donegal St IS N1 4 H4
Doneraile St FUL/PGN SW6 48 K14
Dongola Rd PLSTW E13 52 D1
TOTM N17 38 J1
WCHPL E1 51 Q3
Dongola Rd West PLSTW E13 52 D1
Donington Av BARK/HLT IG6 41 L3
Donkey Aly EDUL SE22 63 L5
Donkey La EN EN1 16 A14
EYN DA4 79 P7
WDR/YW UB7 45 N9
Donnay Cl CFSP/GDCR SL9 32 B4
Donnefield Av EDGW HA8 23 U11
Donne Gdns WOKS/MYFD GU22 80 J5
Donne Pl CHEL SW3 7 P7
MTCM CR4 73 V2
Donne Rd BCTR RM8 41 S7
Donnington Rd KTN/HRWW/WS HA3 35 T4
WLSDN NW10 36 H13
WPK KT4 72 G7
Donnybrook Rd STRHM/NOR SW16 62 B12
Donoghue Cottages POP/IOD E14 * 51 Q3
Donovan Av MUSWH N10 25 V14
Donovan Cl HOR/WEW KT19 72 D14
Donovan Pl WCHMH N21 26 D3
Don Phelan Cl CMBW SE5 50 H13
Don Wy ROM RM1 30 E12
Doods Park Rd REIG RH2 93 P9
Doods Pl REIG RH2 * 93 Q9
Doods Rd REIG RH2 93 Q9
Doods Wy REIG RH2 93 R9
Doone Cl TEDD TW11 59 Q11
Doon St STHWK SE1 8 J1
Dorado Gdns ORP BR6 77 T8
Doral Wy CAR SM5 73 T10
Dorando Cl SHB W12 * 48 H5
Doran Dr REDH RH1 93 R10
Doran Gdns REDH RH1 * 93 R10
Doran Gv WOOL/PLUM SE18 53 N12
Dora Rd WIM/MER SW19 61 N10
Dora St POP/IOD E14 51 R4
Dora Wy BRXN/ST SW9 50 E14
Dorchester Av BXLY DA5 65 T6
PLMGR N13 26 G9
RYLN/HDSTN HA2 35 L4
Dorchester Cl DART DA1 67 M6
NTHLT UB5 34 K10
STMC/STPC BR5 65 R12
Dorchester Ct CRICK NW2 36 J8
HNHL SE24 62 G3
RKW/CH/CXG WD3 * 21 U3
STHGT/OAK N14 25 V5
WOKS/MYFD GU22 80 E6
Dorchester Dr EBED/NFELT TW14 58 A4
HNHL SE24 62 G3
Dorchester Gdns CHING E4 27 S9
GLDGN NW11 * 37 N2
Dorchester Gv CHSWK W4 48 F10
Dorchester Ms TWK TW1 59 S4
Dorchester Pde STRHM/NOR SW16 * 62 C7
Dorchester Rd MRDN SM4 73 Q5
NTHLT UB5 34 K10
WEY KT13 69 T8
WPK KT4 72 J6
Dorchester Ter HDN NW4 * 24 K14
Dorchester Wy KTN/HRWW/WS HA3 35 V4
Dorchester Waye YEAD UB4 46 E4
Dorcis Av BXLYHN DA7 53 U14
Dordrecht Rd ACT W3 48 E6
Dore Av MNPK E12 40 J10
Doreen Av CDALE/KGS NW9 36 D6
Dore Gdns MRDN SM4 73 P5
Dorell Cl STHL UB1 46 H3
Dorian Ct WARL CR6 * 87 M9
Dorian Rd HCH RM12 42 G6
Doria Rd FUL/PGN SW6 49 M14
Doric Dr KWD/TDW/WH KT20 85 M10
Doric Wy CAMTN NW1 4 C5
Dorie Ms NFNCH/WDSPK N12 25 P9
Dorien Rd RYNPK SW20 60 K14
Dorin Ct WARL CR6 87 M10
WOKS/MYFD GU22 80 J5
Doris Av ERITH DA8 54 C13
Doris Rd ASHF TW15 57 V11
FSTGT E7 40 C12
Dorking Cl DEPT SE8 51 R11
WPK KT4 72 K7
Dorking Ri HARH RM3 30 K9
Dorking Rd ASHTD KT21 84 B5
HARH RM3 30 K9
KWD/TDW/WH KT20 92 F4
LHD/OX KT22 83 R13
Dorking Wk HARH RM3 30 K10
Dorkins Wy UPMR RM14 43 S6
Dorlcote Rd WAND/EARL SW18 61 R5
Dorling Dr EW KT17 84 F2
Dorly Cl SHPTN TW17 70 A2
Dorman Pl ED N9 27 L7
Dormans Cl NTHWD HA6 21 V12
Dorman Wy STJWD NW8 3 L1
Dormay St WAND/EARL SW18 61 P3
Dormer Cl BAR EN5 24 K3
SRTFD E15 40 B11
Dormer's Av STHL UB1 46 J4
Dormers Ri STHL UB1 46 K5
Dormer's Wells La STHL UB1 46 J4
Dormywood RSLP HA4 34 B3
Dornberg Cl BKHTH/KID SE3 52 C12
Dornberg Rd BKHTH/KID SE3 * 52 D12
Dorncliffe Rd FUL/PGN SW6 49 L14
Dornels SLN SL2 44 A4
Dorney Gv WEY KT13 69 T7
Dorney Ri STMC/STPC BR5 77 P2
Dorney Wy HSLWW TW4 58 G3
Dornfell St KIL/WHAMP NW6 37 M10
Dornford Gdns COUL/CHIP CR5 86 G9
Dornton Rd BAL SW12 61 V7
SAND/SEL CR2 74 J10
Dorothy Av ALP/SUD HA0 35 U12
Dorothy Evans Cl BXLYHN DA7 66 B2
Dorothy Gdns BCTR RM8 41 R9
Dorothy Rd BTSEA SW11 61 T1
Dorrell Pl BRXN/ST SW9 62 E1
Dorrington Gdns HCH RM12 42 K7
Dorrington St HCIRC EC1N 4 J9
Dorrington Wy BECK BR3 75 U3
Dorrit Ms UED N18 26 K9
Dorrit St STHWK SE1 * 9 P3
Dorrit Wy CHST BR7 65 L11
Dorrofield Cl RKW/CH/CXG WD3 21 U3
Dors Cl CDALE/KGS NW9 36 D6
Dorset Av NWDGN UB2 46 J9
ROM RM1 42 D1
WELL DA16 65 P2
YEAD UB4 46 A1
Dorset Buildings EMB EC4Y * 5 L12
Dorset Cl CAMTN NW1 3 Q9
YEAD UB4 * 46 A1
Dorset Dr EDGW HA8 23 V11
WOKS/MYFD GU22 80 F7
Dorset Gdns MTCM CR4 74 D2
Dorset Ms FNCH N3 25 N13
KTBR SW1X 7 U5
Dorset Pl SRTFD E15 39 V11
Dorset Ri EMB EC4Y 4 K12
Dorset Rd ASHF TW15 57 P8
BECK BR3 75 P1
BELMT SM2 73 N14
EA W5 47 T8
ELTH/MOT SE9 64 G7
FSTGT E7 40 E12
HRW HA1 35 L4
MTCM CR4 61 S14
SEVS/STOTM N15 38 H2
WDGN N22 26 C13
WIM/MER SW19 61 N13
Dorset Sq CAMTN NW1 3 Q8
Dorset St MHST W1U 3 R10
Dorset Wy BF/WBF KT14 81 P1
HGDN/ICK UB10 33 R14
WHTN TW2 59 L6
Dorset Waye HEST TW5 46 H12
Dorton Cl PECK SE15 9 T14
Dorton Dr BGR/WK TN15 91 M12
Dorton Wy RPLY/SEND GU23 81 M11
Dorville Crs HMSMTH W6 48 H8
Dorville Rd LEE/GVPK SE12 64 C3
Dothill Rd WOOL/PLUM SE18 53 L12
Douai Gv HPTN TW12 59 L13
Doubleday Rd LOU IG10 29 L1
Doughty Ms BMSBY WC1N 4 G8
Doughty St BMSBY WC1N 4 G7
Douglas Av ALP/SUD HA0 35 U12
HARH RM3 31 L14
NWMAL KT3 72 H2
WALTH E17 27 S13
WATN WD24 11 R11
Douglas Cl BARK/HLT IG6 28 K12
STAN HA7 23 Q10
WLGTN SM6 74 C11
Douglas Ct CTHM CR3 * 86 G12
Douglas Crs YEAD UB4 46 E2
Douglas Dr CROY/NA CR0 75 S8
Douglas Est IS N1 * 38 G11
Douglas La STWL/WRAY TW19 56 D3
Douglas Ms BNSTD SM7 85 M6
CRICK NW2 37 L8
Douglas Pth POP/IOD E14 51 U10
Douglas Pl POP/IOD E14 * 51 U10
Douglas Rd ADL/WDHM KT15 69 M8
CAN/RD E16 52 C3
CHING E4 28 A5
ESH/CLAY KT10 70 K7
GDMY/SEVK IG3 41 Q5
HSLW TW3 58 K1
IS N1 38 G12
KIL/WHAMP NW6 2 C1
KUT/HW KT1 60 B14
REIG RH2 93 N9
ROM RM1 42 F4
STWL/WRAY TW19 57 P4
SURB KT6 71 V7
WDGN N22 26 E13
WELL DA16 53 R13
Douglas Rd North IS N1 38 G11
Douglas Rd South IS N1 * 38 G11
Douglas St WEST SW1P 8 C8
Douglas Ter WALTH E17 27 R13
Douglas Vls KUT/HW KT1 * 59 V14
Douglas Wy DEPT SE8 51 S12
Doulton Ms KIL/WHAMP NW6 37 P11
The Doultons STA TW18 57 L11
Dounesforth Gdns WAND/EARL SW18 61 P6
Douro Pl KENS W8 6 H5
Douro St BOW E3 39 S14
Douthwaite Sq WAP E1W 51 L6
Dove Ap EHAM E6 52 G3
Dove Cl MLHL NW7 24 G12
NTHLT UB5 46 F2
SAND/SEL CR2 87 P1
WLGTN SM6 74 D12
Dovecot Cl PIN HA5 34 E3
Dovecote Cl WEY KT13 69 T8
Dove Ct LOTH EC2R * 5 Q12
Dovedale Av CLAY IG5 28 J14
KTN/HRWW/WS HA3 35 S4
Dovedale Cl DEN/HRF UB9 21 N14
WELL DA16 53 Q13
Dovedale Ri MTCM CR4 61 T12
Dovedale Rd EDUL SE22 63 M3
RDART DA2 67 Q6
Dovedon Cl STHGT/OAK N14 26 C7
Dove House Gdns CHING E4 27 S7
Dovehouse Gn WEY KT13 69 V9
Dovehouse Md BARK IG11 41 M14
Dovehouse St CHEL SW3 7 M9
Dove La POTB/CUF EN6 14 E8
Dove Ms ECT SW5 6 J8
Doveney Cl STMC/STPC BR5 77 S1
Dove Pk PIN HA5 22 H12
RKW/CH/CXG WD3 20 G3
Dover Cl CRICK NW2 36 K7
CRW RM5 30 C14
Dovercourt Av THHTH CR7 74 E2
Dovercourt Est IS N1 38 H11
Dovercourt Gdns STAN HA7 23 U10
Dovercourt La SUT SM1 73 Q8
Dovercourt Rd EDUL SE22 62 K4
Doverfield CHESW EN7 15 S3
Doverfield Rd BRXS/STRHM SW2 62 C5
Dover Gdns CAR SM5 73 T8
Dover House Rd PUT/ROE SW15 60 G2
Doveridge Gdns PLMGR N13 26 F9
Dove Rd IS N1 38 H11
Dove Rw BETH E2 39 L14
Dover Park Dr PUT/ROE SW15 60 H4
Dover Patrol BKHTH/KID SE3 52 D14
Dover Rd ED N9 27 N7
MNPK E12 40 E7
NRWD SE19 62 H11
WOOL/PLUM SE18 52 K14
Dovers Green Rd REIG RH2 93 P14
Dover St CONDST W1S 3 V14
Dover Ter RCH/KEW TW9 * 48 A14
Dover Wy RKW/CH/CXG WD3 21 U2
Dover Yd MYFR/PICC W1J 7 V1
Doves Cl HAYES BR2 76 G7
Doves Yd IS N1 4 J2
Doveton Rd SAND/SEL CR2 74 H10
Doveton St WCHPL E1 51 N2
Dowanhill Rd CAT SE6 63 V6
Dowd Cl FBAR/BDGN N11 25 U7
Dowdeswell Cl PUT/ROE SW15 60 E2
Dowding Cl HCH RM12 42 H12
Dowding Pl STAN HA7 23 Q11
Dowding Rd BH/WHM TN16 88 F5
HGDN/ICK UB10 33 R12
Dowding Wy GSTN WD25 11 M8
Dowdney Cl KTTN NW5 38 A10
Dower Av WLGTN SM6 73 V13
Dowgate Hl CANST EC4R 5 Q13
Dowland St NKENS W10 2 B5
Dowlas St CMBW SE5 9 S13
Dowlerville Rd ORP BR6 77 P11
Dowman Cl WIM/MER SW19 61 P13
Downage HDN NW4 36 J1
Downalong BUSH WD23 23 M6
Downbank Av BXLYHN DA7 54 D14
Down Barns Rd RSLP HA4 34 F9
Down Cl NTHLT UB5 46 D1
Downderry Rd BMLY BR1 63 V8
Downe Av RSEV TN14 89 L2
Downe Cl WELL DA16 53 S12
Downend WOOL/PLUM SE18 52 K12
Downe Rd HAYES BR2 76 G13
MTCM CR4 61 T14
ORP BR6 89 L4
Downer's Cottages CLAP SW4 62 A2
Downes Cl TWK TW1 59 R4
Downes Ct WCHMH N21 26 E6
Downfield WPK KT4 72 F6
Downfield Cl MV/WKIL W9 2 G8
Downfield Rd CHES/WCR EN8 16 E5
Down Hall Rd KUT/HW KT1 59 T13
Downham Cl CRW RM5 30 A12
Downham Ct WOT/HER KT12 * 70 E8
Downham Rd IS N1 38 H12
Downham Wy BMLY BR1 64 A10
Downhills Av TOTM N17 38 H1
Downhills Park Rd TOTM N17 38 H1
Downhills Wy TOTM N17 26 G14
Downhurst Av MLHL NW7 24 D10
Downing Cl RYLN/HDSTN HA2 35 L1
Downing Dr GFD/PVL UB6 35 N13
Downing Rd DAGW RM9 41 V13
Downings EHAM E6 52 J4
Downing St WHALL SW1A 8 E3
Downings Wd RKW/CH/CXG WD3 20 H10
Downland Cl COUL/CHIP CR5 85 V4
EPSOM KT18 84 H8
TRDG/WHET N20 25 Q6
Downland Gdns EPSOM KT18 84 H8
Downlands WAB EN9 17 L8
Downlands Rd PUR/KEN CR8 86 C3
Downland Wy EPSOM KT18 84 H8
Downleys Cl ELTH/MOT SE9 64 G7
Downman Rd ELTH/MOT SE9 64 G1
Down Pl HMSMTH W6 48 H10
Down Rd TEDD TW11 59 R11
Downs Av CHST BR7 64 H10
DART DA1 67 N5
EPSOM KT18 84 F5
PIN HA5 34 H4
Downs Bridge Rd BECK BR3 63 V13
Downs Court Pde HACK E8 * 39 M10
Downs Court Rd PUR/KEN CR8 86 G3
Downsell Rd SRTFD E15 39 V9
Downsfield Rd WALTH E17 39 Q4
Downshall Av GDMY/SEVK IG3 41 N4
Downs Hl BECK BR3 63 V13
Downs Hill Rd EPSOM KT18 * 84 E5
Downshire Hl HAMP NW3 37 R9
Downside BECK BR3 * 63 S13
CHERT KT16 * 68 K6
EPSOM KT18 84 E4
SUN TW16 58 C13
TWK TW1 59 P8
Downside Bridge Rd COB KT11 82 D5
Downside Cl WIM/MER SW19 61 Q11
Downside Common COB KT11 82 D8
Downside Common Rd COB KT11 82 E8
Downside Crs HAMP NW3 37 S10
WEA W13 47 Q2
Downside Orch WOKS/MYFD GU22 80 E7
Downside Rd BELMT SM2 73 R11
COB KT11 82 D8
Downs La CLPT E5 39 M9
LHD/OX KT22 83 R13
Downs Lodge Ct EW KT17 * 84 E4
Downs Park Rd HACK E8 39 L10
Downs Rd BECK BR3 63 T14
BELMT SM2 85 P1
CLPT E5 39 M9
COUL/CHIP CR5 86 B8
DTCH/LGLY SL3 44 B7
EN EN1 26 J2
EPSOM KT18 84 C10
EPSOM KT18 84 E5
PUR/KEN CR8 86 F1
THHTH CR7 62 G13
Downs Side BELMT SM2 85 M1
The Downs RYNPK SW20 60 K12
Down St E/WMO/HCT KT8 70 J3
MYFR/PICC W1J 7 U2
Downs Vw ISLW TW7 47 P13
KWD/TDW/WH KT20 84 H11
Downsview Av WOKS/MYFD GU22 80 D11
Downs View Cl ORP BR6 77 S14
Downsview Cl COB KT11 82 D9
SWLY BR8 78 F1
Downsview Gdns NRWD SE19 62 G12
Downsview Rd NRWD SE19 62 G12
Downs Wy EPSOM KT18 84 F6
KWD/TDW/WH KT20 84 H11
OXTED RH8 96 A3
Downsway CTHM CR3 86 K6
ORP BR6 77 N10
SAND/SEL CR2 86 J1
Downsway Cl KWD/TDW/WH KT20 84 G11
The Downsway BELMT SM2 73 Q13
Downs Wd EPSOM KT18 84 H7
Downswood REIG RH2 93 R8
Downton Av BRXS/STRHM SW2 62 D7
Downtown Rd BERM/RHTH SE16 51 Q7
Downway NFNCH/WDSPK N12 25 S12
Down Wy NTHLT UB5 46 D1
Dowrey St IS N1 * 4 J1
Dowry Wk WAT WD17 11 M12
Dowsett Rd TOTM N17 27 L14
Dowson Cl CMBW SE5 * 62 H2
Doyce St STHWK SE1 * 9 N3
Doyle Cl ERITH DA8 54 E13
Doyle Gdns WLSDN NW10 36 H13
Doyle Rd SNWD SE25 75 L2
D'Oyley St BGVA SW1W 7 S7
Doynton St ARCH N19 * 37 V7
Draco Ga PUT/ROE SW15 * 60 J1
Draco St WALW SE17 9 N11
Dragonfly Cl PLSTW E13 52 D1
Dragon La WEY KT13 81 S1
Dragon Rd LBTH SE11 8 H8
PECK SE15 9 T12
Dragoon Rd DEPT SE8 51 R10
Dragor Rd WLSDN NW10 48 C2
Drake Av CTHM CR3 86 G12
DTCH/LGLY SL3 44 B9
STA TW18 56 K10
Drake Cl BERM/RHTH SE16 51 P7
Drake Crs THMD SE28 53 S4
Drakefell Rd NWCR SE14 51 P14
Drakefield Rd TOOT SW17 61 U8
Drake Ms HAYES BR2 76 E2
HCH RM12 42 G12
Drake Rd BROCKY SE4 63 S1
CHSGTN KT9 72 A10
CROY/NA CR0 74 D5
MTCM CR4 73 U4
RYLN/HDSTN HA2 34 H7
Drakes Cl CHES/WCR EN8 16 D2
ESH/CLAY KT10 70 J10
Drakes Ctyd KIL/WHAMP NW6 37 M12
Drakes Dr NTHWD HA6 21 T13
Drake St ENC/FH EN2 15 T13
FSBYW WC1X 4 G10
Drakes Wy WOKS/MYFD GU22 80 B12
Drakewood Rd STRHM/NOR SW16 62 B12
Draper Cl BELV DA17 53 V9
ISLW TW7 47 M14
Draper Est STHWK SE1 9 M7
Draper Pl IS N1 5 M1
Drapers Cnr CHONG CM5 19 U4
Drapers Rd ENC/FH EN2 15 R14
SRTFD E15 39 U9
TOTM N17 38 K1
Drappers Wy BERM/RHTH SE16 51 L9
Draven Cl HAYES BR2 76 B5
Drawell Cl WOOL/PLUM SE18 53 N10
Drax Av RYNPK SW20 60 G12
Draxmont WIM/MER SW19 61 L11
Draycot Rd SURB KT6 72 A6
WAN E11 40 D4
Draycott Av CHEL SW3 7 P8
KTN/HRWW/WS HA3 35 R4
Draycott Cl CMBW SE5 9 R13
CRICK NW2 36 K8
KTN/HRWW/WS HA3 35 R4
Draycott Pl CHEL SW3 7 Q8
Draycott Ter CHEL SW3 7 Q7
Dray Ct ALP/SUD HA0 * 35 S11
Drayford Cl MV/WKIL W9 2 D7
Dray Gdns BRXS/STRHM SW2 62 D3
Draymans Ms PECK SE15 50 K14
Draymans Wy ISLW TW7 59 P1
Drayson Cl WAB EN9 16 K6
Drayson Ms KENS W8 6 F4
Drayton Av LOU IG10 28 H5
ORP BR6 76 K6
POTB/CUF EN6 14 A6
WEA W13 47 Q5
Drayton Bridge Rd HNWL W7 47 P5
Drayton Cl HSLWW TW4 58 H3
IL IG1 41 M6
LHD/OX KT22 83 N13
Drayton Ct WDR/YW UB7 * 45 R9
Drayton Court Chambers WEA W13 * 47 R5
Drayton Gdns WBPTN SW10 6 K9
WCHMH N21 26 F5
WDR/YW UB7 45 P7
WEA W13 47 Q5
Drayton Gn WEA W13 47 Q5
Drayton Green Rd WEA W13 47 R5
Drayton Gv WEA W13 47 Q5
Drayton Pk HBRY N5 38 E10
Drayton Park Ms HOLWY N7 * 38 E10
Drayton Rd BORE WD6 24 A2
CROY/NA CR0 74 F7
TOTM N17 26 J14
WAN E11 39 V6
WEA W13 47 Q5
WLSDN NW10 36 F13
Dreadnought St GNWCH SE10 52 A8
Drenon Sq HYS/HAR UB3 46 B5
Dresden Cl KIL/WHAMP NW6 37 P11
Dresden Rd ARCH N19 38 A6
Dresden Wy WEY KT13 69 U10
Dressington Av BROCKY SE4 63 S4
Drew Av MLHL NW7 25 L11
Drewery Ct BKHTH/KID SE3 * 64 A1
Drew Gdns GFD/PVL UB6 35 P11
Drew Pl CTHM CR3 86 H13
Drew Rd CAN/RD E16 52 G6
Drews Cottages STRHM/NOR SW16 * 62 B7
Drewstead Rd STRHM/NOR SW16 62 B7
The Drey CFSP/GDCR SL9 20 C10
Driffield Rd BOW E3 39 Q14
The Drift EHSLY KT24 82 A14
HAYES BR2 76 F8
Drift Wy DTCH/LGLY SL3 44 G13
The Driftway BNSTD SM7 84 J5
LHD/OX KT22 83 S13
MTCM CR4 61 U13
Driftwood Dr PUR/KEN CR8 86 G7
Drill Hall Rd CHERT KT16 69 L5
Drinkwater Rd RYLN/HDSTN HA2 34 K7
Drive Ct EDGW HA8 * 24 A10
Drive Md COUL/CHIP CR5 86 C4
Drive Rd COUL/CHIP CR5 86 A10
Drive Sp KWD/TDW/WH KT20 85 P11
The Drive ACT W3 48 C4
ASHF TW15 57 V12
BAR EN5 25 L1
BAR EN5 25 Q4
BARK IG11 41 P12
BECK BR3 63 S14
BELMT SM2 85 M2
BKHH IG9 28 E5
BNSTD SM7 85 L7
BXLY DA5 65 T5
CFSP/GDCR SL9 20 C12
CHESW EN7 15 R2
CHESW EN7 16 B2
CHING E4 27 V5
CHST BR7 65 P13
CHST BR7 77 P1
COB KT11 82 G4
COUL/CHIP CR5 86 C4
CRW RM5 30 D13
DTCH/LGLY SL3 44 C7
EBED/NFELT TW14 58 E5
EDGW HA8 24 A10
ENC/FH EN2 15 T13
ERITH DA8 54 B12
ESH/CLAY KT10 71 L6
FBAR/BDGN N11 26 A11
FNCH N3 25 N12
GLDGN NW11 37 L5
HARH RM3 31 L13
HGDN/ICK UB10 33 Q9
HGT N6 37 T3
HOLWY N7 38 D11
HOR/WEW KT19 72 F11
HSLW TW3 47 M14
IL IG1 40 G4
KUTN/CMB KT2 60 C12
KWD/TDW/WH KT20 * 85 N14
LHD/OX KT22 83 N12
LHD/OX KT22 83 U13
LOU IG10 28 G1
MRDN SM4 73 Q3
NTHWD HA6 22 A13
ORP BR6 77 P7
POTB/CUF EN6 14 B7
RAD WD7 12 E8
RKW/CH/CXG WD3 21 M3
RYLN/HDSTN HA2 34 J5
RYNPK SW20 60 J12
SCUP DA14 65 R8
SEV TN13 90 H14
STWL/WRAY TW19 56 B3
SURB KT6 71 U5
SWFD E18 40 C1
THHTH CR7 74 H2
VW GU25 68 D3
WALTH E17 39 T1
WAT WD17 10 K11
WBLY HA9 36 C7
WLGTN SM6 74 A14
WWKM BR4 75 V5
The Driveway POTB/CUF EN6 15 N2
Dr Johnson Av TOOT SW17 61 V8
Droitwich Cl SYD SE26 63 L8
Dromey Gdns KTN/HRWW/WS HA3 23 P12
Dromore Rd PUT/ROE SW15 61 L4
Dronfield Gdns BCTR RM8 41 S10
Droop St NKENS W10 2 A7
Drop La LCOL/BKTW AL2 11 V5
Drovers Md BRW CM14 31 V9
Drovers Pl PECK SE15 51 M12
Drovers Rd SAND/SEL CR2 74 H10
Druce Rd DUL SE21 62 J4
Drudgeon Wy RDART DA2 67 V8
Druid's Cl ASHTD KT21 83 V10
Druid St STHWK SE1 9 U3
Druids Wy HAYES BR2 75 V2
Drumaline Rdg WPK KT4 72 E7
Drummond Av ROMW/RG RM7 42 D2
Drummond Cl ERITH DA8 54 E13
Drummond Crs CAMTN NW1 4 C5
Drummond Dr STAN HA7 23 P12
Drummond Ga PIM SW1V 8 D9
Drummond Rd BERM/RHTH SE16 51 M8
CROY/NA CR0 74 G7
ROMW/RG RM7 42 C2
WAN E11 40 D4
Drummonds Pl RCH/KEW TW9 59 U2
The Drummonds EPP CM16 18 E4
Drummond St CAMTN NW1 4 A7
Drum St WCHPL E1 5 V11
Drury Crs CROY/NA CR0 74 E7
Drury La COVGDN WC2E 4 F12
Drury Rd HRW HA1 35 L5
Drury Wy WLSDN NW10 36 D10
Dryad St PUT/ROE SW15 60 K1
Dryburgh Gdns CDALE/KGS NW9 36 A1
Dryburgh Rd PUT/ROE SW15 60 H1
Dryden Av HNWL W7 47 P4
Dryden Cl BARK/HLT IG6 29 P11
Dryden Rd EN EN1 26 J4
KTN/HRWW/WS HA3 23 P13
WELL DA16 53 P13
WIM/MER SW19 61 Q11
Dryden St COVGDN WC2E 4 F12
Dryden Wy ORP BR6 77 Q6
Dryfield Cl WLSDN NW10 36 C11
Dryfield Rd EDGW HA8 24 C11
Dryhill La RSEV TN14 90 B13
Dryhill Rd BELV DA17 53 V11
Dryland Av ORP BR6 77 P9
Drylands Rd CEND/HSY/T N8 38 C4
Drynham Pk WEY KT13 70 A8
Drysdale Av CHING E4 27 T4
Drysdale Cl NTHWD HA6 22 A12
Drysdale Dwellings HACK E8 * 38 K10
Drysdale Pl IS N1 5 T5
Drysdale St IS N1 5 T6
Dublin Av HACK E8 39 L13
Du Burstow Ter HNWL W7 47 N7
Ducal St BETH E2 5 V6
Du Cane Cl SHB W12 * 48 J4
Du Cane Rd SHB W12 48 H4
Duchess Cl FBAR/BDGN N11 25 V10
SUT SM1 73 Q9
Duchess Ct WEY KT13 69 V8
Duchess Gv BKHH IG9 * 28 D7
Duchess Ms CAVSQ/HST W1G 3 V10
Duchess of Bedford's Wk KENS W8 6 E4
Duchess St REGST W1B 3 V10
Duchy Rd EBAR EN4 14 F12
Duchy St STHWK SE1 8 K1
Ducie St CLAP SW4 62 C2
Duckett Rd FSBYPK N4 38 F4
Ducketts Rd DART DA1 66 F3
Duckett St WCHPL E1 51 P3
Ducking Stool Ct ROM RM1 42 E2
Duck La SOHO/CST W1F 4 C12
Duck Lees La PEND EN3 27 Q2
Ducks Hill Rd NTHWD HA6 21 S14
Du Cros Dr STAN HA7 23 T11
Du Cros Rd ACT W3 48 E6
Dudden Hill La WLSDN NW10 36 F10
Dudden Hill Pde WLSDN NW10 * 36 F9
Duddington Cl ELTH/MOT SE9 64 F9
Dudley Av CHES/WCR EN8 16 D6
KTN/HRWW/WS HA3 35 S1
Dudley Cl ADL/WDHM KT15 69 N8
Dudley Dr MRDN SM4 73 L6
RSLP HA4 34 D10
Dudley Gdns RYLN/HDSTN HA2 35 M6
WEA W13 47 R7
Dudley Gv EPSOM KT18 84 C4
Dudley Pl HYS/HAR UB3 45 V9
Dudley Rd ASHF TW15 57 R10
EBED/NFELT TW14 57 V6
FNCH N3 25 P14
HARH RM3 30 K11
IL IG1 40 K9
KIL/WHAMP NW6 2 B3
KUT/HW KT1 71 V1
NWDGN UB2 46 F7
RCH/KEW TW9 47 V14
RYLN/HDSTN HA2 35 L7
WALTH E17 27 S14
WIM/MER SW19 61 N11
WOT/HER KT12 70 C4
Dudley St BAY/PAD W2 * 3 L10
Dudley Whf IVER SL0 * 44 G6
Dudlington Rd CLPT E5 39 N7
Dudmaston Ms CHEL SW3 7 M9
Dudrich Ms EDUL SE22 62 K3
Dudsbury Rd DART DA1 66 H4
Dudset La HEST TW5 46 C13
Dufferin Av STLK EC1Y 5 Q8
Dufferin St STLK EC1Y 5 P8
Duffield Cl HRW HA1 35 P3
Duffield Dr SEVS/STOTM N15 38 K2
Duffield Rd KWD/TDW/WH KT20 84 H14
Duffins Orch CHERT KT16 68 G12
Duff St POP/IOD E14 51 T4
Dufour's Pl SOHO/CST W1F 4 B12
Dugard Wy LBTH SE11 9 L8
Dugdale Hill La POTB/CUF EN6 14 A7
Dugdales RKW/CH/CXG WD3 21 S2
Duggan Dr CHST BR7 64 G11
Dugolly Av WBLY HA9 36 B8
Duke Humphrey Rd BKHTH/KID SE3 52 A14
Duke of Cambridge Cl WHTN TW2 59 M4
Duke of Edinburgh Rd SUT SM1 73 R7
The Duke of Wellington Av
WOOL/PLUM SE18 52 K8
Duke of Wellington Pl KTBR SW1X 7 T4
Duke of York Sq CHEL SW3 7 R9
Duke of York St STJS SW1Y 8 B1
Duke Rd BARK/HLT IG6 41 M2
CHSWK W4 48 D10
Duke's Av CHSWK W4 48 D10
EDGW HA8 23 V11
EPP CM16 18 C9
FNCH N3 25 P13
HRW HA1 35 N2
HSLWW TW4 58 G2
MUSWH N10 38 A1
NTHLT UB5 34 G12
NWMAL KT3 72 E1
PIN HA5 34 H4
RCHPK/HAM TW10 59 S9
Dukes Cl ASHF TW15 57 U9
CFSP/GDCR SL9 32 B6
EPP CM16 19 M1
HPTN TW12 58 H10
Dukes Ga CHSWK W4 * 48 C9
Dukes Green Av EBED/NFELT TW14 58 C4
Dukes Hl CTHM CR3 87 Q10
Dukes Kiln Dr CFSP/GDCR SL9 32 A7
Dukes La KENS W8 6 G3
Duke's Ms MHST W1U 3 T11
MUSWH N10 37 V1
Dukes Orch BXLY DA5 66 C6
Duke's Pl HDTCH EC3A 5 U12
Dukes Point HGT N6 37 V6
Dukes Ride CFSP/GDCR SL9 32 C6
HGDN/ICK UB10 33 Q9
Dukes Rd ACT W3 48 A2
CAMTN NW1 4 D6
EHAM E6 40 J13
WOT/HER KT12 70 F10
Dukesthorpe Rd SYD SE26 63 P9
Duke St MHST W1U 3 T11
RCH/KEW TW9 59 T2
SUT SM1 73 R9
WAT WD17 22 E1
WOKN/KNAP GU21 80 D7
Duke Street Hl STHWK SE1 9 R1
Duke Street St James's
MYFR/PICC W1J 8 B1
Dukes Wy UX/CGN UB8 33 M13
WWKM BR4 76 A8
Dukes Wood Av CFSP/GDCR SL9 32 C6
Dukes Wood Dr CFSP/GDCR SL9 32 B6
Duke's Yd MYFR/PKLN W1K 3 T13
Dulas St FSBYPK N4 38 D6
Dulford St NTGHL W11 2 A13
Dulka Rd BTSEA SW11 61 T3
Dulverton Rd ELTH/MOT SE9 65 L7
HARH RM3 30 K11
RSLP HA4 34 C7
SAND/SEL CR2 75 N14
Dulwich Common DUL SE21 62 H6
The Dulwich Oaks DUL SE21 * 62 K8
Dulwich Rd HNHL SE24 62 E3
Dulwich Village DUL SE21 62 H4
Dulwich Wy RKW/CH/CXG WD3 21 S3
Dulwich Wood Av NRWD SE19 62 K10
Dulwich Wood Pk NRWD SE19 62 J9
Dumbarton Av CHES/WCR EN8 16 D8
Dumbarton Rd BRXS/STRHM SW2 62 C4
Dumbleton Cl KUT/HW KT1 60 B13
Dumbletons RKW/CH/CXG WD3 20 J9
Dumbreck Rd ELTH/MOT SE9 64 J2
Dumfries Cl OXHEY WD19 22 C8
Dumont Rd STNW/STAM N16 38 J8
Dumpton Pl CAMTN NW1 37 U12
Dumville Dr GDST RH9 95 M7
Dunally Pk SHPTN TW17 69 V5
Dunbar Av BECK BR3 75 Q2
DAGE RM10 42 A8
STRHM/NOR SW16 62 E14
Dunbar Cl YEAD UB4 46 C3
Dunbar Ct WOT/HER KT12 70 E7
Dunbar Gdns DAGE RM10 42 A10
Dunbar Rd FSTGT E7 40 C11
NWMAL KT3 72 C2
WDGN N22 26 E13
Dunbar St WNWD SE27 62 G8
Dunblane Rd ELTH/MOT SE9 64 G1
Dunboe Pl SHPTN TW17 69 U5
Dunboyne Rd HAMP NW3 37 T10
Dunbridge St BETH E2 51 L2
Duncan Cl BAR EN5 25 Q2
Duncan Gdns STA TW18 57 L11
Duncan Gv ACT W3 48 E4
Duncannon St CHCR WC2N 4 E14
Duncan Rd HACK E8 39 M13
KWD/TDW/WH KT20 85 L9
RCH/KEW TW9 59 U2
Duncan St IS N1 5 L3
Duncan Ter IS N1 5 L4
Duncan Wy BUSH WD23 11 T14
Dunch St WCHPL E1 51 M4
Duncombe Hl FSTH SE23 63 Q5
Duncombe Rd ARCH N19 38 B6
Duncrievie Rd LEW SE13 63 V4
Duncroft WOOL/PLUM SE18 53 N12
Duncroft Cl REIG RH2 93 M10
Dundalk Rd BROCKY SE4 63 Q1
Dundas Gdns E/WMO/HCT KT8 70 K1
Dundas Rd PECK SE15 51 N14
Dundee Rd PLSTW E13 40 D14
SNWD SE25 75 M3
Dundee St WAP E1W 51 M6
Dundee Wy PEND EN3 27 Q1
Dundela Gdns WPK KT4 72 H9
Dundonald Cl EHAM E6 52 G4
Dundonald Rd WIM/MER SW19 61 M12
WLSDN NW10 36 K13
Dundrey Crs REDH RH1 94 C5
Dunedin Dr CTHM CR3 94 J1
Dunedin Rd IL IG1 41 L6
LEY E10 39 T8
RAIN RM13 54 F1
Dunedin Wy YEAD UB4 46 E2
Dunelm St WCHPL E1 51 P4
Dunfee Wy BF/WBF KT14 81 Q2
Dunfield Rd CAT SE6 63 T10
Dunford Br CHERT KT16 80 F1
Dunford Rd HOLWY N7 38 D9
Dungarvan Av PUT/ROE SW15 60 G2
Dungates La BRKHM/BTCW RH3 92 G10
Dunheved Cl THHTH CR7 74 E4
Dunheved Rd North THHTH CR7 74 E4
Dunheved Rd South THHTH CR7 74 E4
Dunheved Rd West THHTH CR7 74 E4
Dunholme Gn ED N9 26 K8
Dunholme La ED N9 26 K8
Dunholme Rd ED N9 26 K8
Dunkeld Rd BCTR RM8 41 R7
SNWD SE25 74 H2
Dunkellin Gv SOCK/AV RM15 55 U4
Dunkellin Wy SOCK/AV RM15 55 U4
Dunkery Rd ELTH/MOT SE9 64 F9
Dunkin Rd DART DA1 67 N2
Dunkirk St WNWD SE27 * 62 G9
Dunlace Rd CLPT E5 39 N10
Dunleary Cl HSLWW TW4 58 H5
Dunley Dr CROY/NA CR0 75 U11
Dunloe Av TOTM N17 38 H1
Dunloe St BETH E2 5 V4
Dunlop Pl BERM/RHTH SE16 9 V6
Dunmail Dr PUR/KEN CR8 86 J4
Dunmore Rd KIL/WHAMP NW6 2 A2
RYNPK SW20 60 J13
Dunmow Cl CHDH RM6 41 S3
FELT TW13 * 58 G9
LOU IG10 28 G4
Dunmow Dr RAIN RM13 42 F13
Dunmow Rd SRTFD E15 39 V9
Dunmow Wk IS N1 * 5 N1
Dunnage Crs BERM/RHTH SE16 51 Q9
Dunning Cl SOCK/AV RM15 55 U4
Dunningford Cl HCH RM12 42 F10
Dunn Md CDALE/KGS NW9 24 F12
Dunnock Cl BORE WD6 24 A2
ED N9 27 P6
Dunnock Rd EHAM E6 52 G4
Dunn St HACK E8 38 K10
Dunnymans Rd BNSTD SM7 85 M5
Dunollie Pl KTTN NW5 38 A10
Dunollie Rd KTTN NW5 38 A10
Dunoon Gdns FSTH SE23 * 63 P5
Dunoon Rd FSTH SE23 63 N5
Dunottar Cl REDH RH1 93 R12
Dunraven Dr ENC/FH EN2 15 Q14
Dunraven Rd SHB W12 48 G6
Dunraven St MYFR/PKLN W1K 3 R13
Dunsany Rd HMSMTH W6 48 K8
Dunsbury Cl BELMT SM2 73 P13
Dunsfold Ri COUL/CHIP CR5 86 B3
Dunsfold Wy CROY/NA CR0 75 T12
Dunsford Wy PUT/ROE SW15 60 H5
Dunsmore OXHEY WD19 * 22 F7
Dunsmore Cl BUSH WD23 23 M4
YEAD UB4 46 F2
Dunsmore Rd WOT/HER KT12 70 D3
Dunsmore Wy BUSH WD23 23 M4
Dunsmure Rd STNW/STAM N16 38 J6
Dunspring La CLAY IG5 28 K14
Dunstable Ms CAVSQ/HST W1G 3 T9
Dunstable Rd E/WMO/HCT KT8 70 H2
HARH RM3 30 K11
RCH/KEW TW9 59 U2
Dunstall Rd RYNPK SW20 60 H11
Dunstall Wy E/WMO/HCT KT8 70 K1
Dunstall Welling Est WELL DA16 * 53 R14
Dunstan Cl EFNCH N2 * 37 Q1
Dunstan Gld STMC/STPC BR5 * 77 M4
Dunstan Houses WCHPL E1 * 51 N3
Dunstan Rd COUL/CHIP CR5 86 B7
GLDGN NW11 37 M6
Dunstan's Gv EDUL SE22 63 M4
Dunstan's Rd EDUL SE22 63 L5
Dunster Av MRDN SM4 72 K6
Dunster Cl BAR EN5 24 K2
CRW RM5 30 C14
DEN/HRF UB9 21 M13
Dunster Ct BORE WD6 24 D1
MON EC3R 5 S13
Dunster Crs EMPK RM11 43 N7
Dunster Dr CDALE/KGS NW9 36 C6
Dunster Gdns KIL/WHAMP NW6 37 M12
Dunsterville Wy STHWK SE1 9 R4
Dunster Wy RYLN/HDSTN HA2 34 G8
Dunston Rd BTSEA SW11 49 U14
HACK E8 5 U2
Dunston St HACK E8 5 T1
Dunton Cl SURB KT6 71 U6
Dunton Rd LEY E10 39 T5
ROM RM1 42 E2
STHWK SE1 9 U8
Duntshill Rd WAND/EARL SW18 61 P6
Dunvegan Cl E/WMO/HCT KT8 70 K2
Dunvegan Rd ELTH/MOT SE9 64 H2
Dunwich Rd BXLYHN DA7 53 V13
Dunworth Ms NTGHL W11 2 C12
Duplex Ride KTBR SW1X 7 R4
Dupont Rd RYNPK SW20 60 K14
Duppas Av CROY/NA CR0 74 F9
Duppas Cl SHPTN TW17 69 V3
Duppas Hill Rd CROY/NA CR0 74 F9
Duppas Hill Ter CROY/NA CR0 74 F8
Duppas Rd CROY/NA CR0 74 E8
Dupree Rd CHARL SE7 52 D10
Dura Den Cl BECK BR3 63 T12
Durand Gdns BRXN/ST SW9 50 D13
Durand Wy WLSDN NW10 36 C12
Durant Rd SWLY BR8 66 G12
Durants Park Av PEND EN3 27 P2
Durants Rd PEND EN3 27 N2
Durant St BETH E2 39 L14
Durban Gdns DAGE RM10 42 C12
Durban Rd BECK BR3 63 R14
GNTH/NBYPK IG2 41 N6
SRTFD E15 52 A1
TOTM N17 26 K11
WALTH E17 27 R13
WNWD SE27 62 G9
Durban Rd East WATW WD18 22 C2
Durban Rd West WATW WD18 22 C2
Durbin Rd CHSGTN KT9 71 U9
Durdans Rd STHL UB1 46 H4
Durell Gdns DAGW RM9 41 T10
Durell Rd DAGW RM9 41 T10
Durfey Pl CMBW SE5 9 R14
Durfold Dr REIG RH2 93 Q10
Durford Crs PUT/ROE SW15 60 H6
Durham Av GPK RM2 42 J2
HAYES BR2 76 B2
HEST TW5 46 H11
WFD IG8 28 F10
Durham Hl BMLY BR1 64 B9
Durham House St CHCR WC2N * 4 F14
Durham Pl CHEL SW3 7 Q10
Durham Ri WOOL/PLUM SE18 53 L10
Durham Rd BORE WD6 24 C1
CAN/RD E16 52 A2
DAGE RM10 42 C10
EA W5 47 T8
EBED/NFELT TW14 58 E5
ED N9 27 L7
EFNCH N2 37 S1
HAYES BR2 76 C2
HOLWY N7 38 D7
HRW HA1 34 K3
MNPK E12 40 F9
RYNPK SW20 60 H13
SCUP DA14 65 R10
Durham Rw WCHPL E1 51 P3
Durham St LBTH SE11 8 G10
Durham Ter BAY/PAD W2 2 G11
PGE/AN SE20 * 63 M12
Durham Wharf Dr BTFD TW8 47 S12
Durham Yd BETH E2 * 51 M1
Duriun Wy ERITH DA8 54 H12
Durleston Park Dr GT/LBKH KT23 83 L14
Durley Av PIN HA5 34 G4
Durley Gdns ORP BR6 77 R9
Durley Rd STNW/STAM N16 38 J5
Durlston Rd CLPT E5 39 L7
KUTN/CMB KT2 59 U11
Durnell Wy LOU IG10 28 J1
Durnford St SEVS/STOTM N15 38 J3
Durning Rd NRWD SE19 62 H10
Durnsford Av WIM/MER SW19 61 N7
Durnsford Rd FBAR/BDGN N11 26 B12
WIM/MER SW19 61 N8
Durrants Cl RAIN RM13 42 J14
Durrants Dr RKW/CH/CXG WD3 21 U1
Durrant Wy ORP BR6 77 M10
Durrell Rd FUL/PGN SW6 49 L14
Durrell Wy SHPTN TW17 69 V4
Durrington Av RYNPK SW20 60 J13
Durrington Park Rd RYNPK SW20 60 J13
Durrington Rd CLPT E5 39 Q9
Dursley Cl BKHTH/KID SE3 52 E14
Dursley Gdns BKHTH/KID SE3 52 F13
Dursley Rd BKHTH/KID SE3 52 E14
Durward St WCHPL E1 51 M3
Durweston Ms MHST W1U * 3 R9
Durweston St MBLAR W1H 3 Q10
Dury Falls Cl EMPK RM11 43 N6
Dury Rd BAR EN5 14 B13
Dutch Barn Cl STWL/WRAY TW19 57 P4
Dutch Gdns KUTN/CMB KT2 60 B11
Dutch Yd WAND/EARL SW18 61 N3
Duthie St POP/IOD E14 51 U5
Dutton St GNWCH SE10 51 U13
Dutton Wy IVER SL0 44 J4
Duxberry Cl HAYES BR2 76 G3
Duxford Cl HCH RM12 42 J11
Dwight Rd WATW WD18 21 V5
Dye House La BOW E3 39 S13
Dyer's Buildings FLST/FETLN EC4A 4 J10
Dyers Hall Rd WAN E11 39 V7
Dyer's La PUT/ROE SW15 60 H1
Dyers Wy HARH RM3 30 G12
Dyke Dr STMC/STPC BR5 77 S5
Dykes Pth WOKN/KNAP GU21 80 G5
Dykes Wy HAYES BR2 76 B1
Dykewood Cl BXLY DA5 66 D8
Dylan Cl BORE WD6 * 23 T5
Dylan Rd BELV DA17 54 A8
HNHL SE24 62 F2
Dylways CMBW SE5 62 H2
Dymchurch Cl CLAY IG5 40 J1
ORP BR6 77 N9
Dymock St FUL/PGN SW6 61 P1
Dymoke Rd EMPK RM11 42 F5
Dyneley Rd LEE/GVPK SE12 64 E9
Dyne Rd KIL/WHAMP NW6 37 M12
Dynes Rd BGR/WK TN15 91 L7
Dynevor Rd RCHPK/HAM TW10 59 U3
STNW/STAM N16 38 J8
Dynham Rd KIL/WHAMP NW6 37 N12
Dyott St LSQ/SEVD WC2H 4 E11
Dyrham La BAR EN5 13 S10
Dysart Av KUTN/CMB KT2 59 S10
Dysart St SDTCH EC2A 5 R8
Dyson Ct ALP/SUD HA0 35 Q9
Dyson Rd SRTFD E15 40 B11
WAN E11 40 A4
Dysons Cl CHES/WCR EN8 16 D7
Dyson's Rd UED N18 27 M11
Dytchleys Rd BRW CM14 31 M2

E

Eade Rd FSBYPK N4 38 G5
Eagans Cl EFNCH N2 * 37 R1
Eagle Av CHDH RM6 41 U4
Eagle Cl BERM/RHTH SE16 51 M11
HCH RM12 42 H11
PEND EN3 27 N2
WAB EN9 17 N8
WLGTN SM6 74 C11
Eagle Ct FARR EC1M 5 L9
Eagle Dr CDALE/KGS NW9 24 E14
Eagle Hl NRWD SE19 62 H11
Eagle House Ms CLAP SW4 62 A3
Eagle La WAN E11 40 C2
Eagle Ms IS N1 38 J11
Eagle Pl SKENS SW7 6 K9
Eagle Rd ALP/SUD HA0 35 T12
HTHAIR TW6 58 B1
Eagles Dr BH/WHM TN16 88 F8
Eaglesfield Rd WOOL/PLUM SE18 52 K13
Eagles Rd RDART DA2 67 V2
Eagle St GINN WC1R 4 G10
Eagle Ter WFD IG8 28 D12
Eagle Wharf Rd IS N1 5 P3
Eagling Cl BOW E3 51 S1
Ealdham Sq ELTH/MOT SE9 64 E2
Ealing Cl BORE WD6 13 P13
Ealing Golf Course GFD/PVL UB6 * 47 Q1
Ealing Gn EA W5 47 T6
Ealing Park Gdns EA W5 47 S9
Ealing Rd ALP/SUD HA0 35 U11
BOW E3 51 T1
EA W5 47 T9
NTHLT UB5 34 J13
Ealing Village EA W5 47 U4
Eamont Cl RSLP HA4 33 T5
Eamont St STJWD NW8 3 N3
Eardemont Cl DART DA1 66 F2
Eardley Crs ECT SW5 6 F9
Eardley Rd BELV DA17 54 A10
SEV TN13 90 H14
STRHM/NOR SW16 62 A11
Earl Cl FBAR/BDGN N11 25 V10
Earldom Rd PUT/ROE SW15 60 J2
Earle Gdns KUTN/CMB KT2 59 U12
Earleswood COB KT11 82 F2
Earlham Gv FSTGT E7 40 B10
WDGN N22 26 D12
Earlham St LSQ/SEVD WC2H 4 D12
Earl Ri WOOL/PLUM SE18 53 M10
Earl Rd MORT/ESHN SW14 60 C2
Earlsbrook Rd REDH RH1 93 T12
Earls Cnr POTB/CUF EN6 * 13 S7
Earl's Court Gdns ECT SW5 6 G8
Earl's Court Rd ECT SW5 6 F7
Earl's Court Sq ECT SW5 6 G9
Earls Crs HRW HA1 35 N2
Earlsferry Wy IS N1 38 C12
Earlsfield Rd WAND/EARL SW18 61 Q6
Earlshall Rd ELTH/MOT SE9 64 H2
Earls La POTB/CUF EN6 13 Q6
Earlsmead RYLN/HDSTN HA2 34 H9
Earlsmead Rd SEVS/STOTM N15 38 K3
WLSDN NW10 48 J1
Earls Ms WAND/EARL SW18 61 Q5
Earl's Pth LOU IG10 28 E1
Earls Ter KENS W8 6 E6
Earlsthorpe Ms BAL SW12 61 U4
Earlsthorpe Rd SYD SE26 63 P9
Earlstoke Est FSBYE EC1V 5 L5
Earlstoke St FSBYE EC1V 5 L5
Earlston Gv HOM E9 39 M13
Earl St SDTCH EC2A 5 S9
WAT WD17 22 E1
Earls Wk BCTR RM8 41 R9
KENS W8 6 E6
Earlswood Av THHTH CR7 74 E3
Earlswood Gdns CLAY IG5 40 J1
Earlswood Rd REDH RH1 93 T12
Earlswood St GNWCH SE10 52 A10
Early Ms CAMTN NW1 3 V1
Earnshaw St NOXST/BSQ WC1A 4 D11
Earsby St WKENS W14 6 B7
Easby Crs MRDN SM4 73 P4
Easebourne Rd BCTR RM8 41 S10
Easedale Dr HCH RM12 42 H10
Easington Wy SOCK/AV RM15 55 U3
Easleys Ms MHST W1U 3 T11
East Acton Ar ACT W3 * 48 F4
East Acton La ACT W3 48 E5
East Arbour St WCHPL E1 51 P4
East Av EHAM E6 40 G12
HYS/HAR UB3 46 C6
STHL UB1 46 H5
WALTH E17 39 T3
WLGTN SM6 74 D10
East Bank STNW/STAM N16 38 J5
Eastbank Rd HPTN TW12 59 L10
East Barnet Rd BAR EN5 25 Q2
Eastbourne Av ACT W3 48 D4
Eastbourne Gdns MORT/ESHN SW14 60 C1
Eastbourne Ms BAY/PAD W2 2 K11
Eastbourne Rd BTFD TW8 47 T10
CHSWK W4 48 C11
EHAM E6 52 J1
FELT TW13 58 F7
GDST RH9 95 N8
SEVS/STOTM N15 38 J4
SRTFD E15 40 A13
TOOT SW17 61 U11
Eastbourne Ter BAY/PAD W2 2 K11
Eastbournia Av ED N9 27 N8
Eastbrook Av DAGE RM10 42 C9
ED N9 27 N5
Eastbrook Cl WOKN/KNAP GU21 80 E6
Eastbrook Dr ROMW/RG RM7 42 E8
Eastbrook Rd BKHTH/KID SE3 52 D13
WAB EN9 17 L7
Eastbury Av BARK IG11 41 N13
EN EN1 15 U13
NTHWD HA6 22 A10
Eastbury Ct OXHEY WD19 * 22 E5
Eastbury Gv CHSWK W4 48 E10
Eastbury Rd EHAM E6 52 J2
KUTN/CMB KT2 59 U12
NTHWD HA6 22 A11
OXHEY WD19 22 E5
ROMW/RG RM7 42 D4
STMC/STPC BR5 77 M4
Eastbury Sq BARK IG11 41 P13
Eastbury Ter WCHPL E1 51 P2
Eastcastle St GTPST W1W 4 A11
Eastcheap FENCHST EC3M 5 R13
East Churchfield Rd ACT W3 48 D6
Eastchurch Rd HTHAIR TW6 58 A1
East Cl EA W5 48 A2
EBAR EN4 25 U2
GFD/PVL UB6 35 L14
RAIN RM13 54 H2
Eastcombe Av CHARL SE7 52 D11
East Common CFSP/GDCR SL9 32 C4
Eastcote ORP BR6 77 P6
Eastcote Av E/WMO/HCT KT8 70 H3
GFD/PVL UB6 35 Q10
RYLN/HDSTN HA2 34 K7
Eastcote La RYLN/HDSTN HA2 34 H9
Eastcote La North NTHLT UB5 34 H11
Eastcote Rd RSLP HA4 34 A5
RYLN/HDSTN HA2 35 L8
WELL DA16 53 M14
Eastcote St BRXN/ST SW9 50 C14
Eastcote Vw PIN HA5 34 E2
East Ct ALP/SUD HA0 35 S7
East Crs EN EN1 26 J3
FBAR/BDGN N11 25 T9
Eastcroft Rd HOR/WEW KT19 72 E12
East Cross Route HOM E9 39 R12
Eastdean Av EPSOM KT18 84 B3
East Dene Dr HARH RM3 30 K10
Eastdown Pk LEW SE13 63 V2
East Dr CAR SM5 73 S13
GSTN WD25 11 P10
NTHWD HA6 22 A7
STMC/STPC BR5 77 R4
East Duck Lees La PEND EN3 27 R2
East Dulwich Gv EDUL SE22 62 J3
East Dulwich Rd EDUL SE22 62 K2
East End Rd FNCH N3 25 N14
East End Wy PIN HA5 34 G1
East Entrance DAGE RM10 42 B14
Eastern Av CHERT KT16 69 L1
CHES/WCR EN8 16 F7
GNTH/NBYPK IG2 41 L4
PIN HA5 34 F5
SOCK/AV RM15 55 Q7
WAN E11 40 E4
WTHK RM20 55 T11
Eastern Av East ROM RM1 30 E14
Eastern Av West CHDH RM6 41 U2
Eastern Gtwy CAN/RD E16 52 E5
Eastern Perimeter Rd HTHAIR TW6 46 A14
Eastern Rd BROCKY SE4 63 S2
EFNCH N2 37 T1
PLSTW E13 40 D14
ROM RM1 42 F3
WALTH E17 39 U3
WDGN N22 26 C13
Eastern Vw BH/WHM TN16 88 E7
Easternville Gdns GNTH/NBYPK IG2 41 L4
Eastern Wy THMD SE28 53 Q7
Easter Wy GDST RH9 95 R14
East Ferry Rd POP/IOD E14 51 T9
Eastfield Av WATN WD24 11 R13
Eastfield Gdns DAGE RM10 42 A9
Eastfield Rd CEND/HSY/T N8 38 C1
CHES/WCR EN8 16 F6
DAGE RM10 42 A9
PEND EN3 16 D12
REDH RH1 93 V11
WALTH E17 39 S2
Eastfields PIN HA5 34 E3
Eastfields Av WAND/EARL SW18 61 N2
Eastfields Rd ACT W3 48 C3
MTCM CR4 61 U14
Eastfield St POP/IOD E14 51 Q3
East Gdns TOOT SW17 61 S11
WOKS/MYFD GU22 80 G7
Eastgate BNSTD SM7 85 M4
Eastgate Cl THMD SE28 53 T4
Eastglade NTHWD HA6 22 A10
PIN HA5 34 H1
East Hall La RAIN RM13 54 K4
East Hall Rd STMC/STPC BR5 77 U5
Eastham Cl BAR EN5 25 M3
East Ham Manor Wy EHAM E6 52 J4
East Harding St FLST/FETLN EC4A 4 K11

East Heath Rd HAMP NW3 37 R8
East Hl BH/WHM TN16 88 D8
DART DA1 67 M5
EYN DA4 67 R13
OXTED RH8 96 B5
SAND/SEL CR2 74 J14
WAND/EARL SW18 61 Q3
WBLY HA9 36 A7
WOKS/MYFD GU22 80 G6
East Hill Dr DART DA1 67 M5
East Hill Rd BGR/WK TN15 91 P2
OXTED RH8 96 A5
Eastholm GLDGN NW11 37 P2
East Holme ERITH DA8 54 D13
Eastholme HYS/HAR UB3 46 C6
East India Dock Rd POP/IOD E14 51 S4
East India Wy CROY/NA CR0 74 K6
Eastlake Rd CMBW SE5 50 F14
Eastlands Cl OXTED RH8 95 V3
Eastlands Crs EDUL SE22 62 K4
Eastlands Wy OXTED RH8 95 V3
East La ABLGY WD5 11 N2
ALP/SUD HA0 35 S8
BERM/RHTH SE16 51 L7
KUT/HW KT1 71 T1
Eastlea Av GSTN WD25 11 S11
Eastlea Ms CAN/RD E16 52 A2
Eastleigh Av RYLN/HDSTN HA2 34 K7
Eastleigh Cl BELMT SM2 73 P12
CRICK NW2 36 E8
Eastleigh Rd BXLYHN DA7 54 C14
WALTH E17 27 R14
Eastleigh Wy EBED/NFELT TW14 58 C6
East Lodge La ENC/FH EN2 15 M10
Eastman Rd ACT W3 48 D7
East Md RSLP HA4 34 F8
Eastmead Av GFD/PVL UB6 46 K1
Eastmead Cl BMLY BR1 64 G14
Eastmearn Rd DUL SE21 62 G7
Eastmont Rd ESH/CLAY KT10 71 N7
Eastmoor Pl CHARL SE7 52 F8
Eastmoor St CHARL SE7 52 F8
East Mount St WCHPL E1 51 M3
Eastney Rd CROY/NA CR0 74 F6
Eastney St GNWCH SE10 51 V10
Eastnor Pl REIG RH2 * 93 N12
Eastnor Rd ELTH/MOT SE9 65 L6
REIG RH2 93 M12
Easton Gdns BORE WD6 24 E2
Easton St FSBYW WC1X 4 J7
East Park Cl CHDH RM6 41 T3
East Parkside GNWCH SE10 52 A7
WARL CR6 87 S6
East Pas STBT EC1A 5 N9
East Pl WNWD SE27 62 G9
East Pole Cottages STHGT/OAK N14 * 26 B2
East Poultry Av FARR EC1M 5 L10
East Rp HTHAIR TW6 45 T13
East Ridgeway POTB/CUF EN6 15 N3
East Rd CHDH RM6 41 U3
CHEL SW3 7 S10
EBAR EN4 25 U6
EBED/NFELT TW14 57 V5
EDGW HA8 24 C13
IS N1 5 R5
KUTN/CMB KT2 59 U13
PEND EN3 16 C12
REIG RH2 93 M9
ROMW/RG RM7 42 D5
SRTFD E15 40 C13
WDR/YW UB7 45 R9
WELL DA16 53 R14
WEY KT13 69 V13
WIM/MER SW19 61 Q11
East Rochester Wy BFN/LL DA15 65 N3
DART DA1 66 D5
East Rw NKENS W10 2 B8
WAN E11 40 C4
Eastry Av HAYES BR2 76 B4
Eastry Rd ERITH DA8 54 A12
East Sheen Av MORT/ESHN SW14 60 D3
East Side SHB W12 * 48 J7
Eastside Rd GLDGN NW11 37 M2
East Smithfield WAP E1W 5 V14
East St BARK IG11 41 L12
BMLY BR1 64 C14
BTFD TW8 47 S12
BXLYHN DA7 66 A2
EW KT17 84 E2
WALW SE17 9 P9
East Surrey Gv PECK SE15 9 U14
East Tenter St WCHPL E1 5 V12
East Ter BFN/LL DA15 * 65 N6
East Towers PIN HA5 34 F4
East V ACT W3 * 48 F6
East Vw BAR EN5 14 B14
BAR EN5 25 M1
CHING E4 27 U10
Eastview Av WOOL/PLUM SE18 53 N12
Eastville Av GLDGN NW11 37 M4
East Wk EBAR EN4 25 U6
HYS/HAR UB3 46 C7
REIG RH2 93 P10
East Wy CROY/NA CR0 75 Q7
HYS/HAR UB3 46 C6
RSLP HA4 34 C6
WAB EN9 16 K10
Eastway HAYES BR2 76 C5
HOM E9 39 Q13
HOR/WEW KT19 84 C2
LEY E10 39 S9
MRDN SM4 72 K3
WAN E11 40 D3
WLGTN SM6 74 A9
Eastway Crs RYLN/HDSTN HA2 34 K7
Eastwell Cl BECK BR3 63 Q13
Eastwick Crs RKW/CH/CXG WD3 20 K7
Eastwick Dr GT/LBKH KT23 82 K14
Eastwick Park Av GT/LBKH KT23 82 K14
Eastwick Rd WOT/HER KT12 70 D11
Eastwood Cl HOLWY N7 38 E10
SWFD E18 28 C14
TOTM N17 * 27 M12
Eastwood Dr RAIN RM13 54 H4
Eastwood Rd GDMY/SEVK IG3 41 Q5
MUSWH N10 25 U14
SWFD E18 28 C14
WDR/YW UB7 45 S7
Eastwood St STRHM/NOR SW16 62 A11
Eastworth Rd CHERT KT16 68 K6
Eatington Rd LEY E10 39 V3
Eaton Cl BGVA SW1W 7 S7
STAN HA7 23 R9
Eaton Dr BRXN/ST SW9 62 F2
CRW RM5 30 B12
KUTN/CMB KT2 60 A12
Eaton Gdns DAGW RM9 41 U12
Eaton Ga BGVA SW1W 7 S7
NTHWD HA6 21 U11
Eaton La BGVA SW1W 7 V6
Eaton Ms North KTBR SW1X 7 T6
Eaton Ms South BGVA SW1W 7 T7
Eaton Ms West BGVA SW1W 7 T7
Eaton Pk COB KT11 82 G4
Eaton Park Rd COB KT11 82 H4
PLMGR N13 26 E7
Eaton Pl KTBR SW1X 7 S7
Eaton Ri EA W5 47 T4
WAN E11 40 E3
Eaton Rd BELMT SM2 73 R11
EN EN1 26 J1
HDN NW4 36 J3
HSLW TW3 59 M2
SCUP DA14 65 T7
UPMR RM14 43 S7
Eaton Rw BGVA SW1W 7 U5
Eatons Md CHING E4 27 S7
Eaton Sq BGVA SW1W 7 U6
Eaton Ter BGVA SW1W 7 S7
BOW E3 * 51 Q1
Eaton Terrace Ms BGVA SW1W 7 S7
Eatonville Rd TOOT SW17 61 T7
Eatonville Vls TOOT SW17 61 T7
Eaton Wy BORE WD6 12 K13
Eaves Cl ADL/WDHM KT15 69 N11
Ebba's Wy EPSOM KT18 84 B5
Ebbisham Dr VX/NE SW8 8 G11
Ebbisham La KWD/TDW/WH KT20 84 F11
Ebbisham Rd EPSOM KT18 84 B5
WPK KT4 72 J7
Ebbsfleet Rd CRICK NW2 37 L10
Ebdon Wy BKHTH/KID SE3 64 D1
Ebenezer St FSBYE EC1V 5 Q5
Ebenezer Wk STRHM/NOR SW16 62 A13
Ebley Cl PECK SE15 9 U12
Ebner St WAND/EARL SW18 61 P3
Ebor St WCHPL E1 5 U7
Ebrington Rd KTN/HRWW/WS HA3 35 S4
Ebsworth St FSTH SE23 63 P5
Eburne Rd HOLWY N7 38 C8
Ebury Ap RKW/CH/CXG WD3 21 P6
Ebury Br BGVA SW1W 7 U9
Ebury Bridge Rd BGVA SW1W 7 T10
Ebury Cl HAYES BR2 76 G8
NTHWD HA6 21 U10
Ebury Ms BGVA SW1W 7 T7
Ebury Ms East BGVA SW1W 7 U7
Ebury Rd RKW/CH/CXG WD3 21 P6
WAT WD17 22 F1
Ebury Sq BGVA SW1W 7 U8
Ebury St BGVA SW1W 7 T8
Ecclesbourne Cl PLMGR N13 26 E10
Ecclesbourne Gdns PLMGR N13 26 E10
Ecclesbourne Rd IS N1 38 G12
THHTH CR7 74 G3
Eccles Rd BTSEA SW11 61 T2
Eccleston Cl EBAR EN4 25 T3
ORP BR6 * 77 M6
Eccleston Crs CHDH RM6 41 R5
Ecclestone Ct WBLY HA9 35 U10
Ecclestone Ms WBLY HA9 35 U10
Ecclestone Pl WBLY HA9 35 V10
Eccleston Ms KTBR SW1X 7 T6
Eccleston Pl BGVA SW1W 7 U7
Eccleston Rd WEA W13 47 Q5
Eccleston Sq PIM SW1V 7 V8
Eccleston Square Ms PIM SW1V 7 V8
Eccleston St BGVA SW1W 7 T6
Echelforde Dr ASHF TW15 57 S9
Echo Hts CHING E4 * 27 T6
Eckford St IS N1 4 J3
Eckstein Rd BTSEA SW11 61 S2
Eclipse Rd PLSTW E13 52 D3
Ecton Rd ADL/WDHM KT15 69 M9
Ector Rd CAT SE6 64 A7
Edans Ct SHB W12 48 F7
Edbrooke Rd MV/WKIL W9 2 E8
Eddiscombe Rd FUL/PGN SW6 49 M14
Eddy Cl ROMW/RG RM7 42 B4
Eddystone Rd BROCKY SE4 63 Q3
Ede Cl HSLW TW3 58 H1
Edenbridge Cl BERM/RHTH SE16 51 M10
STMC/STPC BR5 77 T2
Edenbridge Rd EN EN1 26 J4
HOM E9 * 39 P12
Eden Cl ADL/WDHM KT15 69 M14
ALP/SUD HA0 35 T13
BXLY DA5 66 D9
DTCH/LGLY SL3 44 E10
HAMP NW3 37 N7
KENS W8 6 F5
PEND EN3 16 G12
Edencourt Rd STRHM/NOR SW16 61 V11
Edendale Rd BXLYHN DA7 54 D13
Edenfield Gdns WPK KT4 72 F8
Eden Gn SOCK/AV RM15 55 V3
Eden Gv HOLWY N7 38 D10
WLSDN NW10 36 H11
Eden Grove Rd BF/WBF KT14 81 Q3
Edenhall Rd HARH RM3 30 J10
Edenham Wy NKENS W10 2 C9
Edenhurst Av FUL/PGN SW6 61 M1
Eden Pde BECK BR3 * 75 Q2
Eden Park Av BECK BR3 75 S2
Eden Rd BECK BR3 75 Q2
BXLY DA5 66 C9
CROY/NA CR0 74 H9
WALTH E17 39 T3
WNWD SE27 62 F10
Edenside Rd GT/LBKH KT23 82 H14
Edensor Rd CHSWK W4 48 E12
Eden St KUT/HW KT1 59 T14
Edenvale CHESW EN7 16 B3
Edenvale Rd MTCM CR4 61 U12
Edenvale St FUL/PGN SW6 49 P14
Eden Wk KUT/HW KT1 * 59 U14
Eden Wy BECK BR3 75 S3
BOW E3 39 R13
WARL CR6 87 Q8
Ederline Av STRHM/NOR SW16 74 D1
Edes Cottages ASHTD KT21 * 83 T9
Edgar Cl SWLY BR8 78 F1
Edgar Kail Wy CMBW SE5 62 J1
Edgarley Ter FUL/PGN SW6 * 49 L13
Edgar Rd BGR/WK TN15 91 L7
BH/WHM TN16 88 F11
BOW E3 51 T1
HSLWW TW4 58 H5
SAND/SEL CR2 74 H14
WDR/YW UB7 45 Q5
Edgbaston Dr RAD WD7 12 J6
Edgeborough Wy BMLY BR1 64 F13
Edgebury CHST BR7 64 K9
Edge Cl WEY KT13 69 S12
Edgecombe Cl KUTN/CMB KT2 60 D12
Edgecoombe SAND/SEL CR2 75 P13
Edgecote Cl ACT W3 48 C6
Edgefield Av BARK IG11 41 P12
Edgefield Cl DART DA1 67 P6
Edge Hl WIM/MER SW19 60 K12
WOOL/PLUM SE18 52 K11
Edge Hill Av FNCH N3 37 N2
Edge Hill Ct WIM/MER SW19 60 K12
Edgehill Ct WOT/HER KT12 * 70 E6
Edgehill Gdns DAGE RM10 42 A9
Edgehill Rd CHST BR7 65 L8
MTCM CR4 61 V13
PUR/KEN CR8 74 E14
WEA W13 47 S4
Edgeley GT/LBKH KT23 82 G14
Edgeley La CLAP SW4 62 B1
Edgeley Rd CLAP SW4 62 A1
Edgell Cl VW GU25 68 D1
Edgell Rd STA TW18 56 K11
Edgel St WAND/EARL SW18 61 P3
Edge Point Cl STRHM/NOR SW16 62 F10
Edgepoint Cl WNWD SE27 * 62 F10
Edge St KENS W8 6 F1
Edgewood Dr ORP BR6 77 P10
Edgewood Gn CROY/NA CR0 75 P6
Edgeworth Av HDN NW4 36 G3
Edgeworth Cl CTHM CR3 87 L8
HDN NW4 36 G3
Edgeworth Crs HDN NW4 36 G3
Edgeworth Rd EBAR EN4 25 S2
ELTH/MOT SE9 64 E2
Edgington Rd STRHM/NOR SW16 62 B11
Edgington Wy SCUP DA14 65 S12
Edgwarebury Gdns EDGW HA8 24 A10
Edgwarebury La BORE WD6 23 V5
Edgware Rd BAY/PAD W2 3 L8
CDALE/KGS NW9 36 D1
CRICK NW2 36 J8
Edgware Rd Burnt Oak Broadway
EDGW HA8 24 B12
Edgware Rd High St EDGW HA8 24 A11
Edgware Rd The Hyde CDALE/KGS NW9 36 E2
Edgware Road Wy CRICK NW2 36 F7
Edgware Wy (Watford By-Pass)
EDGW HA8 23 U7
Edinburgh Av RKW/CH/CXG WD3 21 L5
Edinburgh Cl BETH E2 39 N14
HGDN/ICK UB10 33 T9
PIN HA5 34 G5
Edinburgh Ct KUT/HW KT1 * 71 U1
Edinburgh Crs CHES/WCR EN8 16 E7
Edinburgh Dr ABLGY WD5 11 N6
HGDN/ICK UB10 33 T9
STA TW18 57 P11
Edinburgh Ga DEN/HRF UB9 32 K4
KTBR SW1X 7 Q3
Edinburgh Rd HNWL W7 47 P7
PLSTW E13 40 D14
SUT SM1 73 Q7
UED N18 * 27 L10
WALTH E17 39 S3
Edington Rd ABYW SE2 53 R8
PEND EN3 16 C14
Edison Av HCH RM12 42 F6
Edison Cl HCH RM12 42 F6
WDR/YW UB7 45 R7
Edison Dr STHL UB1 46 K4
WBLY HA9 35 U7
Edison Gv WOOL/PLUM SE18 53 P12
Edison Rd CEND/HSY/T N8 38 B4
HAYES BR2 64 C14
PEND EN3 16 F14
WELL DA16 53 P13
Edis St CAMTN NW1 3 S1
Edith Cavell Wy WOOL/PLUM SE18 52 G13
Edith Gdns BRYLDS KT5 72 B5
Edith Gv WBPTN SW10 6 J12
Edithna St BRXN/ST SW9 62 C1
Edith Nesbit Wk ELTH/MOT SE9 64 G2
Edith Neville Cottages CAMTN NW1 4 C5
Edith Rd CHDH RM6 41 T5
EHAM E6 40 F12
FBAR/BDGN N11 26 B12
ORP BR6 77 Q10
SNWD SE25 74 H3
SRTFD E15 39 V10
WIM/MER SW19 61 P11
WKENS W14 6 B8
Edith Rw FUL/PGN SW6 49 P13
Edith St BETH E2 5 V3
Edith Ter WBPTN SW10 6 J13
Edith Vls WKENS W14 6 C8
Edith Yd WBPTN SW10 7 L13
Edlson Cl WALTH E17 39 S3
Edmansons Cl TOTM N17 26 K14
Edmeston Cl HOM E9 39 Q11
Edmund Gv FELT TW13 58 H7
Edmund Halley Wy GNWCH SE10 52 A7
Edmund Hurst Dr EHAM E6 52 K3
Edmund Ms KGLGY WD4 10 G3
Edmund Rd MTCM CR4 73 S1
RAIN RM13 54 E1
STMC/STPC BR5 77 S4
WELL DA16 65 Q1
Edmunds Av STMC/STPC BR5 77 T1
Edmunds Cl YEAD UB4 46 E3
Edmund St CMBW SE5 9 Q13
Edmunds Wk EFNCH N2 37 S2
Edna Rd RYNPK SW20 60 K14
Edna St BTSEA SW11 49 S13
Edrick Rd EDGW HA8 24 C11
Edrick Wk EDGW HA8 24 C11
Edric Rd NWCR SE14 51 P12
Edridge Cl BUSH WD23 22 K3
HCH RM12 42 K10
Edridge Rd CROY/NA CR0 74 G8
Edulf Rd BORE WD6 13 M14
Edward Amey Cl GSTN WD25 11 Q10
Edward Av CHING E4 27 T10
MRDN SM4 73 R3
Edward Cl ABLGY WD5 11 M6
ED N9 26 K5
GPK RM2 42 J1
HPTN TW12 59 L10
Edward Ct CAN/RD E16 52 C3
STA TW18 57 N11
WAB EN9 17 M7
Edwardes Pl KENS W8 * 6 D6
Edwardes Sq KENS W8 6 E6
Edward Gv EBAR EN4 25 R3
Edward II Av BF/WBF KT14 81 R4
Edward Mann Cl East WCHPL E1 * 51 P4
Edward Mann Cl West WCHPL E1 * 51 P4
Edward Ms CAMTN NW1 * 3 V5
Edward Pl DEPT SE8 51 R11
Edward Rd BH/WHM TN16 88 G8
BMLY BR1 64 D12
CHDH RM6 41 U4
CHST BR7 64 K10
COUL/CHIP CR5 86 B5
CROY/NA CR0 74 J5
EBAR EN4 25 R3
EBED/NFELT TW14 57 V3
HPTN TW12 59 L10
NTHLT UB5 34 E14
PGE/AN SE20 63 P12
RYLN/HDSTN HA2 35 L1
WALTH E17 39 P2
Edwards Av RSLP HA4 34 E10
Edwards Cl WPK KT4 72 K7
Edward's Cottages IS N1 * 38 F12
Edwards Ct EYN DA4 79 L8
Edwards Dr FBAR/BDGN N11 26 B12
Edwards Gdns SWLY BR8 78 D2
Edward's La STNW/STAM N16 38 H7
Edwards Ms IS N1 38 F12
MHST W1U 3 S12
Edwards Pl FBAR/BDGN N11 26 B12
Edward Sq IS N1 4 G2
Edwards Rd BELV DA17 54 A9
Edward St CAN/RD E16 52 C2
DEPT SE8 51 R11
Edward's Wy BROCKY SE4 63 S3
Edward Temme Av SRTFD E15 40 B12
Edward Tyler Rd LEE/GVPK SE12 64 D7
Edward Wy ASHF TW15 57 R7
Edwina Gdns REDBR IG4 40 G3
Edwin Av EHAM E6 52 J1
Edwin Cl BXLYHN DA7 53 V11
RAIN RM13 54 F1
Edwin Hall Pl LEW SE13 63 V4
Edwin Petty Pl RDART DA2 * 67 Q5
Edwin Pl CROY/NA CR0 74 H6
Edwin Rd EDGW HA8 24 D11
RDART DA2 66 H8
WHTN TW2 59 N6
Edwin's Md HOM E9 39 Q9
Edwin St CAN/RD E16 52 C3
WCHPL E1 51 N2
Edwin Ware Ct PIN HA5 * 22 E14
Edwyn Cl BAR EN5 24 J4
Effie Rd FUL/PGN SW6 6 F14
Effingham Cl BELMT SM2 73 P12
Effingham Ct WOKS/MYFD GU22 * 80 C9
Effingham Rd CEND/HSY/T N8 38 E3
CROY/NA CR0 74 D5
LEE/GVPK SE12 64 A3
REIG RH2 93 P11
SURB KT6 71 R5
Effort St TOOT SW17 61 S10
Effra Pde BRXS/STRHM SW2 62 E3
Effra Rd BRXS/STRHM SW2 62 E2
WIM/MER SW19 61 P11
Egan Cl PUR/KEN CR8 86 H10
Egan Wy HYS/HAR UB3 46 A5
Egbert St CAMTN NW1 3 S1
Egerton Av SWLY BR8 66 F13
Egerton Cl DART DA1 66 H6
PIN HA5 34 C2
Egerton Crs CHEL SW3 7 P7
Egerton Dr GNWCH SE10 51 T13
Egerton Gdns CHEL SW3 7 N7
GDMY/SEVK IG3 41 P8
HDN NW4 36 H2
WEA W13 47 R4
WLSDN NW10 * 36 J13
Egerton Gardens Ms CHEL SW3 7 P6
Egerton Pl CHEL SW3 * 7 P6
WEY KT13 69 U11
Egerton Rd ALP/SUD HA0 35 V12
NWMAL KT3 72 F2
SNWD SE25 74 J1
STNW/STAM N16 38 K5
WEY KT13 69 U11
WHTN TW2 59 N5
Egerton Ter CHEL SW3 7 P6
Egerton Wy HYS/HAR UB3 45 T12
Egg Farm La KGLGY WD4 10 J4
Egg Hall EPP CM16 18 E3
Egham By-Pass EGH TW20 56 D9
Egham Cl CHEAM SM3 73 L7
Egham Crs CHEAM SM3 72 K8
Egham Hl EGH TW20 56 C10
Egham Rd PLSTW E13 52 D3
Eglantine La EYN DA4 79 P4
Eglantine Rd WAND/EARL SW18 61 Q3
Egleston Rd MRDN SM4 73 P4
Egley Dr WOKS/MYFD GU22 80 B12
Egley Rd WOKS/MYFD GU22 80 B12
Eglington Rd CHING E4 27 V5
Eglinton Hl WOOL/PLUM SE18 52 K11
Eglinton Rd WOOL/PLUM SE18 52 J11
Eglise Rd WARL CR6 87 Q7
Egliston Ms PUT/ROE SW15 60 J1
Egliston Rd PUT/ROE SW15 60 J1
Eglon Ms CAMTN NW1 37 T12
Egmont Av SURB KT6 71 V6
Egmont Park Rd KWD/TDW/WH KT20 92 G1
Egmont Rd BELMT SM2 73 Q12
NWMAL KT3 72 F2
SURB KT6 71 V6
WOT/HER KT12 70 D5
Egmont St NWCR SE14 51 P12
Egmont Wy KWD/TDW/WH KT20 85 L9
Egremont Rd WNWD SE27 62 E8
Egret Wy YEAD UB4 46 F3
Eider Cl SRTFD E15 40 B10
Eighteenth Rd MTCM CR4 74 C2
Eighth Av HYS/HAR UB3 46 C6
KWD/TDW/WH KT20 * 93 M2
MNPK E12 40 H9
Eileen Rd SNWD SE25 74 H3
Eindhoven Cl CAR SM5 73 U6
WIM/MER SW19 61 R13
Eisenhower Dr EHAM E6 52 G3
Elaine Gv KTTN NW5 37 U10
Elam Cl CMBW SE5 50 F14
Elam St CMBW SE5 50 F14
Eland Rd BTSEA SW11 61 T1
CROY/NA CR0 74 F8
Elan Rd SOCK/AV RM15 55 U3
Elba Pl WALW SE17 * 9 P7
Elberon Av CROY/NA CR0 74 A4
Elbe St FUL/PGN SW6 49 Q14
Elborough Rd SNWD SE25 75 L3
Elborough St WAND/EARL SW18 61 N6
Elbow Meadow DTCH/LGLY SL3 * 44 K13
Elbury Dr CAN/RD E16 52 C4
Elcho St BTSEA SW11 7 N14
Elcot Av PECK SE15 51 M12
Elder Av CEND/HSY/T N8 38 C3
Elderbeck Cl CHESW EN7 16 A2
Elderberry Cl BARK/HLT IG6 28 K12
Elderberry Rd EA W5 47 U7
Elderberry Wy GSTN WD25 11 P9
Elder Cl BFN/LL DA15 65 P6
TRDG/WHET N20 25 P7
WDR/YW UB7 45 Q5
Elder Ct BUSH WD23 23 N7
Elderfield Rd CLPT E5 39 P9
Elderfield Wk WAN E11 40 D3
Elderflower Wy SRTFD E15 40 A12
Elder Oak Cl PGE/AN SE20 63 M13
Elder Rd WNWD SE27 62 G10
Eldersley Cl REDH RH1 93 T8
Eldersley Gdns REDH RH1 93 T8
Elderslie Cl BECK BR3 75 T4
Elderslie Rd ELTH/MOT SE9 64 J3
Elder St WCHPL E1 5 U9
Elderton Rd SYD SE26 63 Q9
Eldertree Wy MTCM CR4 61 V13
Elder Wk IS N1 5 N1
Elder Wy DTCH/LGLY SL3 * 44 D7
RAIN RM13 54 K1
Eldon Av BORE WD6 13 L14
CROY/NA CR0 75 N7
HEST TW5 46 J12
Eldon Gv HAMP NW3 37 R10
Eldon Pde WDGN N22 * 26 F13
Eldon Pk SNWD SE25 75 M2
Eldon Rd CTHM CR3 86 H11
ED N9 27 N6
KENS W8 6 H6
WALTH E17 39 R2
WDGN N22 26 F13
Eldon St LVPST EC2M 5 R10
Eldon Wy WLSDN NW10 36 B14
Eldred Dr STMC/STPC BR5 77 T7
Eldred Gdns UPMR RM14 43 S5
Eldridge Cl EBED/NFELT TW14 58 C6
Eleanora Ter SUT SM1 * 73 Q10
Eleanor Av HOR/WEW KT19 72 D14
Eleanor Cl BERM/RHTH SE16 51 P7
SEVS/STOTM N15 38 K1
Eleanor Crs MLHL NW7 24 K10
Eleanor Cross Rd CHES/WCR EN8 16 E8
Eleanor Gdns BAR EN5 24 K3
BCTR RM8 41 V8
Eleanor Gv BARN SW13 60 E1
HGDN/ICK UB10 33 T8
Eleanor Rd CFSP/GDCR SL9 20 A13
CHES/WCR EN8 16 E7
FBAR/BDGN N11 26 C11
HACK E8 39 M12
SRTFD E15 40 B11
Eleanor St BOW E3 51 S1
Eleanor Wy CHES/WCR EN8 16 F8
Electra Av HTHAIR TW6 58 B1
Electric Av BRXN/ST SW9 62 E2
PEND EN3 16 F10
Electric La BRXN/ST SW9 * 62 E2
Electric Pde SURB KT6 71 T4
Elephant & Castle STHWK SE1 9 M7
Elephant La BERM/RHTH SE16 51 N7
Elephant Rd WALW SE17 9 N7
Elers Rd HYS/HAR UB3 45 U9
WEA W13 47 S7
Eleven Acre Ri LOU IG10 28 H1
Eleventh Av KWD/TDW/WH KT20 * 93 M2
Eley Rd UED N18 27 P10
Elfindale Rd HNHL SE24 62 G3
Elfin Gv TEDD TW11 59 P10
Elford Cl BKHTH/KID SE3 64 E2
Elfort Rd HBRY N5 38 E9
Elfrida Crs CAT SE6 63 S9
Elfrida Rd WATW WD18 22 E3
Elf Rw WAP E1W 51 N5
Elfwine Rd HNWL W7 47 N3
Elgal Cl ORP BR6 76 K10
Elgar Av BRYLDS KT5 72 B6
EA W5 47 U7
STRHM/NOR SW16 74 C1
WLSDN NW10 36 D11
Elgar Cl BKHH IG9 28 F7
BORE WD6 23 S5
DEPT SE8 51 S12
HGDN/ICK UB10 33 S7
PLSTW E13 40 E14
Elgar St BERM/RHTH SE16 51 Q7
Elgin Av ASHF TW15 57 U11
HARH RM3 31 P12
KTN/HRWW/WS HA3 23 R14
MV/WKIL W9 2 G7
SHB W12 48 H8
Elgin Cl SHB W12 48 H7
Elgin Crs CTHM CR3 87 L12
HTHAIR TW6 46 A14
NTGHL W11 2 C12
Elgin Dr NTHWD HA6 22 A12
Elgin Est MV/WKIL W9 2 E8
Elgin Ms NTGHL W11 2 B12
Elgin Ms North MV/WKIL W9 2 H5
Elgin Ms South MV/WKIL W9 2 H6
Elgin Pl WEY KT13 * 69 U11
Elgin Rd CHES/WCR EN8 16 C4
CROY/NA CR0 74 K7
GDMY/SEVK IG3 41 N6
SUT SM1 73 Q8
WDGN N22 26 A14
WEY KT13 69 S11
WLGTN SM6 74 A11
Elgood Av NTHWD HA6 22 C12
Elgood Cl NTGHL W11 2 A14
Elham Cl BMLY BR1 64 F12
Elia Ms IS N1 5 L4
Elias Pl VX/NE SW8 8 J12
Elia St IS N1 5 L4
Elibank Rd ELTH/MOT SE9 64 J2
Elim St STHWK SE1 9 S5
Elim Wy PLSTW E13 52 B1
Eliot Bank FSTH SE23 63 M7
Eliot Dr RYLN/HDSTN HA2 34 K7
Eliot Gdns PUT/ROE SW15 60 G2
Eliot Hl LEW SE13 51 U14
Eliot Ms STJWD NW8 2 J4
Eliot Pk LEW SE13 51 U14
Eliot Pl BKHTH/KID SE3 52 A14
Eliot Rd DAGW RM9 41 T9
DART DA1 67 P3
Eliot V BKHTH/KID SE3 51 V14
Elizabethan Wy STWL/WRAY TW19 57 P5
Elizabeth Av ENC/FH EN2 26 F1
IL IG1 41 M7
IS N1 38 G12
STA TW18 57 N11
Elizabeth Barnes Ct FUL/PGN SW6 * 49 P14
Elizabeth Br BGVA SW1W 7 U8
Elizabeth Cl BAR EN5 24 K1
MV/WKIL W9 * 2 K8
ROMW/RG RM7 30 B13
SUT SM1 73 M9
Elizabeth Clyde Cl SEVS/STOTM N15 38 J2
Elizabeth Cottages RCH/KEW TW9 47 V13
Elizabeth Dr EPP CM16 18 C10
Elizabeth Fry Pl WOOL/PLUM SE18 52 G13
Elizabeth Gdns ACT W3 48 F6
ISLW TW7 59 Q2
STAN HA7 23 S11
SUN TW16 70 E1
Elizabeth Ms HAMP NW3 37 S11
Elizabeth Pl EYN DA4 * 79 M4
SEVS/STOTM N15 38 H2
Elizabeth Ride ED N9 27 M5
Elizabeth Rd BRWN CM15 31 V4
EHAM E6 40 F13
RAIN RM13 54 H3
SEVS/STOTM N15 38 J3
Elizabeth Sq BERM/RHTH SE16 51 Q5
Elizabeth St BGVA SW1W 7 T7
RDART DA2 67 S3
Elizabeth Wy FELT TW13 58 E9
NRWD SE19 62 H12
STMC/STPC BR5 77 S3
Eliza Cook Cl SWCM DA10 67 V2
Elkanette Ms TRDG/WHET N20 25 Q7
Elkington Rd PLSTW E13 52 D2
The Elkins ROM RM1 30 E14
Elkstone Rd NKENS W10 2 C9
Ellaline Rd HMSMTH W6 48 K11
Ella Ms HAMP NW3 37 T9
Ellanby Crs UED N18 27 M10
Elland Rd PECK SE15 63 N2
WOT/HER KT12 70 F7
Ella Rd CEND/HSY/T N8 38 C5
Ellement Cl PIN HA5 34 F3
Ellenborough Pl PUT/ROE SW15 60 G2
Ellenborough Rd SCUP DA14 65 T11
WDGN N22 26 G13
Ellenbridge Wy SAND/SEL CR2 74 J13
Ellenbrook Cl WATN WD24 * 11 Q13
Ellen Cl BMLY BR1 76 F1
Ellen Ct ED N9 27 N7
Ellen St WCHPL E1 51 L4
Ellen Webb Dr KTN/HRWW/WS HA3 35 N1
Elleray Rd TEDD TW11 59 P11
Ellerby St FUL/PGN SW6 48 K13
Ellerdale Cl HAMP NW3 37 Q10
Ellerdale Rd HAMP NW3 37 Q10
Ellerdale St LEW SE13 63 T2
Ellerdine Rd HSLW TW3 59 L2
Ellerker Gdns RCHPK/HAM TW10 59 U4
Ellerman Av WHTN TW2 58 H6
Ellerslie Rd SHB W12 48 H6
Ellerton Gdns DAGW RM9 41 S12
Ellerton Rd BARN SW13 * 48 G13
DAGW RM9 41 S12
RYNPK SW20 60 G12
SURB KT6 71 V7
WAND/EARL SW18 61 R6
Ellery Rd NRWD SE19 62 H12
Ellery St PECK SE15 51 M14
Ellesborough Cl OXHEY WD19 22 E10
Ellesmere Av BECK BR3 63 T14
MLHL NW7 24 D8
Ellesmere Cl RSLP HA4 33 U5
WAN E11 40 B3
Ellesmere Dr SAND/SEL CR2 87 M4
Ellesmere Gdns REDBR IG4 40 G4
Ellesmere Gv BAR EN5 25 M3
Ellesmere Pl WOT/HER KT12 70 A10
Ellesmere Rd BOW E3 39 Q14
GFD/PVL UB6 47 L2
TWK TW1 59 S4
WEY KT13 70 A11
WLSDN NW10 36 G10
Ellesmere St POP/IOD E14 51 T4
Ellice Rd OXTED RH8 96 B5
Ellies Ms ASHF TW15 57 Q7
Ellingfort Rd HACK E8 39 M12
Ellingham Rd CHSGTN KT9 71 T11
SHB W12 48 G7
SRTFD E15 39 V9
Ellington Rd FELT TW13 58 B9
HSLW TW3 46 K14
MUSWH N10 37 V2
Ellington St HOLWY N7 38 E11
Ellington Wy EPSOM KT18 84 H7
Elliot Cl SRTFD E15 40 A12
WBLY HA9 35 V8
WFD IG8 28 F11
Elliot Rd HDN NW4 36 H4
Elliott Av RSLP HA4 34 D7
Elliott Ct WOKN/KNAP GU21 * 80 E6
Elliott Gdns HARH RM3 30 H13
SHPTN TW17 69 S2
Elliott Rd BRXN/ST SW9 9 L14
CHSWK W4 48 E9
HAYES BR2 76 F2
STAN HA7 23 Q11
THHTH CR7 74 F2
Elliotts La BH/WHM TN16 89 S14
Elliott's Pl IS N1 5 M2
Elliott Sq HAMP NW3 37 S12
Elliott's Rw LBTH SE11 9 M7
Ellis Av CFSP/GDCR SL9 20 D13
RAIN RM13 54 G3
Ellis Cl COUL/CHIP CR5 86 D10
EDGW HA8 24 E11
ELTH/MOT SE9 65 L7
SWLY BR8 78 D2
WLSDN NW10 36 J11
Elliscombe Mt CHARL SE7 * 52 E11
Elliscombe Rd CHARL SE7 52 E11
Ellis Farm Cl WOKS/MYFD GU22 80 B12
Ellisfield Dr PUT/ROE SW15 60 F5
Ellison Gdns NWDGN UB2 46 H9
Ellison Rd BARN SW13 48 F14
BFN/LL DA15 65 M6
STRHM/NOR SW16 62 B12
Ellis Rd COUL/CHIP CR5 86 D10
MTCM CR4 73 T4
NWDGN UB2 47 L6
Ellis St KTBR SW1X 7 R7
Ellis Waterton Cl SWLY BR8 78 D2
Ellis Wy DART DA1 * 67 M7
Ellmore Cl HARH RM3 30 H13
Ellora Rd STRHM/NOR SW16 62 B10
Ellsworth St BETH E2 * 51 M1
Ellwood Gdns GSTN WD25 11 P8
Ellwood Ri CSTG HP8 20 A7
Elmar Rd SEVS/STOTM N15 38 H2
Elm Av EA W5 47 U6
OXHEY WD19 22 G5
RSLP HA4 34 C6
UPMR RM14 43 P8
Elmbank STHGT/OAK N14 26 C5
Elmbank Av BAR EN5 24 J2
Elmbank Dr BMLY BR1 64 F14
Elm Bank Gdns BARN SW13 48 E14
Elmbank Wy HNWL W7 47 M3
Elmbourne Dr BELV DA17 54 B9
Elmbourne Rd TOOT SW17 61 V8
Elmbridge Av BRYLDS KT5 72 C4
Elmbridge Cl RSLP HA4 34 C4
Elmbridge Dr RSLP HA4 34 C4
Elmbridge La WOKS/MYFD GU22 80 D9
Elmbridge Rd BARK/HLT IG6 29 Q11
Elmbridge Wk HACK E8 * 39 L12
Elmbrook Cl SUN TW16 58 D13
Elmbrook Gdns ELTH/MOT SE9 64 G2
Elmbrook Rd SUT SM1 73 M9
Elm Cl BKHH IG9 28 F7
BRYLDS KT5 72 C5
CAR SM5 73 T6
DART DA1 66 J6
HDN NW4 36 K3
HYS/HAR UB3 46 C4
KWD/TDW/WH KT20 92 C6
LHD/OX KT22 83 R12
ROMW/RG RM7 30 B13
RPLY/SEND GU23 81 L14
RYLN/HDSTN HA2 34 K4
RYNPK SW20 72 J2
SAND/SEL CR2 74 H11
STWL/WRAY TW19 57 P6
WAB EN9 16 K8
WAN E11 40 D4
WARL CR6 87 P7
WHTN TW2 58 K7
WOKN/KNAP GU21 80 B5
Elmcote Wy RKW/CH/CXG WD3 21 R4
Elm Cottages GDST RH9 * 95 M6
MTCM CR4 * 61 T14
Elm Ct WAT WD17 * 22 D1
Elmcourt Rd WNWD SE27 62 F7
Elm Crs EA W5 47 U7
KUTN/CMB KT2 59 U13
Elmcroft CEND/HSY/T N8 38 D3
Elm Cft DTCH/LGLY SL3 44 A13
Elmcroft GT/LBKH KT23 * 82 J14
Elmcroft Av BFN/LL DA15 65 P5
ED N9 27 M4
GLDGN NW11 37 M5
WAN E11 40 D3
Elmcroft Cl CHSGTN KT9 * 71 U8
EA W5 47 T4
EBED/NFELT TW14 58 B4
Elmcroft Crs GLDGN NW11 36 K5
RYLN/HDSTN HA2 34 J1
Elmcroft Dr ASHF TW15 * 57 S10
CHSGTN KT9 71 U8
Elmcroft Gdns CDALE/KGS NW9 36 A3
Elmcroft Rd ORP BR6 77 Q5
Elmcroft St CLPT E5 39 N9
Elmcroft Ter UX/CGN UB8 * 45 S4
Elmdale Rd PLMGR N13 26 D10
Elmdene BRYLDS KT5 72 C6
Elmdene Av EMPK RM11 43 M3
Elmdene Cl BECK BR3 75 R3
Elmdene Ct WOKS/MYFD GU22 80 C9
Elmdene Rd WOOL/PLUM SE18 52 K10
Elmdon Rd HSLWW TW4 46 F14
HTHAIR TW6 58 B1
SOCK/AV RM15 55 U3
Elm Dr CHES/WCR EN8 16 E2
LHD/OX KT22 83 R12
RYLN/HDSTN HA2 34 K4
SUN TW16 58 E14
SWLY BR8 66 D14
Elmer Av ABR/ST RM4 30 E8
Elmer Cl ENC/FH EN2 26 D1
RAIN RM13 42 G12
Elmer Cottages LHD/OX KT22 * 83 Q13
Elmer Gdns EDGW HA8 24 B12
ISLW TW7 59 M1
RAIN RM13 42 G12
Elmer Ms LHD/OX KT22 83 Q13
Elmer Rd CAT SE6 63 U5
Elmer's Dr TEDD TW11 59 R11
Elmers End Rd BECK BR3 75 N1
PGE/AN SE20 63 N14
Elmerside Rd BECK BR3 75 Q2
Elmers Rd SNWD SE25 75 L5
Elmfield GT/LBKH KT23 82 J13
Elmfield Av CEND/HSY/T N8 38 C3
MTCM CR4 61 U13
TEDD TW11 59 P10
Elmfield Cl HRW HA1 35 N7
POTB/CUF EN6 14 A7
Elmfield Pk BMLY BR1 76 C1
Elmfield Rd BMLY BR1 76 C1
CHING E4 27 U7
EFNCH N2 37 R1
NWDGN UB2 46 G8
POTB/CUF EN6 14 A7
TOOT SW17 61 V7
WALTH E17 39 P4
Elmfield Wy MV/WKIL W9 2 D7
SAND/SEL CR2 74 K13
Elm Friars Wk CAMTN NW1 38 B12
Elm Gdns EFNCH N2 37 Q1
ENC/FH EN2 15 T12
EPSOM KT18 84 J9
ESH/CLAY KT10 71 P11
MTCM CR4 74 B2
Elmgate Av FELT TW13 58 D8
Elmgate Gdns EDGW HA8 24 C10
Elm Gn ACT W3 48 E4
Elmgreen Cl SRTFD E15 40 A13
Elm Gv CEND/HSY/T N8 38 C4
CRICK NW2 36 K9
CTHM CR3 86 J12
EMPK RM11 43 L4
EPSOM KT18 84 C4
ERITH DA8 54 D12
KUTN/CMB KT2 59 U13
ORP BR6 77 P6
PECK SE15 51 L14
RYLN/HDSTN HA2 34 J5
SUT SM1 73 P9
WATN WD24 11 N11
WDR/YW UB7 45 R5
WIM/MER SW19 61 L12
Elmgrove Crs HRW HA1 35 P3
Elmgrove Gdns HRW HA1 35 Q3
Elm Grove Pde CAR SM5 73 U8
Elm Grove Rd BARN SW13 48 G14
COB KT11 82 F6
Elmgrove Rd CROY/NA CR0 75 M6
Elm Grove Rd EA W5 47 U7
Elmgrove Rd HRW HA1 35 P3
WEY KT13 69 T8
Elm Hall Gdns WAN E11 40 D4
Elm Hatch PIN HA5 22 H12
Elmhurst BELV DA17 53 U11
Elmhurst Av EFNCH N2 * 37 R1
MTCM CR4 61 U12
Elmhurst Cl BUSH WD23 22 G2
Elmhurst Crs EFNCH N2 37 R1
Elmhurst Dr EMPK RM11 42 J5
SWFD E18 28 C14
Elmhurst Rd DTCH/LGLY SL3 44 E8
ELTH/MOT SE9 64 G7
FSTGT E7 40 D12
PEND EN3 16 C11
TOTM N17 26 J14
Elmhurst St CLAP SW4 62 B1
Elmhurst Wy LOU IG10 28 H5
Elmington Cl BXLY DA5 66 B5
Elmington Est WALW SE17 9 Q14
Elmington Rd CMBW SE5 9 R14
CMBW SE5 50 H13
Elmira St LEW SE13 63 T1
Elm La CAT SE6 63 R7
RPLY/SEND GU23 81 R9
Elm Lawn Cl UX/CGN UB8 33 Q12
Elmlee Cl CHST BR7 64 H11
Elmley St WOOL/PLUM SE18 53 M9
Elmore Cl ALP/SUD HA0 35 U14
Elmore Rd COUL/CHIP CR5 85 T11
PEND EN3 16 D13
WAN E11 39 U8
Elmores LOU IG10 28 J1
Elmore St IS N1 38 H12
Elm Pde SCUP DA14 * 65 Q9
Elm Pk BRXS/STRHM SW2 62 D4
STAN HA7 23 R10
Elm Park Av HCH RM12 42 H9
SEVS/STOTM N15 38 K3
Elm Park Gdns HDN NW4 36 K3
Elmpark Gdns SAND/SEL CR2 75 N14
Elm Park Gdns WBPTN SW10 7 L10
Elm Park La CHEL SW3 7 L11
Elm Park Rd CHEL SW3 7 L11
FNCH N3 25 M12
LEY E10 39 Q6
PIN HA5 34 F1
SNWD SE25 74 K1
WCHMH N21 26 G5
Elm Pl SKENS SW7 7 L9
Elm Rd BAR EN5 25 M2
BECK BR3 63 R14
BH/WHM TN16 97 N1
CHSGTN KT9 71 U9
DART DA1 66 K6
EBED/NFELT TW14 57 V6
ERITH DA8 54 G13
ESH/CLAY KT10 71 P11
EW KT17 72 F11
FSTGT E7 40 B11
KUTN/CMB KT2 59 V13
LHD/OX KT22 83 R12
MORT/ESHN SW14 60 C1
NWMAL KT3 72 D1
ORP BR6 77 Q12
PUR/KEN CR8 86 F3
RDART DA2 67 S4
REDH RH1 93 S10
ROMW/RG RM7 30 B14
SCUP DA14 65 Q9
SOCK/AV RM15 55 R6
THHTH CR7 74 G2
WALTH E17 39 U3
WARL CR6 87 P7
WBLY HA9 35 U10
WDGN N22 26 F13
WLGTN SM6 73 U6
WOKN/KNAP GU21 80 B8
WOKN/KNAP GU21 80 D5
Elm Rd West CHEAM SM3 73 M5
Elm Rw HAMP NW3 37 Q8
Elmroyd Av POTB/CUF EN6 14 B7
Elmroyd Cl POTB/CUF EN6 14 B7
Elms WAB EN9 17 Q9
Elms Av HDN NW4 36 J3
MUSWH N10 37 V1
Elmscott Gdns WCHMH N21 26 G4
Elmscott Rd BMLY BR1 64 B10
Elms Ct ALP/SUD HA0 35 P9
Elms Crs CLAP SW4 62 A4
Elmscroft Gdns POTB/CUF EN6 14 B6
Elmsdale Rd WALTH E17 39 R2
Elms Farm Rd HCH RM12 42 J10
Elms Gdns ALP/SUD HA0 35 Q9
DAGW RM9 41 V9
Elmshaw Rd PUT/ROE SW15 60 G3
Elmshorn EW KT17 84 J6
Elmshurst Crs EFNCH N2 37 Q2
Elmside CROY/NA CR0 75 T11
Elmside Rd WBLY HA9 36 A8
Elms La ALP/SUD HA0 35 Q9
Elmsleigh Av KTN/HRWW/WS HA3 35 R2
Elmsleigh Rd STA TW18 56 K10
WHTN TW2 59 M7
Elmslie Cl EPSOM KT18 84 D4
WFD IG8 28 H11
Elms Ms BAY/PAD W2 3 L13
Elms Park Av ALP/SUD HA0 35 Q9
Elms Rd CFSP/GDCR SL9 20 C12
CLAP SW4 62 A3
KTN/HRWW/WS HA3 23 N12
Elmstead Av CHST BR7 64 H10
WBLY HA9 35 U6
Elmstead Cl HOR/WEW KT19 72 E10
TRDG/WHET N20 25 N7
Elmstead Gdns WPK KT4 72 G8
Elmstead Gld CHST BR7 64 H11
Elmstead La CHST BR7 64 G12
Elmstead Rd BF/WBF KT14 81 L3
ERITH DA8 54 E13
GDMY/SEVK IG3 41 N7
Elmsted Crs WELL DA16 53 S11
The Elms BARN SW13 60 F1
BORE WD6 * 13 L13
ESH/CLAY KT10 * 71 P12
LOU IG10 * 17 M14
NFNCH/WDSPK N12 * 25 S10
TOOT SW17 * 61 U8
WARL CR6 87 N5
WLGTN SM6 * 74 A9
Elmstone Rd FUL/PGN SW6 49 N13
Elmstone Ter STMC/STPC BR5 * 77 S2
Elm St FSBYW WC1X 4 H8
Elmsway ASHF TW15 57 R10
Elmswood GT/LBKH KT23 82 H14
Elmsworth Av HSLW TW3 46 K14
Elm Ter CRICK NW2 37 N8
ELTH/MOT SE9 64 J4
KTN/HRWW/WS HA3 23 M12
WTHK RM20 55 V11
Elmton Wy CLPT E5 39 L8
Elm Tree Av ESH/CLAY KT10 71 M5
Elm Tree Cl ASHF TW15 57 T10
Elmtree Cl BF/WBF KT14 81 R3
Elm Tree Cl CHERT KT16 68 J7
NTHLT UB5 46 H1
STJWD NW8 3 L5
Elm Tree Ct CHARL SE7 * 52 E11
Elm Tree Rd STJWD NW8 3 L6
Elmtree Rd TEDD TW11 59 N10
Elm Tree Wk RKW/CH/CXG WD3 * 20 K2
Elm Vls HNWL W7 * 47 N5
Elm Wk GPK RM2 42 G1
HAMP NW3 37 N7
ORP BR6 76 H8
RAD WD7 12 D10
RYNPK SW20 72 J2
Elm Wy BRW CM14 31 U8
FBAR/BDGN N11 25 U11
HOR/WEW KT19 72 D10
RKW/CH/CXG WD3 21 M6
WLSDN NW10 36 E9
WPK KT4 72 J8
Elmwood CHIG IG7 29 M11
Elmwood Av BORE WD6 24 B2
FELT TW13 58 D8
KTN/HRWW/WS HA3 35 Q3
PLMGR N13 26 C10
Elmwood Cl EW KT17 72 G12
WLGTN SM6 73 V7
Elmwood Ct ASHTD KT21 83 T7
Elmwood Crs CDALE/KGS NW9 36 C2
Elmwood Dr BXLY DA5 65 U5
EW KT17 72 G12
Elmwood Gdns HNWL W7 47 N4
Elmwood Pk CFSP/GDCR SL9 32 C6
Elmwood Rd CHSWK W4 48 C11
CROY/NA CR0 74 F5
HNHL SE24 62 H3
MTCM CR4 73 T1
REDH RH1 93 U6
Elmworth Gv DUL SE21 62 H7
Elnathan Ms MV/WKIL W9 2 H8
Elphinstone Rd WALTH E17 27 R14
Elphinstone St HBRY N5 38 F9
Elrick Cl ERITH DA8 54 E11
Elrington Rd HACK E8 39 L11
WFD IG8 28 C10
Elruge Cl WDR/YW UB7 45 P8
Elsa Cottages POP/IOD E14 * 51 Q3
Elsa Rd WELL DA16 53 S14
Elsa St WCHPL E1 * 51 Q3
Elsdale St HOM E9 39 N11
Elsden Ms BETH E2 * 39 N14
Elsden Rd TOTM N17 26 K13
Elsenham Rd MNPK E12 40 H10
Elsenham St WAND/EARL SW18 61 M6
Elsham Rd WAN E11 40 A8
WKENS W14 6 A4
Elsham Ter WKENS W14 6 A4
Elsiedene Rd WCHMH N21 26 G5
Elsie Lane Ct BAY/PAD W2 2 G10
Elsiemaud Rd BROCKY SE4 63 R3
Elsie Rd EDUL SE22 62 K2
Elsinge Rd EN EN1 16 B10
Elsinore Av STWL/WRAY TW19 * 57 Q5
Elsinore Gdns CRICK NW2 * 37 L8
Elsinore Rd FSTH SE23 63 Q6
Elsinore Wy RCH/KEW TW9 60 B1
Elsley Rd BTSEA SW11 61 T1
Elspeth Rd ALP/SUD HA0 35 U10
BTSEA SW11 61 T2
Elsrick Av MRDN SM4 73 N3
Elstan Wy CROY/NA CR0 75 Q5
Elsted St WALW SE17 9 R8
Elstow Cl ELTH/MOT SE9 64 H3
RSLP HA4 34 F5
Elstow Gdns DAGW RM9 41 U13
Elstow Rd DAGW RM9 41 U12
Elstree Cl HCH RM12 42 H12
Elstree Gdns BELV DA17 53 U9
ED N9 27 M6
IL IG1 41 L10
Elstree Ga BORE WD6 * 13 P14
Elstree Hl BMLY BR1 64 A12
Elstree Hl North BORE WD6 23 T3
Elstree Hl South BORE WD6 23 T5
Elstree Pk BORE WD6 * 24 D4
Elstree Rd BORE WD6 23 Q4
BUSH WD23 23 M6
Elstree Wy BORE WD6 13 N14
Elswick Rd LEW SE13 51 T14
Elswick St FUL/PGN SW6 49 Q14
Elsworth Cl EBED/NFELT TW14 58 A6
Elsworthy THDIT KT7 71 N4
Elsworthy Ri HAMP NW3 37 S12
Elsworthy Rd HAMP NW3 3 N1
Elsworthy Ter HAMP NW3 37 S12
Elsynge Rd WAND/EARL SW18 61 R3
Eltham Gn ELTH/MOT SE9 64 E3
Eltham Green Rd ELTH/MOT SE9 64 E3
Eltham High St ELTH/MOT SE9 64 H4
Eltham Hl ELTH/MOT SE9 64 F3
Eltham Palace Rd ELTH/MOT SE9 64 F4
Eltham Park Gdns ELTH/MOT SE9 64 J2
Eltham Rd ELTH/MOT SE9 64 E3
Elthiron Rd FUL/PGN SW6 49 N13
Elthorne Av HNWL W7 47 P7
Elthorne Ct FELT TW13 58 E6
Elthorne Park Rd HNWL W7 47 P8
Elthorne Rd ARCH N19 38 B7
CDALE/KGS NW9 36 D5
UX/CGN UB8 33 P14
Elthorne Wy CDALE/KGS NW9 36 D4
Elthruda Rd LEW SE13 63 V4
Eltisley Rd IL IG1 40 K9
Elton Av BAR EN5 25 M3
GFD/PVL UB6 35 P11
Elton Cl KUT/HW KT1 59 S12
Elton Pk WAT WD17 11 N14
Elton Pl STNW/STAM N16 38 J10
Elton Rd KUTN/CMB KT2 59 V13
PUR/KEN CR8 86 A2
Eltringham St WAND/EARL SW18 61 Q2
Elvaston Ms SKENS SW7 6 K6
Elvaston Pl SKENS SW7 6 K6
Elveden Cl WOKS/MYFD GU22 81 M7
Elveden Pl WLSDN NW10 36 A14
WOKS/MYFD GU22 * 81 M7
Elveden Rd COB KT11 82 E2
WLSDN NW10 36 A14
Elvedon Rd FELT TW13 58 B8
Elvendon Rd FBAR/BDGN N11 26 C11
Elver Gdns BETH E2 51 L1
Elverson Ms DEPT SE8 * 51 R12
Elverson Rd DEPT SE8 51 T14
Elverton St WEST SW1P 8 C7
Elvet Av GPK RM2 42 J2
Elvington Gn HAYES BR2 76 B3
Elvington La CDALE/KGS NW9 24 E13
Elvino Rd SYD SE26 63 P10
Elvis Rd CRICK NW2 36 J11
Elwell Cl EGH TW20 56 E11
Elwill Wy BECK BR3 75 V2
Elwin St BETH E2 51 L1
Elwood St HBRY N5 38 F8
Elwyn Gdns LEE/GVPK SE12 64 C5
Ely Cl ERITH DA8 54 F14
NWMAL KT3 60 F14
Ely Cottages VX/NE SW8 * 8 G14
Ely Gdns BORE WD6 24 D3
DAGE RM10 42 C8
Elyne Rd FSBYPK N4 38 E4
Ely Pl HCIRC EC1N 4 K10
WFD IG8 28 J10
Ely Rd CROY/NA CR0 74 H3
HSLWW TW4 58 E1
HTHAIR TW6 46 B14
LEY E10 39 U4
Elysian Av STMC/STPC BR5 77 N4
Elysium Pl FUL/PGN SW6 49 M14
Elysium St FUL/PGN SW6 49 M14
Elystan Cl WLGTN SM6 74 A13
Elystan Pl CHEL SW3 7 P9
Elystan St CHEL SW3 7 N8
Elystan Wk IS N1 4 J2
Emanuel Av ACT W3 48 C4
Embankment PUT/ROE SW15 60 K1
Embankment Gdns CHEL SW3 7 R11
Embankment Pl CHCR WC2N 8 F1
The Embankment STWL/WRAY TW19 56 A5
TWK TW1 59 Q6
Embassy Ct SCUP DA14 65 R8
WLGTN SM6 * 73 V11
Emba St BERM/RHTH SE16 51 L7
Ember Cl ADL/WDHM KT15 69 Q10
STMC/STPC BR5 77 L5
Embercourt Rd THDIT KT7 71 N4
Ember Farm Av E/WMO/HCT KT8 71 M4
Ember Farm Wy E/WMO/HCT KT8 71 M3
Ember Gdns THDIT KT7 71 N5
Ember La ESH/CLAY KT10 71 M6
Ember Rd DTCH/LGLY SL3 44 F8
Emblem Ct EDUL SE22 63 L3
Embleton Rd LEW SE13 63 T2
OXHEY WD19 22 C8
Embry Cl STAN HA7 23 Q9
Embry Dr STAN HA7 23 Q11
Embry Wy STAN HA7 23 Q10
Emden Cl WDR/YW UB7 45 S7
Emden St FUL/PGN SW6 49 P13
Emerald Cl CAN/RD E16 52 G4
Emerald Gdns BCTR RM8 41 V6
Emerald Sq NWDGN UB2 46 F8
Emerald St BMSBY WC1N 4 G9
Emerson Dr EMPK RM11 42 K5
Emerson Gdns KTN/HRWW/WS HA3 35 V4
Emerson Rd IL IG1 40 J5
Emersons Av SWLY BR8 66 F12
Emerson St STHWK SE1 9 N1
Emerton Cl BXLYHS DA6 65 U2
Emerton Rd LHD/OX KT22 83 L10
Emery Hill St WEST SW1P 8 B6
Emery St STHWK SE1 8 K5
Emes Rd ERITH DA8 54 C12
Emilia Cl PEND EN3 27 M3
Emily Davison Dr EPSOM KT18 84 H8
Emily St CAN/RD E16 52 B4
Emley Rd ADL/WDHM KT15 69 M9
Emlyn La LHD/OX KT22 83 Q12
Emlyn Rd REDH RH1 93 U12
SHB W12 48 E7
Emmanuel Rd BAL SW12 62 A6
NTHWD HA6 22 B12
Emma Rd PLSTW E13 40 B14
Emma St BETH E2 39 M14
Emma Ter RYNPK SW20 * 60 J12
Emmaus Wy CHIG IG7 28 J10
Emmetts Cl WOKN/KNAP GU21 80 B7
Emmetts Rd BH/WHM TN16 97 S6
Emmitt Cl RAD WD7 12 J7
Emmott Av BARK/HLT IG6 41 L3
Emmott Cl GLDGN NW11 37 Q4
WCHPL E1 51 Q2
Emperor's Ga SKENS SW7 6 J7
Empire Av UED N18 26 G11
Empire Centre WATN WD24 * 11 Q13
Empire Pde UED N18 * 26 H11
WBLY HA9 * 36 A8
Empire Rd GFD/PVL UB6 35 S13
Empire Sq STHWK SE1 9 Q4
Empire Wy WBLY HA9 35 V9
Empire Wharf Rd POP/IOD E14 51 V9
Empress Av CHING E4 27 T12
IL IG1 40 J7
MNPK E12 40 E7
WFD IG8 28 B12
Empress Dr CHST BR7 64 K11
Empress Pde CHING E4 * 27 S12
Empress Pl FUL/PGN SW6 6 E10
Empress St WALW SE17 9 P11
Empson St BOW E3 51 T2
Emsworth Cl ED N9 27 N6
Emsworth Rd BARK/HLT IG6 28 K14
Emsworth St BRXS/STRHM SW2 62 D7
Emu Rd VX/NE SW8 49 V14
Ena Rd STRHM/NOR SW16 74 C1
Enborne Gn SOCK/AV RM15 55 U3
Enbrook St NKENS W10 2 B6
Enclave Ct FSBYE EC1V 5 M7
Endale Cl CAR SM5 73 T7
Endeavour Rd CHES/WCR EN8 16 E1
Endeavour Wy BARK IG11 41 Q14
CROY/NA CR0 74 C5
WIM/MER SW19 61 P9
Endell St LSQ/SEVD WC2H 4 E11
Enderby St GNWCH SE10 52 A10
Enderley Rd KTN/HRWW/WS HA3 23 M13
Endersby Rd BAR EN5 24 J3
Endersleigh Gdns HDN NW4 36 G2
Endlebury Rd CHING E4 27 U7
Endlesham Rd BAL SW12 61 U5
Endsleigh Cl SAND/SEL CR2 75 N14
Endsleigh Gdns IL IG1 40 H6
STPAN WC1H 4 C7
SURB KT6 71 S4
WOT/HER KT12 70 E10
Endsleigh Pl STPAN WC1H 4 D7
Endsleigh Rd NWDGN UB2 46 H9
REDH RH1 94 A5
WEA W13 47 Q5
Endsleigh St STPAN WC1H 4 D7
Endway BRYLDS KT5 72 A5
Endwell Rd BROCKY SE4 51 Q14
Endymion Rd BRXS/STRHM SW2 62 D5
FSBYPK N4 38 F5
Energen Cl WLSDN NW10 36 E11
Enfield Cl UX/CGN UB8 33 P14
Enfield Rd ACT W3 48 B7
BTFD TW8 47 T10
ENC/FH EN2 26 B2
HTHAIR TW6 46 A14
IS N1 38 J12
Enford St CAMTN NW1 3 Q9
Engadine Cl CROY/NA CR0 74 K8
Engadine St WAND/EARL SW18 61 M6
Engate St LEW SE13 63 U2
Engayne Gdns UPMR RM14 43 P6
Engel Pk MLHL NW7 24 J11
Engineer Cl WOOL/PLUM SE18 52 J11
Engineers Wy WBLY HA9 36 A9
England's La HAMP NW3 37 T11
LOU IG10 17 U14
England Wy NWMAL KT3 72 B2
Englefield Cl CROY/NA CR0 74 G4
EGH TW20 56 A11
ENC/FH EN2 15 Q14
STMC/STPC BR5 77 P2
Englefield Crs STMC/STPC BR5 77 Q3
Englefield Pth STMC/STPC BR5 77 Q2
Englefield Rd IS N1 38 H12
Engleheart Dr EBED/NFELT TW14 58 B4
Engleheart Rd CAT SE6 63 T5
Englehurst EGH TW20 56 A11
Englemere Pk COB KT11 82 K4
Englewood Rd BAL SW12 61 V4
Engliff La WOKS/MYFD GU22 80 K6
English Gdns STWL/WRAY TW19 56 B2
English St BOW E3 51 R2
Enid Cl LCOL/BKTW AL2 11 T5
Enid St BERM/RHTH SE16 9 V5
Enmore Av SNWD SE25 75 L3
Enmore Gdns MORT/ESHN SW14 60 D3
Enmore Rd PUT/ROE SW15 60 J2
SNWD SE25 75 L3
STHL UB1 46 J2
Ennerdale Av HCH RM12 42 G10
STAN HA7 35 S1
Ennerdale Cl EBED/NFELT TW14 58 B6
SUT SM1 73 M9
Ennerdale Dr CDALE/KGS NW9 36 E3
Ennerdale Gdns WBLY HA9 35 S6
Ennerdale Rd BXLYHN DA7 54 A13
RCH/KEW TW9 47 V14
Ennersdale Rd LEW SE13 63 V3
Ennismore Av CHSWK W4 48 E9
GFD/PVL UB6 35 N11
Ennismore Gdns SKENS SW7 7 N5
THDIT KT7 71 N4
Ennismore Gardens Ms SKENS SW7 7 N5
Ennismore Ms SKENS SW7 7 N5
Ennismore St SKENS SW7 7 N5
Ennis Rd FSBYPK N4 38 E6
WOOL/PLUM SE18 53 M11
Ensign Cl PUR/KEN CR8 74 E14
STWL/WRAY TW19 57 P6
Ensign Dr PLMGR N13 26 G8
Ensign St WCHPL E1 51 L5
Ensign Wy STWL/WRAY TW19 57 P6
WLGTN SM6 74 C12
Enslin Rd ELTH/MOT SE9 64 J4
Ensor Ms SKENS SW7 7 L9
Enstone Rd HGDN/ICK UB10 33 R8
PEND EN3 27 Q1
Enterdent Rd GDST RH9 95 N10
Enterprise Cl CROY/NA CR0 74 E7
Enterprise Rw SEVS/STOTM N15 38 K3
Enterprise Wy TEDD TW11 59 P10
WAND/EARL SW18 61 N2
WLSDN NW10 48 F1
Enterprize Wy DEPT SE8 * 51 R9
Eothen Cl CTHM CR3 87 L14
Epcot Ms WLSDN NW10 * 48 K1
Epirus Ms FUL/PGN SW6 6 E13
Epirus Rd FUL/PGN SW6 6 D13
Epping Cl POP/IOD E14 51 S9
ROMW/RG RM7 42 B1
Epping Gld CHING E4 27 U4
Epping La ABR/ST RM4 18 F14
Epping New Rd LOU IG10 17 R12
LOU IG10 28 D2
Epping Pl IS N1 38 E11
Epping Rd EPP CM16 17 T9
EPP CM16 18 H2
EPP CM16 19 N4
Epping Wy CHING E4 27 T4
Epple Rd FUL/PGN SW6 49 M13
Epsom Cl BXLYHN DA7 66 B1
NTHLT UB5 34 H10
Epsom College EW KT17 * 84 G4
Epsom La North EPSOM KT18 84 H9
Epsom La South KWD/TDW/WH KT20 84 J12
Epsom Rd ASHTD KT21 83 V8
CROY/NA CR0 74 E9
EW KT17 84 F1
GDMY/SEVK IG3 41 P4
LEY E10 39 U4
LHD/OX KT22 83 R11
MRDN SM4 73 M4
Epsom Wy HCH RM12 43 M9
Epstein Rd THMD SE28 53 R6
Epworth Rd ISLW TW7 47 R13

FUL/PGN SW6 * 49 M14
Field Ct GINN WC1R 4 H10
OXTED RH8 96 A4
Field End BAR EN5 24 H2
COUL/CHIP CR5 86 B4
RSLP HA4 34 F11
Fieldend TEDD TW11 59 P9
Field End Cl OXHEY WD19 22 G5
Field End Rd PIN HA5 34 D4
RSLP HA4 34 G8
Fieldend Rd STRHM/NOR SW16 62 A13
Fielders Cl EN EN1 26 J2
RYLN/HDSTN HA2 35 M6
Fielders Wy RAD WD7 12 J7
Fieldfare Rd THMD SE28 53 S5
Fieldfares LCOL/BKTW AL2 12 H1
Fieldgate St WCHPL E1 51 L3
Fieldhouse Cl SWFD E18 28 D13
Fieldhouse Rd BAL SW12 62 A6
Fieldhouse Vls BNSTD SM7 * 85 S5
Field Hurst DTCH/LGLY SL3 44 D10
Fieldhurst Cl ADL/WDHM KT15 69 M10
Fielding Av WHTN TW2 59 L8
Fielding Gdns DTCH/LGLY SL3 44 A7
Fielding La HAYES BR2 76 E2
Fielding Rd CHSWK W4 48 E8
WKENS W14 48 K8
Fieldings Rd CHES/WCR EN8 16 F3
The Fieldings BNSTD SM7 85 M7
FSTH SE23 63 N6
Fielding St WALW SE17 9 N11
Fielding Ter EA W5 * 47 V5
Field La BTFD TW8 47 S12
TEDD TW11 59 Q10
Field Md CDALE/KGS NW9 24 E12
Fieldpark Gdns CROY/NA CR0 75 Q6
Field Pl NWMAL KT3 72 F4
Field Rd DEN/HRF UB9 32 J9
EBED/NFELT TW14 58 D4
FSTGT E7 40 C9
HMSMTH W6 6 A11
OXHEY WD19 22 G4
SOCK/AV RM15 55 Q6
TOTM N17 38 H1
Fieldsend Rd CHEAM SM3 73 L10
Fields Est HACK E8 * 39 L12
Fieldside Cl ORP BR6 77 L9
Fieldside Cottages TRDG/WHET N20 * 25 M5
Fieldside Rd BMLY BR1 63 V10
Fields Park Crs CHDH RM6 41 T3
Field St FSBYW WC1X 4 G5
Field Vw EGH TW20 56 G10
FELT TW13 57 V9
Fieldview WAND/EARL SW18 61 R6
Fieldview Cottages STHGT/OAK N14 * 26 B7
Field View Ri LCOL/BKTW AL2 11 S3
Field View Rd POTB/CUF EN6 14 C7
Field Wy CFSP/GDCR SL9 20 B12
CROY/NA CR0 75 T12
GFD/PVL UB6 34 K13
RKW/CH/CXG WD3 21 M6
RSLP HA4 33 U6
UX/CGN UB8 45 P2
WLSDN NW10 36 C12
Fieldway BCTR RM8 41 R9
STMC/STPC BR5 77 M4
Fieldway Crs HBRY N5 38 E10
Fiennes Cl BCTR RM8 41 S6
Fiesta Dr RAIN RM13 54 C2
Fifehead Cl ASHF TW15 57 Q11
Fife Rd CAN/RD E16 52 C3
KUT/HW KT1 59 U14
MORT/ESHN SW14 60 C3
WDGN N22 26 F13
Fife Ter IS N1 4 H3
Fifield Pth FSTH SE23 63 P8
Fifteenth Av KWD/TDW/WH KT20 * 93 M2
Fifth Av GSTN WD25 11 R9
HYS/HAR UB3 46 B6
KWD/TDW/WH KT20 * 93 M2
MNPK E12 40 H9
NKENS W10 2 A6
WTHK RM20 55 U11
Fifth Cross Rd WHTN TW2 59 M7
Fifth Wy WBLY HA9 36 B9
Figge's Rd MTCM CR4 61 U12
Figgswood COUL/CHIP CR5 86 A12
Fig Tree Cl WLSDN NW10 36 E13
Filby Rd CHSGTN KT9 71 V11
Filey Av STNW/STAM N16 39 L6
Filey Cl BELMT SM2 73 Q12
BH/WHM TN16 88 D9
Filey Waye RSLP HA4 34 C7
Fillebrook Av EN EN1 15 U14
Fillebrook Rd WAN E11 39 V6
Filmer Chambers FUL/PGN SW6 * 49 M13
Filmer La RSEV TN14 91 L11
Filmer Rd FUL/PGN SW6 6 C14
FUL/PGN SW6 49 M13
Filston La RSEV TN14 90 D6
Filton Cl CDALE/KGS NW9 24 E14
Finborough Rd TOOT SW17 61 T12
WBPTN SW10 6 H11
Finchale Rd ABYW SE2 53 R8
Fincham Cl HGDN/ICK UB10 33 U8
Finch Av WNWD SE27 62 H9
Finch Cl BAR EN5 25 N3
Finch Dr EBED/NFELT TW14 58 F5
Finch Gdns CHING E4 27 S10
Finch Gn RKW/CH/CXG WD3 20 K2
Finchingfield Av WFD IG8 28 E12
Finch La BANK EC3V 5 R12
BUSH WD23 22 J3
Finchley Cl DART DA1 67 N4
Finchley La HDN NW4 36 K2
Finchley Pk NFNCH/WDSPK N12 25 Q9
Finchley Pl STJWD NW8 3 L3
Finchley Rd HAMP NW3 37 N9
STJWD NW8 3 L2
Finchley Vls NFNCH/WDSPK N12 * 25 R9
Finchley Wy FNCH N3 25 N11
Finch Ms PECK SE15 * 50 K13
Finden Rd FSTGT E7 40 E10
Findhorn Av YEAD UB4 46 D3
Findhorn St POP/IOD E14 51 U4
Findon Cl RYLN/HDSTN HA2 * 34 K8
WAND/EARL SW18 61 N4
Findon Gdns RAIN RM13 54 G3
Findon Rd ED N9 27 M6
SHB W12 48 G7
Fine Bush La DEN/HRF UB9 33 T4
Fingal St GNWCH SE10 52 B10
Finglesham Cl STMC/STPC BR5 77 T6
Finians Cl HGDN/ICK UB10 33 R12
Finland Rd BROCKY SE4 63 Q1
Finland St BERM/RHTH SE16 51 Q8
Finlay Gdns ADL/WDHM KT15 69 N9
Finlays Cl CHSGTN KT9 72 A10
Finlay St FUL/PGN SW6 48 K13
Finnart Cl WEY KT13 69 U9
Finney La ISLW TW7 47 Q13
Finnis St BETH E2 51 M1
Finnymore Rd DAGW RM9 41 U12
Finsbury Av LVPST EC2M * 5 R10
Finsbury Circ LVPST EC2M 5 R10
Finsbury Cottages WDGN N22 26 C12
Finsbury Est CLKNW EC1R 4 K6
FSBYE EC1V * 5 L6
Finsbury Market SDTCH EC2A 5 S8
Finsbury Park Av FSBYPK N4 38 G4
Finsbury Park Rd FSBYPK N4 38 F8
Finsbury Pavement LVPST EC2M 5 R9
Finsbury Rd WDGN N22 26 D13
Finsbury Sq SDTCH EC2A 5 R9
Finsbury St STLK EC1Y 5 Q9
Finsbury Wy BXLY DA5 65 V4
Finsen Rd CMBW SE5 62 G2
Finstock Rd NKENS W10 48 K4
Finucane Dr STMC/STPC BR5 77 S5
Finucane Gdns RAIN RM13 42 G11
Finucane Ri BUSH WD23 23 L7
Finway Ct WATW WD18 * 22 B3
Fiona Cl GT/LBKH KT23 82 J14
Fiona Ct ENC/FH EN2 * 26 F1
Firbank Cl CAN/RD E16 52 F3
ENC/FH EN2 26 G2
Firbank Dr OXHEY WD19 22 G5
Firbank Rd CRW RM5 30 B10
PECK SE15 51 M14
Fir Cl WOT/HER KT12 70 C5
Fircroft Cl WOKS/MYFD GU22 80 D8
Fircroft Ct WOKS/MYFD GU22 * 80 D8
Fircroft Gdns HRW HA1 35 N8
Fircroft Rd CHSGTN KT9 71 V9
EGH TW20 56 A12
TOOT SW17 61 T8
Firdene BRYLDS KT5 72 C6
Fir Dene ORP BR6 76 H8
Fire Bell Aly SURB KT6 71 U4
Firebell Ms SURB KT6 71 U4
Firecrest Dr HAMP NW3 37 P8
Firefly Cl WLGTN SM6 * 74 C12
Firefly Gdns EHAM E6 52 G2
Firethorn Cl EDGW HA8 24 C9
Firfield Rd ADL/WDHM KT15 69 L9
Firfields WEY KT13 69 T12
Fir Grange Av WEY KT13 69 T10
Fir Gv NWMAL KT3 72 F4
Fir Grove Rd BRXN/ST SW9 * 50 E14
Firham Park Av HARH RM3 31 N12
Firhill Rd CAT SE6 63 S8
Firlands WEY KT13 70 A11
Firle Ct EW KT17 * 84 F2
Firle Pl WAND/EARL SW18 61 Q5
Firmingers Rd ORP BR6 78 C10
Firmin Rd DART DA1 66 J3
Fir Rd CHEAM SM3 73 M6
FELT TW13 58 F10
Firs WAB EN9 17 Q9
Firs Av FBAR/BDGN N11 25 U11
MORT/ESHN SW14 60 C2
MUSWH N10 37 U1
Firsby Av CROY/NA CR0 75 P6
Firsby Rd STNW/STAM N16 38 K6
Firs Cl ESH/CLAY KT10 71 N11
FSTH SE23 63 P5
IVER SL0 32 G12
MTCM CR4 61 V14
MUSWH N10 37 U1
Firscroft PLMGR N13 26 G8
Firsdene Cl CHERT KT16 68 H11
Firs Dr DTCH/LGLY SL3 44 D6
HEST TW5 46 D13
LOU IG10 17 U13
Firsgrove Crs BRW CM14 31 V9
Firside Gv BFN/LL DA15 65 P6
Firs La PLMGR N13 26 G8
POTB/CUF EN6 14 D7
Firs Park Av WCHMH N21 26 H6
Firs Park Gdns WCHMH N21 26 H6
Firs Rd PUR/KEN CR8 86 F5
First Av ACT W3 48 F6
ADL/WDHM KT15 69 M13
BXLYHN DA7 53 S12
CHDH RM6 41 S3
DAGE RM10 42 B14
E/WMO/HCT KT8 70 H2
EN EN1 26 K3
GSTN WD25 11 Q9
HDN NW4 36 J2
HOR/WEW KT19 72 E13
HYS/HAR UB3 46 B6
KWD/TDW/WH KT20 * 93 M2
MNPK E12 40 G9
MORT/ESHN SW14 48 E14
NKENS W10 2 C7
PLSTW E13 52 C1
UED N18 27 N9
WALTH E17 39 T3
WBLY HA9 35 T7
WOT/HER KT12 70 D4
WTHK RM20 55 U11
First Cl E/WMO/HCT KT8 71 L2
First Cross Rd WHTN TW2 59 N7
First Dr WLSDN NW10 36 C12
The Firs BF/WBF KT14 * 81 P2
BRWN CM15 31 U4
BXLY DA5 66 D6
CHESW EN7 15 U1
EA W5 47 T3
EBED/NFELT TW14 * 58 A4
EDGW HA8 * 24 D9
ORP BR6 * 78 A11
TRDG/WHET N20 25 R6
First Quarter HOR/WEW KT19 * 84 E1
First St CHEL SW3 7 P7
Firstway RYNPK SW20 60 J14
First Wy WBLY HA9 36 B9
Firs Wk NTHWD HA6 21 V11
WFD IG8 28 C10
Firswood Av HOR/WEW KT19 72 E10
Firth Gdns FUL/PGN SW6 49 L13
Firtree Av MTCM CR4 61 U14
Fir Tree Av WDR/YW UB7 45 S8
Fir Tree Cl EA W5 47 U4
ESH/CLAY KT10 71 L10
EW KT17 84 J5
HOR/WEW KT19 72 F9
LHD/OX KT22 83 S13
ORP BR6 77 P10
ROM RM1 42 D1
STRHM/NOR SW16 62 A10
Fir Tree Ct BORE WD6 23 V2
Fir Tree Gdns CROY/NA CR0 75 S9
Fir Tree Gv CAR SM5 73 T12
Fir Tree Hl RKW/CH/CXG WD3 10 G11
Fir Tree Pl ASHF TW15 * 57 S9
Fir Tree Rd EW KT17 84 H6
HSLWW TW4 58 G2
LHD/OX KT22 83 S13
Fir Trees ABR/ST RM4 29 R1
Fir Trees Cl BERM/RHTH SE16 51 Q6
Fir Tree Wk EN EN1 26 J1
REIG RH2 93 R10
Fir Wk CHEAM SM3 72 K11
Fisher Cl CROY/NA CR0 74 K6
GFD/PVL UB6 46 J1
KGLGY WD4 10 G3
PEND EN3 16 G11
WOT/HER KT12 70 D9
Fisherdene ESH/CLAY KT10 71 Q12
Fisherman Cl RCHPK/HAM TW10 59 S9
Fishermans Dr BERM/RHTH SE16 51 P7
Fisher Rd KTN/HRWW/WS HA3 23 P14
Fishers Cl BUSH WD23 22 G2
CHES/WCR EN8 16 G8
STRHM/NOR SW16 62 B8
Fishers Ct NWCR SE14 51 P13
Fisher's La CHSWK W4 48 D9
Fisher St CAN/RD E16 52 C3
HHOL WC1V 4 G10
Fisher's Wy BELV DA17 54 C6
Fisherton St STJWD NW8 3 L8
Fishguard Wy CAN/RD E16 52 K6
Fishponds Rd HAYES BR2 76 F10
TOOT SW17 61 S9
Fish Street Hl MON EC3R 5 R14
Fisk Cl SUN TW16 58 B11
Fisons Rd CAN/RD E16 52 C6
Fitzalan Rd ESH/CLAY KT10 71 N12
FNCH N3 37 L1
Fitzalan St LBTH SE11 8 H7
Fitzgeorge Av NWMAL KT3 60 D13
WKENS W14 6 A8
Fitzgerald Av MORT/ESHN SW14 60 E1
Fitzgerald Rd MORT/ESHN SW14 60 D1
THDIT KT7 71 Q4
WAN E11 40 C3
Fitzhardinge St MBLAR W1H 3 S11
Fitzhugh Gv WAND/EARL SW18 61 R4
Fitzilian Av HARH RM3 31 M13
Fitzjames Av CROY/NA CR0 75 L7
WKENS W14 6 B8
Fitzjohn Av BAR EN5 25 L3
Fitzjohn's Av HAMP NW3 37 R10
Fitzmaurice Pl MYFR/PICC W1J * 7 V1
Fitzneal St SHB W12 48 F4
Fitzrobert Pl EGH TW20 56 E11
Fitzroy Cl HGT N6 37 T6
Fitzroy Crs CHSWK W4 * 48 D12
Fitzroy Gdns NRWD SE19 62 J12
Fitzroy Ms FITZ W1T 4 A8
Fitzroy Pk HGT N6 37 T6
Fitzroy Pl REIG RH2 93 R10
Fitzroy Rd CAMTN NW1 3 S1
Fitzroy Sq FITZ W1T 4 A8
Fitzroy St FITZ W1T 4 A8
Fitzstephen Rd BCTR RM8 41 R10
Fitzwarren Gdns HGT N6 38 A6
Fitzwilliam Av RCH/KEW TW9 47 V14
Fitzwilliam Ms CAN/RD E16 52 C6
Fitzwilliam Rd CLAP SW4 62 A1
Fitz Wygram Cl HPTN TW12 59 L10
Five Acre CDALE/KGS NW9 24 F14
Fiveacre Cl CROY/NA CR0 74 E4
Five Acres KGLGY WD4 10 F3
Five Acres Av LCOL/BKTW AL2 11 T3
Five Elms Rd DAGW RM9 41 V8
HAYES BR2 76 E8
Five Fields Cl OXHEY WD19 22 H8
Five Oak Ms BMLY BR1 64 C8
Five Oaks La CHIG IG7 29 U11
Fiveways Cnr ELTH/MOT SE9 64 K7
Five Ways Jct HDN NW4 24 G13
Fiveways Rd BRXN/ST SW9 50 E14
Five Wents SWLY BR8 66 G14
Fladbury Rd SEVS/STOTM N15 38 H4
Fladgate Rd WAN E11 40 A4
Flag Cl CROY/NA CR0 75 P6
Flagstaff Cl WAB EN9 16 H7
Flagstaff Rd WAB EN9 16 H7
Flag Wk PIN HA5 34 C4
Flambard Rd HRW HA1 35 Q4
Flamborough Cl BH/WHM TN16 88 D9
Flamborough Rd RSLP HA4 34 C8
Flamborough St POP/IOD E14 51 Q4
Flamborough Wk POP/IOD E14 * 51 Q4
Flamingo Wk HCH RM12 42 G12
Flamstead End Rd CHES/WCR EN8 16 B2
Flamstead Gdns DAGW RM9 41 S12
Flamstead Rd DAGW RM9 41 S12
Flamsted Av WBLY HA9 36 A11
Flamsteed Rd CHARL SE7 52 G10
Flanchford Rd REIG RH2 92 J13
SHB W12 48 F8
Flanders Crs TOOT SW17 61 T12
Flanders Rd CHSWK W4 48 E9
EHAM E6 40 H14
Flanders Wy HOM E9 39 P11
Flandrian Cl PEND EN3 16 G13
Flank St WCHPL E1 51 L5
Flash La ENC/FH EN2 15 S11
Flask Wk HAMP NW3 37 Q9
Flather Cl STRHM/NOR SW16 62 A11
Flavell Ms GNWCH SE10 52 A10
Flaxen Cl CHING E4 27 T8
Flaxen Rd CHING E4 27 T8
Flaxley Rd MRDN SM4 73 P4
Flaxman Rd CMBW SE5 50 F14
Flaxman Ter STPAN WC1H 4 D6
Flaxton Rd WOOL/PLUM SE18 53 M13
Flecker Cl STAN HA7 23 P10
Fleece Dr ED N9 27 L9
Fleece Rd SURB KT6 71 S6
Fleece Wk HOLWY N7 * 38 C11
Fleeming Cl WALTH E17 27 R14
Fleeming Rd WALTH E17 27 R14
Fleet Av RDART DA2 67 Q6
UPMR RM14 43 R4
Fleet Cl E/WMO/HCT KT8 70 H3
RSLP HA4 33 U4
UPMR RM14 43 R4
Fleetdale Pde RDART DA2 * 67 Q6
Fleet Pl FLST/FETLN EC4A 5 L11
Fleet Rd HAMP NW3 37 S10
RDART DA2 67 Q6
Fleetside E/WMO/HCT KT8 70 H4
Fleet Sq FSBYW WC1X 4 G6
Fleet St EMB EC4Y 4 K12
Fleet Street Hl WCHPL E1 * 51 L2
Fleet Ter CAT SE6 * 63 U5
Fleetway EGH TW20 68 G1
Fleetwood Cl CAN/RD E16 52 F3
CHSGTN KT9 71 T12
CROY/NA CR0 74 K8
KWD/TDW/WH KT20 84 K11
Fleetwood Ct BF/WBF KT14 81 L3
Fleetwood Rd KUT/HW KT1 72 B1
WLSDN NW10 36 G10
Fleetwood Sq KUT/HW KT1 72 B1
Fleetwood St STNW/STAM N16 38 J7
Fleetwood Wy OXHEY WD19 22 E9
Fleming Cl CHESW EN7 16 A1
MV/WKIL W9 2 E8
Fleming Ct CROY/NA CR0 74 E10
Fleming Dr WCHMH N21 26 D3
Fleming Md MTCM CR4 61 S12
Fleming Rd STHL UB1 46 K4
WAB EN9 16 H9
WALW SE17 9 M11
Fleming Wk CDALE/KGS NW9 * 24 E14
Fleming Wy ISLW TW7 59 P1
THMD SE28 53 T5
Flemish Flds CHERT KT16 69 L5
Flemming Av RSLP HA4 34 D7
Flempton Rd LEY E10 39 Q6
Fletcher Cl CHERT KT16 68 J11
EHAM E6 52 K5
Fletcher La LEY E10 39 U5
Fletcher Rd CHERT KT16 68 H11
CHIG IG7 29 P10
CHSWK W4 48 C8
Fletchers Cl HAYES BR2 76 D2
Fletcher St WCHPL E1 51 L5
Fletching Rd CHARL SE7 52 F11
CLPT E5 39 N8
Fletton Rd FBAR/BDGN N11 26 C12
Fleur De Lis St WCHPL E1 5 U8
Fleur Gates WIM/MER SW19 60 K5
Flexmere Rd TOTM N17 26 H13
Flight Ap CDALE/KGS NW9 * 24 F13
Flimwell Cl BMLY BR1 64 A10
Flint Cl BNSTD SM7 85 P4
ORP BR6 * 77 P11
REDH RH1 93 T9
SRTFD E15 40 B11
Flint Cottages LHD/OX KT22 * 83 R11
Flint Down Cl STMC/STPC BR5 * 65 Q13
Flintlock Cl STWL/WRAY TW19 57 L2
Flintmill Crs BKHTH/KID SE3 64 G1
Flinton St WALW SE17 9 T9
Flint St WALW SE17 9 R8
WTHK RM20 55 V11
Flitcroft St LSQ/SEVD WC2H 4 D12
Floathaven Cl THMD SE28 53 Q6
The Floats SEV TN13 90 E11
Flock Mill Pl WAND/EARL SW18 61 P6
Flockton St BERM/RHTH SE16 51 L7
Flodden Rd CMBW SE5 50 G13
Flood La TWK TW1 * 59 Q6
Flood St CHEL SW3 7 P10
Flood Wk CHEL SW3 7 P11
Flora Cl POP/IOD E14 51 T4
STAN HA7 23 T8
Flora Gdns CHDH RM6 41 S4
CROY/NA CR0 87 U1
Floral Pl IS N1 38 H10
Floral St COVGDN WC2E 4 F13
Flora St BELV DA17 53 V10
Florence Av ADL/WDHM KT15 81 L1
ENC/FH EN2 26 G1
MRDN SM4 73 Q3
Florence Cl GSTN WD25 11 N9
HCH RM12 43 L7
WOT/HER KT12 70 D5
Florence Ct WAN E11 40 D2
Florence Dr ENC/FH EN2 26 G1
Florence Elson Cl MNPK E12 40 J9
Florence Gdns CHSWK W4 48 C11
STA TW18 57 M12
Florence Rd ABYW SE2 53 S9
BECK BR3 63 P14
BMLY BR1 64 C13
CHSWK W4 48 D8
EA W5 47 U5
FELT TW13 58 D6
FSBYPK N4 38 D5
KUTN/CMB KT2 59 V12
NWCR SE14 51 R13
NWDGN UB2 46 F9
PLSTW E13 40 C14
SAND/SEL CR2 74 H13
WIM/MER SW19 61 P11
WOT/HER KT12 70 D5
Florence St CAN/RD E16 52 B2
HDN NW4 36 J2
IS N1 38 F12
Florence Ter NWCR SE14 51 R13
Florence Vls HGT N6 * 37 V5
Florence Wy BAL SW12 61 T6
UX/CGN UB8 33 N12
Florey Sq WCHMH N21 26 D3
Florfield Rd HACK E8 39 M11
Florian Av SUT SM1 73 R9
Florian Rd PUT/ROE SW15 61 L2
Florida Cl BUSH WD23 23 M7
Florida Rd THHTH CR7 62 F13
Florida St BETH E2 51 M1
Florin Ct UED N18 26 J9
Floris Pl CLAP SW4 62 A1
Floriston Av HGDN/ICK UB10 33 U12
Floriston Cl STAN HA7 23 R13
Floriston Gdns STAN HA7 23 R13
Floss St PUT/ROE SW15 48 J14
Flower Crs CHERT KT16 68 F11
Flower & Dean Wk WCHPL E1 5 V10
Flowerfield RSEV TN14 90 F7
Flower La GDST RH9 95 P5
MLHL NW7 24 F10
Flower Ms GLDGN NW11 37 L4
Flowerpot Cl SEVS/STOTM N15 38 K4
Flowers Cl CRICK NW2 36 G8
Flowers Ms ARCH N19 38 A7
Floyd Rd CHARL SE7 52 E10
Floyds La WOKS/MYFD GU22 81 L6
Floyer Cl RCHPK/HAM TW10 59 V3
Fludyer St LEW SE13 64 A2
Flux's La EPP CM16 18 E7
The Flyers Wy BH/WHM TN16 97 M2
Fogerty Cl PEND EN3 16 H11
Foley Ms ESH/CLAY KT10 71 N11
Foley Rd BH/WHM TN16 88 F8
ESH/CLAY KT10 71 N12
Foley St GTPST W1W 4 A10
Folgate St WCHPL E1 5 T9
Foliot St SHB W12 48 F4
Folkes La UPMR RM14 43 T3
Folkestone Ct DTCH/LGLY SL3 44 E10
Folkestone Rd EHAM E6 40 J14
UED N18 27 L9
WALTH E17 39 T2
Folkingham La CDALE/KGS NW9 24 D13
Folkington Cnr NFNCH/WDSPK N12 25 M10
Follett Dr ABLGY WD5 11 M5
Follett St POP/IOD E14 51 U4
Folly Cl RAD WD7 12 D10
Follyfield Rd BNSTD SM7 85 N4
Folly La CHING E4 27 R12
Folly Pathway RAD WD7 12 D9
Folly Wall POP/IOD E14 51 U7
Fontaine Rd STRHM/NOR SW16 62 D11
Fontarabia Rd BTSEA SW11 61 U2
Fontayne Av CHIG IG7 29 L9
RAIN RM13 42 E12
ROM RM1 30 E14
Fontenoy Rd BAL SW12 61 V7
Fonteyne Gdns WFD IG8 28 F14
Fonthill Ms FSBYPK N4 38 D7
Fonthill Rd FSBYPK N4 38 D7
Font Hills EFNCH N2 25 Q14
Fontley Wy PUT/ROE SW15 60 G5
Fontmell Cl ASHF TW15 57 S10
Fontmell Pk ASHF TW15 57 R10
Fontwell Cl KTN/HRWW/WS HA3 23 N12
NTHLT UB5 34 J11
Fontwell Dr HAYES BR2 76 J3
Fontwell Park Gdns HCH RM12 43 L9
Foord Cl RDART DA2 67 S7
Football La HRW HA1 35 P6
Footbury Hill Rd ORP BR6 77 Q5
The Footpath PUT/ROE SW15 * 60 G3
Foots Cray High St SCUP DA14 65 S11
Foots Cray La SCUP DA14 65 S6
Footscray Rd ELTH/MOT SE9 64 J4
Forbes Av POTB/CUF EN6 14 F7
Forbes Cl CRICK NW2 36 G8
HCH RM12 42 H6
Forbes St WCHPL E1 51 L4
Forbes Wy RSLP HA4 34 D7
Forburg Rd STNW/STAM N16 39 L6
Force Green La BH/WHM TN16 89 M14
Fordbridge Cl CHERT KT16 69 M6
Fordbridge Rd ASHF TW15 57 R10
SUN TW16 70 A4
Ford Cl ASHF TW15 57 Q11
BUSH WD23 23 L2
HRW HA1 35 M5
RAIN RM13 42 F12
SHPTN TW17 69 S3
THHTH CR7 74 F4
Fordcroft Rd STMC/STPC BR5 77 R3
Forde Av BMLY BR1 76 E1
Fordel Rd CAT SE6 63 V6
Ford End DEN/HRF UB9 32 K7
WFD IG8 28 D11
Fordham Cl EMPK RM11 43 N5
Fordham Rd EBAR EN4 25 R1
Fordham St WCHPL E1 51 L4
Fordhook Av EA W5 47 V5
Fordingbridge Cl CHERT KT16 * 69 M6
Fordingley Rd MV/WKIL W9 2 D6
Fordington Rd HGT N6 37 T2
Ford La IVER SL0 45 L4
RAIN RM13 42 F12
Fordmill Rd CAT SE6 63 S7
Ford Rd ASHF TW15 57 R9
BOW E3 39 Q14
CHERT KT16 69 M6
DAGE RM10 42 A12
DAGW RM9 41 V12
WOKS/MYFD GU22 80 F10
Ford's Gv WCHMH N21 26 G6
Fords Park Rd CAN/RD E16 52 C4
Ford Sq WCHPL E1 51 M3
Ford St BOW E3 39 Q13
CAN/RD E16 52 B4
Fordwater Rd CHERT KT16 69 M6
Fordwich Cl ORP BR6 77 P5
Fordwych Rd CRICK NW2 37 L10
Fordyce Cl EMPK RM11 43 N5
Fordyce Rd LEW SE13 63 U4
Fordyke Rd BCTR RM8 41 U7
Forefield LCOL/BKTW AL2 11 U1
Foreland Ct HDN NW4 25 L13
Foreland St WOOL/PLUM SE18 53 M9
Foremark Cl BARK/HLT IG6 29 P11
Foreshore DEPT SE8 51 R10
Forest Ap CHING E4 28 A5
WFD IG8 28 C12
Forest Av CHIG IG7 28 J10
CHING E4 28 A5
Forest Cl CHST BR7 64 J14
WAB EN9 17 P11
WAN E11 40 B3
WFD IG8 28 D9
WOKS/MYFD GU22 80 H5
Forest Ct CHING E4 28 B6
WAN E11 40 A2
Forest Crs ASHTD KT21 84 A6
Forestdale STHGT/OAK N14 26 B9
Forest Dr EPP CM16 18 C10
HAYES BR2 76 G9
KWD/TDW/WH KT20 85 N11
MNPK E12 40 F8
SUN TW16 58 B12
WFD IG8 27 V12
Forest Dr East WAN E11 39 V5
Forest Dr West WAN E11 39 U5
Forest Edge BKHH IG9 28 E8
Forester Rd PECK SE15 63 M2
Foresters Cl CHESW EN7 15 U1
WLGTN SM6 74 B12
Foresters Crs BXLYHN DA7 66 B2
Foresters Dr WALTH E17 39 V2
WLGTN SM6 74 B12
Forest Gdns TOTM N17 26 K14
Forest Ga CDALE/KGS NW9 36 E2
Forest Gld CHING E4 28 A10
EPP CM16 18 J1
WAN E11 40 A4
Forest Gv HACK E8 38 K11
Forest Hill Rd EDUL SE22 63 M4
Forestholme Cl SYD SE26 * 63 N10
Forest La CHIG IG7 28 J10
EHSLY KT24 82 B14
FSTGT E7 40 C10
RAD WD7 12 F5
Forest Mount Rd WFD IG8 27 V12
Fore St BARB EC2Y 5 Q10
PIN HA5 34 C3
UED N18 27 L9
Forest Rdg BECK BR3 75 S1
HAYES BR2 76 G9
Forest Ri WALTH E17 39 V2
Forest Rd BARK/HLT IG6 29 N13
CHEAM SM3 73 N6
CHES/WCR EN8 16 D3
ED N9 27 M6
EHSLY KT24 82 C13
EPP CM16 17 V8
ERITH DA8 54 G13
FELT TW13 58 E8
FSTGT E7 40 C9
GSTN WD25 11 P7
HACK E8 38 K11
LOU IG10 28 F2
PEND EN3 16 E10
RCH/KEW TW9 48 A12
ROMW/RG RM7 42 B1
TOTM N17 39 N2
WALTH E17 27 V14
WAN E11 39 V5
WFD IG8 28 C8
WOKS/MYFD GU22 80 H5
Forest Side CHING E4 28 B5
EPP CM16 18 B7
FSTGT E7 40 D9
WPK KT4 72 F6
Forest St FSTGT E7 40 C10
The Forest WAN E11 40 A2
Forest Vw CHING E4 27 V5
WAN E11 40 B5
Forest View Av LEY E10 39 V3
Forest View Rd LOU IG10 28 F2
MNPK E12 40 G9
WALTH E17 27 U13
Forest Wk BUSH WD23 11 T13
Forest Wy ASHTD KT21 84 A7
BFN/LL DA15 65 M5
LOU IG10 28 G1
STMC/STPC BR5 77 Q3
WAB EN9 17 S5
WFD IG8 28 D9
Forfar Rd BTSEA SW11 49 U13
WDGN N22 26 F13
Forge Av COUL/CHIP CR5 86 E10
Forge Bridge La COUL/CHIP CR5 85 V12
Forge Cl HAYES BR2 76 C6
KGLGY WD4 10 A5
Forge Cottages EA W5 * 47 T6
Forge Dr ESH/CLAY KT10 71 Q12
Forge End WOKN/KNAP GU21 80 C7
Forgefield BH/WHM TN16 88 F6
Forge La BGR/WK TN15 79 U14
CHEAM SM3 73 L12
EYN DA4 79 Q2
FELT TW13 58 G10
NTHWD HA6 22 A12
RCHPK/HAM TW10 59 U6
SUN TW16 70 C1
Forge Ms CROY/NA CR0 75 S10
SUN TW16 * 70 C1
Forge Pl CAMTN NW1 37 U11
Forge Wy RSEV TN14 90 F1
Forman Pl STNW/STAM N16 38 K9
Formby Av KTN/HRWW/WS HA3 35 S1
Formby Cl DTCH/LGLY SL3 44 G9
Form Cl RAD WD7 12 J5
Formosa St MV/WKIL W9 2 H8
Formunt Cl CAN/RD E16 52 B3
Forres Gdns GLDGN NW11 37 N4
Forrester Pth SYD SE26 63 N9
Forrest Gdns STRHM/NOR SW16 74 D1
Forris Av HYS/HAR UB3 46 B6
Forset St MBLAR W1H 3 P11
Forstal Cl HAYES BR2 76 C1
Forster Cl CHING E4 27 V12
Forster Rd BECK BR3 75 Q1
BRXS/STRHM SW2 62 C5
TOTM N17 38 K1
WALTH E17 39 Q4
Forsters Cl CHDH RM6 41 V4
Forston St IS N1 5 P3
Forsyte Crs NRWD SE19 62 J13
Forsyth Gdns WALW SE17 9 M11
Forsythia Cl IL IG1 40 K10
Forsyth Pl EN EN1 26 J3
Forsyth Rd WOKN/KNAP GU21 80 G5
Forterie Gdns GDMY/SEVK IG3 41 Q8
Fortescue Av WHTN TW2 59 L8
Fortescue Rd EDGW HA8 24 D13
WEY KT13 69 R9
WIM/MER SW19 61 R12
Fortess Gv KTTN NW5 38 A10
Fortess Rd KTTN NW5 37 V10
Fortess Wk KTTN NW5 37 V10
Forthbridge Rd BTSEA SW11 61 U2
Forth Rd UPMR RM14 43 R4
Fortin Cl SOCK/AV RM15 55 U5
Fortin Wy SOCK/AV RM15 55 U5
Fortis Cl CAN/RD E16 52 E4
Fortis Gn EFNCH N2 37 T1
Fortis Green Av EFNCH N2 37 U1
Fortis Green Rd MUSWH N10 37 U1
Fortismere Av MUSWH N10 37 U1
Fort La REIG RH2 93 P6
Fortnam Rd ARCH N19 38 B7
Fortnums Acre STAN HA7 23 P11
Fort Rd KWD/TDW/WH KT20 92 C8
NTHLT UB5 34 J12
RSEV TN14 90 C5
STHWK SE1 9 V8
Fortrose Cl POP/IOD E14 51 V4
Fortrose Gdns BRXS/STRHM SW2 62 C6
Fort St CAN/RD E16 52 D6
WCHPL E1 * 5 T10
Fortuna Cl HOLWY N7 * 38 D11
Fortunegate Rd WLSDN NW10 36 F12
Fortune Green Rd KIL/WHAMP NW6 37 N10
Fortune La BORE WD6 23 T4
Fortune Pl STHWK SE1 9 V10
Fortunes Md NTHLT UB5 34 G11
Fortune St STLK EC1Y 5 P8
Fortune Wy WLSDN NW10 48 G1
Forty Acre La CAN/RD E16 52 C3
Forty Av WBLY HA9 35 V8
Forty Cl WBLY HA9 35 V7
Fortyfoot Rd LHD/OX KT22 83 T12
Forty Hl ENC/FH EN2 15 V11
Forty La WBLY HA9 36 C7
Forum Cl BOW E3 39 S13
Forum Magnum Sq STHWK SE1 8 G3
Forumside EDGW HA8 24 A11
The Forum E/WMO/HCT KT8 70 K2
Forum Wy EDGW HA8 24 A11
Forval Cl MTCM CR4 73 T3
Forward Dr KTN/HRWW/WS HA3 35 Q2
Fosbury Ms BAY/PAD W2 2 H14
Foscote Ms MV/WKIL W9 2 F9
Foscote Rd HDN NW4 36 H4
Foskett Rd FUL/PGN SW6 49 M14
Foss Av CROY/NA CR0 74 E10
Fossdene Rd CHARL SE7 52 D10
Fossdyke Cl YEAD UB4 46 G3
Fosse Wy BF/WBF KT14 80 K3
WEA W13 47 Q3
Fossil Rd LEW SE13 63 S1
Fossington Rd BELV DA17 53 T9
Foss Rd TOOT SW17 61 R9
Fossway BCTR RM8 41 S7
Foster Cl CHES/WCR EN8 16 D4
Fosterdown GDST RH9 95 M5
Foster La CITYW EC2V 5 N11
Foster Rd CHSWK W4 48 D10
PLSTW E13 52 C2
Fosters Cl CHST BR7 64 H10
SWFD E18 28 D13
Foster St HDN NW4 36 J2
Foster Wk HDN NW4 36 J2
Fothergill Cl PLSTW E13 40 C13
Fothergill Dr WCHMH N21 26 C3
Fotheringham Rd EN EN1 26 K2
Fotherley Rd RKW/CH/CXG WD3 20 K7
Fouberts Pl SOHO/CST W1F 4 A12
Foulden Rd STNW/STAM N16 38 K9
Foulden Ter STNW/STAM N16 38 K9
Foulis Ter SKENS SW7 7 L8
Foulser Rd TOOT SW17 61 T8
Foulsham Rd THHTH CR7 74 G1
Foundary Ga CHES/WCR EN8 16 E7
Foundation Pl ELTH/MOT SE9 * 64 J3
Founder Cl EHAM E6 52 K4
Founders Cl NTHLT UB5 46 H1
Founders Gdns NRWD SE19 62 G12
Foundry Cl BERM/RHTH SE16 51 Q6
Foundry Ct CHERT KT16 69 L5
Foundry La DTCH/LGLY SL3 56 F1
Foundry Ms CAMTN NW1 4 B7
HSLW TW3 58 K2
Foundry Pl WAND/EARL SW18 * 61 P5
Fountain Cl UX/CGN UB8 45 U3
Fountain Dr CAR SM5 73 T13
NRWD SE19 62 K9
WLGTN SM6 85 V1
Fountain Green Sq BERM/RHTH SE16 51 L7
Fountain Ms HAMP NW3 37 T11
Fountain Pl BRXN/ST SW9 50 E13
WAB EN9 16 J8
Fountain Rd REDH RH1 93 S12
THHTH CR7 62 G14
TOOT SW17 61 R10
Fountains Av FELT TW13 58 H8
Fountains Cl FELT TW13 58 H7
Fountains Crs STHGT/OAK N14 26 C5
Fountayne Rd SEVS/STOTM N15 38 K2
Fount St VX/NE SW8 8 D14
Four Acres COB KT11 82 G3
Fouracres PEND EN3 16 E13
Fourland Wk EDGW HA8 24 C11
Fournier St WCHPL E1 5 U9
Four Seasons Cl BOW E3 39 S14
Four Seasons Crs CHEAM SM3 73 M7
Fourteenth Av KWD/TDW/WH KT20 * 93 M2
Fourth Av GSTN WD25 11 R9
HYS/HAR UB3 46 B6
KWD/TDW/WH KT20 * 93 M2
MNPK E12 40 H9
NKENS W10 2 A7
ROMW/RG RM7 42 C6
WTHK RM20 55 U11
Fourth Cross Rd WHTN TW2 59 M7
Fourth Dr COUL/CHIP CR5 86 B6
Fourth Wy WBLY HA9 36 C9
The Four Tubs BUSH WD23 23 M5
Four Wents COB KT11 82 D3
The Four Wents CHING E4 27 V7
Fowey Av REDBR IG4 40 F3
Fowey Cl WAP E1W 51 M6
Fowler Cl BTSEA SW11 61 R1
SCUP DA14 65 U10
Fowler Rd BARK/HLT IG6 29 S10
FSTGT E7 40 C9
IS N1 5 M1
Fowler's Wk EA W5 47 T2
Fowley Cl CHES/WCR EN8 16 F8
Fowley Mead Pk CHES/WCR EN8 * 16 F8
Fownes St BTSEA SW11 61 S1
Fox & Knot St FARR EC1M * 5 M9
Foxacre CTHM CR3 86 J12
Foxberry Rd BROCKY SE4 63 Q2
Foxborough Cl DTCH/LGLY SL3 44 E10
Foxborough Gdns BROCKY SE4 63 S4
Foxbourne Rd TOOT SW17 61 U7
Fox Burrow Rd BARK/HLT IG6 29 S10
Foxbury Av CHST BR7 65 M11
Foxbury Cl BMLY BR1 64 D11
ORP BR6 77 Q10
Foxbury Dr ORP BR6 77 Q11
Foxbury Rd BMLY BR1 64 C11
Fox Cl BORE WD6 23 T4
BUSH WD23 22 K3
CAN/RD E16 52 C3
CRW RM5 30 B10
ORP BR6 77 Q10
WCHPL E1 51 N2
WEY KT13 69 V10
WOKS/MYFD GU22 80 H5
Foxcombe CROY/NA CR0 75 T11
Fox Covert LHD/OX KT22 83 M14
Foxcroft Rd WOOL/PLUM SE18 52 K13
Foxdell NTHWD HA6 21 V11
Foxdell Wy CFSP/GDCR SL9 20 C10
Foxearth Cl BH/WHM TN16 88 G8
Foxearth Rd SAND/SEL CR2 75 N14
Foxearth Sp SAND/SEL CR2 75 N13
Foxes Dl BKHTH/KID SE3 64 C1
HAYES BR2 75 V1
Foxes Dr CHESW EN7 15 V3
Foxes La POTB/CUF EN6 15 N2
Foxes Pde WAB EN9 * 16 J7
Foxfield Cl NTHWD HA6 22 B11
Foxfield Rd ORP BR6 77 M7
Foxglove Cl BFN/LL DA15 65 Q4
ED N9 27 N6
STHL UB1 46 G5
STWL/WRAY TW19 57 P6
Foxglove Gdns PUR/KEN CR8 86 C1
WAN E11 40 E2
Foxglove La CHSGTN KT9 72 A9
Foxglove Pth THMD SE28 53 N7
Foxglove Rd ROMW/RG RM7 42 E7
Foxglove St ACT W3 48 F5
Foxglove Wy WLGTN SM6 73 U6
Foxgrove STHGT/OAK N14 26 C8
Fox Gv WOT/HER KT12 70 D5
Foxgrove Av BECK BR3 63 T12
Foxgrove Dr WOKN/KNAP GU21 80 E5
Foxgrove Pth OXHEY WD19 22 F10
Foxgrove Rd BECK BR3 63 T12
Foxhall Rd UPMR RM14 43 Q10
Foxham Rd ARCH N19 38 B8
Foxhanger Gdns WOKS/MYFD GU22 80 E7
Foxherne DTCH/LGLY SL3 44 A7
Fox Hl HAYES BR2 76 E10
NRWD SE19 62 K12
Foxhill WATN WD24 11 N10
Fox Hill Gdns NRWD SE19 62 K12
Foxhill Ms CHERT KT16 68 F8
Foxhills WOKN/KNAP GU21 80 A8
Foxhills Cl CHERT KT16 68 F11
Fox Hills Rd CHERT KT16 68 F10
Foxhole Rd ELTH/MOT SE9 64 G3
Foxholes WEY KT13 69 V10
Fox Hollow Cl WOOL/PLUM SE18 53 N10
Fox Hollow Dr BXLYHN DA7 65 T1
Foxholt Gdns WLSDN NW10 36 C12
Foxhome Cl CHST BR7 64 J11
Fox House Rd BELV DA17 54 B9
Foxlake Rd BF/WBF KT14 81 R2
Foxlands Cl GSTN WD25 11 N8
Foxlands Crs DAGE RM10 42 C10
Foxlands Rd DAGE RM10 42 C10
Fox La EA W5 47 U3
GT/LBKH KT23 82 H14
HAYES BR2 76 D10
PLMGR N13 26 D7
REIG RH2 93 P7
Fox La North CHERT KT16 68 K6
Fox La South CHERT KT16 * 68 K6
Foxlees ALP/SUD HA0 35 Q9
Foxley Cl HACK E8 39 L10
Foxley Gdns PUR/KEN CR8 86 F3
Foxley Hill Rd PUR/KEN CR8 86 E2
Foxley La PUR/KEN CR8 74 C14
PUR/KEN CR8 86 E1
Foxley Rd BRXN/ST SW9 8 K13
PUR/KEN CR8 86 F4
THHTH CR7 74 F2
Foxleys OXHEY WD19 22 G8
Fox Manor Wy WTHK RM20 55 V11
Foxmead Cl ENC/FH EN2 26 D1
Foxmore St BTSEA SW11 49 T13
Foxoak Hl WOT/HER KT12 70 A14
Foxon Cl CTHM CR3 86 J11
Foxon La CTHM CR3 86 H11
Foxon Lane Gdns CTHM CR3 86 J11
Fox Rd CAN/RD E16 52 B3
DTCH/LGLY SL3 44 B9
Foxton Gv MTCM CR4 61 R14
Foxwarren ESH/CLAY KT10 71 P13
Foxwell St BROCKY SE4 63 Q1
Fox Wd WOT/HER KT12 70 B12
Foxwood Cha WAB EN9 16 J10
Foxwood Cl FELT TW13 58 D8
MLHL NW7 24 E9
Foxwood Green Cl EN EN1 26 J4
Foxwood Gv ORP BR6 77 S14
Foxwood Rd BKHTH/KID SE3 64 B2
RDART DA2 67 V8
Foyle Dr SOCK/AV RM15 55 U4
Foyle Rd BKHTH/KID SE3 52 B11
TOTM N17 27 L13
Frailey Cl WOKS/MYFD GU22 80 F6
Frailey Hl WOKS/MYFD GU22 80 F6
Framewood Rd SLN SL2 32 A12
Framfield Cl NFNCH/WDSPK N12 25 N9
Framfield Rd HBRY N5 38 F10
HNWL W7 47 P4
MTCM CR4 61 U12
Framlingham Crs ELTH/MOT SE9 64 G9
Frampton Cl BELMT SM2 73 N12
Frampton Park Rd HOM E9 39 N11
Frampton Rd EPP CM16 18 E2
HSLWW TW4 58 G3
POTB/CUF EN6 14 E4
Frampton St STJWD NW8 3 M8
Francemary Rd LEW SE13 63 S3
Frances Gdns SOCK/AV RM15 55 T5
Frances Rd CHING E4 27 S11
Frances St WOOL/PLUM SE18 52 H9
Franche Court Rd TOOT SW17 61 Q8
Francis Av BXLYHN DA7 54 A14
FELT TW13 58 C8
IL IG1 41 M7
Francis Barber Cl STRHM/NOR SW16 * 62 D9
Franciscan Rd TOOT SW17 61 U9
Francis Chichester Wy BTSEA SW11 * 49 U13
Francis Cl HOR/WEW KT19 72 D9
SHPTN TW17 69 S2
Francis Gv WIM/MER SW19 61 M12
Francis Ms LEE/GVPK SE12 * 64 B4
Francis Rd CROY/NA CR0 74 F5
CTHM CR3 86 H12
DART DA1 66 K3
EFNCH N2 * 37 T2
GFD/PVL UB6 35 S14
HRW HA1 35 Q3
HSLWW TW4 46 F14
LEY E10 39 U7
PIN HA5 34 E3
STMC/STPC BR5 77 T1
WATW WD18 22 D2
WLGTN SM6 74 A11
Francis St SRTFD E15 40 A10
WEST SW1P 8 B7
Francis Ter ARCH N19 38 A8
Francis Wk IS N1 4 G1
Francklyn Gdns EDGW HA8 24 A8
Francombe Gdns ROM RM1 42 G4
Franconia Rd CLAP SW4 62 A3
Frank Burton Cl CHARL SE7 52 D10
Frank Dixon Cl DUL SE21 62 J5
Frank Dixon Wy DUL SE21 62 J6
Frankfurt Rd HNHL SE24 62 G3
Frankham St DEPT SE8 51 S12
Frankland Cl BERM/RHTH SE16 51 M8
RKW/CH/CXG WD3 21 S5
WFD IG8 28 E10
Frankland Rd CHING E4 27 S10
RKW/CH/CXG WD3 21 T4
SKENS SW7 7 L6
Franklands Dr ADL/WDHM KT15 68 K12
Franklin Av CHESW EN7 16 A4
Franklin Cl KUT/HW KT1 72 A1
LEW SE13 51 T13
TRDG/WHET N20 25 Q5
WNWD SE27 62 F9
Franklin Crs MTCM CR4 74 A2
Franklin Rd BXLYHN DA7 53 U13
HCH RM12 42 J11
PGE/AN SE20 63 N12
RDART DA2 66 E7
WAT WD17 11 P14
Franklins Ms RYLN/HDSTN HA2 35 L7
Franklin Sq WKENS W14 6 D10
Franklins Rw CHEL SW3 7 R9
Franklin St BOW E3 51 T1
SEVS/STOTM N15 38 J4
Franklin Wy CROY/NA CR0 74 C6
Franklyn Gdns BARK/HLT IG6 29 M11
Franklyn Rd WLSDN NW10 36 F12
WOT/HER KT12 70 D4
Frank Martin Ct CHESW EN7 16 A4
Franks Av NWMAL KT3 72 C2
Franks La EYN DA4 79 P3
Franks Wood Av STMC/STPC BR5 76 K3
Frankswood Av WDR/YW UB7 45 R4
Franlaw Crs PLMGR N13 26 G9
Franmil Rd HCH RM12 42 F5
Fransfield Gv SYD SE26 63 M8
Franshams BUSH WD23 * 23 N7
Frant Cl PGE/AN SE20 63 N12
Frant Rd THHTH CR7 74 F3
Fraser Cl BXLY DA5 66 C6
Fraser Rd CHES/WCR EN8 16 E2
ED N9 27 M8
ERITH DA8 54 C10
GFD/PVL UB6 35 S13
WALTH E17 39 T3
Fraser St CHSWK W4 48 E10
Frating Crs WFD IG8 28 C11
Frays Av WDR/YW UB7 45 P7
Frays Cl WDR/YW UB7 45 P8
Frayslea UX/CGN UB8 33 N14
Fray's Waye UX/CGN UB8 33 N13
Frazer Av RSLP HA4 34 E10
Frazer Cl ROM RM1 42 F5
Frazier St STHWK SE1 8 K4
Frean St BERM/RHTH SE16 51 L8
Freda Corbett Cl PECK SE15 51 L12
Frederica Rd CHING E4 27 V5
Frederica St HOLWY N7 38 D12
Frederick Cl BAY/PAD W2 3 P13
SUT SM1 73 M9
Frederick Crs BRXN/ST SW9 9 L14
PEND EN3 16 C14
Frederick Gdns CROY/NA CR0 74 F4
SUT SM1 73 M10
Frederick Pl WOOL/PLUM SE18 52 K10
Frederick Rd RAIN RM13 42 D14
SUT SM1 73 M10
WALW SE17 * 9 M10
Frederick's Pl LOTH EC2R * 5 Q12
NFNCH/WDSPK N12 25 Q9
Frederick Sq BERM/RHTH SE16 51 Q5
Frederick's Rw FSBYE EC1V 5 L5
Frederick St FSBYW WC1X 4 G6
Frederick Ter HACK E8 * 38 K12
Frederic Ms KTBR SW1X * 7 S4
Frederic St WALTH E17 39 Q3
Fredora Av YEAD UB4 46 B2
Freeborne Gdns RAIN RM13 42 G11
Freedom Cl WALTH E17 39 P2
Freedom Rd TOTM N17 38 H1
Freedom St BTSEA SW11 49 T14
Freedown La BNSTD SM7 85 P3
Freegrove Rd HOLWY N7 38 C10
Freeland Pk HDN NW4 25 L14
Freeland Rd EA W5 47 V5
Freelands Av SAND/SEL CR2 75 P13
Freelands Gv BMLY BR1 64 D13
Freelands Rd BMLY BR1 64 D13
COB KT11 82 D4
Freeland Wy ERITH DA8 54 G13
Freeling St IS N1 38 D12
Freeman Cl NTHLT UB5 34 G12
SHPTN TW17 70 A2
Freeman Dr E/WMO/HCT KT8 70 H2
Freeman Rd MRDN SM4 73 R3
Freemans La HYS/HAR UB3 46 A5
Freemantle Av PEND EN3 27 P3
Freemantle St WALW SE17 9 S9
Freeman Wy EMPK RM11 43 L4
Freemasons Pl CROY/NA CR0 74 J6
Freemasons Rd CAN/RD E16 52 D4
CROY/NA CR0 74 J6
Free Prae Rd CHERT KT16 69 L6
Freesia Cl ORP BR6 77 P10
Freestone Yd DTCH/LGLY SL3 * 44 H12
Freethorpe Cl NRWD SE19 62 J13
Freezeland Wy HGDN/ICK UB10 33 T11
Freightmaster Est RAIN RM13 * 54 G9
Freke Rd BTSEA SW11 61 U1
Fremantle Rd BARK/HLT IG6 28 K14
BELV DA17 54 A9
Fremont St HOM E9 39 N13
Frenchaye ADL/WDHM KT15 69 N10
Frenches Rd REDH RH1 93 V7
The Frenches REDH RH1 93 U8
French Gdns COB KT11 82 E4
French Pl SDTCH EC2A 5 T6
French St SUN TW16 58 E14
Frendsbury Rd BROCKY SE4 63 Q2
Frensham CHESW EN7 15 V1
Frensham Cl STHL UB1 46 H2
Frensham Dr CROY/NA CR0 75 U12
PUT/ROE SW15 60 G8
Frensham Rd ELTH/MOT SE9 65 M7
PUR/KEN CR8 86 F4
Frensham St PECK SE15 51 L11
Frensham Wy EW KT17 84 J6
Frere St BTSEA SW11 49 S14
Freshfield Av HACK E8 38 K12
Freshfield Cl LEW SE13 63 V2
Freshfield Dr STHGT/OAK N14 25 V5
Freshfield Flats KWD/TDW/WH KT20 * 93 M3
Freshfields CROY/NA CR0 75 R5
Freshfields Av UPMR RM14 43 Q10
Freshford St TOOT SW17 61 Q8
Freshmount Gdns HOR/WEW KT19 84 B1
Freshwater Cl TOOT SW17 61 U11
Freshwater Rd BCTR RM8 41 T6
TOOT SW17 61 U11
Freshwell Av CHDH RM6 41 S2
Fresh Wharf Rd BARK IG11 40 K13
Freshwood Cl BECK BR3 63 T13
Freshwood Wy WLGTN SM6 74 A13
Freston Gdns EBAR EN4 25 U3
Freston Pk FNCH N3 25 M14
Freston Rd NKENS W10 48 K5
Freta Rd BXLYHS DA6 65 V3
Frewin Rd WAND/EARL SW18 61 R6
Friar Ms WNWD SE27 62 F8
Friar Rd STMC/STPC BR5 77 Q3
YEAD UB4 46 F2
Friars Av PUT/ROE SW15 60 F8
TRDG/WHET N20 25 S8
Friars Cl CHING E4 27 U8
IL IG1 41 M6
NTHLT UB5 46 E1
STHWK SE1 * 9 M1
Friars Gdns ACT W3 48 D4
Friars Gate Cl WFD IG8 28 C9
Friars La RCH/KEW TW9 59 T3
Friars Md POP/IOD E14 51 U8
Friars Ms ELTH/MOT SE9 64 J3
Friars Orch LHD/OX KT22 83 M11
Friars Place La ACT W3 48 E5
Friars Ri WOKS/MYFD GU22 80 E8
Friar's Rd EHAM E6 40 F13
VW GU25 68 B2
Friars Stile Rd RCHPK/HAM TW10 59 U4
The Friars CHIG IG7 29 N9
Friars Wk ABYW SE2 53 T10
STHGT/OAK N14 25 V6
Friars Wy ACT W3 48 D4
BUSH WD23 11 T13
CHERT KT16 69 L4
KGLGY WD4 10 G4
Friars Wd CROY/NA CR0 75 Q13
Friary Cl NFNCH/WDSPK N12 25 S10
Friary Est PECK SE15 * 51 L12
Friary Island STWL/WRAY TW19 56 A4
Friary La WFD IG8 28 C9
Friary Pk NFNCH/WDSPK N12 * 25 S9
Friary Park Ct ACT W3 * 48 C4
Friary Rd ACT W3 48 C4
NFNCH/WDSPK N12 25 R9
PECK SE15 51 L12
STWL/WRAY TW19 56 A4
The Friary CHES/WCR EN8 * 16 F7
WDSR SL4 56 A5
Friary Wy NFNCH/WDSPK N12 25 S9
Friday Hl CHING E4 28 A8
Friday Hl East CHING E4 28 A8
Friday Hl West CHING E4 28 A7
Friday Rd ERITH DA8 54 D10
MTCM CR4 61 T12
Friday St STP EC4M 5 N13
Frideswide Pl KTTN NW5 38 A10
Friendly Pl LEW SE13 51 T13
Friendly St DEPT SE8 51 S13
Friendly Street Ms DEPT SE8 51 S14
Friends Av CHES/WCR EN8 16 D6
Friendship Wy SRTFD E15 * 39 U13
Friends' Rd CROY/NA CR0 74 H8
PUR/KEN CR8 86 F2
Friend St FSBYE EC1V 5 L5
Friern Barnet La TRDG/WHET N20 25 S9
Friern Barnet Rd FBAR/BDGN N11 25 U10
Friern Mount Dr TRDG/WHET N20 25 Q5
Friern Pk NFNCH/WDSPK N12 25 R10
Friern Rd EDUL SE22 63 L4
Friern Watch Av NFNCH/WDSPK N12 25 R9
Frigate Ms DEPT SE8 51 S11
Frimley Av EMPK RM11 43 N6
WLGTN SM6 74 C10
Frimley Cl CROY/NA CR0 75 U12
WIM/MER SW19 61 L7
Frimley Ct SCUP DA14 65 S10
Frimley Crs CROY/NA CR0 75 U12
Frimley Gdns MTCM CR4 73 S1
Frimley Rd CHSGTN KT9 71 T10
GDMY/SEVK IG3 41 N8
Frimley Wy WCHPL E1 * 51 P2
Fringewood Cl NTHWD HA6 21 T13
Frinstead Gv STMC/STPC BR5 77 T2
Frinsted Rd ERITH DA8 54 D12
Frinton Cl OXHEY WD19 22 D7
Frinton Dr WFD IG8 27 V12
Frinton Ms GNTH/NBYPK IG2 40 J4
Frinton Rd CRW RM5 30 A12
EHAM E6 52 F1
SCUP DA14 65 U7
SEVS/STOTM N15 38 J4
TOOT SW17 61 U11
Friston St FUL/PGN SW6 49 P14
Friswell Pl BXLYHN DA7 66 A2
Fritham Cl NWMAL KT3 72 E4
Frith Ct MLHL NW7 25 L12
Frith Knowle WOT/HER KT12 70 D11
Frith La MLHL NW7 25 L11
Frith Manor Farm Cotts MLHL NW7 * 25 L10
Frith Rd CROY/NA CR0 74 G7
WAN E11 39 U9
Friths Dr REIG RH2 93 P7
Frith St SOHO/SHAV W1D 4 C12
Frithville Gdns SHB W12 48 J6
Frithwald Rd CHERT KT16 68 K5
Frithwood Av NTHWD HA6 22 B11
Frizlands La DAGE RM10 42 B8
Frobisher Cl BUSH WD23 22 J4
PIN HA5 34 F5
PUR/KEN CR8 86 G7
Frobisher Crs BARB EC2Y * 5 P9
STWL/WRAY TW19 57 Q5
Frobisher Gdns LEY E10 * 39 T4
Frobisher Ms ENC/FH EN2 26 H2
Frobisher Rd CEND/HSY/T N8 38 E2
EHAM E6 52 H4
ERITH DA8 54 G12
Frobisher Wy RDART DA2 67 V2
Froggy La DEN/HRF UB9 32 H8
Froghole La EDEN TN8 97 N9
Frogley Rd EDUL SE22 62 K2
Frogmoor La RKW/CH/CXG WD3 21 P7
Frogmore LCOL/BKTW AL2 12 C1
WAND/EARL SW18 61 N3
Frogmore Av YEAD UB4 46 A2
Frogmore Cl CHEAM SM3 72 K8
Frogmore Est HBRY N5 * 38 G9
Frogmore Gdns CHEAM SM3 73 L9
YEAD UB4 46 A2
Frognal HAMP NW3 37 Q10
Frognal Av HRW HA1 35 P2
SCUP DA14 65 Q11
Frognal Cl HAMP NW3 37 Q10
Frognal Gdns HAMP NW3 37 Q9
Frognal La HAMP NW3 37 P10
Frognal Man HAMP NW3 * 37 Q9
Frognal Pde HAMP NW3 37 Q11
Frognal Pl SCUP DA14 65 R10
Frognal Ri HAMP NW3 37 Q8
Frognal Wy HAMP NW3 37 Q9
Froissart Rd ELTH/MOT SE9 64 G3
Frome Rd SEVS/STOTM N15 38 F1
Frome St IS N1 5 N3
Fromondes Rd CHEAM SM3 73 L10
Fromows Cnr CHSWK W4 * 48 C10
Front La UPMR RM14 43 S7
Frostic Wk WCHPL E1 5 V10
Froude St VX/NE SW8 49 V14
Frowycke Crs POTB/CUF EN6 13 S6
Fruen Rd EBED/NFELT TW14 58 B5
Fryatt Rd TOTM N17 26 H12
Fry Cl CRW RM5 30 A10
Fryday Grove Ms BAL SW12 62 A5
Fryent Cl KTN/HRWW/WS HA3 36 A4
Fryent Crs CDALE/KGS NW9 36 E4
Fryent Flds CDALE/KGS NW9 36 E4
Fryent Gv CDALE/KGS NW9 36 E4
Fryent Wy CDALE/KGS NW9 36 A4
Fryern Wd CTHM CR3 86 G14
Frying Pan Aly WCHPL E1 5 T10
Fry Rd EHAM E6 40 F12
WLSDN NW10 36 F13
Fryston Av COUL/CHIP CR5 85 V4
CROY/NA CR0 75 L7
Fuchsia Cl ROMW/RG RM7 42 E7
Fuchsia St ABYW SE2 53 R10
Fulbeck Dr CDALE/KGS NW9 24 E13
Fulbeck Wy RYLN/HDSTN HA2 23 L14
Fulbourne Cl REDH RH1 93 S8
Fulbourne Rd WALTH E17 27 U14
Fulbourne St WCHPL E1 51 M3
Fulbrook La SOCK/AV RM15 55 T5
Fulbrook Ms ARCH N19 38 A9
Fulbrook Rd ARCH N19 38 A9
Fulford Gv OXHEY WD19 22 D7
Fulford Rd CTHM CR3 86 H11
HOR/WEW KT19 72 D12
Fulford St BERM/RHTH SE16 51 M7
Fulham Cl HGDN/ICK UB10 45 U2
Fulham Est FUL/PGN SW6 6 D11
Fulham High St FUL/PGN SW6 49 L14
Fulham Palace Rd FUL/PGN SW6 48 K13
Fulham Park Gdns FUL/PGN SW6 49 M14
Fulham Park Rd FUL/PGN SW6 49 M14
Fulham Rd FUL/PGN SW6 6 G14
FUL/PGN SW6 49 L14
WBPTN SW10 6 K11
Fullarton Crs SOCK/AV RM15 55 T4
Fullbrook Av ADL/WDHM KT15 81 L1
Fullbrooks Av WPK KT4 72 F6
Fuller Cl BETH E2 * 51 L2
BUSH WD23 23 M5
ORP BR6 77 P10
Fuller Gdns WATN WD24 11 P11
Fuller Rd BCTR RM8 41 S8
WATN WD24 11 P11
Fullers Av SURB KT6 71 V7
SWFD E18 28 B12
Fullers Cl CRW RM5 30 C12
WAB EN9 17 N7
Fullers Hl BH/WHM TN16 97 M2
Fuller's Rd SWFD E18 28 B13
Fuller St HDN NW4 36 J2
Fullers Wy North SURB KT6 71 V8
Fullers Wy South CHSGTN KT9 71 U9
Fuller's Wd CROY/NA CR0 75 S10
Fullers Wood La REDH RH1 94 A10
Fullerton Cl BF/WBF KT14 81 R4
Fullerton Dr BF/WBF KT14 81 Q4
Fullerton Rd BF/WBF KT14 81 Q4
CAR SM5 73 S13
CROY/NA CR0 74 K5
WAND/EARL SW18 61 Q3
Fullerton Wy BF/WBF KT14 81 Q4
Fuller Wy HYS/HAR UB3 46 B10
RKW/CH/CXG WD3 21 S3
Fullmer Wy ADL/WDHM KT15 68 K14
Fullwell Av CLAY IG5 28 J13
Fullwood Pl GINN WC1R 4 H10
Fullwood's Ms IS N1 5 R5
Fulmar Ct BRYLDS KT5 71 V4
Fulmar Rd HCH RM12 42 H12
Fulmead St FUL/PGN SW6 49 P13
Fulmer Cl HPTN TW12 58 G10
Fulmer Common Rd DTCH/LGLY SL3 32 D11
Fulmer Cnr CFSP/GDCR SL9 * 32 F6
Fulmer Dr CFSP/GDCR SL9 32 C7
Fulmer La DTCH/LGLY SL3 32 D8
Fulmer Pl DTCH/LGLY SL3 * 32 C9
Fulmer Rd CAN/RD E16 52 F3
DTCH/LGLY SL3 32 C9
Fulmer Wy CFSP/GDCR SL9 32 C4
WEA W13 47 R8
Fulready Rd LEY E10 39 V3
Fulstone Cl HSLWW TW4 58 H2
Fulthorp Rd BKHTH/KID SE3 52 B14
Fulton Ms BAY/PAD W2 2 J13
Fulton Rd WBLY HA9 36 A8
Fulwell Park Av WHTN TW2 59 L7
Fulwell Rd TEDD TW11 59 M9
Fulwich Rd DART DA1 67 M4
Fulwood Av ALP/SUD HA0 35 V14
Fulwood Gdns TWK TW1 59 P4
Fulwood Wk WIM/MER SW19 61 L6
Furber St HMSMTH W6 48 H8
Furham Fld PIN HA5 22 J12
Furley Rd PECK SE15 51 L12
Furlong Cl WLGTN SM6 73 V6
Furlong Rd HOLWY N7 38 E11
The Furlough WOKS/MYFD GU22 80 E7
Furmage St WAND/EARL SW18 61 P5
Furneaux Av WNWD SE27 62 F10
Furner Cl DART DA1 66 F1
Furness Rd FUL/PGN SW6 49 P14
MRDN SM4 73 P4
RYLN/HDSTN HA2 34 K6
WLSDN NW10 36 G14
Furness Wy HCH RM12 42 G10
Furnival Cl VW GU25 68 B4
Furnival St FLST/FETLN EC4A 4 J11
Furrow La HOM E9 39 N10
Furrows Pl CTHM CR3 86 K13
The Furrows WOT/HER KT12 70 E7

Fursby Av FNCH N3 25 N11
Further Acre CDALE/KGS NW9 24 F14
Furtherfield ABLGY WD5 11 L6
Furtherfield Cl CROY/NA CR0 74 E4
Further Green Rd CAT SE6 64 A5
Furze Cl OXHEY WD19 22 E10
REDH RH1 93 T9
Furzedown Cl EGH TW20 56 C11
Furzedown Dr TOOT SW17 61 V10
Furzedown Rd BELMT SM2 85 Q1
TOOT SW17 61 V10
Furze Farm Cl CHDH RM6 29 U14
Furzefield CHES/WCR EN8 16 B2
Furze Fld LHD/OX KT22 83 M3
Furzefield Cl CHST BR7 64 K11
Furzefield Ct POTB/CUF EN6 * 14 A5
Furzefield Crs REIG RH2 93 Q12
Furzefield Rd BKHTH/KID SE3 52 D11
REIG RH2 93 Q12
Furzeground Wy STKPK UB11 45 U7
Furze Gv KWD/TDW/WH KT20 85 M11
Furzeham Rd WDR/YW UB7 45 Q7
Furze Hl KWD/TDW/WH KT20 85 M11
PUR/KEN CR8 86 C1
Furzehill REDH RH1 93 S9
Furzehill Pde BORE WD6 * 24 A2
Furzehill Rd BORE WD6 24 C3
Furzehill Sq STMC/STPC BR5 77 R2
Furze La PUR/KEN CR8 86 C1
Furze Pl REDH RH1 * 93 T9
Furze Rd ADL/WDHM KT15 68 K11
THHTH CR7 74 G1
Furze St BOW E3 * 51 S3
Furze Vw RKW/CH/CXG WD3 20 G4
Furzewood SUN TW16 58 C13
Fusedale Wy SOCK/AV RM15 55 T5
Fye Foot La BLKFR EC4V 5 N13
Fyfe Wy BMLY BR1 64 C14
Fyfield Cl HAYES BR2 75 V2
Fyfield Dr SOCK/AV RM15 55 T5
Fyfield Rd BRXN/ST SW9 62 E1
EN EN1 26 J1
RAIN RM13 42 F13
WALTH E17 39 V1
WFD IG8 28 E12
Fynes St WEST SW1P 8 C7

G

Gabion Av PUR RM19 55 R9
Gable Cl ABLGY WD5 11 L6
DART DA1 66 G3
PIN HA5 22 J12
Gable Ct SYD SE26 63 M9
Gable Ms HAYES BR2 76 G7
Gables Av ASHF TW15 57 R10
BORE WD6 23 V1
Gables Cl CFSP/GDCR SL9 20 C9
CMBW SE5 50 J13
LEE/GVPK SE12 64 C6
WOKS/MYFD GU22 80 D10
The Gables BNSTD SM7 85 M7
LHD/OX KT22 83 L2
NRWD SE19 * 62 J13
WBLY HA9 35 V8
WEY KT13 69 U10
WOKS/MYFD GU22 * 80 B9
Gables Wy BNSTD SM7 85 M6
Gabriel Cl CRW RM5 30 C12
FELT TW13 58 G9
Gabrielle Cl WBLY HA9 35 V8
Gabrielspring Rd HART DA3 79 R7
Gabriel Spring Road (East) HART DA3 79 T7
Gabriel St FSTH SE23 63 P5
Gabriel's Whf STHWK SE1 8 J1
Gad Cl PLSTW E13 52 D1
Gaddesden Av WBLY HA9 35 V11
Gaddesden Crs GSTN WD25 11 R8
Gade Av WATW WD18 22 A2
Gade Bank RKW/CH/CXG WD3 21 V2
Gade Cl HYS/HAR UB3 46 D6
WATW WD18 22 A2
Gadesden Rd HOR/WEW KT19 72 C11
Gade Valley Cl KGLGY WD4 10 G2
Gade View Gdns KGLGY WD4 10 J6
Gadsbury Cl CDALE/KGS NW9 36 F4
Gadsden Cl UPMR RM14 43 S4
Gadswell Cl GSTN WD25 11 S10
Gadwall Cl CAN/RD E16 52 D4
Gage Rd CAN/RD E16 52 A3
Gage St BMSBY WC1N 4 F9
Gainford St IS N1 4 J1
Gainsboro Gdns GFD/PVL UB6 35 N10
Gainsborough Av DART DA1 66 J3
MNPK E12 40 J10
Gainsborough Cl BECK BR3 63 S12
ESH/CLAY KT10 71 N6
Gainsborough Ct SHB W12 48 J7
WOT/HER KT12 70 C9
Gainsborough Dr SAND/SEL CR2 87 L3
Gainsborough Gdns EDGW HA8 23 V14
GLDGN NW11 37 M5
HAMP NW3 37 R8
HSLW TW3 59 M3
Gainsborough Ms DUL SE21 62 G6
SYD SE26 * 63 M8
Gainsborough Pl CHIG IG7 29 P8
Gainsborough Rd BCTR RM8 41 R9
CHSWK W4 48 F9
HOR/WEW KT19 72 C14
NFNCH/WDSPK N12 25 P10
NWMAL KT3 72 D4
RAIN RM13 42 G13
RCH/KEW TW9 47 V14
SRTFD E15 52 A1
WAN E11 40 A5
WFD IG8 28 G11
YEAD UB4 33 U14
Gainsborough Sq BXLYHS DA6 65 T1
Gainsborough St HOM E9 39 R11
Gainsborough Ter BELMT SM2 * 73 M12
Gainsford Rd WALTH E17 39 R2
Gainsford St STHWK SE1 9 U2
Gairloch Rd CMBW SE5 50 J14
Gaisford St KTTN NW5 38 A11
Gaist Av CTHM CR3 87 M12
Gaitskell Rd ELTH/MOT SE9 65 L6
Gaitskell Wy STHWK SE1 9 N3
Galahad Rd BMLY BR1 64 C8
ED N9 27 L8
Galata Rd BARN SW13 48 G12
Galatea Sq PECK SE15 63 M1
Galbraith St POP/IOD E14 51 U8
Galdana Av BAR EN5 25 Q1
Galeborough Av WFD IG8 27 V12
Gale Cl HPTN TW12 58 G11
MTCM CR4 73 R1
Gale Crs BNSTD SM7 85 N7
Galena Rd HMSMTH W6 48 H9
Galen Cl HOR/WEW KT19 84 A1
Galen Pl NOXST/BSQ WC1A 4 F10
Galesbury Rd WAND/EARL SW18 61 Q4
Gales Gdns BETH E2 51 M1
Gale St BOW E3 51 S3
DAGW RM9 41 T11
Gales Wy WFD IG8 28 G12
Galey Gn SOCK/AV RM15 55 V3
Galgate Cl WIM/MER SW19 60 K6
Gallants Farm Rd EBAR EN4 25 T6
Galleon Bvd RDART DA2 67 R3
Galleon Cl BERM/RHTH SE16 51 N7
ERITH DA8 54 D9
Galleon Rd CDW/CHF RM16 55 V9
Galleons Dr BARK IG11 53 Q1
Galleons La DTCH/LGLY SL3 44 B1
The Galleries IS N1 * 5 L3
Gallery Gdns NTHLT UB5 34 F14
Gallery Rd DUL SE21 62 H6
Galleyhill Rd WAB EN9 17 L7
Galley La BAR EN5 13 S12
Galleymead Rd DTCH/LGLY SL3 44 K13
Galleywall Rd BERM/RHTH SE16 51 M9
Galleywood Crs CRW RM5 30 D11
Galliard Rd ED N9 27 L5
Gallia Rd HBRY N5 38 F10
Gallions Cl BARK IG11 53 Q1
Gallions Rd CAN/RD E16 52 K5
CHARL SE7 52 D9
Gallions View Rd THMD SE28 53 N7
Gallon Cl CHARL SE7 52 E9
The Gallop BELMT SM2 73 R13
SAND/SEL CR2 75 M12
Gallosson Rd WOOL/PLUM SE18 53 N9
Galloway Dr DART DA1 66 E5
Galloway Pth CROY/NA CR0 74 H9
Galloway Rd SHB W12 48 G6
Gallows Hl KGLGY WD4 10 J5
Gallows Hill La ABLGY WD5 10 K5
Gallus Cl WCHMH N21 26 D4
Gallus Sq BKHTH/KID SE3 64 D1
Galpin's Rd THHTH CR7 74 C2
Galsworthy Av CHDH RM6 41 R5
POP/IOD E14 51 Q4
Galsworthy Cl THMD SE28 53 R6
Galsworthy Crs BKHTH/KID SE3 52 E13
Galsworthy Rd CHERT KT16 69 L5
CRICK NW2 37 L9
KUTN/CMB KT2 60 B13
Galton St NKENS W10 2 A6
Galva Cl EBAR EN4 25 U2
Galveston Rd PUT/ROE SW15 61 M3
Galway Cl BERM/RHTH SE16 51 M10
Galway St FSBYE EC1V 5 P6
Gambetta St VX/NE SW8 49 V14
Gambia St STHWK SE1 9 M2
Gambole Rd TOOT SW17 61 S9
Games Rd EBAR EN4 25 S1
Gamlen Rd PUT/ROE SW15 60 K2
Gammons Farm Cl WATN WD24 11 M10
Gammons La WATN WD24 11 N11
Gamuel Cl WALTH E17 39 S4
Gander Green Crs HPTN TW12 58 K13
Gander Green La CHEAM SM3 73 L7
Ganders Ash GSTN WD25 11 N7
Gandhi Cl WALTH E17 39 S4
Gandhi Ct WATN WD24 11 R14
Gandolfi St PECK SE15 9 S13
Gangers Hl GDST RH9 95 R3
Gant Ct WAB EN9 17 M8
Ganton St REGST W1B 4 A13
Ganton Wk OXHEY WD19 * 22 G9
Gantshill Crs GNTH/NBYPK IG2 40 J3
Gap Rd WIM/MER SW19 61 N10
Garage Rd ACT W3 48 A4
Garbrand Wk EW KT17 72 F13
Garbutt Pl MHST W1U * 3 T9
Garbutt Rd UPMR RM14 43 Q7
Garden Av BXLYHN DA7 65 V1
MTCM CR4 61 V12
Garden City EDGW HA8 24 A11
Garden Cl ADL/WDHM KT15 69 P9
ASHF TW15 57 U11
BAR EN5 24 J2
BH/WHM TN16 97 S8
BNSTD SM7 85 N5
CHING E4 27 S10
HPTN TW12 58 H10
LEE/GVPK SE12 64 D8
LHD/OX KT22 83 S14
NTHLT UB5 34 G13
PUT/ROE SW15 60 H5
RSLP HA4 34 A7
WAT WD17 11 M14
WLGTN SM6 74 C10
Garden Ct CHSWK W4 48 C8
EMB EC4Y * 4 J13
HPTN TW12 58 H10
SEV TN13 * 90 K12
Gardeners Rd CROY/NA CR0 74 F6
Garden Flats HMSMTH W6 * 48 K11
Gardenia Rd BMLY BR1 76 J1
EN EN1 26 J4
Gardenia Wy WFD IG8 28 C11
Garden La BMLY BR1 64 E11
BRXS/STRHM SW2 62 D6
Garden Lodge Ct EFNCH N2 * 37 R1
Garden Pl HACK E8 5 U1
RDART DA2 66 K8
Garden Reach CSTG HP8 20 B1
Garden Rd ABLGY WD5 11 L5
BMLY BR1 64 D12
PGE/AN SE20 63 N13
RCH/KEW TW9 60 A1
SEV TN13 90 K12
STJWD NW8 2 K5
WOT/HER KT12 70 D4
Garden Rw STHWK SE1 9 L6
The Gardens BECK BR3 63 U14
BRKMPK AL9 14 A1
CEND/HSY/T N8 * 38 C2
CLPT E5 * 38 K5
COB KT11 * 81 U9
EBED/NFELT TW14 57 V4
EDUL SE22 63 L2
ESH/CLAY KT10 70 J9
HGDN/ICK UB10 33 Q7
HRW HA1 35 L4
PIN HA5 * 34 H4
WAT WD17 11 M14
Garden St WCHPL E1 51 P3
Garden Studios BAY/PAD W2 * 2 J10
Garden Ter PIM SW1V 8 C9
Garden Vls ESH/CLAY KT10 * 71 P12
Garden Wk BECK BR3 63 R13
COUL/CHIP CR5 85 V13
SDTCH EC2A 5 S7
Garden Wy LOU IG10 17 U12
WLSDN NW10 36 C11
Gardiner Av CRICK NW2 * 36 J10
Gardiner Cl BCTR RM8 41 T9
PEND EN3 27 P4
STMC/STPC BR5 65 S14
Gardiner House CHARL SE7 * 52 G12
Gardner Cl WAN E11 40 D4
Gardner Pl EBED/NFELT TW14 58 D4
Gardner Rd PLSTW E13 52 D2
Gardners Cl FBAR/BDGN N11 25 U7
Gardners La BLKFR EC4V 5 N13
Gardnor Rd HAMP NW3 37 R9
Gard St FSBYE EC1V 5 M5
Garendon Gdns MRDN SM4 73 P5
Garendon Rd MRDN SM4 73 P5
Gareth Cl WPK KT4 72 K7
Gareth Dr ED N9 27 L8
Gareth Gv BMLY BR1 64 C9
Garfield Ms BTSEA SW11 61 V1
Garfield Rd ADL/WDHM KT15 69 N10
BTSEA SW11 61 U1
CHING E4 27 V6
PEND EN3 27 N2
PLSTW E13 52 B2
TWK TW1 59 Q6
WIM/MER SW19 61 Q11
Garfield St WATN WD24 11 P12
Garford St POP/IOD E14 51 S5
Garganey Wk THMD SE28 53 T5
Garibaldi Rd REDH RH1 93 T11
Garibaldi St WOOL/PLUM SE18 53 N9
Garland Cl CHES/WCR EN8 16 E5
Garland Dr HSLW TW3 47 L14
Garland Rd STAN HA7 23 T13
WOOL/PLUM SE18 53 M12
Garlands Rd LHD/OX KT22 83 R11
REDH RH1 93 T10
Garland Wy CTHM CR3 86 H12
EMPK RM11 43 L2
Garlichill Rd EPSOM KT18 84 H7
Garlick Hl BLKFR EC4V 5 P13
Garlies Rd FSTH SE23 63 Q8
Garlinge Rd CRICK NW2 37 M11
Garman Cl UED N18 26 H10
Garman Rd TOTM N17 27 N12
Garnault Ms CLKNW EC1R 4 K6
Garnault Pl CLKNW EC1R 4 K6
Garnault Rd EN EN1 15 V12
Garner Cl BCTR RM8 41 T6
Garner Rd WALTH E17 27 U13
Garners Cl CFSP/GDCR SL9 20 C11
Garners End CFSP/GDCR SL9 20 C11
Garners Rd CFSP/GDCR SL9 20 C11
Garner St BETH E2 39 L14
Garnet Rd THHTH CR7 74 G2
WLSDN NW10 36 E11
Garnet St WAP E1W 51 N5
Garnett Cl ELTH/MOT SE9 64 H1
WATN WD24 11 R11
Garnett Dr LCOL/BKTW AL2 11 T3
Garnett Rd HAMP NW3 37 T10
Garnham St STNW/STAM N16 38 K7
Garnies Cl PECK SE15 9 U13
Garnon Md EPP CM16 18 H2
Garrad's Rd STRHM/NOR SW16 62 B8
Garrard Cl BXLYHN DA7 66 A1
CHST BR7 64 K10
Garrard Rd BNSTD SM7 85 N6
Garrard Wk WLSDN NW10 * 36 E11
Garratt Cl CROY/NA CR0 74 C9
Garratt La WAND/EARL SW18 61 P3
Garratt Rd EDGW HA8 24 A12
Garratts La BNSTD SM7 85 M6
Garratts Rd BUSH WD23 23 L5
Garratt Ter TOOT SW17 61 S9
Garrett Cl ACT W3 48 D3
Garrett St STLK EC1Y 5 N7
Garrick Av GLDGN NW11 37 M4
Garrick Cl EA W5 47 U2
RCH/KEW TW9 59 S3
STA TW18 57 L12
WAND/EARL SW18 61 Q2
WOT/HER KT12 70 D9
Garrick Crs CROY/NA CR0 74 J7
Garrick Dr HDN NW4 24 J14
THMD SE28 53 M8
Garrick Gdns E/WMO/HCT KT8 70 J1
Garrick Pk HDN NW4 24 K14
Garrick Rd CDALE/KGS NW9 36 F4
GFD/PVL UB6 46 K2
RCH/KEW TW9 48 A14
Garrick St COVGDN WC2E 4 E13
Garrick Wy HDN NW4 36 K2
Garrick Yd CHCR WC2N 4 E13
Garrison Cl HSLWW TW4 58 H3
WOOL/PLUM SE18 52 J12
Garrison La CHSGTN KT9 71 U12
Garrison Rd BOW E3 39 S13
Garrolds Cl SWLY BR8 66 D14
Garron La SOCK/AV RM15 55 T4
Garry Cl ROM RM1 30 E12
Garry Wy ROM RM1 30 E12
Garside Cl HPTN TW12 58 K12
THMD SE28 53 M8
Garsington Ms BROCKY SE4 63 R1
Garsmouth Wy GSTN WD25 11 R10
Garson La STWL/WRAY TW19 56 B5
Garson Rd ESH/CLAY KT10 70 H11
Garston Crs GSTN WD25 11 Q8
Garston Dr GSTN WD25 11 Q8
Garston La GSTN WD25 11 R9
PUR/KEN CR8 86 H5
Garter Wy BERM/RHTH SE16 51 P7
Garth Cl KUTN/CMB KT2 59 V10
MRDN SM4 72 K5
RSLP HA4 34 F6
Garthland Dr BAR EN5 24 H3
Garth Ms EA W5 * 47 U2
Garthorne Rd FSTH SE23 63 P5
Garth Rd CHSWK W4 48 D10
CRICK NW2 37 M7
KUTN/CMB KT2 59 V10
MRDN SM4 72 K6
Garthside KUTN/CMB KT2 59 U10
The Garth ABLGY WD5 10 K7
COB KT11 82 G3
HPTN TW12 58 K11
KTN/HRWW/WS HA3 35 V4
NFNCH/WDSPK N12 * 25 P10
Garthway NFNCH/WDSPK N12 25 S11
Gartlet Rd WAT WD17 22 E1
Gartmoor Gdns WIM/MER SW19 61 M6
Gartmore Rd GDMY/SEVK IG3 41 P6
Garton Pl WAND/EARL SW18 61 Q4
Gartons Cl PEND EN3 27 N3
Gartons Wy BTSEA SW11 61 Q1
Garvary Rd CAN/RD E16 52 D4
Garway Rd BAY/PAD W2 2 G12
Gascoigne Gdns WFD IG8 28 A12
Gascoigne Pl BETH E2 5 U6
Gascoigne Rd BARK IG11 41 L13
CROY/NA CR0 75 U14
WEY KT13 69 T8
Gascony Av KIL/WHAMP NW6 37 N12
Gascoyne Cl HARH RM3 30 K13
POTB/CUF EN6 13 S6
Gascoyne Dr DART DA1 66 F1
Gascoyne Rd HOM E9 39 P12
Gaselee St POP/IOD E14 51 U5
Gasholder Pl LBTH SE11 8 H10
Gaskarth Rd BAL SW12 61 V4
EDGW HA8 24 C14
Gaskell Rd HGT N6 37 T4
Gaskell St CLAP SW4 50 C14
Gaskin St IS N1 5 L1
Gaspar Cl ECT SW5 * 6 H7
Gaspar Ms ECT SW5 6 H7
Gassiot Rd TOOT SW17 61 T9
Gassiot Wy SUT SM1 73 R8
Gastein Rd HMSMTH W6 48 K11
Gaston Bell Cl RCH/KEW TW9 59 V1
Gaston Bridge Rd SHPTN TW17 69 V4
Gaston Rd MTCM CR4 73 U1
Gaston Wy SHPTN TW17 69 V3
Gataker St BERM/RHTH SE16 51 M8
Gatcombe Ms EA W5 47 V5
Gatcombe Rd ARCH N19 38 B8
Gatcombe Wy EBAR EN4 25 T1
Gate Cl BORE WD6 13 N13
Gate Cottages EDGW HA8 * 24 A7
Gate End NTHWD HA6 22 C12
Gateforth St STJWD NW8 3 N8
Gatehill Rd NTHWD HA6 22 C12
Gatehope Dr SOCK/AV RM15 55 T4
Gatehouse Cl KUTN/CMB KT2 60 C12
Gatehouse Ldg REDH RH1 93 U13
Gatehouse Sq STHWK SE1 9 P1
Gateley Rd BRXN/ST SW9 62 D1
Gate Ms SKENS SW7 7 P4
Gater Dr ENC/FH EN2 15 T13
Gatesden Cl LHD/OX KT22 83 L13
Gatesden Rd LHD/OX KT22 83 L13
Gates Green Rd WWKM BR4 76 C9
Gateshead Rd BORE WD6 12 K14
Gateside Rd TOOT SW17 61 T8
Gatestone Rd NRWD SE19 62 J11
Gate St HOL/ALD WC2B 4 G11
Gateway WALW SE17 9 P11
Gateway Ar IS N1 * 5 L3
Gateway Cl NTHWD HA6 21 U11
Gateway Gdns EHAM E6 52 H1
Gateway Ms HACK E8 * 38 K10
The Gateways CHESW EN7 15 T2
RCH/KEW TW9 * 59 T2
The Gateway WATW WD18 22 A3
WOKN/KNAP GU21 80 G3
Gatfield Gv FELT TW13 58 J7
Gathorne Rd WDGN N22 26 E14
Gathorne St BETH E2 39 P14
Gatley Av HOR/WEW KT19 72 B10
Gatliff Rd BGVA SW1W 7 U11
Gatling Rd ABYW SE2 53 Q10
Gatonby St PECK SE15 50 K13
Gatting Wy UX/CGN UB8 33 Q11
Gatton Bottom REIG RH2 93 T4
Gatton Cl BELMT SM2 * 73 P13
REIG RH2 93 Q7
Gatton Park Rd REIG RH2 93 R7
Gatton Rd REIG RH2 93 Q7
TOOT SW17 61 S9
Gattons Wy SCUP DA14 65 V9
Gatward Cl WCHMH N21 26 F4
Gatward Gn ED N9 26 K7
Gatwick Rd WAND/EARL SW18 61 M5
Gauden Cl CLAP SW4 62 B1
Gauden Rd CLAP SW4 62 B1
Gaumont Ap WAT WD17 22 D1
Gaumont Ter SHB W12 * 48 J7
Gauntlet Cl NTHLT UB5 34 G12
Gauntlet Crs COUL/CHIP CR5 86 H10
Gauntlett Ct ALP/SUD HA0 35 R10
Gauntlett Rd SUT SM1 73 R10
Gaunt St STHWK SE1 9 M5
Gautrey Rd PECK SE15 51 N14
Gavell Rd COB KT11 82 C3
Gavel St WALW SE17 * 9 R7
Gavenny Pth SOCK/AV RM15 55 T4
Gaverick St POP/IOD E14 51 S9
Gaveston Cl BF/WBF KT14 81 R3
Gavestone Crs LEE/GVPK SE12 64 D6
Gavestone Rd LEE/GVPK SE12 64 D5
Gaveston Rd LHD/OX KT22 83 Q10
Gavina Cl MRDN SM4 73 S3
Gaviots Cl CFSP/GDCR SL9 32 D6
Gaviots Gn CFSP/GDCR SL9 32 C6
Gaviots Wy CFSP/GDCR SL9 32 C5
Gawain Wk ED N9 27 L8
Gawber St BETH E2 51 N1
Gawsworth Cl SRTFD E15 40 B10
Gawthorne Av MLHL NW7 25 L10
Gawton Crs COUL/CHIP CR5 86 A11
Gay Cl CRICK NW2 36 H10
Gaydon La CDALE/KGS NW9 24 E13
Gayfere Rd CLAY IG5 40 H1
EW KT17 72 G10
Gayfere St WEST SW1P 8 E6
Gayford Rd SHB W12 48 F7
Gay Gdns DAGE RM10 42 C9
Gayhurst Rd HACK E8 39 L12
Gayler Cl REDH RH1 94 K10
Gaylor Rd NTHLT UB5 34 H10
Gaynes Ct UPMR RM14 43 P9
Gaynesford Rd CAR SM5 73 T12
FSTH SE23 63 P7
Gaynes Hill Rd WFD IG8 28 G12
Gaynes Park Rd UPMR RM14 43 N9
Gaynes Rd UPMR RM14 43 P7
Gay Rd SRTFD E15 39 V14
Gaysham Av GNTH/NBYPK IG2 40 J3
Gayton Cl ASHTD KT21 83 U8
Gayton Crs HAMP NW3 37 R9
Gayton Rd HAMP NW3 37 R9
HRW HA1 35 Q4
Gayville Rd BTSEA SW11 61 T4
Gaywood Av CHES/WCR EN8 16 D4
Gaywood Cl BRXS/STRHM SW2 62 D6
Gaywood Rd ASHTD KT21 83 V8
WALTH E17 39 S1
Gaywood St STHWK SE1 9 M6
Gaza St WALW SE17 9 L10
Geariesville Gdns BARK/HLT IG6 40 K2
Gearing Cl TOOT SW17 61 V9
Geary Rd WLSDN NW10 36 G10
Geary St HOLWY N7 38 D10
Geddes Pl BXLYHS DA6 66 A2
Geddes Rd BUSH WD23 * 23 L2
Gedeney Rd TOTM N17 26 G13
Gedling Pl STHWK SE1 9 U5
Geere Rd SRTFD E15 40 B13
Gees Ct MHST W1U 3 T12
Gee St FSBYE EC1V 5 N7
Geffrye Est IS N1 5 T4
Geffrye St BETH E2 5 U3
Geisthorp Ct WAB EN9 17 N7
Geldart Rd PECK SE15 51 M12
Geldeston Rd CLPT E5 39 L7
Gellatly Rd NWCR SE14 51 N14
Gelsthorpe Rd CRW RM5 30 B12
Gemmell Cl PUR/KEN CR8 86 D4
General Gordon Pl WOOL/PLUM SE18 52 K8
The Generals Wk PEND EN3 16 E11
General Wolfe Rd GNWCH SE10 51 V13
Genesis Cl STWL/WRAY TW19 57 R6
Genesta Rd WOOL/PLUM SE18 52 K11
Geneva Cl SHPTN TW17 58 A14
Geneva Dr BRXN/ST SW9 62 E2
Geneva Gdns CHDH RM6 41 U3
Geneva Rd KUT/HW KT1 71 U2
THHTH CR7 74 G3
Genever Cl CHING E4 27 S10
Genista Rd UED N18 27 M10
Genoa Av PUT/ROE SW15 60 J3
Genoa Rd PGE/AN SE20 63 N13
Genotin Rd EN EN1 26 H1
Gentleman's Rw ENC/FH EN2 26 G1
Geoffrey Av HARH RM3 31 N11
Geoffrey Cl CMBW SE5 50 G14
Geoffrey Gdns EHAM E6 40 G14
Geoffrey Rd BROCKY SE4 63 R1
George Beard Rd DEPT SE8 51 R9
George Crs MUSWH N10 25 U12
George Downing Est
STNW/STAM N16 38 K7
George Gange Wy
KTN/HRWW/WS HA3 35 N1
George Green Dr DTCH/LGLY SL3 44 D4
George Green Rd DTCH/LGLY SL3 44 C4
George Groves Rd PGE/AN SE20 63 L13
Georgelands RPLY/SEND GU23 81 M11
George La HAYES BR2 76 D6
LEW SE13 63 U4
SWFD E18 28 C14
George Lovell Dr PEND EN3 16 G11
George Lowe Ct BAY/PAD W2 2 G9
George Mathers Rd LBTH SE11 * 9 L7
George Ms BRXN/ST SW9 50 E14
CAMTN NW1 4 A6
George Rd CHING E4 27 S11
KUTN/CMB KT2 60 C12
NWMAL KT3 72 F3
George Rw BERM/RHTH SE16 51 L7
Georges Dr BRWN CM15 31 T3
Georges Md BORE WD6 23 U4
George's Rd BH/WHM TN16 88 F10
HOLWY N7 38 D11
Georges Ter CTHM CR3 86 H12
George St BARK IG11 41 L12
CAN/RD E16 52 B4
CROY/NA CR0 74 H7
HNWL W7 47 N6
HSLW TW3 46 H14
MBLAR W1H 3 Q11
NWDGN UB2 46 G9
RCH/KEW TW9 59 T3
ROM RM1 42 F4
STA TW18 56 K9
UX/CGN UB8 33 P12
WATW WD18 22 E2
Georgetown Cl NRWD SE19 62 J10
Georgette Pl GNWCH SE10 51 U12
George V Av PIN HA5 22 H14
PIN HA5 34 J1
Georgeville Gdns BARK/HLT IG6 40 K2
George V Wy GFD/PVL UB6 35 R12
RKW/CH/CXG WD3 10 A10
George Wyver Cl WIM/MER SW19 61 L5
George Yd BANK EC3V 5 R12
MYFR/PKLN W1K 3 T13
Georgiana St CAMTN NW1 4 B1
Georgian Cl HAYES BR2 76 D6
HGDN/ICK UB10 33 Q9
STA TW18 57 M9
STAN HA7 23 Q12
Georgian Ct WBLY HA9 36 A11
Georgian Wy HRW HA1 35 M7
Georgia Rd NWMAL KT3 72 C2
THHTH CR7 62 F13
Georgina Gdns BETH E2 * 5 V5
Geraint Rd BMLY BR1 64 C8
Geraldine Rd CHSWK W4 48 A11
WAND/EARL SW18 61 Q3
Geraldine St LBTH SE11 9 L6
Gerald Rd BCTR RM8 41 V7
BGVA SW1W 7 T7
CAN/RD E16 52 B2
Gerald's Gv BNSTD SM7 84 K4
Gerard Av HSLWW TW4 58 J5
Gerard Gdns RAIN RM13 42 E14
Gerard Rd BARN SW13 48 F13
HRW HA1 35 Q4
Gerards Cl BERM/RHTH SE16 51 N11
Gerda Rd ELTH/MOT SE9 64 K7
Gerdview Dr RDART DA2 66 J9
Germander Wy SRTFD E15 52 A1
Gernon Cl RAIN RM13 42 K14
Gernon Rd BOW E3 39 Q14
Geron Wy CRICK NW2 36 J7
Gerpins La RAIN RM13 43 M14
Gerrard Gdns PIN HA5 34 C3
Gerrard Pl SOHO/SHAV W1D * 4 D13
Gerrard Rd IS N1 5 L3
Gerrards Cl STHGT/OAK N14 26 A3
Gerrards Md BNSTD SM7 85 M6
Gerrard St SOHO/SHAV W1D 4 D13
Gerridge St STHWK SE1 8 K4
Gertrude Rd BELV DA17 54 A9
Gertrude St WBPTN SW10 6 K12
Gervase Cl WBLY HA9 36 C8
Gervase Rd EDGW HA8 24 C13
Gervase St PECK SE15 51 M12
Gew's Cnr CHES/WCR EN8 16 D3
Ghent St CAT SE6 63 S7
Ghent Wy HACK E8 38 K11
Giant Arches Rd HNHL SE24 62 G5
Giant Tree Hl BUSH WD23 23 M7
Gibbfield Cl CHDH RM6 41 U1
Gibbins Rd SRTFD E15 39 U12
Gibbon Rd ACT W3 48 E5
KUTN/CMB KT2 59 U13
PECK SE15 51 N14
Gibbons Cl BORE WD6 12 J13
Gibbons Ms GLDGN NW11 37 M3
Gibbons Rd WLSDN NW10 36 D12
Gibbon Wk PUT/ROE SW15 * 60 G2
Gibbs Av NRWD SE19 62 H11
Gibbs Brook La OXTED RH8 95 V10
Gibbs Cl CHES/WCR EN8 16 D3
NRWD SE19 * 62 H10
Gibbs Couch OXHEY WD19 22 F8
Gibbs Gn EDGW HA8 24 C9
WKENS W14 6 C9
Gibbs Green Cl WKENS W14 6 C9
Gibbs Rd UED N18 27 N9
Gibbs Sq NRWD SE19 * 62 H10
Gibraltar Crs HOR/WEW KT19 72 E14
Gibraltar Wk BETH E2 5 V6
Gibson Cl CHSGTN KT9 71 S10
ISLW TW7 59 M1
WCHMH N21 26 E4
WCHPL E1 51 N2
Gibson Ct DTCH/LGLY SL3 44 D10
Gibson Gdns STNW/STAM N16 * 38 K7
Gibson Pl STWL/WRAY TW19 57 N4
Gibson Rd BCTR RM8 41 S6
HGDN/ICK UB10 33 R9
LBTH SE11 8 H8
SUT SM1 73 P10
Gibson's Hl STRHM/NOR SW16 62 E12
Gibson Sq IS N1 4 K1
Gibson St GNWCH SE10 52 A10
Gidd Hl COUL/CHIP CR5 85 U6
Gidea Av GPK RM2 42 G1
Gidea Cl GPK RM2 42 G1
Gideon Cl BELV DA17 54 B9
Gideon Ms EA W5 * 47 T7
Gideon Rd BTSEA SW11 61 U1
Gidian Ct LCOL/BKTW AL2 12 B1
Giesbach Rd ARCH N19 38 A7
Giffard Rd UED N18 26 J10
Giffin St DEPT SE8 51 S12
Gifford Gdns HNWL W7 47 M3
Gifford St IS N1 38 C12
Gift La SRTFD E15 40 A13
Giggs Hl STMC/STPC BR5 65 Q14
Giggs Hill Gdns THDIT KT7 71 Q6
Giggs Hill Rd THDIT KT7 71 Q6
Gilbert Cl WIM/MER SW19 * 61 P13
WOOL/PLUM SE18 52 H13
Gilbert Gv EDGW HA8 24 C13
Gilbert Pl NOXST/BSQ WC1A 4 E10
Gilbert Rd BELV DA17 54 A8
BMLY BR1 64 C12
DEN/HRF UB9 21 P14
LBTH SE11 8 K7
PIN HA5 34 F2
ROM RM1 42 F2
WIM/MER SW19 61 Q12
Gilbert St HSLW TW3 59 L1
MYFR/PKLN W1K 3 T12
PEND EN3 16 C11
SRTFD E15 40 A9
Gilbey Cl HGDN/ICK UB10 33 T9
Gilbey Rd TOOT SW17 61 S9
Gilbeys Yd CAMTN NW1 37 U12
Gilbourne Rd WOOL/PLUM SE18 53 P11
Gilda Av PEND EN3 27 Q3
Gilda Crs STNW/STAM N16 39 L6
Gildea Cl PIN HA5 22 J12
Gildea St GTPST W1W 3 V10
Gilden Crs KTTN NW5 37 U10
Gildenhill Rd SWLY BR8 66 J12
Gildersome St WOOL/PLUM SE18 52 J11
Gilders Rd CHSGTN KT9 71 V12
Giles Cl RAIN RM13 42 K14
Giles Coppice NRWD SE19 62 K9
Giles Md EPSOM KT18 * 84 E4
Giles Travers Cl EGH TW20 68 G1
Gilfrid Cl UX/CGN UB8 45 T4
Gilham's Av BNSTD SM7 84 K2
Gilhams Cottages BNSTD SM7 * 85 L2
Gilkes Crs DUL SE21 62 J4
Gilkes Pl DUL SE21 62 J4
Gillam Wy RAIN RM13 42 G11
Gillan Gn BUSH WD23 23 L7
Gillards Ms WALTH E17 39 S2
Gillards Wy WALTH E17 39 S2
Gill Av CAN/RD E16 52 C4
Gill Cl WATW WD18 21 U4
Gillender St BOW E3 51 U2
Gillespie Rd HBRY N5 38 E8
Gillett Av EHAM E6 40 G14
Gillett Pl HACK E8 38 K10
Gillett Rd THHTH CR7 74 H2
Gillett St STNW/STAM N16 38 J10
Gillham Ter TOTM N17 27 L11
Gilliam Gv PUR/KEN CR8 74 E14
Gillian Crs GPK RM2 30 J14
Gillian Park Rd CHEAM SM3 73 M6
Gillian St LEW SE13 63 T3
Gillian Ter BRYLDS KT5 * 71 V4
Gilliat's Gn RKW/CH/CXG WD3 20 H2
Gilliatt Cl IVER SL0 44 J4
Gillies Rd BGR/WK TN15 79 S10
Gillies St KTTN NW5 37 U10
Gillingham Ms PIM SW1V 7 V7
Gillingham Rd CRICK NW2 37 L8
Gillingham Rw PIM SW1V 8 A7
Gillingham St PIM SW1V 7 V8
Gillison Wk BERM/RHTH SE16 * 51 L8
Gillman Dr SRTFD E15 40 A13
Gillmans Rd STMC/STPC BR5 77 R6
Gills Hl RAD WD7 12 D9
Gills Hill La RAD WD7 12 D10
Gills Hollow RAD WD7 12 D10
Gill's Rd EYN DA4 67 S13
Gill St POP/IOD E14 51 R4
Gillum Cl EBAR EN4 25 T6
Gilmore Cl DTCH/LGLY SL3 44 A7
HGDN/ICK UB10 33 S8
Gilmore Crs ASHF TW15 57 S10
Gilmore Rd LEW SE13 63 V2
Gilmour Cl CHESW EN7 16 A9
Gilpin Av MORT/ESHN SW14 60 D2
Gilpin Cl BAY/PAD W2 2 K10
MTCM CR4 61 S14
Gilpin Crs UED N18 26 K10
WHTN TW2 58 K5
Gilpin Rd CLPT E5 39 Q9
Gilpin Wy HYS/HAR UB3 45 V12
Gilroy Cl RAIN RM13 42 F11
Gilroy Wy STMC/STPC BR5 77 R5
Gilsland WAB EN9 17 L9
Gilsland Rd THHTH CR7 74 H2
Gilson Ct WDSR SL4 56 A5
Gilstead Rd FUL/PGN SW6 49 P14
Gilston Rd WBPTN SW10 6 K10
Gilton Rd CAT SE6 64 A8
Giltspur St STBT EC1A 5 M11
Gilwell Cl CHING E4 27 T2
Gilwell La CHING E4 27 V2
Gimcrack Hl LHD/OX KT22 83 R12
Gippeswyck Cl PIN HA5 22 F13
Gipsy Hl NRWD SE19 62 J10
Gipsy La PUT/ROE SW15 60 G1
Gipsy Rd WELL DA16 53 T14
WNWD SE27 62 H9
Gipsy Road Gdns WNWD SE27 62 G9
Giralda Cl CAN/RD E16 52 F3
Giraud St POP/IOD E14 51 T4
Girdlers Rd HMSMTH W6 48 K9
Girdwood Rd WAND/EARL SW18 61 L5
Girling Wy EBED/NFELT TW14 58 C1
Gironde Rd FUL/PGN SW6 6 D14
Girtin Rd BUSH WD23 22 K3
Girton Av CDALE/KGS NW9 36 A1
Girton Cl NTHLT UB5 35 L11
Girton Ct CHES/WCR EN8 16 E4
Girton Gdns CROY/NA CR0 75 S8
Girton Rd NTHLT UB5 35 L11
SYD SE26 63 P10
Girton Wy RKW/CH/CXG WD3 21 U3
Gisbourne Cl WLGTN SM6 74 B8
Gisburne Wy WATN WD24 11 N11
Gisburn Rd CEND/HSY/T N8 38 D2
Gissing Wk IS N1 * 38 E12
Gittens Cl BMLY BR1 64 B9
Glacier Wy ALP/SUD HA0 35 T14
Gladbeck Wy ENC/FH EN2 26 G2
Gladding Rd MNPK E12 40 F9
Glade Cl SURB KT6 * 71 T7
Glade Gdns CROY/NA CR0 75 Q5
Glade La NWDGN UB2 46 K7
Gladeside CROY/NA CR0 75 P5
WCHMH N21 26 D5
Gladesmore Rd SEVS/STOTM N15 38 K4
Glade Sp KWD/TDW/WH KT20 85 P11
The Glade BELMT SM2 73 L13
BF/WBF KT14 80 J3
BMLY BR1 64 F14
CFSP/GDCR SL9 32 B6
CHARL SE7 52 E12
CLAY IG5 28 H14
COUL/CHIP CR5 86 E9
CROY/NA CR0 75 Q4
ENC/FH EN2 26 E1
EW KT17 72 G11
HACK E8 * 38 K11
KWD/TDW/WH KT20 85 P11
LHD/OX KT22 82 K12
NFNCH/WDSPK N12 * 25 R9
SEV TN13 90 H13
SHB W12 48 H7
STA TW18 57 M12
UPMR RM14 43 Q10
WCHMH N21 26 D4
WFD IG8 28 D8
WWKM BR4 75 T8
The Gladeway WAB EN9 16 K7
Gladiator St FSTH SE23 63 Q5
Glading Ter STNW/STAM N16 38 K8
Gladioli Cl HPTN TW12 58 J11
Gladsdale Dr PIN HA5 34 C2
Gladsmuir Cl WOT/HER KT12 70 E7
Gladsmuir Rd ARCH N19 38 A6
BAR EN5 14 A14
Gladstone Av EBED/NFELT TW14 58 C4
MNPK E12 40 G12
WDGN N22 26 F14
WHTN TW2 59 M5
Gladstone Gdns HSLW TW3 47 L13
Gladstone Ms KIL/WHAMP NW6 37 M11
PGE/AN SE20 63 N12
WDGN N22 26 E14
Gladstone Pde CRICK NW2 * 36 J8
Gladstone Park Gdns CRICK NW2 36 H8
Gladstone Pl BAR EN5 * 24 K2
E/WMO/HCT KT8 * 71 N3
Gladstone Rd ASHTD KT21 83 T8
BKHH IG9 28 E6
CHSWK W4 * 48 D8
CROY/NA CR0 74 H5
DART DA1 67 M4
KUT/HW KT1 72 A1
NWDGN UB2 46 G7
ORP BR6 77 L10
SURB KT6 71 T7
WAT WD17 22 E1
WIM/MER SW19 61 N12
Gladstone St STHWK SE1 9 L5
Gladstone Ter VX/NE SW8 49 V13
WNWD SE27 * 62 G9
Gladstone Wy KTN/HRWW/WS HA3 35 N1
Gladwell Rd BMLY BR1 64 C11
CEND/HSY/T N8 38 D4
Gladwyn Rd PUT/ROE SW15 60 K1
Gladys Rd KIL/WHAMP NW6 37 N12
Glaisher St DEPT SE8 51 T11
Glaisyer Wy IVER SL0 32 G14
Glamis Cl CHESW EN7 16 A3
Glamis Crs HYS/HAR UB3 45 U8
Glamis Dr EMPK RM11 43 L6
Glamis Pl WAP E1W 51 N5
Glamis Rd WAP E1W 51 N5
Glamis Wy NTHLT UB5 35 L11
Glamorgan Cl MTCM CR4 74 C1
Glamorgan Rd KUT/HW KT1 59 S12
Glandford Wy CHDH RM6 41 R3
Glanfield Rd BECK BR3 75 R2
Glanleam Rd STAN HA7 23 T9
The Glanty EGH TW20 56 G9
Glanville Dr EMPK RM11 43 M6
Glanville Ms STAN HA7 23 Q10
Glanville Rd BRXS/STRHM SW2 62 C3
HAYES BR2 76 D1
Glasbrook Av WHTN TW2 58 H6
Glasbrook Rd ELTH/MOT SE9 64 F5
Glaserton Rd STNW/STAM N16 38 J5
Glasford St TOOT SW17 61 T11
Glasgow Rd PLSTW E13 40 D14
UED N18 27 M10
Glasgow Ter PIM SW1V 8 A10
Glaskin Ms HOM E9 39 Q11
Glasse Cl WEA W13 47 Q5
Glasshill St STHWK SE1 9 M3
Glasshouse Cl UX/CGN UB8 45 T3
Glasshouse Flds WAP E1W 51 P5
Glasshouse St REGST W1B 4 B14
Glasshouse Wk LBTH SE11 8 F9
Glasshouse Yd FARR EC1M 5 N8
Glasslyn Rd CEND/HSY/T N8 38 B3
Glassmill La HAYES BR2 76 B1
Glass St BETH E2 * 51 M2
Glass Yd WOOL/PLUM SE18 52 J8
Glastonbury Av WFD IG8 28 F12
Glastonbury Cl STMC/STPC BR5 77 S6
Glastonbury Pl WCHPL E1 51 N4
Glastonbury Rd ED N9 27 L6
MRDN SM4 73 N5
Glastonbury St KIL/WHAMP NW6 37 M10
Glaston Ct EA W5 * 47 T6
Glaucus St BOW E3 51 T3
Glazbury Rd WKENS W14 6 B9
Glazebrook Cl DUL SE21 62 H7
Glazebrook Rd TEDD TW11 59 P12
Glebe Av ENC/FH EN2 26 F1
HGDN/ICK UB10 33 U9
KTN/HRWW/WS HA3 35 U1
MTCM CR4 61 S14
RSLP HA4 34 D11
WFD IG8 28 C11
Glebe Cl CFSP/GDCR SL9 20 B13
CHSWK W4 * 48 E10
HGDN/ICK UB10 33 U9
SAND/SEL CR2 86 K2
Glebe Ct BKHTH/KID SE3 * 64 A1
EA W5 * 47 T6
STAN HA7 23 S10
Glebe Crs HDN NW4 36 J2
KTN/HRWW/WS HA3 35 U1
The Glebefield SEV TN13 90 F13
Glebe Gdns BF/WBF KT14 81 P4
NWMAL KT3 72 E5
Glebe House Dr HAYES BR2 76 D6
Glebe Hyrst SAND/SEL CR2 86 K2
Glebeland Gdns SHPTN TW17 69 U4
Glebelands CHIG IG7 29 R8
DART DA1 66 F2
E/WMO/HCT KT8 70 K3
ESH/CLAY KT10 71 P13
Glebelands Av GNTH/NBYPK IG2 41 M5
SWFD E18 28 C14
Glebelands Cl NFNCH/WDSPK N12 25 R13
WALW SE17 62 J1
Glebelands Rd EBED/NFELT TW14 58 C5
Glebe La BAR EN5 24 G4
KTN/HRWW/WS HA3 35 U2
Glebe Pth MTCM CR4 73 T1
Glebe Pl CHEL SW3 7 N11
EYN DA4 79 Q2
Glebe Rd ASHTD KT21 83 T8
BARN SW13 48 G14
BELMT SM2 73 L13
BMLY BR1 64 C13
CAR SM5 73 T11
CEND/HSY/T N8 38 D2
CFSP/GDCR SL9 20 A13
DAGE RM10 42 B11
EGH TW20 56 G11
FNCH N3 25 Q13
HACK E8 * 38 K12
RAIN RM13 54 H1
REDH RH1 85 U14
STA TW18 57 M10
STAN HA7 23 S10
UX/CGN UB8 33 N14
WARL CR6 87 P7
WLSDN NW10 36 G11
Glebe Side TWK TW1 59 P4
Glebe Sq MTCM CR4 * 73 T1
Glebe St CHSWK W4 48 D10
The Glebe BKHTH/KID SE3 64 A1
CHST BR7 65 L13
GSTN WD25 11 Q7
KGLGY WD4 10 G3
STRHM/NOR SW16 * 62 B9
WDR/YW UB7 45 Q9
WPK KT4 72 F6
Glebe Wy EMPK RM11 43 L5
ERITH DA8 54 E11
FELT TW13 58 J8
SAND/SEL CR2 86 K2
Glebeway WFD IG8 28 E10
Glebe Wy WWKM BR4 75 V7
Gledhow Gdns ECT SW5 6 J8
Gledhow Wd KWD/TDW/WH KT20 85 P12
Gledstanes Rd WKENS W14 6 B10
Gledwood Av YEAD UB4 46 B3
Gledwood Crs YEAD UB4 46 B3
Gledwood Dr YEAD UB4 46 B3
Gledwood Gdns YEAD UB4 46 C3
Gleed Av BUSH WD23 23 M7
Gleeson Dr ORP BR6 77 P10
Gleeson Ms ADL/WDHM KT15 69 N9
Glegg Pl PUT/ROE SW15 * 60 K2
Glenaffric Av POP/IOD E14 51 U9
Glen Albyn Rd WIM/MER SW19 60 K7
Glenalla Rd RSLP HA4 34 B5
Glenalmond Rd KTN/HRWW/WS HA3 35 U2
Glenalvon Wy WOOL/PLUM SE18 52 G9
Glena Mt SUT SM1 73 Q9
Glenarm Rd CLPT E5 39 N9
Glen Av ASHF TW15 57 S9
Glenavon Cl ESH/CLAY KT10 71 Q11
Glenavon Gdns DTCH/LGLY SL3 44 A9
Glenavon Rd SRTFD E15 40 A12
Glenbarr Cl ELTH/MOT SE9 64 K1
Glenbow Rd BMLY BR1 64 A11
Glenbrook North ENC/FH EN2 26 D2
Glenbrook Rd KIL/WHAMP NW6 37 N10
Glenbrook South ENC/FH EN2 26 D2
Glenbuck Rd SURB KT6 71 T4
Glenburnie Rd TOOT SW17 61 T8
Glencairn Dr EA W5 47 S3
Glencairne Cl CAN/RD E16 52 F3
Glencairn Rd STRHM/NOR SW16 62 C12
Glen Cl KWD/TDW/WH KT20 85 L13
SHPTN TW17 69 S2
Glencoe Av GNTH/NBYPK IG2 41 N5
Glencoe Rd BUSH WD23 22 J4
DAGE RM10 42 A9
WEY KT13 69 S8
YEAD UB4 46 G3
Glencorse Gn OXHEY WD19 * 22 F9
Glen Ct ADL/WDHM KT15 * 68 K10
Glen Crs WFD IG8 28 D11
Glendale SWLY BR8 78 F3
Glendale Av CHDH RM6 41 S5
EDGW HA8 23 V9
WDGN N22 26 E12
Glendale Cl ELTH/MOT SE9 64 J1
WOKN/KNAP GU21 80 A8
Glendale Dr WIM/MER SW19 61 M10
Glendale Gdns WBLY HA9 35 T6
Glendale Ms BECK BR3 63 T13
Glendale Ri PUR/KEN CR8 86 F5
Glendale Rd ERITH DA8 54 C9
Glendale Wy THMD SE28 53 S6
Glendall St BRXN/ST SW9 62 D1
Glendarvon St PUT/ROE SW15 60 K1
Glendevon Cl EDGW HA8 24 B8
Glendish Rd TOTM N17 27 L13
Glendor Gdns MLHL NW7 24 D9
Glendower Crs ORP BR6 77 Q4
Glendower Gdns MORT/ESHN SW14 60 D1
Glendower Pl SKENS SW7 7 L7
Glendower Rd CHING E4 27 V6
MORT/ESHN SW14 60 D1
Glendown Rd ABYW SE2 53 Q10
Glendun Rd ACT W3 48 E5
Gleneagle Ms STRHM/NOR SW16 62 B10
Gleneagle Rd STRHM/NOR SW16 62 B10
Gleneagles STAN HA7 23 R11
Gleneagles Cl BERM/RHTH SE16 51 M10
HARH RM3 31 M12
ORP BR6 77 M6
OXHEY WD19 * 22 F10
STWL/WRAY TW19 57 N4
Gleneldon Ms STRHM/NOR SW16 62 C10
Gleneldon Rd STRHM/NOR SW16 62 C9
Glenelg Rd BRXS/STRHM SW2 62 C3
Glenesk Rd ELTH/MOT SE9 64 J2
Glenfarg Rd CAT SE6 63 V6
Glenfield Cl BRKHM/BTCW RH3 92 B14
Glenfield Crs RSLP HA4 33 V5
Glenfield Rd ASHF TW15 57 T11
BAL SW12 62 A6
BNSTD SM7 85 P5
BRKHM/BTCW RH3 92 B14
WEA W13 47 R7
Glenfinlas Wy CMBW SE5 9 M13
Glenforth St GNWCH SE10 52 B9
Glengall Br POP/IOD E14 51 T8
Glengall Gv POP/IOD E14 51 T8
Glengall Rd BXLYHN DA7 65 U1
EDGW HA8 24 B8
KIL/WHAMP NW6 2 D2
PECK SE15 9 V11
WFD IG8 28 C11
Glengall Ter PECK SE15 9 V11
Glen Gdns CROY/NA CR0 74 E8
Glengarnock Av POP/IOD E14 51 U9
Glengarry Rd EDUL SE22 62 J2
Glenham Dr GNTH/NBYPK IG2 40 K3
Glenhaven Av BORE WD6 24 A1
Glenhead Cl ELTH/MOT SE9 64 K1
Glenheadon Cl LHD/OX KT22 83 T13
Glenheadon Ri LHD/OX KT22 83 T13
Glenhill Cl FNCH N3 25 N14
Glenhouse Rd ELTH/MOT SE9 64 J3
Glenhurst Av BXLY DA5 65 V6
KTTN NW5 37 U9
RSLP HA4 33 U6
Glenhurst Ri NRWD SE19 62 G12
Glenhurst Rd BTFD TW8 47 S11
NFNCH/WDSPK N12 25 R10
Glenilla Rd HAMP NW3 37 S11
Glenister Park Rd STRHM/NOR SW16 62 B12
Glenister Rd GNWCH SE10 52 B10
Glenlea Rd ELTH/MOT SE9 64 J3
Glenlee WOKS/MYFD GU22 80 A9
Glenloch Rd HAMP NW3 37 S11
PEND EN3 16 C14
Glen Luce CHES/WCR EN8 16 D5
Glenluce Rd BKHTH/KID SE3 64 D1
Glenluge Rd BKHTH/KID SE3 52 C11
Glenlyon Rd ELTH/MOT SE9 64 J3
Glenmere Av MLHL NW7 24 G12
Glenmill HPTN TW12 58 H10
Glenmore Cl ADL/WDHM KT15 69 M8
Glenmore Gdns ABLGY WD5 11 N5
Glenmore Lawns WEA W13 * 47 Q4
Glenmore Pde ALP/SUD HA0 * 35 U13
Glenmore Rd HAMP NW3 37 S11
WELL DA16 53 P13
Glenmore Wy BARK IG11 53 Q1
Glenn Av PUR/KEN CR8 86 F1
Glennie Rd WNWD SE27 62 E8
Glenny Rd BARK IG11 41 L11
Glenorchy Cl YEAD UB4 46 G3
Glenparke Rd FSTGT E7 40 D11
Glen Ri WFD IG8 28 D11
Glen Rd CHSGTN KT9 71 U8
PLSTW E13 52 E2
WALTH E17 39 R3
Glen Rd End WLGTN SM6 73 V13
Glenrosa St FUL/PGN SW6 49 Q14
Glenroy St SHB W12 48 J4
Glensdale Rd BROCKY SE4 63 R1
Glenshiel Rd ELTH/MOT SE9 64 J3
Glenside CHIG IG7 28 K11
Glenside Cl PUR/KEN CR8 86 H5
Glentanner Wy TOOT SW17 61 R8
Glentham Cottages BARN SW13 * 48 G11
Glentham Gdns BARN SW13 48 H11
Glentham Rd BARN SW13 48 G11
The Glen ADL/WDHM KT15 68 K10
BELMT SM2 * 73 Q11
CROY/NA CR0 75 P8
DTCH/LGLY SL3 44 A9
ENC/FH EN2 26 F2
HAYES BR2 64 A14
NTHWD HA6 21 V12
NWDGN UB2 46 H10
ORP BR6 76 H8
PIN HA5 34 D3
PIN HA5 34 G5
RAIN RM13 54 J2
WBLY HA9 35 T9
Glenthorne Av CROY/NA CR0 75 N6
Glenthorne Cl CHEAM SM3 73 N6
Glenthorne Gdns BARK/HLT IG6 40 J1
CHEAM SM3 73 N6
Glenthorne Rd FBAR/BDGN N11 25 T10
HMSMTH W6 48 J9
KUT/HW KT1 71 V2
WALTH E17 39 Q3
Glenthorpe Rd MRDN SM4 72 K3
Glenton Cl ROM RM1 30 E12
Glenton Rd LEW SE13 64 A2
Glenton Wy ROM RM1 30 E12
Glentrammon Av ORP BR6 77 P11
Glentrammon Cl ORP BR6 77 P11
Glentrammon Gdns ORP BR6 77 P11
Glentrammon Rd ORP BR6 77 P11
Glentworth St CAMTN NW1 3 R8
Glenure Rd ELTH/MOT SE9 64 J3
Glenview ABYW SE2 53 T11
Glen View Rd BMLY BR1 64 F14
Glenville Av ENC/FH EN2 15 S12
Glenville Gv DEPT SE8 51 R12
Glenville Ms WAND/EARL SW18 61 P5
Glenville Rd KUTN/CMB KT2 60 A13
Glen Wy WAT WD17 11 L12
Glenwood Av CDALE/KGS NW9 36 E6
RAIN RM13 54 G2
Glenwood Cl HRW HA1 35 P3
Glenwood Dr GPK RM2 42 G3
Glenwood Gdns GNTH/NBYPK IG2 40 J3
Glenwood Gv CDALE/KGS NW9 36 C6
Glenwood Rd CAT SE6 63 R6
EW KT17 72 G11
HSLW TW3 59 M1
MLHL NW7 24 E8
SEVS/STOTM N15 38 F3
Glenwood Rw NRWD SE19 * 62 K13
Glenwood Wy CROY/NA CR0 75 P4
Glenworth Av POP/IOD E14 51 V9
Gliddon Dr CLPT E5 39 M9
Gliddon Rd WKENS W14 6 A9
Glimpsing Gn ERITHM DA18 53 U8
Glisson Rd HGDN/ICK UB10 33 S14
Gload Crs STMC/STPC BR5 77 T7
Globe Pond Rd BERM/RHTH SE16 51 Q6
Globe Rd EMPK RM11 42 G4
SRTFD E15 40 B10
WCHPL E1 51 N1
WFD IG8 28 E11
Globe St STHWK SE1 9 Q4
Globe Ter BETH E2 51 N1
Glossop Rd SAND/SEL CR2 74 H13
Gloster Rd NWMAL KT3 72 E2
WOKS/MYFD GU22 80 E10
Gloucester Av BFN/LL DA15 65 N7
CAMTN NW1 37 U12
CHES/WCR EN8 16 E7
EMPK RM11 43 N3
WELL DA16 65 P3
Gloucester Circ GNWCH SE10 51 U12
Gloucester Cl THDIT KT7 * 71 Q6
WLSDN NW10 36 D12
Gloucester Ct MTCM CR4 * 74 C3
RCH/KEW TW9 * 48 A12
Gloucester Crs CAMTN NW1 3 U1
STA TW18 57 P11
Gloucester Dr FSBYPK N4 38 F7
GLDGN NW11 37 N2
STA TW18 56 G8
Gloucester Gdns BAY/PAD W2 2 J11
EBAR EN4 25 U2
GLDGN NW11 37 M5
IL IG1 40 G5
SUT SM1 73 P7
Gloucester Ga CAMTN NW1 3 U3
Gloucester Gate Ms CAMTN NW1 3 U3
Gloucester Gv EDGW HA8 24 D13
Gloucester Ms BAY/PAD W2 2 K12
LEY E10 39 S5
Gloucester Ms West BAY/PAD W2 2 J12
Gloucester Pde BFN/LL DA15 * 65 Q3
HYS/HAR UB3 * 45 U8
Gloucester Pl CAMTN NW1 3 Q7
Gloucester Place Ms MBLAR W1H 3 R10
Gloucester Rd ACT W3 48 C7
BAR EN5 25 P3
BELV DA17 53 V10
BRWN CM15 31 V3
CROY/NA CR0 74 H5
DART DA1 66 H4
EA W5 47 S7
ENC/FH EN2 15 S12
FELT TW13 58 E6
HPTN TW12 58 K12
HRW HA1 34 K3
HSLWW TW4 58 G2
KUT/HW KT1 60 A14
LEY E10 39 S5
MNPK E12 40 H8
RCH/KEW TW9 48 A12
REDH RH1 93 T9
ROM RM1 42 F4
SKENS SW7 6 J5
TEDD TW11 59 N10
TOTM N17 38 H1
UED N18 26 K10
WALTH E17 27 P14
WAN E11 40 E3
WHTN TW2 59 L6
Gloucester Sq BAY/PAD W2 3 M12
BETH E2 39 L13
Gloucester St PIM SW1V 8 A10
Gloucester Ter BAY/PAD W2 2 J11
STHGT/OAK N14 * 26 B6
Gloucester Wk KENS W8 6 F3
Gloucester Wy CLKNW EC1R 4 K6
Glover Cl ABYW SE2 53 S9
CHESW EN7 * 15 V1
Glover Dr UED N18 27 N11
Glover Rd PIN HA5 34 F4
Glovers Cl BH/WHM TN16 88 D6
Glovers Gv RSLP HA4 33 T5
Glover's Rd REIG RH2 93 P11
Glycena Rd BTSEA SW11 61 T1
Glyn Av EBAR EN4 25 R2
Glyn Cl EW KT17 72 G13
SNWD SE25 62 J14
Glyn Ct STAN HA7 23 R11
Glyn Davies Cl SEV TN13 90 E10
Glyndebourne Pk ORP BR6 76 K8
Glynde Ms CHEL SW3 7 P6
Glynde Rd BXLYHN DA7 65 T1
Glynde St BROCKY SE4 63 R4
Glyndon Rd WOOL/PLUM SE18 53 L9
Glyn Dr SCUP DA14 65 R9
Glynfield Rd WLSDN NW10 36 E12
Glynne Rd WDGN N22 26 E14
Glyn Rd CLPT E5 39 P9
PEND EN3 27 N2
WPK KT4 72 K7
Glyn St LBTH SE11 8 G10
Glynswood CFSP/GDCR SL9 20 D12
Glynswood Pl NTHWD HA6 21 T13
Goat La EN EN1 15 V12
Goat Rd MTCM CR4 73 U5
Goatsfield Rd BH/WHM TN16 88 E10
Goatswood La ABR/ST RM4 30 H5
Goat Whf BTFD TW8 47 U11
Gobions Av CRW RM5 30 D12
Gobions Wy POTB/CUF EN6 14 D2
Godalming Av WLGTN SM6 74 C10
Godalming Rd POP/IOD E14 51 T3
Godbold Rd SRTFD E15 52 A2
Goddard Cl SHPTN TW17 69 R1
Goddard Pl ARCH N19 38 A8
Goddard Rd BECK BR3 75 Q2
Goddards Wy IL IG1 41 M6
Goddington Cha ORP BR6 77 R9
Goddington La ORP BR6 77 Q8
Godfrey Av NTHLT UB5 34 G13
WHTN TW2 59 M5
Godfrey Hl WOOL/PLUM SE18 52 G9
Godfrey Rd WOOL/PLUM SE18 52 H9
Godfrey St CHEL SW3 7 P9
SRTFD E15 39 U14
Godfrey Wy HSLWW TW4 58 G5
Goding St LBTH SE11 8 F10
Godley Rd BF/WBF KT14 81 R3
WAND/EARL SW18 61 R6
Godliman St BLKFR EC4V 5 M12
Godman Rd PECK SE15 * 51 M14
Godolphin Cl BELMT SM2 85 M1
PLMGR N13 26 F11
Godolphin Pl ACT W3 48 D5
Godolphin Rd SHB W12 48 H7
WEY KT13 69 V11
Godric Crs CROY/NA CR0 75 V14
Godson Rd CROY/NA CR0 74 E8
Godson St IS N1 4 J3
Godstone Green Rd GDST RH9 95 M7
Godstone Hl GDST RH9 95 M4
Godstone Mt PUR/KEN CR8 * 86 F2
Godstone Rd CTHM CR3 95 M2
OXTED RH8 95 S7
PUR/KEN CR8 86 F3
REDH RH1 94 J9
SUT SM1 73 Q9
TWK TW1 59 R4
Godstow Rd ABYW SE2 53 S7
Godwin Cl CHING E4 16 J12
HOR/WEW KT19 72 C11
IS N1 5 P3
Godwin Rd FSTGT E7 40 D9
HAYES BR2 76 E1
Goffers Rd BKHTH/KID SE3 52 A14
Goffs Crs CHESW EN7 15 S3
Goff's La CHESW EN7 15 T3
Goff's Oak Av CHESW EN7 15 S2
Goffs Rd ASHF TW15 57 V11
Gogmore Farm Cl CHERT KT16 68 J5
Gogmore La CHERT KT16 69 L5
Goidel Cl WLGTN SM6 74 B9
Golborne Gdns NKENS W10 2 C8
Golborne Ms NKENS W10 * 2 B9
Golborne Rd NKENS W10 2 B9
Golda Cl BAR EN5 24 K4
Goldbeaters Gv EDGW HA8 24 E12
Goldcliff Cl MRDN SM4 73 N5
Goldcrest Cl CAN/RD E16 52 F3
THMD SE28 53 S5
Goldcrest Ms EA W5 * 47 T3
Goldcrest Wy BUSH WD23 23 L6
CROY/NA CR0 75 V13
PUR/KEN CR8 74 B14
Golden Ct HSLW TW3 47 M14
Golden Crs HYS/HAR UB3 46 B6
Golden Cross Ms NTGHL W11 2 C11
Golden Hind Pl DEPT SE8 * 51 R9
Golden Jubilee Br STHWK SE1 8 G1
Golden La STLK EC1Y 5 N7
Golden Lane Est STLK EC1Y 5 N8
Golden Mnr HNWL W7 47 N5
Golden Pde WALTH E17 * 39 U1
Golden Plover Cl CAN/RD E16 52 C4
Golden Sq SOHO/CST W1F 4 B13
Golden Yd HAMP NW3 37 Q9
Golders Cl EDGW HA8 24 B10
Golders Gdns GLDGN NW11 37 L5
Golders Green Crs GLDGN NW11 37 M5
Golders Green Rd GLDGN NW11 37 L4
Golders Hl HAMP NW3 * 37 P7
Goldersiea GLDGN NW11 * 37 N6
Golders Manor Dr GLDGN NW11 36 K4
Golders Park Cl GLDGN NW11 37 N6
Golders Ri HDN NW4 36 K3
Golders Wy GLDGN NW11 37 M5
Goldfinch Cl ORP BR6 77 Q10
Goldfinch Rd SAND/SEL CR2 75 Q14
THMD SE28 53 M8
Goldfinch Wy BORE WD6 24 A2
Goldhawk Ms SHB W12 48 H7
Goldhawk Rd HMSMTH W6 48 F9
Goldhaze Cl WFD IG8 28 F12
Gold Hl EDGW HA8 24 D11
Gold Hl East CFSP/GDCR SL9 20 B14
Gold Hl North CFSP/GDCR SL9 20 B13
Gold Hl West CFSP/GDCR SL9 20 A14
Goldhurst Ter KIL/WHAMP NW6 37 Q11
Goldingham Av LOU IG10 18 A14
Golding Rd SEV TN13 90 J12
Golding's Hl LOU IG10 17 T12
Goldings Ri LOU IG10 17 U13
Goldings Rd LOU IG10 17 U13
Golding St WCHPL E1 51 L4
Goldington Crs CAMTN NW1 4 B3
Goldington St CAMTN NW1 4 C3
Gold La EDGW HA8 24 D11
Goldman Cl BETH E2 51 L2
Goldney Rd MV/WKIL W9 2 E8
Goldrill Dr FBAR/BDGN N11 25 U7
Goldrings Rd LHD/OX KT22 83 L3
Goldsboro Rd VX/NE SW8 50 B13
Goldsborough Crs CHING E4 27 T7
Goldsdown Cl PEND EN3 16 E14
PEND EN3 27 Q1
Goldsdown Rd PEND EN3 16 D14
Goldsel Rd SWLY BR8 78 E2
Goldsmid St WOOL/PLUM SE18 53 N10
Goldsmith Av ACT W3 48 D5

CDALE/KGS NW9 36 E3
MNPK E12 40 G11
ROMW/RG RM7 42 A5
Goldsmith Cl RYLN/HDSTN HA2 34 J6
Goldsmith La CDALE/KGS NW9 36 C2
Goldsmith Pl KIL/WHAMP NW6 * 2 G2
Goldsmith Rd ACT W3 48 D6
FBAR/BDGN N11 25 T10
LEY E10 39 T6
PECK SE15 51 L13
WALTH E17 27 P14
Goldsmiths Cl ACT W3 * 48 D6
WOKN/KNAP GU21 80 A8
Goldsmith's Rw BETH E2 39 L13
Goldsmith St CITYW EC2V 5 P11
Goldsworth Rd WOKN/KNAP GU21 80 A8
Goldwell Rd THHTH CR7 74 D2
Goldwing Cl CAN/RD E16 52 C4
Golf Cl BUSH WD23 22 F1
STAN HA7 23 S12
THHTH CR7 62 E13
WOKS/MYFD GU22 80 J4
Golf Club Dr KUTN/CMB KT2 60 D12
Golf Club Rd WEY KT13 69 U14
Golfe Rd IL IG1 41 M8
Golf House La OXTED RH8 96 E5
Golf Ride ENC/FH EN2 15 Q9
Golf Rd BMLY BR1 76 J1
EA W5 * 47 V4
PUR/KEN CR8 86 H8
Golf Side BELMT SM2 85 L1
WHTN TW2 59 M8
Golf Side Cl NWMAL KT3 60 E14
Golfside Cl TRDG/WHET N20 25 S8
Gollogly Ter CHARL SE7 52 E10
Gomer Gdns TEDD TW11 59 Q11
Gomer Pl TEDD TW11 59 Q11
Gomm Rd BERM/RHTH SE16 51 N8
Gomshall Av WLGTN SM6 74 C10
Gomshall Gdns PUR/KEN CR8 86 J5
Gomshall Rd BELMT SM2 72 J14
Gondar Gdns CRICK NW2 37 M10
Gonson St DEPT SE8 51 T11
Gonston Cl WIM/MER SW19 61 L7
Gonville Av RKW/CH/CXG WD3 21 T4
Gonville Crs NTHLT UB5 34 K11
Gonville Rd THHTH CR7 74 D3
Gonville St FUL/PGN SW6 61 L1
Goodacre Cl POTB/CUF EN6 14 D6
Goodall Rd WAN E11 39 U8
Goodbury Rd BGR/WK TN15 91 P3
Gooden Ct HRW HA1 35 N8
Goodenough Cl COUL/CHIP CR5 86 E10
Goodenough Rd WIM/MER SW19 61 M12
Goodenough Wy COUL/CHIP CR5 86 D10
Goodey Rd BARK IG11 41 P12
Goodge Pl FITZ W1T 4 B10
Goodge St FITZ W1T 4 B10
Goodhall Cl STAN HA7 23 R11
Goodhall St WLSDN NW10 48 F1
Goodhart Wy WWKM BR4 76 A4
Goodhew Rd CROY/NA CR0 75 L4
Gooding Cl NWMAL KT3 72 C2
Goodinge Cl HOLWY N7 38 C11
Goodinge Rd HOLWY N7 38 C11
Goodison Cl BUSH WD23 23 L3
Goodlake Ct DEN/HRF UB9 32 K5
Goodley Stock Rd BH/WHM TN16 96 K5
Goodman Ct ALP/SUD HA0 * 35 T9
Goodman Crs BRXS/STRHM SW2 62 C7
Goodman Pk SLN SL2 44 A7
Goodman Rd LEY E10 39 U5
Goodmans Ct ALP/SUD HA0 35 T9
Goodman's Yd TWRH EC3N 5 U13
Goodmayes Av GDMY/SEVK IG3 41 Q6
Goodmayes La GDMY/SEVK IG3 41 Q9
Goodmayes Rd GDMY/SEVK IG3 41 Q6
Goodmead Rd ORP BR6 77 R4
Goodrich Cl GSTN WD25 11 N9
Goodrich Rd EDUL SE22 62 K4
Goodson Rd WLSDN NW10 36 E12
Goods Wy CAMTN NW1 4 E3
Goodway Gdns POP/IOD E14 51 V4
Goodwin Cl BERM/RHTH SE16 9 V6
MTCM CR4 73 R1
Goodwin Ct CHES/WCR EN8 16 E2
Goodwin Dr SCUP DA14 65 T7
Goodwin Gdns CROY/NA CR0 74 F11
Goodwin Rd CROY/NA CR0 74 F10
ED N9 27 N6
SHB W12 48 G7
Goodwins Ct CHCR WC2N 4 E13
Goodwin St FSBYPK N4 38 E7
Goodwood Av HCH RM12 43 L9
PEND EN3 16 C11
WATN WD24 11 L9
Goodwood Cl MRDN SM4 73 N2
Goodwood Dr NTHLT UB5 34 J11
Goodwood Pde BECK BR3 * 75 Q2
Goodwood Rd NWCR SE14 51 Q12
REDH RH1 93 T8
Goodwyn Av MLHL NW7 24 E10
Goodwyn's V MUSWH N10 25 U13
Goodyers Av RAD WD7 12 D8
Goodyers Gdns HDN NW4 36 K3
Goosander Wy THMD SE28 53 M8
Gooseacre La KTN/HRWW/WS HA3 35 T3
Goosefields RKW/CH/CXG WD3 21 N4
Goose Green Cl STMC/STPC BR5 65 Q14
Gooseley La EHAM E6 52 J1
Gooshays Dr HARH RM3 31 L11
Gooshays Gdns HARH RM3 31 L11
Goossens Cl SUT SM1 73 Q10
Gophir La CANST EC4R * 5 Q13
Gopsall St IS N1 5 R2
Goral Md RKW/CH/CXG WD3 21 P6
Gordon Av CHING E4 28 A11
HCH RM12 42 F7
MORT/ESHN SW14 60 E2
SAND/SEL CR2 74 G14
STAN HA7 23 P11
TWK TW1 59 Q3
Gordonbrock Rd BROCKY SE4 63 S3
Gordon Cl CHERT KT16 68 J8
STA TW18 57 M11
WALTH E17 39 S4
Gordon Ct REDH RH1 * 93 T12
Gordon Crs CROY/NA CR0 74 J6
HYS/HAR UB3 46 C9
Gordondale Rd WIM/MER SW19 61 N7
Gordon Dr CHERT KT16 68 J8
SHPTN TW17 69 V4
Gordon Gdns EDGW HA8 24 B14
Gordon Gv CMBW SE5 50 F14
Gordon Hl ENC/FH EN2 15 S13
Gordon House Rd KTTN NW5 37 U9
Gordon Pl KENS W8 6 F3
Gordon Rd ASHF TW15 57 Q8
BARK IG11 41 N13
BECK BR3 75 R1
BELV DA17 54 C9
BFN/LL DA15 65 N3
BRYLDS KT5 71 V5
CAR SM5 73 T11
CHDH RM6 41 V4
CHING E4 28 A5
CHSWK W4 48 B11
CTHM CR3 86 H11
DART DA1 66 K5
EA W5 47 S5
ED N9 27 M7
ENC/FH EN2 15 T13
ESH/CLAY KT10 71 N12
FBAR/BDGN N11 26 B12
FNCH N3 25 M12
HSLW TW3 59 L2
IL IG1 41 M8
KTN/HRWW/WS HA3 35 N1
KUTN/CMB KT2 59 V13
NWDGN UB2 46 G9
PECK SE15 51 M14
RCH/KEW TW9 47 V14
REDH RH1 93 U7
SHPTN TW17 69 V4
SRTFD E15 39 U9
STA TW18 56 G9
SWFD E18 28 D13
WAB EN9 16 G8
WAN E11 40 C4
WDR/YW UB7 45 Q5
Gordon Sq STPAN WC1H 4 D7
Gordon St PLSTW E13 52 C1
STPAN WC1H 4 C7
Gordons Wy OXTED RH8 95 V4
Gordon Wy BAR EN5 25 M2
BMLY BR1 64 C13
Gore Cl DEN/HRF UB9 33 M2
Gorefield Pl KIL/WHAMP NW6 2 E3
Gorelands La CSTG HP8 20 C7
Gore Rd HOM E9 39 N13
RDART DA2 67 R7
RYNPK SW20 60 J14
Goresbrook Rd DAGW RM9 41 S13
Gore St SKENS SW7 6 K5
Gorham Pl NTGHL W11 2 A14
Goring Cl CRW RM5 30 C13
Goring Gdns BCTR RM8 41 S9
Goring Rd DAGE RM10 42 D11
FBAR/BDGN N11 * 26 C11
STA TW18 56 H10
Goring St HDTCH EC3A 5 T11
Goring Wy GFD/PVL UB6 35 L14
Gorle Cl GSTN WD25 11 N8
Gorleston Rd SEVS/STOTM N15 38 H3
Gorleston St WKENS W14 6 B7
Gorman Rd WOOL/PLUM SE18 52 H9
Gorringe Av EYN DA4 67 R14
Gorringe Park Av MTCM CR4 61 T12
Gorse Cl CAN/RD E16 52 C4
KWD/TDW/WH KT20 84 H10
Gorse Hill La VW GU25 68 B2
Gorse Hill Rd VW GU25 68 B2
Gorselands Cl BF/WBF KT14 81 N1
Gorse Ri TOOT SW17 61 U10
Gorse Rd CROY/NA CR0 75 S8
STMC/STPC BR5 78 A7
Gorse Wk WDR/YW UB7 45 Q4
Gorseway ROMW/RG RM7 42 E7
Gorst Rd BTSEA SW11 61 T4
WLSDN NW10 48 C2
Gorsuch Pl BETH E2 5 U5
Gorsuch St BETH E2 5 U5
Gosberton Rd BAL SW12 61 T6
Gosbury Hl CHSGTN KT9 71 U9
Gosfield Rd BCTR RM8 42 A6
HOR/WEW KT19 84 D2
Gosfield St GTPST W1W 3 V9
Gosford Gdns REDBR IG4 40 H3
Gosforth La OXHEY WD19 22 C8
Gosforth Pth OXHEY WD19 22 C8
Goshawk Gdns YEAD UB4 46 A1
Goslett Yd SOHO/SHAV W1D 4 D12
Gosling Cl GFD/PVL UB6 46 J1
Gosling Gn DTCH/LGLY SL3 44 C8
Gosling Rd DTCH/LGLY SL3 44 C8
Gosling Wy BRXN/ST SW9 50 E13
Gospatrick Rd TOTM N17 26 G13
Gosport Dr HCH RM12 42 J11
Gosport Rd WALTH E17 39 R3
Gosport Wy PECK SE15 * 9 U13
Gossage Rd HGDN/ICK UB10 33 R12
WOOL/PLUM SE18 53 M10
The Gossamers GSTN WD25 11 S9
Gosset St BETH E2 51 L1
Goss Hl RDART DA2 66 J11
Gosshill Rd BMLY BR1 64 J14
Gossington Cl CHST BR7 64 K9
Gosterwood St DEPT SE8 51 Q11
Gostling Rd WHTN TW2 58 J6
Goston Gdns THHTH CR7 74 E1
Goswell Pl FSBYE EC1V 5 M6
Goswell Rd FSBYE EC1V 5 M5
Gothic Cl DART DA1 66 K8
Gothic Ct HYS/HAR UB3 45 V11
Gothic Rd WHTN TW2 59 M7
Gottfried Ms KTTN NW5 38 A9
Goudhurst Rd BMLY BR1 64 B10
Gough Rd EN EN1 16 B14
SRTFD E15 40 B9
Gough Sq FLST/FETLN EC4A 4 K11
Gough St FSBYW WC1X 4 H7
Goulding Gdns THHTH CR7 62 G14
Gould Rd EBED/NFELT TW14 58 A5
WHTN TW2 59 N6
Goulds Gn UX/CGN UB8 45 T5
Gould Ter HACK E8 39 M10
Goulston St WCHPL E1 5 U11
Goulton Rd CLPT E5 39 M10
Gourley Pl SEVS/STOTM N15 38 J3
Gourley St SEVS/STOTM N15 38 J3
Gourock Rd ELTH/MOT SE9 64 J3
Govan St BETH E2 39 L13
Government Rw PEND EN3 16 G11
Governors Av DEN/HRF UB9 32 K3
Govett Av SHPTN TW17 * 69 U3
Govier Cl SRTFD E15 40 A12
Gowan Av FUL/PGN SW6 49 L13
Gowan Rd WLSDN NW10 36 H12
Gowar Fld POTB/CUF EN6 13 S5
Gower Cl CLAP SW4 62 A4
Gower Ms GWRST WC1E 4 D10
Gower Pl GWRST WC1E 4 B7
Gower Rd FSTGT E7 40 C11
ISLW TW7 47 P11
WEY KT13 69 V11
Gower St GWRST WC1E 4 C8
Gower's Wk WCHPL E1 51 L4
The Gower EGH TW20 68 F1
Gowland Pl BECK BR3 63 R14
Gowlett Rd PECK SE15 63 L1
Gowlland Cl CROY/NA CR0 75 L5
Gowrie Pl CTHM CR3 86 G12
Gowrie Rd BTSEA SW11 61 U1
Graburn Wy E/WMO/HCT KT8 71 M1
Grace Av BXLYHN DA7 53 V14
RAD WD7 12 J7
Gracechurch St BANK EC3V 5 R13
Grace Cl BARK/HLT IG6 29 P11
BORE WD6 13 P13
EDGW HA8 24 C12
ELTH/MOT SE9 64 F8
Gracedale Rd STRHM/NOR SW16 61 V10
Gracefield Gdns STRHM/NOR SW16 62 C8
Grace Jones Cl HACK E8 38 K11
Grace Pl BOW E3 51 T1
Grace Rd CROY/NA CR0 74 G4
Graces Aly CMBW SE5 50 H14
WCHPL E1 * 51 L5
Graces Ms STJWD NW8 * 2 K4
Grace's Rd CMBW SE5 50 J14
Grace St BOW E3 51 T1
Gracious Lane Br BGR/WK TN15 91 N6
Gracious Pond Rd CHOB/PIR GU24 68 A11
The Gradient SYD SE26 63 L9
Graduate Pl STHWK SE1 9 S5
Graeme Rd EN EN1 15 U14
Graemesdyke Av MORT/ESHN SW14 60 B1
Grafton Cl BF/WBF KT14 80 K3
DTCH/LGLY SL3 44 C4
HSLWW TW4 58 G6
WEA W13 47 Q4
WPK KT4 72 E8
Grafton Ct EBED/NFELT TW14 57 V6
Grafton Crs CAMTN NW1 37 V11
Grafton Gdns BCTR RM8 41 U7
FSBYPK N4 38 G4
Grafton Ms FITZ W1T 4 A8
Grafton Park Rd WPK KT4 72 E7
Grafton Pl CAMTN NW1 4 D6
Grafton Rd ACT W3 48 C5
BCTR RM8 41 U7
CROY/NA CR0 74 F6
ENC/FH EN2 26 D1
HRW HA1 35 L3
KTTN NW5 37 U10
WPK KT4 72 D8
Grafton Sq CLAP SW4 62 A2
Grafton St CONDST W1S 3 V14
Grafton Ter HAMP NW3 37 T10
Grafton Wy E/WMO/HCT KT8 70 H2
FITZ W1T 4 B8
Grafton Yd KTTN NW5 37 V11
Graham Av MTCM CR4 61 U13
WEA W13 47 R7
Graham Cl CROY/NA CR0 75 S7
Grahame Park Wy MLHL NW7 24 F12
Graham Gdns SURB KT6 71 U6
Graham Rd BXLYHS DA6 65 V2
CHSWK W4 48 D8
HACK E8 39 L11
HDN NW4 36 H4
HPTN TW12 58 J9
KTN/HRWW/WS HA3 35 N1
MTCM CR4 61 U13
PLSTW E13 52 C2
PUR/KEN CR8 86 E3
SEVS/STOTM N15 38 F1
WIM/MER SW19 61 M12
Graham St IS N1 5 M4
Graham Ter BFN/LL DA15 * 65 R4
BGVA SW1W 7 T8
Grainger Cl NTHLT UB5 35 L10
Grainger Rd ISLW TW7 47 P14
WDGN N22 26 G13
Gramer Cl WAN E11 39 V7
Grampian Cl BELMT SM2 73 Q12
HYS/HAR UB3 45 V12
ORP BR6 77 P4
Grampian Gdns CRICK NW2 37 L6
Grampian Wy DTCH/LGLY SL3 44 E10
Gramsci Wy CAT SE6 63 T8
Granada St TOOT SW17 61 T10
Granard Av PUT/ROE SW15 60 H3
Granard Rd BTSEA SW11 61 T5
The Granaries WAB EN9 17 L8
Granary Cl ED N9 27 N5
Granary Rd WCHPL E1 51 M2
Granary Sq IS N1 38 E11
Granary St CAMTN NW1 4 C2
Granby Park Rd CHESW EN7 15 V2
Granby Rd ELTH/MOT SE9 52 H14
WOOL/PLUM SE18 52 K8
Granby St BETH E2 5 V7
Granby Ter CAMTN NW1 4 A4
Grand Av BRYLDS KT5 72 B4
FARR EC1M 5 M9
MUSWH N10 37 U2
WBLY HA9 36 A10
Grand Av East WBLY HA9 36 B10
Grand Depot Rd WOOL/PLUM SE18 52 J10
Grand Dr NWDGN UB2 47 L7
RYNPK SW20 72 J1
Granden Rd STRHM/NOR SW16 * 62 C14
Grandfield Av WAT WD17 11 M13
Grandison Rd BTSEA SW11 61 T3
WPK KT4 72 J7
Grand Junction Whf IS N1 * 5 N4
Grand Pde FSBYPK N4 * 38 F4
MORT/ESHN SW14 * 60 C2
SURB KT6 * 72 A6
WBLY HA9 * 36 B7
Grand Stand Rd EPSOM KT18 84 G7
Grand Union Canal Wk BTFD TW8 47 S11
DEN/HRF UB9 33 M1
DTCH/LGLY SL3 44 B6
HGDN/ICK UB10 33 N8
HNWL W7 47 N8
HYS/HAR UB3 46 C8
IVER SL0 44 G6
KGLGY WD4 10 H3
NKENS W10 2 B7
NWDGN UB2 46 D8
RKW/CH/CXG WD3 21 L10
STHL UB1 46 H2
UX/CGN UB8 33 M14
WAT WD17 10 K13
WDR/YW UB7 45 T7
WLSDN NW10 36 B14
Grand Union Cl MV/WKIL W9 2 D9
Grand Union Crs HACK E8 * 39 L13
The Grand Union Office Pk
UX/CGN UB8 * 45 N4
Grand Union Wk CAMTN NW1 * 37 V12
Grand View Av BH/WHM TN16 88 E7
Grand Wk WCHPL E1 * 51 Q2
Granfield St BTSEA SW11 * 49 R13
Grange Av KTN/HRWW/WS HA3 23 R14
NFNCH/WDSPK N12 25 Q10
SNWD SE25 62 J14
TRDG/WHET N20 25 L5
WFD IG8 28 C11
WHTN TW2 59 N7
Grangecliffe Gdns SNWD SE25 62 J14
Grange Cl BFN/LL DA15 65 Q8
BH/WHM TN16 97 M2
CFSP/GDCR SL9 20 C13
E/WMO/HCT KT8 70 K2
HYS/HAR UB3 46 A3
LHD/OX KT22 83 T10
REDH RH1 93 V4
REDH RH1 94 H9
STWL/WRAY TW19 56 C4
WAT WD17 11 N13
WFD IG8 28 C12
Grange Ct ALP/SUD HA0 * 35 S10
BELMT SM2 * 73 P12
EGH TW20 * 56 D10
GDST RH9 95 Q14
HRW HA1 * 35 P8
NTHLT UB5 34 E14
PIN HA5 * 34 G1
WAB EN9 16 J8
WLGTN SM6 * 73 V8
WOT/HER KT12 70 C7
Grangecourt Rd STNW/STAM N16 38 J6
Grange Crs CHIG IG7 29 M10
RDART DA2 67 P4
THMD SE28 53 S4
Grangedale Cl NTHWD HA6 22 A13
Grange Dr CHST BR7 64 G11
ORP BR6 77 S13
REDH RH1 93 V4
WOKN/KNAP GU21 80 C5
Grange Farm Cl RYLN/HDSTN HA2 35 L7
Grange Flds CFSP/GDCR SL9 20 C13
Grange Gdns BNSTD SM7 85 P3
HAMP NW3 37 P8
PIN HA5 34 H2
SNWD SE25 62 J14
STHGT/OAK N14 26 B6
Grange Gv IS N1 38 G11
Grange Hl EDGW HA8 24 C10
SNWD SE25 62 J14
Grangehill Pl ELTH/MOT SE9 64 H1
Grangehill Rd ELTH/MOT SE9 64 H2
Grange Houses HBRY N5 * 38 G9
Grange La DUL SE21 62 K7
GSTN WD25 12 B13
Grange Meadow BNSTD SM7 85 P3
Grange Ms FELT TW13 * 57 V8
Grangemill Rd CAT SE6 63 S8
Grangemill Wy CAT SE6 63 S7
Grangemount LHD/OX KT22 83 T10
Grange Pk EA W5 47 U6
WOKN/KNAP GU21 * 80 D4
Grange Park Av WCHMH N21 26 G5
Grange Park Pl RYNPK SW20 60 H12
Grange Park Rd LEY E10 39 T7
THHTH CR7 74 H1
Grange Pl KIL/WHAMP NW6 37 N12
STA TW18 57 N14
WOT/HER KT12 70 C7
Grange Rd ADL/WDHM KT15 69 L14
BARN SW13 48 G13
BELMT SM2 73 N12
BORE WD6 23 V3
BUSH WD23 22 G3
CFSP/GDCR SL9 20 C13
CHSGTN KT9 71 U9
CHSWK W4 48 B10
CTHM CR3 94 K1
E/WMO/HCT KT8 70 K2
EA W5 47 T6
EDGW HA8 24 D11
EGH TW20 56 D10
HARH RM3 30 H11
HGT N6 37 U4
HRW HA1 35 Q4
HYS/HAR UB3 46 A4
IL IG1 41 L9
KUT/HW KT1 71 U1
LEY E10 39 S6
LHD/OX KT22 83 T10
ORP BR6 77 L7
PLSTW E13 52 B1
RYLN/HDSTN HA2 35 M7
SAND/SEL CR2 74 G14
SNWD SE25 74 H2
SOCK/AV RM15 55 Q6
STHL UB1 46 G7
STHWK SE1 9 T6
TOTM N17 27 L11
WALTH E17 39 Q3
WLSDN NW10 36 H11
WOKN/KNAP GU21 80 C5
WOT/HER KT12 70 G9
Granger Wy EMPK RM11 42 G4
Grange St IS N1 5 R2
The Grange ALP/SUD HA0 36 A12
BGR/WK TN15 79 T13
CROY/NA CR0 75 R7
EYN DA4 67 R13
NWMAL KT3 * 72 G3
STHWK SE1 9 U5
WIM/MER SW19 60 K11
WOT/HER KT12 70 D7
WPK KT4 72 D9
Grange V BELMT SM2 73 P12
Grangeview Rd TRDG/WHET N20 25 Q6
Grange Wk STHWK SE1 9 U6
Grange Walk Ms STHWK SE1 9 T6
Grange Wy ERITH DA8 54 H12
IVER SL0 44 K4
Grangeway KIL/WHAMP NW6 37 N12
NFNCH/WDSPK N12 25 P9
WFD IG8 28 E9
Grangeway Gdns REDBR IG4 40 G3
The Grangeway WCHMH N21 26 F4
Grangewood BXLY DA5 65 V6
DTCH/LGLY SL3 44 A3
POTB/CUF EN6 14 D4
Grangewood Av RAIN RM13 54 J2
Grangewood Cl PIN HA5 34 C3
Grangewood La BECK BR3 63 R11
Grangewood St EHAM E6 40 F13
Grange Yd STHWK SE1 9 U6
Granham Gdns ED N9 26 K7
Granite St WOOL/PLUM SE18 53 P10
Granleigh Rd WAN E11 40 A7
Gransden Av HACK E8 39 M12
Gransden Rd SHB W12 48 F7
Grantbridge St IS N1 5 M3
Grantchester KUT/HW KT1 * 60 A14
Grantchester Cl HRW HA1 35 P8
Grant Cl SHPTN TW17 69 T4
STHGT/OAK N14 26 A5
TOTM N17 26 J14
Grantham Cl EDGW HA8 23 U8
Grantham Gdns CHDH RM6 41 V4
Grantham Gn BORE WD6 24 C3
Grantham Pl MYFR/PKLN W1K 7 U2
Grantham Rd BRXN/ST SW9 50 C14
CHSWK W4 48 E12
MNPK E12 40 J8
Grantley Pl ESH/CLAY KT10 70 K10
Grantley Rd HSLWW TW4 46 E14
Grantley St WCHPL E1 51 P1
Grantock Rd WALTH E17 27 V13
Granton Av UPMR RM14 43 M7
Granton Rd GDMY/SEVK IG3 41 Q6
SCUP DA14 65 S11
STRHM/NOR SW16 62 A13
Grant Pl CROY/NA CR0 74 K6
Grant Rd BTSEA SW11 61 S1
CROY/NA CR0 74 K6
KTN/HRWW/WS HA3 35 N1
Grants Cl MLHL NW7 24 J12
Grants La EDEN TN8 96 F13
OXTED RH8 96 E9
Grant St IS N1 4 J3
PLSTW E13 52 C1
Grant Ter STNW/STAM N16 * 39 L5
Grantully Rd MV/WKIL W9 2 G6
Grant Wy ISLW TW7 47 Q11
Granville Ar BRXN/ST SW9 * 62 E2
Granville Av ED N9 27 N8
FELT TW13 58 C7
HSLW TW3 58 J3
Granville Cl BF/WBF KT14 81 R3
CROY/NA CR0 74 J7
WEY KT13 69 U11
Granville Gdns EA W5 47 V6
STRHM/NOR SW16 62 D13
Granville Gv LEW SE13 63 U1
Granville Ms SCUP DA14 65 Q9
Granville Pk LEW SE13 63 U1
Granville Pl FUL/PGN SW6 6 G14
NFNCH/WDSPK N12 * 25 Q12
OXSTW W1C 3 S12
PIN HA5 34 F1
Granville Rd BAR EN5 24 J2
BH/WHM TN16 97 L2
CEND/HSY/T N8 38 D4
CRICK NW2 37 M7
EPP CM16 18 F3
HGDN/ICK UB10 33 T11
HYS/HAR UB3 46 B9
IL IG1 40 K6
KIL/WHAMP NW6 2 E4
NFNCH/WDSPK N12 25 Q12
OXTED RH8 96 B5
PLMGR N13 26 D11
SCUP DA14 65 Q9
SEV TN13 90 G14
SWFD E18 28 D14
WALTH E17 39 T4
WAND/EARL SW18 61 M5
WATW WD18 * 22 E2
WDGN N22 26 F13
WELL DA16 65 S1
WEY KT13 69 U12
WIM/MER SW19 61 N12
WOKS/MYFD GU22 80 D10
Granville Sq PECK SE15 9 T13
Granville St FSBYW WC1X 4 H6
Grape St LSQ/SEVD WC2H 4 E11
Graphite Sq LBTH SE11 8 G9
Grapsome Cl CHSGTN KT9 71 S12
Grasdene Rd WOOL/PLUM SE18 53 Q12
Grasholm Wy DTCH/LGLY SL3 44 G9
Grasmere Av ACT W3 48 C5
HSLW TW3 58 K4
ORP BR6 76 K8
PUT/ROE SW15 60 D9
RSLP HA4 33 U5
WBLY HA9 35 T5
WIM/MER SW19 73 N1
Grasmere Cl EBED/NFELT TW14 58 B6
EGH TW20 56 F12
GSTN WD25 11 P6
LOU IG10 17 T14
Grasmere Ct WDGN N22 26 D11
Grasmere Gdns KTN/HRWW/WS HA3 23 Q14
ORP BR6 76 K8
REDBR IG4 40 G3
Grasmere Rd BMLY BR1 64 B13
BXLYHN DA7 54 C13
MUSWH N10 25 V13
ORP BR6 76 K8
PLSTW E13 40 C14
PUR/KEN CR8 86 F1
SNWD SE25 75 M4
STRHM/NOR SW16 62 D10
TOTM N17 27 L11
Grasmere Wy BF/WBF KT14 81 R2
Grassfield Cl COUL/CHIP CR5 85 V9
Grasshaven Wy THMD SE28 53 P6
Grassingham End CFSP/GDCR SL9 20 C12
Grassingham Rd CFSP/GDCR SL9 20 C12
Grassington Cl FBAR/BDGN N11 25 U11
LCOL/BKTW AL2 1 U4
Grassington Rd SCUP DA14 65 Q9
Grassmere Rd EMPK RM11 43 M2
Grassmount FSTH SE23 63 M7
WLGTN SM6 74 A14
Grass Pk FNCH N3 25 M13
Grassway WLGTN SM6 74 A9
Grasvenor Av BAR EN5 25 N4
Grately Wy PECK SE15 9 U13
Gratton Rd WKENS W14 6 A6
Gratton Ter CRICK NW2 36 K8
Gravel Cl CHIG IG7 29 Q7
Graveley Av BORE WD6 24 C3
Gravel Hl BXLYHS DA6 66 B3
CFSP/GDCR SL9 20 C12
CROY/NA CR0 75 Q11
FNCH N3 25 M14
LHD/OX KT22 83 Q11
UX/CGN UB8 33 P10
Gravel Hill Cl BXLYHS DA6 66 B4
Gravel La CHIG IG7 29 Q4
WCHPL E1 5 U11
Gravelly Hl CTHM CR3 94 K4
Gravel Pit Wy ORP BR6 77 Q7
Gravel Rd EYN DA4 67 P12
HAYES BR2 76 G7
WHTN TW2 59 N6
Gravelwood Cl CHST BR7 65 L8
Gravenel Gdns TOOT SW17 * 61 S10
Graveney Gv PGE/AN SE20 63 N12
Graveney Rd TOOT SW17 61 S9
Gravesend Rd SHB W12 48 G5
Gray Av BCTR RM8 41 V6
Gray Gdns RAIN RM13 42 G11
Grayham Crs NWMAL KT3 72 D2
Grayham Rd NWMAL KT3 72 D2
Grayland Cl BMLY BR1 64 F13
Graylands WOKN/KNAP GU21 80 C6
Graylands Cl WOKN/KNAP GU21 80 C6
Grayling Cl CAN/RD E16 52 A2
Grayling Ct EA W5 * 47 T6
Grayling Rd STNW/STAM N16 38 H7
Grayling Sq BETH E2 * 51 L1
The Graylings ABLGY WD5 10 K7
Gray Pl CHERT KT16 68 H11
Grays Cottages STMC/STPC BR5 * 65 S13
Grayscroft Rd STRHM/NOR SW16 62 B12
Grays Farm Rd STMC/STPC BR5 65 R13
Grayshott Rd BTSEA SW11 61 U1
Gray's Inn Rd FSBYW WC1X 4 F5
Gray's Inn Sq GINN WC1R 4 J9
Grays La ASHF TW15 57 T9
ASHTD KT21 83 V9
Grays Rd BH/WHM TN16 88 K11
HGDN/ICK UB10 33 Q12
Grayswood Gdns RYNPK SW20 60 H14
Gray's Yd MHST W1U * 3 T12
Graywood Ct NFNCH/WDSPK N12 25 Q12
Grazebrook Rd STNW/STAM N16 38 H7
Grazeley Cl BXLYHS DA6 66 C3
Great Benty WDR/YW UB7 45 Q9
Great Brownings DUL SE21 62 K9
Great Bushey Dr TRDG/WHET N20 25 P6
Great Cambridge Jct PLMGR N13 26 G10
Great Cambridge Rd CHES/WCR EN8 16 C8
EN EN1 27 L4
UED N18 26 H10
Great Castle St REGST W1B 4 A11
Great Central Av RSLP HA4 34 E10
Great Central St CAMTN NW1 3 Q9
Great Central Wy WBLY HA9 36 C10
Great Chapel St SOHO/SHAV W1D 4 C11
Great Chart St BTSEA SW11 61 Q1
Great Chertsey Rd CHSWK W4 48 D13
FELT TW13 58 H8
Great Church La HMSMTH W6 48 K10
Great College St WEST SW1P 8 E5
Great Cross Av GNWCH SE10 52 A12
Great Cullings ROMW/RG RM7 42 E7
Great Cumberland Ms MBLAR W1H 3 Q12
Great Cumberland Pl MBLAR W1H 3 Q11
Great Dover St STHWK SE1 9 Q5
Greatdown Rd HNWL W7 47 P3
Great Eastern Rd SRTFD E15 39 V12
Great Eastern St SDTCH EC2A 5 S7
Great Eastern Whf BTSEA SW11 7 P13
Great Ellshams BNSTD SM7 85 N6
Great Elms EW KT17 * 84 F1
Great Elms Rd HAYES BR2 76 E2
Great Fld CDALE/KGS NW9 24 E13
Greatfield Av EHAM E6 52 H2
Greatfield Cl ARCH N19 38 A9
BROCKY SE4 63 S2
Greatfields Dr UX/CGN UB8 45 S3
Greatfields Rd BARK IG11 41 M13
Great Galley Cl BARK IG11 53 R1
Great Gardens Rd EMPK RM11 42 J4
Great Gatton Cl CROY/NA CR0 75 Q5
Great George St STJSPK SW1H 8 D4
Great Gregories La EPP CM16 18 C7
Great Gv BUSH WD23 22 K2
Great Groves CHESW EN7 15 U2
Great Guildford St STHWK SE1 9 N2
Greatham Rd BUSH WD23 22 F1
Great Harry Dr ELTH/MOT SE9 64 J9
Great James St BMSBY WC1N 4 H9
Great Marlborough St REGST W1B 4 A12
Great Maze Pond STHWK SE1 9 R2
Great Nelmes Cha EMPK RM11 43 M3
Greatness La RSEV TN14 90 J11
Greatness Rd RSEV TN14 90 J11
Great New St FLST/FETLN EC4A * 4 K11
Great North Leisure Pk
NFNCH/WDSPK N12 * 25 R12
Great North Rd BAR EN5 14 B14
BAR EN5 25 P4
EFNCH N2 37 S3
Great North Wy (Barnet By-Pass)
HDN NW4 24 H13
Great Oaks CHIG IG7 29 L9
Greatorex St WCHPL E1 51 L3
Great Ormond St BMSBY WC1N 4 F9
Great Owl Rd CHIG IG7 28 J8
Great Pk KGLGY WD4 10 G4
Great Percy St FSBYW WC1X 4 H5
Great Peter St WEST SW1P 8 D6
Great Portland St GTPST W1W 3 V9
Great Pulteney St SOHO/CST W1F 4 B13
Great Queen St DART DA1 67 M4
HOL/ALD WC2B 4 F11
Great Ropers La RBRW/HUT CM13 31 V11
Great Russell St NOXST/BSQ WC1A 4 E10
Great St Thomas Apostle BLKFR EC4V 5 P13
Great Scotland Yd WHALL SW1A 8 E2
Great Slades POTB/CUF EN6 14 B7
Great Smith St WEST SW1P 8 D5
Great South-West Rd
EBED/NFELT TW14 58 C1
Great Spilmans EDUL SE22 62 J3
Great Strd CDALE/KGS NW9 24 F14
Great Suffolk St STHWK SE1 9 M3
Great Sutton St FSBYE EC1V 5 M8
Great Swan Aly LOTH EC2R 5 Q11
Great Tattenhams EPSOM KT18 84 J9
Great Thrift STMC/STPC BR5 77 L2
Great Till Cl RSEV TN14 90 F6
Great Titchfield St GTPST W1W 3 V9
Great Tower St MON EC3R 5 S14
Great Trinity La BLKFR EC4V 5 P13
Great Turnstile HHOL WC1V * 4 H10
Great Warley St RBRW/HUT CM13 31 V14
Great Western Rd NTGHL W11 2 D10
Great West Rd HEST TW5 46 G14
HMSMTH W6 48 H10
ISLW TW7 47 N12
Great West Rd Chiswick CHSWK W4 48 F11
Great West Rd Ellesmere Rd
CHSWK W4 48 C11
Great West Rd Hogarth La
CHSWK W4 48 D11
Great Westwood KGLGY WD4 * 10 E9
Great Winchester St OBST EC2N 5 R11
Great Windmill St SOHO/SHAV W1D 4 C14
Greatwood CHST BR7 64 J12
Greatwood Cl CHERT KT16 68 G13
Great Woodcote Dr PUR/KEN CR8 74 B14
Great Woodcote Pk PUR/KEN CR8 74 C14
Great Yd STHWK SE1 9 T3
Greaves Cl BARK IG11 41 N12
Greaves Cottages POP/IOD E14 * 51 Q3
Greaves Pl TOOT SW17 61 S9
Grebe Av YEAD UB4 46 F4
Grebe Cl BARK IG11 53 Q2
FSTGT E7 40 B10
WALTH E17 27 Q12
Grebe Ct SUT SM1 73 M10
Grebe Crest WTHK RM20 55 U9
Grebe Ter KUT/HW KT1 * 71 U1
Grecian Crs NRWD SE19 62 F11
Greek St SOHO/SHAV W1D 4 D12
The Green WIM/MER SW19 60 K10
Greenacre Cl BAR EN5 14 B12
NTHLT UB5 34 H10
SWLY BR8 78 E2
Greenacre Ct EGH TW20 * 56 A11
Greenacre Gdns WALTH E17 39 U2
Greenacre Pl WLGTN SM6 73 V7
Greenacres BUSH WD23 23 M7
Green Acres CROY/NA CR0 74 K8
Greenacres ELTH/MOT SE9 64 J4
EPP CM16 18 D2
GT/LBKH KT23 82 J14
KWD/TDW/WH KT20 93 M4
OXTED RH8 96 A3
Green Acres SCUP DA14 * 65 P9
Greenacres Av HGDN/ICK UB10 33 S8
Greenacres Cl ORP BR6 77 L9
RAIN RM13 55 L1
Greenacres Dr STAN HA7 23 R12
Greenacre Sq BERM/RHTH SE16 * 51 P7
Greenacre Wk STHGT/OAK N14 26 B8
Greenall Cl CHES/WCR EN8 16 E4
Green Arbour Ct STBT EC1A * 5 L11
Green Av MLHL NW7 24 D9
WEA W13 47 R8
Greenaway Gdns HAMP NW3 37 P9
Greenbank CHES/WCR EN8 16 B2
Green Bank NFNCH/WDSPK N12 25 P9
WAP E1W 51 M6
Greenbank Av ALP/SUD HA0 35 Q10
Greenbank Cl CHING E4 27 U7
HARH RM3 30 K8
Greenbank Crs HDN NW4 37 L2
Greenbank Rd WAT WD17 10 K10
Greenbanks DART DA1 67 L7
UPMR RM14 43 S7
Greenbay Rd CHARL SE7 52 F12
Greenberry St STJWD NW8 3 N4
Greenbrook Av EBAR EN4 14 E13
Greenbury Cl RKW/CH/CXG WD3 20 G1
Green Chain Wk BMLY BR1 63 U10
BMLY BR1 64 A12
ELTH/MOT SE9 64 F10
HAYES BR2 63 V12
SYD SE26 63 P11
THMD SE28 53 T6
WOOL/PLUM SE18 52 H11
Green Cl CAR SM5 73 T7
CDALE/KGS NW9 36 C4
CHES/WCR EN8 16 E6
FELT TW13 58 G10
GLDGN NW11 37 Q5
HAYES BR2 76 A1
Greencoat Pl WEST SW1P 8 B7
Greencoat Rw WEST SW1P 8 B6
Green Court Av CROY/NA CR0 75 M7
Greencourt Av EDGW HA8 24 B13
Green Court Gdns CROY/NA CR0 75 M7
Greencourt Rd STMC/STPC BR5 77 N3
Green Court Rd SWLY BR8 78 D4
Greencroft EDGW HA8 24 C10
Greencroft Av RSLP HA4 34 E7
Greencroft Gdns EN EN1 26 J1
KIL/WHAMP NW6 37 P12
Greencroft Rd HEST TW5 46 H13
Green Curve BNSTD SM7 85 M5
Green Dl EDUL SE22 62 J3
Green Dragon La BTFD TW8 47 U10
WCHMH N21 26 D3
Green Dragon Yd WCHPL E1 51 L3
Green Dr RPLY/SEND GU23 80 K13
STHL UB1 46 J6
Greene Fielde End STA TW18 57 P12
Green End CHSGTN KT9 71 T9
WCHMH N21 26 F7
Greenend Rd CHSWK W4 48 E7
Green Farm Cl ORP BR6 77 P10
Greenfell Man DEPT SE8 * 51 R10
Greenfield Av BRYLDS KT5 72 C4
OXHEY WD19 22 G7
Greenfield Ct ELTH/MOT SE9 64 G8
Greenfield Dr BMLY BR1 64 E14
EFNCH N2 37 T2
Greenfield End CFSP/GDCR SL9 20 D12
Greenfield Gdns CRICK NW2 37 L7
DAGW RM9 41 S13
STMC/STPC BR5 77 L5
Greenfield Link COUL/CHIP CR5 86 C5
Greenfield Rd DAGW RM9 41 T13
RDART DA2 66 D10
SEVS/STOTM N15 38 J3
WCHPL E1 51 L4
Greenfields LOU IG10 28 J2
POTB/CUF EN6 * 15 N4
STHL UB1 46 J5
Greenfield St WAB EN9 16 J8
Greenfield Wy RYLN/HDSTN HA2 34 K1
Greenford Av HNWL W7 47 N3
STHL UB1 46 H5
Greenford Gdns GFD/PVL UB6 46 K1
Greenford Rd GFD/PVL UB6 35 N12
STHL UB1 47 L5
SUT SM1 73 P9
Green Gdns ORP BR6 77 L10
Greengate GFD/PVL UB6 35 R11
Greengate St PLSTW E13 40 D14
Green Gld EPP CM16 18 C11
Green Glades EMPK RM11 43 M4
Greenhalgh Wk EFNCH N2 37 Q2
Greenham Cl STHWK SE1 8 J4
Greenham Crs CHING E4 27 R11
Greenham Rd MUSWH N10 25 U14
Greenham Wk WOKN/KNAP GU21 80 A8
Greenhaven Dr THMD SE28 53 S4
Greenhayes Av BNSTD SM7 85 N5
Greenhayes Cl REIG RH2 93 Q10
Greenhayes Gdns BNSTD SM7 85 N5
Greenheys Cl NTHWD HA6 22 A13
Greenheys Dr SWFD E18 40 B1
Greenheys Pl WOKS/MYFD GU22 80 D8
Green Hl ORP BR6 88 G2
WOOL/PLUM SE18 52 H10
Greenhill BKHH IG9 28 E6
HAMP NW3 37 R9
SUT SM1 73 Q7
WBLY HA9 36 B7
Greenhill Av CTHM CR3 87 M11
Greenhill Ct BAR EN5 * 25 P3
Greenhill Crs WATW WD18 22 A4
Greenhill Gdns NTHLT UB5 34 H14
Greenhill Gv MNPK E12 40 G9
Greenhill La WARL CR6 87 Q7
Greenhill Pde BAR EN5 * 25 P3
Greenhill Pk BAR EN5 25 Q3
WLSDN NW10 36 E13
Greenhill Rd HRW HA1 35 N4
RSEV TN14 90 J5
WLSDN NW10 36 E13
Greenhills Cl RKW/CH/CXG WD3 21 M3
Greenhill's Rents FARR EC1M * 5 L9
Greenhills Ter IS N1 38 H11
Greenhill Ter NTHLT UB5 * 34 H14
WOOL/PLUM SE18 52 H10
Greenhill Wy HRW HA1 35 N4
WBLY HA9 36 B7
Greenhithe Cl BFN/LL DA15 65 N5
Greenholm Rd ELTH/MOT SE9 64 K3
Green Hundred Rd PECK SE15 51 L11
Greenhurst La OXTED RH8 96 C8
Greenhurst Rd WNWD SE27 62 E10
Greening St ABYW SE2 53 S9
Greenlake Ter STA TW18 * 57 L12
Greenland Crs NWDGN UB2 46 E8
Greenland Ms DEPT SE8 51 P10
Greenland Pl CAMTN NW1 3 V1
Greenland Quay BERM/RHTH SE16 51 Q9
Greenland Rd BAR EN5 24 J4
CAMTN NW1 4 A1
Greenlands CHERT KT16 68 G8
HOR/WEW KT19 72 B10
Greenlands Rd BGR/WK TN15 91 N9
STA TW18 57 L9
WEY KT13 69 T8
Greenland St CAMTN NW1 3 V1
Greenland Wy CROY/NA CR0 74 B5
Green La ASHTD KT21 83 S7
BCTR RM8 41 V7
BF/WBF KT14 81 R2
BRW CM14 31 U12
CHERT KT16 68 J7
CHIG IG7 29 L6
CHING E4 * 28 A1
CHSGTN KT9 71 U13
COB KT11 82 G2
CTHM CR3 86 G13
E/WMO/HCT KT8 70 K3
EDEN TN8 97 S12
EDGW HA8 23 V9
EGH TW20 56 F10
ELTH/MOT SE9 64 K7
FELT TW13 58 G10
HDN NW4 36 K3
HNWL W7 47 N7
HSLWW TW4 58 E3
IL IG1 41 M7
KWD/TDW/WH KT20 93 M2
LHD/OX KT22 83 T11
MRDN SM4 73 P5
NTHWD HA6 21 V12
NWMAL KT3 72 C3
OXHEY WD19 22 E6
PGE/AN SE20 63 P12
PUR/KEN CR8 86 A1
REIG RH2 93 M10
RKW/CH/CXG WD3 21 R3
RPLY/SEND GU23 81 T14
SHPTN TW17 69 V4
STA TW18 56 J13
STAN HA7 23 R9
SUN TW16 58 B12
THHTH CR7 62 F13
UX/CGN UB8 45 U3
WAB EN9 17 R9
WOT/HER KT12 70 D10
WPK KT4 72 H5
Green Lane Av WOT/HER KT12 70 D10
Green Lane Cl BF/WBF KT14 81 R2
CHERT KT16 68 J7
Green Lane Cottages STAN HA7 * 23 R9
Green Lane Gdns THHTH CR7 62 G14
Green Lanes HOR/WEW KT19 72 E13
PLMGR N13 26 D10
SEVS/STOTM N15 38 F1
WCHMH N21 26 G6
Greenlaw Ct EA W5 * 47 T4
Greenlaw Gdns NWMAL KT3 72 F5
Greenlawn La BTFD TW8 47 T10
Green Lawns NFNCH/WDSPK N12 * 25 P11
RSLP HA4 * 34 E6
Greenlaw St WOOL/PLUM SE18 52 J8
Green Leaf Av WLGTN SM6 74 B9
Greenleaf Cl BRXS/STRHM SW2 * 62 E5
Greenleafe Dr BARK/HLT IG6 40 K1
Greenleaf Rd EHAM E6 40 E13
WALTH E17 39 R1
Greenlea Pk WIM/MER SW19 * 61 S13
Green Leas SUN TW16 58 B12
Green Leas Cl SUN TW16 58 B11
Greenleaves Ct ASHF TW15 * 57 T11
Greenleigh Av STMC/STPC BR5 77 R2
Greenlink Wk RCH/KEW TW9 48 B13
Green Man La EBED/NFELT TW14 58 C2
WEA W13 47 Q5
Greenman St IS N1 38 G12
Green Md ESH/CLAY KT10 70 H11
Greenmead Cl SNWD SE25 75 L3
Green Meadow POTB/CUF EN6 14 C4
Greenmeads WOKS/MYFD GU22 80 C12
Green Moor Link WCHMH N21 26 F5
Greenmoor Rd PEND EN3 16 C14
Greenoak Pl EBAR EN4 14 H14
Greenoak Ri BH/WHM TN16 88 E8
Green Oaks NWDGN UB2 * 46 F9
Greenoak Wy WIM/MER SW19 60 K9
Greenock Rd ACT W3 48 B8
STRHM/NOR SW16 62 B13
Greenock Wy ROM RM1 30 E12
Greeno Crs SHPTN TW17 69 S3
Green Pde HSLW TW3 * 58 K4
Green Pk STA TW18 56 J8
Greenpark Wy GFD/PVL UB6 35 N13
Green Pond Cl WALTH E17 39 R1
Green Pond Rd WALTH E17 39 Q1
Green Ride CHING E4 28 C4
Green Rd EGH TW20 68 F2
TRDG/WHET N20 25 Q8
Greenroof Wy GNWCH SE10 52 B8
Greensand Cl REDH RH1 94 B4
Greensand Rd REDH RH1 93 U9
Greensand Wy BH/WHM TN16 97 M3
BRKHM/BTCW RH3 92 G10
EDEN TN8 97 L6
GDST RH9 95 P10
OXTED RH8 96 A2
REDH RH1 94 C11
REDH RH1 95 M11
REIG RH2 93 L8
The Greens Cl LOU IG10 17 U14
Greens Ct NTGHL W11 * 6 C2
SOHO/CST W1F 4 C13
Greens End WOOL/PLUM SE18 52 K9
Greenshank Cl WALTH E17 27 Q12
Greenshaw BRW CM14 31 V6
Greenside BCTR RM8 41 S7
BORE WD6 13 L12
BXLY DA5 65 U6
RPLY/SEND GU23 * 81 N11
SWLY BR8 66 D14
Greenside Cl CAT SE6 63 V7
TRDG/WHET N20 25 R7
Greenside Dr ASHTD KT21 83 R8
Greenside Rd CROY/NA CR0 74 E5
SHB W12 48 G8
Greenslade Rd BARK IG11 41 N12
Green Sleeves Dr BRW CM14 31 V10
Greenstead Av WFD IG8 28 E11
Greenstead Gdns PUT/ROE SW15 60 G3
WFD IG8 28 E11
Greensted Rd CHONG CM5 19 S2
LOU IG10 28 H5
Greenstone Ms WAN E11 40 C4
Green St BORE WD6 13 L11
FSTGT E7 40 D10
MYFR/PKLN W1K 3 R13
PEND EN3 27 P1
SUN TW16 58 C13
Green Street Green Rd RDART DA2 67 R9
Greenstreet Hl NWCR SE14 * 63 P1
Greensward BUSH WD23 22 K4
Green Ter CLKNW EC1R 4 K6
The Green ACT W3 48 E4
ASHF TW15 * 57 P10
BGR/WK TN15 * 79 T14
BH/WHM TN16 * 89 S14
BH/WHM TN16 97 M2
BKHH IG9 * 28 D6
BXLYHN DA7 54 A13
CAR SM5 * 73 U9
CHES/WCR EN8 16 C2
CROY/NA CR0 75 R13
CTHM CR3 87 S13
ED N9 27 L7
EGH TW20 56 A9
EPP CM16 18 C11
EW KT17 84 G2
FELT TW13 58 D7
GDST RH9 95 M8
HARH RM3 30 J8
HAYES BR2 76 C5
HEST TW5 46 J11
HGDN/ICK UB10 33 U7
HRW HA1 35 Q7
KWD/TDW/WH KT20 84 K13
KWD/TDW/WH KT20 85 L9
LCOL/BKTW AL2 * 12 H1
LHD/OX KT22 83 M14
MRDN SM4 73 L2
NWDGN UB2 46 H7
NWMAL KT3 72 C1
ORP BR6 * 77 S14
RAIN RM13 55 L5
RCH/KEW TW9 59 T3
RDART DA2 67 R7
RKW/CH/CXG WD3 21 R4
SCUP DA14 65 Q10
SEV TN13 90 K12
SRTFD E15 40 B11
STHGT/OAK N14 26 B8
STMC/STPC BR5 65 R12
STWL/WRAY TW19 56 C4
SUT SM1 73 P8
TOTM N17 26 G11
WAB EN9 16 J8
WAN E11 40 D4
WCHMH N21 26 E5
WDR/YW UB7 45 P8
WELL DA16 65 N2
WHTN TW2 59 N6
WLGTN SM6 73 U7
Green Tiles DEN/HRF UB9 * 32 K5
Green Tiles La DEN/HRF UB9 32 K4
Green Trees EPP CM16 18 E5
Green V BXLYHS DA6 65 T3
EA W5 47 V4
Greenvale Rd ELTH/MOT SE9 64 H2
Green Verges STAN HA7 23 T12
Green Vw CHSGTN KT9 71 V12
Greenview Av BECK BR3 75 Q4
Greenview Cl ACT W3 48 E6
Green Wk DART DA1 66 F2
HDN NW4 36 K3
NWDGN UB2 46 J10
RSLP HA4 34 B6
STHWK SE1 9 S6
WFD IG8 28 G11
The Green Wk CHING E4 27 U6
Green Wy ELTH/MOT SE9 64 F3
HAYES BR2 76 G4
REDH RH1 93 S8
SUN TW16 70 C2
Greenway BCTR RM8 41 S7
BH/WHM TN16 88 E10
CHST BR7 64 J10
GT/LBKH KT23 82 K13
HARH RM3 31 P11
KTN/HRWW/WS HA3 35 U3
PIN HA5 22 D14
RYNPK SW20 72 J2
STHGT/OAK N14 26 C7
TRDG/WHET N20 25 N7
WLGTN SM6 74 A9
YEAD UB4 46 D2
Greenway Av WALTH E17 39 V2
Greenway Cl SEVS/STOTM N15 38 K2
BF/WBF KT14 81 L3
CDALE/KGS NW9 24 D14
FBAR/BDGN N11 25 U11
FSBYPK N4 38 G7
TRDG/WHET N20 25 N7
Greenway Ct IL IG1 40 J6
SRTFD E15 40 A14
Greenway Dr STA TW18 57 N13
Greenway Gdns CDALE/KGS NW9 24 C14
CROY/NA CR0 75 R8
GFD/PVL UB6 46 K1
Green Way Gdns KTN/HRWW/WS HA3 23 N14
Greenways ABLGY WD5 10 K5
BECK BR3 63 S14
CHESW EN7 15 R3
EGH TW20 56 C11
ESH/CLAY KT10 71 N9
KWD/TDW/WH KT20 92 G1
NFNCH/WDSPK N12 * 25 Q11
The Greenways TWK TW1 * 59 Q4
The Green Wy KTN/HRWW/WS HA3 23 N13
The Greenway CDALE/KGS NW9 24 D14
CFSP/GDCR SL9 32 B1
EPSOM KT18 84 A5
HGDN/ICK UB10 33 T7
HSLWW TW4 * 58 H2
OXTED RH8 96 C9
PEND EN3 16 D9
PIN HA5 34 H4
POTB/CUF EN6 14 C7
RKW/CH/CXG WD3 21 L5
UX/CGN UB8 33 P14
Greenwell Cl GDST RH9 95 M6
Greenwell St GTPST W1W 3 V8
Greenwich Church St GNWCH SE10 * 51 U11
Greenwich Crs EHAM E6 52 G3
Greenwich Foot Tnl GNWCH SE10 51 U10
Greenwich Hts CHARL SE7 * 52 G12
Greenwich High Rd GNWCH SE10 51 T12
Greenwich Park St GNWCH SE10 * 51 V11
Greenwich Quay DEPT SE8 51 T11
Greenwich South St GNWCH SE10 51 T13
Greenwich Vw POP/IOD E14 51 T8
Greenwich Wy WAB EN9 16 K10
Greenwood Av CHESW EN7 16 B5
DAGE RM10 42 B9
PEND EN3 16 E13
Greenwood Cl ADL/WDHM KT15 80 K1
BFN/LL DA15 65 Q7
CHESW EN7 16 B5
MRDN SM4 73 L2
STMC/STPC BR5 77 N4
THDIT KT7 71 Q6
Greenwood Dr CHING E4 27 U10
GSTN WD25 11 P8
Greenwood Gdns BARK/HLT IG6 29 L12
CTHM CR3 95 L1
OXTED RH8 96 C10
PLMGR N13 26 F8
RAD WD7 12 J7
Greenwood La HPTN TW12 58 K10
Greenwood Pk KUTN/CMB KT2 60 E12
Greenwood Pl KTTN NW5 37 V10
Greenwood Rd BXLY DA5 66 D9
CHIG IG7 29 R9
HACK E8 39 L11
ISLW TW7 59 N1
MTCM CR4 74 B1
PLSTW E13 40 B14
THDIT KT7 71 Q6
Greenwood Ter WLSDN NW10 * 36 D13
Green Wrythe Crs CAR SM5 73 S6
Green Wrythe La CAR SM5 73 R4
Green Yd FSBYW WC1X 4 H7
Greenyard WAB EN9 16 J7
Greer Rd KTN/HRWW/WS HA3 23 L13
Greet St STHWK SE1 8 K3
Greg Cl LEY E10 39 U4
Gregor Ms BKHTH/KID SE3 52 C12
Gregory Av POTB/CUF EN6 14 E7
Gregory Cl WOKN/KNAP GU21 80 A7
Gregory Crs ELTH/MOT SE9 64 F5
Gregory Ms WAB EN9 16 H6
Gregory Pl KENS W8 6 G3
Gregory Rd CHDH RM6 41 T2
NWDGN UB2 46 K8
Gregson Cl BORE WD6 13 N14
Greig Cl CEND/HSY/T N8 38 C3
Greig Ter WALW SE17 9 M11
Grenaby Av CROY/NA CR0 74 H5
Grenaby Rd CROY/NA CR0 74 H5
Grenada Rd BKHTH/KID SE3 52 E12
Grenade St POP/IOD E14 51 R5
Grenadier Pl CTHM CR3 86 G12
Grenadier St CAN/RD E16 52 J6
Grenadine Cl CHESW EN7 15 V1
Grena Gdns RCH/KEW TW9 59 V2
Grenard Cl PECK SE15 * 51 L12
Grena Rd RCH/KEW TW9 59 V2
Grendon Gdns WBLY HA9 36 A7
Grendon St STJWD NW8 3 N7
Grenfell Av HCH RM12 42 F6
Grenfell Cl BORE WD6 13 N13
Grenfell Ct MLHL NW7 * 24 H11
Grenfell Gdns KTN/HRWW/WS HA3 35 U5
Grenfell Rd NTGHL W11 48 K5
TOOT SW17 61 T11
Grennell Cl SUT SM1 73 R7
Grennell Rd SUT SM1 73 Q7
Grenoble Gdns PLMGR N13 26 E11
Grenside Rd WEY KT13 69 T8
Grenville Cl BRYLDS KT5 72 C6
CHES/WCR EN8 16 D6
COB KT11 82 F3
FNCH N3 25 M13
Grenville Gdns WFD IG8 28 E12
Grenville Ms ARCH N19 38 C6
HPTN TW12 58 K10
Grenville Pl MLHL NW7 24 D10
SKENS SW7 6 J7
Grenville Rd ARCH N19 38 C6
CDW/CHF RM16 55 V10
CROY/NA CR0 75 U14
Grenville St BMSBY WC1N 4 F8
Gresham Av TRDG/WHET N20 25 T9
WARL CR6 87 Q8
Gresham Cl BXLY DA5 65 U4
ENC/FH EN2 26 G1
OXTED RH8 96 B5
Gresham Dr CHDH RM6 41 R3
Gresham Gdns GLDGN NW11 37 L6
Gresham Rd BECK BR3 63 Q14
BRXN/ST SW9 62 E1
CAN/RD E16 52 D4
EDGW HA8 23 V11
EHAM E6 40 H14
HGDN/ICK UB10 33 S14
HPTN TW12 58 J11
HSLW TW3 47 L13
OXTED RH8 96 B5
SNWD SE25 * 75 L2
STA TW18 56 K10
WLSDN NW10 36 D10
Gresham St CITYW EC2V 5 N11
Gresham Wy WIM/MER SW19 61 N8
Gresley Cl SEVS/STOTM N15 * 38 H2
WALTH E17 39 Q4
Gresley Rd ARCH N19 38 A6
Gressenhall Rd WAND/EARL SW18 61 M4
Gresse St FITZ W1T 4 C10
Gresswell Cl SCUP DA14 65 Q8
Greswell St FUL/PGN SW6 48 K13
Gretton Rd TOTM N17 26 J12
Greville Av SAND/SEL CR2 75 P14
Greville Cl ASHTD KT21 83 U9
TWK TW1 59 R5
Greville Ms KIL/WHAMP NW6 2 G2
Greville Park Av ASHTD KT21 83 U8
Greville Park Rd ASHTD KT21 83 U8
Greville Pl KIL/WHAMP NW6 2 H3
Greville Rd KIL/WHAMP NW6 2 G2
RCHPK/HAM TW10 59 V4
WALTH E17 39 U2
Greville St HCIRC EC1N 4 K10
Grey Alders BNSTD SM7 84 J4
Greycaine Rd WATN WD24 11 R11
Grey Cl GLDGN NW11 37 Q4
Greycoat Pl WEST SW1P 8 C6
Greycoat St WEST SW1P 8 C6
Greycot Rd BECK BR3 63 S10
Grey Eagle St WCHPL E1 5 V8
Greyfell Cl STAN HA7 23 R10
Greyfields Cl PUR/KEN CR8 86 F3
Greyfriars Rd RPLY/SEND GU23 81 L14
Greyhound Hl HDN NW4 36 G1
Greyhound La POTB/CUF EN6 13 S7
STRHM/NOR SW16 62 C11
Greyhound Rd HMSMTH W6 48 K11
SUT SM1 73 Q10
TOTM N17 38 J1
WLSDN NW10 48 H1
Greyhound Ter STRHM/NOR SW16 62 A13
Greyhound Wy DART DA1 66 E3
Greyladies Gdns GNWCH SE10 * 51 U14
Greys Park Cl HAYES BR2 76 E10
Greystead Rd FSTH SE23 63 N5
Greystoke Av PIN HA5 34 J1
Greystoke Cottages EA W5 * 47 U2
Greystoke Dr RSLP HA4 33 T5
Greystoke Gdns EA W5 47 U2
ENC/FH EN2 26 B2
Greystone Cl SAND/SEL CR2 87 N1
Greystone Gdns BARK/HLT IG6 29 L14
KTN/HRWW/WS HA3 35 S4
Greystone Pk RSEV TN14 97 U1
Greystones Cl BGR/WK TN15 91 L7
REDH RH1 93 R12
Greystones Dr REIG RH2 93 Q8
Greyswood St STRHM/NOR SW16 61 V11
Grey Towers Av EMPK RM11 42 K6
Grey Towers Gdns EMPK RM11 42 J6
Grice Av BH/WHM TN16 88 D3
Gridiron Pl UPMR RM14 43 P7
Grierson Rd FSTH SE23 63 Q4
Griffin Av UPMR RM14 43 S4
Griffin Centre EBED/NFELT TW14 * 58 D4
Griffin Cl WLSDN NW10 36 H10
Griffin Ct ASHTD KT21 * 83 U9
Griffin Manor Wy THMD SE28 53 M8
Griffin Rd TOTM N17 26 J14
WOOL/PLUM SE18 53 M10
Griffins Cl WCHMH N21 26 H6
Griffin Wk RDART DA2 67 T3
Griffin Wy SUN TW16 58 C14
THMD SE28 53 N8
Griffith Cl BCTR RM8 41 S5
Griffiths Rd WIM/MER SW19 61 N12
Griffon Wy GSTN WD25 11 M8
Griggs Ap IL IG1 41 L7
Griggs Gdns HCH RM12 42 J10
Grigg's Pl STHWK SE1 9 T6
Griggs Rd LEY E10 39 U4
Grimsby Gv CAN/RD E16 52 K7
Grimsby St BETH E2 5 V7
Grimsdyke Crs BAR EN5 24 J1
Grimsdyke Rd PIN HA5 22 G12
Grimsel Pth WALW SE17 9 M13
Grimshaw Cl HGT N6 * 37 U5
Grimshaw Wy ROM RM1 42 E3
Grimston Rd FUL/PGN SW6 49 M14
Grimwade Av CROY/NA CR0 75 L8
Grimwade Cl PECK SE15 51 M14
Grimwood Rd TWK TW1 59 P5
Grindall Cl CROY/NA CR0 74 F9
Grindal St STHWK SE1 8 J4
Grindleford Av FBAR/BDGN N11 25 U7
Grindley Gdns CROY/NA CR0 * 74 K4
Grinling Pl DEPT SE8 51 S11
Grinstead Rd DEPT SE8 51 Q10
Grisedale Cl PUR/KEN CR8 86 J4
Grisedale Gdns PUR/KEN CR8 86 J4
Grisle Cl ED N9 27 M9
Grittleton Av WBLY HA9 36 B11
Grittleton Rd MV/WKIL W9 2 E7
Grobars Av WOKN/KNAP GU21 80 A5
Grocers' Hall Ct LOTH EC2R * 5 Q12
Groombridge Cl WELL DA16 65 Q3
WOT/HER KT12 70 D10
Groombridge Rd HOM E9 39 P12
Groom Cl HAYES BR2 76 D2
Groom Crs WAND/EARL SW18 61 R5
Groomfield Cl TOOT SW17 61 U9
Groom Pl KTBR SW1X 7 T5

Grooms Dr PIN HA5 34 C3
Grosmont Rd WOOL/PLUM SE18 53 P10
Grosse Wy PUT/ROE SW15 60 H4
Grosvenor Av CAR SM5 73 T11
HBRY N5 38 G10
KGLGY WD4 10 J2
MORT/ESHN SW14 60 E1
RYLN/HDSTN HA2 34 K5
YEAD UB4 34 B14
Grosvenor Br PIM SW1V 7 V11
Grosvenor Cl LOU IG10 17 V13
Grosvenor Cottages KTBR SW1X 7 S7
Grosvenor Ct RKW/CH/CXG WD3 * 21 V3
Grosvenor Crs CDALE/KGS NW9 36 A2
DART DA1 66 K3
HGDN/ICK UB10 33 T12
KTBR SW1X 7 T4
Grosvenor Crescent Ms KTBR SW1X 7 T4
Grosvenor Dr EMPK RM11 42 J6
LOU IG10 17 V14
Grosvenor Gdns BGVA SW1W 7 V6
CRICK NW2 36 J11
GLDGN NW11 37 M4
KUTN/CMB KT2 59 T11
MORT/ESHN SW14 60 E1
MUSWH N10 38 A1
STHGT/OAK N14 26 B3
UPMR RM14 43 R7
WFD IG8 28 C11
WLGTN SM6 74 A12
Grosvenor Gardens Ms East
BGVA SW1W * 7 V5
Grosvenor Gardens Ms North
BGVA SW1W 7 U6
Grosvenor Ga MYFR/PKLN W1K 3 R14
Grosvenor Hl MYFR/PKLN W1K 3 U13
WIM/MER SW19 61 L11
Grosvenor Ms REIG RH2 93 P13
Grosvenor Pde EA W5 * 48 A6
Grosvenor Pk CMBW SE5 9 N12
Grosvenor Park Rd WALTH E17 39 T3
Grosvenor Pl KTBR SW1X 7 T3
WEY KT13 69 V8
Grosvenor Ri East WALTH E17 39 T3
Grosvenor Rd BCTR RM8 41 V6
BELV DA17 53 V11
BORE WD6 24 A1
BTFD TW8 47 T11
BXLYHS DA6 65 T3
CHSWK W4 48 C10
ED N9 27 M6
EPSOM KT18 84 E9
FNCH N3 25 M12
FSTGT E7 40 D11
HNWL W7 47 Q6
HSLWW TW4 58 H1
IL IG1 41 L8
LEY E10 39 U6
MUSWH N10 25 V13
NTHWD HA6 22 B10
NWDGN UB2 46 H8
PIM SW1V 7 V11
PIM SW1V 8 D10
RCHPK/HAM TW10 59 U3
ROMW/RG RM7 42 D5
SNWD SE25 75 L2
STA TW18 57 L12
STMC/STPC BR5 77 N4
TWK TW1 59 Q5
WAN E11 40 D3
WAT WD17 22 E2
WLGTN SM6 73 V11
WWKM BR4 75 T7
Grosvenor Sq KGLGY WD4 10 J2
MYFR/PKLN W1K 3 T13
Grosvenor St MYFR/PKLN W1K 3 T13
Grosvenor Ter CMBW SE5 9 N12
Grosvenor V RSLP HA4 34 B7
Grosvenor Wy CLPT E5 39 N7
Grosvenor Wharf Rd POP/IOD E14 51 V9
Grote's Buildings BKHTH/KID SE3 52 A14
Grote's Pl BKHTH/KID SE3 52 A14
Groton Rd WAND/EARL SW18 61 P7
Grotto Ct STHWK SE1 * 9 N3
Grotto Pas MHST W1U 3 S9
Grotto Rd TWK TW1 59 P7
WEY KT13 69 U9
Grove Av EW KT17 84 E3
HNWL W7 47 N4
MUSWH N10 26 A14
PIN HA5 34 G2
SUT SM1 73 N11
TWK TW1 59 P6
Grove Bank OXHEY WD19 * 22 F6
Grovebury Cl ERITH DA8 54 D11
Grovebury Ct STHGT/OAK N14 26 A5
Grovebury Gdns LCOL/BKTW AL2 12 A1
Grovebury Rd ABYW SE2 53 R7
Grove Cl CFSP/GDCR SL9 20 A13
FSTH SE23 63 P6
HAYES BR2 76 C7
HGDN/ICK UB10 33 S10
HOR/WEW KT19 72 A14
KUT/HW KT1 71 V2
STHGT/OAK N14 * 25 V5
Grove Cottages CHEL SW3 7 P11
CHSWK W4 * 48 E11
COB KT11 * 82 F6
Grove Ct E/WMO/HCT KT8 71 M3
EA W5 * 47 U6
EGH TW20 56 E10
WAB EN9 16 H7
Grove Crs CDALE/KGS NW9 36 C2
FELT TW13 58 G9
KUT/HW KT1 71 U1
RKW/CH/CXG WD3 21 S2
SWFD E18 28 B14
WOT/HER KT12 70 D5
Grove Crescent Rd SRTFD E15 39 V11
Grovedale Cl CHESW EN7 15 V4
Grovedale Rd ARCH N19 38 B7
Grove Dwellings WCHPL E1 * 51 N3
Grove End CFSP/GDCR SL9 20 A13
KTTN NW5 37 V9
SWFD E18 28 B14
Grove End La ESH/CLAY KT10 71 M6
Grove End Rd STJWD NW8 3 L5
Grove Farm Pk NTHWD HA6 21 V10
Grove Footpath BRYLDS KT5 71 U2
Grove Gdns HDN NW4 * 36 G3
PEND EN3 16 D13
STJWD NW8 3 P6
TEDD TW11 59 Q9
Grove Green Rd WAN E11 39 U8
Grove Hall Rd BUSH WD23 22 G2
Grove Heath La RPLY/SEND GU23 81 N14
Grove Heath North RPLY/SEND GU23 81 M13
Grove Heath Rd RPLY/SEND GU23 81 M13
Groveherst Rd DART DA1 67 M1
Grove Hl CFSP/GDCR SL9 20 A12
HRW HA1 35 N5
SWFD E18 28 B14
Grove Hill Rd CMBW SE5 62 J1
HRW HA1 35 P5
Grovehill Rd REDH RH1 93 S10
Grove House Rd CEND/HSY/T N8 38 C2
Groveland Av STRHM/NOR SW16 62 D12
Groveland Ct STP EC4M 5 P12
Groveland Rd BECK BR3 75 R1
Grovelands E/WMO/HCT KT8 70 J2
LCOL/BKTW AL2 11 V1
Grovelands Cl CMBW SE5 50 J14
RYLN/HDSTN HA2 34 K8
Grovelands Ct STHGT/OAK N14 26 B5
Grovelands Rd PLMGR N13 26 D9
PUR/KEN CR8 86 D2
SEVS/STOTM N15 39 L4
STMC/STPC BR5 65 R12
Groveland Wy NWMAL KT3 72 C3
Grove La CHIG IG7 29 P8
CMBW SE5 50 H13
COUL/CHIP CR5 85 V5
EPP CM16 18 E4
KUT/HW KT1 71 U2
UX/CGN UB8 45 R2
Groveley Rd SUN TW16 58 B10
Grove Market Pl ELTH/MOT SE9 * 64 H4
Grove Ms HMSMTH W6 48 J8
Grove Mill La RKW/CH/CXG WD3 10 J12
Grove Mill Pl CAR SM5 73 U8
Grove Pk CDALE/KGS NW9 36 C2
CMBW SE5 50 J14
WAN E11 40 D3
Grove Park Av CHING E4 27 T12
Grove Park Br CHSWK W4 48 C12
Grove Park Gdns CHSWK W4 48 C12
Grove Park Rd CHSWK W4 48 C12
ELTH/MOT SE9 64 G7
RAIN RM13 42 G13
SEVS/STOTM N15 38 J2
Grove Park Ter CHSWK W4 48 B12
Grove Pl ACT W3 48 C6
BAL SW12 61 V4
GSTN WD25 * 11 V13
HAMP NW3 37 R8
WEY KT13 69 U10
Grove Rd ACT W3 48 C6
ASHTD KT21 83 V8
BARN SW13 48 F14
BELV DA17 53 V11
BGR/WK TN15 91 N12
BH/WHM TN16 88 E10
BORE WD6 13 L13
BOW E3 39 Q14
BTFD TW8 47 S10
BXLYHN DA7 66 C2
CHDH RM6 41 S5
CHERT KT16 68 K4
CHING E4 27 U8
CRICK NW2 36 J11
E/WMO/HCT KT8 71 M2
EA W5 47 T5
EBAR EN4 25 S1
EDGW HA8 24 A11
EW KT17 84 E3
FBAR/BDGN N11 25 V10
HOM E9 39 P13
HSLW TW3 58 K2
ISLW TW7 47 N13
MTCM CR4 61 V14
NFNCH/WDSPK N12 25 R10
NTHWD HA6 21 V10
OXTED RH8 95 U9
PIN HA5 34 H3
RCHPK/HAM TW10 59 V4
RKW/CH/CXG WD3 21 L7
RSEV TN14 90 J11
SEVS/STOTM N15 38 J3
SHPTN TW17 69 U4
SURB KT6 71 T3
SUT SM1 73 N11
SWFD E18 28 B14
THHTH CR7 74 E2
UX/CGN UB8 33 P12
WALTH E17 39 T3
WAN E11 40 B6
WHTN TW2 59 M8
WIM/MER SW19 61 Q12
WOKN/KNAP GU21 80 D6
Grove Rd West PEND EN3 16 C11
Grover Rd OXHEY WD19 22 F4
Grovers Farm Cottages
ADL/WDHM KT15 * 80 J1
Groves Cl SOCK/AV RM15 55 T5
Grove Shaw KWD/TDW/WH KT20 85 L14
Groveside Cl ACT W3 48 A4
CAR SM5 73 S7
Groveside Rd CHING E4 28 A8
Grovestile Waye EBED/NFELT TW14 57 V6
Grove St BERM/RHTH SE16 51 R9
UED N18 26 K11
Grove Ter KTTN NW5 37 U8
STHL UB1 * 46 J5
TEDD TW11 59 Q9
Grove Terrace Ms KTTN NW5 37 V8
The Grove ADL/WDHM KT15 69 M10
BGR/WK TN15 79 T14
BH/WHM TN16 88 F8
BRKMPK AL9 14 C1
BRW CM14 31 T9
BXLYHS DA6 65 T2
CDALE/KGS NW9 36 D3
CEND/HSY/T N8 38 B3
COUL/CHIP CR5 86 B5
CTHM CR3 86 F11
EA W5 47 T6
EDGW HA8 24 B9
EGH TW20 56 E10
ENC/FH EN2 15 Q14
EW KT17 84 E3
FNCH N3 25 N12
FSBYPK N4 38 D5
GFD/PVL UB6 47 L4
GLDGN NW11 37 L5
HGDN/ICK UB10 33 S10
HGT N6 37 U6
ISLW TW7 47 N13
KGLGY WD4 * 10 C4
PLMGR N13 26 E9
POTB/CUF EN6 14 E6
RAD WD7 12 E8
RKW/CH/CXG WD3 * 21 S2
SCUP DA14 65 U9
SRTFD E15 40 A12
SWLY BR8 78 F1
TEDD TW11 59 Q9
UPMR RM14 43 N9
WOKN/KNAP GU21 80 D6
WOT/HER KT12 70 D5
WWKM BR4 75 U8
Grove V CHST BR7 64 J11
EDUL SE22 62 J2
Groveway BCTR RM8 41 T9
BRXN/ST SW9 50 D13
Grove Wy ESH/CLAY KT10 71 L6
RKW/CH/CXG WD3 20 F3
UX/CGN UB8 33 P12
WBLY HA9 36 C10
Grovewood Cl RKW/CH/CXG WD3 20 F3
Grove Wood Hl COUL/CHIP CR5 86 B4
Grovewood Pl WFD IG8 28 H11
Grub St OXTED RH8 96 E4
Grummant Rd PECK SE15 50 K13
Grundy St POP/IOD E14 51 T4
Gruneisen Rd FNCH N3 25 P12
Guardian Cl EMPK RM11 42 H7
Guards Av CTHM CR3 86 G12
Gubbins La HARH RM3 31 M13
Gubyon Av HNHL SE24 62 G3
Guernsey Cl HEST TW5 46 J13
Guernsey Farm Dr
WOKN/KNAP GU21 * 80 B5
Guernsey Gv HNHL SE24 62 G5
Guernsey Rd IS N1 38 G11
LEY E10 39 V6
Guibal Rd LEE/GVPK SE12 64 D6
Guildables La EDEN TN8 96 G12
Guildersfield Rd STRHM/NOR SW16 62 C12
Guildford Av FELT TW13 58 C7
Guildford Gv GNWCH SE10 51 T13
Guildford Rd CHERT KT16 68 F14
CROY/NA CR0 74 H4
EHAM E6 52 G4
GDMY/SEVK IG3 41 N7
HARH RM3 31 L11
LHD/OX KT22 83 N14
VX/NE SW8 50 C13
WALTH E17 27 U13
WOKS/MYFD GU22 80 B12
Guildford St CHERT KT16 68 K6
STA TW18 57 L11
Guildford Wy WLGTN SM6 74 C10
Guildhall Buildings CITYW EC2V 5 P11
Guildhall Yd CITYW EC2V 5 P11
Guildhouse St PIM SW1V 8 A8
Guildown Av NFNCH/WDSPK N12 25 P9
Guild Rd CHARL SE7 52 F10
ERITH DA8 54 F12
Guildsway WALTH E17 27 R13
Guileshill La RPLY/SEND GU23 81 Q12
Guilford Av BRYLDS KT5 71 V3
Guilford Pl BMSBY WC1N 4 G8
Guilford St BMSBY WC1N 4 G8
Guillemot Pl WDGN N22 * 26 D14
Guilsborough Cl WLSDN NW10 36 E12
Guinevere Gdns CHES/WCR EN8 16 D4
Guinness Cl HOM E9 39 Q12
HYS/HAR UB3 45 V8
Guinness Ct CROY/NA CR0 * 74 K7
Guinness Sq STHWK SE1 9 S7
Guinness Trust STNW/STAM N16 * 38 K6
Guinness Trust Est CHEL SW3 7 Q8
SRTFD E15 * 40 B13
Guion Rd FUL/PGN SW6 49 M14
Gulland Cl BUSH WD23 23 L3
Gulland Wk IS N1 * 38 G11
Gullet Wood Rd GSTN WD25 11 N9
Gulliver Cl NTHLT UB5 34 H13
Gulliver Rd BFN/LL DA15 65 M7
Gulliver St BERM/RHTH SE16 51 R8
Gumleigh Rd EA W5 47 S9
Gumley Gdns ISLW TW7 59 Q1
Gumping Rd STMC/STPC BR5 77 L7
Gundulph Rd HAYES BR2 76 E1
Gunmakers La BOW E3 39 Q13
Gunnell Cl CROY/NA CR0 74 K4
SYD SE26 * 63 L9
Gunner Dr PEND EN3 16 G11
Gunner La WOOL/PLUM SE18 52 J10
Gunnersbury Av ACT W3 48 A9
Gunnersbury Av (North Circular Rd)
ACT W3 48 A8
EA W5 47 V5
Gunnersbury Cl CHSWK W4 * 48 B10
Gunnersbury Crs ACT W3 48 A7
Gunnersbury Dr EA W5 47 V7
Gunnersbury Gdns ACT W3 48 A7
Gunnersbury La ACT W3 48 B6
Gunnersbury Ms CHSWK W4 48 B10
Gunners Gv CHING E4 27 U8
Gunners Rd TOOT SW17 61 R7
Gunning St WOOL/PLUM SE18 53 N9
Gunstor Rd STNW/STAM N16 * 38 J9
Gun St WCHPL E1 5 U10
Gunter Gv EDGW HA8 24 D13
WBPTN SW10 6 J12
Gunters Md LHD/OX KT22 * 83 L1
Gunterstone Rd WKENS W14 6 B9
Gunthorpe St WCHPL E1 5 V10
Gunton Rd CLPT E5 39 M8
TOOT SW17 61 U11
Gunwhale Cl BERM/RHTH SE16 51 P6
Gunyard Ms WOOL/PLUM SE18 * 52 G12
Gurdon Rd CHARL SE7 52 C10
Gurnard Cl WDR/YW UB7 45 P5
Gurnell Gv WEA W13 47 P2
Gurney Cl BARK IG11 40 K11
SRTFD E15 40 A10
WALTH E17 27 P13
Gurney Crs CROY/NA CR0 74 D6
Gurney Dr EFNCH N2 37 R2
Gurney Rd CAR SM5 73 U9
FUL/PGN SW6 61 Q1
NTHLT UB5 46 D1
SRTFD E15 40 A10
Gurney's Cl REDH RH1 93 T11
Guthrie St CHEL SW3 7 N9
Gutteridge La ABR/ST RM4 30 C4
Gutter La CITYW EC2V 5 N11
Guyatt Gdns MTCM CR4 61 U14
Guy Barnett Gv BKHTH/KID SE3 64 C1
Guy Rd WLGTN SM6 74 C8
Guyscliff Rd LEW SE13 63 U3
Guysfield Cl RAIN RM13 42 G13
Guysfield Dr RAIN RM13 42 G13
Guy St STHWK SE1 9 R3
Gwalior Rd PUT/ROE SW15 60 K2
Gwendolen Av PUT/ROE SW15 60 K3
Gwendoline Av PLSTW E13 40 D13
Gwendwr Rd WKENS W14 6 B9
Gweneth Cottages EDGW HA8 * 24 A11
Gwent Cl GSTN WD25 11 R8
Gwillim Cl BFN/LL DA15 65 Q4
Gwydor Rd BECK BR3 75 P1
Gwydyr Rd HAYES BR2 76 B1
Gwyn Cl FUL/PGN SW6 6 J14
Gwynne Av CROY/NA CR0 75 P5
Gwynne Park Av WFD IG8 28 H11
Gwynne Rd BTSEA SW11 49 R14
CTHM CR3 86 H13
Gwynne Whf CHSWK W4 48 F11
Gylcote Cl CMBW SE5 62 H2
Gyles Pk STAN HA7 23 S13
Gyllyngdune Gdns GDMY/SEVK IG3 41 P8
Gypsy La KGLGY WD4 10 K9
Gywnne Pl FSBYW WC1X 4 H6

H

Haarlem Rd WKENS W14 48 K8
Haberdasher Pl IS N1 5 R5
Haberdasher St IS N1 5 R5
Habgood Rd LOU IG10 28 G1
Habitat Cl PECK SE15 51 M14
Haccombe Rd WIM/MER SW19 61 Q11
Hackbridge Park Gdns CAR SM5 73 T7
Hackbridge Rd CAR SM5 73 U7
Hacketts La WOKS/MYFD GU22 80 K5
Hackford Rd BRXN/ST SW9 50 D13
Hackford Wk BRXN/ST SW9 50 D13
Hackforth Cl BAR EN5 24 H3
Hackington Crs BECK BR3 63 S11
Hackney Cl BORE WD6 24 D3
Hackney Gv HACK E8 * 39 M11
Hackney Rd BETH E2 5 U5
Hackney Wick HOM E9 39 R11
Hacton Dr HCH RM12 43 L9
Hacton La UPMR RM14 43 M10
Hadar Cl TRDG/WHET N20 25 N6
Haddenham Ct OXHEY WD19 * 22 F8
Hadden Rd THMD SE28 53 N8
Hadden Wy GFD/PVL UB6 35 M11
Haddington Rd BMLY BR1 63 V8
Haddon Cl BORE WD6 13 L14
BORE WD6 24 A1
EN EN1 27 L4
NWMAL KT3 72 F3
WEY KT13 70 A8
Haddon Gv BFN/LL DA15 65 Q5
Haddon Rd RKW/CH/CXG WD3 20 G3
STMC/STPC BR5 77 T3
SUT SM1 73 P9
Haddo St GNWCH SE10 51 T11
Hadfield Cl STHL UB1 46 H1
Hadfield Rd STWL/WRAY TW19 57 P5
Hadleigh Cl RYNPK SW20 61 M14
WCHPL E1 51 N2
Hadleigh Dr BELMT SM2 73 N13
Hadleigh Rd ED N9 27 M5
Hadleigh St BETH E2 51 N2
Hadley Cl BORE WD6 23 V3
WCHMH N21 26 E4
Hadley Common BAR EN5 14 E14
Hadley Gdns CHSWK W4 48 D10
NWDGN UB2 46 H10
Hadley Gn BAR EN5 25 M1
Hadley Green Rd BAR EN5 14 B14
Hadley Gn West BAR EN5 14 A14
Hadley Gv BAR EN5 14 A14
Hadley Highstone BAR EN5 14 B13
Hadley Pde BAR EN5 * 25 L1
Hadley Pl WEY KT13 69 S12
Hadley Rdg BAR EN5 25 M1
Hadley Rd BAR EN5 25 P2
BELV DA17 53 V9
EBAR EN4 14 J12
MTCM CR4 74 B2
Hadley St KTTN NW5 37 V11
Hadley Wy WCHMH N21 26 E4
Hadley Wood Ri PUR/KEN CR8 86 F5
Hadley Wood Rd BAR EN5 14 C14
Hadlow Pl NRWD SE19 63 L12
Hadlow Rd SCUP DA14 65 Q9
WELL DA16 53 S12
Hadrian Cl BOW E3 39 S13
STWL/WRAY TW19 57 Q5
Hadrian Est BETH E2 * 39 L14
Hadrian's Ride EN EN1 26 K3
Hadrian St GNWCH SE10 52 A10
Hadrian Wy STWL/WRAY TW19 57 Q5
Hadyn Park Rd SHB W12 48 G7
Hafer Rd BTSEA SW11 61 T2
Hafton Rd CAT SE6 64 A6
Hagden La WATW WD18 22 C3
Haggard Rd TWK TW1 59 R5
Hagger Ct WALTH E17 * 39 V1
Haggerston Rd BORE WD6 12 J12
HACK E8 38 K12
Hague St BETH E2 51 L1
Ha-ha Rd WOOL/PLUM SE18 52 H11
Haigh Crs REDH RH1 93 V12
Haig Rd BH/WHM TN16 88 G7
STAN HA7 23 S10
UX/CGN UB8 45 T3
Haig Rd East PLSTW E13 52 E1
Haig Rd West PLSTW E13 52 E1
Haigville Gdns BARK/HLT IG6 40 K2
Hailes Cl WIM/MER SW19 61 Q11
Haileybury Av EN EN1 26 K4
Haileybury Rd ORP BR6 77 Q9
Hailey Rd ERITHM DA18 54 A7
Hailsham Av BRXS/STRHM SW2 62 D7
Hailsham Cl HARH RM3 30 J10
SURB KT6 71 T5
Hailsham Dr HRW HA1 35 M1
Hailsham Rd HARH RM3 30 J10
TOOT SW17 61 U11
Hailsham Ter UED N18 * 26 H10
Haimo Rd ELTH/MOT SE9 64 F3
Hainault Buildings LEY E10 * 39 U6
Hainault Gore CHDH RM6 41 U3
Hainault Gv CHIG IG7 29 L9
Hainault Rd BARK/HLT IG6 29 R12
CHDH RM6 41 R1
CHIG IG7 29 L9
CRW RM5 42 C1
WAN E11 39 U6
Hainault St ELTH/MOT SE9 64 K6
IL IG1 40 K7
Haines Ct WEY KT13 69 V10
Haines Wk MRDN SM4 73 P5
Haines Wy GSTN WD25 11 N8
Hainford Cl PECK SE15 63 P2
Haining Cl CHSWK W4 48 A10
Hainthorpe Rd WNWD SE27 62 F8
Hainton Cl WCHPL E1 51 M4
Halberd Ms CLPT E5 39 M7
Halbutt St DAGW RM9 41 V9
Halcomb St IS N1 5 S2
Halcot Av BXLYHS DA6 66 B3
Halcrow St WCHPL E1 51 N3
Halcyon Wy EMPK RM11 43 M6
Haldane Cl MUSWH N10 25 V12
PEND EN3 16 H12
Haldane Pl WAND/EARL SW18 61 P6
Haldane Rd EHAM E6 52 F1
FUL/PGN SW6 6 D13
STHL UB1 47 L5
THMD SE28 53 T5
Haldan Rd CHING E4 27 U11
Haldon Rd WAND/EARL SW18 61 M4
Hale Cl CHING E4 27 U8
EDGW HA8 24 C10
ORP BR6 77 L9
Hale Dr MLHL NW7 24 C11
Hale End HARH RM3 30 H11
Hale End Cl RSLP HA4 34 C4
Hale End Rd WALTH E17 27 V13
Halefield Rd TOTM N17 27 L13
Hale Gdns ACT W3 48 A6
SEVS/STOTM N15 39 L2
Hale Grove Gdns MLHL NW7 24 D10
Hale House WOOL/PLUM SE18 * 52 G12
Hale La EDGW HA8 24 C10
RSEV TN14 90 F7
Hale Rd EHAM E6 52 G2
TOTM N17 39 L1
Halesowen Rd MRDN SM4 73 P5
Hales St DEPT SE8 51 S12
Hale St POP/IOD E14 51 T5
STA TW18 56 J9
Haleswood COB KT11 82 D4
Halesworth Cl HARH RM3 31 L12
Halesworth Rd HARH RM3 31 L11
LEW SE13 63 T1
The Hale CHING E4 27 V12
TOTM N17 39 L1
Haley Rd HDN NW4 36 J4
Half Acre BTFD TW8 47 T11
Halfacre Hl CFSP/GDCR SL9 20 D13
Half Acre Ms BTFD TW8 47 T12
Half Acre Rd HNWL W7 47 N6
Halfhide La CHES/WCR EN8 16 D1
Halfhides WAB EN9 16 K7
Half Moon Crs IS N1 4 H3
Half Moon La EPP CM16 18 D5
HNHL SE24 62 H4
Half Moon Pas WCHPL E1 5 V12
Halfmoon Pas WCHPL E1 * 5 V12
Half Moon St MYFR/PICC W1J 7 V1
Halford Cl EDGW HA8 24 B14
Halford Rd FUL/PGN SW6 6 F12
HGDN/ICK UB10 33 S10
LEY E10 39 V3
RCHPK/HAM TW10 59 U3
Halfway Ct PUR RM19 55 N9
Halfway Gn WOT/HER KT12 70 D8
Halfway St BFN/LL DA15 65 N6
Haliburton Rd TWK TW1 59 Q3
Haliday Wk IS N1 38 H11
Halidon Ri HARH RM3 31 P11
Halifax Cl GSTN WD25 11 M8
LCOL/BKTW AL2 11 T5
TEDD TW11 59 N11
Halifax Rd ENC/FH EN2 15 S14
GFD/PVL UB6 34 K13
RKW/CH/CXG WD3 20 G5
Halifax St SYD SE26 63 M8
Halifield Dr BELV DA17 53 U8
Haling Gv SAND/SEL CR2 74 G12
Haling Park Gdns SAND/SEL CR2 74 F11
Haling Park Rd SAND/SEL CR2 74 G11
Haling Rd SAND/SEL CR2 74 H11
Halings La DEN/HRF UB9 32 J2
Halkin Ar KTBR SW1X 7 S5
Halkingcroft DTCH/LGLY SL3 44 A7
Halkin Ms KTBR SW1X * 7 S5
Halkin Pl KTBR SW1X 7 S5
Halkin St KTBR SW1X 7 T4
Hallam Cl CHST BR7 64 H10
WATN WD24 11 Q14
Hallam Gdns PIN HA5 22 G12
Hallam Ms GTPST W1W 3 V9
Hallam Rd BARN SW13 60 H1
SEVS/STOTM N15 38 F2
Hallam St GTPST W1W 3 V9
Halland Wy NTHWD HA6 21 V11
Hall Av SOCK/AV RM15 55 Q6
Hall Cl EA W5 47 U3
RKW/CH/CXG WD3 21 L6
Hall Ct TEDD TW11 59 P10
Hall Crs SOCK/AV RM15 55 Q7
Hall Dr DEN/HRF UB9 21 N13
SYD SE26 63 N10
Halley Gdns LEW SE13 63 V2
Halley Rd FSTGT E7 40 E11
WAB EN9 16 H10
Halley St POP/IOD E14 51 Q3
Halley's Wk ADL/WDHM KT15 69 N12
Hall Farm Cl STAN HA7 23 R9
Hall Farm Dr WHTN TW2 59 M5
Hallfield Est BAY/PAD W2 2 H12
Hallford Wy DART DA1 66 J4
Hall Gdns CHING E4 27 R9
Hall Ga STJWD NW8 2 K6
Hall Hl BGR/WK TN15 91 P13
OXTED RH8 95 V8
The Halliards WOT/HER KT12 70 C4
Halliday Cl RAD WD7 12 J6
Halliday Sq NWDGN UB2 47 M6
Halliford Cl SHPTN TW17 70 A1
Halliford Rd SHPTN TW17 70 A3
Halliford St IS N1 38 G12
Hallillo Valley Rd CTHM CR3 87 R10
Halliwell Rd BRXS/STRHM SW2 62 D4
Halliwick Court Pde
NFNCH/WDSPK N12 * 25 T10
Halliwick Rd MUSWH N10 25 U13
Hall La CHING E4 27 R10
HDN NW4 24 G14
HYS/HAR UB3 45 V12
UPMR RM14 43 Q1
Hallmead Rd SUT SM1 73 P8
Hall Oak Wk KIL/WHAMP NW6 37 M11
Hallowell Av CROY/NA CR0 74 C9
Hallowell Cl MTCM CR4 73 U1
Hallowell Rd NTHWD HA6 22 A12
Hallowes Crs OXHEY WD19 22 C8
Hallowfield Wy MTCM CR4 73 R1
Hallows Gv SUN TW16 58 B10
Hall Park Rd UPMR RM14 43 Q10
Hall Pl BAY/PAD W2 3 L8
WOKN/KNAP GU21 80 E6
Hall Place Crs BXLY DA5 66 C3
Hall Place Dr WEY KT13 70 A10
Hall Rd CHDH RM6 41 S4
DART DA1 67 M2
EHAM E6 40 H13
GPK RM2 42 H1
ISLW TW7 59 M3
MV/WKIL W9 2 K6
SOCK/AV RM15 55 Q7
SRTFD E15 39 V9
WLGTN SM6 73 V13
Hallside Rd EN EN1 15 V12
Hallsland Wy OXTED RH8 96 B9
Halls Ter HGDN/ICK UB10 * 45 T2
Hall St FSBYE EC1V 5 M5
NFNCH/WDSPK N12 25 Q10
Hallsville Rd CAN/RD E16 52 B4
Hallswelle Pde GLDGN NW11 * 37 M3
Hallswelle Rd GLDGN NW11 37 M3
Hall Ter SOCK/AV RM15 55 R7
The Hall BKHTH/KID SE3 64 C1
Hall Vw ELTH/MOT SE9 64 F7
Hallywell Crs EHAM E6 52 H3
Halons Rd ELTH/MOT SE9 64 J5
Halpin Pl WALW SE17 9 R8
Halsbrook Rd BKHTH/KID SE3 64 E1
Halsbury Cl STAN HA7 23 R10
Halsbury Rd SHB W12 48 H6
Halsbury Rd East NTHLT UB5 35 L9
Halsbury Rd West NTHLT UB5 34 K10
Halsend HYS/HAR UB3 * 46 D6
Halsey Pk LCOL/BKTW AL2 12 K1
Halsey Pl WATN WD24 * 11 P12
Halsey Rd WATW WD18 22 D1
Halsey St CHEL SW3 7 Q7
Halsham Crs BARK IG11 41 P11
Halsmere Rd CMBW SE5 50 F13
Halstead Cl CROY/NA CR0 74 G8
Halstead Gdns WCHMH N21 26 H6
Halstead Hl CHESW EN7 15 U4
Halstead La RSEV TN14 89 U5
Halstead Rd ERITH DA8 54 E13
WAN E11 40 D3
WCHMH N21 26 H6
Halston Cl BTSEA SW11 61 T4
Halstow Rd GNWCH SE10 52 C10
WLSDN NW10 48 K1
Halsway HYS/HAR UB3 46 C6
Halter Cl BORE WD6 24 D3
Halton Cl FBAR/BDGN N11 25 T11
LCOL/BKTW AL2 12 A2
Halton Cross St IS N1 * 5 M1
Halton Pl IS N1 * 5 N1
Halton Rd IS N1 38 F12
PUR/KEN CR8 86 J10
Halt Pde CDALE/KGS NW9 * 36 D2
Halt Robin Rd BELV DA17 54 B9
Hambalt Rd CLAP SW4 62 A3
Hamble Cl RSLP HA4 34 A7
Hambledon Cl UX/CGN UB8 45 T2
Hambledon Ct EA W5 * 47 U5
Hambledon Gdns SNWD SE25 74 K1
Hambledon Hl EPSOM KT18 84 C6
Hambledon Pl DUL SE21 62 K6
GT/LBKH KT23 82 J13
Hambledon Rd CTHM CR3 86 H13
WAND/EARL SW18 61 M5
Hambledon V EPSOM KT18 84 C6
Hambledown Rd BFN/LL DA15 * 65 M5
Hamble La SOCK/AV RM15 55 T3
Hamble St FUL/PGN SW6 61 P1
Hambleton WDSR SL4 * 56 A6
Hambleton Cl WPK KT4 72 J7
Hamblings Cl RAD WD7 12 H7
Hambro Av HAYES BR2 76 C6
Hambrook Rd SNWD SE25 75 M1
Hambro Rd STRHM/NOR SW16 62 B11
Hambrough Rd STHL UB1 46 G6
Hamburgh Ct CHES/WCR EN8 16 D2
Ham Common RCHPK/HAM TW10 59 T8
Ham Croft Cl FELT TW13 58 C8
Hamden Crs DAGE RM10 42 B8
Hamel Cl KTN/HRWW/WS HA3 35 T2
Hameway EHAM E6 52 J2
Ham Farm Rd RCHPK/HAM TW10 59 T9
Hamfield Cl OXTED RH8 95 U3
Hamfrith Rd SRTFD E15 40 B11
Ham Gate Av RCHPK/HAM TW10 59 V9
Hamilton Av BARK/HLT IG6 40 K2
CHEAM SM3 73 L7
COB KT11 82 C3
ED N9 27 L5
ROM RM1 30 D14
SURB KT6 72 A7
WOKS/MYFD GU22 80 J6
Hamilton Cl BERM/RHTH SE16 51 Q7
CHERT KT16 68 K6
EBAR EN4 25 S2
FELT TW13 58 B10
HOR/WEW KT19 84 C2
LCOL/BKTW AL2 11 U5
POTB/CUF EN6 13 S7
PUR/KEN CR8 86 F2
STJWD NW8 3 L6
TEDD TW11 59 R11
TOTM N17 38 K1
Hamilton Ct EA W5 47 V5
Hamilton Crs HSLW TW3 58 K3
PLMGR N13 26 E9
RYLN/HDSTN HA2 34 H8
Hamilton Dr HARH RM3 31 L14
Hamilton Gdns STJWD NW8 2 K5
Hamilton La HBRY N5 38 F9
Hamilton Ms MYFR/PICC W1J 7 U3
WEY KT13 * 69 S9
Hamilton Pde FELT TW13 * 58 C9
Hamilton Pk HBRY N5 38 F9
Hamilton Pk West HBRY N5 38 F9
Hamilton Pl KWD/TDW/WH KT20 85 M13
MYFR/PKLN W1K 7 T2
SUN TW16 58 D12
Hamilton Rd BTFD TW8 47 T11
BXLYHN DA7 53 U14
CHSWK W4 48 E8
EA W5 47 U5
EBAR EN4 25 S2
ED N9 27 L5
EFNCH N2 37 Q1
FELT TW13 58 A10
GLDGN NW11 36 K5
GPK RM2 42 H3
HRW HA1 35 N3
HYS/HAR UB3 46 D5
IL IG1 40 K9
KGLGY WD4 10 J7
OXHEY WD19 22 D8
SCUP DA14 65 Q9
SRTFD E15 52 A1
STHL UB1 46 H6
THHTH CR7 74 H1
UX/CGN UB8 45 P2
WALTH E17 27 Q14
WHTN TW2 59 N6
WIM/MER SW19 61 P12
WLSDN NW10 36 G10
WNWD SE27 62 H9
Hamilton Road Ms WIM/MER SW19 61 P12
Hamilton Sq NFNCH/WDSPK N12 * 25 Q11
Hamilton St DEPT SE8 51 S11
WATW WD18 22 E3
Hamilton Ter STJWD NW8 2 J4
Hamilton Wy FNCH N3 25 N11
PLMGR N13 26 F9
WLGTN SM6 74 B13
Ham La WDSR SL4 56 A2
Hamlea Cl LEE/GVPK SE12 64 C3
Hamlet Cl CRW RM5 30 A12
LCOL/BKTW AL2 11 T4
LEW SE13 64 A2
Hamlet Gdns HMSMTH W6 48 G9
Hamlet Rd CRW RM5 30 A12
NRWD SE19 62 K12
Hamlet Sq CRICK NW2 37 L8
Hamlets Wy BOW E3 51 R2
The Hamlet WALW SE17 62 H1
Hamlet Wy STHWK SE1 9 R4
Hamlin Crs PIN HA5 34 E3
Hamlin Rd SEV TN13 90 E11
Hamlyn Cl EDGW HA8 23 U8
Hamlyn Gdns NRWD SE19 62 J12
Hamm Ct WEY KT13 69 R8
Hamm Court Est WEY KT13 69 R7
Hammelton Rd BMLY BR1 64 C13
Hammer Pde GSTN WD25 * 11 N7
Hammers La MLHL NW7 24 G9
Hammersmith Br HMSMTH W6 48 H10
Hammersmith Bridge Rd BARN SW13 48 H11
Hammersmith Broadway
HMSMTH W6 48 J9
Hammersmith Emb HMSMTH W6 * 48 J11
Hammersmith Flyover HMSMTH W6 48 J10
Hammersmith Gv HMSMTH W6 48 J9
Hammersmith Rd HMSMTH W6 48 K9
Hammersmith Ter HMSMTH W6 * 48 G10
Hammerton Cl BXLY DA5 66 E8
Hammet Cl YEAD UB4 46 F3
Hammett St TWRH EC3N 5 U13
Hamm Moor La ADL/WDHM KT15 69 Q10
Hammond Av MTCM CR4 61 V14
Hammond Cl BAR EN5 25 M3
GFD/PVL UB6 35 M10
HPTN TW12 58 J13
WOKN/KNAP GU21 80 A5
Hammond Rd EN EN1 27 M1
NWDGN UB2 46 G8
WOKN/KNAP GU21 80 A5
Hammonds Cl BCTR RM8 41 S8
Hammonds La RBRW/HUT CM13 31 V11
Hammond St KTTN NW5 38 A11
Hamond Cl SAND/SEL CR2 74 F13
Hamonde Cl EDGW HA8 24 B7
Hamond Sq IS N1 5 S3
Ham Park Rd FSTGT E7 40 C12
Hampden Av BECK BR3 63 Q14
Hampden Cl CAMTN NW1 4 D4
EPP CM16 19 L1
Hampden Crs CHESW EN7 16 B5
Hampden Gurney St MBLAR W1H 3 Q12
Hampden La TOTM N17 26 K13
Hampden Pl LCOL/BKTW AL2 12 C3
Hampden Rd ARCH N19 38 B7
BECK BR3 63 Q14
CEND/HSY/T N8 38 E2
CFSP/GDCR SL9 20 B13
DTCH/LGLY SL3 44 D8
KTN/HRWW/WS HA3 23 L13
KUT/HW KT1 72 A1
MUSWH N10 25 U12
TOTM N17 27 L13
Hampden Wy STHGT/OAK N14 25 V6
WAT WD17 11 L10
Hampermill La OXHEY WD19 22 C6
Hampshire Cl UED N18 27 M10
Hampshire Hog La HMSMTH W6 * 48 H9
Hampshire Rd EMPK RM11 43 N2
WDGN N22 26 D12
Hampshire St KTTN NW5 * 38 B11
Hampson Wy VX/NE SW8 50 D13
Hampstead Av WFD IG8 28 J12
Hampstead Cl LCOL/BKTW AL2 11 T5
THMD SE28 53 R6
Hampstead Gdns GLDGN NW11 37 N4
Hampstead Ga HAMP NW3 37 Q10
Hampstead Gn HAMP NW3 37 S10
Hampstead Gv HAMP NW3 37 Q9
Hampstead Hill Gdns HAMP NW3 37 S9
Hampstead La HGT N6 37 T5
Hampstead Rd CAMTN NW1 4 A4
Hampstead Sq HAMP NW3 37 Q8
Hampstead Wy GLDGN NW11 37 N3
Hampton Cl BORE WD6 24 C3
FBAR/BDGN N11 25 U10
KIL/WHAMP NW6 2 E6
RYNPK SW20 * 60 J12
Hampton Ct IS N1 38 F11
Hampton Court Av E/WMO/HCT KT8 71 M4
Hampton Court Crs
E/WMO/HCT KT8 * 71 M1
Hampton Court Est THDIT KT7 * 71 N3
Hampton Court Rd E/WMO/HCT KT8 59 M14
E/WMO/HCT KT8 71 N1
Hampton Court Wy THDIT KT7 71 N6
Hampton Gv EW KT17 84 F1
Hampton La FELT TW13 58 G9
Hampton Ri KTN/HRWW/WS HA3 35 U4
Hampton Rd CHING E4 27 R10
CROY/NA CR0 74 G4
FSTGT E7 40 D10
IL IG1 41 L9
TEDD TW11 59 M10
WAN E11 39 V6
WPK KT4 72 G7
Hampton Rd East FELT TW13 58 H9
Hampton Rd West FELT TW13 58 G7
Hampton St WALW SE17 9 M8
Ham Ridings RCHPK/HAM TW10 59 V10
Hamsey Green Gdns WARL CR6 87 N6
Hamsey Wy SAND/SEL CR2 87 M5
Ham Shades Cl BFN/LL DA15 65 P8
Ham St RCHPK/HAM TW10 59 S7
The Ham BTFD TW8 47 S12
Ham Vw CROY/NA CR0 75 Q4
Ham Yd SOHO/SHAV W1D * 4 C13
Hanameel St CAN/RD E16 52 C6
Hanbury Cl CHES/WCR EN8 16 D4
HDN NW4 36 J1
Hanbury Ct HRW HA1 * 35 P4
Hanbury Dr BH/WHM TN16 88 D3
WCHMH N21 26 D2
Hanbury Rd ACT W3 48 B7
TOTM N17 27 M14
Hanbury St WCHPL E1 5 V9
Hancock Ct BORE WD6 13 N13
Hancock Rd BOW E3 51 U1
NRWD SE19 62 H11
Handa Wk IS N1 38 G11
Hand Ct HHOL WC1V 4 H10
Handcroft Rd CROY/NA CR0 74 F6
Handel Cl EDGW HA8 23 V11
Handel Pde EDGW HA8 * 24 A11
Handel Pl WLSDN NW10 36 D11
Handel St BMSBY WC1N 4 E7
Handel Wy EDGW HA8 24 A12
Handen Rd LEE/GVPK SE12 64 A3
Handforth Rd BRXN/ST SW9 8 J13
IL IG1 40 K8
Handley Gv CRICK NW2 36 K8
Handley Page Rd WLGTN SM6 74 D12
Handley Page Wy LCOL/BKTW AL2 12 D4
Handley Rd HOM E9 39 N12
Handowe Cl HDN NW4 36 G2
Handside Cl WPK KT4 72 K6
Handsworth Av CHING E4 27 V11
Handsworth Cl OXHEY WD19 22 C8
Handsworth Rd TOTM N17 38 H1
Handtrough Wy BARK IG11 40 K14
Hanford Cl WAND/EARL SW18 61 N6
Hanford Rd SOCK/AV RM15 55 Q6
Hangar Rd DEN/HRF UB9 32 J2
Hangar Ruding OXHEY WD19 22 H8
Hanger Gn EA W5 48 A2
Hanger Hl WEY KT13 69 T10
Hanger La EA W5 47 U1
Hanger Lane (North Circular Road)
EA W5 47 U1
Hanger Vale La EA W5 47 V4
Hanger View Wy ACT W3 48 A4
Hang Grove Hl ORP BR6 88 K3
Hankey Pl STHWK SE1 9 R4
Hankins La MLHL NW7 24 E7
Hanley Gdns FSBYPK N4 38 D6
Hanley Pl BECK BR3 63 S12
Hanley Rd FSBYPK N4 38 C6
Hanmer Wk HOLWY N7 38 D7
Hannah Cl BECK BR3 75 T1
WLSDN NW10 36 C9
Hannah Mary Wy STHWK SE1 * 51 L9
Hannards Wy BARK/HLT IG6 29 R10
Hannay La ARCH N19 38 B5
Hannell Rd FUL/PGN SW6 6 B13
Hannen Rd WNWD SE27 * 62 F8
Hannibal Rd STWL/WRAY TW19 57 Q5
WCHPL E1 51 N3
Hannibal Wy CROY/NA CR0 74 D10
Hannington Rd CLAP SW4 61 V1
Hanover Av CAN/RD E16 52 C6
FELT TW13 58 C6
Hanover Cir HYS/HAR UB3 45 U4
Hanover Cl CHEAM SM3 73 L9
RCH/KEW TW9 48 A12
REDH RH1 94 A4
Hanover Ct WOKS/MYFD GU22 80 C9
Hanover Dr CHST BR7 65 L10
Hanover Gdns ABLGY WD5 * 11 M4
BARK/HLT IG6 29 L12
LBTH SE11 8 J12
Hanover Pk PECK SE15 51 L13
Hanover Pl BRW CM14 31 V10
COVGDN WC2E 4 F12
Hanover Rd SEVS/STOTM N15 38 K2
WIM/MER SW19 61 Q12
WLSDN NW10 36 J12
Hanover Sq CONDST W1S 3 V12
Hanover Steps BAY/PAD W2 * 3 P12
Hanover St CONDST W1S 3 V12
CROY/NA CR0 74 F8
Hanover Ter CAMTN NW1 3 Q6
Hanover Terrace Ms CAMTN NW1 3 Q6
Hanover Wk WEY KT13 69 V8
Hanover Wy BXLYHS DA6 65 T1
Hanover Yd IS N1 * 5 M3
Hansard Ms WKENS W14 48 K7
Hansart Wy ENC/FH EN2 15 Q13
Hans Crs KTBR SW1X 7 Q5
Hanselin Cl STAN HA7 23 P10
Hansen Dr WCHMH N21 26 D3
Hanshaw Dr EDGW HA8 24 D13
Hansler Gv E/WMO/HCT KT8 71 M3
Hansler Rd EDUL SE22 62 K3
Hansol Rd BXLYHS DA6 65 U3
Hansom Ter BMLY BR1 * 64 D13
Hanson Cl BAL SW12 61 V5
BECK BR3 * 63 T11
MORT/ESHN SW14 60 C1
WDR/YW UB7 45 R8
Hanson Dr LOU IG10 18 A14
Hanson Gdns STHL UB1 46 G7
Hanson St GTPST W1W 4 A9
Hans Pl KTBR SW1X 7 Q5
Hans Rd CHEL SW3 7 Q5
Hans St KTBR SW1X 7 R6
Hanway Pl FITZ W1T 4 C11
Hanway Rd HNWL W7 47 M4
Hanway St FITZ W1T 4 C11
Hanworth La CHERT KT16 68 K6
Hanworth Rd HPTN TW12 58 H9
SUN TW16 58 C12
Hanworth Ter HSLW TW3 58 K2
Hanyards La POTB/CUF EN6 15 M2
Hapgood Cl GFD/PVL UB6 35 M10
Harben Pde HAMP NW3 * 37 R12
Harben Rd KIL/WHAMP NW6 37 Q12
Harberson Rd BAL SW12 61 V6
SRTFD E15 40 B13
Harbert Gdns LCOL/BKTW AL2 11 V3
Harberton Rd ARCH N19 38 A6
Harbet Rd BAY/PAD W2 3 M10
UED N18 27 P10
Harbex Cl BXLY DA5 66 B5
Harbinger Rd POP/IOD E14 51 T9
Harbledown Pl STMC/STPC BR5 77 S2
Harbledown Rd FUL/PGN SW6 49 N13
SAND/SEL CR2 87 L1
Harbord Cl CMBW SE5 50 H14
Harbord St FUL/PGN SW6 48 K13
Harborne Cl OXHEY WD19 22 E10
Harborough Av BFN/LL DA15 65 N5
Harborough Rd STRHM/NOR SW16 62 D9
Harbour Av WBPTN SW10 49 Q13
Harbourer Rd BARK/HLT IG6 29 R10
Harbour Exchange Sq POP/IOD E14 51 T7
Harbourfield Rd BNSTD SM7 85 P5
Harbour Rd CMBW SE5 62 G1
Harbour Yd WBPTN SW10 * 49 Q13
Harbridge Av PUT/ROE SW15 60 F5
Harbury Rd CAR SM5 73 S13
Harbut Rd BTSEA SW11 61 R2
Harcastle Cl YEAD UB4 46 G2
Harcombe Rd STNW/STAM N16 38 J8
Harcourt STWL/WRAY TW19 56 C4
Harcourt Av BFN/LL DA15 65 S4
EDGW HA8 24 C8
MNPK E12 40 H9
WLGTN SM6 73 V9
Harcourt Buildings EMB EC4Y * 4 J13
Harcourt Cl EGH TW20 56 G11
ISLW TW7 59 Q1
Harcourt Fld WLGTN SM6 73 V9
Harcourt Ms GPK RM2 42 F3
Harcourt Rd BROCKY SE4 63 R2
BUSH WD23 23 L3
BXLYHS DA6 65 U2
SRTFD E15 40 B14
THHTH CR7 74 D4
WDGN N22 26 B13
WIM/MER SW19 61 N12
WLGTN SM6 73 V9
Harcourt St MBLAR W1H 3 P10
Harcourt Ter WBPTN SW10 6 H10
Harcourt Wy GDST RH9 95 Q13
Hardcastle Cl CROY/NA CR0 75 L4
Hardcourts Cl WWKM BR4 75 T9
Hardell Cl EGH TW20 56 E10
Hardel Wk BRXS/STRHM SW2 62 E5
Harden Farm Cl COUL/CHIP CR5 86 A11
Hardens Manorway
WOOL/PLUM SE18 52 F8
Harders Rd PECK SE15 51 M14
Hardess St HNHL SE24 62 G1
Hardie Cl WLSDN NW10 36 D10
Hardie Rd DAGE RM10 42 C8
Harding Cl CROY/NA CR0 74 K8
GSTN WD25 11 Q7
KUTN/CMB KT2 59 V13
WALW SE17 9 N12
Hardinge Rd UED N18 26 J10
WLSDN NW10 36 J13
Hardinge St WCHPL E1 51 N4
WOOL/PLUM SE18 52 K8
Harding Rd BXLYHN DA7 53 V14
EPSOM KT18 84 E9
Hardings La PGE/AN SE20 63 P11
Harding Sp DTCH/LGLY SL3 44 D10
Hardings Rw IVER SL0 44 H1
Hardley Crs EMPK RM11 42 K2
Hardinge Crs WOOL/PLUM SE18 53 L8
Hardman Rd CHARL SE7 52 D10
KUTN/CMB KT2 59 U14
Hardres Ter STMC/STPC BR5 * 77 T7
Hardwick Cl LHD/OX KT22 83 L5
STAN HA7 23 S10
Hardwick Crs RDART DA2 67 P4
Hardwicke Av HEST TW5 * 46 J13
Hardwicke Ms FSBYW WC1X * 4 H6
Hardwicke Pl LCOL/BKTW AL2 12 H1
Hardwicke Rd CHSWK W4 48 C9
PLMGR N13 26 C10
RCHPK/HAM TW10 59 S9
REIG RH2 93 N9
Hardwicke St BARK IG11 41 L13
Hardwick Gn WEA W13 47 R3
Hardwick La CHERT KT16 68 G5
Hardwick Pl STRHM/NOR SW16 62 A12
Hardwick Rd REDH RH1 93 R12
Hardwick St CLKNW EC1R 4 K6
Hardwick's Wy WAND/EARL SW18 61 N3
Hardwidge St STHWK SE1 9 S3
Hardy Av CAN/RD E16 52 C6
RSLP HA4 34 D10
Hardy Cl BAR EN5 25 L3
BERM/RHTH SE16 51 P7
PIN HA5 34 F5
Hardy Cottages GNWCH SE10 * 51 V11
Hardy Gv DART DA1 67 N2
Hardy Pas WDGN N22 26 D13
Hardy Rd BKHTH/KID SE3 52 B11
CHING E4 27 R11
WIM/MER SW19 61 P12
Hardys Ms E/WMO/HCT KT8 71 N2
Hardy Wy ENC/FH EN2 15 Q13
Harebell Dr EHAM E6 52 J3
Harebell Hl COB KT11 82 F4
Harebell Wy HARH RM3 30 K12
Hare & Billet Rd BKHTH/KID SE3 51 V13
The Harebreaks WATN WD24 11 N11
Hare Ct EMB EC4Y * 4 J12
Harecourt Rd IS N1 38 G11
Hare Crs GSTN WD25 11 N6
Harecroft LHD/OX KT22 82 K13
Haredale Rd HNHL SE24 62 G2
Haredon Cl FSTH SE23 63 N5
Harefield ESH/CLAY KT10 71 N8
Harefield Av BELMT SM2 73 L13
Harefield Cl ENC/FH EN2 15 Q13
Harefield Ms BROCKY SE4 63 R1
Harefield Rd BROCKY SE4 63 R1
CEND/HSY/T N8 38 B3
RKW/CH/CXG WD3 21 Q7
SCUP DA14 65 T8
STRHM/NOR SW16 62 D12
UX/CGN UB8 33 P11
Hare Hall La GPK RM2 42 H2
Hare Hl ADL/WDHM KT15 68 K11
Hare Hill Cl WOKS/MYFD GU22 81 L5
Harelands Cl WOKN/KNAP GU21 80 A7
Hare La ESH/CLAY KT10 71 N11
Hare Marsh BETH E2 51 L2
Harendon KWD/TDW/WH KT20 84 J11
Hare Rw BETH E2 39 M14
Hares Bank CROY/NA CR0 75 V14
Haresfield Rd DAGE RM10 42 A11
Harestone Dr CTHM CR3 94 K1
Harestone Hl CTHM CR3 94 K2
Harestone La CTHM CR3 94 J1
Harestone Valley Rd CTHM CR3 94 K1
Hare St WOOL/PLUM SE18 52 J8
Hare Wk IS N1 5 T4
Harewood RKW/CH/CXG WD3 21 N3
Harewood Av NTHLT UB5 34 G12
STJWD NW8 3 P7
Harewood Cl NTHLT UB5 34 H12
REIG RH2 93 Q8
Harewood Dr CLAY IG5 28 H14
Harewood Gdns SAND/SEL CR2 87 M5
Harewood Hl EPP CM16 18 C9
Harewood Pl CONDST W1S 3 V12
Harewood Rd BRWN CM15 31 V4
CSTG HP8 20 A1
ISLW TW7 47 P12
OXHEY WD19 22 D8
SAND/SEL CR2 74 J11
WIM/MER SW19 61 S11
Harewood Rw CAMTN NW1 3 P9
Harewood Ter NWDGN UB2 46 H9
Harfield Gdns CMBW SE5 * 62 J1
Harfield Rd SUN TW16 58 F14
Harford Cl CHING E4 27 T5
Harford Dr WAT WD17 11 L12
Harford Rd CHING E4 27 T5
Harford St WCHPL E1 51 Q2
Harford Wk EFNCH N2 37 R2
Harfst Wy SWLY BR8 66 C13
Harglaze Ter CDALE/KGS NW9 * 36 E1
Hargood Cl KTN/HRWW/WS HA3 35 U4
Hargood Rd BKHTH/KID SE3 52 E13
Hargrave Pk ARCH N19 38 A7
Hargrave Pl KTTN NW5 38 B10
Hargrave Rd ARCH N19 38 A7
Hargreaves Av CHESW EN7 16 B5
Hargreaves Cl CHESW EN7 16 B5
Hargwyne St BRXN/ST SW9 62 D1
Haringey Pk CEND/HSY/T N8 38 C4
Haringey Rd CEND/HSY/T N8 38 C2
Harington Ter UED N18 * 26 H9
Harkett Cl KTN/HRWW/WS HA3 23 P14
Harkness CHESW EN7 16 B3
Harkness Cl EW KT17 84 J6
HARH RM3 31 M10
Harland Av BFN/LL DA15 65 M8
CROY/NA CR0 74 K8
Harland Cl WIM/MER SW19 73 P1
Harland Rd LEE/GVPK SE12 64 C6
Harlands Gv ORP BR6 76 K9
Harlech Gdns HEST TW5 46 F11
PIN HA5 34 F5
Harlech Rd ABLGY WD5 11 N5
STHGT/OAK N14 26 C8
Harlequin Av BTFD TW8 47 Q11
Harlequin Cl ISLW TW7 59 N3
YEAD UB4 46 F3
Harlequin Ct EA W5 * 47 S5
Harlequin Rd TEDD TW11 * 59 R12
The Harlequin WAT WD17 * 22 E2
Harlescott Rd PECK SE15 63 P2
Harlesden Cl HARH RM3 31 M12
Harlesden Gdns WLSDN NW10 36 F13
Harlesden Rd HARH RM3 31 M11
WLSDN NW10 36 H13
Harley Cl ALP/SUD HA0 * 35 T11
Harley Crs HRW HA1 35 M2
Harleyford BMLY BR1 64 E13
Harleyford Rd LBTH SE11 8 G11
Harleyford St LBTH SE11 8 J12
Harley Gdns ORP BR6 77 N9
WBPTN SW10 6 K10
Harley Gv BOW E3 51 R1
Harley Pl CAVSQ/HST W1G 3 U10
Harley Rd HAMP NW3 37 R12
HRW HA1 35 M2
WLSDN NW10 36 E14
Harley St CAVSQ/HST W1G 3 U8
Harley Vls WLSDN NW10 * 36 E14
Harlinger St WOOL/PLUM SE18 52 G8
Harlington Cl HYS/HAR UB3 45 U12
Harlington Rd BXLYHN DA7 65 V1
UX/CGN UB8 45 S1
Harlington Rd East
EBED/NFELT TW14 58 D5
Harlington Rd West
EBED/NFELT TW14 58 D4
Harlow Gdns CRW RM5 30 C11
Harlow Rd PLMGR N13 26 H8
RAIN RM13 42 F13
Harlyn Dr PIN HA5 34 D1
Harman Av WFD IG8 28 B12
Harman Cl CHING E4 27 V9
CRICK NW2 37 L8
STHWK SE1 * 51 L10
Harman Dr BFN/LL DA15 65 P4
CRICK NW2 37 L8
Harman Pl PUR/KEN CR8 86 F1
Harman Rd EN EN1 26 K3
Harmondsworth La WDR/YW UB7 45 Q11
Harmondsworth Rd WDR/YW UB7 45 Q9
Harmony Cl GLDGN NW11 37 L3
WLGTN SM6 74 C13
Harmony Pl STHWK SE1 9 V9
Harmony Wy BMLY BR1 64 C14
HDN NW4 36 J2
Harmood Gv CAMTN NW1 37 V12
Harmood St CAMTN NW1 37 V11
Harmsworth Ms STHWK SE1 8 K6
Harmsworth St WALW SE17 9 L10
Harmsworth Wy TRDG/WHET N20 25 M6
Harness Rd THMD SE28 53 Q7
Harnetts Cl SWLY BR8 * 78 D5
Harold Av BELV DA17 53 V10
HYS/HAR UB3 46 B8
Harold Court Rd HARH RM3 31 P11
Harold Crs WAB EN9 16 J6
Harold Rd CEND/HSY/T N8 38 D3
CHING E4 27 U8
NRWD SE19 62 H12
PLSTW E13 40 D13
RDART DA2 67 M9
SEVS/STOTM N15 38 K3
SUT SM1 73 R9
SWFD E18 28 C13
WAN E11 40 A6
WLSDN NW10 48 D1
Haroldstone Rd WALTH E17 39 P3
Harold Vw HARH RM3 31 M14
Harpenden Rd MNPK E12 40 E7
WNWD SE27 62 F7
Harper Cl STHGT/OAK N14 26 A3
Harper La RAD WD7 12 E5
Harper Rd EHAM E6 52 H4
STHWK SE1 9 P5
Harpers Yd ISLW TW7 * 47 P14
TOTM N17 26 K13
Harpesford Av VW GU25 68 A3
Harp Island Cl WLSDN NW10 36 D7
Harp La MON EC3R 5 S14
Harpley Sq WCHPL E1 51 N2
Harpour Rd BARK IG11 41 L11
Harp Rd HNWL W7 47 P2
Harpsden St BTSEA SW11 49 U13
Harps Oak La REDH RH1 93 U1
Harpswood Cl COUL/CHIP CR5 86 A12
Harpur Ms BMSBY WC1N 4 G9
Harpurs KWD/TDW/WH KT20 84 K11
Harpur St BMSBY WC1N 4 G9
Harraden Rd BKHTH/KID SE3 52 E13
Harrier Cl HCH RM12 42 H11
Harrier Ms THMD SE28 53 M7
Harrier Rd CDALE/KGS NW9 24 E14
Harriers Cl EA W5 47 U5
Harrier Wy EHAM E6 52 H3
WAB EN9 17 N8
Harriescourt WAB EN9 17 N6
Harries Rd YEAD UB4 46 E2
Harriet Cl HACK E8 39 L13
Harriet Gdns CROY/NA CR0 75 L7
Harriet St KTBR SW1X 7 R4
Harriet Tubman Cl BRXS/STRHM SW2 62 E5
Harriet Wk KTBR SW1X 7 R4
Harriet Walker Wy RKW/CH/CXG WD3 20 K5
Harriet Wy BUSH WD23 23 M5
Harringay Gdns CEND/HSY/T N8 38 F2
Harringay Rd SEVS/STOTM N15 38 F3
Harrington Cl CROY/NA CR0 74 C7
WLSDN NW10 36 D8
Harrington Ct NKENS W10 2 C5
Harrington Gdns SKENS SW7 6 J8
Harrington Hl CLPT E5 39 M6
Harrington Rd SKENS SW7 7 L7
SNWD SE25 75 L2
WAN E11 40 A6
Harrington Sq CAMTN NW1 4 A3
Harrington St CAMTN NW1 4 A5
Harrington Wy WOOL/PLUM SE18 52 F8
Harriott Cl GNWCH SE10 52 B9
Harriotts Cl ASHTD KT21 83 T10
Harriotts La ASHTD KT21 83 S9
Harris Cl ENC/FH EN2 15 R13
HARH RM3 31 L12
HSLW TW3 46 J13
Harris La RAD WD7 13 L8
Harrison Cl NTHWD HA6 21 U11
REIG RH2 93 P11
TRDG/WHET N20 25 S6
Harrison Ct SHPTN TW17 * 69 T3
Harrison Rd DAGE RM10 42 B11
WAB EN9 16 J9
WLSDN NW10 36 D13
Harrison's Ri CROY/NA CR0 74 F8
Harrison St STPAN WC1H 4 F6
Harrisons Whf PUR RM19 55 N10
Harrison Wk CHES/WCR EN8 16 D4
Harrison Wy SEV TN13 90 G12
SHPTN TW17 69 T3
Harris Rd BXLYHN DA7 53 U13
DAGW RM9 41 V10
GSTN WD25 11 N9
Harris St CMBW SE5 9 R14
WALTH E17 39 R5
Harris Wy SUN TW16 58 A13
Harrods Gn EDGW HA8 24 A10
Harrogate Ct DTCH/LGLY SL3 44 E10
Harrogate Rd OXHEY WD19 22 E8
Harrold Rd BCTR RM8 41 R10
Harrow Av EN EN1 26 K4
Harroway Rd BTSEA SW11 49 R14
Harrow Bottom Rd VW GU25 68 D4
Harrowby St MBLAR W1H 3 Q11
Harrow Cl ADL/WDHM KT15 69 M7
CHSGTN KT9 71 T12
Harrow Crs HARH RM3 30 H12
Harrowdene Cl ALP/SUD HA0 35 T9
Harrowdene Gdns TEDD TW11 59 Q12
Harrowdene Rd ALP/SUD HA0 35 T9
Harrow Dr ED N9 26 K6
EMPK RM11 42 J5
Harrowes Meade EDGW HA8 24 A8
Harrow Fields Gdns HRW HA1 35 N8
Harrow Gdns ORP BR6 77 R9
WARL CR6 87 R6
Harrowgate Rd HOM E9 39 Q12
Harrow Gn WAN E11 40 A8
Harrow La POP/IOD E14 51 U5
Harrow Manor Wy ABYW SE2 53 S6
Harrow Pk HRW HA1 35 N7
Harrow Pl WCHPL E1 5 T11
Harrow Rd ALP/SUD HA0 35 Q9
CAR SM5 73 S11
DTCH/LGLY SL3 44 D8
EBED/NFELT TW14 57 S7
IL IG1 41 L9
RSEV TN14 89 U5
WAN E11 40 B8
WARL CR6 87 R5
WBLY HA9 35 V10
WLSDN NW10 48 H1
Harrow Rd F/O BAY/PAD W2 3 M10
Harrow St CAMTN NW1 * 3 P9
Harrow Vw HGDN/ICK UB10 45 U1
HYS/HAR UB3 46 C5
RYLN/HDSTN HA2 35 M1
Harrow View Rd EA W5 47 R2
Harrow Wy OXHEY WD19 22 G8
SHPTN TW17 57 U14
Harrow Weald Pk
KTN/HRWW/WS HA3 23 M11
Harston Dr PEND EN3 16 G12
Hartcliff Ct HNWL W7 * 47 P7
Hart Cl REDH RH1 94 K9
Hart Crs CHIG IG7 29 P10
Hart Dyke Rd STMC/STPC BR5 77 S7
SWLY BR8 78 D2
Harte Rd HSLW TW3 46 H14
Hartfield Av BORE WD6 24 A2

NTHLT UB5 34 D14
Hartfield Cl BORE WD6 24 A3
Hartfield Crs WIM/MER SW19 61 M12
WWKM BR4 76 C8
Hartfield Gv PGE/AN SE20 63 M13
Hartfield Rd CHSGTN KT9 71 T10
WIM/MER SW19 61 M12
WWKM BR4 76 C9
Hartfield Ter BOW E3 39 S14
Hartford Av KTN/HRWW/WS HA3 35 Q1
Hartforde Rd BORE WD6 13 L14
Hartford Rd BXLY DA5 66 A4
HOR/WEW KT19 72 B11
Hart Gv EA W5 48 A6
STHL UB1 46 J3
Harthall La KGLGY WD4 10 J2
Hartham Cl HOLWY N7 38 C10
ISLW TW7 47 Q13
Hartham Rd HOLWY N7 38 C10
ISLW TW7 47 P13
TOTM N17 26 K14
Harting Rd ELTH/MOT SE9 64 G9
Hartington Cl HRW HA1 35 N9
ORP BR6 77 L10
REIG RH2 93 N8
Hartington Pl REIG RH2 * 93 N8
Hartington Rd CAN/RD E16 52 D4
CHSWK W4 48 C13
NWDGN UB2 * 46 G8
TWK TW1 59 R5
VX/NE SW8 50 C13
WALTH E17 39 Q4
WEA W13 47 R5
Hartismere Rd FUL/PGN SW6 6 D13
Hartlake Rd HOM E9 39 P11
Hartland Cl ADL/WDHM KT15 69 N14
EDGW HA8 24 A7
WCHMH N21 26 G4
Hartland Dr EDGW HA8 24 A7
RSLP HA4 34 D8
Hartland Rd ADL/WDHM KT15 69 L12
CAMTN NW1 * 37 V12
CHES/WCR EN8 16 D4
EPP CM16 18 E5
FBAR/BDGN N11 25 T10
HCH RM12 42 G7
HPTN TW12 58 K9
ISLW TW7 59 Q1
KIL/WHAMP NW6 2 C3
MRDN SM4 73 N5
SRTFD E15 40 B12
Hartland Rd Arches CAMTN NW1 * 37 U12
Hartlands Cl BXLY DA5 65 V4
The Hartlands HEST TW5 46 D11
Hartland Wy CROY/NA CR0 75 Q7
MRDN SM4 73 N5
Hartley Av EHAM E6 40 G13
MLHL NW7 24 F10
Hartley Cl BMLY BR1 64 H14
MLHL NW7 24 F10
SLN SL2 32 A13
Hartley Down PUR/KEN CR8 86 D4
Hartley Farm PUR/KEN CR8 86 D5
Hartley Hl PUR/KEN CR8 86 D5
Hartley Old Rd PUR/KEN CR8 86 D4
Hartley Rd BH/WHM TN16 97 M1
CROY/NA CR0 74 G5
WAN E11 40 B6
WELL DA16 53 S12
Hartley St BETH E2 51 N1
Hartley Wy PUR/KEN CR8 86 D5
Hartmann Rd CAN/RD E16 52 F6
Hartmoor Ms PEND EN3 16 D11
Hartnoll St HOLWY N7 38 D10
Harton Cl BMLY BR1 64 F13
Harton Rd ED N9 27 M7
Harton St DEPT SE8 51 S13
Hart Rd BF/WBF KT14 81 Q3
Hartsbourne Av BUSH WD23 23 L7
Hartsbourne Cl BUSH WD23 23 M7
Hartsbourne Rd BUSH WD23 23 M7
Harts Cl BUSH WD23 11 U14
Hartscroft CROY/NA CR0 75 Q13
Harts Gv WFD IG8 28 C10
Hartshill Cl HGDN/ICK UB10 33 S11
Hartshorn Gdns EHAM E6 52 J2
Hartsland Rd SEV TN13 90 J13
Harts La BARK IG11 40 K12
GDST RH9 95 P12
NWCR SE14 51 Q12
Hartslock Dr ABYW SE2 53 T7
Hartsmead Rd ELTH/MOT SE9 64 H7
Hartspiece Rd REDH RH1 93 V12
Hartspring La BUSH WD23 11 U14
Hart Sq MRDN SM4 * 73 P3
Hart St MON EC3R 5 T13
Hartsway PEND EN3 27 M2
Hartswood Av REIG RH2 93 N14
Hartswood Gdns SHB W12 * 48 F8
Hartswood Gn BUSH WD23 23 M7
Hartswood Rd SHB W12 48 F8
Hartsworth Cl PLSTW E13 40 B14
Hartville Rd WOOL/PLUM SE18 53 N9
Hartwell Dr CHING E4 27 U11
Hartwell St HACK E8 38 K11
Harvard Hl CHSWK W4 48 B10
Harvard Rd CHSWK W4 48 B10
ISLW TW7 47 N13
LEW SE13 63 U3
Harvel Cl CHST BR7 77 Q1
Harvel Crs ABYW SE2 53 T10
Harvest Bank Rd WWKM BR4 76 C8
Harvest End GSTN WD25 11 R10
Harvester Rd HOR/WEW KT19 72 D14
Harvesters Cl ISLW TW7 59 M3
Harvest La LOU IG10 28 F5
THDIT KT7 71 Q4
Harvest Rd BUSH WD23 22 K2
EGH TW20 56 B10
FELT TW13 58 C9
Harvest Wy SWLY BR8 78 C5
Harvey Dr HPTN TW12 58 K13
Harveyfields WAB EN9 16 J8
Harvey Gdns CHARL SE7 52 E10
LOU IG10 28 K1
Harvey Rd CEND/HSY/T N8 38 D3
CMBW SE5 50 H13
HGDN/ICK UB10 33 S14
HSLWW TW4 58 H5
IL IG1 40 K10
NTHLT UB5 34 E12
RKW/CH/CXG WD3 21 S4
WAN E11 40 A6
WOT/HER KT12 70 C5
Harvey's La ROMW/RG RM7 42 E7
Harvey St IS N1 5 R2
Harvill Rd SCUP DA14 65 T10
Harvil Rd DEN/HRF UB9 33 N2
Harvington Wk HACK E8 * 39 L12
Harwater Dr LOU IG10 17 T14
Harwell Cl RSLP HA4 33 V6
Harwood Av BMLY BR1 64 D14
EMPK RM11 43 L1
MTCM CR4 73 S1
Harwood Cl ALP/SUD HA0 35 T9
NFNCH/WDSPK N12 25 S11
Harwood Dr HGDN/ICK UB10 33 R13
Harwood Hall La UPMR RM14 43 P11
Harwood Rd FUL/PGN SW6 6 F14
Harwoods Rd WATW WD18 22 C2
Harwood Ter FUL/PGN SW6 49 P13
Hascombe Ter CMBW SE5 * 50 H14
Haselbury Rd ED N9 26 J8
Haseley End FSTH SE23 * 63 N5
Haselrigge Rd CLAP SW4 62 B2
Haseltine Rd SYD SE26 63 R9
Haselwood Dr ENC/FH EN2 26 F2
Haskard Rd DAGW RM9 41 T9
Hasker St CHEL SW3 7 P7
Haslam Av CHEAM SM3 73 L6
Haslam Cl HGDN/ICK UB10 33 U7
IS N1 38 E12
Haslam St PECK SE15 9 V14
PECK SE15 50 K13
Haslemere Av EBAR EN4 25 T6
HDN NW4 36 K4
HEST TW5 46 E14
HNWL W7 47 Q8
MTCM CR4 61 R14
WAND/EARL SW18 61 P7
Haslemere Cl HPTN TW12 58 H10
WLGTN SM6 74 C10
Haslemere Gdns FNCH N3 37 L2
Haslemere Heathrow Est
HSLWW TW4 * 46 D14
Haslemere Rd BXLYHN DA7 53 V14
CEND/HSY/T N8 38 C5
GDMY/SEVK IG3 41 P7
THHTH CR7 74 F3
WCHMH N21 26 F7
Hasler Cl THMD SE28 53 S5
Haslett Rd SHPTN TW17 58 A14
Hasluck Gdns BAR EN5 25 Q4
Hassard St BETH E2 5 V4
Hassendean Rd BKHTH/KID SE3 52 D11
Hassett Rd HOM E9 39 P11
Hassocks Cl SYD SE26 63 M8
Hassocks Rd STRHM/NOR SW16 62 B13
Hassock Wd HAYES BR2 76 F9
Hassop Rd CRICK NW2 36 K9
Hasted Rd CHARL SE7 52 F10
Hastings Av BARK/HLT IG6 41 L2
Hastings Cl ALP/SUD HA0 35 S9
BAR EN5 25 Q2
PECK SE15 * 51 L12
Hastings Dr SURB KT6 71 S4
Hastings Pl CROY/NA CR0 74 K6
Hastings Rd CROY/NA CR0 74 K6
FBAR/BDGN N11 26 A10
GPK RM2 42 H3
HAYES BR2 76 G7
TOTM N17 * 38 H1
WEA W13 47 R5
Hastings St STPAN WC1H 4 E6
Hastings Ter SEVS/STOTM N15 * 38 G3
Hastings Wy BUSH WD23 22 G2
RKW/CH/CXG WD3 21 T2
Hastings St WOOL/PLUM SE18 53 L8
Hastoe Cl YEAD UB4 46 G2
Hatcham Park Ms NWCR SE14 51 P13
Hatcham Park Rd NWCR SE14 51 P13
Hatcham Rd PECK SE15 51 N11
Hatchard Rd ARCH N19 38 B7
Hatch Cl ADL/WDHM KT15 69 M8
Hatchcroft HDN NW4 36 H1
Hatchers Ms STHWK SE1 9 T4
Hatchett Rd EBED/NFELT TW14 57 U6
Hatch Gdns KWD/TDW/WH KT20 84 K10
Hatch Gv CHDH RM6 41 U2
Hatch La BNSTD SM7 85 U5
CHING E4 27 V9
RPLY/SEND GU23 81 T10
WDR/YW UB7 45 P12
Hatch Pl KUTN/CMB KT2 59 V10
Hatch Rd BRWN CM15 31 U3
STRHM/NOR SW16 62 C14
Hatch Side CHIG IG7 28 J10
The Hatch PEND EN3 16 D13
Hatchwoods WFD IG8 28 B9
Hatcliffe Cl BKHTH/KID SE3 64 B1
Hatcliffe St GNWCH SE10 52 B10
Hatfield Cl BARK/HLT IG6 40 K1
BELMT SM2 73 N13
BF/WBF KT14 * 81 M2
HCH RM12 42 K10
MTCM CR4 * 73 R2
Hatfield Ct BKHTH/KID SE3 * 52 C12
Hatfield Rd ASHTD KT21 83 V9
CHSWK W4 48 D7
HNWL W7 47 Q6
POTB/CUF EN6 14 E5
SRTFD E15 40 A10
WATN WD24 11 P13
Hatfields LOU IG10 28 K1
STHWK SE1 8 K1
Hathaway Cl BARK/HLT IG6 28 K11
HAYES BR2 76 H6
RSLP HA4 34 B9
STAN HA7 23 Q10
Hathaway Crs MNPK E12 40 H11
Hathaway Gdns CHDH RM6 41 T3
WEA W13 47 Q3
Hathaway Rd CROY/NA CR0 74 F5
Hatherleigh Cl CHSGTN KT9 71 T10
EBAR EN4 14 D13
MRDN SM4 73 N2
Hatherleigh Gdns POTB/CUF EN6 14 F6
Hatherleigh Rd RSLP HA4 34 C7
Hatherleigh Wy HARH RM3 30 K13
Hatherley Crs BFN/LL DA15 65 Q7
Hatherley Gdns CEND/HSY/T N8 38 C4
EHAM E6 52 F1
Hatherley Gv BAY/PAD W2 2 G11
Hatherley Ms WALTH E17 39 S2
Hatherley Rd RCH/KEW TW9 47 V13
SCUP DA14 65 Q8
WALTH E17 39 R2
Hatherley St WEST SW1P 8 B8
Hathern Gdns ELTH/MOT SE9 64 J9
Hatherop Rd HPTN TW12 58 H12
Hatherwood LHD/OX KT22 83 T11
Hathorne Cl PECK SE15 51 M14
Hathorne Ter ARCH N19 * 38 B6
Hathway St PECK SE15 51 N14
Hatley Av BARK/HLT IG6 41 L2
Hatley Cl FBAR/BDGN N11 25 T10
Hatley Rd FSBYPK N4 38 D7
Hat & Mitre Ct FARR EC1M 5 M8
Hatteraick St BERM/RHTH SE16 51 N7
Hattersfield Cl BELV DA17 53 V9
Hatters La WATW WD18 21 V4
WATW WD18 22 A3
Hatton Cl WOOL/PLUM SE18 53 M12
Hatton Cross Est HTHAIR TW6 * 58 B2
Hatton Gdn HCIRC EC1N 4 K9
Hatton Gdns MTCM CR4 73 T3
Hatton Gn EBED/NFELT TW14 58 C2
Hatton Gv WDR/YW UB7 * 45 P7
Hatton Pl HCIRC EC1N 4 K8
Hatton Rd CHES/WCR EN8 16 D3
CROY/NA CR0 74 E6
EBED/NFELT TW14 57 U5
HTHAIR TW6 58 B2
Hatton Rw STJWD NW8 * 3 M8
Hatton St STJWD NW8 3 M8
Hatton Wall HCIRC EC1N 4 J9
Haunch of Venison Yd OXSTW W1C * 3 U12
Havana Cl ROM RM1 42 E3
Havana Rd WIM/MER SW19 61 N7
Havannah St POP/IOD E14 51 S7
Havant Rd WALTH E17 39 U1
Havelock Cl SHB W12 * 48 H5
Havelock Pl HRW HA1 35 N4
Havelock Rd BELV DA17 * 53 V9
CROY/NA CR0 74 K7
DART DA1 66 H5
HAYES BR2 76 E2
KGLGY WD4 10 G2
KTN/HRWW/WS HA3 35 N1
NWDGN UB2 46 G8
TOTM N17 27 L14
WIM/MER SW19 61 Q10
Havelock St IS N1 4 F1
Havelock Ter VX/NE SW8 7 V14
Havelock Wk FSTH SE23 63 N6
Haven Cl ELTH/MOT SE9 64 H8
SCUP DA14 65 S11
SWLY BR8 66 F14
WIM/MER SW19 60 K8
YEAD UB4 46 A3
Haven Ct BRYLDS KT5 * 71 V4
Havenfield KGLGY WD4 10 B5
Haven Gn EA W5 47 T5
Havenhurst Ri ENC/FH EN2 15 Q14
Haven La EA W5 47 U4
Haven Rd ASHF TW15 57 T9
Havens Ms BOW E3 51 R3
Haven St CAMTN NW1 37 V12
Havenswood Ct KUTN/CMB KT2 60 B11
The Haven RCH/KEW TW9 60 A1
SUN TW16 58 C12
Havenwood WBLY HA9 36 B8
Haverfield Est BTFD TW8 47 U11
Haverfield Gdns RCH/KEW TW9 48 A12
Haverfield Rd BOW E3 51 P1
Haverford Wy EDGW HA8 23 V13
Havergal Vls SEVS/STOTM N15 * 38 F2
Haverhill Rd BAL SW12 62 A6
CHING E4 27 U6
Havering Dr ROM RM1 42 E2
Havering Gdns CHDH RM6 41 S3
Havering Rd ROM RM1 30 D14
ROM RM1 42 D1
Havering St WCHPL E1 51 P4
Havering Wy BARK IG11 53 R1
Havers Av WOT/HER KT12 70 F10
Haversham Cl TWK TW1 59 T5
Haversham Pl HGT N6 37 T7
Haverstock Hl HAMP NW3 37 S11
Haverstock Pl FSBYE EC1V 4 K4
Haverstock Rd KTTN NW5 37 U10
Haverstock St IS N1 5 M4
Haverthwaite Rd ORP BR6 77 M8
Havil St CMBW SE5 9 S14
CMBW SE5 50 J13
Havisham Pl NRWD SE19 62 F11
Hawarden Gv HNHL SE24 62 G5
Hawarden Hl CRICK NW2 36 G8
Hawarden Rd CTHM CR3 86 G11
WALTH E17 39 P2
Hawbridge Rd WAN E11 39 V6
Hawes Cl NTHWD HA6 22 B12
Hawes La CHING E4 16 J12
WWKM BR4 75 V7
Hawes Rd BMLY BR1 64 D13
KWD/TDW/WH KT20 84 K10
UED N18 27 M11
Hawes St IS N1 38 F12
Haweswater Dr GSTN WD25 11 Q7
Hawfield Bank ORP BR6 77 S8
Hawgood St BOW E3 51 S3
Hawk Cl WAB EN9 17 N8
Hawkdene CHING E4 27 T4
Hawke Park Rd WDGN N22 38 F1
Hawke Pl BERM/RHTH SE16 * 51 P7
Hawke Rd NRWD SE19 62 H11
Hawker Rd CROY/NA CR0 74 E11
Hawkesbury Cl BARK/HLT IG6 29 R9
Hawkesbury Rd PUT/ROE SW15 60 H3
Hawkesfield Rd FSTH SE23 63 R7
Hawkesley Cl TWK TW1 59 Q9
Hawkesley Ct RAD WD7 12 D9
Hawkes Rd EBED/NFELT TW14 58 C5
MTCM CR4 61 S13
Hawkesworth Cl NTHWD HA6 22 A12
Hawkewood Rd SUN TW16 70 C1
Hawkhirst Rd PUR/KEN CR8 86 H6
Hawkhurst COB KT11 82 J4
Hawkhurst Gdns CRW RM5 30 D11
Hawkhurst Rd STRHM/NOR SW16 62 B13
Hawkhurst Wy NWMAL KT3 72 D3
WWKM BR4 75 T7
Hawkinge Wy HCH RM12 42 J11
Hawkins Cl BORE WD6 13 N14
EDGW HA8 24 D10
HRW HA1 35 M5
Hawkins Rd TEDD TW11 59 R11
WLSDN NW10 36 E12
Hawkins Ter CHARL SE7 52 G10
Hawkins Wy CAT SE6 63 S10
Hawkley Gdns WNWD SE27 62 F8
Hawkridge Cl CHDH RM6 41 S4
Hawksbrook La BECK BR3 75 T4
Hawkshaw Cl BRXS/STRHM SW2 62 C5
Hawkshead Cl BMLY BR1 64 A12
Hawkshead La BRKMPK AL9 14 A2
Hawkshead Rd CHSWK W4 48 E8
POTB/CUF EN6 14 C3
WLSDN NW10 * 36 F12
Hawks Hl EPP CM16 19 L1
LHD/OX KT22 83 P13
Hawkshill Cl ESH/CLAY KT10 70 J11
Hawks Hill Cl LHD/OX KT22 83 P13
Hawks Hill Ct LHD/OX KT22 83 P13
Hawkshill Pl ESH/CLAY KT10 * 70 J11
Hawkshill Wy ESH/CLAY KT10 70 H11
Hawkslade Rd PECK SE15 63 P3
Hawksley Rd STNW/STAM N16 38 H8
Hawksmead Cl PEND EN3 16 D10
Hawks Ms GNWCH SE10 * 51 U12
Hawksmoor RAD WD7 13 L7
Hawksmoor Cl EHAM E6 52 G4
WOOL/PLUM SE18 53 N10
Hawksmoor Ms WCHPL E1 51 M5
Hawksmoor St HMSMTH W6 48 K11
Hawksmouth CHING E4 27 T5
Hawks Rd KUT/HW KT1 59 V14
Hawkstone Est BERM/RHTH SE16 51 N9
Hawkstone Rd BERM/RHTH SE16 51 N9
Hawksview COB KT11 82 H3
Hawksway STA TW18 56 K8
Hawkswood Gv DTCH/LGLY SL3 32 D11
Hawkswood La DTCH/LGLY SL3 32 D10
Hawkwell Wk IS N1 * 5 P1
Hawkwood Crs CHING E4 27 T4
Hawkwood La CHST BR7 65 L13
Hawkwood Mt CLPT E5 39 M6
Hawlands Dr PIN HA5 34 G5
Hawley Cl HPTN TW12 58 H11
Hawley Crs CAMTN NW1 37 V12
Hawley Ms CAMTN NW1 37 V12
Hawley Rd CAMTN NW1 37 V12
DART DA1 67 L7
UED N18 27 P10
Hawley Ter RDART DA2 * 67 N9
Hawley V RDART DA2 * 67 N10
Hawley Wy ASHF TW15 57 S10
Hawstead La ORP BR6 77 V10
Hawstead Rd CAT SE6 63 T4
Hawsted BKHH IG9 28 D5
Hawthorn Av PLMGR N13 26 C10
RAIN RM13 54 H2
THHTH CR7 62 F13
Hawthorn Centre HRW HA1 35 P2
Hawthorn Cl ABLGY WD5 11 N6
BNSTD SM7 85 L4
HEST TW5 46 D12
HPTN TW12 58 J10
IVER SL0 32 G14
IVER SL0 44 G1
STMC/STPC BR5 77 M4
WAT WD17 11 M12
WOKS/MYFD GU22 80 C10
Hawthorn Ct ASHF TW15 57 U12
Hawthorn Crs SAND/SEL CR2 87 N1
TOOT SW17 61 U10
Hawthornden Cl NFNCH/WDSPK N12 25 S11
Hawthorndene Cl HAYES BR2 * 76 B7
Hawthorndene Rd HAYES BR2 76 C7
Hawthorn Dr DEN/HRF UB9 33 N11
RYLN/HDSTN HA2 34 J4
WWKM BR4 76 A9
Hawthorne Av BH/WHM TN16 88 F5
BOW E3 39 R13
CAR SM5 73 U12
CHESW EN7 16 B4
HRW HA1 35 Q4
MTCM CR4 61 R14
RSLP HA4 34 D4
Hawthorne Cl BMLY BR1 76 H1
CHESW EN7 16 B5
IS N1 38 J11
Hawthorne Ct STWL/WRAY TW19 * 57 P5
Hawthorne Crs WDR/YW UB7 45 R7
Hawthorne Gv CDALE/KGS NW9 36 C5
Hawthorne Pl EW KT17 84 E2
Hawthorne Rd BMLY BR1 76 H1
RAD WD7 12 E8
STA TW18 56 G10
UED N18 26 K11
WALTH E17 39 S1
Hawthorne Wy ED N9 26 K7
STWL/WRAY TW19 57 P5
Hawthorn Farm Av NTHLT UB5 34 G13
Hawthorn Gdns EA W5 47 T8
Hawthorn Gv ENC/FH EN2 15 T12
PGE/AN SE20 63 M13
Hawthorn Hatch BTFD TW8 47 R12
Hawthorn La SEV TN13 90 F12
Hawthorn Ms MLHL NW7 25 L13
Hawthorn Pl ERITH DA8 54 C10
HYS/HAR UB3 * 46 B5
Hawthorn Rd BTFD TW8 47 R12
BXLYHS DA6 * 65 V2
CEND/HSY/T N8 38 B1
DART DA1 66 K7
FELT TW13 58 C6
RPLY/SEND GU23 80 K14
SUT SM1 73 R10
WFD IG8 28 E9
WLGTN SM6 73 V12
WLSDN NW10 36 G12
WOKS/MYFD GU22 80 C10
Hawthorns WFD IG8 28 C8
The Hawthorns DTCH/LGLY SL3 44 K13
EW KT17 72 F11
OXTED RH8 96 C9
RKW/CH/CXG WD3 20 H10
Hawthorn Ter BFN/LL DA15 65 P4
WEY KT13 * 81 S1
Hawthorn Wk NKENS W10 2 A7
Hawthorn Wy ADL/WDHM KT15 69 M14
REDH RH1 93 V12
SHPTN TW17 69 V2
Hawtrees RAD WD7 12 D9
Hawtrey Av NTHLT UB5 34 F14
Hawtrey Dr RSLP HA4 34 C5
Hawtrey Rd HAMP NW3 37 S12
Haxted Rd BMLY BR1 64 D13
Hayburn Wy HCH RM12 42 F6
Hay Cl BORE WD6 13 N14
SRTFD E15 40 A12
Haycroft Cl COUL/CHIP CR5 86 F9
Haycroft Gdns WLSDN NW10 36 G13
Haycroft Rd BRXS/STRHM SW2 62 C3
SURB KT6 71 T7
Hay Currie St POP/IOD E14 51 T4
Hayday Rd CAN/RD E16 52 C3
Hayden Ct ADL/WDHM KT15 69 M14
Hayden Dell BUSH WD23 22 H4
Hayden Rd WAB EN9 16 J9
Haydens Cl STMC/STPC BR5 77 S5
Hayden's Pl NTGHL W11 2 C11
Hayden Wy CRW RM5 30 C14
Haydn Av PUR/KEN CR8 86 E5
Haydock Av NTHLT UB5 34 J11
Haydock Cl HCH RM12 43 M9
Haydock Gn NTHLT UB5 34 J11
Haydon Cl CDALE/KGS NW9 36 C2
EN EN1 26 J4
HARH RM3 30 H12
Haydon Dell Farm BUSH WD23 * 22 H5
Haydon Dr PIN HA5 34 C2
Haydon Park Rd WIM/MER SW19 61 N10
Haydon Rd BCTR RM8 41 S7
OXHEY WD19 22 G4
Haydon's Rd WIM/MER SW19 61 P10
Haydon St TWRH EC3N 5 U13
Haydon Wk WCHPL E1 5 U12
Haydon Wy WAND/EARL SW18 61 Q2
Hayes Barton WOKS/MYFD GU22 80 H6
Hayes Cha WWKM BR4 75 V4
Hayes Cl HAYES BR2 76 C7
Hayes Crs CHEAM SM3 72 K9
GLDGN NW11 37 M3
Hayes Dr RAIN RM13 42 H12
Hayes End Dr YEAD UB4 45 V3
Hayes End Rd YEAD UB4 45 V3
Hayesford Park Dr HAYES BR2 76 B3
Hayes Gdn HAYES BR2 76 C7
Hayes Gv EDUL SE22 62 K2
Hayes Hl HAYES BR2 76 A6
Hayes Hill Rd HAYES BR2 76 B6
Hayes La BECK BR3 75 V1
HAYES BR2 76 D2
PUR/KEN CR8 86 F6
Hayes Mead Rd HAYES BR2 76 A6
Hayes Pl CAMTN NW1 3 P8
Hayes Rd HAYES BR2 76 C2
NWDGN UB2 46 E9
RDART DA2 67 S5
Hayes St HAYES BR2 76 D6
The Hayes EPSOM KT18 84 D9
Hayes Wy BECK BR3 75 U2
Hayes Wood Av HAYES BR2 76 D6
Hayfield Cl BUSH WD23 22 K2
Hayfield Pas WCHPL E1 51 N2
Hayfield Rd STMC/STPC BR5 77 Q3
Haygarth Pl WIM/MER SW19 60 K10
Haygreen Cl KUTN/CMB KT2 60 B11
Hay Hl MYFR/PICC W1J 3 V14
Hayland Cl CDALE/KGS NW9 36 D2
Hay La CDALE/KGS NW9 36 D2
DTCH/LGLY SL3 32 B9
Hayles St LBTH SE11 9 L7
Haylett Gdns KUT/HW KT1 * 71 T2
Hayling Av FELT TW13 58 C8
Hayling Cl STNW/STAM N16 38 J10
Hayling Rd OXHEY WD19 22 B8
Hayman Crs YEAD UB4 33 V14
Haymarket STJS SW1Y 4 C14
Haymeads Dr ESH/CLAY KT10 71 L11
Haymer Gdns WPK KT4 72 G8
Haymerle Rd PECK SE15 51 L11
Haymill Cl GFD/PVL UB6 47 P1
Hayne Rd BECK BR3 63 R14
Haynes Cl BKHTH/KID SE3 64 A1
DTCH/LGLY SL3 44 D10
FBAR/BDGN N11 25 U8
RPLY/SEND GU23 81 M12
TOTM N17 27 M12
Haynes Dr ED N9 27 M8
Haynes La NRWD SE19 62 J11
Haynes Rd ALP/SUD HA0 35 U12
EMPK RM11 42 K3
Hayne St STBT EC1A 5 M9
Haynt Wk RYNPK SW20 73 L1
Hay Pl SWLY BR8 * 78 C4
Hay's La STHWK SE1 9 S1
Haysleigh Gdns PGE/AN SE20 63 L14
Hay's Ms MYFR/PICC W1J 7 U1
Haysoms Cl ROM RM1 42 E2
Haystall Cl YEAD UB4 34 A14
Hay St BETH E2 39 L13
Hays Wk BELMT SM2 72 K14
Hayter Rd BRXS/STRHM SW2 62 C3
Hayton Cl HACK E8 38 K11
Haywain CTHM CR3 86 G12
The Haywain OXTED RH8 95 V6
Hayward Cl DART DA1 66 D3
WIM/MER SW19 61 P12
Hayward Dr DART DA1 67 M8
Hayward Gdns PUT/ROE SW15 60 J4
Hayward Rd THDIT KT7 71 P6
TRDG/WHET N20 25 Q7
Haywards Cl CHDH RM6 41 S3
Hayward's Pl CLKNW EC1R * 5 L8
Haywood Cl PIN HA5 22 F14
Haywood Copse RKW/CH/CXG WD3 21 P2
Haywood Ct WAB EN9 17 M8
Haywood Dr RKW/CH/CXG WD3 20 K3
Haywood Pk RKW/CH/CXG WD3 20 K3
Haywood Ri ORP BR6 77 N10
Haywood Rd HAYES BR2 76 F2
Hazel Av WDR/YW UB7 45 S8
Hazelbank BRYLDS KT5 72 C6
Hazelbank Rd CAT SE6 63 V7
CHERT KT16 69 N5
Hazelbourne Rd BAL SW12 61 V4
Hazelbrouck Gdns BARK/HLT IG6 29 M12
Hazelbury Av ABLGY WD5 10 J6
Hazelbury Cl WIM/MER SW19 61 N14
Hazelbury Gn ED N9 26 J8
Hazelbury La ED N9 26 J8
Hazel Cl BTFD TW8 * 47 R12
CDALE/KGS NW9 24 F14
CROY/NA CR0 75 P5
HCH RM12 42 H8
MTCM CR4 74 B2
PLMGR N13 26 H8
REIG RH2 93 Q12
WHTN TW2 59 M5
Hazel Ct COB KT11 82 C3
RKW/CH/CXG WD3 * 20 J9
Hazelcroft PIN HA5 22 J11
Hazelcroft Cl HGDN/ICK UB10 33 R12
Hazeldean Rd WLSDN NW10 36 D12
Hazelden Cl BGR/WK TN15 79 U13
Hazeldene ADL/WDHM KT15 69 N10
CHES/WCR EN8 16 E6
Hazeldene Ct PUR/KEN CR8 86 H5
Hazeldene Dr PIN HA5 34 E1
Hazeldene Gdns HGDN/ICK UB10 33 U13
Hazeldene Rd GDMY/SEVK IG3 41 R7
WELL DA16 53 S14
Hazeldon Rd BROCKY SE4 63 Q3
Hazel Dr ERITH DA8 54 H13
Hazeleigh Gdns WFD IG8 28 G11
Hazel End SWLY BR8 78 E3
Hazel Gdns EDGW HA8 24 B9
Hazelgreen Cl WCHMH N21 26 F6
Hazel Gv ALP/SUD HA0 35 U13
CHDH RM6 41 U1
EN EN1 * 27 L4
GSTN WD25 11 P9
ORP BR6 76 K7
STA TW18 57 M11
SYD SE26 63 P9
Hazelhurst BECK BR3 63 V13
Hazelhurst Rd TOOT SW17 61 Q9
Hazel La BARK/HLT IG6 28 K12
Hazell Crs CRW RM5 30 B13
Hazellville Rd ARCH N19 38 B5
Hazel Md BAR EN5 24 H3
EW KT17 72 G14
Hazelmere Cl EBED/NFELT TW14 57 V4
LHD/OX KT22 83 R9
NTHLT UB5 34 H14
Hazelmere Dr NTHLT UB5 34 H14
Hazelmere Gdns EMPK RM11 42 H3
Hazelmere Rd KIL/WHAMP NW6 2 D1
NTHLT UB5 34 H14
STMC/STPC BR5 77 L2
Hazelmere Wk NTHLT UB5 34 H14
Hazelmere Wy HAYES BR2 76 C4
Hazel Pde LHD/OX KT22 * 83 L12
Hazel Ri EMPK RM11 42 J4
Hazel Rd BF/WBF KT14 81 L4
DART DA1 66 K7
ERITH DA8 54 G13
LCOL/BKTW AL2 11 V2
REIG RH2 93 Q13
SRTFD E15 * 40 A10
WLSDN NW10 36 H1
Hazel Rw NFNCH/WDSPK N12 * 25 R10
Hazeltree La NTHLT UB5 46 G1
Hazel Tree Rd WATN WD24 11 P11
Hazel Wk HAYES BR2 76 J4
Hazel Wy CHING E4 27 R11
COUL/CHIP CR5 85 T9
LHD/OX KT22 83 L12
STHWK SE1 9 U7
Hazelway Cl LHD/OX KT22 83 L13
Hazelwood Av MRDN SM4 73 P2
Hazelwood Cl CLPT E5 39 Q8
EA W5 47 U7
RYLN/HDSTN HA2 34 K2
Hazelwood Ct SURB KT6 71 U4
Hazelwood Dr PIN HA5 22 D14
Hazelwood Gdns BRWN CM15 31 U3
Hazelwood Gv SAND/SEL CR2 87 M4
Hazelwood Hts OXTED RH8 96 C7
Hazelwood La ABLGY WD5 10 K6
COUL/CHIP CR5 85 T9
PLMGR N13 26 E9
Hazelwood Park Cl CHIG IG7 29 N10
Hazelwood Rd EN EN1 26 K4
OXTED RH8 96 D8
RKW/CH/CXG WD3 21 U4
RSEV TN14 89 M2
WALTH E17 39 Q3
Hazlebury Rd FUL/PGN SW6 49 P14
Hazledean Rd CROY/NA CR0 74 H7
Hazledene Rd CHSWK W4 48 C11
Hazlemere Gdns WPK KT4 72 G6
Hazlewell Rd PUT/ROE SW15 60 J3
Hazlewood Crs NKENS W10 2 B8
Hazlitt Cl FELT TW13 58 G9
Hazlitt Ms WKENS W14 6 A6
Hazlitt Rd WKENS W14 6 A6
Hazon Wy HOR/WEW KT19 84 D2
Heacham Av HGDN/ICK UB10 33 U8
Headcorn Rd BMLY BR1 64 B10
THHTH CR7 74 D2
TOTM N17 26 K12
Headfort Pl KTBR SW1X 7 T4
Headingley Cl RAD WD7 12 J6
Headington Rd WAND/EARL SW18 61 Q6
Headlam Rd CLAP SW4 62 B5
Headlam St WCHPL E1 51 M2
Headley Ap GNTH/NBYPK IG2 40 J3
Headley Av WLGTN SM6 74 D10
Headley Cl CHSGTN KT9 72 A11
Headley Common RBRW/HUT CM13 31 V12
Headley Common Rd EPSOM KT18 92 D4
Headley Dr CROY/NA CR0 75 U12
EPSOM KT18 84 J9
GNTH/NBYPK IG2 40 K4
Headley Gv EPSOM KT18 92 D4
KWD/TDW/WH KT20 84 H10
Headley Heath Ap
KWD/TDW/WH KT20 92 B7
Headley Pde EPSOM KT18 * 84 D9
Headley Rd EPSOM KT18 84 C10
LHD/OX KT22 83 S12
Heads Ms NTGHL W11 2 E12
Headstone Dr HRW HA1 35 N1
Headstone Gdns RYLN/HDSTN HA2 35 L2
Headstone La KTN/HRWW/WS HA3 22 K13
Headstone Pde HRW HA1 * 35 M2
Headstone Rd HRW HA1 35 N4
Head St WCHPL E1 51 P4
Headway Cl RCHPK/HAM TW10 59 S9
The Headway EW KT17 72 F13
Heald St NWCR SE14 51 R13
Healey Rd WATW WD18 22 B4
Healey St CAMTN NW1 * 37 V11
Healy Dr ORP BR6 77 P9
Hearne Rd CHSWK W4 48 A10
Hearn Ri NTHLT UB5 34 F13
Hearn Rd ROM RM1 42 F4
Hearn's Buildings WALW SE17 9 R8
Hearns Cl STMC/STPC BR5 77 S2
Hearnshaw St POP/IOD E14 51 Q4
Hearns Rd STMC/STPC BR5 77 S2
Hearn St SDTCH EC2A 5 T8
Hearnville Rd BAL SW12 61 U6
Heatham Pk WHTN TW2 59 P5
Heath Av BXLYHN DA7 53 T11
Heathbourne Rd BUSH WD23 23 N7
Heathbridge WEY KT13 * 69 S11
Heath Brow HAMP NW3 37 Q8
Heath Cl BNSTD SM7 85 P4
EA W5 47 V2
GLDGN NW11 37 P5
GPK RM2 42 G1
HYS/HAR UB3 45 V12
POTB/CUF EN6 14 D4
SAND/SEL CR2 74 F11
STMC/STPC BR5 77 S4
STWL/WRAY TW19 57 N4
SWLY BR8 66 E14
VW GU25 68 B2
Heathclose Av DART DA1 66 H5
Heathclose Rd DART DA1 66 G6
Heathcote KWD/TDW/WH KT20 84 K12
Heathcote Av CLAY IG5 28 H14
Heathcote Gv CHING E4 27 U8
Heathcote Rd EPSOM KT18 84 D4
TWK TW1 59 R4
Heathcote St BMSBY WC1N 4 G7
Heathcote Wy WDR/YW UB7 45 P6
Heathcroft EA W5 47 V2
Heathcroft Av SUN TW16 58 B12
Heathcroft Gdns WALTH E17 27 V13
Heathdale Av HSLWW TW4 58 G1
Heathdene KWD/TDW/WH KT20 85 L9
Heathdene Dr BELV DA17 54 B9
Heathdene Mnr WAT WD17 * 11 M13
Heathdene Rd STRHM/NOR SW16 62 D12
WLGTN SM6 73 V12
Heathdown Rd WOKS/MYFD GU22 80 H5
Heath Dr BELMT SM2 73 Q13
EPP CM16 18 C9
GPK RM2 30 G13
HAMP NW3 37 P9
KWD/TDW/WH KT20 92 H2
POTB/CUF EN6 14 C4
RPLY/SEND GU23 80 F13
RYNPK SW20 72 J2
Heathedge SYD SE26 * 63 M7
Heathend Rd BXLY DA5 66 E6
Heather Av ROM RM1 30 D14
Heatherbank CHST BR7 64 J14
ELTH/MOT SE9 52 H14
Heatherbank Cl COB KT11 82 F1
DART DA1 66 E4
Heather Cl ABLGY WD5 11 N6
ADL/WDHM KT15 69 M14
BRWN CM15 31 V3
EHAM E6 52 K4
HPTN TW12 58 H13
ISLW TW7 59 M3
KWD/TDW/WH KT20 85 L12
LEW SE13 63 V4
REDH RH1 93 V7
ROM RM1 30 D13
UX/CGN UB8 45 R3
VX/NE SW8 61 V1
WOKN/KNAP GU21 80 A5
Heatherdale Cl KUTN/CMB KT2 60 A11
Heatherdene Cl MTCM CR4 73 R2
NFNCH/WDSPK N12 25 Q13
Heatherden Gn IVER SL0 32 G13
Heather Dr DART DA1 66 G5
ENC/FH EN2 15 R14
ROM RM1 30 D14
Heather End SWLY BR8 78 D3
Heatherfold Wy PIN HA5 34 B1
Heather Gdns BELMT SM2 73 N11
GLDGN NW11 37 L4
ROM RM1 30 D14
WAB EN9 16 J10
Heather Gln ROM RM1 30 D14
Heatherlands SUN TW16 58 C11
Heather La WDR/YW UB7 45 Q4
Heatherley Dr CLAY IG5 40 H1
Heather Park Dr ALP/SUD HA0 36 A13
Heather Park Pde ALP/SUD HA0 * 35 V12
Heather Pl ESH/CLAY KT10 70 K9
Heather Ri BUSH WD23 11 T14
Heather Rd CHING E4 27 R11
CRICK NW2 36 F7
LEE/GVPK SE12 64 C7
Heatherset Cl ESH/CLAY KT10 71 L10
Heatherset Gdns STRHM/NOR SW16 62 D12
Heatherside Cl GT/LBKH KT23 82 G14
Heatherside Rd HOR/WEW KT19 72 D12
SCUP DA14 65 S8
The Heathers STWL/WRAY TW19 57 R5
Heathervale Rd ADL/WDHM KT15 69 M14
Heathervale Wy ADL/WDHM KT15 69 N14
Heather Wk EDGW HA8 24 B10
NKENS W10 2 B7
Heather Wy POTB/CUF EN6 14 B6
ROM RM1 30 D13
SAND/SEL CR2 75 P13
STAN HA7 23 P11
Heatherwood Cl MNPK E12 40 D7
Heatherwood Dr YEAD UB4 33 V14
Heathfield CHING E4 27 U8
CHST BR7 65 L11
COB KT11 82 J4
HRW HA1 * 35 P5
Heathfield Av WAND/EARL SW18 61 R5
Heathfield Cl ASHTD KT21 83 S9
CAN/RD E16 52 F3
HAYES BR2 76 E10
OXHEY WD19 22 E5
POTB/CUF EN6 14 D4
WOKS/MYFD GU22 80 E8
Heathfield Dr MTCM CR4 61 S13
Heathfield Gdns CHSWK W4 48 C10
CROY/NA CR0 * 74 G9
GLDGN NW11 36 K4
WAND/EARL SW18 61 R4
Heathfield La CHST BR7 65 L11
Heathfield North WHTN TW2 59 N5
Heathfield Pk CRICK NW2 36 J11
Heathfield Park Dr CHDH RM6 41 R3
Heathfield Ri RSLP HA4 33 U5
Heathfield Rd ACT W3 48 B7
BMLY BR1 64 B12
BUSH WD23 22 G2
BXLYHS DA6 65 V2
HAYES BR2 76 E10
SAND/SEL CR2 74 H10
SEV TN13 90 F12
WAND/EARL SW18 61 Q4
WOKS/MYFD GU22 80 E8
WOT/HER KT12 70 G9
Heathfield South WHTN TW2 59 P5
Heathfield Sq WAND/EARL SW18 61 R5
Heathfield Ter CHSWK W4 48 C10
SWLY BR8 * 66 D14
WOOL/PLUM SE18 53 N11
Heathfield V SAND/SEL CR2 75 P13
Heath Gdns DART DA1 * 66 J6
TWK TW1 59 P6
Heathgate GLDGN NW11 37 P4
Heathgate Pl HAMP NW3 37 T9
Heath Gv PGE/AN SE20 63 N12
SUN TW16 58 B12
Heath Hurst Rd HAMP NW3 37 S9
Heathhurst Rd SAND/SEL CR2 74 J13
Heathland Rd STNW/STAM N16 38 J6
Heathlands KWD/TDW/WH KT20 84 K12
Heathlands Cl SUN TW16 58 C14
TWK TW1 59 P7
WOKN/KNAP GU21 80 C4
Heathlands Ct HSLWW TW4 58 G3
Heathlands Ri DART DA1 66 H5
Heathlands Wy HSLWW TW4 58 G3
Heath La BKHTH/KID SE3 51 V14
DART DA1 66 H6
Heathlee Rd BKHTH/KID SE3 64 B2
DART DA1 66 E4
Heathley End CHST BR7 65 L11
Heath Ldg BUSH WD23 * 23 M6
Heathman's Rd FUL/PGN SW6 49 M13
Heath Md WIM/MER SW19 60 K8
Heath Ms RPLY/SEND GU23 81 M13
Heath Park Dr BMLY BR1 76 G1
Heath Park Rd GPK RM2 42 G3
Heath Ridge Gn COB KT11 82 J3
Heath Ri HAYES BR2 76 C4
PUT/ROE SW15 60 K4
Heathrise RPLY/SEND GU23 81 M13
Heath Ri VW GU25 68 B2
Heath Rd BXLY DA5 66 C6
CHDH RM6 41 T5
CTHM CR3 86 H13
DART DA1 66 F4
HGDN/ICK UB10 45 U2
HRW HA1 35 L5
HSLW TW3 59 L2
LHD/OX KT22 83 L2
OXHEY WD19 22 F5
POTB/CUF EN6 14 D4
THHTH CR7 74 G1
TWK TW1 59 P6
VX/NE SW8 49 V14
WEY KT13 69 S10
WOKN/KNAP GU21 80 D5
Heathrow Cl WDR/YW UB7 45 M13
Heath's Cl EN EN1 15 T14
Heathside ESH/CLAY KT10 71 N8
HAMP NW3 37 R9
HSLWW TW4 58 H5
Heath Side STMC/STPC BR5 77 M6
Heathside WEY KT13 69 T10
Heathside Av BXLYHN DA7 53 U14
Heathside Cl ESH/CLAY KT10 71 N8
GNTH/NBYPK IG2 41 M3
NTHWD HA6 21 V10
Heathside Ct KWD/TDW/WH KT20 84 H13
Heathside Crs WOKS/MYFD GU22 80 D7
Heathside Gdns WOKS/MYFD GU22 80 E7
Heathside Park Rd WOKS/MYFD GU22 80 D8
Heathside Pl EPSOM KT18 84 K8
Heathside Rd NTHWD HA6 21 V9
WOKS/MYFD GU22 80 D8
Heathstan Rd SHB W12 48 G4
Heath St DART DA1 66 K5
HAMP NW3 37 Q8
The Heath CTHM CR3 86 G14
HNWL W7 * 47 N7
RAD WD7 12 E7
Heath Vw EFNCH N2 37 Q2
Heathview Av DART DA1 66 E4
Heath View Cl EFNCH N2 37 Q2
Heathview Crs DART DA1 66 G5
Heath View Dr ABYW SE2 53 T11
Heathview Gdns PUT/ROE SW15 60 J5
Heathview Rd THHTH CR7 74 E2
Heath Vls WAND/EARL SW18 * 61 Q6
WOOL/PLUM SE18 53 P10
Heathville Rd ARCH N19 38 C5
Heathwall St BTSEA SW11 61 T1
Heath Wy ERITH DA8 54 C13
IVER SL0 32 H14
RAD WD7 12 G4
Heathway BKHTH/KID SE3 52 C12
CROY/NA CR0 75 R8
CTHM CR3 94 G1
DAGW RM9 41 V10
EHSLY KT24 82 B14
NWDGN UB2 * 46 F9
WFD IG8 28 E9
Heathwood Gdns CHARL SE7 52 H10
SWLY BR8 66 C14
Heathwood Pde SWLY BR8 * 66 C14
Heathwood Wk BXLY DA5 66 E6
Heaton Av HARH RM3 30 H12
Heaton Cl CHING E4 27 U8
HARH RM3 30 J12
Heaton Grange Rd GPK RM2 30 F13
Heaton Rd MTCM CR4 61 U12
PECK SE15 63 M1
Heaton Wy HARH RM3 30 J12
Heaven Tree Cl IS N1 38 G10
Heaverham Rd BGR/WK TN15 91 P7
Heaver Rd BTSEA SW11 * 61 R1
Heavitree Cl WOOL/PLUM SE18 53 M10
Heavitree Rd WOOL/PLUM SE18 53 M10
Hebden Ter TOTM N17 26 J11
Hebdon Rd TOOT SW17 61 S8
Heber Rd CRICK NW2 36 K10
EDUL SE22 62 K4
Hebron Rd HMSMTH W6 48 H8
Hecham Cl WALTH E17 27 Q14
Heckfield Pl FUL/PGN SW6 6 E14
Heckford Cl WATW WD18 21 U4
Heckford St WAP E1W 51 P5
Hector St WOOL/PLUM SE18 * 53 N9
Heddington Gv HOLWY N7 38 D10
Heddon Cl ISLW TW7 59 Q2
Heddon Court Av EBAR EN4 25 T3
Heddon Court Pde EBAR EN4 * 25 U3
Heddon Rd EBAR EN4 25 T3
Heddon St CONDST W1S 4 A14
Hedge Hl ENC/FH EN2 15 R13
Hedge La PLMGR N13 26 G9
Hedgeley REDBR IG4 40 H2
Hedgemans Rd DAGW RM9 41 T12
Hedgemans Wy DAGW RM9 41 U11
Hedge Place Rd RDART DA2 67 T4
Hedgerley Ct WOKN/KNAP GU21 80 A7
Hedgerley Gdns GFD/PVL UB6 35 L14
Hedgerow CFSP/GDCR SL9 20 C11
Hedgerow La BAR EN5 24 H3
Hedgerow Wk CHES/WCR EN8 16 D4
Hedger's Gv HOM E9 * 39 Q11
Hedger St LBTH SE11 9 L7
Hedgewood Gdns CLAY IG5 40 J3
Hedgley St LEE/GVPK SE12 64 B3
Hedingham Cl IS N1 38 G12
Hedingham Rd BCTR RM8 41 R10
EMPK RM11 43 N6
Hedley Rd WHTN TW2 58 J5
Hedley Rw HBRY N5 38 H10
Hedworth Av CHES/WCR EN8 16 D7
Heenan Cl BARK IG11 41 L11
Heene Rd ENC/FH EN2 15 T14
Heidegger Crs BARN SW13 48 H12
Heigham Rd EHAM E6 40 G12
Heighton Gdns CROY/NA CR0 74 F10
Heights Cl BNSTD SM7 85 L6
RYNPK SW20 60 H12
The Heights BECK BR3 * 63 U12
CHARL SE7 52 E10
LOU IG10 17 T14
NTHLT UB5 34 J10
SEV TN13 * 90 E12
WEY KT13 * 69 S14
Heiron St WALW SE17 9 M12
Helby Rd CLAP SW4 62 B4
Helder Gv LEE/GVPK SE12 64 B5
Helder St SAND/SEL CR2 74 H11
Heldmann Cl HSLW TW3 59 M2
Helegan Cl ORP BR6 77 P9
Helena Cl EBAR EN4 14 F11
Helena Pl HACK E8 39 M13
Helena Rd EA W5 47 T3
PLSTW E13 40 B14
WALTH E17 39 S3
WLSDN NW10 36 H10
Helena Sq BERM/RHTH SE16 51 Q5
Helen Av EBED/NFELT TW14 58 D5
Helen Cl DART DA1 66 H5
E/WMO/HCT KT8 70 K2
EFNCH N2 37 Q1
Helen Rd EMPK RM11 42 K1
Helenslea Av GLDGN NW11 37 M6
Helen's Pl BETH E2 51 N1
Helen St WOOL/PLUM SE18 * 52 K9
Helford Cl RSLP HA4 34 A7
Helford Wy UPMR RM14 43 R4
Helgiford Gdns SUN TW16 58 A12
Helios Rd WLGTN SM6 73 U6
Helix Gdns BRXS/STRHM SW2 62 D4
Helix Rd BRXS/STRHM SW2 62 D4
Hellings St WAP E1W 51 L6
Helm Cl HOR/WEW KT19 84 A2
Helme Cl WIM/MER SW19 61 M10
Helmet Rw FSBYE EC1V 5 P7
Helmore Rd BARK IG11 41 P12
Helmsdale Cl ROM RM1 30 E12
YEAD UB4 * 46 G2
Helmsdale Rd ROM RM1 30 E12
STRHM/NOR SW16 62 A13
Helmsley Pl HACK E8 39 M12
Helmsley St HACK E8 39 M13
Helperby Rd WLSDN NW10 36 E12
Helsinki Sq BERM/RHTH SE16 51 R8
Helston Cl PIN HA5 22 H12
Helston Pl ABLGY WD5 11 M6
Helvellyn Cl EGH TW20 56 F12
Helvetia St CAT SE6 63 R7
Hemans St VX/NE SW8 8 D14
Hemans Street Est VX/NE SW8 8 D14
Hemery Rd GFD/PVL UB6 35 M10
Hemingford Cl NFNCH/WDSPK N12 25 R10
Hemingford Rd CHEAM SM3 72 J9
IS N1 4 H1
WAT WD17 11 L10
Heming Rd EDGW HA8 24 B11
Hemington Av FBAR/BDGN N11 25 T10
Hemlock Cl KWD/TDW/WH KT20 85 L13
Hemlock Rd SHB W12 48 F5
Hemmen La HYS/HAR UB3 46 B5
Hemming Cl HPTN TW12 58 J13
Hemmings Cl SCUP DA14 65 R7
Hemmingsmead HOR/WEW KT19 72 C11
Hemming St WCHPL E1 51 L2
Hemming Wy GSTN WD25 11 N9
Hemmingway Cl KTTN NW5 37 U9
Hemnall St EPP CM16 18 D5
Hempshaw Av BNSTD SM7 85 T6
Hempson Av DTCH/LGLY SL3 44 A8
Hempstead Cl BKHH IG9 28 C7
Hempstead Rd KGLGY WD4 10 G2
WALTH E17 39 V1
WAT WD17 22 C1
Hemp Wk WALW SE17 9 R7
Hemsby Rd CHSGTN KT9 71 V11
Hemstal Rd KIL/WHAMP NW6 37 N12
Hemsted Rd ERITH DA8 54 E13
Hemswell Dr CDALE/KGS NW9 24 E13
Hemsworth St IS N1 5 S3
Henbit Cl KWD/TDW/WH KT20 84 H9
Henbury Wy OXHEY WD19 22 F8
Henchman St SHB W12 48 F4
Hendale Av HDN NW4 36 G1
Henderson Cl EMPK RM11 42 H7
WLSDN NW10 36 C11
Henderson Dr DART DA1 67 N2
STJWD NW8 3 L7
Henderson Pl ABLGY WD5 11 M1
Henderson Rd BH/WHM TN16 88 E2
CROY/NA CR0 74 H4
ED N9 27 M6
FSTGT E7 40 E11
WAND/EARL SW18 61 S5
YEAD UB4 46 C1
Hendham Rd TOOT SW17 61 S7
Hendon Av FNCH N3 25 L14
Hendon Gdns CRW RM5 30 C11
Hendon Gv HOR/WEW KT19 72 A13
Hendon Hall Ct HDN NW4 * 36 K1
Hendon La FNCH N3 37 L1
Hendon Park Rw GLDGN NW11 * 37 M4
Hendon Rd ED N9 27 L7
Hendon Ter ASHF TW15 * 57 V11
Hendon Wy CRICK NW2 36 K5
STWL/WRAY TW19 57 P3
Hendon Wood La MLHL NW7 24 G6
Hendren Cl GFD/PVL UB6 35 M10
Hendre Rd STHWK SE1 9 T8
Hendrick Av BAL SW12 61 T4
Heneage Crs CROY/NA CR0 75 U14
Heneage La HDTCH EC3A 5 T12
Heneage St WCHPL E1 5 V9
Henfield Cl ARCH N19 38 A6
BXLY DA5 66 A4
Henfield Rd WIM/MER SW19 61 M13
Hengelo Gdns MTCM CR4 73 R2
Hengist Rd ERITH DA8 54 C12
LEE/GVPK SE12 64 D5
Hengist Wy HAYES BR2 75 V2
Hengrave Rd FSTH SE23 63 N5
Hengrove Ct BXLY DA5 65 U6
Hengrove Crs ASHF TW15 57 P8
Henley Av CHEAM SM3 73 L8
Henley Cl BERM/RHTH SE16 * 51 N7
GFD/PVL UB6 * 35 L14
ISLW TW7 47 P13
Henley Ct WOKS/MYFD GU22 80 E10
Henley Dr KUTN/CMB KT2 60 F12
STHWK SE1 9 V7
Henley Gdns CHDH RM6 41 U3
PIN HA5 34 D1
Henley Rd CAN/RD E16 52 H7
IL IG1 41 L9
UED N18 26 J9
WLSDN NW10 36 J13
Henley St BTSEA SW11 49 U14
Henley Wy FELT TW13 58 F10
Hennel Cl FSTH SE23 63 N8
Hennessy Ct WOKN/KNAP GU21 80 G3
Hennessy Rd ED N9 27 N7
Henniker Gdns EHAM E6 52 F1
Henniker Ms CHEL SW3 7 L11
Henniker Rd SRTFD E15 39 V10
Henningham Rd TOTM N17 26 H13
Henning St BTSEA SW11 49 S13
Henrietta Cl DEPT SE8 51 S11
Henrietta Ms BMSBY WC1N 4 F7
Henrietta Pl CAVSQ/HST W1G 3 U12
Henrietta St COVGDN WC2E 4 F13
SRTFD E15 39 U10
Henriques St WCHPL E1 51 L4
Henry Addlington Cl EHAM E6 52 K3
Henry Cl ENC/FH EN2 15 U12
Henry Cooper Wy ELTH/MOT SE9 64 F8
Henry Darlot Dr MLHL NW7 24 K10
Henry Dent Cl CMBW SE5 62 H1
Henry Dickens Ct NTGHL W11 48 K5
Henry Doulton Dr TOOT SW17 61 U9
Henry Jackson Rd PUT/ROE SW15 60 K1
Henry Macaulay Av KUTN/CMB KT2 59 T13
Henry Peters Dr TEDD TW11 59 N10
Henry Rd EBAR EN4 25 R3
EHAM E6 40 G14
FSBYPK N4 38 G6
Henry's Av WFD IG8 28 B10
Henryson Rd BROCKY SE4 63 S3
Henry St BMLY BR1 64 D13
Henry Tate Ms STRHM/NOR SW16 62 E10
Hensford Gdns SYD SE26 63 M9
Henshall St IS N1 38 H11
Henshawe Rd BCTR RM8 41 T8
Henshaw St WALW SE17 9 Q7
Henslowe Rd EDUL SE22 63 L3
Henslow Wy WOKN/KNAP GU21 80 H4
Henson Av CRICK NW2 36 J10
Henson Cl ORP BR6 76 K7
Henson Pl NTHLT UB5 34 E13
Henstridge Pl STJWD NW8 3 N3
Hensworth Rd ASHF TW15 57 P11
Henty Cl BTSEA SW11 7 P14
Henty Wk PUT/ROE SW15 60 H3
Henville Rd BMLY BR1 64 E13
Henwick Rd ELTH/MOT SE9 64 F1
Henwood Side WFD IG8 28 H11
Hepburn Gdns HAYES BR2 76 B6
Hepple Cl ISLW TW7 47 R14
Hepscott Rd HOM E9 39 S11
Hepworth Gdns BARK IG11 41 Q10
Hepworth Rd STRHM/NOR SW16 62 C12
Hepworth Wy WOT/HER KT12 70 B6
Heracles Cl LCOL/BKTW AL2 12 A2
Herald Gdns WLGTN SM6 73 V8
Heralds Pl LBTH SE11 9 L7
Herald St BETH E2 51 M2
Herbal Hl CLKNW EC1R 4 K8
Herbert Crs KTBR SW1X 7 R5
Herbert Gdns CHDH RM6 41 T5
CHSWK W4 48 B11
WLSDN NW10 36 H14
Herbert Ms BRXS/STRHM SW2 62 E4
Herbert Pl ISLW TW7 47 M14
WOOL/PLUM SE18 52 K11
Herbert Rd BXLYHN DA7 53 U14
CDALE/KGS NW9 36 G4
EMPK RM11 43 L5
FBAR/BDGN N11 26 C12
GDMY/SEVK IG3 41 N7
HAYES BR2 76 F3
KUT/HW KT1 71 V1
MNPK E12 40 G9
SEVS/STOTM N15 38 K3
STHL UB1 46 H6
SWLY BR8 66 H11
WALTH E17 39 R5
WIM/MER SW19 61 M12
WOOL/PLUM SE18 52 K12
Herbert St KTTN NW5 37 U11
PLSTW E13 40 C14
Herbrand St BMSBY WC1N 4 E7
Hercies Rd HGDN/ICK UB10 33 R11
Hercules Pl HOLWY N7 38 C8
Hercules Rd STHWK SE1 8 H6
Hercules St HOLWY N7 38 C8
Hereford Av EBAR EN4 25 T6
Hereford Cl EPSOM KT18 84 D3
STA TW18 57 M13
Hereford Gdns IL IG1 40 G5
PIN HA5 34 G3
WHTN TW2 * 59 L6
Hereford Ms BAY/PAD W2 2 F11
Hereford Pl NWCR SE14 * 51 R12
Hereford Retreat PECK SE15 51 L12
Hereford Rd ACT W3 48 C5
BAY/PAD W2 2 F12
BOW E3 39 R14
EA W5 47 S8
FELT TW13 58 E6
WAN E11 40 D3
Hereford Sq SKENS SW7 6 K8
Hereford St BETH E2 51 L2
Hereford Wy CHSGTN KT9 71 S10
Herent Dr CLAY IG5 40 H1
Heretage Cl BRXN/ST SW9 62 F1
Hereward Av PUR/KEN CR8 74 E14
Hereward Cl WAB EN9 16 J6
Hereward Gdns PLMGR N13 26 E10
Hereward Gn LOU IG10 18 A13
Hereward Rd TOOT SW17 61 T9
Herga Ct WAT WD17 11 N14
Herga Rd KTN/HRWW/WS HA3 35 P2
Heriot Av CHING E4 27 S7
Heriot Rd CHERT KT16 69 L5
HDN NW4 36 J3
Heriots Cl STAN HA7 23 Q9
Heritage Cl SUN TW16 58 C13
UX/CGN UB8 45 N2
Heritage Ct EGH TW20 56 D10
Heritage Hl HAYES BR2 76 E10
Heritage Pl WAND/EARL SW18 * 61 R4
Heritage Vw HRW HA1 35 P8
Heritage Wk RKW/CH/CXG WD3 * 20 J1
Herkomer Cl BUSH WD23 22 K4
Herkomer Rd BUSH WD23 22 J3
Herlwyn Av RSLP HA4 34 A8
Herlwyn Gdns TOOT SW17 61 T9
Herm Cl ISLW TW7 47 L12
Hermes Cl MV/WKIL W9 2 E8
Hermes St IS N1 4 J4
Hermes Wy WLGTN SM6 74 B12
Hermiston Av CEND/HSY/T N8 38 C3
Hermitage Cl ABYW SE2 53 S8
DTCH/LGLY SL3 44 A8
ENC/FH EN2 15 R14
ESH/CLAY KT10 71 Q11
RCHPK/HAM TW10 * 59 T3
SHPTN TW17 69 S2
SWFD E18 40 B2
Hermitage Cottages STAN HA7 * 23 N10
Hermitage Ct POTB/CUF EN6 14 E7
Hermitage Gdns CRICK NW2 37 N8
NRWD SE19 62 G12
Hermitage La CRICK NW2 37 N8
CROY/NA CR0 74 K5
STRHM/NOR SW16 62 D12
UED N18 26 H10
Hermitage Rd FSBYPK N4 38 G5
NRWD SE19 62 H11
PUR/KEN CR8 86 G6
Hermitage Rw HACK E8 * 39 L10
Hermitage St BAY/PAD W2 3 L10
The Hermitage BARN SW13 * 48 F13
FELT TW13 * 58 B8
FSTH SE23 63 N6
KUT/HW KT1 * 71 T2
LEW SE13 * 51 U14
RCHPK/HAM TW10 59 T3
UX/CGN UB8 * 33 P11
Hermitage Wk SWFD E18 40 B2
Hermitage Wall WAP E1W 51 L6
Hermitage Wy STAN HA7 23 Q13
Hermit Pl KIL/WHAMP NW6 2 G2
Hermit Rd CAN/RD E16 52 B3
Hermit St FSBYE EC1V 5 L5
Hermon Gv HYS/HAR UB3 46 C6
Hermon Hl WAN E11 40 C2
Herndon Cl EGH TW20 56 E9
Herndon Rd WAND/EARL SW18 61 Q3
Herne Cl HYS/HAR UB3 46 B4
WLSDN NW10 36 D10
Herne Ct BUSH WD23 * 23 L6
Herne Hl HNHL SE24 62 G3
Herne Hill Rd HNHL SE24 62 G2
Herne Ms UED N18 27 L9
Herne Pl HNHL SE24 62 F3
Herne Rd BUSH WD23 22 K4
SURB KT6 71 T7
Heron Cl BKHH IG9 28 C6
RKW/CH/CXG WD3 21 P7
UX/CGN UB8 33 P11
WALTH E17 27 R14
WLSDN NW10 36 E11
Heron Ct HAYES BR2 76 E2
KUT/HW KT1 * 71 U1
Heron Crs SCUP DA14 65 N9
Heron Dl ADL/WDHM KT15 69 P10
Herondale SAND/SEL CR2 75 P13
Herondale Av WAND/EARL SW18 61 R6
Heron Dr DTCH/LGLY SL3 44 F9
FSBYPK N4 38 G7
Heronfield POTB/CUF EN6 14 E4
Heron Flight Av HCH RM12 42 G12
Herongate Rd CHES/WCR EN8 16 E1
MNPK E12 40 E7
SWLY BR8 66 E11
Heron Hl BELV DA17 53 V9
Heron Md PEND EN3 16 G12
Heron Ms IL IG1 40 K7
Heron Pl DEN/HRF UB9 21 L11
Heron Quays POP/IOD E14 51 S6
Heron Rd CROY/NA CR0 * 74 J6
HNHL SE24 62 G2
TWK TW1 59 R2
The Heronry WOT/HER KT12 70 C11
Herons Cft WEY KT13 69 U11
Heronsforde WEA W13 47 S4
Heronsgate EDGW HA8 24 A10
Heronsgate Rd RKW/CH/CXG WD3 20 F4
Heronslea GSTN WD25 11 Q10
Herons Lea HGT N6 * 37 T4
Heronslea Dr STAN HA7 23 U10
Herons Pl ISLW TW7 59 R1
Herons Ri EBAR EN4 25 S2
Heron Wk NTHWD HA6 22 A9
Heron Wy EBED/NFELT TW14 58 C2
UPMR RM14 43 S6
WTHK RM20 55 V10
Herrick Rd HBRY N5 38 G8
Herrick St WEST SW1P 8 D8
Herries St NKENS W10 2 B4
Herringham Rd CHARL SE7 52 E8
Herrings La CHERT KT16 69 L4
Herrongate Cl EN EN1 15 V14
Hersant Cl WLSDN NW10 36 G13
Herschell Rd FSTH SE23 63 P5
Hersham Centre WOT/HER KT12 * 70 F10
Hersham Cl PUT/ROE SW15 60 G5
Hersham Gdns WOT/HER KT12 70 D9
Hersham Pl WOT/HER KT12 * 70 F10
Hersham Rd WOT/HER KT12 70 D7
Hershell Ct MORT/ESHN SW14 * 60 B2
Hertford Av MORT/ESHN SW14 60 D3
Hertford Cl EBAR EN4 25 R1
Hertford Ct STAN HA7 * 23 T12
Hertford End Ct NTHWD HA6 * 22 A10
Hertford Pl FITZ W1T 4 B8
Hertford Rd BARK IG11 40 J12
EBAR EN4 25 Q1
ED N9 27 M6
EFNCH N2 37 S1
GNTH/NBYPK IG2 41 N4
IS N1 5 T1
IS N1 38 J12
PEND EN3 16 C14
Hertford Road High St PEND EN3 27 N3
Hertford St MYFR/PICC W1J 7 U2
Hertford Wy MTCM CR4 74 C2

Hertslet Rd HOLWY N7 38 D8
Hertsmere Rd POP/IOD E14 51 S6
Hertswood Ct BAR EN5 * 25 L2
Hervey Cl FNCH N3 25 N13
Hervey Park Rd WALTH E17 39 Q2
Hesa Rd HYS/HAR UB3 46 C4
Hesewall Cl CLAP SW4 50 A14
Hesiers Hl WARL CR6 88 A7
Hesiers Rd WARL CR6 88 A6
Hesketh Av RDART DA2 67 P6
Hesketh Pl NTGHL W11 2 A14
Hesketh Rd FSTGT E7 40 C8
Heslop Rd BAL SW12 61 T6
Hesper Ms ECT SW5 6 G9
Hesperus Crs POP/IOD E14 51 T9
Hessel Rd WEA W13 47 Q7
Hessel St WCHPL E1 51 M4
Hesselyn Dr RAIN RM13 42 H12
Hessle Gv EW KT17 84 F1
Hestercombe Av FUL/PGN SW6 49 L14
Hesterman Wy CROY/NA CR0 74 C6
Hester Rd BTSEA SW11 7 N14
UED N18 27 L10
Hester Ter RCH/KEW TW9 60 A1
Heston Av HEST TW5 46 G12
Heston Grange La HEST TW5 46 H11
Heston Rd HEST TW5 46 J12
Heston St DEPT SE8 51 S13
Heswell Gn OXHEY WD19 * 22 C8
Hetherington Rd CLAP SW4 62 C2
SHPTN TW17 57 U14
Hetherington Wy HGDN/ICK UB10 33 Q9
Hethersett Cl REIG RH2 93 R7
Hetley Rd SHB W12 48 H6
Heton Gdns HDN NW4 36 G2
Hevelius Cl GNWCH SE10 52 B10
Hever Av BGR/WK TN15 79 S12
Hever Cft ELTH/MOT SE9 64 J9
Hever Gdns BMLY BR1 64 J14
Heverham Rd WOOL/PLUM SE18 53 N9
Hever Rd BGR/WK TN15 79 S11
Heversham Rd BXLYHN DA7 54 A14
Hever Wood Rd BGR/WK TN15 79 T11
Hevingham Dr CHDH RM6 41 S4
Hewens Rd HGDN/ICK UB10 45 U1
Hewer St NKENS W10 48 K3
Hewers Wy KWD/TDW/WH KT20 84 H10
Hewett Cl STAN HA7 23 R9
Hewett Pl SWLY BR8 78 D2
Hewetts Quay BARK IG11 40 K13
Hewett St SDTCH EC2A 5 T8
Hewins Cl WAB EN9 17 L6
Hewish Rd UED N18 26 J9
Hewison St BOW E3 39 R14
Hewitt Av WDGN N22 26 F14
Hewitt Cl CROY/NA CR0 75 S8
Hewitt Rd CEND/HSY/T N8 38 E3
Hewitts Rd ORP BR6 77 V12
Hewlett Rd BOW E3 39 Q14
The Hexagon HGT N6 37 T6
Hexal Rd CAT SE6 64 A8
Hexham Gdns ISLW TW7 47 Q12
Hexham Rd BAR EN5 25 P2
MRDN SM4 73 P6
WNWD SE27 62 G7
Hextalls La REDH RH1 94 H4
Heybourne Rd TOTM N17 27 M12
Heybridge Av STRHM/NOR SW16 62 D11
Heybridge Dr BARK/HLT IG6 41 M1
Heybridge Wy LEY E10 39 R6
Heyford Av RYNPK SW20 73 M1
VX/NE SW8 8 F13
Heyford End LCOL/BKTW AL2 12 B1
Heyford Rd MTCM CR4 61 S14
RAD WD7 12 D11
Heyford Ter VX/NE SW8 8 F13
Heygate Est WALW SE17 9 P7
Heygate St WALW SE17 9 N8
Heymede LHD/OX KT22 83 S13
Heynes Rd BCTR RM8 41 S9
Heysham Dr OXHEY WD19 22 E10
Heysham La HAMP NW3 37 Q8
Heysham Rd SEVS/STOTM N15 38 H4
Heythorp St WAND/EARL SW18 61 M7
Heythrop Dr HGDN/ICK UB10 33 R9
Heywood Av CDALE/KGS NW9 24 E13
Heyworth Rd CLPT E5 39 M9
SRTFD E15 40 B10
Hibbert Av WATN WD24 11 R12
Hibbert Rd KTN/HRWW/WS HA3 23 P14
WALTH E17 39 R5
Hibbert St BTSEA SW11 61 Q1
Hibberts Wy CFSP/GDCR SL9 32 C1
Hibbs Cl SWLY BR8 66 D14
Hibernia Gdns HSLW TW3 58 J3
Hibernia Rd HSLW TW3 58 J2
Hichisson Rd PECK SE15 63 N3
Hickin Cl CHARL SE7 52 F9
Hickin St POP/IOD E14 51 U8
Hickling Rd IL IG1 40 K10
Hickman Av CHING E4 27 U11
Hickman Cl CAN/RD E16 52 F3
Hickman Rd CHDH RM6 41 S5
Hickmans Cl GDST RH9 95 N8
Hickory Cl ED N9 27 L5
Hicks Av GFD/PVL UB6 47 M1
Hicks Cl BTSEA SW11 61 S1
Hicks St DEPT SE8 51 Q10
Hidcote Cl WOKS/MYFD GU22 80 F6
Hidcote Gdns RYNPK SW20 72 H1
The Hideaway ABLGY WD5 11 M5
Hide Pl WEST SW1P 8 C8
Hide Rd HRW HA1 35 M2
Higgins Rd CHESW EN7 15 T1
High Acres ABLGY WD5 10 K6
Higham Hill Rd WALTH E17 27 Q14
Higham Ms NTHLT UB5 46 H2
Higham Pl WALTH E17 39 Q1
Higham Rd TOTM N17 38 H1
WFD IG8 28 C11
Highams Hill Cottages WARL CR6 * 88 C2
Higham Station Av CHING E4 27 T11
The Highams WALTH E17 * 27 U13
Higham St WALTH E17 39 Q1
Highbank Pl WAND/EARL SW18 * 61 P6
Highbanks Cl WELL DA16 53 Q12
Highbanks Rd PIN HA5 22 K11
Highbank Wy CEND/HSY/T N8 38 E4
Highbarrow Rd CROY/NA CR0 74 K6
High Beech SAND/SEL CR2 74 J12
High Beeches BNSTD SM7 84 K4
CFSP/GDCR SL9 32 B6
ORP BR6 77 Q11
SCUP DA14 65 U10
WEY KT13 70 A11
High Beeches Cl PUR/KEN CR8 74 B14
High Beech Rd LOU IG10 28 G2
Highbridge Rd BARK IG11 40 K13
Highbridge St WAB EN9 16 H7
Highbrook Rd BKHTH/KID SE3 64 F1
High Broom Crs WWKM BR4 75 T5
Highbury Av THHTH CR7 62 E14
Highbury Cl NWMAL KT3 72 C2
WWKM BR4 75 T7
Highbury Cnr HBRY N5 38 F11
Highbury Crs HBRY N5 38 F10
Highbury Est HBRY N5 38 G10
Highbury Gdns GDMY/SEVK IG3 41 N7
Highbury Gra HBRY N5 38 G9
Highbury Gv HBRY N5 38 F10
Highbury Hl HBRY N5 38 F9
Highbury New Pk HBRY N5 38 G10
Highbury Pk HBRY N5 38 F9
Highbury Pl HBRY N5 38 F11
Highbury Qd HBRY N5 38 G8
Highbury Rd WIM/MER SW19 61 L10
Highbury Station Pde HBRY N5 * 38 F11
Highbury Station Rd IS N1 * 38 E11
Highbury Ter HBRY N5 38 F10
Highbury Terrace Ms HBRY N5 38 F10
High Canons BORE WD6 13 N11
High Cedar Dr RYNPK SW20 60 H12
Highclere Cl PUR/KEN CR8 86 G5
Highclere Rd NWMAL KT3 72 D1
Highclere St SYD SE26 63 Q9
Highcliffe Dr PUT/ROE SW15 60 F4
Highcliffe Gdns REDBR IG4 40 G3
High Cl RKW/CH/CXG WD3 21 N3
Highcombe CHARL SE7 52 D11
Highcombe Cl ELTH/MOT SE9 64 G7
High Coombe Pl KUTN/CMB KT2 60 D12
Highcroft CDALE/KGS NW9 36 E3
Highcroft Av ALP/SUD HA0 35 V12
Highcroft Ct GT/LBKH KT23 82 J13
Highcroft Gdns GLDGN NW11 37 M4
Highcroft Rd ARCH N19 38 C5
High Cross GSTN WD25 12 B11
High Cross Rd TOTM N17 39 L1
Highcross Wy PUT/ROE SW15 60 G6
Highdaun Dr STRHM/NOR SW16 74 D2
Highdown WPK KT4 72 E7
High Down La BELMT SM2 85 Q1
Highdown Rd PUT/ROE SW15 60 H4
High Dr CTHM CR3 87 R12
LHD/OX KT22 83 M4
NWMAL KT3 60 C13
High Elms CHIG IG7 29 N9
UPMR RM14 43 S6
WFD IG8 28 C10
High Elms Cl NTHWD HA6 21 U11
High Elms La GSTN WD25 11 P5
High Elms Rd ORP BR6 77 L13
Higher Dr BNSTD SM7 84 K3
PUR/KEN CR8 86 E3
Higher Gn EW KT17 84 G3
Highfield BNSTD SM7 85 S7
CSTG HP8 20 B7
KGLGY WD4 10 E2
OXHEY WD19 22 H8
Highfield Av CDALE/KGS NW9 36 C3
ERITH DA8 54 C11
GFD/PVL UB6 35 N10
GLDGN NW11 36 K5
ORP BR6 77 P11
PIN HA5 34 H3
WBLY HA9 35 U8
Highfield Cl BF/WBF KT14 81 L3
CDALE/KGS NW9 36 C3
CRW RM5 30 C11
LEW SE13 63 V5
LHD/OX KT22 83 M1
NTHWD HA6 22 A13
SURB KT6 71 S6
WDGN N22 26 E13
Highfield Cottages RDART DA2 * 66 H11
Highfield Ct EGH TW20 56 A11
STHGT/OAK N14 26 A4
Highfield Crs HCH RM12 43 M7
NTHWD HA6 22 A13
Highfield Dr HAYES BR2 76 A2
HGDN/ICK UB10 33 Q8
HOR/WEW KT19 72 F12
WWKM BR4 75 T8
Highfield Gdns EPP CM16 18 C5
GLDGN NW11 37 L4
Highfield Hl NRWD SE19 62 H12
Highfield Link CRW RM5 30 C11
Highfield Pl EPP CM16 18 C5
Highfield Rd ACT W3 48 C3
BF/WBF KT14 81 L3
BGR/WK TN15 91 L6
BH/WHM TN16 88 E7
BMLY BR1 76 H2
BRYLDS KT5 72 C5
BUSH WD23 22 G3
BXLYHS DA6 65 V3
CHERT KT16 69 L6
CHST BR7 77 P1
CRW RM5 30 C11
CTHM CR3 87 L12
DART DA1 66 K5
EGH TW20 56 B11
FELT TW13 58 C6
GLDGN NW11 * 37 L4
HCH RM12 43 M7
ISLW TW7 47 P13
NTHWD HA6 22 A13
PUR/KEN CR8 74 D14
SUN TW16 70 B3
SUT SM1 73 S10
WCHMH N21 26 F7
WFD IG8 28 G12
WOT/HER KT12 70 C6
Highfield Rd North DART DA1 66 K4
Highfield Rd South DART DA1 66 K6
Highfields ASHTD KT21 83 T9
KGLGY WD4 * 10 E2
LHD/OX KT22 83 M14
POTB/CUF EN6 15 N2
RAD WD7 12 D9
Highfields Gv HGT N6 37 U6
Highfields Rd EDEN TN8 97 L14
Highfield Wy POTB/CUF EN6 14 D6
RKW/CH/CXG WD3 21 L4
High Firs RAD WD7 12 E9
SWLY BR8 78 E2
High Foleys ESH/CLAY KT10 71 R12
High Garth ESH/CLAY KT10 71 L11
Highgate Av HGT N6 37 V5
Highgate Cl HGT N6 37 U5
Highgate Edge EFNCH N2 * 37 S3
Highgate High St HGT N6 37 U6
Highgate Hl ARCH N19 37 V6
Highgate Rd KTTN NW5 37 U8
Highgate Spinney CEND/HSY/T N8 * 38 B4
Highgate Wk FSTH SE23 63 N7
Highgate West Hl HGT N6 37 U6
High Gv BMLY BR1 64 E13
Highgrove BRWN CM15 31 V4
High Gv WOOL/PLUM SE18 53 M12
Highgrove Cl CHST BR7 64 G13
FBAR/BDGN N11 25 U10
Highgrove Ms CAR SM5 73 S8
Highgrove Rd BCTR RM8 41 S10
Highgrove Wy RSLP HA4 34 C5
High Hill Ferry CLPT E5 39 M6
High Hill Rd WARL CR6 87 V4
High Holborn HHOL WC1V 4 F11
Highland Av DAGE RM10 42 C8
HNWL W7 47 N4
LOU IG10 28 H4
Highland Cottages WLGTN SM6 * 73 V9
Highland Cft BECK BR3 63 T11
Highland Dr BUSH WD23 22 K5
Highland Pk FELT TW13 58 B9
Highland Rd BMLY BR1 64 B13
BXLYHS DA6 66 A3
NRWD SE19 62 J11
NTHWD HA6 22 C14
PUR/KEN CR8 86 E4
RSEV TN14 90 B1
Highlands OXHEY WD19 22 E6
Highlands Av ACT W3 48 C5
LHD/OX KT22 83 S12
WCHMH N21 26 D3
Highlands Cl CFSP/GDCR SL9 20 D12
HSLW TW3 46 K13
LHD/OX KT22 83 R12
Highlands End CFSP/GDCR SL9 20 D12
Highlands Gdns IL IG1 40 H6
Highlands Hl SWLY BR8 66 G14
Highlands La CFSP/GDCR SL9 20 D11
WOKS/MYFD GU22 80 C12
Highlands Pk BGR/WK TN15 91 L11
LHD/OX KT22 83 T13
Highlands Rd BAR EN5 25 N3
LHD/OX KT22 83 S12
REIG RH2 93 R9
STMC/STPC BR5 77 R5
The Highlands BAR EN5 25 N3
EDGW HA8 24 B14
POTB/CUF EN6 14 E5
RKW/CH/CXG WD3 21 M5
Highland Ter LEW SE13 * 63 T1
High La CTHM CR3 87 R9
HNWL W7 47 M4
Highlea Cl CDALE/KGS NW9 24 E13
High Level Dr SYD SE26 63 L9
Highlever Rd NKENS W10 48 J3
High Limes NRWD SE19 * 62 J11
High Md CHIG IG7 29 L7
HRW HA1 35 N3
Highmead WOOL/PLUM SE18 53 P12
High Md WWKM BR4 75 V7
Highmead Crs ALP/SUD HA0 35 V12
High Meadow Cl PIN HA5 34 D2
High Meadow Crs CDALE/KGS NW9 36 D3
High Meadow Pl CHERT KT16 68 K4
High Mdw CHIG IG7 29 M10
High Meads Rd CAN/RD E16 52 F4
Highmore Rd BKHTH/KID SE3 52 A12
High Mt HDN NW4 * 36 G4
High Oaks ENC/FH EN2 15 P12
The High Pde STRHM/NOR SW16 * 62 C8
High Park Rd RCH/KEW TW9 48 A13
High Pth WIM/MER SW19 61 P13
High Pine Cl WEY KT13 69 U10
High Pines WARL CR6 87 N9
High Point ELTH/MOT SE9 64 K8
Highpoint WEY KT13 69 S10
High Rdg MUSWH N10 * 25 V13
POTB/CUF EN6 15 N1
Highridge Cl EPSOM KT18 * 84 E5
Highridge Pl ENC/FH EN2 * 15 P12
High Rd BF/WBF KT14 81 R3
BKHH IG9 28 D7
BUSH WD23 23 M6
CHDH RM6 41 V4
CHIG IG7 28 K8
COUL/CHIP CR5 85 S14
EFNCH N2 25 R14
EPP CM16 18 A7
EPP CM16 19 M1
FBAR/BDGN N11 25 V10
GDMY/SEVK IG3 41 Q6
GSTN WD25 11 N7
KTN/HRWW/WS HA3 23 N13
LEY E10 39 T4
LOU IG10 28 G1
NFNCH/WDSPK N12 25 Q12
RDART DA2 66 J8
SEVS/STOTM N15 38 K3
TRDG/WHET N20 25 Q5
UX/CGN UB8 45 N3
WBLY HA9 35 U10
WDGN N22 26 D12
WLSDN NW10 36 G11
High Rd Eastcote PIN HA5 34 E2
High Rd Ickenham HGDN/ICK UB10 33 U8
High Rd Leyton LEY E10 39 U8
High Rd Leytonstone WAN E11 40 A8
High Rd Woodford Gn WFD IG8 28 C10
Highshore Rd PECK SE15 50 K14
High Silver LOU IG10 28 F2
High St IVER SL0 44 K4
High Standing CTHM CR3 94 G1
Highstead Crs ERITH DA8 54 E13
Highstone Av WAN E11 40 C4
High St ABLGY WD5 11 M4
ACT W3 48 C6
ADL/WDHM KT15 69 M9
BAR EN5 25 M2
BARK/HLT IG6 29 L14
BECK BR3 63 S14
BGR/WK TN15 91 M11
BH/WHM TN16 89 S14
BH/WHM TN16 97 L3
BMLY BR1 76 C1
BNSTD SM7 85 N5
BORE WD6 23 T4
BTFD TW8 47 U11
BUSH WD23 22 J4
CAR SM5 73 T10
CEND/HSY/T N8 38 C2
CFSP/GDCR SL9 20 C13
CHEAM SM3 73 L11
CHES/WCR EN8 16 D7
COB KT11 82 D5
CROY/NA CR0 74 G8
CSTG HP8 20 A8
CTHM CR3 86 J13
DART DA1 67 L5
DEN/HRF UB9 21 N14
DTCH/LGLY SL3 44 G12
E/WMO/HCT KT8 70 J2
EA W5 47 T5
EGH TW20 56 E10
EPP CM16 18 D5
ESH/CLAY KT10 70 K10
EW KT17 72 G13
EYN DA4 79 L7
FBAR/BDGN N11 25 V10
FELT TW13 58 C7
GDST RH9 95 N7
HCH RM12 42 K6
HEST TW5 46 D12
HOR/WEW KT19 84 D3
HPTN TW12 58 K13
HRW HA1 35 N7
HSLW TW3 58 K1
HYS/HAR UB3 45 V11
IVER SL0 44 K4
KGLGY WD4 10 G3
KTN/HRWW/WS HA3 35 N1
KUT/HW KT1 59 S13
KUT/HW KT1 71 T1
KWD/TDW/WH KT20 84 J13
LHD/OX KT22 83 M3
MLHL NW7 24 H10
NTHWD HA6 22 B13
NWMAL KT3 72 E2
ORP BR6 77 L10
ORP BR6 77 R5
ORP BR6 88 J1
OXTED RH8 95 V6
OXTED RH8 96 D4
PGE/AN SE20 63 N12
PIN HA5 34 G1
PLSTW E13 40 C14
POTB/CUF EN6 14 D7
PUR RM19 55 N10
PUR/KEN CR8 86 E1
RDART DA2 67 V2
REDH RH1 94 D10
REIG RH2 93 N10
RKW/CH/CXG WD3 21 Q6
ROM RM1 42 E3
RPLY/SEND GU23 81 N11
RSEV TN14 78 F14
RSEV TN14 90 G6
RSLP HA4 34 A6
SCUP DA14 65 Q9
SEV TN13 90 C12
SHPTN TW17 69 U4
SNWD SE25 74 K2
SOCK/AV RM15 55 Q6
SRTFD E15 39 V12
STA TW18 56 K9
STHGT/OAK N14 26 B6
STMC/STPC BR5 77 S2
STWL/WRAY TW19 57 P4
SUT SM1 73 P11
SWLY BR8 78 E1
TEDD TW11 59 Q10
THDIT KT7 71 Q5
THHTH CR7 74 G2
UX/CGN UB8 33 N12
UX/CGN UB8 45 N3
WALTH E17 39 R2
WAN E11 40 D4
WAT WD17 22 E2
WBLY HA9 35 V9
WDR/YW UB7 45 P11
WEY KT13 69 S9
WHTN TW2 59 L5
WIM/MER SW19 60 K10
WOKN/KNAP GU21 80 A6
WOT/HER KT12 70 C6
WWKM BR4 75 T6
High St Collier's Wd WIM/MER SW19 61 R12
High St Harlesden WLSDN NW10 36 F14
High St Harlington HTHAIR TW6 45 V13
High Street Ms WIM/MER SW19 61 L10
High St North MNPK E12 40 G11
High St South EHAM E6 52 H1
High Timber St BLKFR EC4V 5 N13
High Tor Cl BMLY BR1 64 D12
High Tree Cl ADL/WDHM KT15 69 L10
High Trees BRXS/STRHM SW2 62 E6
CROY/NA CR0 75 Q6
EBAR EN4 25 S3
RDART DA2 67 P4
High Trees Cl CTHM CR3 86 K12
High Trees Rd REIG RH2 93 R11
High Vw BELMT SM2 85 M1
CSTG HP8 20 B7
PIN HA5 34 E2
RKW/CH/CXG WD3 21 L2
WATW WD18 22 B4
Highview CTHM CR3 86 J14
Highview Av EDGW HA8 24 C9
High View Av WLGTN SM6 74 D10
High View Cl LOU IG10 28 E3
NRWD SE19 62 K14
Highview Cl POTB/CUF EN6 14 E7
High View Ct REIG RH2 * 93 R10
Highview Gdns EDGW HA8 24 C10
FBAR/BDGN N11 26 A10
FNCH N3 37 L1
POTB/CUF EN6 14 E7
UPMR RM14 43 P7
High View Rd NRWD SE19 62 H11
SWFD E18 28 B14
Highview Rd SCUP DA14 65 R9
WEA W13 47 Q4
Highview Ter DART DA1 * 66 K3
The Highway BELMT SM2 73 Q13
ORP BR6 77 R10
STAN HA7 23 P13
WCHPL E1 51 L5
Highwold COUL/CHIP CR5 85 U8
Highwood Av BUSH WD23 11 T13
NFNCH/WDSPK N12 25 Q9
Highwood Cl BRW CM14 31 V5
FSTH SE23 63 L6
ORP BR6 77 L7
PUR/KEN CR8 86 G7
Highwood Dr ORP BR6 77 L7
Highwood Gdns CLAY IG5 40 H3
Highwood Gv MLHL NW7 24 D10
Highwood Hl MLHL NW7 24 F8
Highwood La LOU IG10 28 K4
Highwood Rd ARCH N19 38 C8
Highwoods CTHM CR3 94 J1
LHD/OX KT22 83 S11
High Worple RYLN/HDSTN HA2 34 G5
Highworth Rd FBAR/BDGN N11 26 B11
Highworth St CAMTN NW1 * 3 P9
Hilary Av MTCM CR4 73 U1
Hilary Cl ERITH DA8 54 B13
FUL/PGN SW6 * 6 G13
HCH RM12 42 K10
Hilary Rd SHB W12 48 F5
Hilberry Ct BUSH WD23 * 22 K5
Hilbert Rd CHEAM SM3 72 K9
Hilborough Cl WIM/MER SW19 61 Q12
Hilborough Rd HACK E8 38 K12
Hilborough Wy ORP BR6 77 M10
Hilda Lockert Wk BRXN/ST SW9 50 F14
Hilda May Av SWLY BR8 78 E1
Hilda Rd CAN/RD E16 52 A2
EHAM E6 40 F12
Hilda Ter BRXN/ST SW9 * 50 E14
Hilda Vale Rd ORP BR6 76 J9
Hildenborough Gdns BMLY BR1 64 A11
Hilden Dr ERITH DA8 54 H12
Hildenlea Pl HAYES BR2 64 A14
Hildenley Cl REDH RH1 94 B4
The Hilders ASHTD KT21 84 B7
Hildreth St BAL SW12 61 V6
Hildyard Rd FUL/PGN SW6 6 F11
Hiley Rd WLSDN NW10 48 J1
Hilfield La GSTN WD25 11 V13
GSTN WD25 23 M1
Hilgrove Rd KIL/WHAMP NW6 37 Q12
Hiliary Gdns STAN HA7 23 S14
Hiljon Crs CFSP/GDCR SL9 20 C13
Hillars Heath Rd COUL/CHIP CR5 86 C5
Hillary Crs WOT/HER KT12 70 E6
Hillary Dr ISLW TW7 59 P2
Hillary Ri BAR EN5 25 N2
Hillary Rd DTCH/LGLY SL3 44 C8
NWDGN UB2 46 J8
Hillbarn SAND/SEL CR2 86 J1
Hillbeck Cl PECK SE15 51 N12
Hillbeck Wy GFD/PVL UB6 35 M13
Hillborne Cl HYS/HAR UB3 46 C10
Hillborough Cl WIM/MER SW19 * 61 Q12
Hillbrook Gdns WEY KT13 69 S12
Hillbrook Rd TOOT SW17 61 T8
Hill Brow BMLY BR1 64 F13
DART DA1 66 F4
Hillbrow NWMAL KT3 72 F1
Hillbrow Cl BXLY DA5 66 D9
Hillbrow Rd BMLY BR1 64 A12
ESH/CLAY KT10 71 L9
Hillbury Av KTN/HRWW/WS HA3 35 R3
Hillbury Cl WARL CR6 87 M8
Hillbury Gdns WARL CR6 87 N8
Hillbury Rd TOOT SW17 61 V8
WARL CR6 87 L7
Hill Cl BAR EN5 24 J3
CHST BR7 64 K10
COB KT11 82 J2
CRICK NW2 36 H8
GLDGN NW11 37 N4
HRW HA1 35 N8
PUR/KEN CR8 86 G3
STAN HA7 23 R9
WOKN/KNAP GU21 80 B6
Hillcote Av STRHM/NOR SW16 62 E12
Hillcourt Av NFNCH/WDSPK N12 25 P11
Hillcourt Rd EDUL SE22 63 M4
Hill Crs BRYLDS KT5 71 V3
BXLY DA5 66 C6
EMPK RM11 42 J4
HRW HA1 35 Q3
TRDG/WHET N20 25 P7
WPK KT4 72 J7
Hill Crest BFN/LL DA15 65 Q5
POTB/CUF EN6 14 E8
SEV TN13 90 G12
SURB KT6 * 71 U5
Hillcrest EDEN TN8 97 R14
HGT N6 37 U5
HNHL SE24 * 62 H2
KWD/TDW/WH KT20 * 92 B7
WCHMH N21 26 F5
WEY KT13 69 T9
Hillcrest Av CHERT KT16 68 J8
EDGW HA8 24 B9
GLDGN NW11 37 L3
PIN HA5 34 F2
WTHK RM20 55 U11
Hillcrest Cl BECK BR3 75 R4
EPSOM KT18 84 F5
SYD SE26 63 L9
Hillcrest Dr RDART DA2 67 U3
Hill Crest Gdns CRICK NW2 36 G8
Hillcrest Gdns ESH/CLAY KT10 71 P9
FNCH N3 37 L2
Hill Crest Rd CHONG CM5 19 Q4
Hillcrest Rd ACT W3 48 A6
BH/WHM TN16 88 F6
BMLY BR1 64 C9
CTHM CR3 86 K7
DART DA1 66 F5
EA W5 47 U3
EMPK RM11 42 G5
LOU IG10 28 F4
ORP BR6 77 Q7
PUR/KEN CR8 74 D14
RAD WD7 13 L7
WALTH E17 27 V14
Hillcrest Vw BECK BR3 75 R4
Hillcrest Wy EPP CM16 18 E5
Hillcroft LOU IG10 17 U14
Hillcroft Av PIN HA5 34 H4
PUR/KEN CR8 86 A3
Hillcroft Crs EA W5 47 T4
OXHEY WD19 22 D6
RSLP HA4 34 F8
WBLY HA9 35 V9
Hillcroft Rd EHAM E6 52 K3
Hillcroome Rd BELMT SM2 73 R11
Hillcross Av MRDN SM4 73 L4
Hilldale Rd SUT SM1 73 M9
Hilldeane Rd PUR/KEN CR8 74 E14
Hilldene Av HARH RM3 30 J11
Hilldene Cl HARH RM3 30 K10
Hilldown Rd HAYES BR2 76 A6
STRHM/NOR SW16 62 C12
Hill Dr STRHM/NOR SW16 74 D1
WBLY HA9 36 B6
Hilldrop Crs HOLWY N7 38 B10
Hilldrop Est HOLWY N7 38 B10
Hilldrop La HOLWY N7 38 B10
Hilldrop Rd BMLY BR1 64 D11
HOLWY N7 38 B10
Hill End ORP BR6 77 P7
WOOL/PLUM SE18 52 J13
Hill End Rd DEN/HRF UB9 21 M11
Hillersdon Av BARN SW13 48 G14
EDGW HA8 23 V10
Hillery Cl WALW SE17 9 R8
Hilley Field La LHD/OX KT22 83 M12
Hill Farm Av GSTN WD25 11 N7
Hill Farm Rd CFSP/GDCR SL9 20 C12
NKENS W10 48 J3
Hillfield Av ALP/SUD HA0 35 U12
CDALE/KGS NW9 36 E3
CEND/HSY/T N8 38 D2
MRDN SM4 73 S4
Hillfield Cl REDH RH1 93 U10
RYLN/HDSTN HA2 35 L2
Hillfield La South BUSH WD23 23 N4
Hillfield Ms CEND/HSY/T N8 38 D2
Hillfield Pde MRDN SM4 * 73 R4
Hillfield Pk MUSWH N10 37 V2
WCHMH N21 26 E7
Hillfield Park Ms MUSWH N10 37 V1
Hillfield Pl SEV TN13 90 D10
Hill Field Rd HPTN TW12 58 H12
Hillfield Rd CFSP/GDCR SL9 20 C12
KIL/WHAMP NW6 37 M10
REDH RH1 93 U10
SEV TN13 90 E10
Hillfield Sq CFSP/GDCR SL9 20 C12
Hillfoot Av CRW RM5 30 C13
Hillfoot Rd CRW RM5 30 C13
Hill Gardens Craven BAY/PAD W2 * 2 J13
Hillgate Pl BAL SW12 61 V4
KENS W8 6 E1
Hillgate St KENS W8 6 E1
Hill Gv FELT TW13 58 H7
ROM RM1 42 E1
Hillhouse WAB EN9 17 M7
Hill House Av STAN HA7 23 P12
Hill House Cl CFSP/GDCR SL9 20 C12
WCHMH N21 26 E5
Hill House Dr HPTN TW12 58 J13
REIG RH2 93 P12
WEY KT13 81 S1
Hill House Rd RDART DA2 67 Q5
STRHM/NOR SW16 62 D10
Hillhurst Gdns CTHM CR3 86 J10
Hilliard Rd NTHWD HA6 22 B13
Hilliard's Ct WAP E1W * 51 N6
Hilliards Rd UX/CGN UB8 45 P4
Hillier Cl BAR EN5 25 P4
Hillier Gdns CROY/NA CR0 74 E10
Hillier Pl CHSGTN KT9 71 T11
Hillier Rd BTSEA SW11 61 T4
Hilliers Av UX/CGN UB8 45 S1
Hillier's La CROY/NA CR0 74 C8
Hillingdale BH/WHM TN16 88 D8
Hillingdon Av SEV TN13 90 J11
STWL/WRAY TW19 57 Q6
Hillingdon Hl HGDN/ICK UB10 45 R1
Hillingdon Pde HGDN/ICK UB10 * 45 T2
Hillingdon Ri SEV TN13 90 K12
Hillingdon Rd BXLYHN DA7 66 C1
GSTN WD25 11 N8
HGDN/ICK UB10 33 Q13
Hillingdon St WALW SE17 9 M12
Hillingdon Trail DEN/HRF UB9 33 P1
HYS/HAR UB3 46 C10
Hill La KWD/TDW/WH KT20 85 L11
RSLP HA4 33 U6
Hill Leys POTB/CUF EN6 15 N2
Hillman Cl EMPK RM11 42 K1
Hillman Dr NKENS W10 48 J2
Hillman St HACK E8 39 M11
Hillmarton Rd HOLWY N7 38 C10
Hillmarton Ter HOLWY N7 * 38 C10
Hillmead Dr BRXN/ST SW9 62 F2
Hillmont Rd ESH/CLAY KT10 71 N8
Hillmore Gv SYD SE26 63 P10
Hillmount WOKS/MYFD GU22 * 80 C8
Hill Pk LHD/OX KT22 * 83 Q9
Hill Park Ct LHD/OX KT22 * 83 P9
Hill Park Dr LHD/OX KT22 83 P9
Hillpoint RKW/CH/CXG WD3 21 N3
Hillreach WOOL/PLUM SE18 52 H10
Hill Ri CFSP/GDCR SL9 20 C14
Hillrise DTCH/LGLY SL3 44 E11
Hill Ri ED N9 27 M4
ESH/CLAY KT10 71 R7
FSTH SE23 63 M6
GFD/PVL UB6 35 L12
GLDGN NW11 37 P2
POTB/CUF EN6 14 E8
POTB/CUF EN6 15 N2
RCHPK/HAM TW10 59 T3
RDART DA2 67 R10
RKW/CH/CXG WD3 21 M5
RSLP HA4 33 U6
UPMR RM14 43 N7
Hillrise Av WATN WD24 11 R12
Hill Rise Crs CFSP/GDCR SL9 20 C14
Hillrise Rd ARCH N19 38 C5
CRW RM5 30 C11
Hill Rd ALP/SUD HA0 35 R8
BRW CM14 31 U8
CAR SM5 73 S11
EPP CM16 18 C11
HRW HA1 35 Q3
LHD/OX KT22 82 K12
MTCM CR4 61 V13
MUSWH N10 25 T13
NTHWD HA6 21 V11
PIN HA5 34 G4
PUR/KEN CR8 86 D2
RDART DA2 67 L7
STJWD NW8 2 K4
SUT SM1 73 P10
Hillsboro Rd EDUL SE22 62 J3
Hillsborough Gn OXHEY WD19 * 22 C8
Hillsgrove Cl WELL DA16 53 S12
Hill Side BAR EN5 25 Q3
Hillside BAR EN5 * 24 G3
BNSTD SM7 85 L5
CDALE/KGS NW9 36 D2
DEN/HRF UB9 33 N3
ESH/CLAY KT10 * 70 K10
EYN DA4 79 M5
RDART DA2 67 S10
VW GU25 68 A4
WIM/MER SW19 60 K11
WLSDN NW10 36 C13
WOKS/MYFD GU22 80 B10
Hillside Av BORE WD6 24 C1
CHES/WCR EN8 16 D5
FBAR/BDGN N11 25 T11
PUR/KEN CR8 86 F3
WBLY HA9 35 V9
WFD IG8 28 E10
Hillside Cl ABLGY WD5 11 L6
BNSTD SM7 85 L6
BRKHM/BTCW RH3 92 A11
CFSP/GDCR SL9 20 C11
MRDN SM4 73 L2
STJWD NW8 2 H3
WFD IG8 28 E10
Hillside Cottages BNSTD SM7 * 85 T3
Hillside Ct SWLY BR8 78 G2
Hillside Crs CHES/WCR EN8 16 D5
ENC/FH EN2 15 T12
NTHWD HA6 22 C13
OXHEY WD19 22 F4
RYLN/HDSTN HA2 35 L7
Hillside Dr EDGW HA8 24 A11
Hillside Gdns ADL/WDHM KT15 68 K10
BAR EN5 25 L3
BRKHM/BTCW RH3 92 A10
BRXS/STRHM SW2 * 62 E7
EDGW HA8 23 V9
FBAR/BDGN N11 * 26 A11
HGT N6 37 U4
KTN/HRWW/WS HA3 35 U5
NTHWD HA6 22 C12
WALTH E17 39 V1
WLGTN SM6 74 A12
Hillside Gv MLHL NW7 24 G12
STHGT/OAK N14 26 B5
Hillside La HAYES BR2 76 C7
Hillside Ri NTHWD HA6 22 C12
Hillside Rd ASHTD KT21 83 V7
BELMT SM2 73 M12
BGR/WK TN15 91 M7
BH/WHM TN16 88 G9
BRXS/STRHM SW2 62 D7
BUSH WD23 22 G3
COUL/CHIP CR5 86 C8
CROY/NA CR0 74 F10
CTHM CR3 87 L8
DART DA1 66 G4
EA W5 47 U3
EW KT17 72 J14
HAYES BR2 76 B1
NTHWD HA6 22 C12
RAD WD7 12 F9
RKW/CH/CXG WD3 20 G3
SEV TN13 90 K13
SEVS/STOTM N15 38 J5
STHL UB1 46 J2
The Hillside ORP BR6 77 R13
Hillside Wk BRW CM14 31 U8
Hills La BGR/WK TN15 91 P2
NTHWD HA6 22 A13
Hillsleigh Rd KENS W8 6 D1
Hillsmead Wy SAND/SEL CR2 87 L4
Hills Ms EA W5 * 47 U5
Hills Pl SOHO/SHAV W1D 4 A12
Hill's Rd BKHH IG9 28 D6
Hillstowe St CLPT E5 39 N7
Hill St MYFR/PICC W1J 7 U1
RCH/KEW TW9 59 T3
Hillswood Dr CHERT KT16 68 G9
The Hill CTHM CR3 86 K14
Hill Top CHEAM SM3 73 M5
GLDGN NW11 37 P2
LOU IG10 28 J1
Hilltop WALTH E17 * 39 T1
Hilltop Av WLSDN NW10 36 C12
Hilltop Cl LHD/OX KT22 83 S13
Hill Top Cl LOU IG10 28 J1
Hilltop Cottages SYD SE26 * 63 M9
Hilltop Gdns DART DA1 67 M3
HDN NW4 24 H14
ORP BR6 77 N7
Hilltop La CTHM CR3 94 E1
Hilltop Rd CTHM CR3 86 J7
KGLGY WD4 10 K1
KIL/WHAMP NW6 37 N12
REIG RH2 93 P12
WTHK RM20 55 U11
Hill Top Vw WFD IG8 * 28 H11
Hilltop Wk CTHM CR3 87 Q10
Hilltop Wy STAN HA7 23 Q8
Hillview CTHM CR3 86 K7
RYNPK SW20 60 H13
Hillview Av EMPK RM11 42 J4
KTN/HRWW/WS HA3 35 U3
Hill View Cl KWD/TDW/WH KT20 84 J11
PUR/KEN CR8 86 F1
Hillview Cl PIN HA5 22 H11
WBLY HA9 35 V7
Hillview Ct WOKS/MYFD GU22 * 80 C8
Hillview Crs IL IG1 40 H4
ORP BR6 77 N6
Hillview Dr REDH RH1 93 U11
Hill View Dr THMD SE28 53 N6
WELL DA16 53 N14
Hill View Gdns CDALE/KGS NW9 36 D3
Hillview Gdns CHES/WCR EN8 16 E1
HDN NW4 36 K2
RYLN/HDSTN HA2 34 J1
Hill View Rd ESH/CLAY KT10 71 Q12
ORP BR6 77 P6
STWL/WRAY TW19 56 B4
TWK TW1 59 Q4
WOKS/MYFD GU22 80 D8
Hillview Rd CHST BR7 64 J10
MLHL NW7 24 K9
PIN HA5 22 H12
SUT SM1 73 Q8
Hillway CDALE/KGS NW9 36 E6
HGT N6 37 U7
Hill Waye CFSP/GDCR SL9 32 D4
Hillworth BECK BR3 * 63 T14
Hillworth Rd BRXS/STRHM SW2 62 E5
Hillyard Rd HNWL W7 47 N3
Hillyard St BRXN/ST SW9 50 E13
Hillydeal Rd RSEV TN14 90 J5
Hillyfield WALTH E17 27 Q14
Hillyfield Cl HOM E9 39 Q10
Hilly Flds BROCKY SE4 * 63 S2
Hillyfields LOU IG10 17 U14
Hilly Fields Crs BROCKY SE4 63 S2
Hilsea St CLPT E5 39 N9
Hilton Av NFNCH/WDSPK N12 25 R10
Hilton Cl UX/CGN UB8 33 M14
Hilton Wy SAND/SEL CR2 87 M5
Himalayan Wy WATW WD18 22 B4
Himley Rd TOOT SW17 61 S10
Hinchley Cl ESH/CLAY KT10 71 P8
Hinchley Dr ESH/CLAY KT10 71 P8
Hinchley Wy ESH/CLAY KT10 71 Q8
Hinckley Rd EDUL SE22 63 L2
Hind Cl CHIG IG7 29 P10
Hind Ct FLST/FETLN EC4A 4 K12
Hind Crs ERITH DA8 54 C12
Hinde Ms MHST W1U * 3 T11
Hindes Rd HRW HA1 35 N3
Hinde St MHST W1U 3 T11
Hind Gv POP/IOD E14 51 S4
Hindhead Cl UX/CGN UB8 45 T3
Hindhead Gdns NTHLT UB5 34 G13
Hindhead Gn OXHEY WD19 22 E10
Hindhead Wy WLGTN SM6 74 C10
Hindmans Rd EDUL SE22 63 L3
Hindmans Wy DAGW RM9 53 V2
Hindmarsh Cl WCHPL E1 * 51 L5
Hindrey Rd CLPT E5 39 M10
Hindsley's Pl FSTH SE23 63 N7
Hine Cl COUL/CHIP CR5 86 A12
Hinkler Rd KTN/HRWW/WS HA3 35 T1
Hinkley Cl DEN/HRF UB9 33 N2
Hinksey Cl DTCH/LGLY SL3 44 F8
Hinksey Pth ABYW SE2 53 T8
Hinstock Rd WOOL/PLUM SE18 53 L12
Hinton Av HSLWW TW4 58 F2
Hinton Cl ELTH/MOT SE9 64 G6
Hinton Rd BRXN/ST SW9 62 F1
UED N18 26 J9
UX/CGN UB8 33 N13
WLGTN SM6 74 A11
Hipley St WOKS/MYFD GU22 80 F10
Hippodrome Pl NTGHL W11 2 A14
Hirst Crs WBLY HA9 35 U8
Hitcham Rd WALTH E17 39 R5
Hitchcock Cl SHPTN TW17 69 R1
Hitchen Hatch La SEV TN13 90 H13
Hitchin Cl HARH RM3 30 J9
Hitchings Wy REIG RH2 93 N14
Hitherbroom Rd HYS/HAR UB3 46 C6
Hither Farm Rd BKHTH/KID SE3 64 E1
Hitherfield Rd BCTR RM8 41 U7
STRHM/NOR SW16 62 D7
Hither Green La LEW SE13 63 U3
Hither Meadow CFSP/GDCR SL9 * 20 C13
Hithermoor Rd STWL/WRAY TW19 57 L4
Hitherwell Dr KTN/HRWW/WS HA3 23 M13
Hitherwood Cl HCH RM12 42 K9
REIG RH2 93 R8
Hitherwood Dr NRWD SE19 62 K9
Hive Cl BRW CM14 31 U7
BUSH WD23 23 M7
Hive Rd BUSH WD23 23 M7
Hoadly Rd STRHM/NOR SW16 62 B8
Hobart Cl TRDG/WHET N20 25 S7
YEAD UB4 46 F2
Hobart Dr YEAD UB4 46 F2
Hobart Gdns THHTH CR7 74 H1
Hobart La YEAD UB4 46 F2
Hobart Pl BGVA SW1W 7 U6
RCHPK/HAM TW10 59 V5
Hobart Rd BARK/HLT IG6 29 L14
DAGW RM9 41 T9
WPK KT4 72 H8
YEAD UB4 46 F2
Hobarts Dr DEN/HRF UB9 32 K4
Hobbayne Rd HNWL W7 47 M4
Hobbes Wk PUT/ROE SW15 60 H3
Hobbs Cl BF/WBF KT14 81 M3
CHES/WCR EN8 16 D3
Hobbs Cross Rd EPP CM16 18 G9
Hobbs Gn EFNCH N2 37 Q1
Hobbs Pl IS N1 5 S2
Hobbs Place Est IS N1 5 S3
Hobbs Rd WNWD SE27 62 G9
Hobby St PEND EN3 27 P3
Hobday St POP/IOD E14 51 T4
Hoblands End CHST BR7 65 N11
Hobsons Pl WCHPL E1 * 51 L3
Hobury St WBPTN SW10 6 K12
Hockenden La SWLY BR8 78 A1
Hockering Gdns WOKS/MYFD GU22 80 F8
Hockering Rd WOKS/MYFD GU22 80 E8
Hocker St BETH E2 * 5 U6
Hockley Av EHAM E6 40 G14
Hockley Dr GPK RM2 30 J14
Hockley Ms BARK IG11 41 N14
Hocroft Av CRICK NW2 37 M8
Hocroft Rd CRICK NW2 37 M9
Hocroft Wk CRICK NW2 37 M8
Hodder Dr GFD/PVL UB6 35 P14
Hoddesdon Rd BELV DA17 54 A10
Hodes Rw HAMP NW3 37 T9
Hodford Rd GLDGN NW11 37 M6
Hodges Wy WATW WD18 22 C4
Hodgkins Cl THMD SE28 53 T5
Hodgkins Ms STAN HA7 23 R10
Hodister Cl WALW SE17 9 P14
Hodson Cl RYLN/HDSTN HA2 34 H8
Hodson Crs STMC/STPC BR5 77 T4
Hodson Pl PEND EN3 16 G12
Hoebrook Cl WOKS/MYFD GU22 80 C11
Hoe La ABR/ST RM4 29 R1
EN EN1 16 B12
Hoe St WALTH E17 39 S3
The Hoe OXHEY WD19 22 F7
Hoffmann Gdns SAND/SEL CR2 75 L11
Hoffman Sq IS N1 * 5 R5
Hogan Ms BAY/PAD W2 3 L9
Hogarth Av ASHF TW15 57 U11
Hogarth Cl CAN/RD E16 52 F3
EA W5 47 U3
UX/CGN UB8 45 N1
Hogarth Crs CROY/NA CR0 74 G5
WIM/MER SW19 61 R13
Hogarth Gdns HEST TW5 46 J12
Hogarth Hl GLDGN NW11 37 M2
Hogarth Pl ECT SW5 * 6 G8
Hogarth Reach LOU IG10 28 H3
Hogarth Rd BCTR RM8 41 R10
ECT SW5 6 G8
EDGW HA8 24 A14
Hogarth Ter CHSWK W4 * 48 E11
Hogarth Wy HPTN TW12 59 L13
Hogg La BORE WD6 23 Q2
Hog Hill Rd CRW RM5 29 V12
Hogscross La COUL/CHIP CR5 85 T12
Hogshead Pas WAP E1W * 51 M5
Hogshill La COB KT11 82 E4
Hogsmill Wy HOR/WEW KT19 72 C10
Hogtrough Hl BH/WHM TN16 89 Q12
Hogtrough La OXTED RH8 95 T4
REDH RH1 94 B11
Holbeach Cl CDALE/KGS NW9 24 E13
Holbeach Gdns BFN/LL DA15 65 N4
Holbeach Rd CAT SE6 63 T5
Holbeck Rw PECK SE15 51 L12
Holbein Ga NTHWD HA6 22 A10
Holbein Ms BGVA SW1W 7 S9
Holbein Pl BGVA SW1W 7 S8
Holberton Gdns WLSDN NW10 48 H1
Holborn HCIRC EC1N 4 J10
Holborn Circ HCIRC EC1N 4 K10
Holborn Pl HHOL WC1V 4 G10
Holborn Rd PLSTW E13 52 D3
Holborn Viad STBT EC1A 5 L11
Holborn Wy MTCM CR4 61 T14
Holbreck Pl WOKS/MYFD GU22 80 D8
Holbrook Cl EN EN1 15 V13
Holbrooke Ct HOLWY N7 38 C8
Holbrook Gdns GSTN WD25 11 V10
Holbrook La CHST BR7 65 M12
Holbrook Meadow EGH TW20 56 G11
Holbrook Rd SRTFD E15 40 B14
Holbrook Wy HAYES BR2 76 H4
Holburn GINN WC1R 4 J10
Holburne Cl BKHTH/KID SE3 52 E13
Holburne Gdns BKHTH/KID SE3 52 F13
Holburne Rd BKHTH/KID SE3 52 E13
Holcombe Cl BH/WHM TN16 97 M2
Holcombe Hl MLHL NW7 24 G8
Holcombe Rd IL IG1 40 J5
TOTM N17 38 K1
Holcombe St HMSMTH W6 48 H10
Holcon Ct REDH RH1 93 U7
Holcote Cl BELV DA17 53 U8
Holcroft Rd HOM E9 39 N12
Holdbrook Wy HARH RM3 31 M14
Holden Av CDALE/KGS NW9 36 C6
NFNCH/WDSPK N12 25 P10
Holdenby Rd BROCKY SE4 63 Q3
Holden Cl BCTR RM8 41 R8
Holdenhurst Av FNCH N3 25 P12
Holden Rd NFNCH/WDSPK N12 25 P9
Holden St BTSEA SW11 49 U14
Holden Wy UPMR RM14 43 R6
Holdernesse Rd ISLW TW7 47 Q13
TOOT SW17 61 T8
Holderness Wy WNWD SE27 62 G10
Holders Hill Av HDN NW4 24 K14
Holders Hill Crs HDN NW4 24 K14
Holders Hill Dr HDN NW4 24 K14
Holders Hill Gdns HDN NW4 24 K14
Holders Hill Pde MLHL NW7 * 25 L13
Holders Hill Rd HDN NW4 25 L14
Holecroft WAB EN9 17 L8
Hole La EDEN TN8 96 J13
Holford Ms FSBYW WC1X * 4 G5
Holford Rd HAMP NW3 37 Q8
Holford St FSBYW WC1X 4 J5
Holford Yd FSBYW WC1X * 4 J4
Holgate Av BTSEA SW11 61 R1
Holgate Rd DAGE RM10 42 A10
Holgate St CHARL SE7 52 F8
Holland Av BELMT SM2 73 N12
RYNPK SW20 60 F13
Holland Cl BAR EN5 25 R5
HAYES BR2 76 B7
REDH RH1 93 T10
ROMW/RG RM7 42 C3
STAN HA7 23 R10
Holland Crs OXTED RH8 96 C9
Holland Dr FSTH SE23 63 Q8
Holland Gdns BTFD TW8 47 V10
EGH TW20 56 K14
GSTN WD25 11 Q9
WKENS W14 6 B5
Holland Gv BRXN/ST SW9 8 K14
Holland La OXTED RH8 96 C9
Holland Pk NTGHL W11 6 C3
Holland Park Av GDMY/SEVK IG3 41 N4
NTGHL W11 6 A3
Holland Park Gdns NTGHL W11 6 A2
Holland Park Ms NTGHL W11 6 C2
Holland Park Rd WKENS W14 6 C6
Holland Park Ter NTGHL W11 6 B2
Holland Pas IS N1 5 N1
Holland Pl KENS W8 6 G3
Holland Rd ALP/SUD HA0 35 T11
EHAM E6 40 H13
OXTED RH8 96 C11
SNWD SE25 75 L3
SRTFD E15 52 A1
WKENS W14 6 A4
WKENS W14 48 K7
WLSDN NW10 36 G13
The Hollands WOKS/MYFD GU22 80 C8
WPK KT4 72 F6
Holland St KENS W8 6 F4
STHWK SE1 9 M1
Holland Villas Rd WKENS W14 6 B4
Holland Wk STAN HA7 23 Q10
Holland Wy HAYES BR2 76 B7
Hollar Rd STNW/STAM N16 38 K8
Hollen St SOHO/CST W1F 4 B12
Holles Cl HPTN TW12 58 J11
Holles St CAVSQ/HST W1G 3 V11
Holley Rd ACT W3 48 E7
Hollickwood Av NFNCH/WDSPK N12 25 T11
Holliday Sq BTSEA SW11 61 R1
Hollidge Wy DAGE RM10 42 B12
Hollies WAB EN9 17 Q9
Hollies Av BF/WBF KT14 80 K3
BFN/LL DA15 65 P7
Hollies Cl STRHM/NOR SW16 62 E11
TWK TW1 59 P7
Hollies Ct ADL/WDHM KT15 69 N10
Hollies End MLHL NW7 24 H10
Hollies Rd EA W5 47 S9
The Hollies ADL/WDHM KT15 * 69 N10
BAR EN5 * 24 G3
KTN/HRWW/WS HA3 35 Q2
OXTED RH8 96 D9
Hollies Wy BAL SW12 * 61 U5
POTB/CUF EN6 14 E5
Holligrave Rd BMLY BR1 64 C13
Hollingbourne Av BXLYHN DA7 53 V13
Hollingbourne Gdns WEA W13 47 R3
Hollingbourne Rd HNHL SE24 62 G3
Hollingsworth Rd CROY/NA CR0 75 M11
Hollington Crs NWMAL KT3 72 F4
Hollington Rd EHAM E6 52 H1
TOTM N17 27 L14
Hollingworth Cl E/WMO/HCT KT8 70 H2
Hollingworth Rd STMC/STPC BR5 76 K5
Hollingworth Wy BH/WHM TN16 97 M2
Hollis Rw REDH RH1 * 93 T12
Hollman Gdns STRHM/NOR SW16 62 F11
Holloway Cl WDR/YW UB7 45 Q10
Holloway Dr VW GU25 68 C2
Holloway Hl CHERT KT16 68 G8
Holloway La WDR/YW UB7 45 R10
Holloway Rd ARCH N19 38 B7
EHAM E6 52 H1
WAN E11 39 V8
Holloway St HSLW TW3 58 K1
Hollow Hill La IVER SL0 44 F5
Hollow La VW GU25 68 A1
The Hollow WFD IG8 28 B9
Holly Av ADL/WDHM KT15 69 L14
STAN HA7 23 U14
WOT/HER KT12 70 F6
Holly Bank MUSWH N10 * 38 A2
Hollybank Cl HPTN TW12 58 J10
Hollybank Rd BF/WBF KT14 81 L4
Hollybrake Cl CHST BR7 65 M12
Hollybush Cl KTN/HRWW/WS HA3 23 N13
OXHEY WD19 22 E5
SEV TN13 90 J14
WAN E11 40 C3
Hollybush Gdns BETH E2 51 M1
Hollybush Hl WAN E11 40 B5
Hollybush La DEN/HRF UB9 32 G7
Holly Bush La HPTN TW12 58 H12
Hollybush La IVER SL0 44 F4
ORP BR6 78 A11
Holly Bush La SEV TN13 90 J14
Hollybush Pl BETH E2 51 M1
Hollybush Rd KUTN/CMB KT2 59 U11
Hollybush St PLSTW E13 52 D1
Hollybush Ter NRWD SE19 * 62 J11
Holly Bush V HAMP NW3 * 37 Q9
Hollybush Wy CHESW EN7 16 A2
Holly Cl BECK BR3 75 U2
BKHH IG9 28 F8
FELT TW13 58 G10
WLGTN SM6 73 V12
WLSDN NW10 36 E12
Hollycombe EGH TW20 56 B9
Holly Crs BECK BR3 75 R3
WFD IG8 27 V12
Hollycroft Av HAMP NW3 37 N8
WBLY HA9 35 U7
Hollycroft Cl SAND/SEL CR2 74 J10
WDR/YW UB7 45 S11
Hollycroft Gdns WDR/YW UB7 45 S11
Hollydale Cl NTHLT UB5 34 K10
Hollydale Dr HAYES BR2 76 H8
Hollydale Rd PECK SE15 51 N14
Hollydown Wy WAN E11 39 V8
Holly Dr CHING E4 27 T5
POTB/CUF EN6 14 D7
Holly Farm Rd NWDGN UB2 46 G10
Hollyfield Av FBAR/BDGN N11 25 T10
Hollyfield Rd BRYLDS KT5 71 V5
Holly Gdns BXLYHN DA7 66 C2
WDR/YW UB7 45 R7
Holly Gn WEY KT13 69 V9
Hollygrove BUSH WD23 23 M5
Holly Gv CDALE/KGS NW9 36 C5
PECK SE15 50 K14
PIN HA5 22 G13
Hollygrove Cl HSLW TW3 58 H2
Holly Hedge Rd COB KT11 82 D4
Holly Hedge Ter LEW SE13 63 U3
Holly Hl HAMP NW3 37 Q9
WCHMH N21 26 D4
Holly Hill Rd BELV DA17 54 B10
Holly Hough KWD/TDW/WH KT20 92 B6
Holly La BNSTD SM7 85 R8
Holly La East BNSTD SM7 85 P6
Holly La West BNSTD SM7 85 P7
Holly Lodge Gdns HGT N6 37 U7
Holly Lodge (Mobile Home Park)
KWD/TDW/WH KT20 93 L1
Hollymead CAR SM5 73 T8
Hollymead Rd COUL/CHIP CR5 85 U8
Holly Ms WBPTN SW10 6 K10
Hollymoor La HOR/WEW KT19 72 D14
Holly Mt HAMP NW3 * 37 Q9
Hollymount Cl GNWCH SE10 51 U13
Holly Pde COB KT11 82 D5
Holly Pk FNCH N3 37 M1
FSBYPK N4 38 D5
Holly Park Gdns FNCH N3 37 N1
Holly Park Rd FBAR/BDGN N11 25 U10
HNWL W7 47 P6
Holly Rd CHSWK W4 * 48 D9
DART DA1 66 K6
HPTN TW12 59 L11
HSLW TW3 58 K2
ORP BR6 77 Q12
PEND EN3 16 D10
REIG RH2 93 P12
TWK TW1 59 Q6
WAN E11 40 B5
Holly St HACK E8 38 K12
Hollytree Av SWLY BR8 66 E14
Hollytree Cl CFSP/GDCR SL9 20 C10
WIM/MER SW19 60 K6
Hollytree Pde SCUP DA14 * 65 S10
Holly Tree Rd CTHM CR3 86 J12
Hollyview Cl HDN NW4 36 G4
Holly Vls HMSMTH W6 * 48 H8
Holly Wk HAMP NW3 37 Q9
Holly Wy MTCM CR4 74 B2
Hollywood Gdns YEAD UB4 46 D4
Hollywood La BGR/WK TN15 91 T1
Hollywood Ms WBPTN SW10 6 J11
Hollywood Rd CHING E4 27 Q10
WBPTN SW10 6 J11
Hollywoods CROY/NA CR0 75 R14
Hollywood Wy ERITH DA8 54 H13
WFD IG8 27 V12
Holman Ct EW KT17 * 72 G13
Holman Rd BTSEA SW11 49 R14
HOR/WEW KT19 72 C10
Holmbank Dr SHPTN TW17 70 A2
Holmbridge Gdns PEND EN3 27 P2
Holmbrook Dr HDN NW4 36 K3
Holmbury Cl BUSH WD23 23 N7
Holmbury Ct WIM/MER SW19 61 S12
Holmbury Gdns HYS/HAR UB3 46 B6
Holmbury Gv CROY/NA CR0 75 R12
Holmbury Mnr SCUP DA14 * 65 Q9
Holmbury Pk BMLY BR1 64 G12
Holmbury Vw CLPT E5 39 M6
Holmbush Rd PUT/ROE SW15 61 L4
Holm Cl ADL/WDHM KT15 80 J2
Holmcote Gdns HBRY N5 38 G10
Holmcroft KWD/TDW/WH KT20 92 H1
Holmcroft Wy HAYES BR2 76 H3
Holmdale Cl BORE WD6 12 K14
Holmdale Gdns HDN NW4 36 K3
Holmdale Rd CHST BR7 65 L10
KIL/WHAMP NW6 37 N10
Holmdale Ter SEVS/STOTM N15 38 J4
Holmdene Av HNHL SE24 62 G3
MLHL NW7 24 G11
RYLN/HDSTN HA2 34 K1
Holmdene Cl BECK BR3 63 U14
Holmdene Ct BMLY BR1 76 G1
Holmead Rd FUL/PGN SW6 6 H14
Holmebury Cl BUSH WD23 * 23 N7
Holme Cl CHES/WCR EN8 16 E5
WEY KT13 69 U11
Holme Ct ISLW TW7 59 Q1
Holmedale SLN SL2 44 A5
Holme Lacey Rd LEE/GVPK SE12 64 B4
Holme Lea GSTN WD25 11 Q8
Holme Pk BORE WD6 12 K14
Holme Rd EHAM E6 40 G13
EMPK RM11 43 N6
Holmes Av MLHL NW7 25 L10
WALTH E17 39 R1
Holmes Cl EDUL SE22 63 L2
PUR/KEN CR8 86 D3
WOKS/MYFD GU22 80 D11
Holmesdale CHES/WCR EN8 16 C9
Holmesdale Av MORT/ESHN SW14 60 B1
Holmesdale Cl SNWD SE25 74 K1
Holmesdale Hl EYN DA4 67 R13
Holmesdale Pk REDH RH1 * 94 D10
Holmesdale Rd BXLYHN DA7 53 T14
EYN DA4 67 Q13
HGT N6 37 V5
RCH/KEW TW9 47 V13
REDH RH1 94 D12
REIG RH2 93 P9
SNWD SE25 74 H3
TEDD TW11 59 S12
Holmesley Rd FSTH SE23 63 Q4
Holmes Rd KTTN NW5 37 V11
TWK TW1 59 P7
WIM/MER SW19 61 Q12
Holmes Ter STHWK SE1 8 J3
Holmethorpe Av REDH RH1 93 V7
Holme Wy STAN HA7 23 P11
Holmewood Gdns BRXS/STRHM SW2 62 D5
Holmewood Rd BRXS/STRHM SW2 62 C5
SNWD SE25 74 J1
Holmfield Av HDN NW4 36 K3
Holm Gv HGDN/ICK UB10 33 S12
Holmhurst Rd BELV DA17 54 B10
Holmlea Rd DTCH/LGLY SL3 44 B13
Holmlea Wk DTCH/LGLY SL3 44 A13
Holmleigh Av DART DA1 66 J2
Holmleigh Rd STNW/STAM N16 38 J6
Holm Oak Cl PUT/ROE SW15 61 M4
Holm Oak Pk WATW WD18 * 22 C3
Holmsdale Cl IVER SL0 44 K4
Holmsdale Gv BXLYHN DA7 54 E14
Holmshaw Cl SYD SE26 63 Q9
Holmshill La BORE WD6 13 R11
Holmside Ri OXHEY WD19 22 D8
Holmside Rd BAL SW12 61 U4
Holmsley Cl NWMAL KT3 72 F4
Holmstall Av CDALE/KGS NW9 36 C1
EDGW HA8 24 C14
Holmstall Pde EDGW HA8 * 24 C14
Holmwood Av SAND/SEL CR2 86 K3
Holmwood Cl ADL/WDHM KT15 69 L10
BELMT SM2 72 K13
NTHLT UB5 34 K11
RYLN/HDSTN HA2 35 L1
Holmwood Gdns FNCH N3 25 N14
WLGTN SM6 73 V11
Holmwood Gv MLHL NW7 24 D10
Holmwood Rd BELMT SM2 72 J13
CHSGTN KT9 71 U10
GDMY/SEVK IG3 41 N7
PEND EN3 16 D10
Holne Cha EFNCH N2 37 Q4
MRDN SM4 73 N4
Holness Rd SRTFD E15 40 B11
Holroyd Rd ESH/CLAY KT10 71 Q13
PUT/ROE SW15 60 J2
Holsart Cl KWD/TDW/WH KT20 84 H12
Holstein Av WEY KT13 69 S9
Holstein Wy ERITHM DA18 53 T8
Holstock Rd IL IG1 41 L7
Holsworth Cl RYLN/HDSTN HA2 35 L3
Holsworthy Sq FSBYW WC1X 4 H8
Holsworthy Wy CHSGTN KT9 71 S10
Holt Cl BORE WD6 23 V2
CHIG IG7 29 P10
MUSWH N10 37 U2
THMD SE28 53 R5
Holton St WCHPL E1 51 P2
Holt Rd ALP/SUD HA0 35 R8
CAN/RD E16 52 G6
HARH RM3 31 L12
Holtsmere Cl GSTN WD25 11 Q9
The Holt BARK/HLT IG6 29 L11
MRDN SM4 * 73 N2
WLGTN SM6 74 A9
Holt Wy CHIG IG7 29 P10
Holtwhite Av ENC/FH EN2 15 S14
Holtwhite's Hl ENC/FH EN2 15 S14
Holtwood Rd LHD/OX KT22 83 L3
Holwell Pl PIN HA5 34 G2
Holwood Cl WOT/HER KT12 70 E7
Holwood Park Av ORP BR6 76 H9
Holwood Pl CLAP SW4 62 B2
Holybourne Av PUT/ROE SW15 60 G5
Holyfield Rd WAB EN9 16 J3
Holyhead Cl BOW E3 51 S1
Holyoake Av WOKN/KNAP GU21 80 A7
Holyoake Ct BERM/RHTH SE16 51 Q7
Holyoake Crs WOKN/KNAP GU21 80 A7
Holyoake Ter SEV TN13 90 G14
Holyoake Wk EA W5 47 S2
EFNCH N2 37 Q1
Holyoak Rd LBTH SE11 9 L7
Holyport Rd FUL/PGN SW6 48 J12
Holyrood Av RYLN/HDSTN HA2 34 G9
Holyrood Gdns EDGW HA8 24 B14
Holyrood Ms CAN/RD E16 52 C6
Holyrood Rd BAR EN5 25 Q4
Holyrood St STHWK SE1 9 S3

K

MTCM CR4 73 U1
ORP BR6 77 P9
PLSTW E13 40 E13
RCHPK/HAM TW10 59 V3
ROM RM1 42 G3
RYLN/HDSTN HA2 34 H7
SNWD SE25 75 L1
SURB KT6 71 S6
TEDD TW11 59 M10
TOTM N17 26 K13
TWK TW1 59 R4
UED N18 * 27 L10
UX/CGN UB8 33 P14
WAN E11 40 A5
WBPTN SW10 7 L12
WDGN N22 26 D13
WDR/YW UB7 45 R7
WIM/MER SW19 61 N11
WLSDN NW10 36 H12
WOKN/KNAP GU21 80 E6
WOT/HER KT12 70 D7
King's Scholars' Pas PIM SW1V 8 A7
Kings Shade Wk HOR/WEW KT19 * 84 D3
King Stairs Cl BERM/RHTH SE16 51 M7
King's Ter CAMTN NW1 4 A2
Kingsthorpe Rd SYD SE26 63 P9
Kingston Av CHEAM SM3 73 L8
EBED/NFELT TW14 58 A4
LHD/OX KT22 83 R11
WDR/YW UB7 45 R5
Kingston By-Pass ESH/CLAY KT10 71 N8
RYNPK SW20 60 F11
Kingston Cl CHDH RM6 41 U1
NTHLT UB5 34 H12
TEDD TW11 59 R11
Kingston Crs ASHF TW15 57 N10
BECK BR3 63 R13
Kingston Gdns CROY/NA CR0 74 C8
Kingston Hall Rd KUT/HW KT1 71 T1
Kingston Hl KUTN/CMB KT2 60 A13
Kingston Hill Av CHDH RM6 41 U1
Kingston Hill Pl KUTN/CMB KT2 60 C9
Kingston House Est SURB KT6 * 71 R4
Kingston House Gdns LHD/OX KT22 * 83 R11
Kingston La TEDD TW11 59 R11
UX/CGN UB8 45 Q1
Kingston Ldg NWMAL KT3 72 E2
Kingston Pl KTN/HRWW/WS HA3 23 P12
Kingston Ri ADL/WDHM KT15 69 L14
Kingston Rd ASHF TW15 57 R11
BRYLDS KT5 72 B7
EBAR EN4 25 R3
ED N9 27 L7
HOR/WEW KT19 72 D9
IL IG1 41 L9
KUT/HW KT1 72 B1
LHD/OX KT22 83 Q11
NWDGN UB2 46 H7
NWMAL KT3 72 D2
PUT/ROE SW15 60 H6
ROM RM1 42 F2
RYNPK SW20 61 L14
STA TW18 57 L9
TEDD TW11 59 R11
WIM/MER SW19 61 N12
Kingston Sq NRWD SE19 62 H10
Kingston V PUT/ROE SW15 60 D9
Kingstown St CAMTN NW1 3 S1
King St ACT W3 48 C6
CHERT KT16 69 L6
CITYW EC2V 5 P12
COVGDN WC2E 4 E13
EFNCH N2 37 R1
HMSMTH W6 48 G9
NWDGN UB2 46 G8
PLSTW E13 52 C2
RCH/KEW TW9 59 T3
TOTM N17 26 K13
TWK TW1 59 Q6
WATW WD18 22 E2
WHALL SW1A 8 B2
King St Cloisters HMSMTH W6 * 48 H9
King St Pde TWK TW1 * 59 Q6
Kings Wk SAND/SEL CR2 87 M4
Kings Warren LHD/OX KT22 83 L1
Kingswater Pl BTSEA SW11 * 7 N14
Kings Wy CROY/NA CR0 74 D10
HRW HA1 35 N2
Kingsway CFSP/GDCR SL9 32 C1
HOL/ALD WC2B 4 G12
HYS/HAR UB3 45 U3
MORT/ESHN SW14 60 B1
NFNCH/WDSPK N12 25 Q11
NWMAL KT3 72 J2
PEND EN3 27 M3
POTB/CUF EN6 15 N4
STMC/STPC BR5 77 M3
STWL/WRAY TW19 57 P6
WBLY HA9 35 U9
WOKN/KNAP GU21 80 B8
WWKM BR4 76 B8
Kingsway Av SAND/SEL CR2 75 N13
WOKN/KNAP GU21 80 B8
Kingsway Crs RYLN/HDSTN HA2 35 L2
Kingsway North Orbital Rd
GSTN WD25 11 N8
Kingsway Pde STNW/STAM N16 * 38 H8
Kingsway Pl CLKNW EC1R * 4 K7
Kingsway Rd CHEAM SM3 73 L12
Kingsway Ter WEY KT13 69 S13
The Kingsway EW KT17 72 F14
Kingswear Rd KTTN NW5 37 V8
RSLP HA4 34 C7
Kingswell Ride POTB/CUF EN6 15 N4
Kingswood Av BELV DA17 53 V9
HAYES BR2 76 A1
HPTN TW12 58 K11
HSLW TW3 46 H14
KIL/WHAMP NW6 2 A2
SAND/SEL CR2 87 N5
SWLY BR8 78 F2
THHTH CR7 74 E3
Kingswood Cl ASHF TW15 57 U9
BAR EN5 25 Q4
DART DA1 66 J4
EGH TW20 56 B9
EN EN1 26 J3
NWMAL KT3 72 F4
STMC/STPC BR5 77 M5
SURB KT6 71 U5
VX/NE SW8 8 F14
WEY KT13 69 T12
Kingswood Ct LEW SE13 63 V4
Kingswood Creek STWL/WRAY TW19 56 B3
Kingswood Dr BELMT SM2 73 P13
CAR SM5 73 T6
DUL SE21 62 J9
Kingswood La WARL CR6 87 N5
Kingswood Pk FNCH N3 25 M14
Kingswood Pl LEW SE13 64 A2
Kingswood Ri EGH TW20 56 B10
Kingswood Rd BRXS/STRHM SW2 62 C4
CHSWK W4 48 C8
GDMY/SEVK IG3 41 Q6
GSTN WD25 11 P8
HAYES BR2 76 A1
KWD/TDW/WH KT20 84 H11
PGE/AN SE20 63 N11
SEV TN13 90 E11
WAN E11 40 A5
WBLY HA9 36 A8
WIM/MER SW19 61 M13
Kingswood Ter CHSWK W4 48 C8
Kingswood Wy SAND/SEL CR2 87 P2
WLGTN SM6 74 C10
Kingsworth Cl BECK BR3 75 Q3
Kingsworthy Cl KUT/HW KT1 71 V1
Kings Yd PUT/ROE SW15 * 60 K2
RKW/CH/CXG WD3 * 21 Q6
SRTFD E15 * 39 S11
Kingthorpe Rd WLSDN NW10 36 D12
Kingthorpe Ter WLSDN NW10 * 36 D12
Kingwell Rd EBAR EN4 14 F12
Kingweston Cl CRICK NW2 37 L8
King William Ct WAB EN9 * 16 J9
King William La GNWCH SE10 52 A10
King William St CANST EC4R 5 R14
King William Wk GNWCH SE10 51 U11
Kingwood Rd FUL/PGN SW6 6 A14
Kinlet Rd WOOL/PLUM SE18 53 L13
Kinloch Dr CDALE/KGS NW9 36 E5
Kinloch St HOLWY N7 38 D8
Kinloss Gdns FNCH N3 37 M1
Kinloss Rd CAR SM5 73 Q5
Kinnaird Av BMLY BR1 64 B11
CHSWK W4 48 C12
Kinnaird Cl BMLY BR1 64 B11
Kinnaird Wy WFD IG8 28 H11
Kinnear Rd SHB W12 48 F7
Kinnerton Pl North KTBR SW1X * 7 R4
Kinnerton Pl South KTBR SW1X * 7 R4
Kinnerton St KTBR SW1X 7 S4
Kinnerton Yd KTBR SW1X * 7 S4
Kinnoul Rd HMSMTH W6 6 A11
Kinross Av WPK KT4 72 G7
Kinross Cl KTN/HRWW/WS HA3 35 V3
SUN TW16 58 B10
Kinross Dr SUN TW16 58 B10
Kinross Ter WALTH E17 27 R14
Kinsale Rd PECK SE15 63 L1
Kinsella Gdns WIM/MER SW19 60 H11
Kintyre Cl STRHM/NOR SW16 62 D14
Kinveachy Gdns CHARL SE7 52 G10
Kinver Rd SYD SE26 63 N9
Kipings KWD/TDW/WH KT20 84 K12
Kipling Cl BRW CM14 31 V10
Kipling Dr WIM/MER SW19 61 R11
Kipling Est STHWK SE1 9 R4
Kipling Rd BXLYHN DA7 53 U13
DART DA1 67 P3
Kipling St STHWK SE1 9 R4
Kipling Ter ED N9 * 26 H8
Kippington Cl SEV TN13 90 F14
Kippington Dr ELTH/MOT SE9 64 F6
Kippington Rd SEV TN13 90 F14
Kirby Cl BARK/HLT IG6 29 N11
HARH RM3 31 N10
HOR/WEW KT19 72 F10
LOU IG10 28 G5
NTHWD HA6 22 B11
Kirby Est BERM/RHTH SE16 * 51 M8
WDR/YW UB7 * 45 P5
Kirby Gv STHWK SE1 9 S3
Kirby Rd RDART DA2 67 Q5
WOKN/KNAP GU21 80 B7
Kirby St HCIRC EC1N 4 K9
Kirchen Rd WEA W13 47 R5
Kirkcaldy Gn OXHEY WD19 22 E8
Kirkdale SYD SE26 63 M7
Kirkdale Cnr SYD SE26 * 63 N9
Kirkdale Rd WAN E11 40 A6
Kirkfield Cl WEA W13 47 R6
Kirkham Rd EHAM E6 52 G4
Kirkham St WOOL/PLUM SE18 53 N11
Kirkland Av CLAY IG5 28 J14
Kirkland Cl BFN/LL DA15 65 N4
Kirkland Drive ENC/FH EN2 15 S13
Kirkland Ter BECK BR3 63 S11
Kirkland Wk HACK E8 38 K11
Kirk La WOOL/PLUM SE18 53 L11
Kirkleas Rd SURB KT6 71 U6
Kirklees Rd BCTR RM8 41 S10
THHTH CR7 74 E3
Kirkley Rd WIM/MER SW19 61 N13
Kirkly Cl SAND/SEL CR2 74 J13
Kirkmichael Rd POP/IOD E14 51 U4
Kirk Rd WALTH E17 39 R4
Kirkside Rd BKHTH/KID SE3 52 C11
Kirkstall Av SEVS/STOTM N15 38 H2
Kirkstall Gdns BRXS/STRHM SW2 62 B6
Kirkstall Rd BRXS/STRHM SW2 62 C6
Kirksted Rd MRDN SM4 73 P6
Kirkstone Wy BMLY BR1 64 A12
Kirkton Rd SEVS/STOTM N15 38 J2
Kirkwall Pl BETH E2 * 51 N1
Kirkwood Rd PECK SE15 51 M14
Kirn Rd WEA W13 47 R5
Kirrane Cl NWMAL KT3 72 F3
Kirtley Rd SYD SE26 63 Q9
Kirtling St VX/NE SW8 8 A13
Kirton Cl CHSWK W4 48 D9
HCH RM12 42 J11
Kirton Gdns BETH E2 5 V6
Kirton Ldg WAND/EARL SW18 * 61 P4
Kirton Rd PLSTW E13 40 E14
Kirton Wk EDGW HA8 24 C12
Kirwyn Wy CMBW SE5 9 N13
Kitcat Ter BOW E3 51 S1
Kitchener Rd EFNCH N2 37 S1
FSTGT E7 40 D11
THHTH CR7 74 H1
TOTM N17 38 J1
WALTH E17 27 T13
Kite Pl BETH E2 * 51 L1
Kite Yd BTSEA SW11 * 49 T13
Kitley Gdns NRWD SE19 62 K13
Kitsmead La CHERT KT16 68 B7
Kitson Rd BARN SW13 48 G13
CMBW SE5 9 P13
Kitswell Wy RAD WD7 12 D7
Kittiwake Cl SAND/SEL CR2 75 Q14
Kittiwake Rd NTHLT UB5 46 F1
Kittiwake Wy YEAD UB4 46 F3
Kitto Rd NWCR SE14 51 P14
Kitt's End Rd BAR EN5 14 A11
Kiver Rd ARCH N19 38 C7
Kiwi Ter EHAM E6 52 J1
Klea Av CLAP SW4 62 A4
Knapdale Cl FSTH SE23 63 M7
Knapmill Rd CAT SE6 63 S7
Knapmill Wy CAT SE6 63 S7
Knapp Cl WLSDN NW10 36 E11
Knapp Rd ASHF TW15 57 R9
BOW E3 51 S2
Knapton Ms TOOT SW17 61 U11
Knaresborough Dr WAND/EARL SW18 61 P6
Knaresborough Pl ECT SW5 6 G8
Knatchbull Rd WALW SE17 50 G13
WLSDN NW10 36 D13
Knatts La BGR/WK TN15 91 S1
Knatts Valley Rd BGR/WK TN15 79 R12
Knave Wood Rd BGR/WK TN15 91 L7
Knebworth Av WALTH E17 27 S13
Knebworth Pth BORE WD6 24 D2
Knebworth Rd STNW/STAM N16 * 38 J9
Knee Hl ABYW SE2 53 S10
Knee Hill Crs ABYW SE2 53 S9
Kneller Gdns ISLW TW7 59 M4
Kneller Rd BROCKY SE4 63 Q2
NWMAL KT3 72 E5
WHTN TW2 59 L4
Knevett Ter HSLW TW3 58 J2
Knifton Ct POTB/CUF EN6 * 13 V5
Knight Cl BCTR RM8 41 S7
Knighten St WAP E1W 51 M6
Knighthead Point POP/IOD E14 * 51 S7
Knightland Rd CLPT E5 39 M7
Knighton Cl ROMW/RG RM7 42 D4
SAND/SEL CR2 74 F13
WFD IG8 28 D9
Knighton Dr WFD IG8 28 D9
Knighton La BKHH IG9 28 D7
Knighton Park Rd SYD SE26 63 P10
Knighton Rd FSTGT E7 40 C8
REDH RH1 93 U12
ROMW/RG RM7 42 C4
RSEV TN14 90 F7
Knighton-Way La DEN/HRF UB9 33 M10
Knightrider Ct BLKFR EC4V * 5 M12
Knightrider St BLKFR EC4V 5 N13
Knight's Av EA W5 47 U7
Knightsbridge SKENS SW7 7 P4
Knightsbridge Crs STA TW18 57 M12
Knightsbridge Gdns ROMW/RG RM7 42 D3
Knightsbridge Gn KTBR SW1X * 7 Q4
Knights Chambers ED N9 * 27 L8
Knights Cl E/WMO/HCT KT8 70 H3
EGH TW20 * 56 H11
Knightscote Cl DEN/HRF UB9 21 P14
Knights Hl WNWD SE27 62 F10
Knight's Hill Sq WNWD SE27 62 F9
Knight's La ED N9 27 L8
Knights Manor Wy DART DA1 67 M4
Knight's Pk KUT/HW KT1 71 U1
Knights Pl REDH RH1 93 U9
WHTN TW2 59 N6
Knights Rdg ORP BR6 77 R10
Knights Rd CAN/RD E16 52 C6
STAN HA7 23 S9
Knights Wk ABR/ST RM4 29 R1
LBTH SE11 9 L8
Knights Wy BARK/HLT IG6 29 L11
Knightswood Cl EDGW HA8 24 C7
Knightswood Rd RAIN RM13 42 F14
Knightwood Cl REIG RH2 93 N12
Knightwood Crs NWMAL KT3 72 E4
Knipp Hl COB KT11 82 H3
Knivet Rd FUL/PGN SW6 6 E12
Knobs Hill Rd SRTFD E15 39 T13
Knockholt Cl BELMT SM2 73 P14
Knockholt Rd ELTH/MOT SE9 64 F3
RSEV TN14 89 V4
Knock Mill La BGR/WK TN15 91 V4
Knole Cl CROY/NA CR0 * 75 N4
Knole Rd DART DA1 66 G5
SEV TN13 90 K13
The Knole ELTH/MOT SE9 64 J9
Knoll Crs NTHWD HA6 22 B14
Knoll Dr STHGT/OAK N14 25 U5
Knollmead BRYLDS KT5 72 C6
Knoll Park Rd CHERT KT16 68 K6
Knoll Ri ORP BR6 77 P6
Knoll Rd BXLY DA5 66 A5
SCUP DA14 65 R10
WAND/EARL SW18 61 P3
Knolls Cl WPK KT4 72 H8
The Knolls EW KT17 84 J6
The Knoll BECK BR3 63 T13
CHERT KT16 68 K6
COB KT11 82 J3
EA W5 47 S3
HAYES BR2 76 C7
LHD/OX KT22 83 S11
PIN HA5 * 22 F14
Knollys Cl STRHM/NOR SW16 62 F8
Knolly's Rd STRHM/NOR SW16 62 E8
Knolton Wy SLN SL2 44 A4
Knottisford St BETH E2 51 P1
Knotts Green Ms LEY E10 39 T4
Knotts Green Rd LEY E10 39 T4
Knotts Pl SEV TN13 90 G14
Knowle Av BXLYHN DA7 53 U12
Knowle Cl BRXN/ST SW9 62 E1
Knowle Gdns BF/WBF KT14 80 K3
Knowle Gn STA TW18 57 L10
Knowle Gv VW GU25 68 A5
Knowle Grove Cl VW GU25 68 A5
Knowle Pk COB KT11 82 G5
Knowle Park Av STA TW18 57 M11
Knowle Rd HAYES BR2 76 G7
WHTN TW2 59 N6
Knowles Cl WDR/YW UB7 45 Q6
Knowles Hill Crs LEW SE13 63 V3
The Knowle KWD/TDW/WH KT20 * 84 H11
Knowl Hl WOKS/MYFD GU22 80 F9
Knowlton Gn HAYES BR2 76 B3
Knowl Wy BORE WD6 23 V3
Knowsley Av STHL UB1 46 K6
Knowsley Rd BTSEA SW11 49 T14
Knox Rd FSTGT E7 40 C11
Knox St CAMTN NW1 3 Q9
Knoyle St NWCR SE14 51 Q11
Knutsford Av WATN WD24 11 R12
Kohat Rd WIM/MER SW19 61 Q10
Koh-i-Noor Av BUSH WD23 22 J4
Koonowla Cl BH/WHM TN16 88 F5
Kooringa WARL CR6 87 M9
Korda Cl SHPTN TW17 69 R1
Korea Cottages COB KT11 * 82 F6
Kossuth St GNWCH SE10 52 A10
Kramer Ms ECT SW5 6 F10
Kreedman Wk HACK E8 * 39 L10
Kuala Gdns STRHM/NOR SW16 62 D13
Kydbrook Cl STMC/STPC BR5 77 L5
Kylemore Cl EHAM E6 40 F14
Kylemore Rd KIL/WHAMP NW6 37 N12
Kymberley Rd HRW HA1 * 35 N4
Kyme Rd ROM RM1 42 F4
Kynance Cl HARH RM3 30 J9
Kynance Gdns STAN HA7 23 S13
Kynance Ms SKENS SW7 6 H6
Kynance Pl KENS W8 6 J6
Kynaston Av THHTH CR7 74 G3
Kynaston Cl KTN/HRWW/WS HA3 23 M12
Kynaston Ct CTHM CR3 94 J1
Kynaston Crs THHTH CR7 74 G3
Kynaston Rd BMLY BR1 64 C10
ENC/FH EN2 15 T13
STMC/STPC BR5 77 R5
STNW/STAM N16 38 J8
THHTH CR7 74 G3
Kynaston Wd KTN/HRWW/WS HA3 23 M12
Kynersley Cl CAR SM5 73 T8
Kynoch Rd UED N18 27 P9
Kyrle Rd BTSEA SW11 61 U4
Kytes Dr GSTN WD25 11 R7
Kyverdale Rd STNW/STAM N16 38 K5

L

Laburnham Cl UPMR RM14 43 U5
Laburnham Gdns UPMR RM14 43 T5
Laburnum Av DART DA1 66 J6
ED N9 26 J7
HCH RM12 42 G7
SUT SM1 73 S8
SWLY BR8 78 D1
TOTM N17 26 H12
WDR/YW UB7 45 R5
Laburnum Cl ALP/SUD HA0 36 A13
CHES/WCR EN8 16 D5
CHING E4 27 R11
PECK SE15 51 N12
Laburnum Ct STAN HA7 23 S9
Laburnum Crs SUN TW16 58 D13
Laburnum Gdns CROY/NA CR0 75 P5
Laburnum Gv CDALE/KGS NW9 36 C5
DTCH/LGLY SL3 44 E11
HSLW TW3 58 H2
NWMAL KT3 60 D14
RSLP HA4 33 V4
STHL UB1 46 H2
WCHMH N21 26 G7
Laburnum Pl ELTH/MOT SE9 * 64 J3
Laburnum Rd CHERT KT16 69 L6
EPP CM16 18 G3
EPSOM KT18 84 E3
HYS/HAR UB3 46 B9
MTCM CR4 61 U14
WIM/MER SW19 61 Q12
WOKS/MYFD GU22 80 B10
Laburnum St BETH E2 5 U2
Laburnum Wk HCH RM12 42 J10
Laburnum Wy CHESW EN7 15 R2
HAYES BR2 76 K5
STWL/WRAY TW19 57 R6
Lacebark Cl BFN/LL DA15 65 P5
Lacewing Cl PLSTW E13 52 C1
Lacey Av COUL/CHIP CR5 86 E10
Lacey Cl ED N9 27 L7
EGH TW20 56 H12
Lacey Dr BCTR RM8 41 S8
COUL/CHIP CR5 86 E10
EDGW HA8 23 U9
HPTN TW12 58 H13
Lackford Rd COUL/CHIP CR5 85 T8
Lackington St SDTCH EC2A 5 R9
Lackmore Rd EN EN1 16 C9
Lacock Cl WIM/MER SW19 61 Q11
Lacon Rd EDUL SE22 63 L2
Lacrosse Wy STRHM/NOR SW16 62 B13
Lacy Gn COUL/CHIP CR5 86 E10
Lacy Rd PUT/ROE SW15 60 K2
Ladas Rd WNWD SE27 62 G10
Ladbroke Crs NTGHL W11 2 B12
Ladbroke Gdns NTGHL W11 2 C13
Ladbroke Gv NKENS W10 2 A10
NKENS W10 48 K2
REDH RH1 93 U9
Ladbroke Ms NTGHL W11 6 B2
Ladbroke Rd EN EN1 26 K4
EPSOM KT18 84 D4
NTGHL W11 6 B1
REDH RH1 93 U8
Ladbroke Sq NTGHL W11 2 D14
Ladbroke Ter NTGHL W11 2 D14
NTGHL W11 6 D1
Ladbroke Wk NTGHL W11 6 D1
Ladbrook Cl PIN HA5 34 H3
Ladbrooke Cl POTB/CUF EN6 14 C6
Ladbrooke Crs SCUP DA14 65 T8
Ladbrooke Dr POTB/CUF EN6 14 C6
Ladbrook Rd SNWD SE25 74 H1
Ladderstile Ride KUTN/CMB KT2 60 B10
Ladderswood Wy FBAR/BDGN N11 26 A10
Ladds Wy SWLY BR8 78 D2
Lady Alesford Av STAN HA7 23 R10
Lady Booth Rd KUT/HW KT1 59 U14
Ladycroft Gdns ORP BR6 77 L10
Ladycroft Rd LEW SE13 63 T1
Ladycroft Wk STAN HA7 23 T13
Ladycroft Wy ORP BR6 77 L10
Ladyfields LOU IG10 28 K2
Lady Forsdyke Wy HOR/WEW KT19 72 A13
Ladygate La RSLP HA4 33 U4
Ladygrove CROY/NA CR0 75 Q13
Lady Harewood Wy HOR/WEW KT19 72 A13
Lady Hay WPK KT4 72 F7
Lady Margaret Rd KTTN NW5 38 A10
STHL UB1 46 H5
Lady Meadow KGLGY WD4 10 D1
Ladymount WLGTN SM6 74 B9
Lady's Cl WATW WD18 22 E2
Ladyship Ter EDUL SE22 * 63 M5
Ladysmith Av EHAM E6 40 G14
GNTH/NBYPK IG2 41 M5
Ladysmith Cl MLHL NW7 24 G12
Ladysmith Rd CAN/RD E16 52 B1
ELTH/MOT SE9 64 J4
EN EN1 15 V14
KTN/HRWW/WS HA3 23 N14
TOTM N17 27 L14
UED N18 27 M10
Lady Somerset Rd KTTN NW5 37 V9
Ladythorpe Cl ADL/WDHM KT15 69 M9
Ladywalk RKW/CH/CXG WD3 20 J10
Ladywell Cl BROCKY SE4 63 S3
Ladywell Rd LEW SE13 63 T3
Ladywell St SRTFD E15 40 B13
Ladywell Water Tower BROCKY SE4 * 63 R1
Ladywood Av STMC/STPC BR5 77 N3
Ladywood Cl RKW/CH/CXG WD3 21 M1
Ladywood Rd RDART DA2 67 S10
SURB KT6 72 A7
Lafone Av FELT TW13 58 E6
Lafone St STHWK SE1 9 U3
Lagado Ms BERM/RHTH SE16 51 P6
Lagham Ct GDST RH9 * 95 Q14
Lagham Pk GDST RH9 95 Q13
Lagham Rd GDST RH9 95 Q14
Laglands Cl REIG RH2 93 Q8
Lagonda Av BARK/HLT IG6 29 P11
Lagonda Wy DART DA1 66 J2
Lagoon Rd STMC/STPC BR5 77 R3
Laidlaw Dr WCHMH N21 26 D3
Laing Cl BARK/HLT IG6 29 M11
Laing Dean NTHLT UB5 34 E13
Laings Av MTCM CR4 61 T14
Lainlock Pl HSLW TW3 46 K13
Lainson St WAND/EARL SW18 61 N5
Lairdale Cl DUL SE21 62 G6
Lairs Cl HOLWY N7 * 38 C11
Laitwood Rd BAL SW12 61 V6
Lake Av BMLY BR1 64 C11
RAIN RM13 42 K14
Lake Cl BCTR RM8 41 T8
BF/WBF KT14 81 P2
Lakedale Rd WOOL/PLUM SE18 53 N10
Lake Dr BUSH WD23 23 L7
Lakefield Rd WDGN N22 26 F14
Lakefields Cl RAIN RM13 42 K14
Lake Gdns DAGE RM10 42 A10
RCHPK/HAM TW10 59 R8
WLGTN SM6 73 V8
Lakehall Gdns THHTH CR7 74 F3
Lakehall Rd THHTH CR7 74 F3
Lake House Rd WAN E11 40 C7
Lakehurst Rd HOR/WEW KT19 72 E10
Lakeland Cl CHIG IG7 29 R9
KTN/HRWW/WS HA3 23 M11
Lakenheath STHGT/OAK N14 26 B3
Lake Ri ROM RM1 42 F1
WTHK RM20 55 U9
Lake Rd CHDH RM6 41 T2
CROY/NA CR0 75 R7
DAGW RM9 54 B1
LEY E10 39 T5
WIM/MER SW19 61 M10
Lakers Ri BNSTD SM7 85 S6
Lakeside BECK BR3 75 T1
ENC/FH EN2 26 B2
HOR/WEW KT19 72 E11
RAIN RM13 43 L14
REDH RH1 93 U8
WEA W13 47 S4
WEY KT13 70 A7
WLGTN SM6 73 V9
Lakeside Av REDBR IG4 40 F2
THMD SE28 53 Q7
Lakeside Cl BFN/LL DA15 65 S3
CHIG IG7 29 P9
RSLP HA4 33 V2
SNWD SE25 63 L14
Lakeside Crs EBAR EN4 25 T4
Lakeside Dr ESH/CLAY KT10 71 L11
HAYES BR2 76 G8
WLSDN NW10 47 V1
Lakeside Gra WEY KT13 69 U8
Lakeside Pl LCOL/BKTW AL2 12 H2
Lakeside Rd CHES/WCR EN8 16 C2
DTCH/LGLY SL3 44 K12
PLMGR N13 26 D9
WKENS W14 48 K8
Lakeside Wy WBLY HA9 36 A9
Lakes Rd HAYES BR2 76 E10
Lakeswood Rd STMC/STPC BR5 76 K4
The Lake BUSH WD23 23 M6
Lake Vw EDGW HA8 23 V10
KGLGY WD4 * 10 H2
POTB/CUF EN6 14 E7
Lake View Est BOW E3 * 39 P14
Lake View Rd SEV TN13 90 G13
Lakeview Rd WELL DA16 65 R2
WNWD SE27 62 F10
Lake View Ter UED N18 * 26 K9
Lakis Cl HAMP NW3 37 Q9
Laleham Abbey STA TW18 * 69 N2
Laleham Av MLHL NW7 24 D8
Laleham Cl STA TW18 57 M13
Laleham Ct SUT SM1 * 73 Q10
WOKN/KNAP GU21 * 80 C6
Laleham Reach CHERT KT16 57 M14
Laleham Rd CAT SE6 63 U5
SHPTN TW17 69 R2
STA TW18 56 K11
Lalor St FUL/PGN SW6 49 L14
Lambarde Av ELTH/MOT SE9 64 J9
Lambarde Dr SEV TN13 90 G13
Lambarde Rd SEV TN13 90 G12
Lambardes Cl ORP BR6 89 S1
Lamb Cl GSTN WD25 11 Q8
NTHLT UB5 46 G1
Lamberhurst Cl STMC/STPC BR5 77 T6
Lamberhurst Rd BCTR RM8 41 V6
WNWD SE27 62 E9
Lambert Av DTCH/LGLY SL3 44 C8
RCH/KEW TW9 60 A1
Lambert Cl BH/WHM TN16 88 F6
Lambert Ct BUSH WD23 22 F2
Lambert Jones Ms BARB EC2Y * 5 N9
Lambert Rd BNSTD SM7 85 N4
BRXS/STRHM SW2 62 C3
CAN/RD E16 52 D4
NFNCH/WDSPK N12 25 R10
Lambert's Pl CROY/NA CR0 74 H6
Lambert's Rd BRYLDS KT5 71 V3
Lambert St IS N1 38 E12
Lambert Wy NFNCH/WDSPK N12 25 Q10
Lambeth Br WEST SW1P 8 F7
Lambeth High St LBTH SE11 8 G7
Lambeth Hl BLKFR EC4V 5 N13
Lambeth Palace Rd STHWK SE1 8 G6
Lambeth Rd CROY/NA CR0 74 E6
STHWK SE1 8 J6
Lambeth Wk LBTH SE11 8 H7
PECK SE15 50 K14
Lambkins Ms WALTH E17 39 U2
Lamb La HACK E8 39 M12
Lamble St KTTN NW5 37 U9
Lambley Rd DAGW RM9 41 R11
Lambly Hl VW GU25 68 C1
Lambolle Pl HAMP NW3 37 S11
Lambolle Rd HAMP NW3 37 S11
Lambourn Cha RAD WD7 12 C10
Lambourn Cl HNWL W7 47 P7
KTTN NW5 * 38 A9
SAND/SEL CR2 74 F13
Lambourne Av WIM/MER SW19 61 M9
Lambourne Cl CHIG IG7 29 R8
Lambourne Ct UX/CGN UB8 33 M13
Lambourne Crs CHIG IG7 29 S7
WOKN/KNAP GU21 80 H3
Lambourne Dr COB KT11 82 E5
Lambourne Gdns BARK IG11 41 P12
CHING E4 27 S7
EN EN1 15 V14
HCH RM12 42 K7
Lambourne Gv BERM/RHTH SE16 51 P10
KUT/HW KT1 60 B14
Lambourne Pl BKHTH/KID SE3 52 D13
Lambourne Rd BARK IG11 41 N12
CHIG IG7 29 P9
GDMY/SEVK IG3 41 N7
WAN E11 39 U5
Lambourn Rd CLAP SW4 61 V1
Lambrook Ter FUL/PGN SW6 49 L13
Lambs Cl ED N9 27 L7
POTB/CUF EN6 15 P3
Lamb's Conduit Pas FSBYW WC1X 4 G9
Lamb's Conduit St BMSBY WC1N 4 G8
Lambscroft Av ELTH/MOT SE9 64 E8
Lambscroft Wy CFSP/GDCR SL9 20 C14
Lambs Gv BARK IG11 41 N12
Lamb's La North RAIN RM13 54 K2
Lamb's La South RAIN RM13 54 J3
Lambs Meadow WFD IG8 28 F14
Lambs Ms IS N1 5 L2
Lamb's Pas STLK EC1Y 5 Q8
Lambs Ter ED N9 * 26 H7
Lamb St WCHPL E1 5 U9
Lambs Wk ENC/FH EN2 15 S14
Lambton Av CHES/WCR EN8 16 D7
Lambton Pl NTGHL W11 2 D13
Lambton Rd ARCH N19 38 C6
RYNPK SW20 60 J14
Lamb Wk STHWK SE1 9 S4
Lamerock Rd BMLY BR1 64 B9
Lamerton Rd BARK/HLT IG6 28 K14
Lamerton St DEPT SE8 51 S11
Lamford Cl TOTM N17 26 H12
Lamington St HMSMTH W6 48 H9
Lamlash St LBTH SE11 9 L7
Lammas Av MTCM CR4 61 U14
Lammas Cl STA TW18 56 J8
Lammas Dr STA TW18 56 H9
Lammas La ESH/CLAY KT10 70 J9
Lammas Park Gdns EA W5 47 S6
Lammas Rd HOM E9 39 P12
LEY E10 39 Q7
RCHPK/HAM TW10 59 S9
WATW WD18 22 E3
Lammermoor Rd BAL SW12 * 61 V5
Lamont Rd WBPTN SW10 6 K12
Lamont Road Pas WBPTN SW10 7 L12
Lamorbey Cl BFN/LL DA15 65 P7
Lamorbey Pk BFN/LL DA15 * 65 R6
Lamorna WOKS/MYFD GU22 * 80 C8
Lamorna Cl ORP BR6 77 Q5
RAD WD7 12 F8
WALTH E17 27 V14
Lamorna Gv STAN HA7 23 T14
Lampard Gv STNW/STAM N16 38 K6
Lampern Sq BETH E2 * 51 L1
Lampeter Cl WOKS/MYFD GU22 80 C8
Lampeter Sq HMSMTH W6 6 A12
Lamplighter Cl WCHPL E1 51 N2
Lamplighters Cl DART DA1 67 M4
WAB EN9 17 N8
Lampmead Rd LEE/GVPK SE12 64 A3
Lamport Cl WOOL/PLUM SE18 52 H9
Lampton Av HSLW TW3 46 J13
Lampton House Cl WIM/MER SW19 60 K9
Lampton Park Rd HSLW TW3 46 K14
Lampton Rd HEST TW5 46 K13
Lamson Rd RAIN RM13 54 F3
Lanacre Av CDALE/KGS NW9 24 E13
Lanark Cl EA W5 47 S3
Lanark Pl MV/WKIL W9 2 K7
Lanark Rd MV/WKIL W9 2 J5
Lanbury Rd PECK SE15 63 P2
Lancashire Ct MYFR/PKLN W1K 3 U13
Lancaster Av BARK IG11 41 N12
EBAR EN4 14 F12
MTCM CR4 74 C3
WAN E11 40 D2
WIM/MER SW19 60 K10
WNWD SE27 62 F7
Lancaster Cl ASHF TW15 57 Q9
BRWN CM15 31 U3
CDALE/KGS NW9 24 F12
EGH TW20 56 B10
HAYES BR2 76 B2
STWL/WRAY TW19 57 Q4
TOTM N17 * 27 L12
WOKN/KNAP GU21 80 E6
WPK KT4 72 H5
Lancaster Ct BAY/PAD W2 2 K13
WOT/HER KT12 70 D5
Lancaster Dr HAMP NW3 37 S11
HCH RM12 42 H10
LOU IG10 28 G3
POP/IOD E14 51 U6
Lancaster Garde BMLY BR1 76 G3
Lancaster Gdn KUTN/CMB KT2 59 T10
Lancaster Gdns KUTN/CMB KT2 59 U10
WIM/MER SW19 61 L10
Lancaster Ga BAY/PAD W2 2 K14
Lancaster Gv HAMP NW3 37 S11
Lancaster House WOOL/PLUM SE18 * 52 G12
Lancaster Ms BAY/PAD W2 2 K13
RCHPK/HAM TW10 59 U4
WAND/EARL SW18 * 61 P3
Lancaster Pk RCHPK/HAM TW10 59 U3
Lancaster Pl COVGDN WC2E 4 G14
TWK TW1 59 Q5
WIM/MER SW19 60 K10
Lancaster Rd UX/CGN UB8 33 P11
EBAR EN4 25 R3
ENC/FH EN2 15 T13
FBAR/BDGN N11 26 B11
FSBYPK N4 38 E5
FSTGT E7 40 C12
NKENS W10 48 K4
NTGHL W11 2 B11
NTHLT UB5 35 L11
RYLN/HDSTN HA2 34 J3
SNWD SE25 62 K14
SNWD SE25 75 L1
STHL UB1 46 G5
UED N18 26 K10
WALTH E17 27 P14
WAN E11 40 A7
WIM/MER SW19 60 K10
WLSDN NW10 36 F10
Lancaster Stables HAMP NW3 * 37 S11
Lancaster St STHWK SE1 9 L4
Lancaster Ter BAY/PAD W2 3 L13
Lancaster Wk HYS/HAR UB3 45 U4
Lancaster Wy ABLGY WD5 11 M5
WPK KT4 72 J5
Lancaster West NTGHL W11 2 A13
Lancastrian Rd WLGTN SM6 74 C12
Lancefield St NKENS W10 2 C6
Lancell St STNW/STAM N16 38 J7
Lancelot Av ALP/SUD HA0 35 T9
Lancelot Crs ALP/SUD HA0 35 T9
Lancelot Gdns EBAR EN4 25 U5
Lancelot Pde ALP/SUD HA0 * 35 U10
Lancelot Pl SKENS SW7 7 Q5
Lancelot Rd ALP/SUD HA0 35 T9
BARK/HLT IG6 29 N11
WELL DA16 65 Q2
Lance Rd HRW HA1 35 L5
Lancer Sq KENS W8 6 G3
Lancey Cl CHARL SE7 52 F9
Lanchester Rd HGT N6 37 T3
Lancing Gdns ED N9 26 K6
Lancing Rd CROY/NA CR0 74 D4
FELT TW13 58 B7
GNTH/NBYPK IG2 41 M4
HARH RM3 31 L12
ORP BR6 77 R7
WEA W13 47 R5
Lancing St CAMTN NW1 4 C6
Lancing Wy RKW/CH/CXG WD3 21 T3
Lancresse Cl UX/CGN UB8 33 P11
Landale Gdns DART DA1 66 J6
Landau Ter HAYES BR2 76 G9
Landau Wy ERITH DA8 54 K10
Landcroft Rd EDUL SE22 62 K4
Landells Rd EDUL SE22 62 K4
Landford Cl RKW/CH/CXG WD3 21 Q7
Landford Rd PUT/ROE SW15 60 J1
Landgrove Rd WIM/MER SW19 61 N10
Landleys Flds HOLWY N7 * 38 B10
Landmann Wy NWCR SE14 51 P11
Landmead Rd CHES/WCR EN8 16 E3
Landon Pl KTBR SW1X 7 Q5
Landons Cl POP/IOD E14 51 U6
Landon Wy ASHF TW15 * 57 T11
Landor Rd BRXN/ST SW9 62 C1
Landor Wk SHB W12 48 G7
Landra Gdns WCHMH N21 26 F4
Landridge Dr EN EN1 16 B12
Landridge Rd FUL/PGN SW6 49 L14
Landrock Rd CEND/HSY/T N8 38 C4
Landscape Rd WARL CR6 87 M9
WFD IG8 28 D12
Landseer Av MNPK E12 40 J10
Landseer Cl EDGW HA8 24 A14
EMPK RM11 42 H6
WIM/MER SW19 61 Q13
Landseer Rd ARCH N19 38 C8
EN EN1 27 L3
NWMAL KT3 72 D5
SUT SM1 73 N11
Lands' End BORE WD6 23 T4
Landstead Rd WOOL/PLUM SE18 53 M12
Landway BGR/WK TN15 91 M10
The Landway BGR/WK TN15 91 N7
STMC/STPC BR5 77 S1
Lane Ap MLHL NW7 25 L10
Lane Cl ADL/WDHM KT15 69 L10
CRICK NW2 36 H8
Lane End BXLYHN DA7 66 B1
EPSOM KT18 84 B4
Lane Gdns BUSH WD23 23 N6
ESH/CLAY KT10 71 P12
Lane Ms MNPK E12 40 H8
Lanercost Gdns STHGT/OAK N14 26 C5
Lanercost Rd BRXS/STRHM SW2 62 E7
Laneside CHST BR7 64 K10
EDGW HA8 24 C10
Laneside Av BCTR RM8 41 V5
The Lane BKHTH/KID SE3 64 C1
CHERT KT16 69 L1
STJWD NW8 2 J4
VW GU25 68 C1
Laneway PUT/ROE SW15 60 H3
Lanfranc Rd BOW E3 39 Q14
Lanfrey Pl WKENS W14 6 C10
Langaller La LHD/OX KT22 82 K11
Langbourne Av HGT N6 37 U7
Langbourne Wy ESH/CLAY KT10 71 Q11
Langbrook Rd BKHTH/KID SE3 64 F1
Lang Cl LHD/OX KT22 82 K13
Langcroft Cl CAR SM5 73 T8
Langdale Av MTCM CR4 73 T1
Langdale Cl BCTR RM8 41 S6
MORT/ESHN SW14 60 B2
ORP BR6 76 K8
WALW SE17 9 N11
WOKN/KNAP GU21 80 A6
Langdale Crs BXLYHN DA7 54 A13
Langdale Dr YEAD UB4 34 A14
Langdale Gdns HCH RM12 42 G10
PEND EN3 16 D9
Langdale Pde MTCM CR4 * 61 T14
Langdale Rd GNWCH SE10 51 U12
THHTH CR7 74 E2
Langdale St WCHPL E1 * 51 M4
Langdale Ter BORE WD6 * 24 D1
Langdon Ct WLSDN NW10 36 E13
Langdon Crs EHAM E6 40 J14
Langdon Dr CDALE/KGS NW9 36 C6
Langdon House WOOL/PLUM SE18 * 52 G12
Langdon Pk TEDD TW11 59 S12
Langdon Park Rd HGT N6 37 V5
Langdon Pl MORT/ESHN SW14 60 C1
Langdon Rd EHAM E6 40 J13
HAYES BR2 76 D1
MRDN SM4 73 Q3
Langdon Shaw SCUP DA14 65 P10
Langdon Wk MRDN SM4 73 Q3
Langdon Wy STHWK SE1 51 L9
Langford Cl HACK E8 39 L10
SEVS/STOTM N15 38 J4
STJWD NW8 2 K3
Langford Crs EBAR EN4 25 T2
Langford Gn CMBW SE5 62 J1
Langford Pl SCUP DA14 65 Q8
STJWD NW8 2 K4
Langford Rd EBAR EN4 25 T2
FUL/PGN SW6 49 P14
WFD IG8 28 E11
Langfords BKHH IG9 28 F7
Langham Ct EMPK RM11 42 K5
RSLP HA4 * 34 D10
Langham Dene PUR/KEN CR8 86 F5
Langham Dr GDMY/SEVK IG3 41 R4
Langham Gdns ALP/SUD HA0 35 S7
EDGW HA8 24 C12
RCHPK/HAM TW10 59 S9
WCHMH N21 26 E3
WEA W13 47 R5
Langham House Cl RCHPK/HAM TW10 59 T9
Langham Pde SEVS/STOTM N15 * 38 F1
Langham Park Pl HAYES BR2 76 B2
Langham Pl CHSWK W4 48 E11
EGH TW20 56 D10
REGST W1B 3 V11
SEVS/STOTM N15 38 F1
Langham Rd EDGW HA8 24 C11
RYNPK SW20 60 J13
SEVS/STOTM N15 38 G2
TEDD TW11 59 R10
Langham St GTPST W1W 4 A10
REGST W1B 3 V10
Langhedge Cl UED N18 26 K11
Langhedge La UED N18 26 K11
Langholm Cl BAL SW12 62 B5
Langholme BUSH WD23 23 L6
Langhorn Dr WHTN TW2 59 N5
Langhorne Rd DAGE RM10 42 A12
Langland Ct NTHWD HA6 21 U12
Langland Crs STAN HA7 23 T14
Langland Dr PIN HA5 22 G12
Langland Gdns CROY/NA CR0 75 R7
HAMP NW3 37 P10
Langlands Dr RDART DA2 67 S10
Langlands Ri HOR/WEW KT19 84 C3
Langler Rd WLSDN NW10 36 J14
Langley Av RSLP HA4 34 D7
SURB KT6 71 T6
WPK KT4 72 K7
Langley Broom DTCH/LGLY SL3 44 D10
Langleybury La KGLGY WD4 10 H9
Langley Cl EPSOM KT18 84 D9
HARH RM3 30 K12
Langley Ct BECK BR3 * 75 T2
CHESW EN7 * 15 S2
COVGDN WC2E 4 E13
Langley Crs DAGW RM9 41 S12
EDGW HA8 24 C8
HYS/HAR UB3 46 B12
KGLGY WD4 10 G4
WAN E11 40 E5
Langley Dr ACT W3 48 B7
BRW CM14 31 U8
WAN E11 40 D5
Langley Gdns DAGW RM9 41 T12
STMC/STPC BR5 76 K4
Langley Gv NWMAL KT3 60 D14
Langley Hl KGLGY WD4 10 F3
Langley Hill Cl KGLGY WD4 10 G3
Langley La ABLGY WD5 11 N6
EPSOM KT18 92 B1
VX/NE SW8 8 F11
Langley Lodge La KGLGY WD4 10 E5
Langley Oaks Av SAND/SEL CR2 75 M14
Langley Pk DTCH/LGLY SL3 * 44 E3
MLHL NW7 24 E11
Langley Park Rd BELMT SM2 73 R12
DTCH/LGLY SL3 44 E6
Langley Pl WPK KT4 72 K7
Langley Quay DTCH/LGLY SL3 * 44 E7
Langley Rd ABLGY WD5 11 L5
BECK BR3 75 P2
DTCH/LGLY SL3 44 A8
ISLW TW7 47 P14
KGLGY WD4 10 C4
SAND/SEL CR2 75 P13
STA TW18 56 K11
SURB KT6 71 U5
WAT WD17 11 N13
WELL DA16 53 S11
WIM/MER SW19 61 M13
Langley Rw BAR EN5 14 B13
Langley St LSQ/SEVD WC2H 4 E12
Langley Vale Rd EPSOM KT18 84 E8
Langley Wy WAT WD17 11 M13
WWKM BR4 75 V6
Langley Whf KGLGY WD4 * 10 G1
Langley Wd BECK BR3 * 76 A3
Langmead Dr BUSH WD23 23 M6
Langmead St WNWD SE27 62 F9
Langport Ct WOT/HER KT12 70 E6
Langridge Ms HPTN TW12 58 H11
Langroyd Rd TOOT SW17 61 T7
Langshott Cl ADL/WDHM KT15 80 J1
Langside Av PUT/ROE SW15 60 G2
Langside Crs STHGT/OAK N14 26 B8
Langston Hughes Cl HNHL SE24 * 62 F2
Langston Rd LOU IG10 29 M2
Lang St WCHPL E1 51 N2
Langthorn Ct LOTH EC2R * 5 R11
Langthorne Rd WAN E11 39 V8
Langthorne St FUL/PGN SW6 48 K13
Langton Av EHAM E6 52 J1
EW KT17 84 F1
TRDG/WHET N20 25 Q5
Langton Cl ADL/WDHM KT15 69 M8
FSBYW WC1X 4 H6
Langton Gv NTHWD HA6 21 U10
Langton Ri EDUL SE22 63 M5
Langton Rd BRXN/ST SW9 9 M14
BRXN/ST SW9 50 F13
CRICK NW2 36 J8
E/WMO/HCT KT8 71 L3
KTN/HRWW/WS HA3 23 L12
Langton St WBPTN SW10 6 K12
Langton Vls TOTM N17 * 27 L13
Langton Wy BKHTH/KID SE3 52 C13
CROY/NA CR0 74 K9
EGH TW20 56 G11
Langtry Pl FUL/PGN SW6 6 F11
Langtry Rd KIL/WHAMP NW6 2 G2
NTHLT UB5 34 F14
Langwood Cha TEDD TW11 59 S11
Langwood Cl ASHTD KT21 84 A7
Langwood Gdns WAT WD17 11 N13
Langworth Cl RDART DA2 66 K8
Langworth Dr YEAD UB4 46 D4
Lanhill Rd MV/WKIL W9 2 E7
Lanier Rd LEW SE13 63 U4
Lanigan Dr HSLW TW3 58 K3
Lankaster Gdns EFNCH N2 25 R13
Lankers Dr RYLN/HDSTN HA2 34 H4
Lankton Cl BECK BR3 63 U13
Lannock Rd HYS/HAR UB3 46 B6
Lannoy Rd ELTH/MOT SE9 65 L6
Lanrick Rd POP/IOD E14 51 V4
Lanridge Rd ABYW SE2 53 T8
Lansbury Av BARK IG11 41 Q12
CHDH RM6 41 U3
EBED/NFELT TW14 58 D4
UED N18 26 H10
Lansbury Cl WLSDN NW10 36 C10
Lansbury Crs DART DA1 67 N3
Lansbury Dr YEAD UB4 46 B1
Lansbury Gdns POP/IOD E14 * 51 V4
Lansbury Rd PEND EN3 16 D13
Lansbury Wy UED N18 26 J10
Lanscombe Wk VX/NE SW8 8 E14
Lansdell Rd MTCM CR4 61 U14
Lansdown Cl WOT/HER KT12 70 E6
Lansdowne Av BXLYHN DA7 53 S12
ORP BR6 76 K6
Lansdowne Cl BRYLDS KT5 72 B7
TWK TW1 59 P6
Lansdowne Copse WPK KT4 * 72 G7
Lansdowne Ct WPK KT4 72 G7
Lansdowne Crs NTGHL W11 2 B14
Lansdowne Dr HACK E8 39 M13
Lansdowne Gdns VX/NE SW8 50 C13
Lansdowne Gn VX/NE SW8 8 E14
Lansdowne Gv WLSDN NW10 36 E9
Lansdowne Hl WNWD SE27 62 F8
Lansdowne La CHARL SE7 52 F10
Lansdowne Ms CHARL SE7 52 F10
NTGHL W11 6 C2
Lansdowne Pl NRWD SE19 62 K12
STHWK SE1 9 R5
Lansdowne Ri NTGHL W11 2 B14
Lansdowne Rd BMLY BR1 64 C12
CHING E4 27 S7
CROY/NA CR0 74 H7
FNCH N3 25 M12
GDMY/SEVK IG3 41 P6
HACK E8 39 L11
HOR/WEW KT19 72 C12
HSLW TW3 58 K1
MUSWH N10 26 A14
NTGHL W11 2 B14
NTGHL W11 6 C1
PUR/KEN CR8 86 E2
RYNPK SW20 60 J12
SEV TN13 90 K12
STA TW18 57 M12
STAN HA7 23 S11
SWFD E18 40 C1
TOTM N17 27 L13
UX/CGN UB8 45 T4
WALTH E17 39 S4
WAN E11 40 B7
Lansdowne Ter BMSBY WC1N 4 F8
Lansdowne Wk NTGHL W11 6 B1
Lansdowne Wy VX/NE SW8 50 C13
Lansdowne Wood Cl WNWD SE27 62 F8
Lansdown Rd CFSP/GDCR SL9 20 B13
FSTGT E7 40 E12
SCUP DA14 65 R8
Lansfield Av UED N18 27 L9
Lantern Cl ALP/SUD HA0 35 T10
ORP BR6 76 K9
PUT/ROE SW15 60 G2
Lanterns LOU IG10 17 T13
Lanterns Ct POP/IOD E14 51 T8
Lantern Wy WDR/YW UB7 45 Q7
Lant St STHWK SE1 9 N3
Lanvanor Rd PECK SE15 51 N14
Lapford Cl MV/WKIL W9 2 D7
La Plata Gv BRW CM14 31 V8
Lapse Wood Wk FSTH SE23 63 M6
Lapstone Gdns KTN/HRWW/WS HA3 35 S4
Lapwing Cl ERITH DA8 * 54 H12
SAND/SEL CR2 75 Q14
Lapwing Pl GSTN WD25 * 11 Q6
Lapwing Ter FSTGT E7 40 F10
Lapwing Wy ABLGY WD5 11 N5
YEAD UB4 46 F4
Lapworth Cl ORP BR6 77 S7
Lapworth Ct BAY/PAD W2 2 H9
Lara Cl CHSGTN KT9 71 U12
LEW SE13 63 U4
Larbert Rd STRHM/NOR SW16 62 A13
Larby Pl EW KT17 72 E14
Larch Av ACT W3 48 E6
LCOL/BKTW AL2 11 S4
Larch Cl BAL SW12 61 V7
CHESW EN7 15 U1
DEPT SE8 51 R11
FBAR/BDGN N11 25 U12
KWD/TDW/WH KT20 85 Q11
REDH RH1 93 Q12
WARL CR6 87 Q9
Larch Crs HOR/WEW KT19 72 B11
YEAD UB4 46 E3
Larch Dene ORP BR6 76 J7
Larch Dr CHSWK W4 * 48 A10
Larches Av EN EN1 16 C9
MORT/ESHN SW14 60 D2
The Larches BUSH WD23 22 G3
HGDN/ICK UB10 33 T14
PLMGR N13 26 G8
WOKN/KNAP GU21 80 C6
Larch Gv BFN/LL DA15 65 P6
Larch Rd CRICK NW2 36 J9
DART DA1 66 K6
LEY E10 39 S7
Larch Tree Wy CROY/NA CR0 75 S8
Larch Wy HAYES BR2 76 J5
Larchwood Av CRW RM5 30 B11
Larchwood Cl BNSTD SM7 85 L6
CRW RM5 30 C11
Larchwood Gdns BRWN CM15 31 U4
Larchwood Rd ELTH/MOT SE9 64 K7
Larcombe Cl CROY/NA CR0 74 K9
Larcom St WALW SE17 9 P8
Larden Rd ACT W3 48 E7
Largewood Av SURB KT6 72 A7
Larissa St WALW SE17 * 9 R8
Lark Av STA TW18 56 K8
Larkbere Rd SYD SE26 63 Q9
Lark Cl BRW CM14 31 V9
Larken Cl BUSH WD23 23 L6
Larken Dr BUSH WD23 23 L6
Larkfield COB KT11 82 C3
Larkfield Av KTN/HRWW/WS HA3 35 R1
Larkfield Rd RCH/KEW TW9 59 U2
SCUP DA14 65 P8
SEV TN13 90 C13
Larkhall Cl WOT/HER KT12 70 E11
Larkhall La CLAP SW4 50 C14
Larkhall Ri CLAP SW4 62 A1
Larkham Cl FELT TW13 58 A8
Larkhill Ter WOOL/PLUM SE18 * 52 J12
Larkin Cl COUL/CHIP CR5 86 D7
Lark Rw BETH E2 39 N13
Larksfield Gv EN EN1 16 B13
Larkshall Crs CHING E4 27 U9
Larkshall Rd CHING E4 27 V11
Larkspur Cl CDALE/KGS NW9 36 B3
ORP BR6 77 S7
RSLP HA4 33 T5
TOTM N17 26 H12
Larkspur Gv EDGW HA8 24 C9
Larkspur Wy HOR/WEW KT19 72 C10
Larkswood Cl ERITH DA8 54 G13
Larkswood Ri PIN HA5 34 E2
Larkswood Rd CHING E4 27 S9
Lark Wy CAR SM5 73 S5
Larkway Cl CDALE/KGS NW9 36 D2
Larmans Rd PEND EN3 16 D10
Larnach Rd HMSMTH W6 48 K11
Larne Rd RSLP HA4 34 B5
Larner Rd ERITH DA8 54 E12
La Roche Cl DTCH/LGLY SL3 44 A8
Larpent Av PUT/ROE SW15 60 J3
Larsen Dr WAB EN9 16 K8
Larwood Cl GFD/PVL UB6 35 M10
Lascelles Av HRW HA1 35 M5
Lascelles Cl BRWN CM15 31 V3
WAN E11 39 V7
Lascott's Rd WDGN N22 26 D11
Lassa Rd ELTH/MOT SE9 64 G3
Lassell St GNWCH SE10 51 V10
Lasseter Pl BKHTH/KID SE3 52 A11
Lasswade Rd CHERT KT16 68 K5
Latchett Rd SWFD E18 28 D13
Latchford Pl CHIG IG7 29 R9
Latchingdon Gdns WFD IG8 28 G11
Latchmere Cl RCHPK/HAM TW10 59 U10
Latchmere La KUTN/CMB KT2 59 V11
Latchmere Rd BTSEA SW11 49 T14
KUTN/CMB KT2 59 U11
Latchmere St BTSEA SW11 49 T14
Latchmoor Av CFSP/GDCR SL9 32 B2
Latchmoor Gv CFSP/GDCR SL9 32 B2
Latchmoor Wy CFSP/GDCR SL9 32 B2
Lateward Rd BTFD TW8 47 T11
Latham Cl BH/WHM TN16 88 E6
EHAM E6 52 G4
RDART DA2 67 S7
Latham Rd BXLYHS DA6 66 A3
TWK TW1 59 P5
Latham's Wy CROY/NA CR0 74 D7
Lathkill Cl EN EN1 27 L5
Lathom Rd EHAM E6 40 H12
Latimer Av EHAM E6 40 H13
Latimer Cl PIN HA5 22 E13
WATW WD18 22 A5
WOKS/MYFD GU22 80 F6
WPK KT4 72 H9
Latimer Ct REDH RH1 93 T12
Latimer Dr HCH RM12 42 K8
Latimer Gdns PIN HA5 22 E13
Latimer Pl NKENS W10 48 J4
Latimer Rd BAR EN5 25 P1
CROY/NA CR0 * 74 F8
FSTGT E7 40 D9
NKENS W10 48 J3
SEVS/STOTM N15 38 J4
TEDD TW11 59 P10
WIM/MER SW19 61 P11
Latona Rd PECK SE15 51 L11
La Tourne Gdns ORP BR6 77 L8
Lattimer Pl CHSWK W4 48 E12
Latton Cl ESH/CLAY KT10 70 K9
WOT/HER KT12 70 H5
Latymer Cl WEY KT13 69 U9
Latymer Gdns FNCH N3 * 25 L14
Latymer Rd ED N9 26 K7
Latymer Wy ED N9 26 H7
Laubin Cl TWK TW1 59 R2
Lauder Cl NTHLT UB5 34 F14
Lauderdale Dr RCHPK/HAM TW10 59 T8
Lauderdale Pde MV/WKIL W9 * 2 G6
Lauderdale Pl BARB EC2Y * 5 P10
Lauderdale Rd KGLGY WD4 10 J7
MV/WKIL W9 2 H6
Laud St CROY/NA CR0 74 G8
LBTH SE11 8 G9
Laughton Rd NTHLT UB5 34 F14
Launcelot Rd BMLY BR1 64 C9
Launcelot St STHWK SE1 8 J4
Launceston RKW/CH/CXG WD3 20 F4
Launceston Cl HARH RM3 30 J13
Launceston Gdns GFD/PVL UB6 35 S13
Launceston Pl KENS W8 6 J5
Launceston Rd GFD/PVL UB6 35 S13
Launch St POP/IOD E14 51 U8
Launders Ga ACT W3 * 48 B7
Launder's La RAIN RM13 55 L3
Laundress La STNW/STAM N16 39 L8
Laundry Rd HMSMTH W6 6 A12
Laura Cl EN EN1 26 J3
WAN E11 40 E3
Lauradale Rd EFNCH N2 37 T2
Laura Dr SWLY BR8 66 G12
Laura Pl CLPT E5 39 N9
Laura Ter FSBYPK N4 * 38 F7
Laurel Av DTCH/LGLY SL3 44 C7
POTB/CUF EN6 14 B6
TWK TW1 59 P6
Laurel Bank NFNCH/WDSPK N12 * 25 Q9
Laurel Bank Gdns FUL/PGN SW6 49 M14
Laurel Bank Rd ENC/FH EN2 15 S13
Laurel Cl BARK/HLT IG6 29 L11
BFN/LL DA15 65 Q8
DART DA1 66 J6
DTCH/LGLY SL3 44 J12
OXHEY WD19 22 F5
TOOT SW17 61 S10
Laurel Ct IVER SL0 * 32 H12
Laurel Crs CROY/NA CR0 75 S8
ROMW/RG RM7 42 E6
WOKN/KNAP GU21 80 G3
Laurel Dr OXTED RH8 96 B7
WCHMH N21 26 E5
Laurel Flds POTB/CUF EN6 14 B5
Laurel Gdns CHING E4 27 T5
HNWL W7 47 N6
HSLWW TW4 58 G2
MLHL NW7 24 D8
Laurel Gv PGE/AN SE20 63 N12
SYD SE26 63 P10
Laurel La WDR/YW UB7 45 Q9
Laurel Pk KTN/HRWW/WS HA3 23 P12
Laurel Rd BARN SW13 48 G14
CFSP/GDCR SL9 20 B13
HPTN TW12 59 M10
RYNPK SW20 60 H13
Laurels Rd IVER SL0 32 H14
The Laurels BNSTD SM7 85 M7
BORE WD6 * 13 L13
BUSH WD23 * 23 N7
CHESW EN7 15 U1
COB KT11 82 G5
RDART DA2 * 66 J8
Laurel St HACK E8 38 K11
Laurel Vw NFNCH/WDSPK N12 25 P8
Laurel Vls HNWL W7 * 47 N7
Laurel Wy SWFD E18 40 B2
TRDG/WHET N20 25 N8
Laurence Ms SHB W12 48 G7
Laurence Pountney Hl CANST EC4R 5 Q13
Laurence Pountney La CANST EC4R 5 Q13
Laurie Gv NWCR SE14 51 Q13
Laurie Rd HNWL W7 47 N3
Laurier Rd CROY/NA CR0 74 K5
KTTN NW5 37 V8
Laurimel Cl STAN HA7 23 R11
Laurino Pl BUSH WD23 23 L7
Lauriston Rd HOM E9 39 P13
WIM/MER SW19 60 K11
Lausanne Rd CEND/HSY/T N8 38 E2
PECK SE15 51 N14
Lauser Rd STWL/WRAY TW19 57 N5
Lavender Av BRWN CM15 31 V3
CDALE/KGS NW9 36 C6
MTCM CR4 61 S13
WPK KT4 72 J8
Lavender Cl CAR SM5 73 U9
CHEL SW3 7 M12
CHESW EN7 15 V1
COUL/CHIP CR5 * 86 A9
CTHM CR3 94 G1
HARH RM3 30 K12
HAYES BR2 76 G4
LHD/OX KT22 83 S12
Lavender Cottages LHD/OX KT22 * 83 S12
Lavender Ct E/WMO/HCT KT8 70 K1
Lavender Gdns BTSEA SW11 61 T2
ENC/FH EN2 15 R12
KTN/HRWW/WS HA3 23 N11
Lavender Ga LHD/OX KT22 82 K4
Lavender Gv HACK E8 39 L12
MTCM CR4 61 S13
Lavender Hl BTSEA SW11 61 T1
ENC/FH EN2 15 R13
SWLY BR8 78 D1
Lavender Park Rd BF/WBF KT14 * 81 L3
Lavender Pl IL IG1 40 K10
Lavender Ri WDR/YW UB7 45 S7
Lavender Rd BERM/RHTH SE16 51 Q6
BTSEA SW11 61 R1
CROY/NA CR0 74 D4
ENC/FH EN2 15 T13
HOR/WEW KT19 72 B11
SUT SM1 73 R9
UX/CGN UB8 45 R3
WLGTN SM6 73 U10
WOKS/MYFD GU22 80 F6
Lavender St SRTFD E15 40 A11
Lavender Sweep BTSEA SW11 61 T2
Lavender Ter BTSEA SW11 * 61 S1
Lavender V WLGTN SM6 74 B11
Lavender Wk BTSEA SW11 61 T2
Lavender Wy CROY/NA CR0 75 P4
Lavengro Rd WNWD SE27 62 G7
Lavenham Rd WAND/EARL SW18 61 M7
Lavernock Rd BXLYHN DA7 54 A14
Lavers Rd STNW/STAM N16 38 J8
Laverstoke Gdns PUT/ROE SW15 60 F5
Laverton Ms ECT SW5 * 6 H8
Laverton Pl ECT SW5 6 H8
Lavidge Rd ELTH/MOT SE9 64 G7
Lavina Gv IS N1 4 G3
Lavington Cl HOM E9 39 R11
Lavington Rd CROY/NA CR0 74 D8
WEA W13 47 R6
Lavington St STHWK SE1 9 M2
Lavinia Av GSTN WD25 11 Q8
Lavinia Rd DART DA1 67 M4
Lavrock La RKW/CH/CXG WD3 21 R5
Lawdon Gdns CROY/NA CR0 74 F9
Lawford Av RKW/CH/CXG WD3 20 G4
Lawford Cl HCH RM12 42 J9
RKW/CH/CXG WD3 20 G4
Lawford Gdns DART DA1 66 J3
PUR/KEN CR8 86 G6
Lawford Rd CHSWK W4 48 C12
IS N1 38 J12
KTTN NW5 38 A11
Lawless St POP/IOD E14 * 51 T5
Lawley Rd STHGT/OAK N14 25 V5
Lawley St CLPT E5 39 N9
Lawn Av WDR/YW UB7 45 N7
Lawn Cl BMLY BR1 64 D12
DTCH/LGLY SL3 44 A12
EN EN1 26 K5
NWMAL KT3 60 E14
RSLP HA4 34 B8
SWLY BR8 66 C14
Lawn Crs RCH/KEW TW9 48 A14
Lawn Farm Gv CHDH RM6 41 U2
Lawn Gdns HNWL W7 47 N6
Lawn House Cl POP/IOD E14 51 U7
Lawn La VX/NE SW8 8 F11
Lawn Rd BECK BR3 63 S12
HAMP NW3 37 T10
UX/CGN UB8 33 N12
Lawns Ct WBLY HA9 * 36 A7

The Lawns BELMT SM2 73 L12
BKHTH/KID SE3 * 64 B1
CHING E4 27 S10
DTCH/LGLY SL3 * 44 J13
NRWD SE19 62 H13
PIN HA5 22 K12
RAD WD7 12 J7
SCUP DA14 65 R9
Lawns Wy CRW RM5 30 C12
Lawnswood BAR EN5 * 25 L3
Lawn Ter BKHTH/KID SE3 64 B1
The Lawn DTCH/LGLY SL3 * 44 A13
NWDGN UB2 46 J10
Lawn V PIN HA5 22 G14
Lawrance Gdns CHES/WCR EN8 16 D2
Lawrence Av MLHL NW7 24 E9
MNPK E12 40 J9
NWMAL KT3 72 E5
PLMGR N13 26 F9
WALTH E17 27 Q13
WLSDN NW10 36 D13
Lawrence Buildings STNW/STAM N16 38 K8
Lawrence Campe Cl TRDG/WHET N20 25 R8
Lawrence Cl SEVS/STOTM N15 38 J2
SHB W12 48 H5
Lawrence Ct MLHL NW7 24 E10
OXHEY WD19 * 22 F8
Lawrence Crs DAGE RM10 42 B8
EDGW HA8 24 A14
Lawrence Dr HGDN/ICK UB10 33 U9
Lawrence Gdns MLHL NW7 24 F8
Lawrence Hl CHING E4 27 S7
Lawrence Hill Gdns DART DA1 66 J4
Lawrence Hill Rd DART DA1 66 J4
Lawrence La BRKHM/BTCW RH3 92 H8
CITYW EC2V 5 P12
Lawrence Pde ISLW TW7 * 59 R1
Lawrence Pl IS N1 4 F1
Lawrence Rd EA W5 47 S9
ERITH DA8 54 B12
GPK RM2 42 H3
HPTN TW12 58 H12
HSLWW TW4 58 E2
PIN HA5 34 F3
PLSTW E13 40 D13
RCHPK/HAM TW10 59 S9
SEVS/STOTM N15 38 J2
SNWD SE25 74 K2
UED N18 27 M9
WWKM BR4 76 C9
YEAD UB4 33 U14
Lawrence St CAN/RD E16 52 B3
CHEL SW3 7 N12
MLHL NW7 24 F9
Lawrence Wy WLSDN NW10 36 C8
Lawrence Yd SEVS/STOTM N15 38 J2
Lawrie Park Av SYD SE26 63 M10
Lawrie Park Crs SYD SE26 63 N10
Lawrie Park Gdns SYD SE26 63 M10
Lawrie Park Rd SYD SE26 63 N11
Laws Cl SNWD SE25 74 H2
Lawson Cl CAN/RD E16 52 E4
IL IG1 41 M10
WIM/MER SW19 60 K8
Lawson Gdns DART DA1 66 K3
PIN HA5 34 D1
Lawson Rd DART DA1 66 K2
PEND EN3 16 C13
STHL UB1 46 H2
Lawson Wk CAR SM5 73 T14
Law St STHWK SE1 9 R5
Lawton Rd BOW E3 51 Q1
EBAR EN4 25 R1
LEY E10 39 U6
LOU IG10 28 K1
Laxcon Cl WLSDN NW10 36 D10
Laxey Rd ORP BR6 77 P11
Laxley Cl CMBW SE5 9 M13
Laxton Gdns REDH RH1 94 B4
Laxton Pl CAMTN NW1 3 V7
Layard Rd BERM/RHTH SE16 51 M9
EN EN1 15 V13
THHTH CR7 62 H14
Layard Sq BERM/RHTH SE16 51 M9
Layborne Av HARH RM3 30 J7
Layburn Crs DTCH/LGLY SL3 44 F11
Laycock St IS N1 38 E11
Layer Gdns ACT W3 48 A5
Layfield Cl HDN NW4 36 H5
Layfield Crs HDN NW4 36 H5
Layfield Rd HDN NW4 36 H5
Layhams Rd HAYES BR2 88 B1
WWKM BR4 76 A9
Laymarsh Cl BELV DA17 53 V8
Laymead Cl NTHLT UB5 34 G11
Laystall St FSBYW WC1X 4 J8
Layter's Av CFSP/GDCR SL9 20 A14
Layter's Av South CFSP/GDCR SL9 20 A14
Layter's Cl CFSP/GDCR SL9 20 A14
Layter's End CFSP/GDCR SL9 20 A14
Layter's Green La CFSP/GDCR SL9 20 A14
Layters Wy CFSP/GDCR SL9 32 B3
Layton Ct WEY KT13 69 T9
Layton Crs CROY/NA CR0 74 E10
Layton Pl RCH/KEW TW9 48 A13
Layton Rd BTFD TW8 47 T10
HSLW TW3 58 K2
Layton's La SUN TW16 58 B14
Layzell Wk ELTH/MOT SE9 64 F6
Lazenby Ct COVGDN WC2E * 4 E13
Leabank Cl HRW HA1 35 N8
Leabank Sq HOM E9 39 S11
Leabank Vw SEVS/STOTM N15 39 L4
Leabourne Rd STNW/STAM N16 39 L4
Lea Bridge Rd LEY E10 39 P7
WALTH E17 39 U3
Lea Bushes GSTN WD25 11 S9
Leachcroft CFSP/GDCR SL9 20 A13
Leach Gv LHD/OX KT22 83 S12
Lea Cl BUSH WD23 22 K3
WHTN TW2 58 H5
Lea Cottages MTCM CR4 * 61 U14
Lea Crs RSLP HA4 34 B9
Leacroft STA TW18 57 M10
Leacroft Av BAL SW12 61 T5
Leacroft Cl PUR/KEN CR8 86 G6
STA TW18 57 M9
WCHMH N21 26 F7
WDR/YW UB7 45 Q5
Leacroft Rd IVER SL0 44 J5
Leadale Av CHING E4 27 S7
Leadale Rd STNW/STAM N16 39 L4
Leadbeaters Cl FBAR/BDGN N11 25 T10
Leadenhall Pl BANK EC3V 5 S12
Leadenhall St BANK EC3V 5 S12
Leader Av MNPK E12 40 J10
The Leadings WBLY HA9 36 C8
Leaf Cl NTHWD HA6 21 V12
THDIT KT7 71 N3
Leaf Gv WNWD SE27 62 E10
Leafield Cl STRHM/NOR SW16 62 F11
Leafield La SCUP DA14 65 V9
Leafield Rd RYNPK SW20 73 M1
SUT SM1 73 N7
Leaford Crs WATN WD24 11 N11
Leaforis Rd CHESW EN7 16 A2
Leafy Gv HAYES BR2 76 E10
Leafy Oak Rd LEE/GVPK SE12 64 E9
Leafy Wy CROY/NA CR0 74 K7
Lea Gdns WBLY HA9 35 V10
Leagrave St CLPT E5 39 N8
Lea Hall Gdns LEY E10 * 39 S6
Lea Hall Rd LEY E10 39 S6
Leaholme Waye RSLP HA4 33 T4
Leahurst Rd LEW SE13 63 V3
Leake St STHWK SE1 8 H3
Lealand Rd SEVS/STOTM N15 38 K4
Leaming Cl MNPK E12 40 G10
Leamington Av BMLY BR1 64 E10
MRDN SM4 73 M2
ORP BR6 77 N9
WALTH E17 39 S3
Leamington Cl BMLY BR1 64 E9
HARH RM3 31 M11
HSLW TW3 59 L3
Leamington Crs RYLN/HDSTN HA2 34 G8
Leamington Gdns GDMY/SEVK IG3 41 P7
Leamington Pk ACT W3 48 D3
Leamington Pl YEAD UB4 46 B2
Leamington Rd HARH RM3 31 N10
NWDGN UB2 46 F9
Leamington Road Vls NTGHL W11 2 D10
Leamore St HMSMTH W6 48 H9
Lea Mt CHESW EN7 15 U2
Leamouth Rd EHAM E6 52 G4
POP/IOD E14 51 V4
Leander Gdns GSTN WD25 * 11 S11
Leander Rd BRXS/STRHM SW2 62 D4
NTHLT UB5 34 J14
THHTH CR7 74 D2
Learner Dr RYLN/HDSTN HA2 34 J7
Lea Rd BECK BR3 63 S14
ENC/FH EN2 15 T13
NWDGN UB2 46 G9
WAB EN9 16 G8
WATN WD24 * 11 P12
Learoyd Gdns EHAM E6 52 J5
Leas Cl CHSGTN KT9 71 V12
Leas Dl ELTH/MOT SE9 64 J8
Leas Dr IVER SL0 44 J4
Leas Gn CHST BR7 65 P11
Leaside GT/LBKH KT23 82 J13
Leaside Av MUSWH N10 37 U1
Leaside Ct HGDN/ICK UB10 45 T1
Leaside Rd CLPT E5 39 N6
Leas La WARL CR6 87 P8
Leasowes Rd LEY E10 39 S6
Leas Rd WARL CR6 87 P8
The Leas BUSH WD23 11 T14
STA TW18 * 57 L9
UPMR RM14 43 R5
Leasway UPMR RM14 43 Q8
Leathart Cl HCH RM12 42 H12
The Lea EGH TW20 56 F12
Leatherbottle Gn ERITHM DA18 53 V8
Leather Cl MTCM CR4 61 U14
Leatherdale St WCHPL E1 * 51 P1
Leather Gdns SRTFD E15 40 A13
Leatherhead By-Pass Rd
LHD/OX KT22 83 R10
Leatherhead Cl STNW/STAM N16 38 J6
Leatherhead Rd ASHTD KT21 83 U10
CHSGTN KT9 71 T12
CHSGTN KT9 83 S1
LHD/OX KT22 83 M5
Leather La CLKNW EC1R 4 J8
EMPK RM11 42 K6
Leathermarket Ct STHWK SE1 9 S4
Leathermarket St STHWK SE1 9 S4
Leather Rd BERM/RHTH SE16 51 P9
Leathersellers Cl BAR EN5 * 25 L1
Leather St WAP E1W 51 P5
Leathsale Rd RYLN/HDSTN HA2 34 K8
Leathwaite Rd BTSEA SW11 61 T2
Leathwell Rd DEPT SE8 51 T14
Lea V DART DA1 66 D2
Lea Valley Rd CHING E4 27 S5
Lea Valley Wk CLPT E5 39 M5
TOTM N17 27 M14
WAB EN9 16 G7
Leaveland Cl BECK BR3 75 S2
Leaver Gdns GFD/PVL UB6 35 M14
Leavesden Rd STAN HA7 23 Q11
WATN WD24 11 P12
WEY KT13 69 T10
Leaves Green Crs HAYES BR2 88 E1
Leaves Green Rd HAYES BR2 76 F14
Leaview WAB EN9 16 H7
Leaway CLPT E5 * 39 N6
Leazes Av CTHM CR3 86 E13
Lebanon Av FELT TW13 58 F10
Lebanon Cl WAT WD17 10 K10
Lebanon Dr COB KT11 82 J3
Lebanon Gdns BH/WHM TN16 88 F7
WAND/EARL SW18 61 N4
Lebanon Pk TWK TW1 59 R6
Lebanon Rd CROY/NA CR0 74 J6
WAND/EARL SW18 61 N3
Lebrun Sq BKHTH/KID SE3 64 D2
Lechmere Ap WFD IG8 28 E14
Lechmere Av CHIG IG7 29 L9
Lechmere Rd CRICK NW2 36 H11
Leckford Rd WAND/EARL SW18 61 Q7
Leckhampton Pl BRXS/STRHM SW2 62 E5
Leckwith Av ABYW SE2 53 U11
Lecky St SKENS SW7 7 L9
Leconfield Av BARN SW13 60 F1
Leconfield Rd HBRY N5 38 H10
Le Corte Cl KGLGY WD4 10 F3
Leda Av PEND EN3 16 D13
Leda Rd WOOL/PLUM SE18 52 H8
Ledbury Ms North NTGHL W11 2 E13
Ledbury Ms West NTGHL W11 * 2 E13
Ledbury Rd CROY/NA CR0 74 H9
NTGHL W11 2 D11
REIG RH2 93 N10
Ledbury St PECK SE15 51 L12
Ledger Dr ADL/WDHM KT15 68 K11
Ledgers Rd WARL CR6 87 T9
Ledrington Rd NRWD SE19 62 K11
Ledway Dr WBLY HA9 35 V5
Lee Av CHDH RM6 41 U4
Leechcroft Av BFN/LL DA15 65 P3
SWLY BR8 78 F1
Leechcroft Rd WLGTN SM6 73 U8
Leech La EPSOM KT18 92 C2
Lee Church St LEW SE13 64 A2
Lee Cl WALTH E17 27 P13
Lee Conservancy Rd HOM E9 39 R9
Leecroft Rd BAR EN5 25 L3
Leeds Cl ORP BR6 77 T7
Leeds Rd IL IG1 41 M6
Leeds St UED N18 27 L10
Leefe Wy POTB/CUF EN6 15 M2
Lee Gardens Av EMPK RM11 43 N6
Lee Gn STMC/STPC BR5 77 Q3
Lee Gv CHIG IG7 28 K7
Lee High Rd LEW SE13 63 V2
Leeke St FSBYW WC1X 4 G5
Leeland Rd WEA W13 47 Q6
Leeland Ter WEA W13 47 Q6
Leeland Wy WLSDN NW10 36 E9
Leeming Rd BORE WD6 12 K13
Leemount Cl HDN NW4 * 36 K2
Lee Pk BKHTH/KID SE3 64 B2
Lee Park Wy UED N18 27 P10
Lee Rd BKHTH/KID SE3 64 B1
EN EN1 27 L4
GFD/PVL UB6 35 S13
MLHL NW7 24 K12
WIM/MER SW19 61 P13
Lees Av NTHWD HA6 22 B13
Leeside BAR EN5 25 L4
POTB/CUF EN6 14 F6
Leeside Crs GLDGN NW11 37 L4
Leeside Rd TOTM N17 27 N12
Leeson Rd HNHL SE24 * 62 E3
Leesons Hl CHST BR7 77 N1
Leesons Wy STMC/STPC BR5 65 P14
Lees Pde HGDN/ICK UB10 * 45 T2
Lees Pl MYFR/PKLN W1K 3 S13
Lees Rd UX/CGN UB8 45 T2
The Lees CROY/NA CR0 75 R7
Lee St HACK E8 5 U1
Lee Ter BKHTH/KID SE3 64 A1
The Lee NTHWD HA6 22 B10
Lee Vw ENC/FH EN2 15 R13
Leeward Gdns WIM/MER SW19 61 M11
Leeway DEPT SE8 51 R10
The Leeways CHEAM SM3 * 73 L11
Leewood Cl LEE/GVPK SE12 * 64 B4
Leewood Pl SWLY BR8 78 D2
Lefevre Wk BOW E3 39 R13
Leffern Rd SHB W12 48 G7
Lefroy Rd SHB W12 48 F7
Left Side STHGT/OAK N14 * 26 B6
Legard Rd HBRY N5 38 F8
Legatt Rd ELTH/MOT SE9 64 F3
Leggatt Rd SRTFD E15 39 U14
Leggatts Cl WATN WD24 11 M10
Leggatts Ri GSTN WD25 11 N9
Leggatts Wy WATN WD24 11 N10
Leggatts Wood Av WATN WD24 11 P10
Legge St LEW SE13 63 U3
Leghorn Rd WLSDN NW10 36 G14
WOOL/PLUM SE18 53 M10
Legion Cl IS N1 38 E11
Legion Ct MRDN SM4 73 N4
Legion Ter BOW E3 39 R13
Legion Wy NFNCH/WDSPK N12 25 S12
Legon Av ROMW/RG RM7 42 C6
Legrace Av HSLWW TW4 46 F14
Leicester Av MTCM CR4 74 C2
Leicester Cl WPK KT4 72 J9
Leicester Gdns GDMY/SEVK IG3 41 N5
Leicester Pl LSQ/SEVD WC2H * 4 D13
Leicester Rd BAR EN5 25 P3
CROY/NA CR0 74 J5
EFNCH N2 37 S1
WAN E11 40 D3
WLSDN NW10 36 D12
Leicester Sq LSQ/SEVD WC2H 4 D14
Leicester St LSQ/SEVD WC2H 4 D13
Leigham Av STRHM/NOR SW16 62 C8
Leigham Cl STRHM/NOR SW16 62 E8
Leigham Court Rd STRHM/NOR SW16 62 D8
Leigham Dr ISLW TW7 47 N12
Leigham Hall Pde
STRHM/NOR SW16 * 62 C8
Leigham V STRHM/NOR SW16 62 E8
Leigh Av REDBR IG4 40 F2
Leigh Cl ADL/WDHM KT15 68 K12
NWMAL KT3 72 D2
Leigh Ct BORE WD6 * 13 P14
RYLN/HDSTN HA2 * 35 N6
Leigh Court Cl COB KT11 82 F4
Leigh Crs CROY/NA CR0 75 T12
Leigh Dr HARH RM3 30 K9
Leigh Gdns WLSDN NW10 36 J14
Leigh Hill Rd COB KT11 82 F4
Leigh Hunt Dr STHGT/OAK N14 26 B7
Leigh Orchard Cl STRHM/NOR SW16 62 D8
Leigh Pk DTCH/LGLY SL3 * 44 A12
Leigh Pl COB KT11 82 E5
FELT TW13 58 E6
RDART DA2 * 67 N10
WELL DA16 53 Q14
Leigh Place La GDST RH9 95 Q8
Leigh Rd COB KT11 82 D3
EHAM E6 40 J12
HBRY N5 38 F9
HSLW TW3 59 M2
LEY E10 39 U5
Leigh Rodd OXHEY WD19 22 G8
Leigh St STPAN WC1H 4 E7
Leigh Ter STMC/STPC BR5 * 77 R1
The Leigh KUTN/CMB KT2 60 E11
Leighton Av MNPK E12 40 J10
PIN HA5 34 G1
Leighton Cl EDGW HA8 24 A14
Leighton Crs KTTN NW5 38 A10
Leighton Gdns SAND/SEL CR2 87 M3
WLSDN NW10 36 J14
Leighton Gv KTTN NW5 38 A10
Leighton Pl KTTN NW5 38 A10
Leighton Rd EN EN1 26 K3
KTN/HRWW/WS HA3 23 M14
KTTN NW5 38 A10
WEA W13 47 Q7
Leighton St CROY/NA CR0 74 F6
Leighton Wy EPSOM KT18 84 D4
Leila Parnell Pl CHARL SE7 52 E11
Leinster Av MORT/ESHN SW14 60 C1
Leinster Gdns BAY/PAD W2 2 J12
Leinster Ms BAY/PAD W2 2 J14
Leinster Pl BAY/PAD W2 2 J12
Leinster Rd MUSWH N10 37 V2
Leinster Sq BAY/PAD W2 2 F13
Leinster Ter BAY/PAD W2 2 J14
Leisure La BF/WBF KT14 * 81 M2
Leisure Wy NFNCH/WDSPK N12 25 R12
Leith Cl CDALE/KGS NW9 36 D6
Leithcote Gdns STRHM/NOR SW16 62 D9
Leithcote Pth STRHM/NOR SW16 62 D8
Leith Hl STMC/STPC BR5 65 Q13
Leith Rd EW KT17 84 E2
WDGN N22 26 F13
Leith Towers BELMT SM2 * 73 P12
Leith Yd KIL/WHAMP NW6 * 2 F1
Lela Av HSLWW TW4 46 E14
Lelitia Cl HACK E8 39 L13
Leman St WCHPL E1 5 V12
Lemark Cl STAN HA7 23 S11
Le May Av LEE/GVPK SE12 64 D8
Lemmon Rd GNWCH SE10 52 A11
Lemna Rd WAN E11 40 A5
Lemonfield Dr GSTN WD25 11 S6
Lemon Field Dr GSTN WD25 11 S7
Lemonwell Dr ELTH/MOT SE9 64 K3
Lemsford Cl SEVS/STOTM N15 39 L4
Lemsford Ct BORE WD6 24 C2
Lena Crs ED N9 27 N7
Lena Gdns HMSMTH W6 48 J8
Lena Kennedy Cl CHING E4 27 U11
Lendal Ter CLAP SW4 62 B1
Lenelby Rd SURB KT6 72 A6
Len Freeman Pl FUL/PGN SW6 6 C12
Lenham Rd BXLYHN DA7 53 V11
LEE/GVPK SE12 64 B2
SUT SM1 73 P9
THHTH CR7 62 H14
Lennard Av WWKM BR4 76 A7
Lennard Cl WWKM BR4 76 A7
Lennard Rd CROY/NA CR0 74 G6
HAYES BR2 76 H6
SEV TN13 90 E10
SYD SE26 63 N11
Lennard Rw SOCK/AV RM15 55 R6
Lennard Ter PGE/AN SE20 * 63 P11
Lennon Rd CRICK NW2 36 J11
Lennox Cl ROM RM1 42 F4
Lennox Gdns CROY/NA CR0 74 F9
IL IG1 40 H6
KTBR SW1X 7 Q7
WLSDN NW10 36 F9
Lennox Gardens Ms CHEL SW3 7 Q6
Lennox Rd FSBYPK N4 38 D7
WALTH E17 39 R4
Lenor Cl BXLYHS DA6 65 U2
Lensbury Cl CHES/WCR EN8 16 E2
Lensbury Wy ABYW SE2 53 T8
Lens Rd FSTGT E7 40 E12
Lenthall Rd HACK E8 38 K12
LOU IG10 29 M2
Lenthorp Rd GNWCH SE10 52 B9
Lentmead Rd BMLY BR1 64 B8
Lenton Ri RCH/KEW TW9 59 U1
Lenton St WOOL/PLUM SE18 53 M9
Lenton Ter FSBYPK N4 * 38 E7
Leof Crs CAT SE6 63 T10
Leominster Rd MRDN SM4 73 Q4
Leominster Wk MRDN SM4 73 Q4
Leonard Av MRDN SM4 73 Q3
ROMW/RG RM7 42 D6
RSEV TN14 90 H6
Leonard Ct KENS W8 * 6 E5
Leonard Pl HAYES BR2 * 76 G8
STNW/STAM N16 38 J9
Leonard Rd CHING E4 27 S11
ED N9 26 K8
FSTGT E7 40 C9
NWDGN UB2 46 F9
STRHM/NOR SW16 62 A13
Leonard St CAN/RD E16 52 G6
SDTCH EC2A 5 S7
Leonard Wy BRW CM14 31 T9
Leontine Cl PECK SE15 51 L12
Leopold Av WIM/MER SW19 61 M10
Leopold Ms HOM E9 39 N13
Leopold Rd EA W5 47 V6
EFNCH N2 37 R1
UED N18 27 M10
WALTH E17 39 S3
WIM/MER SW19 61 M9
WLSDN NW10 36 E12
Leopold St BOW E3 51 R3
Leo St PECK SE15 51 N12
Le Personne Rd CTHM CR3 86 H12
Leppoc Rd CLAP SW4 62 B3
Leret Wy LHD/OX KT22 83 Q11
Leroy St STHWK SE1 9 S7
Lerry Cl WKENS W14 6 D11
Lesbourne Rd REIG RH2 93 P11
Lescombe Cl CAT SE6 63 Q8
Lescombe Rd FSTH SE23 63 Q8
Lesley Cl BXLY DA5 66 B5
SWLY BR8 78 D1
Leslie Gdns BELMT SM2 73 N12
Leslie Gv CROY/NA CR0 74 H6
Leslie Grove Pl CROY/NA CR0 74 J6
Leslie Park Rd CROY/NA CR0 74 J6
Leslie Rd CAN/RD E16 52 D4
EFNCH N2 37 R1
WAN E11 39 V9
Lesney Pk ERITH DA8 54 D11
Lesney Park Rd ERITH DA8 54 D11
Lessar Av CLAP SW4 62 A3
Lessingham Av TOOT SW17 61 T9
Lessing St FSTH SE23 63 Q5
Lessington Av ROMW/RG RM7 42 C4
Lessness Av BXLYHN DA7 53 T12
Lessness Pk BELV DA17 53 V10
Lessness Rd MRDN SM4 73 Q4
Lester Av CAN/RD E16 52 A2
Lestock Cl SNWD SE25 75 L1
Leston Cl RAIN RM13 54 H1
Leswin Pl STNW/STAM N16 38 K8
Leswin Rd STNW/STAM N16 38 K8
Letchford Gdns WLSDN NW10 48 G1
Letchford Ms WLSDN NW10 * 48 G1
Letchford Ter KTN/HRWW/WS HA3 * 22 K13
Letchmore Rd RAD WD7 12 E10
Letchworth Av EBED/NFELT TW14 58 B5
Letchworth Cl HAYES BR2 76 C3
OXHEY WD19 22 F10
Letchworth Dr HAYES BR2 76 C3
Letchworth St TOOT SW17 61 T9
Letterstone Rd FUL/PGN SW6 6 C14
Lettice St FUL/PGN SW6 49 M14
Lett Rd SRTFD E15 39 V12
Leucha Rd WALTH E17 39 Q3
Levana Cl WIM/MER SW19 61 L6
Levehurst Wy CLAP SW4 50 C14
Leven Cl CHES/WCR EN8 * 16 D7
OXHEY WD19 * 22 F10
Levendale Rd FSTH SE23 63 Q7
Leven Dr CHES/WCR EN8 16 D7
Leven Rd POP/IOD E14 51 U3
Leven Wy HYS/HAR UB3 46 A4
Leveret Cl CROY/NA CR0 87 V1
GSTN WD25 11 N8
Leverett St CHEL SW3 7 P7
Leverholme Gdns ELTH/MOT SE9 64 J9
Leverson St STRHM/NOR SW16 62 A11
Lever St FSBYE EC1V 5 N6
Leverton Pl KTTN NW5 38 A10
Leverton St KTTN NW5 38 A10
Leverton Wy WAB EN9 16 J7
Levett Gdns GDMY/SEVK IG3 41 P9
Levett Rd BARK IG11 41 N11
LHD/OX KT22 83 R10
Levine Gdns BARK IG11 41 T14
Levison Wy ARCH N19 38 B7
Lewes Cl NTHLT UB5 34 J11
Lewesdon Cl WIM/MER SW19 60 K6
Lewes Rd BMLY BR1 64 F14
HARH RM3 30 K9
NFNCH/WDSPK N12 25 S10
Leweston Pl STNW/STAM N16 38 K5
Lewes Wy RKW/CH/CXG WD3 21 T2
Lewgars Av CDALE/KGS NW9 36 C4
Lewing Cl ORP BR6 77 N6
Lewin Rd BXLYHS DA6 65 U2
MORT/ESHN SW14 60 D1
STRHM/NOR SW16 62 B11
Lewins Rd CFSP/GDCR SL9 32 B1
EPSOM KT18 84 B4
Lewis Av WALTH E17 27 S13
Lewis Cl ADL/WDHM KT15 69 N9
DEN/HRF UB9 21 N14
STHGT/OAK N14 26 A5
Lewis Crs WLSDN NW10 36 D10
Lewis Gdns EFNCH N2 25 R14
Lewis Gv LEW SE13 63 U2
Lewisham High St LEW SE13 63 T4
Lewisham Hl LEW SE13 51 U14
Lewisham Pk LEW SE13 63 T4
Lewisham Rd LEW SE13 51 U14
Lewisham Wy BROCKY SE4 51 R14
Lewis La CFSP/GDCR SL9 20 C13
Lewis Pl HACK E8 39 L10
Lewis Rd EMPK RM11 42 J4
MTCM CR4 61 S14
RCH/KEW TW9 * 59 T3
SCUP DA14 65 S8
STHL UB1 46 G7
SUT SM1 73 P9
WELL DA16 65 S1
Lewis St CAMTN NW1 37 V12
Lewiston Cl WPK KT4 72 H5
Lewis Wy DAGE RM10 42 B11
Lexden Dr CHDH RM6 41 R4
Lexden Rd ACT W3 48 B5
MTCM CR4 74 B2
Lexden Ter WAB EN9 * 16 J8
Lexham Gdns KENS W8 6 F7
Lexham Ms KENS W8 6 F7
Lexington Cl BORE WD6 23 V1
Lexington Ct POTB/CUF EN6 13 V5
PUR/KEN CR8 74 G14
Lexington St SOHO/CST W1F 4 B12
Lexington Wy BAR EN5 24 K2
UPMR RM14 43 T4
Lexton Gdns BAL SW12 62 B6
Leyborne Av WEA W13 47 S7
Leyborne Pk RCH/KEW TW9 48 A13
Leybourne Av BF/WBF KT14 81 R3
Leybourne Cl BF/WBF KT14 81 R3
HAYES BR2 76 C3
Leybourne Rd CAMTN NW1 * 37 V12
CDALE/KGS NW9 36 A3
HGDN/ICK UB10 33 U13
WAN E11 40 B6
Leybourne St CAMTN NW1 37 V12
Leyburn Cl WALTH E17 39 U2
Leyburn Crs HARH RM3 31 L12
Leyburn Gdns CROY/NA CR0 74 J7
Leyburn Gv UED N18 27 L11
Leyburn House CHARL SE7 * 52 G12
Leyburn Rd HARH RM3 31 L12
UED N18 27 L11
Leycroft Gdns ERITH DA8 54 H13
Leydenhatch La SWLY BR8 66 D13
Leyden St WCHPL E1 5 U10
Leydon Cl BERM/RHTH SE16 51 P6
Leyes Rd CAN/RD E16 52 E5
Leyfield WPK KT4 72 E7
Leyhill Cl SWLY BR8 78 E3
Leyland Av PEND EN3 16 E14
Leyland Cl CHES/WCR EN8 16 C3
Leyland Gdns WFD IG8 28 E10
Leyland Rd LEE/GVPK SE12 64 B3
Leylands La STWL/WRAY TW19 56 K3
Leylang Rd NWCR SE14 51 P12
Leys Av DAGE RM10 42 C13
Leys Cl DAGE RM10 42 C12
DEN/HRF UB9 21 P13
HRW HA1 35 M3
Leysdown Av BXLYHN DA7 66 C2
Leysdown Rd ELTH/MOT SE9 64 G7
Leysfield Rd SHB W12 48 G7
Leys Gdns EBAR EN4 25 U3
Leyspring Rd WAN E11 40 B6
Leys Rd LHD/OX KT22 83 M2
Leys Rd East PEND EN3 16 E13
The Leys EFNCH N2 37 Q2
KTN/HRWW/WS HA3 35 V4
RAD WD7 12 E11
WOT/HER KT12 * 70 G9
Ley St IL IG1 40 K7
Leyswood Dr GNTH/NBYPK IG2 41 N3
Leythe Rd ACT W3 48 C7
Leyton Cross Rd RDART DA2 66 F8
Leyton Gra LEY E10 39 S7
Leyton Green Rd LEY E10 39 U4
Leyton Park Rd LEY E10 39 U7
Leyton Rd SRTFD E15 39 U10
WIM/MER SW19 61 Q12
Leytonstone Rd SRTFD E15 40 A11
Leywick St SRTFD E15 40 A14
Lezayre Rd ORP BR6 77 P11
Liardet St NWCR SE14 51 Q11
Liberia Rd HBRY N5 38 F11
Liberty Av WIM/MER SW19 61 R13
Liberty Cl UED N18 26 K9
Liberty Hall Rd ADL/WDHM KT15 69 L10
Liberty La ADL/WDHM KT15 69 M10
Liberty Ms WDGN N22 * 26 F13
Liberty Ri ADL/WDHM KT15 69 L11
Liberty St BRXN/ST SW9 50 D13
Libra Rd BOW E3 39 R13
PLSTW E13 40 C14
Library Ct SEVS/STOTM N15 38 K1
Library Pde WLSDN NW10 * 36 E13
Library St STHWK SE1 9 M4
Lichfield Cl EBAR EN4 25 T1
Lichfield Gdns RCH/KEW TW9 * 59 U3
Lichfield Gv FNCH N3 25 N13
Lichfield Rd BCTR RM8 41 R9
BOW E3 51 Q1
CRICK NW2 37 L9
ED N9 27 L7
EHAM E6 52 F1
HSLWW TW4 58 E1
NTHWD HA6 34 C1
RCH/KEW TW9 47 V13
WFD IG8 28 A9
Lichfield Ter RCH/KEW TW9 * 59 U3
UPMR RM14 43 S7
Lichfield Wy SAND/SEL CR2 75 P14
Lidbury Rd MLHL NW7 25 L11
Lidcote Gdns BRXN/ST SW9 * 50 E14
Liddall Wy WDR/YW UB7 45 R6
Liddell Cl KTN/HRWW/WS HA3 35 T1
Liddell Gdns WLSDN NW10 36 J14
Liddell Rd KIL/WHAMP NW6 37 N11
Lidding Rd KTN/HRWW/WS HA3 35 T3
Liddington Rd SRTFD E15 40 B13
Liddon Rd BMLY BR1 76 E1
PLSTW E13 52 C1
Liden Cl LEY E10 39 R5
Lidfield Rd STNW/STAM N16 38 H9
Lidgate Rd PECK SE15 * 9 U14
Lidiard Rd WAND/EARL SW18 61 Q7
Lidlington Pl CAMTN NW1 4 B4
Lido Sq TOTM N17 26 H14
Lidyard Rd ARCH N19 38 A6
Lieutenant Ellis Wy CHESW EN7 15 V5
Liffler Rd WOOL/PLUM SE18 53 N10
Lifford St PUT/ROE SW15 60 K2
Lightcliffe Rd PLMGR N13 26 E9
Lighter Cl BERM/RHTH SE16 51 Q9
Lighterman Ms WCHPL E1 51 P4
Lighterman's Rd POP/IOD E14 51 S7
Lightfoot Rd CEND/HSY/T N8 38 C3
Lightswood Cl CHESW EN7 15 T1
Ligonier St BETH E2 5 U7
Lilac Av EN EN1 16 C10
WOKS/MYFD GU22 80 B11
Lilac Cl BRWN CM15 31 V3
CHESW EN7 16 B5
CHING E4 27 R11
Lilac Gdns CROY/NA CR0 75 S8
EA W5 47 T8
HYS/HAR UB3 46 A4
ROMW/RG RM7 42 E6
SWLY BR8 78 D1
Lilac Pl LBTH SE11 8 G8
WDR/YW UB7 45 R5
Lilac St SHB W12 48 G5
Lilah Ms HAYES BR2 64 B14
Lila Pl SWLY BR8 78 E2
Lilburne Gdns ELTH/MOT SE9 64 G3
Lilburne Rd ELTH/MOT SE9 64 G3
Lile Crs HNWL W7 47 N3
Lilestone St STJWD NW8 3 N7
Lilford Rd CMBW SE5 50 F14
Lilian Barker Cl LEE/GVPK SE12 64 C3
Lilian Board Wy GFD/PVL UB6 35 M10
Lilian Gdns WFD IG8 28 D13
Lilian Rd STRHM/NOR SW16 62 A13
Lillechurch Rd BCTR RM8 41 R11
Lilleshall Rd MRDN SM4 73 R3
Lilley Cl BRW CM14 31 T9
WAP E1W 51 L6
Lilley Dr KWD/TDW/WH KT20 85 P12
Lilley La MLHL NW7 * 24 E10
Lillian Av ACT W3 48 A7
Lillian Rd BARN SW13 48 G11
Lillie Rd BH/WHM TN16 88 F8
FUL/PGN SW6 6 A13
FUL/PGN SW6 48 K11
Lillieshall Rd CLAP SW4 61 V1
Lillie Yd FUL/PGN SW6 6 E11
Lillington Gardens Est PIM SW1V 8 B8
Lilliott's La LHD/OX KT22 83 Q9
Lilliput Av NTHLT UB5 34 G13
Lilliput Rd ROMW/RG RM7 42 D5
Lily Cl WKENS W14 6 A8
Lily Dr WDR/YW UB7 45 P9
Lily Gdns ALP/SUD HA0 35 S14
Lily Pl FARR EC1M 4 K9
Lily Rd WALTH E17 39 S4
Lilyville Rd FUL/PGN SW6 49 M13
Limbourne Av BCTR RM8 41 V5
Limburg Rd BTSEA SW11 61 S2
Lime Av UPMR RM14 43 N9
WDR/YW UB7 45 R5
Limeburner La STP EC4M 5 L11
Limebush Cl ADL/WDHM KT15 69 N13
Lime Cl BKHH IG9 28 F7
BMLY BR1 76 G2
KTN/HRWW/WS HA3 23 Q14
OXHEY WD19 22 F5
PIN HA5 34 B1
REIG RH2 93 P13
ROMW/RG RM7 42 C3
WAP E1W 51 L6
Lime Crs SUN TW16 58 E14
Limecroft Cl HOR/WEW KT19 72 D12
Limedene Cl PIN HA5 22 F13
Lime Gv ADL/WDHM KT15 69 L9
BARK/HLT IG6 29 P11
BFN/LL DA15 65 P4
CHING E4 27 R11
HYS/HAR UB3 45 V5
NWMAL KT3 72 D1
ORP BR6 76 K7
RSLP HA4 34 D4
SHB W12 48 J7
TRDG/WHET N20 25 L6
TWK TW1 59 P4
WARL CR6 87 Q9
WOKS/MYFD GU22 80 C11
Limeharbour POP/IOD E14 51 T8
Limehouse POP/IOD E14 * 51 S5
Limehouse Cswy POP/IOD E14 51 R5
Limehouse Link POP/IOD E14 51 Q5
Limehouse Link (Tunnel)
POP/IOD E14 51 R5
Lime Kiln Dr CHARL SE7 52 D11
Limekiln Pl NRWD SE19 62 K12
Lime Meadow Av SAND/SEL CR2 87 M3
Lime Pit La SEV TN13 90 C7
Limerick Cl BAL SW12 62 A5
Limerick Gdns UPMR RM14 43 T5
Lime Rd SWLY BR8 78 D1
Limerston St WBPTN SW10 6 K11
Limes Av BARN SW13 48 F14
CAR SM5 73 T6
CHIG IG7 29 M11
CROY/NA CR0 74 E8
GLDGN NW11 37 L5
MLHL NW7 24 E11
NFNCH/WDSPK N12 25 Q9
PGE/AN SE20 63 M12
WAN E11 40 D2
The Limes Av FBAR/BDGN N11 25 V10
Limes Cl ASHF TW15 57 S10
CAR SM5 73 T7
FBAR/BDGN N11 * 26 A10
Limesdale Gdns EDGW HA8 24 C14
Limes Field Rd MORT/ESHN SW14 60 E1
Limesford Rd PECK SE15 63 P2
Limes Gdns WAND/EARL SW18 61 N4
Limes Gv LEW SE13 63 U2
Limes Rd BECK BR3 63 T14
CHES/WCR EN8 16 D6
CROY/NA CR0 74 H4
EGH TW20 56 D10
WEY KT13 69 S9
Limes Rw ORP BR6 76 K10
The Limes CMBW SE5 * 62 J1
EMPK RM11 42 K1
EYN DA4 * 79 M5
LHD/OX KT22 83 R13
PUR RM19 55 N10
RKW/CH/CXG WD3 * 21 N6
WAND/EARL SW18 * 61 N4
WOKN/KNAP GU21 80 B5
Limestone Wk ERITHM DA18 53 T7
Lime St FENCHST EC3M 5 S13
WALTH E17 39 Q2
Lime Street Pas BANK EC3V * 5 S12
Limes Wk EA W5 47 T7
PECK SE15 * 63 N2
Lime Tree Av ESH/CLAY KT10 71 M6
RDART DA2 67 U6
Limetree Cl BRXS/STRHM SW2 62 D6
Lime Tree Cl GT/LBKH KT23 82 J14
Lime Tree Ct PIN HA5 * 22 J12
Limetree Ct PIN HA5 22 J12
Lime Tree Gv CROY/NA CR0 75 R8
Limetree Pl MTCM CR4 61 V13
Lime Tree Rd HEST TW5 46 K13
Lime Tree Ter CAT SE6 * 63 R6
Lime Tree Wk BUSH WD23 23 N6
ENC/FH EN2 15 S12
RKW/CH/CXG WD3 21 M3
VW GU25 68 C2
WWKM BR4 76 B9
Lime Wk DEN/HRF UB9 33 N10
SRTFD E15 * 40 A13
Lime Wy RAD WD7 12 G4
Limewood Cl BECK BR3 75 U3
WALTH E17 39 R2
WEA W13 47 R4
Limewood Rd ERITH DA8 54 C12
Limpsfield Av THHTH CR7 74 D3
WIM/MER SW19 60 K7
Limpsfield Rd SAND/SEL CR2 87 L2
WARL CR6 87 N6
Linacre Cl PECK SE15 63 M1
Linacre Rd CRICK NW2 36 H11
Linchfield Rd DTCH/LGLY SL3 44 A13
Linchmere Rd LEE/GVPK SE12 64 B5
Lincoln Av ROMW/RG RM7 42 E6
STHGT/OAK N14 26 A8
WHTN TW2 59 L7
WIM/MER SW19 60 K8
Lincoln Cl EMPK RM11 43 N3
ERITH DA8 54 F14
GFD/PVL UB6 35 L13
RYLN/HDSTN HA2 34 H3
Lincoln Ct BORE WD6 24 D3
Lincoln Crs EN EN1 26 J3
Lincoln Dr OXHEY WD19 22 E8
RKW/CH/CXG WD3 21 T2
WOKS/MYFD GU22 80 J5
Lincoln Est BOW E3 51 S2
Lincoln Gdns IL IG1 40 G5
Lincoln Green Rd STMC/STPC BR5 77 P3
Lincoln Ms KIL/WHAMP NW6 2 C1
SEVS/STOTM N15 38 G2
Lincoln Pde EFNCH N2 * 37 S1
Lincoln Rd ALP/SUD HA0 35 T11
CFSP/GDCR SL9 20 C13
EFNCH N2 37 S1
EN EN1 26 J2
ERITH DA8 54 F14
FELT TW13 58 H8
FSTGT E7 40 F11
MTCM CR4 74 C3
NTHWD HA6 34 B1
NWMAL KT3 72 C1
PLSTW E13 52 D2
RYLN/HDSTN HA2 34 H3
SCUP DA14 65 R10
SNWD SE25 75 M1
SWFD E18 28 B13
WPK KT4 72 H6
Lincolns Fld EPP CM16 18 D3
Lincoln's Inn Flds LINN WC2A 4 H11
Lincolns La BRW CM14 31 Q4
The Lincolns MLHL NW7 24 F8
Lincoln St CHEL SW3 7 Q8
WAN E11 40 A7
Lincoln Ter BELMT SM2 * 73 N12
Lincoln Wy EN EN1 27 M3
RKW/CH/CXG WD3 21 T2
SUN TW16 58 A13
Lincombe Rd BMLY BR1 64 B8
Lindal Crs ENC/FH EN2 26 C3
The Lindales TOTM N17 27 L11
Lindal Rd BROCKY SE4 63 R3
Linden Av COUL/CHIP CR5 85 V6
DART DA1 66 J6
EN EN1 16 A13
HSLW TW3 58 K3
RSLP HA4 34 C6
THHTH CR7 74 F2
WATW WD18 22 B2
WBLY HA9 35 V10
WLSDN NW10 36 K14
Linden Chase Rd SEV TN13 90 H12
Linden Cl ADL/WDHM KT15 81 L1
CHESW EN7 16 B4
KWD/TDW/WH KT20 84 K10
ORP BR6 77 Q10
PUR RM19 55 Q11
RSLP HA4 34 C6
STAN HA7 23 R10
STHGT/OAK N14 26 A4
THDIT KT7 71 Q5
Linden Cottages WIM/MER SW19 * 61 L11
Linden Ct LHD/OX KT22 83 R11
Linden Crs GFD/PVL UB6 35 P11
KUT/HW KT1 59 V14
WFD IG8 28 D11
Linden Dr CFSP/GDCR SL9 20 C13
CTHM CR3 86 G14
Lindenfield CHST BR7 64 K14
Linden Gdns BAY/PAD W2 2 F14
CHSWK W4 48 D10
EN EN1 16 A13
LHD/OX KT22 83 S11
Linden Gv NWMAL KT3 72 E1
PECK SE15 63 M1
TEDD TW11 59 P10
WARL CR6 87 Q8
WOT/HER KT12 70 B7
Linden Lea EFNCH N2 37 Q3
GSTN WD25 11 N7
PIN HA5 * 22 H12
Linden Leas WWKM BR4 75 V7
Linden Ms BAY/PAD W2 2 F14
IS N1 38 H10
Linden Pit Pth LHD/OX KT22 83 R11
Linden Pl EW KT17 84 E2
MTCM CR4 73 S2
Linden Rd FBAR/BDGN N11 25 T7
HPTN TW12 58 J13
LHD/OX KT22 83 R11
MUSWH N10 37 V2
SEVS/STOTM N15 38 G2
WEY KT13 69 U13
Lindens WAB EN9 17 Q9
Linden Sq DEN/HRF UB9 21 L11
SEV TN13 90 E12
The Lindens CHSWK W4 48 C13
CROY/NA CR0 75 U11
LOU IG10 28 J3
NFNCH/WDSPK N12 * 25 R10
WAB EN9 * 17 Q9
WALTH E17 * 39 T2
Linden St ROMW/RG RM7 42 D2
Linden Ter UX/CGN UB8 * 45 P4
Linden Wy PUR/KEN CR8 74 A14
RPLY/SEND GU23 80 K14
SHPTN TW17 69 U3
STHGT/OAK N14 26 A4
WOKS/MYFD GU22 80 D11
Lindfield Gdns HAMP NW3 37 Q10
Lindfield Rd CROY/NA CR0 74 K4
EA W5 47 S2
HARH RM3 31 L10
Lindfield St POP/IOD E14 51 S4
Lindfield Ter WOKN/KNAP GU21 * 80 A6
Lindhill Cl PEND EN3 16 D14
Lindisfarne Md HOM E9 39 Q9
Lindisfarne Rd BCTR RM8 41 S8
RYNPK SW20 60 G12
Lindiswara Ct RKW/CH/CXG WD3 * 21 S4
Lindley Est PECK SE15 51 L12
Lindley Pl RCH/KEW TW9 48 A13
Lindley Rd GDST RH9 95 N6
LEY E10 39 U7
WOT/HER KT12 70 G8
Lindley St WCHPL E1 51 N3
Lindore Rd BTSEA SW11 61 T2
Lindores Rd CAR SM5 73 Q6
Lindo St PECK SE15 51 N14
Lind Rd SUT SM1 73 Q10
Lindrop St FUL/PGN SW6 49 Q14
Lindsay Cl CHSGTN KT9 71 U12
HOR/WEW KT19 84 C3
STWL/WRAY TW19 57 P3
Lindsay Dr KTN/HRWW/WS HA3 35 U4
SHPTN TW17 69 V4
Lindsay Pl CHESW EN7 16 B4
Lindsay Rd ADL/WDHM KT15 81 L1
HPTN TW12 58 K9
WPK KT4 72 H7
Lindsay Sq PIM SW1V 8 D9
Lindsell St GNWCH SE10 51 U13
Lindsey Cl BMLY BR1 76 F1
BRW CM14 31 U9
MTCM CR4 74 C2
Lindsey Gdns EBED/NFELT TW14 * 57 V5
Lindsey Ms IS N1 38 G12
Lindsey Rd BCTR RM8 41 S8
DEN/HRF UB9 33 L8
Lindsey St EPP CM16 18 C2
FARR EC1M 5 M9
Lindsey Wy EMPK RM11 42 J3
Lind St DEPT SE8 51 T14
Lindum Rd TEDD TW11 59 S12
Lindvale WOKN/KNAP GU21 80 C5
Lindway WNWD SE27 62 F10
Linfield Cl HDN NW4 36 J1
WOT/HER KT12 * 70 D10
Linford Rd WALTH E17 39 U1
Linford St VX/NE SW8 50 A13
Lingards Rd LEW SE13 63 U2
Lingey Cl BFN/LL DA15 65 P7
Lingfield Av RDART DA2 67 P5
UPMR RM14 43 N8
Lingfield Cl EN EN1 26 J4
NTHWD HA6 22 A12
Lingfield Ct NTHLT UB5 * 34 J14
Lingfield Crs ELTH/MOT SE9 65 M2
Lingfield Gdns COUL/CHIP CR5 86 F9
ED N9 27 M5
Lingfield Rd WIM/MER SW19 60 K11
WPK KT4 72 J8
Lingfield Wy WAT WD17 11 M12
Lingham St BRXN/ST SW9 50 C14
Lingholm Wy BAR EN5 24 K3
Lingmere Cl CHIG IG7 29 L7
Lingmoor Dr GSTN WD25 11 Q7
Ling Rd CAN/RD E16 52 C3
ERITH DA8 54 C11
Lingwell Rd TOOT SW17 61 S8
Lingwood Gdns ISLW TW7 47 N12
Lingwood Rd CLPT E5 39 L5
Linhope St CAMTN NW1 3 Q7
Linkfield E/WMO/HCT KT8 70 J1
Link Fld HAYES BR2 76 C4
Linkfield Cnr REDH RH1 93 S10
Linkfield Gdns REDH RH1 93 S10
Linkfield La REDH RH1 93 T9
Linkfield Rd ISLW TW7 47 P14
Linkfield St REDH RH1 93 S10
Link La WLGTN SM6 74 B11
Linklea Cl CDALE/KGS NW9 24 E12
Link Rd ADL/WDHM KT15 69 Q9
DAGW RM9 42 B14
DTCH/LGLY SL3 44 A12
EBED/NFELT TW14 58 B5
FBAR/BDGN N11 25 U9
WATN WD24 11 R14
WLGTN SM6 73 U6
Links Av GPK RM2 30 H14
MRDN SM4 73 N2
Links Brow LHD/OX KT22 83 N14
Links Cl ASHTD KT21 83 S7
Linkscroft Av ASHF TW15 57 T11
Links Dr BORE WD6 23 V2
RAD WD7 12 E8
TRDG/WHET N20 25 N6
Links Gdns STRHM/NOR SW16 62 E12
Links Green Wy COB KT11 82 J4
Linkside CHIG IG7 29 L10
NFNCH/WDSPK N12 25 M11
NWMAL KT3 60 E14
Linkside Cl ENC/FH EN2 26 D1
Linkside Gdns ENC/FH EN2 26 D1
Links Pl ASHTD KT21 83 T7
Links Rd ACT W3 48 A4
ASHF TW15 57 Q10
ASHTD KT21 83 S7
CRICK NW2 36 F7
EW KT17 84 G3
TOOT SW17 61 U11
WFD IG8 28 C10
WWKM BR4 75 U6
Links Side ENC/FH EN2 26 D1
The Links WALTH E17 39 Q2
WOT/HER KT12 70 C7
Link St HOM E9 39 N11
Links Vw DART DA1 66 J6
FNCH N3 25 M12
Links View Av BRKHM/BTCW RH3 92 A10
Links View Cl STAN HA7 23 Q11
Linksview Ct HPTN TW12 * 59 M9
Links View Rd CROY/NA CR0 75 S8
HPTN TW12 59 L10
Links Wy NTHWD HA6 21 U13
RKW/CH/CXG WD3 21 U1
TOOT SW17 61 T11
BECK BR3 75 S4
Linksway HDN NW4 24 K14
NTHWD HA6 21 V13
Links Yd WCHPL E1 5 V9
The Link ACT W3 48 B4
ALP/SUD HA0 35 S6
CRICK NW2 36 G6
NTHLT UB5 * 34 H10
PEND EN3 16 E13
PIN HA5 34 E4
TEDD TW11 59 P12
Link Wy DEN/HRF UB9 33 L4
EMPK RM11 43 L6
HAYES BR2 76 G5
RCHPK/HAM TW10 59 R7
STA TW18 57 M11
Linkway BCTR RM8 41 S9
FSBYPK N4 38 G5
PIN HA5 22 F13
RYNPK SW20 72 H1
WOKS/MYFD GU22 80 G7
Linkway Rd BRW CM14 31 T8
The Linkway BAR EN5 25 N4
BELMT SM2 73 Q13
Linkwood Wk CAMTN NW1 38 B12
Linley Crs ROMW/RG RM7 42 B1
Linley Rd TOTM N17 26 J14
Linnell Cl GLDGN NW11 37 P4
Linnell Dr GLDGN NW11 37 P4
Linnell Rd CMBW SE5 50 J14
REDH RH1 93 U11
UED N18 27 L10
Linnet Cl BUSH WD23 23 L6
ED N9 27 P6
SAND/SEL CR2 75 P14
THMD SE28 53 S5
Linnet Ms BAL SW12 61 U5
Linnet Rd ABLGY WD5 11 N5
Linnett Cl CHING E4 27 U9
Linnet Wy PUR RM19 55 P10
Linom Rd CLAP SW4 62 C2
Linscott Rd CLPT E5 39 N9
Linsdell Rd BARK IG11 41 L13
Linsey St BERM/RHTH SE16 51 L9
Linslade Cl HSLWW TW4 58 G3
PIN HA5 34 D1
Linslade Rd ORP BR6 77 Q11
Linstead St KIL/WHAMP NW6 37 N12
Linstead Wy WAND/EARL SW18 61 L5
Linster Gv BORE WD6 24 C3
Linthorpe Av ALP/SUD HA0 35 S11
Linthorpe Rd EBAR EN4 25 S1
STNW/STAM N16 38 J5
Linton Av BORE WD6 12 K14
Linton Cl CAR SM5 73 T5
CHARL SE7 52 E10
WELL DA16 53 R13
Linton Ct ROM RM1 30 E14
Linton Gdns EHAM E6 52 G4
Linton Gld CROY/NA CR0 75 Q14
Linton Gv WNWD SE27 62 F10
Linton Rd BARK IG11 41 L12
Linton's La EW KT17 84 E2
Linton St IS N1 5 P2
Lintott Ct STWL/WRAY TW19 57 P4
Linver Rd FUL/PGN SW6 49 M14
Linwood Cl CMBW SE5 50 K14
Linwood Crs EN EN1 16 A13
Linzee Rd CEND/HSY/T N8 38 C2
Lion Av TWK TW1 59 P6
Lion Cl BROCKY SE4 63 S4
SHPTN TW17 69 Q1
Lion Ct BORE WD6 13 N13
Lionel Gdns ELTH/MOT SE9 64 F3
Lionel Ms NKENS W10 2 A9
Lionel Rd ELTH/MOT SE9 64 F3
Lionel Rd North BTFD TW8 47 U8
Lionel Rd South BTFD TW8 47 V10
Lion Gate Gdns RCH/KEW TW9 59 V1
Lion Gate Ms WAND/EARL SW18 61 N5
Lion Green Rd COUL/CHIP CR5 86 B5
Lion Mills BETH E2 * 39 L14
Lion Park Av CHSGTN KT9 72 A9
Lion Rd BXLYHS DA6 65 U2
CROY/NA CR0 74 G3
ED N9 27 L7
EHAM E6 52 H3
TWK TW1 59 P6
Lions Cl LEE/GVPK SE12 64 E8
Lion Wy BTFD TW8 47 T12
Lion Wharf Rd ISLW TW7 59 R1
Liphook Cl HCH RM12 42 F9
Liphook Crs FSTH SE23 63 N5
Liphook Rd OXHEY WD19 22 F9
Lippitts Hl LOU IG10 17 L14
Lipsham Cl BNSTD SM7 85 R3
Lipton Rd WCHPL E1 51 P4
Lisbon Av WHTN TW2 59 L7
Lisbon Cl WALTH E17 27 R14
Lisburne Rd HAMP NW3 37 T9
Lisford St PECK SE15 50 K13
Lisgar Ter WKENS W14 6 C7
Liskeard Cl CHST BR7 65 L11
Liskeard Gdns BKHTH/KID SE3 52 C13
Lisle Cl TOOT SW17 61 V9
Lisle St LSQ/SEVD WC2H 4 D13
Lismore WIM/MER SW19 * 61 M10
Lismore Circ KTTN NW5 37 T10
Lismore Cl ISLW TW7 47 Q14
Lismore Rd SAND/SEL CR2 74 J11
TOTM N17 38 H1
Lismore Wk IS N1 38 G11
Lissant Cl SURB KT6 71 S5
Lissenden Gdns KTTN NW5 37 U9
Lissoms Rd COUL/CHIP CR5 85 U8
Lisson Gv CAMTN NW1 3 N8
Lisson St CAMTN NW1 3 N9
Lister Av HARH RM3 30 K14
Lister Cl ACT W3 48 D3
MTCM CR4 61 S13
Lister Gdns UED N18 26 G10
Lister Rd WAN E11 40 A6
Liston Rd CLAP SW4 62 A1
TOTM N17 27 L13
Liston Wy WFD IG8 28 E12
Listowel Cl BRXN/ST SW9 * 8 K13
Listowel Rd DAGE RM10 42 A8
Listria Pk STNW/STAM N16 38 J7
Litchfield Av MRDN SM4 73 M5
SRTFD E15 * 40 A11
Litchfield Gdns WLSDN NW10 36 G11
Litchfield Rd SUT SM1 73 Q9
Litchfield St LSQ/SEVD WC2H 4 D13
Litchfield Wy GLDGN NW11 37 Q3
Lithgow's Rd HTHAIR TW6 58 A2
Lithos Rd HAMP NW3 37 P11
Little Acre BECK BR3 75 S1
Little Albany St CAMTN NW1 3 V7
Little Argyll St REGST W1B * 4 A12
Little Aston Rd HARH RM3 31 M12
Little Belhus Cl SOCK/AV RM15 55 U2
Little Benty WDR/YW UB7 45 P10
Little Birch Cl ADL/WDHM KT15 69 P13
Little Birches BFN/LL DA15 65 N7
The Little Boltons WBPTN SW10 6 H9
Little Bookham St GT/LBKH KT23 82 H14
Little Bornes DUL SE21 62 J9
Little Borough BRKHM/BTCW RH3 92 A11
Little Britain STBT EC1A 5 N11
Littlebrook Cl CROY/NA CR0 75 P4
Littlebrook Gdns CHES/WCR EN8 16 D4
Littlebrook Manor Wy DART DA1 67 N3
Little Brownings FSTH SE23 63 M7
Littlebury Rd CLAP SW4 * 62 B1
Little Bury St ED N9 26 J5
Little Bushey La BUSH WD23 22 K1
BUSH WD23 23 L1
Little Cedars NFNCH/WDSPK N12 25 Q9
Little Chesters KWD/TDW/WH KT20 92 G1
Little Chester St KTBR SW1X 7 U5
Little Cloisters WEST SW1P 8 E5
Littlecombe Cl PUT/ROE SW15 * 60 K4
Little Common STAN HA7 23 Q8
Little Common La REDH RH1 94 G8
Littlecote Cl WIM/MER SW19 60 K5
Littlecote Pl PIN HA5 22 G13
Little Cottage Pl GNWCH SE10 * 51 T12
Little Ct WWKM BR4 76 A7
Littlecourt Rd SEV TN13 90 G14
Littlecroft ELTH/MOT SE9 64 J1
Littlecroft Rd EGH TW20 56 D10
Littledale ABYW SE2 53 Q11
Little Deans Yd WEST SW1P 8 E5
Little Dimocks BAL SW12 61 V7
Little Dorrit Ct STHWK SE1 9 P3
Little Dragons LOU IG10 28 F2
Little Ealing La EA W5 47 S9
Little East Fld COUL/CHIP CR5 86 B11
Little Edward St CAMTN NW1 * 3 V5
Little Elms HYS/HAR UB3 45 V12
Little Essex St TPL/STR WC2R * 4 J13
Little Ferry Rd TWK TW1 * 59 R6
Littlefield Cl ARCH N19 38 A9
KUT/HW KT1 59 U14
Littlefield Rd EDGW HA8 24 C12
Little Friday Rd CHING E4 28 A7
Little Gaynes Gdns UPMR RM14 43 P9
Little Gaynes La UPMR RM14 43 N9
Little Gearies BARK/HLT IG6 40 K2
Little George St WEST SW1P 8 E4
Little Gerpins Rd RAIN RM13 43 M13
Little Graylings ABLGY WD5 11 L7
Little Green La CHERT KT16 68 J8
RKW/CH/CXG WD3 21 S1
Little Green St KTTN NW5 * 37 V9
Little Gregories La EPP CM16 18 B9
Little Gv BUSH WD23 22 K2
Littlegrove EBAR EN4 25 S4
Little Grove Av CHESW EN7 15 U1
Little Halliards WOT/HER KT12 70 C4
Little Hayes KGLGY WD4 10 G3
Little Heath CHARL SE7 52 G11
CHDH RM6 41 R2
Littleheath La COB KT11 82 J4
Little Heath Rd BXLYHN DA7 53 V13
Littleheath Rd SAND/SEL CR2 75 M13
Little Hl RKW/CH/CXG WD3 20 G4
Little How Cft ABLGY WD5 10 J5
Little Ilford La MNPK E12 40 H9
Littlejohn Rd HNWL W7 47 P4
STMC/STPC BR5 77 Q4
Little London Cl UX/CGN UB8 45 T3
Little Marlborough St REGST W1B * 4 A12
Little Martins BUSH WD23 22 K3
Littlemead ESH/CLAY KT10 71 M9
Littlemede ELTH/MOT SE9 64 H8
Littlemoor Rd IL IG1 41 M8
Littlemore Rd ABYW SE2 53 Q7
Little Moreton Cl BF/WBF KT14 * 81 M2
Little Moss La PIN HA5 22 G14
Little Newport St LSQ/SEVD WC2H 4 D13
Little New St FLST/FETLN EC4A 4 K11
Little Oak Cl SHPTN TW17 69 R2
Little Orch ADL/WDHM KT15 81 L1
WOKN/KNAP GU21 80 E4
Little Orchard Cl ABLGY WD5 10 K5
PIN HA5 * 22 G14
Little Orchards EPSOM KT18 84 E4
Little Oxhey La OXHEY WD19 22 G10
Little Park Dr FELT TW13 58 F7
Little Park Gdns ENC/FH EN2 26 H1
Little Piper's Cl CHESW EN7 15 R3
Little Pluckett's Wy BKHH IG9 28 F6
Little Portland St REGST W1B 3 V11
Little Potters BUSH WD23 23 M5
Little Queens Rd TEDD TW11 59 P11
Little Queen St DART DA1 67 M5
Little Redlands BMLY BR1 64 G14
Little Riding WOKS/MYFD GU22 80 F6
Little Rd HYS/HAR UB3 46 B7
Little Roke Av PUR/KEN CR8 86 F4
Little Roke Rd PUR/KEN CR8 86 G4
Littlers Cl WIM/MER SW19 61 R13
Little Russell St NOXST/BSQ WC1A 4 E10
Little St James's St WHALL SW1A 8 A2
Little St Leonards MORT/ESHN SW14 60 C1
Little Smith St WEST SW1P 8 D5
Little Somerset St TWRH EC3N 5 U12
Littlestone Cl BECK BR3 63 S11
Little Strd CDALE/KGS NW9 24 F14
Little Stream Cl NTHWD HA6 22 A10
Little St WAB EN9 16 J10
Little Sutton La DTCH/LGLY SL3 44 G10
Little Thrift STMC/STPC BR5 77 L2
Little Titchfield St GTPST W1W 4 A10
Littleton Av CHING E4 28 B6
Littleton Crs HRW HA1 35 P7
Littleton La REIG RH2 93 L12
SHPTN TW17 69 Q3
Littleton Rd ASHF TW15 57 U12
HRW HA1 35 P7
Littleton St WAND/EARL SW18 61 Q7
Little Trinity La BLKFR EC4V 5 P13
Little Turnstile HHOL WC1V 4 G10
Littlewick Rd WOKN/KNAP GU21 80 A4
Littlewood LEW SE13 63 U3
Little Wd SEV TN13 90 J12
Little Wood Cl STMC/STPC BR5 65 Q13
Littlewood Cl WEA W13 47 R8
Little Woodcote Est WLGTN SM6 * 73 V14
Little Woodcote La CAR SM5 85 V2
Littleworth Av ESH/CLAY KT10 71 M10
Littleworth Common Rd
ESH/CLAY KT10 71 M9
Littleworth La ESH/CLAY KT10 71 M9
Littleworth Pl ESH/CLAY KT10 71 M9
Littleworth Rd ESH/CLAY KT10 71 M10
Livermere Rd HACK E8 5 V1
Liverpool Gv WALW SE17 9 Q10
Liverpool Rd CAN/RD E16 52 A3
EA W5 47 T7
IS N1 4 K1
KUTN/CMB KT2 60 A12
LEY E10 39 U4
THHTH CR7 74 G1
WATW WD18 22 D3
Liverpool St LVPST EC2M 5 S10
Livesey Cl KUT/HW KT1 71 V1
THMD SE28 53 L8
Livesey Pl STHWK SE1 51 L11
Livingstone Rd BTSEA SW11 61 R1
CTHM CR3 86 H12
HSLW TW3 59 L2
PLMGR N13 26 C11
SRTFD E15 39 U13
STHL UB1 46 F5
THHTH CR7 62 H14
WALTH E17 39 T4
Lizard St FSBYE EC1V 5 P6
Lizban St BKHTH/KID SE3 52 D12
Llanbury Cl CFSP/GDCR SL9 20 D12
Llanelly Rd CRICK NW2 37 M7
Llanover Rd WBLY HA9 35 T8
WOOL/PLUM SE18 52 J12
Llanthony Rd MRDN SM4 73 R4
Llanvanor Rd CRICK NW2 37 M7
Llewellyn St BERM/RHTH SE16 51 L7
Lloyd Av COUL/CHIP CR5 85 U4
STRHM/NOR SW16 62 C13
Lloyd Baker St FSBYW WC1X 4 J6
Lloyd Ct PIN HA5 34 F3
Lloyd Ms PEND EN3 16 G12
Lloyd Park Av CROY/NA CR0 74 K9
Lloyd Rd DAGW RM9 41 V11
EHAM E6 40 H13
WALTH E17 39 P2
WPK KT4 72 J8
Lloyd's Av FENCHST EC3M 5 T12
Lloyd's Pl BKHTH/KID SE3 * 52 A14
Lloyd Sq FSBYW WC1X 4 J6
Lloyd's Rw CLKNW EC1R 4 K6
Lloyd St FSBYW WC1X 4 J5
Lloyds Wy BECK BR3 75 Q3
Lloyd Thomas Ct WDGN N22 * 26 D12
Lloyd Vls BROCKY SE4 51 S14
Loampit Hl LEW SE13 51 S14
Loampit V LEW SE13 63 T1
Loanda Cl HACK E8 5 U1
Loates La WAT WD17 22 E1
Loats Rd BRXS/STRHM SW2 62 C4
Local Board Rd WAT WD17 22 F3
Locarno Rd ACT W3 48 C6
GFD/PVL UB6 47 L2
Lochaber Rd LEW SE13 64 A2
Lochaline St HMSMTH W6 48 J11
Lochan Cl YEAD UB4 46 G2
Lochinvar St BAL SW12 61 V5
Lochmere Cl ERITH DA8 54 B11
Lochnagar St POP/IOD E14 51 U3
Lock Cha BKHTH/KID SE3 64 A1
Lock Cl ADL/WDHM KT15 80 J2
NWDGN UB2 47 L7
Locke Cl RAIN RM13 42 F11
Locke Gdns DTCH/LGLY SL3 44 A7
Locke-King Cl WEY KT13 69 S12
Locke King Rd WEY KT13 69 S12
Lockesley Dr STMC/STPC BR5 77 P4

Lockesley Sq SURB KT6 * 71 T4
Lockestone Cl WEY KT13 69 R11
Locket Rd KTN/HRWW/WS HA3 23 P14
Locket Road Ms KTN/HRWW/WS HA3 23 N14
Locke Wy WOKN/KNAP GU21 80 D7
Lockfield Av PEND EN3 16 E14
Lockfield Dr WOKN/KNAP GU21 80 C7
Lockgate Cl HOM E9 39 R10
Lockhart Cl HOLWY N7 38 D11
PEND EN3 27 M3
Lockhart Rd COB KT11 82 E3
Lockhart St BOW E3 51 R2
Lockhurst St CLPT E5 39 P9
Lockington Rd VX/NE SW8 49 V13
Lock Keepers Cottages TOTM N17 * 39 M2
Lock La WOKS/MYFD GU22 81 M6
Lockmead Rd LEW SE13 63 U1
SEVS/STOTM N15 39 L4
Lock Rd RCHPK/HAM TW10 59 S9
Lock's La MTCM CR4 61 U13
Locksley Est POP/IOD E14 51 R4
Locksley St POP/IOD E14 51 R3
Locksmeade Rd RCHPK/HAM TW10 59 R9
Lockstone WEY KT13 69 R11
Lockton St NTGHL W11 * 48 K5
Lockwell Rd DAGE RM10 41 V8
Lockwood Cl SYD SE26 63 P9
Lockwood Pth WOKN/KNAP GU21 80 J3
Lockwood Pl CHING E4 27 S11
Lockwood Sq BERM/RHTH SE16 51 M8
Lockwood Wy CHSGTN KT9 72 A10
WALTH E17 27 P14
Lockyer Cl PEND EN3 16 H12
Lockyer Pl BH/WHM TN16 * 97 M2
Lockyer Rd PUR RM19 55 Q11
Lockyer St STHWK SE1 9 R4
Locomotive Dr EBED/NFELT TW14 58 C5
Locton Gn BOW E3 * 39 R13
Loddiges Rd HOM E9 39 N12
Loder Cl WOKN/KNAP GU21 80 H3
Loder St PECK SE15 51 N12
Lodge Av BORE WD6 23 V3
CROY/NA CR0 74 E8
DAGW RM9 41 R13
DART DA1 66 J4
GPK RM2 42 G3
KTN/HRWW/WS HA3 35 U2
Lodgebottom Rd RDKG RH5 92 A3
Lodge Cl CHIG IG7 29 Q8
COB KT11 82 H6
EDGW HA8 * 23 V11
EGH TW20 56 B10
EW KT17 72 J14
ISLW TW7 47 R13
LHD/OX KT22 83 M12
ORP BR6 77 R6
UED N18 26 G10
UX/CGN UB8 45 N2
WLGTN SM6 73 U6
Lodge Ct ALP/SUD HA0 * 35 U10
Lodge Crs CHES/WCR EN8 16 D8
ORP BR6 77 R6
Lodge Dr PLMGR N13 26 E9
RKW/CH/CXG WD3 21 N2
Lodge End RAD WD7 12 F8
RKW/CH/CXG WD3 21 V2
Lodge Gdns BECK BR3 75 R3
Lodge Hl PUR/KEN CR8 86 E5
REDBR IG4 40 G2
WELL DA16 53 R12
Lodgehill Park Cl RYLN/HDSTN HA2 34 K7
Lodge La BH/WHM TN16 97 L3
BXLY DA5 65 T4
CROY/NA CR0 75 T12
CRW RM5 30 A11
CSTG HP8 20 D3
NFNCH/WDSPK N12 25 Q10
WAB EN9 16 K9
Lodge Mansions Pde PLMGR N13 * 26 E9
Lodge Ms HBRY N5 * 38 G9
Lodge Pl SUT SM1 73 P10
Lodge Rd BMLY BR1 64 E12
CROY/NA CR0 74 F4
EPP CM16 17 U8
HDN NW4 36 J2
LHD/OX KT22 83 L12
RKW/CH/CXG WD3 21 V2
STJWD NW8 3 M6
SUT SM1 73 P10
WLGTN SM6 73 V10
The Lodge SHB W12 * 48 K7
Lodge Vls WFD IG8 28 B12
Lodge Wk WARL CR6 87 S6
Lodge Wy ASHF TW15 57 Q7
SHPTN TW17 57 U14
Lodore Gdns CDALE/KGS NW9 36 E3
Lodore Gn HGDN/ICK UB10 33 Q8
Lodore St POP/IOD E14 51 U4
Lofthouse Pl CHSGTN KT9 71 S11
Loftie St BERM/RHTH SE16 51 L7
Lofting Rd IS N1 38 E12
Loftus Rd BARK IG11 41 L11
SHB W12 48 H6
Loftus Vls SHB W12 * 48 H6
Logan Cl HSLWW TW4 58 H1
PEND EN3 16 D13
Logan Ms KENS W8 6 E7
ROM RM1 42 E3
Logan Pl ECT SW5 6 E7
Logan Rd ED N9 27 M7
WBLY HA9 35 U7
The Logans BAR EN5 * 24 K1
Logs Hl CHST BR7 64 G13
Logs Hill Cl CHST BR7 64 G13
Lois Dr SHPTN TW17 69 T3
Lolesworth Cl WCHPL E1 5 V10
Lollard St LBTH SE11 8 H7
Loman Pth SOCK/AV RM15 55 T4
Loman St STHWK SE1 9 M3
Lomas Cl CROY/NA CR0 75 U12
Lombard Av GDMY/SEVK IG3 41 N6
PEND EN3 16 C13
Lombard La EMB EC4Y 4 K12
Lombard Rd BTSEA SW11 49 R14
FBAR/BDGN N11 25 V10
WIM/MER SW19 61 P14
The Lombards EMPK RM11 43 M5
Lombard St BANK EC3V 5 R12
EYN DA4 79 Q2
Lombard Vls FBAR/BDGN N11 * 25 V10
Lombard Wall CHARL SE7 52 D8
Lombardy Cl WFD IG8 28 K12
Lombardy Pl BAY/PAD W2 2 G14
Lombardy Wy BORE WD6 12 J13
Lomond Cl ALP/SUD HA0 35 V12
SEVS/STOTM N15 38 J2
Lomond Gdns SAND/SEL CR2 75 Q12
Lomond Gv CMBW SE5 9 Q14
Loncin Mead Av ADL/WDHM KT15 69 N13
Loncroft Rd CMBW SE5 9 T11
Londesborough Rd STNW/STAM N16 38 J9
London Br CANST EC4R 5 R14
London Bridge St STHWK SE1 9 R2
London Bridge Wk STHWK SE1 * 9 R1
London City Airport Link
CAN/RD E16 52 B5
Londonderry Pde ERITH DA8 * 54 D12
London Flds HACK E8 * 39 M12
London Flds East Side HACK E8 39 M12
London Flds West Side HACK E8 39 L12
London La BMLY BR1 64 C12
HACK E8 39 M12
London Loop BNSTD SM7 85 N3
BORE WD6 24 C5
COUL/CHIP CR5 86 C9
CROY/NA CR0 75 P8
ENC/FH EN2 15 N11
ORP BR6 76 K6
PUR/KEN CR8 86 J5
SAND/SEL CR2 75 P13
WARL CR6 87 L5
WWKM BR4 75 V9
London Ms BAY/PAD W2 3 M12
London Rd ABR/ST RM4 19 N13
ABR/ST RM4 29 Q1
BARK IG11 40 K12
BH/WHM TN16 89 L13
BMLY BR1 64 B12
BRW CM14 31 U8
BUSH WD23 22 G4
CHONG CM5 19 V8
CSTG HP8 20 A7
CTHM CR3 86 H13
DART DA1 66 D3
DTCH/LGLY SL3 44 A12
DTCH/LGLY SL3 44 B9
EGH TW20 56 A12
ENC/FH EN2 26 H3
EW KT17 72 H10
EYN DA4 78 K4
FSTH SE23 63 N6
HRW HA1 35 N7
ISLW TW7 47 N14
ISLW TW7 59 Q3
KUTN/CMB KT2 59 V14
MRDN SM4 73 N3
MTCM CR4 61 T12
MTCM CR4 73 S2
MTCM CR4 73 U5
PLSTW E13 40 C14
RAD WD7 12 K7
RDART DA2 67 Q5
REDH RH1 93 U9
REIG RH2 93 N9
ROMW/RG RM7 42 A4
RSEV TN14 77 V13
RSEV TN14 90 C3
SEV TN13 90 E11
SOCK/AV RM15 55 M6
STA TW18 56 K9
STAN HA7 23 S10
STHWK SE1 9 M5
STRHM/NOR SW16 62 D14
SWLY BR8 66 C14
SWLY BR8 78 G2
THHTH CR7 74 E2
WBLY HA9 35 U10
WLGTN SM6 73 V9
London Rd North REDH RH1 85 V14
London Rd Purfleet PUR RM19 55 P11
London Rd South REDH RH1 93 V6
London Rd West Thurrock
WTHK RM20 55 T11
Londons Cl UPMR RM14 43 Q10
London Stile CHSWK W4 48 A10
London St BAY/PAD W2 3 M12
CHERT KT16 69 L5
FENCHST EC3M * 5 T13
London Ter BETH E2 * 39 L14
London Wall CITYW EC2V 5 P10
London Wall Buildings LVPST EC2M 5 R10
Lonesome La REIG RH2 93 Q14
Lonesome Wy MTCM CR4 61 V13
Long Acre COVGDN WC2E 4 E12
ORP BR6 77 T7
Long Acre Ct WEA W13 * 47 Q3
Longacre Pl CAR SM5 * 73 U11
Longacre Rd WALTH E17 27 V13
Long Barn Cl GSTN WD25 11 N6
Longbeach Rd BTSEA SW11 61 T1
Longboat Rw STHL UB1 46 H4
Longbourne Wy CHERT KT16 68 K4
Longboyds COB KT11 82 D4
Longbridge Rd BARK IG11 41 M11
Longbridge Wy LEW SE13 63 U3
UX/CGN UB8 33 M14
Longbury Cl STMC/STPC BR5 77 R1
Longbury Dr STMC/STPC BR5 77 R1
Longcliffe Pth OXHEY WD19 22 C8
Long Copse Cl GT/LBKH KT23 82 K13
Long Ct PUR RM19 55 N9
Longcroft ELTH/MOT SE9 64 J8
Long Cft OXHEY WD19 22 D5
Longcroft Av BNSTD SM7 85 Q4
Long Croft Dr CHES/WCR EN8 16 F8
Longcrofte Rd EDGW HA8 23 T12
Longcroft Ri LOU IG10 28 K3
Long Croft Rd RKW/CH/CXG WD3 20 H10
Longcross Rd CHERT KT16 68 C8
Long Deacon Rd CHING E4 28 A6
Longdon Wd HAYES BR2 76 G9
Longdown La North EW KT17 84 G3
Longdown La South EW KT17 84 G5
Longdown Rd CAT SE6 63 S9
EW KT17 84 G4
Long Dr ACT W3 48 E4
GFD/PVL UB6 34 K13
RSLP HA4 34 F9
WDR/YW UB7 * 45 Q7
Long Elmes KTN/HRWW/WS HA3 22 K13
Long Elms ABLGY WD5 10 K7
Long Elms Cl ABLGY WD5 10 K7
Long Fallow LCOL/BKTW AL2 11 U1
Longfellow Rd WALTH E17 39 R4
WCHPL E1 * 51 Q1
WPK KT4 72 G6
Longfellow Wy STHWK SE1 * 9 V8
Longfield BMLY BR1 64 B13
Long Fld CDALE/KGS NW9 24 E13
Longfield LOU IG10 28 E3
Longfield Av EA W5 47 S5
EMPK RM11 42 F5
MLHL NW7 24 G12
PEND EN3 16 C11
WALTH E17 39 Q2
WBLY HA9 35 U6
WLGTN SM6 73 U6
Longfield Crs KWD/TDW/WH KT20 84 J10
SYD SE26 63 N8
Longfield Dr MORT/ESHN SW14 60 B3
MTCM CR4 61 S13
Longfield Est STHWK SE1 9 V7
Longfield La CHESW EN7 15 V1
Longfield Rd EA W5 47 S4
Longfield St WAND/EARL SW18 61 N5
Longford Av EBED/NFELT TW14 58 B4
STHL UB1 46 J5
STWL/WRAY TW19 57 Q6
Longford Cl FELT TW13 58 G8
YEAD UB4 46 F5
Longford Ct HOR/WEW KT19 72 C9
HPTN TW12 58 K11
Longford Gdns SUT SM1 73 Q8
YEAD UB4 46 F5
Longford Rd WHTN TW2 58 K6
Longford St CAMTN NW1 3 V7
Longford Wy STWL/WRAY TW19 57 Q6
Long Gn CHIG IG7 29 N9
Long Gv HARH RM3 31 L14
Long Grove Rd HOR/WEW KT19 72 C14
PUR/KEN CR8 86 C1
Longhayes Av CHDH RM6 41 T1
Longheath Dr GT/LBKH KT23 82 G14
Longheath Gdns CROY/NA CR0 75 N3
Longhedge St BTSEA SW11 49 U14
Long Hl CTHM CR3 87 Q11
Longhill Rd CAT SE6 63 V7
Longhook Gdns NTHLT UB5 34 C14
NTHLT UB5 46 C1
Longhope Cl PECK SE15 9 T12
Longhurst Rd CROY/NA CR0 75 M4
LEW SE13 64 A3
Longland Dr TRDG/WHET N20 25 P8
Longlands Av COUL/CHIP CR5 85 V4
Longlands Cl CHES/WCR EN8 16 D6
Longlands Park Crs BFN/LL DA15 65 N8
Longlands Rd BFN/LL DA15 65 N8
Long La BXLYHN DA7 53 V13
CROY/NA CR0 75 N4
EFNCH N2 25 Q14
HGDN/ICK UB10 33 S14
RKW/CH/CXG WD3 20 G4
STBT EC1A 5 M9
STHWK SE1 9 R4
STWL/WRAY TW19 57 R4
Longleat Rd EN EN1 26 J3
Longleat Wy EBED/NFELT TW14 57 U5
Longleigh La ABYW SE2 53 S11
Longley Av ALP/SUD HA0 35 V13
Longley Rd CROY/NA CR0 74 F5
HRW HA1 35 M3
TOOT SW17 61 S11
Long Leys CHING E4 27 T11
Longley St STHWK SE1 51 L9
Longley Wy CRICK NW2 36 J8
Long Lodge Dr WOT/HER KT12 70 E8
Longmans Cl WATW WD18 21 U4
Long Mark Rd CAN/RD E16 52 F4
Longmarsh La THMD SE28 53 N6
Longmarsh Vw EYN DA4 67 P13
Long Md CDALE/KGS NW9 24 F13
Longmead CHST BR7 64 J14
Longmead Cl CTHM CR3 86 J12
Longmead Dr SCUP DA14 65 T7
Long Meadow HARH RM3 30 J8
KTTN NW5 * 38 B11
Longmeadow SEV TN13 90 D11
Long Meadow Cl WWKM BR4 75 U5
Longmeadow Rd BFN/LL DA15 65 N6
Longmead Rd HOR/WEW KT19 72 E14
HYS/HAR UB3 46 C5
THDIT KT7 71 N5
TOOT SW17 61 T10
Longmere Gdns KWD/TDW/WH KT20 84 J9
Long Moor CHES/WCR EN8 16 E3
Longmoore St PIM SW1V 8 A8
Longmore Av BAR EN5 25 Q4
Longmore Cl RKW/CH/CXG WD3 20 K9
Longmore Rd WOT/HER KT12 70 G9
Longnor Rd WCHPL E1 51 P1
Long Pond Rd BKHTH/KID SE3 52 A13
Longport Cl BARK/HLT IG6 29 Q11
Long Reach RPLY/SEND GU23 81 T14
Long Reach Rd BARK IG11 53 P2
Longreach Rd ERITH DA8 54 H12
Longridge RAD WD7 12 F8
Longridge Gv WOKS/MYFD GU22 80 J4
Longridge La STHL UB1 46 K5
Longridge Rd ECT SW5 6 E8
Long Rd CLAP SW4 62 A2
Longs Cl WOKS/MYFD GU22 81 L6
Longsdon Wy CTHM CR3 87 L14
Long Shaw LHD/OX KT22 83 Q9
Longshaw Rd CHING E4 27 V8
Longshore DEPT SE8 51 R9
Longside Cl EGH TW20 56 G13
Longspring WATN WD24 11 P11
Longstaff Crs WAND/EARL SW18 61 N5
Longstaff Rd WAND/EARL SW18 61 N4
Longstone Av WLSDN NW10 36 F12
Longstone Rd IVER SL0 32 G14
TOOT SW17 61 V10
Long St BETH E2 5 U5
WAB EN9 17 S4
Longthornton Rd STRHM/NOR SW16 62 A14
Longton Av SYD SE26 63 L9
Longton Gv SYD SE26 63 M9
Longtown Cl HARH RM3 30 J10
Longtown Rd HARH RM3 30 J10
Longview Wy CRW RM5 30 D13
Longville Rd LBTH SE11 9 L7
Long Wk CSTG HP8 20 C1
EPSOM KT18 84 K9
NWMAL KT3 72 C1
STHWK SE1 9 T5
Longwalk Rd STKPK UB11 45 T7
Longwood Av DTCH/LGLY SL3 44 F10
Longwood Cl UPMR RM14 43 Q10
Longwood Ct WPK KT4 72 G7
Longwood Dr PUT/ROE SW15 60 H5
Longwood Gdns CLAY IG5 40 H2
Longwood Rd PUR/KEN CR8 86 H6
Longworth Cl THMD SE28 53 T4
Long Yd BMSBY WC1N 4 G8
The Loning CDALE/KGS NW9 36 F2
PEND EN3 16 C12
Lonsdale Av EHAM E6 52 F2
ROMW/RG RM7 42 C4
WBLY HA9 35 U10
Lonsdale Cl EHAM E6 52 G2
ELTH/MOT SE9 64 F8
UX/CGN UB8 45 U4
Lonsdale Crs GNTH/NBYPK IG2 40 K4
RDART DA2 67 Q7
Lonsdale Dr ENC/FH EN2 26 C3
Lonsdale Dr North ENC/FH EN2 26 C3
Lonsdale Gdns THHTH CR7 74 D2
Lonsdale Ms NTGHL W11 2 D12
RCH/KEW TW9 * 48 A13
Lonsdale Pl IS N1 38 E12
Lonsdale Rd BXLYHN DA7 53 V14
CHSWK W4 48 F9
KIL/WHAMP NW6 2 C3
NWDGN UB2 46 F8
SNWD SE25 75 M2
WAN E11 40 B5
WEY KT13 69 S12
Lonsdale Sq IS N1 * 38 E12
Loobert Rd SEVS/STOTM N15 38 J1
Looe Gdns BARK/HLT IG6 40 K1
Loom La RAD WD7 12 E11
Loop Rd CHST BR7 65 L11
EPSOM KT18 84 C6
WAB EN9 16 H6
WOKS/MYFD GU22 80 D10
Lopen Rd UED N18 26 J9
Loraine Cl PEND EN3 27 N3
Loraine Cottages HOLWY N7 * 38 D9
Loraine Gdns ASHTD KT21 83 U7
Loraine Rd CHSWK W4 48 B11
HOLWY N7 38 D9
Lord Av CLAY IG5 40 H2
Lord Chancellor Wk KUTN/CMB KT2 60 C13
Lord Chatham's Ride RSEV TN14 89 T7
RSEV TN14 89 V9
Lord Gdns CLAY IG5 40 G2
Lord Hills Rd BAY/PAD W2 2 H9
Lord Holland La BRXN/ST SW9 * 50 E14
Lord Knyvett Cl STWL/WRAY TW19 57 P4
Lord Knyvetts Ct STWL/WRAY TW19 * 57 Q4
Lord Napier Pl HMSMTH W6 48 G10
Lord North St WEST SW1P 8 E6
Lord Roberts Ms FUL/PGN SW6 6 G14
Lordsbury Fld WLGTN SM6 74 A14
Lords Cl DUL SE21 62 G7
FELT TW13 58 G7
RAD WD7 12 J6
Lordsgrove Cl KWD/TDW/WH KT20 84 H10
Lordship Gv STNW/STAM N16 38 H7
Lordship La EDUL SE22 62 K4
WDGN N22 26 E14
Lordship Pk STNW/STAM N16 38 H7
Lordship Park Ms STNW/STAM N16 38 G7
Lordship Pl CHEL SW3 7 N12
Lordship Rd CHESW EN7 16 B4
NTHLT UB5 34 G12
STNW/STAM N16 38 H7
Lordship Ter STNW/STAM N16 38 H7
Lordsmead Rd TOTM N17 26 J13
Lord St CAN/RD E16 52 G6
WAT WD17 22 E1
Lords Vw STJWD NW8 3 N6
Lordswood Cl RDART DA2 67 S9
Lord Warwick St WOOL/PLUM SE18 52 H8
Lorenzo St FSBYW WC1X 4 G5
Loretto Gdns KTN/HRWW/WS HA3 35 U2
Lorian Cl NFNCH/WDSPK N12 25 P9
Lorian Dr REIG RH2 93 Q9
Loriners Cl COB KT11 82 C4
Loring Rd ISLW TW7 47 P14
TRDG/WHET N20 25 S7
Loris Rd HMSMTH W6 48 J8
Lorn Ct BRXN/ST SW9 50 E14
Lorne Av CROY/NA CR0 75 P5
Lorne Cl STJWD NW8 3 P6
Lorne Gdns CROY/NA CR0 75 Q5
NTGHL W11 48 K7
WAN E11 40 E2
Lorne Rd FSBYPK N4 38 D6
FSTGT E7 40 D9
KTN/HRWW/WS HA3 23 P14
RCHPK/HAM TW10 59 V3
WALTH E17 39 S3
Lorne Ter FNCH N3 * 25 M14
Lorn Rd BRXN/ST SW9 50 D14
Lorraine Pk KTN/HRWW/WS HA3 23 N12
Lorrimore Rd WALW SE17 9 M12
Lorrimore Sq WALW SE17 9 M11
Loseberry Rd ESH/CLAY KT10 71 M10
Lossie Dr IVER SL0 44 F5
Lothair Rd EA W5 47 T7
Lothair Rd North FSBYPK N4 38 F4
Lothair Rd South FSBYPK N4 38 E5
Lothbury LOTH EC2R 5 Q11
Lothian Av YEAD UB4 46 D3
Lothian Cl ALP/SUD HA0 35 Q9
Lothian Rd BRXN/ST SW9 9 M14
BRXN/ST SW9 50 F13
Lothian Wd KWD/TDW/WH KT20 84 H12
Lothrop St NKENS W10 2 A6
Lots Rd WBPTN SW10 6 J14
Lotus Rd BH/WHM TN16 88 H8
Loubet St TOOT SW17 61 T11
Loudoun Av BARK/HLT IG6 40 K3
Loudoun Rd STJWD NW8 2 K2
Loudwater Cl SUN TW16 70 C2
Loudwater Dr RKW/CH/CXG WD3 21 N2
Loudwater Hts RKW/CH/CXG WD3 21 M1
Loudwater La RKW/CH/CXG WD3 21 N3
Loudwater Rdg RKW/CH/CXG WD3 21 N2
Loughborough Pk BRXN/ST SW9 62 F2
Loughborough Rd BRXN/ST SW9 50 F14
Loughborough St LBTH SE11 8 H9
Lough Rd HOLWY N7 38 D11
Loughton La EPP CM16 18 B11
Loughton Wy BKHH IG9 28 F6
Louisa Cl HOM E9 39 N12
Louisa St WCHPL E1 51 P3
Louis Cl CHST BR7 64 H9
Louise Bennett Cl HNHL SE24 * 62 F2
Louise Gdns RAIN RM13 54 E1
Louise Rd SRTFD E15 40 A11
Louisville Rd TOOT SW17 61 U8
Louvaine Rd BTSEA SW11 61 R2
Louvain Rd RDART DA2 67 S5
Louvain Wy GSTN WD25 11 P6
Lovage Ap EHAM E6 52 G3
Lovat Cl CRICK NW2 36 F8
Lovat La FENCHST EC3M 5 S13
Lovatt Cl EDGW HA8 24 B11
Lovatts RKW/CH/CXG WD3 21 S2
Loveday Rd WEA W13 47 R6
Love Green La IVER SL0 44 J3
Lovegrove St STHWK SE1 51 L10
Lovegrove Wk POP/IOD E14 51 U6
Love Hill La DTCH/LGLY SL3 44 E5
Lovekyn Cl KUTN/CMB KT2 59 V14
Lovelace Av HAYES BR2 76 J4
Lovelace Cl BGR/WK TN15 79 S11
EHSLY KT24 82 C13
Lovelace Dr WOKS/MYFD GU22 80 K5
Lovelace Gdns BARK IG11 41 Q9
SURB KT6 71 T5
WOT/HER KT12 70 E10
Lovelace Gn ELTH/MOT SE9 64 H1
Lovelace Rd DUL SE21 62 G7
EBAR EN4 25 S5
SURB KT6 71 S5
Lovelace Vls THDIT KT7 * 71 R5
Lovelands La KWD/TDW/WH KT20 93 P3
Love La ABLGY WD5 11 M4
BXLY DA5 66 A4
CHEAM SM3 73 L11
CITYW EC2V 5 P11
GDST RH9 95 N8
IVER SL0 44 H4
KGLGY WD4 10 E3
KWD/TDW/WH KT20 92 G2
MRDN SM4 73 N5
PIN HA5 34 G1
SNWD SE25 75 M1
SOCK/AV RM15 55 Q7
SURB KT6 71 T7
TOTM N17 26 K12
WFD IG8 28 H11
WOOL/PLUM SE18 52 J9
Lovel Av WELL DA16 53 Q14
Lovel End CFSP/GDCR SL9 20 A12
Lovelinch Cl PECK SE15 51 N11
Lovell Pl BERM/RHTH SE16 51 Q8
Lovell Rd EN EN1 16 B9
RCHPK/HAM TW10 59 S8
STHL UB1 46 K4
Lovell Wk RAIN RM13 42 G11
Lovel Md CFSP/GDCR SL9 20 A12
Lovelock Cl PUR/KEN CR8 86 G7
Lovel Rd CFSP/GDCR SL9 20 A12
Loveridge Ms KIL/WHAMP NW6 37 M11
Loveridge Rd KIL/WHAMP NW6 37 M11
Lovett Dr CAR SM5 73 Q5
Lovett Rd DEN/HRF UB9 33 N1
STA TW18 56 F9
Lovetts Pl WAND/EARL SW18 61 Q3
Lovett Wy WLSDN NW10 36 C10
Love Wk CMBW SE5 50 H14
Lovibonds Av ORP BR6 76 K8
WDR/YW UB7 45 R4
Lowbell La LCOL/BKTW AL2 12 K1
Lowbrook Rd IL IG1 40 K9
Low Cl RDART DA2 67 U3
Lowdell Cl WDR/YW UB7 45 Q4
Lowden Rd ED N9 27 M6
HNHL SE24 62 F2
STHL UB1 46 G5
Lowe Av CAN/RD E16 52 C3
Lowe Cl CHIG IG7 29 Q10
Lowell St POP/IOD E14 51 Q4
Lowen Rd RAIN RM13 42 D14
Lower Addiscombe Rd CROY/NA CR0 74 H6
Lower Addison Gdns WKENS W14 6 A4
Lower Barn Rd PUR/KEN CR8 86 H3
Lower Bedfords Rd ROM RM1 30 G11
Lower Belgrave St BGVA SW1W 7 U6
Lower Boston Rd HNWL W7 47 N6
Lower Bridge Rd REDH RH1 93 T10
Lower Broad St DAGE RM10 42 A13
Lower Bury La EPP CM16 18 C5
Lower Camden CHST BR7 64 H13
Lower Church St CROY/NA CR0 * 74 F7
Lower Clapton Rd CLPT E5 39 M9
Lower Clarendon Wk NKENS W10 2 A12
Lower Common South
PUT/ROE SW15 60 H1
Lower Coombe St CROY/NA CR0 74 G9
Lower Court Rd HOR/WEW KT19 84 D1
Lower Cft SWLY BR8 78 F2
Lower Derby Rd WAT WD17 22 E2
Lower Downs Rd RYNPK SW20 60 K13
Lower Dunnymans BNSTD SM7 85 M4
Lower Farm Rd EHSLY KT24 82 D14
Lower Gravel Rd HAYES BR2 76 G6
Lower Green Gdns WPK KT4 72 G6
Lower Green Rd ESH/CLAY KT10 70 K7
Lower Gn West MTCM CR4 73 T1
Lower Grosvenor Pl BGVA SW1W 7 U5
Lower Grove Rd RCHPK/HAM TW10 59 V4
Lower Hall La CHING E4 27 Q10
Lower Hampton Rd SUN TW16 58 F14
Lower Ham Rd KUTN/CMB KT2 59 T11
Lower High St WAT WD17 22 F3
Lower Hill Rd HOR/WEW KT19 84 B2
Lower Island Wy WAB EN9 16 H9
Lower James St SOHO/CST W1F * 4 B13
Lower John St SOHO/CST W1F 4 B13
Lower Kenwood Av ENC/FH EN2 26 C3
Lower Kings Rd KUTN/CMB KT2 59 U13
Lower Lea Crossing POP/IOD E14 52 A5
Lower Maidstone Rd
FBAR/BDGN N11 26 A11
Lower Mardyke Av RAIN RM13 42 C14
Lower Marsh STHWK SE1 8 J4
Lower Marsh La BRYLDS KT5 71 V2
Lower Md IVER SL0 44 H1
Lower Meadow CHES/WCR EN8 16 D1
Lower Merton Ri HAMP NW3 37 S12
Lower Morden La MRDN SM4 72 K4
Lower Mortlake Rd RCH/KEW TW9 59 U2
Lower Noke Cl BRW CM14 31 M7
Lower Northfield BNSTD SM7 85 M4
Lower Paddock Rd OXHEY WD19 22 G4
Lower Park Rd BELV DA17 54 A9
COUL/CHIP CR5 85 S8
FBAR/BDGN N11 26 A10
LOU IG10 28 G3
Lower Pillory Down CAR SM5 85 V2
Lower Plantation RKW/CH/CXG WD3 21 N1
Lower Queen's Rd BKHH IG9 28 G7
Lower Richmond Rd PUT/ROE SW15 60 J1
RCH/KEW TW9 60 B1
Lower Rd BELV DA17 54 C8
BERM/RHTH SE16 51 N8
CFSP/GDCR SL9 32 C1
LHD/OX KT22 83 N13
LOU IG10 17 U13
PUR/KEN CR8 86 F3
REDH RH1 93 R12
RKW/CH/CXG WD3 20 H2
RYLN/HDSTN HA2 35 M7
STMC/STPC BR5 77 R4
SUT SM1 73 R10
SWLY BR8 66 H12
Lower Sandfields RPLY/SEND GU23 80 H13
Lower Sand Hills SURB KT6 71 S5
Lower Sawleywood BNSTD SM7 85 M4
Lower Sloane St BGVA SW1W 7 R8
Lower Sq ISLW TW7 59 R1
Lower Station Rd DART DA1 66 E4
Lower Strd CDALE/KGS NW9 24 F14
Lower Sunbury Rd E/WMO/HCT KT8 58 H14
Lower Swaines EPP CM16 18 C4
Lower Tail OXHEY WD19 22 G8
Lower Teddington Rd KUT/HW KT1 59 T13
Lower Ter HAMP NW3 37 Q8
Lower Thames St MON EC3R 5 S14
Lower Tub BUSH WD23 23 M5
Lower Wood Rd ESH/CLAY KT10 71 R11
Lowestoft Rd WATN WD24 11 P13
Loweswater Cl GSTN WD25 11 Q7
WBLY HA9 35 T7
The Lowe CHIG IG7 29 Q10
Lowfield Rd ACT W3 48 C4
KIL/WHAMP NW6 37 N12
Lowfield St DART DA1 67 L5
Low Hall Cl CHING E4 27 S5
Low Hall La WALTH E17 39 Q4
Lowick Rd HRW HA1 35 N2
Lowland Gdns ROMW/RG RM7 42 B4
Lowlands Dr STWL/WRAY TW19 57 P3
Lowlands Rd HRW HA1 35 N5
PIN HA5 34 E5
SOCK/AV RM15 55 Q6
Lowman Rd HOLWY N7 38 D9
Lowndes Cl KTBR SW1X 7 T6
Lowndes Ct SOHO/CST W1F * 4 A12
Lowndes Pl KTBR SW1X * 7 S6
Lowndes Sq KTBR SW1X 7 R4
Lowndes St KTBR SW1X 7 R5
Lowood St WCHPL E1 51 M5
Lowry Cl ERITH DA8 54 D9
Lowry Crs MTCM CR4 61 S14
Lowry Rd BCTR RM8 41 R10
Lowshoe La CRW RM5 30 B13
Lowson Gv OXHEY WD19 22 G5
Lowswood Cl NTHWD HA6 21 U13
Lowther Cl BORE WD6 23 V3
Lowther Dr ENC/FH EN2 26 C2
Lowther Hl FSTH SE23 63 Q5
Lowther Man BARN SW13 * 48 G13
Lowther Rd BARN SW13 48 F13
HOLWY N7 * 38 E10
KUTN/CMB KT2 59 V13
STAN HA7 35 V1
WALTH E17 27 Q14
Lowth Rd CMBW SE5 50 G14
Loxford Av EHAM E6 40 F14
Loxford La IL IG1 41 L10
Loxford Rd BARK IG11 40 K11
CTHM CR3 94 K1
Loxford Wy CTHM CR3 94 K1
Loxham Rd CHING E4 27 T12
Loxham St STPAN WC1H * 4 F6
Loxley Cl SYD SE26 63 P10
Loxley Rd HPTN TW12 58 H9
WAND/EARL SW18 61 R6
Loxton Rd FSTH SE23 63 P6
Loxwood Cl EBED/NFELT TW14 57 V6
STMC/STPC BR5 77 T7
Loxwood Rd SEVS/STOTM N15 38 J1
Lubbock Rd CHST BR7 64 J13
Lubbock St NWCR SE14 51 N12
Lucan Dr STA TW18 57 P12
Lucan Pl CHEL SW3 7 N8
Lucan Rd BAR EN5 25 L1
Lucas Av PLSTW E13 40 D13
RYLN/HDSTN HA2 34 J7
Lucas Ct WAB EN9 17 M7
Lucas Crs SWCM DA10 67 V3
Lucas Gdns EFNCH N2 25 Q14
Lucas Rd PGE/AN SE20 63 N11
Lucas Sq GLDGN NW11 37 N4
Lucas St BROCKY SE4 51 S14
Lucern Cl CHESW EN7 15 U1
Lucerne Cl PLMGR N13 26 C8
WOKS/MYFD GU22 80 C9
Lucerne Gv WALTH E17 39 V2
Lucerne Ms KENS W8 * 6 F1
Lucerne Rd HBRY N5 38 F9
ORP BR6 77 P6
THHTH CR7 74 F3
Lucerne Wy HARH RM3 30 K11
Lucey Rd BERM/RHTH SE16 51 L8
Lucey Wy BERM/RHTH SE16 51 L8
Lucie Av ASHF TW15 57 T11
Lucien Rd WIM/MER SW19 61 P7
Lucknow St WOOL/PLUM SE18 53 N12
Lucorn Cl LEE/GVPK SE12 64 B4
Luctons Av BKHH IG9 28 E6
Luddesdon Rd ERITH DA8 54 A12
Luddington Av VW GU25 56 D14
Ludford Cl CROY/NA CR0 74 F9
Ludgate Broadway BLKFR EC4V * 5 M12
Ludgate Circ STP EC4M 5 L12
Ludgate Hl STP EC4M 5 L12
Ludgate Sq STP EC4M * 5 M12
Ludham Cl BARK/HLT IG6 29 L13
THMD SE28 53 S4
Ludlow Cl HAYES BR2 * 76 C1
RYLN/HDSTN HA2 34 H9
Ludlow Md OXHEY WD19 22 D8
Ludlow Rd EA W5 47 S2
FELT TW13 58 C8
Ludlow St FSBYE EC1V * 5 N7
Ludlow Wy EFNCH N2 37 Q2
RKW/CH/CXG WD3 21 U2
Ludovick Wk PUT/ROE SW15 60 E2
Luffield Rd ABYW SE2 53 R8
Luffman Rd LEE/GVPK SE12 64 D8
Lugard Rd PECK SE15 51 M14
Lugg Ap MNPK E12 40 J8
Luke St SDTCH EC2A 5 S7
Lukin Crs CHING E4 27 V8
Lukin St WCHPL E1 51 N5
Lullarook Cl BH/WHM TN16 88 E6
Lullingstone Av SWLY BR8 78 F1
Lullingstone Cl STMC/STPC BR5 65 R12
Lullingstone Crs STMC/STPC BR5 65 Q12
Lullingstone La EYN DA4 78 J8
LEW SE13 63 V4
Lullingstone Rd BELV DA17 53 V11
Lullington Garth BMLY BR1 64 A12
BORE WD6 * 24 C3
NFNCH/WDSPK N12 25 M10
Lullington Rd DAGW RM9 41 U12
PGE/AN SE20 63 L12
Lulot Gdns ARCH N19 37 V7
Lulworth Av CHESW EN7 15 R3
HEST TW5 46 K13
WBLY HA9 35 S5
Lulworth Cl RYLN/HDSTN HA2 34 H8
Lulworth Crs MTCM CR4 61 S14
Lulworth Dr CRW RM5 30 B10
PIN HA5 34 F5
Lulworth Gdns RYLN/HDSTN HA2 34 G7
Lulworth Rd ELTH/MOT SE9 64 G7
PECK SE15 * 51 M14
WELL DA16 53 P14
Lulworth Waye YEAD UB4 46 D4
Lumen Rd WBLY HA9 35 T7
Lumley Cl BELV DA17 54 A11
Lumley Gdns CHEAM SM3 73 L10
Lumley Rd CHEAM SM3 73 L11
Lumley St OXSTW W1C 3 T12
Lunar Cl BH/WHM TN16 88 F6
Luna Rd THHTH CR7 74 G1
Lundin Wk OXHEY WD19 * 22 F9
Lundy Dr HYS/HAR UB3 46 B9
Lundy Wk IS N1 * 38 G11
Lunedale Rd RDART DA2 67 Q6
Lunghurst Rd CTHM CR3 87 S11
Lunham Rd NRWD SE19 62 J11
Lupin Cl BRXS/STRHM SW2 62 F7
CROY/NA CR0 75 P6
ROMW/RG RM7 42 D7
WDR/YW UB7 45 P10
Lupton Cl LEE/GVPK SE12 64 D9
Lupton St KTTN NW5 38 A9
Lupus St PIM SW1V 7 V10
Lurgan Av HMSMTH W6 48 K11
Lurline Gdns BTSEA SW11 49 U13
Luscombe Wy VX/NE SW8 8 E13
Lushes Ct LOU IG10 28 K3
Lushes Rd LOU IG10 28 K3
Lushington Dr COB KT11 82 D4
Lushington Rd CAT SE6 63 T10
WLSDN NW10 36 H14
Lushington Ter HACK E8 * 39 L10
Lusted Hall La BH/WHM TN16 88 E11
Luther Cl EDGW HA8 24 C7
Luther King Cl WALTH E17 39 R4
Luther Ms TEDD TW11 59 P10
Luther Rd TEDD TW11 59 P10
Luton Pl GNWCH SE10 51 U12
Luton Rd PLSTW E13 52 C2
SCUP DA14 65 S8
WALTH E17 39 Q1
Luton St STJWD NW8 3 M8
Luttrell Av PUT/ROE SW15 60 H3
Lutwyche Rd FSTH SE23 63 R7
Luxborough La CHIG IG7 28 H9
Luxborough St CAMTN NW1 3 S8
Luxembourg Ms SRTFD E15 40 A10
Luxemburg Gdns HMSMTH W6 48 K9
Luxfield Rd ELTH/MOT SE9 64 G6
Luxford St BERM/RHTH SE16 51 P9
Luxmore St BROCKY SE4 51 R13
Luxor St CMBW SE5 62 G1
Luxted Rd ORP BR6 88 J2
Lyall Av DUL SE21 62 J9
Lyall Ms KTBR SW1X 7 S6
Lyall Ms West KTBR SW1X * 7 S6
Lyall St KTBR SW1X 7 S6
Lyal Rd BOW E3 39 Q14
Lycett Pl SHB W12 48 G7
Lych Ga GSTN WD25 11 R7
Lych Gate Rd ORP BR6 77 Q6
Lych Gate Wk HYS/HAR UB3 46 B5
Lych Wy WOKN/KNAP GU21 80 B6
Lyconby Gdns CROY/NA CR0 75 Q5
Lydd Cl BFN/LL DA15 65 N8
Lydden Gv WAND/EARL SW18 61 P5
Lydden Rd WAND/EARL SW18 61 P5
Lydd Rd BXLYHN DA7 53 V12
Lydeard Rd EHAM E6 40 H12
Lydele Cl WOKN/KNAP GU21 80 D5
Lydford Cl STNW/STAM N16 38 J10
Lydford Rd CRICK NW2 36 K11
MV/WKIL W9 2 D7
SEVS/STOTM N15 38 H3
Lydhurst Av BRXS/STRHM SW2 62 D7
Lydia Rd ERITH DA8 54 F11
Lydney Cl WIM/MER SW19 61 L7
Lydon Rd CLAP SW4 62 A1
Lydstep Rd CHST BR7 64 J9
Lye La LCOL/BKTW AL2 11 U2
The Lye KWD/TDW/WH KT20 84 J12
Lyfield LHD/OX KT22 82 K4
Lyford Rd WAND/EARL SW18 61 R5
Lyford St WOOL/PLUM SE18 52 G9
Lygon Pl BGVA SW1W * 7 U6
Lyham Cl BRXS/STRHM SW2 62 C4
Lyham Rd BRXS/STRHM SW2 62 C3
Lyle Cl MTCM CR4 73 U5
Lyle Pk SEV TN13 90 J13
Lymbourne Cl BELMT SM2 73 N14
Lymden Gdns REIG RH2 93 P12
Lyme Farm Rd LEE/GVPK SE12 64 C2
Lyme Gv HOM E9 39 N12
Lymer Av NRWD SE19 62 K10
Lyme Regis Rd BNSTD SM7 85 M7
Lyme Rd WELL DA16 53 R13
Lymescote Gdns SUT SM1 73 N7
Lyme St CAMTN NW1 38 A12
Lyme Ter CAMTN NW1 38 A12
Lyminge Cl SCUP DA14 65 P9
Lyminge Gdns WAND/EARL SW18 61 S6
Lymington Av WDGN N22 26 E14
Lymington Cl STRHM/NOR SW16 62 B14
Lymington Ct GSTN WD25 * 11 N8
Lymington Dr RSLP HA4 33 V7
Lymington Gdns HOR/WEW KT19 72 F10
Lymington Rd BCTR RM8 41 T6
KIL/WHAMP NW6 * 37 P11
Lyminster Cl YEAD UB4 46 G3
Lympstone Gdns PECK SE15 51 L12
Lynbridge Gdns PLMGR N13 26 F9
Lynbrook Cl PECK SE15 9 T13
RAIN RM13 42 D14
Lynbrook Gv PECK SE15 9 T13
Lynceley Gra EPP CM16 18 E3
Lynch Cl UX/CGN UB8 33 N12
Lynchen Cl HEST TW5 46 C13
The Lynch UX/CGN UB8 33 N12
Lyncourt BKHTH/KID SE3 * 51 V14
Lyncroft Av PIN HA5 34 F3
Lyncroft Gdns EW KT17 72 F13
HSLW TW3 59 L3
KIL/WHAMP NW6 37 N10
WEA W13 47 S7
Lyndale CRICK NW2 37 M8
THDIT KT7 71 N5
Lyndale Av CRICK NW2 37 M8
Lyndale Cl BKHTH/KID SE3 52 B11
Lyndale Hampton Court Wy
ESH/CLAY KT10 71 N5
Lyndale Rd REDH RH1 93 U7
Lynden Wy SWLY BR8 78 C1
Lyndhurst Av BRYLDS KT5 72 B6
MLHL NW7 24 E11
NFNCH/WDSPK N12 25 T11
PIN HA5 22 D13
STHL UB1 46 K6
STRHM/NOR SW16 62 B14
SUN TW16 70 C1
WHTN TW2 58 H6
Lyndhurst Cl BXLYHN DA7 66 B1
CROY/NA CR0 74 K8
ORP BR6 76 K9
WLSDN NW10 36 D8
WOKN/KNAP GU21 80 B5
Lyndhurst Ct BELMT SM2 * 73 N12
Lyndhurst Dr EMPK RM11 42 J6
LEY E10 39 U5
NWMAL KT3 72 E4
SEV TN13 90 E14
Lyndhurst Gdns BARK IG11 41 N11
EN EN1 26 J2
FNCH N3 25 L13
GNTH/NBYPK IG2 41 M4
HAMP NW3 37 R10
PIN HA5 22 D13
Lyndhurst Gv CMBW SE5 50 J14
Lyndhurst Leys HAYES BR2 * 63 V14
Lyndhurst Prior SNWD SE25 * 74 J1
Lyndhurst Ri CHIG IG7 28 J9
Lyndhurst Rd BXLYHN DA7 66 B1
CHING E4 27 U12
COUL/CHIP CR5 85 U6
GFD/PVL UB6 46 K2
HAMP NW3 37 R10
REIG RH2 93 N13
THHTH CR7 74 E2
UED N18 27 L9
WDGN N22 26 E11
Lyndhurst Sq PECK SE15 50 K13
Lyndhurst Ter HAMP NW3 37 R10
Lyndhurst Wy BELMT SM2 73 N13
CHERT KT16 68 J8
PECK SE15 50 K13
Lyndon Av BFN/LL DA15 65 P3
PIN HA5 22 G11
WLGTN SM6 73 U8
Lyndon Rd BELV DA17 54 A9
Lyndon Yd TOOT SW17 61 P9
Lyndsey Pl CHESW EN7 * 16 B4
Lyne Cl VW GU25 68 D4
Lyne Crs WALTH E17 27 R13
Lyne Crossing Rd CHERT KT16 68 E4
Lynegrove Av ASHF TW15 57 U10
Lyneham Wk CLPT E5 * 39 Q10
Lyne La EGH TW20 68 E3
Lyne Rd VW GU25 68 C4
Lynette Av CLAP SW4 61 V4
Lynford Cl BAR EN5 24 F3
EDGW HA8 24 C13
Lynford Gdns EDGW HA8 24 B9
GDMY/SEVK IG3 41 P7
Lynford Ter ED N9 * 26 K6
Lynhurst Crs HGDN/ICK UB10 33 U12
Lynhurst Rd HGDN/ICK UB10 33 U12
Lynmere Rd WELL DA16 53 R14
Lyn Ms STNW/STAM N16 * 38 K9
Lynmouth Av EN EN1 26 K4
MRDN SM4 72 K5
Lynmouth Dr RSLP HA4 34 D7
Lynmouth Gdns GFD/PVL UB6 35 R13
HEST TW5 46 F13
Lynmouth Ri STMC/STPC BR5 77 R2
Lynmouth Rd EFNCH N2 37 T1
GFD/PVL UB6 35 R13
STNW/STAM N16 38 K6
WALTH E17 39 Q4
Lynn Cl ASHF TW15 57 V10
KTN/HRWW/WS HA3 23 M14
Lynne Cl ORP BR6 77 P11
SAND/SEL CR2 87 N1
Lynnett Rd BCTR RM8 41 T7
Lynne Wk ESH/CLAY KT10 71 L10
Lynne Wy NTHLT UB5 34 F14
Lynn Ms WAN E11 40 A7
Lynn Rd BAL SW12 61 V5
GNTH/NBYPK IG2 41 M5
WAN E11 40 A7
Lynn St ENC/FH EN2 15 T13
Lynn Wk REIG RH2 93 P14
Lynross Cl HARH RM3 31 L14
Lynscott Wy SAND/SEL CR2 74 F13
Lynstead Cl BMLY BR1 64 E14
Lynsted Cl BXLYHS DA6 66 B3
Lynsted Ct BECK BR3 63 Q14
Lynsted Gdns ELTH/MOT SE9 64 F2
Lynton Av CDALE/KGS NW9 36 F2
NFNCH/WDSPK N12 25 R9
ROMW/RG RM7 30 B13
STMC/STPC BR5 77 R2
WEA W13 47 Q4
Lynton Cl CHSGTN KT9 71 U9
ISLW TW7 59 P2
WLSDN NW10 36 E11
Lynton Crs GNTH/NBYPK IG2 40 K4
Lynton Est STHWK SE1 9 V8
Lynton Gdns EN EN1 26 J5
FBAR/BDGN N11 26 B11
Lynton Md TRDG/WHET N20 25 N8
Lynton Pde CHES/WCR EN8 16 D4
Lynton Rd ACT W3 48 A5
CEND/HSY/T N8 38 B3
CHING E4 27 T10
CROY/NA CR0 74 E4
KIL/WHAMP NW6 2 D2
NWMAL KT3 72 D3
RYLN/HDSTN HA2 34 G7
STHWK SE1 9 V8
Lynton Ter ACT W3 * 48 C4
Lynwood Av COUL/CHIP CR5 85 V5
DTCH/LGLY SL3 44 B8
EGH TW20 56 C11
EW KT17 84 F4
Lynwood Cl CRW RM5 30 B11
RYLN/HDSTN HA2 34 G8
SWFD E18 28 E13
WOKN/KNAP GU21 80 H3
Lynwood Dr CRW RM5 30 B11
NTHWD HA6 22 A13
WPK KT4 72 G7
Lynwood Gdns CROY/NA CR0 74 D9
STHL UB1 46 H4
Lynwood Gv ORP BR6 77 N5
WCHMH N21 26 E6
Lynwood Hts RKW/CH/CXG WD3 21 M3
Lynwood Rd EA W5 47 T1
EW KT17 84 F4
REDH RH1 93 U8
THDIT KT7 71 P7
TOOT SW17 61 T8
Lynwood Ter WIM/MER SW19 * 61 M13
Lyon Meade STAN HA7 23 S13
Lyon Park Av ALP/SUD HA0 35 V12
Lyon Rd HRW HA1 35 P4
ROM RM1 42 F5
WIM/MER SW19 61 Q13
WOT/HER KT12 70 G7
Lyonsdene KWD/TDW/WH KT20 93 M3
Lyonsdown Av BAR EN5 25 Q4
Lyonsdown Rd BAR EN5 25 Q4
Lyons Pl STJWD NW8 3 L8
Lyon St IS N1 38 D12
Lyons Wk WKENS W14 6 A7
Lyon Wy GFD/PVL UB6 35 N13
Lyoth Rd STMC/STPC BR5 77 L7
Lyric Dr GFD/PVL UB6 46 K2
Lyric Ms SYD SE26 63 N9
Lyric Rd BARN SW13 48 F13
Lysander CDALE/KGS NW9 * 24 F13
Lysander Gdns SURB KT6 71 V4
Lysander Gv ARCH N19 38 B6
Lysander Ms ARCH N19 * 38 C6
Lysander Rd CROY/NA CR0 74 D11
RSLP HA4 33 V7
Lysander Wy ABLGY WD5 11 N6
ORP BR6 77 L8
Lysias Rd BAL SW12 61 U4
Lysia St FUL/PGN SW6 48 K12
Lysley Pl BRKMPK AL9 14 E1
Lysons Wk PUT/ROE SW15 * 60 G3
Lyster Ms COB KT11 82 E3
Lytchet Rd BMLY BR1 64 C12
Lytchet Wy PEND EN3 16 C13
Lytchgate Cl SAND/SEL CR2 74 J12
Lytcott Dr E/WMO/HCT KT8 70 H1
Lytcott Gv EDUL SE22 62 K3
Lytham Av OXHEY WD19 22 F10
Lytham Cl THMD SE28 53 U4
Lytham St WALW SE17 9 Q10
Lyttelton Rd EFNCH N2 37 Q3
LEY E10 39 T8
Lyttleton Cl HAMP NW3 37 S12
Lyttleton Rd CEND/HSY/T N8 * 38 E1
Lytton Av PEND EN3 16 E12
PLMGR N13 26 E7
Lytton Cl EFNCH N2 37 R3
LOU IG10 29 M1
NTHLT UB5 34 H12
Lytton Gdns WLGTN SM6 74 B9
Lytton Gv PUT/ROE SW15 60 K3
Lytton Pk COB KT11 82 H2
Lytton Rd BAR EN5 25 Q2
GPK RM2 42 H3
PIN HA5 22 G12
WAN E11 40 A5
WOKS/MYFD GU22 80 F7
Lyveden Rd BKHTH/KID SE3 52 D12
TOOT SW17 61 S11
Lywood Cl KWD/TDW/WH KT20 84 J12

M

Mabbotts KWD/TDW/WH KT20 84 K11
Mabbutt Cl LCOL/BKTW AL2 11 S4
Mabel Rd SWLY BR8 66 G11
Mabel St WOKN/KNAP GU21 80 B8
Maberley Crs NRWD SE19 63 L12
Maberley Rd BECK BR3 75 P1
BMLY BR1 64 B13
NRWD SE19 62 K13
Mabledon Pl CAMTN NW1 4 D6
Mablethorpe Rd FUL/PGN SW6 6 A14
Mabley St HOM E9 39 Q10
Macaret Cl TRDG/WHET N20 25 P5
Macarthur Cl FSTGT E7 40 C11
WBLY HA9 36 B11
Macarthur Ter CHARL SE7 * 52 F11
Macaulay Av ESH/CLAY KT10 71 N7
Macaulay Rd CLAP SW4 61 V1
CTHM CR3 86 J12
EHAM E6 40 F14
Macbean St WOOL/PLUM SE18 52 J8
Macbeth St HMSMTH W6 48 H10
Macclesfield Br STJWD NW8 3 P3
Macclesfield Rd FSBYE EC1V 5 N5
SNWD SE25 75 N3
Macclesfield St SOHO/SHAV W1D * 4 D13
Macdonald Av DAGE RM10 42 B8
EMPK RM11 43 L2
Macdonald Rd ARCH N19 38 A7
FBAR/BDGN N11 25 T10
FSTGT E7 40 C9
WALTH E17 27 U14
Macdonald Wy EMPK RM11 43 L2
Macdonnell Gdns GSTN WD25 11 M9
Macduff Rd BTSEA SW11 49 U13
Mace Cl WAP E1W 51 M6
Mace La RSEV TN14 89 M3
Mace St BETH E2 39 P14
Macfarlane La ISLW TW7 47 P11
Macfarlane Rd SHB W12 48 J6
Mac Farren Pl CAMTN NW1 3 T8
Macgregor Rd CAN/RD E16 52 E3
Machell Rd PECK SE15 63 N1
Mackay Rd VX/NE SW8 61 V1
Mackennal St STJWD NW8 3 P4
Mackenzie Cl SHB W12 48 H5
Mackenzie Rd BECK BR3 63 Q13
HOLWY N7 38 D11
Mackeson Rd HAMP NW3 * 37 T9
Mackie Rd BRXS/STRHM SW2 62 E5
Mackintosh La HOM E9 39 P10
Macklin St HOL/ALD WC2B * 4 F11
Macks Rd BERM/RHTH SE16 51 L9
Mackworth St CAMTN NW1 4 A5
Maclean Rd FSTH SE23 63 Q4
Maclennan Av RAIN RM13 54 K1
Macleod House CHARL SE7 * 52 G12
Macleod Rd WCHMH N21 26 C3
Macleod St WALW SE17 9 P10
Maclise Rd WKENS W14 6 A6
Macmillan Wy TOOT SW17 61 V9
Macoma Rd WOOL/PLUM SE18 53 M11
Macoma Ter WOOL/PLUM SE18 53 M11
Maconochies Rd POP/IOD E14 * 51 T10
Macon Wy UPMR RM14 43 T4
Macquarie Wy POP/IOD E14 51 T9
Macroom Rd MV/WKIL W9 2 D5
Madan Cl BH/WHM TN16 97 N1
Madan Rd BH/WHM TN16 97 M1
Madans Wk EPSOM KT18 84 D4
Mada Rd ORP BR6 76 K8
Maddams St BOW E3 51 T2
Maddesfield Ct RAD WD7 12 J7
Maddison Cl EFNCH N2 25 Q14
TEDD TW11 59 P11
Maddocks Cl SCUP DA14 65 T11
Maddock Wy WALW SE17 9 L12
Maddox La GT/LBKH KT23 82 H14
Maddox Pk GT/LBKH KT23 82 G13
Maddox St CONDST W1S 3 V13
Madeira Av BMLY BR1 64 A13
Madeira Crs BF/WBF KT14 80 K3
Madeira Gv WFD IG8 28 E11
Madeira Rd BF/WBF KT14 80 K3
MTCM CR4 73 T2
PLMGR N13 26 F9
STRHM/NOR SW16 62 C10
WAN E11 39 V7
Madeira Wk EPSOM KT18 84 D4
REIG RH2 93 R9
Madeleine Ct CHDH RM6 41 S4
Madeley Rd EA W5 47 T5
Madeline Gv IL IG1 41 M10
Madeline Rd PGE/AN SE20 63 L12
Madells EPP CM16 18 D5
Madge Gill Wy EHAM E6 40 G13
Madge Hl HNWL W7 * 47 N5
Madinah Rd HACK E8 39 L10
Madison Crs BXLYHN DA7 53 S12
Madison Gdns BXLYHN DA7 53 S12
Madison Wy SEV TN13 90 F13
Madras Pl HOLWY N7 38 E11
Madras Rd IL IG1 40 K10
Madrid Rd BARN SW13 48 G13
Madron St WALW SE17 9 T9
Maesmaur Rd BH/WHM TN16 88 F11
Mafeking Av BTFD TW8 47 U11
EHAM E6 40 F14
GNTH/NBYPK IG2 41 M5
Mafeking Rd CAN/RD E16 52 B2
EN EN1 26 K1
STWL/WRAY TW19 56 F7
TOTM N17 27 L14
Magazine Ga BAY/PAD W2 * 7 P1
Magazine Pl LHD/OX KT22 83 R12
Magazine Rd CTHM CR3 86 F12
Magdala Av ARCH N19 38 A7
Magdala Rd ISLW TW7 59 Q1
SAND/SEL CR2 74 H12
Magdalen Cl BF/WBF KT14 81 Q4
Magdalen Crs BF/WBF KT14 81 Q4
Magdalene Gdns EHAM E6 52 J2
Magdalene Rd SHPTN TW17 69 R2
Magdalen Rd WAND/EARL SW18 61 Q6
Magdalen St STHWK SE1 9 S2
Magdelan Gv ORP BR6 77 R9
Magee St LBTH SE11 8 J11
Magellan Pl POP/IOD E14 51 S10
Magna Carta La STWL/WRAY TW19 56 B6
Magnaville Rd BUSH WD23 23 N5
Magnet Rd WBLY HA9 35 T7
Magnin Cl HACK E8 39 L13
Magnolia Av ABLGY WD5 11 M6
Magnolia Cl KUTN/CMB KT2 60 B11
LEY E10 39 S7
Magnolia Ct HGDN/ICK UB10 * 33 T11
KTN/HRWW/WS HA3 35 V5
Magnolia Dr BH/WHM TN16 88 F6
Magnolia Gdns EDGW HA8 24 C9
Magnolia Pl CLAP SW4 * 62 C3
EA W5 * 47 T3
Magnolia Rd CHSWK W4 48 B11
Magnolia St WDR/YW UB7 45 P9
Magnolia Wy BRWN CM15 31 V3
HOR/WEW KT19 72 C10
Magnolia Whf CHSWK W4 * 48 B11
Magnum Cl RAIN RM13 54 J2
Magpie Bottom BGR/WK TN15 91 L2
Magpie Cl CDALE/KGS NW9 24 E14
COUL/CHIP CR5 86 A8
EN EN1 16 A13
FSTGT E7 40 B10
Magpie Hall Cl HAYES BR2 76 G4
Magpie Hall La HAYES BR2 76 H4
Magpie Hall Rd STAN HA7 23 N7
Magpie Pl GSTN WD25 * 11 Q6
NWCR SE14 * 51 Q11
Magri Wk WCHPL E1 51 N3
Maguire Dr RCHPK/HAM TW10 59 S9
Maguire St STHWK SE1 9 V3
Mahlon Av RSLP HA4 34 D10
Mahogany Cl BERM/RHTH SE16 51 Q6
Mahon Cl EN EN1 15 V13
Maida Av BAY/PAD W2 2 K9
CHING E4 27 T5
Maida Rd BELV DA17 54 A8
Maida V MV/WKIL W9 2 H4
STJWD NW8 3 L7
Maida Vale Rd DART DA1 66 G3
Maida Wy CHING E4 27 T5
Maiden Erlegh Av BXLY DA5 65 U6
Maiden La CAMTN NW1 38 B12
COVGDN WC2E 4 F14
DART DA1 66 G2
STHWK SE1 9 P1
Maiden Rd SRTFD E15 40 A12
Maidens Br ENC/FH EN2 * 16 A11
Maidenshaw Rd HOR/WEW KT19 84 D2
Maidenstone Hl GNWCH SE10 51 U13
Maidstone Av CRW RM5 30 C14
Maidstone Buildings Ms STHWK SE1 9 P2
Maidstone Rd BGR/WK TN15 91 P12
FBAR/BDGN N11 26 B11
SCUP DA14 65 T11
SEV TN13 90 E12
SWLY BR8 66 B13
Main Av EN EN1 26 K3
NTHWD HA6 21 V7
Main Barracks WOOL/PLUM SE18 * 52 H10
Main Dr CFSP/GDCR SL9 32 B3
DTCH/LGLY SL3 44 J8
GFD/PVL UB6 * 47 Q1
WBLY HA9 35 T8
Mainridge Rd CHST BR7 64 J9
Main Rd BH/WHM TN16 88 E3
EDEN TN8 96 K14
EYN DA4 67 P11
EYN DA4 79 L4
GPK RM2 30 J14
ORP BR6 * 77 S13
ROM RM1 42 F2
RSEV TN14 89 Q8
RSEV TN14 89 U14
SCUP DA14 65 N8
STMC/STPC BR5 65 S13
SWLY BR8 66 F13
SWLY BR8 78 C4
Main Road Gorse Hl EYN DA4 79 P6
Main St ADL/WDHM KT15 69 Q8
FELT TW13 58 F10
Maise Webster Cl STWL/WRAY TW19 * 57 P5
Maismore St PECK SE15 51 L11
The Maisonettes SUT SM1 * 73 M10
Maitland Cl BF/WBF KT14 81 L3
GNWCH SE10 51 T12
HSLWW TW4 58 H1
WOT/HER KT12 70 G7
Maitland Park Rd HAMP NW3 37 T11
Maitland Park Vls HAMP NW3 37 T11
Maitland Rd PGE/AN SE20 63 P11
SRTFD E15 40 B11
Maizey Ct BRWN CM15 31 U3
Majendie Rd WOOL/PLUM SE18 53 M10
Major Cl BRXN/ST SW9 62 F1
Major Rd BERM/RHTH SE16 * 51 L8
SRTFD E15 39 V10
Major's Farm Rd DTCH/LGLY SL3 44 C12
Makepeace Av HGT N6 37 U7
Makepeace Rd NTHLT UB5 34 G14
WAN E11 40 C2
Makins St CHEL SW3 7 P8
Malabar St POP/IOD E14 51 S7
Malam Gdns POP/IOD E14 51 T5
Malan Cl BH/WHM TN16 88 G7
Malan Sq RAIN RM13 42 H11
Malbrook Rd PUT/ROE SW15 60 H2
Malcolm Cl PGE/AN SE20 * 63 N12
Malcolm Ct STAN HA7 23 S10
Malcolm Crs HDN NW4 36 G4
Malcolm Dr SURB KT6 71 T6
Malcolm Pl BETH E2 51 N2
Malcolm Rd COUL/CHIP CR5 86 B5
HGDN/ICK UB10 33 R9
PGE/AN SE20 63 N12
SNWD SE25 75 L4
WCHPL E1 51 N2
WIM/MER SW19 61 L11
Malcolms Wy STHGT/OAK N14 * 26 A3
Malcolm Wy WAN E11 40 C3
Malden Av GFD/PVL UB6 35 N11
SNWD SE25 75 M2
Malden Flds BUSH WD23 22 F3
Malden Green Av WPK KT4 72 G6
Malden Hl NWMAL KT3 72 F2
Malden Hill Gdns NWMAL KT3 72 F1
Malden Pk NWMAL KT3 72 F4
Malden Pl KTTN NW5 37 U10
Malden Rd BORE WD6 24 A1
CHEAM SM3 72 K9
KTTN NW5 37 T10
WAT WD17 11 P14
WPK KT4 72 F5
Malden Wy NWMAL KT3 72 D4
Maldon Cl CMBW SE5 * 62 J1
IS N1 5 N1
Maldon Rd ACT W3 48 C5
ED N9 26 K8
ROMW/RG RM7 42 C5
WLGTN SM6 73 V10
Maldon Wk WFD IG8 28 E11
Malet Cl EGH TW20 * 56 H11
Malet St GWRST WC1E 4 C8
Maley Av WNWD SE27 62 F7
Malford Gv SWFD E18 40 B1
Malfort Rd CMBW SE5 62 J1
Malham Cl FBAR/BDGN N11 25 U11
Malham Rd FSTH SE23 63 P6
Malham Ter UED N18 * 27 M11
Malins Cl BAR EN5 * 24 H3
Malkin Wy WATW WD18 22 A2
Mallams Ms BRXN/ST SW9 62 E1
Mallard Cl BAR EN5 * 25 R4
DART DA1 67 M3
HNWL W7 47 N7
KIL/WHAMP NW6 2 F2
REDH RH1 93 U7
UPMR RM14 43 T5
WHTN TW2 58 J5
Mallard Ct WALTH E17 * 39 V1
Mallard Pl TWK TW1 59 Q8
WDGN N22 26 D14
Mallard Rd ABLGY WD5 11 N5
SAND/SEL CR2 75 P14
Mallards Ct OXHEY WD19 22 H8
Mallard's Reach WEY KT13 69 V7
Mallards Rd BARK IG11 53 Q2
WFD IG8 28 D12
The Mallards STA TW18 57 M14
Mallard Wk BECK BR3 75 P3
Mallard Wy CDALE/KGS NW9 36 C5
GSTN WD25 11 S10
NTHWD HA6 21 U12
WLGTN SM6 74 A13
Mall Chambers KENS W8 * 6 F1
Mallet Dr NTHLT UB5 34 H10
Mallet Rd LEW SE13 63 V4
Malling Cl CROY/NA CR0 * 75 N4
Malling Gdns MRDN SM4 73 Q4
Malling Wy HAYES BR2 76 B5
Mallinson Cl HCH RM12 42 J10
Mallinson Rd BTSEA SW11 61 S3
CROY/NA CR0 74 B8
Mallion Ct WAB EN9 17 M7
Mallord St CHEL SW3 7 M11
Mallory Cl BROCKY SE4 63 Q2
Mallory Gdns EBAR EN4 25 U5
Mallory St STJWD NW8 3 P8
Mallow Cl CROY/NA CR0 75 P6
KWD/TDW/WH KT20 84 H9

Mallow Md MLHL NW7 25 L12
The Mallows HGDN/ICK UB10 33 T8
Mallow St FSBYE EC1V 5 Q7
Mallow Wk CHESW EN7 15 T2
Mall Rd HMSMTH W6 48 H10
The Mall BXLYHS DA6 * 66 A2
EA W5 47 U5
EMPK RM11 42 H6
KTN/HRWW/WS HA3 35 V4
LCOL/BKTW AL2 12 A1
MORT/ESHN SW14 60 C3
STHGT/OAK N14 26 C8
SURB KT6 71 T3
WHALL SW1A 8 A3
Mall Vls HMSMTH W6 * 48 H10
Mallys Pl EYN DA4 67 Q13
Malmains Cl BECK BR3 75 V3
Malmains Wy BECK BR3 75 U2
Malm Cl RKW/CH/CXG WD3 21 P7
Malmesbury Cl PIN HA5 34 C2
Malmesbury Rd BOW E3 39 R14
BOW E3 51 R1
CAN/RD E16 52 B3
MRDN SM4 73 Q5
SWFD E18 28 B13
Malmesbury Ter CAN/RD E16 52 B3
Malmesbury West Est BOW E3 51 R1
Malmstone Av REDH RH1 94 A4
Malory Cl BECK BR3 63 Q14
Malpas Dr PIN HA5 34 F3
Malpas Rd BROCKY SE4 51 R14
DAGW RM9 41 T11
HACK E8 39 M11
Malta Rd LEY E10 39 S6
Malta St FSBYE EC1V 5 L7
Maltby Cl ORP BR6 77 Q6
Maltby Dr EN EN1 16 B12
Maltby Rd CHSGTN KT9 72 A11
Maltby St STHWK SE1 9 U5
Malt Hl EGH TW20 56 C10
Malthouse Dr CHSWK W4 48 F11
FELT TW13 58 F10
Malthouse Ms DEN/HRF UB9 * 21 N13
Maltings La EPP CM16 18 E3
Maltings Pl FUL/PGN SW6 49 P13
STHWK SE1 9 T3
The Maltings BF/WBF KT14 81 Q3
KGLGY WD4 10 J7
ORP BR6 77 P6
OXTED RH8 96 B7
ROM RM1 42 F5
SNWD SE25 * 74 J1
STA TW18 56 J9
Malting Wy ISLW TW7 59 P1
Maltmans La CFSP/GDCR SL9 32 A1
Malton Ms NKENS W10 * 2 A11
WOOL/PLUM SE18 53 N11
Malton Rd NKENS W10 2 A11
Malton St WOOL/PLUM SE18 53 N11
Maltravers St TPL/STR WC2R 4 H13
Malt St STHWK SE1 51 L11
Malus Cl ADL/WDHM KT15 68 K12
Malus Dr ADL/WDHM KT15 68 K12
Malva Cl WAND/EARL SW18 61 P3
Malvern Av BXLYHN DA7 53 U12
CHING E4 27 V12
RYLN/HDSTN HA2 34 G8
Malvern Cl BUSH WD23 23 L4
CHERT KT16 68 G11
HGDN/ICK UB10 33 S7
MTCM CR4 74 A1
NKENS W10 2 C10
SURB KT6 71 U6
Malvern Dr FELT TW13 58 F10
GDMY/SEVK IG3 41 P9
WFD IG8 28 E10
Malvern Gdns CRICK NW2 37 L7
KTN/HRWW/WS HA3 35 U2
LOU IG10 28 H4
Malvern Ms KIL/WHAMP NW6 2 E6
Malvern Pl MV/WKIL W9 2 D5
Malvern Rd CEND/HSY/T N8 38 E1
EHAM E6 40 G13
EMPK RM11 42 G4
HACK E8 39 L12
HPTN TW12 58 J13
HYS/HAR UB3 46 A12
KIL/WHAMP NW6 2 E5
ORP BR6 77 R9
PEND EN3 16 E11
SURB KT6 71 U7
THHTH CR7 74 E2
TOTM N17 39 L1
WAN E11 40 A7
Malvern Ter ED N9 26 K6
IS N1 4 J1
Malvern Wy RKW/CH/CXG WD3 21 T3
WEA W13 47 R3
Malwood Rd BAL SW12 61 V4
Malyons Rd LEW SE13 63 T3
SWLY BR8 66 F12
Malyons Ter LEW SE13 63 T3
The Malyons SHPTN TW17 * 69 V4
Managers St POP/IOD E14 * 51 U6
Manaton Cl PECK SE15 63 M1
Manaton Crs STHL UB1 46 J4
Manbey Gv SRTFD E15 40 A11
Manbey Park Rd SRTFD E15 40 A11
Manbey Rd SRTFD E15 * 40 A11
Manbey St SRTFD E15 40 A11
Manbre Rd HMSMTH W6 48 J11
Manbrough Av EHAM E6 52 H1
Manchester Ct CAN/RD E16 52 D4
Manchester Dr NKENS W10 2 A8
Manchester Gv POP/IOD E14 51 U10
Manchester Ms MHST W1U 3 S10
Manchester Rd POP/IOD E14 51 U10
SEVS/STOTM N15 38 H4
THHTH CR7 74 G1
Manchester Sq MBLAR W1H 3 S11
Manchester St MHST W1U 3 S10
Manchester Wy DAGE RM10 * 42 B9
Manchuria Rd BTSEA SW11 61 U4
Manciple St STHWK SE1 9 R4
Mandalay Rd CLAP SW4 62 A3
Mandarin Wy YEAD UB4 46 F4
Mandela Cl WLSDN NW10 36 C12
Mandela Pl WATN WD24 11 R14
Mandela Rd CAN/RD E16 52 C4
Mandela St BRXN/ST SW9 8 J14
CAMTN NW1 4 B1
Mandela Wy STHWK SE1 9 U8
Mandeville Cl WAT WD17 11 M12
WIM/MER SW19 61 L12
Mandeville Ct CHING E4 27 Q9
Mandeville Dr SURB KT6 71 T6
Mandeville Pl MHST W1U 3 T11
Mandeville Rd ISLW TW7 47 Q14
NTHLT UB5 34 J11
PEND EN3 16 E11
POTB/CUF EN6 14 E6
SHPTN TW17 69 S3
STHGT/OAK N14 25 V7
Mandeville St CLPT E5 39 Q8
Mandrake Rd TOOT SW17 61 T8
Mandrake Wy SRTFD E15 * 40 A12
Mandrell Rd BRXS/STRHM SW2 62 C3
Manette St LSQ/SEVD WC2H 4 D12
Manford Cl CHIG IG7 29 R9
Manford Cross CHIG IG7 29 Q10
Manford Wy CHIG IG7 29 N10
Manfred Rd PUT/ROE SW15 61 M3
Manger Rd HOLWY N7 38 C11
Mangold Wy ERITHM DA18 53 T8
Manilla St POP/IOD E14 51 S7
Manister Rd ABYW SE2 53 Q8
Manley Ct STNW/STAM N16 38 K8
Manley St CAMTN NW1 3 S1
Manly Dixon Dr PEND EN3 16 E11
Mannamead EPSOM KT18 84 E9
Mannamead Cl EPSOM KT18 84 E9
Mann Cl CROY/NA CR0 74 G8
Manningford Cl FSBYE EC1V * 5 L5
Manning Gdns KTN/HRWW/WS HA3 35 T5
Manning Pl RCHPK/HAM TW10 59 V4
Manning Rd DAGE RM10 42 A12
STMC/STPC BR5 77 T3
WALTH E17 39 Q2
Manning St SOCK/AV RM15 55 Q6
Manningtree Cl WIM/MER SW19 61 L6
Manningtree Rd RSLP HA4 34 D9
Manningtree St WCHPL E1 51 L4
Mannin Rd CHDH RM6 41 R5
Mannock Dr LOU IG10 18 A14
Mannock Ms SWFD E18 28 E13
Mannock Rd DART DA1 67 M1
WDGN N22 38 F1
Mann's Cl ISLW TW7 59 P3
Manns Rd EDGW HA8 24 A11
Manoel Rd WHTN TW2 59 L7
Manor Av BROCKY SE4 51 R14
CTHM CR3 86 J14
EMPK RM11 42 J3
HSLWW TW4 58 F1
NTHLT UB5 34 H12
Manorbrook BKHTH/KID SE3 64 C2
Manor Cha WEY KT13 69 T10
Manor Cl BAR EN5 25 L2
CDALE/KGS NW9 36 B3
DAGE RM10 42 D11
DART DA1 66 D2
GDST RH9 95 R14
MLHL NW7 * 24 D10
RDART DA2 66 G8
ROM RM1 42 G3
RSLP HA4 34 B6
SOCK/AV RM15 55 Q6
THMD SE28 53 S4
WARL CR6 87 Q7
WOKS/MYFD GU22 80 K6
WPK KT4 72 E6
Manor Cottages NTHWD HA6 22 B13
Manor Cottages Ap EFNCH N2 25 Q14
Manor Ct ACT W3 * 48 A9
CHES/WCR EN8 * 16 D5
DEN/HRF UB9 21 N14
E/WMO/HCT KT8 * 70 J2
EN EN1 16 B10
HRW HA1 * 35 P4
KUTN/CMB KT2 * 60 A13
POTB/CUF EN6 * 14 B6
RAD WD7 12 D11
WBLY HA9 * 35 U10
WEY KT13 69 T9
Manor Court Rd HNWL W7 47 N5
Manor Crs BF/WBF KT14 81 R3
BRYLDS KT5 72 A4
EMPK RM11 42 J3
HOR/WEW KT19 84 A2
Manor Cft EDGW HA8 * 24 A11
Manor Croft Pde CHES/WCR EN8 * 16 D4
Manorcrofts Rd EGH TW20 56 E11
Manordene Cl THDIT KT7 71 Q6
Manordene Rd THMD SE28 53 S4
Manor Dr ADL/WDHM KT15 69 L14
BRYLDS KT5 72 A4
ESH/CLAY KT10 71 P8
FELT TW13 58 F10
HOR/WEW KT19 72 E11
LCOL/BKTW AL2 11 U1
MLHL NW7 24 D10
STHGT/OAK N14 25 V5
SUN TW16 58 C14
TRDG/WHET N20 25 S8
WBLY HA9 35 V9
Manor Dr North NWMAL KT3 72 D5
The Manor Dr WPK KT4 72 F6
Manor Est BERM/RHTH SE16 51 M9
Manor Farm Av SHPTN TW17 69 T4
Manor Farm Cl WPK KT4 72 E6
Manor Farm Ct EGH TW20 * 56 E10
Manor Farm Dr CHING E4 28 A8
Manor Farm La EGH TW20 56 E10
Manor Farm Rd ALP/SUD HA0 35 T14
EN EN1 16 B9
STRHM/NOR SW16 62 E14
Manorfield Cl ARCH N19 38 A9
Manorfields Cl CHST BR7 77 P1
Manor Gdns ACT W3 48 A9
CLAP SW4 * 50 A14
HOLWY N7 38 C8
HPTN TW12 58 K12
RCH/KEW TW9 59 V2
RSLP HA4 34 E10
RYNPK SW20 61 M14
SAND/SEL CR2 74 K11
SUN TW16 58 C13
Manor Ga NTHLT UB5 34 G12
Manorgate Rd KUTN/CMB KT2 60 A13
Manor Green Rd HOR/WEW KT19 84 C2
Manor Gv BECK BR3 63 T14
PECK SE15 51 N11
RCH/KEW TW9 60 A2
Manor Hall Av HDN NW4 24 K14
Manor Hall Dr HDN NW4 24 K14
Manor Hall Gdns LEY E10 39 S6
Manor Hl BNSTD SM7 85 T5
Manor House Ct EPSOM KT18 * 84 C3
SHPTN TW17 69 T5
Manor House Dr KIL/WHAMP NW6 36 K12
NTHWD HA6 21 T12
WOT/HER KT12 70 B10
Manor House Gdns ABLGY WD5 10 K5
Manor House Wy ISLW TW7 59 R1
Manor La CFSP/GDCR SL9 32 C5
FELT TW13 58 C7
HYS/HAR UB3 45 V11
KWD/TDW/WH KT20 93 N5
LEW SE13 64 A3
SUN TW16 58 D14
SUT SM1 73 Q10
Manor Lane Ter LEW SE13 64 A3
Manor Leaze EGH TW20 56 F10
Manor Ms KIL/WHAMP NW6 2 F3
Manor Mt FSTH SE23 63 N6
Manor Pde HRW HA1 * 35 P4
STNW/STAM N16 * 38 K7
Manor Pk CHST BR7 65 M14
LEW SE13 63 V3
RCH/KEW TW9 59 V2
STA TW18 56 H8
Manor Park Cl WWKM BR4 75 T6
Manor Park Crs EDGW HA8 24 A11
Manor Park Dr RYLN/HDSTN HA2 34 K1
Manor Park Gdns EDGW HA8 24 A10
Manor Park Rd CHST BR7 65 L13
EFNCH N2 37 Q1
MNPK E12 40 F9
SUT SM1 73 Q10
WLSDN NW10 36 F13
WWKM BR4 75 T6
Manor Pl BORE WD6 * 24 C1
CHST BR7 65 M14
EBED/NFELT TW14 58 C6
MTCM CR4 74 A1
STA TW18 57 M10
SUT SM1 73 P10
WALW SE17 9 M10
Manor Rd ABR/ST RM4 29 U5
ASHF TW15 57 R10
BAR EN5 25 L2
BARK IG11 41 P11
BECK BR3 63 S14
BELMT SM2 73 M12
BFN/LL DA15 65 P8
BGR/WK TN15 91 T1
BH/WHM TN16 88 G10
BXLY DA5 66 B6
CAN/RD E16 52 A3
CHDH RM6 41 T4
CHIG IG7 28 J11
DAGE RM10 42 C11
DART DA1 66 E2
E/WMO/HCT KT8 71 M2
ENC/FH EN2 15 T14
ERITH DA8 54 F11
HRW HA1 35 Q4
HYS/HAR UB3 46 C4
LEY E10 39 S5
LOU IG10 17 P13
LOU IG10 28 D4
MTCM CR4 74 A1
POTB/CUF EN6 14 B5
RCH/KEW TW9 59 V1
REDH RH1 94 A5
REIG RH2 93 M8
ROM RM1 42 G3
RPLY/SEND GU23 80 K13
RSEV TN14 89 T14
RSLP HA4 33 V6
RYNPK SW20 61 M14
SNWD SE25 75 L2
STNW/STAM N16 38 J6
TEDD TW11 59 Q10
TOTM N17 27 L13
WAB EN9 16 K7
WALTH E17 27 Q14
WAT WD17 11 P13
WDGN N22 26 C11
WEA W13 47 Q5
WHTN TW2 59 L7
WLGTN SM6 73 V9
WOKN/KNAP GU21 80 A6
WOT/HER KT12 70 C5
WWKM BR4 75 T7
Manor Rd North ESH/CLAY KT10 71 P8
WLGTN SM6 73 V9
Manor Rd South ESH/CLAY KT10 71 N9
Manorside BAR EN5 25 L2
Manor Sq BCTR RM8 41 S7
Manor V BTFD TW8 47 S10
Manor Vw FNCH N3 25 P14
Manor Wk WEY KT13 69 T10
Manor Wy BECK BR3 75 S1
BKHTH/KID SE3 64 C2
BNSTD SM7 85 T6
BORE WD6 24 C2
BRW CM14 31 U8
BXLY DA5 66 A6
BXLYHN DA7 66 D1
CDALE/KGS NW9 36 E2
CHING E4 27 V9
EGH TW20 56 D11
Manorway EN EN1 26 J5
Manor Wy HAYES BR2 76 G4
LHD/OX KT22 83 L6
MTCM CR4 74 A1
NWDGN UB2 46 F9
POTB/CUF EN6 14 C4
PUR/KEN CR8 86 C2
RAIN RM13 54 E2
RKW/CH/CXG WD3 21 S2
RSLP HA4 34 B6
RYLN/HDSTN HA2 34 K2
SAND/SEL CR2 74 J11
STMC/STPC BR5 77 L2
Manorway WFD IG8 28 E10
Manor Wy WOKS/MYFD GU22 80 F10
WPK KT4 72 E6
Manor Waye UX/CGN UB8 33 P14
The Manor Wy WLGTN SM6 73 V9
Manor Wood Rd PUR/KEN CR8 86 C3
Manresa Rd CHEL SW3 7 M9
Mansard Beeches TOOT SW17 61 U10
Mansard Cl HCH RM12 42 G7
PIN HA5 34 F1
Manse Cl HYS/HAR UB3 45 V11
Mansel Gv WALTH E17 27 S13
Mansell Rd ACT W3 48 D6
GFD/PVL UB6 46 K3
Mansell St WCHPL E1 5 V12
Mansell Wy CTHM CR3 86 H12
Mansel Rd WIM/MER SW19 61 L11
Mansergh Cl CHARL SE7 52 G12
Manse Rd STNW/STAM N16 38 K8
Manser Rd RAIN RM13 54 E1
Manse Wy SWLY BR8 78 G2
Mansfield Av EBAR EN4 25 T4
RSLP HA4 34 D6
SEVS/STOTM N15 38 H2
Mansfield Cl ED N9 27 L4
STMC/STPC BR5 77 T5
Mansfield Dr REDH RH1 94 B4
YEAD UB4 46 A2
Mansfield Gdns HCH RM12 42 K7
Mansfield Hl CHING E4 27 T6
Mansfield Ms CAVSQ/HST W1G 3 U10
Mansfield Rd ACT W3 48 B2
CHSGTN KT9 71 S10
HAMP NW3 37 T10
IL IG1 40 J7
SAND/SEL CR2 74 H11
SWLY BR8 66 F11
WALTH E17 39 R2
WAN E11 40 D4
Mansfield St CAVSQ/HST W1G 3 U10
Mansford St BETH E2 39 L14
BETH E2 51 M1
Manship Rd MTCM CR4 61 U13
Mansion Cl BRXN/ST SW9 50 E13
Mansion Gdns HAMP NW3 37 P8
Mansion House Pl MANHO EC4N * 5 Q12
Mansion La IVER SL0 44 G6
Manson Ms SKENS SW7 6 K8
Manson Pl SKENS SW7 7 L8
Manstead Gdns CHDH RM6 41 S5
RAIN RM13 54 H4
Manston Av NWDGN UB2 46 J9
Manston Cl CHES/WCR EN8 16 C4
PGE/AN SE20 63 N13
Manstone Rd CRICK NW2 37 L10
Manston Gv KUTN/CMB KT2 59 T10
Manston Wy HCH RM12 42 H11
Manthorpe Rd WOOL/PLUM SE18 53 L10
Mantilla Rd TOOT SW17 61 U9
Mantle Rd BROCKY SE4 63 Q1
Mantlet Cl STRHM/NOR SW16 62 A12
Mantle Wy SRTFD E15 40 A12
Manton Av HNWL W7 47 P7
Manton Cl HYS/HAR UB3 46 A5
Manton Rd ABYW SE2 53 Q9
PEND EN3 16 H12
Manton Ter ADL/WDHM KT15 * 69 N9
Mantua St BTSEA SW11 61 R1
Mantus Cl WCHPL E1 51 N2
Mantus Rd WCHPL E1 51 N2
Manus Wy TRDG/WHET N20 25 Q7
Manville Gdns TOOT SW17 61 V8
Manville Rd TOOT SW17 61 U7
Manwood Rd BROCKY SE4 63 R4
Manwood St CAN/RD E16 52 H6
Manygate La SHPTN TW17 69 U4
Many Gates BAL SW12 61 V7
Mapesbury Ms CDALE/KGS NW9 36 G4
Mapesbury Rd CRICK NW2 37 L11
Mapeshill Pl CRICK NW2 36 J11
Mape St BETH E2 51 M2
Maple Av ACT W3 48 E6
CHING E4 27 R11
RYLN/HDSTN HA2 34 K7
UPMR RM14 43 P8
WDR/YW UB7 45 Q5
Maple Cl BARK/HLT IG6 29 N11
BKHH IG9 28 F8
BUSH WD23 11 S14
CLAP SW4 62 B4
CTHM CR3 86 K7
FNCH N3 25 N11
HCH RM12 42 H8
HPTN TW12 58 H11
MTCM CR4 61 V13
RSLP HA4 34 D4
STMC/STPC BR5 77 M3
STNW/STAM N16 39 L4
SWLY BR8 66 E14
YEAD UB4 46 F1
Maple Ct ASHF TW15 57 V12
HACK E8 * 39 L11
NWMAL KT3 72 D1
Maple Crs BFN/LL DA15 65 Q4
Maplecroft Cl EHAM E6 52 F4
Mapledale Av CROY/NA CR0 75 M8
Mapledene Est HACK E8 * 39 L12
Mapledene Rd HACK E8 38 K12
Maplefield LCOL/BKTW AL2 11 V3
Maple Gdns ASHF TW15 57 Q7
EDGW HA8 24 E12
Maple Ga LOU IG10 17 U14
Maple Gv BTFD TW8 47 R12
CDALE/KGS NW9 36 C5
EA W5 47 T8
STHL UB1 46 H3
WAT WD17 11 N13
WOKS/MYFD GU22 80 C11
Maplehurst LHD/OX KT22 83 M13
Maplehurst Cl KUT/HW KT1 71 U2
Maple Leaf Cl ABLGY WD5 11 N6
BH/WHM TN16 88 F6
Maple Leaf Dr BFN/LL DA15 65 P6
Mapleleafe Gdns BARK/HLT IG6 40 K1
Maple Leaf Sq BERM/RHTH SE16 * 51 P7
Maple Lodge Cl RKW/CH/CXG WD3 20 K9
Maple Ms KIL/WHAMP NW6 * 2 G3
STRHM/NOR SW16 62 D10
Maple Pl BNSTD SM7 84 K4
FITZ W1T 4 B9
TOTM N17 27 L12
WDR/YW UB7 45 R6
Maple Rd ASHTD KT21 83 T9
CTHM CR3 86 K7
DART DA1 66 J6
PGE/AN SE20 63 N12
REDH RH1 93 T14
RPLY/SEND GU23 81 L14
SURB KT6 71 T3
WAN E11 40 A4
YEAD UB4 46 E1
Maples WAB EN9 17 Q9
Maplescombe La EYN DA4 79 N8
Maples Pl WCHPL E1 * 51 M3
Maple Springs WAB EN9 17 N7
Maplestead Rd BRXS/STRHM SW2 62 D5
DAGW RM9 41 R13
The Maples BNSTD SM7 85 P3
CHERT KT16 68 F11
CHESW EN7 15 U2
ESH/CLAY KT10 * 71 Q12
KUT/HW KT1 * 59 S12
Maple St BETH E2 39 L14
FITZ W1T 4 A9
ROMW/RG RM7 42 C2
Maplethorpe Rd THHTH CR7 74 E2
Mapleton Cl HAYES BR2 76 C3
Mapleton Crs PEND EN3 16 C12
WAND/EARL SW18 61 P4
Mapleton Rd BH/WHM TN16 97 N6
CHING E4 27 U9
EDEN TN8 97 Q11
EN EN1 16 B14
WAND/EARL SW18 61 N4
Maple Tree Pl BKHTH/KID SE3 52 G13
Maple Wk NKENS W10 * 48 K2
Maple Wy COUL/CHIP CR5 85 V11
FELT TW13 58 C8
Maplin Cl WCHMH N21 26 D4
Maplin Pk DTCH/LGLY SL3 44 F8
Maplin Rd CAN/RD E16 52 C4
Maplin St BOW E3 51 R1
Mapperley Dr WFD IG8 28 A12
Marabou Cl MNPK E12 40 G10
Maran Wy ERITHM DA18 53 T8
Marathon Wy THMD SE28 53 P7
Marban Rd MV/WKIL W9 2 C5
Marble Cl ACT W3 48 B6
Marble Dr CRICK NW2 36 K6
Marble Hill Cl TWK TW1 59 R5
Marble Hill Gdns TWK TW1 59 R5
Marble Quay WAP E1W 9 V1
Marbles Wy KWD/TDW/WH KT20 84 K9
Marbrook Ct LEE/GVPK SE12 64 E8
Marcella Rd BRXN/ST SW9 50 E14
Marcellina Wy ORP BR6 77 N8
Marcet Rd DART DA1 66 J3
Marchant Rd WAN E11 39 V7
Marchant St NWCR SE14 51 Q11
Marchbank Rd WKENS W14 6 D11
Marchmant Cl HCH RM12 42 J8
Marchmont Rd RCHPK/HAM TW10 59 V3
WLGTN SM6 74 A13
Marchmont St BMSBY WC1N 4 E7
March Rd TWK TW1 59 P5
WEY KT13 69 S10
Marchside Cl HEST TW5 46 F13
Marchwood Cl CMBW SE5 50 T14
Marchwood Crs EA W5 47 T4
Marcia Rd STHWK SE1 9 T8
Marcilly Rd WAND/EARL SW18 61 R3
Marconi Pl FBAR/BDGN N11 25 V9
Marconi Rd LEY E10 39 S6
Marconi Wy STHL UB1 46 K4
Marcon Pl HACK E8 39 M11
Marco Rd HMSMTH W6 48 H8
Marcus Ct WOKS/MYFD GU22 80 D8
Marcuse Rd CTHM CR3 86 H13
Marcus Garvey Ms EDUL SE22 63 M4
Marcus Garvey Wy HNHL SE24 62 E2
Marcus Rd DART DA1 66 G5
Marcus St SRTFD E15 40 A13
WAND/EARL SW18 61 P4
Marcus Ter WAND/EARL SW18 61 P4
Mardale Dr CDALE/KGS NW9 36 D3
Mardell Rd CROY/NA CR0 75 P3
Marden Av HAYES BR2 76 C4
Marden Crs BXLY DA5 66 C3
CROY/NA CR0 74 D4
Marden Rd CROY/NA CR0 74 D4
ROM RM1 42 E4
TOTM N17 26 J14
Marden Sq BERM/RHTH SE16 51 M8
Marder Rd WEA W13 47 Q7
Mardyke Cl RAIN RM13 42 C14
Mardyke Vw PUR RM19 * 55 S8
Marechal Niel Av BFN/LL DA15 65 M8
Marechal Niel Pde SCUP DA14 * 65 M8
Maresfield CROY/NA CR0 74 J8
Maresfield Gdns HAMP NW3 37 Q10
Mare St HACK E8 39 M11
Marfield Cl WPK KT4 72 G6
Marfleet Cl CAR SM5 73 S7
Margaret Av CHING E4 27 T5
Margaret Bondfield Av BARK IG11 41 Q12
Margaret Cl ABLGY WD5 11 M6
GPK RM2 42 H3
POTB/CUF EN6 14 E7
STA TW18 57 P12
WAB EN9 16 K7
Margaret Dr EMPK RM11 43 M6
Margaret Gardner Dr ELTH/MOT SE9 64 H7
Margaret Ingram Cl FUL/PGN SW6 * 6 C12
Margaret Lockwood Cl KUT/HW KT1 * 71 V2
Margaret Rd BXLY DA5 65 T4
EBAR EN4 25 R3
EPP CM16 18 E3
GPK RM2 42 H3
STNW/STAM N16 * 38 K6
Margaret St CAVSQ/HST W1G 3 V11
GTPST W1W 4 A11
Margaretta Ter CHEL SW3 7 N11
Margaretting Rd MNPK E12 40 E7
Margaret Wy COUL/CHIP CR5 86 F9
REDBR IG4 40 G4
Margate Rd BRXS/STRHM SW2 62 C3
Margeholes OXHEY WD19 22 G7
Margery Gv KWD/TDW/WH KT20 93 L5
Margery La KWD/TDW/WH KT20 93 M5
Margery Park Rd FSTGT E7 40 C11
Margery Rd BCTR RM8 41 T8
Margery St CLKNW EC1R 4 J6
Margherita Pl WAB EN9 17 M8
Margin Dr WIM/MER SW19 60 K10
Margravine Gdns HMSMTH W6 48 K10
Margravine Rd HMSMTH W6 48 K11
Marguerite Vls RYNPK SW20 * 60 H12
Marham Gdns MRDN SM4 73 Q4
WAND/EARL SW18 61 S6
Maria Cl STHWK SE1 51 L9
Mariam Gdns HCH RM12 43 M7
Marian Cl YEAD UB4 46 F2
Marian Gdns GSTN WD25 11 P7
Marian Pl BETH E2 39 M14
Marian Rd STRHM/NOR SW16 62 A13
Marian Sq BETH E2 39 M14
Marian St BETH E2 * 39 M14
Marian Wy WLSDN NW10 36 F12
Maria Ter WCHPL E1 51 P3
Maria Theresa Cl NWMAL KT3 72 D3
Maricas Av KTN/HRWW/WS HA3 23 M13
Marie Curie CMBW SE5 * 50 J13
Marie Lloyd Wk HACK E8 * 39 L11
Marie Manor Wy RDART DA2 * 67 Q8
Mariette Wy WLGTN SM6 74 C13
Marigold Aly STHWK SE1 5 L14
Marigold Cl STHL UB1 46 G5
Marigold Rd TOTM N17 27 N13
Marigold St BERM/RHTH SE16 51 M7
Marigold Wy CROY/NA CR0 75 P6
Marina Ap YEAD UB4 46 G3
Marina Av NWMAL KT3 72 H4
Marina Cl CHERT KT16 69 M6
Marina Dr DART DA1 67 N6
WELL DA16 53 N14
Marina Gdns CHES/WCR EN8 16 C4
ROMW/RG RM7 42 B3
Marina Pde STA TW18 * 57 M13
Marina Wy IVER SL0 44 K5
TEDD TW11 59 T12
Marine Ct PUR RM19 55 M9
Marine Dr BARK IG11 53 R1
WOOL/PLUM SE18 52 H9
Marinefield Rd FUL/PGN SW6 49 P14
Mariner Gdns RCHPK/HAM TW10 59 R8
Mariner Rd MNPK E12 40 J9
Mariners Ms POP/IOD E14 51 V9
Marine St BERM/RHTH SE16 51 L8
Marion Av SHPTN TW17 69 T3
Marion Cl BARK/HLT IG6 29 M12
BUSH WD23 11 T13
Marion Crs STMC/STPC BR5 77 R3
Marion Gv WFD IG8 28 A10
Marion Ms DUL SE21 62 H8
Marion Rd MLHL NW7 24 G10
THHTH CR7 74 G3
Marischal Rd LEW SE13 63 V1
Marish La DEN/HRF UB9 32 H2
Marish Whf DTCH/LGLY SL3 * 44 C7
Maritime Cl RDART DA2 67 V3
Maritime Quay POP/IOD E14 51 S10
Maritime St BOW E3 51 R2
Marius Rd TOOT SW17 61 U7
Marjorams Av LOU IG10 17 U14
Marjorie Gv BTSEA SW11 61 T2
Mark Av CHING E4 27 T4
Mark Cl BXLYHN DA7 53 U13
HAYES BR2 76 G9
STHL UB1 46 J6
Mark Dr CFSP/GDCR SL9 20 B9
Markedge La COUL/CHIP CR5 85 T14
REDH RH1 93 T3
Markeston Gn OXHEY WD19 22 F9
Market Chambers ENC/FH EN2 * 26 H1
Market Est HOLWY N7 38 C11
Market Field Rd REDH RH1 93 T9
Marketfield Wy REDH RH1 93 U10
Market La DTCH/LGLY SL3 44 G8
EDGW HA8 24 C13
Market Link ROM RM1 42 E3
Market Meadow STMC/STPC BR5 77 S2
Market Ms MYFR/PICC W1J 7 U2
Market Pde BMLY BR1 * 64 C13
ED N9 * 27 L7
EW KT17 * 72 F13
FELT TW13 * 58 G7
SCUP DA14 * 65 Q9
SNWD SE25 * 75 L2
STNW/STAM N16 * 39 L6
WALTH E17 * 39 R1
Market Pl ABR/ST RM4 29 R1
ACT W3 48 C6
BERM/RHTH SE16 * 51 L9
BTFD TW8 47 S12
BXLYHS DA6 66 A2
CFSP/GDCR SL9 20 B13
DART DA1 67 L5
DTCH/LGLY SL3 * 44 G12
EFNCH N2 37 S1
GTPST W1W 4 A11
KUT/HW KT1 * 59 T14
ROM RM1 42 E3
WAT WD17 22 E2
Market Rd HOLWY N7 38 C11
RCH/KEW TW9 60 A1
Market Sq BH/WHM TN16 97 L3
ED N9 27 M7
Market St EHAM E6 40 H14
WATW WD18 22 D2
WOOL/PLUM SE18 52 J9
Market Ter BTFD TW8 * 47 U11
The Market COVGDN WC2E 4 F13
Market Wy BH/WHM TN16 97 M2
Market Yard Ms STHWK SE1 9 S5
Markfield CROY/NA CR0 75 R14
Markfield Gdns CHING E4 27 T5
Markfield Rd CTHM CR3 95 M2
SEVS/STOTM N15 39 L2
Markham Cl BORE WD6 23 V1
Markham Pl CHEL SW3 * 7 Q9
Markham Sq CHEL SW3 7 Q9
Markham St CHEL SW3 7 P9
Markhole Cl HPTN TW12 58 H12
Markhouse Av WALTH E17 39 Q4
Markhouse Rd WALTH E17 39 R4
Mark La MON EC3R 5 T13
Markmanor Av WALTH E17 39 Q5
Mark Oak La LHD/OX KT22 82 J11
Mark Rd WDGN N22 26 F14
Marksbury Av RCH/KEW TW9 60 A1
Marks Rd ROMW/RG RM7 42 C3
WARL CR6 87 Q8
Markstone Ter ORP BR6 * 77 Q5
Mark St REIG RH2 93 P9
SDTCH EC2A 5 S7
SRTFD E15 40 A12
Mark Ter RYNPK SW20 * 60 J12
Markville Gdns CTHM CR3 95 M1
Markwade Cl MNPK E12 40 F6
Mark Wy SWLY BR8 78 G3
The Markway SUN TW16 58 E14
Markwell Cl SYD SE26 63 M9
Markyate Rd BCTR RM8 41 S10
Marlands Rd CLAY IG5 28 H14
CLAY IG5 40 H1
Marlborogh Rd ISLW TW7 47 R12
Marlborough Av EDGW HA8 24 B8
HACK E8 39 L13
RSLP HA4 33 U4
STHGT/OAK N14 26 A8
Marlborough Cl ORP BR6 77 P5
TRDG/WHET N20 25 T8
UPMR RM14 43 S6
WALW SE17 9 M8
WIM/MER SW19 61 S11
WOT/HER KT12 70 F8
Marlborough Ct REGST W1B * 4 A13
Marlborough Crs CHSWK W4 48 E8
HYS/HAR UB3 45 V12
SEV TN13 90 E14
Marlborough Dr CLAY IG5 40 G1
WEY KT13 69 U8
Marlborough Gdns TRDG/WHET N20 25 T8
UPMR RM14 43 S6
Marlborough Ga BAY/PAD W2 3 L14
Marlborough Gv STHWK SE1 51 L10
Marlborough Hl HRW HA1 35 N2
STJWD NW8 2 K2
Marlborough La CHARL SE7 52 E11
Marlborough Ms BNSTD SM7 85 N5
BRXS/STRHM SW2 62 D2
Marlborough Pde FSBYPK N4 * 38 G6
HGDN/ICK UB10 * 45 T2
Marlborough Park Av BFN/LL DA15 65 Q6
Marlborough Pl STJWD NW8 2 K3
Marlborough Rd ARCH N19 38 C7
ASHF TW15 57 Q10
BCTR RM8 41 S9
BRWN CM15 31 U4
CHING E4 27 T11
CHSWK W4 48 C10
DART DA1 66 J4
DTCH/LGLY SL3 44 B9
EA W5 47 T7
ED N9 26 K6
FELT TW13 58 F7
FSTGT E7 40 E12
HAYES BR2 76 E2
HGDN/ICK UB10 45 T2
HPTN TW12 58 J11
NWDGN UB2 46 E8
RCHPK/HAM TW10 59 V4
ROMW/RG RM7 42 A2
SAND/SEL CR2 74 G12
SRTFD E15 * 40 A9
SUT SM1 73 N8
SWFD E18 40 C1
WATW WD18 22 D2
WDGN N22 26 D12
WELL DA16 65 T1
WHALL SW1A 8 B3
WIM/MER SW19 61 S11
WOKN/KNAP GU21 80 E6
WOOL/PLUM SE18 52 K8
Marlborough St CHEL SW3 7 N8
Marlborough Yd ARCH N19 38 B7
The Marld ASHTD KT21 83 V8
Marle Gdns WAB EN9 16 J6
Marler Rd FSTH SE23 63 R6
Marlescroft Wy LOU IG10 28 K3
Marley Av BXLYHN DA7 53 T11
Marley Cl ADL/WDHM KT15 68 K11
GFD/PVL UB6 46 J1
SEVS/STOTM N15 38 F2
Marley Rd BERM/RHTH SE16 * 51 P9
Marlin Cl SUN TW16 58 A11
Marlingdene Cl HPTN TW12 58 J11
Marlings Cl CHST BR7 77 N2
CTHM CR3 86 J7
Marlings Park Av CHST BR7 77 N1
Marlins Cl SUT SM1 * 73 Q10
Marlins Meadow WATW WD18 21 V4
Marlin Sq ABLGY WD5 11 M5
The Marlins NTHWD HA6 22 B11
Marloes Cl ALP/SUD HA0 35 T9
Marloes Rd KENS W8 6 G5
Marlow Av PUR RM19 55 N9
Marlow Cl PGE/AN SE20 75 M1
Marlow Ct CDALE/KGS NW9 36 F1
Marlow Crs TWK TW1 59 P4
Marlow Dr CHEAM SM3 72 K8
Marlowe Cl BARK/HLT IG6 29 L13
CHST BR7 65 M12
Marlowe Rd WALTH E17 39 U2
Marlowe Sq MTCM CR4 74 A2
The Marlowes DART DA1 66 D2
STJWD NW8 3 L2
Marlowe Wy CROY/NA CR0 74 C7
Marlow Gdns HYS/HAR UB3 45 V8
Marlow Rd EHAM E6 52 H1
NWDGN UB2 46 H8
PGE/AN SE20 75 M1
Marlow Wy BERM/RHTH SE16 51 P7
Marlpit Av COUL/CHIP CR5 86 C7
Marlpit La COUL/CHIP CR5 86 C7
Marl Rd WAND/EARL SW18 61 P2
Marlton St GNWCH SE10 52 B10
Marlwood Cl BFN/LL DA15 65 N7
Marlyon Rd BARK/HLT IG6 29 R10
Marmadon Rd WOOL/PLUM SE18 53 P9
Marmion Ap CHING E4 27 S9
Marmion Av CHING E4 27 R9
Marmion Cl CHING E4 27 R9
Marmion Ms BTSEA SW11 * 61 U1
Marmion Rd BTSEA SW11 61 U2
Marmont Rd PECK SE15 51 L13
Marmora Rd EDUL SE22 63 N4
Marmot Rd HSLWW TW4 58 F1
Marne Av FBAR/BDGN N11 25 V9
WELL DA16 65 Q1
Marnell Wy HSLWW TW4 58 F1
Marne St NKENS W10 2 A5
Marney Rd BTSEA SW11 61 U2
Marneys Cl EPSOM KT18 84 A5
Marnfield Crs BRXS/STRHM SW2 62 D6
Marnham Av CRICK NW2 37 L9
Marnham Crs GFD/PVL UB6 34 K14
Marnham Pl ADL/WDHM KT15 69 N9
Marnock Rd BROCKY SE4 63 R3
Maroon St POP/IOD E14 51 Q3
Maroons Wy CAT SE6 63 S10
Marquess Rd IS N1 38 H11
Marquess Rd North IS N1 38 G11
Marquess Rd South IS N1 * 38 G11
Marquis Cl ALP/SUD HA0 35 V12
Marquis Rd CAMTN NW1 38 B11
FSBYPK N4 38 D6
WDGN N22 26 D11
Marrabon Cl BFN/LL DA15 65 Q6
Marrick Cl PUT/ROE SW15 60 G2
Married Quarters EDGW HA8 * 24 B12
Marrilyne Av PEND EN3 16 F12
Marriner Ct HYS/HAR UB3 * 46 A5
Marriot Rd MUSWH N10 25 T13
Marriott Cl EBED/NFELT TW14 57 V4
Marriott Lodge Cl ADL/WDHM KT15 69 N8
Marriott Rd BAR EN5 24 K1
DART DA1 67 N5
FSBYPK N4 38 D6
SRTFD E15 40 A13
Marriotts Cl CDALE/KGS NW9 36 F4
Marriotts Yd BAR EN5 * 24 K1
Marriott Ter RKW/CH/CXG WD3 20 K2
Marrowells WEY KT13 70 A8
Marryat Cl HSLWW TW4 58 H2
Marryat Pl WIM/MER SW19 61 L9
Marryat Rd EN EN1 16 B9
WIM/MER SW19 60 K10
Marsala Rd LEW SE13 63 T2
Marsden Rd ED N9 27 M7
PECK SE15 62 K1
Marsden St KTTN NW5 37 U11
Marsden Wy ORP BR6 77 P9
Marshall Cl FBAR/BDGN N11 25 V9
HRW HA1 35 M5
HSLWW TW4 58 H3
SAND/SEL CR2 87 L3
WAND/EARL SW18 61 Q4
Marshall Dr YEAD UB4 46 B3
Marshall Est MLHL NW7 * 24 G9
Marshall Pde WOKS/MYFD GU22 * 80 K5
Marshall Pl ADL/WDHM KT15 69 N13
Marshall Rd LEY E10 39 T9
TOTM N17 26 H13
Marshalls Cl HOR/WEW KT19 84 C3
Marshalls Dr ROM RM1 42 E1
Marshalls Gv WOOL/PLUM SE18 52 G9
Marshall's Pl BERM/RHTH SE16 9 V6
Marshalls Rd ROMW/RG RM7 42 D2
SUT SM1 73 P9
Marshall St SOHO/CST W1F 4 B12
Marshalsea Rd STHWK SE1 9 P3
Marsham Cl CHST BR7 * 64 K10
Marsham La CFSP/GDCR SL9 32 D3
Marsham Ldg CFSP/GDCR SL9 32 C4
Marsham St WEST SW1P 8 E8
Marsham Wy CFSP/GDCR SL9 32 C3
Marsh Av HOR/WEW KT19 72 E14
MTCM CR4 61 T14
Marshbrook Cl BKHTH/KID SE3 64 F1
Marsh Cl CHES/WCR EN8 16 F7
MLHL NW7 24 F8
Marshcroft Dr CHES/WCR EN8 16 E4
Marsh Dr CDALE/KGS NW9 36 F4
Marshe Cl POTB/CUF EN6 14 F6
Marsh Farm Rd WHTN TW2 59 P6
Marshfield DTCH/LGLY SL3 44 A13
Marshfield St POP/IOD E14 51 U8
Marshgate La SRTFD E15 39 T13
Marsh Green Rd DAGE RM10 42 A13
Marsh Hl HOM E9 39 Q10
WAB EN9 17 L1
Marsh La ADL/WDHM KT15 69 M9
LEY E10 39 R7
MLHL NW7 24 E8
STAN HA7 23 T11
TOTM N17 27 M12
Marsh Rd ALP/SUD HA0 47 T1
PIN HA5 34 H2
Marshside Cl ED N9 27 N7
Marsh St DART DA1 55 N14
POP/IOD E14 * 51 T9
Marsh Ter STMC/STPC BR5 * 77 T2
Marsh Wall POP/IOD E14 51 S7
Marsh Wy RAIN RM13 54 D1
Marsland Cl WALW SE17 9 M10
Marston HOR/WEW KT19 84 C1
Marston Av CHSGTN KT9 71 U11
DAGE RM10 42 A8
Marston Cl DAGE RM10 42 A8
KIL/WHAMP NW6 37 Q12
Marston Ct WOT/HER KT12 * 70 E6
Marston Dr WARL CR6 87 Q8
Marston Rd CLAY IG5 28 G14
TEDD TW11 59 R10
Marston Wy NRWD SE19 62 F12
Marsworth Av PIN HA5 22 F13
Marsworth Cl WATW WD18 * 22 A4
YEAD UB4 46 G3
Martaban Rd STNW/STAM N16 38 J7
Martello St HACK E8 39 M12
Martell Rd DUL SE21 62 H8
Martel Pl HACK E8 38 K11
Marten Rd WALTH E17 27 S14
Martens Av BXLYHN DA7 66 C2
Martens Cl BXLYHN DA7 66 C2
Martham Cl BARK/HLT IG6 28 K13
THMD SE28 53 T5
Martha Rd SRTFD E15 40 A11
Martha's Buildings FSBYE EC1V 5 Q7
Martha St WCHPL E1 51 N4
Marthorne Crs KTN/HRWW/WS HA3 23 M14
Martin Bowes Rd ELTH/MOT SE9 64 H1
Martin Cl ED N9 27 P6
HGDN/ICK UB10 33 Q14
SAND/SEL CR2 87 P1
WARL CR6 87 M6
Martin Crs CROY/NA CR0 74 D6
Martindale IVER SL0 44 G2
MORT/ESHN SW14 60 C3
Martindale Av CAN/RD E16 52 C5
ORP BR6 77 Q10
Martindale Rd BAL SW12 61 V5
HSLWW TW4 58 G2
Martin Dene BXLYHS DA6 65 V3
Martin Dr NTHLT UB5 34 H10
RAIN RM13 54 H2
RDART DA2 67 Q4
Martineau Cl ESH/CLAY KT10 71 M9
Martineau Dr TWK TW1 59 R2
Martineau Rd HBRY N5 38 F9
Martineau St WCHPL E1 51 N5
Martingale Cl SUN TW16 70 C2
Martingales Cl RCHPK/HAM TW10 59 T8
Martin Gdns BCTR RM8 41 S9
Martin Gv MRDN SM4 73 N1
Martini Dr PEND EN3 16 G11
Martin La CANST EC4R 5 R13
Martin Ri BXLYHS DA6 65 V3
Martin Rd BCTR RM8 41 S9
RDART DA2 66 J8
SOCK/AV RM15 55 R6
Martins Cl RAD WD7 12 C10
STMC/STPC BR5 77 T1
WWKM BR4 75 V7
Martins Dr CHES/WCR EN8 16 E2
Martins Mt BAR EN5 25 N2
Martins Pl THMD SE28 53 N6
Martin's Rd HAYES BR2 64 A14
Martin's Shaw SEV TN13 90 C12
The Martins SYD SE26 63 M10
WBLY HA9 * 35 V8
Martinstown Cl EMPK RM11 43 N4
Martin St THMD SE28 53 N6
Martins Wk MUSWH N10 * 25 U13
THMD SE28 53 N6
Martinsyde WOKS/MYFD GU22 80 G7
Martin Wy MRDN SM4 73 L1
Martlesham Cl HCH RM12 42 J10
Martlet Gv NTHLT UB5 46 F1
Martlett Ct HOL/ALD WC2B 4 F12
Martley Dr GNTH/NBYPK IG2 40 K3
Martock Cl KTN/HRWW/WS HA3 35 Q2
Martock Gdns FBAR/BDGN N11 25 T10
Marton Cl CAT SE6 63 S8
Marton Rd STNW/STAM N16 * 38 J7
Martyrs La WOKN/KNAP GU21 80 F2
Martys Yd HAMP NW3 * 37 R9
Marvell Av YEAD UB4 46 C3
Marvels Cl LEE/GVPK SE12 64 D7
Marvels La LEE/GVPK SE12 64 E8
Marville Rd FUL/PGN SW6 6 C14
Marvin St HACK E8 * 39 M11
Marwell BH/WHM TN16 96 K2
Marwell Cl ROM RM1 42 G4
WWKM BR4 76 B7
Marwood Cl KGLGY WD4 10 F3
WELL DA16 65 R1
Marwood Dr MLHL NW7 24 K12
Mary Adelaide Cl PUT/ROE SW15 60 E9
Mary Ann Buildings DEPT SE8 51 S11
Maryat Sq FUL/PGN SW6 49 L13
Maryatt Av RYLN/HDSTN HA2 34 K7
Marybank WOOL/PLUM SE18 52 H9
Mary Burrows Gdns BGR/WK TN15 91 P7
Mary Cl KTN/HRWW/WS HA3 35 V2
Mary Datchelor Cl CMBW SE5 50 H13
Maryfield Cl BXLY DA5 66 E8
Mary Gn STJWD NW8 * 2 H1
Maryhill Cl PUR/KEN CR8 86 G7
Maryland Pk SRTFD E15 40 A10
Maryland Rd MV/WKIL W9 2 F8
SRTFD E15 39 V10
THHTH CR7 62 F13
WDGN N22 26 E11
Maryland Sq SRTFD E15 40 A10
Marylands Rd MV/WKIL W9 2 G8
Maryland St SRTFD E15 39 V10
Maryland Wk IS N1 * 5 N1
Maryland Wy SUN TW16 58 C14
Mary Lawrencson Pl BKHTH/KID SE3 52 B12
Marylebone F/O BAY/PAD W2 3 N10
Marylebone High St MHST W1U 3 T9
Marylebone La MHST W1U 3 T11
Marylebone Ms CAVSQ/HST W1G 3 T10
Marylebone Pas GTPST W1W 4 B11
Marylebone Rd CAMTN NW1 3 P9
Marylebone St CAVSQ/HST W1G 3 T10
Marylee Wy LBTH SE11 8 H8
Maryon Gv CHARL SE7 52 G9
Maryon Ms HAMP NW3 37 S9
Maryon Rd CHARL SE7 52 G9
Mary Peters Dr GFD/PVL UB6 35 M10
Mary Pl NTGHL W11 2 A14
Mary Rose Cl DART DA1 67 Q2
HPTN TW12 58 J13
Maryrose Wy TRDG/WHET N20 25 R6
Mary Seacole Cl HACK E8 * 5 U1
Mary Secole Cl HACK E8 * 5 U1
Maryside DTCH/LGLY SL3 44 C7
Mary's Ter TWK TW1 59 Q5
Mary St CAN/RD E16 52 B3
IS N1 5 P2
Mary Ter CAMTN NW1 3 V2
Mary Wy OXHEY WD19 22 E9
Masbro' Rd WKENS W14 48 K8
Mascalls Gdns BRW CM14 31 T9
Mascalls La BRW CM14 31 T9
Mascalls Rd CHARL SE7 52 E11
Mascotts Cl CRICK NW2 36 H8
Masefield Av BORE WD6 24 B3
STAN HA7 23 P10
STHL UB1 46 J5
Masefield Cl ERITH DA8 54 F13
HARH RM3 30 H13
Masefield Crs HARH RM3 30 J13
STHGT/OAK N14 26 A3
Masefield Dr UPMR RM14 43 Q5
Masefield Gdns EHAM E6 52 J2
Masefield La YEAD UB4 46 D2
Masefield Rd DART DA1 67 P3
HPTN TW12 58 H9
Masefield Vw ORP BR6 77 L8
Masefield Wy STWL/WRAY TW19 57 R6
Mashie Rd ACT W3 48 E4
Mashiters Hl ROM RM1 30 D13
Mashiters Wk ROM RM1 42 E1
Maskall Cl BRXS/STRHM SW2 * 62 E6
Maskell Rd TOOT SW17 61 Q8
Maskelyne Cl BTSEA SW11 49 S13
Mason Cl BERM/RHTH SE16 51 L10
BORE WD6 13 P14
BXLYHN DA7 66 B1
CAN/RD E16 52 C5
HPTN TW12 58 H13
RYNPK SW20 60 K13
Mason Ct WBLY HA9 * 36 A7
Mason Dr HARH RM3 31 L14
Masonic Hall Rd CHERT KT16 68 K4
Mason Rd SUT SM1 73 P10
WFD IG8 28 A9
Mason's Arms Ms CONDST W1S * 3 V12
Mason's Av CITYW EC2V 5 Q11
CROY/NA CR0 74 G9
KTN/HRWW/WS HA3 35 N1
Masons Ct EW KT17 * 72 G13
Masons Hl BMLY BR1 76 C1
WOOL/PLUM SE18 52 K9
Masons Pde CHESW EN7 * 15 S2
Mason's Pl FSBYE EC1V 5 M5
MTCM CR4 61 T13
Masons Rd EN EN1 16 B10
Mason St WALW SE17 9 R8
Masons Yd FSBYE EC1V 5 N7
STJS SW1Y 8 B1
Mason Wy WAB EN9 17 L7
Massey Cl FBAR/BDGN N11 25 V10
Massie Rd HACK E8 39 L11
Massingberd Wy TOOT SW17 61 V9
Massinger St WALW SE17 9 S8
Massingham St WCHPL E1 51 P2
Masson Av RSLP HA4 34 E11
Master Cl OXTED RH8 96 A5
Masterman Rd EHAM E6 52 G1
Masters Cl STRHM/NOR SW16 62 A11
Masters Dr BERM/RHTH SE16 51 M10
Master's St WCHPL E1 51 P3
Masthead Cl RDART DA2 67 Q2
Mast House Ter POP/IOD E14 * 51 S9
Masthouse Ter POP/IOD E14 51 S9
Mastmaker Rd POP/IOD E14 51 S7
Mast Quay WOOL/PLUM SE18 52 H8
Maswell Park Crs HSLW TW3 59 L3
Maswell Park Rd HSLW TW3 58 K3
Matara Ms WALW SE17 9 N10
Matcham Rd WAN E11 40 A8
Matchless Dr WOOL/PLUM SE18 52 J12
Matfield Cl HAYES BR2 76 C3
Matfield Rd BELV DA17 54 A11
Matham Gv EDUL SE22 62 K2
Matham Rd E/WMO/HCT KT8 71 M3
Matheson Rd WKENS W14 6 C8
Mathews Av EHAM E6 40 J14
Mathews Park Av SRTFD E15 40 B11
Mathews Yd LSQ/SEVD WC2H * 4 E12
Mathias Cl EPSOM KT18 84 C3
Mathieson Ct STHWK SE1 9 M4
Mathisen Wy DTCH/LGLY SL3 44 J14
Matilda Cl NRWD SE19 62 H12
Matilda St IS N1 4 H2
Matlock Cl BAR EN5 24 K3
HNHL SE24 62 G2
Matlock Crs CHEAM SM3 73 L9
OXHEY WD19 22 E8
Matlock Gdns CHEAM SM3 73 L9
HCH RM12 43 L8
Matlock Pl CHEAM SM3 73 L9
Matlock Rd CTHM CR3 86 J12
LEY E10 39 U4
Matlock St POP/IOD E14 51 Q4
Matlock Wy NWMAL KT3 60 D13
Matthew Arnold Cl COB KT11 82 C4
STA TW18 57 N11
Matthew Cl NKENS W10 * 48 K2
Matthew Ct MTCM CR4 74 B3
Matthew's Gdns CROY/NA CR0 87 V1
Matthews La STA TW18 56 K9
Matthews Rd GFD/PVL UB6 35 M10
Matthews St BTSEA SW11 * 49 T14
REIG RH2 93 N14
Matthias Rd STNW/STAM N16 38 H10
Mattingley Wy PECK SE15 9 U13
Mattison Rd FSBYPK N4 38 E4
Mattock La WEA W13 47 S6
Maud Cashmore Wy WOOL/PLUM SE18 52 H8
Maude Crs WATN WD24 11 P12
Maude Rd CMBW SE5 50 J14
SWLY BR8 66 G11
WALTH E17 39 Q3
Maudesville Cottages HNWL W7 47 N6
Maude Ter WALTH E17 39 Q3
Maud Gdns BARK IG11 41 P14
PLSTW E13 40 B14
Maudlins Gn WAP E1W * 51 L6
Maud Rd LEY E10 39 U8
PLSTW E13 40 B14
Maudslay Rd ELTH/MOT SE9 64 H1
Maud St CAN/RD E16 52 B3
Maud Wilkes Cl KTTN NW5 38 A10
Mauleverer Rd BRXS/STRHM SW2 62 C3
Maundeby Wk WLSDN NW10 * 36 E10
Maunder Rd HNWL W7 47 N6
Maunsel St WEST SW1P 8 C7
Maurice Av CTHM CR3 86 H12
WDGN N22 26 F14
Maurice Browne Cl MLHL NW7 24 K10
Maurice St SHB W12 48 H4
Maurice Wk GLDGN NW11 37 Q2
Maurier Cl NTHLT UB5 34 E13
Mauritius Rd GNWCH SE10 52 A9
Maury Rd STNW/STAM N16 39 L7
Mauveine Gdns HSLW TW3 58 J2
Mavelstone Rd BMLY BR1 64 F13
Maverton Rd BOW E3 * 39 S13
Mavis Av HOR/WEW KT19 72 E10
Mavis Cl HOR/WEW KT19 72 E10
Mavis Gv HCH RM12 43 L7
Mawbey Pl STHWK SE1 9 V10
Mawbey Rd CHERT KT16 68 H11
STHWK SE1 9 V10
Mawbey St VX/NE SW8 8 E14
Mawney Cl ROMW/RG RM7 42 B1
Mawney Rd ROMW/RG RM7 30 B14
ROMW/RG RM7 42 B1
Mawson Cl RYNPK SW20 61 L14
Mawson La CHSWK W4 48 F11
Maxey Gdns DAGW RM9 41 U9
Maxey Rd DAGW RM9 41 U9
WOOL/PLUM SE18 53 L9
Maxfield Cl TRDG/WHET N20 25 Q5
Maxilla Wk NKENS W10 48 K4
Maximfeldt Rd ERITH DA8 54 E10
Maxim Rd DART DA1 66 E3
ERITH DA8 54 E10
WCHMH N21 26 E4
Maxted Pk HRW HA1 35 N5
Maxted Rd PECK SE15 62 K1
Maxwell Cl CROY/NA CR0 74 C6
HYS/HAR UB3 46 C5
RKW/CH/CXG WD3 21 L7
Maxwell Dr BF/WBF KT14 81 N1
Maxwell Gdns ORP BR6 77 P8
Maxwell Ri OXHEY WD19 22 G5
Maxwell Rd ASHF TW15 57 U11
BORE WD6 24 B1
FUL/PGN SW6 6 H14
NTHWD HA6 21 V12
WDR/YW UB7 45 Q9
WELL DA16 65 Q2
Maxwelton Av MLHL NW7 24 D10
Maxwelton Cl MLHL NW7 24 D10
Maya Cl PECK SE15 51 M14
Mayall Cl PEND EN3 16 G12
STHWK SE1 9 P2
Mayall Rd HNHL SE24 62 F3
Maya Pl FBAR/BDGN N11 26 B12
Maya Rd EFNCH N2 37 Q2
May Av STMC/STPC BR5 77 R3
Maybank Av ALP/SUD HA0 35 Q9
HCH RM12 42 H10
SWFD E18 28 D14
Maybank Gdns PIN HA5 34 C2
Maybank Rd SWFD E18 28 E13
May Bate Av KUTN/CMB KT2 59 T13
Mayberry Pl BRYLDS KT5 71 V5
Maybourne Cl SYD SE26 63 M11
Maybourne Ri WOKS/MYFD GU22 80 B14
Maybrick Rd EMPK RM11 42 J3
Maybury Av CHES/WCR EN8 16 B2
RDART DA2 67 P6
Maybury Cl EN EN1 16 B12
KWD/TDW/WH KT20 85 L9
STMC/STPC BR5 76 K3
Maybury Gdns WLSDN NW10 36 G12
Maybury Hl WOKS/MYFD GU22 80 F7
Maybury Ms HGT N6 38 A5
Maybury Rd BARK IG11 41 Q14
PLSTW E13 52 E2
WOKN/KNAP GU21 80 E6
Maybury St TOOT SW17 61 S10
Maybush Rd EMPK RM11 43 L5
Maychurch Cl STAN HA7 23 T13
May Cl CHSGTN KT9 71 V11
Maycock Gv NTHWD HA6 22 B11
Maycroft PIN HA5 22 D14
Maycross Av MRDN SM4 73 M2
Mayday Gdns BKHTH/KID SE3 52 G14
Mayday Rd THHTH CR7 74 F4
Maydwell Ldg BORE WD6 12 K14
Mayefield Rd THHTH CR7 74 D2
Mayell Cl LHD/OX KT22 83 S13
Mayerne Rd ELTH/MOT SE9 64 F3
Mayesbrook Rd BARK IG11 41 P13
GDMY/SEVK IG3 41 Q8
Mayes Cl SWLY BR8 78 G2
WARL CR6 87 P8
Mayesford Rd CHDH RM6 41 S5
Mayes Rd WDGN N22 26 D14
Mayeswood Rd LEE/GVPK SE12 64 E9
Mayfair Av BXLYHN DA7 53 T13
CHDH RM6 41 T4
IL IG1 40 H7
WHTN TW2 59 L5
WPK KT4 72 G6
Mayfair Cl BECK BR3 63 T13
SURB KT6 71 U6
Mayfair Ct EDGW HA8 23 V10
Mayfair Gdns TOTM N17 26 H11
WFD IG8 28 C12
Mayfair Ms CAMTN NW1 * 37 T12
Mayfair Pl MYFR/PICC W1J 7 V1
Mayfair Rd DART DA1 66 K3
Mayfair Ter STHGT/OAK N14 26 B5
Mayfare RKW/CH/CXG WD3 21 V3
Mayfield BXLYHN DA7 65 V1
LHD/OX KT22 83 S11
Mayfield Av ADL/WDHM KT15 69 M14
CHSWK W4 48 E9
KTN/HRWW/WS HA3 35 R3
NFNCH/WDSPK N12 25 Q9
ORP BR6 77 P6
STHGT/OAK N14 26 A7
WEA W13 47 R8
WFD IG8 28 C11
Mayfield Cl ADL/WDHM KT15 69 N14
ASHF TW15 57 T11
CLAP SW4 62 B3
HACK E8 38 K12
HGDN/ICK UB10 45 T1
PGE/AN SE20 63 M13
THDIT KT7 71 R6
WOT/HER KT12 70 C9
Mayfield Crs ED N9 27 M4
THHTH CR7 74 D2
Mayfield Dr PIN HA5 34 H2
Mayfield Gdns ADL/WDHM KT15 69 M14
BRW CM14 31 V6
HDN NW4 36 K4
HNWL W7 47 M4
STA TW18 56 K12
WOT/HER KT12 70 C9
Mayfield Rd ACT W3 48 B5
BCTR RM8 41 S6
BELMT SM2 73 R11
BELV DA17 54 C9
BMLY BR1 76 G3
CEND/HSY/T N8 38 D4
CHING E4 27 U7
PEND EN3 16 D14
PLSTW E13 52 B2
SAND/SEL CR2 74 H13
SHB W12 48 E7
WEY KT13 69 R10
WIM/MER SW19 61 M13
WOT/HER KT12 70 C9
Mayfields WBLY HA9 36 A7
Mayfields Cl WBLY HA9 36 A7
Mayfield Vls SCUP DA14 * 65 S11
Mayflower Cl BERM/RHTH SE16 51 P9
RSLP HA4 33 U4
Mayflower Rd BRXN/ST SW9 62 C1
LCOL/BKTW AL2 11 V1
Mayflower St BERM/RHTH SE16 51 N7
Mayfly Cl PIN HA5 34 E5
STMC/STPC BR5 77 T2
Mayford Cl BAL SW12 61 T5
BECK BR3 75 P1
WOKS/MYFD GU22 80 B12
Mayford Gn WOKS/MYFD GU22 80 B12
Mayford Rd BAL SW12 61 T5
May Gdns ALP/SUD HA0 47 S1
BORE WD6 23 T4
Maygoods Cl UX/CGN UB8 45 P3
Maygoods Gn UX/CGN UB8 45 P3
Maygoods La UX/CGN UB8 45 P3
Maygood St IS N1 4 H3
Maygoods Vw UX/CGN UB8 * 45 N3
Maygreen Crs EMPK RM11 42 G5
Maygrove Rd KIL/WHAMP NW6 37 M11
Mayhew Cl CHING E4 27 S8
Mayhill Rd BAR EN5 25 L4
CHARL SE7 52 D11
Mayhurst Av WOKS/MYFD GU22 80 G6
Mayhurst Crs WOKS/MYFD GU22 80 G6
Maylands Av HCH RM12 42 H9
Maylands Dr SCUP DA14 65 T8
UX/CGN UB8 33 P11
Maylands Rd OXHEY WD19 22 E9
Maylands Wy HARH RM3 31 Q11
Maynard Cl ERITH DA8 54 F12
FUL/PGN SW6 6 H14
SEVS/STOTM N15 38 J3
Maynard Pl POTB/CUF EN6 15 N3
Maynard Rd WALTH E17 39 U3
Maynards EMPK RM11 43 L5
Maynards Quay WAP E1W * 51 N5
Maynooth Gdns CAR SM5 73 T5
Mayo Cl CHES/WCR EN8 16 C2
Mayola Rd CLPT E5 39 N9
Mayo Rd CROY/NA CR0 74 H3
WLSDN NW10 36 E11
WOT/HER KT12 70 C5
Mayors La RDART DA2 66 J10
Mayow Rd SYD SE26 63 P9
Mayplace Av DART DA1 66 G2
Mayplace Cl BXLYHN DA7 66 B1
Mayplace La WOOL/PLUM SE18 52 K11
Mayplace Rd BXLYHN DA7 66 C1
Mayplace Rd East BXLYHN DA7 66 C1
Mayplace Rd West BXLYHN DA7 66 A2

New – Oak 129

Newcastle Cl FLST/FETLN EC4A 5 L11
Newcastle Pl BAY/PAD W2 3 M9
Newcastle Rw CLKNW EC1R 4 K8
New Cswy REIG RH2 93 P13
New Cavendish St CAVSQ/HST W1G 3 T10
New Change STP EC4M 5 N12
New Charles St FSBYE EC1V 5 M5
New Church Rd CMBW SE5 * 9 P13
New City Rd PLSTW E13 52 E1
New Cl FELT TW13 58 G10
WIM/MER SW19 73 Q1
New College Ms IS N1 * 38 E12
New College Pde HAMP NW3 * 37 Q11
Newcombe Gdns HSLWW TW4 58 H2
Newcombe Pk ALP/SUD HA0 35 V13
MLHL NW7 24 E10
Newcombe Ri WDR/YW UB7 45 Q4
Newcombe St KENS W8 * 6 F1
Newcome Gdns STRHM/NOR SW16 62 C9
Newcomen Rd BTSEA SW11 61 R1
WAN E11 * 40 B8
Newcomen St STHWK SE1 9 Q3
Newcome Rd RAD WD7 13 L8
New Compton St LSQ/SEVD WC2H * 4 D12
New Cottages BRKMPK AL9 13 V2
REIG RH2 * 92 K8
New Ct EMB EC4Y * 4 J13
NTHLT UB5 34 K10
Newcourt UX/CGN UB8 45 N3
Newcourt St STJWD NW8 3 N4
New Crane Pl WAP E1W * 51 N6
New Crescent Yd WLSDN NW10 * 36 F14
Newcroft Cl UX/CGN UB8 45 R3
New Cross Rd NWCR SE14 51 R12
Newdales Cl ED N9 27 L7
Newdene Av NTHLT UB5 34 F14
Newdigate STRHM/NOR SW16 * 62 E9
Newdigate Gn DEN/HRF UB9 21 P13
Newdigate Rd DEN/HRF UB9 21 N13
Newdigate Rd East DEN/HRF UB9 21 P13
Newell St POP/IOD E14 51 R5
New End HAMP NW3 37 Q9
New End Sq HAMP NW3 37 R9
Newent Cl CAR SM5 73 T6
PECK SE15 9 T13
New Era Est IS N1 5 S2
New Farm Av HAYES BR2 76 C2
New Farm Cl STA TW18 57 N13
New Farm Dr ABR/ST RM4 29 S1
New Farm La NTHWD HA6 22 A13
New Ferry Ap WOOL/PLUM SE18 52 J8
New Fetter La FLST/FETLN EC4A 4 K11
Newfield Cl HPTN TW12 58 J13
Newfield Ri CRICK NW2 36 G8
New Ford Rd CHES/WCR EN8 16 F8
New Forest La CHIG IG7 28 J11
Newgale Gdns EDGW HA8 23 V13
New Garden Dr WDR/YW UB7 45 Q7
Newgate CROY/NA CR0 74 G6
Newgate Cl FELT TW13 58 G7
Newgate St CHING E4 28 A8
STBT EC1A 5 M11
New Globe Wk STHWK SE1 9 N1
New Goulston St WCHPL E1 5 U11
New Green Pl BRXS/STRHM SW2 62 E5
NRWD SE19 62 J11
Newhall Ct WAB EN9 17 M7
New Hall Dr HARH RM3 31 L13
Newhall Gdns WOT/HER KT12 70 E7
Newham's Rw STHWK SE1 9 T4
Newham Wy CAN/RD E16 52 B3
Newhaven Cl HYS/HAR UB3 46 B9
Newhaven Crs ASHF TW15 57 V10
Newhaven Gdns ELTH/MOT SE9 64 F2
Newhaven La CAN/RD E16 52 C3
Newhaven Rd SNWD SE25 74 H3
New Haw Rd ADL/WDHM KT15 69 N11
New Heston Rd HEST TW5 46 H12
Newhouse Av CHDH RM6 41 T1
Newhouse Cl NWMAL KT3 72 E5
Newhouse Crs GSTN WD25 11 Q7
Newhouse Wk MRDN SM4 73 Q5
Newick Cl BXLY DA5 66 B4
Newick Rd CLPT E5 39 N8
Newing Gn BMLY BR1 64 F12
Newington Barrow Wy HOLWY N7 38 D8
Newington Butts WALW SE17 9 M8
Newington Cswy STHWK SE1 9 N5
Newington Gn IS N1 38 H10
Newington Green Rd IS N1 38 H10
New Inn Broadway SDTCH EC2A * 5 T7
New Inn Sq SDTCH EC2A * 5 T7
New Inn St SDTCH EC2A * 5 T7
New Inn Yd SDTCH EC2A 5 T7
New Kelvin Av TEDD TW11 59 N11
New Kent Rd WALW SE17 9 P7
New King's Rd FUL/PGN SW6 49 N13
New King St DEPT SE8 51 S11
Newland Cl PIN HA5 22 H11
Newland Ct WBLY HA9 36 A7
Newland Dr EN EN1 16 B13
Newland Gdns WEA W13 47 Q7
Newland Rd CEND/HSY/T N8 38 C1
Newlands Av RAD WD7 12 D8
THDIT KT7 71 N6
WOKS/MYFD GU22 80 D12
Newlands Cl ALP/SUD HA0 35 S11
EDGW HA8 23 U8
NWDGN UB2 46 C10
WOT/HER KT12 70 G9
Newlands Dr DTCH/LGLY SL3 56 J1
Newlands Pk SYD SE26 63 N11
Newlands Pl BAR EN5 24 K3
Newlands Quay WAP E1W 51 N5
Newlands Rd STRHM/NOR SW16 62 C14
WFD IG8 28 B7
The Newlands WLGTN SM6 74 A12
Newland St CAN/RD E16 52 G6
Newlands Wk GSTN WD25 11 R7
Newlands Wy CHSGTN KT9 71 S10
POTB/CUF EN6 14 D4
Newlands Woods CROY/NA CR0 75 R13
New La RGUE GU4 80 D14
Newling Cl EHAM E6 52 H4
Newling Est BETH E2 5 V6
New Lodge Dr OXTED RH8 96 B4
New London St MON EC3R * 5 T13
New Lydenburg St CHARL SE7 52 E8
Newlyn Cl LCOL/BKTW AL2 11 S4
ORP BR6 77 Q9
UX/CGN UB8 45 S3
Newlyn Gdns RYLN/HDSTN HA2 34 H5
Newlyn Rd BAR EN5 25 M2
TOTM N17 26 K13
WELL DA16 53 P14
New Maltings SOCK/AV RM15 55 R6
Newman Cl EMPK RM11 43 L3
Newman Ms WDGN N22 26 E12
Newman Rd BMLY BR1 64 C13
CROY/NA CR0 74 D5
HYS/HAR UB3 46 D5
PLSTW E13 52 D1
WALTH E17 39 P3
Newmans La LOU IG10 28 J1
SURB KT6 71 T4
Newman's Rw LINN WC2A 4 H10
Newman St FITZ W1T 4 B10
Newman's Wy EBAR EN4 14 E14
Newmarket Av NTHLT UB5 34 J10
Newmarket Wy HCH RM12 43 L9
Newmarsh Rd THMD SE28 53 P6
New Mill Rd STMC/STPC BR5 65 S13
Newminster Ct ENC/FH EN2 * 15 R14
Newminster Rd MRDN SM4 73 Q5
New Mount St SRTFD E15 39 V12
Newnham Av RSLP HA4 34 E6
Newnham Cl LOU IG10 28 F4
NTHLT UB5 35 L11
THHTH CR7 62 G14
Newnham Gdns NTHLT UB5 35 L11
Newnham Gn WDGN N22 * 26 E13
Newnham Pde CHES/WCR EN8 * 16 D4
Newnham Rd WDGN N22 26 D13
Newnhams Cl BMLY BR1 76 H1
Newnham Ter STHWK SE1 8 J5
Newnham Wy KTN/HRWW/WS HA3 35 U3
New North Pl SDTCH EC2A 5 S7
New North Rd BARK/HLT IG6 29 M12
IS N1 5 P1
REIG RH2 93 M13
New North St BMSBY WC1N 4 G9
Newnton Cl FSBYPK N4 38 H5
New Oak Rd EFNCH N2 25 R14
New Oxford St NOXST/BSQ WC1A 4 E11
New Pde ASHF TW15 * 57 R9
RKW/CH/CXG WD3 * 21 R4
WDR/YW UB7 * 45 Q6
New Park Av PLMGR N13 26 H8
New Park Cl NTHLT UB5 34 G11
New Park Est UED N18 27 N10
New Park Rd ASHF TW15 57 U10
BRXS/STRHM SW2 62 C5
DEN/HRF UB9 21 N13
New Peachey La UX/CGN UB8 45 P4
Newpiece LOU IG10 28 K1
New Place Gdns REDH RH1 93 T9
UPMR RM14 43 R7
New Place Sq BERM/RHTH SE16 * 51 M8
New Plaistow Rd SRTFD E15 40 A13
New Pond Pde RSLP HA4 * 34 C8
Newport Av PLSTW E13 52 D2
POP/IOD E14 51 V5
Newport Cl PEND EN3 16 E11
Newport Ct LSQ/SEVD WC2H 4 D13
Newport Md OXHEY WD19 * 22 F9
Newport Pl SOHO/SHAV W1D * 4 D13
Newport Rd BARN SW13 48 G13
HTHAIR TW6 45 S13
LEY E10 39 V7
WALTH E17 * 39 Q2
YEAD UB4 45 V3
Newports SWLY BR8 78 D5
Newport St LBTH SE11 8 G8
Newquay Crs RYLN/HDSTN HA2 34 G7
Newquay Gdns OXHEY WD19 22 D7
Newquay Rd CAT SE6 63 T7
New Quebec St MBLAR W1H 3 R12
New River Av CEND/HSY/T N8 38 D1
New River Crs PLMGR N13 26 F9
New River Wy FSBYPK N4 38 H5
New Rd ABR/ST RM4 29 T4
ABYW SE2 53 T9
BORE WD6 23 T4
BTFD TW8 * 47 T11
CEND/HSY/T N8 38 C3
CHING E4 27 T9
CSTG HP8 20 C1
DAGE RM10 42 A14
DTCH/LGLY SL3 44 B13
DTCH/LGLY SL3 44 E8
E/WMO/HCT KT8 70 J1
EBED/NFELT TW14 57 V4
ED N9 27 M7
ESH/CLAY KT10 71 L9
ESH/CLAY KT10 71 P14
EYN DA4 67 Q14
FELT TW13 58 G10
GDMY/SEVK IG3 41 N7
GSTN WD25 12 C13
HRW HA1 35 P9
HSLW TW3 58 K2
HYS/HAR UB3 45 U12
KUTN/CMB KT2 60 A12
KWD/TDW/WH KT20 84 J13
LHD/OX KT22 83 P1
MLHL NW7 25 L12
MTCM CR4 73 U6
ORP BR6 77 Q5
OXTED RH8 95 S12
OXTED RH8 96 D6
POTB/CUF EN6 13 S7
RAD WD7 12 C10
RAD WD7 13 L8
RAIN RM13 54 G1
RCHPK/HAM TW10 59 S9
RKW/CH/CXG WD3 21 S3
RSEV TN14 89 T14
SHPTN TW17 69 S1
SOCK/AV RM15 55 M6
STA TW18 56 G10
SWLY BR8 66 F12
SWLY BR8 78 F1
UX/CGN UB8 45 U2
WAT WD17 22 F2
WCHPL E1 51 L3
WDGN N22 26 G13
WELL DA16 53 R14
WELL DA16 65 R1
WEY KT13 69 U10
New Road Hl HAYES BR2 76 G13
New Rw CHCR WC2N 4 E13
Newry Rd TWK TW1 59 Q2
Newsam Av SEVS/STOTM N15 38 H3
Newsholme Dr WCHMH N21 26 D3
New Site ADL/WDHM KT15 * 69 Q9
New Spring Gardens Wk STHWK SE1 * 8 F10
New Sq EBED/NFELT TW14 57 U6
LINN WC2A 4 H11
Newstead Av ORP BR6 77 M8
Newstead Cl NFNCH/WDSPK N12 25 S11
Newstead Ct NTHLT UB5 * 46 G1
Newstead Ri CTHM CR3 95 M2
Newstead Rd LEE/GVPK SE12 64 B5
Newstead Wk CAR SM5 73 Q5
Newstead Wy WIM/MER SW19 60 K9
New St BH/WHM TN16 97 L3
LVPST EC2M 5 T10
STA TW18 57 L9
WAT WD17 * 22 E2
New Street Hl BMLY BR1 64 E10
New Street Sq FLST/FETLN EC4A 4 K11
New Tank Hill Rd PUR RM19 55 N8
Newteswell Dr WAB EN9 16 K6
Newton Av ACT W3 48 C7
MUSWH N10 25 U13
Newton Cl DTCH/LGLY SL3 44 D8
RYLN/HDSTN HA2 34 J7
WALTH E17 39 Q4
Newton Crs BORE WD6 24 C2
Newton Gv CHSWK W4 48 E9
Newton Pl POP/IOD E14 51 S9
Newton Rd ACT W3 48 C7
ALP/SUD HA0 35 V12
BAY/PAD W2 2 F12
CRICK NW2 36 J9
ISLW TW7 47 P14
KTN/HRWW/WS HA3 23 N14
PUR/KEN CR8 86 A2
SEVS/STOTM N15 38 K3
SRTFD E15 * 39 V10
WELL DA16 65 Q1
WIM/MER SW19 61 L12
Newtons Cl RAIN RM13 42 E12
Newton's Ct RDART DA2 67 R2
Newton St HOL/ALD WC2B 4 F11
Newton's Yd WAND/EARL SW18 61 N3
Newton Ter HAYES BR2 76 F4
Newton Wk EDGW HA8 24 C13
Newton Wy UED N18 26 G10
Newton Wood Rd ASHTD KT21 83 V6
New Tower Buildings WAP E1W * 51 M6
Newtown Rd DEN/HRF UB9 33 M11
Newtown St BTSEA SW11 49 V13
New Trinity Rd EFNCH N2 37 R1
New Union Cl POP/IOD E14 51 U8
New Union St BARB EC2Y 5 Q10
New Vls TOTM N17 * 27 L13
New Wanstead WAN E11 40 C4
New Way Rd CDALE/KGS NW9 36 F2
New Wharf Rd IS N1 4 F3
New Wickham La EGH TW20 56 E12
Newyears Green La DEN/HRF UB9 33 S4
New Years La RSEV TN14 89 P6
New Zealand Av WOT/HER KT12 70 C6
New Zealand Wy RAIN RM13 54 F1
Niagara Av EA W5 47 S9
Niagara Cl CHES/WCR EN8 16 D3
IS N1 5 P3
Nibthwaite Rd HRW HA1 35 N3
Nicholas Cl GFD/PVL UB6 34 K14
WATN WD24 11 P11
Nicholas Gdns EA W5 47 T6
WOKS/MYFD GU22 80 K6
Nicholas La MANHO EC4N 5 R13
Nicholas Rd BCTR RM8 41 V7
BORE WD6 23 V4
CROY/NA CR0 74 C9
WCHPL E1 51 N2
Nicholas Wy NTHWD HA6 21 U13
Nicholay Rd ARCH N19 38 B6
Nichol Cl STHGT/OAK N14 26 B6
Nicholes Rd HSLW TW3 58 J2
Nichol La BMLY BR1 64 C12
Nicholl Rd EPP CM16 18 D5
Nicholls Av UX/CGN UB8 45 S2
Nichollsfield Wk HOLWY N7 38 C10
Nicholl St BETH E2 39 L13
Nichols Cl FSBYPK N4 * 38 E6
Nichols Gn EA W5 47 U3
Nicholson Dr BUSH WD23 23 L6
Nicholson House CHARL SE7 * 52 G12
Nicholson Ms EGH TW20 * 56 E10
KUT/HW KT1 71 U2
Nicholson Rd CROY/NA CR0 74 K6
Nicholson St STHWK SE1 9 L2
Nicholson Wk EGH TW20 56 E10
Nickelby Cl THMD SE28 53 S4
Nickleby Cl UX/CGN UB8 45 T4
Nickols Wk WAND/EARL SW18 61 P2
Nicola Cl KTN/HRWW/WS HA3 23 M14
SAND/SEL CR2 74 G11
Nicola Ms BARK/HLT IG6 28 K12
Nicol Cl CFSP/GDCR SL9 20 A13
TWK TW1 59 R4
Nicol End CFSP/GDCR SL9 20 A13
Nicoll Pl HDN NW4 36 H4
Nicoll Rd WLSDN NW10 36 E13
Nicolls Cl CTHM CR3 86 G12
Nicoll Wy BORE WD6 24 D3
Nicol Rd CFSP/GDCR SL9 20 A13
Nicolson Rd STMC/STPC BR5 77 S5
Nicosia Rd WAND/EARL SW18 61 S5
Niederwald Rd SYD SE26 63 Q9
Nield Rd HYS/HAR UB3 46 B7
Nigel Cl NTHLT UB5 34 G13
Nigel Fisher Wy CHSGTN KT9 71 T12
Nigel Ms IL IG1 40 K9
Nigel Playfair Av HMSMTH W6 48 H10
Nigel Rd FSTGT E7 40 E10
PECK SE15 63 L1
Nigeria Rd CHARL SE7 52 E12
Nightingale Av CHING E4 28 A10
UPMR RM14 43 T6
Nightingale Cl ABLGY WD5 11 N5
BH/WHM TN16 88 E5
CAR SM5 73 U7
CHING E4 28 A9
CHSWK W4 48 C11
COB KT11 82 F2
HOR/WEW KT19 84 A2
PIN HA5 34 E3
RAD WD7 12 D10
Nightingale Cnr STMC/STPC BR5 * 77 T2
Nightingale Ct SUT SM1 73 Q10
Nightingale Crs HARH RM3 31 L14
Nightingale Dr HOR/WEW KT19 72 B11
Nightingale Gv LEW SE13 63 V3
Nightingale La BAL SW12 61 U4
BMLY BR1 64 E14
CEND/HSY/T N8 38 C2
RCHPK/HAM TW10 59 U5
WAN E11 40 D3
Nightingale Ms KUT/HW KT1 * 71 T1
LBTH SE11 8 K7
Nightingale Pl RKW/CH/CXG WD3 21 P5
WBPTN SW10 6 K11
WOOL/PLUM SE18 52 J11
Nightingale Rd BGR/WK TN15 90 K7
BUSH WD23 22 J3
CAR SM5 73 T8
CLPT E5 39 M8
E/WMO/HCT KT8 70 K3
ED N9 27 N5
ESH/CLAY KT10 70 H10
HNWL W7 47 P6
HPTN TW12 58 J11
RKW/CH/CXG WD3 21 N5
SAND/SEL CR2 87 P1
STMC/STPC BR5 77 L4
WDGN N22 26 C13
WLSDN NW10 36 F14
WOT/HER KT12 * 70 E5
Nightingale Shott EGH TW20 56 D11
Nightingales La CSTG HP8 20 B3
Nightingale Sq BAL SW12 61 U5
The Nightingales STWL/WRAY TW19 57 R6
Nightingale V WOOL/PLUM SE18 52 K11
Nightingale Wk BAL SW12 61 V4
Nightingale Wy DEN/HRF UB9 32 K4
EHAM E6 52 G3
REDH RH1 94 J10
SWLY BR8 78 E1
Nigntingale Av HRW HA1 35 R5
Nile Cl STNW/STAM N16 38 K8
Nile Dr ED N9 27 N7
Nile Rd PLSTW E13 40 E14
Nile St IS N1 5 Q5
Nile Ter PECK SE15 9 V10
Nimbus Rd HOR/WEW KT19 72 D14
Nimmo Dr BUSH WD23 23 M5
Nimrod Cl NTHLT UB5 46 F1
Nimrod Pas IS N1 38 J11
Nimrod Rd STRHM/NOR SW16 61 V11
Nina Mackay Cl SRTFD E15 * 40 A13
Nine Acres Cl MNPK E12 40 G10
Nineacres Wy COUL/CHIP CR5 86 C6
Nine Elms Av UX/CGN UB8 45 P3
Nine Elms Cl EBED/NFELT TW14 58 B6
UX/CGN UB8 45 P3
Nine Elms La VX/NE SW8 8 D12
Ninefields WAB EN9 17 N7
Ninehams Cl CTHM CR3 86 H10
Ninehams Gdns CTHM CR3 86 H10
Ninehams Rd BH/WHM TN16 88 F11
CTHM CR3 86 H11
Nine Stiles Cl DEN/HRF UB9 33 M11
Nineteenth Rd MTCM CR4 74 C2
Ninhams Wd ORP BR6 76 J9
Ninnings Rd CFSP/GDCR SL9 20 D12
Ninnings Wy CFSP/GDCR SL9 20 D12
Ninth Av HYS/HAR UB3 46 C5
KWD/TDW/WH KT20 * 93 M2
Nisbett Wk SCUP DA14 65 Q9
Nithdale Rd WOOL/PLUM SE18 52 K12
Nithsdale Gv HGDN/ICK UB10 33 U8
Niton Cl BAR EN5 24 K4
Niton Rd RCH/KEW TW9 * 60 A1
Niton St FUL/PGN SW6 48 K12
Niven Cl BORE WD6 13 N13
No1 St WOOL/PLUM SE18 52 K8
No2 St WOOL/PLUM SE18 52 K8
Noah's Ark BGR/WK TN15 91 P8
Noak Hill Rd ABR/ST RM4 30 H10
Nobel Dr HYS/HAR UB3 46 A12
Nobel Rd UED N18 27 N9
Noble Cnr HEST TW5 * 46 J13
Noble St CITYW EC2V 5 N11
Nobles Wy EGH TW20 56 C12
Noel Rd ACT W3 48 A4
EHAM E6 52 G2
IS N1 5 L3
Noel St SOHO/CST W1F 4 B12
Noke Dr REDH RH1 93 U9
Noke Side LCOL/BKTW AL2 11 U1
Nolan Wy CLPT E5 39 L9
Nolton Pl EDGW HA8 23 V13
Nonsuch Cl CHIG IG7 28 K11
Nonsuch Court Av EW KT17 72 H14
Nonsuch Pl CHEAM SM3 * 72 K12
Nonsuch Wk BELMT SM2 72 K14
Nora Gdns HDN NW4 36 K2
Norbiton Av KUT/HW KT1 60 A14
Norbiton Common Rd KUT/HW KT1 72 B1
Norbiton Rd POP/IOD E14 51 R4
Norbreck Pde EA W5 47 U1
Norbroke St SHB W12 48 F5
Norburn St NKENS W10 2 A10
Norbury Av HSLW TW3 59 M3
STRHM/NOR SW16 62 D13
WATN WD24 11 Q13
Norbury Cl STRHM/NOR SW16 62 E13
Norbury Court Rd STRHM/NOR SW16 62 C14
Norbury Crs STRHM/NOR SW16 62 E14
Norbury Cross STRHM/NOR SW16 74 C1
Norbury Gdns CHDH RM6 41 T3
Norbury Gv MLHL NW7 24 E8
Norbury Hl STRHM/NOR SW16 62 E12
Norbury Ri STRHM/NOR SW16 74 C1
Norbury Rd CHING E4 27 S10
FELT TW13 58 B8
REIG RH2 93 M10
THHTH CR7 62 G14
Norbury Vls KUT/HW KT1 * 59 V14
Norcombe Gdns KTN/HRWW/WS HA3 35 S4
Norcott Cl YEAD UB4 46 E2
Norcott Rd STNW/STAM N16 39 L7
Norcroft Gdns EDUL SE22 63 L5
Norcutt Rd WHTN TW2 59 N6
Nordenfeldt Rd ERITH DA8 54 D10
Norfield Rd RDART DA2 66 C9
Norfolk Av PLMGR N13 26 F11
SAND/SEL CR2 75 L14
SEVS/STOTM N15 38 K4
WATN WD24 11 Q12
Norfolk Cl DART DA1 67 N4
EBAR EN4 25 U2
EFNCH N2 37 S1
PLMGR N13 26 F11
TWK TW1 * 59 R4
Norfolk Ct BAR EN5 * 25 L2
Norfolk Crs BAY/PAD W2 3 N11
BFN/LL DA15 65 N5
Norfolk Farm Cl WOKS/MYFD GU22 80 H6
Norfolk Farm Rd WOKS/MYFD GU22 80 H6
Norfolk Gdns BORE WD6 24 D2
BXLYHN DA7 53 V13
Norfolk House RKW/CH/CXG WD3 * 21 Q6
Norfolk House Rd STRHM/NOR SW16 62 B8
Norfolk Ms NKENS W10 2 B10
Norfolk Pl BAY/PAD W2 3 M11
WELL DA16 53 Q14
Norfolk Rd BAR EN5 25 N1
BARK IG11 41 N12
DAGE RM10 42 B10
EHAM E6 40 H13
ESH/CLAY KT10 71 N10
FELT TW13 58 E6
GDMY/SEVK IG3 41 N6
HRW HA1 34 K3
PEND EN3 27 M4
RKW/CH/CXG WD3 21 Q6
ROMW/RG RM7 42 C4
STJWD NW8 3 M2
THHTH CR7 74 G1
UPMR RM14 43 N8
UX/CGN UB8 33 P11
WALTH E17 27 P13
WIM/MER SW19 61 S12
WLSDN NW10 36 E12
Norfolk Rw STHWK SE1 8 G7
Norfolk Sq BAY/PAD W2 3 M12
Norfolk Square Ms BAY/PAD W2 3 M12
Norfolk St FSTGT E7 40 C10
Norgrove Pk CFSP/GDCR SL9 32 C2
Norgrove St BAL SW12 61 U6
Norheads La BH/WHM TN16 88 C8
Norhyrst Av SNWD SE25 74 K1
Nork Gdns BNSTD SM7 85 L4
Nork Ri BNSTD SM7 84 K6
Nork Wy BNSTD SM7 84 K5
Norland Pl NTGHL W11 6 B2
Norland Rd NTGHL W11 48 K6
Norlands Crs CHST BR7 64 K13
Norlands Ga CHST BR7 * 64 K13
Norlands La EGH TW20 56 J14
Norland Sq NTGHL W11 6 B2
Norley V PUT/ROE SW15 60 G6
Norlington Rd LEY E10 39 U6
Norman Av EW KT17 84 F2
FELT TW13 58 G7
SAND/SEL CR2 74 G14
STHL UB1 46 G5
TWK TW1 59 R5
WDGN N22 26 G13
Normanby Cl PUT/ROE SW15 61 M3
Normanby Rd WLSDN NW10 36 F10
Norman Cl BGR/WK TN15 90 K7
EPSOM KT18 84 H9
ORP BR6 77 L8
ROMW/RG RM7 30 B14
WAB EN9 16 K7
Norman Colyer Ct HOR/WEW KT19 * 72 D14
Norman Ct POTB/CUF EN6 14 E5
Norman Crs HEST TW5 46 F12
PIN HA5 22 E13
Normand Ms WKENS W14 6 B11
Normand Rd WKENS W14 6 C11
Normandy Av BAR EN5 25 M3
Normandy Cl SYD SE26 63 Q8
Normandy Dr HYS/HAR UB3 45 U4
Normandy Rd BRXN/ST SW9 50 E13
Normandy Ter CAN/RD E16 52 D4
Normandy Wk EGH TW20 * 56 G10
Normandy Wy ERITH DA8 54 E13
Norman Gv BOW E3 39 Q14
Normanhurst Av WELL DA16 53 T13
Normanhurst Dr TWK TW1 59 R3
Normanhurst Rd BRXS/STRHM SW2 62 D7
STMC/STPC BR5 65 R14
WOT/HER KT12 70 F7
Norman Pde SCUP DA14 * 65 U8
Norman Rd ASHF TW15 57 V12
BELV DA17 54 B7
DART DA1 67 L6
EHAM E6 52 H2
EMPK RM11 42 G5
GNWCH SE10 51 T12
IL IG1 40 K10
SEVS/STOTM N15 38 K3
SUT SM1 73 N10
THHTH CR7 74 F3
WAN E11 40 A7
WIM/MER SW19 61 Q12
Normans Cl UX/CGN UB8 45 Q3
WDGN N22 * 26 G13
WLSDN NW10 36 D11
Normansfield Av KUT/HW KT1 59 S12
Normansfield Cl BUSH WD23 22 K5
Normanshire Dr CHING E4 27 S9
Normans Md WLSDN NW10 36 D11
Norman St FSBYE EC1V 5 N6
RSEV TN14 97 U6
Norman Ter KIL/WHAMP NW6 * 37 M10
Normanton Av WAND/EARL SW18 61 N7
Normanton Pk CHING E4 28 A8
Normanton Rd SAND/SEL CR2 74 J11
Normanton St FSTH SE23 63 P7
Norman Wy ACT W3 48 B3
STHGT/OAK N14 26 C7
Normington Cl STRHM/NOR SW16 62 E10
Norrice Lea EFNCH N2 37 R3
Norris St STJS SW1Y 4 C14
Norris Wy DART DA1 66 F1
Norroy Rd PUT/ROE SW15 60 K2
Norrys Cl EBAR EN4 25 T3
Norrys Rd EBAR EN4 25 T2
Norseman Cl GDMY/SEVK IG3 41 R6
Norseman Wy GFD/PVL UB6 34 K13
Norstead Pl PUT/ROE SW15 60 G7
Norsted La ORP BR6 89 R1
North Access Rd WALTH E17 39 Q4
North Acre BNSTD SM7 85 M6
CDALE/KGS NW9 24 E13
North Acton Rd WLSDN NW10 36 D14
Northallerton Wy HARH RM3 30 K10
Northall Rd BXLYHN DA7 54 C14
Northampton Gv IS N1 38 H10
Northampton Pk IS N1 38 G11
Northampton Rd CLKNW EC1R 4 K7
CROY/NA CR0 75 L7
PEND EN3 27 Q2
Northampton Rw CLKNW EC1R * 4 K7
Northampton Sq FSBYE EC1V 5 L6
Northampton St IS N1 * 38 G12
Northanger Rd STRHM/NOR SW16 62 C11
North Ap GSTN WD25 11 N9
NTHWD HA6 21 U7
North Audley St MYFR/PKLN W1K 3 S13
North Av CAR SM5 73 U12
HYS/HAR UB3 46 C5
RAD WD7 12 J6
RCH/KEW TW9 48 A13
RYLN/HDSTN HA2 34 K4
STHL UB1 46 H5
UED N18 27 L9
WEA W13 47 R4
WOT/HER KT12 70 B13
Northaw Pl POTB/CUF EN6 * 14 G4
Northaw Rd West POTB/CUF EN6 14 K5
North Bank STJWD NW8 3 N6
Northbank Rd WALTH E17 27 U14
North Birkbeck Rd WAN E11 39 V8
Northborough Rd
STRHM/NOR SW16 62 C14
Northbourne HAYES BR2 76 C5
Northbourne Rd CLAP SW4 62 B3
Northbrook Dr NTHWD HA6 22 A13
Northbrook Rd BAR EN5 25 L4
CROY/NA CR0 74 H3
IL IG1 40 J7
LEW SE13 63 V3
WDGN N22 26 C12
Northburgh St FSBYE EC1V 5 M8
North Carriage Dr BAY/PAD W2 3 P13
Northchurch Rd IS N1 38 G12
WBLY HA9 36 A11
Northchurch Ter IS N1 38 J12
North Circular PLMGR N13 26 F10
WALTH E17 27 T13
North Circular Rd BARK IG11 40 J12
CHING E4 * 27 Q11
CRICK NW2 36 E8
GLDGN NW11 37 L4
NFNCH/WDSPK N12 25 S12
REDBR IG4 40 E1
WLSDN NW10 35 V14
Northcliffe Cl WPK KT4 72 E8
Northcliffe Dr TRDG/WHET N20 25 M6
North Cl BAR EN5 24 J3
BXLYHS DA6 65 T2
CHIG IG7 29 Q10
DAGE RM10 42 A13
EBED/NFELT TW14 57 V4
MRDN SM4 73 L2
The North Colonnade POP/IOD E14 51 T6
North Common WEY KT13 * 69 U9
North Common Rd EA W5 47 U5
UX/CGN UB8 33 P10
Northcote ADL/WDHM KT15 69 P9
Northcote Av BRYLDS KT5 72 A5
EA W5 47 U5
ISLW TW7 59 Q3
STHL UB1 46 G5
Northcote Rd BTSEA SW11 61 S2
CROY/NA CR0 74 H4
NWMAL KT3 72 C1
SCUP DA14 65 N9
TWK TW1 59 Q3
WALTH E17 39 Q2
WLSDN NW10 36 E12
Northcott Av WDGN N22 26 C13
North Countess Rd WALTH E17 27 R14
Northcourt FITZ W1T 4 B9
RKW/CH/CXG WD3 * 21 L6
North Cray Rd BXLY DA5 66 A7
SCUP DA14 65 U11
North Crs CAN/RD E16 51 V2
FNCH N3 25 M14
GWRST WC1E 4 C9
Northcroft Rd HOR/WEW KT19 72 E12
WEA W13 47 R7
North Cross Rd BARK/HLT IG6 41 L2
EDUL SE22 62 K3
Northdene CHIG IG7 29 M10
North Dene HSLW TW3 46 K13
MLHL NW7 24 D8
Northdene Gdns SEVS/STOTM N15 38 K4
North Down SAND/SEL CR2 86 J1
Northdown Cl RSLP HA4 34 B8
Northdown Ct GDST RH9 95 N6
Northdown Gdns GNTH/NBYPK IG2 41 N3
Northdown Rd BELMT SM2 73 N14
BGR/WK TN15 91 L7
CFSP/GDCR SL9 20 C11
CTHM CR3 95 S1
EMPK RM11 42 H5
WELL DA16 53 R14
North Downs Crs CROY/NA CR0 75 T14
North Downs Rd CROY/NA CR0 75 U14
Northdown St IS N1 4 G4
North Downs Wy BRKHM/BTCW RH3 92 F6
CTHM CR3 94 E2
GDST RH9 95 R4
KWD/TDW/WH KT20 92 B8
KWD/TDW/WH KT20 92 K6
REDH RH1 94 C2
REIG RH2 93 N6
RSEV TN14 90 K5
SEV TN13 90 D8
WARL CR6 88 C13
North Dr BECK BR3 75 T2
GPK RM2 42 J1
HSLW TW3 47 L14
ORP BR6 77 N9
RSLP HA4 34 A5
STRHM/NOR SW16 62 A9
North End BKHH IG9 28 E5
CROY/NA CR0 74 G7
HAMP NW3 37 Q7
HARH RM3 30 J7
North End Av HAMP NW3 37 Q7
North End Crs WKENS W14 6 C8
North End La ORP BR6 76 K13
Northend Rd ERITH DA8 54 F13
North End Rd GLDGN NW11 37 N6
WBLY HA9 36 B8
WKENS W14 6 B8
North End Wy HAMP NW3 37 Q7
Northern Av ED N9 26 K7
Northernhay Wk MRDN SM4 73 L2
Northern Perimeter Rd HTHAIR TW6 45 U13
Northern Perimeter Rd (West)
WDR/YW UB7 45 N13
Northern Relief Rd BARK IG11 41 L12
Northey Av BELMT SM2 72 K14
North Eyot Gdns HMSMTH W6 * 48 F10
Northey St POP/IOD E14 51 Q5
North Farm LOU IG10 28 E4
Northfield Av PIN HA5 34 F2
STMC/STPC BR5 77 S4
WEA W13 47 R7
Northfield Cl BMLY BR1 64 G13
HYS/HAR UB3 46 B8
Northfield Ct STA TW18 57 M13
Northfield Crs CHEAM SM3 73 L9
Northfield Farm Ms COB KT11 82 C3
Northfield Gdns WATN WD24 11 Q11
Northfield Pde HYS/HAR UB3 * 46 B8
Northfield Pk HYS/HAR UB3 46 B8
Northfield Pl WEY KT13 69 T12
Northfield Rd BORE WD6 13 M13
CHES/WCR EN8 16 E6
COB KT11 82 C3
DAGW RM9 41 V9
EBAR EN4 25 S1
ED N9 * 27 M3
EHAM E6 40 H11
HEST TW5 46 F11
STA TW18 57 M13
STNW/STAM N16 38 J5
WEA W13 47 R7
Northfields ASHTD KT21 83 U9
EW KT17 84 E1
WAND/EARL SW18 61 N2
Northfields Rd ACT W3 48 C3
North Gdns WIM/MER SW19 61 R12
Northgate NTHWD HA6 21 U12
Northgate Dr CDALE/KGS NW9 36 E4
Northgate Pth BORE WD6 12 K12
North Gower St CAMTN NW1 4 A6
North Gv CHERT KT16 68 K4
HGT N6 37 U5
SEVS/STOTM N15 38 H3
North Hl HGT N6 37 T4
North Hill Av HGT N6 37 T4
North Hill Dr HARH RM3 30 K9
North Hyde Gdns HYS/HAR UB3 46 C8
North Hyde La NWDGN UB2 46 G10
North Hyde Rd HYS/HAR UB3 46 A8
North Hyde Whf NWDGN UB2 * 46 E9
Northiam NFNCH/WDSPK N12 25 N9
Northiam St HACK E8 39 M13
Northington St BMSBY WC1N 4 G9
Northlands POTB/CUF EN6 14 F5
Northlands Av ORP BR6 77 N9
Northlands St CMBW SE5 50 G14
North La TEDD TW11 59 P11
North Lodge Cl PUT/ROE SW15 * 60 K3
North Looe EW KT17 * 84 J3
North Md REDH RH1 93 T7
North Ms BMSBY WC1N 4 H8
North Mt TRDG/WHET N20 * 25 Q7
Northolm EDGW HA8 24 D9
Northolme Gdns EDGW HA8 24 A13
Northolme Ri ORP BR6 77 N7
Northolme Rd HBRY N5 38 G9
Northolt Av RSLP HA4 34 D10
Northolt Gdns GFD/PVL UB6 35 P10
Northolt Rd RYLN/HDSTN HA2 34 K9
WDR/YW UB7 45 P13
Northolt Wy HCH RM12 42 J10
North Orbital Rd DEN/HRF UB9 32 K3
LCOL/BKTW AL2 11 S4
North Orbital Rd St Albans Rd
GSTN WD25 11 R5
Northover BMLY BR1 64 B9
North Pde CHSGTN KT9 71 V10
EDGW HA8 * 24 A14
STHL UB1 * 46 J4
North Pk CFSP/GDCR SL9 32 C2
DTCH/LGLY SL3 44 J8
ELTH/MOT SE9 64 H4
North Park La GDST RH9 95 L5
North Pas WAND/EARL SW18 61 N3
North Peckham Est PECK SE15 9 U13
North Pl MTCM CR4 61 T12
TEDD TW11 59 P11
WAB EN9 16 H7
Northpoint Cl SUT SM1 73 Q8
North Pole La HAYES BR2 76 C11
North Pole Rd SHB W12 48 J4
Northport St IS N1 5 R2
North Riding LCOL/BKTW AL2 11 U4
North Ri BAY/PAD W2 * 3 P12
North Rd ABR/ST RM4 30 E7
BELV DA17 54 B8
BMLY BR1 64 D13
CHDH RM6 41 U3
CHES/WCR EN8 16 E7
DART DA1 66 F4
EA W5 47 T8
EBED/NFELT TW14 57 V4
ED N9 27 M6
EDGW HA8 24 B13
GDMY/SEVK IG3 41 N7
HEST TW5 46 E11
HGT N6 37 U5
HOLWY N7 38 C11
HYS/HAR UB3 45 V3
PUR RM19 55 Q9
RCH/KEW TW9 48 A14
REIG RH2 93 M13
RKW/CH/CXG WD3 20 H3
STHL UB1 46 J5
SURB KT6 71 T4
WDR/YW UB7 45 R8
WIM/MER SW19 61 R11
WOKN/KNAP GU21 80 E6
WOOL/PLUM SE18 53 N9
WOT/HER KT12 70 E10
WWKM BR4 75 T6
Northrop Rd HTHAIR TW6 46 A13
North Rw DTCH/LGLY SL3 * 32 C9
MYFR/PKLN W1K 3 R13
North Several BKHTH/KID SE3 * 51 V14
Northside Rd BMLY BR1 64 C13
North Side Wandsworth Common
WAND/EARL SW18 61 Q3
Northspur Rd SUT SM1 73 N8
North Sq ED N9 27 M7
GLDGN NW11 37 N4
North Station Ap REDH RH1 * 94 D12
Northstead Rd BRXS/STRHM SW2 62 E7
North St BARK IG11 40 K12
BMLY BR1 64 C13
BXLYHN DA7 66 A2
CAR SM5 73 T9
CLAP SW4 61 V1
DART DA1 66 K5
EGH TW20 56 D10
EMPK RM11 42 K5
HDN NW4 36 J3
ISLW TW7 59 Q1
LHD/OX KT22 83 Q12
PLSTW E13 40 D14
REDH RH1 93 T9
ROM RM1 42 D2
North Tenter St WCHPL E1 5 V12
North Ter CHEL SW3 7 N6
Northumberland Aly FENCHST EC3M * 5 T12
Northumberland Av CHCR WC2N 8 E1
EMPK RM11 42 J3
EN EN1 16 B12
ISLW TW7 47 P13
MNPK E12 40 E6
WELL DA16 65 N2
Northumberland Cl ERITH DA8 54 C12
STWL/WRAY TW19 57 Q4
Northumberland Crs
EBED/NFELT TW14 58 A4
Northumberland Gdns BMLY BR1 76 J2
ED N9 26 K8
MTCM CR4 74 C3
Northumberland Gv TOTM N17 27 M12
Northumberland Pk ERITH DA8 54 C12
TOTM N17 27 L12
Northumberland Pl BAY/PAD W2 2 E11
Northumberland Rd BAR EN5 25 Q4
EHAM E6 52 G4
RYLN/HDSTN HA2 34 H3
WALTH E17 39 S5
Northumberland St CHCR WC2N 8 E1
Northumberland Wy ERITH DA8 54 C13
Northumbria St POP/IOD E14 51 S4
North Verbena Gdns HMSMTH W6 * 48 G10
North Vw EA W5 47 S2
PIN HA5 34 E5
Northview SWLY BR8 66 E14
North Vw WIM/MER SW19 60 H10
North View Crs EPSOM KT18 84 J7
Northview Crs WLSDN NW10 36 F9
Northview Dr WFD IG8 28 F14
Northview Pde HOLWY N7 * 38 C8
North View Rd CEND/HSY/T N8 38 B1
SEV TN13 90 J11
North Vls CAMTN NW1 38 B11
North Wk CROY/NA CR0 75 T11
North Wy CDALE/KGS NW9 36 B1
ED N9 27 N7
FBAR/BDGN N11 26 A11
Northway GLDGN NW11 37 P3
North Wy HGDN/ICK UB10 33 R12
Northway MRDN SM4 73 L1
North Wy PIN HA5 34 E1
Northway RKW/CH/CXG WD3 21 P5
WLGTN SM6 74 A9
Northway Crs MLHL NW7 24 E9
Northway Rd CMBW SE5 62 G1
CROY/NA CR0 74 K4
Northways Pde HAMP NW3 * 37 R12
North Weald Cl HCH RM12 42 H12
North Weald La KUTN/CMB KT2 59 T10
North Western Av WATN WD24 11 M9
North Western Av Coln WATN WD24 11 Q10
North Western Av Gade Side
KGLGY WD4 10 J9
North Western Av Otterspool Wy
GSTN WD25 11 T12
North Wharf Rd BAY/PAD W2 3 L10
Northwick Av KTN/HRWW/WS HA3 35 Q4
Northwick Cir KTN/HRWW/WS HA3 35 S4
Northwick Cl STJWD NW8 3 L7
Northwick Park Rd HRW HA1 35 P4
Northwick Rd ALP/SUD HA0 35 T13
OXHEY WD19 22 E9
Northwick Ter STJWD NW8 3 L7
Northwold Dr PIN HA5 34 E1
Northwold Rd STNW/STAM N16 38 K7
Northwood Av HCH RM12 42 G9
PUR/KEN CR8 86 E3
Northwood Cl CHESW EN7 15 V1
Northwood Gdns CLAY IG5 40 J2
GFD/PVL UB6 35 P10
NFNCH/WDSPK N12 25 R10
Northwood Pl ERITHM DA18 53 V8
Northwood Rd CAR SM5 73 U11
DEN/HRF UB9 21 Q13
FSTH SE23 63 R6
HGT N6 37 V5
HTHAIR TW6 45 P13
THHTH CR7 62 G14
Northwood Wy DEN/HRF UB9 21 P13
NTHWD HA6 22 C13
North Woolwich Rd CAN/RD E16 52 C6
North Worple Wy
MORT/ESHN SW14 60 D1
Nortoft Rd CFSP/GDCR SL9 20 D11
Norton Av BRYLDS KT5 72 B5
Norton Cl BORE WD6 13 L13
CHING E4 27 S10
Norton Folgate WCHPL E1 5 T8
Norton Gdns STRHM/NOR SW16 62 C14
Norton La COB KT11 82 B9
Norton Rd ALP/SUD HA0 35 T11
DAGE RM10 42 D11
LEY E10 39 R6
UX/CGN UB8 45 P1
Norval Gn BRXN/ST SW9 * 50 E14
Norval Rd ALP/SUD HA0 35 R7
Norway Ga BERM/RHTH SE16 51 Q8
Norway Pl POP/IOD E14 51 R4
Norway St GNWCH SE10 51 T11
Norwich Crs CHDH RM6 41 R3
Norwich Ms GDMY/SEVK IG3 41 Q6
Norwich Rd FSTGT E7 40 C10
GFD/PVL UB6 34 K13
NTHWD HA6 34 B1
THHTH CR7 74 G1
Norwich St FLST/FETLN EC4A 4 J11
Norwich Wk EDGW HA8 24 C12
Norwich Wy RKW/CH/CXG WD3 21 T2
Norwood Av ALP/SUD HA0 35 V13
ROMW/RG RM7 42 D5
Norwood Cl CRICK NW2 37 L8
NWDGN UB2 46 J9
WHTN TW2 59 M7
Norwood Dr RYLN/HDSTN HA2 34 H4
Norwood Farm La COB KT11 82 D1
Norwood Gdns NWDGN UB2 46 H9
YEAD UB4 46 E2
Norwood Green Rd NWDGN UB2 46 J9
Norwood High St WNWD SE27 62 G9
Norwood La IVER SL0 44 H2
Norwood Park Rd WNWD SE27 62 G10
Norwood Rd CHES/WCR EN8 16 E4
HNHL SE24 62 F6
NWDGN UB2 46 G8
Notley End EGH TW20 * 56 A12
Notley St CMBW SE5 9 Q13
Notson Rd SNWD SE25 75 M2
Notting Barn Rd NKENS W10 48 K2
Nottingdale Sq NTGHL W11 6 A1
Nottingham Av CAN/RD E16 52 E3
Nottingham Cl GSTN WD25 11 N8
Nottingham Ct LSQ/SEVD WC2H 4 E12
Nottingham Pl CAMTN NW1 3 S8
Nottingham Rd ISLW TW7 47 P14
LEY E10 39 U4
RKW/CH/CXG WD3 20 G6
SAND/SEL CR2 74 G9
TOOT SW17 61 T6
Nottingham St MHST W1U 3 S9
Nottingham Ter CAMTN NW1 3 S8
Notting Hill Ga NTGHL W11 6 F1
Nova Ms CHEAM SM3 73 L5
Novar Cl ORP BR6 77 P5
Nova Rd CROY/NA CR0 74 F6
Novar Rd ELTH/MOT SE9 65 L6
Novello St FUL/PGN SW6 49 N13
Novello Wy BORE WD6 13 P13
Nowell Rd BARN SW13 48 G11
Nower Hl PIN HA5 34 H2
The Nower BH/WHM TN16 89 P10
RSEV TN14 89 T6
Noyna Rd TOOT SW17 61 T8
Nubia Wy BMLY BR1 64 A9
Nuding Cl LEW SE13 63 S1
Nuffield Rd SWLY BR8 66 G11
Nugent Rd ARCH N19 38 C6
SNWD SE25 74 K1
Nugents Ct PIN HA5 * 22 G13
Nugent's Pk PIN HA5 22 H13
Nugent Ter STJWD NW8 2 K4
Numbers Farm KGLGY WD4 * 10 J3
Nunappleton Wy OXTED RH8 96 C8
Nuneaton Rd DAGW RM9 41 T12
Nunhead Crs PECK SE15 63 M1
Nunhead Gv PECK SE15 63 N1
Nunhead La PECK SE15 63 M1
Nunnington Cl ELTH/MOT SE9 64 G8
Nunn's Rd ENC/FH EN2 15 S14
Nuns Wk VW GU25 68 B3
Nupton Dr BAR EN5 24 J4
Nurse Cl EDGW HA8 24 C13
Nursery Av BXLYHN DA7 65 V1
CROY/NA CR0 75 P7
FNCH N3 25 P14
Nursery Cl ADL/WDHM KT15 68 K14
BROCKY SE4 51 R14
CHDH RM6 41 T4
CROY/NA CR0 75 P7
EBED/NFELT TW14 58 D5
EW KT17 72 E14
KWD/TDW/WH KT20 92 H1
ORP BR6 77 P5
OXHEY WD19 22 D6
PEND EN3 16 D13
PUT/ROE SW15 60 K3
RDART DA2 67 Q5
SEV TN13 90 J12
SWLY BR8 66 C14
WFD IG8 28 D10
WOKN/KNAP GU21 80 A6
Nursery Gdns CHESW EN7 15 T2
CHST BR7 64 K11
HPTN TW12 58 H9
HSLWW TW4 58 H3
PEND EN3 16 D13
STA TW18 57 M12
SUN TW16 58 B14
Nursery La BETH E2 5 U2
DTCH/LGLY SL3 44 A6
FSTGT E7 40 C11
NKENS W10 48 J3
Nurserymans Rd FBAR/BDGN N11 25 U7
Nursery Pl SEV TN13 90 D12
Nursery Rd BRXN/ST SW9 62 D2
EFNCH N2 25 R13
HACK E8 39 N11
KWD/TDW/WH KT20 92 H1
LOU IG10 28 F2
MTCM CR4 73 S1
PIN HA5 34 E1
STHGT/OAK N14 26 A5
SUN TW16 58 A14
SUT SM1 73 Q9
THHTH CR7 74 H2
WIM/MER SW19 61 L12
Nursery Rw BAR EN5 * 25 L1
WALW SE17 9 Q8
Nursery St TOTM N17 26 K12
The Nursery ERITH DA8 54 F12
Nursery Wk HDN NW4 36 H1
Nursery Wy OXTED RH8 * 96 A5
STWL/WRAY TW19 56 B4
Nursery Waye UX/CGN UB8 33 P13
Nurstead Rd ERITH DA8 54 A12
Nutbourne St NKENS W10 2 A5
Nutbrook St PECK SE15 62 K1
Nutbrowne Rd DAGW RM9 41 V13
Nutcroft Gv LHD/OX KT22 83 N12
Nutcroft Rd PECK SE15 51 M12
Nutfield Cl CAR SM5 73 S8
UED N18 27 L11
Nutfield Gdns GDMY/SEVK IG3 41 P7
NTHLT UB5 34 E14
Nutfield Marsh Rd REDH RH1 94 B7
Nutfield Pk REDH RH1 94 E14
Nutfield Rd COUL/CHIP CR5 85 U6
CRICK NW2 36 G7
EDUL SE22 62 K3
REDH RH1 93 V10
REDH RH1 94 A6
SRTFD E15 39 U9
THHTH CR7 74 F2
Nutfields BGR/WK TN15 91 V13
Nutfield Wy ORP BR6 76 J7
Nutford Pl MBLAR W1H 3 P11
Nuthatch Cl STWL/WRAY TW19 57 R6
Nuthatch Gdns REIG RH2 93 Q14
THMD SE28 53 M7
Nuthurst Av BRXS/STRHM SW2 62 D7
Nutley Cl SWLY BR8 66 F13
Nutley La REIG RH2 93 M9
Nutley Ter HAMP NW3 37 R11
Nutmead Cl BXLY DA5 66 C6
Nutmeg Cl CAN/RD E16 52 A2
Nutmeg La POP/IOD E14 51 V4
Nuttall St IS N1 5 T3
Nutter La WAN E11 40 E3
Nuttfield Cl RKW/CH/CXG WD3 * 21 T4
Nutt Gv EDGW HA8 23 T7
Nut Tree Cl ORP BR6 77 T8
Nutt St PECK SE15 9 V13
Nutty La SHPTN TW17 69 U2
Nutwell St TOOT SW17 61 S10
Nutwood Av BRKHM/BTCW RH3 92 C11
Nutwood Cl BRKHM/BTCW RH3 92 C11
Nuxley Rd BELV DA17 53 V11
Nyanza St WOOL/PLUM SE18 53 M11
Nyefield Pk KWD/TDW/WH KT20 92 G2
Nylands Av RCH/KEW TW9 48 A14
Nymans Gdns RYNPK SW20 72 H1
Nynehead St NWCR SE14 51 Q12
Nyon Gv CAT SE6 63 R7
Nyssa Cl WFD IG8 28 H11
Nyth Cl UPMR RM14 43 R4
Nyton Cl ARCH N19 38 C6

O

Oakapple Cl SAND/SEL CR2 87 M4
Oak Av CEND/HSY/T N8 38 C2
CROY/NA CR0 75 S7
EGH TW20 56 H12
ENC/FH EN2 15 P13
HEST TW5 46 F12
HGDN/ICK UB10 33 T7
HPTN TW12 58 G10
LCOL/BKTW AL2 11 U4
MUSWH N10 25 V12
TOTM N17 26 H12
UPMR RM14 43 P8
WDR/YW UB7 45 S8
Oakbank CROY/NA CR0 75 U11
LHD/OX KT22 83 L13
WOKS/MYFD GU22 80 C9
Oakbank Av WOT/HER KT12 70 H5
Oakbank Gv HNHL SE24 62 G2
Oakbrook Cl BMLY BR1 64 D9
Oakbury Rd FUL/PGN SW6 49 P14
Oak Cl DART DA1 66 E2
KWD/TDW/WH KT20 92 B6
STHGT/OAK N14 25 V5
WAB EN9 16 K8
Oakcombe Cl NWMAL KT3 60 E13
Oak Cottage Cl CAT SE6 64 A6
Oak Cottages HNWL W7 * 47 N7
ORP BR6 * 78 B10
Oak Crs CAN/RD E16 52 A3
Oakcroft Cl BF/WBF KT14 80 K4
PIN HA5 22 D14
Oakcroft Rd BF/WBF KT14 80 K4
CHSGTN KT9 71 V9
LEW SE13 51 V14
Oakcroft Vls CHSGTN KT9 71 V9
Oakdale STHGT/OAK N14 25 V6
Oakdale Av KTN/HRWW/WS HA3 35 U3
NTHWD HA6 22 C14
Oakdale Cl OXHEY WD19 22 E9
Oakdale Gdns CHING E4 27 U10
Oakdale La EDEN TN8 97 L9
Oakdale Rd FSBYPK N4 38 G4
FSTGT E7 40 D12
HOR/WEW KT19 72 D13
OXHEY WD19 22 E8
PECK SE15 63 N1
STRHM/NOR SW16 62 C10
SWFD E18 28 D14
WAN E11 39 V7
WEY KT13 69 S8
Oakdale Wy MTCM CR4 73 U5
Oakdene CHES/WCR EN8 16 E4
KWD/TDW/WH KT20 85 L10
WEA W13 47 R3
Oakdene Av CHST BR7 64 J10
ERITH DA8 54 C11
THDIT KT7 71 Q6
Oakdene Cl BRKHM/BTCW RH3 92 C12
Oak Dene Cl EMPK RM11 42 H4
Oakdene Cl PIN HA5 22 H12
Oakdene Dr BRYLDS KT5 72 C6
Oakdene Ms CHEAM SM3 73 M6
Oakdene Pk FNCH N3 25 M12
Oakdene Rd BRKHM/BTCW RH3 92 C13
COB KT11 82 D4
GT/LBKH KT23 82 H14
HGDN/ICK UB10 33 T14
REDH RH1 93 T10
SEV TN13 90 G12
STMC/STPC BR5 77 Q4
WATN WD24 11 P10
Oakden St LBTH SE11 8 K7
Oak Dr KWD/TDW/WH KT20 92 C7
Oaken Coppice ASHTD KT21 84 A9
Oak End Dr IVER SL0 32 G14
Oaken Dr ESH/CLAY KT10 71 P11
Oak End Wy ADL/WDHM KT15 80 K2
CFSP/GDCR SL9 32 D3
Oaken La ESH/CLAY KT10 71 N9
Oakenshaw Cl SURB KT6 71 U5
Oakeshott Av HGT N6 37 U7
Oakey La STHWK SE1 8 J5
Oak Farm BORE WD6 24 C3
Oakfield CHING E4 27 T10
RKW/CH/CXG WD3 21 L5
Oakfield Av KTN/HRWW/WS HA3 35 R1
Oakfield Cl NWMAL KT3 72 F3
POTB/CUF EN6 14 B5
RSLP HA4 34 C4
WEY KT13 69 U9
Oakfield Ct BORE WD6 * 24 B2
Oakfield Dr REIG RH2 93 N8
Oakfield Gdns BECK BR3 75 T3
CAR SM5 73 S6
GFD/PVL UB6 47 M2
UED N18 26 J9
Oakfield Gld WEY KT13 69 U9
Oakfield La HAYES BR2 76 E9
RDART DA2 66 G7
Oakfield Park Rd DART DA1 66 K7
Oakfield Pl DART DA1 66 K7
Oakfield Rd ASHF TW15 57 T10
ASHF TW15 57 T9
ASHTD KT21 83 U8
COB KT11 82 D3
CROY/NA CR0 74 G6
EHAM E6 40 G13
FNCH N3 25 P13
FSBYPK N4 38 E4
IL IG1 40 K8
PGE/AN SE20 63 M13
STHGT/OAK N14 26 C7
WALTH E17 27 Q14
WIM/MER SW19 60 K8
Oakfields BF/WBF KT14 81 M4
WOT/HER KT12 70 C6
Oakfields Rd GLDGN NW11 37 L4
Oakfield St WBPTN SW10 6 J11
Oakford Rd KTTN NW5 38 A9
Oak Gdns CROY/NA CR0 75 S7
EDGW HA8 24 C14
Oak Gld EPP CM16 18 H3
NTHWD HA6 21 T13
Oak Gln EMPK RM11 43 L1
Oak Gn ABLGY WD5 11 M6
Oak Gv CRICK NW2 36 K9
RSLP HA4 34 D6
SUN TW16 58 D12
WWKM BR4 75 U7
Oak Grove Rd PGE/AN SE20 63 N13
Oakhall Dr SUN TW16 58 B10
Oak Hall Rd WAN E11 40 D4
Oakham Cl CAT SE6 * 63 R7
Oakham Dr HAYES BR2 76 C2
Oakhampton Rd MLHL NW7 24 K13
Oak Hl EPSOM KT18 84 D6
Oakhill ESH/CLAY KT10 71 Q11
Oak Hl SURB KT6 71 U5
WFD IG8 27 V12
Oakhill Av HAMP NW3 37 P9
PIN HA5 22 G14
Oakhill Cl ASHTD KT21 83 S8
RKW/CH/CXG WD3 20 J9
Oak Hill Crs SURB KT6 71 U5
WFD IG8 28 A12
Oakhill Gdns WEY KT13 70 A7
Oak Hill Gdns WFD IG8 28 A13
Oak Hill Gv SURB KT6 71 U4
Oak Hill Pk HAMP NW3 37 P9
Oak Hill Park Ms HAMP NW3 37 Q9
Oakhill Pl PUT/ROE SW15 61 N3
Oak Hill Rd ABR/ST RM4 30 E6
SURB KT6 * 71 U4
Oakhill Rd ADL/WDHM KT15 68 K11
ASHTD KT21 83 S8
BECK BR3 63 U14
ORP BR6 77 P7
PUR RM19 55 P10
PUT/ROE SW15 61 M3
REIG RH2 93 P11
RKW/CH/CXG WD3 20 H9
STRHM/NOR SW16 62 C13
SUT SM1 73 P8
Oak Hill Wy HAMP NW3 37 Q8
Oakhouse Rd BXLYHS DA6 66 A3
Oakhurst Av BXLYHN DA7 53 U12
EBAR EN4 25 S5
Oakhurst Cl BARK/HLT IG6 29 L13
CHST BR7 64 H13
TEDD TW11 59 N10
WALTH E17 40 A2
Oakhurst Gdns BXLYHN DA7 53 U12
CHING E4 28 B6
WALTH E17 40 A2
Oakhurst Gv EDUL SE22 63 L2
Oakhurst Pl WATW WD18 * 22 B2
Oakhurst Ri CAR SM5 73 S14
Oakhurst Rd HOR/WEW KT19 72 C11
PEND EN3 16 D10
Oakington Av HYS/HAR UB3 45 V9
RYLN/HDSTN HA2 34 J5
WBLY HA9 35 V8
Oakington Cl SUN TW16 58 E14
Oakington Dr SUN TW16 58 E14
Oakington Manor Dr WBLY HA9 36 A10
Oakington Rd MV/WKIL W9 2 F7
Oakington Wy CEND/HSY/T N8 38 C4
Oakland Pl BKHH IG9 28 C7
Oakland Rd SRTFD E15 40 A9
Oaklands GDST RH9 95 Q14
LHD/OX KT22 83 M14
PUR/KEN CR8 86 G4
WCHMH N21 26 D7
Oaklands Av BFN/LL DA15 65 P5
BRKMPK AL9 14 A1
ED N9 27 M4
ESH/CLAY KT10 71 M6
ISLW TW7 47 P11
OXHEY WD19 22 D6
ROM RM1 42 E1
THHTH CR7 74 E2
WWKM BR4 75 T8
Oaklands Cl ALP/SUD HA0 35 T10
BGR/WK TN15 79 S11
BXLYHS DA6 65 V3
CHSGTN KT9 71 S9
STMC/STPC BR5 77 N4
Oaklands Ct ADL/WDHM KT15 69 M8
WAT WD17 11 N13
Oaklands Dr REDH RH1 93 V12
WHTN TW2 59 L5
Oaklands Gdns PUR/KEN CR8 86 G4
Oaklands Ga NTHWD HA6 22 A11
Oaklands Gv SHB W12 48 G6
Oaklands La BAR EN5 24 H2
BH/WHM TN16 88 E5
Oaklands Ms CRICK NW2 36 K9
Oaklands Park Av IL IG1 41 L7
Oaklands Pl CLAP SW4 62 B2
Oaklands Rd BMLY BR1 64 A12
BXLYHS DA6 65 V2
CRICK NW2 36 K9
HNWL W7 47 P7
MORT/ESHN SW14 60 D1
RDART DA2 67 Q6
TRDG/WHET N20 25 M5
Oaklands Wy KWD/TDW/WH KT20 84 J12
WLGTN SM6 74 B12
Oakland Wy HOR/WEW KT19 72 E11
Oak La EFNCH N2 25 R14
EGH TW20 56 A8
FBAR/BDGN N11 26 B11
ISLW TW7 59 N2
POP/IOD E14 51 R5
POTB/CUF EN6 15 P2
WFD IG8 28 B9
WOKS/MYFD GU22 80 F6
Oaklawn Rd LHD/OX KT22 83 N8
Oak Leaf Cl HOR/WEW KT19 84 C2
Oakleafe Gdns BARK/HLT IG6 40 K1
Oakleigh Av EDGW HA8 24 B14
SURB KT6 72 A6
TRDG/WHET N20 25 R6
Oakleigh Cl SWLY BR8 78 E1
TRDG/WHET N20 25 T8
Oakleigh Ct EDGW HA8 * 24 C14
OXTED RH8 * 96 A5
Oakleigh Crs TRDG/WHET N20 25 S8
Oakleigh Dr RKW/CH/CXG WD3 21 U4
Oakleigh Gdns EDGW HA8 23 V10
ORP BR6 77 N9
TRDG/WHET N20 25 Q6
Oakleigh Ms TRDG/WHET N20 25 R7
Oakleigh Park Av CHST BR7 64 J14

Pepper Cl CTHM CR3 94 J1
EHAM E6 52 H3
Peppercorn Cl THHTH CR7 62 H14
Peppermead Sq LEW SE13 63 S3
Peppermint Cl CROY/NA CR0 74 C5
Peppermint Pl WAN E11 40 A8
Pepper St POP/IOD E14 51 T8
STHWK SE1 9 N3
Peppie Cl STNW/STAM N16 38 J7
Pepys Cl ASHTD KT21 84 A7
DTCH/LGLY SL3 44 F11
HGDN/ICK UB10 33 T9
Pepys Crs BAR EN5 24 J3
CAN/RD E16 52 C6
Pepys Est DEPT SE8 51 Q9
Pepys Park Est DEPT SE8 51 R9
Pepys Ri ORP BR6 77 P6
Pepys Rd NWCR SE14 51 P14
RYNPK SW20 60 J14
Pepys St TWRH EC3N 5 T13
Perceval Av HAMP NW3 37 S10
Percheron Rd BORE WD6 24 D4
Perch St HACK E8 38 K9
Percival Cl LHD/OX KT22 82 K1
Percival Ct TOTM N17 26 K12
Percival Gdns CHDH RM6 41 S4
Percival Rd EMPK RM11 42 J4
EN EN1 26 K2
FELT TW13 58 B7
MORT/ESHN SW14 60 C3
ORP BR6 76 K7
Percival St FSBYE EC1V 5 L7
Percival Wy HOR/WEW KT19 72 C9
Percy Av ASHF TW15 57 S10
Percy Bryant Rd SUN TW16 58 A12
Percy Bush Rd WDR/YW UB7 45 R8
Percy Gdns PEND EN3 27 P3
WPK KT4 72 D6
YEAD UB4 46 A1
Percy Ms FITZ W1T 4 C10
Percy Rd BXLYHN DA7 53 U14
CAN/RD E16 52 A3
GDMY/SEVK IG3 41 Q5
HPTN TW12 58 J12
ISLW TW7 59 Q2
MTCM CR4 73 U5
NFNCH/WDSPK N12 25 Q10
PGE/AN SE20 63 P13
ROMW/RG RM7 42 C1
SHB W12 48 G7
SNWD SE25 74 K3
WAN E11 40 A5
WATW WD18 22 D2
WCHMH N21 26 G5
WHTN TW2 58 K6
Percy St FITZ W1T 4 C10
Percy Wy WHTN TW2 59 L6
Peregrine Cl GSTN WD25 11 S8
WLSDN NW10 36 D10
Peregrine Ct WELL DA16 53 P13
Peregrine Gdns CROY/NA CR0 75 Q7
Peregrine Rd BARK/HLT IG6 29 R10
SUN TW16 58 A14
TOTM N17 26 G12
Peregrine Wy WIM/MER SW19 60 J12
Peregrin Rd WAB EN9 17 N8
Perham Rd WKENS W14 6 C10
Peridot St EHAM E6 52 G3
Perifield DUL SE21 62 G6
Perimeade Rd ALP/SUD HA0 35 S14
Periton Rd ELTH/MOT SE9 64 F2
Perivale Gdns GSTN WD25 11 P8
WEA W13 47 R2
Perivale La GFD/PVL UB6 47 Q1
Perivale Village GFD/PVL UB6 * 47 S1
Perkin Cl ALP/SUD HA0 35 R10
HSLW TW3 58 K2
Perkins Cl RDART DA2 67 T3
Perkin's Rents WEST SW1P 8 C5
Perkins Rd BARK/HLT IG6 41 M3
Perkins Sq STHWK SE1 9 P1
Perks Cl BKHTH/KID SE3 52 A14
Permain Cl RAD WD7 12 J7
Perpins Rd ELTH/MOT SE9 65 N4
Perran Rd BRXS/STRHM SW2 62 F7
Perrers Rd HMSMTH W6 48 H8
Perrin Cl ASHF TW15 57 R10
Perrin Ct WOKN/KNAP GU21 80 F5
Perrin Rd ALP/SUD HA0 35 R9
Perrin's Ct HAMP NW3 * 37 Q9
Perrin's Wk HAMP NW3 37 Q9
Perriors Cl CHESW EN7 16 A1
Perry Av ACT W3 48 D4
Perry Cl RAIN RM13 42 D14
UX/CGN UB8 45 T4
Perry Ct SEVS/STOTM N15 * 38 J4
Perryfield Wy CDALE/KGS NW9 36 F4
RCHPK/HAM TW10 59 R8
Perry Gdns ED N9 26 J8
Perry Garth NTHLT UB5 34 E13
Perry Gv DART DA1 67 N2
Perry Hall Cl ORP BR6 77 Q5
Perry Hall Rd ORP BR6 77 Q5
Perry Hl CAT SE6 63 R7
Perry How WPK KT4 72 F6
Perry Mnr CHST BR7 65 N11
Perrymans Farm Rd GNTH/NBYPK IG2 41 M4
Perry Md BUSH WD23 23 L5
ENC/FH EN2 15 R14
Perrymead St FUL/PGN SW6 49 N13
Perryn Rd ACT W3 48 D5
BERM/RHTH SE16 51 M8
Perry Oak Dr HTHAIR TW6 45 M14
Perry Ri FSTH SE23 63 Q8
Perry Rd DAGW RM9 53 V3
DAGW RM9 54 A3
Perrysfield Rd CHES/WCR EN8 16 E1
Perrys La ORP BR6 89 R3
Perry St CHST BR7 65 N11
DART DA1 66 E1
Perry V FSTH SE23 63 N7
Perry Wy SOCK/AV RM15 55 Q5
Persant Rd CAT SE6 64 A8
Perseverance Pl BRXN/ST SW9 8 K14
Persfield Cl EW KT17 72 G14
Persfield Ms EW KT17 * 72 F14
Pershore Cl GNTH/NBYPK IG2 40 K3
Pershore Gv CAR SM5 73 R4
Pert Cl MUSWH N10 25 V12
Perth Av CDALE/KGS NW9 36 D5
YEAD UB4 46 E2
Perth Cl NTHLT UB5 34 J11
NWMAL KT3 60 F14
Perth Rd BARK IG11 41 M14
BECK BR3 63 U14
FSBYPK N4 38 E6
GNTH/NBYPK IG2 40 K4
LEY E10 39 Q6
PLSTW E13 40 D14
WDGN N22 26 F13
Perth Ter GNTH/NBYPK IG2 41 L5
Perwell Av RYLN/HDSTN HA2 34 H6
Petauel Rd TEDD TW11 59 N11
Petavel Rd TEDD TW11 59 N11
Peter Av OXTED RH8 95 V5
WLSDN NW10 36 H12
Peterboat Cl GNWCH SE10 52 A9
Peterborough Av UPMR RM14 43 S6
Peterborough Ms FUL/PGN SW6 49 N14
Peterborough Rd CAR SM5 73 S4
FUL/PGN SW6 49 N14
HRW HA1 35 N6
LEY E10 39 U3
Peterborough Vls FUL/PGN SW6 49 P13
Petergate BTSEA SW11 61 Q2
Peterhead Ms DTCH/LGLY SL3 44 E10
Peterhill Cl CFSP/GDCR SL9 20 C10
Peters Cl BCTR RM8 41 T6
STAN HA7 23 T11
WELL DA16 53 N14
Petersfield Av HARH RM3 31 L11
STA TW18 57 N11
Petersfield Cl HARH RM3 31 N11
UED N18 26 G10
Petersfield Crs COUL/CHIP CR5 86 C5
Petersfield Ri PUT/ROE SW15 60 H6
Petersfield Rd ACT W3 48 C7
STA TW18 57 N10
Petersham Av BF/WBF KT14 81 Q2
Petersham Cl BF/WBF KT14 81 Q2
RCHPK/HAM TW10 59 T7
SUT SM1 73 N10
Petersham Dr STMC/STPC BR5 65 P14
Petersham La SKENS SW7 6 J5
Petersham Ms SKENS SW7 6 J6
Petersham Pl SKENS SW7 6 J6
Petersham Rd RCHPK/HAM TW10 59 T8
Petersham Ter CROY/NA CR0 * 74 C8
Peter's Hl BLKFR EC4V 5 N13
Petersmead Cl KWD/TDW/WH KT20 84 J13
Peterstone Rd ABYW SE2 53 R7
Peterstow Cl WIM/MER SW19 61 L7
Peter St SOHO/CST W1F 4 C13
Peterwood Wy CROY/NA CR0 74 D7
Petherton Rd HBRY N5 38 G10
Petiver Cl HOM E9 * 39 N12
Petley Rd HMSMTH W6 48 J11
Peto Pl CAMTN NW1 3 V7
Peto St North CAN/RD E16 52 B4
Petrie Cl CRICK NW2 * 37 L11
Petros Gdns KIL/WHAMP NW6 * 37 P10
Petro St South CAN/RD E16 52 B5
Pettacre Cl THMD SE28 53 L8
Pett Cl EMPK RM11 42 H7
Petten Cl STMC/STPC BR5 77 T6
Petten Gv STMC/STPC BR5 77 S6
Petters Rd ASHTD KT21 83 V6
Petticoat La WCHPL E1 5 T10
Petticoat Sq WCHPL E1 5 U11
Petticoat Tower WCHPL E1 * 5 U11
Pettits Bvd ROM RM1 30 E14
Pettits Cl ROM RM1 30 E14
Pettits La ROM RM1 30 E14
ROM RM1 42 E1
Pettits La North ROM RM1 30 E13
Pettit's Pl DAGE RM10 42 A10
Pettit's Rd DAGE RM10 42 A10
Pettiward Cl PUT/ROE SW15 60 J2
Pettley Gdns ROMW/RG RM7 42 D3
Pettman Crs THMD SE28 53 M8
Pettsgrove Av ALP/SUD HA0 35 S10
Pett's Hl RYLN/HDSTN HA2 34 K9
Petts La SHPTN TW17 69 S2
Pett St WOOL/PLUM SE18 52 G9
Petts Wood Rd STMC/STPC BR5 77 N3
Petty France WESTW SW1E 8 B5
Pettys Cl CHES/WCR EN8 16 D3
Petty Wales MON EC3R 5 T14
Petworth Cl COUL/CHIP CR5 86 A9
NTHLT UB5 34 H12
Petworth Gdns HGDN/ICK UB10 33 U13
RYNPK SW20 72 H1
Petworth Rd BXLYHS DA6 66 A3
NFNCH/WDSPK N12 25 S10
Petworth St BTSEA SW11 49 S13
Petworth Wy HCH RM12 42 F9
Petyt Pl CHEL SW3 7 N12
Petyward CHEL SW3 7 P8
Pevensey Av EN EN1 15 U14
FBAR/BDGN N11 26 B10
Pevensey Cl ISLW TW7 47 L12
Pevensey Rd FELT TW13 58 G6
FSTGT E7 40 C9
TOOT SW17 61 R9
Peverel EHAM E6 52 J4
Peveret Cl FBAR/BDGN N11 * 25 V10
Peveril Dr TEDD TW11 59 M10
Pewsey Cl CHING E4 27 S10
Peyton Pl GNWCH SE10 51 U12
Pharaoh Cl MTCM CR4 73 T5
Pheasant Cl CAN/RD E16 52 D4
PUR/KEN CR8 86 F3
Pheasant Hl CSTG HP8 20 A7
Pheasants Wy RKW/CH/CXG WD3 21 M5
Pheasant Wk CFSP/GDCR SL9 20 B9
Phelps Cl BGR/WK TN15 79 S11
Phelp St WALW SE17 9 Q11
Phelps Wy HYS/HAR UB3 46 B9
Phene St CHEL SW3 7 P11
Philanthropic Rd REDH RH1 93 V12
Philan Wy CRW RM5 30 D11
Philbeach Gdns ECT SW5 6 E9
Philchurch Pl WCHPL E1 51 L4
Philimore Cl WOOL/PLUM SE18 53 N10
Philip Av ROMW/RG RM7 42 D6
Philip Cl BRWN CM15 31 V4
Philip Gdns CROY/NA CR0 75 R7
Philip La SEVS/STOTM N15 38 H2
Philippa Gdns ELTH/MOT SE9 64 F3
Philip Rd RAIN RM13 54 E1
STA TW18 57 P11
Philips Cl CAR SM5 73 U6
Philip St PLSTW E13 52 C2
Philip Wk PECK SE15 63 L1
Phillida Rd HARH RM3 31 N14
Phillimore Ct RAD WD7 * 12 C10
Phillimore Gdns KENS W8 6 E4
WLSDN NW10 36 J13
Phillimore Gardens Cl KENS W8 * 6 E5
Phillimore Pl KENS W8 6 E4
RAD WD7 12 C10
Phillimore Wk KENS W8 6 E5
Phillip Av SWLY BR8 78 D2
Phillipers GSTN WD25 11 R10
Phillipp St IS N1 5 T2
Phillips Cl DART DA1 66 H4
Philpot La CHOB/PIR GU24 80 A2
FENCHST EC3M 5 S13
Philpots Cl WDR/YW UB7 45 P5
Philpot St WCHPL E1 * 51 M4
Phineas Pett Rd ELTH/MOT SE9 64 G1
Phipp's Bridge Rd MTCM CR4 61 Q14
WIM/MER SW19 73 Q1
Phipps Hatch La ENC/FH EN2 15 S12
Phipp's Ms BGVA SW1W 7 U6
Phipp St SDTCH EC2A 5 S7
Phoebeth Rd LEW SE13 63 S3
Phoenix Cl HACK E8 * 5 U1
HOR/WEW KT19 84 A2
NTHWD HA6 22 B9
WALTH E17 27 R14
WWKM BR4 75 V7
WWKM BR4 76 A7
Phoenix Ct BTFD TW8 47 U10
POP/IOD E14 51 S9
Phoenix Dr HAYES BR2 76 F9
Phoenix Pk BTFD TW8 * 47 T10
Phoenix Pl DART DA1 66 K5
FSBYW WC1X 4 H7
Phoenix Rd CAMTN NW1 4 C5
PGE/AN SE20 63 N11
Phoenix St LSQ/SEVD WC2H 4 D12
Phoenix Wy HEST TW5 46 F11
Phoenix Wharf Rd STHWK SE1 9 V4
The Phygtle CFSP/GDCR SL9 20 C11
Phyllis Av NWMAL KT3 72 H3
Picardy Manorway BELV DA17 54 B8
Picardy Rd BELV DA17 54 A9
Picardy St BELV DA17 54 A8
Piccadilly MYFR/PICC W1J 8 A1
Piccadilly Ar MYFR/PICC W1J 8 A1
Piccadilly Circ REGST W1B 4 B14
Pickard Cl STHGT/OAK N14 26 B6
Pickard St FSBYE EC1V 5 M5
Pickering Av EHAM E6 40 J14
Pickering Gdns CROY/NA CR0 74 K4
FBAR/BDGN N11 25 U11
Pickering Ms BAY/PAD W2 2 H11
Pickering Pl WHALL SW1A * 8 B2
Pickering St IS N1 5 M1
Pickets Cl BUSH WD23 23 M6
Pickets St BAL SW12 61 U5
Pickett Cft STAN HA7 23 T13
Pickett's Lock La ED N9 27 N7
Pickford Cl BXLYHN DA7 53 U14
Pickford Dr DTCH/LGLY SL3 44 D6
Pickford La BXLYHN DA7 53 U14
Pickford Rd BXLYHN DA7 65 U1
Pickfords Whf IS N1 * 5 N4
Pick Hl WAB EN9 17 N6
Pickhurst Gn HAYES BR2 76 B5
Pickhurst La WWKM BR4 76 B4
Pickhurst Md HAYES BR2 76 B5
Pickhurst Pk HAYES BR2 76 A4
Pickhurst Ri WWKM BR4 75 V6
Pickins Piece DTCH/LGLY SL3 44 E14
Pickmoss La RSEV TN14 90 G6
Pickwick Cl HSLWW TW4 58 G3
Pickwick Ms UED N18 26 J10
Pickwick Pl HRW HA1 35 N5
Pickwick Rd DUL SE21 62 H5
Pickwick St STHWK SE1 9 N4
Pickwick Wy CHST BR7 65 L11
Picquets Wy BNSTD SM7 85 M7
Picton Mt WARL CR6 87 L9
Picton Pl MHST W1U 3 T12
Picton St CMBW SE5 9 R14
Pied Bull Yd IS N1 5 L2
Piedmont Rd WOOL/PLUM SE18 53 M10
Pield Heath Av UX/CGN UB8 45 S2
Pield Heath Rd UX/CGN UB8 45 S3
Piercing Hl EPP CM16 18 B9
Pier Head WAP E1W * 51 M6
Piermont Pl BMLY BR1 64 F14
Piermont Rd EDUL SE22 63 M3
Pierrepoint Ar IS N1 * 5 L3
Pierrepoint Rd ACT W3 48 B5
Pierrepoint Rw IS N1 5 L3
Pier Rd CAN/RD E16 52 H7
EBED/NFELT TW14 58 D3
ERITH DA8 54 E11
SWCM DA10 67 V2
Pier St POP/IOD E14 51 U9
Pier Ter WAND/EARL SW18 61 Q2
Pier Wy THMD SE28 53 M8
Pigeonhouse La COUL/CHIP CR5 93 Q1
Pigeon La HPTN TW12 58 J9
Piggy La RKW/CH/CXG WD3 20 F4
Pigott St POP/IOD E14 51 S4
Pike Cl BMLY BR1 64 D10
HGDN/ICK UB10 33 R13
Pike La UPMR RM14 43 T10
Pike Rd MLHL NW7 24 D9
Pike's End PIN HA5 34 D2
Pikes Hl EW KT17 84 E3
Pikestone Cl YEAD UB4 * 46 G2
Pike Wy EPP CM16 19 L1
Pilgrimage St STHWK SE1 9 Q4
Pilgrim Cl GSTN WD25 11 R7
LCOL/BKTW AL2 12 A1
MRDN SM4 73 P5
Pilgrim Hl WNWD SE27 62 G9
Pilgrims Cl BRWN CM15 31 T3
NTHLT UB5 35 L10
PLMGR N13 26 D9
Pilgrims Ct DART DA1 67 N3
Pilgrim's La BRW CM14 31 S2
CTHM CR3 94 D2
HAMP NW3 37 R9
OXTED RH8 88 E14
Pilgrims Ms POP/IOD E14 51 V5
Pilgrims Pl ASHF TW15 * 57 R9
REIG RH2 93 N8
Pilgrim's Ri EBAR EN4 25 S3
Pilgrim St BLKFR EC4V * 5 L12
Pilgrims Wy ARCH N19 38 B6
BGR/WK TN15 91 M6
BH/WHM TN16 88 K13
DART DA1 67 P6
REIG RH2 93 N8
SAND/SEL CR2 74 K11
WBLY HA9 36 B6
Pilgrims Wy East RSEV TN14 90 K6
Pilgrims Wy West RSEV TN14 90 F6
Pilkington Rd ORP BR6 77 L8
PECK SE15 51 M14
Pillar Box La BGR/WK TN15 91 S12
Pilot Cl DEPT SE8 51 R11
Pilsden Cl WIM/MER SW19 * 60 K6
Piltdown Rd OXHEY WD19 22 F9
Pilton Pl WALW SE17 9 P9
Pimlico Rd BGVA SW1W 7 T9
Pinchbeck Rd ORP BR6 77 P11
Pinchfield RKW/CH/CXG WD3 20 H10
Pinchin & Johnsons Yd WCHPL E1 * 51 L5
Pinchin St WCHPL E1 51 L5
Pincott Pl BROCKY SE4 63 P1
Pincott Rd BXLYHS DA6 66 A3
WIM/MER SW19 61 Q13
Pindar St SDTCH EC2A 5 S9
Pindock Ms MV/WKIL W9 2 H8
Pine Apple Ct WESTW SW1E * 8 A5
Pine Av SRTFD E15 39 V10
WWKM BR4 75 T6
Pine Cl ADL/WDHM KT15 81 M1
CHES/WCR EN8 16 C2
LEY E10 39 S7
PGE/AN SE20 63 N13
PUR/KEN CR8 86 G7
STAN HA7 23 R9
STHGT/OAK N14 26 A5
SWLY BR8 78 F2
WOKN/KNAP GU21 80 A7
Pine Coombe CROY/NA CR0 75 P9
Pine Ct UPMR RM14 43 N9
Pine Crs CAR SM5 85 R1
Pinecrest Gdns ORP BR6 76 K9
Pinecroft GPK RM2 42 J2
KTN/HRWW/WS HA3 35 V3
WOOL/PLUM SE18 53 Q12
Pinecroft Crs BAR EN5 25 L2
Pinefield Cl POP/IOD E14 * 51 S5
Pinefields ADL/WDHM KT15 * 69 M9
Pine Gdns BRYLDS KT5 72 A4
RSLP HA4 34 D6
Pine Gld ORP BR6 76 H9
Pine Gv BUSH WD23 11 T13
FSBYPK N4 38 C7
LCOL/BKTW AL2 11 T4
TRDG/WHET N20 25 M6
WEY KT13 69 T10
WIM/MER SW19 61 M10
Pine Grove Ms WEY KT13 * 69 U10
Pine Hl EPSOM KT18 84 D6
Pinehurst RSEV TN14 91 L11
Pinehurst Cl ABLGY WD5 11 L6
KWD/TDW/WH KT20 85 N12
Pinelands Cl BKHTH/KID SE3 * 52 B12
Pinel Cl VW GU25 68 C2
Pinelees Ct MORT/ESHN SW14 * 60 C2
Pinemartin Cl CRICK NW2 36 J8
Pineneedle La SEV TN13 90 H13
Pine Pl BNSTD SM7 84 K4
Pine Rdg CAR SM5 73 U13
Pineridge Cl WEY KT13 70 A9
Pine Rd CRICK NW2 36 J9
FBAR/BDGN N11 25 U7
WOKS/MYFD GU22 80 A10
Pines Av EN EN1 16 C10
Pines Cl NTHWD HA6 22 A11
Pines Rd BMLY BR1 64 G14
The Pines BORE WD6 12 K14
NRWD SE19 * 62 F11
PUR/KEN CR8 86 F3
STHGT/OAK N14 26 A3
SUN TW16 70 C1
WFD IG8 28 C8
WOKN/KNAP GU21 80 D4
Pine St CLKNW EC1R 4 J7
Pinetree Cl CFSP/GDCR SL9 20 A12
Pine Tree Cl HEST TW5 46 D13
Pine Tree Hl WOKS/MYFD GU22 80 H6
Pine Trees STA TW18 * 56 J10
Pine Trees Dr HGDN/ICK UB10 33 Q9
Pine Wk BELMT SM2 73 R14
BNSTD SM7 85 T7
BRYLDS KT5 72 A4
COB KT11 82 F4
CTHM CR3 86 J12
Pine Wd SUN TW16 58 C13
Pinewood Av ADL/WDHM KT15 69 N13
BFN/LL DA15 65 N6
PIN HA5 22 K11
RAIN RM13 54 H2
RSEV TN14 90 K11
UX/CGN UB8 45 R4
Pinewood Cl BORE WD6 13 P13
CFSP/GDCR SL9 32 C5
CROY/NA CR0 75 Q8
IVER SL0 32 G12
NTHWD HA6 22 C10
ORP BR6 77 M6
PIN HA5 22 K11
WAT WD17 11 N13
WOKN/KNAP GU21 80 E5
Pinewood Dr ORP BR6 77 N10
POTB/CUF EN6 14 B5
STA TW18 * 57 L10
Pinewood Gn IVER SL0 32 G12
Pinewood Gv ADL/WDHM KT15 69 M14
EA W5 47 S4
Pinewood Ldg BUSH WD23 * 23 M6
Pinewood Ms STWL/WRAY TW19 57 P4
Pinewood Pk ADL/WDHM KT15 81 M1
Pinewood Pl RDART DA2 66 E7
Pinewood Rd ABR/ST RM4 30 C9
ABYW SE2 53 T11
FELT TW13 58 D8
HAYES BR2 76 C2
IVER SL0 32 F11
Pinfold Rd BUSH WD23 11 T14
STRHM/NOR SW16 62 C9
Pinglestone Cl WDR/YW UB7 45 Q12
Pinkcoat Cl FELT TW13 58 D8
Pinkham Wy North Circular Rd
NFNCH/WDSPK N12 25 T12
Pinks Hl SWLY BR8 78 E3
Pinkwell Av HYS/HAR UB3 45 V9
Pinkwell La HYS/HAR UB3 45 V9
Pinley Gdns DAGW RM9 41 R13
Pinnacle Hl BXLYHN DA7 66 B2
Pinnacle Hl North BXLYHN DA7 66 B1
Pinnacles WAB EN9 17 L8
Pinn Cl UX/CGN UB8 45 P4
Pinnell Rd ELTH/MOT SE9 64 F2
Pinner Ct PIN HA5 34 J2
Pinner Gn PIN HA5 22 E14
Pinner Gv PIN HA5 34 G2
Pinner Hl PIN HA5 22 E12
Pinner Hill Rd PIN HA5 22 E14
Pinner Park Av RYLN/HDSTN HA2 23 L14
Pinner Park Gdns RYLN/HDSTN HA2 23 L14
Pinner Rd NTHWD HA6 22 C14
OXHEY WD19 22 F4
PIN HA5 34 H2
Pinner Vw RYLN/HDSTN HA2 35 L2
Pinn Wy RSLP HA4 33 V5
Pinstone Wy CFSP/GDCR SL9 32 F7
Pintail Cl EHAM E6 52 G3
Pintail Rd WFD IG8 28 D12
Pintail Wy YEAD UB4 46 F3
Pinto Cl BORE WD6 * 24 D4
Pinto Wy BKHTH/KID SE3 64 D2
Pioneer Cl SHB W12 48 H4
Pioneer St PECK SE15 51 L13
Pioneer Wy SHB W12 48 J4
SWLY BR8 78 E1
WATW WD18 22 B4
Piper Cl HOLWY N7 38 D11
Piper Rd KUT/HW KT1 72 A1
Pipers Cl COB KT11 82 F5
Piper's End VW GU25 68 B1
Pipers Gdns CROY/NA CR0 75 Q5
Pipers Gn CDALE/KGS NW9 36 C3
Pipers Green La STAN HA7 23 U8
Piper's Green Rd BH/WHM TN16 97 Q4
Pipers La BH/WHM TN16 97 R3
Piper Wy IL IG1 41 M6
Pipewell Rd CAR SM5 73 S4
Pippin Cl CRICK NW2 36 G8
CROY/NA CR0 75 R6
RAD WD7 12 J7
Pippins Cl WDR/YW UB7 45 P8
Pippins Ct ASHF TW15 57 T11
The Pippins DTCH/LGLY SL3 44 D6
GSTN WD25 * 11 Q8
Piquet Rd PGE/AN SE20 63 N14
Pirbright Crs CROY/NA CR0 75 U11
Pirbright Rd WAND/EARL SW18 61 M6
Pirie St CAN/RD E16 52 D6
Pitcairn Cl ROMW/RG RM7 42 A2
Pitcairn Rd MTCM CR4 61 T12
Pitchfont La OXTED RH8 96 C2
WARL CR6 88 B14
Pitchford St SRTFD E15 39 V12
Pitfield Crs THMD SE28 53 Q6
Pitfield St IS N1 5 S3
Pitfield Wy PEND EN3 16 C13
WLSDN NW10 36 C11
Pitfold Rd LEE/GVPK SE12 64 C5
Pitlake CROY/NA CR0 74 F7
Pitman St CMBW SE5 9 N13
Pitsea Pl WCHPL E1 51 P4
Pitsea St WCHPL E1 51 P4
Pitshanger La EA W5 47 R2
Pitson Cl ADL/WDHM KT15 69 P9
Pitt Crs WIM/MER SW19 61 P9
Pittman Gdns IL IG1 41 L10
Pitt Pl EW KT17 * 84 E4
Pitt Rd EW KT17 84 E4
ORP BR6 77 L9
RYLN/HDSTN HA2 35 L7
THHTH CR7 74 G3
Pitts Head Ms MYFR/PICC W1J 7 U3
Pittsmead Av HAYES BR2 76 C5
Pitt St KENS W8 6 F3
Pittville Gdns SNWD SE25 75 L1
Pit Wood Gn KWD/TDW/WH KT20 84 J10
Pixley St POP/IOD E14 51 R4
Pixton Wy CROY/NA CR0 75 R12
Place Farm Av ORP BR6 77 N6
Place Farm Rd REDH RH1 94 H7
Placehouse La COUL/CHIP CR5 86 D9
The Plain EPP CM16 18 F3
Plaistow Gv BMLY BR1 64 D12
SRTFD E15 40 B13
Plaistow La BMLY BR1 64 C12
Plaistow Park Rd PLSTW E13 40 D14
Plaistow Rd PLSTW E13 40 C14
Plaitford Cl RKW/CH/CXG WD3 21 Q7
The Planes CHERT KT16 69 N5
Plane St SYD SE26 63 M8
Plane Tree Crs FELT TW13 58 D8
Plantaganet Pl WAB EN9 16 H7
Plantagenet Cl WPK KT4 72 D9
Plantagenet Gdns CHDH RM6 41 T5
Plantagenet Pl CHDH RM6 41 T5
Plantagenet Rd BAR EN5 25 Q2
Plantain Gdns WAN E11 * 39 V8
Plantain Pl STHWK SE1 9 Q3
Plantation Cl RDART DA2 67 T4
Plantation Dr STMC/STPC BR5 77 T6
Plantation La FENCHST EC3M 5 S13
WARL CR6 87 Q9
Plantation Rd ERITH DA8 54 G13
SWLY BR8 66 G12
The Plantation BKHTH/KID SE3 52 C14
Plashet Gv EHAM E6 40 E13
Plashet Rd PLSTW E13 40 C13
Plassy Rd CAT SE6 63 T5
Platford Gn EMPK RM11 43 L2
Platina St SDTCH EC2A 5 R7
Plato Rd BRXS/STRHM SW2 62 C2
Platt's La HAMP NW3 37 N8
Platts Rd PEND EN3 16 C13
Platt St CAMTN NW1 4 C3
Plawsfield Rd BECK BR3 63 P13
Plaxtol Cl BMLY BR1 64 E13
Plaxtol Rd ERITH DA8 54 A12
Playfair St HMSMTH W6 * 48 J10
Playfield Av CRW RM5 30 C13
Playfield Crs EDUL SE22 62 J3
Playfield Rd EDGW HA8 24 C14
Playford Rd FSBYPK N4 38 D7
Playgreen Wy CAT SE6 63 S9
Playground Cl BECK BR3 63 P14
Playhouse Ct STHWK SE1 9 N3
Playhouse Yd BLKFR EC4V 5 L12
Plaza Pde ALP/SUD HA0 * 35 U11
Plaza Wk CDALE/KGS NW9 36 C1
Pleasance Rd PUT/ROE SW15 60 H3
STMC/STPC BR5 65 R14
The Pleasance PUT/ROE SW15 60 H2
Pleasant Gv CROY/NA CR0 75 R8
Pleasant Pl IS N1 38 F12
RKW/CH/CXG WD3 * 20 J12
WOT/HER KT12 70 F11
Pleasant Vw ERITH DA8 54 E10
ORP BR6 77 L10
Pleasant Wy ALP/SUD HA0 35 S14
Pleasure Pit Rd ASHTD KT21 84 B8
Plender St CAMTN NW1 4 A2
Pleshey Rd ARCH N19 38 B9
Plesman Wy WLGTN SM6 * 74 C13
Plevna Crs SEVS/STOTM N15 38 J4
Plevna Rd ED N9 27 L8
HPTN TW12 58 K13
Plevna St POP/IOD E14 51 U8
Pleydell Av HMSMTH W6 48 F8
NRWD SE19 62 K12
Pleydell Est FSBYE EC1V 5 P6
Pleydell Gdns NRWD SE19 * 62 K11
Pleydell St EMB EC4Y 4 K12
Plimsoll Cl POP/IOD E14 51 T4
Plimsoll Rd FSBYPK N4 38 F8
Plough Farm Cl RSLP HA4 33 V4
Plough Hl POTB/CUF EN6 15 N4
Plough La COB KT11 82 C6
CROY/NA CR0 74 C9
DEN/HRF UB9 21 N11
EDUL SE22 62 K4
PUR/KEN CR8 74 D14
TEDD TW11 * 59 Q10
WIM/MER SW19 61 P10
Plough Lane Cl WLGTN SM6 74 C10
Ploughmans Cl CAMTN NW1 4 C1
Ploughmans End ISLW TW7 59 M3
Plough Pl FLST/FETLN EC4A 4 K11
Plough Ri UPMR RM14 43 S6
Plough Rd BTSEA SW11 61 R1
HOR/WEW KT19 72 D12
Plough St WCHPL E1 * 51 L4
Plough Ter BTSEA SW11 61 R2
Plough Wy BERM/RHTH SE16 51 P9
Plough Yd SDTCH EC2A 5 T8
Plover Cl STA TW18 56 K8
Plover Gdns UPMR RM14 43 T6
Plover Wy BERM/RHTH SE16 51 Q8
YEAD UB4 46 F4
Plowden Buildings EMB EC4Y * 4 J13
Plowman Cl UED N18 26 H10
Plowman Wy BCTR RM8 41 T6
Plumbers Rw WCHPL E1 51 L3
Plumbridge St GNWCH SE10 * 51 U13
Plum Cl FELT TW13 58 C6
Plum Garth BTFD TW8 47 T9
Plum La WOOL/PLUM SE18 52 K12
Plummer La MTCM CR4 61 T14
Plummer Rd CLAP SW4 62 A4
Plumpton Av HCH RM12 43 M9
Plumpton Wy CAR SM5 73 S8
Plumstead Common Rd
WOOL/PLUM SE18 52 K11
Plumstead High St WOOL/PLUM SE18 53 N9
Plumstead Rd WOOL/PLUM SE18 53 L9
Plumtree Cl DAGE RM10 42 C11
WLGTN SM6 74 B12
Plumtree Ct FLST/FETLN EC4A 4 K11
Plymouth Dr SEV TN13 90 J14
Plymouth Pk SEV TN13 90 J14
Plymouth Rd BMLY BR1 64 D13
CAN/RD E16 52 C4
Plymouth Whf POP/IOD E14 51 V9
Plympton Av KIL/WHAMP NW6 37 M12
Plympton Cl BELV DA17 53 U8
Plympton Pl STJWD NW8 * 3 N8
Plympton Rd KIL/WHAMP NW6 37 M12
Plympton St STJWD NW8 3 N8
Plymstock Rd WELL DA16 53 S12
Pocklington Cl CDALE/KGS NW9 24 E14
Pocock Av WDR/YW UB7 45 R8
Pocock St STHWK SE1 9 L3
Podmore Rd WAND/EARL SW18 61 Q2
Poets Ga CHESW EN7 15 U2
Poet's Rd HBRY N5 38 H10
Poets Wy HRW HA1 35 N2
Pointalls Cl FNCH N3 25 Q14
Point Cl GNWCH SE10 51 U13
Pointer Cl THMD SE28 53 T4
Pointers Cl POP/IOD E14 51 T10
Pointers Rd COB KT11 81 V7
The Pointers ASHTD KT21 83 U10
Point Hl GNWCH SE10 51 U13
Point Pl WBLY HA9 36 B12
Point Pleasant WAND/EARL SW18 61 N2
Point Wharf La BTFD TW8 47 T12
Poland St SOHO/SHAV W1D 4 B11
Polebrook Rd BKHTH/KID SE3 64 E1
Polecroft La CAT SE6 63 R7
Pole Hill Rd CHING E4 27 U5
HGDN/ICK UB10 45 U1
Polesden Gdns RYNPK SW20 60 H14
Polesden La RPLY/SEND GU23 80 K13
Polesteeple Hl BH/WHM TN16 88 F7
Polesworth Rd DAGW RM9 41 V14
Polhill RSEV TN14 90 C5
Police Station Rd WOT/HER KT12 70 E11
Polish War Memorial Rbt RSLP HA4 34 E11
Pollard Av DEN/HRF UB9 32 K4
Pollard Cl CAN/RD E16 52 C5
CHIG IG7 29 Q10
HOLWY N7 38 D10
HOLWY N7 38 D9
Pollard Rd MRDN SM4 73 R3
TRDG/WHET N20 25 S7
WOKS/MYFD GU22 80 F6
Pollard Rw BETH E2 51 L1
Pollards RKW/CH/CXG WD3 20 H10
Pollards Cl CHESW EN7 15 S3
LOU IG10 28 E3
Pollards Crs STRHM/NOR SW16 74 C1
Pollards Hl East STRHM/NOR SW16 74 D1
Pollards Hl North STRHM/NOR SW16 74 D1
Pollards Hl South STRHM/NOR SW16 74 C1
Pollards Hl West STRHM/NOR SW16 74 C1
Pollards Oak Crs OXTED RH8 96 C8
Pollards Oak Rd OXTED RH8 96 C8
Pollard St BETH E2 * 51 L1
Pollards Wood Hl OXTED RH8 96 D7
Pollards Wood Rd OXTED RH8 96 D7
STRHM/NOR SW16 62 C14
Pollen St CONDST W1S 3 V12
Pollitt Dr STJWD NW8 3 L7
Pollyhaugh EYN DA4 79 L8
Polperro Cl ORP BR6 77 P4
Polperro Ms LBTH SE11 8 K7
Polsted Rd CAT SE6 63 R5
Polthorne Gv WOOL/PLUM SE18 53 L9
Polworth Rd STRHM/NOR SW16 62 C10
Polygon Rd CAMTN NW1 4 C4
The Polygon CLAP SW4 * 62 A2
Polytechnic St WOOL/PLUM SE18 52 J9
Pomell Wy WCHPL E1 5 V11
Pomeroy Crs WATN WD24 11 P10
Pomeroy St PECK SE15 51 N12
Pomfret Rd CMBW SE5 62 F1
Pomoja La ARCH N19 38 C7
Pond Cl BKHTH/KID SE3 52 C14
DEN/HRF UB9 21 N14
NFNCH/WDSPK N12 25 S11
WOT/HER KT12 70 C11
Pond Cottage La BECK BR3 75 S6
Ponder St HOLWY N7 * 38 D12
Pond Farm Cl KWD/TDW/WH KT20 84 H14
Pond Farm Est CLPT E5 * 39 N8
Pondfield Rd DAGE RM10 42 B10
HAYES BR2 76 A6
ORP BR6 76 K8
PUR/KEN CR8 86 F6
Pond Gn RSLP HA4 34 A7
Pond Hill Gdns CHEAM SM3 * 73 L11
Pond Lees Cl DAGE RM10 42 D12
Pond Md DUL SE21 62 H4
Pond Piece LHD/OX KT22 82 K3
Pond Pl CHEL SW3 7 N8
Pond Rd BKHTH/KID SE3 64 B1
EGH TW20 56 G11
SRTFD E15 40 A14
Pondside Cl HYS/HAR UB3 45 V12
The Ponds WEY KT13 69 V11
Pond St HAMP NW3 37 S10
Pond Wk UPMR RM14 43 S7
Pond Wy TEDD TW11 59 S11
Pondwood Ri ORP BR6 77 N6
Ponler St WCHPL E1 51 M4
Ponsard Rd WLSDN NW10 48 H1
Ponsford St HOM E9 39 N11
Ponsonby Pl WEST SW1P 8 D9
Ponsonby Rd PUT/ROE SW15 60 H5
Ponsonby Ter WEST SW1P 8 D9
Pontefract Rd BMLY BR1 64 C10
Pontoise Cl SEV TN13 90 F12
Ponton Rd VX/NE SW8 8 C13
Pont St KTBR SW1X 7 Q6
Pont Street Ms KTBR SW1X 7 Q6
Pony Cha COB KT11 82 H3
Pool Cl BECK BR3 63 S10
E/WMO/HCT KT8 70 H3
Pool Ct CAT SE6 63 S7
Poole Cl RSLP HA4 34 A7
Poole Court Rd HSLW TW3 46 G14
Pool End Cl SHPTN TW17 69 S3
Poole Rd EMPK RM11 43 M5
HOM E9 39 P11
HOR/WEW KT19 72 D11
WOKN/KNAP GU21 80 C8
Pooles Buildings FSBYW WC1X 4 J8
Pooles La WBPTN SW10 6 J14
Pooles Pk FSBYPK N4 38 E7
Poole St IS N1 5 Q2
Poole Wy YEAD UB4 * 46 A1
Pooley Av EGH TW20 56 F10
Pooley Dr MORT/ESHN SW14 60 C1
Pooley Green Rd EGH TW20 56 G11
Poolmans St BERM/RHTH SE16 51 P7
Pool Rd E/WMO/HCT KT8 70 H3
HRW HA1 35 M5
Poolsford Rd CDALE/KGS NW9 36 E2
Poonah St WCHPL E1 51 N4
Pootings Rd EDEN TN8 97 P13
Pope Cl EBED/NFELT TW14 58 B6
WIM/MER SW19 * 61 R11
Pope Rd HAYES BR2 76 F3
Pope's Av WHTN TW2 59 N7
Popes Cl DTCH/LGLY SL3 44 G12
Popes Dr FNCH N3 25 N13
Popes Gv CROY/NA CR0 75 R8
WHTN TW2 59 N7
Pope's La EA W5 47 T8
OXTED RH8 96 B11
WATN WD24 11 P11
Pope's Rd ABLGY WD5 11 L5
BRXN/ST SW9 62 E2
Pope St STHWK SE1 9 T4
Popham Cl FELT TW13 58 G8
Popham Gdns RCH/KEW TW9 * 60 B1
Popham Rd IS N1 5 N1
Popham St IS N1 5 N1
Popinjays Rw CHEAM SM3 * 72 K10
Poplar Av LHD/OX KT22 83 S12
MTCM CR4 61 T13
NWDGN UB2 46 K8
ORP BR6 76 K7
WDR/YW UB7 45 R5
Poplar Bath St POP/IOD E14 51 T5
Poplar Cl DTCH/LGLY SL3 44 J13
HOM E9 39 R10
PIN HA5 22 F13
Poplar Court Pde TWK TW1 * 59 S4
Poplar Crs HOR/WEW KT19 72 C11
Poplar Dr BNSTD SM7 84 K4
Poplar Farm Cl HOR/WEW KT19 72 C11
Poplar Gdns NWMAL KT3 60 D14
Poplar Gn WOKS/MYFD GU22 80 C9
Poplar Gv FBAR/BDGN N11 25 U11
HMSMTH W6 48 J7
NWMAL KT3 72 D1
WBLY HA9 36 C8
Poplar High St POP/IOD E14 51 T5
Poplar La BECK BR3 75 T3
Poplar Ms SHB W12 48 J6
Poplar Mt BELV DA17 54 B9
Poplar Pl BAY/PAD W2 2 G13
HYS/HAR UB3 46 C5
THMD SE28 53 S5
Poplar Rd ASHF TW15 57 U10
CHEAM SM3 73 M6
DEN/HRF UB9 33 N11
HNHL SE24 62 G2
LHD/OX KT22 83 R12
WIM/MER SW19 61 N14
Poplar Rd South WIM/MER SW19 73 N1
Poplar Rw EPP CM16 18 C11
Poplars Cl GSTN WD25 11 P6
RSLP HA4 34 A6
Poplar Shaw WAB EN9 17 M7
Poplars Rd WALTH E17 39 T4
The Poplars ABR/ST RM4 29 R1
BORE WD6 * 13 L13
DEN/HRF UB9 * 21 N13
STHGT/OAK N14 25 V3
Poplar St ROMW/RG RM7 42 C2
Poplar Vw WBLY HA9 * 35 T7
Poplar Wk CROY/NA CR0 74 G7
CTHM CR3 86 J13
HNHL SE24 62 G2
Poplar Wy BARK/HLT IG6 41 L2
FELT TW13 58 C8
Poppins Ct FLST/FETLN EC4A 5 L12
Poppleton Rd WAN E11 40 A4
Poppy Cl BELV DA17 54 B8
NTHLT UB5 34 H11
WLGTN SM6 73 U6
Poppy La CROY/NA CR0 75 N5
Poppy Wk CHESW EN7 15 T2
Porchester Cl EMPK RM11 43 L4
Porchester Garden Ms BAY/PAD W2 2 H12
Porchester Gdns BAY/PAD W2 2 H13
Porchester Ga BAY/PAD W2 * 2 J14
Porchester Md BECK BR3 63 T11
Porchester Pl BAY/PAD W2 3 P12
Porchester Rd BAY/PAD W2 2 H11
KUT/HW KT1 60 B14
Porchester Sq BAY/PAD W2 2 H11
Porchester Square Ms BAY/PAD W2 2 H11
Porchester Ter BAY/PAD W2 2 J12
Porchester Ter North BAY/PAD W2 2 H11
Porchfield Cl BELMT SM2 73 P14
Porch Wy TRDG/WHET N20 25 T8
Porcupine Cl ELTH/MOT SE9 64 G7
Porden Rd BRXS/STRHM SW2 62 D2
Porlock Av RYLN/HDSTN HA2 35 L6
Porlock Rd EN EN1 26 K5
Porlock St STHWK SE1 9 R3
Porrington Cl CHST BR7 64 H13
Portal Cl HGDN/ICK UB10 33 R12
RSLP HA4 34 C9
WNWD SE27 62 E8
Portal Wy ACT W3 48 D3
Port Av SWCM DA10 67 V4
Portbury Cl PECK SE15 51 L13
Portchester Cl HNHL SE24 62 G2
Portchester Ga BAY/PAD W2 2 J14
Portcullis Lodge Rd EN EN1 26 H1
Portelet Rd WCHPL E1 51 P1
Porten Rd WKENS W14 6 A6
Porter Rd EHAM E6 52 H4
Porters Av DAGW RM9 41 R11
Porters Cl BRW CM14 31 U6
Porters Park Dr RAD WD7 12 K7
Porter Sq ARCH N19 38 C6
Porter St MHST W1U 3 R9
STHWK SE1 9 P1
Porters Wk WAP E1W * 51 M5
Porters Wy WDR/YW UB7 45 R8
Porteus Rd BAY/PAD W2 2 K10
Portgate Cl MV/WKIL W9 2 D7
Porthallow Cl ORP BR6 77 P9
Porthcawe Rd SYD SE26 63 Q9
Port Hl ORP BR6 89 R2
Porthkerry Av WELL DA16 65 Q2
Portia Wy BOW E3 51 R2
Portinscale Rd PUT/ROE SW15 61 L3
Portland Av BFN/LL DA15 65 Q4
NWMAL KT3 72 F5
STNW/STAM N16 38 K6
Portland Cl CHDH RM6 41 U3
WPK KT4 72 H5
Portland Cottages CROY/NA CR0 * 74 B5
Portland Crs ELTH/MOT SE9 64 G7
FELT TW13 57 V9
GFD/PVL UB6 46 K3
STAN HA7 23 T14
Portland Crs West STAN HA7 35 T1
Portland Dr CHESW EN7 16 A5
ENC/FH EN2 15 U12
REDH RH1 94 B5
Portland Gdns CHDH RM6 41 T3
FSBYPK N4 38 F4
Portland Gv VX/NE SW8 50 D13
Portland Ms SOHO/CST W1F 4 B12
Portland Pk CFSP/GDCR SL9 32 B4
Portland Pl EW KT17 84 E2
REGST W1B 3 U8
SNWD SE25 75 L2
Portland Place Flats EW KT17 * 84 E2
Portland Ri FSBYPK N4 38 F6
Portland Rd ASHF TW15 57 Q8
BMLY BR1 64 E9
ELTH/MOT SE9 64 G7
KUT/HW KT1 71 U1
MTCM CR4 61 S14
NTGHL W11 6 B1
NWDGN UB2 46 H8
SEVS/STOTM N15 38 J2
SNWD SE25 75 M2
YEAD UB4 46 A1
Portland Sq WAP E1W 51 M6
Portland St WALW SE17 9 Q10
Portland Ter RCH/KEW TW9 * 59 T2
Portley La CTHM CR3 86 J11
Portley Wood Rd CTHM CR3 86 K11
Portman Av MORT/ESHN SW14 60 D1
Portman Cl BXLY DA5 66 E6
BXLYHS DA6 65 T1
MBLAR W1H 3 S11
Portman Dr WFD IG8 28 F14
Portman Gdns CDALE/KGS NW9 36 D1
HGDN/ICK UB10 33 S12
Portman Ga CAMTN NW1 3 P8
Portman Ms South MBLAR W1H 3 S12
Portman Pl BETH E2 51 N1
Portman Rd KUT/HW KT1 59 V14
Portman Sq MBLAR W1H 3 S12
Portman St MBLAR W1H 3 S12
Portman Towers MBLAR W1H 3 R11
Portmeadow Wk ABYW SE2 53 T7
Portmeers Cl WALTH E17 * 39 R4
Portmore Gdns CRW RM5 30 A10
Portmore Park Rd WEY KT13 69 S8
Portmore Quays WEY KT13 69 R9
Portmore Wy WEY KT13 * 69 S8
Portnall Rd MV/WKIL W9 2 C5
Portnalls Cl COUL/CHIP CR5 85 V6
Portnalls Ri COUL/CHIP CR5 85 V6
Portnalls Rd COUL/CHIP CR5 85 V7
Portnoi Cl ROM RM1 30 D14
Portobello Ct NTGHL W11 * 2 D13
Portobello Ms NTGHL W11 * 2 E14
Portobello Rd NKENS W10 2 A9
NTGHL W11 2 C12
Portpool La FSBYW WC1X 4 J9
Portree St POP/IOD E14 51 V4
Portsdown Av GLDGN NW11 37 M4
Portsdown Ms GLDGN NW11 37 M4
Portsea Ms BAY/PAD W2 3 P12
Portsea Pl BAY/PAD W2 3 P12
Portslade Rd VX/NE SW8 50 A14
Portsmouth Av THDIT KT7 71 Q5
Portsmouth Ms CAN/RD E16 52 D5
Portsmouth Rd COB KT11 82 C4
ESH/CLAY KT10 70 J11
KUT/HW KT1 71 T1
PUT/ROE SW15 60 J5
RPLY/SEND GU23 81 L14
RPLY/SEND GU23 81 P11
Portsmouth St LINN WC2A 4 G11
Portsoken St TWRH EC3N 5 U13
Portugal Gdns WHTN TW2 * 59 L7
Portugal Rd WOKN/KNAP GU21 80 D6
Portugal St LINN WC2A 4 H12
Portway EW KT17 72 G14
RAIN RM13 42 G13
SRTFD E15 40 B13
Portway Crs EW KT17 72 G14
Portway Gdns WOOL/PLUM SE18 52 F13
Postboys Rw COB KT11 * 82 C4
Postern Gn ENC/FH EN2 15 Q14
The Postern BARB EC2Y * 5 P10
Post La WHTN TW2 59 M6
Post Meadow IVER SL0 44 H1
Postmill Cl CROY/NA CR0 75 N8
Post Office Ap FSTGT E7 40 D10
Post Office La DTCH/LGLY SL3 44 B4
Post Office Wy VX/NE SW8 8 C13
Post Rd NWDGN UB2 46 K8
Postway Ms IL IG1 40 K8
Potier St STHWK SE1 9 R6
Potiphar Pl BRW CM14 31 V9
Potter Cl MTCM CR4 * 61 V14
The Potteries BAR EN5 * 25 N3
CHERT KT16 68 J11
Potterne Cl WIM/MER SW19 60 K5
Potters Bar Station Yd
POTB/CUF EN6 * 14 C5
Potters Cl CROY/NA CR0 75 Q6
LOU IG10 17 S14
PECK SE15 9 T13
Potters Cross IVER SL0 44 J1
Potters Fld EN EN1 * 26 J2
Potters Flds STHWK SE1 9 T2
Potters Gv NWMAL KT3 72 C2
Potters Heights Cl PIN HA5 22 D12
Potter's La BAR EN5 25 N2
BORE WD6 13 N13
STRHM/NOR SW16 * 62 B11
Potter's Rd BAR EN5 25 P2
FUL/PGN SW6 49 Q14
Potter St NTHWD HA6 22 C13
Potter Street Hl PIN HA5 22 D12
Potters Wy REIG RH2 93 Q14
Pottery La NTGHL W11 2 A14
Pottery Rd BTFD TW8 47 U11
BXLY DA5 66 C7
Pottery St BERM/RHTH SE16 * 51 M7
Pott St BETH E2 51 M1
Poulcott STWL/WRAY TW19 56 C4
Poulett Gdns TWK TW1 59 P7
Poulett Rd EHAM E6 40 H14
Poulter Pk MRDN SM4 * 73 S4
Poulters Wd HAYES BR2 76 F10
Poultney Cl RAD WD7 12 K7
Poulton Av SUT SM1 73 R8
Poulton Cl HACK E8 39 M11
Poultry LOTH EC2R 5 Q12
Pound Bank Cl BGR/WK TN15 79 T13
Pound Cl ORP BR6 77 M7
SURB KT6 71 S6
Pound Ct ASHTD KT21 83 V8
Pound Court Dr ORP BR6 77 M7
Pound Crs LHD/OX KT22 83 M11
Pound Farm Cl ESH/CLAY KT10 71 M6
Pound Fld GSTN WD25 11 M9
Poundfield Gdns WOKS/MYFD GU22 80 G10
Poundfield Rd LOU IG10 28 J3
Pound La HOR/WEW KT19 84 D1
RAD WD7 12 K7
RSEV TN14 89 T5
SEV TN13 90 J14
WLSDN NW10 36 G11
Pound Park Rd CHARL SE7 52 F10
Pound Pl ELTH/MOT SE9 64 J4
Pound Rd BNSTD SM7 85 N7
CHERT KT16 69 M5
Pound St CAR SM5 73 T10
Pounsley Rd SEV TN13 90 E11
Pountney Rd BTSEA SW11 61 U1
Poverest Rd STMC/STPC BR5 77 P3
Powder Mill La DART DA1 67 M7
Powdermill La WAB EN9 16 H7
Powder Mill La WHTN TW2 58 H6
Powdermill Ms WAB EN9 16 H7
Powdermill Wy WAB EN9 16 H7
Powell Av RDART DA2 67 S7
Powell Cl EDGW HA8 23 V11
Powell Gdns DAGE RM10 42 A9
Powell Rd BKHH IG9 28 E5
CLPT E5 39 M8
Power Dr PEND EN3 16 F10
Power Rd CHSWK W4 48 A9
Powers Ct TWK TW1 59 T5
Powerscroft Rd CLPT E5 39 N9
SCUP DA14 65 S12
Powis Ct BUSH WD23 * 23 M6
POTB/CUF EN6 14 E8
Powis Gdns GLDGN NW11 37 M5
NTGHL W11 2 D11
Powis Ms NTGHL W11 2 D11
Powis Pl BMSBY WC1N 4 F8
Powis Rd BOW E3 51 T1
Powis Sq NTGHL W11 2 D12
Powis St WOOL/PLUM SE18 52 J8
Powis Ter NTGHL W11 2 D11
Powlett Pl CAMTN NW1 * 37 V12
Pownall Gdns HSLW TW3 58 K2
Pownall Rd HACK E8 39 L13
HSLW TW3 58 K2
Pownsett Ter IL IG1 * 41 L10
Powster Rd BMLY BR1 64 C10
Powys Cl BXLYHN DA7 53 T11
Powys Ct BORE WD6 24 D1
Powys La STHGT/OAK N14 26 C9
Poyle Pk DTCH/LGLY SL3 * 56 J1
Poyle Rd DTCH/LGLY SL3 44 J14
Poynders Rd CLAP SW4 62 A5
Poynings Cl ORP BR6 77 S7
Poynings Rd ARCH N19 38 A8
The Poynings DTCH/LGLY SL3 44 K9
Poynings Wy HARH RM3 31 L13
NFNCH/WDSPK N12 25 N10
Poyntell Crs CHST BR7 65 M13
Poynter Rd EN EN1 26 K3
Poynton Rd TOTM N17 27 L14
Poyntz Rd BTSEA SW11 49 T14
Poyser St BETH E2 39 M14
Praed Ms BAY/PAD W2 3 M11
Praed St BAY/PAD W2 3 M11
Pragel St PLSTW E13 40 E14
Pragnell Rd LEE/GVPK SE12 64 D7
Prague Pl BRXS/STRHM SW2 62 C3
Prah Rd FSBYPK N4 38 E7
Prairie Cl ADL/WDHM KT15 69 M8
Prairie Rd ADL/WDHM KT15 69 M8
Prairie St VX/NE SW8 49 U14
Pratt Ms CAMTN NW1 4 A2
Pratts La WOT/HER KT12 70 F9
Pratt St CAMTN NW1 4 B1
Pratt Wk LBTH SE11 8 H7
Prayle Gv CRICK NW2 36 K6
Prebend Gdns HMSMTH W6 48 F9
Prebend St IS N1 5 N2
Precinct Rd HYS/HAR UB3 46 C5
The Precinct EGH TW20 * 56 E10
IS N1 * 5 N2
Premiere Pl POP/IOD E14 51 S5
Premier Park Rd WLSDN NW10 36 B14
Premier Pl WATW WD18 22 B3
Prendergast Rd BKHTH/KID SE3 64 A1
Prentis Rd STRHM/NOR SW16 62 B9
Prentiss Ct CHARL SE7 52 F9
Presburg Rd NWMAL KT3 72 E3
Prescelly Pl EDGW HA8 23 V13
Prescot St WCHPL E1 5 V13
Prescott Av STMC/STPC BR5 76 K4
Prescott Cl EMPK RM11 42 H6
Prescott Gn LOU IG10 29 L1
Prescott Pl CLAP SW4 62 B1
Prescott Rd CHES/WCR EN8 16 E1
DTCH/LGLY SL3 44 J14
Presentation Ms BRXS/STRHM SW2 62 D7
Presidents Dr WAP E1W 51 M6
President St FSBYE EC1V * 5 N5
Prespa Cl ED N9 27 N7
Press Rd UX/CGN UB8 33 P12
WLSDN NW10 36 D8
Prestage Wy POP/IOD E14 51 U5
Prestbury Crs BNSTD SM7 85 T6
Prestbury Rd FSTGT E7 40 E12
Prestbury Sq ELTH/MOT SE9 64 H9
Prested Rd BTSEA SW11 61 S2
Preston Av CHING E4 27 V11
Preston Cl STHWK SE1 9 S7
WHTN TW2 59 N8
Preston Ct BAR EN5 25 Q2
WOT/HER KT12 70 E6
Preston Dr BXLYHN DA7 53 T13
HOR/WEW KT19 72 E11
WAN E11 40 E3
Preston Gdns IL IG1 40 G4
PEND EN3 16 E11
WLSDN NW10 * 36 E11
Preston Gv ASHTD KT21 83 S7
Preston Hl KTN/HRWW/WS HA3 35 U5
Preston La KWD/TDW/WH KT20 84 J10
Preston Pl CRICK NW2 36 G11
Preston Rd HARH RM3 30 K9
KTN/HRWW/WS HA3 35 U5
NRWD SE19 62 F11
RYNPK SW20 60 G12
SHPTN TW17 69 S3
SLN SL2 44 A5
WAN E11 40 A4
Preston's Rd POP/IOD E14 51 U6
WWKM BR4 76 C8
Preston Vls KUT/HW KT1 * 59 V14
Preston Waye KTN/HRWW/WS HA3 35 U6
Prestwich Ter CLAP SW4 * 62 B3
Prestwick Cl NWDGN UB2 46 G10
Prestwick Rd OXHEY WD19 22 F8
Prestwood OXHEY WD19 * 22 G7
Prestwood Av KTN/HRWW/WS HA3 35 R2
Prestwood Cl KTN/HRWW/WS HA3 35 R2
WOOL/PLUM SE18 53 Q12
Prestwood Dr CRW RM5 30 C10
Prestwood Gdns CROY/NA CR0 74 G5
Prestwood St IS N1 * 5 P4
Pretoria Av WALTH E17 39 Q2
Pretoria Crs CHING E4 27 U6
Pretoria Pde BROCKY SE4 * 51 S14
Pretoria Rd CAN/RD E16 52 B1
CHERT KT16 68 K6
CHING E4 27 U6
IL IG1 40 K9
LEY E10 39 V6
ROMW/RG RM7 42 C2
STRHM/NOR SW16 61 V11
TOTM N17 26 K11
WATW WD18 22 C2
Pretoria Rd North UED N18 26 K11
Pretty La COUL/CHIP CR5 86 A11
Prevost Rd FBAR/BDGN N11 25 U7
Prey Heath Cl WOKS/MYFD GU22 80 A14
Price Cl MLHL NW7 25 L11
TOOT SW17 61 T8
Price Rd CROY/NA CR0 74 F10
Prices La REIG RH2 93 N13
Prices Ms IS N1 4 H1
Price's St STHWK SE1 9 M2
Pricklers Hl BAR EN5 25 P3
Prickley Wd HAYES BR2 76 B6
Priddy's Yd CROY/NA CR0 74 G7
Prideaux Pl ACT W3 48 D5
FSBYW WC1X 4 H5
Prideaux Rd BRXN/ST SW9 62 C1
Pridham Rd THHTH CR7 74 H2
Priestfield Rd FSTH SE23 63 Q8
Priest Hl OXTED RH8 96 D5
WDSR SL4 56 A7
Priestlands Park Rd BFN/LL DA15 65 P8
Priestley Cl STNW/STAM N16 * 38 K5
Priestley Gdns CHDH RM6 41 R4
WOKS/MYFD GU22 80 E10
Priestley Rd MTCM CR4 61 U14
Priestley Wy CRICK NW2 36 G6
WALTH E17 39 P1
Priest Park Av RYLN/HDSTN HA2 34 J7
Priests Av ROM RM1 30 D14
Priests Br MORT/ESHN SW14 60 E1
Prima Rd BRXN/ST SW9 8 J13
Primmett Cl BGR/WK TN15 79 S11
Primrose Av ENC/FH EN2 15 T13
GDMY/SEVK IG3 41 Q5
Primrose Cl BOW E3 39 S14
CAT SE6 63 U10
FNCH N3 25 P14
RYLN/HDSTN HA2 34 H8
WLGTN SM6 73 V6
Primrose Dr WDR/YW UB7 45 P9
Primrose Gdns BUSH WD23 22 K5
HAMP NW3 37 S11
RSLP HA4 34 E10
Primrose Gln EMPK RM11 43 L2
Primrose Hl EMB EC4Y 4 K12
KGLGY WD4 10 H2
Primrose Hill Rd HAMP NW3 3 Q1
Primrose Hill Studios CAMTN NW1 3 S1
Primrose La CROY/NA CR0 75 N6
GSTN WD25 12 B12
Primrose Ms CAMTN NW1 * 37 T12
Primrose Pth CHESW EN7 16 A5
Primrose Pl ISLW TW7 47 P14
Primrose Rd LEY E10 39 T6
SWFD E18 28 D14
WOT/HER KT12 70 E10
Primrose Sq HOM E9 39 N12
Primrose St SDTCH EC2A 5 S9
Primrose Wk EW KT17 72 F12
NWCR SE14 51 Q12
Primrose Wy ALP/SUD HA0 35 T14
Primula St SHB W12 48 G5
Prince Albert Rd STJWD NW8 3 N5
Prince Arthur Ms HAMP NW3 37 Q9
Prince Arthur Rd HAMP NW3 37 Q9
Prince Charles Av EYN DA4 67 R14
Prince Charles Dr HDN NW4 36 J5
Prince Charles Rd BKHTH/KID SE3 52 B13
Prince Charles Wy WLGTN SM6 73 V8
Prince Consort Dr CHST BR7 65 M13
Prince Consort Rd SKENS SW7 7 L5
Princedale Rd NTGHL W11 6 B1
Prince Edward Rd HOM E9 39 R11
Prince George Av STHGT/OAK N14 26 B3
Prince George Rd STNW/STAM N16 38 J9
Prince George's Av RYNPK SW20 60 J14
Prince Georges Rd WIM/MER SW19 61 R13
Prince Henry Rd CHARL SE7 52 F12
Prince Imperial Rd CHST BR7 64 K12
WOOL/PLUM SE18 52 H13
Prince John Rd ELTH/MOT SE9 64 G3
Princelet St WCHPL E1 5 V9
Prince of Orange La GNWCH SE10 * 51 U12
Prince of Wales Cl HDN NW4 36 H2
Prince of Wales Dr BTSEA SW11 49 T13
VX/NE SW8 * 7 V14
Prince of Wales Ga SKENS SW7 7 N3
Prince of Wales Pas CAMTN NW1 * 4 A6
Prince of Wales Rd BKHTH/KID SE3 52 B13
CAN/RD E16 52 E4
KTTN NW5 37 U11
SUT SM1 73 R7
Prince of Wales Ter CHSWK W4 48 E10
KENS W8 6 H4
Prince Regent La PLSTW E13 52 E2
Prince Regent Ms CAMTN NW1 4 A6
Prince Regent Rd HSLW TW3 59 L1
Prince Rd SNWD SE25 74 J3
Prince Rupert Rd ELTH/MOT SE9 64 H2
Princes Ar MYFR/PICC W1J 8 B1
Princes Av ACT W3 48 A8
CAR SM5 73 T12
CDALE/KGS NW9 36 A2
FNCH N3 25 P13
GFD/PVL UB6 46 K4
MUSWH N10 37 V1
PEND EN3 16 E10
PLMGR N13 26 E10
RDART DA2 67 P6
SAND/SEL CR2 87 M5
STMC/STPC BR5 77 N3
SURB KT6 72 A7
WATW WD18 22 C3
WDGN N22 26 B13
WFD IG8 28 D9
Princes Cl CDALE/KGS NW9 36 A2
EDGW HA8 24 A10
FSBYPK N4 38 F6
HPTN TW12 59 M9
SAND/SEL CR2 87 M5
SCUP DA14 65 T8
Princes Ct WAP E1W 51 M5
WBLY HA9 35 U10
Princes Dr HRW HA1 35 N1
LHD/OX KT22 83 N2
Princesfield Rd WAB EN9 17 P7
Princes Gdns ACT W3 48 A4
EA W5 47 S2
SKENS SW7 7 M5
Prince's Ga SKENS SW7 7 N4
Princes Gate Ct SKENS SW7 7 L4
Princes Gate Ms SKENS SW7 7 M5
Princes La MUSWH N10 37 U1
Prince's Ms BAY/PAD W2 2 G13
HMSMTH W6 * 48 H10
HSLW TW3 58 J2
Princes Pde GLDGN NW11 * 37 L4
POTB/CUF EN6 * 14 D7
Princes Pk RAIN RM13 42 G12
Princes Park Av GLDGN NW11 37 L4
HYS/HAR UB3 45 V5
Princes Park Cir HYS/HAR UB3 45 V5
Princes Park Cl HYS/HAR UB3 45 V5
Princes Park La HYS/HAR UB3 45 V5
Princes Park Pde HYS/HAR UB3 45 V5
Princes Pl NTGHL W11 6 A1
Prince's Pln HAYES BR2 76 G5
Princes Ri LEW SE13 51 U14
Princes Riverside Rd
BERM/RHTH SE16 51 P6
Princes Rd ASHF TW15 57 R10
BARK/HLT IG6 41 M2
BKHH IG9 28 E7
DART DA1 66 H6
EGH TW20 56 D11
FELT TW13 58 B8
KUTN/CMB KT2 60 A13
MORT/ESHN SW14 60 D1
PGE/AN SE20 63 P11
RCH/KEW TW9 47 V13
RCHPK/HAM TW10 59 V3
RDART DA2 67 Q6
REDH RH1 93 U13
ROM RM1 42 G3
SWLY BR8 66 G11
TEDD TW11 59 M10
UED N18 27 N9
WEA W13 47 R6
WEY KT13 69 T10
WIM/MER SW19 61 N11
Princess Alice Wy THMD SE28 53 M7
Princess Av WBLY HA9 35 U7
Princess Crs FSBYPK N4 38 F7
Princesses Pde DART DA1 * 66 F3
Princess Gdns WOKS/MYFD GU22 80 F6
Princess La RSLP HA4 34 A6
Princess Louise Cl BAY/PAD W2 3 M9
Princess Mary's Rd ADL/WDHM KT15 69 N9
Princess May Rd STNW/STAM N16 38 J9

Princess Ms HAMP NW3 37 R11
Princess Pde ORP BR6 * 76 J8
Prince's Sq BAY/PAD W2 2 G13
Princess Rd CAMTN NW1 3 S1
CROY/NA CR0 74 G4
KIL/WHAMP NW6 2 E4
WOKS/MYFD GU22 80 F6
Princess St BXLYHN DA7 65 V1
STHWK SE1 9 M6
Prince's St LOTH EC2R 5 Q12
RCH/KEW TW9 59 U2
REGST W1B 3 V12
SUT SM1 73 R9
TOTM N17 26 J11
Princess Wy REDH RH1 93 U9
Prince's Ter PLSTW E13 40 D13
Prince St DEPT SE8 51 R11
WAT WD17 22 E1
Princes Vw DART DA1 67 N6
Princes Wy BKHH IG9 28 E7
CROY/NA CR0 74 D10
RSLP HA4 34 G9
WIM/MER SW19 60 K5
WWKM BR4 76 B9
Prince's Yd NTGHL W11 * 6 B2
Princethorpe Rd SYD SE26 63 P9
Princeton St GINN WC1R 4 G10
Pringle Gdns PUR/KEN CR8 74 D14
STRHM/NOR SW16 62 A9
Printers Inn Ct FLST/FETLN EC4A 4 J11
Printinghouse La HYS/HAR UB3 46 A7
Printing House Yd BETH E2 * 5 T6
Priolo Rd CHARL SE7 52 E10
Prior Av BELMT SM2 73 S12
Prior Bolton St IS N1 38 F11
Prioress Rd WNWD SE27 62 F8
Prioress St STHWK SE1 9 S6
Prior Rd IL IG1 40 J8
Priors Cft WALTH E17 27 Q14
WOKS/MYFD GU22 80 E10
Priors Fld NTHLT UB5 34 G11
Priorsford Av STMC/STPC BR5 77 Q2
Priors Gdns RSLP HA4 34 E10
Priors Md EN EN1 15 U13
Priors Pk HCH RM12 42 J8
The Priors ASHTD KT21 83 T9
Prior St GNWCH SE10 51 U12
Priory Av ALP/SUD HA0 35 P9
CEND/HSY/T N8 38 B2
CHEAM SM3 72 K9
CHING E4 27 R8
CHSWK W4 48 E8
DEN/HRF UB9 33 N2
STMC/STPC BR5 77 M4
WALTH E17 39 S3
Priory Cl ALP/SUD HA0 35 P9
BECK BR3 75 Q1
BRWN CM15 31 U3
CHING E4 27 R8
CHST BR7 64 H13
DART DA1 66 J3
DEN/HRF UB9 33 L8
DEN/HRF UB9 33 M2
FNCH N3 25 M13
HPTN TW12 58 H13
HYS/HAR UB3 46 D5
RSLP HA4 34 B6
STAN HA7 23 P8
STHGT/OAK N14 25 V3
SUN TW16 58 C12
SWFD E18 28 C13
TRDG/WHET N20 25 M5
WIM/MER SW19 * 61 P13
WOKN/KNAP GU21 80 H3
WOT/HER KT12 70 C8
Priory Cottages EA W5 * 47 V3
Priory Ct BLKFR EC4V * 5 M12
VX/NE SW8 50 B13
WALTH E17 27 R14
Priory Crs ALP/SUD HA0 35 Q8
CHEAM SM3 72 K9
NRWD SE19 62 G12
Priory Dr ABYW SE2 53 T10
REIG RH2 93 N12
STAN HA7 23 P8
Priory Field Dr EDGW HA8 24 B9
Priory Flds EYN DA4 79 M7
Priory Gdns ALP/SUD HA0 35 Q9
ASHF TW15 57 V10
BARN SW13 60 F1
CHSWK W4 * 48 E9
DART DA1 66 K3
DEN/HRF UB9 33 N2
HGT N6 37 V4
HPTN TW12 58 H13
SNWD SE25 74 K2
Priory Ga CHES/WCR EN8 16 F1
Priory Gn STA TW18 57 M10
Priory Green Est IS N1 4 G3
Priory Gv HARH RM3 31 L9
VX/NE SW8 50 C13
Priory Hl ALP/SUD HA0 35 Q9
DART DA1 66 K4
Priory La E/WMO/HCT KT8 70 J2
EYN DA4 79 M6
PUT/ROE SW15 60 F3
Priory Leas ELTH/MOT SE9 * 64 G6
Priory Market Pl DART DA1 * 67 L5
Priory Ms HCH RM12 42 H6
STA TW18 57 M10
Priory Pk BKHTH/KID SE3 64 B1
Priory Park Rd ALP/SUD HA0 35 Q9
KIL/WHAMP NW6 2 D1
Priory Pth HARH RM3 31 L8
Priory Pl DART DA1 66 K4
Priory Rd BARK IG11 41 M12
CFSP/GDCR SL9 32 A1
CHEAM SM3 72 K9
CHSGTN KT9 71 U8
CHSWK W4 48 D8
CROY/NA CR0 74 E5
DART DA1 66 K2
EHAM E6 40 F13
HARH RM3 31 L8
HPTN TW12 58 H12
HSLW TW3 59 L3
KIL/WHAMP NW6 2 G1
LOU IG10 28 G2
MUSWH N10 38 A2
RCH/KEW TW9 48 A11
REIG RH2 93 N12
Priory St BOW E3 51 T1
Priory Ter KIL/WHAMP NW6 2 G1
The Priory BKHTH/KID SE3 64 B2
CROY/NA CR0 * 74 E8
GDST RH9 95 M7
ORP BR6 * 77 R5
Priory Vw BUSH WD23 23 N5
Priory Vls FBAR/BDGN N11 * 25 T11
Priory Wk WBPTN SW10 6 K10
Priory Wy CFSP/GDCR SL9 32 B1
NWDGN UB2 46 F8
RYLN/HDSTN HA2 34 K2
WDR/YW UB7 45 Q11
Pritchard's Rd BETH E2 39 L14
Pritchett Cl PEND EN3 16 H11
Priter Rd BERM/RHTH SE16 * 51 L8
Private Rd EN EN1 26 H3
Probert Rd BRXS/STRHM SW2 62 E3
Probyn Rd BRXS/STRHM SW2 62 F7
Procter St GINN WC1R 4 G10
Proctor Cl MTCM CR4 61 U13
Proctors Cl EBED/NFELT TW14 58 C6
Profumo Rd WOT/HER KT12 70 F10
Progress Wy CROY/NA CR0 74 D7
EN EN1 27 L4
WDGN N22 26 E13
Promenade Approach Rd CHSWK W4 48 E12
Promenade De Verdun PUR/KEN CR8 86 B1
The Promenade CHSWK W4 48 E13
EDGW HA8 * 24 A10
Prospect Cl BELV DA17 54 A9
HSLW TW3 46 H13
RSLP HA4 34 F5
SYD SE26 63 M9
Prospect Cottages WAND/EARL SW18 61 N2
Prospect Crs WHTN TW2 59 L4
Prospect Hl WALTH E17 39 T2
Prospect Pl CHSWK W4 48 D10
CRICK NW2 37 M8
CRW RM5 30 C14
EFNCH N2 37 R2
EW KT17 84 E3
HAYES BR2 76 D1
RYNPK SW20 60 H12
STA TW18 56 K10
WAP E1W 51 N6
Prospect Rd BAR EN5 25 N2
CHES/WCR EN8 16 C3
CRICK NW2 37 M8
EMPK RM11 43 M1
SEV TN13 90 J13
SURB KT6 71 S4
WFD IG8 28 E10
Prospect St BERM/RHTH SE16 51 M7
Prospect V WOOL/PLUM SE18 52 G9
Prospero Rd ARCH N19 38 B6
Prossers KWD/TDW/WH KT20 84 K11
Protea Cl CAN/RD E16 52 B2
Prothero Gdns HDN NW4 36 H3
Prothero Rd FUL/PGN SW6 6 B13
Prout Gv WLSDN NW10 36 E9
Prout Rd CLPT E5 39 M8
Provence St IS N1 5 N3
Providence Av RYLN/HDSTN HA2 34 J6
Providence Cl HOM E9 * 39 P13
Providence Ct MYFR/PKLN W1K 3 T13
Providence La HYS/HAR UB3 45 V12
Providence Pl CRW RM5 29 V13
IS N1 5 L2
WOKS/MYFD GU22 * 81 L4
Providence Rd WDR/YW UB7 45 Q6
Providence Row Cl BETH E2 51 M1
Providence Sq STHWK SE1 9 S3
Providence St RDART DA2 67 U3
Providence Yd BETH E2 * 51 L1
Provincial Ter PGE/AN SE20 * 63 P12
Provost Est IS N1 5 Q5
Provost Rd HAMP NW3 37 T12
Provost St IS N1 5 Q4
Prowse Av BUSH WD23 23 L7
Prowse Pl CAMTN NW1 38 A12
Pruden Cl STHGT/OAK N14 * 26 A7
Prune Hl EGH TW20 56 C12
Prusom St WAP E1W 51 M6
Pryor Cl ABLGY WD5 11 M6
Pucknells Cl SWLY BR8 66 C13
Pudding La CHIG IG7 29 N4
MON EC3R 5 R14
Pudding Mill La SRTFD E15 39 T13
Puddle Dock BLKFR EC4V 5 M13
Puddledock La BH/WHM TN16 97 Q8
RDART DA2 66 E10
Puffin Cl BARK IG11 53 R1
BECK BR3 75 P3
Pulborough Rd WAND/EARL SW18 61 M5
Pulborough Wy HSLWW TW4 58 E2
Pulford Rd SEVS/STOTM N15 38 H4
Pulham Av EFNCH N2 37 R2
Puller Rd BAR EN5 13 V14
Pulleyns Av EHAM E6 52 G1
Pullman Gdns PUT/ROE SW15 60 J4
Pullman Ms LEE/GVPK SE12 64 D8
Pullman Pl ELTH/MOT SE9 64 G3
Pullmans Pl STA TW18 57 L10
Pulross Rd BRXN/ST SW9 62 D1
Pulteney Cl BOW E3 39 R13
ISLW TW7 59 Q1
Pulteney Rd SWFD E18 40 D1
Pulton Pl FUL/PGN SW6 6 E14
Puma Ct WCHPL E1 5 U9
Pump Aly BTFD TW8 47 T12
Pump Cl NTHLT UB5 34 J14
Pump Ct EMB EC4Y * 4 J12
Pump Hl LOU IG10 17 T14
Pump House Cl HAYES BR2 64 B14
Pump House Ms WCHPL E1 * 51 L5
Pumping Station Rd CHSWK W4 48 E12
Pump La HYS/HAR UB3 46 C7
NWCR SE14 51 N12
ORP BR6 78 B10
Punchard Crs PEND EN3 16 H12
Punderson's Gdns BETH E2 51 M1
Purbeck Av NWMAL KT3 72 F4
Purbeck Cl REDH RH1 94 B5
Purbeck Dr CRICK NW2 36 K7
WOKN/KNAP GU21 80 D4
Purbeck Rd EMPK RM11 42 G5
Purberry Gv EW KT17 72 F14
Purberry Shot EW KT17 * 72 F14
Purbrock Av GSTN WD25 11 Q10
Purbrook St STHWK SE1 9 T5
Purcell Cl BORE WD6 12 H13
PUR/KEN CR8 86 G4
Purcell Crs FUL/PGN SW6 * 48 K11
Purcell Ms WLSDN NW10 * 36 E12
Purcell Rd GFD/PVL UB6 46 K3
Purcell St IS N1 5 S3
Purcers Cross Rd FUL/PGN SW6 49 M13
Purchese St CAMTN NW1 4 C3
Purdy St BOW E3 51 T2
Purelake Ms LEW SE13 * 63 V1
Purfleet By-Pass PUR RM19 55 P9
Purfleet Deep Whf PUR RM19 * 55 Q11
Purfleet Industrial Access Rd
SOCK/AV RM15 55 N8
Purfleet Rd SOCK/AV RM15 55 P6
Purkis Cl UX/CGN UB8 45 U5
Purland Cl BCTR RM8 41 V6
Purland Rd THMD SE28 53 Q7
Purleigh Av WFD IG8 28 G11
Purley Av CRICK NW2 37 L7
Purley Bury Av PUR/KEN CR8 86 G1
Purley Bury Cl PUR/KEN CR8 86 G1
Purley Cl CLAY IG5 28 J14
Purley Downs Rd SAND/SEL CR2 74 G14
Purley Hl PUR/KEN CR8 86 F2
Purley Knoll PUR/KEN CR8 86 D1
Purley Oaks Rd SAND/SEL CR2 74 J14
Purley Pde PUR/KEN CR8 * 86 E1
Purley Park Rd PUR/KEN CR8 74 G14
Purley Pl IS N1 38 F12
Purley Ri PUR/KEN CR8 86 D2
Purley Rd ED N9 26 H8
SAND/SEL CR2 74 H12
Purley V PUR/KEN CR8 86 F3
Purley Wy CROY/NA CR0 74 D6
PUR/KEN CR8 86 E1
Purlieu Wy EPP CM16 18 C9
Purlings Rd BUSH WD23 22 K3
Purneys Rd ELTH/MOT SE9 64 F2
Purrett Rd WOOL/PLUM SE18 53 P10
Pursers Cross Rd FUL/PGN SW6 * 49 M13
Pursewardens Cl WEA W13 47 S6
Pursey Cl BGR/WK TN15 79 S11
Pursley Gdns BORE WD6 13 L12
Pursley Rd MLHL NW7 24 H12
Purves Rd WLSDN NW10 48 H1
Putney Br PUT/ROE SW15 61 L1
Putney Bridge Ap FUL/PGN SW6 61 L1
Putney Bridge Rd PUT/ROE SW15 61 M2
Putney Common PUT/ROE SW15 60 J1
Putney Ex PUT/ROE SW15 * 60 K2
Putney Gdns CHDH RM6 41 R3
Putney Heath PUT/ROE SW15 60 H4
Putney Heath La PUT/ROE SW15 60 K4
Putney High St PUT/ROE SW15 61 L2
Putney Hl PUT/ROE SW15 60 K5
Putney Park Av PUT/ROE SW15 60 G2
Putney Park La PUT/ROE SW15 60 H2
Putney Rd PEND EN3 16 D10
Puttenham Cl OXHEY WD19 22 E8
Pycombe Cnr NFNCH/WDSPK N12 25 M9
Pycroft Wy ED N9 27 L9
Pye Cl CTHM CR3 86 H13
Pylbrook Rd SUT SM1 73 N8
Pyle Hl WOKS/MYFD GU22 80 B14
Pylon Wy CROY/NA CR0 74 C6
Pym Cl EBAR EN4 25 R3
Pymers Md DUL SE21 62 G6
Pymmes Brook Trail EBAR EN4 25 S3
EBAR EN4 25 T5
PLMGR N13 26 D9
Pymmes Cl PLMGR N13 26 D10
TOTM N17 27 M13
Pymmes Gdns North ED N9 26 K8
Pymmes Gdns South ED N9 26 K8
Pymmes Green Rd FBAR/BDGN N11 25 V9
Pymmes Rd PLMGR N13 26 C11
Pymms Brook Dr EBAR EN4 25 S2
Pym Orch BH/WHM TN16 89 S14
Pynchester Cl HGDN/ICK UB10 33 S7
Pyne Rd SURB KT6 72 A6
Pynest Green La WAB EN9 17 N11
Pynham Cl ABYW SE2 53 Q8
Pynnacles Cl STAN HA7 23 R10
Pyot Pth BORE WD6 13 L11
Pyrcroft La WEY KT13 69 T10
Pyrcroft Rd CHERT KT16 68 K5
Pyrford Common Rd
WOKS/MYFD GU22 80 J6
Pyrford Heath WOKS/MYFD GU22 80 K6
Pyrford Rd BF/WBF KT14 81 L4
Pyrford Woods Cl WOKS/MYFD GU22 80 K5
Pyrford Woods Rd WOKS/MYFD GU22 80 K5
Pyrian Cl WOKS/MYFD GU22 80 H7
Pyrland Rd HBRY N5 38 H10
RCHPK/HAM TW10 59 V4
Pyrles Gn LOU IG10 17 V14
Pyrles La LOU IG10 17 V14
Pyrmont Gv WNWD SE27 62 F8
Pyrmont Rd CHSWK W4 48 A11
Pytchley Crs NRWD SE19 62 G11
Pytchley Rd EDUL SE22 62 J1

Q

The Quadrangle BAY/PAD W2 3 N11
HNHL SE24 * 62 G3
WBPTN SW10 * 49 Q13
Quadrant Ar REGST W1B 4 B14
Quadrant Cl HDN NW4 * 36 H3
Quadrant Gv KTTN NW5 37 T10
Quadrant Rd RCH/KEW TW9 59 T2
THHTH CR7 74 F2
The Quadrant BELMT SM2 73 Q11
BXLYHN DA7 53 T12
EDGW HA8 * 24 A11
NKENS W10 * 48 K1
PUR RM19 55 Q9
RCH/KEW TW9 59 T3
RYLN/HDSTN HA2 * 35 M1
RYNPK SW20 61 L13
Quadrant Wy WEY KT13 69 S9
Quad Rd WBLY HA9 * 35 T8
Quaggy Wk BKHTH/KID SE3 64 C2
Quail Gdns SAND/SEL CR2 75 Q14
Quainton St WLSDN NW10 36 D8
Quaker Cl SEV TN13 90 K13
Quaker La NWDGN UB2 46 J8
WAB EN9 16 J8
Quakers Course CDALE/KGS NW9 24 F13
Quaker's Hall La SEV TN13 90 J13
Quakers La ISLW TW7 47 Q12
POTB/CUF EN6 14 D4
Quakers Pl FSTGT E7 40 F10
Quaker St WCHPL E1 5 U8
Quakers Wk WCHMH N21 26 H4
Quality Ct LINN WC2A 4 J11
Quality St REDH RH1 93 V4
Quantock Cl DTCH/LGLY SL3 44 E10
HYS/HAR UB3 45 V12
Quantock Gdns CRICK NW2 * 36 K7
Quantock Ms PECK SE15 51 L14
Quantock Rd BXLYHN DA7 54 E14
Quarles Cl CRW RM5 30 A12
Quarles Park Rd CHDH RM6 41 R4
Quarrendon St FUL/PGN SW6 49 N14
Quarr Rd CAR SM5 73 R4
Quarry Cl OXTED RH8 96 A6
Quarry Gdns LHD/OX KT22 83 T11
Quarry Hl BGR/WK TN15 90 K13
Quarry Hill Pk REIG RH2 93 Q7
Quarry Ms PUR RM19 55 N9
Quarry Park Rd SUT SM1 73 M11
Quarry Ri SUT SM1 73 M11
Quarry Rd GDST RH9 95 N4
OXTED RH8 96 A6
WAND/EARL SW18 61 Q4
The Quarry BRKHM/BTCW RH3 92 D8
Quartermaine Av WOKS/MYFD GU22 80 D12
Quartermile La LEY E10 39 T9
Quatre Ports CHING E4 * 27 V10
Quay House POP/IOD E14 * 51 S7
Quay La RDART DA2 67 V2
Quebec Av BH/WHM TN16 97 M2
Quebec Ms MBLAR W1H 3 R12
Quebec Rd GNTH/NBYPK IG2 41 L5
YEAD UB4 46 E5
Quebec Wy BERM/RHTH SE16 51 P7
Queen Adelaide Rd PGE/AN SE20 63 N12
Queen Alexandra's Wy
HOR/WEW KT19 84 A1
Queen Anne Av HAYES BR2 76 C1
Queen Anne Dr ESH/CLAY KT10 71 N12
Queen Anne Ga BXLYHN DA7 65 T1
Queen Anne Ms CAVSQ/HST W1G 3 V10
Queen Anne Rd HOM E9 39 P11
Queen Annes Cl WHTN TW2 59 M8
Queen Annes Ct LHD/OX KT22 83 R11
Queen Anne's Gdns CHSWK W4 48 E8
EA W5 47 U7
EN EN1 26 J4
LHD/OX KT22 83 R11
MTCM CR4 * 73 T1
Queen Anne's Ga STJSPK SW1H 8 C4
Queen Anne's Gv CHSWK W4 48 E8
EA W5 47 U7
ED N9 26 H5
Queen Annes Ms LHD/OX KT22 * 83 R11
Queen Anne's Pl EN EN1 26 J4
Queen Anne's Ter LHD/OX KT22 * 83 R11
Queen Anne St CAVSQ/HST W1G 3 U10
Queen Anne Ter WAP E1W * 51 M5
Queen Borough Gdns CHST BR7 65 M11
Queenborough Gdns
GNTH/NBYPK IG2 40 J2
Queen Caroline Est HMSMTH W6 48 J10
Queen Caroline St HMSMTH W6 48 J10
Queen Elizabeth Buildings EMB EC4Y * 4 J13
Queen Elizabeth College
GNWCH SE10 * 51 U12
Queen Elizabeth Ct WAB EN9 * 16 K9
Queen Elizabeth Gdns MRDN SM4 73 N2
Queen Elizabeth II Br RDART DA2 67 Q1
WTHK RM20 55 S14
Queen Elizabeth Rd KUTN/CMB KT2 59 V14
WALTH E17 39 Q1
Queen Elizabeth's Cl STNW/STAM N16 38 H7
Queen Elizabeth's Dr CROY/NA CR0 75 V14
STHGT/OAK N14 26 C6
Queen Elizabeth's Gdns
CROY/NA CR0 75 V14
Queen Elizabeth St STHWK SE1 9 U3
Queen Elizabeth's Wk
STNW/STAM N16 38 H7
WLGTN SM6 74 B9
Queen Elizabeth Wk BARN SW13 48 H13
Queen Elizabeth Wy WOKS/MYFD GU22 80 D9
Queenhill Rd SAND/SEL CR2 75 M14
Queenhithe BLKFR EC4V 5 P14
Queen Isabella Wy STBT EC1A 5 M11
Queen Margaret's Gv IS N1 38 J10
Queen Mary Av RYNPK SW20 72 K3
Queen Mary Cl ROM RM1 42 F4
SURB KT6 72 A8
WOKS/MYFD GU22 * 80 G6
Queen Mary Rd NRWD SE19 62 F11
SHPTN TW17 57 U14
Queen Mary's Av CAR SM5 73 T12
WATW WD18 22 A2
Queen Marys Ct WAB EN9 * 16 J9
Queen Mary's Dr ADL/WDHM KT15 68 K14
Queen Mother Ga MYFR/PICC W1J 7 T2
Queen Mother's Dr DEN/HRF UB9 32 K4
Queens Acre CHEAM SM3 72 K12
Queens Av BF/WBF KT14 81 P2
FELT TW13 58 E9
FNCH N3 25 Q12
GFD/PVL UB6 46 K4
KTN/HRWW/WS HA3 35 R1
MUSWH N10 37 U1
TRDG/WHET N20 25 R7
WATW WD18 22 C3
WCHMH N21 26 F6
WFD IG8 28 D10
Queensberry Ms West SKENS SW7 * 7 L7
Queensberry Pl MNPK E12 40 F10
SKENS SW7 7 L7
Queensberry Wy SKENS SW7 * 7 L7
Queensborough Ms BAY/PAD W2 * 2 J13
Queensborough Pas BAY/PAD W2 2 J13
Queensborough Studios BAY/PAD W2 2 J13
Queensborough Ter BAY/PAD W2 2 J14
Queensbridge Pk ISLW TW7 59 N4
Queensbridge Rd HACK E8 5 V2
Queensbury Rd ALP/SUD HA0 35 V14
CDALE/KGS NW9 36 D5
Queensbury St IS N1 38 G12
Queens Circ VX/NE SW8 7 U14
Queen's Cl EDGW HA8 24 A10
ESH/CLAY KT10 * 70 K9
KWD/TDW/WH KT20 84 G14
WLGTN SM6 73 V10
Queen's Club Gdns WKENS W14 6 B12
Queens Ct WEY KT13 70 A10
WOKS/MYFD GU22 * 80 D8
BELMT SM2 * 85 N1
Queenscourt WBLY HA9 35 U9
Queens Court Ride COB KT11 82 C3
Queen's Crs KTTN NW5 37 U11
RCHPK/HAM TW10 59 V3
Queenscroft Rd ELTH/MOT SE9 64 F3
Queensdale Crs NTGHL W11 48 K6
Queensdale Pl NTGHL W11 6 A2
Queensdale Rd NTGHL W11 6 A2
Queensdale Wk NTGHL W11 6 A2
Queens Down Rd CLPT E5 39 M9
Queens Dr ABLGY WD5 11 M6
BRYLDS KT5 72 A5
CHES/WCR EN8 16 G8
DTCH/LGLY SL3 32 D13
EA W5 47 V4
FSBYPK N4 38 F7
LEY E10 39 S5
LHD/OX KT22 83 L1
RSEV TN14 90 J10
THDIT KT7 71 Q4
The Queen's Dr RKW/CH/CXG WD3 20 K5
Queen's Elm Sq CHEL SW3 7 M10
Queen's Gdns BAY/PAD W2 2 J13
EA W5 47 S3
HDN NW4 36 J3
HEST TW5 46 G13
RAIN RM13 42 D14
RDART DA2 67 P6
UPMR RM14 43 T4
Queens Garth FSTH SE23 * 63 N7
Queensgate COB KT11 82 F2
Queens Ga SKENS SW7 6 K4
Queens Gate Gdns CHST BR7 65 M13
Queensgate Gdns PUT/ROE SW15 60 H2
Queen's Gate Gdns SKENS SW7 6 K6
Queen's Gate Ms SKENS SW7 6 K4
Queensgate Pl KIL/WHAMP NW6 37 N12
Queen's Gate Pl SKENS SW7 6 K6
Queen's Gate Place Ms SKENS SW7 6 K7
Queen's Gate Ter SKENS SW7 6 K5
Queen's Gv STJWD NW8 3 L2
Queen's Grove Rd CHING E4 27 V6
Queen's Head St IS N1 5 M2
Queens Keep TWK TW1 * 59 S4
Queensland Av UED N18 26 G11
WIM/MER SW19 61 P13
Queensland Cl WALTH E17 27 R14
Queensland Rd HOLWY N7 38 E9
Queens La MUSWH N10 37 V1
Queens Md EDGW HA8 23 V11
Queensmead LHD/OX KT22 * 83 L1
STJWD NW8 3 M1
Queensmead Av EW KT17 72 H14
Queen's Mead Rd HAYES BR2 64 B14
Queensmere Cl WIM/MER SW19 60 K7
Queensmere Rd WIM/MER SW19 60 K7
Queen's Ms BAY/PAD W2 2 G13
Queensmill Rd FUL/PGN SW6 48 K12
Queens Pde CEND/HSY/T N8 * 38 F2
CRICK NW2 * 36 J11
EA W5 * 47 V4
FBAR/BDGN N11 * 25 T10
FBAR/BDGN N11 * 26 C12
HDN NW4 * 36 H3
Queens Parade Cl FBAR/BDGN N11 25 T10
Queens Park Gdns FELT TW13 58 B8
Queen's Park Rd CTHM CR3 86 J13
HARH RM3 31 N13
Queen's Pl MRDN SM4 73 N2
WAT WD17 22 E1
WOT/HER KT12 70 A10
Queens Prom KUT/HW KT1 71 T2
Queen Sq BMSBY WC1N 4 F8
Queen's Ride BARN SW13 60 H1
Queen's Ri RCHPK/HAM TW10 59 V4
Queens Rd BAR EN5 24 K1
BARK IG11 41 L12
BECK BR3 63 Q14
BELMT SM2 73 N14
BKHH IG9 28 D7
BMLY BR1 64 C14
CHES/WCR EN8 16 E8
CHST BR7 64 K11
CROY/NA CR0 74 F4
EA W5 47 U4
ED N9 27 M7
EGH TW20 56 D11
EN EN1 26 J2
ERITH DA8 54 E11
FBAR/BDGN N11 26 C12
FELT TW13 58 D6
FNCH N3 25 Q13
HDN NW4 36 J3
HPTN TW12 58 K9
HSLW TW3 58 K1
HYS/HAR UB3 46 A4
KUTN/CMB KT2 60 A12
LOU IG10 28 H1
MORT/ESHN SW14 60 D1
MRDN SM4 73 N2
MTCM CR4 73 R1
NWDGN UB2 46 F7
NWMAL KT3 72 F2
PECK SE15 51 N13
PLSTW E13 40 D13
RCHPK/HAM TW10 59 V4
TEDD TW11 59 P11
THDIT KT7 71 P3
TWK TW1 59 P6
UX/CGN UB8 45 N1
WALTH E17 39 R4
WAN E11 40 A5
WAT WD17 11 Q14
WDR/YW UB7 45 R7
WELL DA16 53 R14
WEY KT13 69 V10
WIM/MER SW19 61 N11
WLGTN SM6 73 V10
Queen's Rd West PLSTW E13 40 C14
Queens Rw WALW SE17 9 Q11
Queens Ter ISLW TW7 59 Q2
PLSTW E13 40 D13
STJWD NW8 3 L2
THDIT KT7 * 71 Q4
WCHPL E1 * 51 N2
Queens Terrace Cottages HNWL W7 * 47 N7
Queensthorpe Ms SYD SE26 * 63 P9
Queensthorpe Rd SYD SE26 63 P9
Queenstown Gdns RAIN RM13 54 F1
Queenstown Rd VX/NE SW8 7 U12
Queen St BXLYHN DA7 65 V1
CHERT KT16 69 L6
CROY/NA CR0 74 G9
ERITH DA8 * 54 E11
KGLGY WD4 10 A6
MYFR/PICC W1J 7 U1
ROMW/RG RM7 42 D4
STP EC4M 5 P12
TOTM N17 26 J11
Queen Street Pl CANST EC4R 5 P14
Queensville Rd BAL SW12 62 B5
Queens Wk ASHF TW15 57 P9
CDALE/KGS NW9 36 C7
CHING E4 27 V6
EA W5 47 S2
HRW HA1 35 N2
RSLP HA4 34 E8
Queens Walk Ter RSLP HA4 * 34 E8
The Queens Wk STHWK SE1 9 T1
Queens Wy CHES/WCR EN8 16 F8
FELT TW13 58 E9
HDN NW4 36 J3
RAD WD7 12 J5
Queensway BAY/PAD W2 2 H12
CROY/NA CR0 74 D11
PEND EN3 27 N2
REDH RH1 93 T9
STMC/STPC BR5 77 L3
SUN TW16 58 D14
WWKM BR4 76 C9
Queensway North WOT/HER KT12 70 E9
Queensway South WOT/HER KT12 70 E10
The Queensway CFSP/GDCR SL9 32 B2
Queens Well Av TRDG/WHET N20 25 S9
Queen's Whf HMSMTH W6 48 J10
Queenswood Av HPTN TW12 58 K11
HSLW TW3 46 H14
THHTH CR7 74 E3
WALTH E17 27 U13
WLGTN SM6 74 B9
Queenswood Crs GSTN WD25 11 N7
Queenswood Gdns WAN E11 40 C6
Queenswood Pk FNCH N3 25 L14
Queenswood Rd BFN/LL DA15 65 P4
FSTH SE23 63 Q8
Queen's Wood Rd HGT N6 37 V4
Queen's Yd FITZ W1T 4 B8
Queen Victoria Av ALP/SUD HA0 35 T12
Queen Victoria St BLKFR EC4V 5 L13
Queen Victoria Ter WAP E1W * 51 M5
Quemerford Rd HOLWY N7 38 D10
Quendon Dr WAB EN9 16 K7
Quennell Cl ASHTD KT21 83 V9
Quentin Pl LEW SE13 64 A1
Quentin Rd LEW SE13 64 A1
Quentins Dr BH/WHM TN16 * 88 K6
Quentins Wk BH/WHM TN16 * 88 K6
Quernmore Cl BMLY BR1 64 C11
Quernmore Rd BMLY BR1 64 C11
FSBYPK N4 38 E4
Querrin St FUL/PGN SW6 49 Q14
Questor DART DA1 * 67 M7
Quex Ms KIL/WHAMP NW6 2 F1
Quex Rd KIL/WHAMP NW6 2 F1
Quickley Brow RKW/CH/CXG WD3 * 20 F4
Quickley La RKW/CH/CXG WD3 20 G4
Quickley Ri RKW/CH/CXG WD3 20 F4
Quickly Brow RKW/CH/CXG WD3 20 F4
Quickmoor La KGLGY WD4 10 B7
Quick Rd CHSWK W4 48 E10
Quicks Rd WIM/MER SW19 61 P12
Quick St IS N1 5 M4
Quickswood HAMP NW3 37 S12
Quickwood Cl RKW/CH/CXG WD3 20 K4
Quiet Cl ADL/WDHM KT15 69 L9
Quiet Nook HAYES BR2 76 F8
The Quillot WOT/HER KT12 70 B10
Quill St EA W5 47 U1
FSBYPK N4 38 E8
Quilp St STHWK SE1 9 N3
Quilter Rd STMC/STPC BR5 77 T6
Quilter St BETH E2 51 L1
WOOL/PLUM SE18 53 P10
Quinbrookes SLN SL2 44 A4
Quince Rd LEW SE13 51 T14
Quincy Rd EGH TW20 56 E10
Quinnell Cl WOOL/PLUM SE18 53 P10
Quinta Dr BAR EN5 24 H3
Quintin Av RYNPK SW20 61 L13
Quinton Cl BECK BR3 75 U1
HEST TW5 46 D12
WLGTN SM6 73 V9
Quinton Rd THDIT KT7 71 Q6
Quinton St WAND/EARL SW18 61 Q7
Quinton Wy WAB EN9 16 J9
Quixley St POP/IOD E14 51 V5
Quorn Rd EDUL SE22 62 J2

R

Rabbit La WOT/HER KT12 70 C12
Rabbit Rw KENS W8 * 6 F1
Rabbits Rd EYN DA4 67 T14
MNPK E12 40 G9
Rabies Heath Rd REDH RH1 95 L10
Rablus Pl EYN DA4 * 79 M4
Rabournmead Dr NTHLT UB5 34 G10
Raby Rd NWMAL KT3 72 D2
Raby St POP/IOD E14 * 51 Q4
Raccoon Wy HSLWW TW4 46 E14
Rachel Cl BARK/HLT IG6 41 M2
Rackham Cl WELL DA16 53 R14
Rackham Ms STRHM/NOR SW16 62 A11
Racton Rd FUL/PGN SW6 6 E12
Radbourne Av EA W5 47 S9
Radbourne Cl CLPT E5 39 P9
Radbourne Ct KTN/HRWW/WS HA3 * 35 R4
Radbourne Crs WALTH E17 39 V1
Radbourne Rd BAL SW12 62 A5
Radcliffe Av ENC/FH EN2 15 S13
WLSDN NW10 36 G14
Radcliffe Gdns CAR SM5 73 S12
Radcliffe Rd CROY/NA CR0 74 K7
KTN/HRWW/WS HA3 23 Q14
STHWK SE1 9 T5
WCHMH N21 26 F6
Radcliffe Sq PUT/ROE SW15 60 K4
Radcliffe Wy NTHLT UB5 46 F1
Radcot Av DTCH/LGLY SL3 44 F8
Radcot St LBTH SE11 8 K10
Raddington Rd NKENS W10 2 B10
Radfield Dr RDART DA2 67 Q5
Radfield Wy BFN/LL DA15 65 M5
Radford Est WLSDN NW10 * 48 E1
Radford Rd LEW SE13 63 U4
Radford Wy BARK IG11 53 P1
Radipole Rd FUL/PGN SW6 49 M13
Radius Pk EBED/NFELT TW14 * 58 B2
Radland Rd CAN/RD E16 52 C4
Radlet Av SYD SE26 63 M8
Radlett Cl FSTGT E7 40 B11
Radlett La RAD WD7 12 H8
Radlett Park Rd RAD WD7 12 F8
Radlett Pl STJWD NW8 3 N2
Radlett Rd GSTN WD25 12 A12
LCOL/BKTW AL2 12 C3
WAT WD17 22 E1
WATN WD24 11 R14
Radley Av GDMY/SEVK IG3 41 P9
Radley Cl EBED/NFELT TW14 58 B6
Radley Ct BERM/RHTH SE16 51 P7
Radley Gdns KTN/HRWW/WS HA3 35 U2
Radley Ms KENS W8 6 F7
Radley Rd TOTM N17 26 K14
Radley's La SWFD E18 28 C14
Radleys Md DAGE RM10 42 B11
Radley Sq CLPT E5 * 39 N7
Radley Ter CAN/RD E16 52 B3
Radlix Rd LEY E10 39 S6
Radnor Av HRW HA1 35 N3
WELL DA16 65 R3
Radnor Cl CHST BR7 65 N11
MTCM CR4 74 C3
Radnor Ct REDH RH1 93 S10
Radnor Crs REDBR IG4 40 H3
WOOL/PLUM SE18 53 Q12
Radnor Gdns EN EN1 15 U13
TWK TW1 59 P7
Radnor Hall BORE WD6 * 23 U3
Radnor Ms BAY/PAD W2 3 M12
Radnor Pl BAY/PAD W2 3 N12
Radnor Rd HRW HA1 35 M3
KIL/WHAMP NW6 2 A2
PECK SE15 51 L12
TWK TW1 59 P7
WEY KT13 69 S8
Radnor St FSBYE EC1V 5 P6
Radnor Ter WKENS W14 6 C7
Radnor Wk CHEL SW3 7 P10
CROY/NA CR0 75 Q5
Radnor Wy DTCH/LGLY SL3 44 C9
WLSDN NW10 48 B2
Radolphs KWD/TDW/WH KT20 84 K12
Radstock Av KTN/HRWW/WS HA3 35 Q1
Radstock Cl FBAR/BDGN N11 25 U10
Radstock St BTSEA SW11 * 7 N14
Radstock Wy REDH RH1 94 C5
Radstone Ct WOKS/MYFD GU22 80 D8
Raebarn Gdns BAR EN5 24 H3
Raeburn Av BRYLDS KT5 72 B4
DART DA1 66 H3
Raeburn Cl GLDGN NW11 37 Q4
KUT/HW KT1 59 T12
Raeburn Rd BFN/LL DA15 65 N4
EDGW HA8 24 A14
YEAD UB4 33 V14
Raeburn St BRXS/STRHM SW2 62 C2
Rafford Wy BMLY BR1 64 D14
Ragge Wy BGR/WK TN15 91 M10
Raggleswood CHST BR7 64 J13
Rag Hill Rd BH/WHM TN16 88 G11
Raglan Av CHES/WCR EN8 16 D8
Raglan Cl HSLWW TW4 58 H3
REIG RH2 93 Q8
Raglan Ct SAND/SEL CR2 74 F10
Raglan Gdns OXHEY WD19 22 D6
Raglan Rd BELV DA17 53 V9
EN EN1 26 K5
HAYES BR2 76 E2
REIG RH2 93 Q8
WALTH E17 39 U3
WOOL/PLUM SE18 53 L10
Raglan St KTTN NW5 37 V11
Raglan Ter RYLN/HDSTN HA2 * 34 K9
Raglan Vls WALTH E17 * 39 U3
Raglan Wy NTHLT UB5 35 L11
Ragley Cl ACT W3 48 C7
Rags La CHESW EN7 15 V1
Ragstones BGR/WK TN15 91 M10
Rahn Rd EPP CM16 18 E5
Raider Cl ROMW/RG RM7 30 B13
Railey Ms KTTN NW5 38 A10
Railshead Rd ISLW TW7 59 R2
Railton Rd HNHL SE24 62 E3
Railway Ap CHERT KT16 * 68 K6
FSBYPK N4 38 E4
HRW HA1 35 P2
STHWK SE1 9 Q1
TWK TW1 59 Q5
WLGTN SM6 * 73 V11
Railway Ar BRXN/ST SW9 * 62 E2
Railway Av BERM/RHTH SE16 51 N7
Railway Cottages BNSTD SM7 * 85 M4
HMSMTH W6 * 48 J7
OXTED RH8 * 96 C9
SRTFD E15 * 40 A14
WIM/MER SW19 * 61 P9
Railway Gv NWCR SE14 51 R12
Railway Pl BELV DA17 54 A8
Railway Ri EDUL SE22 62 J2
Railway Rd CHES/WCR EN8 16 F7
TEDD TW11 59 N9
Railway Side BARN SW13 60 E1
Railway Station Whf LEY E10 * 39 Q6
Railway St BCTR RM8 41 S6
IS N1 4 F4
Railway Ter BH/WHM TN16 97 M1
FELT TW13 58 C6
KGLGY WD4 10 G1
LEW SE13 63 T3
STA TW18 56 H10
WALTH E17 27 U13
Railway Vw DTCH/LGLY SL3 * 56 D1
Rainborough Cl WBLY HA9 36 C11
Rainbow Av POP/IOD E14 51 T10
Rainbow Ct OXHEY WD19 22 E4
Rainbow Quay BERM/RHTH SE16 51 Q8
Rainbow Rd PUR RM19 55 S8
Rainbow St CMBW SE5 9 S13
Rainer Cl CHES/WCR EN8 16 D3
Raine St WAP E1W 51 M6
Rainham Cl BTSEA SW11 61 T4
ELTH/MOT SE9 65 N4
Rainham Rd RAIN RM13 54 G1
WLSDN NW10 48 J1
Rainham Rd North DAGE RM10 42 B7
Rainham Rd South DAGE RM10 42 B9
Rainhill Wy BOW E3 51 S1
Rainsborough Av DEPT SE8 51 Q10
Rainsford Cl STAN HA7 23 S10
Rainsford Rd WLSDN NW10 48 B1
Rainsford St BAY/PAD W2 3 N11
Rainsford Wy HCH RM12 42 G6
Rainton Rd CHARL SE7 52 C10
Rainville Rd HMSMTH W6 48 J11
Raisins Hl PIN HA5 34 E1
Raith Av STHGT/OAK N14 26 B8
Raleigh Av WLGTN SM6 74 B9
YEAD UB4 46 D3
Raleigh Cl ERITH DA8 54 F11
HDN NW4 36 J3
PIN HA5 34 F5
RSLP HA4 34 B7
Raleigh Ct STA TW18 57 L9
Raleigh Dr BRYLDS KT5 72 C6
ESH/CLAY KT10 71 M10
TRDG/WHET N20 25 S8
Raleigh Gdns BRXS/STRHM SW2 62 D4
MTCM CR4 61 T14
Raleigh Ms IS N1 5 M2
ORP BR6 77 P10
Raleigh Rd CEND/HSY/T N8 38 E2
ENC/FH EN2 26 H2
FELT TW13 58 B7
NWDGN UB2 46 G10
PGE/AN SE20 63 P12
RCH/KEW TW9 59 V1
Raleigh St IS N1 5 M2
Raleigh Wy FELT TW13 58 E10
STHGT/OAK N14 26 B6
Ralliwood Rd ASHTD KT21 84 A9
Ralph Perring Ct BECK BR3 75 S2
Ralston St CHEL SW3 7 Q10
Ralston Wy OXHEY WD19 22 F7
Rama Cl STRHM/NOR SW16 62 C12
Ramac Wy CHARL SE7 52 C10
Rama La NRWD SE19 62 K12
Rambler Cl STRHM/NOR SW16 62 A9
Rambler La DTCH/LGLY SL3 44 A8
Rame Cl TOOT SW17 61 U10
Ramilles Cl BRXS/STRHM SW2 62 C4
Ramillies Pl SOHO/CST W1F 4 A12
Ramillies Rd BFN/LL DA15 65 R4
CHSWK W4 48 D8
MLHL NW7 24 E7
Ramillies St SOHO/SHAV W1D 4 A12
Ramney Dr PEND EN3 16 E10
Ramones Ter MTCM CR4 * 74 A2
Ramornie Cl WOT/HER KT12 70 H10
WOT/HER KT12 70 H9
Rampart St WCHPL E1 51 M4
Ram Pas KUT/HW KT1 59 T14
Rampayne St PIM SW1V 8 C9
Rampton Cl CHING E4 27 S8
Ramsay Gdns HARH RM3 30 J13
Ramsay Ms CHEL SW3 7 N11
Ramsay Rd ACT W3 48 C8
FSTGT E7 40 C8
Ramscroft Cl ED N9 26 J5
Ramsdale Rd TOOT SW17 61 U10
Ramsden Cl STMC/STPC BR5 77 S6
Ramsden Dr CRW RM5 30 A12
Ramsden Ga BAL SW12 * 61 V5
Ramsden Rd BAL SW12 61 U5
ERITH DA8 54 D12
FBAR/BDGN N11 25 T10
ORP BR6 77 R5
Ramsey Cl BRKMPK AL9 14 F1
CDALE/KGS NW9 36 F4
GFD/PVL UB6 35 M10
Ramsey Pl CTHM CR3 86 G12
Ramsey Rd THHTH CR7 74 E4
Ramsey St BETH E2 51 L2
Ramsey Wk IS N1 38 H11
Ramsey Wy STHGT/OAK N14 26 A5
Ramsgate Cl CAN/RD E16 52 D6
Ramsgate St HACK E8 * 38 K11
Ramsgill Ap GNTH/NBYPK IG2 41 P2
Ramsgill Dr GNTH/NBYPK IG2 41 P3
Rams Gv CHDH RM6 41 U2
Ramulis Dr YEAD UB4 46 G2
Ramus Wood Av ORP BR6 77 N10
Rancliffe Gdns ELTH/MOT SE9 64 G2
Rancliffe Rd EHAM E6 40 G14
Randal Crs REIG RH2 93 N12
Randall Av CRICK NW2 36 E7
Randall Cl BTSEA SW11 49 S13
DTCH/LGLY SL3 44 D10
ERITH DA8 54 C11
Randall Dr HCH RM12 42 J9
Randall Pl GNWCH SE10 51 U12
Randall Rd LBTH SE11 8 G9
Randall Rw LBTH SE11 8 G8
Randalls Crs LHD/OX KT22 83 Q10
Randalls Park Av LHD/OX KT22 83 Q10
Randalls Park Dr LHD/OX KT22 83 Q11
Randalls Rd LHD/OX KT22 83 N10
Randalls Wk LCOL/BKTW AL2 11 T5
Randalls Wy LHD/OX KT22 83 Q11
Randell's Rd IS N1 4 F1
Randisbourne Gdns CAT SE6 * 63 T8
Randle Rd RCHPK/HAM TW10 59 S9
Randlesdown Rd CAT SE6 63 T8
Randle's La RSEV TN14 89 T4
Randolf Rd HAYES BR2 76 H6
Randolph Ap CAN/RD E16 52 E4
Randolph Av MV/WKIL W9 2 G4
Randolph Cl BXLYHN DA7 66 C1
COB KT11 82 J5
KUTN/CMB KT2 * 60 C10
Randolph Crs MV/WKIL W9 2 J8
Randolph Gdns KIL/WHAMP NW6 2 G4
Randolph Gv CHDH RM6 41 S3
Randolph Ms MV/WKIL W9 2 K8
Randolph Rd DTCH/LGLY SL3 44 C9
EW KT17 84 F4
MV/WKIL W9 2 J8
STHL UB1 * 46 H7
WALTH E17 * 39 T3
Randon Cl RYLN/HDSTN HA2 22 K14
Ranelagh Av BARN SW13 48 G14
FUL/PGN SW6 61 M1
Ranelagh Cl EDGW HA8 24 A9
Ranelagh Dr EDGW HA8 24 A9
TWK TW1 59 R2
Ranelagh Gdns CHSWK W4 48 C12
FUL/PGN SW6 61 L1
IL IG1 40 J6
WAN E11 40 E3
Ranelagh Gv BGVA SW1W 7 T9
Ranelagh Pl NWMAL KT3 72 E3
Ranelagh Rd ALP/SUD HA0 35 T11
EA W5 47 T7
EHAM E6 40 J13
PIM SW1V 8 B10
REDH RH1 93 S10
STHL UB1 46 F6
TOTM N17 38 J1
WAN E11 40 A9
WDGN N22 26 D13
WLSDN NW10 36 F14
Ranfurly Rd SUT SM1 73 N7
Rangefield Rd BMLY BR1 64 A10
Rangemoor Rd SEVS/STOTM N15 38 K3
Rangers Rd BKHH IG9 28 C5
Range Wy SHPTN TW17 69 S5
Rangeworth Pl BFN/LL DA15 65 P8
Rangoon St TWRH EC3N * 5 U12
Rankin Cl CDALE/KGS NW9 36 E1
Ranleigh Gdns BXLYHN DA7 53 V12
Ranmere St BAL SW12 61 V6
Ranmoor Cl HRW HA1 35 M2
Ranmoor Gdns HRW HA1 35 M2
Ranmore Av CROY/NA CR0 74 K8
Ranmore Cl REDH RH1 93 U7
Ranmore Pth STMC/STPC BR5 77 Q2
Ranmore Pl WEY KT13 * 69 U10
Ranmore Rd BELMT SM2 72 K13
Rannoch Cl EDGW HA8 24 B7
Rannoch Rd HMSMTH W6 48 J11
Rannock Av CDALE/KGS NW9 36 E5
Ranskill Rd BORE WD6 13 L13
Ransom Cl OXHEY WD19 22 E5
Ransom Rd CHARL SE7 52 E9
Ranston Cl DEN/HRF UB9 32 K4
Ranston St CAMTN NW1 3 N9
Ranulf Rd CRICK NW2 37 M9
Ranwell Cl BOW E3 * 39 R13
Ranworth Cl ERITH DA8 54 E14
Ranworth Gdns POTB/CUF EN6 13 V5
Ranworth Rd ED N9 27 N7
Ranyard Cl CHSGTN KT9 71 V8
Raphael Av ROM RM1 42 F1
Raphael Cl RAD WD7 12 J6
Raphael Dr THDIT KT7 71 P6
WATN WD24 11 R14
Raphael St SKENS SW7 7 Q4
Rapier Cl PUR RM19 55 M9
Rasehill Cl RKW/CH/CXG WD3 21 N3
Rashleigh Wy EYN DA4 79 Q2
Rasper Rd TRDG/WHET N20 25 Q7
Rastell Av BRXS/STRHM SW2 62 B7
Ratcliffe Cl LEE/GVPK SE12 64 C5
UX/CGN UB8 45 P1
Ratcliffe Cross St WCHPL E1 * 51 P4
Ratcliffe La POP/IOD E14 51 Q4
Ratcliff Rd FSTGT E7 40 E10
Rathbone Market CAN/RD E16 * 52 B3
Rathbone Pl FITZ W1T 4 C10
Rathbone Sq CROY/NA CR0 * 74 G9
Rathbone St CAN/RD E16 52 B3
FITZ W1T 4 B10
Rathcoole Av CEND/HSY/T N8 38 D3
Rathcoole Gdns CEND/HSY/T N8 38 D3
Rathfern Rd CAT SE6 63 R6
Rathgar Av WEA W13 47 S6
Rathgar Cl FNCH N3 25 M14
Rathgar Rd BRXN/ST SW9 62 F1
Rathmell Dr CLAP SW4 62 B4
Rathmore Rd CHARL SE7 52 D10
Rat's La LOU IG10 17 P12
Rattray Rd BRXS/STRHM SW2 62 E2
Raul Rd PECK SE15 51 L14
Raveley St KTTN NW5 38 A9
Ravel Gdns SOCK/AV RM15 55 Q4
Ravel Rd SOCK/AV RM15 55 R4
Raven Cl RKW/CH/CXG WD3 21 N5
Ravencroft Crs ELTH/MOT SE9 64 H8
Ravendale Rd SUN TW16 58 B14
Ravenet St BTSEA SW11 49 V13
Ravenfield Rd TOOT SW17 61 T8
Ravenhill Rd PLSTW E13 40 E13
Ravenna Rd PUT/ROE SW15 60 K3
Ravenoak Wy CHIG IG7 29 N10
Ravenor Park Rd GFD/PVL UB6 46 K1
Raven Rd SWFD E18 28 E14
Raven Rw WCHPL E1 51 M3
Ravens Ait SURB KT6 * 71 T3
Ravensbourne Av HAYES BR2 63 V13
STWL/WRAY TW19 57 R6
Ravensbourne Crs HARH RM3 43 M1
Ravensbourne Gdns CLAY IG5 28 J13
WEA W13 47 R3
Ravensbourne Pk CAT SE6 63 S5
Ravensbourne Park Crs CAT SE6 63 R5
Ravensbourne Pl LEW SE13 51 T14
Ravensbourne Rd BMLY BR1 76 C1
CAT SE6 63 R5
DART DA1 66 G1
TWK TW1 59 S4
Ravensbury Av MRDN SM4 73 Q3
Ravensbury Gv MTCM CR4 73 R2
Ravensbury La MTCM CR4 73 R2
Ravensbury Rd STMC/STPC BR5 77 P2
WAND/EARL SW18 61 P7
Ravensbury Ter WAND/EARL SW18 61 P7
Ravenscar Rd BMLY BR1 64 A9
SURB KT6 71 V7
Ravens Cl CDALE/KGS NW9 24 F14
EN EN1 15 U14
HAYES BR2 64 B14
REDH RH1 93 T9
SURB KT6 71 T4
Ravenscourt SUN TW16 58 B13
Ravenscourt Av HMSMTH W6 48 G9
Ravenscourt Cl DEN/HRF UB9 33 U5
HCH RM12 43 L8
Ravenscourt Dr HCH RM12 43 L8
Ravenscourt Gdns HMSMTH W6 48 F9
Ravenscourt Gv HCH RM12 43 L7
Ravenscourt Pk HMSMTH W6 48 G9
Ravenscourt Pl HMSMTH W6 48 H9
Ravenscourt Rd HMSMTH W6 48 H9
STMC/STPC BR5 77 Q1
Ravenscourt Sq HMSMTH W6 48 G9
Ravenscraig Rd FBAR/BDGN N11 25 V9
Ravenscroft GSTN WD25 11 S9
Ravenscroft Av GLDGN NW11 37 M5
WBLY HA9 35 U6
Ravenscroft Cl CAN/RD E16 52 C3
Ravenscroft Cottages BAR EN5 * 25 N4
Ravenscroft Pk BAR EN5 24 K2
Ravenscroft Rd BECK BR3 63 N14
CAN/RD E16 52 C3
CHSWK W4 48 C9
WEY KT13 81 U1
Ravenscroft St BETH E2 5 V4
Ravensdale Av NFNCH/WDSPK N12 25 Q9
Ravensdale Gdns NRWD SE19 62 H12
Ravensdale Rd HSLWW TW4 58 G1
STNW/STAM N16 38 K5
Ravensdon St LBTH SE11 8 K10
Ravensfield DAGW RM9 41 T9
Ravens Fld DTCH/LGLY SL3 44 B7
Ravensfield Gdns HOR/WEW KT19 72 E10
Ravenshaw St KIL/WHAMP NW6 37 M10
Ravenshead Cl SAND/SEL CR2 87 N1
Ravenshill CHST BR7 64 K13
Ravenshurst Av HDN NW4 36 J2
Ravenside Cl UED N18 27 P10
Ravenslea Rd BAL SW12 61 T5
Ravensleigh Gdns BMLY BR1 64 C10
Ravensmead CFSP/GDCR SL9 20 D10
Ravensmead Rd HAYES BR2 63 V12
Ravensmede Wy CHSWK W4 48 F9
Ravensmere EPP CM16 18 E4
Ravens Ms LEE/GVPK SE12 * 64 C3
Ravenstone Rd CDALE/KGS NW9 * 36 F4
CEND/HSY/T N8 38 D1
Ravenstone St BAL SW12 61 U6
Ravens Wy LEE/GVPK SE12 64 C3
Ravens Wold PUR/KEN CR8 86 G5
Ravenswood BXLY DA5 65 U6
Ravenswood Av SURB KT6 71 V7
WWKM BR4 75 U6
Ravenswood Cl COB KT11 82 F5
CRW RM5 30 B10
Ravenswood Ct KUTN/CMB KT2 60 C11
WOKS/MYFD GU22 * 80 D8
Ravenswood Crs RYLN/HDSTN HA2 34 H7
WWKM BR4 75 U6
Ravenswood Gdns ISLW TW7 47 N13
Ravenswood Pk NTHWD HA6 22 C11
Ravenswood Rd BAL SW12 61 V5
CROY/NA CR0 74 F8
WALTH E17 39 U2
Ravensworth Rd ELTH/MOT SE9 64 H9
WLSDN NW10 * 48 H1
Ravey St SDTCH EC2A 5 S7
Ravine Gv WOOL/PLUM SE18 53 N11
Rav Pinter Cl STNW/STAM N16 38 K5
Rawlings Cl BECK BR3 75 U3
ORP BR6 77 P10
Rawlings Crs WBLY HA9 36 C8
Rawlings St CHEL SW3 7 Q7
Rawlins Cl FNCH N3 37 L1
SAND/SEL CR2 75 R12
Rawnsley Av MTCM CR4 73 R3
Rawreth Wk IS N1 5 P1
Rawson St BTSEA SW11 49 V13
Rawsthorne Cl CAN/RD E16 52 H6
Rawstorne Pl FSBYE EC1V * 5 L5
Rawstorne St FSBYE EC1V 5 L5
Ray Bell Ct BROCKY SE4 * 51 R14
Rayburn Rd EMPK RM11 43 N5
Raydean Rd BAR EN5 25 N3
Raydons Gdns DAGW RM9 41 U9
Raydons Rd DAGW RM9 41 U10
Raydon St ARCH N19 37 V7
Rayfield EPP CM16 18 D4
Rayfield Cl HAYES BR2 76 G4
Rayford Av LEE/GVPK SE12 64 B5
Rayford Cl DART DA1 66 J3
Ray Gdns BARK IG11 41 Q14
STAN HA7 23 R10
Ray Lamb Wy ERITH DA8 54 H11
Raylands Md CFSP/GDCR SL9 32 A3
Rayleas Cl WOOL/PLUM SE18 52 K13
Rayleigh Av TEDD TW11 59 N11
Rayleigh Cl PLMGR N13 26 H8
Rayleigh Ct KUT/HW KT1 60 A14
Rayleigh Ri SAND/SEL CR2 74 J11
Rayleigh Rd CAN/RD E16 52 D6
PLMGR N13 26 G8
WFD IG8 28 E12
WIM/MER SW19 61 M13
Ray Lodge Rd WFD IG8 28 F11
Raymead Av THHTH CR7 74 E3
Raymead Cl LHD/OX KT22 83 N12
Raymead Wy LHD/OX KT22 83 N12
Raymere Gdns WOOL/PLUM SE18 53 N12
Raymond Av SWFD E18 40 B1
WEA W13 47 Q8
Raymond Buildings GINN WC1R * 4 H9
Raymond Cl ABLGY WD5 10 K6
DTCH/LGLY SL3 44 J13
SYD SE26 63 N10
Raymond Gdns CHIG IG7 29 R8
Raymond Rd BECK BR3 75 Q2
DTCH/LGLY SL3 44 E9
GNTH/NBYPK IG2 41 M5
PLSTW E13 40 E12
WIM/MER SW19 61 L11
Raymond Wy ESH/CLAY KT10 * 71 Q11
Raymouth Rd BERM/RHTH SE16 51 N9
Rayne Ct SWFD E18 40 B2
Rayners Cl ALP/SUD HA0 35 T10
DTCH/LGLY SL3 44 G12
Rayners Gdns NTHLT UB5 46 D1
Rayners La PIN HA5 34 H4
Rayner's Rd PUT/ROE SW15 61 L3
Raynes Av WAN E11 40 E5
Raynes Pk RYNPK SW20 60 J14
Raynham Av UED N18 27 L11
Raynham Rd HMSMTH W6 48 H9
UED N18 27 L10
Raynham Ter UED N18 27 L10
Raynor Cl STHL UB1 46 H6
Raynor Pl IS N1 5 P1
Raynton Cl RYLN/HDSTN HA2 34 G6
YEAD UB4 46 B2
Raynton Dr YEAD UB4 34 A14
Raynton Rd PEND EN3 16 D11
Ray Rd CRW RM5 30 B10
E/WMO/HCT KT8 70 K3
Rays Av UED N18 27 N9
Rays Hl EYN DA4 79 Q2
Rays Rd UED N18 27 N9
WWKM BR4 75 U5
Ray St CLKNW EC1R 4 K8
Ray Street Br CLKNW EC1R * 4 K8
Raywood Cl HYS/HAR UB3 45 U12
Reachview Cl CAMTN NW1 38 A12
Read Cl THDIT KT7 71 Q5
Read Ct WAB EN9 17 N7
The Readens BNSTD SM7 85 S6
Reading Arch Rd REDH RH1 93 T10
Reading La HACK E8 39 M11
Reading Rd NTHLT UB5 34 K10
SUT SM1 73 Q10
The Readings RKW/CH/CXG WD3 20 K1
Reading Wy MLHL NW7 24 K10
Read Rd ASHTD KT21 83 T7
Reads Cl IL IG1 40 K8
Reads Rest La KWD/TDW/WH KT20 85 M9
Reapers Cl CAMTN NW1 4 C1
Reapers Wy ISLW TW7 59 M3
Reardon Pth WAP E1W 51 M6
Reardon St WAP E1W 51 M6
Reaston St NWCR SE14 51 N12
Reckitt Rd CHSWK W4 48 E10
Record St PECK SE15 51 N11
Recovery St TOOT SW17 61 S10
Recreation Av HARH RM3 31 M14
ROMW/RG RM7 42 C3
Recreation Rd HAYES BR2 64 B14
NWDGN UB2 46 G9
SYD SE26 63 P9
Recreation Wy MTCM CR4 74 C1
Rectar Pl ARCH N19 37 V7
Rector St IS N1 5 N2
Rectory Cl ASHTD KT21 83 V9
BF/WBF KT14 81 Q3
CHING E4 27 S8
DART DA1 66 E2
FNCH N3 25 M13
RYNPK SW20 60 J14
SCUP DA14 65 R9
SHPTN TW17 69 S1
STAN HA7 23 R11
SURB KT6 71 S7
Rectory Ct LOU IG10 17 T14
Rectory Field Crs CHARL SE7 52 E12
Rectory Gdns BECK BR3 * 63 S13
CEND/HSY/T N8 38 C2
CHST BR7 * 65 L13
NTHLT UB5 34 H13
UPMR RM14 43 R7
Rectory Gn BECK BR3 63 R13
Rectory Gv CLAP SW4 62 A1
CROY/NA CR0 74 F7
HPTN TW12 58 H9
Rectory La ASHTD KT21 83 V9
BF/WBF KT14 81 Q3
BH/WHM TN16 88 G13
BH/WHM TN16 89 S14
BNSTD SM7 85 T5
BRKHM/BTCW RH3 92 F8
BUSH WD23 22 J4
EDGW HA8 24 A11
KGLGY WD4 10 G2
LOU IG10 17 U14
RAD WD7 12 K7
RKW/CH/CXG WD3 21 P6
SCUP DA14 65 R9
STAN HA7 23 R10
SURB KT6 71 S6
TOOT SW17 61 U10
WLGTN SM6 74 A9
Rectory Orch WIM/MER SW19 61 L9
Rectory Pk SAND/SEL CR2 86 J3
Rectory Park Av NTHLT UB5 46 H1
Rectory Pl CHST BR7 * 65 L13
WOOL/PLUM SE18 52 J9
Rectory Rd BARN SW13 48 G14
BECK BR3 63 S13
COUL/CHIP CR5 93 R1
DAGE RM10 42 A12
HAYES BR2 76 F12
HSLWW TW4 46 D14
MNPK E12 40 H10
NWDGN UB2 46 H8
RKW/CH/CXG WD3 21 P5
STNW/STAM N16 38 K8
SUT SM1 73 N8
WALTH E17 39 T2
Rectory Sq WCHPL E1 51 P3
Rectory Wy HGDN/ICK UB10 33 T7
Reculver Ms UED N18 27 L9
Reculver Rd BERM/RHTH SE16 51 P10
Red Anchor Cl CHEL SW3 7 M12
Redan Pl BAY/PAD W2 2 G12
Redan St WKENS W14 48 K8
Redan Ter CMBW SE5 50 F14
Redbarn Cl PUR/KEN CR8 86 F1
Red Barracks Rd WOOL/PLUM SE18 52 H9
Redberry Gv SYD SE26 63 N8
Redbourne Av FNCH N3 25 N13
Redbourne Dr THMD SE28 53 T4
Redbridge Gdns CMBW SE5 9 T14
Redbridge La East REDBR IG4 40 G3
Redbridge La West WAN E11 40 E4
Redburn St CHEL SW3 7 Q11
Redbury Cl RAIN RM13 54 H2
Redcar Cl NTHLT UB5 34 K11
Redcar Rd HARH RM3 31 M10
Redcar St CMBW SE5 9 N14
Redcastle Cl WAP E1W 51 N5
Red Cedars Rd ORP BR6 77 N5
Redchurch St BETH E2 5 U7
Redcliffe Cl ECT SW5 6 G10
Redcliffe Gdns IL IG1 40 J6
WBPTN SW10 6 H10
Redcliffe Ms WBPTN SW10 6 H10
Redcliffe Pl WBPTN SW10 6 J12
Redcliffe Rd WBPTN SW10 6 J10
Redcliffe Sq WBPTN SW10 6 H11
Redcliffe St WBPTN SW10 6 H11
Redclose Av MRDN SM4 73 N3
Redclyffe Rd PLSTW E13 40 E13
Red Cottage Ms DTCH/LGLY SL3 44 A8
Redcourt WOKS/MYFD GU22 80 H5
Redcroft Rd STHL UB1 47 L5
Redcross Wy STHWK SE1 9 P3
Redden Court Rd HARH RM3 43 L1
Redding Cl RDART DA2 67 S7
Reddings Av BUSH WD23 22 K3
Reddings Cl MLHL NW7 24 F9
The Reddings BORE WD6 23 V1
MLHL NW7 24 F8
Reddington Cl SAND/SEL CR2 74 H13
Reddington Dr DTCH/LGLY SL3 44 D9
Reddins Rd PECK SE15 51 L12
Reddons Rd BECK BR3 63 Q12
Reddown Rd COUL/CHIP CR5 86 B8
Reddy Rd ERITH DA8 54 F11
Rede Ct WEY KT13 69 T8
Rede Pl BAY/PAD W2 2 F12
Redesdale Gdns ISLW TW7 47 Q12
Redesdale St CHEL SW3 7 Q11
Redfern Av HSLWW TW4 58 J5
Redfern Cl UX/CGN UB8 33 N13
Redfern Gdns GPK RM2 30 K14
Redfern Rd CAT SE6 63 U5
WLSDN NW10 36 E12
Redfield La ECT SW5 6 G7
Redford Av COUL/CHIP CR5 85 V5
THHTH CR7 74 D2
WLGTN SM6 74 B12
Redford Cl FELT TW13 58 B7
Redford Wk IS N1 * 5 M1
Redford Wy UX/CGN UB8 33 N12
Redgate Dr HAYES BR2 76 D7

Redgate Ter PUT/ROE SW15 60 K4
Redgrave Cl CROY/NA CR0 74 K4
Redgrave Rd PUT/ROE SW15 60 K2
Redgrave Ter BETH E2 * 51 L1
Redhall La RKW/CH/CXG WD3 10 E13
Redhall Ter EA W5 * 48 A5
Redheath Cl GSTN WD25 11 M9
Red Hi CHST BR7 64 J10
Redhill Dr EDGW HA8 24 C14
Redhill Rd COB KT11 81 T3
Redhill St CAMTN NW1 3 V5
Red House La BXLYHS DA6 65 T2
WOT/HER KT12 70 C7
Redhouse Rd BH/WHM TN16 88 E11
Red House Rd CROY/NA CR0 74 B4
Red House Sq IS N1 38 G12
Redington Gdns HAMP NW3 37 P9
Redington Rd HAMP NW3 37 P8
Redland Gdns E/WMO/HCT KT8 * 70 H2
Redlands COUL/CHIP CR5 86 C6
Redlands Rd PEND EN3 16 E15
SEV TN13 90 F14
Redlands Wy BRXS/STRHM SW2 62 C1
Red La ESH/CLAY KT10 71 R11
OXTED RH8 96 D12
Redleaf Cl BXLYHN DA7 54 A11
LHD/OX KT22 83 M14
Redleaves Av ASHF TW15 57 T11
Redlees Cl ISLW TW7 59 Q2
Red Lion Cl GSTN WD25 11 V11
STMC/STPC BR5 77 S4
WALW SE17 9 Q11
Red Lion Ct FLST/FETLN EC4A 4 K11
HSLW TW3 * 58 K1
Red Lion Hl EFNCH N2 25 R14
Red Lion La RKW/CH/CXG WD3 10 A9
WOOL/PLUM SE18 52 G13
Red Lion Pde PIN HA5 * 34 G1
Red Lion Pl WOOL/PLUM SE18 * 52 J13
Red Lion Rd SURB KT6 71 V7
Red Lion Rw CMBW SE5 9 Q14
Red Lion Sq GINN WC1R 4 G10
WAND/EARL SW18 * 61 N3
Red Lion St GINN WC1R 4 G10
RCH/KEW TW9 59 T3
Red Lion Yd MYFR/PKLN W1K * 7 T1
Red Lodge Crs BXLY DA5 66 D8
Red Lodge Rd BXLY DA5 66 D8
WWKM BR4 75 U6
Redman Cl NTHLT UB5 34 E14
Redmans La RSEV TN14 78 F11
Redman's Rd WCHPL E1 51 N3
Redmead La WAP E1W 51 L6
Redmead Rd HYS/HAR UB3 46 E9
Redmore Rd HMSMTH W6 * 48 H9
Red Oak Cl ORP BR6 76 K7
Red Pl MYFR/PKLN W1K 3 S13
Redpoll Wy ERITHM DA18 53 T8
Red Post Hl HNHL SE24 62 G3
Redriffe Rd PLSTW E13 40 B13
Redriff Rd BERM/RHTH SE16 51 Q8
ROMW/RG RM7 30 B14
Red Rd BORE WD6 23 V1
BRW CM14 31 V9
Redroofs Cl BECK BR3 63 T13
Redruth Cl WDGN N22 26 D12
Redruth Rd HARH RM3 31 M10
HOM E9 39 N13
Redstart Cl CROY/NA CR0 75 V14
EHAM E6 52 G3
NWCR SE14 * 51 Q12
Redstone Hl REDH RH1 93 U10
Redstone Hollow REDH RH1 93 U10
Redstone Mnr REDH RH1 93 V10
Redstone Pk REDH RH1 93 U10
Redstone Rd REDH RH1 93 U11
Redston Rd CEND/HSY/T N8 38 B2
Redvers Rd WARL CR6 87 P8
WDGN N22 26 E14
Redvers St IS N1 5 T5
Redwald Rd CLPT E5 39 P9
Redway Dr WHTN TW2 59 L5
Redwell La BGR/WK TN15 91 V13
Redwing Cl SAND/SEL CR2 87 P1
Redwing Ct ORP BR6 77 P5
Redwing Gdns BF/WBF KT14 81 M2
Redwing Gv ABLGY WD5 11 N5
Redwing Ms CMBW SE5 50 G14
Redwing Rd WLGTN SM6 74 C14
Redwood EGH TW20 56 J14
Redwood Cl BERM/RHTH SE16 51 Q6
BFN/LL DA15 65 Q6
BOW E3 39 S14
HGDN/ICK UB10 33 T14
OXHEY WD19 22 E9
PUR/KEN CR8 86 G4
STHGT/OAK N14 26 B5
Redwood Gdns CHIG IG7 29 Q10
CHING E4 * 27 T5
Redwood Gv EA W5 47 S8
Redwood Ms ASHF TW15 * 57 V12
VX/NE SW8 61 V1
Redwood Mt REIG RH2 93 N7
Redwood Ri BORE WD6 13 L11
Redwoods ADL/WDHM KT15 69 R11
Redwood Wy BAR EN5 24 K3
Reece Ms SKENS SW7 7 L7
Reed Av ORP BR6 76 K8
Reed Cl CAN/RD E16 52 C1
IVER SL0 44 J4
LCOL/BKTW AL2 12 H1
LEE/GVPK SE12 64 C3
Reed Dr REDH RH1 93 U13
Reede Rd DAGE RM10 42 A11
Reede Wy DAGE RM10 42 B11
Reedham Cl LCOL/BKTW AL2 11 U4
TOTM N17 39 M2
Reedham Dr PUR/KEN CR8 86 E3
Reedham Park Av PUR/KEN CR8 86 E6
Reedham St PECK SE15 * 51 L14
Reedholm Vls STNW/STAM N16 38 H9
Reed Pl BF/WBF KT14 81 J3
CLAP SW4 61 V2
SHPTN TW17 69 R6
Reed Pond Wk GPK RM2 30 E14
Reed Rd TOTM N17 26 K14
Reeds Crs WAT WD17 11 Q14
Reedsfield Cl ASHF TW15 57 T9
Reedsfield Rd ASHF TW15 57 T9
Reed's Pl CAMTN NW1 38 A12
Reedworth St LBTH SE11 8 K8
Reenglass Rd STAN HA7 * 23 T9
Rees Dr STAN HA7 23 U6
Rees Gdns CROY/NA CR0 74 K8
Reesland Cl MNPK E12 40 J11
Rees St IS N1 5 P2
Reets Farm Cl CDALE/KGS NW9 36 E4
Reeve Rd REIG RH2 93 Q14
Reeves Av CDALE/KGS NW9 36 D5
Reeves Cnr CROY/NA CR0 74 F7
Reeves Crs SWLY BR8 78 D1
Reeves Ms MYFR/PKLN W1K 3 S14
Reeves Rd BOW E3 51 T2
WOOL/PLUM SE18 52 K11
Reform Rw TOTM N17 26 K14
Reform St BTSEA SW11 49 T14
Regal Cl EA W5 47 T3
WCHPL E1 51 L3
Regal Ct MTCM CR4 73 T3
UED N18 26 K10
Regal Crs WLGTN SM6 74 A10
Regal Dr FBAR/BDGN N11 25 V13
Regal La CAMTN NW1 3 T2
Regal Rw PECK SE15 51 N13
Regal Wy KTN/HRWW/WS HA3 35 U5
WATN WD24 11 Q12
Regan Wy IS N1 5 S4
Regarder Rd CHIG IG7 29 R10
Regarth Av ROM RM1 42 E1
Regency Cl BGR/WK TN15 79 N13
CHIG IG7 29 L10
EA W5 47 U1
HPTN TW12 58 H10
Regency Ct ADL/WDHM KT15 * 69 P9
EN EN1 26 H3
Regency Crs HDN NW4 24 J14
Regency Dr BF/WBF KT14 80 K3
RSLP HA4 34 A6
Regency Gdns EMPK RM11 42 J3
WOT/HER KT12 70 F6
Regency Lawn KTTN NW5 * 37 U9
Regency Ms BECK BR3 63 U13
WLSDN NW10 36 G11
Regency Pde HAMP NW3 * 37 P12
Regency Pl WEST SW1P * 8 C7
Regency St WEST SW1P 8 B8
Regency Ter HGT N6 * 37 T4
SEVS/STOTM N15 38 J3
SKENS SW7 * 7 L9
Regency Wk CROY/NA CR0 75 Q4
Regency Wy BXLYHS DA6 65 S2
Regeneration Rd BERM/RHTH SE16 51 P9
Regent Av HGDN/ICK UB10 33 U11
Regent Cl ADL/WDHM KT15 69 N13
HSLWW TW4 46 D13
KGLGY WD4 10 G3
KTN/HRWW/WS HA3 35 U4
NFNCH/WDSPK N12 25 Q10
REDH RH1 94 A5
Regent Crs REDH RH1 93 U11
Regent Gdns GDMY/SEVK IG3 41 Q4
Regent Pde BELMT SM2 * 73 Q11
STNW/STAM N16 * 38 K5
Regent Pk LHD/OX KT22 * 83 M11
Regent Pl CROY/NA CR0 74 K6
WIM/MER SW19 61 Q10
Regent Rd BRYLDS KT5 71 U3
EPP CM16 18 D4
HNHL SE24 62 F3
Regents Av PLMGR N13 26 D10
Regents Bridge Gdns VX/NE SW8 8 F13
Regents Cl CTHM CR3 86 K8
RAD WD7 12 E8
SAND/SEL CR2 74 H11
YEAD UB4 46 A2
Regents Dr HAYES BR2 76 F10
WFD IG8 29 L7
Regents Ms STJWD NW8 2 K4
Regent's Park Rd CAMTN NW1 2 R1
FNCH N3 37 M2
Regent's Park Ter CAMTN NW1 3 U1
Regents Pl LOU IG10 28 F5
Regents Plaza KIL/WHAMP NW6 * 2 C3
Regent Sq BELV DA17 54 B9
BOW E3 51 T1
STPAN WC1H 4 F6
Regent's Rw BETH E2 39 L13
Regent St CHSWK W4 48 A10
REGST W1B 4 A12
WATN WD24 11 P12
WLSDN NW10 48 K1
Regents Whf IS N1 * 4 G3
Regent Whf IS N1 * 4 G3
Reginald Rd DEPT SE8 51 S12
FSTGT E7 40 C12
HARH RM3 31 N13
NTHWD HA6 22 B13
Reginald Sq DEPT SE8 51 S12
Regina Rd FSBYPK N4 38 D6
NWDGN UB2 46 G9
SNWD SE25 75 L1
WEA W13 47 Q6
Regina Ter WEA W13 47 Q6
Regis Rd KTTN NW5 37 V10
Regnart Buildings CAMTN NW1 4 B6
Reid Av CTHM CR3 86 H11
Reid Cl COUL/CHIP CR5 85 V6
HYS/HAR UB3 45 A4
PIN HA5 34 C1
Reidhaven Rd WOOL/PLUM SE18 53 N9
Reigate Av SUT SM1 73 P6
Reigate Hl REIG RH2 93 P5
Reigate Hill Cl REIG RH2 93 N7
Reigate Rd BMLY BR1 64 C8
BRKHM/BTCW RH3 92 E9
EW KT17 72 F14
GDMY/SEVK IG3 41 P7
LHD/OX KT22 83 S13
REDH RH1 93 U14
REIG RH2 93 Q10
Reigate Wy WLGTN SM6 74 C10
Reighton Rd CLPT E5 39 L8
Reinckendorf Av ELTH/MOT SE9 65 L3
Reizel Cl STNW/STAM N16 38 K6
Relay Rd SHB W12 48 K6
Relf Rd PECK SE15 63 L1
Reliance Ar BRXN/ST SW9 * 62 E2
Reliance Sq SDTCH EC2A 5 T7
Relton Ms SKENS SW7 7 P5
Rembrandt Cl BGVA SW1W 7 S9
POP/IOD E14 51 V8
Rembrandt Ct HOR/WEW KT19 72 F11
Rembrandt Rd EDGW HA8 * 24 A14
LEW SE13 64 A2
Rembrandt Wy WOT/HER KT12 70 D7
Remington Rd EHAM E6 52 G4
SEVS/STOTM N15 38 H4
Remington St FSBYE EC1V 5 M4
Remnant St HOL/ALD WC2B 4 G11
Remus Rd BOW E3 39 S12
Rendle Cl CROY/NA CR0 74 K3
Rendlesham Av RAD WD7 12 D11
Rendlesham Rd CLPT E5 39 L9
ENC/FH EN2 15 R13
Rendlesham Wy RKW/CH/CXG WD3 20 G4
Renforth St BERM/RHTH SE16 51 N8
Renfrew Cl EHAM E6 52 J5
Renfrew Rd HSLWW TW4 46 F14
KUTN/CMB KT2 60 C12
LBTH SE11 9 L7
The Renmans ASHTD KT21 85 V6
Renmuir St TOOT SW17 61 T11
Rennell St LEW SE13 63 U1
Renness Rd WALTH E17 39 Q1
Rennets Cl ELTH/MOT SE9 65 M3
Rennets Wood Rd ELTH/MOT SE9 65 M3
Rennie Cl ASHF TW15 57 P8
Rennie Est BERM/RHTH SE16 51 M10
Rennie St STHWK SE1 9 L1
Rennie Ter REDH RH1 93 U11
Renovation Cl CHESW EN7 15 L6
Renown Cl CROY/NA CR0 74 F5
ROMW/RG RM7 30 A13
Rensburg Rd WALTH E17 39 P3
Rensburg Vls WALTH E17 * 39 P3
Renshaw Cl BELV DA17 53 V11
Renters Av HDN NW4 36 J4
Renton Cl BRXS/STRHM SW2 * 62 D4
Renton Dr STMC/STPC BR5 77 T5
Renwick Rd BARK IG11 53 R2
Repens Wy YEAD UB4 45 F2
Rephidim St STHWK SE1 9 S8
Replingham Rd WAND/EARL SW18 61 M6
Reporton Rd FUL/PGN SW6 49 L13
Repository Rd WOOL/PLUM SE18 52 H11
Repton Av ALP/SUD HA0 35 S9
GPK RM2 42 G1
HYS/HAR UB3 46 C9
Repton Cl CAR SM5 73 S10
Repton Ct BECK BR3 63 T13
Repton Dr GPK RM2 42 G1
Repton Gdns GPK RM2 42 G1
Repton Gv CLAY IG5 28 H13
Repton Pl GPK RM2 42 G1
Repton Rd KTN/HRWW/WS HA3 35 V2
ORP BR6 77 L8
Repton St POP/IOD E14 51 Q4
Repton Wy RKW/CH/CXG WD3 21 S3
Repulse Cl CRW RM5 30 B13
Reservoir Cl THHTH CR7 74 H1
Reservoir Rd BROCKY SE4 51 Q14
RSLP HA4 33 S4
STHGT/OAK N14 26 A3
Resham Cl NWDGN UB2 46 E8
Resolution Wy DEPT SE8 51 S12
Restell Cl BKHTH/KID SE3 52 A11
Restmor Wy CAR SM5 73 U7
Reston Cl BORE WD6 13 M12
Reston Pl KENS W8 7 L4
Restons Crs ELTH/MOT SE9 65 M4
Restons Wy CAN/RD E16 52 F5
Restormel Cl HSLW TW3 58 J3
Retford Cl BORE WD6 13 Q12
HARH RM3 31 N11
Retford Pth HARH RM3 31 N11
Retford Rd HARH RM3 31 N11
Retford St BETH E2 5 U5
Retingham Wy CHING E4 27 T7
Retreat Cl KTN/HRWW/WS HA3 35 U5
Retreat Pl HOM E9 39 N11
Retreat Rd RCH/KEW TW9 59 T4
The Retreat BRW CM14 31 V6
BRYLDS KT5 71 V5
CDALE/KGS NW9 36 D4
EGH TW20 56 B11
MORT/ESHN SW14 60 D1
ORP BR6 87 L1
RYLN/HDSTN HA2 34 J5
SEV TN13 * 90 J14
THHTH CR7 74 H2
WPK KT4 72 H7
Retreat Wy CHIG IG7 29 R8
Reunion Rw WAP E1W * 51 M5
Reveley Sq BERM/RHTH SE16 51 Q7
Revell Cl LHD/OX KT22 82 K12
Revell Dr LHD/OX KT22 82 K12
Revell Ri WOOL/PLUM SE18 53 M10
Revell Rd KUT/HW KT1 60 B14
SUT SM1 73 M11
Revelon Rd BROCKY SE4 63 Q2
Revelstoke Rd WAND/EARL SW18 61 M7
WIM/MER SW19 61 L9
Reventlow Rd ELTH/MOT SE9 65 N5
Reverdy Rd STHWK SE1 9 U8
Reverend Cl RYLN/HDSTN HA2 34 K8
Revere Wy HOR/WEW KT19 72 E13
Revesby Rd CAR SM5 73 S5
Review Rd CRICK NW2 36 F7
DAGE RM10 42 B14
Rewell St FUL/PGN SW6 6 J14
Rewley Rd CAR SM5 73 R5
Rex Av ASHF TW15 57 S11
Rex Pl MYFR/PKLN W1K 7 T1
Reydon Av WAN E11 40 E4
Reynard Cl BMLY BR1 76 H1
Reynard Dr NRWD SE19 62 J12
Reynard Pl NWCR SE14 * 51 Q11
Reynardson Rd TOTM N17 26 G12
Reynards Wy LCOL/BKTW AL2 11 T1
Reynolds Gdns CHARL SE7 52 F10
Reynolds Av CHDH RM6 41 S5
CHSGTN KT9 71 U10
MNPK E12 41 L9
Reynolds Cl CAR SM5 73 T5
GLDGN NW11 37 P5
WIM/MER SW19 61 S13
Reynolds Dr EDGW HA8 35 V1
Reynolds Pl BKHTH/KID SE3 52 D12
RCHPK/HAM TW10 59 V6
Reynolds Rd CHSWK W4 48 C8
NWMAL KT3 71 P5
PECK SE15 63 N2
YEAD UB4 46 F1
Reynolds Wy CROY/NA CR0 74 J9
Rhapsody Crs BRW CM14 31 V10
Rheidol Ms IS N1 5 N3
Rheidol Ter IS N1 5 N3
Rheingold Wy WLGTN SM6 74 C13
Rheola Cl TOTM N17 26 J13
Rhoda St BETH E2 5 V7
Rhodes Av WDGN N22 26 A13
Rhodes Cl EGH TW20 56 F10
Rhodes Ct EGH TW20 * 56 E10
Rhodesia Rd BRXN/ST SW9 62 D1
WAN E11 39 V7
Rhodes St HOLWY N7 38 D10
Rhodes Wy WATN WD24 11 R11
Rhodeswell Rd POP/IOD E14 51 R3
Rhodrons Av CHSGTN KT9 71 U10
Rhondda Gv BOW E3 51 Q1
Rhyl Rd GFD/PVL UB6 35 P14
Rhyl St KTTN NW5 37 U11
Rhys Av FBAR/BDGN N11 26 B12
Rialto Rd MTCM CR4 61 U14
Ribble Cl WFD IG8 28 E11
Ribbleside LCOL/BKTW AL2 12 K1
Ribblesdale Av FBAR/BDGN N11 25 U12
NTHLT UB5 35 L13
Ribblesdale Rd CEND/HSY/T N8 38 D2
RDART DA2 67 Q6
STRHM/NOR SW16 61 V10
Ribbon Dance Ms CMBW SE5 50 H13
Ribchester Av GFD/PVL UB6 47 P1
Ribston Cl HAYES BR2 76 H6
RAD WD7 12 H7
Ricardo St POP/IOD E14 51 U4
Ricards Rd WIM/MER SW19 61 M10
Rice Pde STMC/STPC BR5 * 77 M3
Richard Cl WOOL/PLUM SE18 52 G9
Richard House Dr CAN/RD E16 52 F4
Richards Av ROMW/RG RM7 42 C4
Richards Cl BUSH WD23 23 M5
HGDN/ICK UB10 33 S13
HRW HA1 35 Q3
HYS/HAR UB3 45 V11
Richards Cottages CAR SM5 * 73 T10
Richards Fld HOR/WEW KT19 72 D13
Richardson Cl HACK E8 5 U1
LCOL/BKTW AL2 12 J1
RDART DA2 67 T3
Richardson Gdns DAGE RM10 42 B11
Richardson Rd SRTFD E15 * 40 A14
Richardson's Ms FITZ W1T 4 A8
Richard's Pl CHEL SW3 7 P7
WALTH E17 39 S1
Richards Rd COB KT11 82 K4
Richard St WCHPL E1 51 M4
Richbell Cl ASHTD KT21 83 S12
Richbell Pl BMSBY WC1N 4 G9
Richborne Ter VX/NE SW8 8 G13
Richborough Cl STMC/STPC BR5 77 T2
Richborough Rd CRICK NW2 36 K9
Richens Cl HSLW TW3 47 M14
Riches Rd IL IG1 41 L7
Richfield Rd BUSH WD23 23 M5
Richford Ga HMSMTH W6 48 J8
Richford Rd SRTFD E15 40 B13
Richford St HMSMTH W6 48 J7
Richings Pl DTCH/LGLY SL3 44 J8
Richings Wy DTCH/LGLY SL3 44 K8
Richland Av COUL/CHIP CR5 85 U4
Richlands Av EW KT17 72 G10
Richmer Rd ERITH DA8 54 D12
Richmond Av CHING E4 27 V10
EBED/NFELT TW14 58 A5
HGDN/ICK UB10 33 V13
IS N1 4 J1
RYNPK SW20 61 L13
Richmond Br TWK TW1 59 T5
Richmond Buildings SOHO/SHAV W1D 4 C12
Richmond Cl BH/WHM TN16 88 D9
BORE WD6 24 E1
EPSOM KT18 84 E4
LHD/OX KT22 83 L14
WALTH E17 39 R4
Richmond Ct POTB/CUF EN6 * 14 E5
Richmond Crs CHING E4 27 V10
ED N9 27 L8
IS N1 4 H1
STA TW18 * 56 K10
Richmond Dr SHPTN TW17 69 V4
WAT WD17 11 M12
WFD IG8 28 J10
Richmond Gdns HDN NW4 36 G3
KTN/HRWW/WS HA3 23 P12
Richmond Gn CROY/NA CR0 74 C8
Richmond Gv IS N1 38 F12
Richmond Hl RCHPK/HAM TW10 59 U6
Richmond Ms SOHO/CST W1F 4 C12
Richmond Pde TWK TW1 * 59 T5
Richmond Park Rd KUTN/CMB KT2 59 U12
MORT/ESHN SW14 60 C3
Richmond Pl WOOL/PLUM SE18 53 L9
Richmond Rd BAR EN5 25 Q3
CHING E4 27 V6
COUL/CHIP CR5 85 V5
CROY/NA CR0 74 C7
EA W5 47 U7
FBAR/BDGN N11 26 D12
FSTGT E7 40 D10
HACK E8 38 K12
IL IG1 41 L8
ISLW TW7 59 Q2
KUTN/CMB KT2 59 T13
POTB/CUF EN6 14 F6
ROM RM1 42 F4
RYNPK SW20 60 H13
SEVS/STOTM N15 38 J4
STA TW18 56 K10
THHTH CR7 62 F14
TWK TW1 59 S5
WAN E11 39 V8
Richmond St PLSTW E13 40 C14
Richmond Ter WHALL SW1A 8 E3
Richmond Wy GT/LBKH KT23 82 K14
RKW/CH/CXG WD3 10 C12
SHB W12 48 K7
WAN E11 40 C7
Richmount Gdns BKHTH/KID SE3 64 C1
Rich St POP/IOD E14 51 R4
Rickard Cl BRXS/STRHM SW2 62 E6
HDN NW4 36 H2
WDR/YW UB7 45 P8
Rickards Cl SURB KT6 71 U7
Ricketts Hill Rd BH/WHM TN16 88 B10
Rickett St FUL/PGN SW6 6 F11
Rickman Crs ADL/WDHM KT15 69 M8
Rickman Hl COUL/CHIP CR5 85 V7
Rickman Hill Rd COUL/CHIP CR5 85 V8
Rickman St WCHPL E1 * 51 N2
Rickmansworth La CFSP/GDCR SL9 20 D10
Rickmansworth Rd DEN/HRF UB9 21 M14
NTHWD HA6 21 T11
PIN HA5 22 D14
RKW/CH/CXG WD3 10 H9
WATW WD18 22 A1
Rick Roberts Wy SRTFD E15 39 V13
Rickthorne Rd ARCH N19 38 C7
Ridding La GFD/PVL UB6 35 P10
The Riddings CTHM CR3 94 K1
Riddlesdown Av PUR/KEN CR8 86 G4
Riddlesdown Rd PUR/KEN CR8 86 G3
Riddons Rd LEE/GVPK SE12 64 F8
Rideout St WOOL/PLUM SE18 52 H10
Rider Cl BFN/LL DA15 65 P4
Riders Wy GDST RH9 95 N7
The Ride BTFD TW8 47 R10
PEND EN3 27 N1
Ridgdale St BOW E3 51 S1
Ridge Av DART DA1 66 F4
WCHMH N21 26 F6
Ridgebrook Rd BKHTH/KID SE3 64 E2
Ridge Cl BRKHM/BTCW RH3 92 B14
CDALE/KGS NW9 36 E2
HDN NW4 25 L13
THMD SE28 53 M8
WOKS/MYFD GU22 80 A14
Ridge Ct CTHM CR3 87 L8
Ridge Crest ENC/FH EN2 15 P13
Ridgecroft Cl BXLY DA5 66 C6
Ridgefield WAT WD17 11 M9
Ridgegate Cl REIG RH2 93 R5
Ridge Gn REDH RH1 94 C13
Ridge Green Cl REDH RH1 94 C13
Ridge Hl GLDGN NW11 37 L6
Ridgehurst Av GSTN WD25 11 M7
Ridgelands LHD/OX KT22 83 M14
Ridge La WAT WD17 11 L10
Ridge Langley SAND/SEL CR2 75 L14
Ridgemead Cl STHGT/OAK N14 26 C7
Ridgemead Rd EGH TW20 56 B9
Ridgemont Gdns EDGW HA8 24 C9
Ridgemount WEY KT13 70 A10
Ridgemount Av COUL/CHIP CR5 85 V5
CROY/NA CR0 75 P5
Ridgemount Cl PGE/AN SE20 63 M12
Ridgemount End CFSP/GDCR SL9 20 C10
Ridgemount Gdns ENC/FH EN2 15 R13
Ridge Pk PUR/KEN CR8 74 B14
Ridge Rd CEND/HSY/T N8 38 D4
CHEAM SM3 73 L6
CRICK NW2 37 M8
MTCM CR4 61 V12
WCHMH N21 26 F7
Ridges Yd CROY/NA CR0 74 F8
Ridge St WATN WD24 11 R11
The Ridge BAR EN5 * 25 M3
BRYLDS KT5 72 A3
BXLY DA5 65 V5
COUL/CHIP CR5 86 B5
CTHM CR3 96 A1
EPSOM KT18 84 C8
LHD/OX KT22 83 M14
ORP BR6 76 K8
PUR/KEN CR8 74 B14
WHTN TW2 59 M5
WOKS/MYFD GU22 80 F7
Ridge Ter WCHMH N21 * 26 F6
Ridgeview LCOL/BKTW AL2 12 K1
Ridgeview Cl BAR EN5 25 L5
Ridgeview Rd TRDG/WHET N20 25 P8
Ridge Wy DART DA1 66 F4
FELT TW13 58 D8
IVER SL0 44 H6
RKW/CH/CXG WD3 21 M5
VW GU25 68 C3
Ridgeway HAYES BR2 76 C7
HOR/WEW KT19 84 C2
RDART DA2 67 S10
WFD IG8 28 J6
WOT/HER KT12 70 E6
Ridgeway Av EBAR EN4 25 V5
Ridgeway Cl WOKN/KNAP GU21 80 D6
Ridgeway Ct REDH RH1 * 93 U14
Ridgeway Crs ORP BR6 76 K8
Ridgeway Crescent Gdns ORP BR6 77 N7
Ridgeway Dr BMLY BR1 64 D9
Ridgeway East BFN/LL DA15 65 N3
Ridgeway Gdns HGT N6 38 B5
REDBR IG4 40 G3
WOKN/KNAP GU21 80 D5
Ridgeway Rd ISLW TW7 47 N12
REDH RH1 93 U14
Ridgeway Rd North ISLW TW7 47 N12
The Ridge Wy SAND/SEL CR2 74 J14
The Ridgeway ACT W3 48 A8
CDALE/KGS NW9 36 D2
CHING E4 27 U6
CROY/NA CR0 74 D8
FBAR/BDGN N11 25 T9
FNCH N3 25 P12
GPK RM2 42 G2
HARH RM3 31 L13
KTN/HRWW/WS HA3 35 S4
LHD/OX KT22 83 M13
MLHL NW7 24 H9
POTB/CUF EN6 14 H9
POTB/CUF EN6 14 J5
RAD WD7 12 D11
RYLN/HDSTN HA2 34 H5
STAN HA7 23 S13
STHGT/OAK N14 26 C7
WAT WD17 11 L11
Ridgeway West BFN/LL DA15 65 N3
Ridgewell Cl DAGE RM10 42 B13
IS N1 5 P1
SYD SE26 63 R9
Ridgmount Gdns GWRST WC1E 4 C9
Ridgmount Rd WAND/EARL SW18 61 P3
Ridgmount St GWRST WC1E 4 C9
Ridgway RCHPK/HAM TW10 * 59 U4
WIM/MER SW19 60 K11
WOKS/MYFD GU22 80 K5
Ridgway Gdns WIM/MER SW19 60 K12
Ridgway Pl WIM/MER SW19 61 L11
Ridgway Rd BRXN/ST SW9 62 F1
WOKS/MYFD GU22 80 K6
The Ridgway BELMT SM2 73 R12
Riding Court Rd DTCH/LGLY SL3 44 A12
Riding Hl SAND/SEL CR2 87 L4
Riding House St GTPST W1W 3 V10
Ridings Av WCHMH N21 26 F2
Ridings Cl HGT N6 38 A5
The Ridings ADL/WDHM KT15 68 J11
ASHTD KT21 83 T9
BH/WHM TN16 88 G7
BRYLDS KT5 72 A3
COB KT11 82 K3
DTCH/LGLY SL3 44 K9
EA W5 47 V2
EBAR EN4 * 25 S5
EPSOM KT18 84 E5
EW KT17 72 F15
KWD/TDW/WH KT20 85 M10
REIG RH2 93 R8
RPLY/SEND GU23 81 L13
SUN TW16 58 C15
The Riding GLDGN NW11 37 M6
WOKN/KNAP GU21 80 F4
Ridlands Gv OXTED RH8 96 G6
Ridlands La OXTED RH8 96 G6
Ridlands Ri OXTED RH8 96 G6
Ridler Rd EN EN1 15 U12
Ridley Av WEA W13 47 Q8
Ridley Cl BARK IG11 41 Q12
Ridley Ct STRHM/NOR SW16 62 B10
Ridley Rd FSTGT E7 40 F9
HACK E8 38 K11
HAYES BR2 76 B1
WARL CR6 87 N8
WELL DA16 53 S13
WIM/MER SW19 61 P12
WLSDN NW10 36 G14
Ridsdale Rd PGE/AN SE20 63 M13
Riefield Rd ELTH/MOT SE9 65 M2
Riesco Dr CROY/NA CR0 75 N11
Riffel Rd CRICK NW2 36 J10
Rifle Pl NTGHL W11 48 K5
Rifle Range La HRW HA1 * 35 P6
Rifle St POP/IOD E14 51 T3
Rigault Rd FUL/PGN SW6 49 M14
Rigby Cl CROY/NA CR0 74 D8
Rigby La HYS/HAR UB3 45 V7
Rigby Ms IL IG1 40 J7
Rigby Pl PEND EN3 16 G11
Rigden St POP/IOD E14 51 U4
Rigeley Rd WLSDN NW10 48 G1
Rigg Ap LEY E10 39 Q6
Rigge Pl CLAP SW4 62 B2
Riggindale Rd STRHM/NOR SW16 62 B10
Right Side STHGT/OAK N14 * 26 B6
Riley Cl HOR/WEW KT19 72 C14
Riley Rd PEND EN3 16 E11
STHWK SE1 9 U5
Riley St WBPTN SW10 7 L15
Rinaldo Rd BAL SW12 61 V6
Ring Cl BMLY BR1 64 D12
Ringcroft St HOLWY N7 38 E10
Ringers Rd BMLY BR1 76 C1
Ringford Rd WAND/EARL SW18 61 M4
Ringlet Cl CAN/RD E16 52 D4
Ringlewell Cl EN EN1 16 B14
Ringley Park Av REIG RH2 93 R10
Ringley Park Rd REIG RH2 93 R10
Ringmer Av FUL/PGN SW6 49 L13
Ringmer Gdns ARCH N19 * 38 D7
Ringmer Pl WCHMH N21 26 J2
Ringmer Wy BMLY BR1 76 H3
Ringmore Ri FSTH SE23 63 M5
Ringmore Rd WOT/HER KT12 70 F8
Ringshall Rd STMC/STPC BR5 77 Q1
Ringslade Rd WDGN N22 26 D14
Ringstead Rd CAT SE6 63 T5
SUT SM1 73 S10
Ring Wy FBAR/BDGN N11 26 A11
Ringway NWDGN UB2 46 G10
Ringwold Cl BECK BR3 63 Q12
Ringwood Av CROY/NA CR0 74 C5
EFNCH N2 25 T14
HCH RM12 42 H9
ORP BR6 77 S14
REDH RH1 93 T7
Ringwood Cl PIN HA5 * 34 F2
Ringwood Gdns PUT/ROE SW15 60 G7
Ringwood Rd WALTH E17 39 R4
Ringwood Wy HPTN TW12 58 G9
WCHMH N21 26 F5
Ripley Av EGH TW20 56 C11
Ripley Cl BMLY BR1 76 J3
CROY/NA CR0 75 S12
DTCH/LGLY SL3 44 C9
Ripley Gdns MORT/ESHN SW14 60 D1
SUT SM1 73 Q9
Ripley La RPLY/SEND GU23 81 M14
Ripley Ms WAN E11 40 A4
Ripley Rd BELV DA17 54 A9
CAN/RD E16 52 E4
ENC/FH EN2 15 S11
GDMY/SEVK IG3 41 Q7
HPTN TW12 58 J12
RPLY/SEND GU23 81 P14
Ripley Vls EA W5 * 47 S4
Ripley Wy CHESW EN7 16 A1
Riplington Ct PUT/ROE SW15 60 G6
Ripon Cl NTHLT UB5 34 G11
Ripon Gdns CHSGTN KT9 71 U10
IL IG1 40 H4
Ripon Rd ED N9 27 M5
TOTM N17 38 J2
WOOL/PLUM SE18 52 K11
Rippersley Rd WELL DA16 53 Q13
Ripple Rd BARK IG11 41 N13
BARK IG11 53 Q1
Ripplevale Gv IS N1 38 E13
Rippolson Rd WOOL/PLUM SE18 53 P10
Ripston Rd ASHF TW15 57 V10
Risborough Cl MUSWH N10 * 37 U2
Risborough Dr WPK KT4 72 G5
Risborough St STHWK SE1 9 M3
Risdon St BERM/RHTH SE16 51 N6
Risebridge Cha ROM RM1 30 F12
Risebridge Rd GPK RM2 30 F14
Riseholme Rd BXLYHN DA7 * 54 A13
Riseldine Rd FSTH SE23 63 P4
Rise Park Bvd ROM RM1 30 E13
Rise Park Pde ROM RM1 30 E14
The Rise BKHH IG9 28 H5
BORE WD6 23 V3
BXLY DA5 65 S7
CDALE/KGS NW9 36 E6
EDGW HA8 24 B8
EW KT17 72 F14
GFD/PVL UB6 35 Q10
HGDN/ICK UB10 33 U12
KWD/TDW/WH KT20 84 K9
MLHL NW7 24 D9
PLMGR N13 26 E9
SAND/SEL CR2 87 L2
WAN E11 40 B4
WLSDN NW10 36 E10
Risinghill St IS N1 4 J3
Rising Hill Cl NTHWD HA6 * 21 U11
Risingholme Cl BUSH WD23 23 N4
KTN/HRWW/WS HA3 23 P14
Risingholme Rd KTN/HRWW/WS HA3 35 P2
The Risings WALTH E17 39 V2
Rising Sun Ct STBT EC1A * 4 M10
Risley Av TOTM N17 26 H13
Rita Rd VX/NE SW8 8 F13
Ritches Rd SEVS/STOTM N15 38 G3
Ritchie Rd CROY/NA CR0 75 L4
Ritchie St IS N1 4 K3
Ritchings Av WALTH E17 39 Q2
Ritherdon Rd TOOT SW17 61 V8
Ritson Rd HACK E8 38 K11
Ritter St WOOL/PLUM SE18 52 J12
Ritz Pde EA W5 * 36 A14
Rivaz Pl HOM E9 39 N11
Rivenhall Gdns SWFD E18 40 B3
River Av PLMGR N13 26 F5
THDIT KT7 71 Q5
River Bank E/WMO/HCT KT8 71 N1
Riverbank THDIT KT7 71 Q5
WCHMH N21 26 G5
Riverbank Rd BMLY BR1 64 C8
Riverbank Wy BTFD TW8 47 R11
River Barge Cl POP/IOD E14 51 V7
River Cl CHES/WCR EN8 16 D2
NWDGN UB2 47 N7
RAIN RM13 54 E2
RSLP HA4 34 A4
WAN E11 40 E2
River Ct PUR RM19 55 M8
WOKN/KNAP GU21 80 C4
Rivercourt Rd HMSMTH W6 48 H10
Riverdale Dr WAND/EARL SW18 61 N5
WOKS/MYFD GU22 80 E12
Riverdale Gdns TWK TW1 59 S5
Riverdale Rd BXLY DA5 65 V5
ERITH DA8 54 B10
FELT TW13 58 G9
TWK TW1 59 S5
WOOL/PLUM SE18 53 P10
Riverdene EDGW HA8 24 C9
Riverdene Rd IL IG1 40 J8
River Dr UPMR RM14 43 R4
Riverfield Rd STA TW18 56 K11
River Front EN EN1 26 H1
River Gdns CAR SM5 73 U7
EBED/NFELT TW14 58 D4
River Grove Pk BECK BR3 63 R13
Riverhead Cl WALTH E17 27 P14
Riverhead Dr BELMT SM2 73 P14
River Hl COB KT11 82 D5
Riverholme Dr HOR/WEW KT19 72 D13
River Island Cl LHD/OX KT22 83 M10
River La COB KT11 82 E8
LHD/OX KT22 83 N10
RCHPK/HAM TW10 59 T6
Rivermead BF/WBF KT14 81 R3
E/WMO/HCT KT8 71 L1
KUT/HW KT1 * 71 T3
Rivermead Cl ADL/WDHM KT15 * 69 N12
TEDD TW11 59 R10
Rivermead Rd UED N18 * 27 P10
River Meads Av WHTN TW2 58 K8
River Mt WOT/HER KT12 70 B5
Rivernook Cl WOT/HER KT12 70 E4
River Pde SEV TN13 * 90 E12
River Park Av STA TW18 56 H10
Riverpark Gdns HAYES BR2 63 V12
River Park Rd WDGN N22 26 D14
River Park Vw ORP BR6 77 R5
River Pl IS N1 38 G12
River Reach TEDD TW11 59 S11
River Rd BARK IG11 41 N14
BKHH IG9 28 G6
BRW CM14 31 T6
STA TW18 56 K13
Riversdale Rd CRW RM5 30 B12
HBRY N5 38 F8
THDIT KT7 71 Q5
Riversdell Cl CHERT KT16 68 K5
Riversfield Rd EN EN1 15 V12
Riverside CHARL SE7 52 D8
CHERT KT16 * 57 L14
EYN DA4 78 K7
HDN NW4 36 H6
LCOL/BKTW AL2 12 J1
RCH/KEW TW9 * 47 R11
RCH/KEW TW9 59 T3
SHPTN TW17 70 A5
STWL/WRAY TW19 56 A5
SUN TW16 * 70 A2
TWK TW1 59 R6
Riverside Av E/WMO/HCT KT8 71 M3
Riverside Cl CLPT E5 39 N6
HNWL W7 47 N2
KGLGY WD4 10 G1
KUT/HW KT1 71 S3
STA TW18 56 K14
STMC/STPC BR5 65 S14
WLGTN SM6 73 V8
Riverside Ct CHING E4 * 27 S2
Riverside Dr CHSWK W4 48 E13
ESH/CLAY KT10 71 M9
GLDGN NW11 * 37 L4
MTCM CR4 73 T4
RCHPK/HAM TW10 59 R8
RKW/CH/CXG WD3 21 P6
STA TW18 56 J9
Riverside Gdns ALP/SUD HA0 35 U14
ENC/FH EN2 15 S14
HMSMTH W6 48 H11
WOKS/MYFD GU22 80 F11
Riverside Ms CROY/NA CR0 * 74 C8
Riverside Pl FBAR/BDGN N11 * 26 D7
STWL/WRAY TW19 57 N6
Riverside Rd IL IG1 41 Q11
OXHEY WD19 22 D4
SCUP DA14 65 R10
SRTFD E15 39 V14
STA TW18 56 K13
STWL/WRAY TW19 57 P6
TOOT SW17 61 N9
WOT/HER KT12 70 G11
The Riverside E/WMO/HCT KT8 71 M1
Riverside Vls SURB KT6 * 71 S5
Riverside Wk KUT/HW KT1 71 S3
Riverside Wy DART DA1 66 J3
UX/CGN UB8 45 M2
Riverside Yd TOOT SW17 61 P8
Riverstone Cl RYLN/HDSTN HA2 35 M7
River St CLKNW EC1R 4 K5
River Ter HMSMTH W6 48 J10
Riverton Cl MV/WKIL W9 2 D6
River Vw ADL/WDHM KT15 * 69 N10
Riverview Gdns BARN SW13 48 H12
COB KT11 82 C3
River View Gdns TWK TW1 59 P7
Riverview Gv CHSWK W4 48 B11
Riverview Pk CAT SE6 63 T6
Riverview Rd CHSWK W4 48 B12
HOR/WEW KT19 72 C9
RDART DA2 * 67 T2
Riverview Ter PUR RM19 * 55 P10
River Wk DEN/HRF UB9 33 N10
SUN TW16 70 B4
WOT/HER KT12 70 C4
River Wy GNWCH SE10 52 B8
HOR/WEW KT19 72 D10
LOU IG10 28 J4
WHTN TW2 58 J8
Riverway PLMGR N13 26 E10
STA TW18 56 K14
River Whf BELV DA17 * 54 D7
Riverwood La CHST BR7 65 M14
Rivington Av WFD IG8 28 K13
Rivington Crs MLHL NW7 24 F13
Rivington Pl FSBYE EC1V 5 T6
Rivington St SDTCH EC2A 5 S6
Rivington Wk HACK E8 39 L13
Rivulet Rd TOTM N17 26 G12
Rixon Cl DTCH/LGLY SL3 44 C4
Rixon St HOLWY N7 38 E9
Rixsen Rd MNPK E12 40 G10
Roach Rd BOW E3 39 S12
Road House Est WOKS/MYFD GU22 * 80 F11
Roads Pl ARCH N19 38 C7
Roakes Av ADL/WDHM KT15 69 M7
Roan St GNWCH SE10 51 U11
Robarts Cl PIN HA5 34 C4
Robb Rd STAN HA7 23 Q11
Robert Adam St MHST W1U 3 S11
Roberta St BETH E2 51 L1
Robert Cl CHIG IG7 29 P10
MV/WKIL W9 2 K8
POTB/CUF EN6 14 A7
WOT/HER KT12 70 D10
Robert Dashwood Wy WALW SE17 9 N8
Robert Keen Cl PECK SE15 * 51 L14
Robert Lowe Cl NWCR SE14 51 P12
Roberton Dr BMLY BR1 64 E14
Robertsbridge Rd CAR SM5 73 R6
Roberts Cl CHEAM SM3 72 K11
CHES/WCR EN8 16 E4
DAGE RM10 42 B9
ELTH/MOT SE9 65 R6
HARH RM3 31 M13
STMC/STPC BR5 77 S1
STWL/WRAY TW19 57 L5
THHTH CR7 74 H1
WDR/YW UB7 45 Q6
Roberts Ct CHSGTN KT9 71 U10
PGE/AN SE20 63 N13
WLSDN NW10 36 F11
Roberts House WOOL/PLUM SE18 * 52 G12
Roberts La CFSP/GDCR SL9 20 D10
Roberts Ms KTBR SW1X * 7 S6
Robertson Rd SRTFD E15 39 U13
Robertson St VX/NE SW8 62 A1
Robert's Pl CLKNW EC1R * 4 K7
Roberts Rd BELV DA17 54 A10
MLHL NW7 24 H11
WALTH E17 27 U13
WATW WD18 11 Q14
Robert St CAMTN NW1 3 V6
CHCR WC2N 4 F14
CROY/NA CR0 74 G8
WOOL/PLUM SE18 53 M10
Roberts Wy EGH TW20 56 C13
Roberts Wood Dr CFSP/GDCR SL9 20 C10
Robeson St BOW E3 51 R3
Robeson Wy BORE WD6 13 M9
Robina Cl BXLYHS DA6 65 T2
NTHWD HA6 22 B14
Robin Cl ADL/WDHM KT15 69 P11
CDALE/KGS NW9 24 F12
CRW RM5 30 C11
FELT TW13 58 E10
MLHL NW7 24 F8
Robin Ct WLGTN SM6 74 B11
Robin Crs EHAM E6 52 F3
Robin Gv BTFD TW8 47 S11
HGT N6 37 U7
KTN/HRWW/WS HA3 35 V6
Robin Hill Dr CHST BR7 64 H11
Robinhood Cl MTCM CR4 74 A2
Robin Hood Cl WOKN/KNAP GU21 80 B8
Robin Hood Dr BUSH WD23 11 T13
KTN/HRWW/WS HA3 23 R11
Robin Hood Gdns POP/IOD E14 * 51 U5
Robin Hood Gn STMC/STPC BR5 77 R2
Robin Hood La BXLYHS DA6 65 S3
MTCM CR4 74 A2
POP/IOD E14 51 U5
PUT/ROE SW15 60 E9
SUT SM1 73 P10
Robin Hood Rd BRWN CM15 31 U2
PUT/ROE SW15 60 E10
WOKN/KNAP GU21 80 A7
Robin Hood Wy GFD/PVL UB6 35 P13
PUT/ROE SW15 60 E9
Robinia Cl PGE/AN SE20 * 63 M13
Robinia Crs LEY E10 39 T8
Robin La HDN NW4 36 K1
Robin Pl GSTN WD25 * 11 L6
Robins Cl LCOL/BKTW AL2 12 J1
UX/CGN UB8 45 M5
Robins Gv WWKM BR4 76 C8
Robin's La EPP CM16 18 A10
Robinson Av CHESW EN7 15 R2
Robinson Cl ENC/FH EN2 * 15 R1
HCH RM12 42 H12
WAN E11 40 A8
WOKS/MYFD GU22 80 G10
Robinson Crs BUSH WD23 23 L6
Robinson Rd BETH E2 39 N14
DAGE RM10 42 A9
TOOT SW17 61 S11
Robinson's Cl WEA W13 47 Q3
Robinson St CHEL SW3 7 Q11
Robins Orch CFSP/GDCR SL9 20 C11
Robinsway WOT/HER KT12 70 E9
Robin Wy POTB/CUF EN6 15 N4
STA TW18 56 K9
STMC/STPC BR5 77 R1
Robinwood Gv UX/CGN UB8 45 R2
Robinwood Pl PUT/ROE SW15 60 D9
Robsart St BRXN/ST SW9 50 D14
Robson Av WLSDN NW10 36 G13
Robson Cl CFSP/GDCR SL9 20 C8
EHAM E6 52 G4
ENC/FH EN2 15 R14
Robson Rd WNWD SE27 62 G8
Robsons Cl CHES/WCR EN8 16 C3
Robsons Wy SEV TN13 90 F12
Rocastle Rd BROCKY SE4 63 Q3
Roch Av EDGW HA8 23 V14
Rochdale Rd ABYW SE2 53 R10
WALTH E17 39 S5
Rochdale Wy DEPT SE8 51 S13
Rochelle Cl BTSEA SW11 61 R2
Rochelle St BETH E2 5 U6
Rochemont Wk HACK E8 * 5 V2
Roche Rd STRHM/NOR SW16 62 C13
Rochester Av BMLY BR1 64 D14
FELT TW13 58 B7
PLSTW E13 40 E13
Rochester Cl BFN/LL DA15 65 R4
EN EN1 15 U13
STRHM/NOR SW16 * 62 C12
Rochester Dr BXLY DA5 66 A4
GSTN WD25 * 11 P5
PIN HA5 34 F3
Rochester Gdns CROY/NA CR0 74 J8
CTHM CR3 86 J12
IL IG1 40 K5
Rochester Ms CAMTN NW1 38 A12
EA W5 * 47 S9
Rochester Pde FELT TW13 * 58 C8
Rochester Pl CAMTN NW1 38 A11
Rochester Rd CAMTN NW1 38 A11
CAR SM5 73 T9
DART DA1 67 N5
EGH TW20 56 H11
HCH RM12 42 H12
NTHWD HA6 33 U1
Rochester Rw WEST SW1P 8 B7
Rochester Sq CAMTN NW1 38 A12
Rochester St WEST SW1P 8 B7
Rochester Ter CAMTN NW1 38 A11
Rochester Wk STHWK SE1 * 9 Q1
Rochester Wy BKHTH/KID SE3 52 D13
DART DA1 66 E5
RKW/CH/CXG WD3 21 T2
Rochester Wy Relief Rd ELTH/MOT SE9 64 H3
BKHTH/KID SE3 52 F14
Roche Wk CAR SM5 73 S5
Rochford Av CHDH RM6 41 S3
WAB EN9 16 F10
Rochford Cl EHAM E6 40 F14
HCH RM12 42 G11
Rochford Gn LOU IG10 29 L1
Rochfords Gdns SLN SL2 44 A6
Rochford St KTTN NW5 37 T10
Rochford Wy CROY/NA CR0 74 C4
Rockall Ct DTCH/LGLY SL3 45 D10
Rock Av MORT/ESHN SW14 60 D1
Rockbourne Ms FSTH SE23 63 P6
Rockbourne Rd FSTH SE23 63 P6
Rockchase Gdns EMPK RM11 43 L2
Rockcliffe Av KGLGY WD4 10 D3
Rock Cl MTCM CR4 61 R14
Rockells Pl EDUL SE22 63 M4
Rockfield Cl OXTED RH8 96 B7
Rockfield Rd OXTED RH8 96 B6
Rockford Av GFD/PVL UB6 35 R14
Rock Grove Wy BERM/RHTH SE16 51 L9
Rockhall Rd CRICK NW2 36 K9
Rockhampton Rd SAND/SEL CR2 74 J13
STRHM/NOR SW16 62 F8
Rock Hl DUL SE21 62 K9
ORP BR6 78 B11
Rockingham Av EMPK RM11 42 H1
Rockingham Cl PUT/ROE SW15 60 F2
UX/CGN UB8 * 45 M2
Rockingham Ga BUSH WD23 23 M4
Rockingham Pde UX/CGN UB8 33 M14
Rockingham Rd UX/CGN UB8 33 N15
Rockingham St STHWK SE1 9 N6
Rockland Rd PUT/ROE SW15 61 L3
Rocklands Dr KTN/HRWW/WS HA3 23 R14
Rockley Rd SHB W12 48 K7
Rockmount Rd NRWD SE19 62 H12
WOOL/PLUM SE18 53 N11
Rockshaw Rd REDH RH1 94 A3
Rocks La BARN SW13 60 G1
Rock St FSBYPK N4 38 E8
Rockware Av GFD/PVL UB6 35 N14
Rockways BAR EN5 24 F4
Rockwell Gdns NRWD SE19 62 J10
Rockwell Rd DAGE RM10 42 B10
Rockwood Gdns LOU IG10 29 L1
Rockwood Pl SHB W12 48 J7
Rocky La REDH RH1 93 U5
Rocliffe St IS N1 5 L4
Rocombe Crs FSTH SE23 * 63 N5
Rocque La BKHTH/KID SE3 64 C1
Rodborough Rd GLDGN NW11 37 N6
Rodd Est SHPTN TW17 * 69 V7
Roden Gdns CROY/NA CR0 74 J5
Rodenhurst Rd CLAP SW4 62 A4
Roden St HOLWY N7 38 E8
IL IG1 40 J10
Rodeo Cl ERITH DA8 54 H12
Roderick Rd HAMP NW3 37 S9
Roding Av WFD IG8 28 J11
Roding Gdns LOU IG10 29 L1
Roding La BKHH IG9 28 J5
CHIG IG7 28 J6
Roding La South REDBR IG4 40 J3
Roding Ms WAP E1W 51 M5
Roding Rd CLPT E5 39 P9
EHAM E6 52 J2
LOU IG10 28 J4
Rodings Rw BAR EN5 * 25 L2
The Rodings UPMR RM14 43 L3
Roding Vw BKHH IG9 28 H5
Roding Wy RAIN RM13 42 K14
Rodmarton St MHST W1U 3 R10
Rodmell Cl YEAD UB4 46 G3
Rodmell Slope NFNCH/WDSPK N12 25 M10
Rodmere St GNWCH SE10 52 A10
Rodmill La BRXS/STRHM SW2 62 C6
Rodney Cl CROY/NA CR0 74 F6
NWMAL KT3 72 E3
PIN HA5 34 H5
WOT/HER KT12 70 F10
Rodney Gdns PIN HA5 34 D4
WWKM BR4 76 C10
Rodney Pl WALW SE17 9 P7
WALTH E17 27 Q14
WIM/MER SW19 61 Q13
Rodney Rd MTCM CR4 61 S14
NWMAL KT3 72 E3
WALTH E17 40 A1
WAN E11 40 D1
WHTN TW2 58 K5
WOT/HER KT12 70 E7
Rodney St IS N1 4 H3
Rodney Wy DTCH/LGLY SL3 44 D11
ROMW/RG RM7 30 A14
Rodona Rd WEY KT13 81 V1
Rodway Rd BMLY BR1 64 E14
PUT/ROE SW15 60 G5
Rodwell Cl RSLP HA4 * 34 C8
Rodwell Rd EDUL SE22 62 K4
Roebuck Cl ASHTD KT21 83 U10
FELT TW13 58 D9
REIG RH2 93 Q12
Roebuck La BKHH IG9 28 G4
Roebuck Rd CHSGTN KT9 72 A10
Roedean Av PEND EN3 16 D14
Roedean Cl ORP BR6 77 L9
PEND EN3 16 D14
Roedean Crs PUT/ROE SW15 60 D4
Roe End CDALE/KGS NW9 36 C3
Roe Gn CDALE/KGS NW9 36 C3
Roehampton Cl PUT/ROE SW15 60 G2
Roehampton Dr CHST BR7 65 L11
Roehampton Ga PUT/ROE SW15 60 C5
Roehampton High St PUT/ROE SW15 60 E6
Roehampton La PUT/ROE SW15 60 F4
Roehampton V PUT/ROE SW15 60 E8
Roe La CDALE/KGS NW9 36 B2
Roe Wy WLGTN SM6 74 C12
Rofant Rd NTHWD HA6 22 A12
Roffes La CTHM CR3 * 86 J13
Roffey Cl PUR/KEN CR8 86 E6
Roffey St POP/IOD E14 51 V7
Rogers Cl CHESW EN7 15 Q2
COUL/CHIP CR5 86 F7
Rogers Ct SWLY BR8 78 C2
Rogers Gdns DAGE RM10 42 A10
Rogers Mead GDST RH9 95 N11
Rogers Rd CAN/RD E16 52 C4
DAGE RM10 42 A10
TOOT SW17 61 R9
Rogers Ruff NTHWD HA6 21 U13
Roger St BMSBY WC1N 4 H8
Rogers Wk NFNCH/WDSPK N12 25 P8
Rogers Wood La HART DA3 79 S9
Rojack Rd FSTH SE23 63 P6
Rokeby Gdns WFD IG8 28 G14
Rokeby Pl RYNPK SW20 60 H12
Rokeby Rd BROCKY SE4 * 51 R14
Rokeby St SRTFD E15 40 A13
Roke Cl PUR/KEN CR8 86 E4
Roke Lodge Rd PUR/KEN CR8 86 E3
Roke Rd PUR/KEN CR8 86 F4
Roker Park Av HGDN/ICK UB10 33 Q9
Rokesby Cl WELL DA16 53 M14
Rokesby Pl ALP/SUD HA0 35 T10
Rokesly Av CEND/HSY/T N8 38 C3
Roland Gdns SKENS SW7 6 K9
Roland Ms WCHPL E1 * 51 P3
Roland Rd WALTH E17 39 V2
Roland Wy SKENS SW7 6 K9
WALW SE17 9 R10
WPK KT4 72 F7
Roles Gv CHDH RM6 41 T2
Rolfe Cl EBAR EN4 25 S2
Rolinsden Wy HAYES BR2 76 F10
Rolland Rd CHSGTN KT9 71 V11
Rollesby Wy THMD SE28 53 S5
Rolleston Av STMC/STPC BR5 76 K4
Rolleston Cl STMC/STPC BR5 76 K5
Rolleston Rd SAND/SEL CR2 74 H12
Roll Gdns GNTH/NBYPK IG2 40 J3
Rollins St PECK SE15 51 N11
Rollit Crs HSLW TW3 58 J3
Rollit St HOLWY N7 38 E10
Rollo Rd SWLY BR8 66 F12
Rolls Buildings FLST/FETLN EC4A 4 J11
Rollscourt Av HNHL SE24 62 G3
Rolls Pk CHING E4 27 T10
Rolls Park Av CHING E4 27 T10
Rolls Park Rd CHING E4 27 U9
Rolls Rd STHWK SE1 9 V9
Rolls Royce Cl WLGTN SM6 74 C12
Rolt St NWCR SE14 51 Q11
Rolvenden Gdns BMLY BR1 64 F11
Rolvenden Pl TOTM N17 27 L13
Romana Ct STA TW18 * 57 L9
Roman Cl ACT W3 48 A7
DEN/HRF UB9 21 L13
EBED/NFELT TW14 58 E5
RAIN RM13 42 D14
Romanfield Rd BRXS/STRHM SW2 62 E5
Roman Gdns KGLGY WD4 10 H4
Romanhurst Av HAYES BR2 76 A2
Romanhurst Gdns HAYES BR2 76 A2
Roman Ri NRWD SE19 62 H12
Roman Rd BETH E2 39 P14
BRW CM14 31 T14
CHSWK W4 48 E9
EHAM E6 52 E2
IL IG1 41 L10
MUSWH N10 25 V13
RAD WD7 12 E9
RDART DA2 67 V7
Roman Sq THMD SE28 53 Q6
Romans Wy WOKS/MYFD GU22 81 L8
Roman Villa Rd EYN DA4 67 Q11
Roman Wk RAD WD7 * 12 D10
Roman Wy CROY/NA CR0 74 F6
DART DA1 66 E3
EN EN1 16 C13
HOLWY N7 38 E11
WAB EN9 16 H9
Romany Gdns CHEAM SM3 73 L4
Romany Ri STMC/STPC BR5 77 L6
Roma Rd WALTH E17 39 Q1
Romberg Rd TOOT SW17 61 U8
Romborough Gdns LEW SE13 63 U3
Romborough Wy LEW SE13 63 U3
Rom Crs ROMW/RG RM7 42 E5
Romeland BORE WD6 23 T4
WAB EN9 16 J7
Romero Cl BRXN/ST SW9 62 D1
Romero Sq BKHTH/KID SE3 64 F2
Romeyn Rd STRHM/NOR SW16 62 D8
Romford Rd CHIG IG7 29 S8
MNPK E12 40 G10
SOCK/AV RM15 55 Q1
SRTFD E15 40 A11
Romford St WCHPL E1 51 L3
Romilly Dr OXHEY WD19 22 G9
Romilly Rd FSBYPK N4 38 F7
Romilly St SOHO/SHAV W1D 4 C13
Rommany Rd WNWD SE27 62 H9
Romney Cha EMPK RM11 43 M1
Romney Cl ASHF TW15 57 U11
CHSGTN KT9 71 V10
GLDGN NW11 37 Q6
NWCR SE14 51 N12
RYLN/HDSTN HA2 34 J6
TOTM N17 27 M13
Romney Dr BMLY BR1 64 F12
RYLN/HDSTN HA2 34 J6
Romney Gdns BXLYHN DA7 53 V13
Romney Rd GNWCH SE10 51 V11
NWMAL KT3 72 D4
YEAD UB4 33 V14
Romney Rw CRICK NW2 * 36 K7
Romney St WEST SW1P 8 E7
Romola Rd HNHL SE24 62 F6
Romsey Cl DTCH/LGLY SL3 44 E7
ORP BR6 77 L10
Romsey Rd DAGW RM9 41 T13
WEA W13 * 47 P5
Romside Pl ROMW/RG RM7 42 E2
Romulus Ct BTFD TW8 * 47 R12
Ronald Av SRTFD E15 52 A1
Ronald Cl BECK BR3 75 R3
Ronald Rd HARH RM3 31 R11
Ronalds Rd BMLY BR1 64 C13
HBRY N5 38 F10
Ronaldstone Rd BFN/LL DA15 65 N4
Ronan Wy DEN/HRF UB9 33 N1
Ronart St KTN/HRWW/WS HA3 35 R4
Rona Wk IS N1 38 H11
Rondu Rd CRICK NW2 36 K9
Roneleon Rd SURB KT6 71 V8
Roneo Cnr HCH RM12 42 F7
Roneo Link HCH RM12 42 F7
Ronfearn Av STMC/STPC BR5 77 S2
Ron Green Cl ERITH DA8 54 D10
Ron Leighton Wy EHAM E6 40 F13
Ronneby Cl WEY KT13 70 A8
Ronnie La MNPK E12 41 L10
Ronson Wy LHD/OX KT22 83 M14
Ronver Rd LEE/GVPK SE12 64 C6
Roodlands La EDEN TN8 97 T13
Rood La FENCHST EC3M 5 S13
Rookby Ct WCHMH N21 26 F7
Rook Cl RAIN RM13 42 K8
WBLY HA9 36 B8
Rookeries Cl FELT TW13 58 D8
Rookery Cl LHD/OX KT22 83 N14
Rookery Ct WTHK RM20 * 55 V10
Rookery Dr CHST BR7 64 J13
Rookery Gdns STMC/STPC BR5 77 R2
Rookery Hl ASHTD KT21 84 A8
Rookery Md COUL/CHIP CR5 86 B12
Rookery Rd CLAP SW4 62 A2
ORP BR6 76 J12
STA TW18 * 57 L10
The Rookery STRHM/NOR SW16 * 62 D11
WTHK RM20 55 V10
Rookery Wy CDALE/KGS NW9 36 F3
KWD/TDW/WH KT20 84 K14
Rookesley Rd STMC/STPC BR5 77 T3
Rooke Wy GNWCH SE10 52 B10
Rookfield Av MUSWH N10 37 V3
Rookfield Cl MUSWH N10 37 V3
Rook La CTHM CR3 86 E11
Rookley Cl BELMT SM2 73 P14
Rooks Hl RKW/CH/CXG WD3 20 K4
Rooksmead Rd SUN TW16 70 A4
Rookstone Rd TOOT SW17 61 T10
Rooks Ter WDR/YW UB7 45 Q7
Rook Wk CAN/RD E16 52 E4
Rookwood Av NWMAL KT3 72 G4
WLGTN SM6 74 B9
Rookwood Cl REDH RH1 93 U3
Rookwood Gdns CHING E4 * 28 B7
Rookwood Rd STNW/STAM N16 38 K5
Roosevelt Wy DAGE RM10 42 D13
Rootes Dr NKENS W10 48 K3
Ropemaker Rd BERM/RHTH SE16 51 Q7
Ropemaker's Flds POP/IOD E14 * 51 R5
Ropemaker St BARB EC2Y 5 Q9
Roper La STHWK SE1 9 T3
Ropers Av CHING E4 27 U10
Ropers Orch CHEL SW3 * 7 N13
Roper St ELTH/MOT SE9 65 L3
Roper Wy MTCM CR4 61 U14
Ropery St BOW E3 51 R2
Rope St BERM/RHTH SE16 51 Q8
Ropewalk Gdns WCHPL E1 51 L4
Ropewalk Ms HACK E8 * 38 K12
Rope Yard Rails WOOL/PLUM SE18 52 K9
Ropley St BETH E2 51 L1
Rosa Alba Ms HBRY N5 38 G9
Rosa Av ASHF TW15 57 S9
Rosaline Rd FUL/PGN SW6 6 B14
Rosamond St SYD SE26 63 M8
Rosamond Vls MORT/ESHN SW14 * 60 D2
Rosamun St NWDGN UB2 46 G10
Rosamund Cl SAND/SEL CR2 74 H11
Rosary Cl HSLWW TW4 46 G12
Rosary Ct POTB/CUF EN6 14 G5
Rosary Gdns ASHF TW15 57 T9
BUSH WD23 23 Q1
SKENS SW7 6 K8
Rosaville Rd FUL/PGN SW6 6 A14
Roscoe St STLK EC1Y 5 P8
Roscoff Cl EDGW HA8 24 C13
Roseacre OXTED RH8 96 G9
Roseacre Cl EMPK RM11 43 M2
SHPTN TW17 69 V5
WEA W13 47 R3
Roseacre Rd WELL DA16 65 R1
Rose Aly LVPST EC2M 5 T10
STHWK SE1 9 P1
Rose & Crown Yd STJS SW1Y * 8 B1
Rose Av MRDN SM4 73 Q3
MTCM CR4 61 T13
SWFD E18 28 D13
Rosebank EPSOM KT18 84 D4
PGE/AN SE20 63 M12
WAB EN9 16 K8
Rosebank Av ALP/SUD HA0 35 P8
HCH RM12 42 J10
Rosebank Cl NFNCH/WDSPK N12 25 T9
Rosebank Cl TEDD TW11 59 Q11

Rosebank Cottages REIG RH2 * 93 P12
Rosebank Est BOW E3 39 R14
Rosebank Gdns ACT W3 * 48 D4
BOW E3 39 R14
Rosebank Gv WALTH E17 39 R1
Rosebank Rd HNWL W7 47 N7
WALTH E17 39 S4
Rosebank Wk CAMTN NW1 * 38 B12
Rosebank Wy ACT W3 48 D4
Roseberry Cl UPMR RM14 43 T4
Roseberry Ct WAT WD17 11 N13
Roseberry Gdns DART DA1 66 J5
FSBYPK N4 38 F4
ORP BR6 77 N8
UPMR RM14 43 T5
Roseberry Pl HACK E8 38 K11
Roseberry St BERM/RHTH SE16 51 M9
Rosebery Av BFN/LL DA15 65 N5
CLKNW EC1R 4 J8
EW KT17 84 E4
MNPK E12 40 G11
NWMAL KT3 60 F14
RYLN/HDSTN HA2 34 G9
THHTH CR7 62 G14
TOTM N17 27 L14
Rosebery Cl MRDN SM4 72 K4
Rosebery Ct CLKNW EC1R 4 J7
Rosebery Crs WOKS/MYFD GU22 80 D10
Rosebery Gdns CEND/HSY/T N8 * 38 C3
SUT SM1 73 P9
WEA W13 47 Q4
Rosebery Ms MUSWH N10 26 A14
Rosebery Pde EW KT17 * 72 F12
Rosebery Rd BUSH WD23 22 K6
CLAP SW4 62 C4
EPSOM KT18 84 D9
HSLW TW3 59 L3
KUT/HW KT1 60 B14
MUSWH N10 26 A14
SUT SM1 73 M11
Rosebine Av WHTN TW2 59 M5
Rosebriar Cl WOKS/MYFD GU22 81 L6
Rosebriars CTHM CR3 86 J10
ESH/CLAY KT10 71 L10
Rosebriar Wk WATN WD24 11 M10
Rosebury Rd FUL/PGN SW6 49 P14
Rosebury Sq WFD IG8 28 J12
Rosebury V RSLP HA4 34 C7
Rose Bushes EW KT17 84 J6
Rose Cottages HAYES BR2 * 88 E1
Rose Ct CHESW EN7 16 A1
WCHPL E1 5 U10
Rosecourt Rd CROY/NA CR0 74 D4
Rosecroft Av HAMP NW3 37 N8
Rosecroft Cl BH/WHM TN16 88 H8
STMC/STPC BR5 77 S4
Rosecroft Ct NTHWD HA6 * 21 U11
Rosecroft Dr WAT WD17 11 L11
Rose Croft Gdns CRICK NW2 36 G8
Rosecroft Gdns WHTN TW2 59 M6
Rosecroft Rd STHL UB1 46 J2
Rosecroft Wk ALP/SUD HA0 35 T10
PIN HA5 34 F3
Rosedale ASHTD KT21 83 S8
Rose Dl ORP BR6 76 K7
Rosedale Av CHESW EN7 15 V3
HYS/HAR UB3 45 V3
Rosedale Cl ABYW SE2 53 R8
HNWL W7 47 P7
LCOL/BKTW AL2 11 S4
RDART DA2 67 P5
STAN HA7 23 R11
Rosedale Dr DAGW RM9 41 R13
Rosedale Gdns DAGW RM9 41 R12
Rosedale Pl CROY/NA CR0 75 P5
Rosedale Rd DAGW RM9 41 R12
EW KT17 72 G10
FSTGT E7 40 E10
RCH/KEW TW9 59 U2
ROM RM1 42 C1
Rosedale Wy CHESW EN7 16 A1
Rosedene Av CROY/NA CR0 74 C5
GFD/PVL UB6 46 J1
MRDN SM4 73 N3
STRHM/NOR SW16 62 D8
Rosedene Cl DART DA1 66 J5
Rosedene Gdns GNTH/NBYPK IG2 40 J2
Rosedene Ter LEY E10 39 T7
Rosedew Rd HMSMTH W6 48 K11
Rose End WPK KT4 72 K6
Rosefield POP/IOD E14 51 S5
SEV TN13 90 G14
Rosefield Cl CAR SM5 73 S10
Rosefield Gdns CHERT KT16 68 H11
POP/IOD E14 51 S5
Rosefield Rd STA TW18 57 L9
Rose Garden Cl EDGW HA8 23 U11
Rose Gdns EA W5 47 T8
FELT TW13 58 C7
STHL UB1 46 J2
STWL/WRAY TW19 57 P5
WATW WD18 22 C3
Rose Gln CDALE/KGS NW9 36 D2
ROMW/RG RM7 42 E6
Rosehart Ms NTGHL W11 2 E12
Rosehatch Av CHDH RM6 41 T1
Roseheath Rd HSLWW TW4 58 H3
Rosehill ESH/CLAY KT10 71 Q11
HPTN TW12 58 J13
Rose Hl SUT SM1 73 P7
Rosehill Av SUT SM1 73 Q6
WOKN/KNAP GU21 80 A6
Rosehill Court Pde MRDN SM4 * 73 Q5
Rosehill Farm Meadow BNSTD SM7 85 P5
Rosehill Gdns ABLGY WD5 10 K6
GFD/PVL UB6 35 P10
SUT SM1 73 P7
Rose Hill Pk West SUT SM1 73 Q7
Rosehill Rd BH/WHM TN16 88 E7
WAND/EARL SW18 61 Q4
Roseland Cl TOTM N17 26 H12
Rose La CHDH RM6 41 U2
RPLY/SEND GU23 81 P12
Rose Lawn BUSH WD23 23 L6
Roseleigh Av HBRY N5 38 F9
Roseleigh Cl TWK TW1 59 T4
Rosemary Av E/WMO/HCT KT8 70 J1
ED N9 27 M6
ENC/FH EN2 15 T13
FNCH N3 25 P14
HSLWW TW4 46 F14
ROM RM1 42 F1
Rosemary Cl CROY/NA CR0 74 C5
OXTED RH8 96 C9
UX/CGN UB8 * 45 S3
Rosemary Dr POP/IOD E14 51 V4
REDBR IG4 40 F3
Rosemary Gdns BCTR RM8 41 V6
CHSGTN KT9 71 U9
Rosemary La EGH TW20 68 F1
MORT/ESHN SW14 60 C1
Rosemary Rd PECK SE15 9 V13
TOOT SW17 61 P8
WELL DA16 53 P13
Rosemary St IS N1 5 R1
Rosemead CDALE/KGS NW9 36 F5
CHERT KT16 69 M5
Rose Md POTB/CUF EN6 14 E4
Rosemead Av FELT TW13 58 B7
MTCM CR4 74 A1
WBLY HA9 35 U10
Rosemead Cl REDH RH1 93 R12
Rose Ms UED N18 27 M9
Rosemont Av NFNCH/WDSPK N12 25 Q11
Rosemont Rd ACT W3 48 B5
HAMP NW3 37 Q11
NWMAL KT3 72 C1
RCHPK/HAM TW10 59 U4
Rosemoor St CHEL SW3 7 Q8
Rosemount Av BF/WBF KT14 81 L3
Rosemount Cl WFD IG8 28 H11
Rosemount Dr BMLY BR1 76 H2
Rosemount Rd ALP/SUD HA0 35 U13
WEA W13 47 Q4
Rosenau Crs BTSEA SW11 49 T13
Rosenau Rd BTSEA SW11 49 T13
Rosendale Rd DUL SE21 62 G6
Roseneath Av WCHMH N21 26 F6
Roseneath Ct CTHM CR3 * 95 L1
Roseneath Pl STRHM/NOR SW16 62 E9
Roseneath Rd BTSEA SW11 61 U4
Roseneath Wk EN EN1 26 J2
Rosenheath Cl ORP BR6 77 S13
Rosens Wk EDGW HA8 24 B8
Rosenthal Rd CAT SE6 63 T4
Rosenthorpe Rd PECK SE15 63 P3
Rose Park Cl YEAD UB4 46 E3
Roserton St POP/IOD E14 51 U7
The Rosery CROY/NA CR0 75 P4
The Roses WFD IG8 * 28 B12
Rose St COVGDN WC2E 4 E13
Rosethorn Cl BAL SW12 62 A5
Rosetta Cl VX/NE SW8 8 F14
Roseveare Rd LEE/GVPK SE12 64 E9
Rose Vw ADL/WDHM KT15 * 69 N10
Roseville Av HSLW TW3 58 J3
Roseville Rd HYS/HAR UB3 46 C10
Rosevine Rd RYNPK SW20 60 J13
Rose Wk BRYLDS KT5 72 B3
WWKM BR4 75 V7
The Rose Wk RAD WD7 12 F11
Roseway DUL SE21 62 H4
EDGW HA8 24 C9
Rose Wy LEE/GVPK SE12 64 C3
Rosewell Cl PGE/AN SE20 63 M12
Rosewood RDART DA2 66 E9
Rose Wd WOKS/MYFD GU22 80 E9
Rosewood Av GFD/PVL UB6 35 Q10
HCH RM12 42 G10
Rosewood Cl SCUP DA14 65 S8
Rosewood Ct KUTN/CMB KT2 60 A12
Rosewood Dr ENC/FH EN2 15 R9
SHPTN TW17 69 R3
Rosewood Gv SUT SM1 73 Q7
Rosewood Ter PGE/AN SE20 * 63 N12
Rosher Cl SRTFD E15 39 V12
Rosina St HOM E9 39 P11
Roskell Rd PUT/ROE SW15 60 K1
Roslin Rd ACT W3 48 B8
Roslin Wy BMLY BR1 64 C10
Roslyn Cl MTCM CR4 61 R14
Roslyn Gdns GPK RM2 30 F14
Roslyn Ms SEVS/STOTM N15 * 38 J3
Roslyn Rd SEVS/STOTM N15 38 H3
Rosmead Rd NTGHL W11 2 B13
Rosoman Pl CLKNW EC1R 4 K7
Rosoman St CLKNW EC1R 4 K7
Rossall Cl EMPK RM11 42 G4
Rossall Crs WLSDN NW10 47 V1
Ross Av BCTR RM8 41 V7
MLHL NW7 25 L10
Ross Cl HYS/HAR UB3 45 V9
KTN/HRWW/WS HA3 23 L12
NTHLT UB5 35 M9
Ross Crs GSTN WD25 11 N9
Rossdale SUT SM1 73 S10
Rossdale Dr CDALE/KGS NW9 36 C6
ED N9 27 N4
Rossdale Rd PUT/ROE SW15 60 J2
Rosse Ms BKHTH/KID SE3 52 D13
Rossendale Cl ENC/FH EN2 15 R11
Rossendale St CLPT E5 39 M7
Rossetti Gdns COUL/CHIP CR5 86 D7
Rossetti Rd BERM/RHTH SE16 51 M10
Ross House CHARL SE7 * 52 G12
Rossignol Gdns CAR SM5 73 U7
Rossindel Rd HSLW TW3 58 J3
Rossington Av BORE WD6 12 J12
Rossington Cl EN EN1 16 B12
Rossington St CLPT E5 39 M7
Rossiter Cl DTCH/LGLY SL3 44 C9
Rossiter Flds BAR EN5 25 M4
Rossiter Rd BAL SW12 61 V6
Rossland Cl BXLYHS DA6 66 A3
Rosslare Cl BH/WHM TN16 97 M2
Rosslyn Av BARN SW13 60 E1
BCTR RM8 41 V5
CHING E4 28 B7
EBAR EN4 25 S4
EBED/NFELT TW14 58 C4
HARH RM3 31 L14
Rosslyn Cl HYS/HAR UB3 45 V3
SUN TW16 58 A11
WWKM BR4 76 B8
Rosslyn Crs HRW HA1 35 P2
WBLY HA9 35 U8
Rosslyn Hl HAMP NW3 37 R10
Rosslyn Pk WEY KT13 69 V9
Rosslyn Park Ms HAMP NW3 37 R10
Rosslyn Rd BARK IG11 41 M12
TWK TW1 59 S4
WALTH E17 * 39 U2
WATW WD18 22 D1
Rossmore Cl CAMTN NW1 * 3 P8
PEND EN3 27 P2
Rossmore Rd CAMTN NW1 3 P7
Ross Pde WLGTN SM6 73 V11
Ross Rd COB KT11 82 E3
DART DA1 66 G4
SNWD SE25 74 J1
WHTN TW2 59 L6
WLGTN SM6 74 A11
Ross Wy ELTH/MOT SE9 64 G1
NTHWD HA6 22 B9
Rossway Dr BUSH WD23 23 M3
Rosswood Gdns WLGTN SM6 73 V11
Rostella Rd TOOT SW17 61 R9
Rostrever Gdns HYS/HAR UB3 46 A6
Rostrevor Av SEVS/STOTM N15 38 K4
Rostrevor Gdns IVER SL0 32 H14
NWDGN UB2 46 G10
Rostrevor Rd FUL/PGN SW6 49 M13
WIM/MER SW19 61 N10
Roswell Cl CHES/WCR EN8 16 E4
Rotary St STHWK SE1 9 L5
Rothbury Av RAIN RM13 54 H3
Rothbury Cottages GNWCH SE10 52 A9
Rothbury Gdns ISLW TW7 47 Q12
Rothbury Rd HOM E9 39 R12
Rother Cl GSTN WD25 11 Q8
Rotherfield Rd CAR SM5 73 U9
PEND EN3 16 D11
Rotherfield St IS N1 38 G12
Rotherham Wk STHWK SE1 * 9 M2
Rotherhill Av STRHM/NOR SW16 62 B11
Rotherhithe New Rd
BERM/RHTH SE16 51 M10
Rotherhithe Old Rd BERM/RHTH SE16 51 P9
Rotherhithe St BERM/RHTH SE16 51 N7
Rotherhithe Tnl BERM/RHTH SE16 51 N7
Rothermere Rd CROY/NA CR0 74 D10
Rotherwick Hl EA W5 47 V2
Rotherwick Rd GLDGN NW11 37 N5
Rotherwood Cl RYNPK SW20 61 L13
Rotherwood Rd PUT/ROE SW15 60 K1
Rothery St IS N1 * 5 M1
Rothesay Av GFD/PVL UB6 35 M11
RCHPK/HAM TW10 60 B2
RYNPK SW20 61 L14
Rothesay Rd SNWD SE25 74 H2
Rothsay Rd FSTGT E7 40 E12
Rothsay St STHWK SE1 9 S5
Rothschild Rd CHSWK W4 48 C9
Rothschild St WNWD SE27 62 G9
Rothwell Gdns DAGW RM9 41 S12
Rothwell Rd DAGW RM9 41 S13
Rothwell St CAMTN NW1 3 R1
Rotterdam Dr POP/IOD E14 51 U8
Rouel Rd BERM/RHTH SE16 51 L9
Rougemont Av MRDN SM4 73 N4
Roughets La REDH RH1 94 J5
Roughlands WOKS/MYFD GU22 80 J5
The Roughs NTHWD HA6 22 A8
Roughtallys EPP CM16 18 K1
Roughwood Cl WAT WD17 11 L12
Roughwood La CSTG HP8 20 C4
Roundaway Rd CLAY IG5 28 H14
Roundbush La GSTN WD25 12 B12
Roundel Cl BROCKY SE4 63 R2
Round Gv CROY/NA CR0 75 Q5
Roundhay Cl FSTH SE23 63 P7
Roundhedge Wy ENC/FH EN2 15 P12
Round Hl SYD SE26 63 M7
Roundhill WOKS/MYFD GU22 80 F9
Roundhill Dr ENC/FH EN2 26 D2
WOKS/MYFD GU22 80 F8
Roundhills WAB EN9 17 L8
Roundhill Wy COB KT11 82 K1
Roundlyn Gdns STMC/STPC BR5 77 R2
Roundmead Av LOU IG10 28 J1
Roundmead Cl LOU IG10 28 J1
Roundmoor Dr CHES/WCR EN8 16 E3
Round Oak Rd WEY KT13 69 R9
Roundtable Rd BMLY BR1 64 B8
Roundtree Rd ALP/SUD HA0 35 R10
Roundway EGH TW20 56 G10
Roundways RSLP HA4 34 B8
The Roundway ESH/CLAY KT10 71 P11
TOTM N17 26 H13
WATW WD18 22 B5
Roundwood CHST BR7 64 K14
KGLGY WD4 10 E1
Roundwood Av STKPK UB11 45 U7
Roundwood Cl RSLP HA4 * 33 V5
Roundwood Pk WLSDN NW10 * 36 G13
Roundwood Rd WLSDN NW10 36 E11
Roundwood Ter STNW/STAM N16 38 J5
Roundwood Vw BNSTD SM7 84 K5
Roundwood Wy BNSTD SM7 84 K5
Rounton Rd BOW E3 51 S2
WAB EN9 17 L7
Roupell Rd BRXS/STRHM SW2 62 D6
Roupell St STHWK SE1 8 K2
Rousden St CAMTN NW1 38 A12
Rousebarn La RKW/CH/CXG WD3 10 F12
Rouse Ct CFSP/GDCR SL9 * 20 D12
CFSP/GDCR SL9 32 D3
Rouse Gdns DUL SE21 62 J9
Rous Rd BKHH IG9 28 G6
Routemaster Cl PLSTW E13 52 D1
Routh Ct EBED/NFELT TW14 57 V6
Routh Rd WAND/EARL SW18 61 S5
Routh St EHAM E6 52 H3
Rover Av BARK/HLT IG6 29 P11
Rowallan Rd FUL/PGN SW6 6 A14
Rowan Av CHING E4 27 R11
EGH TW20 56 G10
Rowan Cl ALP/SUD HA0 35 Q8
EA W5 47 U7
IL IG1 41 M10
LCOL/BKTW AL2 11 U5
NWMAL KT3 60 E14
REIG RH2 93 Q12
STAN HA7 23 P11
STRHM/NOR SW16 62 A13
Rowan Crs DART DA1 66 J6
STRHM/NOR SW16 62 A13
Rowan Dr CDALE/KGS NW9 36 G1
Rowan Gdns CROY/NA CR0 74 K8
IVER SL0 32 G14
Rowan Gv COUL/CHIP CR5 85 V11
SOCK/AV RM15 55 Q5
Rowan Md KWD/TDW/WH KT20 84 H9
Rowan Pl HYS/HAR UB3 46 B5
Rowan Rd BTFD TW8 47 R12
BXLYHN DA7 65 U1
HMSMTH W6 48 K9
STRHM/NOR SW16 62 A14
SWLY BR8 78 D1
WDR/YW UB7 45 P9
The Rowans CFSP/GDCR SL9 32 A1
PLMGR N13 26 G8
SOCK/AV RM15 55 Q6
SUN TW16 58 B10
WOKS/MYFD GU22 80 C8
Rowans Wy LOU IG10 28 H2
Rowan Ter PGE/AN SE20 * 63 L13
WIM/MER SW19 * 61 L12
Rowantree Cl WCHMH N21 26 H6
Rowantree Ms ENC/FH EN2 15 R14
Rowantree Rd ENC/FH EN2 15 R14
WCHMH N21 26 H6
Rowan Wk EFNCH N2 37 Q4
EMPK RM11 42 K2
HAYES BR2 76 H8
NKENS W10 * 2 A7
Rowan Wy CHDH RM6 41 S1
Rowanwood Av BFN/LL DA15 65 Q6
Rowben Cl TRDG/WHET N20 25 P6
Rowberry Cl FUL/PGN SW6 48 K12
Rowcross St STHWK SE1 9 U9
Rowdell Rd NTHLT UB5 34 J13
Rowden Pde CHING E4 * 27 S11
Rowden Rd BECK BR3 63 Q13
CHING E4 27 T11
HOR/WEW KT19 72 C9
Rowditch La BTSEA SW11 49 U14
Rowdon Av WLSDN NW10 36 H12
Rowdow La BGR/WK TN15 91 L4
RSEV TN14 90 K6
Rowdown Crs CROY/NA CR0 75 V13
Rowdowns Rd DAGW RM9 41 V13
Rowe Gdns BARK IG11 41 Q14
Rowe La HOM E9 39 N10
Rowena Crs BTSEA SW11 49 S14
Rowe Wk RYLN/HDSTN HA2 34 J8
Rowfant Rd TOOT SW17 61 U7
Row Hl ADL/WDHM KT15 68 K11
Rowhill Rd CLPT E5 39 M9
Rowhurst Av ADL/WDHM KT15 69 M11
Rowington Cl BAY/PAD W2 2 G9
Rowland Av KTN/HRWW/WS HA3 35 S1
Rowland Crs CHIG IG7 29 N9
Rowland Gv SYD SE26 63 M8
Rowland Hill Av TOTM N17 26 H12
Rowland Hill St HAMP NW3 37 S10
Rowland Pl NTHWD HA6 * 22 A12
Rowlands Av PIN HA5 22 J11
Rowlands Cl CHES/WCR EN8 16 D4
HGT N6 * 37 U4
MLHL NW7 24 G12
Rowlandsfields CHES/WCR EN8 * 16 D4
Rowlands Rd BCTR RM8 41 V7
Rowland Wy ASHF TW15 57 U12
WIM/MER SW19 61 P13
Rowlatt Cl RDART DA2 66 J9
Rowley Av BFN/LL DA15 65 R5
Rowley Cl ALP/SUD HA0 35 V12
OXHEY WD19 22 G4
WOKS/MYFD GU22 81 L6
Rowley Ct CTHM CR3 86 G12
Rowley Gdns FSBYPK N4 38 G5
Rowley Green Rd BAR EN5 24 G3
Rowley La BAR EN5 24 E2
BORE WD6 13 P14
DTCH/LGLY SL3 32 C14
Rowley Rd SEVS/STOTM N15 38 G3
Rowley Wy STJWD NW8 2 K1
Rowlheys Pl WDR/YW UB7 45 Q8
Rowlls Rd KUT/HW KT1 71 V1
Rowney Gdns DAGW RM9 41 S11
Rowney Rd DAGW RM9 41 S11
Rowntree Clifford Cl PLSTW E13 52 D2
Rowntree Cl KIL/WHAMP NW6 * 37 N11
Rowntree Rd WHTN TW2 59 N6
Rowse Cl SRTFD E15 39 U13
Rowsley Av HDN NW4 36 J1
Rowstock Gdns HOLWY N7 38 B11
Rowton Rd WOOL/PLUM SE18 53 L12
Row Town ADL/WDHM KT15 68 K12
Rowzill Rd SWLY BR8 66 F11
Roxborough Av HRW HA1 35 N5
ISLW TW7 47 P12
Roxborough Pk HRW HA1 35 N5
Roxborough Rd HRW HA1 35 M3
Roxbourne Cl NTHLT UB5 34 F11
Roxburgh Av UPMR RM14 43 Q8
Roxburgh Rd WNWD SE27 62 F10
Roxburn Wy RSLP HA4 34 B8
Roxby Pl FUL/PGN SW6 6 F11
Roxeth Green Av RYLN/HDSTN HA2 34 K8
Roxeth Gv RYLN/HDSTN HA2 34 K9
Roxeth Hl RYLN/HDSTN HA2 35 M7
Roxford Cl SHPTN TW17 70 A3
Roxley Rd LEW SE13 63 T4
Roxton Gdns CROY/NA CR0 75 S10
Roxwell Rd BARK IG11 41 Q14
SHB W12 48 G7
Roxwell Wy WFD IG8 28 E12
Roxy Av CHDH RM6 41 S5
Royal Albert Rd EHAM E6 52 J5
Royal Albert Wy CAN/RD E16 52 G5
Royal Ar CONDST W1S 4 A14
Royal Arsenal West
WOOL/PLUM SE18 * 52 J10
Royal Av CHEL SW3 7 Q9
CHES/WCR EN8 16 E7
WPK KT4 72 E7
Royal Botanic Gdns RCH/KEW TW9 * 47 U12
Royal Circ WNWD SE27 62 E8
Royal Cl DEPT SE8 51 R11
GDMY/SEVK IG3 41 Q5
ORP BR6 76 K9
STNW/STAM N16 38 J6
WDR/YW UB7 45 R4
WIM/MER SW19 60 K7
WPK KT4 72 E7
Royal College St CAMTN NW1 4 B1
Royal Ct BANK EC3V 5 R12
ELTH/MOT SE9 * 64 H6
EN EN1 * 26 J4
Royal Crs GNTH/NBYPK IG2 41 M4
NTGHL W11 48 K7
RSLP HA4 34 G9
Royal Crescent Ms NTGHL W11 48 K7
Royal Docks Rd EHAM E6 52 K3
Royal Dr EPSOM KT18 84 H8
FBAR/BDGN N11 25 U11
Royal Earlswood Pk REDH RH1 93 U14
Royal Herbert Pavilions
WOOL/PLUM SE18 * 52 H13
Royal Hl GNWCH SE10 51 U12
Royal Hospital Rd CHEL SW3 7 R11
Royal La WDR/YW UB7 45 R4
Royal Ms BAL SW12 61 V5
Royal Mint Pl WCHPL E1 5 V13
Royal Mint St WCHPL E1 5 V13
Royal Naval Pl NWCR SE14 51 R12
Royal Oak Centre PUR/KEN CR8 * 74 G14
Royal Oak Ms TEDD TW11 59 Q10
Royal Oak Pl EDUL SE22 63 M4
Royal Oak Rd BXLYHS DA6 65 V3
HACK E8 39 M11
WOKN/KNAP GU21 80 A8
Royal Oak Yd STHWK SE1 9 S4
Royal Opera Ar STJS SW1Y * 8 C1
Royal Orchard Cl WAND/EARL SW18 61 L5
Royal Pde BKHTH/KID SE3 52 B14
CHST BR7 65 L12
Royal Pl GNWCH SE10 51 U12
Royal Rd CAN/RD E16 52 E4
LBTH SE11 9 L11
RDART DA2 67 N10
SCUP DA14 65 T8
TEDD TW11 59 M10
Royal Route WBLY HA9 35 V9
Royal St STHWK SE1 8 H5
Royal Victor Pl BETH E2 39 P14
Royce Gv GSTN WD25 11 M8
Roycraft Av BARK IG11 41 P14
Roycroft Cl BRXS/STRHM SW2 * 62 E6
SWFD E18 28 D13
Roydene Rd WOOL/PLUM SE18 53 N11
Roydon Cl LOU IG10 28 G5
Roydon Ct WOT/HER KT12 70 C9
Roy Gdns GNTH/NBYPK IG2 41 N2
Roy Gv HPTN TW12 58 K11
Royle Cl CFSP/GDCR SL9 20 D12
GPK RM2 42 H3
Royle Crs WEA W13 47 Q2
Roy Rd NTHWD HA6 22 B12
Roy Sq POP/IOD E14 51 Q5
Royston Av BF/WBF KT14 81 Q2
CHING E4 27 S10
SUT SM1 73 R8
WLGTN SM6 74 B9
Royston Cl HEST TW5 46 D13
WOT/HER KT12 70 C6
Royston Gdns IL IG1 40 F4
Royston Gv PIN HA5 22 H11
Royston Park Rd PIN HA5 22 J10
Royston Rd BF/WBF KT14 81 Q2
DART DA1 66 F4
HARH RM3 31 N12
PGE/AN SE20 63 P13
RCHPK/HAM TW10 59 U3
The Roystons BRYLDS KT5 72 B3
Royston St BETH E2 39 N14
Rozel Rd VX/NE SW8 50 A14
Rubastic Rd NWDGN UB2 46 E8
Rubens Pl CLAP SW4 62 C2
Rubens Rd NTHLT UB5 34 E14
Rubens St CAT SE6 63 R7
Rubin Pl PEND EN3 16 G11
Ruby Ms WALTH E17 * 39 S1
Ruby Rd WALTH E17 39 S1
Ruby St PECK SE15 51 M11
WLSDN NW10 36 C12
Ruby Triangle PECK SE15 * 51 M11
Ruckholt Cl LEY E10 39 T8
Ruckholt Rd LEY E10 39 U8
Rucklers La KGLGY WD4 10 A2
Rucklidge Av WLSDN NW10 36 F14
Rudall Crs HAMP NW3 37 R9
Ruddington Cl CLPT E5 39 Q9
Ruddock Cl EDGW HA8 24 C12
Ruddstreet Cl WOOL/PLUM SE18 52 K9
Ruden Wy EW KT17 84 H5
Rudge Ri ADL/WDHM KT15 68 K10
Rudgwick Ter STJWD NW8 * 3 P2
Rudland Rd BXLYHN DA7 66 B1
Rudloe Rd BAL SW12 62 A5
Rudolf Pl VX/NE SW8 8 F12
Rudolph Rd BUSH WD23 22 J4
KIL/WHAMP NW6 2 F4
PLSTW E13 40 B14
Rudsworth Cl DTCH/LGLY SL3 44 H13
Rudyard Gv EDGW HA8 24 C11
Rue De St Lawrence WAB EN9 16 J8
Ruffetts Cl SAND/SEL CR2 75 M12
The Ruffetts SAND/SEL CR2 75 M12
Ruffetts Wy KWD/TDW/WH KT20 85 L8
Ruffle Cl WDR/YW UB7 45 Q7
Rufford Cl KTN/HRWW/WS HA3 35 Q4
WAT WD17 11 M11
Rufford St IS N1 4 F1
Rufford Street Ms IS N1 38 C12
Rufus Cl RSLP HA4 34 F8
Rufus St FSBYE EC1V 5 S6
Rugby Av ALP/SUD HA0 35 S9
ED N9 26 K6
GFD/PVL UB6 35 M11
Rugby Cl HRW HA1 35 N2
Rugby Gdns DAGW RM9 41 S11
Rugby La BELMT SM2 72 K13
Rugby Rd CDALE/KGS NW9 36 A2
CHSWK W4 48 E7
DAGW RM9 41 R12
TWK TW1 59 N4
Rugby St BMSBY WC1N 4 G8
Rugby Wy RKW/CH/CXG WD3 21 T3
Ruggles-Brise Rd ASHF TW15 57 P10
Rugg St POP/IOD E14 51 S5
Ruislip Cl GFD/PVL UB6 46 K2
Ruislip Ct RSLP HA4 * 34 B7
Ruislip Rd NTHLT UB5 34 E13
Ruislip Rd East GFD/PVL UB6 47 M2
Ruislip St TOOT SW17 61 T9
Rumbold Rd FUL/PGN SW6 6 H14
Rum Cl WAP E1W 51 M5
Rumsey Cl HPTN TW12 58 H11
Rumsey Rd BRXN/ST SW9 62 D1
Rumsley CHESW EN7 16 A1
Runbury Cir CDALE/KGS NW9 36 D7
Runciman Cl ORP BR6 77 S14
Runcorn Cl TOTM N17 39 M2
Runcorn Pl NTGHL W11 2 A14
Rundell Crs HDN NW4 36 H3
Runes Cl MTCM CR4 73 R2
Runnelfield HRW HA1 35 N8
Runnemede Rd EGH TW20 56 D10
Runnymede WIM/MER SW19 61 R13
Runnymede Cl WHTN TW2 58 K4
Runnymede Ct EGH TW20 56 E9
Runnymede Crs
STRHM/NOR SW16 62 B13
Runnymede Gdns GFD/PVL UB6 35 M14
HSLW TW3 58 K4
Runnymede Rd WHTN TW2 58 K4
The Runway RSLP HA4 34 D10
Rupack St BERM/RHTH SE16 * 51 N7
Rupert Av WBLY HA9 35 U10
Rupert Ct E/WMO/HCT KT8 * 70 J2
SOHO/SHAV W1D 4 C13
Rupert Gdns BRXN/ST SW9 50 F14
Rupert Rd ARCH N19 38 B8
CHSWK W4 48 E8
KIL/WHAMP NW6 2 D4
Rupert St SOHO/SHAV W1D 4 C14
Rural Cl EMPK RM11 42 H6
Rural Wy REDH RH1 93 U10
STRHM/NOR SW16 61 V12
Rusbridge Cl HACK E8 39 L10
Ruscoe Dr WOKS/MYFD GU22 80 E7
Ruscoe Rd CAN/RD E16 52 B4
Ruscombe Wy EBED/NFELT TW14 58 B5
Rusham Park Av EGH TW20 56 E11
Rusham Rd BAL SW12 61 T4
EGH TW20 56 D11
Rushbrook Crs WALTH E17 27 R13
Rushbrook Rd ELTH/MOT SE9 65 L7
Rush Common Ms
BRXS/STRHM SW2 62 C5
Rushcroft Rd BRXS/STRHM SW2 62 E2
CHING E4 27 T12
Rushden Cl NRWD SE19 62 H12
Rushdene ABYW SE2 53 S8
Rushdene Av EBAR EN4 25 S5
Rushdene Cl NTHLT UB5 34 E14
Rushdene Crs NTHLT UB5 34 D14
Rushdene Rd PIN HA5 34 E4
Rushdene Wk BH/WHM TN16 88 F7
Rushden Gdns CLAY IG5 40 J1
MLHL NW7 24 J11
Rushdon Cl ROM RM1 42 G3
Rush Dr WAB EN9 16 J10
Rushes Md UX/CGN UB8 33 N13
Rushet Rd STMC/STPC BR5 65 Q14
Rushett Cl THDIT KT7 71 R6
Rushett La CHSGTN KT9 83 T2
Rushett Rd THDIT KT7 71 R5
Rushetts Rd BGR/WK TN15 79 R12
REIG RH2 93 Q14
Rushey Cl NWMAL KT3 72 D2
Rushey Gn CAT SE6 63 T5
Rushey Hl ENC/FH EN2 26 D2
Rushey Md BROCKY SE4 63 S3
Rushfield POTB/CUF EN6 13 V7
Rushford Rd BROCKY SE4 63 R4
Rush Green Gdns ROMW/RG RM7 42 C6
Rush Green Rd ROMW/RG RM7 42 C6
Rushgrove Av CDALE/KGS NW9 36 F2
Rushgrove Pde CDALE/KGS NW9 * 36 F3
Rushgrove St WOOL/PLUM SE18 52 H9
Rush Hill Ms BTSEA SW11 61 U1
Rush Hill Rd BTSEA SW11 61 U1
Rushleigh Av CHES/WCR EN8 16 D4
Rushley Cl HAYES BR2 76 F9
Rushmead BETH E2 51 M1
RCHPK/HAM TW10 59 R8
Rushmead Cl CROY/NA CR0 74 K9
Rushmere Av UPMR RM14 43 Q8
Rushmere Ct WPK KT4 72 G7
Rushmere Pl EGH TW20 56 C10
WIM/MER SW19 60 K10
Rushmon Pl CHEAM SM3 * 73 L11
Rushmon Vls NWMAL KT3 * 72 F2
Rushmoor Cl PIN HA5 34 E2
RKW/CH/CXG WD3 21 P7
Rushmore Cl BMLY BR1 76 G1
Rushmore Ct WATW WD18 * 21 V4
Rushmore Hl ORP BR6 77 S14
RSEV TN14 89 T4
Rushmore Rd CLPT E5 39 N9
Rusholme Av DAGE RM10 42 A8
Rusholme Gv NRWD SE19 62 J10
Rusholme Rd PUT/ROE SW15 60 K4
Rushout Av KTN/HRWW/WS HA3 35 R4
Rushton Av GDST RH9 95 N14
GSTN WD25 11 N9
Rushton St IS N1 5 R3
Rushworth Rd REIG RH2 93 N9
Rushworth St STHWK SE1 9 M3
Rushymead BGR/WK TN15 91 N8
Rushy Meadow La CAR SM5 73 S7
Ruskin Av EBED/NFELT TW14 58 B5
MNPK E12 40 H11
RCH/KEW TW9 48 A12
UPMR RM14 43 Q5
WAB EN9 17 L8
WELL DA16 65 Q1
Ruskin Cl GLDGN NW11 37 P4
Ruskin Dr ORP BR6 77 N8
WELL DA16 65 Q1
WPK KT4 72 H7
Ruskin Gdns EA W5 47 T2
HARH RM3 30 H13
KTN/HRWW/WS HA3 35 V3
Ruskin Gv DART DA1 67 N3
WELL DA16 53 Q14
Ruskin Rd BELV DA17 54 A9
CAR SM5 73 U10
CROY/NA CR0 74 F7
ISLW TW7 59 P1
STA TW18 56 K12
STHL UB1 46 G5
TOTM N17 26 K13
Ruskin Wk ED N9 27 L7
HAYES BR2 76 H4
HNHL SE24 62 G3
Ruskin Wy WIM/MER SW19 61 R14
Rusland Av ORP BR6 77 M8
Rusland Park Rd HRW HA1 35 N2
Rusper Cl CRICK NW2 36 J8
STAN HA7 23 S9
Rusper Rd DAGW RM9 41 S11
WDGN N22 26 F14
Russel Cl BECK BR3 75 T1
Russell Av WDGN N22 26 F14
Russell Cl BKHTH/KID SE3 52 E12
BRWN CM15 31 V5
BXLYHN DA7 66 A2
CHSWK W4 48 F11
DART DA1 66 G1
KWD/TDW/WH KT20 92 G1
NTHWD HA6 21 U10
RSLP HA4 34 E7
WLSDN NW10 36 C12
WOKN/KNAP GU21 80 A5
Russell Ct BAR EN5 * 25 Q2
LHD/OX KT22 83 R12
WHALL SW1A 8 B2
Russell Crs GSTN WD25 11 M9
Russell Dr STWL/WRAY TW19 57 P4
Russell Gdns GLDGN NW11 37 L4
RCHPK/HAM TW10 59 S7
TRDG/WHET N20 25 S7
WDR/YW UB7 45 S10
WKENS W14 6 B5
Russell Gardens Ms WKENS W14 6 A5
Russell Green Cl PUR/KEN CR8 74 E14
Russell Gv BRXN/ST SW9 50 E13
MLHL NW7 24 E10
Russell Hl PUR/KEN CR8 74 D14
Russell Hill Pl PUR/KEN CR8 86 E1
Russell Hill Rd PUR/KEN CR8 74 E14
Russell Kerr Cl CHSWK W4 * 48 C12
Russell La TRDG/WHET N20 25 T7
WAT WD17 10 K10
Russell Pde GLDGN NW11 * 37 L4
Russell Pl EYN DA4 67 N13
HAMP NW3 37 S10
Russell Rd BKHH IG9 28 E6
CAN/RD E16 52 C4
CDALE/KGS NW9 36 F4
CEND/HSY/T N8 38 B4
CHING E4 27 R9
EN EN1 15 V12
MTCM CR4 73 S1
NTHLT UB5 35 L10
NTHWD HA6 21 U8
SEVS/STOTM N15 38 J3
SHPTN TW17 69 U5
TRDG/WHET N20 25 S7
WALTH E17 39 R1
WDGN N22 26 D11
WHTN TW2 59 P4
WIM/MER SW19 61 N12
WKENS W14 6 B5
WOKN/KNAP GU21 80 A5
WOT/HER KT12 70 C4
Russells KWD/TDW/WH KT20 84 K12
Russell's Dr CHES/WCR EN8 16 E5
Russell Sq RSQ WC1B 4 E8
Russell's Ride CHES/WCR EN8 16 D5
Russell St HOL/ALD WC2B 4 G12
Russell Ter EYN DA4 * 79 Q2
Russell Wy OXHEY WD19 22 D5
SUT SM1 73 P10
Russet Cl HGDN/ICK UB10 45 U2
STWL/WRAY TW19 56 K4
WOT/HER KT12 70 F8
Russet Crs HOLWY N7 * 38 D10
Russet Dr CROY/NA CR0 75 Q6
RAD WD7 12 J6
Russets Cl CHING E4 27 V9
The Russets CFSP/GDCR SL9 20 B14
Russett Cl ORP BR6 77 R10
Russett Hl CFSP/GDCR SL9 32 C1
Russetts EMPK RM11 43 L2
Russetts Cl WOKN/KNAP GU21 80 D5
Russett Wy SWLY BR8 66 D14
Russia Dock Rd
BERM/RHTH SE16 * 51 Q6
Russia La BETH E2 39 N14
Russia Rw CITYW EC2V 5 P12
Russington Rd SHPTN TW17 69 V4
Rusthall Av CHSWK W4 48 D8
Rusthall Cl CROY/NA CR0 75 N4
Rustic Av STRHM/NOR SW16 61 V12
Rustic Cl UPMR RM14 43 S6
Rustic Pl ALP/SUD HA0 35 T9
Rustington Wk CHEAM SM3 73 M5
Ruston Av BRYLDS KT5 72 B5
Ruston Gdns STHGT/OAK N14 25 U4
Ruston Ms NTGHL W11 2 A12
Ruston Rd WOOL/PLUM SE18 52 G8
Ruston St BOW E3 39 R13
Rust Sq CMBW SE5 9 Q13
Rutford Rd STRHM/NOR SW16 62 C10
Ruth Cl STAN HA7 35 V2
Ruthen Cl EPSOM KT18 84 B4
Rutherford Cl BELMT SM2 73 R11
BORE WD6 13 N14
UX/CGN UB8 45 R2
Rutherford St WEST SW1P 8 C7
Rutherford Wy BUSH WD23 23 N6
WBLY HA9 36 A8
Rutherglen Rd ABYW SE2 53 Q11
Rutherwyke Cl EW KT17 72 G11
Rutherwyk Rd CHERT KT16 68 J5
Ruthin Cl CDALE/KGS NW9 36 E4
Ruthin Rd BKHTH/KID SE3 52 C11
Ruthven Av CHES/WCR EN8 16 D7
Ruthven St HOM E9 39 P13
Rutland Ap EMPK RM11 43 N3
Rutland Av BFN/LL DA15 65 Q5
Rutland Cl ASHTD KT21 83 U7
BXLY DA5 65 T6
CHSGTN KT9 71 V11
DART DA1 66 K5
HOR/WEW KT19 72 D14
MORT/ESHN SW14 60 B1
REDH RH1 93 T9
WIM/MER SW19 61 S12
Rutland Ct CHST BR7 64 J13
SKENS SW7 7 P4
Rutland Dr EMPK RM11 43 N3
MRDN SM4 73 N5
RCHPK/HAM TW10 59 T6
Rutland Gdns BCTR RM8 41 S10
CROY/NA CR0 74 J9
FSBYPK N4 38 F4
SKENS SW7 7 P4
WEA W13 * 47 Q3
Rutland Gardens Ms SKENS SW7 7 P4
Rutland Ga BELV DA17 54 B10
HAYES BR2 76 B2
SKENS SW7 7 N5
Rutland Gate Ms SKENS SW7 * 7 N4
Rutland Gv HMSMTH W6 48 H10
Rutland Ms STJWD NW8 2 H2
Rutland Ms South SKENS SW7 * 7 N5
Rutland Pk CAT SE6 63 R7
CRICK NW2 36 J11
Rutland Pl BUSH WD23 * 23 M6
FARR EC1M * 5 M9
Rutland Rd FSTGT E7 40 F12
HOM E9 39 P13
HRW HA1 35 L4
HYS/HAR UB3 45 V9
IL IG1 40 K9
STHL UB1 46 J2
WALTH E17 39 S4
WAN E11 40 D3
WHTN TW2 59 M7
Rutland St SKENS SW7 7 P5
Rutland Wk CAT SE6 63 R7
Rutland Wy STMC/STPC BR5 77 T4
Rutley Cl WALW SE17 9 L11
Rutlish Rd WIM/MER SW19 61 N13
Rutson Rd BF/WBF KT14 81 R4
Rutter Gdns MTCM CR4 73 R2
Rutters Cl WDR/YW UB7 45 S7
Rutt's Ter NWCR SE14 51 P13
The Rutts BUSH WD23 23 M6
Ruvigny Gdns PUT/ROE SW15 60 K1
Ruxbury Rd CHERT KT16 68 H4
Ruxley Cl HOR/WEW KT19 72 B10
SCUP DA14 65 T11
Ruxley Crs ESH/CLAY KT10 71 R12
Ruxley La HOR/WEW KT19 72 D10
Ruxley Ms HOR/WEW KT19 72 B10
Ruxley Rdg ESH/CLAY KT10 71 Q12
Ruxley Towers ESH/CLAY KT10 * 71 Q12
Ruxton Cl COUL/CHIP CR5 86 A5
SWLY BR8 78 E1
Ruxton Ct SWLY BR8 78 E1
Ryall Cl LCOL/BKTW AL2 11 S3
Ryan Cl BKHTH/KID SE3 64 D2
RSLP HA4 34 D6
Ryan Ct OXHEY WD19 * 22 G5
Ryan Dr BTFD TW8 47 Q11
Ryan Wy WATN WD24 11 Q13
Ryarsh Crs ORP BR6 77 N9
Rycroft Wy TOTM N17 * 38 K1
Ryculff Sq BKHTH/KID SE3 52 B14
Rydal Cl HDN NW4 25 L13
PUR/KEN CR8 86 H3
Rydal Crs GFD/PVL UB6 47 R1
Rydal Dr BXLYHN DA7 54 A13
WWKM BR4 76 A7
Rydal Gdns CDALE/KGS NW9 36 E3
HSLW TW3 58 K4
PUT/ROE SW15 60 E10
WBLY HA9 35 S6
Rydal Mt HAYES BR2 * 76 B2
POTB/CUF EN6 * 14 A7
Rydal Rd STRHM/NOR SW16 62 B10
Rydal Wy EGH TW20 56 F12
PEND EN3 27 N4
RSLP HA4 34 E9
Ryde Cl RPLY/SEND GU23 81 N11
Rydens Av WOT/HER KT12 70 E7
Rydens Cl WOT/HER KT12 70 E7
Rydens Gv WOT/HER KT12 70 F9
Rydens Pde WOKS/MYFD GU22 * 80 F10
Rydens Pk WOT/HER KT12 70 F7
Rydens Rd WOT/HER KT12 70 D8
Rydens Wy WOKS/MYFD GU22 80 E10
Ryde Pl TWK TW1 59 S4
Ryder Cl BUSH WD23 22 K4
Ryder Dr BERM/RHTH SE16 51 M10
Ryder Gdns RAIN RM13 42 F11
Ryder St STJS SW1Y 8 B1
The Ryde STA TW18 57 M13
Ryde Vale Rd BAL SW12 61 V7
Rydon Ms WIM/MER SW19 60 J12
Rydon's La COUL/CHIP CR5 86 G10
Rydon St IS N1 5 P1
Rydon's Wood Cl COUL/CHIP CR5 86 G10
Rydston Cl HOLWY N7 38 D12
Rye Brook Rd LHD/OX KT22 83 Q8
Rye Cl BXLY DA5 66 B4
Ryecotes Md DUL SE21 62 J6
Rye Crs STMC/STPC BR5 77 T6
Ryecroft Av CLAY IG5 28 K14
WHTN TW2 58 K6
Ryecroft Crs BAR EN5 24 H3
Ryecroft Rd LEW SE13 63 U3
RSEV TN14 90 G7
STMC/STPC BR5 77 M4
STRHM/NOR SW16 62 E11
Ryecroft St FUL/PGN SW6 49 P13
Ryedale EDUL SE22 63 M4
Ryedale Ct SEV TN13 90 E11
Rye Fld ASHTD KT21 83 T7
Ryefield Av HGDN/ICK UB10 33 U13
Ryefield Crs PIN HA5 * 22 C14
Ryefield Pde NTHWD HA6 * 22 C14
Ryefield Rd NRWD SE19 62 G11
Rye Hill Pk PECK SE15 63 N2
Ryeland Cl WDR/YW UB7 45 Q4
Ryelands Cl CTHM CR3 86 J11
Ryelands Ct LHD/OX KT22 83 Q8
Ryelands Crs LEE/GVPK SE12 64 E4
Ryelands Pl WEY KT13 70 A8
Rye La PECK SE15 51 L14
RSEV TN14 90 F10
Rye Rd PECK SE15 63 P2
The Rye STHGT/OAK N14 26 A5
Rye Wk PUT/ROE SW15 60 K3
Rye Wy EDGW HA8 23 V11
Ryfold Rd WIM/MER SW19 61 N8
Ryhope Rd FBAR/BDGN N11 25 V9
Ryland Cl FELT TW13 58 B9
Rylandes Rd CRICK NW2 36 G8
SAND/SEL CR2 75 M14
Ryland Rd KTTN NW5 * 37 V11
Rylett Crs SHB W12 48 F8
Rylett Rd SHB W12 48 F7
Rylston Rd FUL/PGN SW6 6 C12
PLMGR N13 26 H8
Rymer Rd CROY/NA CR0 74 J5
Rymer St HNHL SE24 62 F4
Rymill St CAN/RD E16 52 J6
Rysbrack St CHEL SW3 7 Q5
Rysted La BH/WHM TN16 97 L2
Rythe Cl CHSGTN KT9 71 S12
Rythe Ct THDIT KT7 71 Q5
Rythe Rd ESH/CLAY KT10 71 M10
The Rythe ESH/CLAY KT10 70 K14
Ryvers End DTCH/LGLY SL3 44 D8
Ryvers Rd DTCH/LGLY SL3 44 D8
Ryves Cottages MTCM CR4 * 61 U14

S

Sabbarton St CAN/RD E16 52 B4
Sabine Rd BTSEA SW11 61 T1
Sabines Rd ABR/ST RM4 31 M1
Sable Cl HSLWW TW4 58 E1
Sable St IS N1 38 F12
Sach Rd CLPT E5 39 M7
Sackville Av HAYES BR2 76 C6
Sackville Cl RYLN/HDSTN HA2 35 M8
SEV TN13 90 H12
Sackville Crs HARH RM3 31 L13
Sackville Est STRHM/NOR SW16 62 C8
Sackville Gdns IL IG1 40 H6
Sackville Rd BELMT SM2 73 N12
RDART DA2 66 K7
Sackville St CONDST W1S 4 A14
Saddlebrook Pk SUN TW16 58 A12
Saddlers Cl BAR EN5 24 H3
BORE WD6 * 24 D3
PIN HA5 22 J10
Saddlers Hall EYN DA4 * 78 K8
Saddlers Ms KUT/HW KT1 59 S13
Saddler's Pk EYN DA4 78 K8
Saddlers Wk KGLGY WD4 * 10 G3
Saddlers Wy EPSOM KT18 84 D9
Saddlescombe Wy
NFNCH/WDSPK N12 25 N10
Sadler Cl MTCM CR4 61 T14
Sadlers Gate Ms PUT/ROE SW15 60 J1
Sadlers Ride E/WMO/HCT KT8 59 L14
Saffron Av POP/IOD E14 51 V5
Saffron Cl CROY/NA CR0 74 C4
GLDGN NW11 37 M3
Saffron Hl HCIRC EC1N 4 K10
Saffron Rd CRW RM5 30 D14
Saffron St HCIRC EC1N 4 K9
Saffron Wy SURB KT6 71 T6
Sage Cl EHAM E6 52 H3
Sage Ms EDUL SE22 62 K3
Sage St WCHPL E1 51 N5
Sage Wy FSBYW WC1X 4 G6
Sage Yd SURB KT6 * 71 V6
Saigasso Cl CAN/RD E16 52 F4
Sail St LBTH SE11 8 H7
Sainfoin Rd TOOT SW17 61 U7
Sainsbury Rd NRWD SE19 62 J10
St Agatha's Dr KUTN/CMB KT2 59 V11
St Agatha's Gv CAR SM5 73 T6
St Agnes Cl HOM E9 * 39 N13
St Agnes Pl LBTH SE11 8 K12
St Agnes Well STLK EC1Y 5 R7
St Aidan's Rd EDUL SE22 63 M4
WEA W13 47 R7
St Albans Av CHSWK W4 48 D8
EHAM E6 52 H1
FELT TW13 58 F10
UPMR RM14 43 S7
WEY KT13 69 S8
St Albans Crs WDGN N22 26 E13
St Albans Farm EBED/NFELT TW14 * 58 E3
St Alban's Gdns TEDD TW11 59 Q10
St Alban's Gv CAR SM5 73 S5
KENS W8 6 H5
St Albans La GLDGN NW11 37 N6
St Alban's Ms BAY/PAD W2 3 M9
St Alban's Pl IS N1 5 L2
St Albans Rd BAR EN5 13 V12
DART DA1 67 M4
EPP CM16 18 H3
GDMY/SEVK IG3 41 P6
KTTN NW5 37 U8
KUTN/CMB KT2 59 U11
POTB/CUF EN6 13 Q5
REIG RH2 93 N9
SUT SM1 73 M9
WAT WD17 11 P14
WFD IG8 28 C12
WLSDN NW10 36 E13
St Alban's St STJS SW1Y 4 C14
St Albans Ter HMSMTH W6 6 A11
St Alfege Pas GNWCH SE10 51 U11
St Alfege Rd CHARL SE7 52 F11
St Alphage Gdns BARB EC2Y 5 P10
St Alphage Highwalk BARB EC2Y 5 P10
St Alphage Wk EDGW HA8 * 24 C14
St Alphege Rd ED N9 27 N5
St Alphonsus Rd CLAP SW4 62 A2
St Amunds Cl CAT SE6 63 S9
St Andrews Av ALP/SUD HA0 35 Q9
HCH RM12 42 F10
St Andrews Cl BERM/RHTH SE16 51 M10
CRICK NW2 * 36 H8
ISLW TW7 47 N13
NFNCH/WDSPK N12 * 25 Q9
REIG RH2 93 P11
RSLP HA4 34 F7
SHPTN TW17 69 V2
STAN HA7 * 23 S14
STWL/WRAY TW19 56 C4
THDIT KT7 71 R6
THMD SE28 53 T4
WIM/MER SW19 61 P11
WOKN/KNAP GU21 80 A7
St Andrew's Ct WAND/EARL SW18 61 Q7
WAT WD17 * 11 P13
St Andrews Dr STAN HA7 23 S13
STMC/STPC BR5 77 R4
St Andrews Gdns COB KT11 82 E3
St Andrews Ga WOKS/MYFD GU22 80 D8
St Andrew's Gv STNW/STAM N16 38 H6
St Andrew's Hl BLKFR EC4V 5 M12
St Andrews Ms BAL SW12 62 B6
BKHTH/KID SE3 52 C12
STNW/STAM N16 38 J6
St Andrew's Pl CAMTN NW1 3 U7
St Andrew's Rd ACT W3 48 E4
CAR SM5 73 S8
CDALE/KGS NW9 36 D6
COUL/CHIP CR5 85 V6
CROY/NA CR0 74 G9
ED N9 27 N5
EN EN1 26 H1
GLDGN NW11 37 M4
HGDN/ICK UB10 33 Q13
HNWL W7 47 N7
IL IG1 40 H5
PLSTW E13 52 D1
ROMW/RG RM7 42 D4
SCUP DA14 65 T8
SURB KT6 71 T4
WALTH E17 27 P14
WAN E11 40 A4
WKENS W14 6 B11
WLSDN NW10 36 H11
St Andrew's Sq NTGHL W11 * 2 A12
SURB KT6 71 T4
St Andrews Ter OXHEY WD19 * 22 E10
St Andrew St HCIRC EC1N 4 K10
St Andrew's Wk COB KT11 82 D5
St Andrews Wy BOW E3 51 T2
OXTED RH8 96 G7
St Anna Rd BAR EN5 * 24 K3
St Anne's Av STWL/WRAY TW19 57 P5
St Anne's Cl CHESW EN7 15 V2
HGT N6 37 U8
OXHEY WD19 22 E9
St Annes Ct SOHO/CST W1F 4 C12
St Anne's Dr REDH RH1 93 U9
St Annes Dr North REDH RH1 93 U8
St Annes Gdns WLSDN NW10 47 V1
St Annes Mt REDH RH1 * 93 U9
St Anne's Pas POP/IOD E14 * 51 R4
St Annes Ri REDH RH1 93 U9
St Anne's Rd ALP/SUD HA0 35 T10
DEN/HRF UB9 33 N1
LCOL/BKTW AL2 12 H1
LEY E10 39 V7
St Anne's Rw POP/IOD E14 51 R4
St Anne St POP/IOD E14 51 R4
St Annes Wy REDH RH1 * 93 U9
St Ann's BARK IG11 41 L13
WOKS/MYFD GU22 * 80 C8
St Ann's Cl CHERT KT16 68 K4
St Anns Ct HDN NW4 * 36 H1
St Ann's Crs WAND/EARL SW18 61 Q4
St Ann's Gdns KTTN NW5 37 U11
St Ann's Hl WAND/EARL SW18 61 P3
St Ann's Hill Rd CHERT KT16 68 H4
St Ann's Park Rd WAND/EARL SW18 61 Q4
St Ann's Rd BARK IG11 41 L13
BARN SW13 * 48 F14
CHERT KT16 68 K4
ED N9 26 K7
HRW HA1 35 N4
NTGHL W11 48 K5
SEVS/STOTM N15 38 H3
St Ann's St WEST SW1P 8 D6
St Ann's Ter STJWD NW8 3 M3
St Ann's Vls NTGHL W11 48 K6
St Anns Wy BH/WHM TN16 * 88 K6
CROY/NA CR0 74 F11
St Anselms Rd HYS/HAR UB3 46 B7
St Anthony's Av WFD IG8 28 E12
St Anthonys Cl TOOT SW17 61 S7
WAP E1W * 51 L6
St Anthony's Ct ORP BR6 76 K7
St Anthony's Wy EBED/NFELT TW14 58 B2
St Antony's Rd FSTGT E7 40 D12
St Arvans Cl CROY/NA CR0 74 J8
St Asaph Rd BROCKY SE4 63 P1
St Aubyn's Av HSLW TW3 58 J3
WIM/MER SW19 61 M10
St Aubyns Cl ORP BR6 77 P8
St Aubyns Gdns ORP BR6 77 P7
St Aubyn's Rd NRWD SE19 62 K11
St Audrey Av BXLYHN DA7 54 A14
St Augustine's Av EA W5 35 U14
HAYES BR2 76 G3
SAND/SEL CR2 74 G12
WBLY HA9 35 U8
St Augustine's Rd BELV DA17 53 V9
CAMTN NW1 38 B12
St Austell Cl EDGW HA8 23 V14
St Austell Rd LEW SE13 51 U14
St Awdry's Rd BARK IG11 41 M13
St Barnabas Cl BECK BR3 63 U14
EDUL SE22 62 J3
St Barnabas' Gdns E/WMO/HCT KT8 70 J3
St Barnabas Rd MTCM CR4 61 U12
SUT SM1 73 R10
Saint Barnabas Rd WALTH E17 39 S4
St Barnabas Rd WFD IG8 28 D13
St Barnabas St BGVA SW1W 7 T9
St Barnabas Ter HOM E9 39 P10
St Barnabas Vls VX/NE SW8 50 C13
St Bartholomew's Cl SYD SE26 63 N9
St Bartholomew's Rd EHAM E6 40 G13
St Benets Cl TOOT SW17 61 S7
St Benet's Gv CAR SM5 73 Q5
St Benjamins Dr ORP BR6 77 S13
St Bernards CROY/NA CR0 74 J8
St Bernards Cl WNWD SE27 62 H9
St Bernards Rd DTCH/LGLY SL3 44 A8
EHAM E6 40 G13
St Blaise Av BMLY BR1 64 D14
St Botolph's Av SEV TN13 90 G14
St Botolph's Rd SEV TN13 90 H14
St Botolph St TWRH EC3N 5 U11
St Bride's Av EDGW HA8 23 V13
St Brides Cl ERITHM DA18 53 T7
St Bride St FLST/FETLN EC4A 5 L11
St Catherines WEY KT13 * 69 T8
WOKS/MYFD GU22 80 A9
St Catherines Cl CHSGTN KT9 71 T11
TOOT SW17 * 61 S7
St Catherines Ct FELT TW13 58 C6
St Catherine's Cross REDH RH1 94 J10
St Catherine's Dr NWCR SE14 51 P14
St Catherines Ms CHEL SW3 7 Q7
St Catherines Rd CHING E4 27 S7
RSLP HA4 33 U3
St Chads Cl SURB KT6 71 S5
St Chad's Gdns CHDH RM6 41 U5
St Chad's Pl FSBYW WC1X 4 F5
St Chad's Rd CHDH RM6 41 U4
St Chad's St STPAN WC1H 4 F5
St Charles Pl NKENS W10 2 A10
WEY KT13 69 S10
St Charles Rd BRW CM14 31 V7
St Charles Sq NKENS W10 2 A10
St Christopher Rd UX/CGN UB8 45 P4
St Christopher's Cl ISLW TW7 47 N13
St Christophers Ct
RKW/CH/CXG WD3 * 20 H2
St Christophers Dr HYS/HAR UB3 46 D5
St Christopher's Ms WLGTN SM6 74 A10
St Christopher's Pl MHST W1U 3 T12
St Clair Cl CLAY IG5 28 H14
OXTED RH8 95 U6
REIG RH2 93 Q10
St Clair Dr WPK KT4 72 H9
St Clair Rd PLSTW E13 40 D14
St Clair's Rd CROY/NA CR0 74 J7
St Clare St TWRH EC3N 5 U12
St Clement Cl UX/CGN UB8 45 P4
St Clement's Av WTHK RM20 55 U11
St Clements Ct PUR RM19 55 N9
St Clement's La LINN WC2A 4 H12
St Clements St HOLWY N7 38 E12
St Clement's Wy WTHK RM20 55 T12
St Clements Yd EDUL SE22 * 62 K3
St Clere Hill Rd BGR/WK TN15 91 T2
St Cloud Rd WNWD SE27 62 G9
St Crispins Cl HAMP NW3 37 S9
STHL UB1 46 H4
St Crispins Wy CHERT KT16 68 G13
St Cross St HCIRC EC1N 4 K9
St Cuthbert's Cl EGH TW20 56 B11
St Cuthberts Gdns PIN HA5 * 22 H12
St Cuthbert's Rd CRICK NW2 37 M11
PLMGR N13 26 E11
St Cyprian's St TOOT SW17 61 T9
St David Cl UX/CGN UB8 45 P3
St David's COUL/CHIP CR5 86 D7
St Davids Cl BERM/RHTH SE16 * 51 M10
IVER SL0 32 H13
REIG RH2 93 Q9
WBLY HA9 36 C8
WWKM BR4 75 T5
St David's Dr EDGW HA8 23 V13
EGH TW20 56 A12
St Davids Ms BOW E3 51 Q1
St David's Pl HDN NW4 36 H5
St David's Rd SWLY BR8 66 F11
St Davids Sq POP/IOD E14 51 T10
St Denis Rd WNWD SE27 62 G9
St Denys Cl PUR/KEN CR8 74 F14
St Dionis Rd FUL/PGN SW6 49 M14
St Donatt's Rd NWCR SE14 51 R14
St Dunstan's Av ACT W3 48 D5
St Dunstans Cl HYS/HAR UB3 46 B9
St Dunstan's Gdns ACT W3 48 D5
St Dunstan's Hl MON EC3R * 5 S14
SUT SM1 73 L9
St Dunstan's La MON EC3R * 5 S14
St Dunstan's Rd FELT TW13 58 B8
FSTGT E7 40 E11
HMSMTH W6 48 K10
HNWL W7 47 N7
HSLWW TW4 46 E14
SNWD SE25 74 K2
St Edith's Rd BGR/WK TN15 91 N8
St Edmunds Av RSLP HA4 33 V4
St Edmunds Cl ERITHM DA18 53 T7
STJWD NW8 3 Q2
TOOT SW17 61 S7
St Edmunds Dr STAN HA7 23 Q13
St Edmund's La WHTN TW2 58 K5
St Edmunds Rd DART DA1 67 N2
ED N9 27 L5
IL IG1 40 H4
St Edmunds Sq BARN SW13 48 J11
St Edmund's Ter STJWD NW8 3 P2
St Edwards Cl CROY/NA CR0 87 V1
GLDGN NW11 37 N4
St Edwards Wy ROM RM1 42 E2
St Egberts Wy CHING E4 27 U6
St Elizabeth Dr EPSOM KT18 84 C4
St Elmo Rd SHB W12 48 F7
St Elmos Rd BERM/RHTH SE16 51 Q7
St Erkenwald Ms BARK IG11 41 M13
St Erkenwald Rd BARK IG11 41 M13
St Ervans Rd NKENS W10 2 B9
St Faith's Cl ENC/FH EN2 15 S13
St Faith's Rd DUL SE21 62 F6
St Fidelis' Rd ERITH DA8 54 D9
St Fillans WOKS/MYFD GU22 * 80 F6
St Fillans Rd CAT SE6 63 U6
St Francis Cl ORP BR6 77 N4
OXHEY WD19 22 D6
POTB/CUF EN6 14 E7
St Francis Rd DEN/HRF UB9 32 K4
EDUL SE22 62 J2
St Francis Wy IL IG1 41 M9
St Gabriel's Cl WAN E11 40 D6
St Gabriel's Rd CRICK NW2 36 K10
St George's ED N9 27 L8
St George's Av CDALE/KGS NW9 36 C2
EA W5 47 T7
EMPK RM11 43 M5
FSTGT E7 40 D12
HOLWY N7 38 B9
STHL UB1 46 H5
WEY KT13 69 U11
St George's Circ STHWK SE1 9 L4
St Georges Cl ALP/SUD HA0 35 Q8
GLDGN NW11 37 M4
THMD SE28 53 T4
VX/NE SW8 50 A13
WEY KT13 69 U10
St George's Ct STP EC4M * 5 L11
St Georges Dr HGDN/ICK UB10 33 R8
OXHEY WD19 22 G9
PIM SW1V 7 V9
St Georges Flds BAY/PAD W2 3 P13
St George's Gdns EW KT17 84 F4
SURB KT6 72 B7
St George's Gv TOOT SW17 61 R8
St George's Industrial Est
KUTN/CMB KT2 59 T10
St George's La MON EC3R * 5 R13
St George's Ms CAMTN NW1 37 T12
CHSWK W4 * 48 C11
DEPT SE8 51 R9
St Georges Pde CAT SE6 * 63 R7
St Georges Rd ADL/WDHM KT15 69 N9
BECK BR3 63 T13
BMLY BR1 64 H14
CHSWK W4 48 D7
DAGW RM9 41 U10
EN EN1 15 V12
FELT TW13 58 G9
FSTGT E7 40 D12
GLDGN NW11 37 M4
HNWL W7 47 P6
IL IG1 40 H5
KUTN/CMB KT2 59 V12
LEY E10 39 U8
MTCM CR4 73 V1
PLMGR N13 26 D8
RCH/KEW TW9 59 V1
SCUP DA14 65 T11
SEV TN13 90 H12
STHWK SE1 9 L6
STMC/STPC BR5 77 M4
SWLY BR8 78 F3
TWK TW1 59 R3
WATN WD24 11 P12
WEY KT13 69 V11
WIM/MER SW19 61 M11
WLGTN SM6 73 V10
St Georges Rd West BMLY BR1 64 G14
St George's Sq FSTGT E7 40 D12
NWMAL KT3 * 72 E1
PIM SW1V 8 B9
St George's Square Ms PIM SW1V 8 C10
St George's Ter CAMTN NW1 3 R1
PECK SE15 * 51 L12
St George St CONDST W1S 3 V13
St George's Wk CROY/NA CR0 74 G7
St George's Wy PECK SE15 9 T12
St Gerards Cl CLAP SW4 62 A3
St German's Pl BKHTH/KID SE3 52 C14
St German's Rd FSTH SE23 63 Q6
St Giles Av DAGE RM10 42 B12
HGDN/ICK UB10 33 U9
POTB/CUF EN6 13 T7
St Giles Churchyard BARB EC2Y * 5 P10
St Giles Circ SOHO/SHAV W1D 4 D11

Swan Rd BERM/RHTH SE16 51 N7
CHES/WCR EN8 16 D8
FELT TW13 58 G9
IVER SL0 44 K4
STHL UB1 46 K4
WDR/YW UB7 45 P7
WOOL/PLUM SE18 52 F8
Swanscombe Rd NTGHL W11 48 K6
Swansea Rd EBED/NFELT TW14 57 U4
PEND EN3 27 N2
Swanshope LOU IG10 17 V14
Swanston Pth OXHEY WD19 22 E8
Swan St ISLW TW7 59 R1
STHWK SE1 9 P4
The Swansway WEY KT13 * 69 S8
Swanton Gdns WIM/MER SW19 60 K6
Swanton Rd ERITH DA8 54 A12
Swan Wk CHEL SW3 7 Q11
SHPTN TW17 70 A5
Swan Wy PEND EN3 16 D14
Swanwick Cl PUT/ROE SW15 60 F5
Swan Yd IS N1 38 F11
Swanzy Rd RSEV TN14 90 J10
Sward Rd STMC/STPC BR5 77 Q4
Swaton Rd BOW E3 51 S2
Swaylands Rd BELV DA17 54 A11
Swaynesland Rd EDEN TN8 96 H10
Swaythling Cl UED N18 27 M9
Swedenbourg Gdns WCHPL E1 51 L5
Sweden Ga BERM/RHTH SE16 51 Q9
Sweeney Crs STHWK SE1 9 V4
Sweeps Ditch Cl STA TW18 57 M13
Sweeps La EGH TW20 56 D10
STMC/STPC BR5 77 T3
Sweet Briar Gn ED N9 26 K8
Sweet Briar Gv ED N9 26 K8
Sweet Briar Wk UED N18 26 K9
Sweetcroft La HGDN/ICK UB10 33 R12
Sweetmans Av PIN HA5 34 F1
Sweets Wy TRDG/WHET N20 25 R7
Swete St PLSTW E13 40 C14
Sweyn Pl BKHTH/KID SE3 52 C14
Swievelands Rd
BH/WHM TN16 88 D9
Swift Cl HYS/HAR UB3 46 B4
RYLN/HDSTN HA2 34 K7
THMD SE28 53 R5
UPMR RM14 43 S6
WALTH E17 27 Q12
Swift Rd FELT TW13 58 G9
NWDGN UB2 46 H8
Swiftsden Wy BMLY BR1 64 A11
Swift St FUL/PGN SW6 49 L13
Swinbrook Rd NKENS W10 2 B9
Swinburne Crs CROY/NA CR0 75 N5
Swinburne Rd PUT/ROE SW15 60 G3
Swinderby Rd ALP/SUD HA0 35 U11
Swindon Cl GDMY/SEVK IG3 41 N7
Swindon Gdns HARH RM3 31 M10
Swindon La HARH RM3 31 M10
Swindon Rd HTHAIR TW6 57 U3
Swindon St SHB W12 * 48 H6
Swinfield Cl FELT TW13 58 G9
Swinford Gdns BRXN/ST SW9 62 F1
Swingate La WOOL/PLUM SE18 53 N12
Swinnerton St HOM E9 39 Q10
Swinton Cl WBLY HA9 36 B6
Swinton Pl FSBYW WC1X 4 G5
Swinton St FSBYW WC1X 4 G6
Swires Shaw HAYES BR2 76 F9
Swiss Av WATW WD18 22 A2
Swiss Cl WATW WD18 22 A1
Swithland Gdns ELTH/MOT SE9 64 H9
Swyncombe Av EA W5 47 R9
Swynford Gdns HDN NW4 36 G2
Sybil Phoenix Cl DEPT SE8 51 Q10
Sybourn St WALTH E17 39 R5
Sycamore Ap
RKW/CH/CXG WD3 21 U3
Sycamore Av BFN/LL DA15 65 P4
BOW E3 39 R13
EA W5 47 T8
HYS/HAR UB3 46 A5
UPMR RM14 43 N8
Sycamore Cl ACT W3 48 E6
BUSH WD23 11 S14
CAN/RD E16 52 A2
CAR SM5 73 T9
CHESW EN7 15 V1
EBAR EN4 25 R4
ED N9 27 L9
EDGW HA8 24 C9
FELT TW13 58 C8
GSTN WD25 11 P9
LHD/OX KT22 83 P13
NTHLT UB5 34 G13
SAND/SEL CR2 74 J10
WDR/YW UB7 45 R5
Sycamore Ct WEY KT13 70 B8
Sycamore Dr LCOL/BKTW AL2 12 B1
SWLY BR8 66 E14
Sycamore Gdns MTCM CR4 61 R14
SHB W12 48 H7
Sycamore Gv CAT SE6 63 U4
CDALE/KGS NW9 36 C5
GPK RM2 30 G14
NWMAL KT3 72 E1
PGE/AN SE20 63 L13
Sycamore Hl FBAR/BDGN N11 25 U11
Sycamore Ms CLAP SW4 62 A1
ERITH DA8 * 54 D10
Sycamore Ri BNSTD SM7 84 K4
Sycamore Rd DART DA1 66 K5
RKW/CH/CXG WD3 21 U3
WIM/MER SW19 60 J11
The Sycamores GT/LBKH KT23 83 L14
RAD WD7 12 F8
Sycamore St FSBYE EC1V 5 N8
Sycamore Wk DTCH/LGLY SL3 44 C4
NKENS W10 2 A7
REIG RH2 93 Q13
Sycamore Wy TEDD TW11 59 S11
Sydcote DUL SE21 * 62 G7
Sydenham Av SYD SE26 63 M10
Sydenham Cl ROM RM1 42 F2
Sydenham Cottages
LEE/GVPK SE12 * 64 E7
Sydenham Hl FSTH SE23 63 M7
Sydenham Pk SYD SE26 63 N8
Sydenham Park Rd SYD SE26 63 N8
Sydenham Ri FSTH SE23 63 M7
Sydenham Rd CROY/NA CR0 74 H6
SYD SE26 63 P10
Sydenham Station Ap SYD SE26 63 N9
Sydmons Ct FSTH SE23 * 63 N5
Sydner Rd STNW/STAM N16 38 K9
Sydney Av PUR/KEN CR8 86 D2
Sydney Cl SKENS SW7 7 M8
Sydney Crs ASHF TW15 57 T11
Sydney Gv HDN NW4 36 J3
Sydney Ms CHEL SW3 7 M8
Sydney Pl SKENS SW7 7 M8
Sydney Rd ABYW SE2 53 T8
BARK/HLT IG6 29 L14
BXLYHS DA6 65 T2
CEND/HSY/T N8 38 E2
EBED/NFELT TW14 58 C6
ENC/FH EN2 26 H2
MUSWH N10 25 V13
RCH/KEW TW9 59 U2
RYNPK SW20 60 K14
SCUP DA14 65 N9
SUT SM1 73 N9
TEDD TW11 59 P10
WAN E11 40 D4
WATW WD18 22 A3
WEA W13 47 Q6
WFD IG8 28 C10
Sydney St CHEL SW3 7 N9
Sydney Ter ESH/CLAY KT10 * 71 P11
Syke Cluan DTCH/LGLY SL3 44 J7
Syke Ings DTCH/LGLY SL3 44 J8
Sykes Dr STA TW18 57 M10
Sylvana Cl HGDN/ICK UB10 33 R13
Sylvan Av CHDH RM6 41 V4
EMPK RM11 43 M4
MLHL NW7 24 E11
WDGN N22 26 E12
Sylvan Cl OXTED RH8 96 D5
SAND/SEL CR2 75 M14
WOKS/MYFD GU22 80 F8
Sylvan Gdns SURB KT6 71 T5
Sylvan Gv CRICK NW2 36 K9
PECK SE15 51 M11
Sylvan Hl NRWD SE19 62 K13
Sylvan Ms SWCM DA10 67 V2
Sylvan Rd FSTGT E7 40 C11
IL IG1 41 L7
NRWD SE19 62 K13
WALTH E17 * 39 S3
WAN E11 40 C3
Sylvan Ter PECK SE15 * 51 M12
Sylvan Wk BMLY BR1 76 H1
Sylvan Wy BCTR RM8 41 R8
CHIG IG7 29 R8
REDH RH1 93 V11
WWKM BR4 76 A9
Sylverdale Rd CROY/NA CR0 74 F8
PUR/KEN CR8 86 F3
Sylvester Av CHST BR7 64 H11
Sylvester Pth HACK E8 * 39 M11
Sylvester Rd ALP/SUD HA0 35 S10
EFNCH N2 25 Q14
HACK E8 * 39 M11
WALTH E17 * 39 R5
Sylvia Av PIN HA5 22 H11
Sylvia Gdns WBLY HA9 36 B12
Symes Ms CAMTN NW1 4 A3
Symington Ms HOM E9 39 P10
Symister Ms IS N1 * 5 S6
Symonds Cl BGR/WK TN15 79 S10
Symonds Ct CHES/WCR EN8 16 D2
Symons Cl PECK SE15 63 N1
Symons St CHEL SW3 7 R8
Symphony Cl EDGW HA8 24 B12
Symphony Ms NKENS W10 2 B5
Syon Gate Wy BTFD TW8 47 R12
Syon La ISLW TW7 47 P11
Syon Pk ISLW TW7 * 59 R1
Syon Park Gdns ISLW TW7 47 P12
Syracuse Av RAIN RM13 54 K1

T

Tabard Garden Est STHWK SE1 9 Q3
Tabard St STHWK SE1 9 Q5
Tabarin Wy EW KT17 84 J6
Tabernacle Av PLSTW E13 52 C2
Tabernacle St SDTCH EC2A 5 R8
Tableer Av CLAP SW4 62 A3
Tabley Rd HOLWY N7 38 C9
Tabor Gdns CHEAM SM3 73 M11
Tabor Gv WIM/MER SW19 61 L12
Tabor Rd HMSMTH W6 48 H8
Tabrums Wy UPMR RM14 43 S5
Tachbrook Rd EBED/NFELT TW14 58 B5
NWDGN UB2 46 F9
UX/CGN UB8 33 N14
Tachbrook St PIM SW1V 8 B8
Tack Ms BROCKY SE4 63 S1
Tadema Rd WBPTN SW10 6 K14
Tadlows Cl UPMR RM14 43 P10
Tadmor Cl SUN TW16 70 B2
Tadmor St SHB W12 48 K6
Tadorne Rd KWD/TDW/WH KT20 84 J11
Tadworth Av NWMAL KT3 72 F2
Tadworth Cl KWD/TDW/WH KT20 84 K12
Tadworth Pde HCH RM12 42 H9
Tadworth Rd CRICK NW2 36 G7
Tadworth St KWD/TDW/WH KT20 84 J13
Taeping St POP/IOD E14 51 T9
Taffy's How MTCM CR4 73 S1
Tait Rd CROY/NA CR0 74 J5
Takeley Cl CRW RM5 30 D14
WAB EN9 16 K7
Talacre Rd KTTN NW5 37 U11
Talbot Av DTCH/LGLY SL3 44 D8
EFNCH N2 37 R1
OXHEY WD19 22 G5
Talbot Cl REIG RH2 93 P11
SEVS/STOTM N15 38 K2
Talbot Ct BANK EC3V 5 R13
Talbot Crs HDN NW4 36 G3
Talbot Gdns GDMY/SEVK IG3 41 Q7
Talbot Pl BKHTH/KID SE3 52 A14
DTCH/LGLY SL3 44 A13
Talbot Rd ALP/SUD HA0 35 T10
ASHF TW15 57 P10
BAY/PAD W2 2 F11
CAR SM5 73 U10
DAGW RM9 41 V12
EDUL SE22 62 J2
EHAM E6 40 H14
FSTGT E7 40 C9
HGT N6 37 U4
ISLW TW7 59 Q2
KTN/HRWW/WS HA3 23 P14
NTGHL W11 2 D11
NWDGN UB2 46 G9
RKW/CH/CXG WD3 21 Q6
SEVS/STOTM N15 38 K2
THHTH CR7 74 H2
WDGN N22 26 A14
WEA W13 * 47 Q5
WHTN TW2 59 N6
Talbot Sq BAY/PAD W2 3 L12
Talbot Wk NTGHL W11 * 2 A12
WLSDN NW10 * 36 E11
Talbot Yd STHWK SE1 9 Q2
Talbrook BRW CM14 31 T8
Talcott Pth BRXS/STRHM SW2 * 62 E6
Taleworth Cl ASHTD KT21 83 T10
Taleworth Pk ASHTD KT21 83 T10
Taleworth Rd ASHTD KT21 83 T9
Talfourd Pl PECK SE15 50 K13
Talfourd Rd PECK SE15 50 K13
Talfourd Wy REDH RH1 93 U13
Talgarth Rd WKENS W14 6 A9
Talgarth Wk CDALE/KGS NW9 36 E3
Talisman Cl GDMY/SEVK IG3 41 R6
Talisman Sq SYD SE26 63 L9
Talisman Wy EW KT17 84 J6
WBLY HA9 35 V8
Tallack Cl KTN/HRWW/WS HA3 23 N12
Tallack Rd LEY E10 39 R6
Tall Elms Cl HAYES BR2 76 B3
Tallents Cl EYN DA4 67 P12
Tallis Cl CAN/RD E16 52 D4
Tallis Gv CHARL SE7 52 D11
Tallis St EMB EC4Y 4 K13
Tallis Vw WLSDN NW10 36 D11
Tallis Wy BORE WD6 12 H13
BRW CM14 31 V10
Tallow Rd BTFD TW8 47 S11
Tall Trees DTCH/LGLY SL3 44 J13
STRHM/NOR SW16 74 D1
Tall Trees Cl EMPK RM11 42 K4
Tally Rd OXTED RH8 96 G7
Talma Gdns WHTN TW2 59 N5
Talmage Cl FSTH SE23 63 N5
Talman Gv STAN HA7 23 T11
Talma Rd BRXS/STRHM SW2 62 E2
Talus Cl PUR RM19 55 R9
Talwin St BOW E3 51 T1
Tamar Cl BOW E3 * 39 R13
UPMR RM14 43 S4
Tamar Dr SOCK/AV RM15 55 Q4
Tamarind Yd WAP E1W 51 L6
Tamarisk Sq SHB W12 48 F5
Tamar St CHARL SE7 52 G9
Tamar Wy DTCH/LGLY SL3 44 F10
Tamerton Sq WOKS/MYFD GU22 80 C9
Tamesis Gdns WPK KT4 72 E7
Tamian Wy HSLWW TW4 58 E2
Tamworth Av WFD IG8 28 A11
Tamworth La MTCM CR4 73 V1
Tamworth Pk MTCM CR4 73 V2
Tamworth Pl CROY/NA CR0 * 74 G7
Tamworth Rd CROY/NA CR0 74 G7
Tamworth St FUL/PGN SW6 6 E11
Tancred Rd FSBYPK N4 38 F4
Tandridge Dr ORP BR6 77 M6
Tandridge Gdns SAND/SEL CR2 86 K3
Tandridgehill La GDST RH9 95 R4
Tandridge La OXTED RH8 95 S7
Tandridge Rd WARL CR6 87 P9
Tanfield Av CRICK NW2 36 F9
Tanfield Cl CHESW EN7 16 A1
Tanfield Rd CROY/NA CR0 74 G9
Tangent Link HARH RM3 30 K13
Tangent Rd HARH RM3 30 K13
Tangier Rd RCHPK/HAM TW10 60 B1
Tangier Wy KWD/TDW/WH KT20 85 L7
Tangier Wd KWD/TDW/WH KT20 85 L8
Tangleberry Cl BMLY BR1 76 H2
Tangle Tree Cl FNCH N3 25 P14
Tanglewood Cl CROY/NA CR0 75 N8
STAN HA7 23 N8
WOKS/MYFD GU22 80 H6
Tanglewood Wy FELT TW13 58 D8
Tangley Gv PUT/ROE SW15 60 F5
Tangley Park Rd HPTN TW12 * 58 H10
Tanglyn Av SHPTN TW17 69 S3
Tangmere Crs HCH RM12 42 H11
Tangmere Gdns NTHLT UB5 34 E14
Tangmere Gv KUTN/CMB KT2 59 T10
Tangmere Wy CDALE/KGS NW9 24 E14
Tanhouse Fld KTTN NW5 * 38 B10
Tan House La BRW CM14 31 N1
Tanhouse Rd OXTED RH8 95 V8
Tankerton Houses STPAN WC1H * 4 F6
Tankerton Rd SURB KT6 71 V7
Tankerton St STPAN WC1H 4 F6
Tankerton Ter CROY/NA CR0 * 74 D5
Tankerville Rd STRHM/NOR SW16 62 B12
Tank Hill Rd PUR RM19 55 N9
Tank La PUR RM19 55 P9
Tankridge Rd CRICK NW2 36 H7
The Tanneries WCHPL E1 * 51 N2
Tanners Cl WOT/HER KT12 70 D4
Tanners Dean LHD/OX KT22 83 S12
Tanners End La UED N18 26 J9
Tanners Hl ABLGY WD5 11 M5
BRKHM/BTCW RH3 92 B12
DEPT SE8 51 S13
Tanners La BARK/HLT IG6 41 L1
Tanners Meadow BRKHM/BTCW RH3 92 B14
Tanners Ms DEPT SE8 51 R13
Tanner St BARK IG11 41 L11
STHWK SE1 9 U4
Tanners Wood La ABLGY WD5 11 L6
Tannery Cl CROY/NA CR0 75 P3
DAGE RM10 42 B8
Tannery La RPLY/SEND GU23 80 J12
The Tannery REDH RH1 93 S10
Tannington Ter HBRY N5 38 E8
Tannsfeld Rd SYD SE26 63 P10
Tansley Cl HOLWY N7 38 B10
Tanswell St STHWK SE1 * 8 J4
Tansy Cl EHAM E6 52 J4
HARH RM3 31 L11
Tantallon Rd BAL SW12 61 U6
Tant Av CAN/RD E16 52 B4
Tantony Gv CHDH RM6 41 T1
Tanworth Cl NTHWD HA6 21 U11
Tanworth Gdns PIN HA5 22 D14
Tan Yard La BXLY DA5 * 66 A5
Tanza Rd HAMP NW3 37 T9
Tapestry Cl BELMT SM2 73 P12
Taplow Ct MTCM CR4 73 S2
Taplow Rd PLMGR N13 26 G9
Taplow St IS N1 5 P4
Tappesfield Rd PECK SE15 63 N1
Tapping Cl KUTN/CMB KT2 * 60 A12
Tapp St WCHPL E1 51 M2
Tapster St BAR EN5 25 M1
Taransay Wk IS N1 38 H11
Tara Ter BROCKY SE4 * 63 Q1
Tarbert Rd EDUL SE22 62 J3
Tarbert Wk WCHPL E1 51 N5
Target Cl EBED/NFELT TW14 58 A4
Tariff Rd UED N18 27 L11
Tarleton Gdns FSTH SE23 63 M6
Tarling Cl SCUP DA14 65 R8
Tarling Rd CAN/RD E16 52 B4
EFNCH N2 25 Q14
Tarling St WCHPL E1 51 M4
Tarmac Wy WDR/YW UB7 45 M12
Tarnbank ENC/FH EN2 26 C3
Tarn St STHWK SE1 9 N6
Tarnwood Pk ELTH/MOT SE9 64 H6
Tarnworth Rd HARH RM3 31 N10
Tarragon Cl NWCR SE14 * 51 Q12
Tarragon Gv SYD SE26 63 P11
Tarrant Pl BF/WBF KT14 * 80 K3
MBLAR W1H 3 Q10
Tarriff Crs DEPT SE8 51 R9
Tarrington Cl STRHM/NOR SW16 * 62 B9
Tartar Hl COB KT11 82 E3
Tartar Rd COB KT11 82 E3
Tarver Rd WALW SE17 9 M10
Tarves Wy GNWCH SE10 51 T12
Tash Pl FBAR/BDGN N11 * 25 V10
Tasker Cl HYS/HAR UB3 45 U12
Tasker Rd HAMP NW3 37 T10
Tasmania Ter UED N18 26 G11
Tasman Rd BRXN/ST SW9 62 C1
Tasso Rd HMSMTH W6 6 A11
Tate Cl LHD/OX KT22 83 S13
Tate Gdns BUSH WD23 23 N5
Tate Rd CAN/RD E16 52 H6
CFSP/GDCR SL9 20 D10
SUT SM1 73 N10
Tatham Pl STJWD NW8 3 M3
Tatnell Rd FSTH SE23 63 Q4
Tatsfield La BH/WHM TN16 88 H11
Tattenham Corner Rd EPSOM KT18 84 G8
Tattenham Crs EPSOM KT18 84 H8
Tattenham Gv EPSOM KT18 84 H9
Tattenham Wy KWD/TDW/WH KT20 85 L7
Tattersall Cl ELTH/MOT SE9 64 G3
Tatton Crs CLPT E5 38 K5
Tatum Rd WLSDN NW10 36 C12
Tatum St WALW SE17 9 R8
Tauber Cl BORE WD6 23 V2
Tauheed Cl FSBYPK N4 38 G7
Taunton Av CTHM CR3 86 K13
HSLW TW3 47 L14
RYNPK SW20 60 H14
Taunton Cl BARK/HLT IG6 29 P11
BXLYHN DA7 66 D1
CHEAM SM3 73 N6
Taunton Dr EFNCH N2 25 Q14
ENC/FH EN2 26 E1
Taunton La COUL/CHIP CR5 86 E9
Taunton Ms CAMTN NW1 3 Q8
Taunton Pl CAMTN NW1 3 Q7
Taunton Rd GFD/PVL UB6 34 K12
HARH RM3 30 J10
LEE/GVPK SE12 64 A3
Taunton Wy STAN HA7 23 U14
Tavern Cl CAR SM5 73 S5
Taverners Cl NTGHL W11 6 A2
Taverner Sq HBRY N5 * 38 G9
Taverners Wy CHING E4 28 A6
Tavistock Av GFD/PVL UB6 35 Q14
MLHL NW7 24 K12
WALTH E17 39 P1
Tavistock Cl HARH RM3 30 K13
POTB/CUF EN6 14 F5
STA TW18 57 P12
STNW/STAM N16 * 38 J10
Tavistock Ct COVGDN WC2E * 4 F13
Tavistock Crs MTCM CR4 74 C2
NTGHL W11 2 D10
Tavistock Gdns GDMY/SEVK IG3 41 N9
Tavistock Gv CROY/NA CR0 74 H5
Tavistock Ms NTGHL W11 * 2 C11
Tavistock Pl STHGT/OAK N14 * 25 V4
STPAN WC1H 4 D7
Tavistock Rd CAR SM5 73 R6
CROY/NA CR0 74 H6
EDGW HA8 23 V13
FSBYPK N4 38 H4
HAYES BR2 76 C2
HGDN/ICK UB10 33 V10
NTGHL W11 2 C11
WAN E11 40 B9
WATN WD24 11 R13
WDR/YW UB7 45 P5
WELL DA16 53 S13
WLSDN NW10 36 F14
Tavistock Sq STPAN WC1H 4 D7
Tavistock St COVGDN WC2E 4 F13
Tavistock Ter ARCH N19 38 C8
Taviton St STPAN WC1H 4 C7
Tavy Br ABYW SE2 53 S7
Tavy Cl LBTH SE11 8 K9
Tawney Common EPP CM16 19 L6
Tawney La EPP CM16 19 N6
Tawney Rd THMD SE28 53 R5
Tawny Av UPMR RM14 43 P10
Tawny Cl FELT TW13 58 C8
WEA W13 47 R6
Tawny Wy BERM/RHTH SE16 51 P9
Tayben Av WHTN TW2 59 N4
Taybridge Rd BTSEA SW11 61 U1
Tayburn Cl POP/IOD E14 51 U4
Tayfield Cl HGDN/ICK UB10 33 V8
Tayles Hill Dr EW KT17 72 F14
Taylor Av RCH/KEW TW9 48 B14
Taylor Cl CRW RM5 30 A12
DEPT SE8 51 R11
HOR/WEW KT19 84 A1
HPTN TW12 59 L10
HSLW TW3 47 L13
ORP BR6 77 P9
TOTM N17 27 L12
Taylor Rd ASHTD KT21 83 T7
MTCM CR4 61 S12
WLGTN SM6 73 V10
Taylor Rw RDART DA2 66 J8
Taylor's Buildings WOOL/PLUM SE18 52 K9
Taylors Cl SCUP DA14 65 P9
Taylors Ct FELT TW13 58 C7
Taylor's Gn ACT W3 * 48 E4
Taylor's La BAR EN5 14 B13
SYD SE26 63 M9
WLSDN NW10 36 E12
Taylors Md MLHL NW7 * 24 G10
Taymount Ri FSTH SE23 63 N7
Taynton Dr REDH RH1 94 B6
Tayport Cl IS N1 38 D12
Tayside Dr EDGW HA8 24 B8
Tay Wy ROM RM1 30 F13
Taywood Rd NTHLT UB5 46 G2
Teak Cl BERM/RHTH SE16 51 Q6
Teal Av STMC/STPC BR5 77 T2
Teal Cl CAN/RD E16 52 F3
PEND EN3 16 C11
SAND/SEL CR2 87 P1
Teal Dr NTHWD HA6 21 U12
Teale St BETH E2 39 L14
Tealing Dr HOR/WEW KT19 72 D9
Teal Pl SUT SM1 73 M10
Teasel Cl CROY/NA CR0 75 P6
Teasel Crs THMD SE28 53 N6
Teasel Wy SRTFD E15 52 A1
Teather St CMBW SE5 9 S14
Teazlewood Pk LHD/OX KT22 83 Q7
Tebworth Rd TOTM N17 26 K12
Technology Pk CDALE/KGS NW9 * 36 D1
Teck Cl ISLW TW7 47 Q14
Tedder Cl CHSGTN KT9 71 S10
HGDN/ICK UB10 33 R12
RSLP HA4 34 C10
Tedder Rd SAND/SEL CR2 75 P12
Teddington Cl HOR/WEW KT19 72 D14
Teddington Pk TEDD TW11 59 P10
Teddington Park Rd TEDD TW11 59 Q9
Tedworth Gdns CHEL SW3 7 Q10
Tedworth Sq CHEL SW3 7 Q10
Tees Av GFD/PVL UB6 35 N14
Tees Cl UPMR RM14 43 R5
Teesdale Av ISLW TW7 47 Q13
Teesdale Cl BETH E2 39 L14
Teesdale Gdns ISLW TW7 47 Q13
SNWD SE25 62 J14
Teesdale Rd RDART DA2 67 Q6
WAN E11 40 B4
Teesdale St BETH E2 39 M14
Teesdale Yd BETH E2 * 39 M14
Tees Dr HARH RM3 30 K8
The Tee ACT W3 48 E4
Teevan Cl CROY/NA CR0 75 L5
Teevan Rd CROY/NA CR0 75 L5
Tegg's La WOKS/MYFD GU22 80 K6
Teign Ms ELTH/MOT SE9 64 G7
Teignmouth Cl CLAP SW4 62 B2
EDGW HA8 23 V14
Teignmouth Gdns GFD/PVL UB6 35 Q14
Teignmouth Rd CRICK NW2 36 K10
WELL DA16 53 S14
Telcote Wy RSLP HA4 * 34 E5
Telegraph Hl HAMP NW3 37 P8
Telegraph La ESH/CLAY KT10 71 P9
Telegraph Ms GDMY/SEVK IG3 41 P6
Telegraph Pas BRXS/STRHM SW2 62 C5
Telegraph Pl POP/IOD E14 51 T9
Telegraph Rd PUT/ROE SW15 60 H5
Telegraph St LOTH EC2R 5 Q11
Telegraph Tr CAR SM5 73 U14
WLGTN SM6 85 U1
Telephone Pl WKENS W14 6 D11
Telferscot Rd BAL SW12 62 B6
Telford Av BRXS/STRHM SW2 62 C6
Telford Cl GSTN WD25 11 R9
NRWD SE19 62 K11
WALTH E17 39 Q5
Telford Dr WOT/HER KT12 70 E5
Telford Rd CDALE/KGS NW9 36 F4
ELTH/MOT SE9 65 M7
NKENS W10 2 A9
STHL UB1 46 K5
WHTN TW2 58 J5
Telford Rd North Circular Rd
FBAR/BDGN N11 26 A11
Telfords Yd WAP E1W * 51 L5
Telford Ter PIM SW1V 8 A11
Telford Wy ACT W3 48 E3
YEAD UB4 46 G3
Telham Rd EHAM E6 40 J14
Tell Gv EDUL SE22 62 K2
Tellisford ESH/CLAY KT10 70 K9
Tellson Av WOOL/PLUM SE18 52 G13
Telscombe Cl ORP BR6 77 N7
Telston La RSEV TN14 90 F7
Temeraire Pl BTFD TW8 47 V10
Temeraire St BERM/RHTH SE16 51 N7
Tempelhof Av HDN NW4 36 J5
Temperley Rd BAL SW12 61 U5
Tempest Av POTB/CUF EN6 14 F6
Tempest Md EPP CM16 19 M1
Tempest Rd EGH TW20 56 G11
Tempest Wy RAIN RM13 42 G11
Templar Dr THMD SE28 53 T4
Templar Pl HPTN TW12 58 J12
Templars Av GLDGN NW11 37 M4
Templars Ct DART DA1 * 67 N3
Templars Crs FNCH N3 25 N14
Templars Dr KTN/HRWW/WS HA3 * 23 M11
Templar St CMBW SE5 50 F14
Temple Av BCTR RM8 42 A6
CROY/NA CR0 75 R8
EMB EC4Y 4 K13
TRDG/WHET N20 25 R5
Temple Cl CHESW EN7 16 A5
FNCH N3 25 M14
THMD SE28 53 L8
WAN E11 40 A5
WAT WD17 11 M14
Templecombe Ms
WOKS/MYFD GU22 * 80 F6
Templecombe Rd HOM E9 39 N13
Templecombe Wy MRDN SM4 73 L3
Temple Ct POTB/CUF EN6 13 V5
Templedene Av STA TW18 57 M12
Temple Dwellings BETH E2 * 39 M14
Temple Field Cl ADL/WDHM KT15 69 M11
Temple Fortune Hl GLDGN NW11 37 N3
Temple Fortune La GLDGN NW11 37 M4
Temple Gdns BCTR RM8 41 T8
EMB EC4Y * 4 J13
GLDGN NW11 37 M4
RKW/CH/CXG WD3 21 T8
STA TW18 56 K13
WCHMH N21 * 26 F7
Temple Gv ENC/FH EN2 26 F1
GLDGN NW11 37 N4
Temple Hl DART DA1 67 M3
Temple Hill Sq DART DA1 67 M3
Temple La EMB EC4Y 4 K12
Templeman Cl PUR/KEN CR8 86 E6
Templeman Rd HNWL W7 47 P3
Templemead Cl ACT W3 48 E4
Temple Mead Cl STAN HA7 23 R11
Temple Mills La LEY E10 39 T9
Templepan La RKW/CH/CXG WD3 10 E11
Temple Pde BAR EN5 * 25 R5
Temple Pk UX/CGN UB8 45 S1
Temple Pl TPL/STR WC2R 4 H13
Temple Rd BH/WHM TN16 88 F7
CEND/HSY/T N8 38 D2
CHSWK W4 48 C8
CRICK NW2 36 J9
CROY/NA CR0 74 H9
EA W5 47 T8
EHAM E6 40 G13
HOR/WEW KT19 84 D2
HSLW TW3 58 K2
RCH/KEW TW9 47 V14
Temple Sheen Rd MORT/ESHN SW14 60 C2
Temple St BETH E2 39 M14
Temple Ter WDGN N22 * 26 E14
Templeton Av CHING E4 27 S9
Templeton Cl NRWD SE19 62 H13
STNW/STAM N16 * 38 J10
Templeton Pl ECT SW5 6 F8
Templeton Rd FSBYPK N4 38 H4
Temple Wy SUT SM1 73 R8
Templewood WEA W13 47 R3
Templewood Av HAMP NW3 37 P8
Temple Wood Dr REDH RH1 * 93 T7
Templewood Gdns HAMP NW3 37 P8
Temple Yd BETH E2 51 L1
Tempsford Av BORE WD6 24 D2
Tempsford Cl ENC/FH EN2 26 G1
Temsford Cl RYLN/HDSTN HA2 23 L14
Ten Acre La EGH TW20 56 G14
Ten Acres Cl LHD/OX KT22 83 M14
Tenbury Cl FSTGT E7 40 F10
Tenbury Ct BAL SW12 62 B6
Tenby Av KTN/HRWW/WS HA3 23 R14
Tenby Cl CHDH RM6 41 U4
Tenby Gdns NTHLT UB5 34 J11
Tenby Rd CHDH RM6 41 U4
EDGW HA8 23 V13
PEND EN3 27 N1
WALTH E17 39 Q3
WELL DA16 53 T13
Tenchley's La OXTED RH8 96 F7
Tench St WAP E1W * 51 M6
Tenda Rd STHWK SE1 51 M9
Tendring Wy CHDH RM6 41 S3
Tenham Av BRXS/STRHM SW2 62 B7
Tenison Wy STHWK SE1 8 J2
Tenniel Cl BAY/PAD W2 2 J12
Tennison Av BORE WD6 24 B3
Tennison Cl COUL/CHIP CR5 86 F10
Tennison Rd SNWD SE25 74 K2
Tennis St STHWK SE1 9 Q3
Tenniswood Rd EN EN1 15 V13
Tennyson Av CDALE/KGS NW9 36 C1
MNPK E12 40 G12
NWMAL KT3 72 H3
TWK TW1 59 P6
WAB EN9 17 L8
WAN E11 40 C5
Tennyson Cl EBED/NFELT TW14 58 C4
PEND EN3 27 P3
WELL DA16 53 N13
Tennyson Rd ADL/WDHM KT15 69 Q9
ASHF TW15 57 Q10
DART DA1 67 N3
HARH RM3 30 J12
HNWL W7 47 P5
HSLW TW3 47 L14
KIL/WHAMP NW6 2 C1
LEY E10 39 T6
MLHL NW7 24 G10
PGE/AN SE20 63 P12
SRTFD E15 40 A12
WALTH E17 39 R4
WIM/MER SW19 61 Q11
Tennyson St VX/NE SW8 49 V14
Tennyson Wy HCH RM12 42 F6
Tensing Rd NWDGN UB2 46 J8
Tentelow La NWDGN UB2 46 K8
Tenterden Cl ELTH/MOT SE9 64 H9
HDN NW4 36 K1
Tenterden Dr HDN NW4 36 K1
Tenterden Gdns CROY/NA CR0 75 L5
HDN NW4 36 K1
Tenterden Gv HDN NW4 36 J2
Tenterden Rd BCTR RM8 41 V7
CROY/NA CR0 75 M5
TOTM N17 26 K12
Tenterden St CONDST W1S 3 V12
Tenter Gnd WCHPL E1 5 U10
Tenth Av KWD/TDW/WH KT20 * 93 M2
Tent Peg La STMC/STPC BR5 77 L3
Tent St WCHPL E1 51 M2
Tercel Pth CHIG IG7 29 R9
Teredo St LEW SE13 51 T14
Teresa Gdns CHES/WCR EN8 16 C8
Terling Cl WAN E11 40 B8
Terling Rd BCTR RM8 42 A7
The Terlings BRW CM14 31 U8
Terling Wk IS N1 * 5 N1
Terminus Pl BGVA SW1W 7 V6
Tern Gdns UPMR RM14 43 S6
Tern Wy BRW CM14 31 S9
Terrace Gdns BARN SW13 48 F14
WAT WD17 11 P14
Terrace La RCHPK/HAM TW10 59 U4
Terrace Rd HOM E9 39 P12
PLSTW E13 40 C13
WOT/HER KT12 70 D5
The Terraces RDART DA2 67 Q5
The Terrace ADL/WDHM KT15 69 Q10
BARN SW13 48 E14
BETH E2 * 51 N1
CHING E4 * 28 A8
DEPT SE8 * 51 R9
EFNCH N2 * 37 U2
FNCH N3 * 25 M14
FSTH SE23 * 63 Q5
KIL/WHAMP NW6 2 E1
SEV TN13 90 D12
WOKS/MYFD GU22 * 80 E11
Terrace Vls HMSMTH W6 * 48 G10
Terrace Wk DAGW RM9 41 U10
Terra Cotta Rd GDST RH9 95 N14
Terrac St RCH/KEW TW9 59 V2
Terrapin Rd TOOT SW17 61 V8
Terretts Pl IS N1 38 F12
Terrick Rd WDGN N22 26 C13
Terrick St SHB W12 48 H4
Terrilands PIN HA5 34 H1
Terront Rd SEVS/STOTM N15 38 G3
Terry Pl UX/CGN UB8 * 45 N3
Tessa Sanderson Wy GFD/PVL UB6 35 M10
Testers Cl OXTED RH8 96 D8
Testerton Rd NTGHL W11 * 48 K5
Testerton Wk NTGHL W11 * 48 K5
Tetbury Pl IS N1 5 L2
Tetcott Rd WBPTN SW10 6 J14
Tetherdown MUSWH N10 37 U1
Tetty Wy BMLY BR1 64 C14
Teversham La VX/NE SW8 50 C13
Teviot Av SOCK/AV RM15 55 R4
Teviot Cl WELL DA16 53 R13
Teviot St POP/IOD E14 51 U3
Tewkesbury Av FSTH SE23 63 M6
PIN HA5 34 G4
Tewkesbury Cl BF/WBF KT14 81 P1
LOU IG10 28 G4
Tewkesbury Gdns CDALE/KGS NW9 36 B1
Tewkesbury Rd CAR SM5 73 R6
SEVS/STOTM N15 38 H5
WEA W13 47 Q6
Tewkesbury Ter FBAR/BDGN N11 26 A11
Tewson Rd WOOL/PLUM SE18 53 N10
Teynham Av EN EN1 26 H4
Teynham Gn HAYES BR2 76 C3
Teynham Rd RDART DA2 67 Q6
Teynton Ter TOTM N17 26 G13
Thackeray Av TOTM N17 27 L14
Thackeray Cl ISLW TW7 47 Q14
UX/CGN UB8 45 T4
WIM/MER SW19 60 K12
Thackeray Dr CHDH RM6 41 R5
Thackeray Ms HACK E8 39 L11
Thackeray Rd EHAM E6 40 F14
VX/NE SW8 49 V14
Thackeray St KENS W8 6 H5
Thakeham Cl SYD SE26 63 M10
Thalia Cl GNWCH SE10 51 V11
Thame Rd BERM/RHTH SE16 51 P7
Thames Av CHERT KT16 69 L1
DAGW RM9 54 C1
GFD/PVL UB6 35 P14
WBPTN SW10 49 Q13
Thames Bank MORT/ESHN SW14 48 C14
Thamesbank Pl THMD SE28 53 S4
Thames Cir POP/IOD E14 51 S9
Thames Cl CHERT KT16 69 M5
HPTN TW12 58 K14
RAIN RM13 54 H4
Thamesdale LCOL/BKTW AL2 12 K1
Thames Down Link ASHTD KT21 83 V4
ASHTD KT21 84 A7
BRYLDS KT5 72 C3
HOR/WEW KT19 72 C9
Thames Dr RSLP HA4 33 U4
Thames Eyot TWK TW1 * 59 Q7
Thamesfield Ms SHPTN TW17 69 U5
Thames Ga DART DA1 67 N3
Thamesgate STA TW18 57 M14
Thamesgate Cl RCHPK/HAM TW10 59 R9
Thameside TEDD TW11 59 T12
Thameside Centre BTFD TW8 * 47 V11
Thames Lock WEY KT13 * 69 S7
Thames Md WOT/HER KT12 70 C5
Thames Meadow E/WMO/HCT KT8 70 J1
SHPTN TW17 69 V6
Thamesmere Dr THMD SE28 53 Q5
Thames Pth BARN SW13 48 F13
CLPT E5 39 P8
ISLW TW7 47 S14
POP/IOD E14 51 S8
STA TW18 56 K12
STWL/WRAY TW19 56 C7
TWRH EC3N 9 T1
VX/NE SW8 7 T12
WEST SW1P 8 E9
WEY KT13 69 T7
WOT/HER KT12 70 C3
Thames Pl PUT/ROE SW15 60 K1
Thamespoint TEDD TW11 * 59 T12
Thames Quay WBPTN SW10 * 49 Q13
Thames Reach KUT/HW KT1 * 59 T13
Thames Rd BARK IG11 53 Q1
CAN/RD E16 52 F6
CHSWK W4 48 B11
DART DA1 66 G1
DTCH/LGLY SL3 44 F9
Thames Side KUT/HW KT1 59 T13
STA TW18 57 L13
THDIT KT7 71 R4
Thames St GNWCH SE10 51 T11
HPTN TW12 58 K14
KUT/HW KT1 59 T14
STA TW18 56 K10
SUN TW16 70 D1
WEY KT13 69 T7
WOT/HER KT12 70 B5
Thamesvale Cl HSLW TW3 46 J14
Thames Village CHSWK W4 48 C13
Thamley PUR RM19 55 N9
Thanescroft Gdns CROY/NA CR0 74 J8
Thanet Dr HAYES BR2 76 F8
Thanet Pl CROY/NA CR0 74 G9
Thanet Rd BXLY DA5 66 A5
ERITH DA8 54 E12
Thanet St STPAN WC1H 4 E6
Thane Vls HOLWY N7 38 D8
Thant Cl LEY E10 39 T8
Tharp Rd WLGTN SM6 74 B10
Thatcham Gdns TRDG/WHET N20 25 Q5
Thatcher Cl WDR/YW UB7 45 Q7
Thatchers Cl LOU IG10 18 A14
Thatchers Wy ISLW TW7 59 M3
Thatches Gv CHDH RM6 41 U2
Thavies Inn FLST/FETLN EC4A 4 K11
Thaxted Pl RYNPK SW20 60 K12
Thaxted Rd BKHH IG9 28 G5
ELTH/MOT SE9 65 L7
Thaxted Wy WAB EN9 16 K7
Thaxton Rd WKENS W14 6 E11
Thayers Farm Rd BECK BR3 63 Q13
Thayer St MHST W1U 3 T11
Thaynesfield POTB/CUF EN6 14 F5
Theatre Sq SRTFD E15 39 V11
Theatre St BTSEA SW11 61 T1
Theberton St IS N1 4 K1
Theed St STHWK SE1 8 J2
Thellusson Wy RKW/CH/CXG WD3 20 K5
Thelma Gv TEDD TW11 59 Q11
Thelusson Ct RAD WD7 * 12 E9
Theobald Crs KTN/HRWW/WS HA3 22 K13
Theobald Rd CROY/NA CR0 74 F7
WALTH E17 39 R5
Theobald's Cl POTB/CUF EN6 15 P4
Theobald's Gv CHES/WCR EN8 * 16 D6
Theobald's La CHES/WCR EN8 16 C6
Theobalds Park Rd ENC/FH EN2 15 R9
Theobald's Rd GINN WC1R 4 G9
POTB/CUF EN6 15 N4
Theobald St BORE WD6 12 J13
STHWK SE1 9 Q6
Theodora Wy PIN HA5 34 B1
Theodore Rd LEW SE13 63 V4
Thepps Cl REDH RH1 94 D13
Therapia La CROY/NA CR0 74 C5
Therapia Rd EDUL SE22 63 N4
Theresa Rd HMSMTH W6 48 G9
Theresa's Wk SAND/SEL CR2 74 H13
Thermopylae Ga POP/IOD E14 51 T9
Theseus Wk IS N1 5 M4
Thesiger Rd PGE/AN SE20 63 P12
Thessaly Rd VX/NE SW8 8 A14
Thetford Cl PLMGR N13 26 F11
Thetford Rd ASHF TW15 57 Q9
DAGW RM9 41 T12
NWMAL KT3 72 E3
Theydon Ct WAB EN9 17 P7
Theydon Gdns RAIN RM13 42 E12
Theydon Ga EPP CM16 * 18 C10
Theydon Gv EPP CM16 18 E4
WFD IG8 28 E11
Theydon Park Rd EPP CM16 18 C13
Theydon Pl EPP CM16 18 D5
Theydon Rd CLPT E5 39 N7
EPP CM16 18 B8
Theydon St WALTH E17 39 R5
Thicket Crs SUT SM1 73 Q9
Thicket Gv DAGW RM9 41 S11
PGE/AN SE20 63 L12
Thicket Rd PGE/AN SE20 63 M12
SUT SM1 73 Q9
Thicket Ter PGE/AN SE20 * 63 L12
The Thicket WDR/YW UB7 45 Q4
Thickthorne La STA TW18 57 N12
Third Av ACT W3 48 F6
CHDH RM6 41 S4
DAGE RM10 42 B13
EN EN1 26 K3
GSTN WD25 11 R9
HYS/HAR UB3 46 B6
KWD/TDW/WH KT20 * 93 M2
MNPK E12 40 G9
NKENS W10 2 B7
PLSTW E13 52 C1
WALTH E17 39 S3
WBLY HA9 35 T7
WTHK RM20 55 U11
Third Cl E/WMO/HCT KT8 70 K2
Third Cross Rd WHTN TW2 59 M7
Third Wy WBLY HA9 36 B9
Thirleby Rd EDGW HA8 24 D13
WEST SW1P 8 B6
Thirlmere Av GFD/PVL UB6 47 S1
Thirlmere Cl EGH TW20 56 F12
Thirlmere Gdns NTHWD HA6 21 T10
WBLY HA9 35 S6
Thirlmere Ri BMLY BR1 64 B11
Thirlmere Rd BXLYHN DA7 54 C14
MUSWH N10 25 V13
STRHM/NOR SW16 62 B9
Thirsk Cl NTHLT UB5 34 J11
Thirsk Rd BORE WD6 13 L12
BTSEA SW11 61 U1
SNWD SE25 74 H2
Thirteenth Av KWD/TDW/WH KT20 * 93 M2
Thirza Rd DART DA1 67 N4
Thisilefield Cl BXLY DA5 65 T6
Thistlebrook ABYW SE2 53 S8
Thistlecroft Gdns STAN HA7 23 T14
Thistlecroft Rd WOT/HER KT12 70 E9
Thistledene BF/WBF KT14 80 K3
THDIT KT7 71 N4
Thistledene Av CRW RM5 30 B10
RSLP HA4 34 G8
Thistle Gv WBPTN SW10 6 K10
Thistlemead CHST BR7 64 K14
Thistle Md LOU IG10 28 J1
The Thistles LHD/OX KT22 83 S12
Thistlewaite Rd CLPT E5 39 M8
Thistlewood Cl HOLWY N7 38 D7
Thistlewood Crs CROY/NA CR0 87 V2
Thistleworth Cl ISLW TW7 47 M12
Thistley Cl COUL/CHIP CR5 86 B12
NFNCH/WDSPK N12 25 S11
Thomas A Beckett Cl HRW HA1 35 P9
Thomas Av CTHM CR3 86 G11
Thomas Baines Rd BTSEA SW11 61 R1
Thomas Cribb Ms EHAM E6 52 H4
Thomas Dean Rd SYD SE26 * 63 R9
Thomas Dinwiddy Rd LEE/GVPK SE12 64 D7
Thomas Doyle St STHWK SE1 9 L5
Thomas' La CAT SE6 63 T5
Thomas Moore St WAP E1W 51 L5
Thomas Moore Wy EFNCH N2 37 Q1
Thomas More St WAP E1W * 51 L5
Thomas North Ter CAN/RD E16 * 52 B3
Thomas Pl KENS W8 6 G6
Thomas Rd POP/IOD E14 51 R4
Thomas Rochford Wy
CHES/WCR EN8 16 F1
Thomas St WOOL/PLUM SE18 52 J9
Thomas Wall Cl SUT SM1 73 P10
Thompson Av RCH/KEW TW9 60 B1
Thompson Cl CHEAM SM3 73 N6
DTCH/LGLY SL3 44 E9
IL IG1 41 L7
Thompson Rd DAGW RM9 41 V8
EDUL SE22 62 K4
HGDN/ICK UB10 33 Q12
HSLW TW3 58 K2
Thompson's Av CMBW SE5 9 N13
Thompsons Cl CHESW EN7 15 V3
Thompson Wy RKW/CH/CXG WD3 21 L5
Thomson Crs CROY/NA CR0 74 E6
Thomson Rd KTN/HRWW/WS HA3 35 N1
Thorburn Sq STHWK SE1 51 L9
Thorburn Wy WIM/MER SW19 * 61 R13
Thoresby St IS N1 5 P5
Thorkhill Gdns THDIT KT7 71 Q6
Thorkhill Rd THDIT KT7 71 R6
Thorley Cl BF/WBF KT14 81 L4
Thorley Gdns WOKS/MYFD GU22 81 L4
Thornaby Gdns UED N18 27 M11
Thornash Cl WOKN/KNAP GU21 80 A5
Thornash Rd WOKN/KNAP GU21 80 A6
Thornash Wy WOKN/KNAP GU21 80 A5
Thorn Av BUSH WD23 23 L6
Thornbridge Rd IVER SL0 32 G13
Thornbury Av ISLW TW7 47 M12
Thornbury Cl STNW/STAM N16 38 J10
Thornbury Gdns BORE WD6 24 C2
Thornbury Rd CLAP SW4 62 C4
ISLW TW7 47 M12
Thornbury Sq HGT N6 37 V6
Thornby Rd CLPT E5 39 N8
Thorncliffe Rd CLAP SW4 62 C4
NWDGN UB2 46 H10
Thorn Cl HAYES BR2 76 J4
NTHLT UB5 46 H1
Thorncombe Rd EDUL SE22 62 J3
Thorn Ct BELMT SM2 * 73 P12
Thorncroft EGH TW20 56 A12
EMPK RM11 42 H4
Thorncroft Cl COUL/CHIP CR5 86 E9
Thorncroft Rd SUT SM1 73 P9
Thorncroft St VX/NE SW8 8 E14
Thorndean St WAND/EARL SW18 61 Q7
Thorndene Av TRDG/WHET N20 25 T6
Thorndike Av NTHLT UB5 34 F13
Thorndike Cl WBPTN SW10 6 J13
Thorndike Rd IS N1 38 H11
Thorndike St PIM SW1V * 8 C8
Thorndon Cl STMC/STPC BR5 65 P14
Thorndon Gdns HOR/WEW KT19 72 E9
Thorndon Rd STMC/STPC BR5 65 P14
Thorn Dr DTCH/LGLY SL3 44 C4
Thorndyke Ct PIN HA5 22 H12
Thorne Cl ASHF TW15 57 U12
CAN/RD E16 52 C4
ERITH DA8 54 C11
ESH/CLAY KT10 71 Q12
WAN E11 40 A9
Thorneloe Gdns CROY/NA CR0 74 F10
Thorne Rd VX/NE SW8 8 E14
Thorne's Cl BECK BR3 75 U1
Thorne St BARN SW13 60 E1
Thornet Wood Rd BMLY BR1 76 J1
Thorney Crs BTSEA SW11 7 M14
Thorneycroft Cl WOT/HER KT12 70 E4
Thorneycroft Dr PEND EN3 16 G12
Thorney Hedge Rd CHSWK W4 48 B9
Thorney La North IVER SL0 44 K4
Thorney La South WDR/YW UB7 44 K7
Thorney Mill Rd WDR/YW UB7 45 M8
Thorney St WEST SW1P 8 E7
Thornfield Av MLHL NW7 25 L13
Thornfield Pde MLHL NW7 * 25 L12
Thornfield Rd SHB W12 48 H7
Thornford Rd LEW SE13 63 U3
Thorngate Rd MV/WKIL W9 2 F7
Thorngrove Rd PLSTW E13 40 D13
Thornham Gv SRTFD E15 39 V10
Thornham St GNWCH SE10 51 T11
Thornhaugh St STPAN WC1H 4 D8
Thornhill Av SURB KT6 71 V7
WOOL/PLUM SE18 53 N12
Thornhill Bridge Whf IS N1 4 G2
Thornhill Crs IS N1 38 D12
Thornhill Gdns BARK IG11 41 N12
LEY E10 39 T7
Thornhill Gv IS N1 38 D12
Thornhill Rd CROY/NA CR0 74 G5
HGDN/ICK UB10 33 S9
IS N1 38 E12
LEY E10 39 T7
NTHWD HA6 21 U9
SURB KT6 71 U7
Thornhill Wy SHPTN TW17 69 S3
Thorn La RAIN RM13 42 K14
Thornlaw Rd WNWD SE27 62 E9
Thornley Cl TOTM N17 27 L12
Thornley Dr RYLN/HDSTN HA2 34 K7
Thornridge BRW CM14 31 V5
Thornsbeach Rd CAT SE6 63 U6
Thornsett Pl PGE/AN SE20 63 M14
Thornsett Rd PGE/AN SE20 63 M14
WAND/EARL SW18 61 P7
Thornsett Ter PGE/AN SE20 * 63 M14
Thorn's Meadow BH/WHM TN16 89 S13
Thornton Av BRXS/STRHM SW2 62 B7
CHSWK W4 48 E9
CROY/NA CR0 74 D4
WDR/YW UB7 45 R8
Thornton Cl WDR/YW UB7 45 R8
Thornton Crs COUL/CHIP CR5 86 E9
Thornton Dene BECK BR3 63 S14
Thornton Gdns BAL SW12 62 B6
Thornton Gv PIN HA5 22 J11
Thornton Hl WIM/MER SW19 61 L12
Thornton Pl MBLAR W1H 3 Q9
Thornton Rd BAL SW12 62 B5
BAR EN5 25 L1
BELV DA17 * 54 B9
BMLY BR1 64 C10
CAR SM5 73 S5
IL IG1 40 K9
MORT/ESHN SW14 60 D2
POTB/CUF EN6 14 E4
THHTH CR7 74 E3
UED N18 27 N8
WAN E11 39 V7
WIM/MER SW19 60 K11
Thornton Rw THHTH CR7 74 E3
Thorntons Farm Av ROMW/RG RM7 42 C7
Thornton St BRXN/ST SW9 50 E14
Thornton Wy GLDGN NW11 37 P3
Thorntree Rd CHARL SE7 52 F10
Thornville Gv MTCM CR4 61 R14
Thornville St DEPT SE8 51 S13
Thornwood Cl SWFD E18 28 D14
Thornwood Rd EPP CM16 18 F2
LEW SE13 64 A3
Thorogood Gdns SRTFD E15 40 A10
Thorogood Wy RAIN RM13 42 E13
Thorold Cl SAND/SEL CR2 75 Q14
Thorold Rd IL IG1 40 K7
WDGN N22 26 C12
The Thoroughfare
KWD/TDW/WH KT20 84 G14
KWD/TDW/WH KT20 92 G1
Thorparch Rd VX/NE SW8 50 B13
Thorpebank Rd SHB W12 48 G6
Thorpe By-pass EGH TW20 68 F1
Thorpe Cl CROY/NA CR0 87 V1
NKENS W10 2 B11
ORP BR6 77 N7
SYD SE26 * 63 P9
Thorpe Ct TOOT SW17 61 S9
Thorpe Crs OXHEY WD19 22 D5
WALTH E17 27 R14
Thorpedale Gdns GNTH/NBYPK IG2 40 J2
Thorpedale Rd FSBYPK N4 38 C6
Thorpe Hall Rd WALTH E17 27 U13
Thorpe Lea Rd EGH TW20 56 F13
Thorpe Pk CHERT KT16 * 68 K1
Thorpe Rd BARK IG11 41 M12
CHERT KT16 68 H3
EHAM E6 40 H13
FSTGT E7 40 C8
KUTN/CMB KT2 59 U12
SEVS/STOTM N15 38 J4
STA TW18 56 H10
WALTH E17 27 U14
Thorpeside Cl STA TW18 56 J14
Thorpewood Av SYD SE26 63 M7
Thorpland Av HGDN/ICK UB10 33 U8
Thorsden Cl WOKS/MYFD GU22 80 C9
Thorsden Ct WOKS/MYFD GU22 * 80 C8
Thorsden Wy NRWD SE19 * 62 J10
Thorverton Rd CRICK NW2 37 L8
Thoydon Rd BOW E3 39 Q14
Thrale Rd STRHM/NOR SW16 62 A10
Thrale St STHWK SE1 9 P2
Thrasher Cl HACK E8 * 5 U1
Thrawl St WCHPL E1 5 V10
Threadneedle St LOTH EC2R 5 R12
Three Arches Pk REDH RH1 * 93 T14
Three Arch Rd REDH RH1 93 U14
Three Colts La BETH E2 51 M2
Three Colt St POP/IOD E14 * 51 R5
Three Corners BXLYHN DA7 54 B14
Three Forests Wy ABR/ST RM4 19 P11
LOU IG10 17 R13
WAB EN9 17 R10
Three Gates Rd HART DA3 79 U5
Three Kings Yd MYFR/PKLN W1K 3 U13
Three Meadows Ms
KTN/HRWW/WS HA3 23 P13
Three Mill La BOW E3 51 U1
SRTFD E15 39 U14
Three Oak La STHWK SE1 9 U3
Three Oaks Cl HGDN/ICK UB10 33 R8
Three Valleys Wy BUSH WD23 22 F3
Threshers Pl NTGHL W11 2 A13
Threshold Wy CHOB/PIR GU24 68 C14
Thriffwood SYD SE26 63 N8
Thrift Farm La BORE WD6 13 N14
Thrift La RSEV TN14 * 89 N7
Thrifts Md EPP CM16 18 C11
Thrigby Rd CHSGTN KT9 71 V11
Throckmorten Rd CAN/RD E16 52 D4
Throgmorton Av OBST EC2N 5 R11
Throgmorton St OBST EC2N 5 R11
Throstle Pl GSTN WD25 * 11 Q6
Throwley Cl ABYW SE2 53 S8
Throwley Rd SUT SM1 73 P10
Throwley Wy SUT SM1 73 P9
Thrums WATN WD24 11 P11
Thrupp Cl MTCM CR4 61 V14
Thrupps Av WOT/HER KT12 70 F10
Thrupps La WOT/HER KT12 70 F10
Thrush Gn RKW/CH/CXG WD3 21 N5
RYLN/HDSTN HA2 34 J2
Thrush La POTB/CUF EN6 15 N2
Thrush St WALW SE17 9 N9
Thunderer Rd DAGW RM9 53 V2
Thurbarn Rd CAT SE6 63 T10
Thurland Rd BERM/RHTH SE16 51 L8
Thurlby Cl WFD IG8 28 H10
Thurlby Rd ALP/SUD HA0 35 T11
WNWD SE27 62 E9
Thurleigh Av BAL SW12 61 U4
Thurleigh Rd BAL SW12 61 T4
Thurleston Av MRDN SM4 73 L3
Thurlestone Av GDMY/SEVK IG3 41 P9
NFNCH/WDSPK N12 25 T11
Thurlestone Cl SHPTN TW17 * 69 U4
Thurlestone Pde SHPTN TW17 * 69 U4
Thurlestone Rd WNWD SE27 62 E8
Thurloe Cl SKENS SW7 7 N7
Thurloe Gdns ROM RM1 42 E4
Thurloe Pl SKENS SW7 7 N6
Thurloe Place Ms SKENS SW7 * 7 M7
Thurloe Sq SKENS SW7 7 N7
Thurloe St SKENS SW7 7 M7
Thurlow Cl CHING E4 27 T11
Thurlow Gdns ALP/SUD HA0 * 35 T10
BARK/HLT IG6 29 M11
Thurlow Hl DUL SE21 62 G6
Thurlow Park Rd DUL SE21 62 G7
Thurlow Rd HAMP NW3 37 R10
HNWL W7 47 Q7
Thurlow St WALW SE17 9 S10
Thurlow Ter KTTN NW5 37 T10
Thurlow Wk WALW SE17 9 S10
Thurlston Rd RSLP HA4 34 C8
Thurlton Ct WOKN/KNAP GU21 80 C6
Thurnham Wy KWD/TDW/WH KT20 84 K10
Thursland Rd SCUP DA14 65 U11
Thursley Crs CROY/NA CR0 75 V12
Thursley Gdns WIM/MER SW19 60 K7
Thursley Rd ELTH/MOT SE9 64 H8
Thurso Cl HARH RM3 31 P11
Thurso St TOOT SW17 61 R9
Thurstan Rd RYNPK SW20 60 H12
Thurston Rd DEPT SE8 51 T14
STHL UB1 46 H4
Thurtle Rd BETH E2 5 V2
Thwaite Cl ERITH DA8 54 C11
Thyer Cl ORP BR6 77 L9
Thyra Gv NFNCH/WDSPK N12 25 P11
Tibbatt's Rd BOW E3 51 T2
Tibbenham Pl CAT SE6 63 T6
Tibberton Sq IS N1 * 38 G12
Tibbets Cl WIM/MER SW19 60 K6
Tibbet's Ride PUT/ROE SW15 60 K5
Tibbles Cl GSTN WD25 11 S9
Tibbs Hill Rd ABLGY WD5 11 M5
Tiber Cl BOW E3 39 S13
Tiber Gdns IS N1 4 F2
Ticehurst Cl STMC/STPC BR5 65 Q12
Ticehurst Rd FSTH SE23 63 Q7
Tichborne RKW/CH/CXG WD3 20 H10
Tichmarsh HOR/WEW KT19 72 C14
Tickford Cl ABYW SE2 53 S7
Tidal Basin Rd CAN/RD E16 52 B5
Tidenham Gdns CROY/NA CR0 74 J8
Tideswell Rd CROY/NA CR0 75 S8
PUT/ROE SW15 60 J2
Tideway Cl RCHPK/HAM TW10 59 R9
Tidey St BOW E3 51 S3
Tidford Rd WELL DA16 53 P14
Tidworth Rd BOW E3 51 S2
Tidy's La EPP CM16 18 E3
Tiepigs La WWKM BR4 76 A7
Tierney Rd BRXS/STRHM SW2 62 C6
Tierney Ter BRXS/STRHM SW2 * 62 C6
Tiger La HAYES BR2 76 D2
Tiger Wy CLPT E5 39 M9
Tigres Cl ED N9 27 N7
Tilbrook Rd BKHTH/KID SE3 64 E1
Tilburstow Hill Rd GDST RH9 95 N10
Tilbury Cl PECK SE15 9 V13
STMC/STPC BR5 65 R14
Tilbury Rd EHAM E6 40 H14
LEY E10 39 U5
Tilbury Wk DTCH/LGLY SL3 44 F8
Tildesley Rd PUT/ROE SW15 60 J4
Tile Farm Rd ORP BR6 77 M8
Tilehouse Cl BORE WD6 23 V1
Tilehouse La DEN/HRF UB9 32 J3
RKW/CH/CXG WD3 20 J13
Tilehouse Wy DEN/HRF UB9 32 K5
Tilehurst Rd CHEAM SM3 73 L10
WAND/EARL SW18 61 R6
Tilekiln Cl CHESW EN7 15 V3
Tile Kiln La BXLY DA5 66 D8
DEN/HRF UB9 33 T5
HGT N6 37 V6
PLMGR N13 26 G10
Tilers Cl REDH RH1 94 A7
Tiler's Wy REIG RH2 93 Q14
Tileyard Rd HOLWY N7 38 C12
Tilford Av CROY/NA CR0 75 U12
Tilford Gdns WIM/MER SW19 60 K6
Tilgate Common REDH RH1 94 G9
Tilia Cl SUT SM1 73 M10
Tilia Rd CLPT E5 39 M9
Till Av EYN DA4 79 M5
Tiller Rd POP/IOD E14 51 S8
Tillett Cl WLSDN NW10 36 C11
Tillet Wy BETH E2 51 L1
Tilley La EPSOM KT18 84 C13
Tilley Rd FELT TW13 58 C6
Tillingbourne Gdns FNCH N3 37 M1
Tillingbourne Gn STMC/STPC BR5 77 Q3
Tillingbourne Wy FNCH N3 37 M2
Tillingdown Hl CTHM CR3 87 M12
Tillingdown La CTHM CR3 87 M14
CTHM CR3 95 M1
Tillingham Ct WAB EN9 17 N7
Tillingham Wy NFNCH/WDSPK N12 25 N9
Tilling Rd CRICK NW2 36 J5
Tilling Wy WBLY HA9 * 35 T8
Tillman St WCHPL E1 51 M4
Tilloch St IS N1 * 38 D12
Tillotson Rd ED N9 26 K7
IL IG1 40 J5
KTN/HRWW/WS HA3 22 K12
Tilmans Md EYN DA4 79 M5
Tilney Gdns IS N1 38 H11
Tilney Rd DAGW RM9 41 V11
NWDGN UB2 46 E9
Tilney St MYFR/PKLN W1K 7 T1
Tilson Cl CMBW SE5 9 S13
Tilson Gdns BRXS/STRHM SW2 62 C5
Tilson Rd TOTM N17 27 L13
Tilston Cl WAN E11 40 B8
Tilt Cl COB KT11 82 G6
Tilt Meadow COB KT11 82 G6
Tilton St FUL/PGN SW6 6 B12
Tilt Rd COB KT11 82 F6
Tilt Vw COB KT11 * 82 E5
The Tiltwood ACT W3 48 C5
Tilt Yard Ap ELTH/MOT SE9 64 H4
Timber Cl CHST BR7 64 J14
WOKS/MYFD GU22 80 K5
Timbercroft HOR/WEW KT19 72 E9
Timbercroft La WOOL/PLUM SE18 53 N11
Timberdene Av BARK/HLT IG6 29 L13
Timber Hl ASHTD KT21 83 U9
Timber Hill Rd CTHM CR3 87 L14
Timberland Cl PECK SE15 * 51 L12
Timberland Rd WCHPL E1 * 51 M4
Timberling Gdns SAND/SEL CR2 74 H14
Timber Mill Wy CLAP SW4 62 B1
Timber Pond Rd BERM/RHTH SE16 51 P7
Timberridge RKW/CH/CXG WD3 21 N2
Timberslip Dr WLGTN SM6 74 B13
The Timbers CHEAM SM3 * 73 L11
Timber St FSBYE EC1V * 5 N7
Timbertop Rd BH/WHM TN16 88 E8
Timberwharf Rd SEVS/STOTM N15 39 L4
Time Sq HACK E8 * 38 K10
Times Sq SUT SM1 * 73 P10
Timms Cl BMLY BR1 76 H2
Timothy Cl BXLYHS DA6 65 U3
Timperley Gdns REDH RH1 93 S8
Timsway STA TW18 56 K10
Tindale Cl SAND/SEL CR2 86 H1
Tindall Cl HARH RM3 31 M14
Tindall Ms HCH RM12 42 J8
Tindal St BRXN/ST SW9 50 F13
Tine Rd CHIG IG7 29 N10
Tinker Pot La BGR/WK TN15 91 Q4
Tinkerpot Ri BGR/WK TN15 91 Q4
Tinmans Rw COB KT11 * 82 E8
Tinniswood Cl HBRY N5 38 E10
Tinsey Cl EGH TW20 56 F10
Tinsley Cl SNWD SE25 75 M1
Tinsley Rd WCHPL E1 51 N3
Tintagel Cl EW KT17 84 F4
Tintagel Crs EDUL SE22 62 K2
Tintagel Dr STAN HA7 23 T10
Tintagel Rd ORP BR6 77 S7
Tintagel Wy WOKS/MYFD GU22 80 E6
Tintern Av CDALE/KGS NW9 36 B1
Tintern Cl PUT/ROE SW15 61 L3
WIM/MER SW19 61 Q12
Tintern Gdns STHGT/OAK N14 26 C5
Tintern Rd CAR SM5 73 R6
WDGN N22 26 G13
Tintern St CLAP SW4 62 C2
Tintern Wy RYLN/HDSTN HA2 34 K6
Tinto Rd CAN/RD E16 52 C3
Tinwell Ms BORE WD6 24 D3
Tinworth St LBTH SE11 8 F9
Tippendell La LCOL/BKTW AL2 12 A1
Tippetts Cl ENC/FH EN2 15 S13
Tipthorpe Rd BTSEA SW11 61 U1
Tipton Dr CROY/NA CR0 74 J9
Tiptree Cl CHING E4 27 U8
EMPK RM11 43 N6
Tiptree Crs CLAY IG5 28 J14
CLAY IG5 40 J1
Tiptree Dr ENC/FH EN2 26 H2

Column 1

Tiptree Rd RSLP HA4 — 34 D9
Tirlemont Rd SAND/SEL CR2 — 74 D12
Tirrell Rd CROY/NA CR0 — 74 C4
Tisbury Rd STRHM/NOR SW16 — 62 C14
Tisdall Pl WALW SE17 — 9 H8
Titan Ct BTFD TW8 — 47 V10
Titchborne Rw BAY/PAD W2 — 3 P7
Titchfield Rd CAR SM5 — 16 E11
 PEND EN3
 STJWD NW8 — 3 P3
Titchwell Rd WAND/EARL SW18 — 73 R5
Tite Hill EGH TW20 — 56 B10
Tite St CHEL SW3 — 7 N9
Tithe Barn Cl KUTN/CMB KT2 — 59 V13
Tithe Barn Cl WELL — 11 M8
The Tithe Barn — 34 D14
Tithe Barn Wy NTHLT UB5 — 34 C13
Tithe Cl DTCH/LGLY SL3
 HDN NW4
Tithe Farm Av RYLN/HDSTN HA2 — 34 J8
Tithe Farm Cl RYLN/HDSTN HA2 — 34 J9
Tithepit Shaw La WARL CR6 — 87 M5
Tithe Wk MLHL NW7 — 24 G13
 VW GU25
 WOT/HER KT12 — 70 D4
 YEAD UB4 — 46 B3
Titian Av BUSH WD23 — 23 N5
Titley Cl CHING E4 — 27 V10
Titmus Av THMD SE28 — 53 U5
Titmuss Av THMD SE28 — 53 V5
Titmuss St SHB W12 — 48 H7
Titsey Hill WARL CR6 — 88 B14
Titsey Rd OXTED RH8 — 96 D13
Tiverton Av CLAY IG5 — 40 J1
Tiverton Cl CROY/NA CR0 — 74 K5
Tiverton Dr ELTH/MOT SE9 — ...
Tiverton Rd ED N9 — ...
 EDGW HA8 — 24 F5
 HSLW TW3 — 46 K6
 RSLP HA4 — 33 U8
 SEVS/STOTM N15 — 38 H4
 UED N18 — 26 J10
 WBLY HA0 — 35 U14
 WLSDN NW10 — ...
Tiverton St STHWK SE1 — 9 N5
Tiverton Wy CHSGTN KT9 — 71 S10
 MLHL NW7 — ...
Tivoli Gdns WOOL/PLUM SE18 — 52 G9
Tivoli Rd CEND/HSY/T N8 — 38 B3
 HSLWW TW4 — 58 E2
 WNWD SE27 — ...
Toad Rw HSLWW TW4 — 58 H2
Tobago St POP/IOD E14 — 51 S7
Tobin Cl HAMP NW3 — 37 S12
Toby La WCHPL E1 — 51 Q1
Toby Wy SURB KT6 — 72 B7
Todber Cl RAIN WD13 — ...
Tokenhouse Yd LOTH EC2R — 5 Q11
Tokyngton Av WBLY HA9 — 36 A3
Toland Sq PUT/ROE SW15 — 60 G5
Tolcarne Dr PIN HA5 — 22 C14
Toley Av RYLN/HDSTN HA2 — 35 U5
Toll Bar Ct SUT SM2 — ...
Tollbridge Cl NKENS W10 — 2 B5
Tollers La COUL/CHIP CR5 — 86 D9
Tollet St WCHPL E1 — 51 P2
Tollgate Cl RKW/CH/CXG WD3 — 20 K2
Tollgate Dr DUL SE21 — ...
 YEAD UB4 — 46 F5
Tollgate Gdns KIL/WHAMP NW6 — 2 J1
Tollgate Rd CHES/WCR EN8 — 16 C4
 EHAM E6 — 52 C3
 RDART DA2 — ...
Tollhouse La WLGTN SM6 — 74 A13
Tollhouse Wy ARCH N19 — ...
Tollington Pk FSBYPK N4 — 38 C7
Tollington Pl FSBYPK N4 — 38 C7
Tollington Rd HOLWY N7 — ...
Tollington Wy HOLWY N7 — ...
Tolmers Av POTB/CUF EN6 — 15 N2
Tolmers Ms POTB/CUF EN6 — ...
Tolpits Cl WATW WD18 — 22 B3
Tolpits La WATW WD18 — ...
Tolpuddle Av PLSTW E13 — ...
Tolpuddle St IS N1 — 4 J3
Tolsford Rd HACK E8 — 39 M12
Tolson Rd ISLW TW7 — 59 Q1
Tolverne Rd RYNPK SW20 — 60 J13
Tolworth Broadway SURB KT6 — 72 A6
Tolworth Gdns CHDH RM6 — 41 V1
Tolworth Park Rd SURB KT6 — 71 V7
Tolworth Ri North BRYLDS KT5 — 72 C5
Tolworth Ri South BRYLDS KT5 — 72 C6
Tolworth Rd (Kingston By-Pass) BRYLDS KT5 — ...
Tolworth Underpass (Kingston By-Pass) SURB KT6 — 72 A8
Tom Critch Rd THMD SE28 — 53 M8
Tom Groves Cl SRTFD E15 — ...
Tom Hood Cl SRTFD E15 — 39 V10
Tom Jenkinson Rd CAN/RD E16 — 52 C8
Tomkins Cl BORE WD6 — ...
Tomkyns La UPMR RM14 — 43 R1
Tomlin Cl HOR/WEW KT19 — 84 D1
Tomlins Av BOW E3 — 5 T6
Tomlinson Cl BETH E2 — ...
 CHSWK W4 — 48 B10
Tomlins Orch BARK IG11 — 41 L13
Tomlin's Ter POP/IOD E14 — ...
Tom Mann Cl BARK IG11 — ...
Tom Nolan Cl SRTFD E15 — 40 A14
Tompion St FSBYE EC1V — ...
Tom's La KGLGY WD4 — ...
Tomswood Hl BARK/HLT IG6 — 28 K10
Tomswood Rd CHIG IG7 — 28 F5
Tonbridge Cl BNSTD SM7 — ...
Tonbridge Crs KTN/HRWW/WS HA3 — 35 V1
Tonbridge Rd E/WMO/HCT KT8 — 70 C12
 RAIN RM13 — 30 K12
Tonbridge St STPAN WC1H — 4 E6
Tonfield Rd CHEAM SM3 — ...
Tonge Cl BECK BR3 — 75 S4
Tonsley Hl WAND/EARL SW18 — 61 P3
Tonsley Pl WAND/EARL SW18 — 61 P3
Tonsley Rd WAND/EARL SW18 — 61 P3
Tonsley St WAND/EARL SW18 — 61 P3
Tonstall Rd HOR/WEW KT19 — ...
 MTCM CR4 — ...
Tooke Cl PIN HA5 — ...
Tookey Cl KTN/HRWW/WS HA3 — 35 V5
Took's Ct FLST/FETLN EC4A — ...
Tooley St STHWK SE1 — ...
Toorack Rd KTN/HRWW/WS HA3 — 23 M14
Toot Hill Rd CHONG CM5 — 19 R4
Tooting Bec Gdns STRHM/NOR SW16 — ...
Tooting Bec Rd TOOT SW17 — 61 U10
Tooting Gv TOOT SW17 — 61 S10
Tooting High St TOOT SW17 — ...
Tootswood Rd HAYES BR2 — 76 A4
Tooveys Mill Cl KGLGY WD4 — ...
Topcliffe Dr ORP BR6 — 77 M9
Top Dartford Rd SWLY BR8 — ...
Topham Sq TOTM N17 — 26 G14
Topham St CLKNW EC1R — ...
Top House Ri CHING E4 — ...
Topiary Sq RCH/KEW TW9 — ...
The Topiary ASHTD KT21 — 83 U10
Topland Rd CFSP/GDCR SL9 — ...
Toplands Av SOCK/AV RM15 — 55 T6
Topmast Point POP/IOD E14 — 51 S7
Top Pk BECK BR3 — 76 A3
Topping La UX/CGN UB8 — 45 P1
Topsfield Cl CEND/HSY/T N8 — ...
Topsfield Pde CEND/HSY/T N8 — 38 C2
Topsfield Rd CEND/HSY/T N8 — ...
Topsham Rd TOOT SW17 — 61 T8
Tor Av WAB EN9 — ...
Tor Gdns KENS W8 — ...
Tor La WEY KT13 — ...
Torbay Rd KIL/WHAMP NW6 — ...
 RYLN/HDSTN HA2 — ...
Torbay St CAMTN NW1 — 37 V12
Torbitt Wy GNTH/NBYPK IG2 — 41 Q3
Torbridge Cl EDGW HA8 — ...
Torcross Dr FSTH SE23 — 63 N8
Torcross Rd RSLP HA4 — 34 C7
Tor Gdns KENS W8 — 6 D2
Tor Rd WELL DA16 — 53 R14
Toronto Av MNPK E12 — ...
Toronto Rd IL IG1 — ...
 UED N18 — 26 K7
Torquay Gdns REDBR IG4 — 40 F2
Torquay St BAY/PAD W2 — ...
Torrance Cl EMPK RM11 — ...
Torrens Rd BRXS/STRHM SW2 — 62 D3
 SRTFD E15 — ...
Torrens Sq SRTFD E15 — ...
Torrens St FSBYE EC1V — 5 L4
Torre Wk CAR SM5 — 73 T6
Torrey Dr BRXN/ST SW9 — 50 E14
Torriano Av KTTN NW5 — ...
Torriano Cottages KTTN NW5 — 38 A13
Torriano Ms KTTN NW5 — ...
Torridge Gdns PECK SE15 — ...
Torridge Rd DTCH/LGLY SL3 — 44 A11
 THHTH CR7 — ...
Torridon Rd CAT SE6 — ...
Torrington Av NFNCH/WDSPK N12 — 25 S9
Torrington Cl ESH/CLAY KT10 — 71 N14
Torrington Dr LOU IG10 — 29 L2
 POTB/CUF EN6 — ...
 RYLN/HDSTN HA2 — ...
Torrington Gdns FBAR/BDGN N11 — ...
 GFD/PVL UB6 — ...
 LOU IG10 — ...
Torrington Pk NFNCH/WDSPK N12 — 25 S9

Column 2

WAP E1W — ...
 ESH/CLAY KT10 — ...
 GFD/PVL UB6 — ...
 RSLP HA4 — ...
Torrington Sq STPAN WC1H — ...
Tor Rd WELL DA16 — 53 R14
Torver Rd HRW HA1 — ...
Torver Wy ORP BR6 — 77 M8
Torwood La WARL CR6 — ...
Torwood Rd PUT/ROE SW15 — 60 G3
Torworth Rd BORE WD6 — 13 L3
Tothill St STJSPK SW1H — ...
Totnes Rd WELL DA16 — 53 R12
Totnes Vis FBAR/BDGN N11 — 26 A10
Tottan Ter WCHPL E1 — 51 P4
Totteridge Common TRDG/WHET N20 — 25 N7
Totteridge Gn TRDG/WHET N20 — ...
Totteridge La TRDG/WHET N20 — 25 N7
Totteridge Village TRDG/WHET N20 — ...
Totternhoe Cl KTN/HRWW/WS HA3 — ...
Totton Rd THHTH CR7 — ...
Toulmin St STHWK SE1 — 9 N4
Toulon St CMBW SE5 — ...
Tournay Rd FUL/PGN SW6 — ...
Tovil Cl PGE/AN SE20 — 63 L14
Towcester Rd BOW E3 — ...
Tower Br WBPT E1W — ...
Tower Bridge Ap TWRH EC3N — ...
Tower Bridge Ms ALP/SUD HA0 — ...
Tower Bridge Rd STHWK SE1 — ...
Tower Buildings WAP E1W — ...
 ORP BR6 — ...
 PGE/AN SE20 — ...
 WOKN/KNAP GU21 — ...
Tower Cft EYN DA4 — 79 L7
Tower Gdns ESH/CLAY KT10 — ...
Tower Gardens Rd TOTM N17 — 26 C15
Towergate Cl UX/CGN UB8 — ...
Tower Gv WEY KT13 — ...
Tower Hamlets Rd FSTGT E7 — ...
 WALTH E17 — 39 S1
Tower HI WALTH E17 — 39 U14
Tower Hill Ter MON EC3R — ...
Tower Ms WALTH E17 — 39 S1
Tower Park Rd DART DA1 — ...
Tower Pl MON EC3R — ...
Tower Rd BELV DA17 — ...
 BXLYHS DA6 — ...
 DART DA1 — ...
 EPP CM16 — ...
 KWD/TDW/WH KT20 — ...
 TWK TW1 — ...
 WLSDN NW10 — ...
Tower Royal MANHO EC4N — ...
Towers Av HGDN/ICK UB10 — 45 U1
Towers Pl RCH/KEW TW9 — 59 U3
Towers Rd PIN HA5 — ...
 STHL UB1 — ...
The Towers PUR/KEN CR8 — 86 C5
Towers Wk WEY KT13 — 69 T11
Towers Wd EYN DA4 — 79 L7
Tower Ter WDGN N22 — ...
Tower Vw CROY/NA CR0 — ...
Towfield Rd FELT TW13 — ...
Towncourt Crs STMC/STPC BR5 — 77 L5
Towncourt La STMC/STPC BR5 — 77 M4
Towncourt Pth FSBYPK N4 — 38 G6
Townend LITH SE1 — ...
Town End Pde KUT/HW KT1 — 71 T1
Townley Rd BXLYHS DA6 — ...
 EDUL SE22 — ...
Townley St WALW SE17 — 9 R8
Townmead Rd FUL/PGN SW6 — ...
Town Meadow BTFD TW8 — 47 T13
Townmead Rd FUL/PGN SW6 — ...
 RCH/KEW TW9 — ...
 WAB EN9 — ...
Town Quay BARK IG11 — 40 K15
Townsend Av STHGT/OAK N14 — ...
Townsend La CDALE/KGS NW9 — ...
Townsend Ms WAND/EARL SW18 — ...
Townsend Rd ASHF TW15 — ...
 STHL UB1 — ...
 WOOL/PLUM SE18 — ...
Townsend St WALW SE17 — 9 T6
Townsend Yd HGT N6 — ...
Townshend Cl SCUP DA14 — ...
Townshend Est STJWD NW8 — ...
Townshend Rd CHST BR7 — ...
 RCH/KEW TW9 — ...
 STJWD NW8 — ...
Townshend Ter RCH/KEW TW9 — 59 V2
Townson Av NTHLT UB5 — ...
Townson Wy NTHLT UB5 — 34 D13
Town Sq CTHM CR3 — ...
Town Square Crs RDART DA2 — ...
Town Tree Rd ASHF TW15 — ...
Town Wall Wy TWK TW1 — ...
Towpath SHPTN TW17 — ...
 WOT/HER KT12 — ...
Towpath Rd UED N18 — ...
Towpath Wy CROY/NA CR0 — ...
Townson Wy NTHLT UB5 — ...
Toynbec Cl CHST BR7 — ...
Toynbee St WCHPL E1 — ...
Toynbee Wy HGT N6 — ...
Toy's Hill THMD SE28 — ...
The Tracery BNSTD SM7 — ...
Tracey Av CRICK NW2 — ...
Tracy Av DTCH/LGLY SL3 — ...
Trade City WEY KT13 — ...
Trader Rd EHAM E6 — ...
Tradescant Rd VX/NE SW8 — ...
Trading Estate Rd WLSDN NW10 — 48 A3
Trafalgar Av PECK SE15 — ...
 TOTM N17 — ...
 WPK KT4 — ...
Trafalgar Cl THMD SE28 — ...
Trafalgar Ct COB KT11 — ...
Trafalgar Dr WOT/HER KT12 — ...
Trafalgar Gdns WCHPL E1 — ...
Trafalgar Gv GNWCH SE10 — ...
Trafalgar Ms HOM E9 — ...
Trafalgar Pl UED N18 — ...
 WAN E11 — ...
Trafalgar Rd DART DA1 — ...
 GNWCH SE10 — ...
 RAIN RM13 — ...
Trafalgar Sq STJS SW1Y — ...
Trafalgar St WALW SE17 — 9 Q7
Trafalgar Ter HRW HA1 — ...
Trafalgar Wy CROY/NA CR0 — ...
 POP/IOD E14 — ...
Trafford Cl BARK/HLT IG6 — 29 L8
 SRTFD E15 — ...
Trafford Rd THHTH CR7 — ...
Trahorn Cl WCHPL E1 — ...
Tramway Av ED N9 — ...
 SRTFD E15 — ...
Tramway Cl PGE/AN SE20 — ...
Tramway Pth MTCM CR4 — ...
Tranby Ms HOM E9 — ...
Tranley Ms HAMP NW3 — ...
Tranmere Rd ED N9 — ...
 WAND/EARL SW18 — ...
 WHTN TW2 — ...
Tranquil Dl BRKHM/BTCW RH3 — ...
Tranquil Pas BKHTH/KID SE3 — ...
Tranquil Ri ERITH DA8 — ...
Tranquil V BKHTH/KID SE3 — 52 B14
Transept St CAMTN NW1 — ...
Transmere Cl STMC/STPC BR5 — ...
Transmere Rd STMC/STPC BR5 — ...
Transom Cl BERM/RHTH SE16 — ...
Transom Sq POP/IOD E14 — ...
Tranton Rd BERM/RHTH SE16 — ...
Trap's Hl LOU IG10 — ...
Traps La NWMAL KT3 — ...
Travellers Site CHING E4 — ...

Column 3

Travellers Wy HEST TW5 — 46 E14
Travers Cl WALTH E17 — ...
Travers Rd HOLWY N7 — 38 E8
Treacy Cl BUSH WD23 — ...
Treadgold St NTGHL W11 — ...
Treadway St BETH E2 — ...
Treadwell Rd EPSOM KT18 — 84 F5
Treaty St IS N1 — 4 F2
Trebeck St MYFR/PICC W1J — ...
Treborough Dr CTHM CR3 — ...
Treby St BOW E3 — 51 R2
Trecastle Wy HOLWY N7 — 38 B9
Tredegar Rd BOW E3 — 39 R14
 FBAR/BDGN N11 — ...
 RDART DA2 — ...
Tredegar Sq BOW E3 — ...
Tredennick Rd HACK E8 — ...
Tredown Rd SYD SE26 — 63 N10
Tredwell Cl BRXS/STRHM SW2 — ...
 HAYES BR2 — ...
Tredwell Rd WNWD SE27 — ...
Treebourne Rd BH/WHM TN16 — ...
Tree Cl ABR/ST RM4 — ...
 RCHPK/HAM TW10 — 59 T6
Treen Av BARN SW13 — ...
Tree Rd CAN/RD E16 — ...
Treeside Cl WDR/YW UB7 — 45 P9
Tree Top Ms DAGE RM10 — 42 D11
Treetops GDST RH9 — ...
Treetops Cl ABYW SE2 — 53 U10
Tree View Cl NRWD SE19 — ...
Treetops GDST RH9 — ...
Treewall Gdns BMLY BR1 — ...
Trefgarne Rd DAGE RM10 — 42 A7
Trefoil Rd WAND/EARL SW18 — ...
Trefusis Wk WAT WD17 — 11 U3
Tregaron Av CEND/HSY/T N8 — ...
Tregarthen Pl LHD/OX KT22 — ...
Tregarvon Rd BTSEA SW11 — ...
Tregenna Av RYLN/HDSTN HA2 — 34 J3
Tregenna Cl STHGT/OAK N14 — ...
Tregony Rd ORP BR6 — 77 P9
Trego Rd HOM E9 — ...
Tregothnan Rd BRXN/ST SW9 — ...
Tregunter Rd WBPTN SW10 — ...
Trehearn Rd BARK/HLT IG6 — ...
Treherne Ct BRXS/STRHM SW2 — ...
Trehern Rd MORT/ESHN SW14 — 60 D1
Trelawn Cl CHERT KT16 — ...
Trelawney Av DTCH/LGLY SL3 — ...
Trelawney Est HOM E9 — ...
Trelawney Rd BARK/HLT IG6 — 29 M12
Trelawn Rd BRXS/STRHM SW2 — ...
Trellis Sq BOW E3 — ...
Treloar Gdns NRWD SE19 — 62 H11
Tremaine Cl BROCKY SE4 — ...
Tremaine Rd PGE/AN SE20 — 63 M12
Trematon Pl TEDD TW11 — ...
Tremlett Gv ARCH N19 — 38 A8
Tremlett Ms ARCH N19 — ...
Trenance Gdns GDMY/SEVK IG3 — ...
Trenchard Av RSLP HA4 — ...
Trenchard Cl CDALE/KGS NW9 — ...
 STHGT/OAK N14 — ...
Trenchard St GNWCH SE10 — ...
Trenches La DTCH/LGLY SL3 — ...
Trenholme Cl PGE/AN SE20 — 63 M12
Trenholme Ter PGE/AN SE20 — ...
Trenmar Gdns WLSDN NW10 — ...
Trent Av EA W5 — 47 S8
Trent Cl RAD WD7 — 12 J6
Trent Ct WAN E11 — ...
Trentham Gdns STHGT/OAK N14 — 80 E11
Trentham Dr STMC/STPC BR5 — ...
Trentham Rd BRXN/ST SW9 — ...
Trentham St WAND/EARL SW18 — ...
Trent Pk EBAR EN4 — ...
Trent Rd BKHH IG9 — ...
 BRXS/STRHM SW2 — ...
 DTCH/LGLY SL3 — ...
Trent Wy WPK KT4 — 72 J8
 YEAD UB4 — ...
Trentwood Side ENC/FH EN2 — ...
Treport St WAND/EARL SW18 — ...
Tresco Cl BMLY BR1 — 64 A15
Trescoe Gdns CRW RM5 — ...
 RYLN/HDSTN HA2 — ...
Tresco Gdns GDMY/SEVK IG3 — ...
Tresco Rd PECK SE15 — 63 N2
Tresham Crs STJWD NW8 — ...
Tresham Rd BARK IG11 — ...
Tresillian Av WCHMH N21 — ...
Tressell Cl IS N1 — ...
Tressillian Crs BROCKY SE4 — ...
Tressillian Rd BROCKY SE4 — ...
Trestis Cl YEAD UB4 — ...
Treswell Rd DAGW RM9 — ...
Tretawn Gdns MLHL NW7 — ...
Tretawn Pk MLHL NW7 — ...
Trevanion Rd WKENS W14 — ...
Treve Av HRW HA1 — ...
Trevelyan Av GSTN WD25 — 11 V13
Trevelyan Crs KTN/HRWW/WS HA3 — ...
Trevelyan Gdns WLSDN NW10 — ...
Trevelyan Rd SRTFD E15 — ...
 TOOT SW17 — ...
Treveris St STHWK SE1 — ...
Treverton St NKENS W10 — ...
Treville St PUT/ROE SW15 — ...
Treviso Rd FSTH SE23 — ...
Trevithick Cl EBED/NFELT TW14 — ...
Trevithick Dr DART DA1 — ...
Trevithick St DEPT SE8 — ...
Trevone Gdns PIN HA5 — ...
Trevor Cl EBAR EN4 — ...
 HAYES BR2 — ...
 ISLW TW7 — ...
 KTN/HRWW/WS HA3 — ...
 NTHLT UB5 — ...
Trevor Crs RSLP HA4 — ...
Trevor Gdns EDGW HA8 — ...
 NTHLT UB5 — ...
 RSLP HA4 — ...
Trevor Pl SKENS SW7 — 7 P4
Trevor Rd EDGW HA8 — ...
 HYS/HAR UB3 — ...
 WFD IG8 — ...
 WIM/MER SW19 — ...
Trevor Sq SKENS SW7 — 7 P4
Trevor St SKENS SW7 — 7 P4
Trevose Av BR/WBF KT14 — ...
Trevose Rd WALTH E17 — ...
Trewenna Dr CHSGTN KT9 — ...
Trewince Rd RYNPK SW20 — ...
Trewint St WAND/EARL SW18 — ...
Trewsbury Rd SYD SE26 — ...
Triandra Wy YEAD UB4 — ...
Triangle Pas EBAR EN4 — ...
Triangle Pl CLAP SW4 — ...
Triangle Rd HACK E8 — ...
Trigg's Cl WOKS/MYFD GU22 — ...
Trigg's La WOKN/KNAP GU21 — ...
Trigon Rd VX/NE SW8 — ...
Trilby Rd FSTH SE23 — ...
Trimmer Wk BTFD TW8 — ...
Trim St NWCR SE14 — ...
Trinder Gdns ARCH N19 — ...
Trinder Rd ARCH N19 — ...
 EBAR EN4 — ...
Trindles Rd REDH RH1 — 94 D13
Tring Av EA W5 — ...
 STHL UB1 — ...
 WBLY HA9 — ...
Tring Cl GNTH/NBYPK IG2 — ...
Tringham Cl CHERT KT16 — ...
Trinidad Gdns DAGE RM10 — ...
Trinidad St POP/IOD E14 — ...
Trinity Av EN EN1 — ...
 EFNCH N2 — ...
Trinity Buoy Wharf POP/IOD E14 — ...
Trinity Church Rd BARN SW13 — ...
Trinity Church Sq STHWK SE1 — ...
Trinity Cl CLAP SW4 — ...
 HAYES BR2 — ...
 HTHAIR TW6 — ...
 LEW SE13 — ...
 NTHWD HA6 — ...
 SAND/SEL CR2 — ...
 STMC/STPC BR5 — ...
 WAN E11 — ...
Trinity Cots RCH/KEW TW9 — ...
Trinity Crs STHWK SE1 — ...
Trinity Gdns BRXN/ST SW9 — 62 D2
Trinity Gn WCHPL E1 — ...

Column 4

CAN/RD E16 — 52 B3
Trinity La CAT SE6 — ...
Trinity Ms PGE/AN SE20 — ...
Trinity Pde HSLW TW3 — ...
Trinity Pl BXLYHS DA6 — ...
 TWRH EC3N — ...
Trinity Rd BARK/HLT IG6 — 29 L11
 RCH/KEW TW9 — ...
 SEVS/STOTM N15 — ...
 WAND/EARL SW18 — ...
 WDGN N22 — ...
 WIM/MER SW19 — ...
Trinity Sq TWRH EC3N — 5 T14
Trinity St CAN/RD E16 — 52 B3
 ENC/FH EN2 — ...
 STHWK SE1 — ...
Trio Pl STHWK SE1 — 9 Q4
Tristan Ldg BUSH WD23 — 23 N4
Tristan Cl WALTH E17 — ...
Triton Sq CAMTN NW1 — 4 A8
Tritton Av CROY/NA CR0 — ...
Tritton Rd DUL SE21 — 62 K8
Trittons KWD/TDW/WH KT20 — 84 J11
Triumph Cl HYS/HAR UB3 — ...
Triumph Rd EHAM E6 — ...
Trivett Cl RDART DA2 — ...
Trojan Wy CROY/NA CR0 — 74 D7
Trolling Down Hi RDART DA2 — ...
Troon Cl ABR/ST RM4 — ...
 BERM/RHTH SE16 — ...
 THMD SE28 — ...
Troon St WCHPL E1 — 51 S4
Trosley Av GPK RM2 — ...
Trosley Rd BELV DA17 — ...
Trossachs Rd EDUL SE22 — ...
Trothy Rd STHWK SE1 — ...
Trotsworth Av VW GU25 — ...
Trotters Bottom BAR EN5 — 13 S11
Trottsworth Av VW GU25 — ...
Trotts La BH/WHM TN16 — ...
Trotwood CHIG IG7 — ...
Troughton Rd CHARL SE7 — 52 C10
Troutbeck Rd NWCR SE14 — ...
 STMC/STPC BR5 — ...
Trout La WDR/YW UB7 — ...
Trout Ri RKW/CH/CXG WD3 — ...
Trout Rd WDR/YW UB7 — 45 N5
Troutstream Wy RKW/CH/CXG WD3 — ...
Trouville Rd CLAP SW4 — ...
Trowbridge Rd HARH RM3 — ...
 HOM E9 — ...
Trowers Wy REDH RH1 — 93 V7
Trowlock Av TEDD TW11 — ...
Trowlock Wy TEDD TW11 — 59 R11
Troy Ct KENS W8 — ...
Troy Rd NRWD SE19 — 62 H11
Troy Town PECK SE15 — ...
Trubshaw Rd NWDGN UB2 — ...
Trueman Cl EDGW HA8 — ...
Truesdale Dr DEN/HRF UB9 — ...
Truesdale Rd EHAM E6 — 52 K4
Truman's Rd STNW/STAM N16 — ...
Trumpers Wy HNWL W7 — ...
Trumpington Rd FSTGT E7 — ...
Trump St CITYW EC2V — ...
Trumps Green Cl VW GU25 — 68 A5
Trumps Green Rd VW GU25 — ...
Trumpsgreen Rd VW GU25 — ...
Trumps Mill La VW GU25 — ...
Trundlers Wy BUSH WD23 — 23 N6
Trundle St STHWK SE1 — 9 N3
Trundleys Rd DEPT SE8 — ...
Trundleys Ter DEPT SE8 — ...
Truro Gdns IL IG1 — ...
Truro Rd GNTH/NBYPK IG2 — ...
 WALTH E17 — ...
 WDGN N22 — ...
Truro St KTTN NW5 — 37 U11
Truro Wy YEAD UB4 — ...
Truslove Rd WNWD SE27 — ...
Trussley Rd HMSMTH W6 — ...
Trustees Wy DEN/HRF UB9 — ...
Trystings Cl ESH/CLAY KT10 — ...
Tuam Rd WOOL/PLUM SE18 — ...
Tubbenden Cl ORP BR6 — 77 M7
Tubbenden Dr ORP BR6 — 77 M8
Tubbenden La ORP BR6 — 77 M7
Tubbenden La South ORP BR6 — ...
Tubbs Rd WLSDN NW10 — ...
Tubs Hill Pde SEV TN13 — ...
Tucker Rd CHERT KT16 — ...
Tucker St WATW WD18 — 22 B3
Tuckey Gv RPLY/SEND GU23 — ...
Tudor Av HPTN TW12 — ...
 ROM RM1 — ...
 WPK KT4 — ...
Tudor Cl ASHF TW15 — ...
 BNSTD SM7 — ...
 BRXS/STRHM SW2 — ...
 CDALE/KGS NW9 — ...
 CHEAM SM3 — ...
 CHIG IG7 — ...
 CHSGTN KT9 — ...
 CHST BR7 — ...
 COB KT11 — ...
 COUL/CHIP CR5 — ...
 DART DA1 — ...
 GLDGN NW11 — ...
 HPTN TW12 — ...
 PIN HA5 — ...
 SAND/SEL CR2 — ...
 WLGTN SM6 — ...
 WOKS/MYFD GU22 — ...
Tudor Ct North WBLY HA9 — ...
Tudor Ct South WBLY HA9 — ...
Tudor Crs BARK/HLT IG6 — 29 L7
 ENC/FH EN2 — ...
Tudor Dr GPK RM2 — ...
 KUTN/CMB KT2 — ...
 MRDN SM4 — ...
 WATN WD24 — ...
 WOT/HER KT12 — ...
Tudor Est WLSDN NW10 — ...
Tudor Gdns ACT W3 — ...
 BARN SW13 — ...
 CDALE/KGS NW9 — ...
 KTN/HRWW/WS HA3 — ...
 ROM RM1 — ...
 TWK TW1 — ...
 WWKM BR4 — ...
Tudor La WDSR SL4 — ...
Tudor Manor Gdns GSTN WD25 — ...
Tudor Pde CHDH RM6 — ...
 ELTH/MOT SE9 — ...
Tudor Pl MTCM CR4 — ...
 NRWD SE19 — ...
 SOHO/SHAV W1D — ...
Tudor Rd ASHF TW15 — ...
 BAR EN5 — ...
 BECK BR3 — ...
 ED N9 — ...
 HAMP NW3 — ...
 HPTN TW12 — ...
 HRW HA1 — ...
 HYS/HAR UB3 — ...
 KUTN/CMB KT2 — ...
 NWDGN UB2 — ...
 PGE/AN SE20 — ...
 PIN HA5 — ...
Tudors Cl KTN/HRWW/WS HA3 — ...
The Tudors BRKHM/BTCW RH3 — ...
Tudor St EMB EC4Y — ...
Tudor Wk BXLY DA5 — ...
 WATN WD24 — ...
 WEY KT13 — ...
Tudor Wy ACT W3 — ...
 HGDN/ICK UB10 — ...
 RKW/CH/CXG WD3 — ...
 STHGT/OAK N14 — ...
 WAB EN9 — ...
 WDSR SL4 — ...
Tudway Rd BKHTH/KID SE3 — ...
Tufnell Park Rd HOLWY N7 — ...
Tufter Rd CHIG IG7 — ...
Tufton Gdns E/WMO/HCT KT8 — ...
Tufton Rd CHING E4 — ...
Tufton St WEST SW1P — ...
Tugboat St THMD SE28 — 53 N7

Column 5

Tugela Rd CROY/NA CR0 — 74 H4
Tugela St CAT SE6 — 63 R7
Tugmutton Cl ORP BR6 — 76 K9
Tulip Cl CROY/NA CR0 — ...
 EHAM E6 — 52 G5
 HPTN TW12 — ...
 NWDGN UB2 — ...
Tulip Gdns CHING E4 — ...
 IL IG1 — ...
Tulse Cl BECK BR3 — ...
Tulse Hill BRXS/STRHM SW2 — ...
Tulsemere Rd WNWD SE27 — 62 K7
Tulyar Cl KWD/TDW/WH KT20 — 84 H9
Tumber St EPSOM KT18 — 92 C15
Tumbler Rd HARLW CM18 — ...
Tumbling Bay WOT/HER KT12 — 70 C4
Tummons Gdns SNWD SE25 — ...
Tuncombe Rd UED N18 — 26 J8
Tunis Rd SHB W12 — ...
Tunley Gn POP/IOD E14 — ...
Tunley Rd TOOT SW17 — ...
 WLSDN NW10 — ...
Tunmarsh La PLSTW E13 — ...
Tunmers End CFSP/GDCR SL9 — ...
Tunnan Leys EHAM E6 — 52 K5
Tunnel Av GNWCH SE10 — ...
Tunnel Gdns FBAR/BDGN N11 — ...
Tunnel Link Rd HTHAIR TW6 — ...
Tunnel Rd East WDR/YW UB7 — 45 T12
Tunnel Rd West WDR/YW UB7 — ...
Tunnel Wood Rd WAT WD17 — ...
Tunstall Av BARK/HLT IG6 — ...
Tunstall Cl ORP BR6 — 77 N9
Tunstall Rd BRXN/ST SW9 — ...
 CROY/NA CR0 — ...
Tunstock Wy BELV DA17 — ...
Tunworth Cl CDALE/KGS NW9 — ...
Tunworth Crs PUT/ROE SW15 — 60 F4
Tupelo Rd LEY E10 — ...
Tuppy St THMD SE28 — ...
Tupwood La CTHM CR3 — ...
Tupwood Scrubs Rd CTHM CR3 — 95 L2
Turenne Cl WAND/EARL SW18 — 61 Q2
Turin Rd ED N9 — ...
Turin St BETH E2 — ...
Turkey Oak La NRWD SE19 — ...
Turkey St EN EN1 — 16 A10
Turks Cl UX/CGN UB8 — ...
Turks Rw CHEL SW3 — 7 R8
Turle Rd FSBYPK N4 — ...
Turlewray Cl FSBYPK N4 — 38 B6
Turley Cl SRTFD E15 — ...
Turnagain La FLST/FETLN EC4A — 5 L11
Turnant Rd TOTM N17 — ...
Turnberry Ct WATN WD24 — ...
Turnberry Dr LCOL/BKTW AL2 — ...
Turnberry Wy ORP BR6 — ...
Turnbull Cl RDART DA2 — ...
Turnbury Cl THMD SE28 — ...
Turnchapel Ms CLAP SW4 — ...
Turner Av MTCM CR4 — ...
 SEVS/STOTM N16 — ...
 WHTN TW2 — ...
Turner Cl BRXN/ST SW9 — ...
 GLDGN NW11 — ...
 WBLY HA0 — ...
Turner Dr GLDGN NW11 — ...
Turner Ms BELMT SM2 — 73 P12
Turner Rd BUSH WD23 — ...
 EDGW HA8 — ...
 NWMAL KT3 — ...
Turners Cl STA TW18 — 57 M10
Turners Meadow Wy BECK BR3 — ...
Turners Rd POP/IOD E14 — ...
Turner St CAN/RD E16 — ...
 WCHPL E1 — ...
Turners Wy CROY/NA CR0 — 74 E7
Turners Wood GLDGN NW11 — ...
Turneville Rd WKENS W14 — ...
Turney Rd DUL SE21 — ...
Turnford Rd CHES/WCR EN8 — ...
Turnham Green Ter CHSWK W4 — 48 D9
Turnham Rd BROCKY SE4 — ...
Turnmill St CLKNW EC1R — ...
Turnoak Av WOKS/MYFD GU22 — ...
Turnoak La WOKS/MYFD GU22 — ...
Turnpike Cl DEPT SE8 — ...
Turnpike Dr ORP BR6 — ...
Turnpike La CEND/HSY/T N8 — ...
 SUT SM1 — ...
 UX/CGN UB8 — ...
Turnpike Link CROY/NA CR0 — ...
Turnpike Wy ISLW TW7 — ...
Turnstone Cl CDALE/KGS NW9 — ...
 PLSTW E13 — ...
 SAND/SEL CR2 — ...
Turnstones GSTN WD25 — ...
Turp Av GPK RM2 — ...
Turpentine La PIM SW1V — ...
Turpin Av CRW RM5 — ...
Turpington Cl HAYES BR2 — ...
Turpington La HAYES BR2 — ...
Turpin La ERITH DA8 — ...
Turpin Rd EBED/NFELT TW14 — ...
Turpin's La WFD IG8 — ...
Turpin Wy WLGTN SM6 — ...
Turquand St WALW SE17 — ...
Turret Gv CLAP SW4 — ...
Turton Rd ALP/SUD HA0 — ...
Turville St BETH E2 — ...
Tuscan Rd WOOL/PLUM SE18 — ...
Tuskar St GNWCH SE10 — ...
Tussauds Cl RKW/CH/CXG WD3 — ...
Tutsham Wy SCUP DA14 — ...
Tuttlebee La BKHH IG9 — ...
Tweeddale Gv HGDN/ICK UB10 — ...
Tweeddale Rd CAR SM5 — ...
Tweedmouth Rd PLSTW E13 — ...
Tweed Wy ROM RM1 — ...
Tweedy Cl EN EN1 — ...
Tweedy Rd BMLY BR1 — ...
Twelveacre Crs EN EN1 — ...
Twelve Av KWD/TDW/WH KT20 — ...
Twelvetrees Crs BOW E3 — ...
Twentyman Cl WFD IG8 — ...
Twickenham Br TWK TW1 — ...
Twickenham Cl CROY/NA CR0 — ...
Twickenham Gdns GFD/PVL UB6 — ...
 KTN/HRWW/WS HA3 — ...
Twickenham Rd FELT TW13 — ...
 ISLW TW7 — ...
 RCH/KEW TW9 — ...
 WAN E11 — ...
Twig Folly Cl BETH E2 — ...
Twilley St WAND/EARL SW18 — ...
Twigg Cl ERITH DA8 — ...
Twine Cl BARK IG11 — ...
Twine Ct WCHPL E1 — ...
Twineham Gn NFNCH/WDSPK N12 — ...
Twining Av WHTN TW2 — ...
Twinn Rd MLHL NW7 — ...
Twisden Rd KTTN NW5 — ...
Twitton La RSEV TN14 — ...
Twitton Mdw RSEV TN14 — ...
Two Acres EGRIN RH19 — ...
Twybridge Wy WLSDN NW10 — ...
Twyford Abbey Rd WLSDN NW10 — ...
Twyford Av ACT W3 — ...
 EFNCH N2 — ...
Twyford Crs ACT W3 — ...
Twyford Pl LINN WC2A — ...
Twyford Rd CAR SM5 — ...
 IL IG1 — ...
 RYLN/HDSTN HA2 — ...
Twyford St IS N1 — ...
The Tudors BRKHM/BTCW RH3 — ...
Tyas Rd CAN/RD E16 — ...
Tybenham Rd WIM/MER SW19 — ...
Tyberry Rd PEND EN3 — ...
Tyburn La HRW HA1 — ...
Tyburn Wy MBLAR W1H — ...
Tycehurst Hl LOU IG10 — ...
Tycombe Rd TOTM N17 — ...
Tydcombe Rd WARL CR6 — ...
Tye La ORP BR6 — ...
Tyers Est STHWK SE1 — ...
Tyers Gate STHWK SE1 — ...
Tyers St LBTH SE11 — ...
Tyers Ter LBTH SE11 — ...
Tyeshan Av ABYW SE2 — ...
Tyfield Cl CHES/WCR EN8 — ...
Tylecroft Rd STRHM/NOR SW16 — ...
Tylehurst Gdns IL IG1 — ...
Tyler Cl BETH E2 — ...
 CAR SM5 — ...
 ERITH DA8 — ...
Tyler Gdns ADL/WDHM KT15 — 69 M8

Column 6

Tyler Gv GDST RH9 — 95 M6
 KGLGY WD4 — 10 F3
Tylers Cl KGLGY WD4 — 10 J7
Tylersfield ABLGY WD5 — 11 M5
Tylers Ga KTN/HRWW/WS HA3 — 35 U5
Tylers Green Rd SWLY BR8 — 78 C5
Tyler St GNWCH SE10 — 52 A10
Tyler Wy DTCH/LGLY SL3 — 44 V10
Tylney Av NRWD SE19 — 62 K10
Tylney Rd BMLY BR1 — 64 E15
 FSTGT E7 — 40 E9
Tyndale Ct POP/IOD E14 — 51 S11
Tyndale La IS N1 — 38 F12
Tyndale Ter IS N1 — 38 F12
Tyndall Rd LEY E10 — 39 U7
 WELL DA16 — 53 Q14
Tyne Cl UPMR RM14 — 43 R4
Tynedale LCOL/BKTW AL2 — 11 N1
Tynedale Rd BRKHM/BTCW RH3 — 92 G14
Tyne Gdns SOCK/AV RM15 — 55 S10
Tyneham Rd BTSEA SW11 — 61 U1
Tynemouth Cl EHAM E6 — 52 A4
Tynemouth Dr EN EN1 — 16 A12
Tynemouth Rd MTCM CR4 — 61 U12
 SEVS/STOTM N15 — 38 K2
 WOOL/PLUM SE18 — 53 N10
Tyne St WCHPL E1 — 5 V11
Tyne St BETH E2 — 5 S3
Tyrawley Rd FUL/PGN SW6 — 49 P15
Tyre La CDALE/KGS NW9 — 36 C1
Tyrell Cl HRW HA1 — 35 N9
Tyrells Cl UPMR RM14 — 43 M4
Tyrone Rd EHAM E6 — 40 J14
Tyron Wy SCUP DA14 — 65 N9
Tyrrell Av WELL DA16 — 65 Q5
Tyrrell Rd EDUL SE22 — 62 K2
Tyrrell Sq MTCM CR4 — 61 S12
Tyrrell Wy CDALE/KGS NW9 — 24 E15
Tyrwhitt Rd BROCKY SE4 — 63 T1
Tysea Cl HARLW CM18 — 16 F6
Tysea Hill ABR/ST RM4 — 30 G2
Tyson Gdns FSTH SE23 — 63 N5
Tyson Rd FSTH SE23 — 63 N5
Tyssen Rd STNW/STAM N16 — 38 V8
Tyssen St HACK E8 — 38 V8
 IS N1 — 5 T3
Tytherton Rd ARCH N19 — 38 B8

Column 7

U

Uamvar St POP/IOD E14 — 51 U13
Uckfield Gv MTCM CR4 — 61 U13
Uckfield Rd PEND EN3 — 16 D11
Udall Gdns CRW RM5 — 30 D11
Udney Park Rd TEDD TW11 — 59 Q11
Uffington Rd WLSDN NW10 — 36 G13
 WNWD SE27 — 62 G10
Ufford Cl KTN/HRWW/WS HA3 — 22 K12
Ufford Rd KTN/HRWW/WS HA3 — 22 K12
Ufford St STHWK SE1 — 8 K2
Ufton Gv IS N1 — 38 U12
Ufton Rd IS N1 — 38 U12
Uhura Sq STNW/STAM N16 — 38 J8
Ullathorne Rd STRHM/NOR SW16 — 62 C9
Ulleswater Rd STHGT/OAK N14 — 26 C9
Ulleswater Rd WCHMH N21 — 26 E5
Ullin St POP/IOD E14 — 51 U3
Ullswater Cl BMLY BR1 — 64 A13
 PUT/ROE SW15 — 60 A14
 YEAD UB4 — 34 A14
Ullswater Crs COUL/CHIP CR5 — 86 A4
 PUT/ROE SW15 — 60 A14
Ullswater Rd BARN SW13 — 48 G12
 WNWD SE27 — 62 H7
Ulster Gdns PLMGR N13 — 26 H7
Ulster Ter CAMTN NW1 — 4 A7
Ulundi Rd BKHTH/KID SE3 — 52 A11
Ulva Rd PUT/ROE SW15 — 60 K2
Ulverscroft Rd EDUL SE22 — 63 L3
Ulverstone Rd WNWD SE27 — 62 H7
Ulwin Av BF/WBF KT14 — 81 Q4
Ulysses Rd KIL/WHAMP NW6 — 37 N9
Umberston St WCHPL E1 — 51 L4
Umberston St PUT/ROE SW15 — 60 A14
Umfreville Rd FSBYPK N4 — 38 E6
Undercliff Rd LEW SE13 — 63 T1
Underhill BAR EN5 — 25 M3
Underhill Park Rd REIG RH2 — 93 S7
Underhill Rd EDUL SE22 — 63 M3
Underhill St CAMTN NW1 — 3 V1
Underne Av STHGT/OAK N14 — 25 V7
Undershaft HDTCH EC3A — 5 S12
Undershaw Rd BMLY BR1 — 64 A11
Underwood CROY/NA CR0 — 75 T14
Underwood Rd CHING E4 — 27 U11
 HARH RM3 — 31 L8
 WCHPL E1 — 51 L2
Underwood Rw IS N1 — 5 Q5
The Underwood ELTH/MOT SE9 — 64 H7
Underwood St IS N1 — 5 Q5
Undine Rd POP/IOD E14 — 51 T9
Undine St TOOT SW17 — 61 T11
Uneeda Dr GFD/PVL UB6 — 35 N14
Union Cl WAN E11 — 39 U6
Union Cottages SRTFD E15 — 40 A12
Union Ct CLAP SW4 — 62 A1
Union Dr WCHPL E1 — 51 S1
Union Gv VX/NE SW8 — 49 V14
Union Rd ALP/SUD HA0 — 35 T13
 BMLY BR1 — 76 E3
 CLAP SW4 — 49 V14
 CROY/NA CR0 — 74 G5
 NTHLT UB5 — 34 E14
 UED N18 — 26 K9
Union Rd North CHSWK W4 — 48 C7
Union Sq IS N1 — 5 P1
Union St BAR EN5 — 25 L1
 KUT/HW KT1 — 59 S14
 SRTFD E15 — 39 V13
 STHWK SE1 — 9 M1
Union Wk BETH E2 — 5 T5
United Av PLSTW E13 — 40 A14
Unity Cl CROY/NA CR0 — 75 S14
 WLSDN NW10 — 36 H11
Unity Ms CAMTN NW1 — 4 C4
Unity Rd PEND EN3 — 16 E10
Unity Ter RYLN/HDSTN HA2 — 34 G7
Unity Wy WOOL/PLUM SE18 — 52 F8
University Cl BUSH WD23 — 11 S15
 MLHL NW7 — 24 C12
University Gdns BXLY DA5 — 65 V6
University Rd WIM/MER SW19 — 61 S11
University St FITZ W1T — 4 B9
Unwin Av EBED/NFELT TW14 — 57 R1
Unwin Cl PECK SE15 — 50 H12
Unwin Rd ISLW TW7 — 47 N14
 SKENS SW7 — 6 K4
Upbrook Ms BAY/PAD W2 — 3 N12
Upcerne Rd WBPTN SW10 — 6 K12
Updale Cl POTB/CUF EN6 — 14 C5
Updale Rd SCUP DA14 — 65 N9
Upfield CROY/NA CR0 — 75 N8
Upfield Rd HNWL W7 — 47 P3
Upgrove Manor Wy BRXS/STRHM SW2 — 62 E4
Uphall Rd IL IG1 — 40 K10
Upham Park Rd CHSWK W4 — 48 D8
Uphill Dr CDALE/KGS NW9 — 36 C2
 MLHL NW7 — 24 C11
Uphill Gv MLHL NW7 — 24 C11
Uphill Rd MLHL NW7 — 24 C10
Upland Court Rd HARH RM3 — 31 M14
Upland Ms EDUL SE22 — 63 L3
Upland Rd BELMT SM2 — 73 P12
 BXLYHS DA6 — 53 V15
 CTHM CR3 — 87 L14
 EDUL SE22 — 63 L3
 EPP CM16 — 17 T6
 PLSTW E13 — 52 B2
 SAND/SEL CR2 — 74 H11
 WALTH E17 — 39 V2
Uplands BECK BR3 — 75 S1
 RKW/CH/CXG WD3 — 20 K5
Uplands Av WALTH E17 — 27 P14
Uplands Cl MORT/ESHN SW14 — 60 A4
 SEV TN13 — 90 E14
Uplands End WFD IG8 — 28 E14
Uplands Park Rd ENC/FH EN2 — 15 R13
Uplands Rd CEND/HSY/T N8 — 38 D3
 CHDH RM6 — 41 U1
 EBAR EN4 — 25 U6
 KTN/HRWW/WS HA3 — 34 K3
 ORP BR6 — 77 T6
 WARL CR6 — 87 M13
 WFD IG8 — 28 E14
The Uplands CFSP/GDCR SL9 — 20 C10
 LCOL/BKTW AL2 — 11 N3
 LOU IG10 — 28 K1
 RSLP HA4 — 34 B5
Uplands Wy SEV TN13 — 90 E14
 WCHMH N21 — 16 A15
Upney La BARK IG11 — 41 N12
Upnor Wy WALW SE17 — 9 T7
Uppark Dr GNTH/NBYPK IG2 — 41 L5
Upper Abbey Rd BELV DA17 — 53 V9
Upper Addison Gdns WKENS W14 — 6 C3
Upper Austin Lodge Rd EYN DA4 — 79 R8
Upper Bardsey Wk IS N1 — 38 G11
Upper Bank St POP/IOD E14 — 51 T6
Upper Bank St POP/IOD E14 — ...
Upper Belgrave St KTBR SW1X — 7 T5
Upper Berkeley St MBLAR W1H — 3 Q11

Column 8

Upper Beulah Hl NRWD SE19 — 62 J13
Upper Brentwood Rd GPK RM2 — 42 J2
Upper Bridge Rd REDH RH1 — 93 T10
Upper Brighton Rd SURB KT6 — 71 T5
Upper Brockley Rd BROCKY SE4 — 51 R14
Upper Brook St MYFR/PKLN W1K — 3 S13
Upper Butts BTFD TW8 — 47 S12
Upper Caldy Wk IS N1 — 38 G11
Upper Camelford Wk NTGHL W11 — 2 A12
Upper Cavendish Av FNCH N3 — 37 L1
Upper Cheyne Rw CHEL SW3 — 7 N12
Upper Clapton Rd CLPT E5 — 39 M7
Upper Clarendon Wk NTGHL W11 — 2 A12
Upper Court Rd CTHM CR3 — 87 S14
 HOR/WEW KT19 — 84 C1
Upper Dengie Wk IS N1 — 38 G11
Upper Dr BH/WHM TN16 — 88 E8
Upper Dunnymans BNSTD SM7 — 85 M4
Upper Elmers End Rd BECK BR3 — 75 Q5
Upper Fairfield Rd LHD/OX KT22 — 83 R10
Upper Gn East MTCM CR4 — 61 T2
Upper Gn West MTCM CR4 — 61 T2
Upper Grosvenor St MYFR/PKLN W1K — 3 S14
Upper Grotto Rd TWK TW1 — 59 P7
Upper Gnd STHWK SE1 — 4 J15
Upper Gv SNWD SE25 — 74 K1
Upper Grove Rd BELV DA17 — 53 V11
Upper Gulland Wk IS N1 — 38 G11
Upper Halliford Rd SHPTN TW17 — 58 A14
Upper Ham Rd RCHPK/HAM TW10 — 59 T9
Upper Handa Wk IS N1 — 38 H11
Upper Harestone CTHM CR3 — 95 L8
Upper Hawkwell Wk IS N1 — 38 G12
Upper High St EPSOM KT18 — 84 E5
Upper Hitch OXHEY WD19 — 22 G6
Upper Holly Hill Rd BELV DA17 — 54 A12
Upper John St SOHO/SHAV W1F — 4 B13
Upper Lismore Wk IS N1 — 38 G11
Upper Lodge Wy COUL/CHIP CR5 — 86 E9
Upper Marsh STHWK SE1 — 8 G5
Upper Montagu St MBLAR W1H — 3 R10
Upper Mulgrave Rd BELMT SM2 — 73 L12
Upper North St POP/IOD E14 — 51 T4
Upper Paddock Rd OXHEY WD19 — 22 F5
Upper Park Rd BELV DA17 — 54 B9
 BMLY BR1 — 64 E15
 FBAR/BDGN N11 — 25 V9
 HAMP NW3 — 37 T11
 KUTN/CMB KT2 — 60 A10
Upper Phillimore Gdns KENS W8 — 6 D4
Upper Pillory Down CAR SM5 — 86 E5
Upper Pines BNSTD SM7 — 85 T7
Upper Ramsey Wk IS N1 — 38 H11
Upper Rawreth Wk IS N1 — 38 G11
Upper Richmond Rd PUT/ROE SW15 — 60 K2
Upper Richmond Rd West RCHPK/HAM TW10 — 60 A2
Upper Rd DEN/HRF UB9 — 32 H5
 PLSTW E13 — 52 B1
 WLGTN SM6 — 74 B10
Upper Ryle BRW CM14 — 31 V5
Upper St Martin's La LSQ/SEVD WC2H — 4 E13
Upper Sawleywood BNSTD SM7 — 85 M4
Upper Selsdon Rd SAND/SEL CR2 — 74 K13
Upper Sheppey Wk IS N1 — 38 G11
Upper Sheridan Rd BELV DA17 — 54 A9
Upper Spring La BGR/WK TN15 — 91 V12
Upper Sq ISLW TW7 — 59 Q2
Upper Station Rd RAD WD7 — 12 F9
Upper St IS N1 — 4 J3
Upper Sunbury Rd HPTN TW12 — 58 H13
Upper Sutton La HEST TW5 — 46 H12
Upper Swaines EPP CM16 — 18 C5
Upper Tachbrook St PIM SW1V — 8 A7
Upper Tail OXHEY WD19 — 22 G6
Upper Talbot Wk NTGHL W11 — 2 A12
Upper Teddington Rd KUT/HW KT1 — 59 S15
Upper Ter HAMP NW3 — 37 R8
Upper Thames St BLKFR EC4V — 5 N13
Upper Tollington Pk FSBYPK N4 — 38 E6
Upperton Rd SCUP DA14 — 65 Q10
Upperton Rd East PLSTW E13 — 52 D1
Upperton Rd West PLSTW E13 — 52 E2
Upper Tooting Pk TOOT SW17 — 61 T7
Upper Tooting Rd TOOT SW17 — 61 T9
Upper Town Rd GFD/PVL UB6 — 35 L14
Upper Tulse Hl BRXS/STRHM SW2 — 62 E4
Upper Vernon Rd SUT SM1 — 73 R10
Upper Walthamstow Rd WALTH E17 — 39 V2
Upper West St REIG RH2 — 93 M10
Upper Wickham La WELL DA16 — 53 R11
Upper Wimpole St CAVSQ/HST W1G — 3 U9
Upper Woburn Pl CAMTN NW1 — 4 D6
Upper Woodcote Village PUR/KEN CR8 — 86 D7
Uppingham Av STAN HA7 — 23 R13
Upsdell Av PLMGR N13 — 26 F11
Upshire Rd WAB EN9 — 17 N4
Upstall St CMBW SE5 — 50 F14
Upton Av FSTGT E7 — 40 D13
Upton Cl BXLY DA5 — 65 V3
 CRICK NW2 — 36 K8
Upton Court Rd DTCH/LGLY SL3 — 44 E9
Upton Dene BELMT SM2 — 73 P12
Upton Gdns KTN/HRWW/WS HA3 — 35 M3
Upton La FSTGT E7 — 40 D14
Upton Lodge Cl BUSH WD23 — 23 L6
Upton Park Rd FSTGT E7 — 40 E15
Upton Rd BXLY DA5 — 65 V3
 HSLW TW3 — 46 J9
 THHTH CR7 — 62 J15
 UED N18 — 26 K9
 WOOL/PLUM SE18 — 52 K12
Upton Rd South BXLY DA5 — 66 A3
Upway CFSP/GDCR SL9 — 20 C9
 NFNCH/WDSPK N12 — 25 T12
Upwood Rd LEE/GVPK SE12 — 64 C4
 STRHM/NOR SW16 — 62 D13
Urban Av HCH RM12 — 42 J11
Urlwin St CMBW SE5 — 50 E12
Urlwin Wk BRXN/ST SW9 — 50 E13
Urmston Dr WIM/MER SW19 — 61 L5
Ursula Ms FSBYPK N4 — 38 H6
Ursula St BTSEA SW11 — 49 S13
Urswick Gdns DAGW RM9 — 41 V13
Urswick Rd DAGW RM9 — 41 V13
 HOM E9 — 39 M11
Usborne Ms VX/NE SW8 — 50 B12
Usher Rd BOW E3 — 39 R13
Usherwood Cl KWD/TDW/WH KT20 — 92 J2
Usk Rd BTSEA SW11 — 61 R2
 SOCK/AV RM15 — 55 U4
Usk St BETH E2 — 39 P14
Utopia Village CAMTN NW1 — 37 U13
Uvedale Cl CROY/NA CR0 — 75 V14
Uvedale Rd DAGE RM10 — 42 A7
 ENC/FH EN2 — 15 V15
 OXTED RH8 — 96 B5
Uverdale Rd WBPTN SW10 — 6 K13
Uxbridge Rd DTCH/LGLY SL3 — 44 D7
 FELT TW13 — 58 E7
 HGDN/ICK UB10 — 33 S11
 HNWL W7 — 47 P5
 HPTN TW12 — 58 H10
 HYS/HAR UB3 — 46 A4
 KTN/HRWW/WS HA3 — 22 K12
 KTN/HW KT1 — 71 T3
 NWDGN UB2 — 46 H5
 RKW/CH/CXG WD3 — 20 G2
 SHB W12 — 48 F6
 STAN HA7 — 23 L10
 STHL UB1 — 46 H5
Uxbridge Rd (Harrow Weald) KTN/HRWW/WS HA3 — 22 K12
Uxbridge Rd (Pinner) PIN HA5 — 22 A11
Uxbridge Rd High St STHL UB1 — ...
Uxbridge Rd (Pinner) PIN HA5 — 22 A12
Uxbridge Rd The Broadway YEAD UB4 — 46 F5
Uxbridge St KENS W8 — 6 E1
Uxendon Crs WBLY HA9 — 35 V6
Uxendon Hl WBLY HA9 — 35 V6

Column 9

V

Vache La CSTG HP8 — 20 A7
Vache Ms CSTG HP8 — 20 A5
Vaillant Rd WEY KT13 — 69 T8
Valan Leas HAYES BR2 — 76 A2
Vale Cl BRXN/ST SW9 — 31 U11
 CFSP/GDCR SL9 — 20 C10
 COUL/CHIP CR5 — 86 C12
 ORP BR6 — 76 J7
 MV/WKIL W9 — 2 K6
 TWK TW1 — 59 S5
 WCHMH N21 — 26 H5
 WOKN/KNAP GU21 — 80 B6
Vale Cottages PUT/ROE SW15 — 60 B7
Vale Crs PUT/ROE SW15 — 60 B7
Vale Cft ESH/CLAY KT10 — 71 L12
 PIN HA5 — 34 J3
Vale Dr BAR EN5 — 25 M2
Vale Farm Rd WOKN/KNAP GU21 — 80 B6
Vale Gv ACT W3 — 48 D6
 FSBYPK N4 — 38 H5
Valence Av CHDH RM6 — 41 U6
Valence Circ BCTR RM8 — 41 U7
Valence Rd ERITH DA8 — 54 D11

Acknowledgements

Schools address data provided by Education Direct.

Petrol station information supplied by Johnsons

One-way street data provided by © Tele Atlas N.V. Tele Atlas

Garden centre information provided by

Garden Centre Association   Britains best garden centres

Wyevale Garden Centres

The boundary of the London congestion charging zone supplied by Transport for London

The statement on the front cover of this atlas is sourced, selected and quoted from a reader comment and feedback form received in 2004